THE MOTHER
OF ALL
WINDOWS 95™
BOOKS

*A recounting of Mom's intrepid journey
into the depths of Windows 95.
With supporting appearances by Igor, Rush, Erwin, Sarah, and Mao.
Introducing screen sensation Billy95.*

Woody Leonhard & Barry Simon

Addison-Wesley Publishing Company

Reading, Massachusetts • Menlo Park, California • New York
Don Mills, Ontario • Wokingham, England • Amsterdam • Bonn
Sydney • Singapore • Tokyo • Madrid • San Juan
Paris • Seoul • Milan • Mexico City • Taipei

Many of the designations used by manufacturers and sellers to distinguish their products are claimed as trademarks. Where those designations appear in this book and Addison-Wesley was aware of the trademark claim, the designations have been printed in initial capital letters.

The authors and publisher have taken care in preparation of this book, but make no expressed or implied warranty of any kind and assume no responsibility for errors or omissions. No liability is assumed for incidental or consequential damages in connection with or arising out of the uses of the information or programs contained herein.

Library of Congress Cataloging-in-Publication Data
Leonhard, Woody.
    The mother of all Windows 95 books / Woody Leonhard and Barry Simon
       p.   cm.
    Includes index.
    ISBN 0-201-40971-2
    1. Microsoft Windows 95.   2. Operating systems (Computers)
I. Simon, Barry.   II. Title.
QA76.76.063L46   1996
005.4'469—dc20
                                95–44110
                                    CIP

Sponsoring Editor: Kathleen Tibbetts
Cover design by: Suzanne Heiser
Set in 11½ point Times Roman by Pre-Press Company, Inc.

5 6 7 8 9 10 11 12 CRW 0100999897
Fifth printing, June 1997

Addison-Wesley books are available for bulk purchases by corporations, institutions, and other organizations. For more information please contact the Corporate, Government, and Special Sales Department at (800) 238-9682.

Find us on the World-Wide Web at:
http://www.aw.com/devpress/

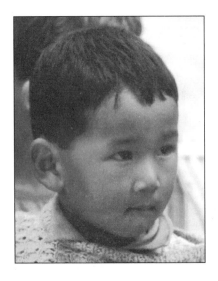

In 1959 the Communist Chinese invaded Tibet, driving its 24-year-old leader, the Dalai Lama, into exile. The Chinese unleashed a pogrom of ethnic and cultural genocide. Millions of Tibetans were imprisoned, tortured, murdered; their artistic, religious, and cultural heritage reduced to rubble. Reliable estimates place the number of Tibetans slaughtered since the Chinese invasion at 3 million. According to Amnesty International and other leading human rights organizations, arbitrary arrest, torture, and Chinese government-sanctioned killings in Tibet continue to this day.

The Dalai Lama settled in northern India. Millions of Tibetans followed him into exile. Most moved into refugee camps scattered throughout Nepal and India. Life in the camps is hard. Few families have more than one room to call their own. Many eke out a hand-to-mouth existence as subsistence farmers, manual laborers, handicraft workers, traders—often with "shops" consisting of no more than a couple of pieces of bamboo and a plastic tarp.

The Tibetan Children's Fund was founded in 1993 to provide food, shelter, and education for Tibetan refugee children living in northern India. TCF's center of operation is in Darjeeling—renowned to Westerners as a source of tea, but better known to Tibetans and many other Asians as a respected center of education. For more than a hundred years, English-language boarding schools in and around Darjeeling have prepared leaders of government, education, and commerce.

As of this writing, TCF sponsors almost a hundred Tibetan children around Darjeeling. The children are chosen for their scholastic ability and financial need. TCF volunteers (who pay for their own trips to India) interview the children and their parents, select the children, and monitor their progress in school each semester. Scholastic evaluation emphasizes proficiency in English, math, the sciences, and humanities.

A little hard currency goes a long way in India. U.S. $60 will sponsor a refugee child for a full year in one of the government-run schools. U.S. $250 covers a full year—including tuition, room, and board—in one of the top English-language schools.

TCF is an all-volunteer organization. Overhead expenses are paid by TCF's corporate sponsors. Every penny donated by individuals goes straight to the children. If you would like to help a deserving Tibetan refugee child, please contact:

Tibetan Children's Fund
P. O. Box 473, Pinecliffe, CO USA 80471
Voice: 303-642-0492, Fax: 303-642-0491

Part of the profits from the sale of this book are donated to the TCF.

Dedicated to our kids
Justin, Rivka, Sanford, Benny, Zvi, Ari, and Chana,
and Tzippy, of course.

Contents

PART 1: PERSPECTIVE

CHAPTER 1—THE BRAVE NEW WORLD   1

Should I Upgrade?   2
System Requirements   5
Setup   9
Is Window 95 New?   9
Counterpoint   12
The Evil Empire   19
Docucentrified and Objectfuscated   22
Interface 95   24
Other Goodies   32
All the World's a Folder   34
What's Missing? What's Broken?   37
Performance   38

CHAPTER 2—WINDOWS CONCEPTS   41

Of Mice and Menus   42
Objection, Your Honor   66
Drag 'til You Drop   68
A First Look Under the Hood   84
And Dots Not All   110
Putting Up a Good Font   118
Winning on the First Palette   149
Putting Windows on a Sound Basis   156
No PC is an Island   172

PART 2: GETTING TO WORK

CHAPTER 3—CORE COMPONENTS   179

Taken to Taskbar   179
Explorering the Great Unknown   187
You Gave Me Such a Start   210

Desktop Dancing	230
Configuring Context Menus and Associations	235
I've Got It Under Control Panel	264
DOS v'danya	280
Mr. Roger's Network	310
A Fair Exchange	310
Helping Those that Help Themselves	360

CHAPTER 4—APPLETS, UTILITIES, MORE   373

Disk 'n Dat	373
Gettin' It Together	383
Gettin' Hitched to the Net	400
Internet Tools	416
Your WordPad or Mine?	433
Draw, Pardner	437
Little 'ns	439
Multimediaaaaahhhhh	448
Da Games	455

PART 3: BEYOND THE BASICS

CHAPTER 5—ADD 'EM ON   457

Mom's Report Card	457
Microsoft Presents	459
Norton	464
Shell Enhancements or Replacements	469
Internet Tools	476
Other Goodies	480

CHAPTER 6—THE HARD STUFF   483

Gotta Know It	483
The Bottom Line on Component Upgrades	484
How Much Is That Hot-Diggity-Dog in the Window?	486
Narrowing the List	488
Multimedia Madness	491
What You Need . . . and Don't	493
The Transaction	495
Hard Times in Win9x	498
Mom's Checklist	502

CHAPTER 7—STAYING ON TOP   505

Prong 1: Mags   506
Prong 2: Conferences   509
Prong 3: Get On-line   510

PART 4: SCOTTY'S SECTION

CHAPTER 8—CRANK 'ER UP   515

Deciding How to Install   516
Preparing for Installation   528
Setup Vérité   533
What Can Go Wrong   550
MS Marines Are Looking For A Few Good Men   558
After the Installation   560
Ferreting More Goodies   572
How Win95 Starts   575
Nonstandard Ways of Starting   583
How Win95 Really Boots   589

CHAPTER 9—TECHIE FILES, TECHIE PROGRAMS   591

Setup   591
Startup   602
An INI Still?   610
Family Jewels   611
Recycology   612
Changing the Splash Screens   614
The Startup Disk   617
CFGBACK—Registry Backup   621
Bad Programs   621
Cleaning Up   624
Other Files   627

CHAPTER 10—(OUT OF) CONTROL PANEL   629

Abbreviations in the Belfry, er, Registry   630
Accessibility Options   630
Add New Hardware   632
Add/Remove Programs   639
Date/Time   641
Display   643

Fonts   669
Internet   669
Joystick   669
Keyboard   671
Mail and Fax   673
Microsoft Mail Postoffice   673
Modems   674
Mouse   677
Multimedia   683
Network   684
Passwords   690
Printers   690
Regional Settings   690
Zounds! Sounds   695
System   696

CHAPTER 11—Oh Registry, My Registry   713

Regedit   714
Care and Feeding of Da Registry   721
Gettin' Around   732
HKCR   738
HKCU   768
HKLM   776
Registry Hacks, Ultimate Power Users' Tricks   784

PART 5: THE END

APPENDIX A—MOM'S CD   799

APPENDIX B—MOM'S ICON CATALOG   821

APPENDIX C—MOM'S TINY BLACK BOOK   835

APPENDIX D—THE MOTHER OF ALL WINDOWS FILE TYPE LISTS   845

APPENDIX E—WHERE THE FILES ARE   851

APPENDIX F—HAAAAAAAALP   889

INDEX   901

Conventions

> Metaphor is of the highest value in both prose and poetry,
> but one must give special attention to the use of metaphor in prose—
> for the resources of prose are less abundant than those of poetry.
>
> —Aristotle, *Rhetoric,* ca. 322 B.C.

Most of *MOM95* is in plain English. Sometimes, though, Mom has to lapse into computer-speak—as infrequently as possible, I promise! When computer terminology comes to the forefront, conventions can't be far behind.

I'll put filenames in a different font, just to warn you that a computer thing is coming. Like this: `system.dat`. Stuff on the menus will receive similar treatment; I might say: Click `File` then `Exit`. Rarely I'll talk about pushing keys (ach! so *pedestrian!*), but if I want you to hold down two or more keys at once I'll use a + plus sign; for example, `Ctrl+Alt+Del`.

So much for the technical gobbledygook.

You might've noticed that these pages are populated—some would say "littered"—with little guys and gals who chime in, spreading wit, wisdom, enlightenment, and more than a little fertilizer. If you've read any of the previous MOM books, you may be acquainted with some of these characters already.

Meet *MOM95*'s eclectic assortment of unfettered icons, the array of literary artifices who will carry you into the depths of this often-intimidating topic. They're here to break up this dry technical stuff with a bit of much-needed humor, bantering with opposing points of view when appropriate. Hmmmmm. . . come to think of it, maybe the techy stuff is here to break up the icons' bone-headed wit. Whatever.

Bowing to the obvious protocol—and an iron-tight contractual restriction—we'll start with Mom herself, the Mother of all. . . well, you get the idea. . . and let her do the introductions. Mom runs the show. What she says goes. *Capice?*

 Windows 95 has generated so much controversy that I figured we really needed someone here, in the book, to present the Microsoft side of things: a Speaker for Mom's Loyal Opposition, as it were. I asked the company to assign an employee to my team. And *boy!* did they assign an important personage.

Our celebrity spokesperson was first announced to the world shortly after he was conceived: his parents figured it would take nine months, and an entire industry went on hold in anticipation of his arrival. The world waited and waited, as he stalled and stalled, unwilling to face the light of day until 400,000 screaming, paying fans declared him ready. Finally the bouncing babushka arrived on August 24, 1995—27 months after he was first announced. Oh well. Late babies are supposed to be smart babies. Besides, 27 months *in utero* ain't bad if you're born in Redmond, home of Microsoft.

Then there was this big flap about his name. Given that his dad was called Trey or III, folks sorta assumed our celebrity would be named IV, but no indeedee. His name skipped 91 points, no doubt in synch with Microsoft's stock. "Make it like a car," they said, as if you or I drive a Ford93 or a Toy87. Yeah, sure.

Anyway, I am proud to introduce to you our quasi-official on-site, in-book Microsoft rep, Billy95. You've probably seen him: he's done all the talk shows, and his Q rating recently surpassed his IQ. Just don't make fun of his name, OK?

Oh, Mom, being here is so cool. I'm glad to have this opportunity to explain the position of America's most forward-looking and user-friendly corporation. People think we have a lot of power, but that's not true. Consumers have the power, when they buy software, to choose whichever products they feel are best. We're always glad to serve in the interest of the industry and our users.

Hey kid, will ya stop pushing those glasses up your nose? Barracudas look forward, too, ya know. As for the interest of the industry, bah, humbug. You can fool Tom Brokaw, after cutting that cushy deal with NBC and your MS Network, but ya can't fool me.

Rush, lay off the poor little guy.

He's here to help us understand the reasoning behind Microsoft's choices, and to shed light on where the folks in Redmond might be heading. He's a mouthpiece, all right! Besides, could anyone with Billy's love of lightbulb jokes be all bad?

I also like top-ten lists and knock-knock jokes. By the way:

Q: How many Microsoft VPs does it take to change a lightbulb?

A: Eight. One to change the bulb, and seven to make sure Microsoft gets two bucks for every lightbulb ever changed anywhere in the world.

Q: How many Windows users does it take to change a lightbulb?

A: One, and he'll swear up and down that it was *just* as easy for him as it would have been for a Macintosh user.

 I see that Rush and Sarah are going to be a handful, once again. Those of you who read *The Mother of All PC Books* probably remember Rush, our token dummy. He's in charge of keeping us toe-to-toe with reality. After all, Rush is Right. Just ask him. Or Pizza Hut. Not many icons can draw six figures for eating a slice of pizza backward on national TV.

Sarah continues in her cameo role of technowonk extraordinaire, delivering the techie goods when the going gets tough. Having busted through the glass ceiling here at my place, she's the head techie. But there is so much technical stuff to talk about in this system, that we need her mentor and my *other* head techie, Mao.

 Thanks for the vote of confidence, Mom. They don't call me CTO Mao for nothing. Oh, and you'll be pleased to know that this time I've brought along my collection of quotations from Amok Singh, the scourge of Cathay—no doubt better known to our readers as Genghis Khan. *MOM95* will be just the third book in history to quote from the wisdom of the mighty Khan.

 Oh, great, Cathay is my favorite strip in da funnies. But who's dis tough Khan guy? He couldn't hold a candle to my Uncle Ducky "Webfoot" Salvatorre. Da San Marino Salvatorres, ya know? Dey been workin' for Microsoft for years. Uncle Webfoot's da one what put da word out on da Justice Department. "Youse wanna see anti-competitive practices?" he says to da broad, real tough-like. "Try ta compete wid *dis!*" an' he hands her a pair a concrete galoshes.

 That's completely untrue. We've never hired anybody to put pressure on the Justice Department, or on any of its employees. It wouldn't be part of the Microsoft vision. Trust me. Ducky was in Washington at the time, giving a demo of Bob to the Central Intelligence Agency—we were pushing for a name change to "Central IntelliSense™ Agency"—and he just happened to catch Bingaman in the hallway.

 Well, I see you've met Igor, my fearless enforcer and defender of Truth and Justice. Igor's a bit disoriented: he still thinks he should be in Chicago. Keeps mumbling something about marrying his Auntie and merging in Cairo. Dear boy. We'll be seeing a lot of Igor.

Oh. I almost forgot our bug expert, Erwin, a.k.a. Schrödinger's cockroach, who returns to warn us all about the creepy-crawlies in Windows 95.

Bugs? In Windows 95? Surely you jest, Mom. Microsoft says Win95 is the most stable system it's ever shipped.

Hmmmmm. . . come to think of it, that may be true. Kinda makes me feel wanted, all over. The buggy warm fuzzies.

Erwin has been with me since my first book, pointing out bugs and warning folks about the unthinkable. He's a dashing eight-legged refuge from the 1930s. The physicists in the audience will no doubt recall Erwin Schrödinger, one of the founders of quantum mechanics, who invented a famous "thought experiment" in which a vial of poison gas might (or might not) kill a cat. Schrödinger's cat became justly famous among the psi-squared crowd. A few years ago, a computer book writer had the temerity to refer to Schrödinger's cat in a book submitted to IBM. The IBM Thought Police wouldn't put up with such an offensive allusion to a cuddly animal, so they changed the manuscript, exorcising Schrödinger's cat and introducing in his stead Schrödinger's cockroach, an animal that could be (presumably) sometimes-dead without offending the more delicate readers of IBM manuals.

Erwin is thus my tribute to IBM's hubris in particular, and the purveyors of the politically correct in general. Bah. Humbug.

As always, Barry and Woody will fade into the background and let the icons take it on the chin: when you've got a good stable of opinionated comic foils, flesh-and-blood authors are b-o-r-i-n-g. Oh. One disclaimer applies. As you've probably guessed, the opinions expressed by any of the icons are not necessarily their own. Unless you happen to agree with them.

It is good to have companions in misery.

—John Gower, *Confessio Amantis*, ca. 1390

What makes *The Mother of All Windows 95 Books*—MOM95 for short—different from the other five hundred or so Windows 95 books on the market? Two reasons. It's the only book that shows you what's really going on inside Win95, from a user's point of view. And it's the only place you'll find hundreds of unique tips—and straightforward, down-to-earth explanations—for configuring Win95 to work *for* you, not against you.

We got tired of reading books and magazine articles that say, "Win95 is great but it won't do this and this and this." We spent months figuring out new ways to make Win95 do *what the experts say it can't,* and making it cookbook-easy to put those tricks to use. Whether you're supporting a company full of Win95 users or simply sitting at home and trying to get the bloody thing to start, *MOM95* will show you hundreds of ways to make Win95 work better, faster, easier, and more reliably, the first time, every time, day after day after day.

And we'll do it all in plain English.

Windows for Dullards—NOT!

If you're looking for a book to show you how to push the Windows 95 "Start" button, well, you're in the wrong place. The Win95 tutorial will show you all you need to know to get started, and the proliferation of built-in Windows wizards can run you through the most common procedures. For nearly all the "click here, drag there" basic stuff, Windows on-line help will show you step by step what you need.

But Windows 95 is such a rich environment and the provided docs and on-line help are so skimpy, you'll need *MOM95* just for its collections of tips and pointers, its plain-language explanation of what's really happening, and its authoritative exploration of Win95's seamier side. The shortcuts you'll find by opening to just about any page of this book will save you lots of frustration every time you boot up.

Manual Labor

At this point you're probably wondering, "Why doesn't Microsoft tell us about all these cool, albeit weird, things?" Or maybe, "Why should I pay for a book when the documentation I already have undoubtedly covers all the important stuff—if I ever get around to reading it. . ." Or, "Why doesn't my favorite aftermarket Windows book give me at least some little hint that all this funky stuff is going on under the covers?" Let me clue you in on a little behind-the-scenes stuff, a few of the dirty secrets of the publishing biz.

First, all of the official Win95 documentation and almost all of the aftermarket Win95 books were written before the final code for Windows 95 was ready. That means that *everything* on the bookstore shelves and in the shrinkwrapped Win95 box— including the official docs, the Help files, and the wizards— every bit of it is based on beta test code and an idealized concept of how Win95 should work, once/if all the problems were resolved.

MOM95, in blazing contrast, was written by, for, and with the final, shipping Win95 product. That made us last on the shelves, and probably hurt *MOM95's* sales, but it was the only way we could be sure you'd get the straight story.

Second, the aftermarket books are based almost entirely on the official documentation. Where the *Windows Resource Kit* or on-line Help is wrong or ambiguous, virtually every book you'll find will gloss over that particular point—or be wrong or ambiguous. Mom wouldn't let us get away with parroting Microsoft, even if we wanted to. She wields a mean rolling pin. We went back to original principles, as the saying goes, and only reported on what we could see: what's really there, as opposed to what somebody thought should be there.

More than that, we had a chance to talk with many of Win95's designers and developers to pull together detailed descriptions of how the final shipping product works, how each individual piece really functions, and how the pieces fit together in the overall scheme of Win95 things. We worked meticulously to make sure all the details are right, so when you have to figure out a solution to your own problems, you can rely on the most accurate information available anywhere—right here on these pages. You won't find these kinds of detailed, accurate, no-bull explanations anywhere else.

Third, the amount of documentation Microsoft produces—and it's the Microsoft documentation that drives the rest of the book-writing industry—has dwindled away. Consider the Decline and Fall of the Windows Manual.

Windows 2.0   568 pages

Windows 3.0   640 pages

Windows 3.1   754 pages   (with 104 in the *Getting Started* booklet)

Windows 3.11 477 pages

Windows 95   95 pages

Do you detect a pattern here? The *Getting Started* booklet for Windows 3.1 is larger than the entire Windows 95 manual, even though the Exchange application alone—a tiny part of Windows 95—is as complicated as all of Windows 3.1.* Mathematical extrapolation has demonstrated conclusively that Windows 01, which we expect should actually ship in the year 2003, will indeed have a one-page manual.

Microsoft claims they are backing away from longer manuals because readers don't want them, but that's a bunch of hooey. Their real goal is to drive down the COG—Cost of Goods. Paper manuals are the single most expensive part of the whole equation. Look at it this way: if shipping a 95-page manual instead of a 750-page manual saves them two dollars a package, and they ship 50 million copies. . . well, that's some nice pocket change, yes?

Mom's Point of View

MOM95 is more than an encyclopedic reference of the reality behind Win95. It's also a book for that proverbial rainy day. The day that Win95 won't boot up at all. The day one of your Registry settings goes haywire. The day you delete or move a program and can't figure out how to get it working again. The day you need to do something Windows' designers didn't think of. . . or the day you want to do something the designers thought you shouldn't be allowed to do.

If you want to get under Windows's skin—whether for the sheer pleasure of understanding what's happening in that box on your desk, or to ward off the sheer terror of a machine that won't work right—this is the book you need.

MOM95 concentrates on the parts of Win95 that are hard to "get"—the tough concepts underlying Win95 font technology, for example, or what a Shortcut really entails. You'll find never-before-seen tips on how to make Win95 work better, on how to customize it to support the way *you* work. You'll see how the Desktop connects to your applications, and how folders

---

* Okay, okay. I exaggerated a bit. So sue me.

control what you see on the screen. You'll learn how Win95 starts itself, and what's really happening in Safe Mode. You'll see where vestiges of Windows 3.1 and even DOS creep into Win95, and how a rudimentary knowledge of those "archaic" operating systems can keep you out of a whole lot of hot water.

And if you've ever tried to understand the Registry—the single repository of all Windows knowledge, where all the bodies are buried—by using the virtually nonexistent official documentation in the *Windows Resource Kit,* or on-line Help, you'll appreciate *MOM95's* unique, detailed report on what we found there, including all sorts of errors in the *WRK,* the Help files, and just about everywhere else we looked. A very large part of Chapter 3, and practically all of Chapters 10 and 11 work directly, down 'n dirty, with the Registry. That's about two hundred pages of Registry stuff, almost all of it previously unpublished. Now you know why we say that *The Mother of All Windows 95 Books* contains *The Mother of All Registry Books.*

Most important of all is what you *won't* see: the Microsoft Party Line. *MOM95* doesn't crib from the official, often erroneous, Windows manuals and books: it's a fresh, untainted look at what's really happening in the Win95 ooze. Mom and the other icons would sooner starve than serve up rehashed Redmond cant.

What you'll find here is the straight story, as best we can tell it, about the most pervasive, most important computer program ever created. In short, we think that every single Windows 95 user beyond the "What is the Start button?" stage needs *MOM95.* Sooner or later, it'll save your butt.

One final caveat. While we do talk a bit about networking, this is not a hard-core networking book—indeed, it would take a book several times this size to cover the nuances of Windows networking alone. *MOM95* will show you how to set up a simple peer-to-peer network and give you a never-before-seen cookbook to make dial-up networking easy, but if you're looking for advice on building a robust mission-critical network, or installation scripts for diskless workstations, you should be looking at books dedicated to the topic— and at NetWare or Windows NT, not Windows 95.

Enjoy!

Iacta alea est.*
Woody Leonhard
Coal Creek Canyon, Colorado

Barry Simon
Los Angeles, California

---

* "The die is cast." Julius Caesar, on crossing the Rubicon, 49 B.C.

Quick, look at the back cover. That shiny frisbee. It's the *Mother of All Windows 95 CDs,* just filled with goodies (hold your breath!):

- Norton Utilities' System Information program, which provides detailed operating statistics for every part of your Windows 95 system.

- Twenty hand-picked Bitstream fonts.

- The entire Official Airline Guide. The whole thing, including detailed information on more than 650,000 flights, worldwide.

- The Pro Phone "Free Phone" 800-number directory. About 200,000 entries cover every toll-free number in the USA.

- The Phone Disk collection of 200,000 phone numbers for all computer dealers, manufacturers, software vendors—virtually every computer-related business in the USA.

- Microsoft's latest and greatest for Windows 95: the Windows Driver Library (more than 10 MB of new, improved drivers, covering hundreds of hardware products); the infamous Hardware Compatibility List; the *User Interface Guide* (which costs $39 in paperback); and the new, greatly improved Microsoft Word Viewer.

- Full working models (not little slide-shows, but get-your-hands-dirty working segments) of many popular Win95 multimedia titles: Arcade America from 7th Level (which includes a page from Monty Python's Compleat Waste of Time); Freddi Fish and Putt-Putt Joins the Zoo from Humongous; Sound Forge; the simulation game Freshwater Fish from AnimaTek; and others.

- The full Public (software) Library collection of shareware and freeware Windows utilities—far and away the largest, most complete set of utilities ever compiled.

- A special collection of bonus shareware and freeware, including Batutil for controlling Windows programs from .BAT files; WS_IRC, an Internet Relay Chat program; MicroAngelo, the most sophisticated icon handler yet; and much more.

- The Windows 95 Supplemental Disk Library. If you bought Win95 on diskette and you've been wondering what you're missing, this is the whole enchilada: QuickView; Character Map; Mouse Pointers; CD Player; Windows On-Line User's Guide; Clipbook; Chat; the old DOS programs that may have been deleted from your disk when you installed Win95; MSD; the Win95 logo wallpaper; Scripting for Dial-Up Networking; System Policy Editor; too much more to list.

I'll forgive you if you take a look at that list and say, "Oh sure. The CD is worth many times as much as the cover price. They're just giving away the book. Can't be done. Besides, it won't all fit on one CD. These guys think I'm awfully gullible."

Well, guess what. It *does* all fit on one CD, and this is it. *PC Magazine* named my last CD one of the Top 100 CDs of all time. This one is many, many times better. And, yes, you *could* buy the book for the shiny plastic frisbee in back, and throw away the dead tree part. I won't be offended. I'll just be. . . crushed.

Wait a minute! That's just half the CD story. As you will see in Appendix A, when you buy this book, you can also send away for a *second* bonus CD—crammed with things we couldn't stuff into the first companion CD, including this entire book on-disk in (searchable!) Adobe Acrobat format and a wealth of additional goodies—for $9.95 (in the USA) to cover our costs for shipping and handling.

Billy95's Road Map

So you're still reading the introduction, eh? Kinda low bandwidth, aren't you?

Anyway, Mom wanted me to say that MOM95 is designed to be read from beginning to end. Or at least beginning to middle.

If you haven't yet installed Win95, go directly to Chapter 8. Do not pass go. Do not shell out another $200. When you're done with Chapter 8, hop back to Chapter 1, and learn what it was that you really did.

Chapter 1 will explain how Windows 95 fits into the larger picture of evolving systems and ever-increasing PC capabilities. It will plunk you down in the middle of Win95 things, and get you oriented. Even if you know Win95 inside and out, you may find the icons' take on things amusing, even insightful.

Chapter 2 takes you through the panoply of Windows concepts, leaving no tern. . . uh, leaving no stone unturned. These are the things you must understand before digging into the belly of Windows itself.

Chapters 3 and 4 show you Windows' components from the inside out—how they work together, how they don't work at all, how they can be molded to get more work done, your way.

Chapter 5 lets you know about Win95 add-ons, from Microsoft and others. A short Chapter 6 covers the basics in buying hardware specifically for Win95 and some of the hardware trends you need to know about. Chapter 7 shows you how to keep on top of new developments in the Windows world—no mean feat!

That's where you should stop reading sequentially. Chapters 8, 9, 10, and 11 are Reference Chapters, with a capital RC, designed to help you diagnose and fix problems: this is the only place you'll find the whole story on installing Win95, on Win95 startup, those odd files that Windows 95 insists on scattering various places, plus the inside scoop on the Control Panel, and most of all details on the Registry and other behind-the-scenes topics crucial to your continued sanity.

In the back of the book, Appendix A will step you through the contents of Mom's Companion Disk—an astounding collection of vital, interesting, and otherwise nice additions to Windows 95 itself. Don't forget to look there also to learn about Mom's Bonus

Disk, which includes (among many other nifty things) the entire text of this book, and can be yours for a paltry additional $9.95. Appendix B presents the ever-popular printed index of icons (try finding that anywhere else!). Appendix C is Mom's little black book, stuffed with addresses and phone numbers you'll need sooner or later. Appendix D is our latest compilation of filename extensions—more important than ever. Appendix E tells you which files sit on what installation diskettes or in what CD .CABs, and how to retrieve them if you run into trouble.

Finally, my favorite, Appendix F gives you a checklist of things to do when all of Windows goes to hell. When you're ready to put your fist through your computer's terminal, look to Appendix F.

That's about it! Remember, you can read straight through the end of Chapter 7, but beyond that point, sequential scanning is only appropriate for people who get a kick out of reading the encyclopedia from cover to cover.

 Like me.

Acknowledgments

No metaphysician ever felt the deficiency of language so much as the grateful.

—C.C. Colton, *Lacon,* 1820

Woody and Barry wanted to thank the Win95 team—Brad Silverberg, in particular, the "Father of Windows 95" who has done more to bring computing power to the people than any other individual in history—and 'Softies Tom Adams, Kurt Eckhardt, Ian Ellison-Taylor, Chris Guzak, Satoshi Nakajima, Peter Pathe, George Pitt, Steve Shaimen, and especially George Moore, who may understand the technical details of Windows 95 better than any human alive.

We also wanted to thank Zvi Simon for several useful insights.

Finally, Woody and Barry wanted to thank Linda and Martha, for putting up with the insanity yet another time. The stress of putting together an enormously complex book like this on a short deadline is hard to imagine. . . or even describe. Writers' spouses, more than any others, feel that stress take its toll every day.

Act I, Scene 1. On the deck of the Starship !nterprise. Close up on Spock.

Spock: I think it's imperative that we start with Windows' psyche, Captain.

Kirk: How do you propose to do that, Mr. Spock?

Spock: I suggest a Vulcan Mind Meld with the CPU.

Bones: C'mon, Jim. I *hate* that stupid plot device. Can't the writers do any better?

Kirk: Hey, it's up to Leonard, er, Spock. He's in charge of technical *deus ex machina* stuff.

Nimoy: I am not Spock. See? It says so on the cover of my book.

Chekov: Vhat? Dayus X. Masheena vas a Roosian!

Bones: If the writers can't do any better than Mind Melds and Russian gags, I'm outta here.

Roddenberry: If you walk, you'll never find work in this universe again!

Barrett: Calm down, dear. I'll talk like a computer. Will that make you feel better?

Kirk: No, don't! I can't *stand* that fakey semi-inflected monotone.

Spock (bending over the PC): Now where is the head on this damn thing?

(Dissolve in a shower of hot white sparks leaping from Spock's fingers.)

Now you know why I didn't trust the Win95 technical evaluation to the crew on the Starship !nterprise. Follow along in the first two chapters as we explore the concepts underlying Windows 95.

The Brave New World

Rolling in the muck is not the best way of getting clean.

—Aldous Huxley, *Brave New World,* 1932

However elegant and memorable, brevity can never, in the nature of things,
do justice to all the facts of a complex situation.

—Aldous Huxley, *Brave New World Revisited,* 1958

 Welcome to my brave new world of Windows 95. In this chapter, all the icons have a chance to tell you the "true facts" about Win95—conflicting and contradictory as they may be.

Huxley's futuristic tome showed us the trappings of society in the sixth century A.F. (*After Ford**). Compare it, if you will, to the vexing problems facing us as we approach the second decade A.W. (*Anno Windowi*). Come along as we join the raging debate consuming Mom's Manor, which is already in progress . . .

---

*No, not the president, the car. Sheesh.

Should I Upgrade?

> Our inventions are wont to be pretty toys, which distract our attention from
> serious things. They are but improved means to an unimproved end.

> —Henry David Thoreau, *Walden,* 1854

 Should you upgrade to Windows 95? What a question you ask! You bet your sweet bippy you should upgrade! It's truly a no brainer.

 Of course you'd say that, Mom. You're under contract to write a whole book about the product. What are you supposed to say? "Buy this 800-page book about a product that I recommend you not waste your money on?"

 Mom's right, Rush. Windows 95 meets Sarah's rule of three. An upgrade to Windows 3.1 has to meet three criteria to be a "must-have" upgrade.

First, it has to solve—or at least vastly improve—the Free System Resources problem. That's the one where users get "out of memory" problems because they run out of space in the System Resources areas—four measly chunks of memory containing just 65,536 bytes apiece.

Second, it has to put an end to the fun message that Windows 3.x often gives when a program hangs: "Although you can use CTRL+ALT+DEL to quit an application that has stopped responding to the system, there is no application in this state." Yeah, sure. More monitors have been broken by users pounding on them in frustration, yelling, "You dummy Windows!! There *is* an application that has stopped responding; the hourglass is frozen and won't let me do a bloody thing! If I can see it, why can't you?"

Third, it has to be at least as stable as Windows 3.1 and has to be close to 100 percent compatible with the array of DOS and Windows programs out there and with the zoo of different kinds of hardware.

That's what a "must-have" upgrade must do. All the rest, my thoroughly recyclable friend, is gravy.

 Not a bad set of criteria, Sarah, and Windows 95 passes each of those points in spades. Free System Resources concerns aren't totally gone; even the best Windows 95–specific programs use some of those silly 65,536 bytes. Behind the curtains, Windows is doing its best to slip objects placed into those regions into other regions of memory—ones that don't suffer the same constraints. So while running Word and Excel and a couple applets would bring Windows 3.1 to its knees, I'm able to load four copies of each under Windows 95 and still have over 30 percent of resources free. Moreover, Windows 95 does a better job of cleaning up after programs that don't free all their resources when they exit, although I still find that running certain programs slowly drops the amount of free resources I have, even in Win95. That passes the first criterion.

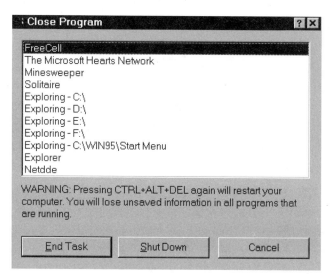

Second, hitting CTRL+ALT+DEL under Windows 95 brings up the Close Program dialog that lists all running programs and gives you three choices for each one (see Figure 1-1):

When you choose an application and hit End Task, Windows tries to send the program a command to exit. If that fails, Windows 95 puts up a second dialog offering to truly end the program.

Figure 1-1. Out, damned program

And, if you tell it to, it does: Windows wraps concrete galoshes around the sucker and tosses it in the deep blue sea. The stalled application disappears. No backtalk. You are the boss. Right, boss?

Right, Igor. Third, Windows 95 is more stable than Windows 3.1, or Windows for Workgroups 3.11. On my system, I typically needed to reboot Windows 3.x once an hour to keep it stable. Under Windows 95, I'm down to once or twice a day.

Yeah, but don't Windows NT and OS/2 also meet Sarah's criteria? I mean, they're both good, solid products.

True, but they both fail to some extent on the compatibility issue, especially for programs that try to cheat the system. Microsoft is trying to force Windows 95 programs to be side-compatible with WinNT by coercing application developers into writing for both WinNT and Win95 simultaneously, but Windows 3.1 compatibility has never been one of WinNT's strong points. OS/2 tries to emulate Windows by making Windows programs think they're running under Windows—but I know of well-behaved Windows 3.1 programs that simply turn belly-up and die when thrust on OS/2.

There are other problems. Neither OS/Who nor WinNT has the array of drivers for weird hardware that you'll find for Windows 95. And while Windows 95 prefers drivers written for it, it will use Windows 3.1 drivers for hardware it doesn't otherwise support.

If you really pressed me, though, I'd have to admit that OS/2 *does* basically meet my three criteria. However, you'll notice I said they were criteria for an upgrade—a compelling reason to shell out the money and spend the time to switch to a new system. If you're talking justification for the upgrade trauma, OS/2 just doesn't cut the mustard.

 There are more than 50 million Windows users worldwide, and the vast majority of them are going to need a more compelling reason to switch to OS/2. When you take into consideration that Windows 95 has fewer hardware requirements (vis-à-vis OS/2), a more friendly interface to new users, and some thoughtful extras, it's going to be irresistible to a significant fraction of current Windows users. And once they switch, the momentum and the fact that OS/2 will have trouble supporting native Windows 95 applications will make OS/2 an unattractive choice.

 Even I've got to admit the care that goes into the little stuff. Take a look at Figure 1-2, which shows what happens to me on the first Sunday in April, when Windows automatically adjusts my clock. Or consider the fact that if some program installs an old version of a critical system file over the ones in the Windows directory, Windows merrily restores the correct files from the C:\windows\sysbckup directory.

Figure 1-2. Spring ahead, fall back

Of course, Rush, the time change adjustment will be different outside the United States, and users in those parts of Indiana and Arizona that don't use daylight saving time will need to be sure to pick the explicit entry for them in the Time Zone dialog that pops up during initial install (it can be accessed by double clicking the time on the Taskbar).

And on top of that, there's a new interface that's a big improvement over Windows 3.1 with oodles of new goodies built in. *Exchange,* the new combined information/mail manager, is likely to revolutionize how we track stuff.

Hey, I'm supposed to be the shill for Microsoft. It says so right here on my job description.

You guys are trying to take my job away. MOMMMMMM!

I know, Bill. Believe me, we are not great lovers of Microsoft at Mom's place. They are a little too in-yer-face, beat-the-competition, win-at-all-costs types. And they have way too much power to be healthy for the industry. We'd have loved to knock this product, but, while there is a lot of stuff to warn my readers about, overall, your minions did a great job on this one.

But great as it is, some tradeoffs were made—a few that we might wish weren't. The interface has been totally revamped, so Windows 3.1 users have to figure anywhere from a day to several weeks of dissonance dislocation after they upgrade and find that even the familiar down arrow to minimize a window has changed. Crash protection isn't as good as it could've been—isn't as good as WinNT's or OS/2's—but better crash protection would've involved performance hits, and a heftier "minimum machine."

System Requirements

There are three kinds of falsehoods: lies, damned lies, and system requirements.

—Erwin's Book of Certainties

Here, according to Microsoft's Windows 95 Resource Kit, are the minimum requirements for Windows 95 (giggle):

Microsoft Minimum Requirements for Win95

Computer:	386 DX or higher
Memory:	4 MB of RAM
Video Display:	VGA (640 × 480 × 16 colors)
Video Monitor:	14 inch
Other:	Mouse
Optional:	Modem, CD ROM, Network Adapter
Sound:	Any sound card (optional)
Free Disk Space:	50 MB (new install)

If you're installing over Windows 3.1x, you can subtract 15 MB from the disk space—less if you want to save a backup of the critical system files to let you uninstall Win95. If you pick the compact install (which reduces network functionality), you can subtract another 10 MB, but if you want a complete custom install, add 15 MB more.

In English, Erwin is saying you'll need to figure on 25 MB to 65 MB of additional disk space when installing Win95 over Windows 3.1. Typical Windows 3.1 users should figure about 50 MB.

So the disk space requirements are about right. Otherwise, Microsoft's numbers are a fairy tale, a pipe dream of some Redmondian marketing types who don't have to use Windows 95 in the real world.

Here are my minimums:

Mom's Absolute Minimum Requirements for Win95

Computer:	486 or higher
Memory:	8 MB of RAM
Video Display:	Accelerated Super VGA (800×600×256)
Video Monitor:	15 inch
Other:	Mouse
Optional:	Modem, CD ROM, Network Adapter
Sound:	16 bit sound card
Free Disk Space:	50 MB (new install)

Mom's minimum requirements are a generation beyond Microsoft's recommended minimum setup. If you try using Windows 95 on a 386, you'll see why! Mom's *recommended* setup is more substantial still:

Mom's Recommended Win95 Machine

Computer:	Pentium
Memory:	16 MB of RAM
Video Display:	PCI bus Super VGA (1024×768×256)
Video Monitor:	17 or 20 inch
Other:	Mouse, Modem, CD ROM
Optional:	Network Adapter
Sound:	16 bit sound card with Wave table MIDI
Disk Space:	65 MB (new complete install)
	55 MB (windows upgrade)

Speaking of the Pentium and the best of the Pentium jokes:

Q: How many Pentium designers does it take to screw in a light bulb?

A: 1.99904274017, but that's close enough for nontechnical people.

Q: What is the successor to the RU-486 birth control drug?

A: The RU-Pentium; it prevents cells from dividing properly.

The one place I'd be most willing to compromise is the CPU. If you have a 386 but 8 MB of RAM and sufficient disk space, go ahead and upgrade to Windows 95. But consider if you wouldn't rather upgrade the whole machine. You can get my recommended setup (except for the monitor) for under $2,500. And that's likely to include Windows 95 in the purchase price.

The place I'd be least willing to compromise and most want to open my wallet for a good cause would be the video; your eyes will be happy. The Taskbar is a little cramped at 640 x 480. At that resolution, you'll want at most one row, and that row will clip program names after three or four programs are running. At 800 x 600, you can give up enough screen space for a two-row Taskbar and each row can hold four or five programs.

The, ahem, official Microsoft position on the 4 MB RAM requirement is that Windows 95 will run the same mix of applications as well and as fast on a 4 MB machine as Windows 3.1 will run on the same machine. And Microsoft explicitly says that if you want to run Exchange or MS Network, you need 8 MB of RAM.

Yeah, right. Windows 3.1 runs like a slug with 4MB, so you can smile and claim that Windows 95 only requires 4 MB to run as well as Windows 3.x does. Pretty good racket you guys have going: Windows 95 may have some resource limitations, but they are much less severe than Windows 3.1. Make a product that is shaky and you can tout the upgrade because it is less shaky. Wotta concept.

Lots of Windows 3.1 applications won't run on 4 MB machines even though their peddlers say they will. I've got a friend who tried to run Turbo Tax for Windows 3.1 on a 4 MB 386. The program ran so slow, he had to file for an extension before he could finish the complete return!

Setup

Many divorces are not really the result of irreparable injury but involve, instead, a desire on the part of the man or woman to shatter the setup, start out from scratch alone, and make life work for them all over again. They want the risk of disaster, want to touch bottom, see where bottom is, and, coming up, to breathe the air with relief and relish again.

—Edward Hoagland, *Harper's,* July 1973

 OK, so you've decided to upgrade. If you haven't yet, er, done the deed, turn right to Chapter 8 and read all my crew's tips on setup. It's a half-hour spent perusing that could well save you hours of frustration in the setup process, not to mention the tufts of hair you might pull out without my tricks.

 Yeah, some fraction of users will go through setup hell but the overwhelming majority will have a relatively smooth experience, so don't be frightened by Mom's warning. Still, if only 1 percent have problems and 40 million people upgrade, that's 400,000 support calls. Hmm. There might be a looooong hold if you try to get through.

 If you count the users who go into cardiac arrest (or at least have their lives flash before their eyes) when they get a frightening error message or just plain crash during the first reboots of the system, it'll probably be a lot more than 1 percent—maybe even the majority! But so long as users persevere and just keep rebooting, setup should be fairly successful for most—maybe not Billy's 99 percent, but I'll bet more than 95 percent.

 Even if you have run Setup, read Chapter 8 for the tips on the cleanup to be sure you go through after setup.

Is Windows 95 New?

There's no certainty for dates. If you take quality as a given, you are always going to have some uncertainty in the date . . . . Look, every date we give, we have this probability. We make clear that what we're going to do is get the product done, get the feedback, and make the decision. Every product is like that. If you're confused about that, then it's a good time for me to straighten that out—the date is not the fixed thing for any of these products, PERIOD. It's not. And everyone else, I think, knows that.

—Bill Gates from *Gates Unguarded,* an interview in *Infoworld,* Nov. 21, 1994

In the early summer of 1994, many trade publications had breathless previews of Windows 95 (then called Chicago) based on the first beta, a hype-filled Microsoft *Reviewers' Guide* and a press tour that, not surprisingly, emphasized the positive and let magazine editors fill in some gaps in the discussion—invariably misunderstanding in Microsoft's favor. For example, the press material from Microsoft used terms like "preemptive multitasking" when in reality the multitasking in Windows 95 is only sorta, kinda preemptive. You get the idea.

According to the propaganda hawked in July 1994, Chicago was an integrated operating system that combined DOS and Windows into a seamless whole. The operating system was built from the ground up to be a true 32-bit operating system that was multithreaded and had fully preemptive multitasking. The shipped product would have close to bulletproof protection so that if one task died it couldn't bring down the whole system. A brand new, 32-bit disk subsystem is added to dynamite performance. Not only did this new Windows have a pretty face, but wow—what a body! Oh, and by the way, Chicago would ship in 1994.

The new millennium had arrived, the brave new world stood at our fingertips. Peace and light and salvation would descend from Chicago, in late 1994. Cool.

Then in the fall of 1994, we learned that Chicago was to be called Windows 95! Its ship date had slipped, but Win95 would still ship in the first half 1995. Of course, as time went on, the date slipped again—but, hey, this is Microsoft, and they always ship late.

Various articles and books written around the time of the Chicago-to-Win95 name change claimed that Windows 95 wasn't really a *new* operating system at all. These folks claimed that Win95 is nothing more than an amalgam of Windows 3.1 and DOS 6.22, smashed together and gussied up for the shareholders. The effluvia hit the on-line fan. Flames engulfed anyone who dared to take a position, and the OS/2 partisans had a field day. The "new" question rapidly became one of the most written-about issues in the history of Windows.

Is Windows 95 really a new product? As you'd expect, the icons debated this issue endlessly. Let's listen in.

 Look, kids, the situation is clear. As far as I'm concerned, Windows 95 is the third brand-new mass market operating system (OS) that's appeared in the history of the PC. The first two were DOS 2.0 and Windows 3.0.

But Mom

  But Mom

 But Mom

 But Mom

 But Mom

 Right on.

 Don't "But Mom" me. I'm not going to let you waste our readers' time with all sorts of folderol. I'm gonna explain the simple truth and let them skip the next two sections, where you guys can prattle on all you want. And any icon that gives me any backtalk in this section is gonna go out to the woodshed for a good whuppin'.

Think about it. From a user's point of view, an OS is its user interface (UI). All the behind-the-scenes things offered to programmers are technical; it's the UI that counts. From that point of view, all DOSs with their infamous `C:>` prompt are the same. Sure, the command line got smarter when Microsoft included Doskey, borrowing the idea from popular utilities like PCED. But it still was basically the command line.

DOS 1.x didn't count. It was hardly mass market, and without support for hard disks, it was more the OS for an exciting toy than a serious computer. DOS 2.0 was the first PC operating system worthy of mention.

Similarly, GEM and Windows 1.0 and 2.x, while exciting for their potential, were niche products touching a small fraction of the market. I won't even mention the nongraphical . . . thing . . . IBM tried to market. The MS-DOS executive behind Windows 2.x was so brain-dead it hardly counted as a UI. No, Windows 3.0 was the first mass-market graphical UI for PCs and, as far as users were concerned, it was an OS.

As of this writing, it remains to be seen if Windows 95 will reach mass market status, but I'll bet that within its first year, tens and tens of millions of users will switch. And the UI is so overhauled that it qualifies as new.

If you look at the other thing that users think of when they hear OS—namely, the included utilities—again, Windows 95 is brand-spanking new. The disk utilities are now graphical, and they actually work under Windows. Built into the OS is a system-reporting module that is competitive with "snoop" products from the likes of CheckIt. There are new communications utilities like Dial-Up Networking, and there is a built-in mail/information organizer. And that's only a small part of the array of utilities that my crew and I will discuss in Chapters 3 and 4.

No question about it, Windows 95 is new.

Counterpoint

The trade press likes to beat up on Microsoft for what seems like its failure to move more rapidly away from real-mode DOS. Yet when Windows *does* take giant steps away from real-mode DOS, as in 32BFA,* the trade press again beats up on Microsoft, or the vendor of the broken DOS utility, or both—only this time, they view such movement away from DOS compatibility as a bug! What everyone wants apparently is DOS compatibility but not DOS.

—Andrew Schulman, *Unauthorized Windows 95,* 1995

 I promised those whippersnappers that I'd let them have their say but I didn't promise them that you'd stick around. So feel free to skip this, er, theological discussion and jump to the section "Docucentrified and Objectfuscated."

The other icons didn't so much disagree totally with what Mom said but they objected to the broad strokes with which she painted the picture. There were essentially three kinds of objections. Mao and Sarah objected to the idea that Windows 95 was new because at a deep technical level, it isn't. Igor and Erwin thought that Mom hadn't looked at enough options when she talked of only three mass-market operating systems, and Rush used the Evil Empire approach.

 To understand the techie objection, you've got to realize that Windows has three levels. First there is the user interface, the pretty face that is obvious to someone sitting at a console. Underneath that is the Windows ooze. There are lots of bits of code loaded in Windows DLLs (dynamic link libraries), drivers, programs, and whatnot, and the ball is being continually passed from one to the next with messages flying back and forth between these chunks of code.

---

* That's 32-bit file access.

But underneath that is the system services layer. This layer processes calls to the disk, the program- and DLL-loading services, and the code that holds up the ooze.

As you burrow deeper, Windows 95 looks less new. The interface has indeed changed. The DLL level has changed in that there are now spiffy new 32-bit versions of the basic libraries `user32.dll`, `gdi32.dll` and `kernel32.dll`. But the old 16-bit versions of `user`, `gdi`, and `kernel` are also there, and even if you only run new 32-bit applications, this 16-bit code gets used.

Sarah, what's this stuff about 16 bits and 32 bits mean? I hear a lot about it, and the obvious conclusion is that 32 bits (being twice as much as 16 bits) must be better. Other than that, I can't make heads nor tails out of it.

Remember that a byte is the basic unit of computer code, enough to store a single character. A byte is 8 bits (or eight 1s and 0s). 16-bit programs treat 2 bytes at a time while 32-bit programs treat 4 bytes at a time. Intel family computers from the 386 onward have been capable of processing 32 bits at a time, but DOS and the earlier Windows only processed 16-bit programs. So most of Windows 3.x sort of makes the processor work with one hand tied behind its back.

One reason 32-bit code is better than 16-bit code is simply that the central processor gets to operate on twice as much data with each step it takes. 32 bits versus 16 bits also comes into play because the Intel computers divide memory into segments, and a program can only work on one segment at a time. 16-bit segments have 2 to the 16th power, or 64K,* in them, while 32-bit segments have 2 to the 32nd power, or 4 GB* of memory in them. That means 16-bit programs have various 64K limitations built in; programs have to fight with the operating system every time they want to work with data that takes more than 64K. The four 64K segments that are the precious system resources in Windows 3.x are just 16-bit limited data segments of two key Windows programs called user.dll and `gdi.dll` (three data segments for `user` and one for `gdi`).

16-bit programs can't be automatically converted to 32-bit, in general, and 32-bit programs commonly take up more room than 16-bit programs. For these and several other reasons, Microsoft decided it wouldn't convert all of the Windows 3.1 16-bit code libraries to 32 bits. One thing that Microsoft overstated in its summer 1994 PR barrage was how great the shift would be to full 32-bit code. They really got hammered when programmers looking under the covers at early versions of Windows 95 expected to see lots of 32-bit programs, but instead discovered old, unmodified 16-bit programs all over the place. That's at the crux of the "Win95 isn't new" debate.

---

* 64K ("kilobytes") is roughly 64,000 bytes. 4 GB ("gigabytes") is about 4,000,000,000 bytes. Quite a difference, eh?

32-bit programming isn't a panacea. Even programs written to be fully 32-bit (in techie parlance, the ones that only call `user32.dll`, `gdi32.dll`, and `kernel32.dll`) wind up having 64K system resource limitations because these 32-bit programs rely on older 16-bit programs.

 Although you will hear some people say that the system resource problem is solved in Windows 95 with the use of 32-bit code, that's not entirely true. It's partially solved with a kludge!* Behind the scenes, Windows 95 is moving stuff that is stored in the claustrophobic 64K regions into the wide open spaces of 32-bit memory segments, and then moving it back when some program needs it. Smoke and mirrors.

 *The compromises that result in 16-bit code still being used so heavily in Windows 95 have two causes. First is compatibility. To avoid breaking programs that sidestep the operating system and to try to directly access the data in the system resource area, we had to keep large chunks of 16-bit code around. In addition, our desire to run on systems with only 4 MB of memory forced us to keep certain components at 16 bits even if they could otherwise have been rewritten as 32-bit programs.*

 Why does 32-bit code take up more memory than 16-bit code?

 It's not so much the code as the data! Some of the data—say, coordinates of windows—are described as a single byte, or 8 bits. If that number were stored to be processed by 16-bit programs, it would be stored as a byte of 0 and the data byte. But if that data were stored for use by 32-bit code you need to store three bytes of 0s plus the data byte. It has been estimated that shifting all the programs in Windows to 32 bits would increase the memory requirements by about 1 MB and prevent Windows 95 from running on 4 MB systems.

 But doesn't that mean that upgrades of applications that are written to support Windows 95 and to be fully 32-bit will take up more memory and that they won't run on a 4 MB system?

---

* kludge /*klooj*/ 1. n. A Rube Goldberg device, whether in hardware or software. *New Hacker's Dictionary,* MIT Press, 1992.

Precisely. That's why Mom's minimum requirement for Windows 95 is 8 MB. You'll be able to run Windows 95 on a 4 MB system about as well as you could run Windows 3.1 but you won't be able to run the Windows 95 upgrades of the applications you are used to at anything resembling a decent pace, so you'll be stuck running your old apps under Windows 95.

So the ooze layer is mixed 16-bit code from Windows 3.1 and new 32-bit code. And the system services code below that is even more reliant on good old DOS and Windows 3.x. Andrew Schulman, in his book *Unauthorized Windows 95,* makes a convincing case based on various experiments with debug code that there is still a certain amount of DOS code running under Windows and that even a 32-bit application that calls Windows for services will have Windows, in turn, make calls to DOS. Moreover, even the 32-bit parts of the system services are based on the VxD architecture that was built into Windows 3.0, but not much used there.

Hey, we said the new operating system was rebuilt from the ground up. We didn't say anything about the basement, did we?

The compromises built into Windows 95 also affect how bulletproof the system is. You can write a simple two-line piece of assembly language code, make it into a `.com` file, run that file in a DOS session, and totally hang Windows. And while Windows is much better about closing down errant Windows applications, they can still crash in a way to bring down the whole system. OS/2 and Windows NT don't have these problems as badly.

As you say, this involves a compromise. One could "virtualize" all code that is run in a DOS session and avoid the hang by that special `.com` file, but to do so would involve a significant performance hit. So we've chosen to improve stability but still run acceptably on platforms where Windows NT wouldn't run.

As for OS/2, it has a similar basic system design to Windows 95. All system code is mapped into each 32-bit process address space and programs can write to it. So an ill-behaved or malicious 32-bit application under OS/2 can crash the entire system, too. There is a `killos2.exe` application available on CompuServe's Canopus forum that illustrates this. Windows NT is immune from such attack because the system code is never visible to end user processes.

Mao, what about the claim that Windows and DOS are now integrated into a seamless whole?

A piece of Microsoft sleight of hand. The "seamless" integration isn't much more than forcing Windows to load after your `autoexec.bat` is run. It's not much different than a user adding `win` as the last line of a Windows 3.1 `autoexec.bat` and declaring that Windows is now integrated into DOS. And if you doubt this, you can hit `F8` while Windows 95 is booting and choose item 6 from the Microsoft Windows 95 Startup Menu. You sure get what looks like a DOS prompt, as if you booted DOS and never loaded Windows. And Windows 95 will still use `config.sys` and `autoexec.bat`.

I pay you guys to do the techie stuff, but you are just plain wrong about this. Windows and DOS are integrated. If truth be told they were already pretty integrated in Windows 3.1, since DOS had code to get out of Windows' way and to work properly with Windows. Moreover, while you can boot Windows 95 to a DOS-like prompt, Windows is not really running over that prompt. It loads true 32-bit disk drivers and 32-bit CD code and all sorts of other stuff that totally replaces the code that runs at, say, a DOS 6.2 prompt. As for processing `config.sys` and `autoexec.bat`, that's for compatibility and is a healthy sign.

You guys may be right that there is more old code in Windows 95 than those reading our literature might think, but if there is, that's a cause for celebration, not sadness. After all, what better way to ensure compatibility than to be using the same code that has been tested on tens of millions of machines?

But if you guys knew that you were overstating your case in the summer of 1994, why did you lie to the media and fool the media into lying to the public?

You have to realize that just as Windows has three levels (UI, winooze, and system services), Microsoft has to be thought of as having three levels. There's Waggener Edstrom, the Microsoft PR firm that puts the pretty face to the outside world. There's the marketing folks—think of them as winooze—and then there is the system services level, the programmers that do the actual coding. The programmers know exactly how much of the code is new and how much is tried and true, but as the story moves up the chain, it tends to get more and more shaded. So what comes out isn't exactly a lie, merely a rather large, uh, overstatement.

Besides, users don't give a fig for these arguments about code and ooze and system services. From their point of view, Windows 95 is a brand new ballgame, a brave new world.

All this techie stuff makes my head spin. It seems to be a draw, Mom. But I can't let stand your assertion that the only previous new mass market operating systems were DOS 2.0 and Windows 3.0. What about the Mac and OS/2? And there are those who claim that Windows isn't really an operating system anyway.

The Mac and OS/2? Those aren't operating systems. They're religions.

Igor, the key is my use of the term "mass market." If an OS doesn't penetrate 20–25 percent of the users, I just don't consider it mass market, and the Mac has consistently had about 10 percent of the market— perhaps as much as 15 percent. OS/2 is even less. That doesn't mean that the Mac OS (or its predecessors at Xerox PARC) hasn't been important historically and dominated some arenas like high-end Desktop publishing. It has, although I think the collapse of prices in the PC world and the undoubted success that Windows 95 will have spell bad news for Apple. As for OS/2, it has appealed to power users waiting for Windows 95. But as dynamite Windows 95 applications come out and it becomes clear that IBM will have a lot of trouble adding Windows 95 support to OS/2, all but the fanatics will jump ship and come back to the Windows 95 fold. Mark my words.

As for those who say Windows isn't a real operating system, horse puckey. It talks like an OS (programs can be written that only make calls to Windows rather than DOS) and it walks like an OS (users can interact only with Windows without knowing DOS is there) so it must be an OS.

During the discussions, a guest at my mansion was quizzing Mao and Sarah and Billy, trying to understand how Windows really started. Figure 1-3, a sketch from Jay Munro, lab project leader at *PC Magazine,* was so informative, I grabbed it for you:

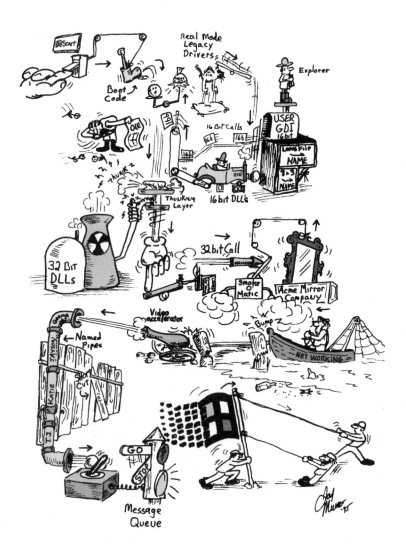

Figure 1-3. Ain't just Armani that makes good boots

Giggle. My favorite is the indication that long filenames sit on top of 8.3 filenames with a bit of spit and ceiling wax.

It's a remarkably accurate picture, except that OLE doesn't load as part of the boot and the Registry, which is a critical part of boot up, isn't to be seen.

Crimony, kid, get a life, will ya? It's a Rube Goldberg-type cartoon, not a learned article in *Microsoft System Journal*.

Er, Mom, you said that the artist was Jay Munro, but the signature clearly says that his name is Jay Munro 95. I wonder if he's related to Billy.

That left the evil empire complaint, which deserves its own section!

The Evil Empire

Most software executives view Microsoft as the meanest shark in the ocean.
That is a mistake. Microsoft is no longer a shark. Microsoft is the ocean
itself in which all the other fish must live.

—Roger McNamee (quoted by Schulman in *Unauthorized Windows 95,* 1995)

I have gotten questions, in a kidding way so far, about the "evil empire," from my
brother and some of my other adult relatives. How long until my kids are asking, or
worse, thinking, about the questions and not asking? How far will it go? Will my
children become victims of taunts and ridicule by the other kids on the playground?

—A Microsoft manager complaining to some friends

If having an inside track on the operating system gives you the edge in
creating applications, it would stand that Claris would be the leading
application vendor in the Macintosh market. Surprise, surprise. It's not Claris,
but Microsoft that holds a commanding lead in Macintosh application sales—
in fact, it has greater market share on the Macintosh than on Windows.

—Fred Davis, letter to the *Wall Street Journal*

Mom, I can accept your analysis, except for one problem. Microsoft wants to take over the world. In 1986 (the last year before Microsoft became the largest microcomputer software company), Lotus had sales of $283 million and Microsoft $260 million. In 1994, Lotus sold $970 million to Microsoft's $5.3 billion. Microsoft controls the operating system, has the leading applications in the major categories, is a major CD ROM vendor, and is moving to take over the personal finance market. They are so big they dominate the industry, and that isn't healthy. And they often play hard ball and use their OS dominance to gain unfair advantage in other areas. And your praise just plays into their hands.

Yes, Rush, Microsoft is big and does play tough. But is that any reason for end users to eschew their products if they find them to be the best available? Besides, I'd remind you that IBM still has sales that are more than ten times those of Microsoft—its software sales alone are $12 billion, so by your reasoning, we should avoid OS/2, also. Are you suggesting we all get old copies of GEM and use that? (Actually, GEM was a Digital Research product and that company was bought by Novell, which is the second largest microcomputer software company with about $2 billion in sales.)

Yeah, but Microsoft is anticompetitive, unlike those other big companies.

Actually, all the big software companies play hardball. Unlike Lotus, which has tried to use the courts to win what it couldn't in the marketplace, Microsoft has succeeded in the market. Maybe Microsoft's growth is six times Lotus's because Bill Gates has better vision than Jim Manzi?*

My opinion on why Microsoft is where it is? We are bottom-up on products. We do work hard. We are smart. We are focused. We have been persistent when we thought we were right. We have changed directions quickly when we were sure we were wrong. We have avoided the big mistakes. We have demonstrated an uncanny talent for falling on our face and landing on our feet. We were in the right place at the right time.

---

* Manzi was the head of Lotus, while Lotus was being swallowed by IBM—and he was the CEO when Lotus changed from the *1-2-3* company to the *Notes* company.

No doubt one part of why Microsoft has been successful is a consistent, intelligent strategy, but that isn't the whole story. Their competition has done stupid things. Long after it was clear that Windows applications were the future, Word Perfect and Lotus were concentrating on DOS and OS/2 products. Microsoft has consistently bet on all horses at once—for example, developing Mac products and PC applications. Microsoft has this amazing ability to produce poor first iterations but to keep plugging and finally getting it right—or at least righter than the competition. They have been very frugal in lots of way. For a long time salaries were low but employees got stock options, which more than made up for that. While Borland paid a lot for Ashton Tate (dBase), Microsoft got the better deal with FoxPro. Even though Microsoft is sitting on a cash horde of more than $4 billion (!!), before the Feds scotched the deal, they proposed to buy Intuit (the makers of Quicken) with stock, not cash. Smart, smart, smart.

But there is another side to the coin. DOS 6.x had utilities from Norton and Central Point, which, if one can believe rumor, were provided to Microsoft at no cost. Microsoft played one company against the other, warning that if they didn't play along they'd miss the opportunity to be in the DOS box and so expose users to their products. Is that unethical use of Microsoft's size or just good business? After all, there is real value to being included in the DOS box.

There are certainly times that Microsoft has gone beyond the bounds of what's right. The Wave Mapper scandal I documented in my Windows 3.x book is a good example. The bundling arrangements that the Justice Department consent decree forbids is another. But on the whole, I think a dispassionate viewer would have to conclude that most of Microsoft's success was won fair and square by duking it out successfully in the marketplace.

That doesn't make their arrogance any easier to deal with. They actually floated the idea of bundling trial versions of Microsoft Office on the Windows 95 CD. And they dropped it because their retail distributors complained about lost sales, not because they were afraid of antitrust implications. Pure chutzpah.

I think we can all agree that Microsoft isn't particularly nice, but then again, the software business is a very tough neighborhood to live in.

And, Mom, consider this. The traditional sign of the beast is the mystical number 666. The ASCII values added up for BILLGATES come to 663 so Bill Gates III is 666, isn't it? And WINDOWS95 is 665, so the first release, I figure, is also 666. Explains a lot, doesn't it?

Docucentrified and Objectfuscated

An object-oriented UI works well for basic tasks but not for complex ones. The general belief is that the more object-oriented a UI is, the easier it is to use. However, this is not the case. Although the direct manipulation of screen objects to achieve logical results is important for basic tasks (such as dragging a file from a folder to the Desktop), direct manipulation to carry out more advanced tasks (such as dragging a file to a printer icon) is not intuitive. On the other hand, selecting an object with a mouse and then browsing menus or buttons for actions to perform on that object is intuitive.

—Microsoft's Windows 95 Reviewer Guide

I took a walk while visiting Los Angeles. The lawns had little signs on them indicating the security service they used (or at least the sign they had to scare away potential burglars): Guardian Security, HiTech Protection, and so on. Then I saw it: "Multimedia Security." Buzzwords are everywhere.

The computer industry is especially guilty of overuse of buzzwords, from *artificial intelligence* to *user-friendly,* so much so that most quickly become meaningless. *Object-oriented* is perhaps the most overused term of recent vintage, although *multimedia* is a close second. But guess what? It's really true that after talking about it for several years, with Windows 95, the Desktop has become document-centered and object-oriented.

One could say that with Windows 95, *New Wave* has finally arrived.

New Wave was a product from Hewlett Packard released in the mid 1980s. Its only success was in drawing the attention of Apple, which included New Wave in its look-and-feel suit against Microsoft Windows. New Wave had three extremely forward-looking elements: compound documents, an object-oriented, document-centered Desktop, and a sophisticated batch language called *agents.* Compound documents entered the mainstream with OLE. Windows 95 has embraced the second element. Agents aren't there yet but I think they will be before too long.

 New Wave failed for two reasons. It couldn't control the whole software universe. It was confusing for the *New Wave* Desktop to have long file names if applications used some crazy name that *New Wave* translated the long name to. And the implementation was too rigid and leaned toward doctrinal purity over usability.

There are a number of ways that Windows 95 conveys its docucentric tilt. Extensions to filenames (the characters at the end, following the period) are usually suppressed, at least by default. This is part and parcel of the shift to long file names. The `doc` makes sense in `annrpt95.doc` but is silly in `annual report for 1995.doc`. So in Explorer, the Windows 95 replacement for File Manager, extensions are dropped unless you take an explicit option to include them.

Applications are also encouraged to drop extensions from the filename displayed in their title bars. A further shift to the idea that the "program" takes a back seat to the "page" is that, according to the official style guidelines, the title bar is supposed to display `Filename - Program Name` rather than `Program Name - Filename` (see Figure 1-4).

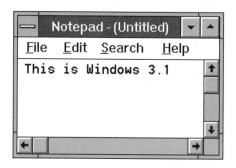 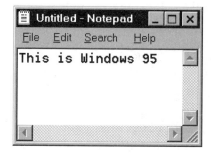

Figure 1-4. A tale of two windows

The document orientation is also seen in the New submenu that cascades from the File/New item in the Explorer menu (or from the New item on the Desktop context menu—I'll discuss context menus in the next section). The menu begins with Folder and Shortcut, two operating system objects, but then lists items that have been registered as document types, as, for example, in Figure 1-5. So rather than start a program and tell it to make a new document, you can make the new document and click on it to launch the program to edit that document.

The second half of the equation is that Windows is now object-oriented. For practical purposes, what that means is you will normally select something and then choose an action on it rather than choose an action and only then select what the action applies to.

Interface 95

A worker may be the hammer's master, but the hammer still prevails. A tool knows exactly how it is meant to be handled, while the user of the tool can only have an approximate idea.

—Milan Kundera, *The Book of Laughter and Forgetting* (1978; tr. 1980)

Windows 95 has a new user interface. I'll discuss it in depth in the first part of Chapter 2 and in Chapter 3, but I want to hit the highlights now. Even the way a windows looks has changed radically, as seen in Figure 1-4.

In terms of functionality and not mere looks, you'll notice that the buttons on the top right of the window have changed. The up/down arrows that minimize and maximize a window have a changed look. The leftmost of the three buttons replaces the down arrow; its supposed to look like a button on the Taskbar, which I'll discuss in a moment. The middle button is supposed to look like a maximized window and the rightmost button closes the application. Double-clicking on the left upper corner, changed to an icon, will still close the application, as it does in Windows 3.1.

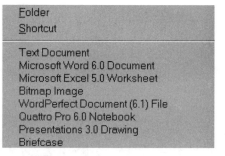

Figure 1-5. The Explorer file/ new dialog

You know, you guys just changed all this to get a new look, sorta like adding fins in one model year and dropping them in the next. Bah, humbug. Millions of hours of lost productivity while folks learn to cope with this new look, and for nothing.

Microsoft did extensive usability testing and the changes are based on what we discovered. New users were baffled about the funny arrows used by the Windows 3.1 model to minimize and maximize windows. They often confused them with the scroll arrows. They wanted to scroll a document downward, hit the minimize arrow, and were totally baffled when the window disappeared. Moreover, the overwhelming majority of users never learned about double clicking to close a window, and some of those that did had trouble perfecting the double click. In fact, much of the design in Windows 95 is intended to avoid the need for double clicking so that the double-click-impaired can still use the system.

 Look closely at Figure 1-4 again. Notice that the Win 3.1 Notepad has a name on its title bar of *Notepad - (untitled)* while the Win95 has the name *Untitled - Notepad*. Know why?

 I know. It's that docucentric stuff you just talked about. But riddle me this, Sarah-man . . . why does Word for Windows 95 insist on keeping its name first? When you crank up Word 95, the title says *Word for Windows - Document1,* not the docucentric politically correct *Document1 - Word for Windows.* If Microsoft can't keep the document-centric ball rolling in its own products, who can?

 There is another advantage to putting the document name first. The Taskbar button might not have room for the entire title bar button, so it shows the start of the title. So if you have three copies of Notepad running, you can easily distinguish them on the Taskbar because the document names are first and so are displayed there.

The Desktop has a new look and new functionality. Figure 1-6 shows a somewhat cluttered Desktop. At the bottom of the screen is the Taskbar, which has three parts. The extreme left is the Start Menu that I'll describe in a bit. At the right is the notification area, which by default shows the date/time and a sound icon. This area is live—I'll discuss it in detail in Chapter 3. The middle area is a kind of combined replacement for the Windows 3.1 Task Manager and the icons that Win 3.1 put at the bottom of the screen.

 But there is an important difference between the tasks on the Taskbar and the Win 3.1 icon row. The icon row only showed minimized applications. The Taskbar shows *all* running programs.

 Once again, the decision was based on usability testing. Users often had trouble finding an open window that was buried underneath a bunch of other windows, so even though a program wasn't minimized it was inaccessible. This was especially so for users who like to run their programs maximized. By default, maximized windows don't take the whole screen; they leave room for the Taskbar at the bottom of the screen so the switching mechanism is always visible.

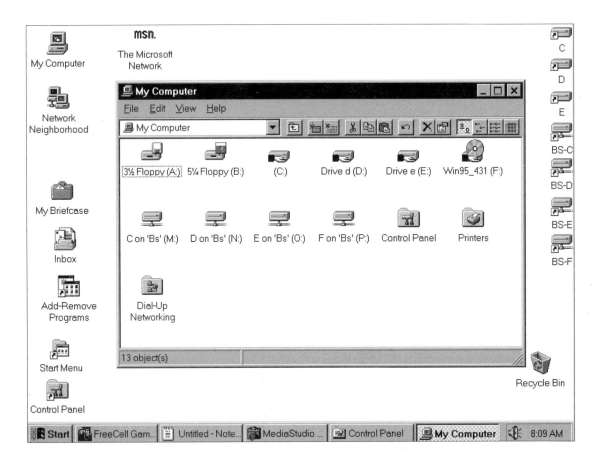

Figure 1-6. The Win95 Desktop

It's unfortunate that no way is given for end users to tell Windows not to display certain programs in the Taskbar that are just background processes. The darned thing gets rather cluttered.

Well, we start by not showing everything there. Wizards and most property sheets aren't shown, and programs like Screen Savers, if they link into Desktop properties, aren't displayed, either. And a program can choose not to display a Taskbar button. For example, Windows System Monitor, when minimized, only shows an icon in the notification area.

If you hit the Start button at the extreme left of the Taskbar, you get the Start Menu shown in Figure 1-7. The Default menu doesn't have the top two items as shown—they were added by Mao. The bottom five items are hard-wired into the Start Menu. I'll discuss them in detail in Chapter 3. The *Programs* item and any others you or Mao might add are for program launching and are the Windows 95 equivalent of the Windows 3.1 Program Manager. This is really a very different paradigm! Program lists can have submenus and launch items and the submenus can have submenus.

Figure 1-8 shows the cascade to the default place where Windows 95 puts the games.

Boss, you remembered da games! But Microsoft sure did their best to make it hard to reach 'em.

**Figure 1-7.
The Start Menu**

If you prefer the Program Manager interface, ProgMan does ship with the product, but it is probably better to use an alternate, which I'll discuss also in Chapter 3.

If you are dismayed at having to grab the mouse to start a program, you access the Start Menu by hitting Ctrl+Esc. And yes, it seems a little weird to me that the lead item in the Start Menu is called Shut Down. Er, I guess it's where you go to *start* to shut down the system.

Returning from the Taskbar to the Desktop, as seen in Figure 1-6, you'll notice lots of icons. These serve a totally different function from the Desktop icons in Windows 3.x. They are quick-launch shortcuts that allow you to place nonrunning programs and quickly start them up.

This one change is likely to confuse more folks than any other one. But once you get used to it, it's really quite handy to have available.

You bet it is! That's why launchable icons were so popular with Norton Desktop users. Hey, I wonder from where Microsoft got the idea to use launch icons on the Desktop?

Figure 1-8. The cascades ain't just in the Pacific Northwest!

The File Manager replacement is called Explorer. Figure 1-9 shows the default look and Figure 1-10 shows how it can be set up for power users with a button bar, status bar, and linked file/tree list with lots of details.

Once again, Microsoft has decided to sock it to power users. They make the default a silly, underpowered version of something that's actually pretty good if set up properly.

Figure 1-9. Explorer dumbed down

 You've got it backwards, Rush, old chap. One size won't fit all, and so long as that is the case, I can guarantee you that we'll set the defaults for the novice and let the power user figure out how to set things up with all the bells and whistles. First of all, the power user, by definition, is better able to figure out how to change away from the default. But more importantly, power users are outnumbered by novices. And the model has changed. Used to be that most novices were power user wannabes. Now we are reaching out to users who just want to balance their checkbook and send off their email and want the darned thing to be as easy to use as their toaster. Heck, Rush, you power users have had a good run. Now, you'd better get used to stuff aimed to the tyro. Besides, Rush, think of it—this way, we give the book writers something to tell power users about, and that's good for you, isn't it, Rush?

Explorer and how to configure it are also discussed in Chapter 3. My quick overview has got to cover two last interface elements: right button menus and property sheets.

In general, the right mouse button is supposed to bring up a menu of choices specific to the current context and so is called a context menu. For example, there are such menus for the

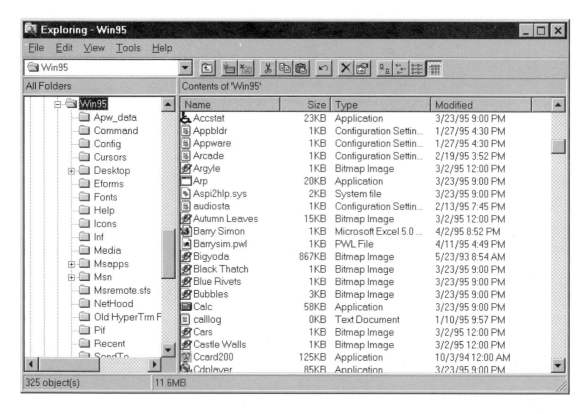

Figure 1-10. Explorer on steroids

Taskbar, for the Start Menu and for the Desktop. Often where
double-clicking or left dragging would produce a default
action, right-clicking will produce a menu of choices, with
the default choice highlighted. If you grab an executable in
Explorer (by pressing and holding the left mouse button) and
drag it to the Desktop, it makes a launchable shortcut. I'll
discuss shortcuts in the section after next, but if you right-
drag and drop—that is, press and hold the right button, and
move to the Desktop—when you release the button, you get

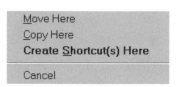

**Figure 1-11. A drag/drop
context menu**

the menu shown in Figure 1-11. This is useful as a learning device since it gets you to
understand what the default action is going to be, but is also useful for the additional
flexibility you gain.

As I explained, Windows is now object centered, and the options and user-accessible
features of an object are called its properties. Virtually every object in the system has a
property sheet. Four of them are shown in Figure 1-12: two for files, a third for a disk drive,
and the last for the display.

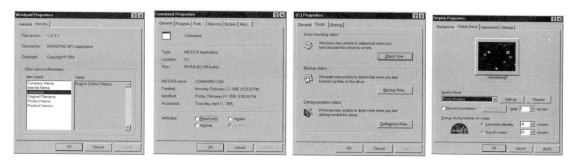

Figure 1-12. More properties than Monopoly

Hey, Mom, does this book come with a magnifying glass?

Actually, Igor, when we discuss a specific property sheet in detail, I'll show a much bigger screen shot and explain a lot more. This is just to expose the beast.

Property sheets are usually tabbed dialogs, with separate tabs for different sets of properties. Thus, the second tab for a DOS executable has much of the information that used to go in PIF files. The disk tab includes information and access to ScanDisk (error checking), backup, and disk defragmentation. The rightmost property sheet for the display includes dialogs to choose the screen saver, wallpaper, and screen resolution.

What kinda mixed up mishmash is this? Any object-oriented honcho will tell you that the properties of an object (intrinsic data) and the methods (code you apply to the object) are different beasts. So what in the blue blazes are defragmentation and ScanDisk doing on the drive properties sheets? Some kind of PC crap, huh?

As Boltzmann* said, "Elegance is for tailors." Sure it offends the object purist, but it provides more functionality to users.

---

*Ludwig Boltzmann was the founder of modern thermodynamics. He is best known for his constant used in statistical mechanics. He also wore off-the-rack . . . .

So how do you access the property sheet of an object? Generally in one of two ways, and sometimes three. First, if the object has a right button context menu, the last item should read Properties. Secondly, if you can select the object, hitting Alt+Enter will normally invoke the property sheet. Finally there may be access via a menu or control panel or some other object specific way.

Other goodies

> In the late 1600s the finest instruments originated from three rural families whose workshops were side-by-side in the Italian village of Cremona. First were the Amatis, and outside their shop the sign read: "The best violins in all of Italy." Not to be outdone, the family Guarnerius hung a bolder sign that proclaimed, "The best violins in all the world!" At the end of the street was the workshop of Anton Stradivarius, and on its front door was a simple notice which read: "The best violins on the block."
>
> —Freda Bright

Here are some of the other notable new features of Windows 95. Most of them will be discussed in great detail later in the book:

☺ DOS sessions have more free memory than under Windows 3.1 because network, CD ROM, and other drivers have been moved to protect mode.

☺ There is support for TrueType fonts in windowed DOS sessions and a button bar in DOS windows.

☺ Support for CDs is vastly enhanced. In prior versions of Microsoft operating systems, CD ROM was an afterthought controlled via an OS extension that took valuable memory space from DOS sessions. Not only is support now built in and provided by a VxD that runs in protect mode and takes no memory from DOS sessions, but the OS can sense when a new CD has been placed in the drive and can take appropriate action. This means on many systems, if you place an audio CD into the drive, Windows automagically loads its CD player applet and starts playing the CD! It also allows CD ROM makers to add an *autorun* file that can start programs as soon as you place the CD in the drive.

☺ An undo feature is built into the operating system. You can rename a file, think better of it, and choose Undo Rename from the Edit menu in Explorer to change the file back. If you choose Minimize All Windows in error from the context menu on the Taskbar, you can instantly choose Undo Minimize All from the context menu.

☺ Peripherals are easier to install, especially those supporting Plug 'n Play.

☺ An improved Help Engine includes full text indexing.

☺ Screen resolution can be changed without rebooting the system.

☺ TCP/IP support is built in to allow Internet access through a variety of third party Internet providers.

☺ Print spooling is vastly improved.

☺ All applications are encouraged to register an uninstall procedure with the operating system and, if they do, the uninstall is available from the Add/Remove Programs Applet in Control Panel. To qualify for the Windows 95 logo, a program *must* have such an uninstall procedure.

☺ A communication driver actually lets you do background communications in DOS sessions! It includes support for 16550 UARTs.

☺ Modem configuration is centralized so you don't have to configure your modem in every communication application.

☺ Dial-Up Networking lets you access a remote file system via modem in a transparent manner.

☺ A universal email client called Exchange, once it is supported by third-party on-line services, will let you put all your email in one place. In the initial shipment, support is provided for CompuServe mail, Microsoft mail, and the new Microsoft Network. And the Plus! Pack includes an Internet mail server.

☺ There is support for UNC (Universal Network Connections) pathnames over networks. This means one can access remote drives without assigning them local letter names. This is possible from the new Open/Save dialogs and by using a new syntax. For example, if a remote computer has the name `george`, and drive C has the sharename `root`, you could access `C:\windows` on that machine by referring to `\\george\root\windows`.

☺ Support for Video is built in, and MIDI support is easier to access.

☺ A new set of routines (WinG, Direct Draw, and Direct Audio) is available for games makers.

☺ Support for oodles of system sounds is provided.

☺ Changing cursors and installing animated cursors are supported.

☺ There are application-specific paths so you'll never again have problems with a too-long path statement.

All the World's a Folder

> After all, the world is not a stage—not to me: nor a theatre: nor a show-house of any sort. And art, especially novels, are not little theatres where the reader sits aloft and watches . . . and sighs, commiserates, condones and smiles.—That's what you want a book to be: because it leaves you so safe and superior, with your two-dollar ticket to the show. And that's what my books are not and never will be. . . . Whoever reads me will be in the thick of the scrimmage, and if he doesn't like it—if he wants a safe seat in the audience—let him read someone else.
>
> —D. H. Lawrence, Letter, 22 Jan. 1925

If you've used PCs for any period of time, you've no doubt made some kind of peace with the notion of *directory,* so you think you understand how they work and what they are good for. You may use a relatively flat directory structure (with everything a subdirectory of the root) or you may have a deep structure with many levels, but you probably thought that directories were one aspect of computing that wouldn't change. Well, it has with Windows 95. There are two changes. First of all, Microsoft has changed the name from *directory* to *folder.*

Oy. We not only need to look like a Mac, we now have to sound like a Mac.

Folders are a familiar metaphor for storing stuff. Directories are techie. So the term had to go to help out the novice.

My gang will try to use the term *folder,* but I'm sure we'll slip and use *directory* a few times. Feel free to think, "Gack, they've screwed up again."

Chapter 1: The Brave New World • 35

Secondly, Windows 95 vastly expands the notion of directory, er, folder.

You can say that again. Even the lousy Desktop is now a folder.

Actually, little friend, one can claim that folders are what directories have always been, a place where files are kept. The difference in Windows 95 is twofold. There is a new file type called *shortcuts,* and the OS is now using folders to store its own data.

Following Mao's lead, I'd better explain shortcuts first. DOS originally had three kinds of executable files: `.com`, `.exe`, and `.bat`. To DOS, all other files were data files, although there was a fourth kind of file with code—the device driver, typically with extension `.sys` or `.dev`. Device drivers could only be loaded by the OS during bootup, and weren't executable by end users. Although the structure of Windows `.exe` files changed, Windows itself added no additional user-executable programs. There were additional code files with extension `.dll` or `.vxd` (dynamic link libraries and virtual drivers), but like device drivers, they couldn't be run directly by the user.

Windows 95 has introduced a new type of user-executable file called a *shortcut,* normally with the extension `.lnk`. As the name implies, shortcuts are, er, *shortcuts* to other actions, most often to executable files. Such shortcuts are essential to the new organization with folders. For example, the launch icons on the Desktop are in one-to-one correspondence with the files in the directory `C:\windows\desktop`. The name under the icon is the name of the file. Rename the icon on the Desktop and you rename the file.

Click on the icon and you run the program. But programs often want their own directory with additional files that you don't want to appear on the Desktop, and a program will sometimes stop working if you rename it. Thus, you'll normally want to place shortcuts on the Desktop. That lets you keep the name and directory of the original program.

It is a slight overstatement that all the icons on the Desktop correspond to files in `C:\windows\desktop`. Two icons are built in: `My Computer` and, on systems with networking turned on, `Network Neighborhood`. In addition, there are up to three icons that Microsoft adds to the Desktop via funny business in the Registry: Inbox, Recycle Bin, and The Microsoft Network. In Chapter 11, I'll explain how to remove them or turn them into files in the Desktop directory. You can name the windows directory anything you want; for example, `C:\win95`, or even `C:\oy vey whata thing` (using long filenames!) and you can rename the Desktop directory to something else. For simplicity, through the book, I'll refer to `C:\windows` even though it could be named something different.

Shortcuts are indicated on the Desktop with a different icon. Figure 1-13 displays the icons used if the actual program Freecell is placed on the Desktop and when a shortcut to it is placed there instead. Notice the little arrow placed as an indication of the shortcut.

Freecell   FreeCell

Figure 1-13. Tale of two icons

You can create shortcuts in a number of ways. If you drag an executable program from an Explorer window to the Desktop, then by default, a shortcut is created. The name of the object on the Desktop will have the words *Shortcut to,* but you can just click on the name and type in whatever alternate you want or delete these words.

On the File menu in Explorer is a submenu called New and one of its items is Shortcut. The Desktop context menu also lets you create a shortcut. These menu creation options invoke a wizard that leads through the setup of the shortcut. Shortcuts can also point to control panel applets—just drag one from the Control Panel window.

While shortcuts will be used most often for executable programs, you can have a shortcut to a folder or even a shortcut to a location on the MS Network or on the Internet. And these shortcuts to the network can be sent by binary email to other Windows 95 users. You can even have a shortcut to a piece of OLE scrap, say a paragraph you often want to be able to drop into your documents, or a shortcut pointing to specific location in a long document. I'll cover these later in the book when I discuss the corresponding concepts.

 While shortcuts are neat, one down side is the disk space they take. On a system with hard disk with 512 MB to 1 GB of space, each file takes a minimum of 16K. If your Start Menu has sixty items, that's a megabyte used for shortcuts. Or are they longcuts?

 Not if you use Drive Space 3, included with Microsoft® Plus! (aka the Plus Pack). The minimal space taken by a file is a mere 512 bytes.

 The same if you use Stacker.

While on the subject of files, Windows 95 has added support for long filenames—up to 255 characters, including spaces. In Chapter 2, I'll discuss how Windows does this and how it handles the fact that older programs don't know how to treat these long filenames.

As for folders, besides `C:\windows\desktop`, there are three other subfolders of `C:\windows` with special meaning to Windows itself:

- `C:\windows\Start Menu` (two words as allowed by long filenames), which is where the Start Menu gets its items from. Submenus correspond to subfolders and launch items to shortcuts, showing once more the utility of shortcuts.

- `C:\windows\fonts`, which is the usual place that fonts will get stored. You can store them elsewhere but the default method for a user to install fonts will be to drag them to this folder in Explorer.

- `C:\windows\system`, as in Windows 3.x stores technical stuff.

 Actually, there are several other subdirectories of `C:\windows` with special meaning to Windows, including SendTo, Recent, and Nethood. See Chapter 2.

Besides this, Windows stores some of its applets in a subfolder of a folder that is called `C:\Program Files`. The setup guidelines suggest all applications store their files as a subfolder of this directory, at least as a default that the user can override.

What's Missing? What's Broken?

> What is broken is broken—and I'd rather remember it as it was at its best
> than mend it and see the broken places as long as I lived.
>
> —Rhett Butler's farewell to Scarlett O'Hara, in *Gone with the Wind*

Users of the DOS 6.x/Windows 3.1x combination have got to wonder what's been removed and not replaced by something equivalent or better. The list isn't too long:

☹ There is no anti-virus software.

☹ Qbasic is gone.

☹ Windows Recorder is gone and the Windows 3.1 version doesn't capture some critical key combinations like the one that invokes Start Menu.

☹ Calendar and Cardfile are gone, although if you upgrade over Windows 3.x, the old versions are retained and work fine in Windows 95.*

---

* Rush: If you could ever say that Cardfile, dog that it is, ever worked fine.

☹ Schedule +, which was included in Windows for Workgroups, has been removed—a Windows 95 version is part of Office 95.

☹ There is no undelete program. Sure, there's a Recycle Bin, but that doesn't work if you delete a file in a DOS window, and there is no way to recover files that you've removed with `Shift+Del`.

 The movement of Schedule + to Office is shameful. Seems like a rather transparent ploy to move to Office those folks who got used to it in Windows 3.11. Once again, Microsoft uses its virtual monopoly in the OS to benefit other parts of the business in a questionable way.

 As for the antivirus, check out my Bonus CD, on which we expect to include a Virus scanner from Norton.

As for what's broken, figure that very few applications are broken, but that most utilities won't work without upgrades or will work in an undesirable way. You don't want to use a file management program that doesn't understand long filenames. Not only won't it display right, but moving a file with an associated long name in such a program will foul up the long name. Similarly, backup programs will clobber long filenames when you restore. Program launchers may still work, but the interface has changed so much, they may not make much sense.

 I threw out three shelves' worth of Windows 3.x utilities that were in Mom's Software testing laboratories. Some will need upgrades and will still find users, but quite a few have been superseded by Windows 95!

Performance

> It provokes the desire but it takes away the performance.
>
> —William Shakespeare, *Macbeth**

---

* Some OS/2 proponents think the Bard was giving an early review of Windows 95 but in fact he was talking about the effect of alcohol on sex. It's terrible how these modern writers focus so much on sex, isn't it?

So you ask: What about performance? Is all the new 32-bit code gonna turbo charge my system the way the magazines reported it would in the summer of 1994 when they based their breathless reviews on Microsoft hype rather than testing real code? Since performance was never viewed as the primary reason for this upgrade, my crew didn't do its own performance testing. But the tests that the weeklies and magazines did on the final Windows 95 code paint a consistent picture. In a sentence, speed considerations are close to a wash. The reason you upgrade won't be because the speed improvement is so great. On the other hand, all the new stuff won't slow your system down significantly.

In more detail, tests of the speed of disk access show a marked improvement over Windows 3.1 but virtually no improvement over Windows for Workgroups 3.11. That's not surprising —the move to 32-bit disk access does remove a bottleneck, but that was already done in the Windows for Workgroups 3.11 upgrade.

Screen benchmarks also showed little improvement, typically by less than 20 percent.

 There are those who would yell that a 20 percent speed improvement in screen drawing is the most important thing since sliced bread. But trust me; you'll hardly notice it. I talk more about speed and benchmark issues in Chapter 6.

What about the Winstone benchmark, based on real-world applications? There the tests seemed to show that Windows 95 was slightly slower, but not by enough to spit at. Of course, it's in real world applications that Windows 95 should show the biggest performance gain once the applications move to 32 bit. The tests done at release were typically 16-bit applications running in both environments to avoid an apples versus oranges. But in the real world, you'll be using 32-bit applications under Windows 95 as you upgrade them.

As Mom said, speed is basically a wash. There are of course other aspects of performance where Windows 95 is a vast improvement. If your system tended to start running like a sludge under Windows 3.1 because you ran low on system resources, that's a heck of a lot less likely under Windows 95. The multitasking, while not as smooth as Windows NT or OS/2 or UNIX, is much better than Windows 3.1. Most particularly, the comm driver in Windows 95 actually works in multitasking situations so that downloading a file in the background in a DOS program is possible without totally giving up other uses of your machine.

So much for the intro. Let's get down to the tough part.

Chapter 2

Windows Concepts

The *Hitchhiker's Guide to the Galaxy* has, in what we laughingly call the past, had a great deal to say on the subject of parallel universes. Very little of this is, however, at all comprehensible to anyone below the level of advanced god. . . .

One encouraging thing the *Guide* does have to say on the subject of parallel universes is that you don't stand the remotest chance of understanding it. You can therefore say "What?" and "Eh?" and even go cross-eyed and start to blither if you like without any fear of making a fool of yourself.

The first thing to realize about parallel universes, the *Guide* says, is that they are not parallel.

It is also important to realize that they are not, strictly speaking, universes either, but it is easiest if you don't try to realize that until a little later, after you've realized that everything you've realized up to that moment is not true.

The reason they are not universes is that any given universe is not actually a thing as such, but is just a way of looking at what is technically known as the WSOGMM, or Whole Sort of General Mish Mash. The Whole Sort of General Mish Mash doesn't actually exist either, but is just the sum total of all the different ways there would be of looking at it if it did. . . .

Please feel free to blither now.

—Douglas Adams, *Mostly Harmless*

 Those other books start by telling you how to click and clack and tip and tap. I won't forget that one of the reasons that you bought *this* book is for that sort of stuff. But my philosophy is that by first understanding some of the ideas that motivate the Windows interface, you'll be able to figure out the tips yourself and—more importantly—remember the ones that I give you. So my gang will start with an overview of the idea behind not only windows, menus, and the common dialogs but also fonts, MIDI, and video.

Listen up, fans. You probably figure this is the chapter you can skip because it deals with abstract stuff, but it's exactly the opposite. If you only read one chapter in this book, read this one! It'll save you time every day and make your computing more pleasant to boot.

Of Mice and Menus

It is with roses and locomotives (not to mention acrobats, Spring, electricity, Coney Island, the 4th of July, the eyes of mice and Niagara Falls) that my "poems" are competing.

—e. e. cummings, Foreword to *is 5* (1926)

No two ways about it; you have to learn the lingo. If you're on the phone to tech support and they tell you to choose the second radio button, you have to know they don't mean to switch from Rush to Howard using the presets you've configured on the portable radio next to your computer. So part of this first section just tells you the names of things. But it's more. I'll also give you the functionality tips that, once you learn them, can save you lotsa time; for example, the title bar double-click.

I had a cross-reference issue to settle because there's so much happening on your screen. I start with simple windows, but when I discuss minimizing, the Taskbar needs to be mentioned. But I've not told you what the Taskbar is! In fact, as part of the basic shell, the Taskbar is only discussed in detail in the next chapter. I decided I'm going to refer to some terms without defining them because you might come to this book with some terminology—if not, the dynamite index should help you out.

Microsoft provides a document to developers called *The Windows Interface Guidelines for Software Design.* It should be the bible for how objects act, for that way the user interface will be consistent across applications. I'll refer to it often, calling it *The Interface Guidelines.* You'll find a copy in help format on Mom's CD.

Anatomy of a Window

Anatomy is destiny.

—Sigmund Freud, 1912

Here's some rocket science for ya. They call it Windows® because it has a lotta windows running around on screen.

Figure 2-1 shows a minimal window with as little extra as possible. There is actually a lot more there than meets the glance. The most obvious features of this window are the three buttons on the right side of the strip at the top. That colored strip at the top is called the *title bar,* and I'll talk about it more in a moment. The extreme right-hand button looks like ✖ . It is called a *close button* and it closes the window—more rocket science, eh? Actually, all it really does is send a message to the window that says, "Hey buddy, boss man says it's time

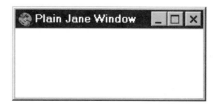

Figure 2-1. Innocent little window

to close shop." The window can then go gentle into that good night, or it can rage, rage against the dying of the light . . . oops, I mean it can post a message back to the user to confirm the action, perhaps giving some additional information. For example, if the window were your word processor, it might first ask about saving some unsaved work.

To the left of the close button are a pair—the *maximize button,* which looks like ❐ , and the *minimize button,* which looks like ▬ . The maximize button is called that because it makes the window as large as it can be. Under Windows 3.1, that normally meant filling the whole screen. Under Windows 95, the window expands to the whole screen except for the Taskbar (the row of buttons at the bottom of the screen).

There are inevitable exceptions. Some users will configure their systems so the toolbar doesn't usually appear (autohidden), and then maximize does take the whole screen. Others will like the Application Bar that ships with Microsoft Office and will place it as a second bar along the right side of the screen, and then maximizing will cover the part of the screen taken by all but *both* bars. Windowed DOS sessions treat maximize in a special way—the window expands to show the standard 80- × -25 character screen in whatever the current font size is.

 While on the subject of exceptions, some applications, like Windows Calculator, will have the maximize button grayed out. (In Windows, an unavailable option appears as totally gray. Interestingly enough, under Windows 3.x, the calculator shows no maximize button at all, but the Windows 95 team decided that consistency was a good idea so a maximize button is shown on all standard windows—it is just sometimes grayed out.)

The minimize button is named so for historical reasons—under Windows 3.1, the window was iconized—that is, replaced with an icon at the bottom of the screen and so replaced by its minimum size object. Under Windows 95, the window disappears even though it is still running. Normally you can tell it is still running because it remains as a button at the bottom of the screen on the Taskbar like so: 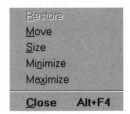. But that button is there even when the window is open. Again, there are exceptions—a program can choose to hide itself totally or can become an icon in the area of the Taskbar where the time appears.

When you maximize a window, the maximize button (▢) is replaced by a different button called the *restore button* that looks like 🗗 . It returns the window to the state it was in before you maximized it.

 The look of the buttons is supposed to be descriptive. The maximize button is supposed to look like a full-screen window, the minimize like a blob on the Taskbar, and the restore button like several windows on the screen rather than a maximized window taking the whole Desktop.

Moving right along, the strip, usually blue at the top of the window, is called the *title bar*. The text in the title bar is called the *window caption,* a holdover from the Windows 3.x days when it appeared underneath the icon as a caption. Now it appears as a title on Taskbar button.

 The title bar is a really useful device to control a window. Double-clicking it is the same as clicking the maximize or restore button; that is, it will toggle between the normal and maximized window state. You can put your mouse pointer over the title bar, press the left button, move the mouse (this is called *click and drag*), and the window moves! Normally, an outline of the window shows as you move it, but the Plus! Pack lets you turn on a mode where the window is drawn as it moves. I'll tell you about right click on the title bar in a moment.

The icon at the extreme left of the window title bar is called the *system menu button.* If you click once on it (or hit Alt+Space), you get the menu shown in Figure 2-2. It's called the window's *system menu.* All the actions on the menu are available with the mouse in more direct ways—we've seen this except for Size, which I'll discuss in a moment. Note two things about the last item on the list. First, it is boldface. That's an indication that if you double-click the system menu button, the boldface action takes place. Double-clicking the icon on the left is the same as single clicking the ✖ button on the right side of the title bar. Second, note that the keystroke Alt+F4 is shown by that choice. It indicates this is a shortcut key to close the window if it is the active window.

Figure 2-2. A system menu

 New with Windows 95, if you right-click on the title bar, the system menu for the window pops up.

The final element of the window in Figure 2-1 is the border. It is shown there in a different color but there are cases where it may not be. As you move your mouse pointer over the border, it changes shape to $\updownarrow$ over the top and bottom borders, to $\leftrightarrow$ over the sides and to $\nearrow$ or $\searrow$ over the corners. At that point, if you press the left mouse button and drag, you resize your window in the obvious way.

 Some windows cannot be resized and they won't have a cursor change over their borders. The calculator is a good example. Also, the pointers can be changed by a user, so the shapes I just described may not be the ones that actually appear on your system.

So much for the simple window. Figure 2-3 shows a window with lots of trimmings—an Explorer window with all its options turned on. Immediately below the title bar is the *menu bar* and below that a *toolbar.* I'll talk about their typical contents later in this chapter.

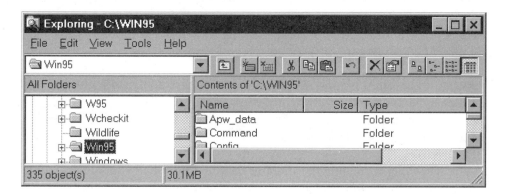

Figure 2-3. A fancy schmancy window

The last general feature I'll point out in this window is the bar at the bottom. It is called the *status bar* and in well-designed applications it gives you information—it might be free disk space (as in this example), a page number in a word processor or the date and time in some applications.

 The toolbar has also been called a lot of other names, such as action bar or button bar.

If you look at the right-hand side of the window in Figure 2-3, you see some objects that look like ◀┃ ▶ . This is called a scroll bar, and it appears when a window or part of a window has more information than can be displayed in the viewport on screen. You can have a vertical scroll bar, a horizontal bar, or, as in this case, both.

This scroll bar has four parts—the scroll arrows on the left and right, the scroll shaft (that's really what *The Interface Guidelines* calls it), which is the long strip between the arrows, and the thingee in the middle. Most folks call that thingee the slider; some call it the elevator (because it moves up and down the shaft on vertical scroll bars); *The Interface Guidelines* calls it the scroll box—no kidding. I'll call it the slider.

Let me describe how vertical scroll bars work. Clicking on the top arrow or bottom arrow is supposed to move the contents of the window up or down by a single line, or single unit if there is one. For a picture, there isn't a natural unit (other than a single line of dots, which is much too small), so the program is supposed to choose its own unit.

 Clicking the top scrolls a line above what was visible into view, so really it moves the viewport up and the content actually moves down. It's the natural thing to do, although if you start saying, "Clicking the up arrow moves the contents down," you'll get a headache, which goes to prove that it sometimes doesn't pay to think.

Clicking an empty part of the shaft is supposed to move the content up by a screenful if you click above the slider and down a screenful if you click below it. Actually, as *The Interface Guidelines* explains, not quite a full screen—a single line of overlap should be preserved (so it moves by a screen minus one line) to keep your bearings.

Finally, you can drag the slider. Dragging the slider to the top of the shaft should take you to the top of the document; dragging to the bottom of the shaft should take you to the end of the document. For something like a spreadsheet that has empty rows at its bottom, dragging to the bottom of the shaft should take you to the end of the data, not the last empty row of the spreadsheet.

If you drag the slider 30 percent of the way down, the document should scroll to the 30 percent mark. As you scroll with the keyboard, for example by using PgUp/PgDn, the slider should move to give you a visual clue of where you are.

In Windows 95, the size of the slider is supposed to indicate the fraction of the document currently on screen, so the slider in a two screenful document would take up half the shaft. On a ten-page document, it would be a tenth of the shaft and on a hundred-page document, it would be a thin line.

Microsoft Word 7.0 shows the kind of innovation in design that my crew applauds—an extra that doesn't disconcert when it is absent in other applications—namely, when you press on the slider, a box pops up with the current page number. I hope this idea is widely copied.

Waiter—Menu, Please

Although our Plain Jane Window doesn't have one, most application windows have a menu underneath the title bar. The menu usually has the names of submenus. Hitting the Alt key with nothing else will move you to the menu bar where you can use the arrow keys and Enter. If a menu item has an underlined letter like File or Edit or Middle, hitting Alt+F or Alt+E or Alt+D (no, you don't need to shift the F to get Alt+F) will pull down the menu, and it's often easier to do that when you have just been typing than to grab the mouse.

The combo like Alt+F is called an *accelerator key*. You'll sometimes see someone write "&File" or "Mi&ddle" because that's what Windows programmers do to tell Windows about accelerator keys. You need to know about this funny & convention because it carries over to quite a few programs that let you build your own menus or customize the ones the program already has. In Windows 95, when you customize the context menu for a file type, if you add a new action (call up View/Options in Explorer, go to the File Types tab, and hit Edit and then New), placing an & in front of a letter in the name makes that letter the accelerator key for the new command.

Select a submenu name with the mouse or accelerator and down pops a submenu. There are many conventions about what symbols in a submenu mean.

- No special symbol means that an immediate action is taken. Since top menu choices normally invoke submenus in those rare programs that take immediate actions from the top menu bar, the sign this is going to happen is an exclamation point. So if a menu item says **Format!** rather than **Format,** you'd better be sure you know what's about to be formatted with no questions asked!

- If the choice is going to just invoke a further submenu, then the symbol ▶ appears to the right of the menu choice. The sub-submenu is called a cascading submenu.

- If the menu choice is going to invoke a dialog box (I'll talk about them later), the choice is followed by an ellipsis—that is, . . .

- If a submenu choice isn't available, it will often still appear, but in a lighter gray color (said to be "grayed out").

- Some menu items act as a toggle—for example, determining whether a toolbar is displayed or not. If the option is toggled on, the menu item will appear with a ✓ to its left (not the right, as for other symbols).

- If there is an accelerator key for a menu option giving you a shortcut to invoke the item without traversing the menus, then the accelerator key is shown to the right of the menu choice; it is right-justified. Not all programs are thoughtful enough to provide this great educational tool in their shortcuts—kudos to those that do. Especial kudos to those programs that let you assign menu items to your own choices of accelerator keys and then display those choices for you on the menus.

The Interface Guidelines discusses five common submenus found on the menu bar of many applications. Although the Windows 3.1 *Interface Guide* goes into these menu items in great detail, Windows 95 *Interface Guidelines* is much more relaxed, probably because the standards for what *Open* and the like mean are so well understood! I'll mainly quote from the Windows 3.1 *Guide* because it still applies. (I've changed *Print* and added a discussion of *Send . . . .*)

The File menu is supposed to have the following entries:

New or New. . .	Ctrl+N	Should always be the first item; should create a new document with a standard name like Untitled; the . . . is for programs that let you set document size, pick a template to base the new document on, or otherwise ask for information first.
Open. . .	Ctrl+O	This should lead to the Windows common dialog, discussed later.
Close		Optional item for programs allowing multiple document to be open. Closes the active document. Note that the "Close" command on the system menu closes the application, so it is like an Exit command on the File menu rather than like the Close command. A certain logic, but confusing nonetheless.
Save	Ctrl+S	If the document has never been saved, this entry should invoke Save As. . . Otherwise, it just saves the file.
Save As		Also should use the Windows common dialog. It allows renaming of document before saving, as well as change of format.
Print or Print. . .	Ctrl+P	This should normally occur with the ellipses and invoke the Windows Common Dialog Print.

P<u>r</u>int Setup	You shouldn't find this command on programs written for Windows 95, since what used to be called Printer Setup has been subsumed into the Properties button in the Print common dialog. You will find this command on the File menu of many Windows 3.x applications.
Send. . .	This should invoke Exchange to let you "print" to a FAX or send the document via email.
E<u>x</u>it	This should be the last command on the <u>F</u>ile menu.

 In the *Mother of All Windows Books,* Mom complained that the Windows 3.1 *Interface Guide* listed no accelerator keys for Save and the other File menu commands. I am pleased to say that Microsoft listens, and with Windows 95 we now list `Ctrl+O, Ctrl+S,` and `Ctrl+P` for <u>O</u>pen, <u>S</u>ave, and <u>P</u>rint. So `Ctrl+S` should save even without reaching for the mouse.

 It's about time, fuzzface. Alas, it is so late that I'll bet we see quite a few programs released for Windows 95 that don't implement them.

The <u>E</u>dit menu largely refers to clipboard-related commands—I'll discuss the clipboard later in detail; for now, I note it's a place that programs can use to exchange data both within the application and between distinct applications. I'll defer the discussion of OLE object commands (like Paste Special, Link, and Object) until my discussion of OLE. Here's what is supposed to be on the Edit menu:

<u>U</u>ndo	`Ctrl+Z`	Not appropriate for all programs, but implementing it most separates the user-friendly program from the pack. Those few programs with a multilevel undo are especially blessed. If the last action can't be undone, this command should be grayed and optionally changed to *Can't Undo.*
Cu<u>t</u>	`Ctrl+X` (`Shift+Del`)	This copies selected data to the Clipboard and deletes it from the application. "Selected" data has a special meaning in Windows that I'll explain in "For the Select Few" later. This command should be grayed out if there is no currently selected data.
<u>C</u>opy	`Ctrl+C` (`Ctrl+Ins`)	Copies the selected data to the clipboard without deleting it from the application. Like Cut, it should be grayed out if nothing is selected.

<u>P</u>aste	`Ctrl+V` `(Shift+Ins)`	Copies data from the clipboard to the current insertion point (for text, where typing would enter text) in your document. If there is selected data, the clipboard contents should replace that data. This item should be grayed out if the clipboard has no data or does not have data in a form appropriate for the current insertion point.
Delete		Like Cut, it removes the current selection from the document, but it doesn't change the clipboard.
Repeat		This repeats the last action.
Find and Replace		This can invoke Windows common dialogs, although some applications need to use specialized dialogs.

The key combination in parentheses are the ones that were standard in Windows 2.x and 3.0. Microsoft, in what I think was a terrible blunder in interface consistency, changed them to something close to the Mac keystrokes (the Macintosh doesn't have a `Ctrl` key, but it has one called `Command`. Paste on a Mac is `Command+V`). I guess they figured they'd rather be like the Mac than like OS/2! *Interface Guidelines* clearly states that while the new keystrokes should be implemented and appear on the Edit menu, the old-style keystrokes should also be implemented but undocumented. Alas, too many vendors don't pay attention, so we have a mishmash—some programs that use only the old keystrokes, some that use only the new, and some that allow both. As usual, we poor users take it on the chin. The moral is that if you are used to one key combination and it doesn't work in some application, try the other or go to the menus rather than assume something is broken. Cheer up—in about five years, it should be cleared up and the new `Ctrl+X`, and others, will be in place.

The View menu, often the third menu, should give us ways to change the view of our data and turn on/off special panels like a toolbox in a paint program. The last menus are the <u>W</u>indow menu, relevant for multiple-document applications, and the Help menu.

Good Dialogs Are the Key to a Healthy Relationship

It's like Britain, only with buttons.

—Ringo Starr describing the United States in a 1965 BBC interview

More terminology. Menu items that end with . . . and a variety of buttons and other actions while you run Windows produce dialog boxes—panels, sometimes without border, that allow you to communicate with the program. The elements of the dialog are called controls. Programs can implement their own custom controls. I'll describe the most common controls to keep you in touch with the lingo.

Figure 2-4 shows a dialog with lots of trimmings. At the right side are what are called *command buttons* or just *buttons*. Most often, you'll execute a button by clicking it. If you look closely, one of the buttons sometimes has a highlight around it. That's the one that will get executed if you hit the Enter key. If a non–button control is highlighted—say, you are typing in a string and there is a button labeled OK, then Enter is supposed to execute it. If there is a button marked Cancel, then the Esc key should enter it.

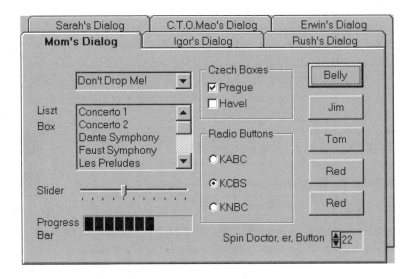

Figure 2-4. Let's dialog personal, like

 Psst, CTO, I get the Belly and the pair of Reds, but what's with Jim and Tom?

 Jim Button is the author of PC File and one of the fathers of shareware. Tom Button is an obscure Microsoft executive in the Visual Basic Group—at least, he used to be obscure.

I'll pay a lot of attention to keyboard ways to drive a dialog box. If the dialog has some places you need to type in a word, moving your hand from the keyboard to mouse and back can be a pain and a half, so it pays to learn the keyboard methods.

Often a button will have an underlined character like menus have. As with a menu, they are indications of accelerator keys. A button called <u>T</u>om with an underlined T can be executed from anywhere by hitting `Alt+T`. But there is one difference with a menu. If you have a menu called Forma<u>t</u>, you can pull it down with either `Alt+T` or by first hitting `Alt` and then `T`. With a button called Forma<u>t</u>, you can only use `Alt+T`, not the two separate keystrokes.

Several controls in a dialog can be grouped together by surrounding them with a big box called a *frame*. It's especially common to group together several check boxes and/or radio buttons, so I'll talk about those next.

One control consists of some text written to the right of a box □ which sometimes appears with an ✓ like so ☑. It is called a check box. When the check is there the box is "checked." Check boxes are for options that are on or off—checked means on. It may be that sometimes when you call up a dialog, it refers to several objects at once; for example, you might select some text in a word processor and call up a character formatting dialog that includes a check box for *Italic*. If all the selected text is italic, the box is checked; if none is, it is unchecked. But what if some of the text is italic and some not? In that case, the box is gray. Clicking once will check it and turn on the option for all selected items and clicking again would turn it off for all.

The keyboard way to toggle a checkbox is to use the `space bar`.

A dialog can have any number of check boxes, grouped or not, and each box can be checked/unchecked independently of the others, even others in the same group.

A *radio button* is a control with some text written to the right of a circle. Sometimes the circle is filled in like KCBS in Figure 2-4. The name comes from the fact that these are supposed to look like the on/off switches on an old radio—talk about obscure! Normally several radio buttons are grouped together inside a single group.

Interface Guidelines calls them *option buttons,* not radio buttons, but the rest of the world uses *radio button.*

Radio buttons are intended for mutually exclusive choices. That means that only a single radio button can be clicked in each group. A dialog can have several groups of radio buttons, each in its own group. If there is a set of related choices to be made that are not mutually exclusive, they'll appear as several check boxes in a single frame. Check boxes are used for true/false questions and radio buttons for multiple-choice questions. (Windows programmers hate grading essay questions, so you won't find many of those.)

Figure 2-4 illustrates a number of other elements of dialog boxes:

- As Windows programs became feature-rich, dialogs became more and more complex or invoked additional dialogs with scores of buttons. Then someone had the idea of the *tabbed dialog,* as shown. The metaphor is like a box of cards in a file with tabs sticking up. Click on the tab you want to access the underlying dialog.

- Dialogs often require you to choose from canned lists. The most common controls for displaying such lists are the list box and the drop-down list, both shown in Figure 2-4.

- Increasing a number is often done with a slider or with a spin button. Both are shown in Figure 2-4.

- A progress bar is a control that a program can use to show, er, progress.

Some of these simple controls are combined with an edit box to provide "combo controls." The most common examples are combo drop-down list boxes and combo edit/spin controls.

For items in a list of alphabetized names, hitting a letter key is supposed to take you to the first item that starts with that letter, hitting the letter a second time will take you to the next item, and so on. That means that the default Windows behavior for drop-down lists won't let you easily get to the first item starting with "St" if you have lots of "S" items. For combo boxes where you'll start entering a full name, "St" should scroll to the first "St" item. This different behavior in the two cases is doubly unfortunate—it means two controls with a similar look behave differently and it prevents an attractive behavior for list boxes of multiletter searches.

Four keystrokes help you navigate dialogs when you don't want to take your hands off the keyboard:

`Tab`	Moves to the next control on the dialog
`Shift+Tab`	Moves to the previous control on the dialog
`Ctrl+Tab`	Moves to the next tab in tabbed dialogs
`Ctrl+Shift+Tab`	Moves to the previous tab in tabbed dialogs

Each dialog has a *tab order* set by the programmer assigning a number to each button, drop-down list, and other control. As you hit Tab, you cycle through successively higher numbers (until you reach the highest number, in which case Tab moves to the control with the lowest tab order number). Shift+Tab cycles in the opposite direction.

The Wizard Behind the Curtain

Toto, we're not in Kansas anymore.

—L. Frank Baum, *Wonderful Wizard of Oz,* 1900

Windows is peopled with wizards to help you through common tasks. Not only that, the Windows SDK makes wizard technology available to application vendors, so you're likely to see these a lot. The main point here is to let you know what the name means so when I or someone else refers to a wizard, you don't think "huh?" A typical wizard screen is shown later in the chapter in Figure 2-17. Wizards take you through a sequence of dialogs that has you fill in the blanks in little steps. Usually there are three buttons on the bottom of each dialog: <Back, Next>, and Cancel. In the first screen <Back is grayed out; in the final screen, Next> becomes Finished. Wizards often branch on what you choose in earlier screens. You get to step back if you realize that you made a mistake in any earlier screen.

There isn't much to say except to point out that using wizards usually is a pleasure and that you'll find a wizard during the installation of Windows 95 and wizards to add a Printer, to add new Hardware, and to do many other actions.

I'm not real fond of Microsoft but I have to admit they did a great job on this wizard stuff. Not only is the basic scheme a good one, but whoever designed the actual wizards in Windows 95 did a great job. Even formerly unpleasant tasks are kinda fun. Hmmm. Maybe they could design a root canal wizard?

Belly Up to the Button Bar

If you press exactly the right buttons and are also lucky, justice may show up.

—Raymond Chandler, *The Long Goodbye,* 1953

User interfaces evolve—no doubt about it. They are not given from on high and set in stone. Vendors experiment with devices that go beyond the defined UI, and users, by their reactions, can cause de facto standards to arise. A great example of this is the tool bar, aka button bar, aka a lot of other names.

Made up of often inscrutable little icons that puzzled users, button bars were nevertheless such an effective shortcut that they became wildly popular, inscrutability and all.

Obviously, the easiest way to avoid inscrutability is to have some standard buttons used by all applications, because that way even the inscrutable can become scrutable. *Interface Guidelines* defines the twenty-four standard icons shown in Figure 2-5. The first thirteen are standard menu functions, the next is appropriate for situations where objects have property sheets, and the next three are font attributes. The eighteenth button is for context-sensitive help and the next for the contents page of the full application help file. The last four have to do with the views available for the common list control, which I'll discuss in the section called "Common Controls."

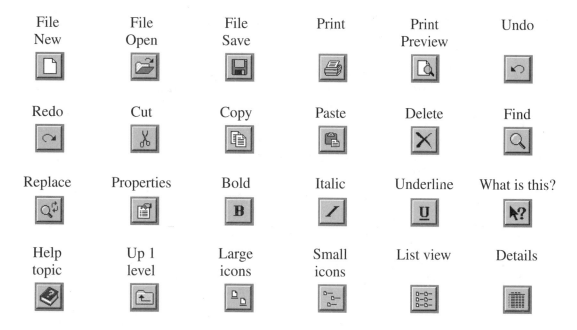

Figure 2-5. Button, button, who's got the button?

The *Guidelines* define three other less-usual icons.

Let's see how the theory of *The Interface Guidelines* stands up against the actual button bars used by Windows 95 itself. Figure 2-6 shows the toolbars of three applications included with Win95.

WordPad

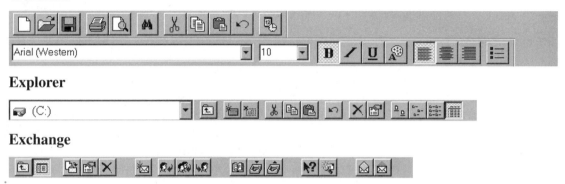

Explorer

Exchange

Figure 2-6. A tale of three toolbars

WordPad is really very close. Of the eleven buttons on the top, all are standard except that the binoculars icon is used for Find and there is a nonstandard `Insert Date/Time`. The more specific formatting buttons on the second line start with three standard ones. Except for two network-specific ones, all the buttons in Explorer are standard. On the other hand, Exchange's buttons are mainly nonstandard. They are not incompatible with the standard— just specialized functions. So Windows does very well meeting the standard of "Do not only what I say but what I do"!

 With one exception. The writer of the *Interface Guidelines* decided that `Find` is a magnifying glass but the rest of the world, not only WordPad but also Word

thinks `Find` is a binoculars, like so: .

Hey, one out of twenty-four is only about a 4 percent error. You guys sure are a tough crowd.

Besides standardized buttons, the other standard help for defeating inscrutable icons is the *Tooltip,* a little floating box of text that explains what a button does (rest the cursor over a button in WordPad to see what I mean). These are arranged not to display until the cursor has rested for a moment, so when trying to figure out what a funny-looking button does, be sure to rest the cursor there for more than a fleeting instant. Also be aware that some applications let you turn tooltips on/off with a check box in an Options dialog. So look for that if an application doesn't have tooltips.

 One last point about toolbars is that the best of breed are customizable and let you determine what functions appear there and in what order. Many Winword users aren't aware that you can customize the toolbars (check out Customize in the Tools menu and the on-line help). Of the three Windows toolbars mentioned, only Exchange lets you customize it and the method isn't nearly as slick as Winword's.

For the Select Few

Many lists in Windows dialogs are single choice lists—that is, lists that only allow you to make a single choice, just as if there were a radio button next to each item. But a few lists are multiple-choice lists—you can choose more than one item. *Interface Guidelines* specifies a convention on using a mouse to select multiple items. When items are chosen, there is one called the anchor that can be the same as the item with focus but can also be different.* The anchor is usually a selected item but not always, as I'll explain shortly. If there are no selected items, the anchor can be regarded as being identical to the item with focus.

Here is a summary:

- Clicking an item deselects any items already selected, selects the clicked item, and moves both the anchor and focus to the clicked item.

- Shift+Clicking—that is, clicking while holding down either shift key, moves the focus to the clicked item. If the anchor is currently selected, all items between the anchor and the clicked item are selected; any other items, even those selected before the Shift+Click, are not selected; the anchor doesn't move. If the anchor is currently not selected, all items are removed from the selection list.

- Ctrl+Clicking moves both the focus and the anchor to the clicked item. It toggles the selection state of the clicked item to the opposite of what it was. If you Ctrl+Click a selected item, the new item becomes an unselected anchor.

- Shift+Ctrl+Clicking (you only like this if you can wiggle your nose and twiddle your thumbs at the same time). If the anchor is currently selected, all items between the anchor and the clicked item are added to the selection list. Items outside that range

---

* The item with focus is the currently active item—it usually has a dotted line around it.

remain selected if they were previously selected. The anchor is not moved. If the anchor is currently not selected, all items between the anchor and the click item are taken off the selected list and the anchor doesn't move.

As an example, suppose you have items 1–10 in order and you do the following: `Click 2`, `Shift+Click 9`, `Ctrl+Click 4`, and finally `Shift+Ctrl+Click 6`. Here's the state after each mouse action:

After Action	Selected items	Focus	Anchor
Click 2	2	2	2
Shift+Click 9	2,3,4,5,6,7,8,9	9	2
Ctrl+Click 4	2,3,5,6,7,8,9	4	4
Shift+Ctrl+Click 6	2,3,7,8,9	6	4

Click and drag will select contiguously; that is, it will act as if you clicked the item where you start the drag and then shift-clicked the item where you stopped the drag.

In Windows 3.x, there was a keyboard method for multiple selection using the `Shift+F8` keyboard combination. It is no longer mentioned in *The Interface Guidelines* and seems not to be supported. Indeed, I could find no way to use the keyboard to make multiple noncontiguous selections in Explorer (although `Ctrl+Click` works fine).

The undocumented `Ctrl+/` and `Ctrl+\`, which worked in Windows 3.x File Manager, don't work in Explorer and presumably have gone the way of the dodo.

Most of these selection techniques work inside applications like your word processor and spreadsheet, except that noncontiguous selection may not always be sensible. For example, Winword doesn't allow noncontiguous selection of text and uses `Ctrl+Click` to select the current sentence.

Keys to the Kingdom

> Giving money and power to government is like
> giving whiskey and car keys to teenage boys.

> —P. J. O'Rourke, *Why God is a Republican and Santa Claus Is a Democrat,* 1991

It pays to remember the reserved keystrokes that Windows uses and that are common to most Winapps, both to avoid inadvertently assigning them to macros and to get into the habit of using these shortcut keys. Later on, in Chapter 3, as I come to specific core components like Desktop and Explorer, I'll discuss keystrokes specific to those components. Remember that in the previous section, "Good Dialogs are the Key to a Healthy Relationship," I described the special use that Tab with various shifts (`Shift`, `Ctrl`, and `Ctrl+Shift`) has in dialogs.

Global Keystrokes

Note: These keys even work in full-screen DOS sessions; however, if some DOS application uses one of them—say, your favorite word processor, *foowrite*, uses `Ctrl+Esc` to access its menus, you can reserve their use for that DOS session on the `Misc.` tab of the application's property sheet.

`Ctrl+Esc` This brings up the Start Menu. Using keystrokes can often be a quick route—for example hitting `Ctrl+Esc`, F, F will bring up the Find Files dialog a lot quicker than mousing around.

`Alt+Tab` This was one of the most underused, neat things in Windows 3.x and it's even neater in Win95! Hitting `Alt+Tab` cycles through your applications without actually cycling through them! Instead it displays a panel like that shown in Figure 2-7 with an icon for each running program and the window caption in text below it. The trick is to hold the `Alt` key down and hit the `Tab` key multiple times. It cycles through the applications. If you start `Alt+Tab` and change your mind, hitting `Esc` while `Alt` is still down will get you out! `Alt+Tab` only visits applications and will not include things like property sheets and wizards.

Figure 2-7. Where do you want to go today?

`Alt+Shift+Tab` This is like `Alt+Tab`, only it cycles in the opposite direction. It's unlikely you'd want to start moving with `Alt+Shift+Tab` (how could you remember which one of the currently open applications you used the longest time ago!), but if you start `Alt+Tab`bing and overshoot, `Alt+Shift+Tab` (remembering to keep the `Alt` down) will let you back up.

`Alt+Esc`

This is like `Alt+Tab`, except for two things. First, rather than showing you just the name of the application, it shifts to it, redrawing the screen and popping up the application. Secondly, unlike `Alt+Tab`, it does visit property sheets and the like. It may be the quickest way to locate a property sheet lost behind some maximized windows.

`Alt+Shift+Esc`

This is like `Alt+Esc`, except it cycles in the opposite direction.

`PrintScreen`

Here's another underused goodie. Did you know that Windows comes with its own Screen Capture utility—you know, the kind of thing you pay $39 to get all by itself? Hit `PrintScreen` (`Shift+PrtScr` on some keyboards) and Windows copies the current screen to the clipboard. When on the Windows Desktop, it is copied as a picture. In DOS text mode, it is copied as text. You do lose the convenience of DOS PrintScreen going to the printer, although by pasting from the clipboard into WordPad, shifting to Courier font, and printing, you can duplicate what DOS PrintScreen does, albeit awkwardly. This is half of the Screen Capture utility—I'll describe the other half shortly.

`Alt+PrintScreen`

In DOS mode, this does what `PrintScreen` does, but on the Windows Desktop, it copies the current window only, to the clipboard (as a bitmap).

`Alt+Spacebar`

This invokes the system menu. There's a change from Windows 3.x in how this key works in full-screen DOS sessions run. Under Windows 3.x, it shifted to a windowed DOS session, pulling down the system menu! Under Windows 95, you get shifted to the Windows Desktop with the Toolbar button for the DOS session highlighted and the system menu for it popped up. But the DOS session is not put into a window.

Other common keystrokes that you need to know about (although they are application-dependent) are the Cut/Copy/Paste commands (discussed earlier in "Waiter—Menu please." The keystrokes are either `Ctrl+X/Ctrl+C/Ctrl+V` or `Shift+Del/Ctrl+Ins/Shift+Ins`, depending on the application), the DOS session `Alt+Enter` (which toggles between full screen and windowed DOS session and which I discuss in Chapter 3), and `Alt+F4` (which closes most applications).

The free screen capture is so useful that I want to describe it in detail. Hit `PrintScreen` or `Alt+PrintScreen` to place the whole screen or the active window on the clipboard. Then start *Paint.* Go to the Image/Attributes . . . menu choice and make sure the height and width are smaller than what you captured (for example, you could pick 400 ✕

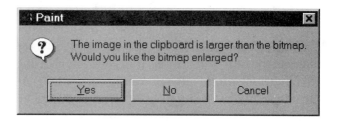

Figure 2-8. A clean capture

300 if you captured an 800 ✕ 600 screen). Now choose Paste from the Edit menu and answer Yes to the dialog in Figure 2-8.

The Interface Guidelines also encourages applications to use these keystrokes where appropriate: `Ctrl+S`, `Ctrl+O`, `Ctrl+P`, and `Ctrl+Z` for the File/Save, File/Open, File/Print, and Edit/Undo menu choices. Also `F1` is the same as Help Topics and

`Shift+F1` is the same as the "What is this?" button ( ). `Shift+F10` brings up an object's context menu just like right-clicking on it.

Hey!! You! Pay attention. Look at me when I talk to you. I'm tired of your skimming the good stuff and missing it. You probably figure keystrokes are boring and you are only looking at this section, hoping for some good jokes but not looking much at what it says. And then I tell you about `Shift+F10` in a single sentence that you could easily miss. This is a REALLY NEAT keyboard shortcut. It works in Windows itself and in well-behaved Windows 95 applications. For example, if you are typing in Winword 7.0 and see a wavy underline indicating a spelling error, no need to reach for the mouse if you remember that `Shift+F10` will do the same thing as a right mouse click.

Super Natural Keyboard

> Whatever the scientists may say, if we take the supernatural out of life,
> we leave only the unnatural.
>
> —Amelia Barr, *All the Days of My Life*

The Microsoft Natural Keyboard includes three keys special to Windows 95. I expect many keyboards will start coming with them. Two are identical and are squeezed in between the two sets of `Ctrl` and `Alt` keys and are marked with the Windows logo. Their behavior is the same—they are called the *Windows key* and I'll call them `Win`. As with `Alt`, `Win` is a shift—that is, it can be used with other keys—you hold down `Win` and press the second key.

The third special key is the *Application key* and is located to the right of the right-hand `Win` key. The Application key pops up the context menu for any active object in the shell—for example, a selected drive or the Desktop as a whole. It thus acts the same as a right mouse click on the object. However, it is *not* a keyboard equivalent of the right mouse button or `Shift+F10` within all applications—the application can define it to have a special meaning if it likes.

Here are the special things that you can do with the `Win` key (the ones after `Shift+Win+M` require that you install version 1.1 or later of the software drivers that come with the keyboard):

`Win`	Pops up Start Menu (same as `Ctrl+Esc`)
`Win+F`	Pops up Find File dialog (same as `Ctrl+Esc, F, F`)
`Win+Ctrl+F`	Pops up Find Computer dialog (same as `Ctrl+Esc, F, C`)
`Win+F1`	Pops up Windows Help topics (same as `Ctrl+Esc, H`)
`Win+R`	Pops up the Run dialog (same as `Ctrl+Esc, R`)
`Win+E`	Pops up Explore My Computer (same as right click on My Computer, Explore)
`Win+M`	Minimizes all windows (same as right click on Taskbar, Minimize...)
`Shift+Win+M`	Undoes Minimize All Windows (same as right click Taskbar, Undo...)
`Win+P`	Opens Printers Folder
`Win+C`	Opens Control Panel
`Win+V`	Views Clipboard
`Win+K`	Opens Keyboard Properties
`Win+I`	Opens Mouse Properties
`Win+A`	Opens Accessibility Options
`Win+Space`	Pops up a list of `Win+` hotkeys
`Win+Break`	Opens System Properties

I didn't much like the Natural Keyboard when I tried it. The feel is mushy and I'm a lover of the IBM/Northgate/Lexmark firm keyboard. And the split and twist was something that I couldn't get used to. But hey, the P in PC stands for something, and some folks probably like these aspects.

Microsoft is encouraging manufacturers to include a Win key with their keyboard, and I suspect all of them will before too long. Windows has built in support for the keys just listed up to Shift+Win+M, but not the Win+P and after. These come from the special drivers in the Natural Keyboard.

When I first tested the Natural Keyboard without its software, I had a problem: when I pressed down the Win key, the Start Menu popped up at the point I released the Win key. That's fine. If I hit Win+F, the File Find dialog popped up right away. But a fair fraction of the time, when I released the Win key, the Start Menu popped up, so I had to hit Esc before accessing the Find dialog.

Investigation showed that this behavior was due to an interesting bug. The Microsoft Mouse software in versions 8.x and 9.x included two files intended for Windows 3.x called pointer.dll and pointer.exe. These provided popular features like Snap To, and also provided support for hitting the Win key on the Natural Keyboard to do the same as Ctrl+Esc. This popped up the Task Manager in Windows 3.x, but pops up the Start Menu in Windows 95.

Because the extra mouse features were popular, the Windows 95 designers updated pointer.* to work with Windows 95. If Windows 95 finds these files on your disk it installs the new versions to work with Windows 95. But because they wanted to encourage keyboard makers to include the Win key, support for it was built into the Windows 95 standard keyboard driver. So when I pressed Win+F, the keyboard driver popped up the Find File dialog and it was smart enough to set a flag to not pop up the Start Menu when I released the Win key. But pointer.dll was also in the system, and it popped up the Start Menu. Oh, how I love a nice bug in the mornin'.

There are two solutions to this problem. The best (if you have the Microsoft keyboard) is to contact Microsoft and update the keyboard software to version 1.1 or later. It has a pointer32.dll replacement for pointer.dll, which fixes the problem and gives you the extra combinations from Win+P onwards listed earlier. Otherwise, you'll have to live with the problem or delete pointer.* (and lose the extra mouse goodies they provide).

Mice Is Nice but MouseKeys Is Slicker

There isn't much to say about mouse actions because there aren't many actions: you can move the beast, you can click (quickly press and release a mouse button) one or both buttons, double-click the buttons, or drag and drop (drag means to press a button down and move the mouse while keeping the button depressed; drop means to then release the button). On three-button mice, you obviously have other options. Logitech told Mom they'd have software to enhance their mice to use the third button beyond the driver that ships with Windows 95 itself, so be sure to contact Logitech if you have one of their mice!

 My favorite obscure mouse trick is habit-forming once you get used to it. If you press down the `Alt` key while double-clicking an object, the property sheet for that object should open. It certainly works for objects controlled by the Windows 95 shell-like icons on the Desktop.

Windows 95 includes a really neat option called MouseKeys that, except for one flaw, is an ultimate version of the kind of programs intended to give mouse functionality to laptop users without mice. It's part of the Accessibility packages, so you might miss it because the other components of Accessibility are of interest to the otherwise enabled. Although MouseKeys is clearly of interest to some users with disabilities, it is also of interest to users who like the keyboard and hate always reaching for the mouse.

When MouseKeys is on and active, the arrow keys on the numeric keypad move the cursor in the direction of the arrows, and the `Home`/`End`/`PgUp`/`PgDn` keys move the cursor diagonally. By holding down the `Ctrl` or `Shift` key while moving the cursor, you can speed up or slow down the cursor motion.

The `Center` key (5 on the keypad) is the same as single click. The number pad `Plus` is the same as double-click. By default, these clicks are with the left mouse button. However, if you hit the `Minus` on the keypad, you shift to mode where `Center`/`Plus` has the effect of clicking the right button. Hitting keypad `Slash` returns to the mode where the left button is simulated.

The `Ins` key is the same as pressing the mouse button and holding it down, so that after pressing `Ins`, moving the cursor keys will drag. After `Ins` is pushed, `Del` has the effect of dropping the object—that is, it simulates releasing the mouse button. Normally, these keys simulate a left drag, but if you've pressed the `Minus` key, they will simulate a right button drag.

To turn MouseKeys on, you need to call up the Accessibility applet in Control Panel and click on the Mouse tab. You'll want to click Settings at least the first time to configure how it works.

When the MouseKeys option is turned on, NumLock toggles between whether the MouseKeys is active or not. If you check the `Show MouseKey status on screen` box in the MouseKeys Settings dialog (Figure 2-9), a `mouse` icon is displayed in the notification area of the Taskbar with a "not" symbol superimposed on it when the option is on but MouseKeys is inactive. A radio button in that dialog determines whether the active state is with NumLock on or off.

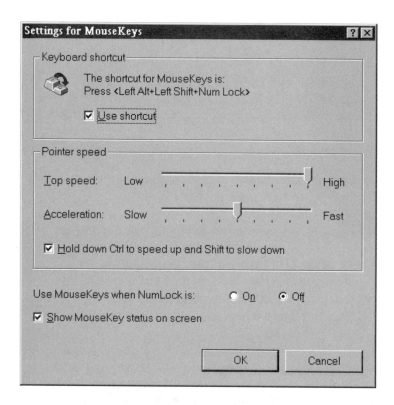

Figure 2-9. Nibble, nibble little MouseKeys

 If you are used to using the cursor keys on the numeric keypad but don't use the number pad much, configure MouseKeys to be active when NumLock is on. If you tend to use the cursor tee for movement of the typewriter cursor, then configure MouseKeys to be active when NumLock is off. When you configure it that way, you get typewriter cursor motion from the cursor keys, mouse cursor motion from the number pad cursor mode, and number pad when you turn NumLock on.

If you check the "Use Shortcut" box you can toggle between MouseKeys being enabled by using the `Left Alt+Left Shift+NumLock` combination.

MouseKeys is incredibly nice for users with full-size keyboards, but it sure does leave laptop users in the lurch. Lots of laptop users would love to have a hotkey that turned on a MouseKey-like feature but applied to the cursor keys on the laptop. Since they don't simulate the numeric keypad but instead the cursor T, MouseKeys as currently implemented doesn't help laptop users a bit. Sigh.

You may think it strange that MouseKeys doesn't do squat on a laptop. But you have to realize that it was originally developed by the hardware group that makes the Natural Keyboard and so was made for that keyboard. The Windows group coopted the software for Accessibility purposes but it was already written. Since several laptop vendors are pressuring Microsoft to make MouseKeys work with a laptop, it is inevitable it will before too long.

Objection, Your Honor

> To *make* oneself an object, to *make* oneself passive,
> is a very different thing from *being* a passive object.

—Simone de Beauvoir, *The Second Sex,* 1953

Everything you see on the screen is an object. That goes for program windows, for dialogs, and for buttons in dialogs, and it goes for the Desktop, the Start button and the Taskbar. To say it is an object means that it is something on which you can perform actions. This idea of objects and actions will be central as we look at some common threads in the Windows 95 UI.

Studies have shown that some users freak out at the mention of objects; they stare off in space and . . . . Well, just relax, it's just a fancy-pants word for a piece of the user interface that you can interact with!

Right On

> Inanimate objects are classified scientifically into three major categories—
> those that don't work, those that break down and those that get lost.

—Russell Baker, *New York Times,* June 18, 1968

If I have any piece of advice to someone who is exploring the interface of Windows 95, or a program written to run with Windows 95, it's, "Don't forget the mouse right button." Especially, don't forget to right-click everywhere to see what pops up.

The Windows 95 Interface is based on the notion that when you right-click on an object, it brings up a menu of actions and options for that object. There is even a right-click menu in the edit boxes that you find in dialogs where you are asked to type in text strings!

This menu is called a *context menu* or sometimes a *right-click menu.* That means, for example, if you open `My Computer` (by double-clicking on it) and right-click on a diskette drive (or even better, drag the drive to your Desktop for easy access), you'll get a menu that includes `Copy Disk . . .` and `Format. . . .` You might like to also find ScanDisk there, but it won't be—at least not on the menu. You can pick properties and get ScanDisk from there. But that's only the default menu. Most context menus can be configured. How that's done will depend on the object and will be a recurring theme as our discussion of the details of the interface picks up speed. In particular, I'll explain how to add ScanDisk to drive menus in Chapter 3. Some menu changes will require editing of the Registry and will be described in Chapters 3 and 11.

Not only can you change most of the built-in context menus, but you can even make some changes to their cascading submenus. File objects (including drives and files on the Desktop and in Explorer windows) have a menu item called `Send To`. I'll explain how to configure that later in this chapter in the section "The Tree-Based Menu." Blank pieces of Explorer windows and the Desktop have a branching submenu called `New`. I'll show you how to configure that in Chapter 11.

Basically, almost anything in Windows can be configured. Of the few exceptions, the most notable is the right-click menu that pops up over the Desktop (where I only know how to change the New submenu). If you think you can configure something but don't know how, look it up in the index to this book!

Keep in mind that what you may think of as a single object might be many and might have many context menus depending on precisely where you right-click. You might think of the Taskbar as a single thingee, but you get separate context menus for the Start button for a blank part of the Taskbar for each task button and for each different icon in the notification area!

At the bottom of each context menu is typically a choice called *Properties,* which lets you change intrinsic aspects of an object. Some objects call up property sheets that you might not expect, but they provide very quick shortcuts. The Properties choice on `My Computer` brings up the Control Panel System applet. The Desktop properties is the same as the Display applet of the Control Panel. The Taskbar properties is the same as hitting Start, then Settings, then Taskbar. Properties of Network Neighborhood is, not too surprisingly, the same as the Network applet of Control Panel. Properties of the `Inbox` icon is the same Mail and Fax applet in Control Panel.

Drag 'til You Drop

> A drawing is always dragged down to the level of its caption.

—James Thurber, *New Yorker*, Aug. 2, 1930

 Oh, you think you're a hotshot, don't you? You heard my advice about right-clicking everywhere and so now you think you know it all. Well, I haven't finished reading you your rights. It's also important to know about right-drag and drop!

Windows 95 is highly drag-and-drop enabled. That means you should expect that, under most circumstances, the shell and well-made programs written for Windows 95 will accept transfer of information via dragging and dropping. This works in cases you might not expect. Open both a windowed DOS session and an Explorer window. Grab a filename in the Explorer window and drag it to the DOS window. When you drop the file, its full pathname will be entered at the DOS command line. This happens also in any DOS program, which can be very handy for dealing with old DOS programs that don't have a "browse for file" capability.

 Yeah, but what about programs that won't take full pathnames? There is no way to enter just the directory name or just the filename. It would be good if a right drag could bring up a menu of choices like "full name," "directory," and "filename," or if `Ctrl` or `Shift` would work. But they don't—you get the full pathname whether you want it or not.

 Yes, but at least we are smart enough not to paste long filenames. The assumption is that DOS programs don't understand long filenames, so if you drag `My long file name.doc` in `D:\My Documents` to a DOS command line, what gets pasted in is something like `D:\MYDOCU~1\MYLONG~1.DOC`.*

---

* I'll discuss how short 8+3 filenames are associated to long filenames a few sections from now.

And of course, the Windows shell is usually Drag-and-Drop enabled. If you open the Run dialog and drag a filename to it from Explorer, the full pathname is pasted in. Since you can run a program by double-clicking it, you won't often use this for programs. However, if a program needs another filename as a parameter, it is often simplest to use Start Menu's Find command to locate the file and then drag it from the Find results window to a Run window. Another time this comes in handy is when you locate a program you want to run in Explorer but you want to run it with parameters. Hit `Ctrl+Esc, R, Del` (the final `Del` blanks the Run box) and drag the name to the Run box and add the parameters.

Ah, but the design team fell down in at least one place. You'd certainly expect that the Target field in a shortcut's property sheet could get a filename by dragging the file from an Explorer window but it can't. That's really a pain if your target has a long path, so it would be a nuisance to either type it in (and risk typos) or navigate through a Browse dialog.

Under such circumstances, I've found it useful to hit `Ctrl+Esc, R, Del`, drag the file to the Run box, hit `Shift+Del, Esc` to cut that filename to the clipboard, close the Run dialog, and finally, paste the name into the shortcut property sheet. It may not be any less effort but you feel more in control!

When dragging and dropping a file from one Explorer window to another or to the Desktop, there are generally three actions that can occur. The file can be moved or copied, or a shortcut to the file can be created. As seen in Figure 2-10, Windows gives subtle feedback to tell you what is going to happen. You see pieces of actual screen shots of dragging a file in suitable ways. If the result of the drag will be to move the file, the cursor "picks up" the filename as seen on the left. If the result is going to be a copy then a plus is added, as in the middle panel. Finally, the standard shortcut symbol is added if a shortcut is going to be made.

Move File   **Copy File**   **Make Shortcut**

   Dragged File   Dragged File   Dragged File

Figure 2-10. A tale of three dragons

The visual clues are important because Explorer isn't consistent about what drag and drop does, in that its action depends on the file type and on whether the source and destination drives are the same or different. The basic rules are that, by default, dragging a program creates a shortcut to the program, dragging another file within the same drive moves it, and dragging it between drives copies it. Such behavior is downright confusing.

Actually Rush, it is disconcerting to the users who always pay attention and feel they have to learn these rules. But if you think about it, you'll agree that the default does what the naïve user wants 90 percent of the time, probably more. And if you don't want the default you can always use right-drag and drop or the `Shift` keys.

I'd better expand on Billy's ways out. The first is the way that Mom mentioned at the start of this section. Targets for a drag-and-drop operation can provide you with several different options when you drag and drop, although one must be the default option. If you drag and drop with the left button, then when you drop, the default action happens. If you right-drag and drop (that is, depress and hold the right mouse button while dragging), then when you drop, a menu of options will pop up with the default option in bold. You then get to pick among the options. For example if you right-drag and drop a program to the Desktop, you'll get the menu shown in Figure 2-11.

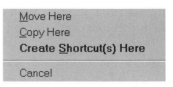

Figure 2-11. Right is better

The second set of methods for controlling what happens on the drop concerns the special meaning of shifts when you left-drag and drop on a target that is part of the Windows 95 shell, such as the Desktop or an Explorer window. If you hold down `Shift`, the object is always moved. If you hold down `Ctrl`, the object is always copied. If you hold down `Ctrl+Shift`, you get the same menu as you would if you right-dragged.

It is especially important to note that you don't need to be holding down the shifts at the time you start to drag, only at the point you drop. This has two important consequences. First, if you forget which of `Ctrl` or `Shift` means copy and which move but you remember that copy gives the plus sign in the icon, you can just try each shift and see what happens to the `drag` icon. Secondly, if you realize in mid-drag that you really wanted to right-drag and drop because you know that the default action is wrong, you can always hold down `Ctrl+Shift` and get the same effect as if you did right-drag and drop.

If you press `Ctrl+Shift`, the icon adds the shortcut symbol, but that only indicates that `Create Shortcut Here` will be the default—you always get the right-drag menu with those shifts down.

But remember that these shifts are only sure to work if the target is a Windows 95 shell object. They may not work in other places, whereas the right drag is always supposed to produce a menu.

Yeah, Mom, maybe that's theory but Winword 7.0 sure didn't understand that. Right-drag a file `*.txt` file to Winword and you should get a menu with Cancel as one of the options, but that ain't what Winword does. It merely inserts it as an OLE object. If Microsoft can't even get it right in their flagship application . . .

It will sometimes happen that you start a drag and realize that you don't want to drag after all. Hitting `Esc` will cancel the drag. You can also look for a target that isn't legal—the mouse cursor turns into the universal NO sign of a circle with a slash—and drop it there, which is the same as aborting the drag.

One final drag-and-drop trick to mention: Suppose you want to drag something to a running application on the toolbar. It might be minimized or it might be behind some other window. For example, suppose you have a `*.doc` file in Explorer that you want to open in a copy of Word that is already running. If the Word window were visible, you could drop the file to the Word titlebar and it would open that document. Instead, drag it to the Word button on the Taskbar and hold it there—do not drop it on the button. After you hold it over the button for a moment, Word will open and you can drop it where you want. This will work for any program, not just Word.

Bah, humbug. Why not just let me drop the filename on the button? Why make me hold it over the button until the application opens?

Because the program may act differently, depending on where the filename is dropped. Word will open the file if you drop the name on the toolbar but will imbed it if you drop it in an open document.

Common Dialogs

The greatest benefit of a GUI has nothing to do with the "graphical" part—it's really something called a CUI. CUI, the Common User Interface, refers to the fact that well-written Windows programs look and behave very similarly.

—Woody Leonhard and Barry Simon, *The Mother of All Windows Books,* 1993

In the Wild West world that was DOS, every time you got a new program, you had to learn its idiosyncratic way of opening files, printing them, saving them, and so on. When Sheriff Windows rode into town, this changed. A new paradigm arose: standard actions in programs should go through a standard series of steps so that once you've learned to open a file in one program, you should be able to open it in all programs. This not only means common menu locations (for example, `File/Open`) and shortcut keys (for example, `Ctrl+O`) but that the same dialog should be used. To this end, Windows, starting with Windows 3.1, provides a set of common dialogs that programs are strongly encouraged to use for a variety of functions:

- **File** functions, most notably for File Open and File Save As, but also for actions like Inset Picture

- **Print** and **Print Setup** (in Windows 3.1 but not Windows 95); **Page Setup** (in Windows 95)

- **Find** and **Find and Replace**

- **Font** picking and **Color** picking

Most of these dialogs are fairly straightforward so they will not be discussed in depth. The main exception is the File functions dialog—there are some tips you need to know for this. I'll also mention the Print dialog. I show the color picker in Figure 2-36 and discuss custom colors in the section "Some of My Friends Are Pals and Some Are Palettes."

Figure 2-12 shows the Windows 95 Open common dialog. A similar dialog is used for Save and Save As. Much of the dialog is obvious—there's a drive drop-down list at the top but it shows more than drives. As you choose directories in the large area, the directory is listed and the drop-down will show the directory and its parents. You can also use the first button (🔼) to go up the tree one step—Backspace will do the same thing.

Figure 2-12. The open common dialog

If you keep going up, at the top you reach Desktop, which is a little strange since Desktop is also `C:\windows\Desktop`. What's worse, if you reach Desktop and it has a drive icon labeled C and you pick that thinking you'll get a directory of C, you may wind up opening `C:\windows\Desktop\c.lnk`!

 There is logic to placing Desktop at the top where it is the most accessible. Users with simple needs are always losing their files. We encourage them to save files on the Desktop where they are "in sight." Such users are likely to access their drive icons through a `My Computer` window, which does act the way you'd expect on the Desktop—that is, choosing it gives you a list of drives to pick from. It is also convenient to have Desktop at the top because it gives you direct access to Network Neighborhood and files on any hard drive shared over the network.

To expand on what Billy says, if you open the drive drop-down, you'll find Network Neighborhood on it—choose it and you'll be able to access files the same as you do from Network Neighborhood. You can also type UNCs directly into the field that says "File name." I'll say more about Network Neighborhood and UNC names at the end of this chapter and in the next.

The other buttons on the top of the Open dialog are also worth noting. will make a new subdirectory. 🔳 shifts from the view in Figure 2-12, where there are several columns of directory/filenames, to a "details view," where there is only one file or folder per row but that row has columns for name, size, file type, and modification date. 🔳 shifts back to the view with lots of rows of files. By the way, in details view, clicking on the column headers sorts on that column and clicking twice sorts in reverse order.

 Just looking at these buttons and the drop-down list misses the power of this dialog. The Open File dialog file list area is essentially a small Explorer window with all the power that entails.

What Mom is saying is that the Open dialog has right-click context menus and that it can be a drag-and-drop source or target. You don't need the New Subdirectory button—if you right-click on a blank space in the file list, you'll get a right-click menu with a New submenu from which you can pick Folder. If you single-click on a file or folder name to select it and then right-click, you get the same kind of context menu that you get in Explorer (I'll describe this in some detail in the next chapter). For example, you can Quick View files that have quick viewers and the entire SendTo menu is accessible to you.

You can also delete files from the Open or Save dialog either with the Del key or by dragging them to the Recycle Bin.

As for drag and drop and the Open dialog, you can move, copy, and so on from an Open dialog to the Desktop or an Explorer window or in the other direction. You could even drag a file in an Open dialog to a Folder icon in the same dialog and thereby move the file from the current folder to the subfolder you dragged it to!

Windows 3.1 programs that are run under Windows 95 will not use the new File Open dialogs. In essence, they use the old common dialogs (Figure 2-13), albeit with a new look (Figure 2-14).

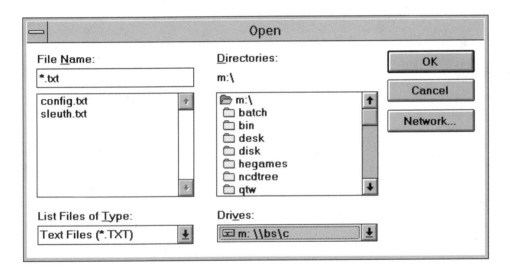

Figure 2-13. The Windows 3.1 common dialog

These Windows 3.1 dialogs not only lack the power of the Windows 95 dialogs but they don't support long filenames.

 Bah, humbug. Microsoft should have included long filename support in the dialogs that Win 3.1 programs use when running under Windows 95. Initially they said they expected to, but then they claimed they were unable to do it. But guess what? Norton has done it in Norton Navigator, as have several other utilities makers. So much for being unable to do it.

Figure 2-14. The Windows 95 common dialog for 16 bit apps

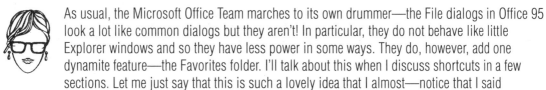

The problem is that Win16 apps are linked with a fixed stack size. Many Win16 applications that use the common dialogs were tested under Windows 3.1 and may possibly be borderline in their usage of stack space when using these dialogs. If we were to change the in-memory size of these dialogs to support long filenames, we might cause existing Win16 apps to run out of stack space. At the very minimum, long filename support would add 260 bytes just for the possible file buffer, plus whatever code was necessary to parse/convert the long filenames into 8+3 filenames. Norton Navigator can get away with adding this support because it is an ancillary product that the user doesn't have to run. If their common dialogs blow up, so what? They don't have to test their shell with 2,500 existing applications. If we add this support into *Windows*, however, then there's nowhere to turn if the app blows up. It would have added a huge extra testing effort to Microsoft and the beta user community.

As usual, the Microsoft Office Team marches to its own drummer—the File dialogs in Office 95 look a lot like common dialogs but they aren't! In particular, they do not behave like little Explorer windows and so they have less power in some ways. They do, however, add one dynamite feature—the Favorites folder. I'll talk about this when I discuss shortcuts in a few sections. Let me just say that this is such a lovely idea that I almost—notice that I said *almost!*—forgive them for deciding they are above the standard. In any event, I'd love to see Windows 95 emulate this feature in a tuneup pack.

The Print common dialog is shown in Figure 2-15. Again, it's pretty straightforward except I'd point out that you can change the printer in the drop-down list (that will just change it temporarily in the current program—I discuss permanent changes when I talk about the Printer Folder in Chapter 3). And by clicking on properties, you can access the Printer settings—for example, whether a color printer prints in black or in color.

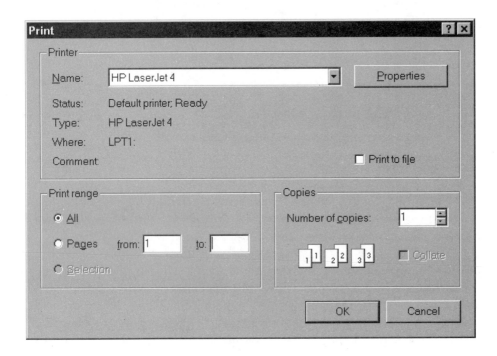

Figure 2-15. The Print common dialog

Common Controls

> Common-looking people are the best in the world:
> that is the reason the Lord makes so many of them.

> —Abraham Lincoln

Windows 95 also introduced a library of common controls beyond the simple stuff like buttons that were provided by Windows 3.x. Most of these new controls needn't concern you much—what do you care if the spin buttons that are used come from common controls or are from third parties?*

---

* Mao: You care because controls taken from the same place look the same and you needn't wonder, "Whazzat?"

You'd also care if you were blind. Our common controls now all support standard internal text labels for all functions that blind access technology screen readers can extract to enunciate to the end user. Many "roll your own" third-party controls do not support this functionality. Hence, the blind user cannot tell that this collection of bitmaps is in reality a toolbar. This is a very big deal in light of the Americans With Disabilities Act that requires equal access in buildings, offices, software, and so on.

There are three controls that you should know about because some of their neat features might not be so obvious:

- **Header Controls** display lists in columns with column names in gray at the top

- **Tree View Controls** display objects in a hierarchy

- **List View Controls** display icon/text combinations in alternate views

Well, header controls are only displayed in gray by default; you can change the color scheme in Windows 95 to your heart's content. Plus! Pack themes will definitely change them for you. Technically, the color called "3D Objects" in the Display applet is used for the column names in header controls.

An Explorer window such as can be seen in Figure 2-3 illustrates all three controls. The right pane in the window shows a header control, the left pane a tree control. The file side (right pane) shows a list view control in details view.

The point about a header control is what you can do with the headers. If you hold the mouse cursor over the gap between two headers, it changes shape to ✛, which indicates that one can change the position of the column separator by pressing and dragging the mouse. Even more important is knowing that pressing a column header will sort on that column in ascending order. If the column is already sorted in that way, pressing on the header will sort it in descending order.

The only thing to remember about Tree View controls is that each branch can be open or closed, and there are different symbols for open/closed in different applications. In Explorer, it is a minus and plus sign, but the tree controls used in Help Contents are an open and closed book.

List View controls can be displayed in four modes that can usually be chosen from a View menu or from a button bar that looks like ⊞⊞⊞⊞ . Taking it from the left, the four views are large icons, small icons, list view, and details view. Small icons and list view show the same icons but sort differently and have windows that scroll differently. Rather than try to put it into words, view a large directory in an Explorer window and you'll see how the views differ.

Clip Bored

> Philosophy will clip an angel's wings

> —John Keats, *Lamia*

The next two sections, on the Clipboard and on Dynamic Date Exchange, aka DDE, have nothing to do with objects but they are preliminary to the discussion of OLE which is object city—think of the clipboard as the delivery van for OLE and DDE as its bill of lading.

The clipboard is an area of memory that Windows sets aside to store data to facilitate data transfer between applications and even within an application. In its simplest form, you select data in an application, *copy* or *cut* it to the clipboard and *paste* it into an application, which can be the same or different.

We'll give both the Windows 3.0 and 3.1 hotkeys for these operations—they changed from one version to the other. Ideally, both will work in applications that follow *The Interface Guidelines*. These guidelines suggest that programs accept the older keys but will not document them! Alas, you need to know both sets of keys because there are applications in which only one of the two sets works; if all else fails, you can use the Edit menu.

Copy (hotkey is Ctrl+Ins or Ctrl+C) leaves the source document alone but places the data on the clipboard. Cut (hotkey is Shift+Del or Ctrl+X) copies to the clipboard and deletes the material from the source. Paste (hotkey is Shift+Ins or Ctrl+V) copies the data from the clipboard to target application.

That's the simple idea, but the question comes up—in what format does the clipboard transfer data? Does it include font information if you copy from one word processor to another? How about spreadsheet formula if you copy between spreadsheets? The answer is, that depends on the source and the target.

The clipboard itself is very flexible. If you have Excel 7.0, open it, load a spreadsheet, mark some data, and copy it to the clipboard. Then run Windows Clipbook viewer (which I'll discuss in Chapter 4). One of the menu items in that viewer is View. Pull it down and it gives you a list of twenty-seven formats—six are black and twenty-one are gray (Figure 2-16 shows the menu split to fit on the page!). What's that mean? The six black formats are actually placed on the clipboard by Excel. For the other twenty-one, it only places a promise on the clipboard. Essentially, it tells target applications, "If you have a need for the data in a promised format, let the clipboard know and it will get that format from me to give to you." By only promising data, not as much memory is taken and the copy is faster.

The downside of promised rather than actual data is that you have to keep the source application open to fulfill the promise. If you close an application before pasting, the clipboard notices and removes the promised formats from the list it offers to transfer. So if you are trying to transfer anything more complex than straight text, be sure to keep the source application open until after you paste.

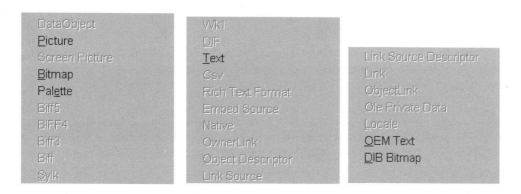

Figure 2-16. Sure is a lot loaded on that clipboard

The clipboard uses terms that may differ from those that applications use. It will say `Picture` for what many applications call `Windows Metafile` or `WMF`, and it will say `Bitmap` for what applications may call `BMP`. If you never look at the viewer, this terminology is irrelevant because the applications and clipboard can talk about these standard formats, but it may confuse you if you do look and aren't aware of the terms.

When you paste into an application, that application will pick the format to use if there are several. The Edit menu sometimes has a Paste Special command—you then get to pick the format used from the ones that are both on the clipboard and understood by the target application.

How well does the clipboard do on the transfer of formatted data? Remarkably well. When Mom tested this in 1993 for *The Mother of All Windows Books,* she was unable to transfer bold attributes on text between any pair of Word, Write, and Word Perfect. Similarly, attempting to paste a column of numbers with a SUM formula at the bottom only pasted the numbers, not the formula, when going in either direction between the then-Excel and Quattro Pro. For this book, Mom tested Office 95 products and the Perfect Office products released in early 1995 and the results were heartening. Pasting formatted text, including font and size and bold/italic information, worked perfectly between all pairs of Word, WordPad, and Word Perfect. Formulae pasted OK from Excel to Quattro, but not the other way.

 Wow. The industry really can get its act together. I'm impressed.

 The key to passing formatted text is the adaptation by all word-processing vendors of a format called RTF (Rich Text Format). It is likely to become the standard for formatted email, also.

For some users, the biggest disappointment in the clipboard is that there is no Append command. If you copy or cut anything to the clipboard, whatever was there is gone, vaporized, moved to the great electron graveyard. What was there is replaced by the new cut. It's unfortunate that Windows doesn't have an Append command built in for the special case where the clipboard has text and what you try to append is also text.

DDE

DDE stands for **Dynamic Data Exchange**. It's a built-in part of the Windows architecture that is of special importance for programmers. Indeed, it was added to the Windows spec in 1989–90 at the request of Aldus and Microsoft's Power Point groups. It impacts end users mainly through a command called *Paste Link*. If you write really fancy macros, you need to know about DDE at the level beyond Paste Link, and we recommend that you look at Woody's *Windows 95 Programming for Mere Mortals.* If you aren't going to do programming (including macro programming), don't worry your pretty head about anything but Paste Link.

 In many ways, DDE as a programming device is regarded as passé—replaced by OLE automation. But that isn't totally true. When you press the Start Menu and choose `Find/File` or `Folder`, the Start Menu actually sends a DDE command to Explorer to tell it to display the Find dialog!

Paste Link extends the idea of promised data to the idea of future promises. Not only does the source provide data now, but it promises to provide data again in the future. Why would you want to do that? Suppose that you are preparing a daily report for your boss in Winword and part of it is a table of data that needs to be computed in Excel. If you link the data rather than just paste it, that data can be updated automatically so that today's data is used without you having to do an explicit copy and paste again.

So, for example, if you have an Excel sheet called `daily.xls` and position R6:C2 is a formula that you want to link into a Word document called `report.doc`, you select the cell in Excel, pick copy from the Edit menu, go to Word, and pick Paste Special from its Edit menu. The dialog that pops up has a pair of radio buttons marked Paste and Paste Link.

Pick the latter and Paste as unformatted text, which means it picks its formatting from Word and not from Excel. Word not only stores and displays the current value of the number in that cell but stores the application it is linked to (Excel), the filename (`daily.xls`) and the topic—the identifying tag it needs to send Excel to get that number back in the future (`R6:C2` in this case).

Links come in two main varieties: **automatic** and **manual**. A manual link is only updated when you explicitly ask for it to be updated; you'd need to use a command in the target file to do the update. Automatic links are updated whenever you open the file with the target link (the Word `.doc` file in the example). With automatic links, the target application also asks the source application to inform it whenever the source of the link is changed; it's impressive to make a link like the Excel/Word link we described and type in changes in Excel while you have the Word window visible on the screen. You see the numbers updated in real time as you change the values in the spreadsheet that are involved in the formula!

If the link is automatic and the source of the DDE link isn't open when the target application loads the file with the target link (for example, if Excel isn't open when Word loads `report.doc`), then the target will offer to open the source and update the links. Either way, Word begins a DDE conversation with Excel that begins, "Hey, Excel, ole buddy, how ya been?" Quite literally, the first step in a DDE exchange is initialization. It continues with asking for and getting the linked data. The line is kept open for Excel to inform Word of further changes in real time. Often, users don't get to determine which kind of link it is—that's set by the target application—but it is important that you understand which kind of link it is so you know whether and when to ask for an explicit update. Civilized applications give you control over the links through a Links . . . command in the Edit menu.

 While you needn't worry about understanding DDE beyond Paste Link if you aren't going to program, you should care a great deal whether your applications support DDE and/or OLE automation because of the potential third-party add-ins possible when they are available.

OLÉ, José

> Every country gets the circus it deserves. Spain gets bullfights.
> Italy gets the Catholic Church. America gets Hollywood.
>
> —Erica Jong, *How To Save Your Own Life,* 1977

Objects truly come into their own with the notion of compound documents. If you had an Ami word-processing file with a piece of an Excel spreadsheet, a photo touched with Picture Publisher, and a Corel Draw graphic in it, Windows 3.0 thought of that as a file made with Ami that happens to have pieces pasted in from other applications. Most likely, the files from Picture Publisher and Corel were saved to disk and just copied into the Ami document, although the Excel spreadsheet fragment might have been Paste Linked.

The object/compound document paradigm would view such a document as one that had a single piece whose parts you would edit and act on with four separate tools—the four programs that made up the pieces. This idea was pioneered by New Wave, an environment from Hewlett Packard that ran over Windows.

New Wave could never reach the critical momentum for its glue to catch on, but it and related ideas in the academic literature and other platforms captured Microsoft's and the industry's imagination. According to Microsoft's version of the history, OLE came out of a proposal of Lotus and the OLE 1.0 spec was formulated by a committee of programmers from Lotus, Word Perfect, Aldus, and Microsoft's application programming group, with input from Micrografx, Samna, Borland, Metaphor, and Iris. About six months before Windows 3.1 shipped, Microsoft released OLE program libraries that third parties could distribute, and these OLE 1.0 spec libraries were included with Windows 3.1. In the middle of 1993, Microsoft released libraries implementing the OLE 2.0 spec based on input from many Software Vendors.

 While there is no doubt that Microsoft has listened to other vendors, it is clearly first among equals. It is a remarkable coincidence that Microsoft's applications and languages seem to be the first ones to have the various versions of OLE implemented.

 Not surprising at all. OLE 2.0 was actually developed by the application division and then ordered by big Bill to turn it over to the Windows group for inclusion in the operating system.

OLE is not automatically built into all applications—the applications have to be supported by code. So you likely have a hybrid collection of applications with no OLE support, a few with OLE 1.0 support, and some with OLE 2.0 support. In order to qualify for the Windows 95 logo, an application (but not a utility) must support OLE 2.0, so you are likely to find more and more programs with OLE support.

OLE stands for "Object Linking and Embedding," although "Object Linking or Embedding" might be clearer. The bitmap that you'd edited with Picture Publisher would be embedded in your Ami document as a picture before OLE. If you didn't like the way it looked, you'd launch Picture Publisher from Program Manager or your favorite launcher, load the on disk file, edit it, save it to disk, and tell Ami to update it. Not hard but sure tedious.

The OLE 1.0 spec presented a better way. If the photo was an on-disk file placed inside the Ami doc, when you place it there, it is linked as a PCX file to Picture Publisher. A database is kept by Windows that OLE PCX objects are to be edited by Picture Publisher (if that happens to be your photo editor). Double-click on the picture in the Ami document and Picture Publisher is loaded with the picture already opened. Edit it and close Picture Publisher; you will be asked if you want to update the linked object. The tedium described earlier is somewhat reduced and you have much more of a feel that you are working on a single document.

It isn't even necessary to have an on-disk file. You can instead "embed" the object in the target document—that is, save the data that Picture Publisher needs to describe a bitmap as part of the Ami document. This is done by creating the object while in Ami by telling it you want to embed a PCX object and have it load Picture Publisher for you.

At a technical level, the difference between Linking and Embedding is that Linking only stores display data in the document and to edit it a file needs to be loaded from disk. Embedding also stores the native data that an editor needs. At the user level, linking is the way to go if you have a file (for example, a company logo) that you want to share among several documents where editing it once affects all documents using it. Embedding is the best thing to use if you want to send the document to someone else without worrying about also sending extra files and about problems with the directory structure being different on the new machine.

While the OLE 1.0 spec started us down the docucentric road, where users are supposed to think more in terms of documents and less of individual applications, there is still a feel of separate programs, because you double-click when you want to edit and editing takes place in a separate window that feels like (and is!) a separate program. OLE 2.0 introduced the idea of "in place editing." Click on a photo inside a word processor `.doc`. If the word processor and photo editor supports OLE 2.0 in place editing, the menus change to those of your photo editor. You have much more the feel of a single application acting on a single document, with menus changing appropriately to part of the document you are editing.

OLE really does pass responsibility for the embedded or linked object to the program that created it. When the larger document is printed and gets to the embedded object, it passes commands to the program that understands that object asking that the object be rendered in a way that can be passed on to the printing subsystem.

A second important element of the OLE 2.0 spec is a protocol for programs to drive each other, called OLE automation. It goes way beyond the DDE spec and allows the potential of universal macro languages. Examples of application programs that support OLE automation are Excel and Visio.

Here are some acronyms related to OLE that you may hear bandied about: **OLE DB** (DB=database) and **distributed OLE** are extensions of the current spec to allow sharing of objects across networks. The grand architecture on which these and other OLE extensions are based is called **COM**, for **Common Object Model**. A competing consortium, including IBM and Novell, wants to wrest control of the object specification away from Microsoft. They have a replacement for OLE called **OpenDoc**, based on an architecture called **CORBA** (for **Common Object Request Broker Architecture**). Given Microsoft's control of the OS and the importance it attaches to specifications, I wouldn't rate CORBA's chance of success very high!

The program doing the driving—either sending the automation commands or asking for the embedded object—is usually called a *client* and one whose strings are being pulled or which is providing the embedded object is usually called a *server.* Microsoft says that with the release of OLE 2.0, the correct terms are not client and server but *container* and *object.*

I think I'll scream if anything else is called an object. I assume some purist at Microsoft, thinking of an object hierarchy, thought themselves really clever to use the word *object* to refer to the controlled program in an OLE 2 conversation. But that's a big mistake. Oy.

There are two new OLE file types that are implemented with Windows 95. The first is known as *scrap* (it has the extension .shs). It allows you to take a fragment of an OLE document and save it to a file—you'd most often save it on your Desktop. For example you could take some text in a Winword 7.0 document, select it and drag it to the Desktop. You can later drag a copy of it into Winword or to any OLE 2.0 client that supports being a drag-and-drop client. Even in Winword, the scrap is treated as a separate object, but since you can edit it, it almost behaves as an intrinsic part of the document. The second new file type is called a *Shortcut into a Document* (and has a filename with the extension .shb). I'll discuss it when I get into the subject of shortcuts in a few sections. If you right-drag and drop some text from Winword to the Desktop, you get a menu that lets you choose whether to make the text into scrap or into a document shortcut or to cancel. As usual, if you start left-dragging, you can hit Ctrl+Shift and have the drop pop up a context menu.

WordPad has implemented scrap with left-drag and drop of selected text. It has no document shortcuts—you can't right-drag and drop selected text at all.

A First Look Under the Hood

Being willing to look under the hood is what distinguishes users who want to squeeze performance from their system from those who don't. Four whole chapters at the end of this book will look in the Engine Room and show you a lot of what is happening. In this group of sections, I'll give a first look at some parts of the Engine Room, in part to expose you to notions that will help in understanding how to optimally use Explorer and the other core components discussed in the next chapter.

 Of course there are those that say being willing to look under the hood is a sure sign of someone who spends too much time fooling with computers rather than getting any work done. But, what the hey—sure beats TV for entertainment.

Directories and Folders, Folders and Directories

> I have been a soreheaded occupant of a file drawer labeled
> "Science Fiction" . . . and I would like out, particularly since so
> many serious critics regularly mistake the drawer for a urinal.
>
> —Kurt Vonnegut, Jr., *Wampeters, Foma and Granfallons,* 1974

I told you in Chapter 1 that Microsoft has started using the term folder instead of directory. That's the truth, but not the whole truth. In some ways it is more accurate to say that *folder* is a term that encompasses what used to be called a directory. Every directory is a folder but not every folder is a directory.

A folder is basically a collection of objects that the operating system understands. Just as a compound document can be thought of a container for objects like pictures and text, so a folder is a container for files and, er, other things. In fact, it is useful to continue to use the term *directory* to refer to a folder whose contents are just disk files. I'll do that in this section.

 Ha! You can look in the Registry to learn what the designers of Windows 95 really think about the names of these things. Classes of objects have both a techie name that you'd never see if you didn't look in the Registry and a public name, which is what is used in the FileTypes tab of Explorer's View/Options dialog. For example, what is publicly called "Microsoft Word Document" has the techie name `Word.Document.6` (presumably because the file format is that of Word 6.0). There is an object with the public name "File Folder" but its techie name is `Directory`.

To give you an idea of a folder that is not a directory, consider the one folder that is on everyone's Desktop—`My Computer`. It is hardwired in. You can change its name. If you have the Plus! Pack (or are adept at editing the Registry; see Chapter 11) you can change its icon, or even make it invisible, but it is hardwired into the Desktop. Open it up and you'll not find a file in sight. You'll find an icon for each drive. These drives should also be thought of as folders—indeed, they correspond to the root directory of the drives. If you doubt it, pop up Run from the Start Menu and type in C:\ and hit OK. The folder that opens is identical to the one that opens if you click the C drive icon in My Computer.

You could argue that since My Computer has folders corresponding to the directories A:\, for example, it is essentially a folder like a directory. But wait a minute. You'll notice that My Computer has some icons that do not correspond to drives—at least two will be there: Control Panel and Printers. If you installed Dial-Up Networking when you ran setup for Win95, there will be a Dial-Up Networking folder also. All three of these are folders that do not correspond to directories—they are folders of a totally different type from file folders. They have objects that don't correspond to files. Of course, this means that My Computer is a kind of hybrid with some objects that are "files" and some that are not.

There are some other hybrid folders, each with its own weird twist on the paradigm. One is the Fonts folder, which can contain objects that are totally virtual. I'll talk about it later at the end of the group of sections on fonts.

Another hybrid folder is Network Neighborhood, which you'll have hardwired* into the Desktop as long as you've installed network drivers. By default all it shows are workgroups and workstations on the network. But you can drag files into it—presumably Microsoft assumes you'll put shortcuts to places on the network there. As soon as you put any files there, Windows makes a directory called C:\windows\nethood and physically places the files in that directory. So Network Neighborhood displays the top level Network nodes and all the files in C:\windows\nethood.

 And then there is The Mother of All Folders. The Desktop. If you don't believe me, run Explorer and keep hitting Backspace. Each one takes you one up the folder hierarchy. You'll likely start in C:\. Backspace will take you to My Computer, the parent of C:\. A second Backspace will take you to its parent, which is Desktop. Further hitting of Backspace does nothing—Desktop is indeed The Mother of All Folders.

In reality, as we'll explore in Chapter 3, the visible Desktop, which shows the contents of the Desktop folder, is another one of these hybrids. It shows one icon for each file or folder in the disk directory C:\windows\desktop. It also shows the two hardwired folders My Computer and Network Neighborhood. Finally, it will display icons that are installed in a special way in the Registry, which is how Windows adds the icons for Inbox, Recycle Bin, The Microsoft Network and, if you install Plus!, The

---

* Actually, in Chapter 11, I'll explain several ways to remove Network Neighborhood from your desktop.

`Internet`. It appears these are hard-coded in and that, except for `The Microsoft Network`,* you can't delete them. But you can: see Chapter 11.

This putting Desktop at the top is just crazy. How can `Desktop\My Computer\C:\Windows\desktop` be contemplated without a bad case of vertigo caused by circular reasoning? And it serves no purpose.

It may be well-known that Rush is right, but this time, Rush is wrong. Putting Desktop at the top is a brilliant coup for two reasons. First, naïve users will like the hierarchical idea of Desktop containing the icons it obviously contains. They'll happily drag to and from it, never knowing there is a directory—a hidden directory, by the way—that holds the files that they drag there. Secondly, the Desktop is a terribly convenient place to place temporary files. Maybe you want to make a zip, send it to someone via email, and delete it. Put it on the Desktop when you make it and you can drag it into the email message and then later drag it to the Recycle Bin. Because the Desktop is the top of the, er, heap, in any File SaveAs dialog, you can just

keep hitting Backspace or keep hitting the button and get to the Desktop—awfully handy if you want to leave stuff there.

Yeah, but you blew it in how you treat any drive shortcuts left on the Desktop. Sensible users will place shortcuts to folders they use all the time and to their drives on the Desktop. If I choose such a shortcut on the Desktop in a File Open dialog, the dialog should move to the folder that the shortcut points toward. Instead it offers to open the actual shortcut file. Dumb! The Office custom file dialogs handle this right, by the way. I hope Windows gets fixed to do that also.

Hidden Pleasures

> The knowingness of little girls
> Is hidden underneath their curls.
>
> —Phyllis McGinley, *What Every Woman Knows*, 1960

Billy95 just referred to the fact that `C:\windows\desktop` is a hidden directory. The name *hidden* makes it sound like some deep, dark secret, and hidden directories sound rather underhanded. In fact, *hidden* isn't very hidden. If you go to Explorer's

---

* Late in the beta process, a Delete option suddenly appeared on the context menu for The Microsoft Network desktop icon. Methinks this was a preemptive strike on the Justice Department.

View/Options dialog, you'll find a pair of items with radio buttons saying Show all files and Hide Files of these types:. The second option is the default when Windows is installed and you'll note the first type in the list is "Hidden Files." When that radio button is picked, C:\windows\desktop won't appear on the directory list under C:\windows when you open Explorer. If the Show all files is picked, it will appear. Similarly, if you do a dir at the DOS command prompt you won't see hidden files, but if you do dir /a:h, you will see (only) hidden files. Using DOS's attrib command or the property sheet of a file in Explorer you can make it hidden or unhide it.

So *hidden* means only from naïve users; don't hold much store by it for real security issues! In fact, it should be thought of more as "kept out of the way of naïve users" than "hidden." Serious users will probably want to be sure that the radio button to show hidden files is picked.

Windows places seven hidden subdirectories in its own directory:*

- inf contains files used to setup additional components of Windows. Most of these files have the extension .inf. They are intended to be run via the Add/Remove Programs applet in Control Panel, but they can also be run by right-clicking on them and choosing Install.

- nethood is discussed in the last section. Even if you have networking turned on, you may not have this directory if you've never dragged a file or folder into Network Neighborhood.

- pif involves PIF files, which I'll discuss in detail in the sections on DOS in Chapter 3. PIFs serve many purposes but, in particular, if you try to run a DOS program directly, Windows 95 will make a PIF for it. If the DOS program is on a local hard drive, the PIF file is placed in the same directory as the program. If the DOS program is on a CD ROM or a network drive, the PIF files are placed in C:\windows\pif.

- recent stores the shortcuts that appear in the Start Menu's Document command.

- shellnew is the default location for templates used in documents made from the New submenu of the Desktop context menu.

- spool is where files waiting to be printed are stored.

- sysbckup stores copies of the most basic Windows system files—if some rogue installation program overwrites them, Windows will try to restore them from here.

---

* The desktop folder is not hidden in the technical sense, but Explorer hides it if you tell it to not show hidden files.

The windows directory also normally stores six hidden files—the two files that make up the Registry (`user.dat` and `system.dat`), their backups (`user.da0` and `system.da0`), a font cache (`ttfcache`), and a cache for icons (`ShellIconCache`).

 It's not unreasonable that these files and directories are hidden, in that all but the most serious users won't need to access them and their presence could confuse naive users.

 Actually, I'll explain in Chapter 11 why some users will want to delete ShellIconCache and force Windows to reconstruct it, but I'll admit only rather sophisticated users will want to do that.

 Expect an explosion of hidden directories. Microsoft's setup recommendation to application developers is to place all the funny binary files in a hidden subdirectory of the main application directory called `system`. No doubt some paranoids will rant and rave about all this hidden stuff on users disks, but you and I know better: *hidden* is just a name, and a user who wants access to these directories can easily get it.

Shortcuts

What Romantic terminology called genius or talent or inspiration is nothing other than finding the right road empirically, following one's nose, taking shortcuts.

—Italo Calvino *Cybernetics and Ghosts,* lecture, Nov. 1969

 I know what a shortcut is. It's one file that points to a program or document so when you double-click on the shortcut, the program gets run or the document gets launched in its associated program. Shortcuts have the extension `.lnk`.

 That's a pretty good summary, and one that many people would agree with, but it's not the whole truth by a long shot. First of all, even shortcuts with the extension `.lnk` can point toward objects in the folder hierarchy that are executable, but not programs in the usual sense. And I'm aware of at least four other extensions used for specialized shortcuts by Windows 95! Also, applications can define their own shortcut types.

A shortcut, as defined by the *Programmer's Guide to Windows 95* (part of the official SDK* documentation) is "a data object that contains information used to access another object in the system such as a file, folder, disk drive, or printer." Double-clicking on the shortcut is supposed to access the object that the shortcut points toward.

---

* Microsoft's official Software Development Kit for software designers.

To understand why the notion was needed, it helps to consider Window 3.x's Program Manager, if you are familiar with it. The main Program Manager window had subwindows called *groups.* The groups contained items (represented by icons), and when you double-clicked one of them it launched the object that the item was supposed to point toward. In a sense, the Program Manager items were already shortcuts, but they were of a very different makeup from the objects to which they pointed. The target objects were always files in the file system. The Program Manager items were bits of binary fluff inside the files that were associated to groups.

Given the folder emphasis in Windows 95, it was natural that Program Manager Groups would evolve into folders of some sort—it turns out that they are folders exactly corresponding to disk directories (namely, subdirectories of `C:\windows\start menu\programs`). But then what happens to the launch items? They couldn't always be the actual executable files because programs often insist on being in a directory with lots of other files. So was born the shortcut: The icons in a Program Manager folder would evolve into shortcuts to executable programs—files that could launch other files. But the designers then pushed the concept to new heights.

That shortcuts are the evolution of Program Manager items is clear in several ways. Just as items had working directories, hot keys, and icons, so do shortcuts. I'll discuss these in detail in Chapter 3. More telling, Windows 95 has a conversion program to turn `.grp` files, the binary files representing groups, into subfolders of `C:\windows\start menu\programs`. Items get translated into `.lnk` files in the folders. This conversion program is automatically run during Windows 95 setup if you install it into the same directory as Windows 3.x. In any event, if you double-click on a `.grp` file in Windows 95 explorer, the conversion program is run.

So far, the picture is exactly like that presented by Igor. But links can point to things other than programs and documents. They can point to folders; for example, the command in a shortcut could be `C:\windows`. The shortcut would then open the folder in Explorer, running in folder view displaying the `C:\Windows` folder. As I'll explain in Chapter 3, drives (i.e., folders like `C:\`) are treated specially.

You can add a link shortcut by dragging an object to the Desktop or from one folder to another in a suitable way. For `.exe` files, making shortcuts is the default action after a drag and drop. For other files you'll need to right drag. To get drive shortcuts by dragging, you can drag from the `My Computer` folder. You can also right-click on the Desktop or on a blank part of an Explorer window, choose New and then Shortcut from the menu, and invoke a Create Shortcut Wizard (see Figure 2-17). This lets you pick the command line by browsing and assigning a name to the shortcut.

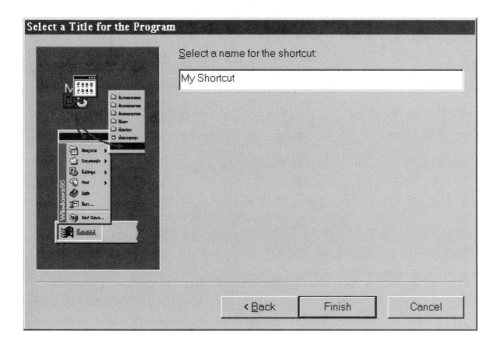

Figure 2-17. The Create Shortcut Wizard

The folder-based object system has other objects besides files. For example, Control Panel, the Printers Folder, Dial-up Networking, and Network Neighborhood have their own types of objects (applets, printers, dial-up connections and computers). The Windows 95 shell is consistent and lets you drag these objects to the Desktop and create shortcuts that launch them.

A second kind of shortcut is the DOS PIF file, which could be used as a launch shortcut under Windows 3.x. I'll discuss it in detail in Chapter 3. It's a clever piece of design that presents link shortcuts and DOS PIF files to the user as conceptually the same thing. That they are different in some ways is shown by the fact that their property sheets are very different. PIF files have the extension `.pif`.

A third kind of shortcut—my favorite—is the shortcut into a document. Programs that fully support the OLE spec (for servers) let you select a piece of a document and drag it to the Desktop (or an Explorer folder) and make that piece into a shortcut (which happens to have the extension `.shb`*). For example, right-drag a piece of a Winword 7.0 document to the Desktop and choose to make a shortcut. When you later double-click that shortcut, Winword will be launched if it is not already running, the document will be loaded if it isn't already loaded, and Winword will scroll to the location of the original text and reselect it.

---

* That's not something you'll need to know very often!

This is ideal for saving a bookmark to where you are currently working on a project like, oh, writing an 800+ page book on Windows 95!

A fourth kind of shortcut is created if you drag a location in The Microsoft Network to your Desktop (or right-click and pick `Create Shortcut`). You get a file with extension `.mcc` that offers to dial up The Microsoft Network if you aren't currently connected and puts you in the bulletin board or file collection or ellipsis that you dragged.

There is a fifth kind of file-based shortcut installed by the Plus! Pack—a shortcut to an Internet Web site with the extension `.url`. Like MSN shortcuts, double-clicking will offer to dial up your Internet connection, launch the Plus! Browser, and connect to the Website that you were visiting when you created the shortcut.

These two kinds of network shortcuts can be emailed to other Windows users, who should be able to access them directly (at least if you use MSN mail), and are the basis of Favorite Places menus.

There is a further kind of phantom shortcut, to a font. I'll discuss why I call it a phantom when I get to fonts a bit later in this chapter.

Well, I think I was basically right at the start. Sure there are other extensions than `.lnk` but who cares? That's techie stuff. And sure, the shortcut can point to objects other than programs, but conceptually they are all the same.

There is one aspect of shortcuts that has caused some complaints from the learned magazine writers; namely, how well shortcuts do at locating the program they point to if that program gets moved. If that happens, you get the dialog shown on the top of Figure 2-18. It does an excellent job of locating the file, as long as it has been moved to the same drive. It searches based on more than name—look at the dialog on the bottom that located the Windows 3.1 `calc.exe` when Windows 95 `calc.exe` was moved to another drive. It didn't just match the names. Moving to a different drive doesn't get automatically fixed but you can use the Browse button.

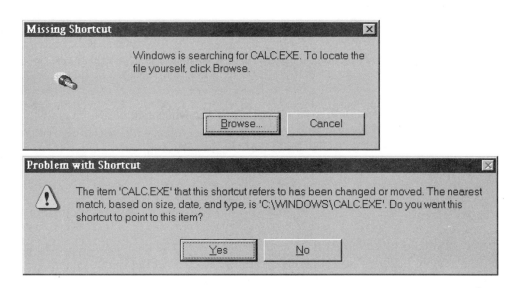

Figure 2-18. It's 10 o'clock. Do you know where your program is?

It's remarkable how often I've heard the anti-Win95 crowd kvetch about this. It is true it would be nice if Windows 95 tracked all shortcut/file pairs, but I'm not sure I'd like the overhead if it did, nor would I like not being able to have shortcuts to nonlocal file systems, such as a Netware server. . . . In any event, on the list of my top-ten peeves with Windows 95, this ranks about a hundred-and-fourth.

Files can be registered with the operating system to never display extensions* and shortcuts are registered so you won't see extensions for any of the shortcut types on the Desktop or in Explorer, even if you uncheck the option in Explorer `Hide MS-DOS extensions for file types that are registered`. You will see them if you do a `dir` at a DOS prompt and in some third-party file managers.

An interesting use of shortcuts is made by the File Open dialogs in the Office 95 applications. If you click on a shortcut to a folder, the dialog switches to that folder. If you click on a shortcut to a file, that file is immediately opened. In contrast, if you do the same in the Windows 95 File Open dialog, the program will try to open the `.lnk` file you clicked on! Office goes further in setting up a special directory, er folder, called Favorites, where you can place shortcuts to the folders and files you often want. The dialogs include buttons to switch to the Favorites folder (which means that the folders whose

---

* This is distinct from the option in the Explorer View/Options dialog; I'll talk about it further in Chapter 11.

shortcuts are in Favorites are at most two clicks away) and to add a shortcut to the current folder to Favorites. I hope Windows steals these ideas from Office (the use of something similar in the Plus! Pack's Internet Browser is a promising sign that it will).

The Tree-Based Menu

> Tree at my window, window tree,
> My sash is lowered when night comes on;
> But let there never be curtain drawn
> Between you and me.

—Robert Frost, *Tree at My Window*

There is one paradigm that is reused several times by Windows 95 and its applications and it is important to understand: a menu that gets built based on a subtree of the folder system. There is a top level of the menu associated to a specific folder, which I'll call the **root folder for the menu**. Items on the menu are associated to files in the root folder. Submenus are associated to subfolders. Items on the submenu associated to a given subfolder are associated to files in that subfolder and sub-submenus to sub-subfolders of the subfolder. This process keeps going on as long as the folders last. The names of the menu items and submenus are precisely the names of the files and subfolders. When a menu item is chosen, the corresponding file is run. It is useful to make the file items shortcuts—they run properly and their names display without their extensions.

The Mother of All Tree-based Menus is the Start Menu. Its root folder is `C:\windows\Start Menu`. Items in its top level are more than what's in the root folder but the `Programs` submenu is precisely built from the `C:\windows\Start Menu\Programs` folder. You can add additional items to the main Start Menu by adding shortcuts to the `C:\windows\Start Menu` folder and you can make additional submenus by putting subfolders in that same folder.

The point of understanding the paradigm is that it tells you how to modify your Start Menu. You want to use Explorer to view this part of the Folder tree and move/add/delete shortcuts and subfolders. This is much, much more efficient than calling up `Start/Settings/Taskbar . . .` from the Start Menu, choosing the `Start Menu Programs` tab, and using the `Add . . .` and `Remove . . .` buttons. One way to access Explorer on these folders is the `Advanced . . .` button in that same dialog, but it is hardly the most efficient. You can right-click on the Start button and choose Explore and get to the folders that way. In Chapter 3, I'll encourage you to make an `Edit Start Menu` item on your Start Menu, which is better still.

A second place that this paradigm is used is for the Send To submenu on the context menu that you get if you right-click on file and folder objects in Explorer. This is a tree-based menu with root folder C:\windows\sendto. Yeah, that's right, there is a space between *send* and *to* in the submenu name but not in the folder name. You can add or remove items from the Send To menu by manipulating the files in the folder. If you want, you can add submenus to Send To by adding subfolders to the sendto folder.

A third place where one would expect Windows to use a tree-based menu is on the Documents submenu of the Start Menu. The items on this submenu are related to shortcuts in the folder C:\windows\recent but it is not a simple tree-based menu—its kinda techie, one might even say irrelevant. Sarah will tell you about it when Start Menu is discussed in Chapter 3.

There is a place that the Plus! Pack uses a tree-based menu. The Web Browser included with the Plus! Pack (called Microsoft Internet Explorer) has a Favorites menu, which is essentially a tree-based menu based on C:\windows\favorites. I say essentially because, while it does use subfolders to get submenus, its items don't correspond to all files in the folders but only to the files that are Shortcuts to the Internet (*.url files). This is a quite reasonable extension of the basic paradigm since, of course, you'd only want to choose Internet shortcuts from within this program. The Open Favorites menu command (and button bar button) opens up C:\windows\favorites in folder view. There should be an Explore Favorites command as well, but there is not! If you weren't familiar with the basic paradigm you might not realize how easy it is to organize your Internet favorites in submenus.

I think the designers of Plus! made a big mistake in using the same C:\windows\favorites folder that Microsoft Office uses for its favorites. Office uses favorites to speed up exploration when in a File Open or File SaveAs dialog. It's true that since Internet Explorer uses *.url's for its items and an application like Word only displays *.docs and shortcuts to *.docs, there won't be a collision of items but the subfolders one wants to use will be very different in the two cases. Moreover, the Folder view of C:\windows\favorites that you open from Internet Explorer shows all the files, including any shortcuts you may have put there with Office.

There is also an interesting buglet in the way the Office install sets up the Favorites directory. It adds a shortcut to C:\windows\My Documents. Problem is that it sets up a My Documents folder in a different place. Oh how I love a nice bug in the mornin'.

Long Filenames

> . . . one needs long arms; it is better to have them too long than too short.

> —Sarah Bernhardt, *Memories of My Life,* 1907

 Hey, what's there to say about long filenames? You can have 'em. That's great, but what more is there to be said? Shortest section in the book, eh?

 Other than the obvious need to explain how long they can be and what characters are allowed. For the curious and to warn readers how fragile the system behind long filenames is, Mao will explain how long filenames are stored. But there are two more important issues to discuss. In a world that suddenly allows spaces and periods in filenames, how do you deal with extensions and multiple parameters in a command line? And how do programs written for 8+3 filenames cope in a world with long filenames?

Filenames under versions of DOS or Windows prior to Windows 95 had extensions of up to 3 characters and prenames up to 8. The full pathname for a file including `C:`, `\`'s and the `.` between the prename and extension was limited to 80 characters. Under Windows 95, filenames can be up to 255 characters and pathnames up to 260. Extensions can be more than 3 characters—because multiple periods are allowed, the extension is the part after the last period.

The following are forbidden characters in filenames and directory: any control character (one with codes below ASCII 32, e.g. ^A=ASCII 001) and the following special characters:

`\ / : * ? " < > |`

In particular, both space and period are allowed, as well as the following characters, which are forbidden in older versions of DOS: `+ , ; = [ ]` .

 I understand why those characters are forbidden. `:` and `\` are for drive and directory names, `/` is for parameters, `*` and `?` are wildcards, `"` is for quoted names and `>` `<` `|` are for DOS redirection.

 Right, but there is a scheme that would allow any character. One could use `$` as an "escape." You could have `*` in a filename and still use `*` for a wildcard. You'd use `$*` when referring to that character as part of a filename. `$$` would mean a single `$` .

Oh, how UNIX-like. One could use an escape character to allow anything in filenames, but what would that gain except to tickle the fancy of the Computer Science crowd? Real users would get confused as all get out. Nope. We made the right decision to just forbid these characters, although some users will no doubt try to use ? or < or > in a name and be puzzled at the error message.

I did find a few buglets in the way that Rename treats an attempt to put a control character (one with an ASCII code below 32) into a name. Explorer pops up a message that says `A filename cannot contain any of the following characters: \ / : * ? " < > |` . That's correct of course, but irrelevant to the case at hand. DOS rename is even worse. If you type `ren config.sys ^G.sys` at the DOS command line (where `^G` is entered as `Ctrl+G`), DOS will reply: `File not found - config.sys`. Oh, how I love a nice bug in the mornin'.

Microsoft says that long filenames are stored in Unicode, which says something about the future.*

For compatibility with programs that don't understand long filenames, Windows 95 assigns each file an 8+3 filename without any of the characters that are illegal in earlier versions of DOS. The short filename is determined by the following rules:

1. If the "long" filename is legal under earlier versions (i.e. no more than 8+3, no more than one period and none of the newly allowed characters: <space> + , ; = [ ]), then the short filename is the same as the "long" filename.

2. If the long filename is illegal under earlier versions of DOS, keep up to three characters after the last period. From the characters before the last period, drop all periods and all spaces. Then keep the first six of the remaining characters, or all of them if there are fewer than six. This gives a preliminary 6+3 name.

3. In the preliminary 6+3 name, replace all the newly allowed characters by _ .

4. Tack ~1 onto the end of the 6 part to get an 8+3 filename. Use this name as the short filename if there isn't already another file in the directory with that name.

5. If the first try already exists, try ~2, ~3, etc. instead of ~1.

---

* Unicode is a scheme for handling multiple alphabets; I'll discuss it in the collection of sections of fonts.

So assuming that a ~1 files doesn't already exist, here are some examples:

LONG NAME	Short Name	LONG NAME	Short Name
winutil.doc	winutil.doc	win util.doc	winuti~1.doc
winutil.do;	winuti~1.do_	A very long.name	Avery1~1.name
winutil.docs	winuti~1.doc	a;;;;;.abc	a_____~1.abc

If you look at these names, you see the convention is rather silly. Why shouldn't `winutil.docs` and `win util.doc` just become `winutil.doc`? You could imagine a saner system where the `~1, ~2, ....` is only used if absolutely necessary. Apparently, so can someone on the Windows 95 team, because there is a back door to shift to that behavior with a secret registry setting. I tell you about it in Chapter 11.

What happens if you use up
`~1, ..., ~9` and add another?

How about if you go over
999,999 files?

Windows uses the first five characters
and appends `~10`.

You are in big trouble!

If you want to refer to a long filename with spaces or other characters that might be confusing (like + or ;), you can use quotes. Thus, to distinguish renaming `this file` to `that file` from `this file that` to `file` at the DOS command line, you could use `ren "this file" "that file"`.

An unusual case where you need to use quotes is the following. Suppose you want to save a file in Notepad to the name `foo.bar`. If you just type that name in the Save dialog, Notepad happily tacks on a `txt` extension and saves it as `foo.bar.txt` (!). To save it as `foo.bar`, you need to type `"foo.bar"` in the Save dialog. Notepad is smart enough not to try to tack `.txt` onto .bat and `.ini` files. Word and WordPad behave similarly, insisting on tagging on their extensions.

I had a tricky situation with using quotes properly. Sarah had to explain it to me. I figure it could be a pointer to you. I wanted to add Norton's antivirus scanner to the programs that get run automatically by the Plus! Pack's System Agent scheduler. If you just run the program, it sits there in interactive mode, but I wanted to run it while I sleep. If you pass the program C: as a parameter it scans drive C and exits if no problems are found. *No problemo,* I figured. Norton was installed in the `C:\Program Files\Norton AntiVirus` folder, so I typed the command line

`C:\Program Files\Norton AntiVirus\Navw32.exe C:`

into System Agent, but it complained that it couldn't find the file. Oh, I figured, it was fooled by the spaces in the directory name, so I typed in

`"C:\Program Files\Norton AntiVirus\Navw32.exe C:"`

but it also complained about that, so I went to Sarah and she fixed me up.

 Igor was right that the space in pathname made System Agent unable to figure out the true program name so quotes were the way to go, but his second try made it appear that `C:` was part of the program name. What he had to do (which worked fine) was type in

`"C:\Program Files\Norton AntiVirus\Navw32.exe" C:`

Alas, old apps—that is, Windows 3.x applications—don't understand long filenames. You might hope that if the application used calls to the Windows 3.1 type Common File dialogs,* then that dialog could display the long filenames for the user but pass the short filename on to the application. Windows 95 doesn't work that way for reasons Billy elucidated earlier.

 I've got a bug to report along these lines. Information for setup is stored in files with the extension `.inf`. Find one of these files in Explorer and right-click on it, and one of the context menu items is `Install`. Choose it and the setup for that program is run. That's cool. Under the covers, routines from a `dll` installed into the Windows95 system directory are run. But guess what happens if the file has a long filename, or even if it lives in a directory with a long filename? Doesn't work. Oh how I love a nice bug in the mornin'. One other warning about Rename. I'll let you decide if it is a bug or not. If you use the DOS `ren` command on a short name associated to a long name, the long name is dropped and the renamed file has its short and long names the same.

When you use a long filename it is likely to be fewer than thirty characters, and I don't see much need for caution in doing that. However, you might be wise to try to avoid total pathnames over eighty characters because that will certainly be a problem with DOS

---

* Common File dialogs were discussed a few sections before this one!

program (at least if there are more than eighty characters after translation to short names for each directory and for the filename itself). It is even a problem for some components of Windows 95.

I discovered that PIF files have serious problems with icon pathnames that are over eighty characters. I copied `shell32.dll` into a directory named `C:\temp\1234567890\1234567890\....\1234567890` (with seven levels of 1234567890). I then browsed to use one of these icons in a DOS program property sheet. I then tried to change the icon and the error message in Figure 2-19. Notice there are exactly eighty characters in the name displayed before the crazy §. When I made the path length over one hundred characters, hitting Change Icon caused a GPF (aka General Protection Fault) in Explorer! Oh, how I love a nice bug in the mornin'.

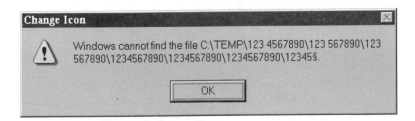

Figure 2-19. Long names? We don't need no steenking long names.

Oy. A path with eighty characters may seem like a lot, but if you download anything from The Microsoft Network, it goes into a directory called `C:\Program Files\The Microsoft Network\Transferred Files`. That's fifty-two characters right there, not so far from the magic eighty. Oy.

I also found that the DOS `move` command didn't much like long path names. I went into a directory with a hundred-character pathname and typed in

`move ..\..\*.dll.`

I got an error message about being unable to move the file and was pushed into the root directory!! It did, in fact, move the files, but my faith in the ability of `move` to react gracefully under the pressure of long pathnames was not enhanced. Oh, how I love a good bug in the mornin'.

To see how Windows 95 stores long filenames, I made a file called `This is a very long file name with a peirod in the middle. Isn't it.txt`. (Hey, I bet you don't spell so good late at night either). The resulting directory is shown in Figure 2-20. Notice that DOS `dir` command shows the associated short name on the left and the long name on the right.

```
C:\Test>dir

 Volume in drive C has no label
 Volume Serial Number is 2E11-11E8
 Directory of C:\Test

.                <DIR>         07-31-95 10:51p .
..               <DIR>         07-31-95 10:51p ..
THISIS~1 TXT            0      07-31-95 10:51p This is a very long file name with a
 peirod in the middle. Isn't it.txt
         1 file(s)              0 bytes
         2 dir(s)      511,623,168 bytes free
```

Figure 2-20. A directory listing

I then fired up Diskedit from Norton Utilities for Windows 95, which has to be run in DOS exclusive mode. The data actually stored in the on-disk directory is displayed in Figure 2-21.* The actual file is shown as the last item before the Unused directory entries. You see it assigned to its short filename. Old DOS and Windows programs will normally only find such entries. But immediately above it appear a whole bunch of entries—six, in this case. They manage to squeeze thirteen characters to a line and put them in order of the name if you read upward from the true file entry.

```
Name     .Ext  ID        Size      Date      Time     Cluster  76 A R S H D V
Cluster 2,533, Sector 81,527
.              Dir         0     7-31-95  10:51 pm    2,533     - - - - D -
..             Dir         0     7-31-95  10:51 pm       0      - - - - D -
ment.txt       Del LFN                                  0      - R S H - V
New Text Docu  Del LFN                                  0      - R S H - V
σEWTEX~1 TXT   Erased      0     7-31-95  10:51 pm       0      A - - - - -
it.txt         LFN                                      0      - R S H - V
iddle. Isn't   LFN                                      0      - R S H - V
irod in the m  LFN                                      0      - R S H - V
ame with a pe  LFN                                      0      - R S H - V
y long file n  LFN                                      0      - R S H - V
This is a ver  LFN                                      0      - R S H - V
THISIS~1 TXT   File        0     7-31-95  10:51 pm       0      A - - - - -
               Unused directory entry
               Unused directory entry
               Unused directory entry
               Unused directory entry
Cluster 2,533, Sector 81,528
               Unused directory entry
               Unused directory entry
```

Figure 2-21. A look at an LFN directory file

---

* The discussion in the rest of this section is a little technical and assumes you know about file attributes, clusters, and a little about how directory entries are stored on disk. Feel free to skip to the next section.

Note the cluster assigned to these entries—it's 0, which is normally used for erased file entries. And if you look to the extreme right where the file attributes are stored, you'll see that each of these babies is a read-only, hidden, system file that happens to be a volume label. This scheme depends on the fact that most programs totally ignore volume labels. Weird, but slick, isn't it?

This scheme is fairly fragile in that the association of long filenames depends on the exact location of the long filename entries. They have to be in the directory immediately prior to the associated short filename. This means if you do something like run a pre–Win95 directory sorting utility (like Norton's DS), you'll lose all your long filenames. In fact, you should assume that any pre–Win95 utility that directly manipulates file directories will foul up long filenames if you run it. Totally foul them up.

If you really do need to run some kind of pre–Win95 utility and want to save long filenames, look at lfnbk, the long filename backup utility. You'll find it on the Windows CD in the directory \admin\apptools\lfnback. You'll find documentation for it in a text file in that directory and also in the Windows 95 Resource Kit. Using it is like a root canal, only less fun.

'Softies sometimes use the abbreviation LFN for a long filename and SFN for the old-fashioned 8+3 name.

Drivers

> KERMIT: Where did you learn to drive?
>
> FOZZIE: I took a correspondence course.
>
> —*The Muppet Movie*

To understand Windows, it sometimes pays to look at the real world, but a somewhat skewed real world. The plumbing industry has settled on standard pipe size and connectors, but suppose it didn't and you wanted a new sink connected to the city lines. The poor plumber would have to ask you exactly what brand and model sink you had and what kind of incoming pipe you have and make sure that he had the right connection to join them. If there were forty kinds of sinks and thirty kinds of pipes, the plumber would need twelve hundred (40 times 30, ya see) connectors to cover all the possibilities.

Pretty heavy toolkit to carry around. A really clever plumber might figure out the following: Develop a special standard intermediate piping. Then the plumber would only need forty connectors to connect the sink to the special intermediate piping and thirty connectors for the other side. Only seventy (the sum) rather than twelve hundred. Big improvement.

A plumber with real clout in the industry would convince the sink makers that *they* should supply the forty connectors for the sinks to the standard. True, with the extra connectors, there would be more chance of leaks, but if handled right, this would simplify everything.

The same idea is central to much in the world of computing. Rather than have everything connect directly to each other and require products of connections, we use a protocol (like the standard pipe) and only need the sum of the possibilities, not the product. This is important to understanding the Windows API and the role of drivers.

 Take printing. Please. The confused world of twelve hundred connectors is the DOS world. Each printer had its own quirks and command set. Each application had to provide its own connector for each printer out there—called printer drivers. Lots of duplicated effort, lots of application programmer time wasted writing drivers, and the people who knew the quirks of individual printers best—the printer manufacturers—were not those who wrote the drivers.

Windows is like the smart plumber. It provides a standard intermediate connector, the Windows API, for printing. The applications talk to the API. The printers connect to the API by providing drivers that are loaded as part of Windows. Not only is this paradigm used for printers, but for monitor adapters (screen drivers), sound cards, and more.

An advantage of this scheme is that the hardware manufacturers who presumably know their products best are responsible for the drivers. Another advantage is that a manufacturer can provide a fancy new piece of hardware and have its features work with most Windows software just by writing the driver. For example, HP could up the printer resolution from 300 dpi to 600 dpi (dots per inch) without waiting for application software to catch up; they supplied a new printer driver and the software automatically caught up!

If you got the impression that drivers are pretty important parts of your system, you'd be right on. Probably no third-party component of Windows is used more than your screen driver. These drivers tended to be unruly stepchildren under Windows 3.1. The hardware vendors didn't always expend the resources they needed to, and Microsoft didn't always provide the help to drivers writers they needed when the companies did take them seriously. As a result, they were responsible for a lot of crashes.

 We realized this and attempted to address the problem in two ways under Windows 95. First, we worked closely with vendors of mainstream hardware to get their drivers stable. And some learned their lessons well. For example, after working with us to write Windows 95 drivers, ATI went back to their Windows 3.1 and improved them. Secondly, we shifted the screen driver over to the unidriver model that worked well with Windows 3.1 for printers. Basically, unidriver, written

by Microsoft, provided the core of functionality that drivers need and a third party wrote minidrivers that are essentially add-ons for the unidriver module. For Windows 95, we created an analog of unidriver but for video—it is called the DIB engine.

You'll see mention of a special driver called a **VxD.** These are virtual device drivers that get loaded as extensions of the windows core and live at the lowest level of the system software. They have the advantage that they can provide services to DOS sessions while taking no conventional memory footprint. They are the key to the increased memory that Windows 95 can provide for such DOS sessions. They also provide improved performance in Windows programs. The 32-bit file system, the CD file system, the protect mode Network clients, the comm port driver, support for file sharing, and the print spooler are all implemented in VxDs.

One more comment on drivers involves the extension of the notion of printer drivers to a heck of a lot of "virtual" printer drivers. "Printing" is just a way of outputting a document from an application, usually as a set of dots. If you want to send that document over the phone lines to someone's fax machine, it's just like printing so one way to implement faxing from Windows is via a printer driver that doesn't print! Instead, the driver pops up a box asking who you want to send the fax to and then it sends the bit pattern out the serial port to your fax modem instead of out a parallel port to your printer! Actually, if Windows fax software finds either another Windows fax program on the receiving end or a stand-alone fax machine that understands Windows fax, then it does something more efficient that just blast a bitmap across the phone line.

Windows 95 prefers to implement fax as part of MAPI* and you'll use a Send or Mail command in mail-enabled applications to send faxes. But while Windows 95 prefers to think of MAPI for programs that are not mail-enabled, when you install Microsoft Fax it also installs a Microsoft Fax print driver. If a program doesn't support MAPI, you can just print to this driver to send a fax to it.

Another interesting example of this philosophy is in the Hijaak Shell extensions for Windows 95, a neat set of graphics utilities that I'll talk about in Chapter 5. They have a Hijaak conversion driver that can take the graphics files produced by any program, even one that Hijaak has never heard of, and convert them to the standard types that Hijaak *does* know like WMF, EMF, CGM, and EPS. How does it do this magic? It uses the fact that programs that print graphics under Windows 95 will send them to the printer as Windows Enhanced Metafiles. By pretending to be the printer, Hijaak gets the program to convert their graphic to an EMF and from there, conversion to the other formats that Hijaak understands is easy!

---

* MAPI is discussed at the end of this chapter.

Similarly, the portable document idea I'll discuss in the section "Portable Documents" later in this chapter depends on "printing" a document to a file. The moral is to keep in mind that printer drivers are really *output drivers* and might not actually print!

The Registry

> History . . . is, indeed, little more than the register of the crimes,
> follies, and misfortunes of mankind.
>
> —Edward Gibbon, *The Decline and Fall of the Roman Empire*, 1776

 `Autoexec.bat`, `config.sys` and all the `ini` files you could imagine are passé, toast, no longer of the slightest relevance to a properly set-up Windows 95 system. At least if you believe what the designers say. "Trust us, the old DOS/Windows files are only there for compatibility." Our testing systematically shows this isn't entirely true; there is some information in the `ini` files that still gets used. But that's an anomaly. It really is true that the oodles of information stored about system details and your preferences is almost entirely in a single *logical* object called the Registry.

Erwin emphasized the word *logical* after *single* because the Registry in most systems is built from two files—`user.dat` and `system.dat` in the `C:\windows` directory. There is even a good reason for this, as I'll explain when the rubber meets the road on the Registry in Chapter 11. I'll leave most of the discussion for there, but I want to note a few general facts here:

* The amount of stuff stored there is overwhelming including OLE registration information, the most intimate details of the life of your hardware and configuration information like what goes on the New submenu of the Desktop context menu and what icon is used for `My Computer`. The windows `ini` files were typically 40,000 to 100,000 bytes. Figure ten times that for the Windows 95 Registry.

* The ini files are ASCII. The Registry files are binary to allow a more elaborate structure and quicker reading by the system. This means a special program is needed to view the Registry. Windows 95 comes with such a program, called `Regedit`. It is installed in the Windows 95 directory but is not added to the Accessories (or any other group) in the Start Menu. You can add it yourself or just type `regedit` into the Run box. So long as you don't use the Add or Modify commands, you can't do anything wrong, so you might want to take a quick look—or better, jump to Chapter 11 and look at it in some detail.

* The structure is more involved than the old `ini` files. These had sections (like `[386Enh]`) and value pairs like `com1autoassign=2` in them. Sections are now

called keys and are hierarchically designed like the folder structure, so believe it or not, if you choose to have your Start Menu directory renamed to Mao's Menu, the information is stored in the key

```
\HKEY_CURRENT_USER\Software\Microsoft\Windows
\CurrentVersion\Explorer\Shell Folders
```

(that's all one long path!) with the value pair `StartMenu=C:\windows\Mao's Menu`.

It takes some getting used to, but once you pick it up it's not as bad as those huge key names look. Besides, the first time you reel off something like that key name, the jaw of the person you are talking to will drop and they'll think, "My, wotta guru."

Plug 'n Whatever

Now the truth can be told about where Plug 'n Play came from. One day big Bill was driving along in one of his souped up sports cars, happy as a clam. He looked in the mirror—whoops, it was a Smokey. Yet another ticket to shove in the glove compartment for Bill Neukom* to take care of. Being the world's richest human being means not having to worry about what a ticket will do to your insurance rates, but still, big Bill was steamed, so he turned on the radio to relax. Then he heard it—an Apple ad called "readings from the Microsoft® Windows™ manual" poking fun at the complications of dealing with comm ports under Windows. Bill stormed onto the corporate campus and let the Windows team have it. Why couldn't a PC be as easy to configure as a Mac? The result was Plug 'n Play.

In 1981, when IBM released the first PCs, configuration of add-ons wasn't hard. First, there weren't many boards you could add to the computer, and those you could add came from IBM, who could arrange for them to have no conflicts. The computers weren't very smart—they were several hundred times slower than current PCs and IBM could assume that most users understood technical stuff about IRQs and DMAs or else would like nothing better than to learn.

But as time went on, add-on hell sprang up. The explosion of wonderful add-on boards appeared, and conflicts could arise. Users were forced to use 1981 technology because the

---

* Bill Neukom is Microsoft's general counsel. He started with the company when he was a junior partner in a prestigious Seattle law firm and his boss asked him to keep an eye on the legal affairs of the boss's son, who had just moved his company from Albuquerque to Seattle. Neukom may not handle Bill's tickets, but Bill does have a reputation for getting them.

industry couldn't get its act together. You'd set some dip switches on the board, turn on your computer, and hope things worked—it was Plug 'n Pray.

Intel and Microsoft decided to put their considerable combined weight behind a specification that has been embraced by the industry and that finally reaches fruition with Windows 95. This spec is called `Plug 'n Play`.

The idea is simplicity itself. Plug 'n Play hardware can be configured by the operating system. When you put a new board in the system, it doesn't grab any system resources, but during boot-up when Windows 95 asks if anyone new is here, the board says, "Me, oh me! Could you set me up to work with the rest of the stuff?" Windows 95 then figures out what settings to use for the board; if it needs to, it adjusts the settings of other Plug 'n Play peripherals to prevent conflicts. It finds out what kind of peripheral it is and if it has drivers for that peripheral it automatically installs them.

That's the theory. I've no doubt within the next few years, that's the way virtually everything will work. For now it often works but not always, because of two issues. First, users still have what is called *legacy hardware*—that is, boards and peripherals that are not Plug 'n Play. Windows 95 provides some help for installing such hardware (as I'll describe in Chapter 10) but it's not transparent. Secondly, Plug 'n Play will have a bit of a shakedown cruise, especially as regards somewhat unconventional hardware.

As an example, take ECP ports—please. This is an enhanced parallel port specification that should make printing shine. High-class laser printers like the HPs have had ECP support as an option for some years and the better PCs like Gateway 2000 have had parallel ports with this capability for at least a while. There was no operating system glue to put them together, but there is now. With suitable Plug 'n Play implementations, you plug the printer in and the port on printer and computer are configured and everything works!

In theory. But not in practice, at least in the summer of 1995. It turns out that while many computers were supposed to have Plug 'n Play ECP support, only one line from one vendor did. You had to configure the port on other ECP computers by hand. And the procedure is quite complex because Windows 95 isn't very smart about getting the normal parallel port support out of the way. But if you turned ECP support on by hand, you'd find that that the printer had problems like buffer overflows because the ECP support had been done in theory without anything to test it with. In fact, as of July 1995, only one laser printer had ECP support that worked—and that was only if you had the latest version of the printer's firmware—Sigh.

 One confusion often occurs. Users assume if their computers don't have a Plug 'n Play BIOS, then Plug 'n Play boards won't work. That's not true for most kinds of plug-ins and certainly not for CDs and sound, the two biggest headaches for most users.

Crash 'em, Bash 'em

A car crash harnesses elements of eroticism, aggression, desire, speed, drama, kinesthetic factors, the stylizing of motion, consumer goods, status—all these in one event. I myself see the car crash as a tremendous sexual event really: a liberation of human and machine libido (if there is such a thing).

—J. G. Ballard , Interview in *Penthouse*

 I wonder what Ballard would think about a crash of Windows?

 Anyone that tells you the program that they've just shipped has no bugs in it is either a liar or a fool. Anyone that tells you the program that they've just shipped has no *known* bugs in it is either a liar or an incompetent. Any modern program is so complex that it is bound to have some kind of glitches, hopefully small. Indeed, vendors of complex programs keep lists of bugs found during the beta test and invariably some wind up on the list of "bugs that won't get fixed before we ship this version." Since fixing one set of bugs can introduce a new set, if a vendor waited until he knew it was bug-free, the product would never ship.

Some fraction of program bugs will result in the program doing something that causes the operating system to close the program down, lock, stock, and barrel. Up pops a message that says `This program has performed an illegal operation and will be shut down.` If you hit the `Details>>` button, you get the view seen in Figure 2-22.

The most common problem is that a program will try to access memory owned by another program. Essentially Mother Windows then says, "Naughty, naughty. That's Johnny's. Put it down and go to your room." The error is not so much that the program is making a power play for someone else's memory but that it passes Windows an address to send data too, and the address is wrong. These kinds of errors are called *protection violation errors.* If the address points to nowhere, the error is called an *invalid page fault.*

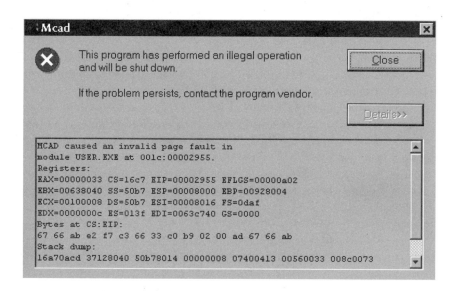

Figure 2-22. It's not my fault

In Windows 3.x, if some program crashed, the best advice was to save your work and reboot. In Windows 95, unless it was Explorer that crashed, you can probably safely continue working without rebooting. If you get a Windows error message with a details tab and you plan on contacting the vendor, be sure to click Details>> button and save the information shown. You can select it with a mouse and hit Ctrl+C to copy it to the clipboard, open Notepad, and paste it in and save it to a file. Saving the information could help the vendor out a lot.

 I always reboot whenever I get an IllOp . . . er, Illegal Operation. I'm still superstitious, and rebooting is such a small price to pay. Besides, I've seen applications crash with an IllOp— then, when restarted, crash with a similar IllOp, and so on, as if something got "stuck" and doesn't shake loose until I reboot. And while we're on the subject of IllOps, why in the blue blazes didn't Microsoft include a Copy or Print button along with Details? I always need to copy or print the information, just so I can yell at the manufacturer.

 You are overly cautious, Sarah. My practice is to save all files in other applications that are running and reload the problem program—if it has a problem reloading, then I do the reboot. Otherwise I continue, happy as a clam.

The other common crash is when the hourglass pops up and won't stop or the program just beeps if you click something. After being sure you haven't missed some message from the program telling you what to do, you can hit `Ctrl+Alt+Del` and wrap the sucker in concrete galoshes and drop it in the deep blue sea (see Figure 1-1 in Chapter 1).

And Dots Not All

> I could never make out what those damned dots meant.
>
> —Winston Churchill (speaking of decimal points)

Well, Blast My Raster

> Beware of Geeks bearing gifs.
>
> —Heard on the net

Run your finger along a piece of glass. GET YOUR FINGER AWAY FROM THAT MONITOR!!! It's a little-known fact that computer monitor screens are treated with special chemicals that draw the grease out of your fingertips. Some advanced models have the ability to draw it out from across the room. So use a window. NO, NOT THAT KIND OF WINDOW.

Is the piece of glass a smooth surface or is it a bunch of tiny bead like atoms spread out in two dimensions? It's "really" a set of atoms, but it's useful to think of it both ways. If you want to understand the sounds made when you hit a glass with a spoon, the smooth surface model may be better, but to understand how the kind of sand used to make the glass affects its strength, the atomic model may be better.

In the same way, what you see on a screen or what is printed out on a piece of paper is really a bunch of dots. And the computer or printer thinks of it that way. Before the display on your screen reaches the monitor it is put into the language of pixels—the color of each and every dot on your screen needs to be specified. (*Pixel* is short for "picture element.") In 1024×768 mode, there are 786,432 pixels on the screen. With that kind of job to do, it's no wonder Windows can be slow! Similarly, when printing a graphics on a 300 dpi laser printer on $11\text{-}\times\text{-}8.5$-inch paper, the computer needs to send 8,415,000 dots to the printer per page!

With those kinds of numbers involved, it is often better to think on an abstract level in terms of lines and suitable curves. Windows-accelerated display cards work on that principle; in detail

this is the line that Windows wants to draw

this is the driver that got passed the line that Windows wants to draw

this is the accelerator chip that understands lines that got one from the driver that got passed the line that Windows wants to draw

this is the adapter RAM where bits were placed by the accelerator chip that understands lines that got one from the driver that got passed the line that Windows wants to draw

this is the monitor that turns on the pixels sent to it by the adapter RAM, where bits were placed by the accelerator chip that understands lines that got one from the driver that got passed the line that Windows wants to draw

all without your CPU worrying its pretty head.

Similarly, if a file can describe a graphic in terms of lines and other objects—say, solid rectangles, text and . . . , it can be a lot smaller than if it has to describe every color. It's called 24-bit color because it takes 3 bytes (24 bits) to describe the color of each pixel. So a 24-bit color, 1024 × 768 file describing bits would require 2,359,296 bytes (1024 × 768 × 3)—that's more than 2MB on disk!

Alas, lines and shapes do have their limits. If you have a solid blue, large, rectangular shape, you can hope to use a description in terms of lines, but if you have a photo of the sky, the subtle changes of shade of blue can't be captured in terms of higher-order graphics, but only via "this here dot is royal blue, that one over there is kinda cyan."

So both descriptions via dots and descriptions with graphics objects have their place. If you ever want to manipulate either, you'd better know which is which, so you have to learn some names and file types.

Files that describe graphics in terms of dots (or pixels) are called bit-mapped files, bitmapped files, or just plain *bitmaps*. They are also called *raster*-based files. Windows has a native bitmapped-file format distinguished by the file extension bmp. Wallpaper has to be a * .bmp file and Windows ships with a whole bunch of them, which it probably installed on your disk. Other bitmapped formats are PC Paintbrush (* .pcx), TIFF (short for Tagged Image File Format—* .tif), CompuServe's Graphics Image Format (* .gif), and the Joint Photographic Expert Group compressed file format (called JPEG with name * .jpg).

Programs that manipulate bitmaps are sometimes called Paint programs, although the higher-class name is Image Editor. Occasionally, the Paint name is for programs that focus on creating bitmaps (*Fractal Painter* is the best example) and the Image Editor is for programs that focus more on Editing a photo you've gotten (by purchase or scanning). Mom's favorite bitmap editor is *Picture Publisher* and the standard for photographic professional is *Adobe Photoshop.* Windows itself comes with *Microsoft Paint,* which is a bitmap manipulation program. Each of the high-end paint programs has its own internal file format, adding to the plethora of formats in this area.

Files that describe graphics in terms of higher order objects are called vector graphics or object graphics. Different formats will support different kinds of objects but almost all support lines, some kinds of curves, and text. Many allow a special kind of complicated curve called a Bezier. Alas, there isn't really anything like a common standard in vector graphics. The closest things are the Windows built-in format called Windows Metafile (or *.wmf) and Encapsulated Postscript (*.eps).

The Windows Metafile format that was used in Windows 3.1 had limitations, such as no support for Bezier curves and limited ability to embed bitmaps. Windows 95 now has an Enhanced Metafile Format (*.emf) that removes these limitations and is likely, over time, to become the standard for vector graphics.

 Ha! Dream on. Vendors like to think they are adding something with their own formats—like trapped customers. There will never be an overwhelming standard in graphics files. If there were, Windows BMP files would have replaced TIFF and PCX—and they haven't.

EPS is intended for use with PostScript Printer's only. Displaying an EPS in native format requires a program to have a full-scale PostScript interpreter built in. However, most EPS files include a TIFF bitmap implementation inside them and programs can read and display those on screen. They can then send the real postscript code on to a postscript printer, even if the program itself doesn't understand postscript. There is a subset of EPS used by Adobe Illustrator (AI) and some programs that can't deal with arbitrary EPS can deal with AI files.

A third common format is a holdover from DOS called Computer Graphics Metafile (*.cgm) and because Word Perfect had so many users, its Word Perfect Graphics (*.wpg) files is a fourth common format.

Programs that manipulate vector graphics are called draw programs, drawing programs, or illustration programs. The leading products are *Adobe Illustrator, Corel Draw,* and *Micrografx Designer.* A draw program with less power but a unique, especially easy-to-use interface is *Visio.* The idea is to provide you with a large library of building blocks out of which to make your drawings.

In addition to solid colors, many vector formats allow gradient fills—a smooth interpolation of colors in a region of the drawing.

For special effects, most vector formats allow a bitmap to be an object as part of their graphic. And several recently released bitmap edit programs (*Adobe Photoshop* and *Picture Publisher,* for example) allow an object layer in their files, so that, for instance, they can leave text as separate letters rather than embedding it as a bunch of pixels.

Many of the high-end bitmap and vector graphics editors have their own file formats, making the area confusing. Even worse, many programs that use `.tif` or `.cgm` files support only some of the files that have that designation!

Generally photographs that you get from third parties and items that you scan in are bitmaps. Most high-end clip art is vector. You want your clip art to be vector because it scales to different sizes (as I'll discuss in the next section) and prints on different printers with no loss of quality. If you upgrade from a 300 dpi printer to a 600 dpi, your vector clip art will automatically use the higher resolution, although bitmaps will effectively print out no better.

So if you get an offer for a wonderful CD with oodles of clip art, find out if it is vector or raster and don't bother to get it if it is raster.

Besides the two basic graphics file families, multimedia has introduced its own graphics types. Most notable are the two main video types: Microsoft audiovisual interleave (`*.avi`) and Apple's Quicktime Movie (`*.mov`). There are also animation files (where the standard is Autodesk Animator— `*.flc`), sound (which I'll discuss later), and 3D graphics.

The Scales of Just Us

Vector graphics has a special advantage because it is scalable. Consider a capital A, shown in Figure 2-23. In a font like Arial, it consists of three straight lines—two forming a tent and one crossbar. TrueType stores it as a vector graphic. Of course, when you type an A on the screen, it has to be shown as bits so the TrueType engine makes the translation. The process of changing from vector to raster is called *rasterization*. Figure 2-23 shows a blowup of a boldface 10-point Arial A shown on a pixel-sized grid to see the rasterization. Suppose we blindly blow it up to double size. Thus, every black pixel becomes a 2 × 2 grid of pixels and

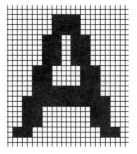

Figure 2-23.

you get the blown-up A on the left in Figure 2-24. In the middle, you see a blowup of the TrueType rasterized 20-point bold cap A in Arial font. Notice that the straight blowup is blocky and ugly compared to the A made directly from the vector rasterized at the higher size. The blockiness is even evident on the right side where the letters are shown (in the same orientation) without the blowup:

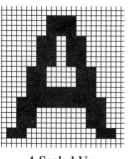
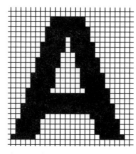

A A

A Scaled Up   Large *A* Rasterized

Figure 2-24. A, A who's got the A

Actually, this particular example involves more than just rasterization of lines—in the 20-point A, the rather delicate (and effective) single-pixel black rows at the bottom and single white row just above the cross bar are a consequence of hinting. We'll see what that means when I discuss "Could you gimme a hint?" soon.

The moral of this is that vector graphics are scalable. Bitmaps are not. If you scan in line art and want to blow it up, try to convert it to a vector graphic, blow that up, and convert back (I'll talk about conversion in a bit).

That's a Cockroach of a Different Color

Another wrinkle in rasterization concerns the use of colors, a process known as antialiasing. Allow me to explain.

If you were computing in the ancient days when VGAs were first introduced, you may recall that it had two "spectacular" new graphics modes. (The modern equivalent of telling your kid about trudging through the snow to school might be recalling the CGA: "Gee, I remember when graphics modes had only four colors"; "Was that before or after the end of the Civil War, Dad?" But I digress.) There were 640 × 400 in 16 colors and 320 × 200 in 256 colors. The remarkable thing was that the lower resolution but higher color mode looked more lifelike and seemed to actually be higher resolution than the 16-color mode.

This is an example of the phenomenon that, as far as perception is concerned, you can often trade color depth for resolution. This can place a monitor that is low resolution (640 × 480 on a 15-inch monitor works out to about 55 dpi) with lots of colors on a closer footing to the latest popular laser printers that are high resolution (600 dpi) with only two colors (black and white!).

In one direction, consider how a laser printer handles gray-scale printing. The printer has no gray ink. It mimics gray by putting down black dots in differing densities. A light gray will print as a few dots among the white background, while darker shades have more dots for the same area. If the resolution is high enough, you don't see the dots but perceive shades of gray. What is effectively a "gray dot" is a mix of several black dots amid white space, so one has less resolution when printing in grays. The printer has traded resolution for extra colors.

 HP III, 4 and 5 printers use variable-sized dots as well to help mimic gray scales, a procedure called RET (resolution enhancement technology) but the idea is the same.

The precise way that grays are translated depends on an algorithm that has to be carefully chosen to avoid banding and other artifacts. Usually your applications and the printer handle this for you, but if you read or hear about halftone frequency and angle, or error diffusion, someone is talking about this gray-to-dot-pattern translation.

On screen, when translating from a vector object like a line at some angle to dots, the problem is that rasterization occurs in block size units—the ideal rasterization might be to take only a third of some block, but pixels don't come in thirds. Or do they? When the object suggests that one take only a third of a pixel, why not use a shade of light gray, roughly one-third of the way from white to black? That's what antialiasing does.

To illustrate this, we looked at a 20-point Arial cap A as entered in the paint program *PhotoMagic* with and without antialiasing, an option that it supports. On the extreme right of Figure 2-25, you see the two A's normal size with the antialiased version on the right. If you look closely, you'll see that the normal A has a more noticeable staircase effect. The antialiased letter is smoother although a little fuzzy. The other two parts of the figure show blowups of the two letters. There are several different gray-scale levels used to produce the effect.

So what does antialiasing mean for you? One option with the Plus! Pack is that you can turn on antialiased screen fonts as long as you are running with at least 256 colors. It should have been turned on by the Plus! Pack Install, but to check that it has and turn it on if it hasn't, go to the Display Properties sheet (right-click on the Desktop and pick properties or run the display applet in Control Panel), go the Plus! tab and check the box labeled `Smooth edges of screen fonts`.

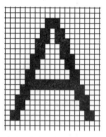

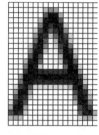

A A

A **in black and white**   **Antialiased** *A*

Figure 2-25. What was the name of that masked A?

 The general rule for the screen enhancements in the Plus! Pack—that means high color themes as well as antialiased fonts—is to do it only if your video is accelerated.

 Call me an aesthetic yahoo if you want—I know antialiased screen fonts are supposed to be the knees bees, but they make the letters look so fuzzy to me I keep thinking I've got to get my eyeglass prescription changed. So I experimented, but then turned the check box off.

In addition, some bitmap editing programs give you antialiased fonts and curves as an option. If you plan to print out a bitmap, if there is any way to keep the font as a vector object (for example, in programs with a vector layer), that is preferable. Rather than turn on gray scale and then have the printer turn those to thinned-out black areas, it is better to have the rasterization done at the higher resolution by the printer. If you are sending a presentation to a service bureau to make slides, the same considerations are true—try to keep anything that can be a vector object as one. But if your goal is to display fonts in an on-screen presentation, it will pay to use antialiasing if it is an option when you prepare the final screens.

Ain't Just Missionaries That Do Conversions

> Domini, domini, domini
> You're all converted now

> —Firesign Theater

Graphics files are a tower of Babel. Not only are there bitmaps and vector graphics but there are oodles of formats for each. You really need a method to transfer between one format and another, a translation utility.

You have to realize that there are four kinds of translations and each faces a different set of problems:

- **Raster to Raster.** This is the most straightforward. The different formats have different headers (the start of bitmapped files contains information like the dimensions, color depth, and so on; it is called a header because it comes at the start of the file) and use different compression schemes (some formats use data compression schemes that allow you to take less space without losing any information), but basically, they list each and every pixel color, one after the other. So translation is relatively straightforward. If you have a decent bitmapped editor, you can usually convert between formats by loading in one and saving in another without the need for a special utility. Most of the time you'll want to keep your files in PCX or TIF format, which are accepted by virtually any program that supports bitmaps at all. If you've installed Microsoft Office, Windows *Paint* will use its graphic importers so you can read a `pcx` or `tif` into *Paint* and save it as a `bmp`.

- **Vector to Raster.** This is the second easiest conversion—it is what we called rasterization and has all the issues of antialiasing. Still, you can expect a decent conversion program (like *Hijaak,* see Chapter 5) to handle this without surprises.

- **Vector to Vector.** This is tricky and fraught with peril. The biggest problem is that different formats support different objects. If a program tries to translate from a format that understands Bezier curves to one that doesn't, the best it can do is use a polyline— something that looks like a curve but is really a bunch of short lines strung together. So the file swells in size and complexity. Avoid such conversions if you possibly can.

 Did you hear about the computer programs they put in tandem—one was supposed to translate from English to Russian and the other from Russian to English, so you put in English and got out English with a twist. In went, "The spirit is willing but the flesh is weak" and back came "The vodka's great but the meat is rotten." If you try to translate from `cgm` to `wmf` and back, you should expect similar results, at best.

- **Raster to Vector.** This is really an art rather than a conversion! It used to be available only in special programs called autotrace programs. Now such capability is available with drawing packages and with Hijaak. If you have a complicated bitmap with subtle colors, successful autotracing is close to impossible. If you want to scan in line art or a logo in a fancy font and blow it up, you can hope to successfully use autotrace, but be prepared to do some correcting of the trace by hand in a drawing program—most likely, the trace will put too many nodes on a polyline and you'll want to smooth that out.

To be clear about blowing up a line art logo you have on paper, you

☞ Scan in the line art. This will produce a TIFF file in bitmapped format. If you can set the scanner for line art or two-color rather than gray scale, do so.

☞ Run the bitmap through an autotrace program. This will change the file to some vector format, for example, `ai` (a variant of `eps`) in *Adobe Illustrator.*

☞ Look at the vector file in a draw program that uses that file as its native format— presumably you'd use *Illustrator, Designer,* or *Corel Draw.* See if you need to clean it up.

☞ Ideally, you'll use the logo in a program that understands your vector format so that blowing it up is as simple as setting dimensions in a dialog or dragging on some handles. If you really need a bitmap, blow up the vector image in a draw program and use a conversion program for vector to bitmap. Your draw program might allow you to save as a bitmap, or you might need to use a program like Hijaak.

Putting Up a Good Font

As soon as he learned that I was writing a Windows book, Igor, who has been taking font lessons from Mao, started bugging me to be sure that when I talked about fonts, he could get a chance to tell you about 'em. So, here's Eeeeegor:

To explain fonts to folks, you print out samples of the good fonts and the bad fonts. Then you hold the page of good fonts up to the light and twirl it. You give a knowing look and remark, "1984 was an exquisite year for Caslons." Then you bring the page of good fonts carefully up to your nose and say, "Quelle arôme, quel bouquet."

Whoops; it appears that Igor mixed up the wine lessons he's been getting from Mao with the font lessons. That's the point. You've probably learned to ignore the wine snobs. That doesn't mean you have to drink rotgut. You can enjoy a good wine and learn some basics, like when to serve a white wine without becoming a wine snob yourself.

But the same folks who don't let the wine snobs and the hifi snobs faze 'em turn to jello in the face of font snobs. Funny thing is that while we know a very few sensible font experts, most font snobs are pompous fools and, if you don't believe me, just ask the other font snobs. So *illigitimus non carborundum.**

Both to cope with the font snobs and to understand the simple do's and don'ts, you need to learn some of the basic language. Forthwith, I'll present the basics, a kind of first course in fonts. An intermediate course will follow. If you want to know more, say, enough to know what it means when you tell a font snob to go kern himself, you'll want the advanced course following that. Then I'll let Mao tell you some of what his Little Red Book says about fonts and I'll talk about font technology in Windows 95. Even if you skip the rest because you decide you don't want to know about the theory of fonts, be sure to read the two sections "Font Tools in Windows 95" and "Installing and Removing Fonts in Windows 95."

In understanding the language of fonts, you need to remember you are dealing with an art that goes back more than five hundred years, so the terms reflect the technology of a hundred years ago more than the changes of the past fifteen, revolutionary though they may be. Most of all, they deal with movable metal type.

 The terminology enters in places you may not realize. A printer once set type by grabbing the letters from two boxes, each with compartments for the individual letters. The boxes were typically laid out with one over the other. The capital letters were in the box on top because they were used less often and the other letters on the bottom. These boxes were called cases and the two of them were the *uppercase* and the *lowercase.* I kid you not.

Fonts 101

Here's the basic terms. The first thing that you have to realize is that what you think is a font—you know, something like Arial or Times or Courier, isn't a font (nor is it a parallel universe). It's a *type family*! A *font* is a set of letter forms (fancy-pants name for shapes of letters) at a given size, weight, style, and type family. The *typeface* is the family of similar-looking fonts. *Size* is a measure of the vertical height of the font (normally the widths scale as the height does, so an 11-point font is not only 10 percent taller than a 10-point font, but also 10 percent wider). *Weight* refers to a measure of how heavy the strokes in the font are—the most common weights are *normal* and *bold,* but you can have an *extra bold* or a *light* at the heavier and lighter ends of the spectrum. *Style* is an expression of orientation—the most common are *Roman* and *italic.*

Fonts are also called typefaces, and as the irreducible typographical unit go back to those cases of type that contained letters from a single font. A set of fonts where all that is varied

---

* Don't let the bast.. er, illegitimate ones get you down.

is the size should have a convenient, simple name given current practice in computer typesetting, but there doesn't seem to be one. I'll call it a *scalable typeface.*

You can also have fonts with the same type family name and weight that are distinguished by how wide the letters are. If the font is made less wide for a given height, it is called *condensed* or *narrow.* If it is made wider, it is called *expanded,* but those are rare. Condensed fonts are useful in situations where you want to squeeze a lot of text into a headline.

Here are typical examples for the Arial font:

Normal: ABCDEFGHIJKLMnopqrstuvwxyz

Bold: **ABCDEFGHIJKLMnopqrstuvwxyz**

Extra Bold: **ABCDEFGHIJKLMnopqrstuvwxyz**

Black (Extra, Extra bold!):   **ABCDEFGHIJKLMnopqrstuvwxyz**

Extra Bold Condensed: **ABCDEFGHIJKLMnopqrstuvwxyz**

Narrow: ABCDEFGHIJKLMnopqrstuvwxyz

Italic: *ABCDEFGHIJKLMnopqrstuvwxyz*

Bold Italic: ***ABCDEFGHIJKLMnopqrstuvwxyz***

Bear in mind that a well-made italic font is not merely the font with a slant added, nor is a condensed font made by blindly scaling the widths—there are subtle design changes that a skillful type designer will make when italicizing or condensing. Of course, if the font is a schlock font made by scanning and autotracing, it is likely that the italic is made by simply skewing the outlines!

Interestingly enough, while a good font design is a work of art, fonts cannot be copyrighted in the United States or directly protected. Some bozo in the copyright office decided years ago that after all, the alphabet is the alphabet, so what's to copyright? That doesn't mean that you can buy a font pack and give the files on it to all your friends. Those files are computer programs and, as such, *are* protected. What it does mean is that if you are a font producer, you can try to make a perfect copy of a fancy new font you see. You can even print out that font, scan it in, autotrace it, and sell that as your own. However, font names can be trademarked, so you have the phenomenon that Helvetica has been called Aristocrat, Claro, Corvus, Europa Grotesk, Geneva, Hamilton, Helios, Holsatia, Megaron, Newton, Spectra, Swiss, Vega, and Video Spectra among other names.

Hehe, Europa Grotesk. I like that. I'll have to remember that name when I next have a run-in with the Swiss gendarmes.

Monotype's Arial is not a copy of Helvetica, as some might think but a separate font with some similar characteristics and arranged to have identical widths to the Adobe Helvetica font. But enough of culture! Let's return to our list of font terminology.

How are sizes measured? Fonts define a number of horizontal lines, all shown in Figure 2-26.

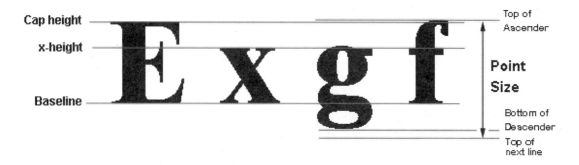

Figure 2-26. The definition of point size for a font

The letters cap E and x are especially regular. The line at their bottoms, which also lies on the bottom of most letters, is called the *baseline.* An imaginary line at the top of the cap E is called the *cap height.* Most caps go up to the same line, but some (like cap S) often extend slightly above. The height of the letter x, called the *x-height*—another one of those obscure technical terms—is the typical height of many lowercase letters but won't really concern us. Any lowercase letter that extends above the x-height is said to have an *ascender.* Typical examples are the letters t, h, and f (note that the t does not extend above the cap height but is still considered to have an ascender since it is higher than the x-height). Lowercase letters that fall below the baseline are said to have a *descender.* Typical are g, j, and y.

The point size of metal type was easy to define; it was the height of the slug of metal that the letter floated on. The type designer would include an extra space below the lowest descender to avoid a too-cramped look. If even more space was desired between lines, a strip of lead was inserted. The practice was called leading.

So *point size* is the distance between baselines of two successive lines of text. It is the distance from the top of the highest ascender to the bottom of the longest descender plus the default spacing that the designer wants.

The space taken by a line of type on a page is not determined only by the point size, because the blank space between the bottom of the descenders of one row and the top of the ascenders of the next can be adjusted. This is called *leading,* after the lead that printers once used to change that space! The term is pronounced to rhyme with "bedding," not with "seeding." With computer type, unlike the metal version, one can even have negative leading!

One often talks of the sum of the extra space and the point size. So a 10-point font with an extra 1-point leading between lines is called a 10-point font with an 11-point spacing, or just "10 on 11."

As the name *point size* suggests, the height is usually measured in a unit called *points.* A point was once about 1/72 inch, but since the United States is the hand that rocks the computer cradle, it is now considered to be exactly 1/72 inch. The rest of the world may be metric, but we continue to impose our weird measurements on them. So an 8-point font is 1/9 of an inch and an 11-point font with 12-point spacing fits six lines to the inch.

 Having told you that a font isn't a font but is a scalable typeface, I'll misuse the terms and talk about fonts unless there is an especial need for clarity. What do vendors do? Why, of course, they use the terms in a way that will let them blazon the largest number of "fonts" in their packages. When fonts were sold in bitmapped form so that size mattered, a vendor could sell you two type families but in the standard four weight/styles (normal, bold, italic, and bold italic) and in seven point sizes (say 6, 8, 10, 11, 12, 14, 18) and yell about having fifty-six fonts!! The two type families blossomed to 56 by multiplying 2 x 4 x 7.

Now that most fonts are outlines, vendors don't get to multiply by the number of font sizes, but you can bet they still count different weights/styles as separate "fonts." So, for example, the *Monotype Value Pack* says it has "57 typefaces." In fact, it has seven type families in the standard four weight/styles, twenty-one display/symbol/script type families in twenty-five combinations, four Arial fonts, and one Times New Roman at weights that supplement the ones in Windows. I'm not sure how they count fifty-seven, since by their rules, I count fifty-eight but it's only a 2 percent error and no doubt it makes Heinz happy, so why complain? However, by what a naive user would think fonts means, this package has thirty "fonts."

Monotype isn't to be singled out. Every vendor counts the way they do and every naive user misunderstands! In the naive terms, it is not atypical for a package that claims *N* fonts to have *N*/2 or *N*/2.5 type families. Indeed, the celebrated thirty-five Postscript fonts are actually eight families of the standard four weight/styles and three specialized fonts, for only eleven type families.

Type families are often grouped together in various ways. The simplest is fixed pitch versus proportional spacing. *Fixed pitch,* aka *monospaced,* fonts have a common width for all letters so that M takes the same space as i. *Proportional fonts* have variable letter widths within the single font. Here is the effect seen with Courier, a fixed-pitch font versus Arial, a proportional one:

Courier: MMMMMMMMMM   Arial: MMMMMMMMMM

iiiiiiiiii   iiiiiiiii

1234567890   1234567890

1111144444   1111144444

To have numbers line up, all numbers have a common width in either fixed pitch or proportional fonts.

Fonts 201

A more complex but useful breakdown is into serif, sans serif, script, display, and symbol. The first two sets are the work horses of typography—the ones you'd normally use for body text. A serif is the funny hook that some fonts have at their edges. Look at the four letters shown in Figure 2-27. The letters on the left are in a sans serif font (Arial) and the ones in the right in a serif font (Times New Roman). Serif fonts are more common and include **Century Schoolbook**, Garamond, Palatino, and Times. Sans serif fonts include Avant Garde, **Futura**, and **Helvetica**.

Figure 2-27. Serif vs. Sans Serif

Script fonts are ones you might use for invitations like *Shelley Allegro*, *Shelley Andante*, and *Shelley Volante*. Display fonts are usually used only in small amounts, mainly in headlines or letterheads. Among the more famous ones are **Cooper Black** and **Bodoni.** Symbol fonts include foreign alphabets—notably Greek ($\alpha\beta\gamma\delta\epsilon\kappa\lambda\mu\nu\pi$)—math symbols ($\int$, $\otimes$, Σ, $\notin$) and dingbats, those little pieces of fluff that make bulleted lists less dull (☎, ✉, ➜, ✍, ☺).

It turns out that making dingbat fonts is fraught with peril! If you take the letters NYC, highlight them, and change the font to Wingdings, you get

A New York-based consultant discovered this shortly after Windows 3.1 shipped and suddenly the *New York Post* blazoned on its front page:

Software Company Vows Death to New York Jews

I kid you not—it really happened. Isn't technology grand?

 If you're really into Microsoft conspiracy theories, there's a better one. This story was short-lived because the Los Angeles riots broke out the next day and moved this story off the front page even in the *Post*.

 It's an interesting sidelight to the story; six high-ranking Microsoft executives met the next day to decide how to react to the *Post* story. Of the six, four were Jewish, including the managers of the font and Windows units.

 Personally, I think what the message really means is, "If you take poison, see a Jewish doctor and you'll feel better." It's also interesting that they didn't complain about Mr. Zapf. In *his* dingbats, $A4 becomes ✂ ✡ ✔. Surely the *Post* could have made something of that.

Fonts 378

Herewith, a primer of some of the more esoteric font terminology:

- **Tracking.** This refers to letter spacing in a font as a whole or in a chunk of text as a whole. Useful only for special situations. Here's an example that should make it clear.

How big did you say that the fish was? It was a real WOPR, sir.	How big did you say that the fish was? It was a real WOPR, sir.	How big did you say that the fish was? It was a real WOPR, sir.
Default tracking	Tracked (too) tight	Tracked (too) loose

- **Kerning.** This refers to spacing between pairs of letters. Without kerning each letter has a fixed width—different width for different letters. In the absence of kerning, all occurrences of one letter have the same width as all other occurrences. The space next to a **T** is the same as for **Th** as for **To**. But there is room to slightly tuck the o under the T, which makes for a more attractive possibility at large point size. Look at the three examples below; the one where the o is nudged under the T is more attractive. High-class fonts come with kerning information—tables to tell programs how to kern if they want to kern automatically. For headlines at large point sizes, you might want to do this hand adjustment.

To	**To**	**To**
No kerning	Kerned Condensed	Kerned Expanded

- **Hanging Indent.** This is the name given to a paragraph where the first line starts to the left of the rest of the paragraph, like the following example:

This text has a hanging indent. You'll notice that the second and subsequent lines start indented. Hanging indents are most naturally used when discussing a list of items. The indentation makes it easy for the eye to see when a new item has begun. Often with such a list, the first line has a bullet or dingbat so the text on line one is actually aligned with the lower lines. Typographers still regard that as having a hanging indent, since the bullet is included in line one!

- **Dropped Caps and Raised Caps**

This is a dropped cap, determined by making the initial letter large and having it dropped down into the text. A few programs allow you to pick dropped caps from a menu but otherwise you need to fool around with frames. Dropped caps should be arranged so that they lie on the base line of a lower line of type. In Microsoft Word, you can get a drop cap by picking the Drop Cap . . . item from the Format menu.

This is a raised cap. It is made by picking a large point size for the initial letter. It isn't as effective as a drop cap.

- **Rules** is Rules; actually, rules are fancy names for lines.

> The most famous kind of rules are ones that are used for *pull quotes,* quotes from your text that you pull out and emphasize by placing lines, I mean rules, above and below.

- **En** and **Em** dashes are font-dependent measures of horizontal space. At one time, the em was the width of the letter M and the en was half an em. Now, an em is a horizontal space exactly equal to the point size and an en is half an em. Most important for referring to dashes of that width, specifically – and —.

- **Small Caps.** If you want an effect like SMALL CAPS, you can try to use a smaller point size for the letters MALL but the proportions aren't quite what a typographic purist would want. Some typefaces have special small caps fonts in their family. These are available in a few PostScript fonts but not in TrueType.

- **Lower case or old style numerals.** The numerals included with modern fonts are called *lining numerals* because they are fixed width and will line up under one another. For a spreadsheet, you want to use these kinds of numerals but they do not look right if you are typing the time where 1:11 should have very different letter widths than 6:00. Quite a few True Type fonts with old style numerals are available.

- **Justification.** Your word processor probably supports four varieties:

  Text squeezed against the left side of the page but not aligned on the right side is often called *ragged right,* or sometimes *left justified.*

  Text that is set to line up on both sides is called *justified.* Your word processor adds extra spaces between words to arrange for the text to line up.

  Text made to line up on the right side is called *right justified.* It is useful only in special circumstances, such as entering the date in a letter.

  Centered text is also only useful in special circumstances.
  Use it sparingly.

- **Widows and Orphans.** Yeah, I know, you gave at the office. To adequately tell you about these terms, I need to talk about my poor friend Sylvia from Boston, who married John from London. One day, Sylvia's parents and John were in a terrible car accident and they were all killed. So Sylvia is a widow in England but an orphan in the United States. In the same way, at one point, a paragraph with a few words straggling onto the next page was called a widow in England and an orphan in the United States. Since then, an array of books on Desktop publishing has so muddied the waters that it is not clear what exactly is a widow and what is an orphan. The thing to avoid is either beginning a paragraph with a single line at the bottom of one page and its bulk on the next or beginning a page with a single line left over from the paragraph on the previous page. When you see either, flip a coin and then knowingly say "Oh my, an orphan," or "Oh my, a widow," depending on whether the coin is heads or tails. Half the know-it-alls will think you right and half wrong. This terminology is also sometimes used to refer to single words on the last line of a paragraph. Desktop publishers need to worry about this. You can safely ignore it for general correspondence.

- **Ligatures.** Certain combinations (namely, fi, fl, ffi, and ffl) are spaced so closely together that they really should be treated as a single character (and the i's dot is wrong if you just kern the letters). In some specialized fonts they are. These characters are called *ligatures.*

- **Panose numbers** are numbers assigned to fonts based on various characteristics so that fonts with nearby Panose numbers are similar to each other. When you list fonts in Win95 by similarity, the ranking is derived from Panose numbers.

 Panose is so named because if you take the measurements of the uppercase P, A, N, O, S, and E characters from any Roman font, you can derive a high fidelity measurement of the overall font's style. For example, the P tells you the basic shape of the B and R since they (generally) share the same upper bowl. The N tells you the shape of the M, X, W, Y, Z and V because they will have the same diagonal strokes in the center. E tells you what the F will look like, while O tells you the basic shape of the Q, C, G, D and lower portion of the U. The system is designed to be mathematically repeatable, meaning that if you teach one hundred monkeys how to measure a font using the Panose method, and lock them in a room, they will all arrive at the same answer for the same font, unlike other font measurement methods that depend on the subjective "feel" from a group of "experts." It's sort of like wine tasting versus using a mass spectrometer.

- **The standard 35 PostScript** fonts are the eleven font families that were included on the earliest printers that licensed PostScript from Adobe, most notably, Apple's LaserWriter. This involved eight families of body fonts in the standard four weights and three symbol (or decorative) fonts. The following table shows the Postscript names and the Monotype equivalents. These equivalents are not the same fonts, or even fonts with precise same shapes. For example, Arial and Helvetica are *not* the same font with different names. But the Monotype equivalents do use the same width tables and so you could replace them on a one-to-one basis.

Postscript Name	Number	Monotype Name
Courier	4	Courier New
Helvetica	4	Arial
Symbol	1	Symbol
Times Roman	4	Times New Roman
Avant Garde	4	Century Gothic
Bookman	4	Bookman Old Style
Helvetica Condensed	4	Arial Narrow
New Century Schoolbook	4	Century Schoolbook
Palatino	4	Book Antiqua
Zapf Chancery	1	Monotype Corsiva
Zapf Dingbats	1	Monotype Sorts

The thirteen fonts above the line are included with Windows (which includes a fourteenth TrueType font—Wingdings). The twenty-two afterwards are among those available in the *Monotype Value Pack* and in *The Microsoft Font Pack.*

Windows TrueType Fonts

Windows comes with fifteen scalable TrueType fonts:

- Arial in four weights/styles: a proportionally spaced sans serif font

- Courier New in four weights/styles: a monospaced serif font

- Times New Roman in four weights/styles: a proportionally spaced serif font.

- Symbol including ΑΒΧΔΕΦΓΗΙϑΚαβχδεφγηιφκ but also math: ≅∃⊥≡ℑ↑∞

- Wingdings including ✌☜☟☝☞☞ ☺☻☐☐📄📄📄⌛⌨️📠🕐💿☐📁✏️✂️✂️✁☎️☐☒☎️◐

- Marlett, of which I'll say more

 Marlett is new with Windows 95; the other fourteen were included with Windows 3.1. But here is a mystery. If you call up WordPad, type some text in, select it and choose Font . . . from the Format menu, you'll find listed a font named Marlett with the TT symbol next to it. Now call up the Fonts Folder from My Computer or Control Panel, which is supposed to list all your fonts, and you won't find Marlett among them!

Marlett is a monospaced font and here are some of the characters (with the corresponding letters in Courier New below them):

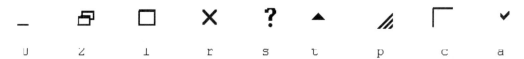

If you look at the buttons on the upper-right of a Windows 95 window, you'll recognize the Marlett characters 02r or 01r on those buttons. The other characters are also used for system drawing. For example, look at the symbol associated to the letter p and at the lower-right corner of an Explorer window.

While it seems to be documented nowhere, Marlett is clearly a system-level font. It seems to be built into one of the kernel files since a search for marlett.ttf on the install hard disk or for Marlett in the fonts section of the Registry draws a blank.

But Microsoft does supply you with a TrueType file with this font, so, for example, Woody and Barry could pass said font file on to their publisher for use on the Macs (gack!), where the book is typeset. The file is `marlett.ttf` and it's in the `Win95_05.cab` file on the CD. If you need it, check out Appendix E for instructions on how to expand from CAB files.

Good Writing Needs Character Development

Simplicity of character is no hindrance to subtlety of intellect.

—John Morely, *Life of Gladstone,* 1903

In addition to the physical characteristics of size, weight, and style, the actual font you use has a character set, the actual mapping of computer codes to symbols, not only for letters like A or x but for special symbols like ™ or ½. The initial starting point for PC character sets is the ASCII* code, a 7-bit assignment of a specific symbol to each number from 0 to 127. This starts with thirty-two control characters (holdovers from the days of Teletypes!) with codes 0 to 31. It is followed by thirty-two symbols starting with space at code 32, punctuation like , and !, and the ten numerals. At code 64 is the character @ followed by the twenty-six uppercase letters in alphabetical order and then five more symbols to round out the third set. The final thirty-two start with ` and then have the twenty-six lowercase letters, each exactly thirty-two codes beyond the corresponding caps. The basic ASCII set is rounded out by five final symbols (see Figure 2-29—the codes from 32 to 127).

When IBM introduced the PC, the architecture of the system CPU made it natural to use 8-bit characters, so IBM extended the ASCII set in two ways. It gave symbols to the codes below 32, strange ones like the playing card suits and the closest that the original PC had to dingbats. In the area above 128, it placed accented letters like ê or á, line-drawing characters to allow the placement of frames, and a pitifully small selection of Greek letters and mathematical symbols. Figures 2-28 and 2-29 give two views of the IBM character set (also called extended ASCII):

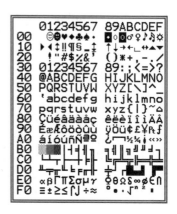

Figure 2-28. ASCII codes in Hexadecimal

---

* ASCII is short for American Standard Codes for Information Interchange

Figure 2-29 is a decimal-labeled table: cap **A** is in the 060 row and the 5 column, so its ASCII code is 65 decimal. Figure 2-28 is a hexadecimal (base 16) table. Here A is in row 40 and column 1, so its code is 41H (the same as 65 decimal, of course).

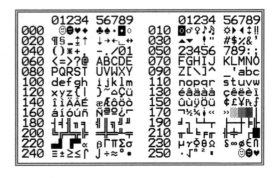

Figure 2-29. ASCII codes in decimal

These character sets are mainly of historical interest, although Windows 95 does supply several fonts that use the Extended IBM sets (in the United States):

- For displaying data pasted from DOS sessions in the clipboard viewer, Windows provides a bitmapped font with "OEM" in its name* (for example, `8514oem.fon` at high screen resolutions).

- Bitmapped fonts for displaying DOS sessions in a window. For weird historical reasons, these are stored in five files: `dosapp.fon`, `ega40woa.fon`, `ega80woa.fon`, `cga40woa.fon`, `cga80woa.fon`. `woa` stands for "Windows Old Apps", i.e., DOS.

- A bitmapped font called terminal for display of terminal mode in communication programs.

- New to Windows 95, Courier New has an extended set of characters that includes the OEM character set. It is these characters that are used in windowed DOS sessions when you choose one of the fonts marked TT. I'll have more to say about extended sets of characters shortly.

- If you have the Plus! Pack, it installs Lucida Console fixed-pitch TrueType font, which you can use instead of Courier. By default, this replaces Courier, although you can restore the use of Courier by calling up the Add/Remove Programs applet in Plus, highlighting and clicking `Microsoft® Plus! for Windows® 95` in the `Install/Uninstall` tab, then clicking `Add/Remove . . .`, choosing Visual Enhancements and removing "Enhanced MS-DOS Font." Which TrueType font is used for DOS sessions is built into the Windows kernel and not something you can change with, say, a Registry setting.

---

* Rush: OEM means "Original Equipment Manufacturer" but it is really Microsoft speak for IBM.

Courier has all those serifs and is kinda feminine. Lucida is a strong masculine font.

Billy, you MCP, you.

Young man, those cheeks are looking a lot less pinchable. Slapping makes more sense!

For other Windows fonts, a different character set is normally used—it is called the Windows ANSI character set. ANSI is short for American National Standards Institute and you'll see their name pop up all the time as you learn about computers. Microsoft has modified the set and makes some refinements as time goes on. In particular, some of the codes in the 140–160 range were not in Windows 3.0 but only added in Windows 3.1. A few of these "new" codes only codified what you could call black market codes—for example, ones for fancy quotes that the main Desktop publishers had set up. Figure 2-30 shows the Windows ANSI set:

	!	"	#	$	%	&	'	(	)	*	+	,	-	.	/	0	1	2	3	4	5	6	7	8	9	:	;	<	=	>	?
@	A	B	C	D	E	F	G	H	I	J	K	L	M	N	O	P	Q	R	S	T	U	V	W	X	Y	Z	[	\	]	^	_
`	a	b	c	d	e	f	g	h	i	j	k	l	m	n	o	p	q	r	s	t	u	v	w	x	y	z	{			}	~	□
□	□	,	ƒ	„	…	†	‡	ˆ	‰	Š	‹	Œ	□	□	□	□	'	'	"	"	•	–	—	˜	™	š	›	œ	□	□	Ÿ
	¡	¢	£	¤	¥	¦	§	¨	©	ª	«	¬	-	®	¯	°	±	¹	³	´	µ	¶	·	¸	¹	º	»	¼	½	¾	¿
À	Á	Â	Ã	Ä	Å	Æ	Ç	È	É	Ê	Ë	Ì	Í	Î	Ï	Ð	Ñ	Ò	Ó	Ô	Õ	Ö	×	Ø	Ù	Ú	Û	Ü	Ý	Þ	ß
à	á	â	ã	ä	å	æ	ç	è	é	ê	ë	ì	í	î	ï	ð	ñ	ò	ó	ô	õ	ö	÷	ø	ù	ú	û	ü	ý	þ	ÿ

Figure 2-30. Windows ANSI characters

It's displayed with thirty-two characters in each row and only starts with character 32, the space. Unassigned codes are shown with a box. The first three rows are the standard ASCII characters from code 32 to 126. The 0 in row one is at position 16, which is a useful marking point so, for example, the box below the 0 in row 4 is at position 128+16=144 and the quotes are at 145–148.

You'll occasionally need to know these character numbers, so we note especially:

Types of Characters	Examples	Codes
Publisher's Quotes	' ' " "	145–148
En and Em Dash	– —	150, 151
Trademark, etc.	™ ® ©	153, 169, 174
Fractions	¼ ½ ¾	188–190
Currency	¢ £ ¥	162, 163, 165
Dots and Daggers	† ‡ •	134, 135, 149
typographic symbols	§ ¶	167, 182
Accented letters	ä Ø ç ñ	192–256

How do you enter these funny ANSI characters? There are three ways:

- you can use the Windows applet *Character Map,* which I'll discuss in Chapter 4

- you can enter a character with code 192, by making sure NumLock is on, and then holding down the `Alt` key and hitting

  `0 1 9 2`

  on the keypad

- Word processors may have automated ways to enter them. For example, Winword automagically replaces " with " at the start of a word and with " at the end. And by default, (c) becomes ©, with similar replacements for ®. I'd recommend you consider going into Winword's autocorrect dialog and replace -- by –, an en dash and == by —, an em dash. To make such specialized setup in Winword, you'll need to know the codes at the time you set up (or use *Character Map*).

Mom, in *The Mother of All Windows Books,* you raved about a utility called Compose that let you easily enter the special Windows ANSI characters. For example, with it `Right Ctrl+c+o` gave ©. Why didn't you mention it here?

Compose was indeed a wonderful free Windows 3.x utility. But it doesn't work in 32-bit Windows 95 applications and crashes sometimes in 16-bit applications. Compose-type utilities will need to be rewritten for Windows 95. For now, I'm anxiously waiting for one to appear!

IBM (whoops, OEM) and Windows ANSI aren't the whole story for the forward-looking Windows maven. Extended ASCII and Windows ANSI are 1-byte character codes, which means only 256 codes. This is stretched already, but if one thinks of the ideographs of Japan and China, it is clearly too restricted. Unicode is a proposed 2-byte scheme that therefore allows 65,536 possible characters. Quite a bit of homework to learn them all, isn't it? The codes are described in two 600+ page volumes, the second devoted solely to East Asian ideographs. Volume 1 starts with ASCII and then includes the Greek, Cyrillic, Armenian, Hebrew, Arabic, Devanagari, Bengali, Gurmukhi, Gujarti, Oriya, Tamil, Telugu, Kannada, Malayalam, Thai, Lao, Tibetan, and Georgian alphabets, as well as assorted dingbats, math symbols, arrows, and currency symbols.

Microsoft has announced its intention to move to Unicode in a future version of Windows. Think of all the symbols you'll have, and think of all the programs that could break! Progress is rarely cheap.

Actually, grasshopper, Windows already supports Unicode to some extent. Every TrueType font that Microsoft has shipped has been internally coded as Unicode. At one point, full Unicode support was promised for Windows 95, but that promise was not fulfilled. Use of some non-Latin alphabets (for example, Hebrew) in English versions of Windows remains a disaster with no standard. Each program that uses such fonts marches to its own drummer. Sigh.

American Windows does have support, though, for variants on the standard English alphabet that involve accented letters, for example, French or Spanish. You can explore this by calling up the keyboard applet in Control Panel and clicking on the Language tab.

Most of the TrueType fonts in Win95 have the option of including multiple character sets inside a single font. Indeed, the Courier New font that comes with Windows includes both the Windows ANSI and OEM sets. By default programs accessing those fonts will get the ANSI set, but a program can request OEM characters, and that is exactly what DOS boxes do.

The windows CD comes with two sets of font files for twelve of the fourteen core fonts (all but Symbol and Wingdings). By default the "small" versions of the fonts are installed taking almost exactly 1 MB, but as I'll explain, you can install "large" versions that take almost 2 MB. The *small* and *large* do not refer to font size (after all, these are scalable fonts), but to the number of extra characters squeezed in. The large fonts include up to 652 characters including Cyrillic, Greek, Turkish, the Baltic States, and all of Eastern Europe and even the Mac character set.

Except we couldn't get permission to include the character in the Mac character set that is the Apple logo. Too bad.

You install these fonts together with keyboard support for central European languages, Cyrillic and/or Greek by calling up the Add/Remove Programs applet in Control Panel, clicking on the Windows Setup tab, scrolling to the entry labeled "Multilanguage Support," and hitting Details. . . .

The Font of All Wisdom

CTO Mao has a whole chapter in his little red book on use and misuse of fonts. He's authorized me to quote liberally from it.

Avoid Ransom Note Typography. It is the biggest type-based sin in a world with hundreds of fonts.

Ransom note typography is the name given to material that uses too many fonts—sort of like the ransom notes that are cut out of magazine ads with each letter in a different Font. There are rules of thumb, but they may be too generous to the fontoholic. The advice is somewhat different for *heading text,* the words used as section titles, and *body text,* the bulk of what you are saying.

Certainly, do not use multiple fonts for body text on a single page. Indeed, consider using a single-body text font in each document. Some of the font etiquette books suggest using a serif font for body text and a sans serif font for headings. That's OK, but it is often more elegant to use the same font for heading and body with the heading in bold and at a larger point size. Normally, you'd want to use the same typeface for heading and for page header/footer but, as this book shows, there can be special reasons to violate that rule.

Boy, the authors of this book should hang their heads in shame. They complain about ransom note typography and just look at the pages where we icons are all talking to each other. Geez!

Consider 11-point text for correspondence.

Ten-point text is more usual but it looks small. Some users jump to 12 point. Before scalable text, many font collections only had 10 and 12 point and skipped 11, but if you are using scalable fonts, 11 is easy. And it's a good compromise.

Pitch out your fixed-pitch fonts.

Well, don't exactly throw them out. Fixed-pitch fonts are a holdover from obsolete technology. Typewriters couldn't handle proportional spacing so fixed pitch was introduced even though it was unknown before then. The two fonts used in IBM typewriters—Courier and Elite—became so much the standard for business correspondence that even now law offices and some other businesses tend to use them. But they are ugly. Avoid their use except for special purposes like our use of a fixed-pitch font for keyboard keys.

Don't think that to get numbers to line up in a column, you need fixed pitch—all fonts use a fixed pitch for their numerals. And a proper use of tabs, especially of right as well as left tabs, is a more effective way to align columns with text.

 Neither a borrower nor a lender be.

 Igor, you cut that one out from the wrong part of the book! Besides, isn't that Tobias, not Mao?

 Well, from someone guilty of Polonius' assault . . .

 As a general rule, set body text in a font with serifs.

The general wisdom is that for large chunks of text a font with serifs is easier to read because the serifs sweep the eyes along. The exception to this rule is the next rule!

 Use sans serif fonts for smaller point sizes.

Eight-point type and certainly anything smaller is more legible without the clutter of serifs. So if you are typing up a legal contract, use Arial for the fine print. This rule is an artifact of computer-generated fonts. Hot metal fonts compensated for smaller sizes by thickening strokes and increasing x-heights. With such fonts, serif fonts were more legible at smaller sizes also, but even with hinting, this is not true for computer generated fonts.

 Think about your audience when using fonts.

This may be obvious, but users caught up in the excitement of the great new font forget it. Fonts are important because, in unseen ways, they really can set the tone of a document. You should use the template/style sheet feature of your word processors to pick the fonts for different kinds of documents and stick with it. You can make exceptions for the announcement of the company picnic.

So he's saying, "To thine own self be true!"

Oy, Billy. The Bard is too much with thee.

Avoid using dingbats and other doohickeys too much. Similarly, avoid using too many rules.

Remember that the point of using fonts is to make your point—to get a message across. You risk having the messenger get in the way if you overload the text with stuff that distracts rather than complements. Again, you can make exceptions for the announcement of the company picnic.

Yo, Mom. Did ya see what he said about avoiding too many rules? Kids would sure like that!

He meant publisher's rules. The lines that make up boxes or break text.

For long documents, use ragged right text. For short business correspondence and memos of less than a page, consider using justified text.

This advice is somewhat controversial. Justified text is definitely harder to read (which is why you want to avoid it in long documents), less elegant to my taste, and enough to make the font snobs wince. But it looks more businesslike.

Use publisher's quotes like ". . ." and '. . .' and the real apostrophe ' rather than the lower ASCII characters ", ' and `. Also, use the en dash – and em dash — rather than a hyphen -, where appropriate. Generally an em dash is used for a major break in a sentence and an en dash for number ranges (e.g., 1–40) and for expressions like New York–London route.

It is a pain to enter these characters from the keyboard so you'll need some method to help. See the discussion in the last section about ways to enter special characters.

Be consistent. A good rule in dealing with children, employees, and type. Use the same font including weight and point size for heading throughout a document.

Avoid too much dense text. If you want people to read and understand what you write, don't have long paragraphs. Be sure to place some white space between paragraphs. Remember that the concentration span of the MTV generation for written text is about three words.

AVOID USING ALL CAPS. They are actually harder to read because the eye prefers variation and they don't even produce the desired emphasis. Besides, needing to use all caps for emphasis is the sign of a limited typographic environment as you'd find with a typewriter or in on-line messages. Use **bold** or *italic* for emphasis.

Use real bold and italic. If you use a font that doesn't have a bold or an italic, Windows will try to fake it and the results are not as fine as you get with a font that has the extra weights/styles. Alas, the only way to know if the bold/italic is real is to remember from the ad for the font (!), or if you are dealing with TrueType fonts, from the Fonts folder.

Don't be cowed by this advice or the advice of others. Do experiment and do consider breaking rules (the rules that get pontificated, not the rules that are really straight lines!). If you've understood the reason for a rule and have reason to break it, you're almost sure to do the right thing.

Could You Gimme a Hint?

That faculty of beholding at a hint the face of his desire and the shape of his dream, without which the earth would know no lover and no adventurer.

—Joseph Conrad, *Lord Jim,* 1900

You want a hint, sonny, I'll give you a hint! If you go to New York and don't call your Aunt Sally, I'll . . . Lemme give ya a hint. It's spelled E-G-O-R-E.

I guess Mom's had a bad day. But when you hear about how good Microsoft's hinting is, most likely, the speaker is not referring to how well their press agency seeds rumors but to the care put into their TrueType fonts.

If you print a 72-point letter on a 2200 dpi Linotronic, the letter will be at least a thousand dots high and a few dots won't matter. But consider a 15-inch monitor running at 800 × 600. A 15-inch diagonal at a 4 × 3 aspect ratio means a 9-inch height, or fewer than 72 dpi, so on screen an 8-point letter could have 5 or 6 dots in it.

 Hey, CTO, how come he didn't say 2200 dots for the Linotronic and 8 dots for the 8 point?

 Remember that point size is measured from the top of the tallest letter to the bottom of the letter that drops down the most plus a default line spacing. So no letter has a height equal to the point size!

The best fonts in Windows are scalable fonts, which are stored as outlines that are rasterized before being displayed on your screen or printer. In case you skipped it, I discussed rasterization earlier in the first part of "And dots not all."

The two main outline formats in terms of usage are TrueType and PostScript Type 1. TrueType is included in Windows 95. To rasterize PostScript fonts on screen, you need a copy of *Adobe Type Manager,* called *ATM.* You can purchase ATM separately or find it bundled with a variety of programs from Adobe.

The dumb algorithm for rasterizing an outline font is to pretend to draw the objects at a much higher resolution on top of a grid representing the available resolution. If a box is more than 50 percent covered, fill in the corresponding dot as black. Otherwise leave it blank. This algorithm could do violence to a letter form. In many fonts, W is left–right symmetric. But if the grid is aligned to the exact character width, using the dumb algorithm could destroy that symmetry. So an intelligent font rasterization scheme allows for information about symmetry. *Hints* are the name given to all information beyond the pure outlines that are included with a font.

Hints include information to be sure serifs aren't dropped and that essential type elements like a cross bar on the t aren't dropped and are uniform from left to right when they need to be. Both TrueType and PostScript Type 1 have hinting engines built into them so that font vendors can supply this extra information.

Hinting has three levels of sophistication. Some fonts in these formats have no hinting because the vendor didn't bother. Some are autohinted. That means that an automated program was used to make the hints. A few have hand-tuned hints—hints added by a professional type designer, usually after autohinting is first done.

Both ATM and TrueType include font caches. They save in memory the raster patterns for recently rasterized letters and don't have to do it again and again. On slower machines you may note a pause the first time you use a font in a session compared to later usage—that's the effect of the font not being in the cache the first time around.

The biggest font vendors have their own programs for internal use. And they will also hand-tune afterward. Microsoft did all the right things when it added TrueType to Windows. First they started with a good specification. Indeed, TrueType hinting is a superset of what is in PostScript.

Second, they introduced new printing technology that substantially sped up printing on HP laser (and related) printers compared to ATM 1.0. That version of ATM rasterized a page of text as dots and sent it to the printer as a graphic. Suppose that page had the letter A two hundred times on the page, all in the precisely identical font. Because of the font cache, ATM would rasterize it only one time and get it the other times from the cache. But because the dot pattern is sent as a graphic, the dot pattern for that A would get sent to the printer two hundred times on that page. Since the parallel port is one of the slowest links on computer, that's a lengthy process.

Windows TrueType engine instead used the ability of laser printers to understand downloadable fonts. It would send the characters needed for that page to the printer as a soft font, sending each dot pattern only once. Then those two hundred could be sent as characters requiring only 1 byte each. ATM added that feature in version 2.0, but the speed boost was a welcome addition for which Microsoft deserves the bulk of the credit.

Third, Microsoft provided fourteen TrueType fonts with Windows—not merely OK fonts but great ones. There were four weights each of three basic typefaces, Times New Roman, Arial, and Courier New. All were licensed from Monotype and all had hand-tuned hints. Times New Roman is certainly my favorite variant of Times and one of the best fonts period. These twelve fonts were supplemented by a symbol font and the Wingdings font.

Finally, Microsoft broke the back of high font prices with its first TrueType font pack, but more of that in the section after the next.

Love Me True (Type)

> The advantage of love at first sight is that it delays a second sight.
>
> —Natalie Clifford Barney

The $64,000 question for fonts is, "Do I need Postscript and ATM if I already have TrueType under Windows?" There's a simple answer and a complicated answer.

The simple answer is: TrueType is a superb engine, there are lots of inexpensive, well-done TrueType fonts available, and it's built into Windows, so you save no memory by not using TrueType. And you can be sure that any application will support it. ATM's font cache will take a significant chunk of memory and will be supported by most but not all applications. So no, you don't need ATM.

The complex answer is: TrueType is a superb engine, there are lots of inexpensive, well-done TrueType fonts available, and it's built into Windows, so you save no memory by not using TrueType. And you can be sure that any application will support it. ATM's font cache will take a significant chunk of memory and will be supported by most but not all applications. So no, you don't need ATM. Except under special circumstances.

The special circumstances mean that you are doing heavy-duty Desktop publishing or need some of the special font families that come from Adobe. Most users don't need to install ATM.

Hmmm, I'll bet John Warnock* never talks to me again but I gotta tell you the truth, don't I?

How Much Is that Font Pack for Windows, the One with the Shiny Ohs?

> The heaping together of paintings by Old Masters in museums is a catastrophe; likewise, a collection of a hundred Great Brains makes one big fathead.
>
> —Carl Jung, *Civilization in Transition,* 1934

There are a few fonts suitable for body text that you'll use most of the time—your bread-and-butter fonts. I want to tell you how I choose those. The name-font foundries really do have better fonts and the advice I'd give you is to go with a top foundry, most notably Monotype or Bitstream. Here's the advice in more detail.

The fonts that come with Windows are so good that you could happily only use those, but they are so common that if you want to show some individuality, you may decide to buy some more fonts. You won't be alone. But be careful, because the font business really is a classic case of Gresham's law: the schlock fonts have come close to driving the class foundries out of business.

---

* The founder and CEO of Adobe.

Fonts used to be a boutique kind of business but in the early '90s they soared. Igor's limited market research suggests that in 1992, fonts did more than $100 million a year business.

I, Igor, figured out this sales figure from two numbers I did know. Bitstream's 1990–92 sales were more than $20 million each year. In 1992, Microsoft offered its font pack as an option for direct mail Windows 3.1 upgrades and about 1 million upgraders got the pack at about $40. So counting Adobe (whose 1992 sales, including not only fonts but also PostScript licenses and their software programs was over $250 million), I figure it must be more than $100 million.

Fonts are the potato chips of the Windows world. You can't eat only one. At least in the old days, a better analogy might have been nicotine or harder drugs. The font companies had their few samples to hook you—their Joey Camels. All sorts of programs were bundled with Bitstream Dutch and Swiss, which vendors got for very little. But if they hooked you, boy, did you have to raid the cookie jar. A single typeface (in four outlines for the standard weight/styles) beyond the basics went for $200–$300. That's $50 or more per font.

The boys'll count fonts the way that the foundries do. If a font pack has the wonderful new Foorific™ font as Foorific™ Roman, Foorific™ Bold, Foorific™ Italic, and Foorific™ Italic Bold, they call it four fonts even though you and I know it is really only one type family. This counting isn't so bad. Decorative typefaces usually come in one weight/style. You'll use the four weight/style typefaces at least four times as much as the decorative one.

But then Microsoft went and spoiled the party! Their Font Pack I gave you forty-four fonts for a street price of under $50. Fonts were suddenly only a buck each. At that price, you could afford to nibble quite a few potato chips. The major font foundries gritted their teeth and, gasp, competed. They kept some of their fonts at the old rate to catch the pathetic guys huddled in the corner shooting up every new font that shows up, but they also produced font packs at the buck-a-font street price. And, surprise, they did quite well, because the volume was enormous compared to what it was for the $50/font market.

The schlock font vendors competed. They blazoned **250 fonts for $49.99,** or some such tease. Those fonts tend to run 20–25 cents each. The high-class fonts should have won, but alas, the difference between schlock and class is subtle and not so easy for the novice to see. So the junk sold and the good stuff didn't. Monotype and Adobe pulled back from the mass market and sold expensive fonts to the cognoscenti. Bitstream competed and put out a superb library of five hundred fonts for $50. That's ten cents apiece. If you feel a need to go out and buy fonts, my top pick is the Bitstream CD if you can find it.

On Mom's companion CD, we've included 20 Bitstream fonts, courtesy of Bitstream. Another 24 are on Mom's bonus CD.

If you get Corel Draw or certain other packages, you'll find hundreds of fonts are included. The Plus! Pack comes with an extra nineteen TrueType fonts and Microsoft Office includes thirty-four fonts. So maybe you don't need to buy more fonts after all!

If you install more than about a hundred fonts, your font list will get enormous and you'll want a font organizer like Ares' Font Minder (415-578-9090).

Portable Documents

> Barbarism is the absence of standards.
>
> —José Ortega y Gasset, *The Revolt of the Masses,* 1930

The only universal format for exchange of textual information is ASCII, a format that has been in place for many years. Clearly, we need a format that supports font information, pictures, and all that so we can transmit "portable documents." There are several competing proprietary standards proposed by differing vendors. Mom is betting on *Adobe Acrobat* as sure to be the winner.

The set of products from Adobe involve a format they call PDF (portable document format) and a set of products under the name Acrobat—specifically *Acrobat Reader, Acrobat Exchange,* and *Acrobat Distiller.* The PDF includes general information on the fonts used in the document and the reader has technology to produce an approximation of the font on your screen and printer even if you don't own the actual font. The output won't make a font lover do cartwheels but it will look a lot like the true original.

Acrobat Exchange for Windows includes a "printer driver" that lets you "print" a document to a PDF file. The Distiller allows you to take PostScript output (as you'd get if you used a PostScript printer driver and printed to a file). Distiller plus Reader combine for one of the best PostScript interpreters currently available! Exchange has a PDF editor that lets you add hyperlinks, annotations, and more to a PDF file.

By using compression technology and settling for approximations of the actual document, PDF files can be much smaller than the original document. In one sample that Adobe talks about, an 80 MB PageMaker document (with lots of big bitmaps) produces a PDF under 2 MB. Impressive technology, well worth watching.

With Adobe's name behind it and such technology, Adobe's format should have won easily, but initially, Adobe used a stupid marketing model where you had to buy the Reader. That meant it couldn't spread on BBS or be used as a universal format. This opened the door to competition, most notably, *Envoy* from Word Perfect.

But Adobe shifted to the right moves before any competitor could get established. First, in 1994, Adobe convinced the IRS to put all IRS forms in PDF format and posted them on CompuServe with a free reader to download. The next year they were posted in many places. You could download the forms and Acrobat Reader and print them out looking as good as the original without trekking to the library or calling the IRS.

Then with version 2.0 of Acrobat, they made the reader free to distribute. In fact, on the bonus CD you'll find a copy of the Acrobat reader and this entire book in Acrobat format.

Finally, Adobe made a deal with Netscape, the makers of Netscape Navigator, which has been the standard-setter in World Wide Web Browsers. Adobe clearly hopes to have Acrobat used on the Web for displaying formatted documents.

Font Tools in Windows 95

> There is a great satisfaction in building good tools for other people to use.
>
> —Freeman Dyson, *Disturbing the Universe,* 1979

The tools for organizing fonts provided in Windows 95 are vastly superior to those in Windows 3.1.

 That ain't saying much, since Windows 3.1 provided almost nothing to organize fonts.

Many of the tools are associated with the Fonts folder, an object found in `My Computer` with a shortcut to it in Control Panel. This folder is an entirely different beast from any other folder in Windows 95 and one that can be a little confusing. Most folders correspond to a directory of on-disk files. Open the `C:\windows` folder and you see the same files that you'd get by opening a DOS window and typing `dir C:\windows` at the DOS command line. There are other folders like the Printers Folder that are entirely virtual. The objects shown do not correspond to files anywhere.

The Fonts Folder is different because there is an on-disk directory—by default, `C:\windows\fonts`, which is associated to it, but there is not a simple one-to-one correspondence between the files that `dir C:\windows\fonts` will turn up and the icons shown when you open the Fonts folder. In the first place, when you open the Fonts folder you will never see any icons but those associated to TrueType fonts (with the extension `.ttf`) and those associated to Windows bitmapped fonts (with extension `.fon`). If you copy a file called `readme.txt` to `C:\windows\fonts`, the DOS `dir` command will show it is there but you'll never see it in a folder view of the directory or with Explorer because those show you the sort of virtual directory that is the Font folder and not the actual contents of `C:\windows\fonts`.

There is another folder that is not entirely virtual nor a disk directory, and that is Network Neighborhood. It shows icons for machines and other resources on the network that don't correspond to local files but it also shows files in the directory `C:\windows\nethood`. The purpose of those files is to place shortcuts to network resources, but if you make a text file in the `C:\windows\nethood` directory, it'll happily show up in Network Neighborhood. Moreover, if you view `C:\windows\nethood` in Folder or Explorer view, you see the actual files in that directory without the virtual objects included in Network Neighborhood. So `C:\windows\nethood`/Network Neighborhood, while neither totally disk-based nor totally virtual, is very different from the Fonts folder.

The story gets even stranger, though. If you or a program installs a font into a directory other than `C:\windows\fonts`, it shows up in the Font folder as a shortcut. I'll explain in the next section how you can install fonts in other directories. But here's the weird part. The font shortcut does not correspond to *any* disk file. Make a shortcut to an executable and a `*.lnk` file is made; make a shortcut to a DOS program and a `*.pif` file is made. Make a font shortcut and no additional file is made. In some sense the shortcut corresponds to an entry in the Registry.

The lack of a file corresponding to font shortcuts is partly a curiosity, but since it is a player in a dangerous removal problem I'll explain in the next section, it is more than a mere curiosity.

And the behavior of the `C:\windows\fonts` directory under the Find Files dialog is weird (to put it in a positive light) and buggy (to be more negative). Call up that dialog and type `C:\windows\fonts\w*.ttf` in the named box and do Find Now. It will find `wingding.ttf`. Now try `C:\w*.ttf` and make sure that the Include subfolders box is checked. It will not find the file in your Windows 95 Fonts folder! Similarly, if you open a DOS window, go to the `C:\windows` directory, and type `dir *.ttf / s`, you'll get no files reported. But try `dir fonts\*.ttf` and lots of files will be reported. Oh, how I love a nice bug in the mornin'.

 Hey, I wouldn't necessarily call that a bug. If you use command `dir /a:d /v` in the `C:\windows` directory, you'll learn that the Fonts folder is marked with the system attribute. As an experiment, use the DOS Attrib command to turn on the system attribute for the Cursors folder. You'll find the same behavior for cursors and `*.ani` files as you did for fonts and `*.ttf` files. Turn the system attribute off for one folder or the other and the behavior is as expected.

The icons in the Fonts folder show either a TT for `*.ttf` TrueType files or an A for bitmapped `*.fon` files. Double-click on either and you pop up a box like that shown in Figure 2-31 with the name of the font, some general samples, the alphabet and samples in 12, 18, 24, 36, 48, 60 and 72 point. You can view the sample on screen or print it by using the handy button provided on the sample.

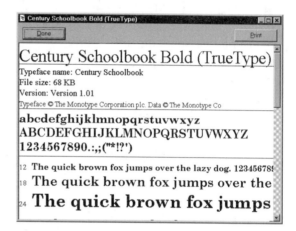

Figure 2-31. Windows font viewer

Here's the neatest thing about this viewer: it works on fonts you haven't yet installed! If you have a CD filled with fonts and want to figure out which to install, you can double-click on the `*.ttf` on that CD and look at samples to help decide which you want to view.

 There is no real magic here. There is a program called `fontview.exe` that you'll find in the Windows directory. Running it is assigned as the default action when you double-click on a `*.ttf` or `*.fon` file. If you just want to print out the sample of the font, you can right-click on the font and choose Print. That just runs fontview with the `/p` switch to get it to print the font and exit.

 I guess the spec sheets you print/display are so much better than what you are used to that I shouldn't complain, but it is a pretty limited applet. How about at least letting us see the full ANSI character set in the font? That would sure be useful for Dingbat and other symbol fonts, for Hebrew fonts, and the like. And, rather than make us look at a bunch of fonts one at a time, how about a way to print out single lines in all the fonts in some directory?

If you want more than the anemic spec sheets that come with Windows 95 font viewer, take a look at Printer's Apprentice, a superb shareware application.

The only other font tools to mention are options in the View menu. Figure 2-32 shows the View menu in a Font folder while Figure 2-33 shows the View menu in a normal folder. The items missing from the Font folder (small icons, icon line up commands) aren't important. What is important are the two items special to Font folders: Hide Variations, which is an on/off check box, and List Fonts By Similarity, which is one of four list options. Hide Variations shows a single font from a family rather than the usual four—normal, italic, bold, and bold italic. It's a useful option when you are trying to

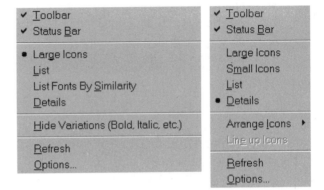

Figure 2-32. The Font Folder View menu

Figure 2-33. A normal Folder View menu

see what fonts are installed. List Fonts By Similarity uses Panose numbers to take any font you choose and list the other fonts in four categories: very similar, fairly similar, not similar, and "No PANOSE information available." The button bar in Font folders has an extra icon to allow quick shift to Similarity view.

Installing and Removing Fonts in Windows 95

Do not use a hatchet to remove a fly from your friend's forehead.

—Chinese proverb

You can install a font in Windows easily. Just open the Fonts folder, locate the `*.ttf` file you want in Explorer, and drag-and-drop the `ttf` to the Fonts folder. The default action (no matter what the source drive) is to copy the `ttf` file to the `C:\windows\fonts` directory and install the font into Windows.

Don't be fooled by how smoothly the install works. If you copy a file to the `C:\windows\fonts` directory at a DOS prompt or in a third-party file manager, the font will *not* be installed. Explorer treats copying to the Fonts folder in a special way. Not only does it do the copying of the file, but it adjusts the Registry in a way that the font is placed on the available font list when Windows is rebooted in the future. It also makes operating system calls so that Windows and any currently running applications add the font to the available list for the current session.

I'll talk about the Registry in Chapter 10. Font information is stored in the key `HKEY_Local_Machine\Software\Microsoft\Windows\CurrentVersion\Fonts`. Fonts whose `ttf` file is in `C:\windows\fonts` just have the name of the `ttf` file listed (without the full pathname). Fonts located elsewhere have their full pathname given.

This method of simply storing directory information in the Registry is much smoother than the procedure used in Windows 3.x. That model used an extra binary file called an `fot` file. `Win.ini` entries pointed toward the `fot` file and the pathname of the `ttf` file was embedded inside the `fot` file.

This change was made only after considerable thought, since it breaks a number of font utilities! Most fonts under Windows 3.x were placed in the system directory. So if you had 400 fonts installed, you have 800 extra files in your system directory—400 `ttf` files and 400 `fot`s. Every time any program wanted a `dll`, it needed to read the system directory and those extra 800 files had a noticeable impact on performance. So we removed the `fot` and moved the fonts to their own directory.

But doesn't this break the installation model for Windows 3.x programs installing under Windows 95? Won't they just put their fonts and `fot` files in the system directory and adjust `win.ini`?

We realized that could be a problem, so when Windows 95 boots, it looks for entries in the `[fonts]` section of `win.ini`. If it finds them, it looks for the `fot` file and uses that to figure out where the corresponding `ttf` file is. It then properly installs the font in the Registry, moving the ttf file to `C:\windows\fonts` if it was in `C:\windows\system`. The entries in `win.ini` and the `fot` file are then deleted.

If you want to install a font in Windows without moving it to `C:\windows\fonts`, you right-drag it to the Fonts folder. On the context menu that pops up, one of the choices will say "Create Shortcut(s) Here." If you choose that, Windows will not copy the `ttf` file but will instead install the font using the full pathname in the Registry. In the Explorer view of the Fonts folder, the font name will appear but with a shortcut symbol indicated. As I mentioned in the last section, there is no file placed in C:\windows\fonts corresponding to the shortcut.

I have lots of fonts installed—more than nine hundred at last count—and I've encountered lots of problems installing new fonts. With one font, I can double-click on a .ttf file and get the full font information, print it, and whatnot. I can install the file by dragging it to the C:\windows\fonts directory. But if I use the File/Install New Fonts option, I get a message that the font file is damaged. With a different font, double-clicking works fine, but dragging into C:\windows\fonts gives the same bogus damaged file message. Oh how I love a nice bug in the middle of nine hundred fonts!

Hey, anyone who tries to install that many fonts gets what they deserve.

Removal of fonts is as easy. If you select a font icon (which is not a shortcut) in the Fonts folder and delete it, the corresponding ttf file is deleted from C:\windows\fonts. And the font will no longer appear on the list of available fonts. If you select an icon corresponding to a shortcut and hit Del, you get exactly the behavior you'd expect: the original ttf file pointed to by the shortcut is unaffected but the font is no longer installed in Windows.

But, if you drag a font shortcut from the Fonts folder to the Recycle Bin, then Windows not only removes the font from the list of installed fonts but deletes the original ttf that the shortcut pointed to.

Ooo! A bug, a big fat juicy squishy one! Gotta be. You drag any other kind of shortcut to the Recycle Bin and only the shortcut is deleted, not the file it points to. And in every other place in Explorer, hitting Del and dragging to the Recycle Bin are the same thing. Bug! Bug! Bug! In fact, this one is so blatant, it could be fixed in one of the tuneup packs by the time some of you read this.

Perhaps not; it may be a design flaw. It seems unlikely that the differing behavior for Del and Recycle drag is accidental. The reasoning may have gone like this. When you hit Del on the shortcut, it uninstalls the font, but since there is no actual file corresponding to the shortcut, there is no file placed in the Recycle Bin. If it started empty, it'll stay empty. If the user dragged the shortcut to an empty bin and the icon didn't change to indicate a bin with something there, the user might get very confused. So the shell designers made the choice to blow away the `ttf` file that could have been a family heirloom to avoid a little confusion. Dumb design—but sorta understandable.

Well, end users hardly care if it's a bug or a bonehead design decision. The bottom line is that if you use the capability to install fonts via shortcuts, you'd better be sure not to delete them by dragging to the Recycle Bin!

Winning on the First Palette

The next few sections are gonna be colorful, that's for sure. Well, at least color-full.

Which One Is Burnt Umber?

> But soft! what light through yonder window breaks?
>
> William Shakespeare, *Romeo and Juliet,* Act II, Scene II

Remember when Mom got you your first 64-crayon Crayola set? Your friend said, "Gimme that brown," but you couldn't figure out which crayon she meant since the one you had was called burnt umber. Well, you're gonna have to pick colors a lot in Winapps if you get at all graphical, so you'd better learn the way colors are named.

Alas, it ain't as simple as remembering which one is burnt umber. Colors are labeled by numbers, and there are at least four different color-numbering standards that are in common use: RGB, CYMK, HSB, and HLS.

RGB stands for Red, Green, Blue. Each can have a level from 0 to 255. It is a model of light, where RGB are the primary colors. As the numbers get higher, the color gets brighter, so that (R=0,G=0,B=0) is black and (R=255,G=255,B=255) is white. The color space is a cube. This is the most common color model used in Windows.

You may have heard that light has a continuous parameter called frequency representing variation in space and time. Light of wavelength midway between Red and Green is Yellow—but how can that also be a mixture of 50 percent Red light and 50 percent Green light? Physically, the two wave trains are very different. The answer is in our eyes. Color is perceived in terms of three types of cones in the retina. Roughly speaking, the cones are sensitive to light frequencies near pure red, near pure green, and near pure blue. True yellow light (that is, light whose frequency is midway between red and green light) will stimulate both the red- and green-sensitive cones in roughly the same way that a combination of red and green light will, so they are perceived similarly even though the physical light waves are different.

CYM (we'll get to K soon) stands for Cyan, Yellow, and Magenta; the complementary colors to Red (Cyan is Green/Blue), Blue, and Green. It is a model of ink; indeed, color printers normally have ink in those exact colors blended to make the rainbow. As an ink model, higher numbers are darker so that (C=0,Y=0,M=0) is white and theoretically, (C=255,Y=255,M=255) is black. In fact, if you mix together those inks in high concentration, you don't get black but instead a kind of muddy dark ooze.

Muddy dark ooze. Sorta sounds like Mom's coffee. Have to remember that—CYM crouches in wait.

Hey, Sonny! You are in big trouble if you knock my coffee.

Because mixing colored inks makes a lousy black, high-class color printers use a fourth ink, namely blacK. Well, Black but then it would be CYMB, so it must be blacK after all. Programs that prepare pictures for actual color printing will often use the CYMK scheme but most users will hardly see it.

HSB stands for Hue, Saturation, and Brightness. It uses a color cone model (Figure 2-34). Think of the cone as upright like an ice cream cone with the apex at the bottom and an axis running through the middle. The colors along that axis are grays. Black is at the apex and white is at the center of the circle that lies at the top of the cone. The B parameter measures the distance along the axis from the apex (brightness 0) toward the brighter colors.

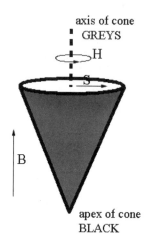

Hue is a discriminator of the pure color. It is connected to the color wheel. Imagine a wheel with pure red (R=255) at 3 o'clock, yellow (R=G=255) at 5 o'clock, green at 7 o'clock (G=255), cyan (R=G=255) at 9 o'clock, with blue (B=255) and magenta (R=G=255) at 11 and 1. As you move around, the red value is 255 from 1 to 5 and 0 from 7 to 11. It changes linearly in the transition areas. Many programs measure H in degrees from 0 to 360. Windows measures from 0 to 240 so that red is H=0, yellow is H=40, green is H=80, and so on.

Figure 2-34. The HSB color model

In the HSB model, the color wheel is put on the circle at the top of the cone and H measures the angle around the axis.

The color wheel is more naturally a hexagon with the colors at the vertices, so the cone should be a hexagonal pyramid (Figure 2-35).

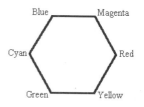

Finally, saturation measures the distance from the axis toward the edge. S=0 is a gray. As saturation increases the color gets purer.

Figure 2-35. The color hexagon

HLS stands for Hue, Saturation, and Luminosity. Its model is a double cone, two cones shaped like the one in HSB with one turned over and put on top of the other so there are points at the top and bottom. L=0 is black while L=24 (in Windows units) is white at the points of the double cone. The pure color wheel is in the middle at L=120. If you fix S=0, you still go through the grays. If you fix S=240 and H=0 (red) and move from L=1 down to 0, you move from white through pink, through red, then dark red to black.

Many color theorists regard the HSB/HLS models as more intuitive. In RGB, pink, which is a mixture of white and red, has RGB values (255,127,127) that say red and half green and half blue, which sure isn't what one thinks of as pink. HSL is pure red hue of luminosity three-fourths of the way from black to white. Moreover, the color wheel is in line with the actual physical wavelength of color light.

Windows standard color dialog uses the HLS model. You'll find it if you run the Display applet in Control Panel (or right-click the Desktop and choose Properties, which is the same thing), click the Appearance tab, hit the Color button and choose Other. It is also used in any program using the common dialog, such as Windows Paint. But it doesn't use cones or circles, only squares (see Figure 2-36). The slider on the right changes the L values. Slide it all the way to the top or bottom and you'll only get white or black no matter what color you pick in the

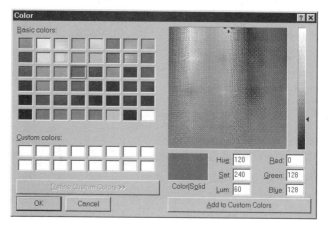

Figure 2-36. The color common dialog

middle area. In that middle area, the top is the pure color wheel if L is 120 (midway). The bottom is a shade of gray no matter how you shift from left to right. That's because the top of the square is really a circle and the bottom is really a single point representing the center of the circle. Leave it to Microsoft to square the circle!

Some of My Friends Are Pals and Some Are Palettes

If you are going to fool around with color schemes (and you may as well confess that you already have!), you should understand how Windows controls what colors you can access. I'll discuss 256 color drivers because that's what many of you will be using. If you have only 16 colors, those are normally hard-coded, although a very few programs will manipulate them. (If you use any program much that does, you really do want to shift to 256 colors even if it requires a new video card!) The 24- and 16-bit color drivers (called *True Color* and *Hi Color* respectively, they have roughly 16 million and 64,000 colors) don't use the palette and dither stuff I'll discuss but represent everything as a pure color, so much of what I'll say is irrelevant if you are running at that number of colors.

 Microsoft is to be commended for using the Plus! Pack to nudge the user community toward Hi Color. Many of its Desktop themes require this number of colors. There is a performance penalty associated with the higher color depth, but on an accelerated video card it is not large. I urge you to seriously consider moving to Hi Color. But for those who won't or can't, I'll discuss 256 colors here.

Drivers that display 256 colors are capable of picking those 256 colors from among either 262,144 colors (2 to the power 18) or 16,777,216 colors (2 to the power 24). VGA cards and older SuperVGA cards have the smaller number while higher-end adapters and cards that have a 24 bit mode have the larger number.

 "Oh, boy," you must be thinking, "I get to pick what color my title bar is from hundreds of thousands of colors." Alas not; read on.

Windows keeps track of which 256 colors of those 262,144 or 16,777,216 are to be displayed, and such an assignment is called a *palette*. If a program asks for a color not in the current palette, Windows fakes it—it uses a *dithered* color that is nearby dots of two different colors, which when blended sorta give the desired colors. Pure colors look great; dithered colors often look awful. For example (assuming you are running at 16 or 256 colors), call up the color common dialog that I described in the last section. I'm sure several of the 48 colors shown don't look like colors but like polka dots. Assuming your screen driver uses the standard colors for 256 color drivers (while a driver can define different colors sets, I'm not aware of any that don't use those supplied in the Windows SuperVGA scheme), it has the worst polka dots in row 2, column 6 and row 1, column 7.

Programs can also attempt to manipulate the palette and tell Windows to change what colors are used. If colors can be manipulated by programs, how does Windows deal with the fact that you want your title bar color to be consistent across applications? It makes a compromise. Twenty colors of the 256 are *reserved* for all 256 color drivers. The other 236 colors can be freely changed by applications that need to. (Actually, programs that really need to are allowed to change 254 of the colors, leaving only black and white alone but that is very rare—indeed, I know of no program that takes advantage of this.)

As you switch from one program to another, Windows changes the palette to the one that the active program has set. Since most programs don't change the default palette, you might not see any changes, but image editors and some other graphics programs will change the palette and then you'll often see funny flashes as you switch—and perhaps fouled-up colors on your wallpaper when you are in certain programs.

Some image editors when displaying several images will adjust the palette to be ideal for the one you are working on; others adjust it so that all the images display in a not-too-bad way but still save most of the 236 colors for the foreground image.

Because Windows is worried about what other programs may do to their 236 colors, it will only let you use the 20 reserved colors for title bars, menu bars, and the like. Moreover, you cannot change those 17 colors: the 16 basic RGB combinations and an extra gray. I'll describe here the 20 colors that get used unless you go to the Screen applet in Control Panel and change the color assigned to 3D objects. If you do, three of the 20 colors are linked to this 3D objects color. I'll provide the full details to that situation when I discuss the Screen applet in Chapter 10. For now I'll focus on the default situation.

I'll use *x/y/z* to indicate R/G/B values so 123/235/68 means RGB values R=123, G=235, B=68. You can ignore them but they will tell you something about the colors if you think in the right way.

The twenty colors include the sixteen that have been standard on the PC since the CGA's text mode. Those sixteen colors are the six primary color wheel colors in dark and light (e.g., red is 255/0/0 and dark red is 128/0/0; magenta is 255/0/255 and dark magenta is 128/0/128) plus white (255/255/255), black (0/0/0), dark gray (128/128/128) and light gray (192/192/192).

How come dark red is R=128 with a smaller value than red at R=255?

Remember that RGB is a model of light so R=255 means more intense red light, which appears brighter!

Besides the sixteen standard colors, there are an extra four colors that must have been picked by Bill Gates's interior decorator: they are shown in Figure 2-37.

I've got a theory that the medium gray should really be 160/160/160, a true gray. First of all, why pick something so close to a gray and not take a real gray? My most compelling reason, though, has to do with Windows 3.1. There, the default colors in the common dialog had nineteen of the twenty reserved colors. The missing one was medium gray. On the other hand, one of the most polka-dotted colors had R/G/B values 160/160/160. I'd have thought that with the adjustments made to powder blue, they would have also fixed medium gray, but they didn't.

Mao's Name	Red	Green	Blue
Medium Gray	160	160	164
Eggshell White	255	251	240
Army Olive	192	220	192
Powder Blue	166	202	240

Figure 2-37. The extra four solid system colors

One mysterious change, though, in the passage from Windows 3.x to Windows 95: They made a slight change in the R/G/B values of powder blue—from 164/200/240 to 166/202/240. I wonder why? Musta been that big Bill's interior decorator came and said, "A smidgen more red and green would be just parfait."

If you go back to the Appearance tab in the Display Properties, if you click on the `Color` button, you get a drop down of exactly twenty colors above the word `Other`. Guess what? Those are precisely the twenty solid colors. Choose them for your Windows colors and you won't get anything dithered. On the other hand, some of the dithered colors don't look too bad; indeed, the default tool tip color is dithered. So you might want to look at the `Other` colors. For those objects like title bars that Windows insists be solid, the dithered colors are grayed out. For all others, you get the 8 × 6 array indicated in the following grid.

The boxes marked BUG are there because those colors are the same.

It's remarkable how many of the dithered colors look pretty good (I marked the good dithered colors with a +) and that they bothered to include the awful ones I marked with a −.

−	+	+	+		−	−	−
red	yellow	+	+	cyan	−	−	magenta
+		green	dark cyan	+	−	+	+
dark red	−	dark green	+	blue	+	dark magenta	
+	+	+	+	dark blue	+	BUG	+
black	brown	+	dark gray	+	light gray	BUG	white

But there sure are a bunch of mysteries in this little corner of Windows land. Most of the solid colors are in the same locations they were in Windows 3.1. So why did they move yellow? And why not fix the duplicate color rather than have some users decide they have gone colorblind?* And why, oh why, didn't they include the extra four solid colors in the forty-eight that are displayed, so they'd be easily accessible in other programs like Paint that use the common color dialog? By the way, Mao, given that it changed from Windows 3.1, how'd you figure out the RGB values for the new, er, improved, powder blue?

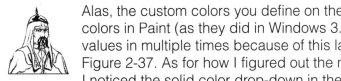

Alas, the custom colors you define on the Desktop don't appear as custom colors in Paint (as they did in Windows 3.1), so you'll need to type the RGB values in multiple times because of this last oversight. Use the numbers in Figure 2-37. As for how I figured out the new RGB values for powder blue, I noticed the solid color drop-down in the Appearance tab, chose the powder blue as a Desktop color, and used Regedit to look at the entry in the Registry where the color is stored (in `HKEY_CURRENT_USER\Control Panel\Colors\ Background`). There it was clear as day: "166 202 240." By the way, powder blue is a particularly good choice for the color of the thing called "3D Objects" in the Item drop-down list on the Appearance tab.

---

* Igor: I have a theory: At a product review, Mr. Gates complimented the designers on how wonderful it was to put two subtly different shades next to each other like that. The product managers were afraid to tell him they were the same color and they've been afraid to change it since.

Putting Windows on a Sound Basis

> The power of sound has always been greater than the power of sense.

> —Joseph Conrad, *A Personal Record,* 1912

Wav and MIDI

IBM included a kludgy speaker in the original PC and, in the interest of compatibility, that's what virtually all PCs since then have used for sound, if you can call it that. Early on, Macs had real sound allowing both voice and music, as did Amigas, Ataris, Suns, NeXT, . . . Until recently, PC Sound solutions going beyond the speaker were largely driven by the needs of games with successive standards set by Ad Lib and then Sound Blaster cards. But sound has even entered the business mainstream with sound annotation, multimedia presentations (whatever that means), and most especially Windows support for sound in version 3.1. And future developments in voice synthesis and recognition will only make sound capabilities more important.

There are two types of sounds you can record and play under Windows. It's rasters and vectors all over again but at the sound level. One kind of sound is *digital,* the analog of a bitmap—the actual sampling or playing of sound levels. Just as the standard Windows bitmap file is the bmp, the Windows digital sound file standard is called a *wave file* with the extension wav. A wav file literally gives directions to a speaker to oscillate in a certain way.

The sound analog of vector graphics is the *synthesized sound* file, under Windows a *MIDI file* with extension mid. Instead of telling the sound card to oscillate in a given way, a MIDI file has commands like "play a middle C for so much time and do it as if you were playing it on a piano."

Microsoft has developed a general header for various kinds of multimedia files. The header contains binary information that can be useful to programs using the files. The header format is call RIFF for "Resource Interchange File Format" and wav files have RIFF headers as part of the spec. MIDI files that predate the RIFF spec do not have RIFF headers. A hybrid file format that has a RIFF header followed by a MIDI file for content is now the format recommended by Microsoft. These RIFF–MIDI files are called RMID files by Microsoft and have the extension .rmi. Windows 95 installs seven superb RMID files in the C:\windows\media directory. I'll say more about them later.

To see the dramatic size difference between MIDI and digital files, consider the following: The RMID of Beethoven's 5th symphony, first movement takes about 90K of disk space for more than six minutes of music. The Utopia Sound Scheme Windows Start sound file is about 150K of disk space, for less than four seconds of sound. That's a factor of about 150. To add to the drama, the wave file in question isn't even of the top quality (it is mono, not stereo, and FM radio quality rather than CD Audio) and uses digital audio compression.

 Of course, since the Utopia Start sound isn't instrumental music, it couldn't be duplicated in MIDI. The point is that each format has its uses but that while orchestral music can be put in digital files, MIDI is much more efficient for such sounds. It boggles the mind to think that an hour of music can be stored in 1 MB of disk space!

Just as it pays to keep in mind whether a graphic is raster or vector, you'll want to bear in mind the difference between digitized and synthesized sounds. Here are more details on the two types.

Riding the Perfect Wav

> . . . here shall thy proud waves be stayed.

> —Job 38:11

Bitmaps files are characterized by the number of colors and sometimes by their intended resolution. In the same way, wav files have some basic parameters that describe the native format of the data. Of course, just as Windows can display a 16 million color file on a 256 color screen by doing its best, it can play a stereo wav file on a mono sound card by merging the two channels. The point of a stereo file is that it can play stereo on appropriate hardware.

Wav files have three basic parameters:

1. **The sound is either *mono* or *stereo*.** You know the difference. Most presentations don't need stereo. Some games do. Stereo sound files run twice the size of mono, for rather obvious reasons.

2. *Sample size* **measures how much information about a single sound sample is kept around.** 4-bit sampling suffices for low fidelity voice recordings and 8-bit does a good job of reproducing speech; but 16 bits—the sample size used in CD audio—is necessary for high quality sound. Basically, sample size measures the number of different sound levels that are distinguished—4 bit has 16 levels (2 to the power 4), 8 bit has 256 levels (2 to the power 8), and 16 bit has 65,536 levels (2 to the power 16).

3. **The *sample rate* measures how often the computer looks at the incoming sound and translates it into numbers.** Sample rate has to do with how high a frequency can be distinguished and how much one can hear differing amounts of harmonic overtones. 11

kHz sampling (sampled 11,000 times per second, natch) sounds like AM radio. 22 kHz sampling sounds like FM radio. And 44 kHz sampling sounds like CD audio—because it *is* CD audio.

Most sound boards nowadays can record 8-bit mono sound at 22 kHz. Few can record at CD audio rates, that is, 16-bit stereo 44 kHz. Even if they could, you probably wouldn't want them to: one minute of 8-bit mono 22 kHz sound generates 1.3 MB of data, hefty by any standard; one minute of 16-bit stereo 44 kHz sound would produce a 10.6 MB file. Fidelity hath its price!

You get 1.3 MB by multiplying 22,000 by 60 seconds (since 8 bits is a byte) and 10.6 MB by multiplying 44,000 by 60 seconds, then by 2 (16 bits is 2 bytes) and then by 2 again for the stereo.

There are other digital sound file types but they are less common than alternate bitmap types because sound has less of a pre–Windows history. The ones you may see are voc (the Sound Blaster standard—PC digitized sound at games player prices started on the Sound Blaster), au (used on NeXT and Sun), snd (used on the Mac and Amiga and the most common pre-wav type), and vox (Dialogic phone-answering system voice files). Just as bitmap to bitmap conversion is straightforward, so is conversion from one digitized sound format to another. One program that will do such conversions for you as well as edit is Sonic Foundry's *Sound Forge* (Voice: 608-256-3133).

There is another source of digitized sound on some systems with both a sound card and CD ROM—so-called *red book audio.* No, not my Red Book, but the standards document used to define audio CDs. Red book audio is essentially audio CD tracks embedded in the middle of a CD ROM. Multimedia CDs will sometimes have sound in that format. One way that you can hear such sounds is if you connect the output jack on your CD (assuming it has one!) to a pair of speakers. If you use that route, you'll need a mixer to use the same speakers on your sound card output. A better solution is to connect the CD output to your sound card and have the sound card send out to the speakers.

Ideally, you should use internal connections on CD and sound card, assuming that the CD is internal. But be warned that the internal connectors are anything but standard. After a year of trying I gave up on finding an internal connector to send the Red Book Audio from my *Toshiba* CD ROM to my *Sound Blaster Pro.* Fortunately, the external connectors are standard, so a modular audio cable I picked up at Radio Shack did the trick. But it sure is silly to have a cable snaking out from the front of my CD around to the external audio input on the back of the Sound Blaster.

'mid the MIDI

MIDI is short for Musical Instrument Digital Interface. It's a standard invented to drive high-end musical devices as might be used in a recording studio, but was already fairly common in non-IBM-compatible computer systems (e.g., the Mac) before its adaptation by Windows in version 3.1. Microsoft is to be complimented for using an external standard rather than rolling its own, although there are Windows-specific modifications in the implementation.

There is considerable confusion surrounding MIDI under Windows. To start with, there are really three separate MIDI devices relevant to a sound setup—the device used to play `mid` and `rmi` files, a MIDI in port, and a MIDI out port.

As a preliminary, you should know there are basically two routes to synthesis on sound cards. One is called FM synthesis, usually based on a Yamaha chip. The chip understands the general features that make something sound like a piano or an organ or a flute, and given a command to play a middle C as a piano would, the chip makes it up, er, synthesizes, the sound on the spot.

The second is wave table lookup. The sound card has actual recorded samples of a piano and other instruments playing various notes and uses the lookup to do the synthesis. Typically, the wave table information is stored in ROM with 2 or even 4 MB of wave tables possible. Some cards are available with wave tables stored on your hard disk and a buffer on card.

The difference between these two sources is dramatic. FM synthesis sounds tinny and wave table lookup sounds rich. It is the same kind of dramatic difference as between a dot matrix and laser printer. Whatever you do, don't listen to a wave table card if your budget can't afford it, or else you'll have a unrequited yearning. The good news is that wave table sound is coming down in price. There was essentially a single card with a street price over $800 in mid-1992, but now wave table is available in all but the very lowest-end sound solutions. Still, not including wave table is a way that some computer vendors cut corners on unsuspecting consumers, so be sure it is on your checklist when you buy a system.

 Although wave table is desirable, don't totally despair if you discover your sound card uses FM synthesis. Most of the sound you play on your computer will be digital or red book audio, so it is only a mild calamity if your MIDI isn't up to snuff.

Any sound card that includes a synthesizer will allow you to play `mid` files directly from the card. If you have a MIDI out port, there is usually a choice between the internal card or the external out port as the place that `mid` files are played. You choose where `mid` files are by calling up the Multimedia applet in Control Panel, shifting to the MIDI tab, and choosing there. Figure 2-38 shows the dialog for a Sound Blaster Pro with a choice of external MIDI and internal FM synthesis.

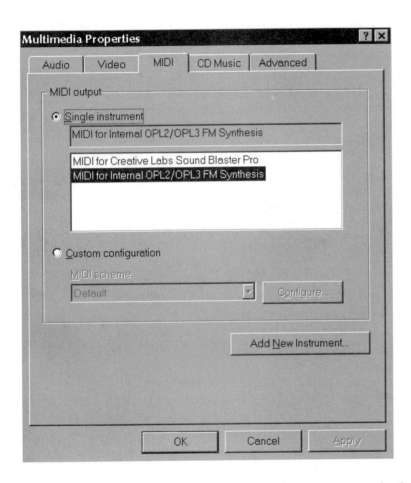

Figure 2-38. Where do you want your MIDI output to go today?

 If you have a card like the Sound Blaster AWE 32 with both FM synthesis and wave table, be sure to call up this dialog and check that the wave table option is picked (the FM synthesis will use the name *FM synthesis* while the term *wave table* may not be mentioned explicitly; try the choices that are not labeled FM synthesis!).

While MIDI in and out ports are part of the MPC spec, for many users they are not as important and they tend to be an extra cost item that you can happily skip (for example, Sound Blaster cards have a box that attaches to their joy stick ports with MIDI in, MIDI out and passes through joy stick port on the box).

MIDI is used attached to a MIDI keyboard or other MIDI instrument. If you want to make your own music, you'll want a MIDI in port. MIDI out ports are for attaching high-end MIDI synthesizers like the *Roland Sound Canvas.* They present one way of adding a wave table output device to a sound card that just has an FM synthesizer, although it is a pricey one.

Other synthesized sound file types include `rol` (the Ad Lib standard, quite popular on BBS at one time), `cmf` (the Sound Blaster attempt to replace `rol`; because `rol`'s worked on Sound Blaster, `cmf`, a subset of `mid` never really took off) and `mod` (an Amiga spec that includes the instrument data as part of the file).

 Windows 95 includes seven `rmi` samples that are so well done they are to kill for! They are an optional component (Multimedia/Sample Sounds in the Add/Remove Programs applet) taking about 350 KB for the following files:

BACH'S~1 RMI	Bach's Brandenburg Concerto No. 3.rmi
BEETHO~1 RMI	Beethoven's 5th Symphony.rmi
BEETHO~2 RMI	Beethoven's Fur Elise.rmi
DANCEO~1 RMI	Dance of the Sugar-Plum Fairy.rmi
DEBUSS~1 RMI	Debussy's Claire de Lune.rmi
INTHEH~1 RMI	In the Hall of the Mountain King.rmi
MOZART~1 RMI	Mozart's Symphony No. 40.rmi

So far, MIDI has played a minor role to most Windows users compared to `wav` files. One reason is that only `wav` files can be assigned to system events and that's what has most captured the public's attention. Secondly, until wave table sound becomes common, `mid` files just don't sound as rich as what you can get with red book Audio or with `wav` files. Finally, the cost of a decent MIDI editor is two to three times what a wav editor costs and requires a lot more knowledge to use.

Wasn't General MIDI in the Battle of the Choral C?

 This section gets into the guts of MIDI and may be more than you want to know. So you can skip it. It's here to show the scope of MIDI. In Windows 3.1, you need this information to cope with the MIDI mapper, which is fortunately a thing of the past!

MIDI used to be a tower of Babel. MIDI instructions refer to instruments by number and exactly which instrument referred to which number was determined by the MIDI device manufacturer and/or software company. In 1991, a consortium of the leading MIDI suppliers—the MIDI Manufacturers Association (write International MIDI Association, 5316 W. 5th St, Los Angeles, CA 90056 for the detailed spec)—produced a standard called *General MIDI Level 1* (sometimes called GM and sometimes just MIDI level 1). Interestingly, the original call for a spec came from a publisher of multimedia titles (Warner New Media), and the key to adopting it was a hardware manufacturer (Roland, whose *Sound Canvas* was the first GM device).

To overwhelm you with how rich the MIDI spec is, let me list the 128 instruments: Acoustic Grand Piano, Bright Acoustic Piano, Electric Grand Piano, Honky-Tonk Piano, Elect. Piano 1 (Rhodes), Elect. Piano 2 (Chorused), Harpsichord, Clav, Celesta, Glockenspiel, Music Box, Vibraphone, Marimba, Xylophone, Tubular Bells, Dulcimer, Hammond Organ, Percussive Organ, Rock Organ, Church Organ, Reed Organ, Accordion, Harmonica, Tango Accordion, Acoustic Guitar (nylon), Acoustic Guitar (steel), Electric Guitar (jazz), Electric Guitar (clean), Electric Guitar (muted), Overdriven Guitar, Distortion Guitar, Guitar Harmonics, Acoustic Bass, Electric Bass (fingered), Electric Bass (picked), Fretless Bass, Slap Bass 1, Slap Bass 2, Synth Bass 1, Synth Bass 2, Violin, Viola, Cello, Contrabass, Tremolo Strings, Pizzicato Strings, Orchestral Harp, Timpani, String Ensemble 1, String Ensemble 2, SynthStrings 1, SynthStrings 2, Choir Aahs, Voice Oohs, Synth Voice, Orchestra Hit, Trumpet, Trombone, Tuba, Muted Trumpet, French Horn, Brass Section, SynthBrass 1, SynthBrass 2, Soprano Sax, Alto Sax, Tenor Sax, Baritone Sax, Oboe, English Horn, Bassoon, Clarinet, Piccolo, Flute, Recorder, Pan Flute, Blown Bottle, Skakuhachi, Whistle, Ocarina, Lead 1 (square), Lead 2 (sawtooth), Lead 3 (calliope), Lead 4 (chiff), Lead 5 (charang), Lead 6 (voice), Lead 7 (fifths), Lead 8 (bass+lead), SynthPad 1 (new age), SynthPad 2 (warm), SynthPad 3 (polysynth), SynthPad 4 (choir), SynthPad 5 (bowed), SynthPad 6 (metallic), SynthPad 7 (halo), SynthPad 8 (sweep), FX 1 (rain), FX 2 (soundtrack), FX 3 (crystal), FX 4 (atmosphere), FX 5 (brightness), FX 6 (goblins), FX 7 (echoes), FX 8 (sci-fi), Sitar, Banjo, Shamisen, Koto, Kalimba, Bagpipe, Fiddle, Shanai, Tinkle Bell, Agogo, Steel Drums, Woodblock, Taiko Drum, Melodic Tom, Synth Drum, Reverse Cymbal, Guitar Fret Noise, Breath Noise, Seashore, Bird Tweet, Telephone Ring, Helicopter, Applause, Gunshot.

Wow! One doesn't think of Helicopter or Gunshot as an instrument. Is Tinkle Bell just Peter Pan's friend in the ladies' room?

And there are 47 drum sounds: Acoustic Bass Drum, Bass Drum 1, Side Stick, Acoustic Snare, Hand Clap, Electric Snare, Low Floor Tom, Closed Hi-Hat, High Floor Tom, Pedal Hi-Hat, Low Tom, Open Hi-Hat, Low-Mid Tom, Hi-Mid Tom, Crash Cymbal 1, High Tom, Ride Cymbal 1, 52, Chinese Cymbal, 53, Ride Bell, 54, Tambourine, 55, Splash Cymbal, 56, Cowbell, 57, Crash Cymbal 2, Vibraslap, Ride Cymbal 2, Hi Bongo, Low Bongo, Mute Hi Conga, Open Hi Conga, Low Conga, High Timbale, Low Timbale, High Agogo, Low Agogo, Cabasa, Maracas, Short Whistle, Long Whistle, Short Guiro, Long Guiro, Claves, Hi Wood Block, Low Wood Block, Mute Cuica, Open Cuica, Mute Triangle, Open Triangle.

MIDI supports polyphony, that is, multiple notes. These notes can be played on multiple instruments that are assigned to distinct channels. General MIDI devices are supposed to allow 32-note polyphony and to respond to sixteen channels with the first nine set for instruments and the tenth for percussion. A GM file can do whatever it wants with channels 11–16, although usually they aren't used.

Windows 3.1 introduced a variant on General MIDI, which many at Microsoft now admit was a dumb mistake. With Windows 95, straight general MIDI rules the waves, er, the MIDIs. Hooray, I say.

Trip the Light Fantastic: Video

> If we see light at the end of the tunnel,
> It's the light of the oncoming train.

> —Robert Lowell, *Since 1939*

In just a few short years, video has gone from an exotic computer add-on to something users expect. The Windows CD even comes with a few sample video clips, including a movie trailer and MTV clip. A video clip is a sequence of pictures with a sound track interleaved. From the point of view of playback, there is no difference between animation and movies although obviously very different tools are needed for their creation. For this reason, there are special animation formats, most notably `*.flc` for files made with Autodesk Animator. But most videos you'll see are in one of two formats: Microsoft Audio-Visual Interleaved (`*.avi`), a RIFF-based type and Quick Time (`*.mov`), and an Apple format developed for the Mac. Mom's favorite tool for converting between video formats is the conversion program in Ulead's Media Studio Pro.

Besides the obvious picture parameters (size and number of colors), videos have one other parameter of importance—their frame rate. Motion pictures have a rate of thirty frames per second but many computer videos have rates of only fifteen frames per second, which makes them rather jerky.

 There are two reasons the frame rate was set low. First, videos take a lot of disk space and halving the frame rate cuts the disk space used by a factor of two for rather obvious reasons. In addition, drawing thirty frames per second on the screen would bring the best PC of several years ago to its knees begging for mercy. As disk storage prices continue to plummet and hardware improves, the fifteen-frames-per-second video will go the way of the dodo or the CGA.

Compression

> A definition is a sack of flour compressed into a thimble.
>
> —Rémy de Gourmont

 A picture is only worth a thousand words if black and white and less than a tenth of a super VGA screen in size.

Why does Sarah say that? Well, a typical word is about 5 bytes counting the space so a thousand words are 5,000 bytes or 40,000 bits. That's enough disk space for a 200×200 black-and-white bitmap.

 A 1024 x 768 True Color picture requires a whooping 2.25 MB of space, so with my, sniff, high standards, I'd like to say a picture is worth 450,000 words.

And if pictures take a lot of space, videos take even more. What often saves the day is compression. Files often have a lot of inefficiently presented data in them. For example if a black-and-white bitmap is represented as a series of bits indicating black-and-white dots as 0s and 1s, that's going to be not too efficient for "typical" pictures. Because pictures are usually made of blobs so that if a given dot is black, it is likely that the next dot will be black. It is clearly more efficient to code most pictures by describing them as "first so many black dots, then so many white dots, then . . . ."

That's a simple compression technique known as Run Length Encoding (RLE). Another set of algorithms, of which the best known is Huffman compression, depends on the fact that something like a text file will use the letter e a lot more often than the letter q, not to mention the ASCII code for ©! Huffman schemes use fewer than 8 bits for e's and more for characters like © and gains space in the bargain.

By far the most common compression algorithms depend on the fact that bit patterns tend to get repeated over and over. It may be more efficient to use shorthand meaning "the three letters that occurred 27 letters ago" than to reuse the word *the*. The mother of all repeating pattern algorithms is Lempel-Ziv and a variant on it called Lempel-Ziv-Welch (LZ and LZW). These algorithms are behind `zip` and `gif` files and Drive Space.

Abraham Lempel and Jacob Ziv are two Israeli academic computer scientists who pioneered the technology in the late 1970s. Terry Welch worked for one of the companies that merged to become Unisys, which claims a patent on LZW. There have been huge arguments over how much of the technology was already in LZ and so in the public domain. Periodically, Unisys tries to assert its claims, most recently demanding royalties on all the `gif` files on the World Wide Web. Sigh.

All these schemes are lossless compression schemes, which means one can recover the original file byte for byte from the compressed file. This is obviously a requirement if you are going to compress programs or highly structured data like that in a spreadsheet. But if the colors of a few pixels in a picture are changed, the eye won't notice. Or, if the high frequency part of a recorded sound is dropped, your dog's ear might notice but yours won't. So multimedia files can use lossy compression schemes where the original file can't be reconstructed byte for byte. JPEG and MPEG (for pictures and videos, respectively) are the two best-known compression schemes.

I had to restrain Mao and Sarah from bending your ears with all the technical details behind these schemes since they find the mathematical ideas so lovely. But I told them that readers could look at the two pieces on compression that Barry wrote for *PC Magazine* in 1993 if they wanted more details.

Programs that play compressed videos or audios have to know how to decompress them or have to have the decompression done for them automagically by the operating system.

Windows is built around the second idea and provides many built-in decompression schemes. When you record something and save it to disk, you may want to compress it, again automagically. The drivers that compress and decompress are called Codecs—get it? COmpress/DECompress.

The Advanced tab of the Multimedia Applet in Control Panel (Figure 2-39) displays the installed Video and Audio Codecs. Windows should have installed them during setup, but if they aren't there and you plan to run any videos or play wav files, you can install them by running Add/Remove Programs, going to Windows Setup, highlighting Multimedia, hitting the Details button, and making sure Audio and Video Compression are checked.

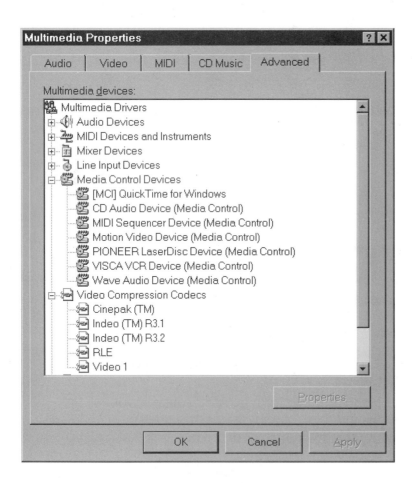

Figure 2-39. The Multimedia Properties Tab

If you read *The Mother of All Windows Books,* you may wonder whatever happened to the Wave Mapper. It's become the Audio Compression Manager. Go to the part of the Advanced Multimedia dialog labeled Audio Compression Codecs, open it, highlight "Microsoft PCM Converter," click Properties and the About. You'll see the bits per sample converter that was at the heart of "Le Scandale du Wave Mapper."

Media Control Interface—Do You Mean DeeDee Meyers?

Windows' support for Multimedia is extensible; drivers written to what Microsoft calls MCI, for Media Control Interface, can be plugged into any program that uses the MCI API. If you get a new multimedia device, say a video disc player, the *Media Player* applet can play files from it if the vendor supplies a driver that supports MCI.

MCI defines the following standard device types:

animation	animation device like an Autodesk flc player
cdaudio	red book audio from a CD
dat	digital audio tape player
digitalvideo	digital video in a window
other	undefined MCI type
overlay	analog video in a window
scanner	image scanner
sequencer	MIDI sequencer to play mid and rmi files
vcr	Video recorder or player
videodisc	Videodisc player
waveaudio	Audio device that plays digitized wav files

An MCI driver has to respond to two types of commands—a *command message interface* and a *command string interface.* The command message interface uses what the Windows API call mciSendCommand and is intended for C programmers. It is much like any other part of the Windows API. The command string interface uses what appears to be English language. Here's a little program written in the command string interface (with comments on each line in brackets):

open tada.wav type waveaudio   {gets control of the wav player; gives it a file to open}

play waveaudio   {tells the driver to play the sound}

close waveaudio   {returns control of the wav player to Windows}

The presence of a command string interface is an indication that Microsoft expects sophisticated users to try to use MCI in macro languages. As a first step, Visual Basic has an MCI custom control that uses a variant of the command string interface. Moreover, when Media Player is paused, you can hit Ctrl+F5 and open a special window that lets you send MCI commands to the current device. For a video, try typing in "status frames skipped" or choose CD Audio in the Device menu and type in "set door open" to eject the CD.

The full documentation for the command string interface is available as part of the Windows 95 SDK. To give you an idea of the power of the command string interface, I note that the commands include: open, close, play, record, pause, resume, seek, stop, status, and (for appropriate types) freeze (for Video) and set tempo (for MIDI).

Windows stores the list of installed MCI types in the Registry (where it stores nearly everything else) in the key*

        HKEY_LOCAL_MACHINE\System\CurrentControlSet\control
                        \MediaResources\mci

You have access to the list in the Advanced Tab of the Control Panel Multimedia applet. Figure 2-39 shows the list with the six MCI drivers built into Windows and with Quick Time added by a program that used Quick Time Video.

Media Player uses a rather involved scheme to get the items it shows on its Device menu and to pick up the file extensions it uses in the File dialog that then pops up. First it looks in the [mci] section of system.ini to find the names of all the MCI drivers. Then it makes calls to the drivers themselves to find out the user-friendly names to use. When it pops up the File Open dialog, it looks in the [mci extensions] section of win.ini to figure out what extensions are associated with the various devices.

---

* Registry keys are explained in Chapter 11.

C'mon Mao, ole buddy. That's quite a whopper you've made up there! Microsoft says `ini` files are no longer used by Windows 95 and its components. Your scheme doesn't even mention the Registry, where we know all this sort of information goes. That's so far-fetched, even the OJ defense wouldn't touch it. Have you any evidence to back up this preposterous theory?

My esteemed Mr. Rush, of course, I wouldn't posit such a theory without an experiment to back it up. I did the following. First I copied the driver `midseq.drv` to `midseq1.drv`. I loaded that copy into a binary file editor I have and located the string `MIDI Sequencer` near the end of the driver. Since that was the name that appeared on Media Player's Device menu but was nowhere to be found in the entire Registry, I figured this might be significant. So I changed it to `IGOR Sequencer`. Then I loaded up sysedit and changed the line in `system.ini`'s `[mci]` section that said `sequencer=mciseq.drv` to instead say `sequencer=mciseq1.drv`. And I added the line `mao=Sequencer` to the [mci extensions] section of `win.ini`. I saved those files and started up Media Player. On the Device menu, what had been "MIDI Sequencer" now said "IGOR Sequencer" and the Open dialog I saw is in Figure 2-40. Look at what it says under "File of type" at the bottom of that dialog.

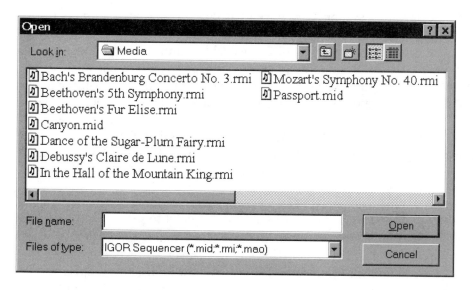

Figure 2-40. Mao's experiment

Bravo! Johnny Cochran, move over. But why, oh why, did Microsoft do that?

 I can only conjecture why it's that way. The interface for Media Player is hardly changed from Windows 3.11, so I'd guess that the guts haven't changed much either. They had a scheme that worked with Windows 3.11 and figured, "Why change it?" Besides, they probably rationalized that changing the old scheme could break the installation method of some programs written for Windows 3.x.

CD Mania

Bill Gates is a CD visionary. In 1986, he organized the first international conference on CD ROM technology, calling it "The New Papyrus." One of the first products on the PC to show what could be done was Microsoft's *Multimedia Beethoven* (which wasn't made by Microsoft, but was successfully marketed by the Redmondians).* Microsoft has been a major player in several types of CD ROMs. For example, *EnCarta,* its encyclopedia, outsells the best-selling print encyclopedia by a factor of more than ten.

Yet, when it came to the operating system, CDs were treated as an afterthought. Support for CDs was not built into the core of DOS but was provided by a program called MSCDEX (for MicroSoft CD EXtensions) that took over 40K of valuable below-1-MB memory address space. Until DOS 6.0, this program wasn't even included with DOS but was provided by CD ROM manufacturers, which meant that users had the hassle of getting a new version from their hardware supplier whenever they got a new version of DOS.

With Windows 95, CD technology is finally being taken seriously. Of course, this is no surprise—the installed base of CD drives has increased almost fivefold in the past two years. Here's what Windows 95 provides for CDs:

- a built-in CD file system that is handled via a VxD

- autoplay for audio CDs. Put an audio CD into the drive and Windows 95 CD Player will pop up and start playing the CD. If you hold down a `Shift` key while popping the CD into the drive, it won't autoplay. In Chapter 3, I'll explain how to disable autoplay so that the CD will not automagically start playing. You'll still be able to start playing by right-clicking the CD icon and choosing Play.

---

* Microsoft's corporate headquarters are in Redmond, Washington, a suburb of Seattle.

- audio CD track support. You can drag a specific track of a specific CD to the Desktop or Start Menu, pick it, and have Windows tell you which CD to put in and have that track played.

- CD Plus support. This is a new, enhanced audio CD specification from SONY and Phillips that allows audio CDs to come with data—the idea is that a music CD could include pictures of the stars, video clips, and more to enhance the experience. The CD could be played on a standard audio CD player but if you load it under Windows 95, you get extra goodies. The spec depends critically on multisession technology, so you'll need a CD drive with multisession support—most single-speed and some very early double-speed CDs don't have this, but any recently manufactured CD drive will.

- autoplay for CD ROMs. A CD maker can arrange that when a CD is placed in the drive the CD will just start playing. This will be ideal for younger kids and also for users who don't want to worry about what drive letter their CD is. As with audio CDs, if you hold down a `Shift` key while popping the CD into the drive, it won't autoplay. Unlike audio CD, there is no way to prevent automatic autoplay while keeping autoplay capability on a context menu.

- Informative CD icons. If you look at a CD drive in `My Computer` or drag a shortcut to a drive onto the Desktop, a CD ROM maker can arrange for a special icon to replace the default and so let you know what CD is in the drive. Place an audio CD in the drive and

  see replaced by . Or pop the Windows CD in and see it become .

Let the Games Begin

Insurance. An ingenious modern game of chance in which the player is permitted to enjoy the comfortable conviction that he is beating the man who keeps the table.

—Ambrose Bierce, *The Devil's Dictionary*

 Boss, you may have forgotten da games, but Microsoft sure didn't.

The joke used to be that the largest software company in Redmond wasn't Microsoft, it was Nintendo (whose U.S. subsidiary is based there). With its incredible growth in sales, Microsoft has passed Nintendo, but it hasn't escaped Bill Gates's notice that games are big business, very big business. Not only hasn't the PC been the premier games machine but games, especially action games, have been the last bastion of DOS. Games makers knew that you just couldn't get the graphics speed and oomph you needed if you used Windows.

So Microsoft has made a big push to make Windows more hospitable to games. Windows 95 has made some additions:

- Game programmers can use a set of code libraries called WinG (G as in Games!) to produce rapid action on the screen. Microsoft touted the fact that the makers of Doom were able to port the product to Windows 95 in just a few days.

- Wintoon is a set of tools that can be used to produce slick animation.

- Some of the CD stuff I discussed in the last section is important for games.

The following were not in the initial release of Windows 95, but are expected to be added in the first few tune-up packs:

- Direct Draw, Direct Sound, Direct Play, and Direct Input (the later for Joysticks) are to be parts of a special games subsystem.

- Software MPEG libraries* will be added.

- Look for surround video for 360 degree panning of photos.

- Reality Lab real time 3-D rendering engine became part of Microsoft when Microsoft bought the British company Reality Lab. The rendering engine will make it possible to quickly produce 3D images on the fly.

No PC Is an Island

Networking Light

> Only connect! That was the whole of her sermon. Only connect the prose and
> the passion, and both will be exalted, and human love will be seen at its height.
> Live in fragments no longer.
>
> —E. M. Forster, *Howards End*, 1910

---

* I'll discuss MPEG in Chapter 6.

If you want to know about using Windows 95 with a "real" network, which these days most often means with Novell Netware or with Windows NT server, you are looking in the wrong place. Dealing with the issues raised by large-scale networks requires a book of its own that is at least the size of this book.

But Windows 95 has built-in peer-to-peer networking that is ideal for a small business or home office with a few machines to connect to each other. It is useful for what we expect to become a common scenario: at least two computers in the home. The modern family will need a computer for the kids to do homework on or play games, while Mom or Dad checks email or scans the on-line services on another computer. So we want to say something about setting up a simple peer-to-peer network in this book.

But even more significantly, even if the idea of ethernet* and peer-to-peer networking gives you the willies and you wouldn't think of using anything but a stand-alone PC, you're going to get brushed pretty hard by networking if you want to connect to the Internet, because the Internet is a network and Windows 95 treats it as such. Dial-Up Networking is the name that Windows 95 gives to network connections over a phone line, be it to an Internet provider or to your corporate network or from your portable computer to a stand-alone machine at home!

I'll give you some of the basic terminology here and discuss Dial-Up Networking and Internet access in Chapter 4.

There are four components to a network as far as Windows 95 is concerned:

1. **Adapters.** This is most typically an ethernet hardware board that needs to be installed through the `Network` applet of Control Panel. But it can also be the virtual adapter called Dial-Up Adapter that you install to do "networking" over the phone line.

2. **Protocols.** These are the methods that networks use to talk to one another. If you are connecting to a large-scale network, you'll likely want to use the protocols that the network's maker provides, but for the kind of networks I'm discussing you'll want the Microsoft protocols: IPX/SP, NetBUI, and TCP/IP. When you install the adapter, the associated protocols should be installed, except that you may need to install TCP/IP support (which I'll discuss further) by hand.

---

* Ethernet is a standard for Local Area Networking hardware.

3. **Client.** This software allows your computer to use the protocols and adapters to actually do stuff over the network. For the kind of connections I'm discussing, you'll want the `Client for Microsoft Networks`. Again, this should be installed when you install the adapter.

4. **Services.** This provides extras. If you want other machines to be able to access files on your machine, you'll need to add `File and printer sharing for Microsoft Networks`. Rather than add this explicitly, you press the File and Printer Sharing button in the `Network` applet. When you hit the check boxes, the necessary service will get turned on. Be sure to check what I say in Chapter 8 about the need to separately turn on sharing for individual drives even after turning on general File and Printer Sharing.

TCP/IP* is the standard protocol of the Internet. When you have an Internet provider that gives you direct access to the net, the provider will normally establish a PPP account for you and you'll need TCP/IP support (a `TCP/IP stack`) on your machine. A Windows `dll` that provides TCP/IP is called a *Winsock*. Before Windows 95 there were lots of third-party Winsocks floating around. You'll want to be sure to replace any one you might have with the one that comes with Windows 95.

Before you worry about installing TCP/IP, you'll want to read about the Internet Signup Wizard, which I talk about in Chapter 4.

A final general networking issue concerns *UNC filenames*,[†] which are fully supported in Windows 95. Every workstation on a network has a name. Newt's machine might be called Aye. If you want to refer to a file in `C:\windows` on that machine, you could type in `\\aye\c\windows`, any place that Windows 95 accepts a filename. Of course, Windows 3.1 applications and DOS applications aren't likely to understand these terminology. But Windows 95 understands it so well that if you type that in the Run box, it will open that folder in folder view!

With this understanding of UNC names, drive mapping becomes a thing of the past. You no longer need to refer to drives with associated letters that you can run out if you link a number of machines together.

---

* TCP/IP = Transmission Control Protocol/Internet Protocol; PPP = point-to-point protocol. Thoroughly useless information, but I knew you'd want to know.

† Universal Naming Convention, if you must know!

MAPI and TAPI

One of Microsoft's ways of controlling the software market is to place high barriers for the entry of small, innovative companies. Their favorite device for making it hard for the small developer is the API of the month.

—A disgruntled programmer

 From the perspective of the programmer, Windows is filled with collections of calls they can make to the operating system and its extensions. These are called APIs, short for Application Programming Interface. Two of these are worth pointing out to readers, because understanding the architecture behind these APIs can help in understanding what is going on. The Messaging API (MAPI) is the architecture beyond email services. The Telephony API (TAPI) is there to provide links to the brave new world of telephone services.

MAPI is intended to provide a universal Inbox, a single place that all your email is collected and stored. At the same time, it provides a uniform place to store name, address, and telephone number information. The MAPI architecture has five components:

1. **A message store provider.** Message stores are files with a specified format that store messages and other personal information. These files have an extension `.pst` and are sometimes referred to a **Personal Information Store.** If you install Exchange under Windows 95, it will make such a file for you.

2. **An address book provider.** MAPI specifies a format for address books and allows other service providers to extend the information stored in an address book record so that, for example, CompuServe can define the formats it requires for email messages sent via CompuServe. **Personal address books** have the extension `.pab`. Again, Exchange will set up such a file for you.

3. **Transport service providers.** These provide the back-end links to various places that mail can be sent. These providers respond to requests from clients and message-aware applications to send or collect mail. Exchange automatically offers to install two transport providers when you install it—Microsoft FAX and The Microsoft Network. The Windows CD has a transport provider supplied by CompuServe. The Plus! Pack installs a fourth provider for Internet Mail. Exchange Server, Microsoft's planned Notes killer, will be network-based databases with a service provider linking the user to these databases.

I hope that America Online, Prodigy, MCI mail, Notes, and the rest all provide MAPI servers soon to give Windows users a complete email solution. But I worry that the angst and anger caused by The Microsoft Network and the way it is included in Windows 95 will cause a knee-jerk reaction against cooperating with anything in Windows 95. CompuServe is to be commended for their inclusion of the MAPI server.

4. **A MAPI client.** This is the basic user interface to the whole shebang. The Client accesses the address book and information store to allow the user to read and compose mail and then calls the transport providers to actually send and collect that mail. Exchange is the MAPI client provided with Windows 95.

5. **Message aware applications.** When they sense that a MAPI client is installed in the system, programs can add a `Send . . .` command to their File menus that will send the current document to the message store and then invoke the client to handle addressing and the actual sending of the messages.

 The Exchange Client is the weakest major component of Windows 95. MAPI itself is so vast that even with a less-than-ideal interface Exchange is exceedingly valuable. But the interface lacks the polish of the Windows 95 shell, and I hope that a revamped Exchange Client is high on the list of things we'll see in one of the Tune-Up packs.

The wonderful thing about this architecture is that it sets standards. Third parties can produce their own MAPI clients with more features than Exchange or with the ability to more easily manipulate the Message Store or the Address book. Since the file specifications are standard, files manipulated with one client should be readable in another. And the transport providers should work with any client.

 That's the theory at least, but this is such a fine opportunity for problems. Everyone will work with Exchange, but I'll bet that we find that third-party clients don't work with files that are manipulated by other third-party clients. And some third-party clients won't work with some third-party transport providers. Expect a rough shakedown cruise if you try to go beyond the basics until the industry figures out what the standards *really* mean!

To me, one of the most exciting parts of the whole specification is the common address book. I don't want to count the number of times I've had to reenter hundreds of address and phone numbers because I changed PIMs* or because my envelope addresser didn't understand my PIMs format. At this point I'm only interested in PIMs that use the MAPI address book to get addresses, phone numbers, and so on.

TAPI provides a common set of calls that allows programs access to the telephone without having to reinvent the wheel. A program can, after installation, offer to register the product by phone without knowing anything about modems. Once the program determines a TAPI provider is present in the system, it just sends commands to dial. A PIM could track incoming phone calls by using caller ID with calls to the TAPI provider. This use of caller ID will need specialized hardware in your computer. Indeed, TAPI is more a promise of things to come than a full-fledged working specification implemented on most Windows 95 systems.

You may hear reference to subsets of these basic APIs that are useful to programmers because they are easier to use. For TAPI, this subset is called *Assisted Telephony*. For MAPI, it is called *Common Message Calls* (CMC).

I have a favorite acronym in these specs, *POTS*, which is sprinkled through the TAPI documentation. What does POTS stand for? "Plain Old Telephone Service." I kid you not.

My favorite is TSAPI, the TAPI competitor offered by Novell. What's so cool about the acronym? Well, unless you live in Ogden (Novell's home turf), it's pronounced "Sappy." Proof positive that engineers have a tin ear for marketing!

---

* PIM = Personal Information Manager, the programs that track phone calls, appointments, to do lists, etc.

PART 2

Act II, Scene 1. Pan to Uhuru at the Communications Console.

Uhuru: I'm receiving a sub-space communication from Star Fleet Command Dot Com, Captain.

Kirk: Put it on the sound track so the audience can hear, Uhuru.

Uhuru: It's mostly gibberish, sir, but....

Disembodied Voice: May Day. May Day. Starship !nterprise, please respond.

Kirk: How do they pronounce "!nterprise," Uhuru?

Uhuru: I don't know sir. Must be one of those exotic sub-Saharan "click" languages.

Kirk: What is the nature of your problem, Star Fleet Command Dot Com?

D. V.: We are being invaded by X-Filers. Repeat. We are being invaded by…

Kirk: Yeah, I heard you the first time. What's an X-Filer?

D. V.: They sit in circles on Friday night, light candles and chant, "Take me to your Muldar."

Kirk: Sounds like an insurrection, Command Dot Com.

D.V.: It wouldn't be so bad if it weren't for all the UFOs that hover during the seances.

Kirk: So what do you want me to do about it? Train our phasers on the UFOs?

D.V.: Naw. Just come down here and kick some butt. Tell 'em to get a haircut. And a shave.

Kirk: I'll bring along the Windows geeks, too. Maybe they can learn a trade.

The next two chapters show you how to put Windows 95 to work, with the built-in components and applications. If you want to master Windows, and make it do your bidding, this is where you must start.

Chapter 3

Core Components

A fierce unrest seethes at the core,
Of all existing things:,
It was the eager wish to soar,
That gave the gods their wings.

—Don Marquis, *Unrest.*

 They call it the Windows 95 shell. It's the console you use to drive spaceship Windows. The most important functions are task management, file manipulation, and program launching. And that's what my crew will start with. Pay particular attention to the discussion in the group of sections called *Configuring the Context Menu* because that's Windows 95 wondrous power feature that seems to have gotten lost in most magazines' meandering on the product. Be sure to check out "Sarah's Smart Setup Step by Step," the power user's preferred way to have folders and drives open. Then, my crew will talk about some of the other core components, including a first brush at Control Panel (continued in Chapter 10), Network Neighborhood, Help, and how DOS sessions are handled by Windows. Finally there's Exchange, which many would argue is an applet, not a core component. But I think it is potentially the most important, most core, component of all.

Taken to Taskbar

. . . the task itself arises only when the material conditions
necessary for its solution already exist . . .

—Karl Marx, *A Contribution to the Critique of Political Economy*

There's no feature of Windows 95 more obvious to a new user sitting down to a new machine than the Taskbar (see Figure 3-1) and the Taskbar will be one of the most obvious new features to experienced Windows 3.1 users—probably the most obvious feature the first few days. So what better place to start than the Taskbar. Besides, the Start button is there (although this is not the group of sections where my team will discuss the Start Menu itself; that'll come after the Taskbar and Explorer discussions).

Figure 3-1. This must be the start of something grand

When someone starts up Windows 95 and there are no programs in the StartUp group they get a `Click here to begin` and arrow bouncing up against the Start Menu as shown in Figure 3-1. Kindy tacky, but it wows them newbies.

The irony of the fancy start is that if the Welcome application runs—the one that pops a message about Windows onto the screen—at startup, then the moving "Click here..." message is not displayed. Speaking of the Welcome messages, you'll find them on Mom's CD in a file in the root directory called `Welcome.doc`. Read them over and be done with them by unchecking "Show this Welcome screen next time you start Windows." Or if you prefer, add your own welcome messages as data to the Registry key `HKEY_LOCAL_MACHINE \SOFTWARE\Microsoft \Windows\CurrentVersion\explorer\Tips`. You'll have to master the Registry by looking in Chapter 11. By the way, if you checked the box in error and want to get the welcome screen back, run `welcome` from Start Menu/Run box and recheck the box!

Taskbar Basics

> The hardest task of a girl's life, nowadays,
> is to prove to a man that his intentions are serious.

> —Helen Rowland, *A Guide to Men*, 1922

The Taskbar has four parts.

Four? I only see three: the Start button, the task buttons and that area on the extreme right with the time and tiny icons.

The area with tiny icons is called the Notification Area. And the fourth part is the blank, unoccupied part of the task button area in the middle. The blank area is important because it lets you do quite a few things. First you can right-click and get the menu shown in Figure 3-2. The first three menu items rearrange all open Windows—Cascade places them overlapping along a diagonal. Tile makes the Windows nonoverlapping. Minimize All Windows gives you access to the Desktop with all the Windows gone.

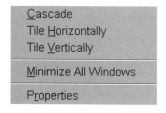

Figure 3-2. The Taskbar context menu

It is important to note the fact that if you pick any of the top four items, the menu picks up an Undo option—with the first three choices, Undo is an extra option; if you pick `Minimize All Windows`, then that option is grayed out and in essence, the `Undo Minimize All` is a replacement. This has two important consequences. First, you can experiment with Tile and Cascade, whose results won't always be to your liking.

Secondly, you can pick `Minimize All Windows` to get at the Desktop, launch an icon on the Desktop and then `Undo Minimize All` since that command stays on the Taskbar context menu for a several actions afterward.

I'll talk about the Taskbar Properties menu (which you can access from the context menu) in a bit. I first want to note that the unoccupied part of the Taskbar is also what you use to move the Taskbar. Click and hold the mouse cursor over a blank part of the Taskbar and experiment with what happens if you drag it. You can repeat the process to drag the Taskbar back. You'll notice that you can place the Taskbar in any of the four edges of the screen. It's as if the blank part of the Taskbar was playing the role played by the title bar of a normal window.

It's clear that most users will leave it at the bottom of the screen, if only because they didn't know you can move it, but sophisticated users are already split into warring camps—much like Swift's bottom enders and top enders, there are the bottom taskers and right side taskers. And, as we'll see, there are also arguments about autohide. Mom doesn't cotton much to theological arguments so we'll let you figure out which you prefer.

Even if you like the Taskbar at the bottom of the screen very much, thank you, there are two reasons you need to know about moving the Taskbar. First, you can move it by mistake. You reach to click a button, your hand slips and suddenly your lovely Taskbar has moved from the bottom to the side and you haven't the foggiest idea how to move it back. Well, you do if you read what I just told you.

Second, there's a neato Stupid Desktop Trick. I like a nice neat column of drive icons along the right edge of my screen. How do I line them up? Simple, I sort of line them up along the right side. Then I drag the Taskbar to the right side and maybe stretch it to be a little wider. It lines the icons up nice and neat to the left side of the Taskbar. Then I just drag the Taskbar back, lasso the column of icons, and move them in bulk.

You can also resize the Taskbar; that is, make it higher when it is horizontal and wider when it is vertical. Just let your cursor hover over the edge of the Taskbar opposite from the screen edge until it changes into a double header arrow; then press down and drag.

 Certainly at 1024 x 768 resolution and maybe at 800 x 600, I recommend that horizontal Taskbar have two rows.

A final remark on getting at the blank part of the Taskbar: If you have a two-row Taskbar, there is always a blank area below the notification area and below the Start button. Even if you only have a one-row Taskbar, there is usually a thin line between the recessed notification area and the rightmost task button and an even thinner line to the right of the recessed notification button. You can right-click on those areas to get at the Taskbar context menu.

There isn't much to say about the buttons on the Taskbar. They'll bring their application to the top when pressed whether the program is minimized or just behind another program. If you right-click on a button, the system menu for that program will pop up. If the full caption for a program won't fit on the button, . . . appears and then if you place the mouse cursor over the button and let it rest for a moment a Tooltip appears with the full caption. This is especially useful for Explorer buttons since they often have long directory names and the Windows designers made the mistake of placing the program name before the directory name.

If you choose Properties from the Taskbar context menu (or Settings/Taskbar . . . from the Start Menu), you get the Property sheet shown in Figure 3-3. I'll talk about the Start Menu tab and about the third checkbox when I discuss the Start Menu. The Show Clock checkbox obviously determines whether the time is shown at the extreme right of the Taskbar. I can't imagine why anyone would want to, but you can turn off the display of the time.

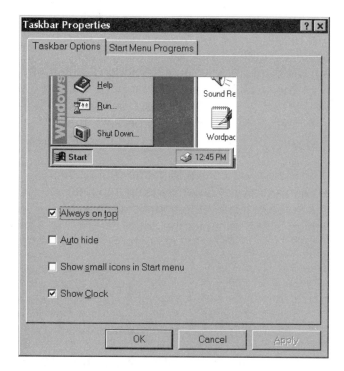

Figure 3-3. The Taskbar Property Sheet

Always on top controls whether the Taskbar can be covered by other windows. If the box is checked (the default) when a program asks Windows to maximize a window, it only fills the part of the screen other than the Taskbar. I can't imagine why anyone would want this option independently of Autohide.

The Autohide choice is an interesting one that causes the Taskbar to normally appear as a single thin line. But move the mouse cursor to the edge with that thin line and the Taskbar pops up to its normal size.

 If you are running at 640 x 480, screen real estate is so valuable that Autohide will be extremely tempting for any user. As resolutions go up, the case is less compelling, so much so that I wouldn't turn it on at 1024 x 768.

 Well, I wouldn't think about running without Autohide on no matter what the resolution and I'd urge all our readers to at least give it a try.

We agree it is something everyone should try. To my taste, it only makes sense at the bottom of the screen because every other edge is used by many programs' windows. For example, if you have a maximized window with a scroll bar on the right side and an autohidden Taskbar on the right, when you reach for the scroll bars, the Taskbar pops out and you can't reach the scroll bars! While the right edge is used the most, the top and left side of main windows are edges you often need to reach. In most programs, the bottom of the window is a status area and you don't need to move your mouse there.

There are programs—Claris's File Maker Pro comes to mind—that place popup menus at the bottom of their windows. If Autohide is on and the File Maker Pro window is maximized, you can't reach the popups without the Taskbar getting in the way. Autohide is a problem for me, too.

The Notification Area

> All publicity is good, except an obituary notice.
>
> —Brendan Behan, *Sunday Express,* Jan. 5, 1964

One of the most innovative ideas in the basic design of the Desktop is the area on the extreme right of the Taskbar called the *Notification Area.* As its name implies, one of its main purposes is for programs to notify you of some situation, for example to inform you that new mail has arrived. But it is also a good place to put background programs so you can access them without their having to take a full button in the middle area of the Taskbar. Icons in the Notification Area can communicate with you in five different ways:

- **Through their icons.** The presence of the icon—for example, to show New Mail has arrived—can convey information but also the icon itself can change. For example, in Figure 3-6, the fourth icon from the left is Windows's own System Monitor and the level changes to indicate the amount of free system resources. The icon two over is the Powertoys audio CD player. The Not sign through it means that there isn't an audio CD in the drive.

- **Through a tooltip.** If you rest your mouse cursor over the time on the notification area, you'll see the day of the week and the date in a tooltip. Some tooltips are just the name of the program—but many convey useful information.

- **Through a single-click action.** Single clicks on a Notification Area icon normally pop up a small interactive control. A typical example is the volume control, which pops up a single master volume slider and mute checkbox (Figure 3-4). But some programs only react to a double click and not a single one (for example, the Plus! Pack's System Agent). And a program can take whatever action it deems appropriate on a single click. For example, the Powertoys* audio CD player uses a single click to start/pause CD playing.

- **Through a double-click action.** This should normally pop up a more extensive interactive control. For example, double-clicking the volume brings up a full-fledged mixer (Figure 3-5).

- **Through a context menu.** Right-clicking an icon can invoke a menu. For example, the Powertoys CD player lets you get to an audio track list that way.

Figure 3-4. Simple minded volume control

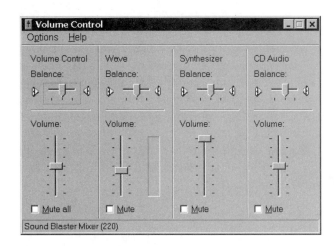

Figure 3-5. Full fledged volume control

Not every icon in the Notification Area will use all five ways—indeed, very few will use all of them—but you need to know of all them. When a new icon appears in the area, you should experiment with it to see which of the methods it uses.

The only notification area icon built into Windows on all systems is the time. On systems with a sound driver, there will be a volume icon (which can be turned off via a checkbox in the Audio tab of the Multimedia Applet of Control panel).

---

* I'll discuss Powertoys in Chapter 5.

Portable computers supporting the Advanced Power Management (APM) version 1.1 specification will display a battery icon in the Notification Area—if you have such a computer and no icon, you'll need to open the Device Manager (it's a tab in the System Applet of Control panel), expand the entry called "System Devices" by hitting the plus and looking for an entry called "Advanced Power Management Support." If it's not there, your portable doesn't support it after all. If it is, double-click on it and check the enable box on the Settings tab.

This is a dangerous thing to tell people to do. We've found many, many laptops that have buggy implementations of the APM BIOS. Most of these machines will crash or hang when you attempt to suspend them from the Start Menu (since the "Suspend" menu will be added when APM 1.1 is enabled). Early on in the beta we were getting tons of bug reports from people saying, "Hey, my machine dies when I choose 'suspend'." It turns out that this machine would have never properly suspended even under Windows 3.1, but because we automatically detected the APM BIOS, we enabled it by default. Starting around May 1995 we changed Setup so that we would only enable APM if the user already had it previously enabled on their machine. Currently I can count on one hand the number of laptop models that will properly support suspend.

Well, excuse me. I was only quoting the Windows 95 help when I gave the advice. But given what you've told me, I'd better warn readers to try this with extreme care.

The Resource Meter accessory (if you installed it, it will be under the `Programs/ Accessories/System Tools` submenu of the Start Menu, but I'd recommend you add it to the StartUp group) displays an icon in the notification area giving you a readout on Free System Resources.

When there are jobs waiting to be printed in the spooler of your Printer an icon will appear that gives you quick access to the Spooler control. When Exchange is up, if you've installed Microsoft Fax, you'll see a small fax icon. Exchange also uses an envelope icon to notify you of new email. Many third-party utilities use the Notification Area.

Figure 3-6. A population explosion

The Notification Area is likely to be so popular that as more utilities appear, there will be an awful population explosion there. For example, Figure 3-6 shows a notification area that is already awfully full.

Reading from the left, we have Norton Anti-Virus, Volume, Plus! Pack's System Agent, Windows Resource Meter, Powertoys QuickRes screen resolution changer, Powertoys FlexiCD, Norton Utilities, Exchange Fax icon, New Mail notification, Modem status, Microsoft Networks icon, and the time. It seems likely that what to do with an overfilled Notification Area will become a power user issue down the road.

Taskman Lives!

Windows installs a program called `Taskman.exe`, aka the Task Manager, into your Windows directory. It has much of the functionality of the Windows 3.1 Task Manager, functionality now built into Windows. You can start it by typing `Taskman` in the Run dialog, or if you really like, you could assign it to a hot key.

 What a cockamamie thing. With the taskbar here, who asked for this piece of fluff?

 Well, I guess Microsoft put it there so the Windows 3.1 lovers wouldn't complain. It is also true that some perverse folks might like to have Taskman floating on top with the Taskbar autohidden.

There is one other time Taskman may be useful, and it is reason enough to keep it on your disk given that it takes less than 4K of disk space. Every once in a while, Windows gets confused during shutdown and leaves you with a totally blank Desktop. At that point, if you double-click or hit `Ctrl+Esc`, up will pop Taskman and you can invoke `Shutdown Windows` from its File menu. See the discussion of "Advanced Start Menu Tips" for a Stupid Desktop Trick that lets you see this behavior for yourself.

 Talk about weird. Under normal circumstances, double-clicking on a blank part of Desktop does nada, even though it might be useful to have Taskman pop up at that point. But have Explorer exit and Windows seems to drag out of its Jungian subconscious the fact that once upon a time, double-clicking on the Desktop invoked Taskman. Truly bizarre.

Explorering the Great Unknown

I seem to have been only like a boy playing on the seashore,
and diverting myself in now and then finding a smoother pebble or a
prettier shell than ordinary, whilst the great ocean of truth lay all undiscovered before me.

—Isaac Newton

You are likely to spend a lot of time with Explorer and folders, so you may as well learn how to interact with the beast efficiently. While the bulk of Explorer tips and tricks are in this section, the program affects so much else that there are important sidelights in a number of other places. I discuss Find File under Start Menu because most users will access it from the Start Menu, but the Find File window is just a special Explorer window. The Desktop is also just a special Explorer window and some of the tips in "Desktop Dancing" are as much Explorer Tips as they are about the Desktop. Finally, there is the mother lode of Explorer customization in the collection of sections titled "Configuring Context Menus and Associations" later in this chapter; check out especially the section "Sarah's Smart Setup Step by Step."

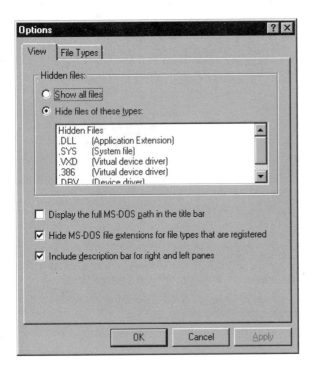

Figure 3-7. Default Explorer options

Fix Explorer Options

The first thing that you want to be sure to do is to fix the default options that Explorer uses. These are in the View tab on the `View/Options` menu (Figure 3-7). The defaults aren't unreasonable for naive users but they are not the best for experienced ones. In many ways the most important change is the Hidden Files radio button. This refers to whether Explorer displays certain files—those whose attributes indicate they are hidden*—and files with five special extensions. You want to be able to see the files and folders hidden by this radio button because some of them are important (e.g. `C:\windows\ desktop`) so change the selected button to Show all files.

---

* I discussed what "hidden" means in Chapter 2 in the section called *Hidden Pleasures.*

Next, be sure to uncheck the box that says "Hide MS-DOS file extensions for the types that are registered." The other two options are matters of taste, but I strongly prefer to have them checked. Note that Figure 3-7 shows the default options that Windows uses initially.

 You're wrong about the Hide MS-DOS. . . checkbox. Why confuse users with inscrutable three-letter extensions that are passé. Registered files normally have their own icons and Type column in Details view gives a more scrutable version of the type than the silly little extension.

 Yup, Billy. We've had real progress. Sometimes inscrutable extensions have been replaced by really inscrutable icons. Yup, real progress. The Type column is nice, but the eye has to move to it while extensions are right there, and extensions show up in List view and the Icon views. Moreover, I want to see the difference between `.gif` and `.tif` files even though on my machine both are registered as the type "Micrografx Picture Publisher Image."

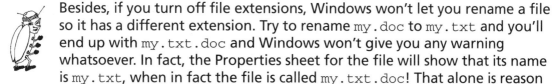 Besides, if you turn off file extensions, Windows won't let you rename a file so it has a different extension. Try to rename `my.doc` to `my.txt` and you'll end up with `my.txt.doc` and Windows won't give you any warning whatsoever. In fact, the Properties sheet for the file will show that its name is `my.txt`, when in fact the file is called `my.txt.doc`! That alone is reason enough for any Win95 user beyond the abject novice stage to show file extensions.

 There are a number of strange elements in the Figure 3-7 dialog. First, the radio button also affects whether `C:\windows\desktop` is visible in Explorer or not. But this directory is not hidden and does not have any of the special extensions. So the dialog doesn't tell the whole truth. Moreover, it seems the list is hard coded to the four file types (and five corresponding extensions) listed.* All four types appear in the Registry with `EditFlags` set equal to `01 00 00 00` and with a value entry named `AlwaysShowExt`. And they are the only types with either of these value entry pairs. But adding a new type with such entries doesn't add the corresponding extension to the list.

 The checkbox that says "Hide MS-DOS file extensions for the types that are registered," doesn't quite mean what it says either. Some types like Shortcut (with extension `.lnk`) have a Registry value pair named `NeverShowExt` and they, er, never show their extension no matter how the checkbox is checked. Similarly, those with a value pair named `AlwaysShowExt` always show their extension.

---

* The rest of Mao's comment is fairly technical and assumes you've mastered Chapter 11!

Views, Filtering, and Sorting

> We shall not cease from exploration
> And the end of all our exploring
> Will be to arrive where we started
> And know the place for the first time.

—T. S. Eliot, *Four Quartets*

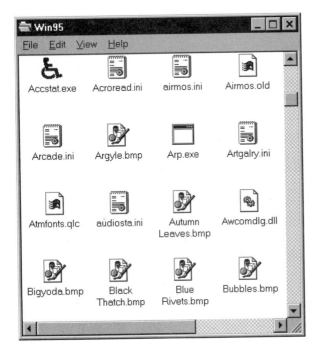

Figure 3-8. Explorer dumbed down

A number of issues involve the view in an Explorer window, including Folder View versus Explorer View, the four possible looks for the right-hand panel in Explorer, issues of sorting, and filtering.

The program Explorer can open a folder in two views. Folder view (Figure 3-8) just shows the contents of the folder. Explorer view (Figure 3-9) has two panes—a tree on the left and content view on the right. The designers of Windows assumed you'd normally want Folder view, which for experienced users is the wrong attitude. I even think it wrong for naive users (who have to be aware of the folder tree to cope with it), although I'd agree that is debatable.

In any event, the defaults in Windows are set up to strongly favor opening lots of Folder views. When you double-click any drive or folder, by default it opens in Folder view. If you do this in Explorer (in the contents pane), it always opens a new window, although if you do it in Folder view it may or may not open a new window, depending on an option you set in the `View/Options . . . Folder` tab. In "Stupid File Types Tricks" and "Sarah's Smart Setup Step by Step" later in this chapter, I'll explain how to change the defaults so that double-clicking a drive or directory on the Desktop or in a Folder window opens Explorer and double-clicking on one in an Explorer window contents pane just shifts Explorer to that drive or directory (without opening a new window). And I'll tell you how to do it while still having My Computer and Control Panel open in Folder view. Even after you set up your system this way, the Folder View choice is available on the right-click context menu for drives and folders.

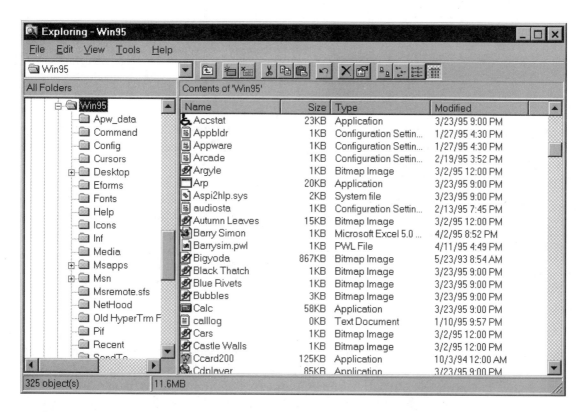

Figure 3-9. Explorer on steroids

Another place that Folder view is preferred by Windows is with the Explorer command!
Indeed, if you type `Explorer C:\` in the Run box it opens in Folder view! To get
Explorer view, you either need to type in `Explorer` with no parameters or `Explorer`
`/e,C:\` (note the comma after the e). I'll discuss the Explorer command line later. There is
no simple way to make `Explorer C:\` bring up Explorer view, but you could make a
batch file `explore.bat` (or even `ex.bat` to keep it short) with the single line `@C:\`
`windows\explorer.exe /e,%1` and with properties set to `Close on Exit` and
`Run Minimized`. Typing in `Explore C:\` without the `r` would bring up Explorer view.

If you insisted on having `Explorer C:\` bring up Explorer view, it can be done, but this is
just a thought experiment—because third party programs will assume `explorer.exe` is
in `C:\windows`. I urge you not to try this at home! You need to move `explorer.exe`
from `C:\windows` to `C:\windows\command`. You can't do that in Windows because
you'll get a complaint that `explorer.exe` is in use! But you can do it if you boot up in
command prompt mode (hit `F8` during startup and choose the Command Prompt option). Windows will still
locate `explorer.exe` because `C:\windows\command` is in your path. You'll next need to

search through your Registry and make sure all references (and there will be a lot!) to `C:\windows\explorer.exe` are changed to `C:\windows\command\explorer.exe`. Now make a batch file like the one just given, but put it in the Windows directory, call it `explorer.bat`, and have the line read `@C:\windows\command\explorer.exe ,e/%1`. This Desktop trick is only worth mentioning to expand your thinking.

The third place that Windows has a preference for Folder view is that when you type in the name of a folder in the run box, Windows opens that folder in Folder view. This, too, can be changed.

 By far the best way to change it is to make all of the changes Sarah recommends in the section "Sarah's Smart Setup Step by Step," later in the chapter. But if you want a quick and dirty way (that will also change the default action when you click on My Computer and Control Panel, something that you may not want), you can open up Regedit, go to the key `HKEY_CLASSES_ROOT\Folders\Shell`, and rename the subkey `Open` to `FolderView` and then `Explore` to `Open`. If you do that, typing in a folder name will open it in Explorer mode.

If you are in Folder view and want to bring up an Explorer view, you can do that easily. The little icon in the upper left corner of any Folder view is "live." Right-clicking on it brings up the context menu (Figure 3-10). It has an entry for Explore (under the default menu scheme). With the simplest version of Sarah's Smart Setup, Explore is absent but you won't see many Folders views if you use Sarah's setup, and it can be added by hand. I also note that the fourth through sixth items on the context menu in Figure 3-10 are there because Mao, on whose machine this screen was shot used three of the "Stupid File Type Tricks."

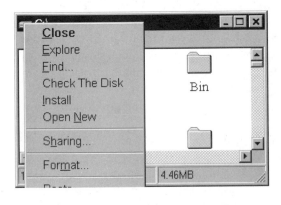

The other parts of view involve the status bar and toolbar—which are on the View menu—and which of the four views you pick for the content panel: Large Icons, Small Icons, List, or Details. You can make the choice in the View menu, or, if you have the toolbar turned on, in the part of the toolbar with four buttons together ( ). Large Icons is the Mac-like view that feels right for Folder view but will rarely make sense in Explorer view. An exception would be when looking at a folder

Figure 3-10. Folder window context menu

with lots of icons (`.ico`), which show as thumbnails. Details shows the filename, size, file type, and date/time modified. This is the most useful view for times when you are managing your files. The entries in Small Icon and List view are the same—file name and small icon. List view lists in multiple columns sorted down column by column with scroll bars to bring more columns into view if needed. The columns adjust if you resize the window. Small Icon view sorts rowwise and normally scrolls to bring additional rows into view, but it doesn't adjust for window resizing. I've found Small Icon view generally useless, although List view is often useful, especially in Open and Save dialogs (which are specialized Explorer windows).

The Arrange Icons submenu of view will sort the items in the Contents window, although in anything but Details view, it seems confusing to sort on anything but name since that's the only sort variable visible. The efficient way to sort in Details view is to click on a column header. That sorts Ascending unless the column is already sorted that way in which case it sorts Descending. So double clicking an unsorted column brings it to a Descending sort. Sorts on name always place subfolders at the top.

Explorer doesn't have a command to filter the view, say to only show `*.ico` files but the Find File command is a most effective substitute because its results are displayed in a window with most Explorer capabilities. F3 from Explorer will bring up a Find File dialog with the current directory name filled in.

The Directory Tree

The left pane in an Explorer window shows a folder tree (Figure 3-11) starting with My Computer and its Drives, and then its idealized folders—Control Panel, Printer, and Dial-Up Networking. At the same level as My Computer you'll have, where appropriate, Network Neighborhood, Recycle Bin, and any folders that you've place on the Desktop.

The tree is displayed in outline format with folders that have subfolders, indicated with either a + or a – to the left. Those with a – have their subfolders displayed (they are open) and those with a + have their subfolders hidden from view (they are closed). Clicking on a folder selects it and changes the display in the Contents window to that folder. Double-clicking does what clicking does and toggles the folder between open and closed.

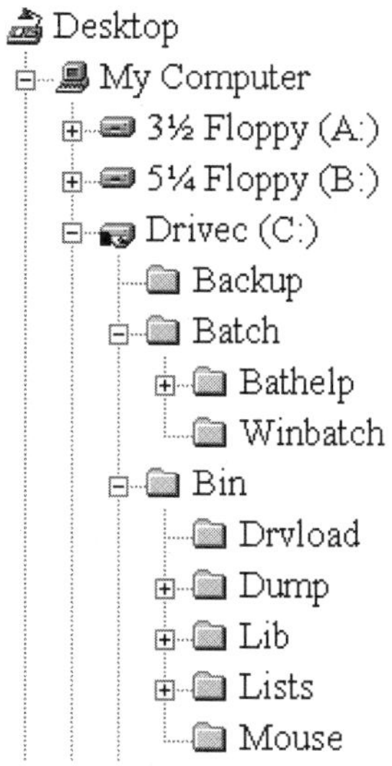

Figure 3-11. The tree

Clicking + or – will toggle between open or closed state without selecting the folder or changing the view in the Contents pane. This is very important for file operations (see "The Two Directory Conundrum" following). Hitting * will open the entire current branch of the tree completely. Backspace or the 🔼 button changes the folder displayed in the Contents window to the parent. That means hitting backspace or that button repeatedly will take you to the Desktop. Backspace and this button work whichever pane is active, but * is only effective if the tree pane is active. There is also a drop-down ⎸📄 Batch ⎸▼⎹ on the toolbar for quick change of the current folder.

Property Sheets

Drives, File Folders, and Files each have their own Property sheets, as shown in Figure 3-12.

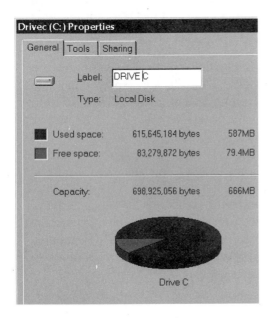

Figure 3-12. Property sheets for Drive, Directory (er, Folder) and File (continued, next page)

Each Explorer object has a Property sheet that is accessible by hitting Alt+Enter or choosing Properties from the context menu or from the File menu. Figure 3-12 shows Property sheets for the three main objects in the file system. The Property sheet of a drive lets you relabel the drive and displays total and available space both graphically and as numbers (too bad that percentages aren't given).

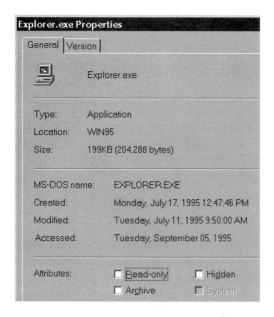

Figure 3-12. Property sheets *continued*

The Property sheet of a directory includes the total size of the files that the directory and its subfolders have with a count of the number of files and folders. You get similar counts if you select multiple files and/or multiple folders and ask for Properties.

Notice the Sharing tabs on the drive and directory Property sheets. Some machines won't have a Sharing tab, even on a network with file sharing enabled. That's because a system administrator could have disabled file-sharing capabilities for that particular machine, or that particular user, via the system policies editor.

Notice that three dates are listed on the Property sheet for the file—the date and time it was created, the date and time it was last modified, and the date it was last accessed. In this case of Windows' `explorer.exe`, the modified time is the time the file was made in Redmond (or what they fudged it to be. Obviously all the Windows 95 files weren't made at precisely 9:50 A.M.), the created time is when it was loaded on Mao's disk and the accessed date is the time it was last run. As contrary as it seems, the modified time is before the creation time, which goes to show the names are less than ideal. Before Windows 95, the only time kept on a file was the modified time. The other two times are new to Windows 95.

 The accessed time is especially neat because it lets there be utilities that will inform you which files on disk have not been used at all in the past six months and are therefore ripe for removal.

You'll notice that the directory and file sheets have four attributes listed at the bottom. I'll not discuss their meaning here.* `System` is grayed out because you can't change that attribute here—you can change the others by checking or unchecking a box.

---

* See, for example, *The Mother of All PC Books.*

Ha! Windows puts up a brave front to indicate that the System attribute is the system's and not the user's to change. But guess what? Using the DOS `attrib` command, included in the Windows package, you can change the system attribute. It's all a show of bravado by good ole Windows.

Hey, boss, I'm puzzled. When I select Drive C and look at its Property sheet, it tells me that the used space is 613,351,424 bytes. When I select all the directories and files in C and hit `Alt+Enter`, it tells me that the size is 507,827,042 in 9,611 files and directories. What gives? Those numbers can't both be right. Do I have a bug to report to Erwin?

Nope. Believe it or not, both numbers are correct! The 500 million-plus number is the sum total of the sizes of all the files and directories. File sizes are the size of the data in the file. But the DOS FAT system must allocate an integral number of clusters of disk space, so the space used by a file is more than its size. The difference, called the slack, is always less than a cluster per file. If all the files were very large and random in size, the average slack would be about half a cluster. Since small files have almost a whole cluster of slack and there are lots of small files around in Windows (shortcuts, for example), the average slack is generally more than half a cluster. On the disk you are asking about, the cluster size is 16K, and if you divide the difference of the two numbers you gave me by 9,611 you get about 10.7 KB—indeed, between a half and a whole cluster. This slack is a serious space drain—it's about 20 percent of the total file size in this case.

If you run ScanDisk, it will tell you the cluster size, although it calls it allocation units. You can also figure it out yourself using the fact that there are at most 64K clusters on a disk and cluster size is always a power of 2. So hard disks between 256 MB and 512 MB have 8K clusters, between 512 MB and 1 GB have 16K clusters, and between 1 GB and 2 GB have 32K clusters. Some of the impressive compression numbers that DriveSpace gets comes from the fact that it organizes files in such a way that the true slack is less than 512 bytes per file.

If you look at the file Property sheet in Figure 3-12, you'll notice a second tab called Version. That's special to `.exe`, `.vxd`, and `.dll` files. Windows or third parties can add extra tabs to Property sheets (in this case, it is Windows). For example, Norton Navigator offers a Dates tab on which you can change any of the times associated to a file.

I'll discuss the tools in the Tools tab for Drives in Chapter 4.

The most important thing to remember about Property sheets for Explorer objects is that they often have useful information.

File Operations

The most common operations you'll do in Explorer are the basic file management operations of Deleting, Copying, Moving, and Renaming. If you select one or more files or folders and hit `Del` or drag them to the Recycle Bin, they'll get moved to the Recycle Bin. Until you explicitly empty that bin or selectively delete some files from it (opening Recycle Bin, selecting some files, and hitting Del deletes them for real), the Recycle Bin fills up. When it gets too large, Windows complains and tells you, "Take out the trash, darn it." The advantage of this method is that recovery of "deleted" files is 100 percent perfect until you remove them from the Recycle Bin. The disadvantage is that Windows forces you to explicitly manage the Recycle Bin. It would be better if it let you specify a time period (I'd pick a week or two) and had the trash automatically deleted after that time—that is, Windows would automatically remove from the Recycle Bin files deleted for real if they'd been "deleted" by the user more than the specified time period ago.

You'll need to empty the Recycle Bin on a regular basis. You can do this by double clicking and picking `Empty Recycle Bin` from the `File` Menu. If you're sure you want to empty the bin and don't need to see what is in it, right click on the Recycle Bin and pick `Empty Recycle Bin`.

 A second disadvantage is that the Recycle Bin only captures files that you delete from a local hard drive using Explorer. If you use a third-party file manager, some program deletes them, you delete them at a DOS prompt, or if you delete them from a floppy, they do not go to the Recycle Bin and Windows provides no recovery tools other than the Recycle Bin.

 The Norton Utilities for Windows 95 addresses all these lacks.

If you have a bunch of files that you are 100 percent sure you want to delete and you don't want them to go to the Recycle Bin, select them in Explorer and hit `Shift+Del` (or hold down `Shift` when choosing Delete from their context menu). If you hold down the `Shift` key and drag something to the Recycle Bin, it also gets deleted for real. There is a difference, though, from using `Shift+Del`. When you use the key combination, you get a warning message. When you `Shift` drag, you don't. Also be aware that if you delete (with plain old `Del` or by dragging to your Recycle Bin) files from a Network or Floppy drive, then they are deleted for real.

If you drag a file on a local hard drive to the Recycle Bin, it eats it silently, storing it away. If you do that from a diskette or network drive where it is going to delete the file without storing in a Recycle Bin, it warns you. That's good. But if you Shift drag to the Recycle Bin where it is going to also delete without storing, it does the deed without warning. That's a bug as far as I'm concerned.

You can copy or move files or folders between two Explorer windows or from one Explorer window and a directory in an Explorer tree. That means one way to copy or move is to go to the source directory, pick the files you want, use the scroll bars on the tree to locate the destination, and drag the files from the contents pane to the destination on the tree. As long as you are careful to hit only the + signs, you can even open directories on the tree side.

Whether a drag produces a copy or a move depends on the type of files, whether you use the left or right mouse button, and whether you hold down various combinations of Ctrl and Shift. I discussed the rules in Chapter 2 in the section called "Drag 'til you Drop."

You can rename a file or folder by selecting it and hitting F2, or selecting it and picking Rename from a context menu or from the File menu. Or you can select it and then click on the name. In all cases, the name in the Explorer window turns into an edit box where you can change by just retyping. The name is initially selected so that if you start typing the name is replaced totally. If you just want to edit the name, click gently a second time or use Home or End and the arrow keys. If you hit Esc, you abort the rename. Hitting Enter or clicking outside the edit box accepts the edit.

After a Rename, you can use Edit/Undo to undo the rename.

This clicking stuff is a pain and a half. If you try to use it to select and rename, you have to noticeably pause in between or else Windows will interpret it as a double-click. And often when you just mean to select, somehow you wind up in rename mode. This click to rename looks neat, but on balance I wish it wasn't there.

You can rename files and folders this way, but not a drive. The drive name, called a label, can be changed from the Property sheet for that drive (see the leftmost sheet in Figure 3-12). You create a new folder by selecting New and then Folder from the File menu or by right-clicking on a blank area of the contents pane of the folder in which you want to create the new subfolder. This is awkward—there should be a single keystroke option to make a new folder (Ins was used in some third-party file managers for Windows 3.1). When you make a new folder it comes in with the name New Folder but ready to rename immediately.

The New submenu of the blank area context menu or of the File menu also lets you create new documents. The application adding its documents to the New menu can arrange for a wizard to pop up to make the document or can arrange for the document to start out as some template. Information in the New menu is contained in the Registry. I'll have a lot to say about it in Chapter 11, where I'll explain how you can remove items you feel you'll never want, and even how you can add some new New entries of your own.

Built into the New menu when you install Windows are six entries: Folder, Shortcut, Text Document, Bitmap Image, Wave Sound, and Briefcase. You may want to remove Bitmap Image and/or Wave Sound using the methods I'll discuss in Chapter 11.

Using the Clipboard

Explorer supports an interesting use of the clipboard for file copying and moving. On the Edit menu in Explorer you'll see items Cut, Copy and Paste. The usual hotkeys work for them and the toolbar has the standard icons ⬚⬚⬚ for the operations, albeit smaller than in other programs such as WordPad.

You can select one or more files and/or folders in the contents pane, or a folder in the tree pane, and hit/pick `Cut` or `Copy`. Then move the focus of Explorer to the destination directory or use second Explorer window, click on a blank area in the contents pane, and hit/pick `Paste`. If the original action was Copy, the files are copied to the destination. If the original action was Cut, they are moved there. You can do multiple Pastes in different Explorer destinations.

When you choose Cut, the file isn't actually deleted. That only happens after you do the Paste. Before then, the icon of the Cut file is grayed out.

You can Copy and Paste to the same location. If you do, the words "Copy of" are prepended to the file names. You can then rename the copies if you want. This is a rather efficient way to make backup copies of `config.sys` and similar files before you edit them.

When there are files that have been placed on the clipboard with Copy (but not with Cut), the Edit menu has an item that says Paste Shortcut. For those who don't much like dragging, this can be an efficient way to make shortcuts on the Desktop or in a Start Menu submenu. Remember that these clipboard options are available when you have several Explorer windows on a crowded screen and you have trouble getting the windows placed to do a simple drag and drop.

Alas, you cannot use this method to paste the names of files into DOS sessions, Open dialogs, or text editors. You can use it to paste OLE packages into applications that are OLE2.0 clients.

Diskettes

Diskettes are a media of the past. I can't wait for the era when kids say "Diskette? What's that? A female hard disk?" With Windows's built-in networking and the advent of decent on-line speeds, you'll need diskettes less often than you used to but you will still use them. Here are some tools for use with diskettes besides the general ScanDisk, Backup, and Defragger that I'll discuss in the next chapter.

A simple Copy Disk program (Figure 3-13) is accessible if you right-click on a diskette icon on the Desktop or in `My Computer`. It's just the Windows version of Disk Copy. It requires you to track which diskette formats are compatible. A Format Utility (Figure 3-14) is also available on a diskette's context menu. You get to pick the diskette capacity and whether to make the diskette bootable. You also choose between Quick format (logical formatting only) or Full (physical formatting also). Bootable diskette means copying only four system files (`io.sys`, `msdos.sys`, `command.com`, and `drvspace.bin` taking a total of 378K). The diskette boots into a command prompt without support for long filenames.

Finally, don't forget to consider using diskettes with Drive Space file compression. I'll discuss Drive Space in Chapter 4. Figure that you'll normally be able to squeeze about 2 MB on a 1.4 MB diskette, maybe as much as 2.5 MB. Since Drive Space is now built into Windows, any Windows 95 user who gets a compressed diskette from you will be able to read it even if they aren't using any disk compression at all.

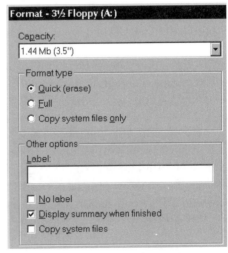

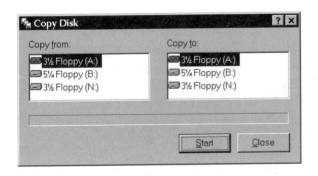

Figure 3-13. Diskcopy redux

Figure 3-14. The Format Utility

The Explorer Command Line

The Explorer command can take some parameters. The syntax is

```
explorer [/n] [/e] [,root,object] [,subobject]
```

Here, I've left out a specialized and not very interesting parameter called /select (which opens Explorer with some files selected) and I'm not discussing the /idlist undocumented parameter (which appears in some Registry entries—I've no idea what it does). The [. . .] in the syntax summary means that the parameter is optional. *Object* and *subobject* are directory names. You can use UNC* path names but not nondirectory filenames. If you try using explorer "My Computer", you'll get an error message. Here's what it all means when run from the Run box or a shortcut (there are special rules for actions run from context menus inside Explorer itself as I'll explain):

- explorer with no parameter opens Explorer in Explorer mode in the folder C:\ (or in the root folder of the drive with your Windows directory if it is not C:).

- explorer *foldername* opens the folder in Folder View, not Explorer mode. The comma that the syntax suggests is needed is optional. If the folder is already open, then a second copy is not opened—instead the open one becomes the active window.

- explorer /e, *foldername* opens an Explorer window with the content pane showing the folder. It is rooted on the Desktop in that repeated Backspaces will take you up to Desktop eventually.

- explorer /n, *foldername* opens the folder in Folder view. A new copy is opened even if the folder is already open. You can use explorer /n, /e, *foldername* but the /n, has no effect whatsoever—a new Explorer window is open whether the /n, is there or not. If you use /n without a comma, you'll get an error message.

Gack! When Windows 95 is installed an item is placed on the Programs submenu called Windows Explorer. The shortcut this points to has the following command line: explorer /n, /e, C:\. The /n, does nothing or rather it does nothing but confuse users who look at it. Even the Redmondians can't keep the syntax straight. Oh, how I love a nice bug in the morning.

---

* Of the form \\network_computer_name\netpath, e.g. \\aye\c\windows

- `explorer /e, /root, foldername` opens Explorer view rooted at the folder and with the folder as the one displayed in the contents pane. Rooted in a certain folder means that you can't go to the parent of the folder with `Backspace`, and the tree pane only shows the rooted folder and its subfolders.

- `explorer /e, /root, foldername, subfoldername` opens in Explorer view rooted at the folder with the subfolder displayed in the contents pane. The `subfoldername` must be a relative path to `foldername`, not absolute. In other words, use `explorer /e, /root,C:\,windows\system`, not `explorer /e, /root, C:\,C:\windows\system`, which would produce an error message.

- The last two commands work without the `/e,` for rooted folders.

There is one special situation where the syntax is slightly different, and this is for actions associated to Folders, File Folders, or Drives and issued from a context menu of an object inside an Explorer window. I'll discuss such actions and how you add them in the sections of File Types below but I'll note the syntax rule here:

- If an object has an action with the underlying command as `explorer /e,` without a `/n,` and if the action is invoked from the context menu inside an Explorer window, then an new Explorer window is *not* opened. If there is an `explorer /e,/n,` then a new window is always opened.

I'll use this explorer command line syntax when I discuss various shortcuts to make in dealing with the Start Menu in the next group of sections and in the "Stupid File Type Tricks" section.

More Tips

- The Undo has multiple steps and works even if you have exited Explorer but not if you reboot.

- You cannot undo a file deletion unless it is to the Recycle Bin; in particular, you can't undo a `Shift+Del` deletion.

- If you have a number of Folder Windows open, `Shift` clicking on the close button on one will close it, its parent, and so on, as long as the parent chain is unbroken.

- If you pick `Tools/Go to . . .` or hit `Ctrl+G`, you get a window offering you to type in a folder name and giving you a drop-down list of previous, er, previous stuff.

This Go to . . . is almost a brilliant, wonderful, fantastic thing. You type in a few complicated paths and there they are for you on the drop down for a long time in the future. Not! For some insane, absurd, ridiculous, ludicrous, preposterous, foolish reason, the drop down list in the Go to . . . box is the same as in the Start Menu Run box. As you run commands there, items you typed in at the Go to . . . box drop off the list. And if you pick one of the commands you ran in the Run box, it doesn't even work from Go to . . . —only folder names work there. Sigh.

Hotkeys

Explorer Shortcut Keys			
F1	Help	F2	Rename
F3	Find File	F4	Drop down folder list
F5	Refresh current Window	F6	Cycle among Tree pane, drop down list and Contents pane
Ctrl+G	Go to	Shift+F10	Context menu
Alt+Enter	Property Sheet	Backspace	Parent

While on the subject of keystrokes, it is worth mentioning two keyboard modifications of the double click action on a folder:

- Shift+double click opens the folder in Explorer view

- Ctrl+double click toggles the Folder View Option action. That is, if you have the "Browse folders using a separate window for each folder" radio button picked, then Ctrl+double click will shift to the new folder without opening a new window, whereas if you pick the radio button marked "Browse folders using a single window that changes as you open each folder," then Ctrl+double click will open a new window.

These two are with the default setup where Windows opens in Folder View when you double-click, but this last Ctrl as toggle also matters if you use Sarah's Smart Setup. If you right-click and pick Folder View on a directory in Sarah's Setup, then the action depends on the radio button choice in the View/Options/Folders dialog and whether you hold down the `Ctrl` key when you click on Folder View in the context menu. Holding down the `Ctrl` key gives the same effect as if you switched the radio button in the dialog.

 Oy, these weird clicks with shift key tricks. I'd better tell our readers about the special `Ctrl+Shift Click` command built into Windows. You have to be pressing on `F10`, `Backspace` and the `Del` key while you do it, but if you do and it is the first Sunday in April between 2:30 A.M. and 2:45 A.M., then Windows 95 turns into OS/2. Don't believe me? Test it out!

The Two Directory Conundrum

> Poor fellow, he suffers from files.
>
> —Aneurin Bevan, referring to a bureaucrat

 If there's one bellyache I've heard in the press most about Windows 95 Explorer, it is that you have to open two copies of Explorer to copy files from one directory to another. They compare this with Windows 3.x File Manager, where it is claimed you could get away with a single copy of File Manager. Of course, you did need two windows within File Manager, but it seemed like less. And in File Manager, you had drive icons just below the menu bar and could drag to diskette icons without a second window. While I think the complaint has been overblown, at its core, there is a real issue—it is more awkward than it has to be to copy or move files from one folder to another. So my team is going to discuss some of the ways to do it.

 First, there are two special methods for copying to diskette without opening a second Explorer window:

- If you choose some files and right-click, there is the Send To submenu and on that you'll find an entry like 3½ `Floppy (A)`. If you choose that, the files are copied there.

- If you drag a diskette drive from My Computer to the Desktop or if you make a shortcut whose command line is `A:\` (and not `Explorer /e,A:\`), the diskette drive that appears on the Desktop is a drag-drop target. If you select some files in an Explorer window and drag them to such an icon, they'll get copied to the diskette. This is my preferred method since I can right-drag and drop and get a `move` option and because it is quicker than Send To.

Actually, neither of these methods is really diskette-specific. If there is a folder on a hard disk you often need to copy files to, you can place a shortcut to it in the `C:\windows\sendto` folder or on the Desktop and have the same capabilities just mentioned. The only difference is that files on the same drive as the folder will get moved and not copied if you do Send To item or a left-drag and drop.

Here are some other ways to easily copy or move files:

- Use the clipboard. Remember that you go to the source directory in an Explorer window, select the files you want, pick Copy or Cut (for file copy or move respectively) from the button bar or Edit menu, change to the destination directory (in the same or different Explorer window) and pick Paste from the button bar or Edit menu. This will copy or move the files.

- Use the fact that you can scroll the tree pane in an Explorer window without changing which folder is displayed in the contents pane. Therefore, you can place the source folder in the content pane, scroll the tree so it shows the destination folder, select files in the contents pane, and drag them to the destination folder in the tree side. While scrolling in the tree pane, you can even expand/contract parts of the tree without changing the folder displayed in the contents pane so long as you use the + / - and don't ever click on a folder name.

- Use the free Power Toys Send To Any Folder . . . Other Folder menu item. I'll discuss Power Toys in detail in Chapter 5, but these are utilities written by the Windows 95 team so we can expect (or at least hope) they'll find their way into a tune-up pack. As shown in Figure 3-15, after you select a bunch of files and choose this item from the Send To menu, you get a dialog with the names of the files and a pair of radio buttons to pick Copy or Move and a place to enter the destination. You can enter the destination in this `To:` field by typing it in, choosing it from a drop-down list of recent destinations, or using a `Browse . . .` button.

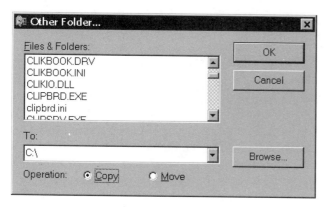

Normally I wouldn't show a picture of a third-party product here, but this is so natural and the third

Figure 3-15. Power Toys Any Folder

party is more like a second-and-a-half party, so I have. I should mention that Norton Navigator adds `Norton Copy. . .` and `Norton Move. . .` items to the context menu of files that provide similar functionality. I'll also discuss Norton Navigator in Chapter 5.

You left out what I've always wanted as the solution—an easy way to load two nonoverlapping Explorer windows side by side, taking up all of the left and right sides of the Desktop area.

I left that out on purpose, Igor, because I've seen it in Winbatch. It lets you easily launch such a setup, but there are two difficulties with it. The windows are a little too narrow, and even after you close both windows, the next one you launch has the same dimensions, which isn't good for browsing. Still, if this appeals to you, check out Winbatch.

If you want to be able to quickly open a second Explorer window in cascade position, check out the section titled "Adding an Open New in Explorer" later in this chapter.

QuickView

It cannot be said that nude sunbathing on a beach is a form of expression likely to be understood by the viewer as an attempt to convey a particular point of view.

—Vito J. Titone, judge, N.Y. State Court of Appeals, Oct. 21, 1986, opinion

One of the options on the context menu of certain files is QuickView. This brings up a set of barebones File Viewers for a limited number of file types. Here is a list of the supported file types and extensions:

Text and Word Processors: `.txt`, `.asc`, `.ini`, `.inf` (ASCII text), `.wri` (Windows 3.x WRITE), `.rtf` (Rich Text Format), `.sam` (Ami, Ami Pro), `.doc` (Winword v1,2,6,7), `.wps` (Works Word Processing)

Spreadsheets: `.xls` (Excel 4 and 5), `.wk1`, `.wks`, `.wk3`, `.wk4` (Lotus 1-2-3 v 1,2,3,4), `.wq1`, `wq2`, `.wb1` (Quattro Pro v4,5 for DOS, v1 for Windows), `.mod` (Multiplan)

Database formats: `.wdb` (Works Database)

Graphics formats: `.bmp`, `.dib`, `.rle` (Windows Bitmaps), .XLC (Excel 4 Chart), `.cdr` (Corel Draw, v4,5), `.drw` (Micrografx Draw), `.wmf` (Windows MetaFile), `.ppt` (Powerpoint, v 4), `.pre` (Freelance)

Executable Files: `.exe`, `.dll`

To say that this has lacks is a huge understatement. No support for Word Perfect, for `.pcx`, `.tif` or `.gif`, for `.wpg`, `.emf`, or `.cgm` or for any common database format. The list is heavy on obscure Microsoft formats (Multiplan?) and viewers for obsolete versions of products (no Excel 6 or Quattro Pro Win 2.0). The text file viewer has no search or copy/paste or print capability and the word processing doesn't show embedded graphics or much formatting.

It's a huge come-on Mom. These viewers are based on technology from Outside In made by System Compatibility Corp. (SCC). Outside In did a lot more than this. Imso, the renamed SCC, is selling a product called QuickView Plus that's pretty good. I'll discuss it in Chapter 5. Given what Microsoft has done in the past, I'll bet dollars to donuts that Microsoft magnanimously allowed SCC/Imso to supply these viewers at no cost to Microsoft for the privilege of being a part of the Windows 95 product.

Bellyaching again, Rush? Where's the beef? Our users come out ahead because they have viewers that, while they may have lacks, aren't exactly chopped liver. Imso comes out ahead because they have an in with tens of millions of potential customers. Third-party vendors come out ahead because we've published the specs for them to add their own QuickView viewers. And MS comes out ahead. So where's the beef?

The supported extensions and file types are stored in the Registry in the keys under `HKEY_CLASSES_ROOT\QuickView`. The viewers themselves are stored in directory `C:\windows\system\viewers` and use `quikview.exe` in that directory and the dynamic library `sccview.dll` in `C:\windows\system`.

You do have some other viewers available to you with some of the Windows add-ons provided by Microsoft—there is a Word viewer (called WordView) on the Windows CD (and a later version on Mom's CD) that views (including graphics and fonts), and will search and print Microsoft Word documents. If you have the Plus! Pack or the Internet Jump

Start Kit, the Internet Explorer, Microsoft's web browser is actually also a viewer for two graphics files types common on the World-Wide Web and not supported by QuickView—.gif and .jpg. To view such files, click on the Internet icon on your Desktop and cancel out of the dialog that wants to dial-up your Internet provider. Then you can either take a .gif or .jpg in Windows Explorer and drag it to the Internet Explorer window or pick File/Open in Internet Explorer and pick the Open File . . . in the resulting dialog.

Explorer Lacks

Here are some of the limitations and problems with Explorer, and a wish list:

- It's crazy that there is no way to switch a Folder View window into an Explorer view, and vice versa. Exchange lets you do this for its analogs. Why can't Explorer?

- The most infuriating aspect of Explorer is that it saves settings for windows only kinda sorta and doesn't give you any access to where it is storing the defaults. I've seen machines that love to load Control Panel and My Computer in list mode even though I prefer them in Large Icons. I switch Control Panel to Large Icons, close the window, and for a while it opens in the right mode but then I don't use it for a few days and bam—list mode. This affects the Desktop, which is after just a special Explorer window in Folder view. It can happen that suddenly Windows loads and it puts your Desktop icons alphabetically in columnwise fashion, forgetting the arrangements you carefully laid out.

 This is probably my greatest complaint in the shell design. The data on Explorer is stored in the Registry. In Chapter 11, I'll give you some insight into how Desktop positions are stored and even a complex way to try to save and later restore the locations of Desktop icons. The data is in what the registry calls Streams. There are twenty-eight sets of binary data in the keys HKEY_CURRENT_USER\Software\Microsoft\Windows\CurrentVersion\Explorer\Streams\ *N* where *N* runs from 1 to 28. These store data for recently used Explorer windows and other items of interest to the shell. When it needs to store data for a new window, Windows throws away the stream it regards as least important according to an algorithm that must make sense to it but certainly not to me.

 Not only does Windows need to be more coherent about settings, but it needs to let you set up styles (to store things like Folder versus Explorer view, the view in the sense of Large Icons versus Details versus . . ., an ordering and width for columns in details view, and window size and position) and let you apply these styles to a given folder (yo, Windows, I always want Control Panel to open like thus) or to a given shortcut.

- Disney might think that the lion is king but Microsoft thinks it's the mouse that is king. So little thought seems to have been given to an intelligent keyboard interface to Explorer and the other parts of Windows. No, I'm not arguing that the mouse is not a requirement for Windows 95—I'd call them stupid if it wasn't. But that doesn't mean that those who use mice reluctantly or those who prefer to use the keyboard for quick stuff shouldn't have a decent set of keyboard methods to do things.

- Explorer should have a configurable button bar. I'd prefer the kinds of configuration interface that Word has, but even the one in Exchange would be OK.

- In particular, there should be a single keystroke and Button Bar icon to make a new folder.

- The Power Toys Copy/Move to Any Folder should be built into Explorer but with hotkey access and directly on the context menu instead of being buried a menu deep in `Send To`.

- They should fix the sort design. If you are sorted on Name and the cursor is on, say, `aardvark.txt`, and you hit the column label to sort Type, the viewport will stay at the top of the list (where `aardvark.txt` was when sorted on Name), even though the selected file is now near the bottom of the list. Clearly when you re-sort, the viewport should move to show the currently selected file.

- And what happened to sort by extension? The Type designations don't bear much relationship to what I want to find—say, all the `.bat` files, or all the `.docs`, in a folder.

- There should be a drop-down of recently accessed folders I can switch back to, where *recently accessed* means ones where I initiated a copy, move, quick view, or delete.

- There should be a button to take me to a Favorite Dirs list that lets me quickly move Explorer to a directory I use often. In the section called "Desktop Dancing," I'll describe a way to get some of this functionality, but it isn't as smooth as it could be if it were built into Explorer.

- Recycle Bin should have a setting to automagically, truly delete files older than a user-set time.

- There should be better viewers than currently provided in Quick View. Certainly, the text viewer needs to include decent search.

- What was one of the biggest complaints about Program Manager? "They won't let me choose separate icons for my Program Manager groups!" Well, groups have become folders, and guess what—they won't let you choose separate icons for your folders! In Chapter 11, I'll discuss how the hooks are there so that a third party could write a program to do this, but it really should be a part of the Windows itself.

- Two compressed formats—`.zip` and `.cab` are so important that Windows Explorer should provide direct support for them. I'll discuss third-party tools for them in Chapter 5.

- Internet's FTP protocol is just a file copy utility. It should be possible to have FTP sites in your directory tree that you copy files from (using FTP in the background) by drag and drop. Norton Navigator's File Manager implements this, as do some Internet utilities like Emissary.

- There should be a GUI file compare rather than just the DOS `fc.exe` that comes with Windows.

You Gave Me Such a Start

> When you start with a portrait and search for a pure form, a clear volume, through successive eliminations, you arrive inevitably at the egg. Likewise, starting with the egg and following the same process in reverse, one finishes with the portrait.

> —Pablo Picasso, 1932

Figure 3-16. Guess what?

If the Start button is the most famous symbol in Windows 95, then the menu you get when you press it (the default form is shown in Figure 3-16) is the most notable source of user control. Rather than go through the seven choices in spatial order (starting from the bottom, of course!), I'll discuss them in what I regard as their order of significance. That means beginning with the `Programs` submenu and, more importantly, how to configure things to have more launch options than just the `Programs` submenu. I'd be remiss while discussing launching if I didn't discuss hotkey launching, one of Windows 3.x's most underused goodies made more powerful in Windows 95. Then I'll jump down to the `Find` command, one of Windows 95 most wonderful features. Next I'll talk together about `Documents` and `Run`, which are two sides of the same coin. Only then will I turn to `Shutdown`, where I'll bet you are in for some surprises. I'll end this collection of sections with some advanced topics. You may note two players as missing in action. `Help` brings up the central Windows help file which is best discussed when I talk about the help engine in general at the end of the chapter. `Settings` brings up the submenu in Figure 3-17. There isn't much to say about it. The first two launch the Control Panel and Printers folders—I'll give you a better way to do that when I discuss

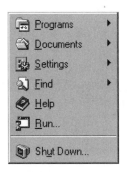

**Figure 3-17.
Set 'em up**

**Figure 3-18.
Demure Start
Menu**

configuring the Start Menu. Of course, there is a lot to say about the actual Printers and Control Panel folders—indeed, they'll be the major themes of the central part of this chapter and of chapter 10. The `Taskbar . . .` submenu item has two tabs—one I discussed when I talked about the Taskbar and the other will be mentioned in the very next section.

By checking the box labeled `Show small icons in Start Menu` in the Taskbar Properties sheet (Figure 3-3), you can shift the look of the Start Menu from that shown in Figure 3-16 to the more demure look of Figure 3-18. And the ad for Windows 95 is gone, too! I strongly recommend this setting at 640 × 480 resolution.

 If you have a portable with properly implemented Advanced Power Management support, the Start Menu will include a Suspend item that puts the machine in a very low power consumption state that saves the system—a Resume button on the keyboard will reawaken the system. Depending on the laptop expect the suspended state to persist for several hours to several days but never much longer than a week (assuming you don't plug the system into the wall!).

Configuring the Start Menu

> A journey of a thousand miles
> Starts from beneath one's feet.

> —Lao-Tzu, *Tao-te-ching*

If you want to manipulate the Start Menu, go to Chapter 2 and reread the section "The Tree-based Menu." The Programs submenu of Start Menu and items above it in the Start Menu that you can add are a reflection of the files and subfolders of the folder `C:\windows\Start Menu`.

 A suitable picture really is worth a thousand words. In the left side of Figure 3-19, you see the top of Mao's Start Menu from Programs on up. Notice that he has added three additional submenus (you know they are submenus by the ▶ to the right) and one item that runs a shortcut when you choose it. Now look at the right side of the figure at the Explorer

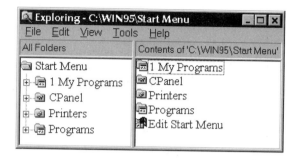

Figure 3-19. Extra Start Menu items reflect a Directory structure

view of Mao's `C:\windows\Start Menu` folder.* You'll notice the folder has four subfolders whose names are precisely the names of the four submenus on the left. In addition, the file panel on the extreme right has one file besides the four subfolders— a shortcut whose name is identical to the Start Menu item.

 You may notice three strange aspects of the extra folders I put in. First, there are folders named Cpanel and Printers, with the Control Panel and Printer folder symbols next to them. Since their setup is a little bit techie, I'll tell you about them later in the section called "Advanced Start Menu Tips." Second, my other folder is called `1 My Programs`. Why did I use that 1? Simple—you don't get to choose the ordering of the submenus above Programs. They are alphabetical, and 1 happens to come before any letter in the alphabet (in the ASCII code list, which is what counts) so it lets me be sure that the menu is always at the very top. Some folks label subfolders starting with 1, 2, . . . to control their ordering.

 Don't let Mao's use of the words *techie* and *advanced* frighten you away. The trick to put a dynamic Control Panel on the Start Menu is simple if you are careful. Check it out.

This paradigm extends to submenus and subsubmenus. Figure 3-20 shows a third level submenu branching off the Start Menu, while Figure 3-21 shows the Explorer view of the corresponding folders and subfolders. This should make it clear that the way to arrange and reorganize your Start Menu and the way to add and remove submenus and items is exactly the way you organize your files and folders. Since I strongly urged you to use Explorer mode

---

* Yeah, yeah, I know it says `C:\win95\start menu`, not `C:\windows\start menu`. That's because Mao's windows directory is `C:\win95`. But I'll continue the convention of always using `C:\windows` for the windows directory.

Figure 3-20. A third level submenu

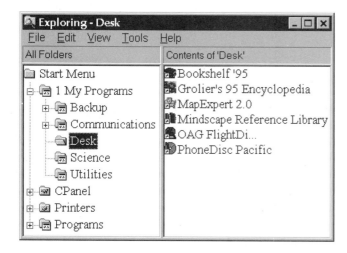

Figure 3-21. The corresponding third level subfolder

to manipulate files, you won't be surprised that I encourage you to use Explorer to manage your Start Menu. You'll find Add. . . and Remove. . . buttons in the Start Menu Programs tab of the Taskbar Properties sheet. They may be useful for those who don't understand the menu/folder paradigm, but since you do, you'll not be interested in them!

There are two built-in ways to access Explorer to manage your Start Menu program items, but I'll recommend you use a third! First, if you right-click on the Start button and pick Explore, you'll get Explorer opened up with C:\windows\Start Menu as the current folder. Second, if you pick Advanced . . . from the Start Menu Programs tab of the Taskbar Properties sheet, you get a rooted Explorer starting at C:\windows\Start Menu. (I discussed rooted Explorers and the Explorer command line earlier in this chapter.)

The rooted Explorer you get from the `Advanced . . .` button is more natural for this manipulation than the unrooted Explorer that you get from right-clicking on the Start button, but it is a pain to have to choose Start, then Settings, then Taskbar and then click a second tab and then a button to reach Advanced. . . . So I strongly recommend you set up a Shortcut to do essentially what the Advanced . . . button does. Right-click on a blank part of the Desktop, pick New, and then Shortcut. This will invoke the New Shortcut wizard. For the command line, enter:

```
C:\WINDOWS\EXPLORER.EXE /e, /root, C:\windows\Start Menu
```

and hit Next. You can use anything for the name of the shortcut. I doubt you'll like the one Windows suggests, which is `explorer.exe`. You might want to use `Edit Start Menu` the way Mao does, but you're the boss. You might want to double-click on it to make sure it works. If you get an error message, you may have forgotten the two commas, which are important. You might also want to change the icons—right click on the shortcut, choose `Properties`, go to the `Shortcut` tab and pick `Change Icon . . .` .

Once the icon is on your Desktop, you can assign a hotkey to it if you want and/or place it on the main Start Menu the way Mao does by dragging the shortcut and dropping it on the Start button. Once you have quick access to `Edit Start Menu`, you can easily manage the Start Menu. Removing an item is as simple as finding it in the folder tree and hitting `Del`. Adding a new item is as easy as setting Explorer to display the folder corresponding to the submenu you want the item on, opening another Explorer window, locating the executable, and dragging it to the `Edit Start Menu` window. (Dragging an `.exe` creates a shortcut; if you are dragging a document or an existing shortcut, you may want to right-drag and drop, and pick `Create Shortcut Here`.) Adding a new submenu is just creating a New Folder and rearranging items, even whole submenus, is just drag-and-drop file or folder moving.

A few final remarks on organizing the program menus in Start Menu:

- There is a special subfolder in the Programs subfolder of Start Menu called StartUp. Items in this folder (i.e. in `C:\windows\Start Menu\programs\startup`) are run when Windows starts up (unless you hold the `Shift` key down). As I'll discuss in Chapter 11, there are at least eight other places that program names can be placed and have those be run when Windows starts up. So if some package is installed and the result is a new program that runs automagically, don't suppose that necessarily the entry for it is in the StartUp group.

- You can add an item to the top level of the Start Menu by dragging it to the Start button. Even if you don't want the item at the top level, this can be a quick way to get an item on the Desktop into the Start Menu, where you can use Edit Start Menu to move it to a submenu below the top.

- If a Windows 3.1 package is installed but makes the proper DDE calls to Program Manager to add a new group, then Windows 95 intercepts them and instead makes a new subfolder in the `Programs` subfolder of Start Menu. But some installs may not work quite right. If that happens you may be able to add the subfolder by hand.

- Consider rearranging any folders you inherited from Windows 3.1 that had to have all groups as subgroups of the top level. With multiple level submenus, you can move some infrequently used programs to a deeper level. And consider moving (or better, copying) some of the Accessories and Games folder items that you use often to a higher level in the hierarchy.

- If you install Windows 95 to a new directory, it won't translate your old Windows 3.1 Program Groups to Start Menu subfolders (as it does if you install Windows 95 over Windows 3.1). But you can accomplish that on a group-by-group basis by double-clicking the `.grp` files. This is discussed in detail in Chapter 8.

- You can rename or move the Start Menu folder. As long as you do so in Explorer, Explorer is smart enough to adjust the Registry entries necessary to make sure that Start Menu (and the StartUp group still work). But I recommend against this—some dumb program may just blithely assume your Start Menu is in the Start Menu subfolder of the Windows folder.

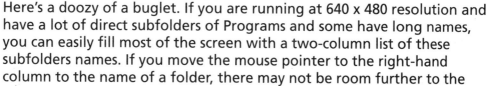

Here's a doozy of a buglet. If you are running at 640 x 480 resolution and have a lot of direct subfolders of Programs and some have long names, you can easily fill most of the screen with a two-column list of these subfolders names. If you move the mouse pointer to the right-hand column to the name of a folder, there may not be room further to the right for the submenu that wants to pop up. But there will likely be room for it above the Start Menu to the left, so it pops up there. Now move the mouse to reach it and you go over the left column and the submenu disappears. Boom—catch 22. Oh, how I love a nice bug in the mornin'.

No, no. If you move your mouse really fast, at least some of the time, you can reach that submenu before it disappears—so think of this as a video game. Doom, not Boom. Besides, if you hit the right arrow key after the menu submenu pops up, it'll move the cursor to the popup on the, er, left.

If this problem plagues you, you should reorganize your menu to have fewer first-order submenus to Programs. That's something you should do in any event.

I'm Hot for Hotkeys

A woman is like a teabag—only in hot water do you realize how strong she is.

—Nancy Reagan

Hey, listen up. I've had enough. In *The Mother of All Windows Books* I told you to start using Program Manager hotkeys, but I'm on to you, wiseguy. A lot of you didn't. Well, the feature has gotten better in Windows 95, so pay attention—use launch hotkeys. You'll be glad you did.

Mom's right. In the Property sheet of a shortcut, there is a field shown in Figure 3-22 for entering hotkeys. It's in the `Shortcut` tab of a Windows shortcut (`.lnk` file) and in the Program tab of a DOS shortcut (`.pif` file). For some strange reason Internet shortcuts (`.url` files) don't support hotkeys.

**Figure 3-22.
Hokey hotkeys**

Hotkeys either shift to a running program or start a program that isn't running. They work under two circumstances:

• If a program was launched from a shortcut with an assigned hotkey either directly (you double-clicked on the shortcut) or indirectly (you launched it from Start Menu or via a hotkey), then hitting the hotkey will restore the program window (if minimized) and switch to the program in question. These hotkeys work no matter where the shortcut is located.

• If the shortcut is in the Desktop directory or one of its subfolders (or subsubfolders or . . .) or in the Start Menu directory or one of its folders (or sub . . .), then the program associated to the shortcut will get launched.

This second item means that the program gets launched no matter where you are, even inside a full-screen DOS window. It does sometimes take a little while for the hotkey to do the launch, which is unfortunate.

The official documentation for hotkeys (what you get if you hit the ▣ in the dialog and press the words `Shortcut key`) says: "Shortcut keys must include CTRL and/or ALT and another key, for example CTRL+Y. You cannot use ESC, ENTER, TAB, SPACEBAR,

PRINTSCREEN or BACKSPACE." That's not totally true—you can use `Shift+Function` keys. `Alt+` combinations don't work although `Ctrl+Alt+` combinations do. `Ctrl+Shift+` combinations and `Alt+Shift+` combinations mostly work. You can also use `Ctrl+Alt+Shift+` combinations if your fingers are limber enough and you want to get some violin practice in.

You assign a hotkey by placing the cursor in the `Shortcut Key` field and hitting the hotkey. To blank an assigned hotkey, hit `Backspace` in the same field. You won't normally be able to assign the same hotkey to two shortcuts because attempting to hit the hotkey to define the second one won't work but will instead invoke the first program assigned with the hotkey. If a hotkey is assigned to an action, figuring out exactly where the shortcut is that is producing the action may not be so easy. Alas, I know of no place where Windows stores this information.

Using FileFind

> What affects men sharply about a foreign nation is not so much finding or not finding
> familiar things; it is rather not finding them in the familiar place.
>
> —G. K. Chesterton, *Generally Speaking*

 Windows File Find is one of its shining moments. Not only does it have intelligent wildcard and multiple filespec support and the ability to search within files, but it's very speedy. Third-party unindexed file search utilities are a thing of the past.

It's deceptively simple looking (Figure 3-23) but exceedingly powerful. You have to understand the capabilities of the entry fields in the main `Name & Location` tab, of the additional options and what you can do with the results of a search.

While the main place you'll probably invoke File Find is off the Start Menu Find/File menu item (hit `Ctrl+Esc, F, F` real fast!), it can also be invoked by hitting `F3` in any Explorer window (including the Desktop). And I'll explain how to assign it to a hotkey later. There is no executable that invokes the dialog—rather, it is so much a part of Explorer that it is called via DDE commands to Explorer.

The two fill-in fields on the main tab are called `Named:` and `Look in:`. Here is the power of entry you have:

- The named field is for filenames. You can use the standard DOS filenames `*` and `?` but with more flexibility than in DOS. `*a?b*.*` would look for files with an a and b in the middle, separated by a single letter.

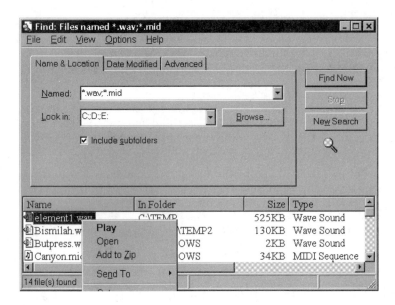

Figure 3-23. Finders, keepers

- If you enter a string with no wildcards and no period, then it looks for names with that string anywhere in the middle, for example, win is the same as *win* and would find both win.ini and topwin.exe.

- You can enter multiple file names in the Named: field separated by spaces, commas, or semicolons, and the search will be for all of the types (i.e., the union of the lists for each of the types). I'd suggest remembering semicolons for reasons that will become clear in a second. Note that one cannot search for explicit filespecs with a space in them—names in quotes don't work. You can use ? in place of the space (e.g. start?menu) to at least find the file, but you may find others.

- Look in: will specify the target directory. By default an Include subfolders box is checked that can turn a search of C:\ into a search of an entire drive.

- There are two obvious ways to enter choices in the Look in: box. There is a drop-down list with all your drive names and any recent single directories you've searched in. Also, Browse . . . lets you search for a particular directory whose name can be entered. One of the drop-down choices is My Computer. Pick that and all the local drives and any mapped network drives will be searched (at least if Include subfolders is checked).

- You can type a full pathname into the `Named:` box. If you type `C:\windows\*.exe`, when you hit `Enter`, `C:\windows` will magically get transferred to `Look in:` and `*.exe` will remain in `Named:`. This does not work properly with multiple specs (separated by `,` `;` or space).

- The true power is that the `Look in:` is a combo box—that is, you can type multiple drives or directories into it, separated by semicolons, but not by spaces or commas. This works as you expect if you also use multiple filespaces in the `Named:` field. For example, if you type `*.exe;*.com` in the Named field and `C:\windows;D:\msoffice`, you'll get a list of all `.exe` and `.com` files in either directory (or their subdirectories). You'll most often just do a multiple drive search, e.g. `C:;D:`.

- The directories you type into `Look in:` can be UNC pathnames as well as local drives.

 This is totally crazy. The last three features are wonderful, but I've not found them mentioned in any Microsoft documentation or in any prior books or magazine articles. Some programmer at Microsoft musta felt really good when he wrote the code for these goodies and then they get hidden from the world. What gives, Billy?

 Ah, you've discovered the MGS—the Microsoft Goody Specification. One key idea behind the committee that formulated this specification is that there can be no documentation errors if there is no documentation. If we'd documented this neat File Find stuff, the writer might have made a small error—maybe he'd have said that comma worked in `Look in:`. If he had, you guys in the press would have made a bigger deal about the error than about the feature. And you'd have forgotten about it being so great in a few weeks. But under the MGS, the goodies dribble out slowly. Instead of a few lines in the *Resource Kit*, maybe we'll get a whole column by Brian Livingston on the power of the Find dialog. And it'll last for months after the rollout. Yes sirree—the MGS is one of our marketing teams' most brilliant ploys. And I've even better news for you—the same team that wrote the MGS is working on the MGAPI.

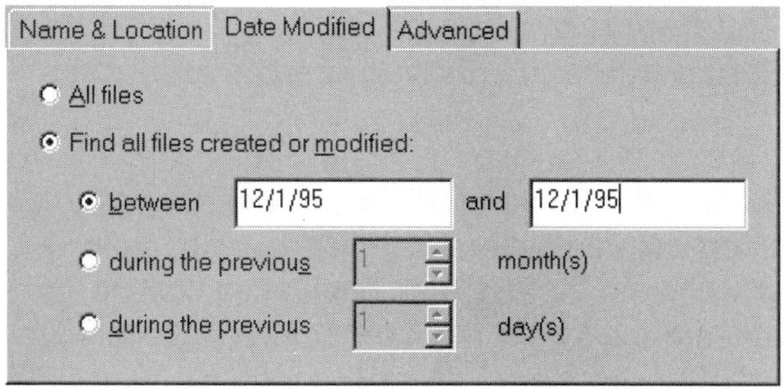

The Date Modified tab (Figure 3-24) is pretty straightforward. The only thing to note is that the designer fouled up here. You'll often want to search on

Figure 3-24. Finding by date

files made today but the `during the previous N day(s)` means today and the *N* days before that, so that a 1 there means "yesterday" and "today." Alas, you can't make that 1 into a 0. But you can fool the designer and use the `between` option. It defaults to today's date in the final date—type in the same date in the first beginning date and you can search just for today's files. The Advanced tab is also straightforward. `Of type` refers to the File Types that I'll discuss extensively later in this chapter. And `Containing text` is the true power of File Find. It'll even search for text effectively inside binary files if you need it to.

Once you've done the search, bear in mind that the resulting list is essentially a full-fledged Explorer window with a very few lacks. As shown in Figure 3-23, you can select a filename and right-click to get the full context menu. You can launch the default action by double-clicking. You can delete files (not just from the list but from the disk), rename them, and move or copy them to an Explorer window or the Desktop. If you have lots of folders under a Games folder, you could search for `C:\games\*.exe` and then drag the files to a Start Menu subfolder window to get shortcuts to all your games at once. If you want, you can use the View menu to change to large icons and you can resize the window to see more rows of columns. The File menu includes the full context menu for selected file(s) together with a command to open the folder containing the selected file.

The final Find tip you need to know about is that you can save a find with the `File/Save Search` menu item. Depending on whether you've checked the `Save Results` item on the `Option` menu, either the search criterion or the criterion and results get saved. If you pick this item, you get no feedback, no choice of file in which the data is saved, and no indication that the menu item did a darned thing. Ah well, you think, something else broken. In fact, the search is saved in a file on the Desktop with extension `.fnd` and name based on the title in the find window, e.g. `All Files.fnd` or `@.exe.fnd`. Since * and ? aren't allowed characters in a filename, they are replaced with @ and !, respectively.

 Note that you must run the Find once (at least to the point of clicking Stop) before the search parameters "take." It isn't enough to type, say, `c:;d:` in the `Look in:` box, and then click `File`, then `Save Search`. If you want the `c:;d:` to be included in the `.fnd` saved search, you must press `Find Now` first.

 As I'll explain soon, I'm all for using the Desktop as a convenient repository, but this silent use of the Desktop violates several cardinal rules of good UI design—give the user feedback when something has been accomplished, let the user pick a meaningful filename, and warn the user before you overwrite one of their files—instead, `File/Save Search` just overwrites any prior search with the name it feels it should use. The moral is to be sure to move and or rename any saved finds you want to keep.

One useful thing to do with saved searches is to place shortcuts to them on the Desktop or Start Menu and then assign a hotkey to the shortcut. On one machine with four local drives, C..F, I saved a search with a blank `Named:` and a `Look in:` of `C:;D:;E:;F:`. I ran the Search, but clicked Stop before it looked at all the files. I then made a shortcut to that and assigned a hotkey to it. Because calling up a `.fnd` file makes a DDE call to Explorer and DDE can be slow or even flakey, the response to the hotkey is sometimes slow, and occasionally doesn't do anything at all, but by and large it's great.

 Find does have two limitations in its full text search. The searches are unindexed—that is, from scratch each time rather than based on the previous creation of indices to some or all of your files. While the search will locate text within proprietary file types if the text is stored in pure ASCII format as soon as any formatting codes or other binary junk intervenes, the search will fail. For the Office 95 file types, its Fast Find (built into the Office 95 Open dialog) doesn't have either of these limitations.

The Run Box and the Documents Menu

> Of all the thirty-six alternatives, running away is best.

> —Chinese Proverb

The `Run . . .` command and the `Documents` submenu have in common access to a history of your recent actions. The documents menu normally lists the last fifteen documents you used. A document is any file with an extension that has an associated Open command. Such files will be displayed in Explorer with an icon next to them although not every file with an icon next to it is considered a document for the purposes of the document menu.

 To get supertechie, in the language of ProgIDs that I'll describe in the sections on File Types later, the extensions that are considered to be documents are precisely those that have an associated ProgID listed in the registry with a `shell\open` subkey. There, aren't you sorry you asked?

Files can get listed in the Documents menu in several ways:

- If you double-click on a document in Explorer, it gets listed in this list.

- If you have a shortcut to a document and you double-click on that, the document is placed in the list.

- If you use a Windows 95 application and either open or save a document (using the Win95 common dialogs), then the document appears on the list.

- If some program wants to, it can add a document to the list. For example, the Office 95 applications don't use the Windows 95 common dialogs but they still list their document files in this list—presumably by using custom code.

Surprisingly, if you type in the full pathname of a document (or the name of a document in the DOS path, for example, `win.ini`) into the Run box, it does not appear in the documents list. It may be that this was done on purpose because the entry will appear in the Run history, but it sounds like a bug to me.

The files in the Documents menu are associated to shortcuts in the directory `C:\windows\recent`. You can delete an individual document from the list by deleting the shortcut from that directory but you cannot add a document to the menu by adding a shortcut to that directory. That's because the Documents menu also involves the Registry entries in the Registry key `HKEY_CURRENT_USER\Software\Microsoft\CurrentVersion\Explorer\RecentDocs`. This key tracks the order in which the documents were used so Windows knows which of the fifteen to remove when a new one needs to be added. There, aren't you sorry you asked?

You can also clear the Documents list completely from the Start Menu Programs tab of the Taskbar Properties sheet.

The `Run. . .` box has a drop down list of the last twenty-six commands you issued from the run box. (Well, it turns out to be a drop up list most of the time!) You can type in the full path to a command or `Browse. . .` for it. The command can be an executable or the name of a document (extension with an Open command as Mao just explained). You can drag a file from Explorer to the Run box and have the full path name entered there. As I explained in Chapter 2, this can be an efficient way to get a complicated pathname onto the clipboard.

The number 26 isn't random—it's the number of letters in the alphabet. The list is stored in the Registry (in a key similar to the one for documents but it ends with `\RunMRU` instead of `\RecentDocs`). There are twenty-seven items in this Registry key. Twenty-six have the names a,b,. . .,z with values equal to the command and the last is called `MRUlist` and has the twenty-six letters in the order that the commands were run. The indirection of this list makes for efficiency in the code to change it. If the order were fixed to be commands a,b,c,. . ., then every time a new command was run, Windows would have to change twenty-six Registry entries, moving y to z, w to y,. . ., a to b and putting the new command in slot a. With this indirect method, Windows looks at the last letter in the MRUlist string, places the new command in the key for that letter, and moves the last letter in the

MRUlist string to the first place. Only two Registry entries are changed. And if a command is rerun to move it to the top of the list, all that need be done is reorder the letters in the MRUlist string.

I'll spare you repeating the diatribe I had when I discussed Explorer about the Run... history list being the same as the Go to... list in Explorer but it is, and it's dumb that it is.

I'm Gonna Shut You Down

> I hope, when I stop, people will think that somehow I mattered.
>
> —Martina Navratilova, *International Herald Tribune,* July 22, 1986

 What's there to say about the Shut Down option? It stops Windows, and that's that.

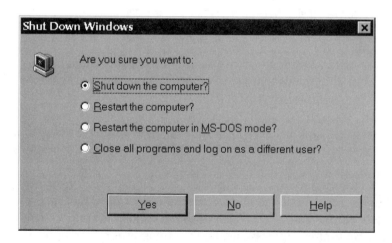

Figure 3-25. Adios, baby

But Igor, there are actually four options in the Shut Down dialog box shown in Figure 3-25. And as I'll explain, there are secretly five options there! The point is that the Shut Down option isn't just to Shut Down. It's also for restart, and there are many kinds of restarts. Besides, I have to emphasize to the readers how important it is to shut down the system and not just turn it off. There is sometimes important information to be stored in the Registry when Windows exits, and it won't be if you just turn off the machine. For example, programs can restore themselves after a reboot if you give them a chance to save their state by going through Shutdown, which informs each program that the system is about to shutdown. For the same reason, don't just hit the reset button to restart Windows—go through one of the levels of restart that I'll discuss in a moment.

That said, don't freak out if your kid trips over the wire and pulls the plug from the wall so you don't have a proper shutdown. Well, don't freak out because you are concerned about the lack of a proper shutdown. If you have six hours of unsaved work, you do have my permission to say gently: "I wish you wouldn't do that!" Anyhow, the consequences of not shutting down properly are most likely going to be the loss of some option you changed that wasn't properly saved, not the end of civilization as we know it.

The last option on the menu in Figure 3-25, viz. `Close all programs and log on as a different user?` is not present on all systems. For it to be there, you either have to have turned on multiple user profiles (a procedure discussed later in this chapter) or you need to have some kind of networking turned on. I find the restart option associated with it (that I'll discuss momentarily) so useful, that I think users might want to install Dial-Up Networking just to get this menu option! You can install Dial-Up Networking on any computer—you don't need a modem or a network card!

There are, in essence, four ways to restart Windows 95 itself. As a preliminary, I note there are normally three user-made files of commands that get run during a complete boot up of Windows: `C:\config.sys`, `C:\autoexec.bat` and `C:\windows\winstart.bat`. These files and all aspects of the startup of Windows 95 are discussed extensively in Chapter 8. The four levels of restart (in order of how thoroughly they start over) are:

1. **Cold reboot.** The system goes through POST,* of which the most noticeable symptom is the memory count. Memory is zeroed out and all three user configuration files are processed. The only absolutely sure way to accomplish this is to choose "Shut down the computer?", wait for the "It's now safe . . ." message and then hit a reset button or turn the machine on and off. (In reality, one could argue that this is two options, since reset is subtly different from power off/on, especially if you wait a minute or two between turning the machine off and on. Under Windows 3.x, I once saw the SCSI controller get so confused that hitting reset didn't help, although power off/on did).

---

* POST=Power On Self Test

2. **Warm reboot.** This is what happened in prior DOS versions if you hit `Ctrl+Alt+Del`. There is no POST and memory isn't zeroed out (but the operating system assumes all memory can be used by any program), but otherwise it is just like a cold reboot. There may or may not be a way to cause a cold reboot. On all the systems I've seen choosing "Restart the computer?" and choosing Shut down . . . , waiting for "It's now safe . . ." and then hitting `Ctrl+Alt+Del` did the same thing. But what that same thing was seems to be system-dependent. On some systems, they cause a cold reboot. On other they cause a warm reboot—in which case I'm not aware of any simple way to force a cold reboot short of hitting the Reset button.

3. **Restarting Windows . . .** This is the undocumented fifth option in the Shutdown dialog. If you choose the radio button that says "Restart the computer?", hold down the `Shift` key and choose `Yes`, and keep the `Shift` key down until you see the message "Windows is now restarting. . . ." What occurs is essentially the Windows 3.1 equivalent of exiting Windows and typing `win` at the DOS command line. Windows itself and the program loaded in it are closed but the programs you loaded in `config.sys` and `autoexec.bat` remain in memory. `Winstart.bat` is run again (but what was previously in it is unloaded). Please note that if the `Shift` key is held down through the loading of Windows itself, then your StartUp group is skipped. So you have to be careful to remove your finger from the `Shift` when you see the message (assuming you do want the program in StartUp loaded up).

4. **Relogging Windows.** The option that reads "Close all programs and log in as a different user?" is primarily intended for situations where you've set up multiple user profiles, an option I'll discuss later in this chapter. In that case, it does what the question suggests. But you can use this option even if you are a single user to quickly unload all the running winapps without unloading Windows itself or rerunning `winstart.bat`. If you are a single user with no login password, you get the dialog that is shown in Figure 3-26. Just hit `OK` and you'll preserve your no login status.

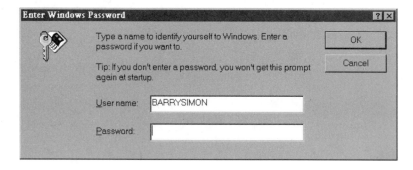

Figure 3-26. Will the next guest sign in?

If you have a program that is eating resources or otherwise need to "start afresh," this last option is probably enough and is by far the quickest restart. Under some circumstances it isn't enough, in which you should see if option 3 is. Given the amount of time that it takes to boot up from Scratch, options 3 and 4 are definitely worth trying first.

That leaves the option that says "Restart the computer in MS-DOS mode?". This normally involves what is called MS-DOS exclusive mode, an option I'll talk about more extensively in the section called "The Penalty Box" later in this chapter. Exactly what happens when you choose this option depends on whether there is a file called `Exit to DOS.pif` in the `C:\Windows` directory. If there is no such file, Windows 95 makes one and runs it. This default `Exit to DOS.pif` is set to run DOS Exclusive mode with the choice of `Use current MS-DOS configuration`. If Windows just runs, this standard `.pif`, why does it bother to make it? Because it gives you control over what this menu choice does. If you want it to restart in a configuration that has your real mode CD-ROM drivers present, change `Exit to DOS.pif` to use a custom MS-DOS configuration that loads them. If you want to disable this Shutdown entry, you can make `Exit to DOS.pif` run a batch file that displays a message saying "DOS Exclusive Mode not allowed on this machine." A sophisticated user wouldn't get fooled but another might. Heck, if you were a system administrator concerned that some user was booting this mode too often to play some DOS game, you could have `Exit to DOS.pif` run a batch file that first sent a notification to your computer and then ran another `.pif` file that really did exit to Exclusive DOS mode.

An interesting fact to note. If you call up the Shutdown dialog and answer No, then Windows saves the Desktop icon position information in the Registry. You might want to do this right after a lot of Desktop rearranging as insurance against a crash before you've had a chance to properly Shutdown.

Advanced Start Menu Tips

My interest in desperation lies only in that sometimes I find myself having become desperate.
Very seldom do I start out that way. I can see of course that,
in the abstract, thinking and all activity is rather desperate.

—Willem de Kooning

Here's one important tip and one Stupid Desktop Trick.

You can easily add a shortcut to Control Panel to the Start Menu by just dragging it from `My Computer` to the Start button. This opens a Control Panel window and forces you to click on a second icon and close Control Panel afterward. You could make a subfolder of Start Menu called CPanel and laboriously make shortcuts to each and every applet. That's not only time-consuming, but if a new applet gets added, you'll have to explicitly update the Start Menu. There's a better way.

To get a dynamic Control Panel on the Start Menu at the top level, you need to open an Explorer window on the `C:\windows\Start Menu` directory, make a new folder, and then name that folder with the following strange name (see Figure 3-27):

```
CPanel.{21EC2020-3AEA-1069-A2DD-08002B30309D}
```

Figure 3-27. Making a dynamic Control Panel   **Figure 3-28. A dynamic Control Panel**

You can put anything you want before the `.` in place of `CPanel`, say `Control Panel` or `Applets`. But the funny string of thirty-two characters with the braces and dashes must be exactly as it appears here. When you hit `Enter` to complete the rename, the extension will no longer appear in Explorer (but it will be there, for example in a DOS directory). If you choose that menu item from the Start Menu, you get a submenu with the names of all the Control Panel Applets (a part of the flyout menu is shown in Figure 3-28).

You can get similar flyout lists of the Printers and Dial-Up Networking Folders using the magic strings given here:

	Magic CLSIDs
Control Panel	{21EC2020-3AEA-1069-A2DD-08002B30309D}
Printers	{2227A280-3AEA-1069-A2DE-08002B30309D}
Dial-Up Networking	{992CFFA0-F557-101A-88EC-00DD010CCC48}

The thirty-two-character strings are hex* digits and these numbers are called CLSIDs. I'll have a lot more to say about them in Chapter 11. Basically, they are just identifying numbers for shell objects and the specific number tells you as much about the object as your Social Security number says about you. The Registry tells windows what code library to use to deal with objects with a particular CLSID.

I dunno what all the hoopla is. I don't set things up with a dynamic Control Panel on my top level Start Menu. There are two problems with this. First, if my mouse passes over that choice on my way to some other choice, there can be a noticeable pause while Windows reads the names of the applets from disk. Secondly, the menu is long and includes applets like `Mouse` and `Date/Time` that I use once in a blue moon. Instead, I have a subfolder of Start Menu called `CP Applets`. Inside, I've put shortcuts to the few applets I use all the time (Add/Remove Programs, Display, Fonts, Mail and Fax, System) and a shortcut to Control Panel, which I call Other Applets. I considered putting a dynamic Control Panel in that folder and would have if I could have figured out a way for it to go at the bottom of the menu but Start Menu insists on putting submenus at the top of any menu, and so I'd still have that pause when my mouse brushes over the dynamic Control Panel.

So much for the important tip. Here's a weird trick, mainly a curiosity. Call up the Shutdown dialog from Start Menu. Hold down the `Ctrl`, `Alt`, and `Shift` keys at the same time and click `No`. Explorer will unload itself totally. No Taskbar, no Desktop icon, and no Explorer windows, but all other programs will be running. Double-clicking the Desktop will call up Taskman, from which you can shutdown.

Ye Olde Shell Game

There's no accounting for tastes. Some people actually like Program Manager and miss it when faced with the rather dry and nongraphical Start Menu Programs submenu. Windows 95 does ship with a version of Program Manager and you can install it as your shell (I'll tell you how in a moment), but even if you like the Program Manager shtick, I urge you to stick with Explorer, but use the psuedo Program Manager I'll also describe here.

The `shell=` setting from Windows 3.1 is alive and well. I assume you have no interest in this if you aren't familiar with Windows 3.1, and I'll assume you know the syntax for `system.ini` settings. Within `system.ini` there is a section called `[boot]`. You can have a line there saying

        shell=*shellname*

---

* hex means base 16 and has the "digits" 0-9 and A-F with A=ten, B=eleven, . . . , F=fifteen

If *shellname* is progman.exe, you'll get the Windows 95 version of Program Manager as your shell. If it is winfile.exe, you'll get the Windows 95 version of File Manager. Just for kicks, I placed the Windows 3.1 version of Dashboard in a directory C:\dash, placed the directory in my path and set *shellname* to C:\dash\dash.exe. It worked fine. It appears that you can use just about any valid Windows 3.1 shell here but I didn't do extensive testing since I think you'd have to be crazy to use this option! You get wallpaper but no Taskbar, no Desktop icons, and no Start Menu. Progress it ain't. By the way, if you pick an invalid program for *shellname*, you get the heartening message from Windows:

Error loading *shellname*. You must reinstall Windows.

Jolly fellow, that Windows. Of course, you don't really need to reinstall Windows. Hit F8 during bootup, pick command prompt, use Edit C:\windows\system.ini to remove the shell line, save, reboot, and you'll be fine.

Here's how you make a Folder View that will look and act a lot like Program Manager. Right-click on the Desktop, pick New and Shortcut to invoke the new shortcut wizard. Type in the command line C:\windows\explorer.exe /root,C:\windows\Start Menu\programs and then name it whatever strikes your fancy, say Progman strikes back. Next, double-click on the icon, go to the View menu, and make sure that Large Icons are checked and that Toolbar and Status Bar are not. Go to Options . . . and make sure Display the Full . . . is not checked. Close the program. When you reopen that icon, it will remember these settings, at least most of the time. What you get looks a lot like Program Manager (Figure 3-29).

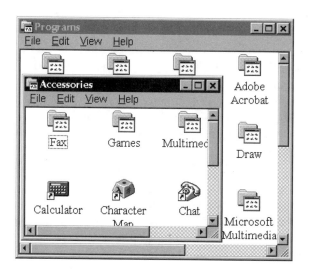

Figure 3-29. Progman impersonator

Desktop Dancing

> Custom has made dancing sometimes necessary for a young man;
> therefore mind it while you learn it, that you may learn to do it well,
> and not be ridiculous, though in a ridiculous act.
>
> —Lord Chesterfield, *The Letters of the Earl of Chesterfield to His Son*

 I've always considered calling the computer screen a Desktop as slightly weird. First, the monitor is usually on your Desktop so there's a wheels within wheels phenomenon. More significantly, at least to Windows 3.x users, it sure didn't resemble how I use my Desktop—as the repository of all sorts of things that I want to keep handy. Windows 95 has changed that.

If this section has one lesson you should take away from it, it is that the Windows Desktop is the ideal place to put stuff while you are working with it, especially files that you need for awhile but that you want to toss out when some project is done or some email is sent, for example. Tossing it out is easy—just drag it to the Recycle Bin. Accessing it is easy if the file is a document associated to a program—just double-click on it.

So if you are saving a new file, ask yourself if you are going to need to access it again in the next day. If so, put it on your Desktop.

Windows actually makes it easy to save stuff on the Desktop and to access the Desktop in Explorer, because the Desktop is the Mother of All Folders. Literally. Figure 3-30 shows the right panel of Explorer when My Computer is closed. Your disk drives appear on the Explorer tree because they are children of My Computer and My Computer is a child of Desktop, which is at the top. Since Desktop is the ultimate parent, its easy to get there in Explorer—just hit Backspace or ⬆ repeatedly and you are guaranteed to wind up there. The same is true in the Windows 95 Open and Save As dialogs.

Figure 3-30. The Mother of All Folders

Alas, Windows 3.x Open and Save As dialogs don't work that way, and those dialogs don't understand the folder structure above individual drives. So to save a file on the Desktop in a Windows 3.1 program you need to know that it's "the same" as the file folder C:\windows\desktop.

If you are wondering how Recycle Bin appears on Igor's machine (see Figure 3-30) as `Ye Olde Recycle Bin`, I'll tell you how to rename the Recycle Bin in Chapter 11.

Free the `My Computer` Four

> My desk, most loyal friend
> thank you. You've been with me on
> every road I've taken.
> My scar and my protection.

> —Marina Tsvetaeva, *Desk*

It's the hallmark of the Mac, but what the heck, it's a good idea. You want to place icons for each of your disk drives on your Desktop. But you'll have to choose which of two ways to do it.

There are two ways to add icons representing disk drives on your Desktop.

1. You can drag the drives from `My Computer` to the desktop and make shortcuts—you'll get a dialog saying you can't move or copy the icon, but it offers to make a shortcut. Alternately, you can right-click on the Desktop and pick `New Shortcut`. If you type in `C:\` for the command line, you'll get a shortcut equivalent to dragging the C drive from `My Computer`. You can type in `C:` instead and Windows will change it to `C:\`. Do this for each of your drives, which for many people means three icons—for floppy, hard drive, and CD. While you're at it, free a fourth icon from the confines of `My Computer`. Drag Control Panel to the Desktop. It's true that I gave you a method for putting a dynamic Control Panel on Start Menu, but I like also having this quick access around.

2. Go through the New Shortcut wizard specifying the command line as `C:\windows\explorer.exe /e, A:\`. You'll get the Explorer icon so you'll need to right-click, choose Properties, go to the Shortcut tab and choose `Change Icon. . . `. It will display icons from `C:\WIN95\SYSTEM\SHELL32.DLL`. If you scroll you'll get a bunch of appropriate ones for disks: . Pick the right one for your floppy, hard drive, and CD as you set up things for your different drives.

Once set up, I suggest putting the icons on the extreme right of your Desktop with the drive icons at the top and Recycle Bin on the lower right—but hey, you hardly need me as your interior decorator. Put 'em where you want.

I strongly recommend you use the first method, which has several advantages but one huge down side. One advantage is that you can copy by dragging files to icons set up by the first method but not the second. Another plus is that the drive icons automatically adjust to the type of drive. Finally, the icons shown for a CD drive can be adjusted by Windows or by the CD itself. Figure 3-31 shows the default CD icon, the one used for audio CDs, and the ones taken from the Windows 95 and Plus! Pack CDs when they are in the drive. The disadvantage is that with the default Windows setup, if you double-click on a drive icon set up by the first method, it opens in Folder view while those set up by the second open in Explorer view.

The solution to the downside is easy—if you shift over to Sarah's Smart Setup, which she explains later in this chapter, then icons set up by the first method open in Explorer mode. So I say you should use Sarah's setup and the direct icon method.

Plain	Audio	Win95	Plus!

Figure 3-31. CD icons

Desktop Tips and Tricks

> When one wanted one's interests looking after whatever the cost, it was not so well for a lawyer to be over honest, else he might not be up to other people's tricks.
>
> —George Eliot, *Felix Holt, The Radical,* Introduction

Here are a bunch of suggestions for using your Desktop:

- You can click down the mouse on the Desktop and drag to lasso several icons, which you can then move together. You can also select multiple icons with Ctrl+Click. But, be careful—it is easy to drag several icons and wind up with some of them off screen by accident! If you do, picking Line Up Icons from the Desktop's context menu will bring the icons in from the cold but could do some other icon rearranging you aren't so happy about.

- I'll repeat the tip I gave when I discussed the Taskbar, on how to align icons in a column. Sort of line them up at one side or the other. Then drag the Taskbar to that side and make the now-columnar Taskbar so wide it covers up your column of icons. Instead the icons will jump to the side and line up in a neat column. Now drag the Taskbar back to the bottom of the screen. Lasso the now neat column of icons and move it where you want. You can also use Line Up Icons but you'll probably want to adjust the icon spacing options in the Appearance tab of the Desktop Property sheet—Icon Spacing (Horizontal) and Icon Spacing (Vertical) are on the Item drop down.

- There is no easy way to restore the location of all your Desktop icons if Windows or you should foul up (a single Arrange Icons from the Desktop menu can ruin your whole day—it cannot be undone with Undo). But there is a complicated way that I'll tell you about in Chapter 11.

- Consider placing a shortcut to a folder that is under Start Menu on the Desktop. For example, you might make a subfolder called `Current Projects` in the `C:\Windows\Start Menu` folder. Then using Explorer, right-drag that folder to the Desktop and pick Create Shortcut (or use the Create Shortcut wizard or Cut and Paste Shortcut from Explorer). By double-clicking* on the shortcut, open a Folder view of the folder. Keep the view open and quite small. You can drag shortcuts to documents you are working on to this open folder window. They'll then be available on the Current Projects submenu of Start Menu.

- Mao's office has two PCs in it that he uses for different projects. They are networked together. He's placed shortcuts to each machine's Desktop on the other machine's Desktop. The two machines are called `mao1` and `mao2`. On the Desktop of `mao1` he used the Create Shortcut wizard to make a shortcut with command line `\\mao2\c\windows\Desktop`. He can send files to the other machine by just dragging them to this shortcut. A boss and her secretary could use a similar shortcut to the Desktop.

- This idea works as well with Dial-Up Networking as with direct networking. Mom had Igor working out of her Chicago office at one point. Igor had Windows 95 on his Mom's mansion machine with the Remote Access Server[†] from the Plus! pack. The first time he made a Dial-Up connect from his Chicago machine to home base, he dragged a shortcut of the Desktop on homebase to the Chicago machine. Now, when he's at the Chicago office and he drags a file to this icon, Windows offers to use Dial-Up Networking. When he answers yes, it makes the connection and copies the file.

- Consider making a Folder on your Desktop called `Favorite Dirs`. In it, place shortcuts to the directories you use a lot. While you are in Explorer, hitting Backspace or 🔼 repeatedly will take you to Desktop. You can click on `Favorite Dirs` and then a shortcut to move Explorer's focus to the directory in question.

---

* If you use Sarah's Smart Setup, you right click and pick FolderView from the Context menu.
[†] I'll discuss the Remote Access Server in Chapter 4 when I talk about Dial-Up Networking.

The Mother of All Easter Eggs

> The cocks may crow, but it's the hen that lays the egg.

> —Margaret Thatcher

Faberge made elaborately jeweled Easter eggs for the last czars of Russia. So credit screens for programs that were reached by elaborate steps came to be called Easter eggs also. Frankly, I call them Rube Goldberg eggs. In *The Mother Of All Windows Books,* Mom gave Easter eggs the disdain they deserve as In Crowd tricks. But I know you don't care what Mom thinks about Easter eggs—you just want to know how to find the one that's in Windows 95. So here goes:

1. Right-click on the Desktop and select New . . . Folder from the context menu.

2. You'll have New Folder in the Edit Box for the name. Type in `and now, the moment you've all been waiting for` instead and hit `Enter`.

3. Click once on the name and rename it to `we proudly present for your viewing pleasure` and hit `Enter`.

4. Click once on the name and rename it to `The Microsoft Windows 95 Product Team!` and hit `Enter`.

5. Double-click the folder to open it.

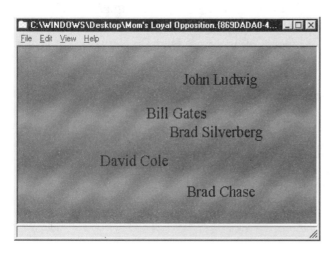

You'll get a window like that shown in Figure 3-32 with clouds and lots of names flying across the screen. Once you go through this nonsense, you'll have a folder on your Desktop called "The Microsoft Windows 95 Product Team!" but you can rename it to anything you want, for example "OS-2 Boosters of America." If you have the option to show full DOS pathnames on in Explorer, you'll see the CLSID `{869DADA0-42A0-1069-A2E7-08002B30309D}`

Figure 3-32. Take a big bow

as the extension, but darned if I can figure out where this is registered. It appears that rebooting your machine causes the folder to stop working as an Easter egg. I'll bet the CLSID is only put in memory and not in the on disk registration database.

However, the sound file used during the Easter egg is left behind—it is called `clouds.mid` and is placed in your `C:\windows\media` directory. If you'd like a different background music while watching the names, just put any `.mid` or `.rmi` file there and call it `clouds.mid`. I kinda like the Bach Brandenburg Concerto that ships with Windows 95 myself. You can do this either before typing in the Easter Egg codes or afterward.

Configuring Context Menus and Associations

Hors d'oeuvres have always had a pathetic interest for me; they remind me of one's childhood that one goes through wondering what the next course is going to be like— and during the rest of the menu one wishes one had eaten more of the hors d'oeuvres.

—H. H. Munro, *Reginald*

A columnist in one of the big magazines, and we won't mention *PC/Computing* by name, complained that you couldn't change the right-click menu for drives and, in particular, you couldn't arrange to have ScanDisk a direct option on this menu (rather than have to click through the Properties menu). This set of sections will let you in on the secret of changing the context menu for most objects in the Windows 95 shell (but alas, not the context menu for a blank part of the Desktop). In particular, using some fancy footwork, we'll show you how to place a ScanDisk option on your Drive menu, which is a little tricky.

It's remarkable how poorly Microsoft has documented this power user stuff that lets you do things like change the context menu. They didn't even let the press in on it so the magazines didn't discuss this sort of thing in their first set of articles. And it is too bad that for some stuff you need to use Regedit, which can be a bit daunting.

Piece 'o cake, Mom, piece 'o cake. And if you didn't sometimes need Regedit, we wouldn't have supplied it, now would we? As for the lack of documentation for the power user stuff, we wanted to give the magazine and book writers something to discover and talk about. Think of it as the Mao and Sarah Full Employment Act of 1995.

Send To, which does have some limited uses, was too often presented in the press as a cure-all when it was often a poor substitute for what is better and more flexibly done with File Types.

The thorough treatment of File Types in the next section can get a little hairy at times, so you'll want to look ahead to the section titled "Stupid File Type Tricks" to see lots of examples of the theory in practice.

The File Types Dialog: An Overview

To put it rather bluntly, I am not the type who wants to go back to the land;
I am the type who wants to go back to the hotel.

—Fran Lebowitz, *Social Studies*

Before I explain how you change actions associated with file extensions and shell objects, I need to give you a few terms that will come up again and again. You may think that .txt files are directly associated to Notepad. That was true under Windows 3.0. But in Windows 95 (and already in some cases under Windows 3.1) there are several layers between .txt and Notepad! Inside the Registry, extensions are assigned to hidden things called **application identifier keys.** I'll use the techie name **ProgID** taken from the OLE technical docs to save ink. These keys cannot contain spaces. I call them hidden because you won't ever see them unless you look in the Registry. Several extensions can be assigned to a single ProgID. ProgIDs have associated to them three things of relevance for our discussion here—an **application description** (I'll call them *public names*), an icon, and one or more actions that can be applied to the files whose extensions are assigned to that ProgID. The actions themselves come in two parts—a name and the command that performs the action. One of the actions is normally the default action—it is run if you left-double-click on the object and is the boldface item on the right-click menu. The icons are used to represent the associated files in Explorer or Folder windows, either as large icons or the tiny icons that appear in the margin in the other three views.

For example, .txt has an associated ProgID of txtfile. The public names for txtfile is "Text Document." The default icon is not that for Notepad but an icon taken from the collection in shell32.dll. There are two actions assigned to txtfile, namely Open (the default) with action C:\windows\notepad.exe %1 and Print with command C:\windows\notepad.exe /p %1.

somefile.txt

Open
Print
Quick View
Add to Zip
Send To ▶
Cut
Copy
Create Shortcut
Delete
Rename
Properties

**Figure 3-33.
The .txt context
menu**

The result is the context menu shown in Figure 3-33. The two actions assigned to the `ProgID txtfile` appear at the top. `Add to Zip` is added by the program Winzip using a Context Menu Handler, something I'll discuss in Chapter 11. All the other choices are built into the Windows shell.

There are also `Shell Identifier Keys` (I'll also use `ProgID` for them!). These are objects with special meaning to the Windows shell, such as AudioCD, Drive, and Directory, which do not have an associated file extension but otherwise have all the properties of a `ProgID`, including a public name, icon, and actions.

 Mom made me promise not to say much about Regedit outside Chapter 11, but you get such a good idea of what I'm talking about by looking there that I will say something—but see that chapter for a lot more. Run Regedit (for example, by typing `regedit` in a Run box). Click on the plus sign in front of `HKEY_CLASSES_ROOT`. Scroll down and you'll see a bunch of `.abc` type entries at the start. If you highlight one you'll see the words `(Default)` and the associated `ProgID` on the right. That's where extensions are associated to a `ProgID`. Now scroll down to a `ProgID` and highlight it. The associated `public names` with the familiar `(Default)` will be on the right. Look at `.txt` and follow it to `txtfile`. Highlight that and hit the star key on your keyboard and you'll open up keys that show you how the icon and actions are stored.

You could change and add Actions here. But this is only for educational purposes! Windows provides a more humane way to adjust this using the File Types dialog you'll see in Figure 3-34. You get to this by opening an

Options	? ✕

View | **File Types**

Registered file types:

Cursor
DAT File
DBF File
Drive
Fax Viewer Document
File Folder
File Set for Microsoft Backup
Folder
Font file
Help File

[New Type...]
[Remove]
[Edit...]

File type details

Extension: HLP

Opens with: WINHLP32

[OK] [Cancel] [Apply]

Figure 3-34. The File Types dialog

Explorer or Folder window, dropping down the View menu, and picking Options . . . .
The View tab is displayed—the other tab is File Types!

If you've installed the Plus! pack, this panel and some of the others will look slightly
different—I'll explain how and why later.

The most obvious thing is a scrolling list of items. What shows are the public names of
the various ProgIDs. This is something of a pain as you might not guess that the name
associated to batch files is "MS-DOS Batch File" or that directory has become the
politically correct "File Folder." It can be a real pain to scroll through a long list. If you
can't locate something that must be there, run Regedit and trace from the extension(!).

If you highlight an item on the list you get several pieces of information displayed in the
File type details panel, including the associated extension(s), the icon for the
ProgID, and the name and icon of the program that "opens" the object. Normally, this is
the program in the command for the default action.

From the main file types dialog you can take three actions that involve new and current File
Types. Remove blows away the highlighted item from the list. It removes at least two sets
of keys from the Registry—the one defining the ProgID and the one or more defining the
associated extension(s). Exercise extreme care—look at the discussion in Chapter 11 about
making backups of your Registry before fooling with *any* of the options in the File Types
dialog.

New Type. . . gives you a dialog almost identical to the Edit. . . option I'll discuss
next. The main difference is that you can and must supply a Description of type
and you have the option to fill in extensions. When you make a new File Type, Windows
chooses the ProgID—it takes the first listed extension, say *foo,* and turns it into the
ProgID *foofile.* Brilliant, no? This is not the place to change the program associated to a
given extension—the dialog complains and won't let you assign your new type to an already
taken extension. I'll talk about how to do that in the next section.

If you hit the Edit. . . button, you get the dialog shown in Figure 3-35. At the top, you
get to change the icon that is used when files with the extensions associated to this new type
appear in the shell. If you pick the button you get the standard Change Icon. . . dialog
(Figure 3-62) that I'll discuss when I talk about PIF files in "Take a Deep PIF" later in this
chapter. The Description of type allows you to change the public name. It appears
grayed out here, which means you can't change the name of Drive. I'll talk more about this
later. Normally you can change that name and it can be a name with spaces.

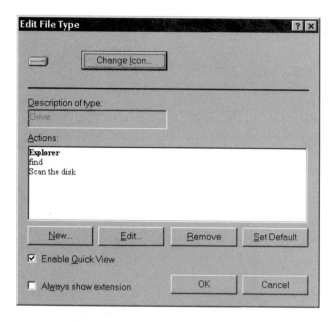

Figure 3-35. The Edit File Types dialog

The `Actions` box lists the various actions assigned to the File Type with the default action in bold. If you highlight an action and hit `Set Default`, it changes the default to the highlighted action if another action was the default. If you highlight a bold action and hit `Set Default`, it unbolds and you may be fooled into thinking that there is no default action. But that's false— there's a complex algorithm that determines the default action if nothing is highlighted— I'll describe it in Chapter 11. For an example of where you might like to change the default, look at my discussion of AudioCD in the section on "Stupid File Types Tricks."

All this stuff with `Set Default` only affects the context menu. It doesn't affect what happens if you just type the document name in the Start Menu Run box. When you type in a document name, Windows looks for a command called `Open` and runs it whether or not `Open` is the default. And if there is no command called `Open` then Windows complains "No application is associated with the specified file. Create an association by using the Explorer." Type in `C:\windows\win.ini` in the Run box and Notepad opens the file even if you've made Print the default action that takes place when you double-click the file. Double click a `.cpl` file and it opens the first control panel applet in that file. Type the name of that file into the Run box and you get an error message. Why? Because the action isn't called `Open` but `Open with Control Panel`. Not quite. `Open with Control Panel` is the public name, and what counts is the name buried in the Registry, which isn't `Open` but `cplopen`.

Of all the crazy conventions. It makes no sense that double-clicking and "running" the application can do different things. Anyhow, you can at least fix the behavior of `.cpl` files. Open the Registry, go to the key `HKEY_CLASSES_ROOT\cplfile\shell\cplopen`, right-click on it, pick rename, and change the name to open. When you run `.cpl` files, what you'd expect to happen does.

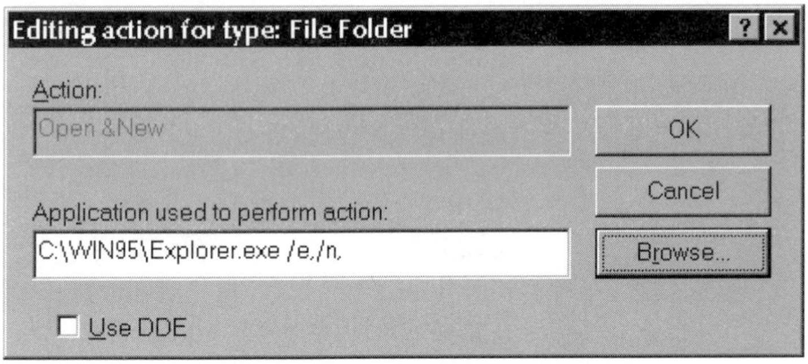

Figure 3-36. The Edit Actions dialog

The Edit. . . button calls up the dialog shown in Figure 3-36. The Action name is grayed out—the only ways of changing that are to do it in the Registry or else to delete the action and reset it using New. . . . The second edit field lets you change the command issued by the action. When you change actions this way, Windows automatically tacks a %1 onto the command before storing it in the Registry. That means the filename that you clicked on to reach the context menu with this action gets passed to the command as an action. If done this way, the name is always tacked on after any other parameters. This is usually what you want, but if you don't want a %1 or you need to place it before some parameters, you can arrange that but only by directly editing the Registry—see Chapter 11.

The New. . . button in the Figure 3-35 brings up an identical dialog to Edit. . . except that the action field isn't grayed out and you can enter a name for the new Action.

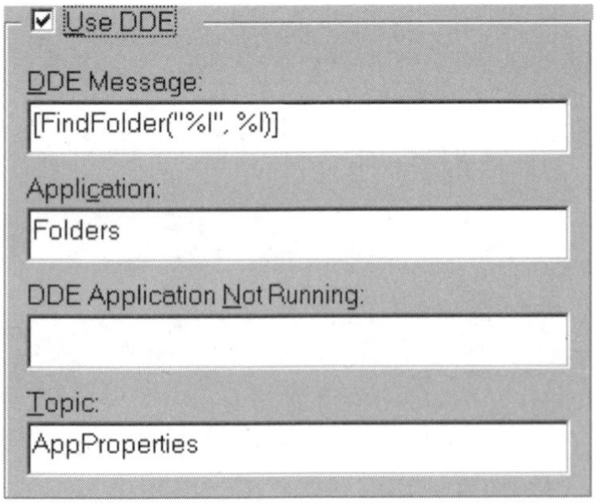

Figure 3-37. DDE fields

If you check the Use DDE field in the New. . . /Edit. . . dialog or if you Edit an action that has it checked the dialog expands to include what is shown in Figure 3-37. The fields shown in that figure come from the Find command, which pops up the Find dialog (which I explained earlier was launched via DDE commands to Explorer). DDE is stuff for gurus. I doubt you'll ever want to look at this dialog for your own use.

The Enable Quick View check box in Figure 3-35 adds a Quick View item to the context menu that will try to pass the files of the given file type to Quick View; for most files that means opening it in an ASCII text viewer. The checkbox marked `Always show extension` does what you'd expect: even if you've checked the box marked `Hide MS-DOS file extensions for file types that are registered`, the extensions are shown if you check the `Always. . .` box for that type. Of course, since you followed my advice earlier in the chapter to uncheck `Hide. . . registered`, this is irrelevant to you.

 You may find that as you use the File Types and Edit Action dialogs that some buttons are mysteriously grayed out. You can't change the batch file default from `Open` to `Edit` even if you want to. Bah, humbug.

 We've placed keys called EditFlags in the Registry to stop you from doing stuff that might harm you. Think of it as a chastity belt to prevent you from screwing around with important entries.

 Microsoft might not trust you but of course I do, so I'll give you the keys to the chastity belt. In Chapter 11, Mao will describe these flags in loving detail. But for now, I'll give you the simple method. For any file type that has grayed out items you don't like being grayed out, note the public name for the type in the File Type dialog. Then call up Regedit and search for the name. For example, for batch files you'd search on "MS-DOS Batch File." When you locate that name, you should find on the right side of the display the word `EditFlags` and to its right eight hex digits, such as `d0 04 00 00` for batch files. You want to double-click on the word `EditFlags` and change the value. For types like `batfiles` that are associated to an extension, change the flags to `00 00 00 00`. For types like File Folder (aka `directory`) that don't have an associated extension, use `02 00 00 00`. It's important that you not use all zeros for entries like this because Windows only displays File Types in the dialog if they have an associated file type or if the seventh bit in the edit flags is turned on.

 Two ProgIDs have special meaning: `*` applies to all files and `unknown` applies to files with extensions that are not registered. You can add them to File Types, and then add actions by running Regedit, opening `HKEY_CLASSES_ROOT`, scrolling down to `unknown`, and highlighting it. Choose `Edit\New\Binary Value` from the Regedit menu. Type in the name `EditFlags` (with no space between Edit and Flags), then double-click on that name and enter the data `02 00 00 00`. Do the same with `*`, which is first on the list under this key.

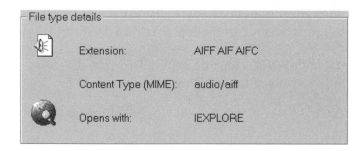

Figure 3-38. The Plus! File Type Details panel

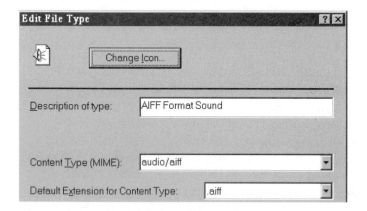

Figure 3-39. The Plus! Edit File Type dialog

Finally, we note that if you installed the Plus! Pack or the Internet Jump Start Kit, you'll find that it has added an extra field called `Content Type (MIME)` (Figure 3-38) to the main File Types panel in the file type details frame and a corresponding pair of fields labeled `Content Type (MIME)` and `Default Extension for Content Type` (Figure 3-39). MIME* is the Internet equivalent of file extensions. What Windows would call `.gif`, Internet calls `image/gif`. The MIME names are used by Web Browsers and when sending Internet mail via MIME enabled systems. These fields provide a translation from Internet to Windows and, not coincidentally, allow Web Browsers to know what application to use to display files they don't understand.

---

* You do insist on filling up your memory with the useless translations of acronyms, don't you? Since you insist, MIME = multipurpose Internet mail extensions

The Open With Dialog

> Man has lost the basic skill of the ape, the ability to scratch its back.
> Which gave it extraordinary independence, and the liberty to associate
> for reasons other than the need for mutual back-scratching.

—Jean Baudrillard, *Cool Memories*

If you double-click on a file with an extension that has no associated file type, you get the dialog shown in Figure 3-40. So long as you leave the checkbox that says "Always use this program to open this file" checked (and that's the default) you have a back door for the creation of a new File Type. If the extension is `foo`, the `ProgID` for the new File Type will be `foo_auto_file`. The public name will be whatever you fill in. (If you don't fill one in, it will pick `FOO File`.) The programs you get to choose from are precisely those that are associated with the Open command for already existent File Types. The exact command line for the existing `Open` command is transfered to be the command line for an `Open` command associated to the new `ProgID`. If you uncheck the bottom check box, the

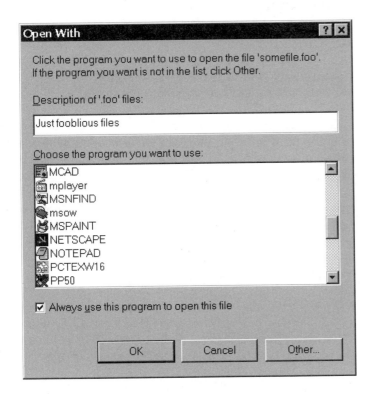

Figure 3-40. The Open With dialog

program is used this one time but no permanent file association is made. Note the Other. . . button, which lets you browse for a program in case the one you want isn't in the list.

This is a natural for opening ASCII text files, which often pop up with random extensions. But that's the point. For 99 out of 100 users, 99 out of 100 times the program they'll want to use is Notepad. So why the heck did the designers of Windows 95 make you scroll halfway through a huge list? They shoulda treated Notepad as special. Even better, they should have let you choose a default editor somewhere and given that special treatment in Open With.

Oh, Rush! You dummy. Of course there's a way to make Notepad the first program on the Open With list. Go into Explorer, click once on \windows\notepad.exe, click Edit, then Copy. Then click Edit and Paste. Scroll down to the bottom of the list and rename Copy of notepad.exe to _notepad.exe. Then click View, Options, bring up the File Types tab, and click New Type. . . . In Description of Type use Mom's Magical Mystery and in Associated Extension type, oh, mom. Click New. . . . In the box marked Action type Open, in the box marked Application used to perform action type c:\windows_Notepad.exe, and click OK all the way back out. Heh heh heh. If you want you can delete the .mom subkey from the HKCR key of the Registry. The key that is needed for this trick is the other one that is created, which will be called momfile.

If a program has an Open command (which is the default), you can add an Open With. . . item to the context menu if you hold down the Shift key when you right-click.

What is this with the Shift key producing weird, but useful, alternate actions all the time? The designers of the shell seem to be Shift fixated. And why the heck isn't Open With. . . available if Open is a nondefault action or if there is no Open command at all? Truly bizarre.

It gets worse, grasshopper. The default if you use Open With. . . when an Open command exists is to have the "Always use this program. . ." option unchecked. That's sensible. But if you check the box, what you get may be unexpected. You might think it would act the way the dialog works when there is no Open command and create a new File Type. Instead it changes the command line for the File Type already associated to files with the clicked extension. If only one extension is assigned to the File Type, that could be desirable but it often won't be if there are multiple extensions assigned to one File Type.

So, for example, if you have a general bitmap program that handles .pcx, .tif and .gif and you get some kind of great .gif handler, there is no way using File Types or Open With to just change the assignment for .gif and leave .pcx and .tif alone. You can do it with the Registry, but that'll be hair-raising for many users.

The design of the Windows shell is normally so good that only so-so components stick out like a sore thumb. And `Open With. . .` is so-so at best.

 There actually is a program that ships with Windows 95 that will let you assign an individual extension, breaking out a single extension from a situation where several are assigned to a single `ProgID`. The program is called File Manager and you run it by typing `winfile` in the Run box or by double-clicking on the program in Explorer. It is a pretty brain-dead upgrade of the Windows 3.11 File Manager! It does not understand long filenames and it is still 16 bit. But it does have a `File/Associate` that can be useful.

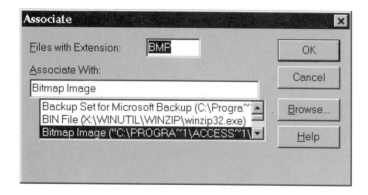

Figure 3-41. File Manager to the rescue!

Figure 3-41 shows the dialog that results when you pick Associate from Fileman's File menu. It will normally fill in the extension of the highlighted file (BMP here) but you can type in another choice. You then scroll down to the File Type you want—the public name and the program that is run are shown. File Manager acts exactly as you might expect it to (and have expected `Open With. . .` to). It takes only the extension you picked and assigns it to the `ProgID` that you pointed to in the Associate dialog. It leaves any other extensions assigned to the same program as your extension used to be assigned to. You can even assign a new program to the extension and make a `ProgID` on the fly.

 Because of some new features in Windows 95, what File Manager does might not be precisely what you want. Commands in the Registry as subkeys of the entry for an extension can set up an item on the New submenu for the context menu for the Desktop and any folders. When you change the `ProgID` using File Manager it leaves the old New items in place—if you find a spurious entry for the old file type on the New submenu, you'll need to go into the Registry and delete by hand the subkey of the extension called `ShellNew`. The advantage of not deleting these subkeys is that if you make a mistake and reassign the wrong extension, you can easily recover.

 If you use the old PC Tools File Manager, it takes the other tack and removes the subkeys for the New submenu. I had a vivid example of this kind of problem when I visited my brother's house. When I arrived there was terrible turmoil. It seems that bro's number-one son had mistakenly used PC Tools File Manager to make an association. He'd intended to assign a particular file to Write (so that Word Pad would open it) and his hand had slipped and he'd instead assigned a Shortcut to Write! So all the shortcuts on the Desktop had `.lnk` visible, they were all displaying the Write icon, and when you double-clicked on them, they started WordPad! I was asked to fix this little problem. One part was easy—I merely went into the Registry to change the `ProgID` assigned to `.lnk` from `wrifile` to `lnkfile`—the extension, icon, and click to launch were restored. But Shortcut was gone from the New menu!! Fortunately, I had my emergency disk, which has a complete Registry in text format (using the Export command in Regedit), and was able to restore the necessary ShellNew command. The moral is to be careful if you use PC Tools File Manager to make changes in file associations.

 While on the subject of warnings, you should note that all this File Type and association stuff is stored in the part of the Registry that is machine-dependent, not the part that is user-dependent. So if you are using mulitple User Profiles (which I'll discuss later in this chapter), changes one user makes in these things will affect all users. So on such a machine, you may need to consult your fellow users before making changes.

If you assign an extension to an `Open` command using File Manager or `Open With. . . ,` there is no default icon. In that case, as in any other where there is no document icon specified but there is an `Open` command whose associated program has an icon, Windows does a good job of faking it. It shrinks the program's icon and places it inside a document. To the left, you see Notepad's icon and the document icon made on the fly for a document assigned to Notepad. On the right, you see the generic icon Windows 95 uses if it can't figure out anything else to use. This ultimate default icon is used for extensions with no registration or if there is no default icon and no `Open` command.

Stupid File Types Tricks

People who make puns are like wanton boys that put coppers on the railroad tracks. They amuse themselves and other children, but their little trick may upset a freight train of conversation for the sake of a battered witticism.

—Oliver Wendell Holmes, Sr., *The Autocrat of the Breakfast-Table*

 Here my crew is going to show you some explicit ways to use File Types to usefully configure your context menus. First, there will be the ScanDisk caper, where I'll show how to add the item that the *PC/Computing* columnist complained about. Then there will be a bunch of tips about various individual changes. Finally, Sarah will tell you how she organizes her Folder and Drive menus. In doing so she'll need to explain the File Types hierarchy that Microsoft has built for folders. In the next section, "Sarah's Smart Setup, Step by Step," she'll give you a step-by-step method summarizing how to put in place those tricks from this section involving context menus of various folder types.

ScanDisk

Running ScanDisk for Windows on a drive isn't hard but it sure is tedious. You can open `My Computer`, locate the drive, right-click, find Properties, and then switch to the Tools tab or you can click the Start Menu, move to `Programs`, then `Accessories`, then `System Tools` and only then get ScanDisk. And if you go about it this way, you'll have to scroll to the right drive after startup. What a drag.

If you followed my advice earlier in this chapter, you have shortcuts to drive icons for each of your drives on the Desktop. Running ScanDisk with the default menus isn't helped by these icons since their Property sheets are for the shortcut and don't have the Tools tab that true drives have. Clearly, you'd like to add a context menu item called `Check the Disk` that runs ScanDisk with the right drive letter.

There is an obvious first try. Call up `View/Options` in an Explorer window, click on the File Types tab, find Drive on the list, hit `Edit. . .` and then `New. . .` for a new action. Call the action "Check the Disk," and browse to find ScanDisk for Windows—it is called `scandskw.exe` and is found in your Windows directory.

 Ah, my little chickadee, when you do that and try it, ScanDisk gives you an error dialog titled "ScanDisk Cannot Start" with the explanation, "You typed parameters that are invalid for ScanDisk for Windows." The problem is that the Folder names "`C:\`" was passed to ScanDisk which is happy with "`C:`" but sure doesn't like that "`\`". Yo, Mao, can we get around that?

But of course, my sometimes moribund friend. One way around it is to change the Registry. I'll discuss the Registry and Regedit in all its glory in Chapter 11, but I can tell you now what to do. Call up the Run dialog from Start Menu and type in `Regedit`. Choose `Find` from the `Edit` menu and look for *scandskw*. When it is found, you see on the right panel, the data "`C:\WINDOWS\Scandskw.exe %1`". It's that `%1` that is passing "`C:\`" to ScanDisk. Double-click on the word (`Default`) in the right-hand panel and remove the `%1` from the Value data box. Click OK and exit Regedit and the Check item in the drive menu will invoke ScanDisk. Alas, it will start out highlighting the last drive you used on ScanDisk rather than the drive you right-clicked—that's because by deleting the `%1`, you dropped any link to the particular drive letter.

```
@echo off

if %1==A:\ scandskw A:

if %1==B:\ scandskw B:

if %1==C:\ scandskw C:

if %1==D:\ scandskw D:
```

Figure 3-42. Listing of Checkup.bat

But there is a better way. I'll assume that your hard drives are C: and D: and that you have two diskette drives. Using Notepad, make a batch file called `Checkup.bat` like that in Figure 3-42.

I'll suppose you place it in `C:\batfiles`. Now go back to the actions for Drives dialog, highlight `Check The Disk`, and choose `Edit. . . .` Make the command `C:\batfiles\checkup.bat`. Instant ScanDisk!

If you've just gotten the impression that Windows has a built in macro language—namely, the DOS batch language, you're right. This is a theme I'll discuss in some detail later. For now, though, I want to note that for the `Checkup.bat` batch file and for the Quick Install example we'll see momentarily, you want to be sure to set the Properties as shown in Figure 3-43. Be sure to explicitly check `Close on exit` and to pick `Minimized` in the Run dropdown. If you don't check `Close. . .` the DOS window will stay open marked as Finished until you explicitly close it. By running it minimized, you'll only see a flash on the Taskbar.

You can set properties by either running it once and setting the properties from the System menu in the Inactive DOS session or by copying the batch file to a shortcut in the same directory (by right-drag and drop) and picking Properties from the Shortcut's context menu.

Disabling Autoplay of CDs

It's kinda neat to pop in an audio CD and have Windows automagically start the Windows 95 Audio CD player. But what if you have your own favorite CD player program that you want

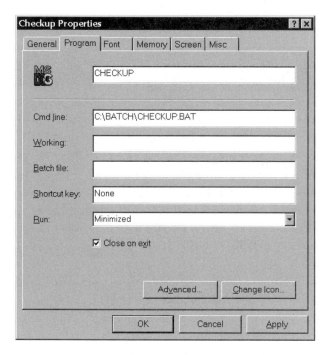

Figure 3-43. Configuring Batch File Properties

to use instead, or suppose you'd like to disable this Autoplay but still have playing a right-click away. You'll notice that one of the built-in file types is Audio CD. If you look at its action you'll see it has exactly one called Play that is boldface and for which the command is C:\WINDOWS\ cdplayer.exe /play. You can Edit the action to replace the Windows CD player with your favorite or disable autoplay by highlighting Play and hitting Set Default, which turns the default into a command that opens the CD in folder view. If you do that rather than delete the command, you have a setup where you don't have autoplay but you can still play the CD by right-clicking the CD drive (or the shortcut to it I told you to put on the Desktop!).

There's no question you want to chuck the Windows CD player and use the PowerToys player (FlexiCD) instead.* When FlexiCD is loaded, you don't want the CD player to pop up because even if it does, it can't play the CD—it will tell you another application has gotten to the CD first. So when you install FlexiCD you want to be sure to toggle CD Player off.

What's crazy is that there is a way to toggle off Audio CD Autoplay, but you can't do the same for CD ROM Autorun.

You can avoid Autorun by holding down the Shift while the CD loads, or you can totally disable Autorun by going to Device Manager, expanding CD-ROM, highlighting your drive letter, hitting Properties, going to the Settings Tab and unchecking Auto insert notification.

---

* I talk about Power Toys in Chapter 5.

I know about that well, Bill, but that's a very different thing from toggling off Autoplay. It's like the difference between tossing out the bath water and tossing out both the baby and the bath water—something I'll bet you're pretty sensitive about. Because when you just untoggle Play as the default, Play is still available from the context menu. If you insert a CD-ROM and hold down `shift`, Autorun is still available from the context menu. But if you turn off Auto insert notification, the context menu has no idea there is a CD with autorun capability or an Audio CD in the drive.

Editing Batch Files

To me, it doesn't make sense that batch files are run by double-clicking on them. If I want to run a batch file, often I have a shortcut to it (a PIF file) that I can double-click on. In fact, if you've ever run the batch file and it is on a local hard drive, you'll have a shortcut there automatically. The only sensible default is to have `Edit` be the default action. `Open` (i.e. run the file) is still on the right-click menu in any event.

Alas, Mother Windows doesn't let you change the default for `MS-DOS Batch Files` in the File Types dialog. It's got the chastity belt on. So you'll need to first call up the Registry, search on `batfile`, and then double-click on `EditFlags` and change the value to `00 00 00 00`.

Editing Generic Files

More often than not a file with an unregistered extension will be an ASCII text file like `readme.1st` or `read.me`. Assuming you followed Mao's advice to add the unknown File Type to the list of types you can edit, you can add an action called `Notepad` with command `C:\windows\notepad`.

Quick Install

Here's a useful device for quickly getting to the setup for a new program. It is true that you can always call up the `Add/Remove Programs` applet in Control Panel and get at an install that way, but it's a heck of a lot quicker to just right-click on the drive icon for the diskette drive or CD drive that you know has an install program on it. You make a batch file called `C:\batfiles\inst.bat`, shown in Figure 3-44.

```
@echo off

if exist %1setup.exe goto setup

if exist %1install.exe goto install

Mommess No Valid Install or Setup located in %1

goto end

:setup

%1setup

goto end

:install

%1install

:end
```

Figure 3-44. Listing of inst.bat

This assumes you use Mom's Message Center, the program we've included on the CD that lets you pop up Windows messages from a DOS batch file, and have placed it in your path or in the batfiles directory. Now go to the drives entry in the File Types list, hit Edit. . . , then New. . . , and enter an action called Install that invokes this batch file.

Converting a .doc File

So far, I've shown you how to use batch files to add neat context menu commands. Macros in programs can also be useful. Here's an example. Suppose you often want to convert a Winword .doc file into an ASCII .txt file. Open Winword, go to Tools/Macro, name the new macro SaveAsText, and click Create. Then type in the macro in Figure 3-45 based on one on page 300 in *Woody's Hacker's Guide to Word for Windows* (written with Vince Chen and Scott Krueger).

```
Sub MAIN

    fn$ = FileNameFromWindow$()

    fn$ = FileNameInfo$(fn$, 5) + FileNameInfo$(fn$, 4)

    FileSaveAs fn$ + ".txt", .Format = 3

    DocClose 2

    If CountWindows() = 0 Then FileExit

End Sub
```

Figure 3-45. Listing of SaveAsText Macro

Now go to File Types, highlight `Microsoft Word Document`, choose `Edit. . .`, then `New. . . .` Call the Action `Convert to Text` and use the command line

    C:\msoffice\winword\winword.exe /mSaveAsText

Now you have an extra menu item on the right-click menu for your `.doc` files. This sure is fun.

Not quite so fast. In testing out your idea I stumbled upon a subtle but disturbing design flaw in the way Windows 95 handles Actions made in File Types. I had a `.doc` file called `My Red Book.doc`. I set up your macro and context menu item, right-clicked on this file and chose `Convert to Text`. Instead of converting it, Winword popped up three errors messages saying it couldn't locate `my.doc`, `red.doc`, and `book.doc`. The problem is that when it stores the command in the Registry, Windows appends a `%1` to it. But in order to accommodate long filenames with spaces, it should have appended a `"%1"` (with the quotes). You can go into the Registry and fix this by hand. It's a shame Windows doesn't do that automatically.

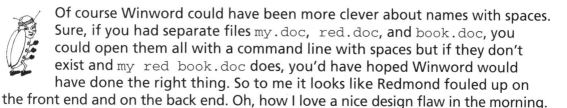 Of course Winword could have been more clever about names with spaces. Sure, if you had separate files `my.doc`, `red.doc`, and `book.doc`, you could open them all with a command line with spaces but if they don't exist and `my red book.doc` does, you'd have hoped Winword would have done the right thing. So to me it looks like Redmond fouled up on the front end and on the back end. Oh, how I love a nice design flaw in the morning.

Adding A Local DOS

Sometimes you can't beat DOS for some quick actions. Here is a way to add a menu item to the context menu for directories that will open a DOS box with that directory as the current one. Open up the File Types dialog, scroll down to `File Folder`, and add a new Action called `Local-DOS`. For the action, type in `C:\command.com`.

 If you do this, the box will start fine but there will be a complaint from the system on the top of the DOS screen that says `Specified COMMAND search directory bad`. It's harmless but inelegant. To get rid of it, call up Regedit, search on "local-dos," and when you find the command, remove the `%1` that Windows appended to `C:\command.com`.

Printing a Directory Listing

 Windows 95 can't do this. Windows 95 can't do that. It gets so tiresome to hear the critics who haven't bothered to understand the power of DOS as a batch language for Windows and of File Types. One learned book complained Windows couldn't print a directory listing and while you could use DOS, by typing `dir > prn`, you'd have to eject the last page by hand. Mind you, Explorer should have some built-in directory smarts, but lacking that you can still do pretty well.

Make a batch file * `C:\batfiles\dirlist.bat` which reads

```
dir %1 /-p /o:gn > "C:\temp\Directory Listing"
start /m /w notepad /p "C:\temp\Directory Listing"
del "C:\temp\Directory Listing"
```

Figure 3-46. Listing of Dirlist.bat

---

* It can be in any directory you want! This also assumes `C:\temp` exists. If you are distributing this to a bunch of users you could use `%temp%` in place of `C:\temp`.

Then do the same steps I told you about in discussing ScanDisk to run the batch file minimized and set to close after running. Next call up the File Types dialog, scroll down to `File Folder`, hit `Edit. . .` and then `New. . .` and call the action `Print Directory Listing` and the command is `C:\batfiles\dirlist.bat`.

This is an interesting batch file. The `/-p` switch on `dir` is just to overcome any default `/p` that the user might have to normally have output pause every screenful. The `/o:gn` sorts with directories first and by name. The need for the `start` command is especially interesting and comes from the fact that Windows is multitasking. Without it, Notepad loads but before it can grab the file the directory output was saved in, the batch file has finished and erased that file. The `/w` after `start`, says to wait for the program being started to finish to continue the batch file. The `/m` runs Notepad minimized and is only for cosmetic reasons.

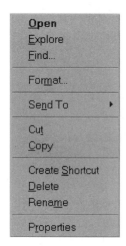

**Figure 3-47.
The Default Drive
menu**

Looking at the Folders Hierarchy

If you right-click on a drive icon, you get the menu shown in Figure 3-47. As usual the default action is boldface, so double-clicking opens up the drive in Folder view, that is dumb Explorer mode. We already know how to change context menus for objects if the object is listed in the `File Type` tab of the dialog that pops up when you choose `View/Options` from the Explorer menus.

Scroll down the list of File Types and you'll find Drive as a type. Aha. We only need to click `Edit. . .`, get the expected list of actions—Open, Explore, and Find—highlight Explorer, hit the `Set Default` button and change the default. But that doesn't work! Despite the fact that the top of the context menu should come from the Action list, the Action List for Drive has a single entry—find.

Hmm. Remember that a drive icon is just a special kind of Folder. Folder is also a legitimate File Type. Scroll down to it on the File type list, pick `Edit. . .` and you get two actions—Explore and Open.

It is indeed true that the Drive context menu is picking up the actions for *both* Folder objects and Drive objects. You can see this by adding an action to the Folder actions—you'll see it appear on the Drive context menu. There is a kind of hierarchy of objects and Drive is treated as a type of Folder. In the best spirit of object-oriented programs, it picks up the actions for both Drives and the parent of Drive, that is, Folder. File Folder, aka Directory and Drive are the only children of Folder. Drive has a child called AudioCD that is only active if the drive is a CD drive and an audio CD is in it. This four object set is the only hierarchy within the set of shell objects. An abstract folder like My Computer or Control Panel picks up only the actions of Folder, drives pick up the actions of Folder and Drive, directories pick up the actions of Folder and File Folder, and audio CDs pick up the actions of Folder, Drive, and AudioCD.

It's too bad they didn't push the hierarchy further to have diskette drive, CD, hard and network drives as subobjects of drive. At some level Windows is already doing that. It uses different icons for the different kinds of drives and of all drives, only diskette drives have a `Copy Disk...` option on their context menus. But this level is not accessible to the end user fooling with File Types.

Adding an Open New in Explorer

I'd suggest adding an action to both Drive and File Folder called `Open New` with the command `C:\WIN95\Explorer.exe /e,/n,`. Note the commas after both `/e` and `/n`. What this does is open a new Explorer window starting from the current drive or directory. If you really want to you could add a `/root,`—see the discussion of Explorer earlier in this chapter to see what that does.

This is a useful command when copying a lot of files from one place to another. Find the source or destination first in Explorer and use this command. That opens a second Explorer window. Then go to the other of the source or destination and you have the windows you need to drag and drop between.

Sarah's Context Menus

I'm particular about how I want the context menus for drives, directories, and other folders to work. After all, I figure a lot of my interaction with the shell will be through those objects. I like the special folders like Control Panel and `My Computer` to open in Folder view with large icons. I've seen Control Panel in Explorer mode and it seems weird. On the other hand, there is no question that I want my Drives and Directories to open in Explorer mode with details, not large icons showing.

I couldn't just call up the Edit File Type dialog for Folder and change the default from Open to Explore, because that would open Control Panel and similar folders in Explorer mode. Being well-versed in the theory of objects, I knew what to do. I'd just add an action to Drive and an action to File Folder called Explore and make that the Default for those types.

But of all the dumb behaviors of Windows! When Sarah did that, she got a context menu with `Explore` shown twice! It is well-known that if the same action is defined for both an object and its parents, the parent definition is supposed to be ignored. Oh well, maybe they'll get it right in one of the tuneups.

So Sarah was caught between a rock and hard place.

I decided that since I didn't care if I never used Explorer on the special folders, I was able to change things so that double-clicking on a special folder would open that folder in Folder view, but double-clicking on a drive or directory would open it in Explorer view.

FolderView
Open
Find...
Check The Disk
Install
Open New
Sharing...
Format...
Paste
Create Shortcut
Properties

Figure 3-48. Sarah's Drive menu

With the other tricks from this section, Sarah's drive context menu looks like Figure 3-48 as opposed to the default Figure 3-47. And Open means to open in Explorer view, not Folder, as it does in the Figure 3-47 menu. Setting this up is a little tricky but the result is so worthwhile I've asked Sarah to explain what she did in the section after this one titled "Sarah's Smart Setup Step by Step." Please check it out.

The Send To Menu

> Tell me what brand of whiskey that Grant drinks. I would like to send a barrel of it to my other generals.
>
> —Abraham Lincoln, responding to tales that his most successful general was a drunk

Many context menus contain a cascading submenu marked Send To. All drives, directories, and file objects do. It appears that objects that are folders but neither directories or drives (like the Control Panel icon in `My Computer`) do not have a Send To submenu, but shortcuts to such objects do. The hardcoded Desktop icons do not. But most objects do.

As I discussed in Chapter 2, the Send To menu is built up with the same paradigm as the Start Menu but is rooted in the directory `C:\windows\SendTo`—yeah, it is Send To on the menu but `SendTo` in the directory. As we'll see, the designer of this part of the shell isn't big on consistency. As with Start Menu, subdirectories of the top directory (`C:\windows\SendTo` in this case) produce submenus of the Send To menu.

On systems where Exchange and Fax have been installed there are normally four or five shortcuts preinstalled in the `SendTo` directory: shortcuts to your floppy drive(s) and to My Briefcase on the Desktop and shortcuts to executables that are labeled `Mail Recipient` and `Fax Recipient`.

Menu items will mainly correspond to shortcuts but can include other files. Shortcuts to folders and drives are given special treatment, as follows:

• If one or more files on drive X are selected and a shortcut to a folder is picked from Send To and the folder is on a different drive Y, then the files are all copied there. This is true for any file including executable files. For folders, a copy of the folder is made in the target.

• If one or more files on drive X are selected and a shortcut to a folder is picked from Send To and the folder is on the same drive X, then all files and folders are moved to the new location except for executables, which pop up a message saying they cannot be moved or copied and offer to make a shortcut.

Of all the crazy . . . Why tell the user the file cannot be copied or moved when it clearly can be? And why treat it differently from dragging and dropping, which just makes a shortcut quietly without popping up a message?

If the item on the Send To menu corresponds to anything but a shortcut to a folder, Windows runs the item passing to it the selected filenames as parameters. If there are multiple files, they are passed as multiple parameters separated by spaces. The full pathnames are passed but with their shortname versions with the ~1s and not the long filenames.

Multiple selected files are treated very differently by general context menu commands and by Send To. For context menu items, the command is executed multiple times, once for each selected file with the different selected files passed as parameters for each running of the command. `Send To` runs the command only once with all the filenames passed in a long string. I'd not claim that either behavior is wrong, but it is unfortunate that their behaviors aren't consistent since, after all, `Send To` command does cascade off of the context menu. Why should users have to keep straight these different behaviors?

When I tested what happens with parameters on the Shortcut command line, I found more inconsistent behavior that I'd have to regard as a bug. Both DOS shortcuts (`.pif`) and Windows shortcuts (`.lnk`) have a place you enter the command to be executed and both allow you to include parameters to the basic executable. If you double-click on the shortcut or run it from the Run box, the command gets executed with the included parameters passed to it. It is clear what the behavior should be if you run a shortcut with internal parameters with extra parameters on the command line to the shortcut: Both the internal parameters and the command line parameters should get passed to the executable. But that ain't the way it is! For Send To menu items, all internal parameters get dropped, which is a crimp on what you can do with `Send To`. It's even worse when you use the Run box from Start Menu. Internal parameters are passed for `.lnk` shortcuts but not for `.pif` shortcuts. Oh, how I love a nice bug in the mornin'.

It's remarkable that you see a lot more ink in the magazines and books on `Send To` than on the File Types dialog. Maybe not—it's easier to find `Send To` and too many writers prefer to complain that you can't modify the context menus instead of finding out what the story really is. But don't let those writers fool you into thinking that `Send To` is the cure for all that ails you. It's a pretty limited thing and is broad-based in that it applies to all files rather than being extension-based. I think you'll want to add an Edit item, which is a shortcut to Notepad, but that's probably it.

There is one other item that all users will want added to their Send To menu, and that is the `AnyFolder...OtherFolder` command in PowerToys.*

While I agree with the assessment that `Send To` is limited and that File Types is often more useful, you shouldn't lose sight of the incredible usefulness of the built in items on the Send To menu. In particular, the Send To diskette and Send To briefcase commands are the quickest way to copy files to those locations.

Sarah's Smart Setup Step by Step

The secret of the demagogue is to appear as dumb as his audience so that these people can believe themselves as smart as he is.

—Karl Kraus, *Sprüche und Widersprüche*

---

* I discuss PowerToys in Chapter 5.

I'm so pleased and proud. Sarah, my head of technical support, has broken into Windows' inner sanctum and figured out how to change the Registry so Windows' default behavior is to work in "smart" Explorer mode rather than the "dumb" Folder view. She also figured out how to keep Windows from producing more and more windows when you click on a drive or folder. And the good news is, if you follow the steps outlined here, you can do it yourself. The default user-configured parts of the context menus for drive and directory are shown in Figure 3-49 and Sarah's smart menus in Figure 3-50. See Figure 3-47 and Figure 3-48 for the full menus.

- In "dumb" Windows, if you type the name of a folder or drive into the Start/Run box, or put a folder or drive in a shortcut, that drive or directory opens in "dumb" Folder View. Sarah's smart setup makes the drive or folder open in "smart" Explorer View.

- In "dumb" Windows, if you double-click a drive or folder, it opens in "dumb" Folder View. With Sarah's setup, it will open up in "smart" Explorer View. (In "dumb" Windows, you can right-click on a drive or folder to open it in Explorer View. In "smart" Windows, you can right-click to open in "dumb" Folder View).

Figure 3-49. Dumb drive menu

- In "dumb" Windows, if you double-click on a drive or folder in the right-hand pane of an Explorer window, you get a new window with that drive or folder—in "dumb" Folder View. With Sarah's "smart" Windows, double-clicking just changes the active directory in Explorer, and you don't get that stupid extra window.

- In cases where you want that extra window, you can use the context menu where FolderView will give you a new window in Folder View while Open New will give you a new Explorer window.

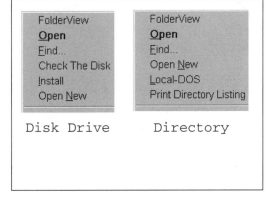

Figure 3-50. Sarah's smart menus

Step 1. <u>Make a Binary Backup of the Registry.</u> Call me ultra-careful. But since you're going to be fooling around in your Registry, I recommend your first step is to make a binary backup of the Registry. In Explorer, make sure you are configured to display hidden files. Then go to the C:\windows directory, sort on Type, and look for system.dat and user.dat. Their type will be DAT File. Select them, copy to

the clipboard, and paste from the clipboard. Scroll down to the bottom of the folder and you'll find files named `Copy of system.dat` and `Copy of user.dat`. Rename them to `system.bac` and `user.bac`. You'll get a coupla warnings about each rename. Just answer `Yes` to them.

Step 2. <u>Get used to working with the Registry.</u> If you are already a Regedit maven, skip this step. Otherwise, you'll need to get used to working with it. Go to the Run box and type `Regedit`. You should keep it running until the process is finished, but if you close it in error, just restart it from the Run box. You might want to read the beginning of Chapter 11, but here's a quick summary. You get a display that is much like Explorer with a tree on the left and a contents pane on the right. Be warned that there is no File Save here. Basically, as soon as you make any changes Windows saves them to the Registry. And there is no built-in Undo!

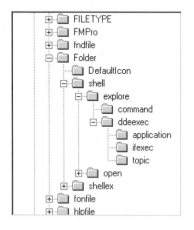

Figure 3-51. Register today

We'll need to worry about the top key (what the Registry calls the analog of folders), which you'll see in the Regedit window. It is called `HKEY_CLASSES_ROOT` and I'll abbreviate it `HKCR`. Double-click on it (or click once on the + next to it) to open `HKCR`. There will be a long list of subkeys starting with * and a bunch that begin with a period. Scroll past them. We'll be interested in three subkeys that are near to each other, called Directory, Drive, and Folder. Scroll down to Folder and open the keys `shell`, `explore` under it, and `ddeexec` under that. You should see something much like in Figure 3-51.

Right-click on Folder and pick Rename. Then hit Esc. This was just for practice. Click on Folder and look at the right-hand pane. You should see EditFlags. Double-click on it and hit `Cancel`. Double-click on `(Default)` and then `Cancel`. This is how you'll later edit some values—although, of course, you'll hit `OK` instead of `Cancel`!

Step 3. <u>Make a .reg file to Restore the Initial Setup.</u> Now Click on Folder again, go to the Registry Menu item, and choose `Export Registry File. . . .` In the resulting dialog make sure the Selected branch radio button is selected and save the file on the Desktop as `folder.txt`. Similarly, scroll up and select Drive and Export to `drive.txt` and select Directory and export to `dir.txt`.

Now minimize Regedit and double-click on each of the `.txt` files to open three Notepad windows. In the `drive.txt` window delete the first line (`REGEDIT4`) and the blank line below it, then choose Edit/Select All and Edit/Copy to put the rest of the file on the clipboard. Click on the `folder.txt` window, hit `Ctrl+End` to go to the bottom of the file, and then Edit/Paste. Repeat the operation with `dir.txt` (delete `REGEDIT4. . .`).

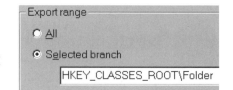

You should now have in the `Folder.txt` window a file that is the combination of the three `.txt` files, except that there is only one `REGEDIT4` line and it is at the top of the file. Now click File, then SaveAs, and save on the Desktop as `dumbwin.reg`. You can delete the old `folder.txt`, `drive.txt`, and `dir.txt`.

`dumbwin.reg` is your bailout file: if something goes wrong in the middle of the following steps, or if you find that "smart" Windows isn't to your liking after all, it's easy to bring back the old "dumb" version of Windows. In Regedit, delete the Folder, Directory, and Drive keys by selecting each one in turn and hitting the `Del` key, then double-click on `dumbwin.reg` to restore Windows 95 to its original dumb state.

As two last checks, first double-click on `dumbwin.reg` to make sure the Regedit says it successfully updated the Registry. Then delete the Folder key in Regedit and double-click on `dumbwin.reg` and confirm that the Folder key was indeed restored.

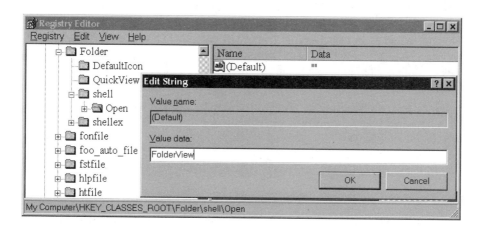

Figure 3-52. Editing the Folder key (step 4)

Step 4. <u>Adjustments in the HKCR\Folder\Shell Key.</u> Now return to or restart Regedit and open up and scroll down to the `HKCR\Folder\Shell` and open it up so you can see its two subkeys `open` and `explore`. Do the following:

1. Rename the `open` key to `temp`.

2. Rename the `explore` key to `open`.

3. Select the new `open` key (that used to be called `explore`) and export it to a file you place on your Desktop, named `sarah.txt`.

4. Delete the key that is now called `open`.

5. Rename the `temp` key to `open`.

6. Select the open key and look at the right-hand pane, where you should see a single name (`Default`) with an empty value (which appears as `""`). Double-click on the word (`Default`) and type in the value `FolderView`. Hit OK. See Figure 3-52.

Step 5. <u>Adjustments in Directory and Drive subkeys.</u> Now you need to load `sarah.txt` into WordPad since you need to do a search and replace and Notepad won't do that. Type `WordPad` in the Run box and then open `sarah.txt`. Then:

1. Inside WordPad, click on `Edit`, then `Replace` and change occurrences of `\Folder` to `\Drive`. **WARNING!! It is very important to include the "\" in the search and replace strings because the file has two occurrences of the string "Folder" (without the \ ) and they must not be changed.**

2. Click File, then SaveAs, and save the file with the name `drive.reg`. It is important when you do SaveAs that you leave the format as Text Document. Don't exit WordPad yet.

3. Do a search and replace in the entire Word Pad document changing `Drive` to `Directory`, and use `SaveAs` to save the new file on your Desktop as `dir.reg`. Close WordPad.

4. Double-click on each of the files `drive.reg` and `dir.reg`. After each Windows should claim that the Registry was successfully updated.

5. Delete the three files `sarah.txt`, `drive.reg`, and `dir.reg`.

Step 6. <u>Optional extra commands.</u> There are five extra commands on my sample menus seen in Figure 3-50. Here's a table that shows where you can find them:

Menu Command	Drv	Dir	Batch File	Subsection
Check The Disk	✓		`checkup.bat` (Figure 3-42)	Scan disk
Install	✓		`inst.bat` (Figure 3-44)	Quick Install
Local-DOS		✓		Adding a Local DOS
Open New	✓	✓		Adding an Open New in Explorer
Print Dir. Listing		✓	`dirlist.bat` (Figure 3-46)	Printing a Directory Listing

The subsection column refers to subsections of the section called "Stupid File Types Tricks." The figures give the places you'll find the listing of required batch files.

Step 7. <u>Fix Edit Flags (optional).</u> While you're fooling with these keys anyway, you may as well change the `EditFlags`. Select the key `HKCR\Directory` in Regedit. One of the value entries on the right side will have name `EditFlags` and value `d2 01 00 00`. Double-click on `EditFlags` and replace it with the value `02 00 00 00`. Now do the same with the keys `HKCR\Drive` and `HKCR\Folder`. Edit Flags are discussed in Chapter 11.

Step 8. <u>Make a Windows "smart pill" .reg file.</u> Repeat all the steps in the third step, except name the combined file `Smartwin.reg`.

Remember, if you ever need to dumb down Windows 95, go into Regedit and delete the three HKCR subkeys `Folder`, `Directory`, and `Drive`, then double-click on `dumbwin.reg`. To make Windows 95 smart again, delete those three keys and double-click on `smartwin.reg`.

Hey Boss' boss, mind if I ask some questions? Why didn't you just do it all with a `.reg` our readers could import?

Please do. Two reasons. You can't delete/rename keys from a `.reg` file. I don't know the path to Explorer since the Windows directory might be `C:\win95` or `D:\windows` or . . .

Why did you name the key left under Folder `Open` and have to fool with (`Default`)? Why not name the key `FolderView` instead of `Open`?

Because of a Windows weirdness. When you click on the Fonts or Printers shortcut in Control Panel, it doesn't run the default command but looks for an `Open` command. If you don't have an open command, you get an error message!

How does calling (`Default`) FolderView work?

When it makes the context menu, Windows looks first to see if (Default) has a nonempty value. If it does, that name is used on the menu; otherwise the name of the key is used. This was put in to support foreign languages but I can use it, also.

I've Got It Under Control Panel

Who controls the past controls the future: who controls the present controls the past.

—George Orwell, *Nineteen Eighty-Four,* 1949

 As in Windows 3.x, an enormous number of user configuration options are encapsulated into Control Panel. Even more than in earlier versions, you have information-gathering utilities inside Control Panel—most notably, the Device Manager. Control Panel is so important it has its own chapter (Chapter 10) dealing with its more technical aspects and applets. Here, I'll give you an overview and discuss three of the more basic and less technical applets in detail.

A Fistful of Applets

It is now quite lawful for a Catholic woman to avoid pregnancy by a resort to mathematics, though she is still forbidden to resort to physics and chemistry.

—H. L. Mencken, speaking of birth control

You can access Control Panel in a variety of different ways. There is a `Control Panel` icon in `My Computer`. You can drag this icon to the Desktop or Start Menu and get another route. Or you can follow my advice in the section on Start Menu and add a dynamic list of Control Panel applets to the Start Menu. You can also type `Control` into a `Run` box or make a shortcut to the program `control.exe` in the `C:\windows` directory. In any event, Control Panel is merely a listing of individual programs called applets, each with its own icon.

In principle, Control Panel reads in its list of applets from three places:

1. Dynamic link libraries with the extension `.cpl` in the `C:\windows\system` folder.

2. `.cpl` files in the directory from which `control.exe` is loaded, normally `C:\windows`.

3. Programs entered in the Registry key `HKEY_CURRENT_USER\MMCPL`.

 That's the theory, but all the applets that come with Windows 95 and every third-party applet that I've seen use the first method. This is a big change from Windows 3.1, where it was possible to add an applet by having a routine in a driver file. Another difference from Windows 3.1 is that third-party programs can add their own tabs to Applet Property Sheets—for example, a mouse with three buttons could add an extra property sheet to the Mouse applet, the Microsoft Natural Keyboard adds some tabs to the Keyboard applet and the Plus! pack adds a sheet to Display Properties.

The applets installed with Windows 95 are normally among nineteen standard ones in fourteen `.cpl` files—four applets are in `main.cpl` and two each in `mmsys.cpl` and `sysdm.cpl`. The install diskettes also include `.cpl` files for TAPI if you have specialized telephony hardware and for the HP Jet Admin hardware. Here are the standard nineteen applets together with a twentieth that will be standard for users of the Internet who get the Internet Jump Start Kit:*

	Accessibility Options	Loaded from `access.cpl`. This optional module is mainly for the otherwise enabled. I discuss MouseKeys in Chapter 2. I discuss the applet in Chapter 10.
	Add New Hardware	Loaded from `sysdm.cpl`. This is the Hardware Installation wizard, which I'll discuss extensively in Chapter 10.
	Add/Remove Programs	Loaded from `appwiz.cpl`. Installation, Uninstall, StartUp Disk and more. This is the subject of the next section.
	Date/Time	Loaded from `timedate.cpl`. This is also accessible from the Time in the Notification Area. It sets the date, time, and time zone. See Chapter 10.
	Display	Loaded from `desk.cpl`. This is also accessible if you right-click on the Desktop and pick Properties. This controls display drivers, wallpaper, screen saver, and more. See Chapter 10.
	Fonts	Loaded from `main.cpl`. This is also accessible in My Computer. This is a shortcut to the Fonts Folder. I discussed it in Chapter 2.

---

* The Internet Jump Start Kit is included in the Plus! Pack and can be downloaded from the Microsoft World-Wide Web site. I discuss it in Chapter 4.

	Internet	Loaded from `inetcpl.cpl`. This is there if you load the Internet Jump Start kit. I discuss it in Chapter 4.
	Joystick	Loaded from `joy.cpl`. Discussed in Chapter 10.
	Keyboard	Loaded from `main.cpl`. Discussed in Chapter 10.
	Mail and Fax	Loaded from `mlcfg32.cpl`. This is also accessible if you right-click on the `Inbox` icon and pick Properties. This is the MS Exchange Settings Properties used to configure Exchange. I discuss it later in this chapter when I talk about Exchange.
	Microsoft Mail Postoffice	Loaded from `wgpocpl.cpl`.* Only relevant if you administer an MS Mail Post Office. I'll discuss it in the group of sections on Exchange. If you've never administered MS Mail and never expect to, just delete this file and the icon will disappear from Control Panel.
	Modems	Loaded from `modem.cpl`. Discussed in Chapter 10.
	Mouse	Loaded from `main.cpl`. Discussed in Chapter 10.
	Multimedia	Loaded from `mmsys.cpl`. Has tabs for Audio, Video, MIDI, CD Music, and Advanced. The Audio tab alone is accessible if you right-click on the volume icon in the Notification Area and choose Adjust Audio Properties. Discussed in Chapter 10.
	Network	Loaded from `netcpl.cpl`. This is also accessible if you right-click on Network Neighborhood and pick Properties. Discussed in Chapter 10.

---

* wgpo = WorkGroup PostOffice

	Passwords	Loaded from `password.cpl`. This controls multiple user profiles and is discussed three sections from now. If you are on a single user machine and forced to login when you don't want to, the way to turn it off is in the Network applet and not this applet (discussed in Appendix F).
	Printers	Loaded from `main.cpl`. This is also accessible in `My Computer`. This is a shortcut to the Printers Folder. I'll discuss it in the section after next.
	Regional Settings	Loaded from `intl.cpl`. Controls formatting of numbers, currency, date, and time. Discussed in Chapter 10.
	Sound	Loaded from `mmsys.cpl`. This is where you can waste an inordinate amount of time trying to figure out what kind of whoosh you want to hear every time you minimize a window. Discussed in Chapter 10.
	System	Loaded from `sysdm.cpl`. This is also accessible if you right-click on `My Computer` and pick Properties. The Mother of All Applets, this includes Device Manager and it's where you go to set up multiple hardware profiles. Discussed extensively in Chapter 10.

It is worth repeating that a number of applets are the Property sheets of system objects and so accessible by choosing `Properties` from a context menu or by `Alt+Double Click`. Explicitly, Display is Desktop properties, System is `My Computer` properties, Mail and Fax is Inbox properties, Network is Network Neighborhood properties and Date/Time Settings are accessible by double-clicking the Time.

Besides these applets, the Plus! Pack installs a second applet: **Desktop Themes** (in `themes.cpl`) in addition to **Internet.** Office 95 installs **Find Fast** (in `findfast.cpl`) and many database programs including Office 95 install **32 bit ODBC** (in `odbccp32.cpl`). Many other programs will no doubt add their own applets. Some Win 3.1 drivers have Win 3.1 `.cpl` files that can be read by Windows 95.

We owe to Matt Koenig (as reported in Livingston and Staub's *Windows 95 Secrets*) the command line syntax for loading a particular tab of a particular applet. This syntax is useful if you want to place it in a shortcut to use on the Desktop or in the Start Menu.

The syntax for starting an applet is

```
control cpl-name applet-name,number
```

where *cpl-name* is the name (including the extension) of the `.cpl` file that contains the applet. I listed the `.cpl` for each applet in the earlier list. *Applet* is the name as it appears under the icon and in the list with spaces and all if the name is "Mail and Fax" or "Regional Settings." *Number* is the number of the tab you want with labeling starting with zero. So, for example, if you want to start up Device Manager (which is the second tab and so numbered 1 with zero-based counting), you place the following as the command in a shortcut

```
control sysdm.cpl system,1
```

and the Appearance tab in Display Properties would be

```
control desk.cpl display,2
```

The Plus! Pack adds a tab to the Display applet but you ignore this in the tab count. Indeed, I don't know how to load this applet with the `Plus!` tab in front. The tab shift doesn't seem to work with the Mail and Fax applet.

Software Installation

> An autobiography is an obituary in serial form with the last installment missing.
>
> —Quentin Crisp, *The Naked Civil Servant*

The `Add/Remove Programs` Applet (see Figure 3-55) serves many purposes:

- There is a `StartUp disk` tab that can be used to try to start your system in case of emergency. You probably made one when you installed Windows. I talk about what's on that disk in Chapter 8. One warning—you'll need the original diskettes 1 and 2 or the CD (and if you have Drive Space 3 installed, you'll need the Plus CD or diskettes) to make the StartUp disk. You'll be asked for them. You'd think there would at least be an option to store the files you need for the StartUp disk on your hard disk.

- There's an `Install . . .` button on the `Install/Uninstall` tab. All this does is look successively in the root directory of any diskette and CD drives you have for a program called `setup.exe` or `install.exe` and then offer to run it. This should successfully locate about 80 percent of programs, but figure 20 percent will do something silly like put the setup in a subdirectory or name it something like `foostall.exe`. You may want to look at the section on "Stupid File Type Tricks" for an alternate, more efficient way to handle installs.

- There's an Uninstall list on the `Install/Uninstall` tab. Highlight a program in it and choose `Add/Remove. . . .` At a minimum you should be offered a complete Uninstall. Some programs will take the `Add` part in the button seriously and also let you install extra components from this list. By the way, don't be fooled into thinking that the Uninstall list is limited to programs that you installed through the `Install. . .` button or that any program installed via that button will have an Uninstall. Uninstall routines and their registration with the system is a function of the Setup program and will work or not equally well if Setup is run from the `Install. . .` button, by hand, or by an Autorun program when you pop the CD into the drive. The good news is that for a program to get the Windows 95 logo, it is required to have an Uninstall routine that it registers with the system.

- The `Windows Setup` tab can be used to add or remove programs that are part of the core of Windows itself. But it can also be used to install some of the extra goodies on the Windows CD and other programs that will tell you to install components that way.

 The procedure for installing extras from the Windows CD is a little tricky, so let me explain how to install one of my favorite little tools for talking across the network—Winchat.

1. Look through the CD for installable components. They will have the extension `.inf` so Find File on that will be useful. In this case if your CD is D:, you'll find `winchat.inf` in `D:\other\chat`. If you are installing from a diskette you can skip step 2.

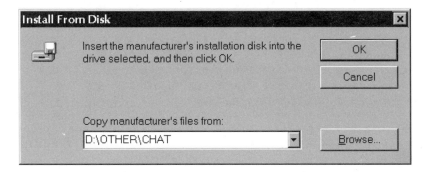

Figure 3-53. Picking the directory

2. Be sure to use Explorer to look at a file in the directory with the `.inf`. For example, you might double-click on the `.txt` file in that directory. This action is necessary to be sure that the system thinks that `D:\other\chat` is the current directory on `D:`. If it doesn't when it comes time to copy files, setup will get royally confused!*

3. Call up the `Add/Remove` Programs applet, jump to the `Windows Setup` tab and hit the `Have Disk. . .` button. Browse to the directory `D:\other\chat` and double-click on the `.inf` file and pick OK (Figure 3-53). In the resulting dialog (Figure 3-54) you may be tempted to just click OK since the listed program is what you want but you must first check the box next to the program you want!

4. You've completed the install but you might think that since you installed the program from the Windows Setup and it is from the Windows CD after all, that the Uninstall is also done through that tab. Nope. Chat is added to the same list where third-party programs go on the `Install/Uninstall` tab (see Figure 3-55).

It can't be emphasized too strongly how revolutionary the logo requirement for Uninstall routines is. The installing program is the right one to do the Uninstall. It will know a lot more than some special "Uninstall" utility. Within a short period, these utilities will be a less than fond memory of worse days past. Bravo, Microsoft!

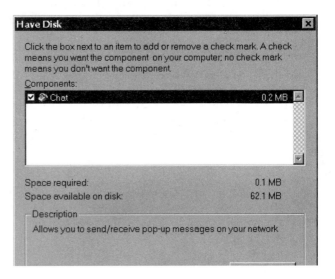

Figure 3-54. Check the box!

Printers

An editor is someone who separates the wheat from the chaff and then prints the chaff.

—Adlai Stevenson

---

* Erwin: Oh, goody, a bug!

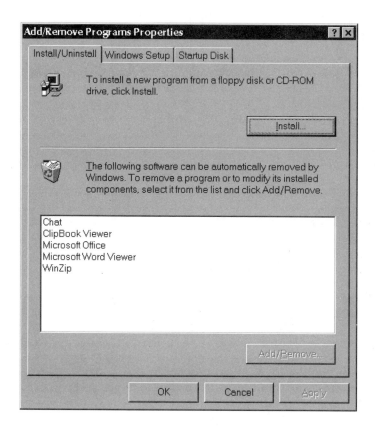

Figure 3-55. The Uninstall list

The Printers Folder allows you to install printers and to access individual printer controls that let you adjust parameters and to control the way documents spool. If you drag a Printer icon to the Desktop and then drag a document to that icon or to the icon within the Printers Folder, the document will print, assuming the program that made the document registered a print routine.

I'm going to explain to you how to install a Printer. To illustrate some of the good stuff in Windows 95 and because local printer installation is similar, I'll install a Network Printer.

1. Open the Printers Folder and click on the `Add Printers` icon. This invokes the Add Printer wizard. You `OK` through the first introductory panel.

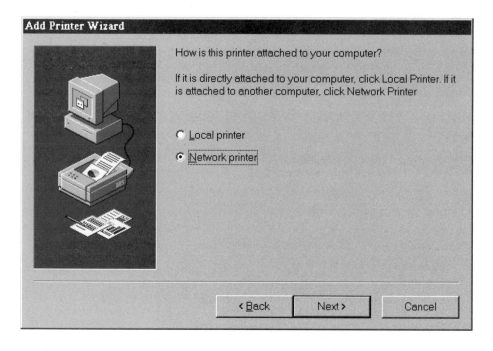

2. In the next dialog you need to pick whether the Printer is a local printer—that is, attached to your machine—or a network printer, that is, a separate network node or a printer attached to another machine on the network. If you pick local printer, Windows pauses to construct a database of printers and then displays a list of manufacturer/models to choose from.

3. If you pick Network Printer, you get a dialog that asks for the Printer name and also asks "Do you print from MS-DOS based programs?" You can browse the network to find the network printer as shown here. For a printer to show, the owner of the machine it is attached to has to have turned on sharing for it.

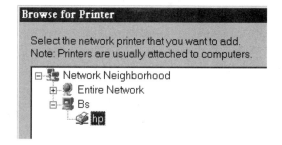

4. If you answered Yes to the print from DOS query, you next get a panel explaining your need to "capture" a printer port; that is, assign a real port to it to fool DOS programs into sending output that Windows captures and shuffles off to the Network. You hit a Capture Printer Port... button to actually pick the port as shown here. For a local printer, instead of capturing a port, you get a dialog where you assign a port to the printer.

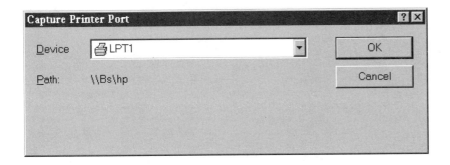

5. In the next to last panel of the Add Printer wizard, you get to name the Printer. This is the caption that appears in the Printers folder and the name that appears in the drop-down list in File/Print dialogs. By all means use a descriptive name like "Fourth-Floor Broom Closet Printer." Be sure to choose the radio button at the bottom asking for a test printer page. If the network printer is also attached to a Windows 95 machine, the drivers are copied from the other machine! Otherwise, you'll need to pick manufacturer/model to get the right driver!

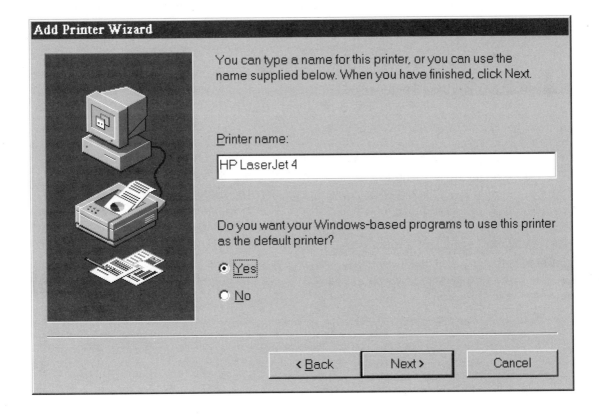

6. Success!! Be sure to adjust the parameters in the Printer Property sheet (which I'll get to in a moment). If you answer No to the question on this panel, you're thrown into the Print Troubleshooting part of Windows help. If that doesn't solve your problem, try the Enhanced Print Troubleshooter. It's on the Windows CD in the directory \Other\Misc\EPTS. If you have printer problems later, call up Windows help, go to the Index tab, and find Print Troubleshooting.

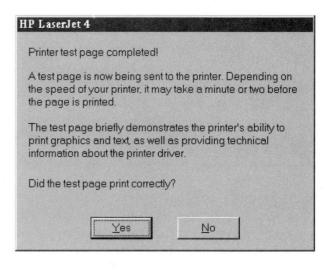

You'll want to check your Printer's Property sheet as soon as you install it. You can invoke it by choosing Properties from the Printer icon's context menu, from the File menu in the Printers folder, or from the File menu of the window that opens if you double-click on as printer. These are also the places you find an item marked Set as Default, which lets you change which printer is the default.

The actual dialog is shown in Figure 3-56 with one of the subdialogs superimposed. Looking at the tabs will give you an idea of the kinds of options there are. Device Options is where you go if you have a nonstandard amount of memory or other hardware enhancements.

These days, with True Type fonts, font cartridges are about as common as the passenger pigeon, so you can probably ignore that tab. The Sharing tab is where you turn on the ability of other users on the network to use that printer. The General tab has one important choice for users of a shared printer—you can specify a special page to be used as a separator between print jobs. The one place you certainly want to look is the dialog on the top in Figure 3-56, which you get by hitting the Spool Settings. . . button on the Details tab. If your goal is to get your machine back as soon as possible rather than to get output as soon as possible make sure that the radio button marked "Start printing after last page is spooled" is chosen.

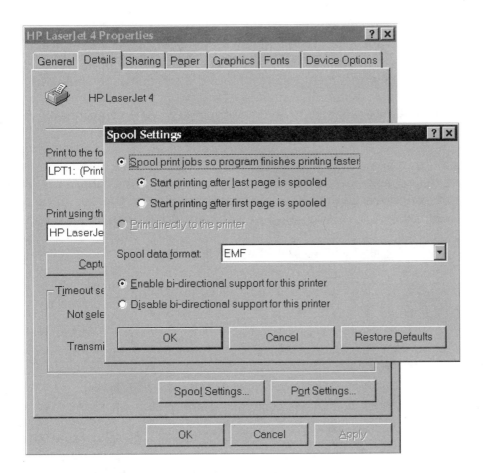

Figure 3-56. The Printer properties and Spooler Settings dialogs

 The Spool data format drop-down involves an interesting enhancement in Windows 95. Print data is now normally spooled in a metafile format,* which allows the driver to send as much data as possible in a high-level format that lets the printer do the translation to dots rather than sending everything over the parallel port as individual dots.

---

* EMF = Enhanced MetaFile

One final printer tip: Be sure to install the Generic/Text printer. The Manufacturer is `Generic` and the model is `Generic/Text Only`. You'll want to be sure to assign it to the port `FILE:`. It allows you print the ASCII text part of a document to a text file and is sometimes the only way to get such output. It doesn't always do exactly what you'd like, but it is a vast improvement over the similarly named driver in Windows 3.1. When you choose this printer to print, you'll get a dialog asking you what file you want to print to.

But the dialog that you get to choose the file to print to is the Windows 3.1 File Save dialog without support for long filenames or the other goodies in the Windows 95 dialog. Given that this is part of the operating system, I'd call the fact that this dialog isn't the Windows 95 dialog a bug.

I realize that it can sometimes be foolish to demand consistency, but it seems a bit strange to me that if you go to install a modem, the first manufacturer is `(Standard Modem Types)` and if you install a video driver, the first choice is `(Standard Display Types)` but that the `Generic/Text` printer driver is buried under that well-known manufacturer `Generic`.

User Profiles

> Teenage boys . . . have only a brief season of exhilarating liberty between control by their mothers and control by their wives.

> —Camille Paglia, in *Esquire,* Oct. 1991

Windows 95 has an optional feature called Multiple User Profiles. When it is set up appropriately, users can have their own Desktop, their own Start Menu, their own list of recently used documents, and their settings for things like wallpaper and Desktop colors. Moreover, third-party programs can save their options in a way that the ones that should be user-specific can be different for different users. This is obviously useful in a business setting where some computer may be used by multiple people, but it is also useful for home users, where each of your teenage boys can have the exhilarating liberty of choosing their own wallpaper!

The first step in turning on User Profiles is to invoke the Passwords applet in Control Panel and shift to the tab marked `User Profiles` (Figure 3-57). Pick the bottom radio button, which lets the user customize settings. By doing this, those settings stored in the HKEY_CURRENT_USER key of the Registry, which includes Desktop wallpaper, colors, sound schemes, and so on, can be made user-dependent. The two checkboxes let you decide whether the Desktop icons and the Start Menu are user-dependent.

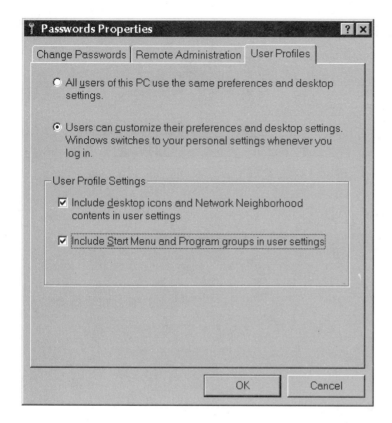

Figure 3-57. Turning on User Profiles

You should give some thought to the issue of letting the Start Menu be user-dependent, because some programs will only install themselves in the current user's Start Menu and someone may need to take responsibility for updating the Start Menu's other users by hand. I'll explain what is involved in a moment.

Once you've turned on this option and rebooted, you'll be greeted by the dialog in Figure 3-58. Each user must pick a user name and a password upon logging on the first time.

It is important that the question in Figure 3-59 be answered correctly. The users are asked if they want to have individualized settings on the machine. They should answer Yes if you turned on User Profiles for them. Anyone answering No will wind up with common default settings so that changes any user makes affects all other users with these default options.

Welcome to Windows   ? ☒

Type a user name and password to log on to Windows.   OK

User name: CTO Mao   Cancel

Password: ✶✶✶✶✶✶✶✶

Figure 3-58. The Windows Logon

Windows Networking   ☒

You have not logged on at this computer before. Would you like this computer to retain your individual settings for use when you log on here in the future?

Yes   No

Figure 3-59. Psst—Answer Yes

Since I answered `Yes` to this question, this very first time I logged on Windows 95 did the following. It made a directory called `C:\windows\profiles\cto mao` using my login name as part of the directory name. In that directory, it placed two hidden files and four subdirectories. The hidden files are `user.dat` and its backup `user.da0`. These are the user half of the Registry. Initially they are just the default `user.dat` files with some obvious changes—for example, the entries that tell Windows where my Start Menu is will be adjusted to the new Start Menu location. Any changes I make while I'm running will get stored in the `user.dat` in my directory, which is why I can have different wallpaper from Sarah.

The four directories correspond to the Desktop, the collection of Recent Documents, the user shortcuts in Network Neighborhood, and the Programs in Start Menu. Windows no longer builds my Start Menu from the directory `C:\windows\Start Menu`. Instead, it uses `C:\windows\profiles\cto mao\Start Menu`. It does some copying from the default but not all files. For example, it only copies the shortcuts from the default Desktop to mine and not any documents that might have been there. Finally, a password file `ctomao.pwl` is created in the `C:\windows` directory.

This is a great first step in giving multiple users on a PC control over their environment, but there are several gotchas you need to be aware of:

- There is no effective password protection, in that all users have access to all files on the machine. Thus, a savvy user could modify another user's setup with ease.

Unless, of course, you enable system policies and prevent your teenagers from running an MS-DOS prompt, or executing any Windows app (except for the ones that you allow ahead of time). You could also prevent them from changing the Desktop, rooting around in My Computer, changing the resolution, and so on.

Gimme a break, Billy. If I tried that with my teenager, she'd get a boot diskette and delete the darned .pol files that enforce system policies. Windows 95 security may be effective against confused corporate drones, but it is not serious enough to defeat a determined teenager.

- There is no built-in way to remove a user once one has left. Instead, you need to delete the user's directory under C:\windows\profiles and the *.pwl file. Remembering the .pwl file is important if you want to restore a system to a single user setup not requiring logins. Windows 95 will allow bootup with no login only if you have it set up to use Windows passwords, the Windows password is blank, and there is at most one .pwl file.

- You are likely to need to install the same program multiple times, once for each user—you can use the same program directory so you won't have many duplicate files. Otherwise, you'll need to copy the Start Menu items from one user's Start Menu to another's by hand. For example if foowrite installs Start Menu items in C:\windows\profiles\cto mao\Start Menu\programs\foowrite, you may need to copy the shortcuts by hand to a new directory called C:\windows\profiles\sarah\Start Menu\ programs\foowrite if Sarah also wants them on her menu.

- There are some other subtle gotchas. For example, while most directories are user-specific, SendTo is not, and if one user renames the SendTo directory, the feature won't even work on other user's setups until their Registries are modified by hand.

One thing really bugs me. The option on whether Recycle Bin collects deleted files has to be the same for all users. I'm so competent (ahem!) that I prefer having it off, but Sarah insists that for the sake of Rush and Igor, it needs to be on. There are lots of other settings that are systemwide that I think should be user-specific.

Hey, boss. I often come to a machine with the password dialog up and want to turn the machine off. Do I have to login and then pick Shutdown from the Start Menu? Or can I just turn it off?

 If possible, you should always run Shutdown but there is no need to login. Hit `Ctrl+Alt+Del` and you get a dialog you can pick Shutdown from!

DOS v'danya

> DOS is like the faithful worker who's agreed to delay retirement.
> He'd love it if the company would bring in some younger blood,
> but they can't seem to find anyone to replace him.

—Scott Spanbauer

 The Mother of All Windows Books, my tome on Windows 3.1, had twenty-two pages on DOS over Windows. Now that DOS is integrated into Windows and Windows's DOS support has substantial improvements from the ability to start Windows applications from the DOS prompt, to the windowed DOS button bar, to scalable fonts, to MS-DOS exclusive mode, to a comprehensive Property sheet, you'd think that I'd have at least forty pages. Instead you'll find fifteen (not counting the discussion of DOS commands), fewer than in the earlier book! How come? Isn't DOS important? That's the right question. DOS isn't so important any more. I have a few DOS applications I've lived with for ten years or more. I suspect you may have some also, but they tend to run fine with Windows 95, and I'll bet there are a lot fewer than there were two or even one year ago.

 One reason that problems with DOS sessions are less an issue than they used to be is that there is just more memory available. A lot of programs that used to take valuable DOS memory are run from protected mode even in DOS sessions and take zero DOS memory: network, CD, and mouse drivers come to mind. On the three machines I currently have running in my office, all have almost exactly 600K (that's about 614,000 bytes, not 600,000 since 1 KB is 1,024 bytes) free in a fresh DOS box. Under Windows 3.1, 600K would be regarded as spectacular. And all of those systems have compressed disk and network support at the DOS prompt, two have CDs and sound cards, and one of those two has a scanner.

My gang is going to start by talking about the Property sheet for DOS programs—the Windows 95 repository for what used to be in a PIF (Program Information file). Then we'll talk about DOS commands and the DOS batch language. The surprise is that with the new `start` command, DOS batch language has become a bare-bones but fairly useful batch language for all of Windows. Finally, I'll talk about DOS exclusive mode.

Even if you don't use DOS programs, you should care about DOS for two reasons—for certain kinds of file operations, by far the fastest way to do what you want is to use the DOS command line. And DOS batch language can be useful even for winapps.

Take a Deep Pif

Program Information Files (`.pif`) were first introduced with IBM's Topview, a clunky text-based task switcher that IBM tried to foist on the world in the mid-80s. Its sole lasting legacy is the PIF, which has gone through many changes since. Windows 95 expands the information that can be stored in PIFs and replaced the gangly Windows PIF editor with a Property Sheet metaphor (hooray).

Whenever you run a DOS program or batch file directly, Windows first looks for a `.pif` file with the same name in the program's directory. If that fails, it looks in the `C:\windows\pif` directory, then `C:\windows`, then `C:\windows\system`, and finally the directories in the DOS path in order.

If it fails to find an existing `.pif`, it makes a `.pif` for the program giving it the same name but the extension `pif`. If Windows has to make a `.pif`, it looks for the name of the `.exe` in the ASCII text file `C:\windows\inf\apps.inf` in the [PIF95] section of that file and uses that information to make a `.pif`—I'll discuss the format of `apps.ini` later. If it doesn't find an entry there, it looks for a `_default.pif` file in the same sequence of directories it originally looked for a `.pif`. Failing that, it uses some defaults built into Windows itself. You'll have a `_default.pif` if you upgraded over Windows 3.x—otherwise, you'll likely not have one. If you care about the defaults, you can copy a convenient `.pif` like the `dosprmpt.pif` that you'll find in `C:\windows` and customize that.

That a `dosprmpt.pif` is still there is a weird sort of compatibility. Under Windows 3.1, the MS-DOS entry in the Main Program Manager group pointed to that `.pif` file (although even there it was otherwise not used). Under Windows 95, there is still a `dosprmpt.pif`, but it is *never* used (unless you explicitly click on it of course). The MS-DOS Prompt entry on the Start Menu, of course corresponds to its own `.pif` file, namely `C:\windows\Start`

Figure 3-60. A DOS session

`Menu\programs\MS-DOS Prompt.pif`. By the way, if you just type in `command.com`, Windows uses an entry in `dosapps.inf` unless you've previously run command and have a `command.pif` in the right place.

Once Windows makes a `.pif`, you can customize it to your heart's content. If you'd like to make a `.pif` directly, you can copy the DOS program or batch file in Explorer to the same directory, and it will make a `.pif` (although you'll have to remove the extra `Shortcut to MS-DOS` that it prepends to the program name if you want this shortcut to get used when you double-click on the program). If a `.pif` exists that would get used for the program if you double-clicked on it, a copy of that `.pif` is used for the new shortcut.

And of course, if you double-click on a `.pif` itself, no matter where it is, or what its name, it runs the program it is a shortcut to.

Following is the structure of the tabs in a `.pif`.

General Settings

> Never let the other fellow set the agenda.
>
> —James Baker

If you look at the Properties sheet of a running application, the first tab is the one shown in Figure 3-61. If you ask for the Properties of an actual PIF file, there is a General tab in first place with the standard ability to change attributes, see file date, and so on, and this is the second tab. I'll number tabs using the count that puts `Program` first.

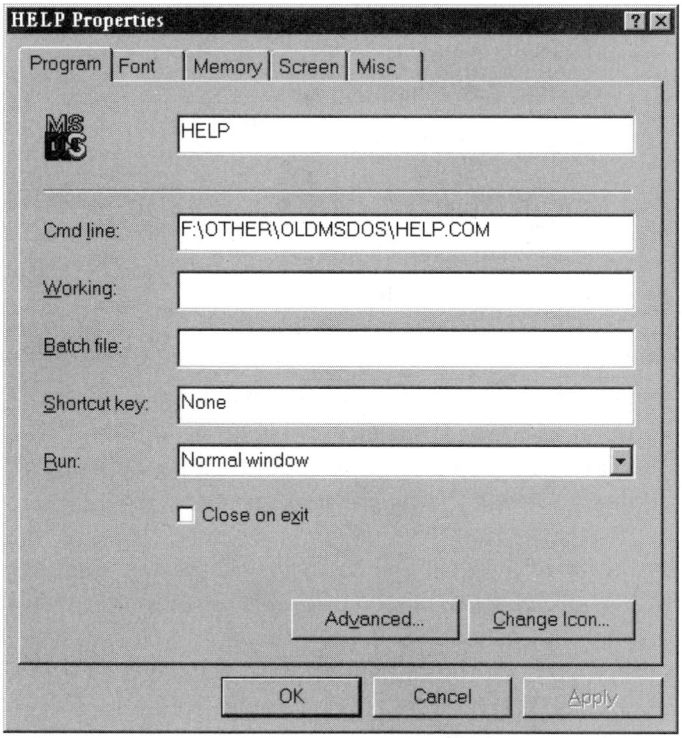

Figure 3-61. PIF Program tab

The top of the tab shows the icon used (more on this later) and the name used in the caption. The caption is both used when the program is running in a windowed DOS session and on the Taskbar. Actually, Windows is so smart that if a program other than the initial one is running in the session, it adds the program name—see, for example, Figure 3-60, where Windows knows that DOS 6.22 Help loaded Qbasic to do its thing.

Four of the next five fields (`Cmdline`, `Working`, `Shortcut key`, and `Run`) are essentially identical to the fields in a Windows shortcut (`Target`, `Start in`, `Shortcut key`, and `Run`). When the `.pif` is run, either directly or by running a program that associates to the `.pif`, Windows switches to the directory in Working and tries to run the command in `Cmdline`. If you include a ? in the command in `Cmdline`, when the .pif is run, Windows will pop up a box inviting you to type in parameters for the command.

 But of all the dumb things, this parameter box takes the cake. It doesn't have a browse button to let you search for a file, but I was hoping that it would be a drag-drop target so I could at least drag and drop a filename from Explorer. Not only isn't it that, but the dialog is system modal—that's a fancy way of saying that you can't access *any* other program until you fill in the parameters Windows is asking for. Not only can't you drag and drop anything to the dialog, you can't even consult Explorer once the dialog is up!

The kind of window the program runs in (normal, minimized, or maximized) is mainly determined by the `Run` drop-down in the Program tab, but is also impacted by choices in the Font and Screen tabs. The `Batch file` field lets you fill in a batch file to load before the program is run. You might want to load `doskey` that way. Actually, if all you want to load is doskey, just put `C:\windows\command\doskey` in this field; it may say `Batch file` but it'll run any command.

The checkbox called `Close on exit` determines whether the window closes when the program is finished or stays open with the word `Finished` prepended to the window caption. For DOS programs that just display some information on the screen (like mem) you'd want to leave the box unchecked, but you want to check it for most DOS programs.

If you want to change the icon used by the `.pif`, you hit the `Change Icon...` button and get the dialog shown in Figure 3-62. This elegant dialog is also used for shortcuts and in the Edit File Type Actions dialog. It displays all the icons in numeric order. If you ever need to place an icon number in a Registry entry, you can count them off in this dialog, remembering that the first entry is number 0. The `Browse...` button lets you look for another source of icons. The standard sources are `.ico` files, `.dll`s and `.exe`s.

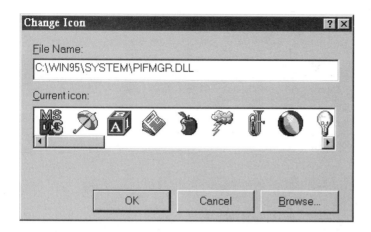

Figure 3-62. The Change Icon Dialog

Faking 'em Out

> Sincerity: if you can fake it, you've got it made.

> —Daniel Schorr, journalist

The Advanced. . . button on the Program tab leads to an Advanced Programs Setting dialog (Figure 3-67) that is mainly concerned with DOS Exclusive mode, something I'll discuss in "The Penalty Box." But, here I want to note one checkbox on the dialog that you might miss. It says ☑ Prevent MS-DOS-based programs from detecting Windows . Its intention is to fool DOS programs, mainly games, that will run fine under Windows 95, but refuse to run because they have code that tests for Windows and posts a message that says, "I don't do no steenkin' Windows," if you try. The code is there because there are problems with Windows 3.x, sometimes only memory problems, and the vendor wants to preempt tech support calls. If you have a program that gives such a message, at least try this option before resorting to DOS exclusive mode.

Fonts

The Font tab concerns the font used to display the text in the DOS session when it is running in a window. The sessions can use one of nine bitmap fonts or one of eight sizes of Courier New TrueType font. If you have installed the Plus! Pack, there are seventeen sizes of Lucida Console TrueType in place of Courier New. All the fonts have the full IBM-extended ASCII character set. The nine bitmapped fonts come in sizes 4×6, 5×12, 6×8, 7×12, 8×8, 8×12, 10×18, 10×20, and 12×16, listed as width by height. That means that a DOS screen with 80 columns and 25 lines with a 10×20 font will be 800×500 pixels—too

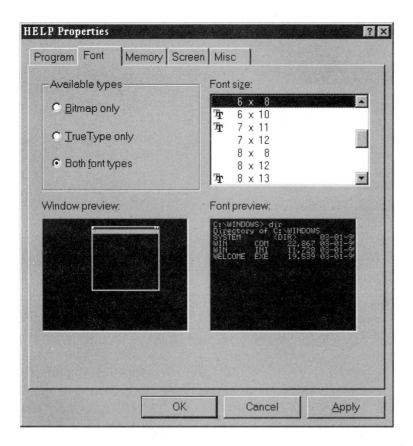

Figure 3-63. PIF font tab

big for a 640 × 480 screen and even too large for 800 × 600 if you remember the space needed for the title bar and toolbar. The bitmapped fonts are Terminal fonts designed by Bitstream and used for DOS sessions over Windows for many, many years. These fonts are all stored in a single file called `dosapp.fon`.

 This is a big improvement over the five files used for DOS's bitmapped fonts in Windows 3.1 as documented in *The Mother of All Windows Books.* Don't be surprised if you look really hard for this font file on disk and can't find it. It's in a hidden, system file in the `C:\windows\fonts` directory, which is itself marked with the system attribute. Since the font is not installed into Windows as a font accessible to Windows applications, it won't appear in the Fonts folder (many of the other `.fon` files that are also hidden and system files are installed as fonts for winapps and will appear in the fonts folder). To see it, you'll need to go to a DOS prompt and use the right switches on the `dir` command.

The DOS TrueType font with straight Windows comes in sizes $5 \times 12, 6 \times 12, 7 \times 14,$
$7 \times 15, 8 \times 16, 10 \times 18, 10 \times 20,$ and 12×22. Since there is a bitmapped 10×18
font, the Courier is not used unless you have only TrueType selected. If you have the Plus!
pack, its DOS TrueType font has sizes $2 \times 4, 3 \times 5, 4 \times 6, 4 \times 7, 5 \times 8, 5 \times 9, 6 \times 10,$
$7 \times 11, 7 \times 12, 8 \times 13, 8 \times 14, 9 \times 15, 10 \times 16, 11 \times 18, 12 \times 20, 13 \times 22,$ and
$16 \times 27.$

Gimme a break, 2 x 4, 3 x 5, 4 x 6, and 16 x 27 are ludicrous—added for
demos and marketing purposes, not for real users.

The extremely small sizes are very handy sometimes. If you have a compile
running in a DOS box, you can make the font really small and place it down in the
corner of your screen. Seeing the little lines down there scrolling away lets you
know that your compile is proceeding OK. If they stop, then you can quickly
Alt+Enter to a full-screen mode to see what the problem might be. The larger
sizes can be helpful for people who don't see well.

You'll notice that the Lucida options include many small pixel heights—eight sizes smaller
than the twelve-pixel-high smallest Courier font. That's no coincidence. Courier is a font
with serifs and Lucida is sans serif (see the samples in Figure 3-64 taken from actual screen
shots). The serifs are untenable at small pixel counts.

from the Help menu, Courier	from the Help menu, Lucida Console	from the Help menu, Terminal

Figure 3-64. A Tale of three fonts

Courier is a remarkably ugly font created to work with typewrite-sized type and typewriter
technology. Although Lucida is better, it just doesn't look as good as the hand-tuned bitmapped
Terminal fonts. I tend to run my DOS sessions in the bitmapped 10 x 18 font. Works well on a
1024 x 768 screen.

The `Auto` font choice adjusts the font size to fit the window as you adjust the screen size. This is a great idea in principle but doesn't work well in practice. First, as you resize, the screen jerks all over the place because the height-to-width ratio jumps all over the place (unless you have TrueType only chosen). Secondly, when auto is turned on, I'm sometimes totally unable to resize the screen.

You'd think if Microsoft was going to bother to do autofont, they'd do it right, the way it is done on several other computer systems. You need a font that allows independent scaling in the two directions and then the font just resizes to fit the stretched screen.

Memory Settings

Figure 3-65 shows the last three tabs with a miscellany of settings.

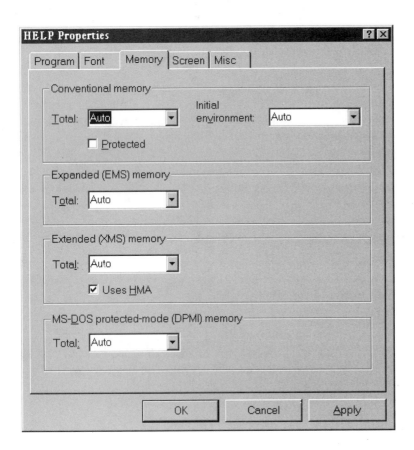

Figure 3-65. A tale of three tabs

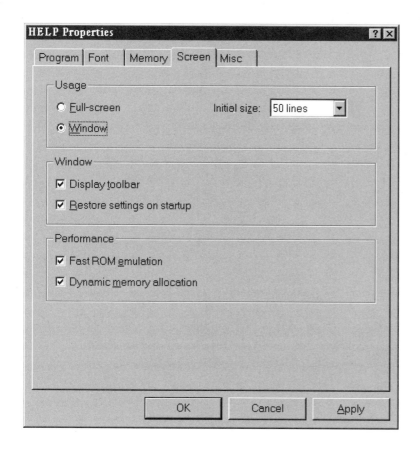

Figure 3-65. *(continued)*

 Finally, with Windows 95, we see the beginning of the end of the DOS reliance on weird memory schemes with weird names to overcome the 640K barrier built into the first PC. No more EMS. No more XMS. No more UMB. No more IRT. No more HMA. Hooray!

 Igor, there's no IRT memory spec.

 Sure there is, boss. Hearing about IRT brings back memories of taking da subway from my mom's house in Benhoist to da Bronx.

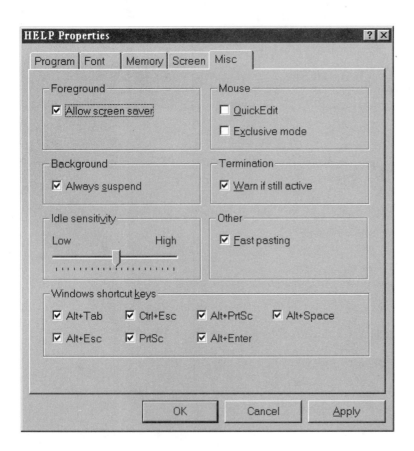

Figure 3-65. *(continued)*

As long as you run DOS programs, you can't totally ignore these arcane memory issues, but Windows will usually handle them pretty well for you. The default settings (first part of Figure 3-65) for memory usage is set at `Auto`, which allows Windows to dole out memory resources as needed. A few rude programs will grab all the free EMS and XMS memory when they load and so should be given a fixed ration, but mainly, you can ignore this tab.

The Toolbar

New to Windows 95, windowed DOS sessions come with a toolbar, which provides considerable functionality and which integrates well with the window (see Figure 3-60). You

can turn the display of the toolbar on/off with a checkbox in the Screen tab and by a choice on the Title bar context menu. The functions are shown in Figure 3-66.

⊤T 6 x 10 ▾ Font dropdown	▢ Mark	▤ Copy	▤ Paste
✛ Full screen	▤ Properties	▱ Background	A Font Tab

Figure 3-66. The DOS session toolbar buttons

The Mark/Copy/Paste buttons work in concert—Mark brings up a cursor so you can mark a block with the mouse, Copy copies the text to the clipboard, and Paste will send text from the clipboard to the DOS program through the keyboard. The Full Screen button jumps you to full screen mode, as does `Alt+Enter`. The only easy way to get from full screen back to windowed mode is to use `Alt+Enter`, although from the Windows screen, you can call up the Property sheet of a full screen DOS session by right-clicking on the Taskbar button for that session and shift to windowed mode there. There are two ways to change the font from the toolbar—with the drop-down and with the button to the Property sheet with the Font tab up. The switched on Background button lets the program run in the Background; otherwise it will be suspended when you switch away from it.

Screen Setting

The Screen tab (the second part of Figure 3-65) has three panels: `Usage` lets you choose whether the initial display is a Full screen session or windowed DOS and pick the number of screen lines. `Window` has a checkbox on whether you want the toolbar (I can't believe you wouldn't!) and one called `Restore settings on startup` that I'll discuss in a moment.

I dunno, sure seems to me like the names of the `Window` and `Usage` got switched.

Nope. The checkboxes in `Window` only matter if you are in a windowed session.

The Performance panel means what it means so often in Windows—it's really a panel about troubleshooting. There are two options here that enhance performance and are turned on by default. If a DOS program is being flaky, try unchecking these and see if it helps.

 I can imagine the meeting that musta gone on in the office of Brad Silverberg, the head of the Windows 95 project. One of the engineers said, "You know, boss, we've got all these neat performance-boosting features that could cause problems under unusual circumstances. We should have Troubleshooting dialogs that let you check off options to turn them off." So the marketing guys said, "The public will think that if they have Troubleshooting dialogs, it must be because they have trouble. Lets call the dialogs Performance and have the options checked by default so the user unchecks them to turn them off. Whadya think, boss?" Brad started to sing, "You have to accentuate the positive. . ." and wondered if he could get Cole Porter to write an ad for Windows 95.

That leaves the "Restore settings on startup" option. You have to realize it means exactly what it says—the settings in question (we'll see which ones in a moment) are stored in the PIF file when the program exits. If the box is not checked, it also stores the settings in effect the last time you started up. If you don't check the box in the `.pif` before reloading the program, it will reload in the same place it was when last loaded, but if you do check it in the meantime, it will load with the settings in effect when the program exited.

Which settings? Well, let's see what happens when you press [?] and point at that option. You are informed "Restores window settings when you quit this program, including window size, position and font."

 Oy. I guess what the help writer meant was that it restores the settings to what they were when you last quit the program, but that isn't what it says.

 Worse, it's got the information wrong on what is saved. The window position is affected by this checkbox, and as long as you have the Run setting on the Program tab at Normal, so is the window size. But the window font, together with settings like Background and Run state, are saved when you exit and restored when you restart whether this box is checked or not. Oh, how I love a nice bug in the mornin'.

Not quite, my not-quite-living bug. If the font is set to Auto, then the font size is adjusted according to the window size, so in that case, the font is restored. In others cases, well, er . . ., er . . . oh, how I love a nice bug in the mornin'.

Other Settings

The final tab (last part of Figure 3-65) is called `Misc`—it is a hodgepodge of leftovers including:

Foreground: Windows 95 screen savers can even kick off from a full-screen DOS session. If the box here is unchecked and the program in question has focus (is the active application), then the screen saver won't; otherwise it will.

Background: If the item labeled `Always suspend` is unchecked, then the program will continue to run in the background; if it is checked it will stop running when you switch away from it.

Talk about poor design. There is a Background button on the toolbar whose meaning is the opposite of this checkbox. If the button is pushed in the box is unchecked, and if the box is unchecked the button is pushed out.

Idle Sensitivity: Oh, how the mighty have fallen. A fair number of Windows technical experts based their reputation on being able to compute the exact interplay of all the time-slice stuff built into Windows 3.1, and now they are reduced to a single slider. And guess what? Even it doesn't matter very often. Just leave it in the middle.

Mouse: `Quick Edit` is neat. When it is on, you can start marking by just pressing on the mouse. It would be neater if the right mouse button pasted, but—hey, what's there is good to have. Basically, if a DOS program doesn't support the mouse, you want this box checked. `Exclusive mode` turns off the mouse in all other programs including Windows. Avoid it if you possibly can.

Termination: Another neat setting. If `Warn if still active` is checked, you will be sent to the DOS program when you try to shutdown Windows. That's an improvement over Windows 3.x, since this actually takes you to the relevant DOS sessions. But even more is the option you should use with care to uncheck the box and have the DOS session automatically closed when you shutdown Windows. This setting also comes into play if you click the DOS windows close button. If it is unchecked, that will close the application; otherwise, it will issue a warning.

Other: Talk about ignominy. To be an Other setting on a Misc tab, you must be pretty random. In fact, Fast pasting is pretty simple and is one of those performance/troubleshooting things. Usually a program can accept keystrokes fast enough to keep up with the Fast Paste method. But sometimes it will beep or even go bananas when you try to paste in text from the clipboard. If that happens, try unchecking the box and see if it helps. The difference of speed of entry with the two methods is normally more than a factor of ten.

Windows shortcut keys: There are seven keys here that Windows normally wants for itself. Uncheck any key you want to go to the application instead.

The Apps.inf file

As a final topic in `.pif` files I want to discuss the somewhat technical issue I alluded to at the start of the section: If a premade `.pif` can't be found for a program, Windows uses information in `C:\windows\inf\apps.inf`. This file has the structure of a Windows 3.x `.ini` file—there are sections with names inside [ ] and items in the sections of the form `name=value`. There are two generic sections in the file called [`PIF95`] and [`Strings`] and other program-dependent sections. The syntax of the items in the [`PIF95`] section is

> `program=%title%,icon,icon_number,X,section,Y,Z`

where X,Y,Z are technical entries you can read about in the Windows Resource Kit. The entries can stop without specifying all options, and an option can be left blank by placing two commas next to each other. Here `%title%` is an indirect reference to an item in [`Strings`] that is used for the title bar caption for the program, `icon,icon_number` is the usual specification of an icon by giving a filename and the number of the icon in the file (starting with number 0), and `section` is a reference to a section of the `apps.inf` with additional information.

As an example, consider the references to Qbasic in the supplied `apps.inf` file:

```
[PIF95]
        QBASIC.EXE=%QBASIC.EXE%,moricons.dll,15,,QBASIC.EXE
[QBASIC.EXE]
        Params="?"
        LowMem=330
        EMSMem=None
        XMSMem=None
        Disable=win
[Strings]
        QBASIC.EXE="Microsoft QuickBASIC"
```

The first item says that caption title will be found in the Strings section and so the caption `Microsoft QuickBASIC` will get used. The sixteenth icon in `moricons.dll` is used and additional `.pif` information comes from the `section [QBASIC.EXE]`.

There is nothing sacred about these entries. If you try to run the old shareware program PC-Write whose name is `ed.exe` and the PIF insists on setting itself up as WPOffice Editor, just go ahead and edit the PIF. Alternatively, you can add your own entries to `apps.inf`. You wouldn't for a single machine but might if you were responsible for supporting a group of users.

Mom's Favorite DOS Commands

> Windows '95 requires so much in the way of system resources,
> it should be called HOGG'IN DOS.
>
> —Heard on the Net

 Here I get to talk about DOS commands. I can't help it—I'm a command line kinda gal. Sometimes the quickest way to get something done is to start up a DOS prompt and just do it. First, my top-ten list. Then a few more useful commands, but I'm not going to attempt complete lists of available and now-missing DOS commands. Also, DOS programs like `ftp`, which are really Internet utilities, will be discussed in Chapter 4.

Help

I'm not going to give you detailed syntax of all the commands. Help is available for any DOS command by typing its name followed by `/?`. There's also the full screen DOS help engine from DOS 6.2. You'll find it on the Windows CD in the directory `\other\oldmsdos`. Copy `help.com` and `help.hlp` to your `C:\windows\command` directory. You'll also need to copy `qbasic.exe`, since the 1K executable `help.com` is only a wrapper to load `qbasic` in a special read-only mode.

Mem

Sometimes you need to know how much free memory you have in your DOS sessions, if only for bragging rights. `Mem` is a great tool for that. The `/c` and `/d` parameters give impressive amounts of detail. `/p` tells it to pause after each screenful.

Start

This is new with Windows 95 and probably the most important new DOS element. The syntax is

```
start [options] prog_or_doc
```

where the options are /m for minimized, /max for maximized, and /w for wait. Normally when you run start it immediately returns to the DOS prompt or runs the next line in the batch file. With the /w switch it waits for the program it started to exit before continuing. See Figure 3-46 and the discussion of that batch file for an example of where the /w switch is needed. What appears after the options can be anything you could type into the Windows Run box—that means either a program with parameters or a doc file.

You can start any Windows program from the DOS prompt by typing its name. Start is more powerful in the following ways:

• It can start a new DOS session.

• You can specify a /m or /max switch.

• The command line gets passed to Windows without prior interpretation by DOS. That means you can have doc files, can refer to the system directory* (which is not normally in the DOS path), and can use apppaths and other Windows goodies.

The real use of start is in batch files, as I'll discuss shortly.

Edit

DOS and Windows have a tradition of bare-bones editors starting with edlin and continuing through Notepad. Edit has been a cludgy shell for qbasic until now, but it has suddenly blossomed. I'll discuss it in detail in the next chapter when I discuss Notepad and Wordpad. Check it out.

Edit isn't bad, but why did they name its help file, edit.hlp? It is not a Windows help file, and you'll get an error message if you double-click on it.

---

* Try typing sysedit and then start sysedit when your current directory is C:\.

Doskey

It's hard to figure out why Microsoft didn't build this into DOS rather than make it a program you have to know to run. Basically, if you are going to use the DOS command line, you want `doskey` loaded, which gives you standard editing and recall of previous commands. You can load `doskey` in your `autoexec.bat` and have it available in all DOS sessions. The command recall is independent in each window. If you use DOS a lot, check out `doskey`'s macro feature.

xcopy

`xcopy` has long been one of DOS's gems. There are so many options, they won't fit on a single twenty-five-line screen. It will not only copy files but whole directories, preserving the subdirectory structure. It uses extended memory to enable it to copy more efficiently. It understands long filenames (you have to put them in quotes to settle ambiguities if there are spaces). It understands UNC names. It's great for complicated copy actions that would be awkward using GUI tools.

 Here's a weird one. If you look in `C:\windows\command`, you'll find `xcopy.exe` and `xcopy32.exe`. The syntax and capabilities are identical (books that claim `xcopy32` understands long filenames and xcopy doesn't are wrong). `xcopy` is clearly just a shell that calls `xcopy32`. Why have two programs? To brag that `xcopy` is 32 bit? Weird, weird, weird.

dir

Don't forget the lowly `dir`. It, too, has a fistful of options, and because of redirection, it can do some useful things like send the contents of a directory to a file. I'd suggest that you add

```
set dircmd=/o/p
```

to your `autoexec.bat`. Check out the DOS 6.22 Help under `dir` and look at its Notes to see about `dircmd`. To have a directory of all files including hidden and system use `/a` with no :.

deltree

This does what the name advertises—it puts concrete galoshes around a whole branch of a tree and drops it in the deep blue sea. None of this wimpy Recycle Bin to rescue you if you foul up (the Norton utilities can save you by the way, usually even after the fact). Useful if used with extreme care. A single `deltree C:\` can ruin your whole day.

move and copy

Don't forget these two standbys.

 One advantage of using DOS to copy/move is that you are spared the graphic of the paper floating between folders. That graphic is really neat the first time you see it, but it gets old fast. Some vendor will make a mint selling randomized replacements for it—maybe dart throwing at a poster of big Bill.

Other DOS Commands

> Those who lord it over their fellows and toss commands in every direction
> and would boss the grass in the meadow about which way to bend in the wind
> are the most depraved kind of prostitutes.

— P. J. O'Rourke, *Parliament of Whores*

Ansi.sys

If you want to add color to full-screen DOS sessions, you want to place `ansi.sys` in your `config.sys`. There's a complete discussion of all the options and how to produce really fancy prompts in *The Mother of All PC Books*. For now, I note that you can turn DOS session text to yellow on blue by doing the following. First in `config.sys` add:

```
device=C:\windows\command\ansi.sys
```

In your `autoexec.bat` replace `prompt=$p$g` by

```
prompt=$e[1;33;44m$p$g
```

Memmaker

If you have DOS 6.22 on your disk, Windows install places `memmaker.exe` in your `C:\windows` directory, together with a DOS exclusive mode `.pif` for it. Otherwise, it is on the Windows CD in `\other\oldmsdos`. In theory, you can run `memmaker` to have it adjust your `config.sys` and `autoexec.bat` to increase free memory in a DOS session over Windows. It can't hurt to try if you have quite a bit in your `config.sys` and `autoexec.bat`, but keep your old system files, since you may not gain anything. On one test system, I started with 568K free in a DOS session over Windows. When I ran `memmaker`, it assured me that it had gained 20K but I now had 553K in my DOS sessions over Windows! The problem was that `memmaker` (being a DOS 6.22 program) doesn't understand anything about Windows. It wound up placing so much in UMB space that

Windows didn't have enough room for some of its critical buffers, and it had to take memory from below 640K. This is not to say that `memmaker` will never gain space but that it *might* not.

Attrib.exe

For several years, DOS has included a command to change file attributes (hidden, read only, archive, system) that complements the ability to change attributes in the Property sheets of files. The DOS command line program has several uses: First, you can use it to change the system attribute, which you can't do with Explorer. Second, its wildcards are often easier to use than the equivalent with Explorer—although you can use a wildcarded search in `Find File`, select all, pick Properties from the context menu, and change attributes there for even more power. The one place you are likely to most need `attrib` (or the equivalent in Explorer) is after copying files from a CD to a hard disk. They will have the Read Only attribute set, and you'll probably want to change that.

fc

Windows 95 needs a decent File Compare utility. Failing that, there's `fc.exe`. Mind you, as a comparison engine, `fc` is superb. It will compare ASCII files and show line differences and will then resynch the files to find more similarities and differences. The problem is that the DOS screen display of results is almost unusable if the differences are extensive. Microsoft has done the hard work. How about putting a decent interface on it?

Debug, Sort, Find

These are all clunky, venerable DOS utilities that have been around since DOS 2.x. You'll find old books and articles with all sorts of neat tricks that use them. Some venerable debug tricks might cause Windows to shut debug down with a protect mode violation but other than that, the tricks should work. And these programs are there in `C:\windows\command`.

Fdisk, Format

If you need to set up a new hard drive, you'll need to use `Fdisk` and `Format`. To do so, make a startup disk and copy these two programs to it. Then use them to partition and format the hard disk. If it is a replacement hard drive, you'll need to install Windows 95 on it.

Interlink

On the CD, in the directory `\other\oldmsdos`, you'll find `interlnk.exe` and `intersvr.exe`. These can be used to set up a parallel port connection between two computers vastly inferior to what you get with Windows 95's Direct Cable Connection (discussed in Chapter 4). So why do I mention it? Because it will work with earlier versions of DOS. If you have a laptop without CD for which you've purchased a valid license to upgrade to Windows 95 and you have the CD, you could use `interlnk` to transfer the contents of the `\win95` directory on the CD to the laptop and then run the install from there.

MSCDEX

When running under Windows 95, the protect mode CDFS should be in place and MSCDEX will be irrelevant. However, you'll need to know the syntax of MSCDEX if you plan to run a CD in the penalty box (our name for custom MS-DOS Exclusive mode, which I'll discuss soon). You'd use

```
C:\windows\command\mscedex /D:name /L:letter
```

where `letter` is the letter you want to assign to the drive (feel free to ignore this option if you don't mind the next available letter getting picked), and `name` is the name specified in the `config.sys` line loading the hardware driver for the CD.

Qbasic

Qbasic, aka Microsoft Quick Basic, found in `\other\oldmsdos` on the CD, is great to throw at a bright high school student. Visual Basic would be even better, but it isn't included free with Windows!

Windows Batch Language

Now, as always, the most automated appliance in a household is the mother.

—Beverly Jones, *The Florida Paper on Women's Liberation*

The DOS batch language is pretty primitive but you can do a lot with it. There's a whole chapter in *The Mother of All PC Books* about it, and you'll find more tricks in books on DOS. With the ability to launch Windows applications from batch files and the start command (which I described earlier), you can use DOS batch files to do Windows tasks. Somewhat complicated examples appeared earlier in this chapter in the listings in Figure 3-42, Figure 3-44, and Figure 3-46. As a simpler example, if you have a project where you want to open Winword on a particular file, say `bookprop.doc` and Excel in `booksale.xls`, you'd just make a batch file that reads

```
start bookprop.doc
start booksale.xls
```

and assign it to a shortcut set to run minimized and to close when done. The important point is to remember that the batch language is there.

I found one disturbing compatibility problem with old batch files and the new DOS built into Windows 95. There is a way under DOS to strip off the end of a string of fixed length, for example, pull the C out of C:\. It uses the fact that DOS command lines are only 127 characters long so if a line in an old DOS batch file is more than 127 characters, then DOS only uses the first 127 characters. But they broke this part of the batch processor in Windows 95. First, while the DOS command line can still be only 127 characters long, DOS will happily process commands from within batch files that are up to 1023 characters. In addition, they totally changed the order of processing of %1 parameter replacement so that DOS will process an even longer command line if it only gets longer after %1 replacement. The bottom line is that the batch trick doesn't work.

Ahem. We didn't break the batch language. We enhanced it. We figured with long filenames, batch files might actually need to deal with command lines longer than 127 characters. So we fixed them. If, in doing that, we broke some of the tricks that the DOS weenies so love, well, er, progress does have its costs, doesn't it?

The Penalty Box

Come children, let us shut up the box and the puppets, for our play is played out.

—William Makepeace Thackeray, *Vanity Fair,* 1848

Windows 95's enhanced support for DOS sessions over Windows is supposed to be so good that just about any DOS program will run in one. This is pretty much true. With the large memory typically available there, the ability to fool programs and make them think Windows isn't running (see *Faking 'em out,* above) and more stable hardware drivers, Windows 95 can run a lot of DOS programs, especially games, that couldn't begin to run under Windows 3.x. But there are still some recalcitrant DOS programs, mainly games that just won't run in a DOS session over Windows. For such programs, Windows 95 offers DOS-exclusive mode where you can load a DOS environment without Windows.

Actually, there are two rather different DOS-exclusive modes that could be called standard and custom. The custom mode is so ghastly to set up that I tend to think of it as a penalty box.

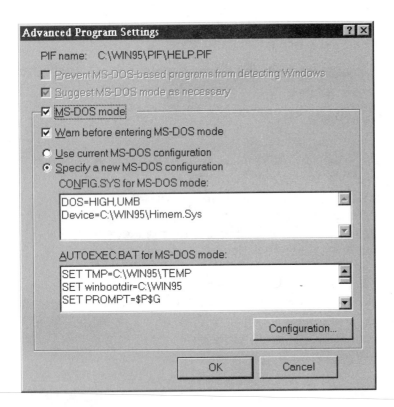

Figure 3-67. Advanced Program settings

You set up MS-DOS exclusive mode by clicking the `Advanced...` button in the Program tab of a DOS Property sheet. The key dialog is in Figure 3-67. You turn on the MS-DOS exclusive mode capability by checking the box denoted `MS-DOS mode`. That turns on the check box and the pair of radio buttons immediately below it. I'd urge you to always have the box marked "Warn before entering MS-DOS mode" checked since you don't want to click on such a `.pif` in error and wind up in MS-DOS mode.

The radio button determines whether you go into standard MS-DOS mode or into the penalty box. If you pick "Use current MS-DOS configuration" you go into standard mode when you run the `.pif`, while "Specify a new MS-DOS configuration" puts you in custom mode.

Standard MS-DOS Exclusive Mode

If you run a `.pif` that starts up standard mode, including choosing "Restart the computer in MS-DOS mode?" from the Shutdown menu (assuming you've not customized `Exit to DOS.pif`), the following happens:

- All programs running under Windows are closed down.

- Windows exits, leaving only 4K in memory. Basically, the machine is returned to the state it was when `autoexec.bat` was run and before `winstart.bat` was run but with an additional 4K still controlled by Windows.

- The batch file `C:\windows\dosstart.bat` is run if it is present. More on this later.

- The program specified in the `.pif` is run. If you specified `command.com` and did not check "Close on exit," (and in particular, if you picked "Restart the computer in MS-DOS mode?" from the Shutdown menu), you wind up at the DOS prompt.

- When you exit the program you're running, Windows is restarted. If you've loaded no resident programs (either directly or through `dosstart.bat`), just Windows is loaded (similar to picking "Restart the computer?" with the `Shift` key held down). Otherwise, a reboot and reload of `autoexec.bat` and `config.sys` is performed (similar to picking "Restart the computer?" without the `Shift` key). You can tell which of these Windows has picked because in the former case it says "Restarting Windows 95" and in the latter it says "Starting Windows 95."

When you install Windows 95, it makes a `dosstart.bat` file for commands in your `autoexec.bat` that it thinks you might want in DOS-exclusive mode but it doesn't want run before Windows. The two typical examples are a real mode mouse driver and `mscdex`, the real mode CD file system. Of course, `mscdex` won't do you much good if you haven't kept a real-mode hardware driver for your CD in `config.sys`.

Custom MS-DOS Exclusive Mode, aka the Penalty Box—How It Works

The problem is that the drivers you want in `config.sys` when you are running Windows are not likely to be the drivers you want for running DOS in exclusive mode. For example, you might want a real-mode hardware CD driver when running DOS but you won't need it with Windows—while Windows won't use it, it also won't free up the memory it takes. A second problem is that, depending on the DOS program, you may have different needs for what you need loaded—say, a CD ROM driver for one program and not for some other that needs every bit of RAM it can lay its hands on. For these reasons, there is the penalty box. It lets you specify a custom `config.sys` and `autoexec.bat`. I'll talk about how and where you specify them soon.

When you try to run a `.pif` with penalty box setup, Windows does the following:

- It renames your `config.sys` and `autoexec.bat` to `config.wos` and `autoexec.wos`. If you see such files on your disk during a custom exclusive session, *do not* erase or move them!

- It creates a new `config.sys` that starts with the line `dos=single` and then has all the lines in your custom `config.sys`. It creates a new `autoexec.bat` consisting of the lines of your custom `autoexec.bat`, followed by the three lines

    ```
    cd working-dir
    call program-name
    C:\windows\win.com /wx
    ```

    where *working-dir* and *program-name* are specified in the `.pif` as `Working` and `Cmd line`, respectively.

- It sets a flag somewhere deep in the kernel that tells the system it is set for custom MS-DOS exclusive mode.

- It reboots the system.

When the reboot takes place, the first thing that you see is "Windows 95 is now starting your MS-DOS based Program. Press Esc now to Cancel MS-DOS mode and Restart Windows 95." This message shows before the F8 Startup Menu is looked for, before `drvspace` processing takes place and before `config.sys` or `autoexec.bat` is loaded and is the result of the conjectured flag deep inside the kernel.

If you hit `Esc`, then Windows resets the flag, and copies `config.wos` over `config.sys` and `autoexec.wos` over `autoexec.bat` and continues a normal boot process.

Otherwise it runs the custom `config.sys` and `autoexec.bat` and loads your program. When you are done with the program, the `autoexec.bat` file runs `win` with the `/wx` parameter, which resets the flag, does the `config/autoexec` renaming, and reboots.

This scheme as described has important consequences:

- If you don't properly exit the program when you are done you will need to watch for the `Press Esc. . .` prompt when you next start up and hit `Esc`.

- With this fooling with `autoexec.bat` and `config.sys`, it is a good idea to make frequent backups of them if you run in the Penalty Box often.

- If disaster strikes and you get into some kind of loop in Exclusive mode, just hit `F8` and go to confirm each step mode.

Setting Up the Penalty Box

If you pick the radio button for "Specify a new MS-DOS configuration," small edit boxes open up where you can type in your custom `config.sys` and `autoexec.bat` files. I call this mode the penalty box because the setup is so awkward:

1. The edit boxes only show three lines at a time so you don't get a chance to see the entire files if they get very involved. There should at least be a way to specify which files get used that you could edit with notepad.

2. The width of the panels is not a fixed number of characters (since the font is proportional), but it is narrow enough that complex paths or command lines won't fit without scrolling (and jerky scrolling at that) in the horizontal direction.

3. Under DOS 6, there was finally memmaker to help optimize upper memory usage for DOS configuration files, but here you are back to having to optimize by hand if you need just a little bit more memory for that DOS game. And the process between successive reboot/edits of the configuration files is lengthy, since it require Windows to load.

4. As I'll explain, there are some simple options Windows helps you set up, but they don't include some of the most important ones. Your CD and sound card commands aren't there, which I can forgive since they depend on your hardware so Windows could be clueless. But neither is a command to set up UMBs, nor a command to move `drvspace` into UMB memory. Fear not—I'll at least partly remedy this!

 Suddenly, you need to become an expert on obscure DOS 6.22 commands. You didn't throw out the old DOS manuals and books, did you? None of this is discussed in the Windows 95 documentation.

When you first pick this mode, Windows normally sets up a simple starting `config.sys` consisting of the two lines:

```
DOS=HIGH,UMB
Device=C:\windows\Himem.sys
```

and an `autoexec.bat` consisting entirely of `set` commands. Indeed, if you open a fresh windowed MS-DOS prompt and type `set` at the DOS command line, you'll get a list of environmental variables identical to the set commands in this initial `autoexec.bat`,

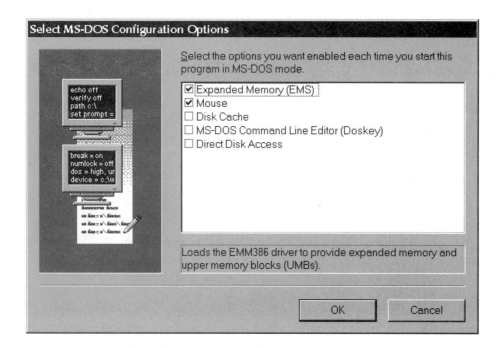

Figure 3-68. The Advanced Configuration Dialog

including the order, except that two variables are dropped—COMSPEC and windir. You are free to edit these initial templates.

As an additional aid, in adding items to your custom configurations, there is a button marked Configuration. . . that brings up the panel shown in Figure 3-68. Too bad such an elegant graphic is buried here! Two of the five items are checked, but you are free to pick and choose. The panel at the bottom provides a tip about the selected item. I'll have a lot to say about the tip for EMS memory currently displayed in that figure.

Actually, this is what happens normally. But it can be changed by entries in the Registry key HKLM\Software\Microsoft\Windows\ CurrentVersion\MS-DOSOptions. I'll discuss this in Chapter 11 and we'll see which items are checked and where the commands come both in the Advanced Configuration Dialog and in the initial templates. In particular, a hardware vendor can add items to both the initial templates and to the dialog in Figure 3-68.

The five options that are by default in the Figure 3-68 dialog set up EMS memory, Mouse, Smartdrv (the disk cache), Doskey, and a special mode that allows programs like Norton Disk Editor to access the hard drive directly. As I said, there are some important options missing.

Microsoft's intentions are made clear in the Registry key Mao mentioned. Three subkeys there are turned off and without specific commands: CD-ROM, Net, and VESA.* Clearly the Redmondians hope that vendors selling new hardware for Windows 95 users will arrange that those keys have the right commands to turn on support for those three options and that the hardware vendors will then arrange choices in the Figure 3-68 dialog to turn on these options. So maybe you are lucky and you have a CD-ROM option in the list in Figure 3-68.

Here is some information for dealing with the items that Microsoft left out.

Turning on UMBs

The Tip Text for the item `Expanded Memory (EMS)` in the list in Figure 3-68 says `Loads the EMM386 driver to provide expanded memory and upper memory blocks (UMBs)`. But that's false for the command that is actually placed in `Config.sys` if you select that item. The command is `DeviceHigh=C:\windows\emm386.exe`. (I'll ignore the fact that it should be device not `devicehigh`, since the high is ignored.) This form of the command loads EMS support but not UMB support. Here's the correct syntax:

UMB and EMS	`device=C:\windows\emm386.exe RAM`
EMS only	`device=C:\windows\emm386.exe`
UMB only	`device=C:\windows\emm386.exe NOEMS`

You must make sure this line is loaded immediately after the `himem` line, which should be the second line in `config.sys after DOS=High,UMB`.

To remind you, UMB, aka Upper Memory Blocks, is the name given to the memory area that can be addressed in real mode but is above the DOS 640K limit. Some of that is used for hardware ROM but usually 100–200K can be used to shoehorn in device drivers and resident programs that otherwise take memory space less than 640K. If UMB support is turned on, and you use `devicehigh` for device drivers and `loadhigh` for `autoexec.bat` resident programs, then these programs will go into the UMB area. Juggling programs into the limited space can be a bear. That's why it is called the penalty box (sigh!). EMS (Expanded Memory) is used by a very few programs to store buffers and other data, but it takes 64K of valuable UMB space, so it is usually not worth it to use EMS.

---

* The VESA spec is a Video scheme for high-resolution DOS modes that some DOS game makers use. Many video cards require special programs be run in `autoexec.bat` to turn on VESA support.

Most of you will want to have UMB only support turned on and a sizable minority will want both UMB and EMS. None of you will want EMS only turned on, which is precisely what the default check mark set up by Windows does. Oh, how I love a nice bug in the morning.

Dealing with CD-ROM drives and Sound Cards

For CD ROM support, you need one or two lines in your `config.sys` and one in `autoexec.bat`. I can't tell you the precise syntax for the `config.sys` lines but on Mao's system it reads:

```
DEVICE=C:\SYSTEM\SCSI\ASPI7DOS.SYS /D
DEVICE=C:\SYSTEM\SCSI\ASPICD.SYS /D:ASPICD0
```

Basically, you want to look at a pre-Windows 95 `config.sys` for lines something like this. The CD driver will be a device line with the word CD in the name of the driver and usually a `/D:`*name* afterward. Your old `autoexec.bat` should tell you what is after the `/D:` as I'll explain. If your CD controller is SCSI (and that is true of many controllers included on sound cards), you'll probably also have a device line in that old `config.sys` with `ASPI` in it; you want that driver also. Mao's old `autoexec.bat` has

```
C:\SYSTEM\DOS\MSCDEX.EXE /V /D:ASPICD0 /M:12 /L:G
```

It's no coincidence that this line has `/D:ASPICD0`, as does the device line. The names have to be the same, and you can use the `mscdex` line to help locate the driver.

To be explicit, here's how you figure out how to add CD support to a penalty box.

1. Try to locate an old matched `config.sys`/`autoexec.bat` that supported your CD. If you have dual boot under Windows 95, look for `config.dos` and `autoexec.dos`. Otherwise, look for `config` and `autoexec` files with extensions like `syd` or `001`.

2. In the old `autoexec.bat`, you'll find a line with `mscdex`. You want almost the identical line your custom `autoexec.bat`. The only change will be the path in front of `mscdex`, which should read `C:\windows\command`. To add the line, open the old file in notepad and cut and paste to the `.pif` dialog.

3. Using the name after /D: in the `mscdex` line, locate your CD driver in the old `config.sys` and also check for a driver with the string ASPI in its name. Copy those lines with no changes to your custom `config.sys`. You might check the drivers are still where they are supposed to be.

4. After making sure this all works, make sure you've added UMB support and then experiment with putting a `loadhigh` in front for the `mscdex` command and `devicehigh` in place of `device` in the `config.sys` device line(s).

For the sound card, try to locate the needed drivers in the old configuration files. They'll usually be in a directory that has something to do with the name of the card or the maker of the card. For example, the drivers for Mao's old Sound Blaster Pro were in `\SBPRO`. Copy the driver load lines verbatim to your custom files if you need sound support.

If you have a brand new Windows 95 computer, you won't have old configuration files and maybe you won't even have the drivers. Check—maybe you lucked out and your vendor has arranged that the Figure 3-68 dialog has entries for CDROM and sound. If so, send them a love letter and tell your friends how wonderfully thoughtful they are. If not, you'll need to get on the phone or Online service to them.

DriveSpace

One final tip about setting up penalty boxes: You may very well have `drivespace` loaded when you run in DOS exclusive mode. Running `mem /c/p` should tell you. If you do, be sure to add UMB support to your `config.sys` and the line

```
devicehigh=C:\windows\command\drvspace.sys /move
```

there also. That'll move almost 60K of memory-hogging space into UMBs.

Don't assume because you have no compressed hard drives, that you aren't loading `drvspace`. I've found that once a system has mounted a single compressed diskette, `drvspace` is there forever. The only way to get rid of it is to delete the hidden files `drvspace.bin` and `dblspace.bin` from the root directory which feels rather extreme.

Penalty boxes are the pits—a fitting punishment for the audacity to continue using unfriendly DOS programs. Keep cool and use my tips. On one of my systems, I had more than 620K free at an exclusive DOS prompt—that was with `drvspace` and cd drivers loaded into UMBs.

Mr. Roger's Network

Few things are more revolting than the spectacle of a normally reasonable father and husband gowned in one of those hot, massive aprons inscribed with disgustingly corny legends, presiding over a noisome brazier as he destroys huge hunks of good meat and fills the neighborhood with greasy, acrid smoke: a Boy Scout with five o'clock shadow.

—Donald Rogers, NY *Herald Tribune,* July 21, 1961

There isn't much to say about Network Neighborhood. If you're here to figure out how to stop it from showing up on your Desktop, you are in the wrong place—that's discussed in Chapter 11 (Hint to the Regedit literate: you'll need to add a DWord key to `HKCU\Software\Microsoft\Windows\CurrentVersion\Policies\Explorer` called `NoNetHood`, give it the value 1, and reboot).

If you are on a large network, Network Neighborhood can be a wonderful tool in ferreting out resources, although trying to browse the entire network can take a long time. If your immediate workgroup is medium-sized—large enough that you may not keep up with all the available computing resources but small enough that you needn't go out for lunch during a browse of all resources, Network Neighborhood can be exceedingly useful.

With a small network, say in a small office with fewer than five employees or in a home peer-to-peer network, Network Neighborhood is probably useless and even counterproductive. If you are in a situation where you know all the resources that are available, it is probably most efficient to set up a Desktop folder with these resources in it. You can add drive icons to network drives you often access and place them on the Desktop. Once you've done that, play the Registry game to blow Nethood away.

 When you set this up, I recommend you use UNC type names rather than mapped drives as long as you're sure your programs will understand them. Mapped drives should be used merely as a convenience for aliasing very long UNCs.

A Fair Exchange

The exchange program is the thing that reconciles me to all the difficulties of political life.

—J. William Fulbright, *New Yorker,* May 10, 1958

My, that Senator Fulbright sure was smart. Forty years ago, he already realized that Windows 95's Exchange Program was going to revolutionize the world of communications.

I don't know about Senator Fulbright but I think that in the long run, Exchange could be the most revolutionary and permanently significant part of Windows 95. If you've used a PIM for a while, either you are slave to its proprietary file formats or else you've switched PIMs at some point and spent hours reentering name and address data. Your PIM may talk to Winword because of special routines the PIM maker wrote, but probably not to many other programs. With a universal address book that any PIM or any application can access, the whole world of tracking names and addresses has changed. And the Address book is but a tiny part of Exchange.

You're right, Mom, that Exchange is a very big deal, but more because of its promise than anything else. A universal address book is exciting, but so much in the current implementation of the address book is brain-dead that its main function for now is as an email address book only. The email client is better, but my relation to it is definitely love–hate (and other users I've talked to feel the same way). But the architecture is solid, Microsoft seems committed to the component, and I'm sure it'll get a whole lot better.

The weeklies have said that the Exchange client was written by the same team that is working on Exchange Server, Microsoft's vehicle for killing Lotus Notes. It lacks the UI polish of the Windows shell. I can only hope the Windows team takes over responsibility for the Exchange client that ships with Windows and that it is upgraded rapidly.

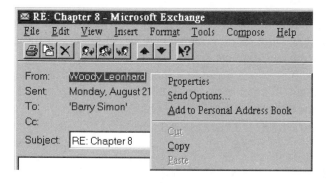

Figure 3-69. You can too save addresses!

Every Exchange user I've talked to has the same complaint. How could they have forgotten to provide a way to directly add to your address book the addresses of people who send you mail? They haven't—it's there, just very well hidden. When reading any message look at the header information at the top. It's black on gray, which is usually a sign that it is inaccessible information, but right-click on the name in the From field and up pops a menu (Figure 3-69) that includes Add to

Personal Address Book!! I figured that I'd better tell you about this one up front! This item violates one of the cardinal rules of application design—every command accessible from context menus should be accessible in other ways, especially via the drop down menu system. As far as I know, this right-click menu and a button you get after double-clicking an address are the only places you can save an address from.

If you're here because Internet mail will receive but not send messages, see the section called "Hoping for an Easy Delivery."

Exchange Overview

> Ants are so much like human beings as to be an embarrassment. They farm fungi,
> raise aphids as livestock, launch armies into war, use chemical sprays to
> alarm and confuse enemies, capture slaves, engage in child labor,
> exchange information ceaselessly. They do everything but watch television.
>
> —Lewis Thomas, *The Lives of a Cell*

Exchange provides a universal email box (for now supporting mail through CompuServe, Internet Providers, The Microsoft Network, and MSMail), a universal address book, the central repository of Windows 95's fax capabilities, and a place to organize your mail, faxes, and any other files you'd like to.

Exchange has a reputation of being complex and confusing. This is in part because its design is one of the weaker parts of Windows 95, but also because Exchanges does so much and has so many kinds of options that you have to have a big picture in mind to understand the details. With this in mind, you'll find the product so useful and, in some ways, so powerful, that you'll want to learn it.

If you plan to use Exchange, the first thing that you need to do is go back to Chapter 2 and read my discussion of MAPI because first and foremost, Exchange is a MAPI client. Of the five components I described there, you can ignore Message Aware Applications when using Exchange. Such applications will invoke Exchange when you call their `File/Send. . .` menu item. In addition, if you set up Windows 95's fax software, you'll have a printer called `Microsoft Fax` and if you "print" to that printer, Exchange will pop up. So these applications can call Exchange, but aren't lurking in the background whenever you use Exchange.

The other three players (plus the MAPI client, which is Exchange itself) are lurking near the surface. The Address Book is what its name implies. You can invoke it with a button ( ) or menu item but you'll mainly use it indirectly. The Personal Information Store is what stares you in the face in Exchange, and manipulating that is an important part of Exchange. The

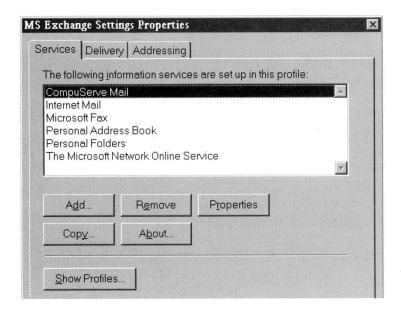

Figure 3-70. The Mail and Fax applet

actual links to the outside word will be through the Transport Service providers. Organizing them is through the `Tools/Services` menu item in Exchange or the `Mail and Fax` applet of control panel, which is shown in Figure 3-70. It should be set up for you during initial Windows setup and be setup for the various components themselves. Nonetheless, you may need to access this control, which is the subject of the section on "Better Profiles Than Mount Rushmore."

Listen up, sonny and girlie, because what I'm about to tell you is very important. If you make changes in the `Mail and Fax` applet or through the `Services. . .` and `Options. . .` items on the `Tools` menu in Exchange itself, you are warned that the changes won't take effect until you exit Exchange. That's the truth, but not the whole truth. I've found that many changes don't take effect until you exit and reboot Windows. A quick Restart (that is, holding down `Shift` while choosing Restart from the Shutdown menu) will suffice, but don't assume that any changes you make will get made until you restart Windows.

Figure 3-71 shows a schematic of what MAPI and Exchange is all about!

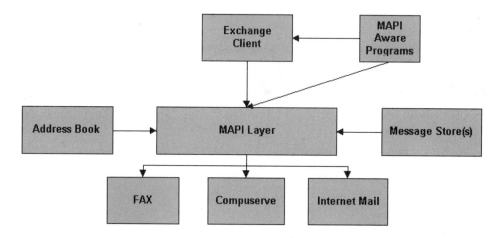

Figure 3-71. A MAPI they could all understand

 Besides the MAPI components, you need an editor to read and write mail. Exchange comes with a built-in editor, but there is a better choice. If you have Office 95, you can install Winword as your email editor. I don't know anyone who has used Wordmail (as this editor is called) who doesn't find it habit-forming. I'll talk more about it later.

 Exchange is a vast system, so you might miss some of its goodies. The next few sections give some of the high points. You can set up mailing lists—sets of addresses you send to be entering a single address. They are called PDLs (for Personal Distribution Lists) and discussed at the end of the section called "The Address Book." When composing a message, you can use partial names and hit 🔍—this is discussed just before PDLs. Also, when entering addresses in messages, if you have Internet or MSN installed as a Service Provider, you can type in an Internet address in the form `someone@domain.ext` and have it properly understood. Ways of directly entering addresses without their being in your address book are discussed in the middle of the section on "Reading and Composing Mail." How you can transfer messages to an archive or transfer messages from a portable to your main Desktop setup is described in the section titled "Using Multiple Message Stores." How to collect mail if you have multiple accounts on one service is discussed in "Better Profiles than Mount Rushmore." The complete local email system included in Windows 95, which is adequate for small- to medium-sized businesses and workgroups, is discussed in "Microsoft Mail Postoffice." Setting up the Fax software included with Windows 95 and, in particular, setting it to receive incoming faxes, is discussed in the section called "Fax is Fax."

The Address Book

There's nothing that makes you so aware of the improvisation of human existence
as a song unfinished. Or an old address book.

—Carson McCullers, *The Ballad of the Sad Cafe*

 The Address Book system has three distinct parts. First there is the
capability of the address book files (.pab files) themselves as defined by
MAPI. Next there are the individual address record entry forms, and finally
there is the address book viewer. I'd give them grades of A, C- and F and
regard the C- as a generous grade.

The specification allows records in the address book to have multiple forms associated with
them. The people in the book are thought of as objects and the forms are pages on the
Property sheet of the object. Service providers can provide multiple forms that can be added
to an addressee object. Indeed, CompuServe provides—count 'em—twenty-one different
possible address forms from straight CompuServe to Internet over CompuServe to Deutsche
Bundespost! Since forms appear as Tabs on the Property Sheet I'll call them Tabs.

Address entries created by Exchange have three basic Tabs, plus a fourth Tab that is
provided by a Service Provider with the person's email address. The main Tab, shown in

Business	Phone Numbers	Notes	COMPUSERVE - CompuServe Mail

Name
First: Igor Guido   Last: Salvatorre

Address: Mom's Place
12345 Mom St.

Title: Cheif Enforcer and Gofer
Company: The Mother of All Companies
Department: Gofer, Gophers and Loafers

City: Momville   Office:
State: ZY   Assistant: C.T.O. Mao (I wish)
Zip code: 98765
Country: USA   Phone number: Dial...
Business ▼ 123-456-7890

Figure 3-72. The main tab of an Address Book item

Figure 3-72, contains a plethora of information such as name, address, title, and company. There is a phone drop down whose full range of possibilities is seen on the Phone Numbers Tab and includes up to two business numbers, an assistant's numbers, fax, up to two home numbers, mobile and pager.

 The phone number fields don't have separate places for area code and extension. The Dial button has problems if you want to include an extension for information purposes.

So much for the good news on the individual address entries. What's bad?

- There is no way to import non-Exchange phone directories you might have, nor are there ways to export the Exchange address directory in a standard database or comma delimited format.

- Each "person" can only have a single email Tab and that Tab totally determines the method used to contact the person. Joe Jones can have a fax number entered in the Phone Number Tab, but if the fourth Tab is a CompuServe address, there is no way to send Joe a fax unless you make a duplicate entry called Joe Jones—Fax or something similar. Indeed, even if Joe's entry has a fax entry and you "print" a document to the fax printer and say Joe is the recipient, the message will go to Exchange as a CompuServe message. Ideally, address entries could have multiple email address pages with a default service and the possibility of changing the service provider on a message by message basis.

- There is the First Name bug that Erwin will detail in a moment.

- There is no way to copy one record to another as a head start for entering numbers of multiple people from the same company. If you have seventeen people to enter from XYZ Company, be prepared to enter their street address seventeen times.

- When I say there is no way to do something, I only *think* that's the case. The help for addresses is so execrable that I can't tell for sure.

 Ah yes, the First Name bug—it's so dumb it is one of my favorites. The main tab has separate fields called Last and First. The distinction is important because there is an option in Exchange itself to display names as First Last or as Last, First. When you enter a new address, the first field on the email address tab is called Display Name. If you enter First and Last names in the main tab, the display name will be gotten by concatenating the two. If you enter a two-word display name, the Address form handler dumps both into the First name field. Parsing seems to be beneath its dignity. Worse, if you carefully enter a First and Last name and then make the smallest editing change in the Display name field on the Email tab, the whole thing is dumped into First name. For example, if I enter Erwin in the First field and Schrodinger in the Last and then in the display field, add "'s Cockroach" at the end, it is all dumped into First name. I love a good bug in the mornin', but this bug is so annoying I hate it in the mornin' also.

If you have a complete `.pab` file that you want to add wholesale to your own Personal Address book, you can use `File/Import` on the Exchange menus. I've found no way to take your friend's Personal Address Book and selectively import some of the entries into your Personal Address Book other than the absurd route of copying that book, changing what Exchange thinks is your PAB to this copy, deleting the entries you don't want, changing back to your own PAB, and importing the copy of your friend's PAB with the deletions. Bah, humbug!

Then there's the Address Book Viewer. If Exchange is the low point of Windows from a UI point of view, the Address Book viewer is the low point of Exchange. It makes the individual address viewer look good.

The addresses are displayed in columns showing name, first business number, office, title, company, email provider, and email address. The columns aren't even labeled, have fixed width and order, and you can't sort on anything but the default name sort. The window size is fixed so you have to scroll to see the last column. You can't search on any field except for name. Particularly galling is that Windows 95 includes a Common Control called a header control that programmers can easily call. This control automatically allows change of column width, column labels, and sorting on any column. But the Address Book Viewer doesn't use it. I can't think of anything nice to say about the Address Book Viewer.

I can think of something nice to say about it. While you need it for entry, you can avoid the Address Book completely when sending messages.

Igor is talking about the wondrous ![button] button that you'll find in the button bar of the Create Message window. You can type in part of one or more names separated by semicolons in the `To:` and/or in the `Cc:` box and hit this button. Exchange then searches the names in the address book for matches. If it finds a unique match it replaces the partial name with the full name (underlined, which means there is address information underneath it). If it finds several matches, Exchanges pops up a list of names for you to choose from. If you have multiple entries (by using semicolons), it does this for each entry, popping up multiple matching name boxes as needed. There is even a hotkey for Check Names (`Ctrl+K` in the Exchange Email editor; `Alt+K` in Word Mail). This clever handling of address matching almost makes up for the awful Address Book.

Actually, boss, you don't need the button. If you type in the names separated by semicolons the way you said, when you hit the send message button (⊠), it resolves the addresses just as if you hit the button.

 Be careful if you trust Exchange to resolve the addresses sight unseen. One time, I was sure I'd put my buddy Jonathan Winters in the address book, so I just typed "jon," assuming Exchange would fix it. But I hadn't put Jonathan in there and the message wound up going to James Earle Jones, who wrote back asking if I'd turned to the dark side of the farce.

One hidden goodie in the Address Book is **Personal Distribution Lists,** aka **PDLs.** If you go to the Address Book and hit the button for new entry (or pick `New Entry` from the `File` Menu), you'll find "Personal Distribution List" at the bottom of the list. Pick it and you get a dialog that lets you name the list and pick its members from your address book. Lists then appear in the Address Book Viewer with a distinctive icon (📇) next to them.

 Be warned that while the individual entries in the address book have room for a lot more than email addresses—for example, for lots of phone numbers, for now that information is hardly used unless you have Word 7! Within Exchange, only the Fax Cover Page engine uses that information to fill in fields for your faxes like `{Recipient's Street Address}`. That even Microsoft doesn't always take the Exchange Address Book seriously for anything other than email is seen by Office 95's Schedule +. The format of it's contact list entries is almost identical to that of Exchange Address Book entries, but Schedule + won't use Exchange for contacts or even import your Exchange Address Book. Word's insert address button *will* use your current MAPI address book to get name, street, city, and state.

 The bottom line is that the address book is barely adequate for email and is inadequate as the basis of a PIM until some third party or Microsoft makes better tools. But the underlying MAPI spec is so strong and the likely installed base (all Windows 95 users!) so large that I've no doubt those better tools will come.

Organizing Mail

> One man was so mad at me that he ended his letter:
> "Beware. You will never get out of this world alive."
>
> —John Steinbeck

Exchange lets you organize your mail into folders that can form a multilevel hierarchical tree. Four folders have special meaning to Exchange: `Inbox`, where it puts messages that come in, `Outbox`, where it stores messages waiting to get sent, `Sent Items`, where it moves messages after sending them, and `Deleted Items`, which is Exchange's Recycle Bin where messages get moved when you "delete" them. You have to explicitly delete from the Deleted Items Folder later. Just as you need to clear out your Recycle Bin on a regular basis, you'll need to clean out your Deleted Items folder. There is no equivalent of the Recycle Bin's `Shift+Del` to directly delete a message without sending it to the Deleted Items folder.

That's with the default settings. The `Tools/Options` dialog lets you change this default behavior for Deleted Items (you can have it emptied every time you exit) in the `General` tab and you can choose to have mail deleted after you send it rather than saved in Sent Items by unchecking the box at the bottom of the `Send` tab.

I can't imagine deleting mail as you send it. Most messages don't take much space and you can always delete them later. By saving them, you won't wonder the next day if you remembered to answer Aunt Tilly's message. And when Aunt Tilly replies to your message, you'll have the message she's replying to in case she makes a reference to it that baffles you. Besides, computers are great at searching, and searching messages is one of Exchange's strong points. But, hey, it's your machine—if you want to delete messages as they are sent, go ahead. Spoil my day.

Another option you may want to change from the default is on the `Read` tab. It's the one that says `Include the original text when replying`. This involves a clash of cultures. It's traditional for UNIX mail users, which pretty much means traditional Internet users, to include the original message in their reply. CompuServe users don't. Other users are mixed. This convention made sense in the old UNIX days where you couldn't just open a window with your original message. I never quote the original in full because I don't like getting a one-sentence reply with a long quoted original filling the screen. If it is appropriate I'll quote a few lines from the original using cut and paste. So I uncheck the box.

The Exchange team fouled up on how they handle quoting the original message. By default, Exchange distinguishes the original by putting it in blue. If the whole world had RTF mail, using blue would be fine, but it doesn't and most people will get messages where it is unclear where the original starts. Worse, many older mail systems start lines quoted from an earlier message with `>>`, but that isn't an option with Exchange. Sigh.

RTF is short for **Rich Text Format,** an ASCII-based text scheme that allows universal descriptions of formatting. In Word, I typed in `Mao's little red book`. I made the size of `little` 6 points and put `red` in bold, colored red. I saved the file in RTF format and opened in Notepad. It was a pure ASCII file with ASCII codes only under 128, so even 7-bit that Internet mail systems could transfer. This little message blossomed to almost 1500 characters, most of that header setting up fonts and color tables. The actual text part of the message became `Mao \rquote s {\fs12 little} {\b\cf6 red} book`. Note how the upper ASCII apostrophe in `Mao's` becomes `\rquote`. The `\fs12` is a reference to the twelfth font in the font table and `\cf6` to the sixth entry in the color table. RTF is a rich enough protocol that it is ideal as a universal vehicle for email formatting. I hope it catches on.

As with the file hierarchy, you'll want to look both at your folders in a tree and the messages in a given folder, much as you want to use Explorer for file management rather than Folder View. Exchange comes configured out of the box to just show messages in a single folder. The first thing you want to do is to turn on the analog of Explorer View, which Exchange calls `Show Folders`. Either pull down the View menu and make sure that `Folders` is checked or else push down the second button from the left in the button bar (see Figure 3-74).

If you don't use much email and think you can get away with just using the Inbox and Sent Items, you may not need to create many folders, but if you use email a lot you are bound to want other folders. Indeed, may people prefer to use their Inbox for messages they still need to answer and to move messages out of it when they are taken care of. There is no `New Folder` option on the context menu for a folder—you need to choose `New Folder` from the File menu to make a new folder in the currently displayed folder. If you have to make a lot of new subfolders, repeatedly hitting `Alt+F`, `F` works fine. You can rename a folder from the right-click menu (or from the File menu), but you can't just click and type as you do in Explorer. It's a shame that the Exchange window looks a lot like Explorer, but a lot of functionality is accessed in subtly different ways.

Controlling the view in the message list window is one of Exchange's strong points. You can change column widths by dragging the divider between the heading names. You can sort on any column by clicking on the column. You need to right-click on the column to switch between sorting ascending and sorting descending. Or you can `Ctrl+Click` on a column to sort in the opposite order. Alas, it doesn't use the click twice to change the sort direction that the Windows common control does—once again, Exchange has to be subtly different.

You can choose what columns are displayed from among forty-four possibilities by using the dialog in Figure 3-73, which is invoked with the `Columns . . .` choice in the View menu. The buttons at the extreme right let you change column order. It's a shame that there

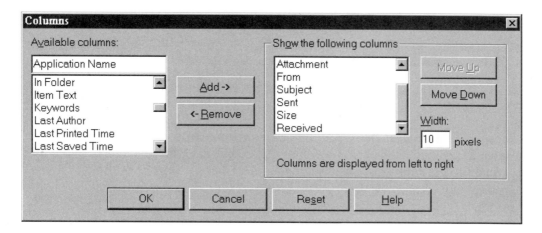

Figure 3-73. Exchange's Columns dialog

is no way to change the default columns used for new folders, nor any way to give a certain array of columns a name to let you easily reuse a configuration. Every time you make a new folder you'll have to futz with the columns.

 There are two columns that supply date and time—one called Sent and one called Received. The latter is included in the default view (for all folders but Sent Items) and so it is probably what you are using. But the former, especially if you are using Internet mail, may make more sense for you. Experiment with them to decide which you want displayed.

 You may be surprised to see column names like Last Author and Keywords in the list of columns. They are there because you can store files in Exchanges as well as messages! So long as the files follow the OLE specs for placing information like Last Author in the OLE header, Exchange can read and display that information. You should consider organizing correspondence using Exchange even for memos and letters that get hard copies.

Moving messages is as easy as dragging from the right message pane to the right folder in the left pane. If you prefer, there is a Move Item button on the button bar to bring up a dialog. It is sometimes useful to use the `View/New Window` menu item to make multiple Exchange windows to drag messages between.

Speaking of the button bar, it's another of Exchange's strong points, because you can modify it using the `Customize Toolbar. . .` option in the Tools menu. Figure 3-74 shows the default toolbar and the one that Igor has set up.

Default Button Bar

Igor's Button Bar

Figure 3-74. A tale of two button bars

Figure 3-75 shows the buttons in both bars and their functions. Note especially the pair to mark a message as read/unread. When a new message comes in, it appears in bold in the list until you've read it. These pairs of buttons shift a message from/to appearing as bold. If you read messages quickly and then want to mark some to be sure to answer, the Mark as Unread is useful. If a folder has any messages that are marked as unread, it will appear as bold in the folder list.

📁 Move to parent folder	📋 Show Folder Pane	📂 Move Message/Folder
📝 Message Properties	✕ Delete Message/Folder	📧 Compose New Message
📨 Reply to Sender	📨 Reply to All	📨 Forward Message
📖 Address Book Viewer	📥 Inbox	📤 Outbox
📌 What's this? (Help)	🔍 Find	📧 Mark Message as Read
📧 Mark as Unread	🖨 Print	

Figure 3-75. Button, button, who's got the button?

 I agree there is a lot to like about the button bar, but the Customize Toolbar mode in Winword is far superior to that in Exchange. And worse, there is no available button for the menu action that many users will most need—the command to dial a single service. There is one to dial up all your services, but that isn't what you'll necessarily want, and it doesn't work so well anyway, as I'll describe.

Notice that one of the buttons that Igor added was Find, the same as Find. . . from the Tools menu. This tool is so wonderful that it lets me almost forget the parts of Exchange that aren't so wonderful. You can search on sender, recipient, or subject, or do a full text search of the message body. You can search on a single folder and subfolder or on all folders. I suggest making sure that Personal Folders is highlighted in the folder part of the window when you invoke Find or else be sure to pick the `Folder. . .` button in the Find dialog.

One great thing about the Find dialog in Exchange is that, like the File Find dialog in Windows itself, Exchange's Find results are a live message window. That means you can drag files from it to a single folder. Using this capability with Find's ability to look for all messages received in a certain date range make find an ideal tool for archiving messages. Another nice thing is the speed of the search. On a Pentium-90, full text search through more than 10 MB of messages took less than a minute.

Speaking of large message files, you should be aware of two tools for dealing with the message files themselves. First, if disaster should strike and a message file becomes corrupted, there is an Inbox Repair Tool (the file is call `scanpst.exe`, an analog for `.pst` files of `scandsk` for disks; it is located in `C:\Program Files\Microsoft Exchange`). A shortcut to it is added to the Start Menu in `Programs\Accessories\System Tools`.

The second tool involves compressing the `.pst` file. As you delete messages and/or delete embedded message attachments, the `.pst` file can develop pockets of unused space. You'll have to explicitly compact the file to regain that space. To access the compact tool, pick `Services. . .` from the `Tools` menu, highlight `Personal Folders` in the resulting dialog, hit `Properties. . .` and then choose the `Compact Now` button in the next dialog.

Hey, boss. I'm puzzled by this whole Exchange shtick. They call them folders. They act like non-file folder objects. They are closer in spirit to directories than the shell's virtual folders like Printers or Dial-Up Networking. Why is Exchange a separate program? Shouldn't Personal Folders just appear on an Explorer folder list under Desktop at the same level as `My Computer` and Network Neighborhood? If that happened, the methods for organizing email would be the same as for organizing files.

Very penetrating, grasshopper. In fact, Microsoft produced a series of white papers on their plans for Exchange in the fall of 1994. In Figure 3-76, I reproduce a part of one of their pictures that shows what they planned for the Exchange client for Windows 95. You'll notice they didn't call it Personal Folders, but rather, InfoCenter. Otherwise, it looks as you thought it should. That suggests we look a little at Microsoft's greater vision for Exchange and how the Windows 95 Exchange client is one piece of a much larger picture.

Microsoft's Vision

The main concept behind Microsoft Exchange is to provide a product that integrates email, scheduling, electronic forms, document sharing, and applications such as customer tracking to make it altogether easier to turn information into a business advantage.

—From Messaging to Information Exchange—A White Paper, Microsoft Corp., fall 1994

 Since I'm going to mention Exchange Server here, let me first set the record straight. The head of campus computing at a university using Internet mail told me that they were considering setting users up with the Exchange client in Windows 95, but they were quite happy with Internet mail for delivery purposes and weren't sure they wanted to invest in Exchange Server. That confusion is inevitable given the names that Microsoft is using, but the impression is 180 degrees from reality. Not only isn't Exchange Server needed to use the Exchange Client in Windows 95, that client won't even work with Exchange Server.*

In April 1994 Microsoft announced a family of products called Exchange. In the Microsoft vision, Exchange gives users control over all sorts of information, including email and files. In addition, through a specialized product called Exchange Server, medium to large companies can provide access and control over companywide information, including setting up threaded discussion groups (essentially BBS!), databases of customer contacts, computer-based forms, and other structured information.

 Gee, it sure sounds a lot like Lotus Notes.

Although the 'softies will bristle at the suggestion, it is clear that in part Exchange is a response to the phenomenal success of Notes in the large corporate marketplace. Notes was there first and lots of companies have spent a lot of time, money, and effort moving data to Notes format. For that reason, it will be hard for Microsoft (or for Novell's Groupwise, which has a similar ambition) to displace Notes. But Microsoft has several things going for it. First, some kind of version of the Exchange client will be built into the operating system; indeed,

---

* Mao: To be precise, Exchange Server isn't shipping at the time this book is written. Microsoft has stated clearly that Exchange Server will include a site license to an enhanced client with special features linked to the Server. It seems likely that the client that ships with Windows won't even work with the Exchange Server, but we can't be sure yet.

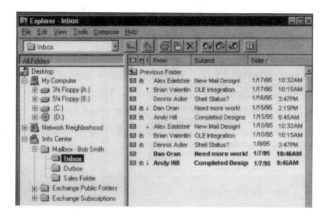

Figure 3-76. The Fall 1994 plan for Exchange

as Figure 3-76 shows, it could be very tightly integrated with the operating system. Second, it is clear that Microsoft regards this general groupware category as essential to its future, and when Microsoft is after a strategic objective it is a fierce competitor. But most of all, while Notes is a grand concept, the implementation is not. Notes tends to crap out on networks with more than 10,000 or 20,000 users. And its user interface is so bad that one editor, who is usually a Lotus fan, when asked his opinion of the Notes UI, replied "UI? What UI?"

All this means, though, that Exchange is serving two masters—the Exchange group in Microsoft, whose goal is to push Exchange Server, and the Windows group who wants a component of Windows itself that supports email, address databases, and other personal information needs. The real reason that the user interface in Exchange doesn't quite match that in Explorer is that the Windows 95 Exchange client was written by the Exchange team, not by the Windows 95 team.

Until late in the beta process, the Exchange client for Windows had or, according to the help file, had planned, some neat features that were dropped at the last minute because of a fear that users would find them confusing. One of the neatest involved saving named folder views, which not only let you save an arrangement of columns but also a filtering of a folder to only display certain messages, such as those no more than a month old. There was the ability to define grouped views in which, for example you could group by subject and have a subject-based collapsible outline. There was the ability to assign multiple delivery addresses to one person. There were high-class security options for mail, including password protection, digital signatures, and encryption on individual messages.

To hear the howls of outrage from the computer press, you'd think what was left was chopped liver, when in fact it's a great program. We felt we had to pull the fancy stuff until we could get it right.

Yes, what's left is very good, but the original concept was great. I expect that before too long, the Windows team will turn attention to the Exchange client and we'll see a much improved interface. I worry, though, that it'll have stuff that even the home user would find useful but that will get labeled for high-end corporate users and only kept in the client that ships with Exchange Server.

Reading and Composing Mail

*Politeness is as much concerned in answering letters within a reasonable time
as it is in returning a bow, immediately.*

—Lord Chesterfield, *Letter of Sept. 15, 1768 to His Godson*

Exchange uses the same editor to both read and compose mail. If you have Microsoft Office 95 or Winword 7.0, you have a basic decision to make. Should you replace Exchange's mail editor with Wordmail, the special configuration of Winword that supports messages? I'll talk about both editors in this section.

It's a no brainer. Winword is, well, Winword—arguably the best word processor ever written. This version has a feature that makes it worth its weight in gold as an email editor for the spelling impaired.* As you type along, misspelled words get a little wavy underline—if you right-click on such a word, you get spelling alternatives. But be warned: Wordmail is terribly habit forming: I've yet to meet anyone who has used it who feels they could switch to a more pedestrian email editor.

If you installed Office 95 and Exchange isn't using something that looks like Winword, you'll have to go back and install WordMail. It is an optional component under the Winword setup. Explicitly, you need to select on Microsoft Word in the main setup dialog, click on the `Change Options. . .` button, and make sure that `WordMail` is checked off. Once you've installed WordMail, you control how it behaves from the `WordMail Options. . .` choice on the `Compose` menu in Exchange. A checkbox there can be unchecked to return to Exchange's email editor. You can't do things like define macros when reading or composing email. For that you need to go to this dialog and choose `Edit. . .` or else run Word and load `email.dot` and make the changes there.

---

* Igor: Gee, if it really is worth its weight in gold, I'll bet Microsoft is sorry it cut down on the printed docs so much.

WordMail is missing an Insert Message command and the ability to mark the mail as urgent. The menu item to add a `Bcc:` box for Blind carbon copies, which is part of the `Options` menu in the Exchange editor, is buried under `File/Properties. . .` in WordMail. You can turn the `Bcc` on in the Exchange editor or in WordMail, and you'll get a `Bcc:` in either.

 Yeah, no doubt about it, WordMail is great. But will we see a WordPerfectMail or a WordProMail? I'll bet the Winword group got undocumented hooks from the Exchange people to be able to do this. And if they did, Microsoft is using its OS monopoly to help out Office.

 Rush, baby. We have a virtual monopoly in both areas. So all we're doing is helping our users.

If you don't have Word, do not despair; the built-in editor shown in Figure 3-77 is quite good with support for fancy text attributes like color, choice of font, and so on. All the remarks I make in the rest of this section apply to either editor. You can attach files to a message (use the paper clip button). Messages can have multiple recipients and they can be

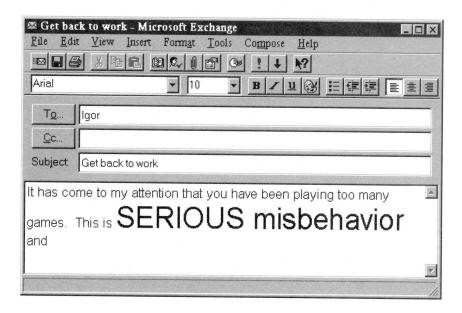

Figure 3-77. Exchange's email editor

associated with multiple service providers, so one and the same message can go to Bill by fax and to John via Internet mail. You can enter recipients that are in your Address Book in the To: or Cc: lists in two ways:

1. Hit the buttons with those words that bring up an Address List scroll box from which you can choose to add people.

2. Type in partial names, separated by semicolons. You can then hit the 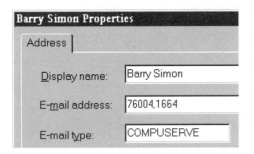 button or just wait for Exchange to check the names when you hit the Send ( ) button.

My advice is to use the second method unless you really can't recall the name you gave someone or even if they are in your list, in which case you can fall back on the first.

Figure 3-78. Generic Mail Addresses

There is a way to add addresses of people who aren't in your address book and who you don't want to put in there. For example, to send to CompuServe, at the To: prompt, type in [Compuserve:1] and hit the checkbox. Magically, it will be replaced by 1. Now double-left-click (or right-click on it and pick Properties) and get a box (Figure 3-78) that will let you type in both the name you want to use as the recipient and the person's CompuServe number. If you prefer, you could type in the person's ID directly, for example [CompuServe:76004,1664].

 There is nothing magical about the use of CompuServe here. If you type [Junk:1], you'll get a box just like Figure 3-78 with the email type called JUNK. But when you try to send such a message, instead of it going to the Outbox, it goes to Sent Items (which seems a strange place to go) and your Inbox gets a message from "System Administrator" announcing that your message didn't reach some of its recipients because no transport provider was available. That means you have some confidence that the invisible, er, System Administrator will protect you. When I talk about faxing later, I'll explain how you can resend messages that are bounced by your friendly System Administrator.

 Alas, a few times when I was experimenting with this a message addressed to the email type JUNK did wind up in Mao's Outbox, where it presumably would have stayed forever. Oh, how I love a nice bug in the mornin'.

Besides `CompuServe`, possible email types you can fill in with the `[E-MAIL TYPE:number]` address syntax are `FAX`, `SMTP`, and `MSN` (SMTP is for Internet and MSN is for The Microsoft Network). When typing in fax numbers in the United States, you have to put the 1 before an area code. Windows is smart enough to strip your local area code off a number if it is proceeded by a 1 but isn't smart enough to add a 1 in front of any area code or to strip off your area code if it is not proceeded by a 1. Local fax numbers can be typed in without a 1 or an area code.

You don't need to remember the SMTP keyword and funny `[. . .]` syntax if you are using Internet mail. Type in any Internet address, like `bsimon@cis.compuserve.com`, and Exchange will automatically interpret it as Internet mail. The rule seems to be that Exchange accepts any address of the form `X@Y.Z` with `X Y Z` strings—the key is the `@` before the period. Since MSN will accept SMTP mail, this trick will also work if you have MSN but not Internet mail. While CompuServe can send mail via Internet, it isn't by supporting SMNP addressing, so this won't work with CompuServe.

Underlined names can be moved from To: to Cc: or between messages with drag and drop or with cut/copy and paste.

Exchange itself does not come with a spelling checker, but it has hooks to use a 32-bit spelling checker if it exists. I can vouch that when you install Office 95, the spell checking is automagically enabled even in the Exchange editor. There is an implication that this will be true when you install any 32-bit spell checker, but darned if I can figure out where this information is stored. Once there is an installed spelling checker, then by default it is only a menu choice in the Exchange Editor. However, you can add it to the button bar, which can be customized. You can also configure the built-in editor (use the `Spelling` tab in `Tools/Options` dialog) to do a spell check when you hit the Send button.

Although you can add colors and fancy fonts to your messages and attach files, depending on your email service, the attempt may or may not be successful. The Microsoft Network handles both fancy text and attachments with aplomb. CompuServe ignores fancy text* and sends attachments as separate messages. How Internet mail will treat this feature is heavily dependent on how the mail provider has set things up. Attachments may be ignored, may get translated into a lower ASCII format using a method called Unencoding, or they may get sent using a recently introduced specification called MIME (for multipurpose Internet mail extensions). Fancy text attributes will be ignored unless the provider has full MIME support. Whatever your mail provider does, you'd better hope that the recipient of the mail has a reader that understands MIME (if that was used) or has software to Undecode (if that method was used).

---

* At the time that I'm writing, there are persistent rumors that support for RTF in CompuServe mail is coming.

The Exchange Editor supports three kinds of insertions (via its `Insert` menu). There is a neat dialog to insert any message either as text or an attachment (Figure 3-79); alas, this is gone if you install WordMail. You can insert any file as an attachment. Finally, the editor is an OLE 2.0 container supporting in place editing, so you insert an Object and edit it inside the document. For example, you could insert an Excel worksheet fragment (if you have Excel!) and use the Excel menus to format it while inside the mail editor.

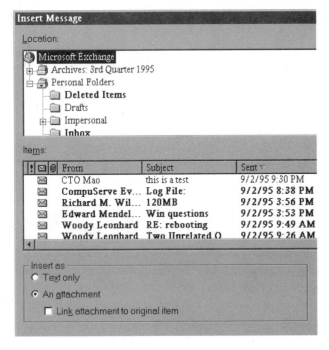

Figure 3-79. Inserting a message

How attachments and inserted objects are handled will depend on the mail service. For example, CompuServe will send them as separate messages. If the recipient is also using Exchange, the OLE objects, even though they are in separate messages, will appear with OLE objects in those separate messages, i.e., with their formatting intact.

Messages waiting to be sent are stored in the Outbox folder, where you can call them up to edit before sending. If you do call up a message in the Outbox, even if only to read it, be sure to hit the `Send` button when you exit the editor. If you exit in any other way (for example, by clicking the close button on the window), then the message will remain in the Outbox and will not be marked to send. Visually, messages in the Outbox that are going to be sent appear in the mail list in italics, and those that will not be sent are in nonitalics. To change a message listing from nonitalics to italics, just double-click on it and pick the `Send` button.

Although you can leave drafts of messages in the Outbox by calling them into the editor and not hitting the Send button, my advice is to make a folder called Drafts to store drafts of messages you aren't ready to send.

There isn't much to say about the message reader except to note the three buttons I already mentioned in the Exchange Toolbar—namely `Reply`, `Reply to All`, and `Forward`. And the two arrow buttons take you to the previous/next message in the list in the main Exchange Windows. All five of these buttons are also in WordMail.

If you didn't notice it at the start of the overall discussion of Exchange, in the Reader, the various addressees have context menus (see Figure 3-69) that will let you add names to your address list or access address entries to check out a company name, for example, if the sender is in your address book.

In either the message reader or the editor, you can double-click on an underlined name to bring up its Property sheet, including the full email address.

Sending and Receiving Mail

In a man's letters you know, Madam, his soul lies naked, his letters are only the mirror of his breast, whatever passes within him is shown undisguised in its natural process.

—Samuel Johnson, *Letter of Oct. 27, 1777, to Hester Thraler*

At this point in time I'm aware of five service providers for Exchange, although it is to be hoped that others get on board—I'd hope to see Prodigy, America Online, MCI Mail, ccMail, and Notes before too long:

- Microsoft Fax; this isn't exactly email and I'll discuss it in a separate section (two after next)

- The Microsoft Network, natch

- Microsoft Mail, natch (see the next section)

- CompuServe (of which more follows)

- Internet Mail using SMTP and POP3 servers*

During the initial setup of Windows 95, if you ask to have Exchange installed, you'll have a chance to include the first three of the providers just listed (as well as specifying an address book and personal store). The CompuServe Exchange Service Provider is on the Windows CD in the directory `Drivers\Other\Exchange\Compusrv`.

---

* SMTP = Simple Mail Transfer Protocol; POP3 = Post Office Protocol—version 3. These are the current standards for Internet Mail servers.

Gee, Billy, couldn't you guys do a better job of hiding it than putting it only four levels deep in the CD directory structure?

Hey, you press guys are always talking about a level playing field, aren't you? We figured that given that CompuServe has more than two million members and MSN had zero before it opened, putting a fully functioning MSN icon on the desktop with CompuServe (and only mail at that!) four levels deep would level the playing field. Besides, this way it's clear that support is CompuServe's responsibility, not ours.

CompuServe is to be commended for writing an Exchange Service Provider. Alas, file transfers with this provider are glacial—less than 50 percent the rate I get with WinCIM, another CompuServe product. And on Mao's system, the client sometimes fails to hang up the phone and has even been known to crash.

Internet Mail is part of the Internet Jump Start Kit which is included with the Plus! Pack and available on Microsoft's web site. If your Internet mail will collect but won't send, look at the section called "Hoping for an Easy Delivery."

If you have multiple accounts on a single service, I'll tell you what to do in "Better Profiles Than Mount Rushmore."

The variety of services and possible user scenarios makes for a melange of ways to collect and send mail. The most common way will be to choose `Deliver Now Using` on the Tools menu. The name is confusing, to say the least. You'd expect that command would send mail you've written, but in fact it *both* sends what you've written and collects mail from your mailbox. Even if you have nothing to send, it will connect and collect your mail. It will then log out—disconnect you from the service you connected to. Someone really should teach the meaning of the word *deliver* to the designer of the Exchange UI.

If you have a single Service Provider, `Deliver Now Using` will do just that. If you have multiple Providers installed, then that menu item passes to a cascading menu that starts with All Services and then lists the individual services for you. In the section called "Hoping for an Easy Delivery," I'll discuss where the ordering of the services on this list comes from.

I never could get All Services to work without one provider tromping over another.

As long as I put The Microsoft Network at the top, CompuServe in the middle and Internet at the end, I could get All Services to work.

You might hope to have a command line option to load Exchange and dial a particular provider (or all providers). Then you could use a scheduler like the Plus! Pack's System Agent to pick up your mail just before you arrived in the office. Exchange does have some command line switches listed in its help, but they are basically useless* and dialing a provider is not one of them.

The second method of collecting mail is `Remote Mail`, a potentially cascading menu of Tools just like `Deliver Now Using`. It calls up the Remote Mail window shown in Figure 3-80. Most of the important actions are accessible with the buttons listed in Figure 3-81.

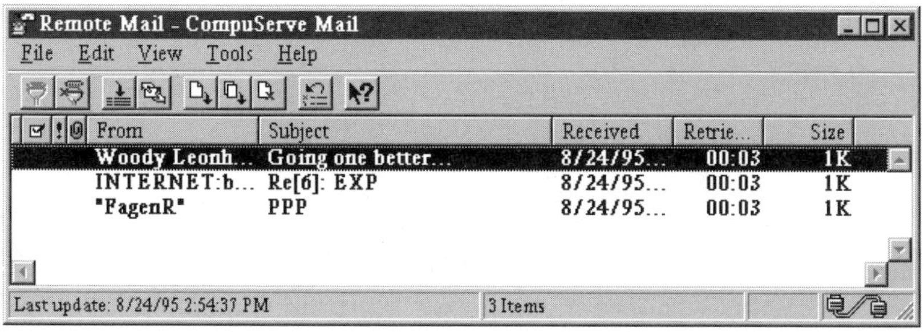

Figure 3-80. Remote Mail

Connect (grayed out if currently connected)	Disconnect (gray if not currrently connected)	Update headers
Collect marked and send	Mark to retrieve and delete	Mark to retrieve but leave in mailbox
Mark to delete	Unmark All	Explain this

Figure 3-81. The right buttons to push

---

* Useless for your typing in at the command line. They are there for the Mail Recipient item on the SendTo menu.

Basically, you update headers, then take one of four actions for each message: mark it for downloading with or without deletion, delete without downloading, or wait for another time to take any action. Finally, you click a button that does the requested actions on the headers that you've marked and sends any messages waiting to go out.

You'd use remote mail in the following situations:

- You have reason to believe you've a large binary file to download but you don't have time and only want to pick up your messages.

- You keep your main message store at the office but want to quickly check messages from home. You can use Remote Mail, mark messages to retrieve, but leave them there to pick up for placement in your main message store when you next collect mail from the office.

- You're checking your box for the first time after an absence and want to pick the most important mail to download first.

- Your mailbox is on a local network, and you prefer to be logged into the mail machine at all times, updating headers when the mood strikes you.

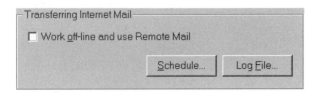

Figure 3-82. Internet Mail options

The final method only applies to Internet Mail and is mainly useful for those whose mail is on a local network. If you call up `Services. . .` from the `Tools` menu (or access the same dialog though the `Mail and Fax` Control Panel applet), highlight `Internet Mail`, click `Properties`, and choose the `Connection` tab, and you get a dialog that includes the panel in Figure 3-82. The checkbox titled "Work off-line and use Remote Mail" may not be what you think. It is not a choice of whether to use Remote Mail. Rather, that check box determines if you are using the third method of scheduled access. The key is the button marked Schedule. . ., which is grayed out if the checkbox is checked. It determines how often your mailbox is automatically polled—the default is every fifteen minutes.

So, if you want to access Internet Mail on demand by choosing from the Tools menu as you would access CompuServe or MSN mail, make sure the checkbox in Figure 3-82 is checked. If you access Internet Mail over the phone through a service provider, that's presumably what you want to do. But if your Internet access is through a local network and your email is a corporate mail system using UNIX pop-servers, then you might want to have Exchange automatically look for email every fifteen minutes or so. To do that just uncheck the box.

 If Windows offers to dial up your Internet network provider every time that Windows restarts and you can't figure out why it does, it's because the option to automatically poll is turned on. Check the box in this dialog and it will stop trying to dial at startup time.

 Of all the cockamamie checkboxes. Why the heck didn't they say "Enable automatic polling of mailbox."? That way people would be able to understand what the silly box meant and checking it would turn on automatic polling instead of turning it off.

 Take a look at the `General` tab of the `Tools/Option` dialog. The panel in Figure 3-83 is especially useful if you are using scheduled polling. Besides these three optional methods of notification, when new mail arrives, a 🔲 icon appears in the Notification area on the Taskbar.

You can have a message addressed to multiple users on different mail services. It remains in your outbox until you have logged on to each service that has recipients. It's quite efficient, but has one huge lack. There should be an easy way to tell from a message in your outbox which service providers it needs and which recipients remain to be contacted. Exchange keeps track of this very well but doesn't let you in on the secret. This is more than annoying—sometimes you'll be at a loss to figure out why some message is remaining in your Outbox, whom it has been delivered to, and whom not.

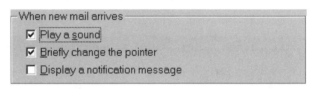

Figure 3-83. Mail for me? How nice!

Microsoft Mail Postoffice

The post-office had a great charm at one period of our lives. When you have lived to my age, you will begin to think letters are never worth going through the rain for.

—Jane Austen, *Emma,* 1816

 Included in Windows 95 is the Workgroup edition of Microsoft Mail, but you'd hardly know it. It isn't mentioned in the Windows 95 documentation or the on-line help for Windows or Exchange. It is discussed in the Resource Kit, but that's it.

This version of Microsoft Mail sets up a common Postoffice and allows sharing of mail among those with accounts with that Postoffice. The access can be via direct LAN connection or via Dial-Up Networking. You need to get an upgrade to the full Microsoft Mail Server (or when its available to Exchange Server) to send mail between Workgroup Postoffices or via Gateways to supported services like MCI mail, Novell MHS, and IBM PROFS.

For a small or even medium-sized office, this workgroup version may well be enough, and the support for Dial-Up Networking makes this especially useful if you have workers out on the road who have to check in. If a company is using Internet mail for its main email service, it might make sense for workgroups to use MSMail for their local mail, because transfer of mail is instantaneous if both sender and recipient are running Exchange, and the Exchange client makes it transparent whether you are sending MS Mail to your fellow workgroup members or Internet mail to someone else in the company. I can also see this being used on a single family machine with multiple user profiles—at a minimum, the kids will have fun sending messages to each other.

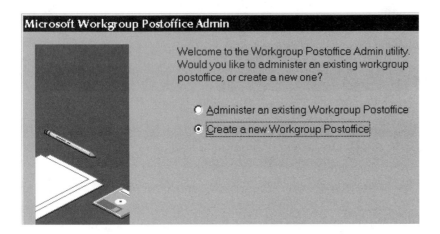

The first step is to click on the `Microsoft Mail Postoffice` icon in Control Panel to start the Postoffice Admin wizard. Be sure that the Create a new Workgroup Postoffice radio button is picked and click on `Next`.

In the next panel (not shown) you pick the location of the Postoffice. If you pick `C:\`, the directory used will be `C:\wpgo0000`. Believe it or not, this directory is made with more than fifty subdirectories!

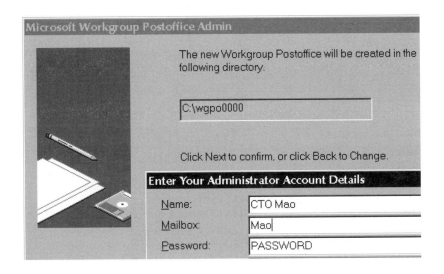

You are asked to confirm the directory; when you hit Next, you have to enter the name of the Administrator, mailbox name, and Password. The Postoffice Administrator has to set up new accounts and can deal with forgotten passwords. It is obviously important that you as the Administrator remember your password or else the Postoffice will need to be deleted, and you'll have to start over! This will complete the setup wizard but not the setup of the Postoffice.

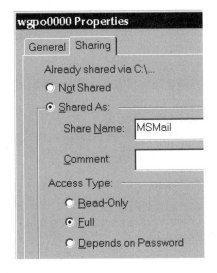

Next you'll need to turn on sharing for the Postoffice directory—go to Explorer, right-click on the directory, and pick Sharing. . . . You might consider giving a friendly sharename to the directory (the default is the wgpo0000 directory name) since users will need to enter that name when they set up their local Exchanges.

The last administrator step is to set up the accounts for all your users. You again invoke the Microsoft Mail Postoffice icon in Control Panel, but

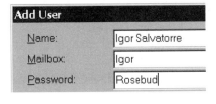

this time you choose Administer an existing. . . . After entering your password, you get to Add new users.

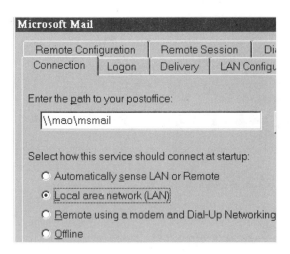

Once the Postoffice is created and the accounts are set-up, each user needs to call up his or her Exchange Profile (either from the `Mail and Fax` applet in Control Panel or `Tools/Services. . .` in the Exchange menus). Pick `Add. . .` and the `Microsoft Mail`. The first critical tab (left) requires you to enter the path to the Postoffice. UNC names can be used, and you'll want the sharename set up earlier by the administrator. If you are going to access the Postoffice over a LAN all the time, say so. The off-line option lets a remote user compose mail without having to log in.

Another important tab is `Logon`, which lets you decide whether you have to type in your password every time or not. If your network supports the Netbios protocol (most do), go to the `Delivery` tab and check `Immediate notification`. If that box is checked, Exchange polls the MS Mailbox frequently and your mail arrives automagically. If it is not checked, you have to use `Remote Mail` or `Deliver Now Using. . .` to get your mail.

While you are looking at the Delivery tab, you may happen to look at the `Address Types. . .` button and see a puzzling long list of services that it appears MS Mail will use. Those are only relevant if you have the upgraded server with gateways and, in fact, once you fire up Exchange and connect to the Postoffice the first time, the list will shrink to one item: Network/Postoffice. You also may be puzzled that `Change Password. . .` is grayed out on the Logon tab if you are accessing the Property sheet outside Exchange (using the `Mail and Fax` applet). That's because you need to be connected to the Postoffice to make that change—it will be working if you invoke the Microsoft Mail Property Sheet from the `Tools/Services. . .` menu in Exchange or via Control Panel when Exchange is loaded and connected to the Postoffice.

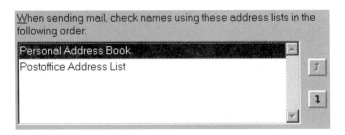

Figure 3-84. How shall I address you?

A final aspect of MS Mail you need to be aware of involves the Address Book. As with so much else in the Address Book, it isn't designed quite right. First, you'll want to be sure the MS Mail Address Book is added to the list of books you access. To be sure it is, go to the `Tools/Options...` menu item in Exchange and look at the list of address lists. If Postoffice Address List isn't included, hit the `Add...` button and add it. You'll notice little arrows next to the list (Figure 3-84) that allow you to change the ordering of your address lists. This concerns the rules used to search for matches when you hit or send mail with unresolved addresses. It looks through the first address list and displays only matches from that list—only if there are no matches in the first address list will it go to the second. There is no way to tell the program to always look through several of your lists.

> This is crazy. The only work-around I've come up with is to copy the names from the Postoffice list to your Personal Address Book (there is a button on the button bar when you are looking at any list but the Personal Address list in the Address Book viewer). This defeats the purpose of the Postoffice list, which is kept up to date as users are added and subtracted.

Hoping for an Easy Delivery

Every accent, every emphasis, every modulation of voice, was so perfectly well turned and well placed, that, without being interested in the subject, one could not help being pleased with the discourse; a pleasure of much the same kind with that received from an excellent piece of music. This is an advantage itinerant preachers have over those who are stationary, as the latter can not well improve their delivery of a sermon by so many rehearsals.

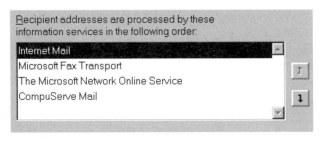

Figure 3-85. Improving your Delivery

—Benjamin Franklin, *Autobiography*

Buried in the Exchange options is one that can cause an interesting problem if you don't know where to look. It also is the secret way to customize something you might want to. The dialog fragment that controls the option, shown in Figure 3-85, is on the `Delivery` tab of the `Mail and Fax` applet and also in the `Delivery` tab of the dialog invoked by the `Tools/Options` menu choice in Exchange itself.

The problem is that you install Internet Mail and you find that you have no trouble receiving mail, but the messages you've marked to send just sit in your Outbox and aren't sent. There are several possible reasons this can happen, and I'll come back to another at the end of this section. But the most common reason is the list in Figure 3-85 and the fact that the mail type used for Internet Mail—called SMTP—is understood by both Internet Mail and The Microsoft Network Online Service, aka MSN. If you want your Internet Mail to get sent via your direct Internet provider, you need to use the arrows next to the list and move up the Internet Mail entry, so it is above the MSN entry.

The other place the list in Figure 3-85 is used is so bizarre, it still surprises me. You may wonder where the ordering of services in the Tools/Deliver Now Using menu comes from. It is precisely the list in Figure 3-85, but in the reverse order!

The last shall be first and first shall be last—eh, grasshopper? You can change the ordering of services in that menu by using the arrows in the dialog in Figure 3-85.

It is not only bizarre to link these two lists, but by doing it in the opposite order and placing new services at the bottom of the list, the designers made this choice inconvenient for those who use the keyboard. (You could use `Ctrl+1` to launch the first service, for example.) Adding a service puts that service in the `Ctrl+1` position and changes the hotkeys for all the others. Of course, if that bothers you, you now know how to fix it!

The other common cause for messages not going out over Internet even though you can receive them is that you are using the wrong address type because both CompuServe and MSN have Internet address forms that are different from the one specifically needed for an Internet Mail provider. Anyone you want to send mail to over a standard Internet provider needs an email tab that says `SMTP-Internet`.

The Fax is The Fax

> Fax is email for the computer otherwise enabled.
>
> —*Igor's book of Bulgarian Witticisms*

 The good is the enemy of the best and the very good is even more an enemy. The Fax software my team built into Windows 95 is so good that the stuff you pay for, while often better, is toast.

 Yes, indeed. Already in Windows for Workgroups, the MS Fax driver was the best I'd seen at connecting to unruly fax machines, but the software was pretty poor. You've fixed that problem in spades!

Nothing but the Fax

> The facts: nothing matters but the facts: worship of the facts leads to everything, to happiness first of all, and then to wealth.

> —Edmond de Goncourt and Jules de Goncourt, *The Goncourt Journals,* entry for July 30, 1861

I'll discuss installation and then talk about some of the basic options and send procedures. Call up the `Mail and Fax` applet and see if Microsoft Fax is listed—it will be if you added Fax when you originally set up Exchange. If not, you need to install the software.

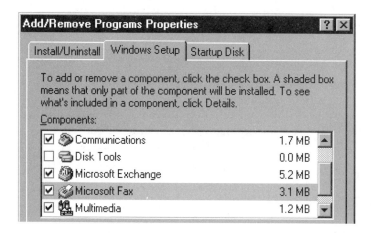

First, you've got to be sure the fax software is on your disk. Call up the `Add/Remove` applet from Control Panel and go to the `Windows Setup` tab. No, it isn't under Communications or Microsoft Exchange. It's got its own entry that you have to scroll to see at 640 × 480 resolution. If the box isn't checked, check it and hit `OK`. It takes 3.1 MB of disk space. If you have Win95 on diskette, #5 should be ready.

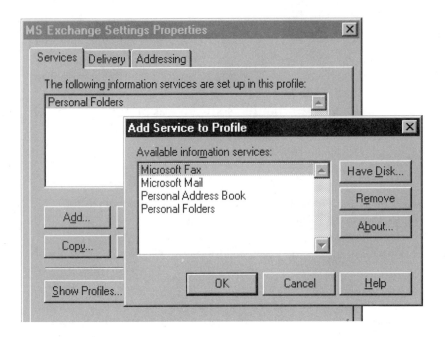

Installing Microsoft Fax doesn't install the fax software, as you might think. You've got to attach it to Exchange. So call up the Mail and Fax applet in Control Panel and click the Add. . . button, highlight Microsoft Fax, and hit OK.

Then say Yes and give it your name and fax number and then hit OK and accept its offer to install a Fax modem (unless you have a Network Fax Server, discussed later).

That will invoke a wizard within a wizard to install your fax modem. It'll both search out the modem and set it as the default for faxes. In these final stages, you've seen the Fax Property sheet (Figure 3-86), which will come up again and again as I discuss faxes. It can be invoked directly by picking Tools/Microsoft Fax Tools/Options. . . in the Exchange menus, by picking Tools/Services. . . from those menus, highlighting Microsoft Fax and hitting Properties, or doing the equivalent from the Mail and Fax applet in Control Panel.

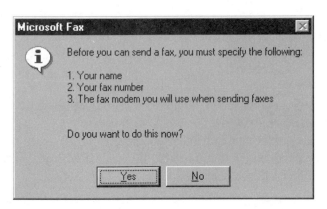

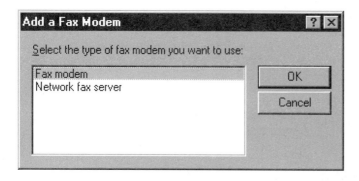

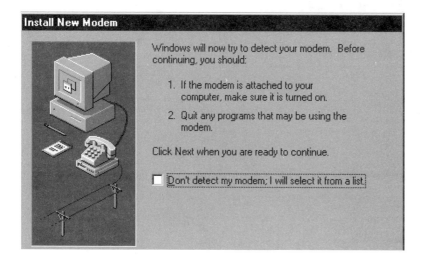

The `Message` tab is so important I'll prominently discuss each of its three main parts later. It only sets defaults: using the `File/Send Options` menu item in the message editor, you can change these items on a Fax-by-Fax basis.

`Dialing` and `Modem` do what you'd think, except auto answer is buried on the `Modem` page. The `User` tab fields other than name and fax number are only used for cover pages with send fields. If you use such pages, you'll need to fill it in!

When you first install, you have two main things to be sure to set. One involves whether you want the Fax modem to accept incoming faxes. Don't bother looking for the option on any of the tabs of the Fax Property sheet. This is considered a fax *modem* property, so you need to go to the `Modem` tab of the Fax property dialog, highlight the Fax modem, hit `Properties . . .` and look at the `Answer mode` panel in the resulting dialog (Figure 3-87). The default is `Don't answer`, so the fact that this dialog is buried isn't likely to burn you.

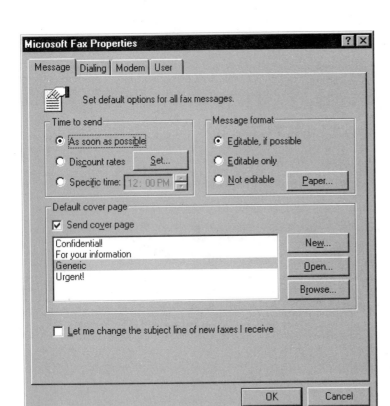

Figure 3-86. The Fax Properties sheet

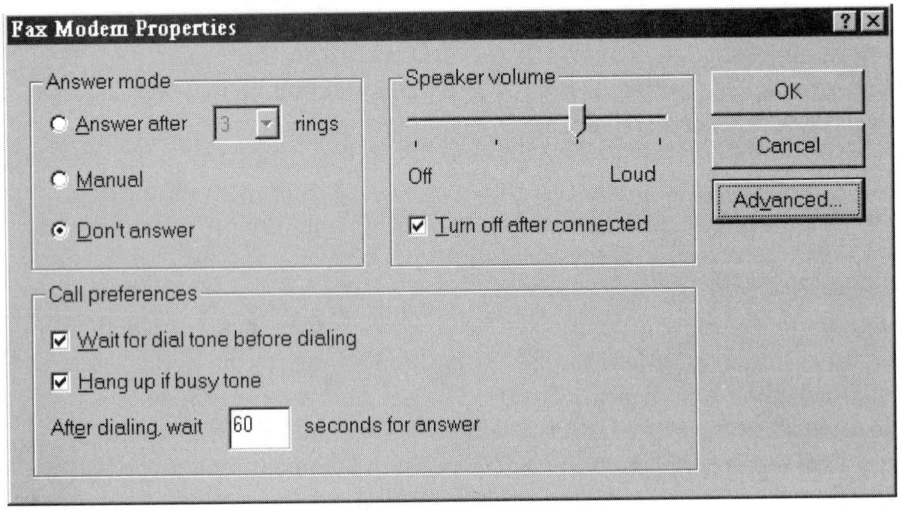

Figure 3-87. Important Answer option

Figure 3-88. Important Send option

The second important item to set is the part of the `Message` tab of the Fax Properties dialog shown in Figure 3-88 that determines when outgoing faxes get sent by default. The initial setting is "As soon as possible," which means that pretty much as soon as you hit the Send button, the fax processing starts. The other two options involve a delayed send. When you have outgoing faxes pending, the fax icon on the notification area of the Taskbar picks up the extra outgoing paper icon shown on the right. If you

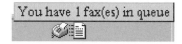

rest the mouse over that icon, it tells you the number of faxes in the queue, as seen here.

 One strange thing is that if you add Fax to an existing Exchange profile, you have to fill in the dialogs and know to go to the Fax Modem Properties box to set up Fax autoanswer. But, if you set up a brand new profile and check off Fax as one of the services you want included, it goes through a Setup Fax wizard that makes the fill-ins painless and has an explicit panel where you get to decide on Fax autoanswer capability. The question, though, is why the Setup Fax wizard isn't invoked when you add to an existing profile.

The settings you make in the Message tab of the Fax Property sheet can be overridden as long as you do so before you hit the Send button. When composing a Fax Message in either Exchange's built-in editor or in WordMail, you can call up the `Send Options` item on the File menu and get what looks exactly* like the `Message` tab in Fax Properties, but this tab lets you set the options for this particular message.

 Ah, but suppose you change your mind after you hit the Send button and, in particular, suppose that you want to send a fax right away that was originally scheduled to get sent later? I may be missing something, but as far as I can tell the only way to do that is a set of steps that even Rube Goldberg would find bizarre.

---

* Well, not exactly exactly! Individual Send options include the Advanced Security I'll discuss at the end of this section.

You might expect that if you went to the Exchange Tools menu and picked `Deliver Now Using Microsoft Fax` that it would, er, deliver now using Microsoft Fax. But no such luck. You might expect that when you double-clicked on the Fax page on the notification bar and got a listing of outgoing faxes, that you could access the properties (i.e., send options) of any fax in the queue, but you can't.

Get this—Mom's patented method for rescheduling fax transmissions. In Exchange, go to the Outbox. Until the fax is sent, the message remains in the Outbox, so double-click on it to bring it into the editor, call up the `Send Options` from the File menu, and change the send time to, for example, `As soon as possible`. Then hit the Send button. But don't think you are done! You'll get a notification of a new message, and indeed, you'll find a missive in your Inbox from your old friend and mine—Exchange's virtual System Administrator. Good ole Sys (as she's known to her friends) informs you, "The fax was not sent because you or the system administrator cancelled it." And indeed, Sys has removed the fax from the queue. But don't despair. In Sys's message there is a button marked `Send Again`. That will bring up a panel that includes a `Send` button. Hit that and the fax gets sent with the new options. Rube's brother must work for Microsoft.

So much for setting up the fax software. There are essentially three ways of sending faxes:

- Think like Igor that Fax is just email for the computer phobic. You can compose it as an email message as you'd compose any other message but the email type in your address book is FAX and the "address" is a Fax number. If you do that you might want a cover page—I'll discuss those in a little while.

Don't get confused by the fact that any email type has a place for you to enter fax numbers in the Phone Numbers tab. In its current incantation, Exchange ignores fax numbers that you enter in that tab unless the email type is FAX.

- Pick `New Fax` from the `Compose` menu in Exchange and get a rather elegant wizard. This lets you type in a little message—if you use a cover page with room for it and your message is short, you can even include the message on the cover page. You don't need to load Exchange to access the New Fax wizard. From the Start Menu, `Programs/Accessories/Fax` has a `Compose New Fax` item that will call up the wizard and send the Fax without starting up Exchange itself. Despite not loading Exchange, the Fax is stored in your Personal Folders. There is a third way to invoke the New Fax wizard.

Right-click on a file in Explorer and choose Fax Recipient from the Send To menu. In the wizard panel where you choose the cover page to use, you'll also find an easily missed `Options. . .` button that lets you override the default for the time the Fax is sent.

- From an application, print to the Fax Printer or use the Send item in the File menu, if it has one. I'll discuss this after I talk about cover pages. If you prepare the document properly in your application, you might not want a cover page.

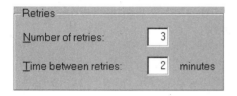

Figure 3-89. Try, try again

The Dialing tab of the Fax Property sheet has the panel shown in Figure 3-89. The fields seem pretty obvious, but what *retries* means might not be. If Exchange tries to send a Fax and it gets a busy signal, then it retries. If it gets no answer or a voice reply, then it does *not* retry. Instead, our buddy Exchange's virtual System Administrator removes the fax from the queue and sends a message that says, "No one answered your call, or the receiving device is not a fax machine." A Send Again button brings up a dialog where you can resend with a change of fax number if need be. To check or change the fax number, you right-click on the recipient's name in the Resend dialog, and pick Properties from the context menu. Given that you don't need to worry about making an error and ringing a voice line multiple times, you may want to increase the number of retries from the default 3.

 I'm the System Administrator on Mom's LAN, and I sure don't like Exchange pretending to be me. The services of the virtual System Administrator are great, but why use a name that could get users confused between the real SysAdmin and the virtual one? I also think it's a big mistake that messages that get canceled by you or the virtual System Administrator still wind up in the Sent Items folder. Either there should be a special folder for canceled items or they shouldn't be saved as messages at all (since they are saved in the message from the virtual System Administrator).

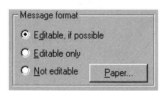

Figure 3-90. Total Quality Control

You may want to save money on fax transmissions by using draft quality (200 × 100 dpi). You do that in the `Message format` frame of the `Message` tab in the Fax Property sheet. `The Paper. . .` button has a drop-down for `Image Quality`. Unless you want to trade quality for cost, the default "Best Available" option is probably the best choice. For sending to European machines or a legal office with different paper size, you also use the `Paper. . .` button. I'll explain what `Not editable` means later.

I've Got the Answer For You

Figure 3-87 shows the three options you can set for having your fax modem answering the phone. The meaning is fairly clear: If you choose Manual, when the fax line rings a box will pop up offering to let you receive the incoming fax.

 But there's a doozy of a bug associated to the "Answer after *N* rings" option. If you have that option picked, when the fax line rings, you get the dialog shown in Figure 3-91. You'd think that hitting the button that says "Answer Now" would do just that. But instead, it *doesn't answer at all* within the roughly ten rings that many fax machines try (including Microsoft Fax!). So "Answer Now" becomes "don't answer"! Worse, after a couple of minutes, it does initialize the modem and try to pick it up. Oh, how I love a nice bug in the 'mornin.

Figure 3-91. Answer Now—NOT!

There are several things you've got to realize about either of the options that will let your modem accept incoming faxes. First, you have to have Exchange running for them to have any effect. This is strange, because the New Fax wizard seems quite capable of driving the Fax without Exchange loaded. You'd think that there could be a way to load a small fax-receiving stub without making you keep Exchange (which is a memory and resource hog) always up. Second, if you have these modes turned on and Exchange loaded, then your modem won't be usable by many other programs. Basically, any DOS and any Windows 3.1 program will think that the serial port is unavailable. Windows 95 communication programs that are TAPI aware (that includes Dialer, Hyperterminal, and Dial-up Networking) will able to use the modem when the fax isn't actually in use. Of course, you can exit Exchange if you need to and then the Windows 3.1 or DOS programs will able to access the modem. Third, you might expect that your modem's autoanswer light would go on if you had Fax Autoanswer in effect. But it doesn't with most modems that use the Autoanswer light to indicate that the modem is set to pick up the line *as a modem,* not as a fax machine.

As I'll explain at the end of this section, some faxes will come in as editable objects. But you'll get bitmaps for faxes sent to you by fax machines, from computers using other fax software, and from Microsoft Fax users who have chosen to send their fax to you in noneditable form. Such faxes appear in the Exchange Inbox with a subject that begins Fax from. . . . Double-click such a message and it is loaded into the fax viewer. This viewer isn't bad, but it is the weakest component of the Fax package. You can view and print out faxes and export them into a Fax Viewer–specific file format. There is a zoom function and you can display a mixed thumbnail/text view. But there is a lot missing that you'll find in the high-class packages—there is no OCR to turn an incoming noneditable fax into text. There is no ability to annotate pages or rearrange them. There is no thumbnail only view.

You can forward an incoming noneditable fax by using the standard forward function in Exchange.

Not exactly standard incoming fax but related is the Request a Fax wizard that you'll find off the Start Menu in `Programs\Acessories\Fax` and in the Exchange menus under `Tools\Microsoft Fax Tools\Request a Fax`. In its own words, "This wizard lets you call a fax information service and retrieve a document or file. After your call is finished, the retrieved information will appear in your Inbox." Exchange need not be running when you use the wizard, although you'll need to load Exchange to read any fax sent in response to the request.

Request a Fax is something with great potential, but at the time of Windows 95 launch, it is only that. It is intended for use with special fax servers that can talk directly to your Microsoft Fax. You'd call in once with a generic request and the object retrieved would be a master list of documents. Subsequent calls would allow you to retrieve specific documents. A company called Ibex Technology seems to have the lead in producing the hardware/software components that a business would need to set up a Fax on Demand server that talks to Windows 95. If you want to see the technology in action, you can use the Request a Fax wizard to phone their Fax Server at (916) 939–9650.

One issue that remained to be settled when I spoke with Ibex is whether a single phone number could be used by a company to both act as an automated server for Win95 Request a Fax and act as the traditional choose-from-the-menu-from-hell voice line Fax back service. But either way, if this idea catches on, you'll eventually find the technology so useful that I'll bet you'll put an icon to the wizard on your Desktop. For the moment, this idea is waiting for the world to catch up with it. Once the world does, it'll be wonderful.

The True Fax about Networks

The social kiss is an exchange of insincerity between two combatants on the field of social advancement. It places hygiene before affection and condescension before all else.

—*Sunday Correspondent* of London, Aug. 12, 1990

You can share a fax modem over a network. More precisely, you can use a fax connected to another Windows 95 computer on the network to send (but not receive) faxes. You aren't actually using the modem over the network (so, for example, you can't use a comm program on one computer to drive a modem on another, at least with only the native Windows 95 software). Rather, you send the faxes to a shared directory and software on the computer with the modem actually sends out.

First, on the computer that has the fax modem, you need to call up the Fax Property sheet and pick the `Modem` tab. You'll find a panel like the one shown in Figure 3-92. Check the box that says, "Let other people on the network use my modem to send faxes." It will then ask you to "Select the drive the network fax service will use." There is a drop-down of local drives only. The default share name is FAX, but you can change that by using the `Properties. . .` button.

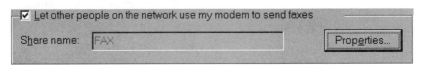

Figure 3-92. Share and share alike

When you make these choices, Windows makes a directory `\netfax` in the root of the directory you pick and places two files, `netfax2.q` and `netfax2.sta`. When Exchange is running, a third file called `netfax2.inf` is also placed there. Even if the whole host drive is shared, the directory `\netfax` is shared with the specified sharename.

Before you install the remote fax modem, make sure that Exchange is running on the machine to which the modem is attached. Then on the machine you want to remotely access that modem, call up the Fax Property sheet, go to the `Modem` tab and hit the `Add. . .` button, highlight `Network Fax Server`, hit OK, and get the `Connect to Network Fax Server` dialog shown in Figure 3-93. You need to type in the path to the network fax directory using `\\`*name*`\`*sharename*.

In this UNC pathname, *name* is the name of the computer to which the fax modem is attached and *sharename* is FAX or the replacement you picked when you turned on sharing of the modem. That's it—you should now be able to print faxes to the remote network fax server.

You must use the directory sharename, not an indirect one. For example, if the computer is called `maos_marvel` and drive c is shared and `C:\netfax` is shared as `fax`, then in the Figure 3-93 dialog, you *must* use `\\maos_marvel\fax` and not `\\maos_marvel\c\netfax`. I think this is a bug, but the powers that be might shrug and say that's just the way networks work.

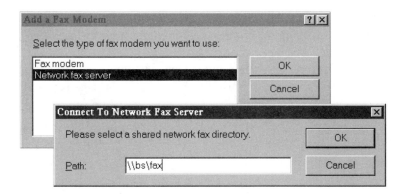

Figure 3-93. Alike share and share

Behind the scenes, when you send a fax from a client computer via the modem on the fax server computer, what really happens is that Exchange on the client computer places a file (with the extension `.fax`) in the `netfax` directory on the server computer. Exchange on the server computer notices the file there, sends it out over the modem, deletes it, and places an `.ack` acknowledgment file in the `netfax` directory. The client Exchanges notices that file, uses it to process the sending data (puts on the right date time stamp and moves the file from Outgoing to Sent Items), and deletes it.

Exchange must be running on the server computer when the fax is sent. If not and you try to send a fax from the client machine, you are advised that the fax server is unavailable and you get an offer to work off-line. If you do that, the next time you reboot Windows and start up Exchange, the pending faxes will be sent if the fax server has become available.

The model for sharing a printer over a network is simple and intuitive—you pick Sharing. . . from the Printer's context menu on the server to turn on sharing and then go through a simple Printer install on the client where you browse the network to see available printers. Fax is associated to a virtual print driver to Microsoft Fax. It's unfortunate that the same paradigm isn't used for faxes as for printers with the virtual printer used, but it isn't. In fact Sharing. . . is not a choice for fax printers.

I've Got You Covered

The covers of this book are too far apart.

—a one-sentence book review by Ambrose Bierce

There are some circumstances where you want a cover page for a fax or want a single-page fax with cover page information and room for a note. Windows 95 includes a cover page editor that you invoke from `Start Menu/Programs/Accessories/Fax/Cover Page Editor`. It's not the slickest program you've seen, but it serves its purpose well. There are four sample cover pages provided that you can use for templates. The page is made up of regions where you can place simple objects, including vector graphics using the program's primitive drawing tools, text areas, special fields, and (because the program is an OLE 2 in place editing application) any object made by an OLE server—for example, bitmaps using MS Paint.

The fields can include the following information about the recipient: name, fax number, company, address, city, state, zip, country, title, department, office location, home and office telephone number, to and cc lists. Except for the last two items (which are taken from the names you put in at the time you send), the items come from the Address Book entry for the recipient. This is the only place in the programs that ship with Windows 95 where the General tab fields in the Address Book are used.

Fields for the sender can include name, fax number, company, title, department, office location, and home and office phone number. This information is obtained from what is filled in on the `User` tab in the Fax Property sheet. Obviously, if you are making a cover page for your use alone, you can just use your information instead of the sender fields, but they are useful for cover pages made for workgroups or companies. If such a cover sheet is used, make sure that users fill in their `User` tab! Finally, you can provide the number of pages (including the cover page) and other message-specific information in fields.

You get to decide on cover pages in many places. In the Message tab of the Fax Property sheet there's a panel that lets you choose whether to send a cover page and which to use (see Figure 3-94). You can change it in Send Options for messages created in the editor. If you use the Create Fax wizard, you get to choose the cover page. Only with this wizard can you send a single-page fax with cover page, including a brief note.

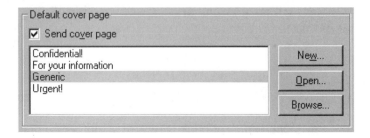

Figure 3-94. Cover me, partner

One final cover page issue concerns a most annoying bug that afflicts one of the machines in Mom's stable. Sometimes the list of available cover pages disappears and the Send Cover Page options are grayed out. I try to add cover pages, but I get the complaint they are already installed. The only solution I've found is to use `Add/Remove Software` to remove the fax software and then reinstall it. Fortunately, all the Exchange settings are remembered, so this process is mainly a reboot. Oh, how I love a nice bug in the mornin'.

The So-Called Microsoft Fax Printer

> Email is Fax is for the computer savvy.
>
> *—Igor's book of Bulgarian Syllogisms*

Like Voltaire's bon mot about the Holy Roman Empire, the Microsoft Fax Printer is neither a printer nor is it for faxes alone. Hmm—but it is from Microsoft.

Was Voltaire that guy in the Batman movie who kept shouting Holy Roman Empire, Batman? I wonder how much it would cost to get Batman to use the word Microsoft instead of holy?

The Send option that you'll find in many Windows 95 programs from Visio to Winword to WordPad sends the current document as an attachment to an email message. If you then fax that message to a fax machine, the attachment gets printed. What about Windows 3.1 programs? For that, you need to use a "printer" called Microsoft Fax.

Oh, I get it. If you pick "Microsoft Fax" as your printer, and print from an application, then the file is faxed—sorta using the other guy's fax machine as a remote printer. Cool.

Not quite, grasshopper. "Microsoft Fax" means roughly the same as Send. It calls the "printed" document into Exchange, where you can email it as an attachment or fax, as you'd like. This can be confusing because a user might expect that if someone is in your address book with their email address but their address book entry also has a fax number, then printing to the Microsoft Fax Printer would fax to them. Not so; it emails to them. The only way to fax to them is to make a second entry in your address book of fax type and use that address.

Windows Secret File Transfer Program

Windows 95 Fax is cheap file-transfer software.

—Igor's book of Bulgarian Quips

 Happens to me all of the time. Someone needs to get a file to me urgently and I'm on CompuServe while they are on Internet or AOL or . . . and they ask if we can't try a direct modem hookup. So I call up ProComm and go to host mode. Depending on their modem, it can go smoothly or roughly— but more often than not, we wind up having to try multiple Xmodem, Kermit, yeechy binary protocols. And it's not only the hassle—I'm not happy that someone I don't know well gets some kind of direct access to my disk. So one of my favorite Windows 95 secrets is the really neat direct modem transfers that are built in. One requires special hardware—Voice View capable modems—I'll discuss it in Chapter 4. Here I'll discuss the secret method that anyone with a Faxmodem can use.

One of the reasons it is a secret is that it's not networking where you'll find talk of direct Cable Connection and Dial-Up Networking, subjects I'll discuss in the next chapter. Rather, it's part of faxing! The key is the panel several pages back in Figure 3-90 (part of the Message tab in the Fax Property sheet) and the difference between editable and noneditable formats. Editable format is just a name for sending files instead of the usual bitmaps that Fax machines use. If you pick Editable only or Editable, if possible and the Windows 95 fax software finds Windows 95 fax software on the receiving end, then Windows doesn't send a fax bitmap, it sends a binary file.

This has three huge advantages. The first advantage involves the amount of data sent over the phone line. As a trial I sent the same seven-page Word document—purely text with a little formatting—between the same two Windows 95 machines with fax modem, but in one case I marked the message as Not editable, forcing the file to get sent as a Fax bitmap. I had the "paper" option set to Best available, so it was sent as 300 dpi. The Fax bitmap was 282K while the editable version was 27K. Not surprisingly, it took about ten times as long to send the fax bitmap.

The second advantage concerns text messages that are, er, editable, when sent in editable format. If you've prepared a message in Word, it'll arrive as a Word file with all its formatting and the text in a format that can be manipulated. To do that with a bitmap Fax you'd need OCR and have some rate of errors.

The third advantage is that this can be used to send binary files. If someone who has Windows 95 wants to send you a bunch of files and you both have fax modems, have them zip them up using PKZIP or Winzip, have them address a Fax message to you and drag the zip into the message. Then you need to turn on Fax Autoanswer (manual is fine) and they phone you. The transfer is painless and rather quick, given one restriction—even if your modems support higher speeds as modems, as faxes they will probably be limited to 9600 bps. In a test, it took almost exactly three minutes to transfer a 187K file, which is close to maximum efficiency for 9600 bps.

Believe it or not, Windows 95 has some heavy-duty security options available for binary fax transfers. Go to the `Tools\Microsoft Fax Tools\Advanced Security. . .` dialog. There are passwords, encryption, public key RSA encryption, digital signatures—the whole nine yards. In fact, one could say nine times nine yards. I didn't test any of this.

This is triply bizarre! Why is Microsoft putting RSA encryption—something sure to raise the hackles of the government snoops—into Windows 95, which is, in part, a consumer product? Why is there such heavy-duty stuff in a system whose password protection is so light that it can be overcome if you hit `Esc` at the login prompt? And, if Exchange is going to offer encryption, why of fax and not email? Truly bizarre.

Better Profiles Than Mount Rushmore

> There is something tragic about the enormous number of young men there are
> in England at the present moment who start life with perfect profiles,
> and end by adopting some useful profession.
>
> Oscar Wilde, *Phrases and Philosophies for the Use of the Young*

Exchange stores its basic settings in what it calls profiles. An important feature of Exchange is that you can have multiple profiles. Why should you ever want more than one?

- If you have more than one account on a single service, say a CompuServe account paid for by your employer and one you use for personal use, you'll need to use multiple profiles. To avoid confusion, Exchange only allows a single account from a given provider in a given profile. I'll explain how to handle this in detail later. Profiles can share the same message store, so by switching profiles, you can collect a message in one account and answer it in another.

- On a machine shared by several users, whether or not you've turned on multiple user profiles for Desktop settings, you can use multiple Exchange profiles. By combining the ability to set up a forced choice of Profile upon starting Exchange with password protection for profiles (explained later) you can set up an effective shared mail program for the multiple users.

- If you use the same machine in several locations, multiple profiles may help. For example, if you take a portable to several different cities and use CompuServe to collect your mail, you could copy the same profile several times, give these profiles the names of the cities, and change the phone numbers in the CompuServe Properties Sheet Connection tab to the proper ones for that city. If you do that, you'll want to set up the multiple profiles to prompt you for which one to use when you start Exchange.

 If you are using multiple profiles like this, one of the really annoying quirks of Exchange is that there isn't any direct way to tell what the current profile is. There is a hidden way to do so, though. The name of your Personal Message Store and the name of the file are disconnected. So you can have the different profiles share the same message file but still name the store something like `Los Angeles Profile` and `New York Profile`. Since the name appears at the second place in the Exchange Folders tree, you have this information immediately at your fingertips. You can rename the message store in three ways: by right-clicking on it in the folder tree and picking rename, by selecting it in the tree and choosing File/Rename. . . from the menus, or by choosing the Message Store from the Profile Property sheet and invoking its set of Properties.

- If you have a portable with a docking station, you might want different profiles for when you are connected to the network and when you are on the road and need to use DialUp networking to access your mailbox.

- Let's suppose that you use several machines on a network, say in different offices you have—I'll call then machine1 and machine2. You can arrange for them to normally share the same Personal Folders and Address Book, say on machine1. But that means that if you leave Exchange running on machine1 and then try to log in on machine2, you'll have a problem caused by the shared files. If you just want to use machine2 for, say, a quick fax, you could set up two profiles on machine2—one with your usual files and one with only the fax service and local address book and personal store. When using the second profile, there'll be no problem of shared files.

You can set up multiple profiles in several ways. In the main `Mail and Fax` applet of Control Panel (recall Figure 3-70), if you hit `Show Profiles. . .` you get the dialog shown in Figure 3-95. The `Add. . .` button calls up the New Profile wizard with subwizards to set up the individual services. The `Copy. . .` button lets you make a new

Figure 3-95. The Profile Manager

profile based on an existing one. You can then modify it at the main `Mail and Fax` applet screen, which you can get back to (with the new profile selected if appropriate). In a drop-down, you get to pick what is Exchange's default profile. This default choice is used in several places. It is the Property sheet for the default profile that shows up when you start the `Mail and Fax` applet. To get to the Property sheet of another profile, you hit `Show Profiles. . .`, highlight the one you want, and hit `Properties`.

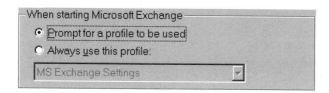

Figure 3-96. Turn right to show your best profile

The default is also used in one of two possible ways when you start Exchange, depending on the radio button chosen in Figure 3-96. That's a panel in `General` tab in the `Tools/Options` menu choice in Exchange. If you make the default "Always use this profile," then the default profile is used when you start Exchange. If you check "Prompt for a profile to use," you'll get the dialog in Figure 3-97.

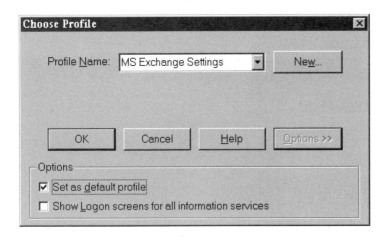

Figure 3-97. Making a good choice

 Hummph! A lotta poor design here. The text above the drop-down in the Profile Manager (Figure 3-95) says, "When starting Microsoft Exchange use this profile." But that's not what it means if you have the top radio button in the Figure 3-96 dialog selected. Moreover, the choice made in dialog fragment in Figure 3-96 is so important it shouldn't just be buried in Options inside Exchange but should be part of the Profile Manager and of the multiple profile login screen (Figure 3-97).

 My advice if you use multiple profiles depends on how you use them. If you use one profile almost all the time, set it as the one to use automatically. When you need to access one of the others, you can change the default profile in the General tab of the Tools/Options Exchange menu or in the Profile Manager and then change it back. If you switch profiles often, use the option that lets you choose the option when Exchange starts up.

Using Multiple Message Stores

> You can have multiple message stores, although one is plenty.
>
> —Brian Livingston and Davis Straub, *Windows 95 Secrets*

One feature of Exchange that will be used and be most welcome by users that know of the feature is its ability to place multiple message stores in a single Profile. If you try to add any other service but "Personal Folders," Exchange will complain, "You cannot create a second copy of this messaging service in your profile." But you can tell it to add additional Personal

Figure 3-98. Adding a second
message store

Folders. The dialog that pops up lets you pick the file that is used. It can be an existing `.pst` file or a new one. I'll explain situations where you might want one or the other. The default directory for the second `.pst` file is `C:\windows`, which makes no sense if the original store is placed in `C:\Exchange`. But since it is a standard open dialog you can navigate to `C:\Exchange`.

The dialog that comes next (Figure 3-98) lets you name the store—that's the name that appears in the folder listing in Exchange itself (Figure 3-99). You can always change this name later, either in the Properties sheet for the message store or by selecting the name in Exchange, right-clicking, and picking Rename (or using File/Rename from the Exchange menus). The dialog in Figure 3-98 also lets you set password and other options.

When you add a second message store as a new file, it only makes a Deleted Items folder and does not make Inbox, Outbox, and Sent Items folders for that store. But if you load a second store that comes from elsewhere, it may have an Inbox, etc., already, which means that your total Exchange folder hierarchy can have multiple Inbox folders, multiple Outbox folders, and multiple Sent Items Folders. Under this circumstance, the ones that are actually used are determined by the `Delivery` tab of the Exchange `Tools/Options. . .` menu. The dialog says "Deliver new mail to the following location," which might make you think that the choice only affected which Inbox is used, but it affects all three folders. Normally, if you do nothing, your original choice is used.

Figure 3-99. Multiple
message stores

 Be careful of accidentally choosing a secondary store without Inbox and other folders as either your primary or secondary location for new mail because if you do, Exchange will create Inbox, Outbox, and Sent Items folders as subfolders. If that happens, I haven't figured out how to delete these unwanted folders, except by making a new store and transferring messages to the new store and deleting the old one.

The reason multiple stores are so important is that you can move messages from one store inside a single profile to another by merely dragging. You can drag whole folders. You can even drag multiple folders, which are subsets of a single parent, if you select them on the right pane with `Ctrl+Click` and drag them. If you have a lot of messages you are moving, it can take a long time.

Here are some situations for which you'll find multiple stores useful:

- If you use email extensively and want to save old messages, you'll want to make monthly or quarterly archives. You move messages from the active store to an archive where they remain available for searching. Then, when more time has passed, you can delete the older archives from your active profile. This only deletes the connection to the profile but leaves the corresponding `.pst` on disk. You can move this file to archival storage or leave it on disk and reattach it to your profile if you want to consult it.

- If you normally use a Desktop machine but take a portable on the road occasionally, you can pick up your messages from Exchange on the portable while you are on the road and, when you return, copy the message store to your Desktop's hard disk, add it to the profile of your Desktop's exchange and copy the messages you received and sent on the road to your main message store. Then copy the portable message back to the portable so you won't have confusion in the future. If you have a docking station or use a direct cable connection (discussed in Chapter 4), you don't need to copy the message stores from the portable but instead can read them directly off the portable's drive!

- If you use Exchange to store both documents and mail, it is cleaner if you put them in separate stores.

One annoying limitation with multiple Message Stores is that even if several are loaded you can only search one at a time.

Helping Those that Help Themselves

Historically, we've focused on documenting our products—that is, explaining how they work . . . This motivated us to rethink our approach . . . We realize that you have a job to do; you need to get from point A to point B. Our job is to provide you with a "map" and steer you in the right direction so that you can get there as quickly and efficiently as possible.

—Pete Higgins, Microsoft Group Vice President in *What Have We Done to Your Manual,* an Introduction to the Office 95 printed documentation

The Windows 3.1 help engine was one of the product's unsung heroes. It had hypertext links, support for simple graphics, and extensibility for third parties wanting to make specialized addins. The Windows 95 help engine has turned a good component into a superb one. Added are the ability to include video and 256 color bitmaps, the ability to load multiple help files into a single master help and the biggie: full text search.

I've got to agree that the new Help engine is a work of art—kudos to the Help team, which, according to rumor, is a single, obviously smart, programmer. But the Windows Help itself makes me very unhappy. There is a trend in all the help and documentation from Microsoft to task-based user assistance. The philosophy, as enunciated in the quote above from Pete Higgins, is to focus on "how do I?" for explicit tasks. This is often useful, but just as often, you find that the task in the Help is subtly different from the one you want to do and you have little recourse, because the products don't come with documentation in the sense that they used to—that is, something explaining how they work. This task-based frustration is what you'll find through most of the Help System for Windows itself.

Microsoft is a market-driven company. If your readers don't like this new format or want real documentation as well, they need to let us know loud and clear. We made the change because users complained that they needed task-based help. Besides, Microsoft Press offers numerous books to fill in the gaps.

Bah, humbug. The bottom line on this shift toward task-based help and documentation without any real "explaining how they work" is, er, the bottom line. COGs, aka Cost of Goods, drove this decision. By far the most expensive part of the Software Packages from Microsoft is the printed documentation. Eliminate that and you save big bucks.

Besides, think how many bugs were eliminated in one fell swoop. It used to be if there was a bug, a user could point out that it didn't work the way the documentation said it should. Now that there is no documentation to explain how it should work, there can't be as many bugs. Brilliant!

As a book author, I should be pleased at the opportunities that Microsoft has given not only to Microsoft Press but to the computer book market in general. But I'm not. Users have gotten the shaft. I've no doubt that users have asked for task-based help, but I'm sure they didn't say they wanted it *instead* of real documentation rather than *in addition to* it. That was Microsoft's decision. If COGs are an issue, at least make real documentation available on disk as an option that users can install.

But enough of this philosophy. My gang will first focus on the basics, most notably, the options on setting up full text search. Then they'll talk about less used Help features like annotations. Finally, Mao will discuss some of the technical ins and outs about what kinds of files are part of the help system.

We'll focus entirely on the ins and outs of the Windows 95 help command (and the help files you invoke from the Help menu of applications), but I note that you should be aware of and use the little ⁇ box you'll find in the upper right-hand corner of the dialog boxes of most Windows 95 components and Windows 95 applications. That produces a `what's this` mouse cursor. Pressing that cursor on a part of the dialog box should get you a popup panel explaining what the component is. Some applications have a `What's This?` command if you right-click on an object and give you a little help panel there. An example is the Windows Calculator.

Help Basics

> . . . most programs are like Verdi operas. They communicate in a foreign language and require reading notes in advance to have any idea of what is happening.

> —Paul Heckel

When you start up a help file in stand-alone mode, one of three things is displayed:

1. If it is a help file made for Windows 95 and it has a contents file, the Help Topics Window appears either with the Contents tab displayed (Figure 3-100) or with the last tab you looked at. There are three tabs shown, as in that figure: Contents, Index, and Find.

2. If it is a help file made for Windows 95 and there is no contents file (or one didn't get properly copied to your hard disk), the Help Topics Index tab is displayed. There are only two tabs: Index and Find.

3. If it is a Window 3.1 help file, the opening page of that file, often contents in the Help window, is displayed. But you can get to a Help Topics window with Index and Find tabs by hitting the Search button on the Windows 3.1 Help window. One of the neat things about the Windows 95 Help Engine is that it even adds full text search to Windows 3.1 help files! A Windows 95 Help system can be written so that the initial display is also a specific opening page for the Help file rather than the Index tab. By doing that and not providing Help Topics, Index, Find, or Search buttons, the Help author can lock you out of doing a full text search.

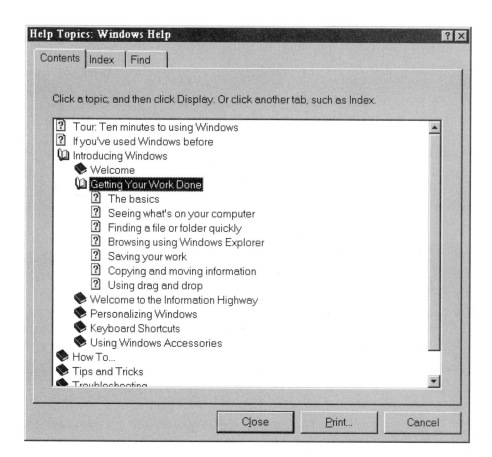

Figure 3-100. The Help Topics Window

If you access Help from within a program, it will either display the same initial window as if you ran stand alone help, or, if the help is context-sensitive, you'll get a Help window specific to the situation. That window should have a button called Search or Index that will take you to the main Help Topic screen. If there is a Contents button and it is a help file written for Windows 95, that button should also go to Help Topics. If you get the idea that Help Topics is the cockpit for accessing help features you are right.

Contents has a collapsible outline form—books indicate nodes that have subtopics and ? pages show topics you can open. Index lists the topics under keywords chosen by the author of the Help system. If the help file is well made, the index and subindex topics will be invaluable. The Find tab is where you can search on individual words and phrases. You shouldn't assume that every Help Topic is accessible through the Contents. Some can only be accessed through the other tabs.

Before you can do a full text search, the Help engine needs to make an index and save it to disk. The first time you access the `Find` tab, you invoke the Find Setup Wizard (Figure 3-101). If you want to change options, you can invoke it again by hitting the Rebuild. . . button on that tab. To illustrate the options and the sizes of the indices produced, let's consider the main Windows Help file, the one that is invoked when you pick Help from the Start Menu. It illustrates another feature of the new Help Engine—it is built not from a single help but from eleven files totaling 1,071,163 bytes, namely `31users.hlp`, `access.hlp`, `common.hlp`, `expo.hlp`, `license.hlp`, `mouse.hlp`, `network.hlp`, `overview.hlp`, `server.hlp`, `windows.hlp`, and `winhlp32.hlp`. If they are present, several other help files will be added, including `plus!.hlp` (for the Plus! Pack), `oem.hlp` (for computer-maker-specific help), and `pen.hlp`, for pen-based machines.

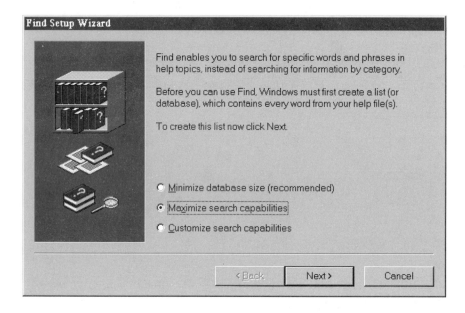

Figure 3-101. The Find Setup Wizard

 Isn't it interesting that Microsoft Exposition help is included? Exposition is just a demo of Microsoft Consumer products that is on the CD. Talk about using their operating system monopoly to push their other businesses!

Returning to full text search, when you start the process of indexing (Figure 3-101) you have to make one of three choices: `Minimize database size`, `Maximize search capabilities`, or `Customize search capabilities`. Windows recommends the first while Mom recommends the second if you have the disk space. What's the difference? I thought you'd never ask.

As a preliminary, you need to know that Help Files are divided into topics—each panel or popup window is a separate topic. Some topics are assigned titles and some, which are usually accessed indirectly, are not. What fraction of topics have titles is a function of the Help file, but most files have mainly titled topics. If you choose `Minimize database size`, then only topics with titles are indexed and all that is indexed is the individual words, not their position in the topic, so you cannot search on phrases. If you pick `Maximize search capabilities`, then still only titled topics are included, but three other capabilities are added:

1. You can search on phrases—that is, sequences of words in the exact order you type them.

2. You can have matching phrases typed in as you look for them.

3. You can turn on a `Find Similar` feature that I'll describe in a moment.

`Customize search capabilities` lets you choose which help files are indexed for cases where there are multiple files (normally all of them are), lets you pick which of the three extras just mentioned is included, and allows you to include untitled topics that then appear in lists as `Untitled topic #1`, for example. I won't say anything more about this last option.

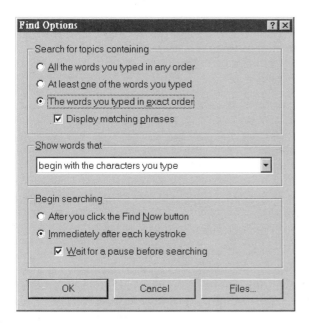

Figure 3-102. The Find Options dialog

 Except . . . except . . . there is this one bug. If you have built the `Maximize search capabilities` index and then choose Rebuild. . . and pick all options on, including to include untitled topics, the Help Engine decides, "Been there, done that," and doesn't rebuild and so doesn't pick up the untitled topics. Oh, how I love a nice bug in the mornin'.

If you hit the `Options. . .` button, you get the dialog in Figure 3-102. The option currently chosen in the first group, "The words you typed in the exact order," is not available if you choose the minimum option or customized and didn't choose to include phrase matching. The display matching phrases checkbox is there because on slow machines Windows claims it can be very slow to have it turned on.

It is important to note that unless you have the `exact order` radio button chosen in `Options` (and it is not the default!), typing in several words will just search for those words in any location in the topic. The `Files...` button option on this dialog is another place to exclude files that would otherwise be included.

The `Find` tab indicates the current options in a text box just over the buttons; the first word, which is `All`, `One+`, or `Phrase`, indicates the first set of radio buttons.

If `Find Similar...` is turned on, and it is with the Maximum choice that I recommend, then each topic has a checkbox next to it. Check one or more of the topics and hit the `Find Similar...` button, and a list pops up of those topics with significant word overlap with the checked topics.

I did some tests on sizes. Recall that the combined `.hlp` files that make up the main Windows Help are about 1.1 MB. When I chose the `Minimize Size` option, the index files totaled 470K. The Maximize Capabilities option came to 1.5 MB, and when untitled topics were included it swelled to a whopping 2.9 MB. On a 486/66, it only took thirty seconds to make the index itself.

If you pick the Maximize option for a given help file, be sure to go into `Options...` and check the `exact words` radio button.

Esoteric Help

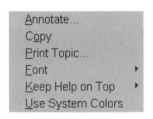

**Figure 3-103.
Topic Context Menu**

What *do* girls do who haven't any mothers to help them through their troubles?

—Jo March speaking in Louisa May Alcott's *Little Women,* 1868

Many of the help extras involve the context menu that pops up inside any individual topic (but not inside the main Help Topics window, where there is no useful context menu). The menu is also accessible from the Options button in Windows 95 help files. This menu (see Figure 3-103) pops up in help files written for both Windows 95 and Windows 3.1. The `Annotate...` choice was an underused goody in Windows 3.1 help. With it users can add comments and notes to any help page. The page then shows a paper clip icon in the corner. Clicking on that clip will bring back the comment.

`Copy` will copy the selected text to the clipboard or the whole topic if nothing is selected. `Print Topic. . .` only lets you print an entire topic, not a selection, but it does let you choose which printer. While Help authors can choose their own fonts, most Help Systems use default fonts. Despite what you might hope, the `Font` menu item doesn't let you choose which font. That seems to be hard wired as MS San Serif, a bitmapped (not TrueType) font included with Windows. There are three choices—large, which is 10 point, medium, which is 8 point, and small, which seems to also be 8 point but with a smaller leading. `Keep Help on Top` has three options. The default has the status determined by the help author, who can specify some topic panels to keep on top and others not to. You can override this setting and globally determine what happens—for that particular help file. The last item determines whether the Help Topic windows use the default color—a motley-looking dithered yellow polka dots on white (yuck)—or the same color used by the system for the background in windows. The latter is the color you can change in the `Appearance` tab of Display Properties by changing the `Item` to `Window`.

 The weird thing is that this last `Use System Colors` choice is absent if you run with more than 256 colors. I guess big Bill's interior decorator must have approved the color that appears if a system has 64K colors but then saw the color used when you only have 256 colors and exclaimed, "Yuck, you must give them a way to change it." Weirder still, there were undocumented but well-known ways to change the colors used by Windows 3.1 Help, but I haven't found anything you can do in the Registry for Windows 95 Help.

 Speaking of the Registry, I'm not sure the author of Windows 95 Help knows about it. Every bloody one of the context menu's options is stored in the configuration file (`.gid`) for that help system and only holds for that system. There is no way to change the defaults used by all Help systems. Boo, hiss!

 Oy. It's two steps forward but one step back. If you run a Windows 3.1 Help System under Windows 95, it uses the Help Topics dialog in place of the old search. Otherwise, it uses the Windows 3.1 windows, which included two invaluable menu items that are no longer automatically included in Windows 95 help systems. Indeed, both are absent from the help you invoke from the Start Menu! You could open a history window and look at where you've been and easily return. You could put a book mark on any topic and later return there. But now Windows 95 Help seems to say, "Menus? We don't need no steenkin' menus," and those options are gone. Sigh.

Help Under the Covers

Self-help books are making life downright unsafe. Women desperate to catch a man practice all the ploys recommended by these authors. Bump into him, trip over him, knock him down, spill something on him, scald him, but *meet him.*

—Florence King, *Reflections in a Jaundiced Eye*

Help under the covers!!! I knew you guys would get to the pornography eventually. Wait until my buddy Senator Exxon hears about this. This book has a mother on the cover, so it can pretend to be family fare. But the truth comes out, doesn't it?

But Bill, didn't The Microsoft Network announce it would have adults only areas? What's that? Chopped liver?

Hey, that's entirely different. We have customers who want to pay for that stuff. Don't we owe it to our stockholders to take their money? 'Course, we'll mark it so parents can keep kids out.

The section title is there because Mao is going to tell you some of the technical stuff behind Windows Help. But don't necessarily run away. I'll also tell you how you can combine several help files into one with a common index and full text search, all by yourself.

Normally help vendors ship two kinds of files for their help systems and Windows Help makes up to five more. Here's the lowdown:

Extension	Location	Purpose and Comment
.hlp	Home Directory	The basic Help file(s)
.cnt	Home Directory	Contents file in ASCII format, discussed shortly (.cnt=CoNTents)
.gid	Home or Help Directory but hidden	Help configuration file. Stores information like which tab was active when the user last quit.

Extension	Location	Purpose and Comment
`.fts`	Home or Help Directory	Index for Full Text Search, hence `.fts`.
`.ftg`	Home or Help Directory	Information for FTS Groups
`.ann`	`C:\windows\help`	Annotations are saved here
`.bmk`	`C:\windows\winhlp32.bmk`	Bookmarks are saved here

The basic files have the extension `.hlp`. They are documents associated to the executable file `winhlp32.exe` in the `C:\windows` directory. Help files written for Windows 95 should also have a *contents* file with the extension `.cnt`. If this file is missing, then when you start the help file you'll get the Help Topics dialog with the Contents tab missing. If you run a Windows 3.x help file, it normally has a contents built into the file, and that's what you see when you start up as a separate panel, not as a part of Help Topics. Windows 3.x help files do not have a separate `.cnt` file.

As we'll see, the Contents tab is built from the `.cnt` file. Normally, these are the only two files shipped with a help system. Up to three additional files are built during the basic help operations. They are normally put in the same directory as the `.hlp` and `.cnt` files—I called this the home directory in the chart. If Windows can't put the files there (for example, if you run a help file from a CD or from a network drive where you don't have write privileges) then these files are put in `C:\windows\help`—which I called the help directory.

The first time you run a help file, you might see a message that Windows is preparing to run the help file for the first time. What it is doing is making the `.gid` file,* which contains the following information:

- Binary representation of the `.cnt` file. This allows for faster loading and means that if you delete a `.cnt` file after running help the first time, the Contents tab is still displayed.

---

* The *Help Author's Guide*—the official documentation for writers of help—is silent on what the letters gid stand for.

- The names of all help files referenced in the master .cnt file—as we'll see, a single running of help can load multiple help files.

- A list of all the keywords for quicker loading of the Index tab.

- A list of associated .fts and .ftg files.

- The size and location of any other files such as video or special dialog boxes called by the help file.

 It's the .gid file that allows for quick loading of the Contents and Index tabs. But that means if you install a new version of the basic .hlp file without the .gid being updated, you won't have access to the new topics! When a program installs a new version of help, it is supposed to regenerate the .gid file, but if it seems as if you can't get help on the new features in a new version of a program, the problem might be that the updating wasn't done. If you suspect that, just delete the .gid file. It will be regenerated the first time you run the corresponding help file.

 You may think that because the information in it is stored in the .gid file, you can delete the .cnt file once the .gid is made. But that's dangerous if you ever need to regenerate the .gid. The .cnt files are small, so I say leave 'em where they are.

When you generate a full text search index, it is stored as a .fts file in the home directory, or, if that is unavailable, in C:\windows\help. Similarly, if you generate an index from a help system built from multiple .hlp files, an extra .ftg file is built.

Any annotations you make for a given help file, say one called *name*.hlp, are stored, not in the Home directory but always in C:\windows\help in a binary file called *name*.ann. Bookmarks for all help files are stored in a single file winhlp32.bmk, stored in C:\windows.

 Open up Explorer and find C:\windows\help\windows.cnt and double-click on it. In the Open With dialog, choose Notepad. Make sure that the Always use this program to open this type of file is checked because .cnt files are text and you'll want to use Notepad. You'll see a text file that gives you considerable insight into how Windows 95 help can build help systems based on multiple .hlp files.

When you first look at windows.cnt, skip past the lines that start with a :. You'll see a bunch of lines with numbers. They correspond precisely to the levels in the Contents tab you'll see if you pick Help from the Start Menu. There may be a single entry at the top about the Windows Tour that you don't see in the text file in front of you—that comes from `:include w_tour.cnt` in the text file.

 After you've run the Windows Tour once my advice is to be sure that you've not got it installed (check the Accessories group in the Windows Setup tab of Add/Remove Programs) and then delete this include line. If you uninstall the tour but don't delete this include line and you later pick this help page by mistake, you'll find that the Help file looks for the CD. Also, while cleaning up, check out the `.avi` files in `C:\windows\help`. You may have 7 MB of them there. Look at them once (by double-clicking on them) and erase them—the worst you'll get are some `missing graphics` boxes in Help. I wish freeing up 7 MB were always so easy.

Two of those lines with a dot in front will concern us. `:Index` lets you add extra help files to the `Index` and `Find` Tabs and `:Include` lets you add extra entries to the `Contents` tab. Search through the file looking for `:Index` lines. You'll find the names of all the `.hlp` files that I said are combined to make Windows 95 master help. `:Include` lines insert subsidiary contents entries into the middle of `Contents`.

You can use these lines to make your own combined help files. For example, suppose you want to take the UI Guidelines Help file you'll find on Mom's CD and combine it with the Help Author's Guide, which we expect will be available on CompuServe. You'll need to be sure the four basic files `uiguide.hlp`, `uiguide.cnt`, `hcw.cnt`, and `hcw.hlp` are in a single directory. Load `uiguide.cnt` into Notepad and add the following line before the first entry without a colon in front:

        `:Index Help Author's Guide =hcw.hlp`

and add

        `:Include hcw.cnt`

at the very end.

Now delete `uiguide.gid` if it is there and start `uiguide.hlp`. Go to the Find tab and choose `Rebuild. . .` if you haven't been asked to explicitly rebuild it. You've made the two help files into one with a combined contents, index, and full text search index! The general method should be clear to you when you want to use it yourself. You can add multiple files this way.

 You can add extra files to the Index and Find tabs even if they are in a different directory, but it seems that to have them added to Contents, both the `.cnt` and `.hlp` files need to be in the same directory as the master `.hlp` file.

Chapter 4

Applets, Utilities, and More

PCs are the world's greatest medium for futzing around. They're computational catnip for
obsessives, keyboard crack for neurotics and seductive time sinks for ordinary folks who
just want to make sure that they've reasonably examined all their options.
Why do you think we call them "users"?

—Michael Schrage

 In this chapter, I cover all the parts of Windows 95 that didn't make it
into the last chapter. The high points are the networking and Internet
components. I faced a difficult decision on how to handle the Plus! Pack,
which was built by the Windows team but isn't exactly part of Windows. I
compromised—the Internet Jumpstart Kit, which is also available for
downloading, is such a central part of the picture I treat it in full. Items like DriveSpace
3, which fit right into the discussion of disk compression, are also here. But some other
components are in the next chapter on third-party programs.

Disk 'n Dat

It is a capital mistake to theorize before one has data.

—Sir Arthur Conan Doyle, *The Adventures of Sherlock Holmes*

 In order to understand the function of Windows disk tools, you need to
know a little bit about the system DOS and Windows use to organize
data on disk. For the full low down, you can read *The Mother of All PC
Books*. Here's a brief summary.

Files are allocated space in units called *clusters* (ScanDisk calls them *allocation units*). A
disk is limited to 64K of clusters. Cluster size can be as small as 512 bytes (that's what it is
on a diskette) and is always a power of two times this basic half-kilobyte unit. So cluster
sizes are ½, 1, 2, 4, 8, 16 or 32 kilobytes. You can find cluster size on most media by
dividing the size by 64K and rounding up to the next possible cluster size. Thus, a 1 GB

disk will have 16K clusters, but above 1 GB to 2 GB disks will have 32K clusters. The maximum drive size supported by Windows 95 is thus 2 GB (64K clusters × 32K/cluster). Above that, you must partition disks into multiple drives.

 This 2 GB barrier will start to be a problem soon, and Microsoft will need to address it. I remember in the mid-1980s when there was a 32 MB barrier based on the fact that at a lower level than clusters, disks are divided into 512-byte sectors and there was a limit of 64K sectors. The shift to allow a larger number of sectors was made with DOS 4.0 and broke a fair number of third-party disk utilities. The shift that breaks the 2 GB barrier shouldn't be so traumatic, unless Microsoft uses it as an excuse to shift away from the basic FAT system that has been used by DOS since its beginning.

The operating system keeps a database, called the *File Allocation Table,* aka *FAT* of clusters. For each cluster, this database indicates one of three things:

- The cluster is not in use and can be assigned to a file if needed.

- The cluster is the final cluster in a file.

- The cluster is in use by a file, in which case the number of the next cluster in the file is indicated.

The directory entry for a file indicates the first cluster in the file. Then the FAT entries let the operating system successively figure out all the clusters in a file and their order. Notice that a file need not have all its clusters be consecutive. This is useful—imagine having a 10 MB file and adding a few bytes that make the file need another cluster. If the very next cluster isn't available, the operating system would have to move the full 10 MB file. Of course, as files spread out over the disk in noncontiguous pieces, the drive has to do more to retrieve them and performance can plummet. A file that is in noncontiguous pieces is called fragmented. Defragmentation software rearranges the clusters on which the data lives (by physically moving the data) so that files are no longer fragmented.

Most of the logical ills that can befall a disk are sicknesses of the FAT. *Lost* or *orphaned* clusters refer to clusters that the FAT has marked as in use but that are not assigned to any file in any directory on the disk. *Cross-linked files* are situations where more than one file lays claim to the same cluster.

Disk Tools: ScanDisk and Defrag

A computer lets you make more mistakes faster than any other invention in human history, with the exception of handguns and tequila.

—Heard on the Net

ScanDisk and Disk Defragmenter are two utilities that you'll find on the `Programs/Accessories/System Tools` menu, but it is probably easier to get them by selecting a drive in Explorer (or `My Computer`), asking for `Properties`, and going to the `Tools` tab.

You should consider calling up the `Advanced` tab in ScanDisk and setting the options as shown in Figure 4-1. For crosslinked files, this makes copies of both files even though it is certain that at least

Figure 4-1. ScanDisk options

one of them is wrong. You should also turn on logging and one of the options that reports errors. So if you have a report of crosslinked files you'll know to check them out. The `Lost file fragments` choice throws the information in the lost clusters away and frees up the clusters as unused.

No doubt this advice to throw away lost clusters will cause howls from some quarters. I used to carefully save all such clusters to files and check them out. Under normal circumstances I never once found anything of value in these clusters, nor has anyone else I know. Notice I said "under normal circumstances." I've had horrendous crashes (in the DOS days before Windows 3.x) that turned a directory into chopped liver. That meant that the lost clusters were associated to real files and saving them as such was invaluable. So, if you pick "Free," you'll need to be sure to change it when there is a crisis. If you worry that you won't, better set it to `Convert to files` and delete the ones produced under normal circumstances by hand.

Crosslinked files are a rarity and almost always indicate at least some lost data and perhaps a more serious underlying problem. Lost clusters are fairly common, a symptom of some program that didn't properly close a temporary file. They don't cause happiness, but if you occasionally get some with no apparent missing data, they shouldn't cause much concern, either.

If you get to Disk Defragmenter from the Tools tab of a drive's Property sheet, and you ask to Defragment now, you'll get a dialog like that in Figure 4-2 that reports on the degree of defragmentation with advice on whether you need to run the program. If you do run the program, you get a progress bar like that shown in Figure 4-3. If there is disk activity while this dialog is running, the process will seem to begin all over. But as you can see by watching the process in detail, when it does start over, it quickly reads through the part of the disk that it has already done before the interruption.

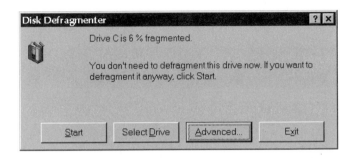

Figure 4-2. Defragment now?

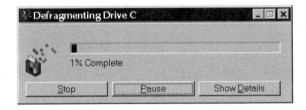

Figure 4-3. Defragmenter running

If you have any curiosity about defragging, I urge you to hit the `Show Details` button. You'll get a full screen display that is lovely to watch, although it will be hard to understand until you go to Legend for an explanation of what is going on (Figure 4-4). The screen shot in this book is gray scale but the true panel is color-coded.

You're probably wondering how often to run ScanDisk and Defrag. It is probably adequate if you run them once a month, although given that ScanDisk can be an early warning and only takes a few minutes to run, I aim to run it at least once a week. However, such a schedule has the defect that it will get forgotten. If you have the Plus! Pack, use the System Agent that comes with it—then you may as well run these programs on a more regular basis.

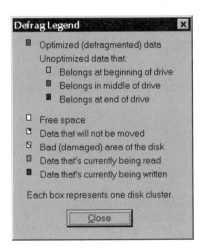

Figure 4-4. A Legend in its own time

 I have my machine configured to run a daily backup at 3 A.M. and ScanDisk on all my drives at 4:30 A.M. Defrag and Norton Virus Scan run on alternate mornings at 5:00 A.M.

Several final remarks about ScanDisk:

1. The executable that runs ScanDisk for Windows is called `scandskw.exe`, not `scandisk.exe`. It resides in your Windows directory.

2. As a tool in case you have a disaster that prevents your running Windows, there is a program called `scandisk.exe` in `C:\windows\command` that runs outside Windows as a DOS program. If loaded from Windows (whether from the Run box or at a DOS prompt in a DOS session over Windows), it loads `scandskw.exe` and exits. It's an interesting test to load it from the Run box, see a DOS session load, see ScanDisk for Windows pop up over it, and then see the DOS session close. The important thing is to remember that there is this DOS tool if complete disaster does strike.

3. If you installed the Plus! Pack, it replaced both your versions of ScanDisk. The originals will be `C:\windows\scandskw.w95` and `C:\windows\command\scandisk.w95` with dates of 7/11/95. The new version installed by Plus! will be `C:\windows\scandskw.exe` and `C:\windows\command\scandisk.exe` with a date of 7/14/95. The new versions are needed to support Plus's improved compressed drives. If you have Plus!, add ScanDisk to the list of programs that System Agents automatically runs.

4. You might consider including `scandskw` in your startup group so that your disk is checked every time you start up. If you do that, you'll be interested in the following command line parameters:

   `X:`   checks drive X; can use multiple drives

   `/a`   checks all drives

   `/p`   reports errors but doesn't correct them

   `/n`   closes ScanDisk when it is done (if there are no errors)

5. In the `C:\windows\command` directory, you'll find a file called `scandisk.ini` with options for further controlling the behavior of ScanDisk. The documentation for this `ini` file command is inside the file itself.

 Oy. Not only is the printed documentation essentially nonexistent, but the on-line help doesn't discuss this. The user is reduced to stumbling on an `.ini` file that isn't even in the same directory as the executable. Instead of behaving like a billion-dollar-a-year corporation, Microsoft is acting like a $100,000 garage operation.

You've got that wrong, Rush. The garage operation would have too much pride in its product to pull that kind of shtick.

DriveSpace

> Space isn't remote at all.
> It's only an hour's drive away if your car could go straight upwards.
>
> —Fred Hoyle, *London Observer,* Sept. 9, 1979

Disk compression is the closest thing the computer world has to a free lunch, at least with the release of Windows 95, because now:

- The compression built into the operating system is close to best of breed (and the upgrade that comes with Plus! *is* best of breed).

- When running in Windows or DOS sessions over Windows, the memory cost of loading the software to handle compressed drives is negligible. If you have to use DOS-exclusive mode often, that isn't true, although you may be able to load the necessary drivers in UMB space.

- Processor speeds are now fast enough that there is virtually no performance penalty.

- The technology is now mature enough and tested enough that even many of us who were nervous with it early on are now quite comfortable with it.

DriveSpace does its magic in using two tricks. First, behind the scenes, it allocates space to files in 512 byte sectors instead of clusters, which, as I explained earlier in the chapter, are

256 MB to 512 MB hard drive	8K clusters
512 MB to 1 GB hard drive	16K clusters
1 GB to 2 GB hard drive	32K clusters

That means that a 768-byte icon file suddenly takes only 1K of space instead of 8–32K. Second, it uses a compression scheme based on the fact that bit patterns tend to repeat in files. The bottom line is that one should expect DriveSpace (the version that comes with Windows) to increase effective storage by a factor of about 2 while DriveSpace 3 (the version that comes with Plus!) will compress by a factor of about 2.5 if you choose the option that heavily compresses (at something of a performance cost).

An element of the magic is that the original drive becomes a host and the compressed drive appears as a huge file on the host. The compressed drive then acts a virtual new drive. The operating system in a masterful sleight of hand then remaps the host to a new letter so that the compressed drive can take over the old drive letter. For example, you might have an uncompressed drive C on a portable. After the compression what was drive C becomes drive D, and the compressed drive is called C. From the user's point of view, D is irrelevant and may even get hidden and the drive that files are put on is still called C.

To compress a drive, you run DriveSpace from the `Programs\Accessories\ System Tools` menu. The dialog that results lets you choose a drive. If you then pick `Compress` from the `Drive` menu, it will offer to totally compress the drive. Another option is to only compress the free space on the drive to make a new compressed drive. You do that via `Create Empty` on the `Advanced` menu.

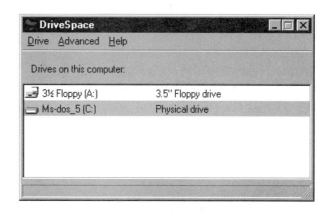

If you go the `File/Compress` route, you are shown the current situation and estimates after the compression. The amount of free space afterward can only be an estimate because until you actually place files there, no one can know how effectively they can be compressed. You should at least look at the compression options dialog (shown below). It lets you determine to what letter the old host drive will be remapped. Normally, you'd take the choice made by the system (a complex algorithm), but you might choose to bump it higher if, for example, you planned to install a **CD-ROM** drive soon and wanted it to get the next letter.

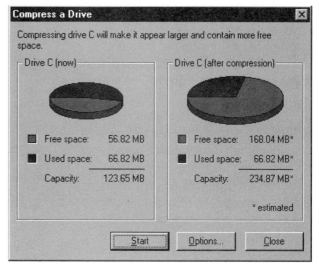

After you pick start, Windows will reboot to a special mode. It can take several hours to do the initial compression but this is a one-time operation.

The built-in compression only supports drives that after compression are up to 512 MB, which might prevent you from fitting everything on a single compressed drive. DriveSpace 3 supports drives up to 2 GB after compression (which means you'll need to create two drives if your uncompressed drive is more than about 800 MB!).

The DriveSpace 3 menus are almost identical to those for DriveSpace except that in addition to `Compress` on the File menu there is an `Upgrade` choice for changing a DriveSpace compressed drive to a DriveSpace 3 compressed drive. As you can see, the prediction of the change may not be optimistic, but in reality it improved by about 10 MB. Moreover, this doesn't take into account two special compression schemes—HiPacked and UltraPacked—that DriveSpace 3 supports. It doesn't automatically use them because there is a small performance penalty when accessing such compressed files and the compression times are lengthy. Indeed, on-the-fly compression of new files is always in Standard mode; the special modes require special processing.

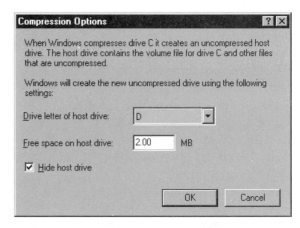

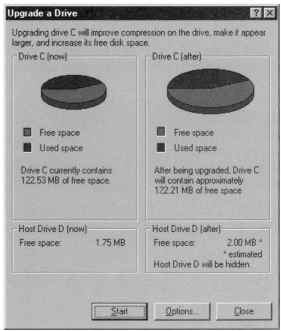

You get to pick these special modes in one of two ways. When using DriveSpace 3, the Property sheet for a compressed drive picks up an extra tab called `Compression`, shown here. The Compression Agent you can call from here does the change to better modes. Or, you can schedule the Compression Agent overnight using the System Agent program of automatic scheduling. You'll find the default choices on when to use which type of compression quite reasonable, although you can adjust them through the `Advanced...` button.

You can also compress floppy disks with Drive Space or Drive Space 3. Even with Drive Space 3, you can compress a floppy with Drive Space only. You'll want to do that if you are sending the floppy to someone who hasn't got the Plus! Pack. You can configure Drive Space (through the `Advanced/Settings...` menu item) to automatically read compressed floppies—and there is no reason you wouldn't want to once you are using disk compression.

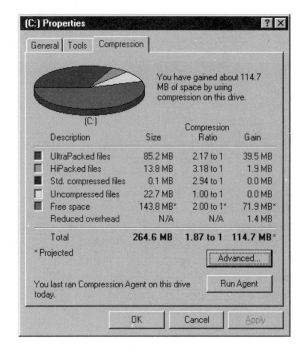

If you use DriveSpace, Windows will copy `drvspace.bin` from `C:\windows\command` to the root directory twice, once as `drvspace.bin` and once as `dblspace.bin`. There are two copies there for compatibility with prior versions of DOS. These files provide access to the compressed drives only until Windows 95 itself loads. Then a protect mode driver called `drvspacx.vxd` in `C:\windows\system\iosubsys` takes over. There is a file in the root directory called `dblspace.ini`, but it does not seem to be documented anywhere.

`Drvspace.sys` (or its copy `dblspace.sys`) is only used to move the real mode driver into UMB space, and is only useful for MS-DOS exclusive mode. I discussed it in Chapter 3. The Resource Kit documents a lot of command line switches you can use with the Windows application `drvspace.exe`, which is what gets run from the Start Menu.

If you have the Plus! Pack, it renames `dblspace.bin` to `dblbin.w95`, `drvspace.bin` to `drvbin.w95`, `drvspacex.vxd` to `drvvxd.w95`, `drvspace.exe` to `drvexe.w95`, `drvspace.sys` to `drvsys.w95` and places its own versions of these files on the disk. Again, you can use file dates (7/11/95 for Win 95 vs. 7/14/95 for Plus!) to tell the difference.

One warning. If you decide to look at the host drive, you'll find a huge, hidden file there with extension `.cvf` (=Compressed Volume File). That's your compressed drive. Fool with that file at your extreme peril.

Backup

> Let's have the Union restored as it was, if we can;
> but if we can't, I'm in favor of the Union as it wasn't.

—Artemus Ward, *Artemus Ward: His Travels*

By the standard of previous DOS backup programs, the one that comes with Windows 95 is heaven—and it looks pretty good, too (Figure 4-5). DOS Backup had a knack of incompatibility between DOS versions. Until DOS 6, the command line interface was for the birds. And even when a decent interface was added in DOS 6 (by licensing the program from Symantec, makers of Norton Backup!), it only supported backup to floppies.

This version of backup is written by Colorado Memory Systems (CMS), the leading maker of QIC backup drives. It supports some QIC tape

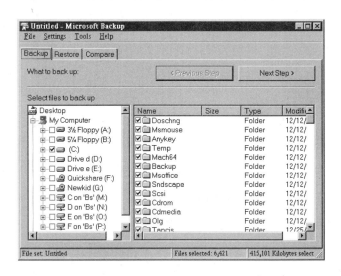

Figure 4-5. Backup

backup systems, not surprisingly, especially those from CMS. The wizard-like interface is fairly easy to use.

But viewed in absolute terms or in comparison with the other disk applets, Backup only rates a so-so. The tape support is limited to QIC 40, 80, or 3010 drives from CMS, Conner, Iomega, and Wangtek that are connected to primary floppy controllers or from CMS to the parallel port. Drives from Archive, Irwin, Mountain, and Tarvan, drives connected to an IDE controller, SCSI controller, or tape controller are not supported. (Adaptec sells a version of Backup enhanced to support SCSI tape drives.)

While the transfer to tape is speedy enough, the program is slow at reading the drive directories. On one test Mao did with a Pentium-90 machine with gobs of memory and a speedy hard disk, doing a Start Menu Find File for all files on a drive with 6500 files took eighteen seconds, but it took Backup seventy-two seconds to read the same disk. That means if you have a huge file system, an incremental backup can take a long time. In addition, the amount of information that backup provides while you are backing up is not extensive. The program is acceptable (if your hardware is supported), but far from great!

A few warnings are in order:

- Heed the message (Figure 4-6) you get when Backup starts about not using the Full Backup set provided to do partial restores. If you restore even a single file, the saved Registry is merged with your current Registry. (It's crazy to do a full backup and not be able to do a partial restore!)

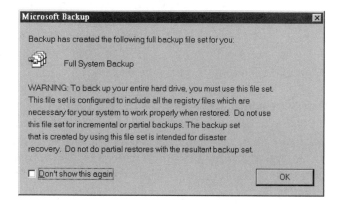

Figure 4-6. You vuz warned

- If you try to use pre-Windows 95 backup software, you'll lose long filename information.

- If you use pre-Windows 95 backup software, be very careful about restoring the Registry files (`user.dat` and `system.dat`) because that will wipe out any Registry changes made since the backup. I've heard horror stories about users being unable to reboot after such a restore. Windows 95 Backup and any competent third-party program will treat the Registry specially and do some sort of merge.

But by far the most important warning about backing up is to do it! And often. It isn't a question of whether backup will ever save you but when. There are too many gremlins out there not to properly protect yourself.

Gettin' It Together

> A home theater would, within two decades, let people dial up symphonies,
> presidential speeches, and three dimensional Shakespeare plays . . .
> Novels, orchestras, and movie theaters would vanish.
>
> —1912 prediction

In the mid-1980s, pundits kept predicting that "this year will be the year of the LAN," the year that local area networking finally took off. Just when the pundits seemed to be silly repeating the same prediction, it became true in spades. Within the space of two or three years, the bulk of large- to medium-sized corporations went from stand-alone setups to fully networked. Small businesses took a little longer, but by now, the overwhelming bulk of PCs in office environments are connected to LANs. The mid-1990s have seen a dramatic explosion in the Internet both via network connections in the office and via dial-up connection from home. The designers of Windows 95 realized that networking is now a central part of computing. Network protocols are not only built into the system for computers on LANs but are part of Internet Dial-Up connections and even Laplink-style parallel cable connections between PCs.

Part of Windows Networking is the registration/installation of a network adapter in your hardware tree. If you are on a LAN via a physical connection, you have an installed hardware network adapter. If you are using one of the other forms of networking, you need a virtual adapter, which Windows calls a Dial-Up Adapter. The software and options for it get installed on your computer when you install Dial-Up Networking or Direct Cable Connection. Networking is so vast that my discussion of it is spread throughout this book. General concepts, including the notion of UNC names, are found in Chapter 2. Email, which is separate from, but related to, networking, is discussed in Chapter 3 under the discussion of Exchange. The Network applet in control panel and how to set up a simple peer-to-peer network is in Chapter 10. If you are here because you don't want to have to sign on when you start up your PC, see Appendix F.

That still leaves lots to cover in the few collections of sections of this chapter. First, I'll discuss the Dial-Up Networking (aka DUN)—both the client built into Windows and the server that comes with the Plus! Pack. Then I'll discuss Direct Cable Connection, which should really be called Direct Parallel Port Connection since performance on the Serial version is so awful. Then I'll discuss the Briefcase, followed by several modem based applets (Hyperterminal and Dialer), several miscellaneous applications, and a word about Online Services, including The Microsoft Network. That leaves the Internet, something that has been the subject of acres of books. First I'll discuss how to set up Windows 95 to do Internet connections over the phone or LAN, and then the broad array of Internet tools that are included with Windows or with the Internet Jumpstart Kit.

Dial-Up Networking

> Information networks straddle the world. Nothing remains concealed. But the sheer volume of information dissolves the information. We are unable to take it all in.
>
> —Günther Grass, *New Statesman & Society,* June 22, 1990

You'll need to setup a Dial-Up Networking (aka DUN) connection before you can use DUN. If you are using the Internet Setup Wizard to make an Internet connection, it will set up the DUN connection for you. So you'll need to roll your own only if you are setting up a Dial-Up Internet connection manually or you are dialing in to a remote LAN.

To set up a DUN connection, you need to open the Dial-Up Networking folder you'll find in `My Computer` and click on `New Connection` to invoke the wizard shown here. You get to choose the name for the connection, the modem you'll use for the connection (Figure 4-7) and the telephone number you'll dial in to (Figure 4-8). When you're done, the DUN folder will show all the connections you've made (Figure 4-9).

When you double-click on a DUN connection (or launch it from a shortcut) you get the login screen shown in Figure 4-10. This lets you enter a Username and Password (why you aren't given an opportunity to enter this information in the wizard, as you can in the Internet Setup Wizard, is beyond me). You can even tell the screen to remember your Password—but bear in mind if you do that it blocks some of the protection that Passwords offer.

Under some circumstances, `Dial Properties. . .` on the Login Screen can be important. It brings up the dialog

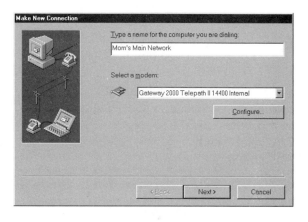

Figure 4-7. New Connection—1

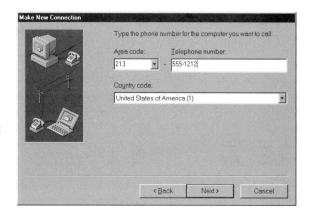

Figure 4-8. New Connection—2

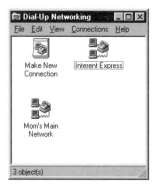

Figure 4-9. DUN folder

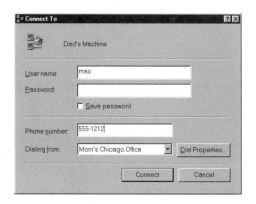

Figure 4-10. DUN login screen

shown in Figure 4-11. This lets you
define locations to dial from, which is
especially useful if you don't always
dial up from the same area code. This
is also where you can automate Credit
Card dialing—Windows understands
many of the standard Telephone Credit
Cards and even has the 800 number for
MCI and Sprint built in!

Once you've made a Dial-Up
connection to a LAN, you can do all
the usual things you can do on a LAN,
including setting up shortcuts to
programs and folders on the LAN.

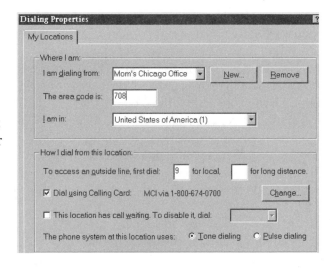

Figure 4-11. Dialing Properties

If you double-click on such a shortcut
when you are not connected, you get a
dialog like that in Figure 4-12. If you
check the checkbox, then forever afterward
when you click on the Desktop folder in
future, it will pop up the DUN login screen
and connect you. As soon as you are
connected, it will open the folder or run the
program that the shortcut was to. This is an
elegant interface to Dial-Up Networking.

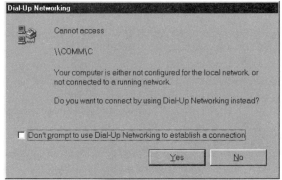

Figure 4-12. Offering to automate dial-up

Most often you'll use DUN with some
corporate LAN with specialized servers
that support remote access. But if you want
to use it with a home machine or small
office network, you may want to use the
Remote Access Server (aka RAS), which comes
with the Plus! Pack. Microsoft has done a good
job of hiding it. After you install Plus!, the DUN
folder picks up an extra item called `Dial-Up`
`Server. . .` on its `Connections` menu.
That's where you can turn the server on and off
and where you get to set a login password. An
especially important option is invoked by the
`Server Type. . .` button, which leads to the
drop-down shown in Figure 4-13.

Figure 4-13. RAS Server type

If the RAS is a stand-alone machine or is on a network with a Browse Master, you can choose what seems to be the obvious choice for server type—PPP: Windows 95, Windows NT 3.5, Internet. But if the server is on a small peer-to-peer network, you need to choose Windows for Workgroups and Windows NT 3.1. With that choice the Dial-Up client will only be able to access the machine the server software is on (as opposed to the rest of the network) but performance with the PPP choice is unacceptable at best and unreliable at worst when connecting to a peer-to-peer network.

The underlying technology of DUN is neat. The ability to click on a remote folder and invoke remote dial-up login is wonderful, but much of the interface is confused and inconsistent. The RAS is hidden and the DUN Setup Wizard doesn't let you put in a user name/password while the Internet Setup Wizard does, even though that part of the Internet wizard is setting up a DUN connection. The connection options are spread in two different places. Some you get to by double-clicking the connection and hitting Dial Properties. . . in the DUN logon screen. Others you reach by selecting but not double-clicking a connection and picking Properties from the context menu (or the File menu) and then choosing to Configure. These last configurations are allowed to be modem-dependent (for no good reason!) and the dialog that chooses them lists the modem name rather than the connection name (see Figure 4-20 in the section on setting up the Internet). Finally, there is a third set of options involving how to redial if a line is busy under Connections/Settings.

While DUN is adequate for small file transfers and checking email, given typical modem speeds, it is not an efficient way to run programs remotely. If you have such a need, look into a Remote Control product like *Reach Out* or *PC Anywhere.*

I found a really strange gotcha on the Save password checkbox in Figure 4-10. If you have no Network client installed and haven't enabled multiple user profiles, then that checkbox is grayed out. If you either install a client (like Client for Microsoft Networks) or turn on multiple user profiles, then magically, you'll have an enabled checkbox. Oh, how I love a nice bug in the mornin'.

That's not a bug. It was put there on purpose to punish someone so antisocial as to have neither a shared PC or a network. Actually, the problem seems to be that there is no password file if neither of those options are available and we weren't clever enough to make one if you checked that box.

If you have no network and don't use multiple user profiles or direct cable connection, then when you install Internet support with the Plus! Pack you'll wind up with DUN with no network clients and so DUN won't be able to remember your passwords. You're right, Billy—it is punishment. Any readers in that bind should consider installing the Microsoft Client for Microsoft networks. You can get rid of the Network Neighborhood icon that will appear by following my direction in Chapter 11.

Direct Cable Connection

A book is like a piece of rope;
it takes on meaning only in connection with the things it holds together.

—Norman Cousins, *Saturday Review,* April 15, 1978

In the mid-1980s, when laptop computers were just coming into vogue, a program called *The Brooklyn Bridge* appeared that let you use a parallel cable to transfer files between computers. One computer was the *slave,* and during the process, it had to be dedicated to the other computer called the *master.* During the transfer, the slave couldn't be used for anything other than to listen to the master's voice. The master had to be rebooted after it was connected to the slave and the slave was put into slave mode. It was an awkward procedure, but useful enough that many purchased and used it. We've come a long way, baby!

The category was taken over by *Laplink* from Traveling Software, which over time became elegant and even supported serial linkups at respectable speeds. Some versions of DOS 6.0 had a pair of programs called *Interlink* that allowed transfers over cable, but they were very much in the slave/master mode of the original Brooklyn Bridge: one computer had to be totally dedicated to the link while the other had to be rebooted. It had a slightly prettier face than *The Brooklyn Bridge* but it wasn't much more functional. And it was certainly no *Laplink.*

Windows 95 includes a program called Direct Cable Connection, aka DCC, that is finally a serious cable connection program—certainly competitive with *Laplink.* In one way, it is much worse than *Laplink* in that its serial support is a joke, whereas *Laplink*'s is pretty good (although even its serial speeds aren't as good as its parallel port speeds). But in another way Windows 95's way is superior because it connects as a network using the Dial-Up Networking adapter.

The networking comes via the DUN virtual adapter, but DCC is not run via the DUN folder! You use a menu item installed under `Programs/Accessories` in the Start Menu. You can, of course, place a shortcut to the executable (`directcc.exe`) on your Desktop or assign a hotkey to it. If DCC isn't under your Start Menu, it probably isn't installed—go to the `Add/Remove Programs` applet of Control Panel, go to the `Windows Setup` tab, highlight `Communications`, and hit `Details. . . .` You'll find `Direct Cable Connection` there. If you pick it and you don't already have DUN installed, it will install DUN also.

You'll also need a cable to connect the two computers you want to talk to each other. You may lean toward the serial cable choice because you are more likely to have free serial ports than free parallel ports, but DON'T DO IT! Serial port rates will be 1-3 KB/sec,* while a simple parallel connection should be ten to twenty times better.

Using special enhanced parallel ports and a special cable called a Universal Cable Modem, there have been reports of speeds in excess of 100K/sec (sold for $70 by the supplier listed in Windows Help).

You may have a suitable parallel cable left over from an earlier brush with file transfer software; if not, your local computer store should have them—they may refer to them as Laplink cables. Windows Help lists a supplier from whom you can order a cable for $20.

Before you start, here are some things to keep in mind:

1. Both machines need to have the Dial-Up Networking Adapter installed with the same protocol on both sides (I'd recommend you install both NetBEUI and IPX/SPX on both machines), and both need to have the Client for Microsoft Networks installed. See the discussion of the Network applet in Chapter 10 on installing Network protocols and clients.

2. In a certain sense, the connection is one way in that one machine (usually the portable) is designated the guest and the other the host. The guest computer can access the drives on the Host and not vice versa. However, the guest computer can transfer files in either direction, so in that sense, the communication is two way. Note that both the guest and the host can run DCC in the background.

3. The host computer will need to have Printer and File Sharing turned on and the drives the guest wants to access will need to have sharing turned on for them explicitly. This is also discussed in Chapter 10.

---

* This means you should figure a 1 MB file will take close to fifteen minutes on a serial connection, while a parallel connection should be about one minute.

First you need to decide which machine is going to be the Guest and which the host. The Guest is the machine you'll be using to do the file transfers and so on. If one machine is a Laptop, it is traditionally the Guest. If you're using this to transfer files from one Desktop computer to another because you just bought a new computer, you'll probably want the new computer to be the Guest.

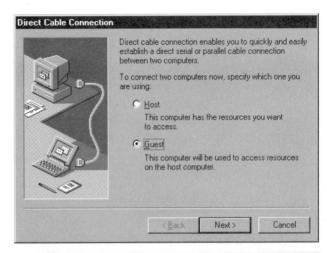

You need to run DCC on both machines; I'll describe the Guest setup.

You need to tell it what ports to use. Of course, having read what I just said, you picked Parallel ports, didn't you? It says to plug in the cable at this point but, of course, you could have plugged it before you began.

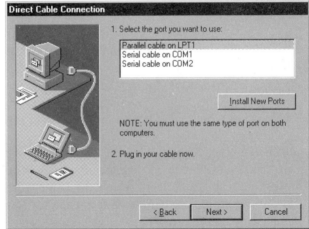

After you've gotten this far on each machine, hit Next on each.

You should get a notice that the machines are trying to connect.

You'll then be asked to type in the name of the Host computer. Success!!

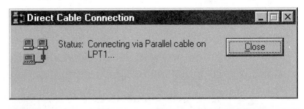

Once you are connected, the host computer will be accessible from the

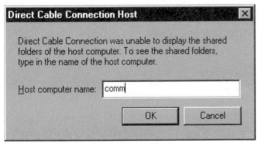

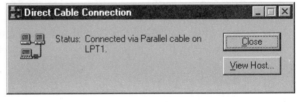

guest. Indeed, if you hit `View Host. . .`, a folder window should open on the guest with folders for each shared drive on the host. If it doesn't or you close it, you can access drives on the host using UNC pathnames. For example, if the host computer's name is `aye`, you could open its C drive by typing `\\aye\c` in the Run box. You can copy, move files via the standard Explorer methods.

DOS commands understand UNC pathnames, so once I've established a DCC connection, I often open a DOS box on the guest and use xcopy and move to transfer files.

Because DCC is networking, it can be used to install software you only have on CD to a laptop without CD. Make the laptop the guest to a host that has a CD. You can then run the setup program on the CD which will act like a drive, admittedly a slow drive, on the laptop.

Because DCC is networking, all programs can use the host's drives. So for this book, when I needed a screen shot from the portable, I used `PrtSc` and Paint to capture the screen and then used `File\Save` in Paint to save the file in `\\aye\c\windows\desktop` on the Desktop of the, er, Desktop machine.

Once you've set up a Direct Cable Connection, the next time you try to run DCC, it offers to restore the connection last used so you don't have to pick Guest/Host and port type. Surprisingly, though, it didn't remember the name of the host, which has to be entered each time.

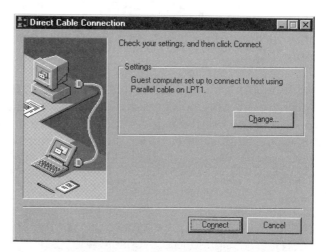

Another disappointment is that it doesn't handle shortcuts to the host machine as slickly as DUN does. If you use a modem DUN connection, then as I've explained, if you double-click on a shortcut to the remote machine when you aren't connected, DUN offers to connect you. With DCC if you make a shortcut to the other machine while connected and then double-click it while you are not, you just get the error panel shown here.

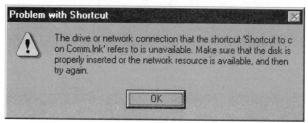

Floppy Briefcase

A lawyer with his briefcase can steal more than a hundred men with guns.

—Don Corleone speaking in Mario Puzo's *The Godfather,* 1969

 Windows provides a device for keeping files in two places in synch, called a *briefcase*—it's just a special kind of folder. There are two very different kinds of briefcases, with two very different modes of operation. Although their icons look the same and their technical guts are the same, their operations are different. One is floppy-based and one is network-based. Think of them as different, because if you don't, you'll use the methods for one in the context of the other and the files will lose synch. It's too bad that except for one vague reference in Windows Help, Microsoft hasn't bothered to clearly explain the fact that there are two different modes.

 As soon as Sarah told Mom that it reminded her of the theory of relativity, Mom said that I had to be the one to explain the modes since my mentor was buddies with "Dear Albert." Basically, in the floppy-based mode, the briefcase doesn't move while in the network mode it does. That is to say, in floppy mode, the floppy moves from one machine to another but the briefcase doesn't move—it stays in one place on the floppy. In this mode, there are three versions of each file—one on each computer and one in the briefcase on the floppy.

In the network mode the briefcase is moved to another location on the network and there are only two versions of the files—the one on the original machine and the one in the briefcase, located somewhere on the network. It's important that in this mode, on machines other than the original, files be accessed directly from the briefcase.

 The system knows that a folder is really a briefcase because of two hidden files that are in the briefcase folder—a text file called `Desktop.ini` and a binary file called `Briefcase Database`. The first has a CLSID,* the one assigned to briefcases, and it's what tells the system what icon to use via information in the Registry under that CLSID. I'm not sure how the system distinguishes between what I'm calling the network and floppy modes—it might be that if it finds a briefcase on a movable medium, it assumes it is a floppy briefcase.

---

* CLSID = CLaSs ID; I discuss these in Chapter 11.

Here's the basic idea—you make a briefcase on a floppy disk. The briefcase cannot span floppies but you can obviously have multiple floppies, each with its own briefcase. If you prefer, you can make the briefcase on your Desktop, copy some files there, and then move the briefcase to the floppy. But once you've got the briefcase on the floppy you shouldn't move the briefcase to another location.

 Windows is pretty intelligent about the defaults for dragging to briefcases and for dragging briefcases. If you drag a briefcase to a drive icon, the briefcase is moved (i.e., copied and deleted). If you drag a file to a briefcase, even from the same drive, it is copied. This is different from the behavior of any other kind of folder.

I'll imagine using a floppy-based briefcase to move files between computers you have at the office and home. Each file has three copies:

1. The one in the briefcase

2. The one on the office machine

3. The one on your home machine

You set this up by creating the file on the office machine and dragging it to the briefcase. Then when you get home, you drag it from the briefcase to a convenient folder on your home machine. Once you have these three copies in place, do not drag them to or from the briefcase. That's so important I'll shout it: **With floppy-based briefcases, you only drag files to and from the briefcase during the initial setup.** Once the three copies of files are in place, you don't even think about dragging them to/from the briefcase, or, for that matter dragging them between folders on your office or home PC because the briefcase will then lose track of them! Of course, if you've been using a given file (in three copies) for months and need to synch another file, you can do the create and drag routine on that new file without affecting the existing files.

Once set up, the key command for briefcase is called Update. If you open a briefcase in Folder view or view it in Explorer, an extra `Briefcase` menu appears between `View` and `Help`. It includes commands to update all or to update selected files (Figure 4-14). Alternatively, you can right-click on a closed briefcase and pick `Update All` from the context menu.

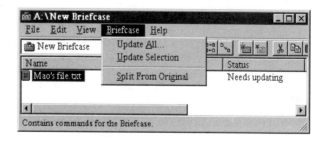

Figure 4-14. Briefcase in Folder view

If there are no files out of synch, you'll get a message saying that. Otherwise you'll get the dialog in Figure 4-15—although if you've done everything right, the recommendation will always be a replace arrow rather than the skip arrow shown here. If you right-click on a line you can override the recommendation, as shown here. Once you've checked all the recommendations, you just click Update.

This means that if you want to do some work at home on some files from the office, and you've already set up the three copies, you'd follow these steps:

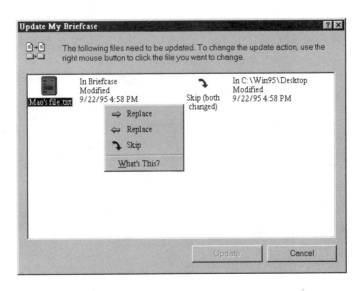

Figure 4-15. Briefcase update dialog

1. Before leaving the office, put the floppy briefcase(s) in your floppy drive, open the floppy in Folder view or Explorer, right-click on the briefcase, and pick Update All. Take the floppy out of the drive and put it in whatever you'll be using to take it home—most likely a, er, briefcase (so you have a briefcase on a floppy in a briefcase).

2. Before starting work at home, put the floppy in the drive, right-click on the briefcase inside the floppy folder, and Update All. The three copies of the file are now in synch.

3. After finishing your homework, do another Update All.

4. After you get the floppy back to the office again, Update All. All three copies will again be in synch.

Network Briefcase

The network briefcase is even simpler in concept than the floppy briefcase. You want to lend out some of your files to someone else or take them elsewhere in a situation where the elsewhere is accessible via the network at least via Dial-Up Networking or Direct Cable Connection. The procedure is simple:

1. Make a briefcase on your system. It's easiest to do this on your Desktop, but it can be anywhere you want. There's a New Briefcase command on the Desktop Context menu.

2. Drag the files you want to synch to the briefcase. Windows will make copies there.

3. Move the Briefcase folder to some other location on the network—for example, to a laptop currently connected via a docking station.

4. The files in the briefcase can be accessed and changed by the person working at the location of the briefcase—for example, on the laptop that is now out on the road. But here's the important proviso—the files have to be accessed from the briefcase. **In Network Briefcase mode, while in the secondary location, do not move or copy files into and out of the briefcase.** If you've dragged `budget.xls` to `Budget Briefcase` and then moved `Budget Briefcase` to `C:\` on the laptop, then on the laptop, you'd tell Excel to open `C:\Budget Briefcase\budget.xls`.

5. Once the briefcase is on the network in a place where the originals are accessible, you right-click on the briefcase and do an `Update All`, and it will put things back in synch. If you've used Dial-Up Networking to move the Briefcase, it will offer to make the call for you when you do an `Update All`.

Briefcases work well if you've only changed one of the pair of files involved in an update. If you've changed both, you'll normally get the message in Figure 4-15 warning you that both have changed, and you'll need to resolve the changes by hand. But programs can register a merge procedure with briefcase.

For example, if you drag an MS Access 7 database to a briefcase, you get a message (Figure 4-16) offering to set up a replica (in my test, a 2.5 MB blossomed to 3.6 MB after replication). Then if you change both, Briefcase offers to merge them, and Access has a Resolve Conflicts menu item to complete the merge.

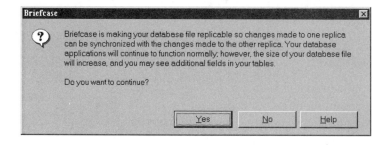

Figure 4-16. Access and briefcases

Hyperterminal

Like everyone else, I hate modems. They are infuriating, complicated, obscure, etc., etc.
But mostly, they are slow. No matter how fast they are, they are slow.
And slowness is the ultimate crime in computing.

—Stewart Alsop

Hyperterminal is, in the spirit of Windows 3.x Terminal, a fairly bare-bones modem communications program. It would do poorly on most magazine roundups, although better than Terminal would have because it does support Zmodem transfers and ANSI-BBS terminal emulation (the two biggest lacks in Terminal).

You save connections as icons in the Hyperterminal folder. These include a name and phone number and settings obtained from various dialogs. Don't overlook the button that says `Configure`. . . next to the modem. That's where you set communication parameters. Despite the implication that these settings are for the modem, they are for a specific connection.

There is no CompuServe B protocol and no scripting language at all.

 I take the position that because of the advent of Internet, this program is becoming irrelevant. It was already true that to access on-line services, you wanted or even were required to use a service-specific program. But a terminal program was important for vendor BBS and for accessing the vast BBS culture. That's changed. Vendor BBS are being replaced by websites and some general purpose BBS have Telnet access. What is missing from Hyperterminal is a Telnet mode. Some Telnet-accessible ANSI-BBS bulletin boards won't respond well to Windows Telnet program (which doesn't understand ANSI BBS) nor to Hyperterminal (which doesn't understand Telnet).

Dialer

The Englishman's telephone box is his castle. Like the London taxi,
it can be entered by a gentleman in a top hat. It protects the user's privacy,
keeps him warm and is large enough for a small cocktail party.

—Mary Blume, *International Herald Tribune*, Aug. 30, 1985

Phone Dialer is a fairly simple way of dialing your phone through the modem but with more functionality than you might think because it is a TAPI dialer, which means that other programs can link to it.

The program has eight-speed dial tabs, a number pad to enter numbers with, and a drop-down of recently dialed numbers (Figure 4-17). When you dial, Dialer will pop up a box where you can tell it the name of the person you are calling and let it know when you stopped. It then stores this name, the number, date, time, and duration of the call in a log.

The log is an ASCII text files `C:\windows\calllog.txt`. You can turn off call logging by first picking `Show Log` from the `Tools` menu in Dialer and then `Log/Options` from the menu in the log window that results.

The true importance of dialer comes from the checkbox in the dialog of `Tools/Connect Using...` in the main menu system. It says "`Use Phone Dialer to handle voice call requests from other programs`" and is enabled by default. If enabled, Dialer is the TAPI voice provider that means, for example, that the Dial button on the Phone Tab of items in Exchanges Address Book will invoke Dialer passing it a name as well as phone numbers. Dialer is functional as is, but will be more important because of these links.

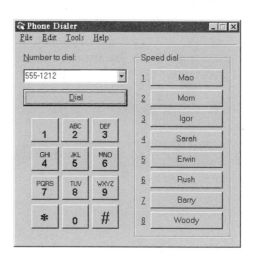

Figure 4-17. Roll your dex

File Transfer

> The average Ph.D. thesis is nothing but a transference of bones
> from one graveyard to another.

—J. Frank Dobie, *A Texan in England*

Windows 95 has special support for VoiceView modems. These modems, which should be available from a variety of vendors, have special technology to allow file transfers while you are talking on the phone—using the unused bandwidth. When you install a Voice View modem, Windows installs a program called Microsoft File Transfer (file name: `filexfer.exe`) in the `C:\windows` folder, adds it to the Accessories submenu

Figure 4-18. Microsoft File Transfer

and to the StartUp group and makes a directory called `C:\windows\received files` (see Figure 4-18). The program starts up minimized and handles files received transparently. You can use the program to send files. You can set an option for the `Received Files` folder open automagically whenever a new file is received.

 If you and the folks you transfer files with have a VoiceView modem, this is definitely the way to go, but if not, don't forget how to transfer files with Fax modems, as I described in Chapter 3 in "Windows Secret File Transfer Program."

WinChat and Winpopup

Many of the quests for status symbols—the hot automobile, the best table in a restaurant or a private chat with the boss—are shadowy reprises of infant anxieties. . . . The larger office, the corner space, the extra window are the teddy bears and tricycles of adult office life.

—Dr. Willard Gaylin, *The Rage Within*

 I get a big kick out of WinPopup. Any time I want to send a note to somebody on the network, I just push the button and away it goes. The trick with WinPopup is that both you and the person you are sending to have to have it running—typically, by putting it in your StartUp folder—before it will respond to messages.

Figure 4-19. WinPopup in action

If you installed either Client for Netware Networks or Client for Microsoft Networks, and installed from a CD, you'll find `winpopup.exe` in your `\windows` folder. If not, click Start, Settings, Control Panel. Double-click on Add/Remove Programs, and bring up the Windows `Setup tab`, click `Accessories`, and add it by clicking on WinPopup.

Add it to your StartUp group if you plan to use it.

Oh creepy one, you are showing your network naiveté! Windows for Workgroups has a similar program called Chat, and it works better than WinPopup. If a message comes in, Chat rings a little bell. You can use it to talk to up to seven different people at once. Other people can dial in and catch the conversation in progress. To install it, use Explorer to look at your Win95 CD's `\other\chat` folder. Right-click on `winchat.inf` and choose Install.

Blecccch. I tried WinChat, and I hate it. Where WinPopup lets you send a message to a specific user, computer I.D., or workgroup, WinChat requires you to know the computer I.D. of the people you want to talk to. You have no control over who else on the network sees your messages. Turning it off is a pain in the neck.

Oh well. Guess that's what makes a horserace . . . er, cockroachrace.

The On-line Bazaar

You may wonder why the other books tell you about MSN, aka The Microsoft Network, and I don't. It's because I object to Microsoft using Windows 95 to launch its admittedly impressive new on-line service. Using a monopoly in one part of the business to benefit another is something I don't cotton to.

Right on, Mom. The Department of Justice shoulda made 'em pull MSN from the box when they were looking at this in August 1995.

Not at all, Rush. If Justice had something in January 1995, I'd have said fair enough, but to do something at the last minute, after the beta test was done and the code had gone gold, would have been ludicrous, given that Justice and MSN's competitors knew about this for a year before that.

Hey, it's a checkbox during install. The user can choose not to install MSN. So where's the beef?

Horse, er cockroach pucky, Billy. Even if the user says no, an icon is still installed that tells you to click there to install MSN. And according to press reports, Microsoft required hardware vendors to install MSN when they were installing Windows.

In my previous job, I sent people to sleep with the sharks, so I may as well swim with them now. Prodigy shipped preinstalled on more than half the PCs sold last year. So what's the big deal if MSN is preinstalled? Let Microsoft's competitors, all big corporations, compete with them by making a good product instead of getting their lawyers to kvetch to Justice.

Well, I believe in choice for my readers. So I'm going to try to get the software for AOL, Prodigy, and CompuServe on my bonus CD. And to keep the field level, I'm not going to talk a lot about MSN.

Gettin' Hitched to the Net

> Always marry a short woman;
> Her clothes will cost you less.

—Moroccan Proverb

If you want to get your PC working on the Internet, you'll be miles ahead to get the Internet Jumpstart Kit (IJK). There are several ways to get this. First, you can buy the Windows Plus! Pack, which includes IJK. Second, if you've gotten a new PC recently, check that it isn't included—some hardware manufacturers licensed the IJK from Microsoft. Third, the program is available on-line under the file name `msie10.exe` (the 10, which stands for version 1.0 may change). You'll find it on CompuServe (go to the Microsoft File Finder and search for `msie*.*`) and it can be downloaded from the Microsoft Website (`http://www.windows.microsoft.com/windows`). Yes, it is sorta self-referential to need to be connected to the Web and a Web Browser to download Microsoft's Web connection tools and their Web Browser, but I'm giving you this information in case you've a friend with a working Web setup or in case you are on one of the on-line services and want to switch to a plain Internet provider.

While it's true that you can set things up manually—and I'll give you instructions on how to do so, later in this section—Internet Jumpstart Kit contains something called the Internet Setup Wizard. That wizard will save you lots of time and frustration. In addition, the IJK has programs that will let you receive, read, and send Internet email with Exchange.

By the way, if you're trying to get your computer at work connected to the Internet, you can also use the IJK to get set up. I'll focus first on Dial-Up connections but then say something about LAN connections.

Net 101

> Net: Anything reticulated or decussated at equal distances,
> with interstices between the intersections.
>
> —Samuel Johnson, *Dictionary*, 1755

First, a little tutorial. I promise to keep this painless, even if you're a Net Newbie. The Internet, as you probably know, is a network that connects computers all over the world. If you're running Win95 and have a modem, you already have almost everything you need to get on the Net. The one part that's missing is a "service provider," and (unless you have a cushy deal with a University or a research group) service providers are not free.

A service provider has a computer that's connected to the Net. Your PC dials into the service provider's computer and is thus connected to the Net. You pay the service provider for use of its computer, for the fee it pays for access to the Internet, and (in theory, anyway) for their help and support when your attempts to connect to the Net are invariably thwarted. A few providers may try to sell you so-called "Shell" accounts, which essentially turn your PC into a big, dumb monitor connected to their UNIX machines—with a "Shell" account your only access is through a series of character-mode menus. Blecccch. What you want for full-fledged Net action—and the only type of connection supported by the IJK, Exchange, Internet Explorer, and the rest of the Win95 goodies—is a PPP account.* There is an older kind of direct net access account called a SLIP account—you want PPP, not SLIP, but most accounts these days are PPP accounts.

It probably won't surprise you to discover that Microsoft is a service provider through The Microsoft Network. You can dial into Microsoft's computers and have them connect you to the Net. If you're willing to pay Microsoft its current hourly fee for Internet access, the Internet Setup Wizard is supposed to do almost everything for you. On the other hand, if you want to use a different service provider—and there are

---

* PPP = Point-to-Point Protocol

hundreds of 'em—you'll need to set up an account with that service provider, get an I.D., and the telephone number for tech support and whatnot, before you run the Internet Setup Wizard.

CompuServe can also act as a general-purpose PPP provider using the Dial-Up Networking Scripting Tool. I'll show you later how to effortlessly arrange that (in the section *Logon scripts for CompuServe*). Prodigy and America Online do not (at this writing, anyway) provide direct PPP connections, so you are limited to accessing the Internet with their tools.

Mom, don't leave your readers with the impression that Microsoft is necessarily the best Internet service provider. It might not even be the easiest to set up. Providing a good "Internet On-Ramp" is a whole lot more involved than hanging out a shingle and attaching a phone line. There are big questions about tech support and capacity. Shop around! No need for Microsoft to get all the marbles.

Microsoft has endeavored to provide a top-quality service at a rock-bottom price—a price certainly competitive with most other service providers. At this moment, we offer a standard plan that costs $4.95/month and includes three hours of usage per month (whether on MS Network or on the Net), with extra hours at $2.50. We also offer a Junkies . . . uh, Frequent User's Plan that gives twenty hours of usage (again, either MSN or Internet, doesn't matter) for $19.95, and extra hours are $2.00.

Well, that means that your prices are just about even with CompuServe, America Online and Prodigy, give or take a dollar here and an hour there. What about the local companies that provide Internet connections, all over the world? Can your physical installation keep up with the demand? What about your phone line capacity? And how well will you support your users? Those are the questions users have to ask when choosing a service provider. Microsoft does not have a clear advantage in any of those areas, as far as I can see.

Except they get to give their hook-up a special place in the IJK. Talk about using a monopoly in one area to advance business interests in another.

Internet Setup Wizard

Whatever befalls the earth befalls the sons of the earth. Man did not weave the web of life: he is merely a strand in it. Whatever he does to the web, he does to himself.

—Seattle, Indian Chief, *Letter to President Franklin Pierce,* 1854

 Got that? If you're going to use Microsoft as a service provider, you can run the wizard now. If you already have an account with a service provider (and have the tech support line's phone number!), you can run the wizard as soon as you get some simple information together. But if you don't want to use Microsoft, and you don't already have an account with a service provider, you have to get one set up before you continue.

Don't get the willies. The Internet Setup Wizard really is the simplest Internet setup routine I've ever seen—and I've sweated through a bunch of 'em. Start by checking your documentation or calling your service provider for all of the following information:

- The telephone number you dial to get into their machine.

- Whether you have an explicit IP address and, if so, what the address is (four numbers, each up to three digits—each always 255 or less). If you have an explicit IP address, find out if you also need a subnet mask.

- Your provider's DNS ("Domain Name Server") address (four numbers); if there's a "Secondary DNS," get its address, too (another four numbers).

- The name of your provider's mail system (something like daemon.microsoft.com); the mail server is also commonly called a POP-server, but don't tell Mom that, OK?

In addition, there are a few things you'll need to know, but probably won't be able to get over the phone. With a little luck they're tucked away somewhere in the material the provider sent to you. You need your logon user name and password (the ones you use to log on to the provider's computer) and your email address, if you have one (like, oh, billg@microsoft.com).

For a LAN setup, you'll need a Gateway Address instead of a phone number.

Let's step through the wizard now and take a look at the things you'll need to figure out.

When you install the Plus! Pack it will offer to take you through Internet setup. If you say no but installed the Plus! Pack's Internet Tools or you installed a downloaded IJK, you should have an icon on your Desktop called `The Internet`. Once you are set up, that icon will launch Microsoft's Web Browser but until you are set up, it will launch the Internet Setup Wizard. You should also find `Internet Setup Wizard` off the Start Menu under `Programs\ Acessories\Internet Tools`.

As, I mentioned, I'm going to assume that you're setting up Internet access for your PC only, from a modem attached to your computer. I'll talk about LAN setup afterward.

If you're going to use Microsoft as your service provider, click "Use The Microsoft Network" here and follow the instructions (have your credit card number handy). If you're connecting to your own service provider, click the lower button. The wizard will tell you that it's installing files. You'll probably need to dig out your Win95 installation CD to get all of them.

Think of a good name for this connection to the service provider and type it in here. (The name can be anything you want.) The wizard will create a new Dial-Up Networking entry with this name. You can see it or modify it later by double-clicking on `My Computer`, then double-clicking on Dial-Up Networking, right-clicking the name of the provider and choosing Properties.

Here's where you type in the service provider's phone number. Most service providers have logon programs that can automatically negotiate with Windows 95 to log you on. Many, though, aren't that smart—you have to type in your logon user

name and password every time you log on, and
manually enter a command like `ppp` or `slip` to
get the two computers to talk to each other. We're
going to assume that your service provider is hip
to the Win95 connection scene, and not check that
box at the bottom. If your service provider doesn't
speak Win95 connection, we'll find out, and
correct the problem shortly.

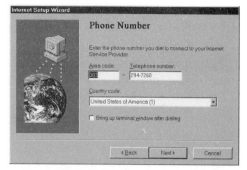

Next, the wizard wants to know which I.D. and
password you use when you first log onto the
service provider's computer. Typically, they're the
two things you type in immediately after getting
attached to the service provider's computer.

The IP address is a series of four numbers that
identifies your computer on the Net. If you set up
your account fairly recently, chances are good you
have a "Dynamic SLIP/PPP" account, which
means the service provider's computer
automatically assigns your computer a new IP
address every time you dial up. If you have a
permanently assigned IP address, you have to
enter it here, as well as a subnet mask, if need be.

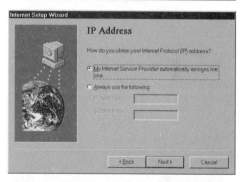

When you work on the Net, you use easy-to-
remember addresses like billg@microsoft.com or
http://www.wopr.com/wopr. Net computers aren't
so smart; they route things by using numeric
addresses like 129.187.121.1. Domain Name
Servers (DNSs) are just computers that translate
the "human" addresses we use to four-number
addresses the computers can use. Your service
provider will give you the (numeric!) addresses of
one or two DNSs nearby that can do the
translation quickly. Enter their numbers here.

Your service provider will assign you an email
address like sarah@mom.com. Assuming you
want to use Exchange for email (and it's a quite
capable mail droid), this is where you tell it your
email I.D. In addition, your service provider will
be running email off a specific machine called an
Internet Mail Server or a POP-server. Get the
name of the Mail Server from the service provider,
and type it in here.

Congratulations! You're almost done. Unless
you're really, uh, fastidious about such things,
you're going to want to use the standard Exchange
Profile, so just click Next> here. The next wizard
panel will tell you that it's done. Double-click
"The Internet" on your Desktop and see if you get
connected to the World-Wide Web. You'll probably
find that everything works right the first time. If
not, see Erwin's admonishments coming up next.

If you are using a LAN connection, you won't
need a name for the service provider or telephone
number (natch), but you'll need to get a Gateway
address (usually a four-number address) from your
LAN administrator. The wizard will skip the
panels asking for the number and phone number of
your Internet provider but will slip in this panel
after asking for a DNS.

Behind the scenes, the Setup wizard will also
install TCP/IP support and `winsock.dll` for
your Dial-Up Networking Adapter or for your LAN adapter.

Can't Get Connected

The most common interconnection problem is a phone line that just sits
there and does nothing. You double-click on "The Internet," wait a minute
or two, hear the modem being dialed and the other end picking up, they
squeal for a bit, and then absolutely nothing happens. After a while you
might get a message saying you were disconnected, or that the computers
were unable to establish a compatible protocol. That's all hogwash.

If you got all the entries in the wizard right, and you can log on to your service provider manually (you should double-check both, of course), the most likely source of the problem lies *with your service provider's computer* and its inability to automatically log on Win95 users. Here's how you can check and see if that's what's keeping you from getting on (see Figure 4-20). Double-click on `My Computer`, double-click on Dial-Up Networking. Right-click on the name of the connection you typed into the wizard and pick `Properties`. Click `Configure`. Click on the `Options` tab, and check the box marked "Bring up terminal window after dialing."

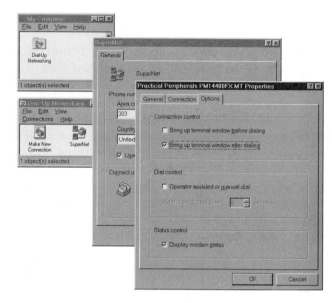

Figure 4-20. Bring up terminal window after dialing

Click `OK` all the way back out. That checkbox tells Win95, "Go ahead and dial the phone, but when the computer on the other end asks for a logon User Name and Password, let me type them in."

 Now double-click on "The Internet" on your Desktop. You'll hear the modem dialing and the squeal that typifies happy cyberconnections. As soon as the connection is established, a window will pop up and you'll have a chance to go through your usual logon sequence. You'll probably have to enter your logon user name and password, and some sort of command like `ppp` or `slip`. Your service provider can give you the details. When the screen starts to spout gibberish, hit `F7` to see if the two computers can sort out their differences and get connected.

If that solves the problem, get on the phone with your service provider and yell bloody murder: they'd better get with the system, according to Windows 95, or they're gonna lose your business!

If that *doesn't* solve your problem, try running through the manual installation steps described later and see if you can find anything obviously wrong. If all else fails, call your service provider. They should be quite accustomed to Win95 questions by now. Remember that Microsoft charges $35 a pop (or $1.95 a minute) to answer network questions.

Can't Get Your Mail

The second most common problem occurs when you can log on. "The Internet" browses the Web just fine, but for some unknown reason, Exchange ("Inbox" on your Desktop) won't retrieve your Internet mail. Again, if you got the settings in the wizard right and you can retrieve your mail with some other program (and you should double-check both), the fault might lie with your service provider—but in this case, it really isn't the service provider's fault.

Some service providers require a separate Internet email user name and password, one that's different from your usual logon user name and password (Figure 4-21). That's not necessarily a bad thing, but it does require some extra effort on your part to get Windows to use it—for some unknown reason, the wizard can't handle it.

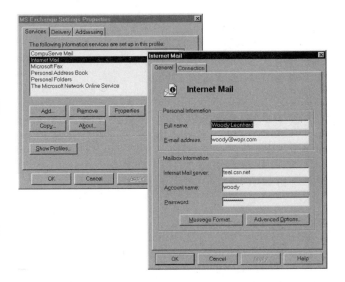

Start by finding out what your Internet email user name and password are. You may have to rummage through the settings of your current email

Figure 4-21. Email user name and password

package; you may have to call your service provider once again. When you have the user name and password, click on Start, Settings, Control Panel, and double-click on the `Mail and Fax` applet. Click once on Internet Mail, click `Properties`. Put your user name in the "Account Name" box and your password in the "Password" box. Click OK all the way back out.

Now go back to your Desktop, double-click on Inbox, click `Tools`, then `Deliver Now Using`, then `Internet Mail`. Does the connection get established? Does your mail get downloaded? Good. If not, gripe at your service provider and see what else can be done.

If you can receive Internet mail but not send it, see the section in Chapter 3, "Hoping for an Easy Delivery."

Manual Installation

> O, what a tangled web we weave,
> When first we practice to deceive!

— Sir Walter Scott, *Marmion*

 If you're not in the mood to buy the Plus! Pack, can't get the Internet Jumpstart Kit, or you just don't have the time to run out and get it right now, everything the Internet Setup Wizard does can also be accomplished by hand. I've done it several times, but it is a little tricky: Here's the condensed version of what you need to do to get Win95 up to the same point that the wizard accomplishes automatically.

 Remember, you need the Plus! Pack or IJK to use Exchange for Internet Mail. If you're going to need it for that, get it before you even set up your Internet connection, and save yourself the hassle. But if your Internet Provider has its own email program that they've given you and you think you'll be happy with it, you can get Internet email by non-Exchange means without Plus! or IJK.

 I think it's pretty chintzy of Microsoft to put Internet Mail in the IJK rather than in Windows itself. A sneaky ploy to head you toward The Microsoft Network and/or into buying Plus! In fact, the whole IJK shoulda been on the Windows CD.

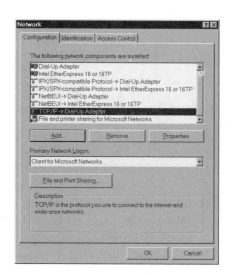

Figure 4-22. The TCP/IP Connection

If you used the Internet Setup Wizard and you can get on the Net—say, you click on Inbox and can retrieve your Internet email—do not muck with any of this!

- First you want to make sure your modem can speak TCP/IP, the Net's language. Click Start, Settings, Control Panel. Double-click on the `Network` applet and bring up the Configuration tab. You're looking for two entries. One says Dial-Up Adapter and the other says TCP/IP -> Dial-Up Adapter (Figure 4-22).

- If you're missing the Dial-Up Adapter entry, click on Add, double-click Adapter. On the left pick Microsoft, on the right pick Dial-Up Adapter, and click OK. If you're missing the TCP/IP -> line, click on Add, double-click Protocol. On the left, click Microsoft; on the right, click TCP/IP. Click OK. You may have to insert your Win95 CD to retrieve some files. Double-click on Dial-Up Adapter. Click on the Bindings tab and make sure the TCP/IP box is checked. Click OK. The line TCP/IP -> Dial-Up Adapter should appear.

- Double-click on TCP/IP -> Dial-Up Adapter. There are six tabs; you'll probably only need to change one, the "DNS Configuration." As explained in the Wizard discussion, you'll need one or two DNS addresses—sets of four numbers, separated by periods. Your service provider will give them to you. Type them in here and click Add. If you've been assigned a permanent IP address (unusual, and getting more unusual every day; see the earlier discussion), you'll have to click the IP Address tab and type it in. Click OK to get out of TCP/IP Properties. You'll probably be asked if you want to reboot your machine. Go ahead and reboot.

- After Windows has restarted itself, double-click on My Computer, double-click on Dial-Up Networking, double-click on Make New Connection. You'll get the "Make New Connection Wizard." Click Configure, then the Options tab. Don't check "Bring up terminal window after dialing." (As in the Network Setup Wizard, that would allow you to manually log on to your service provider.) Finish off the Make New Connection Wizard. You'll ultimately get a new icon in the Dial-Up Networking window. Congratulations! You're done: Double-clicking on that icon will connect you to the Net.

 Chasing and swatting bugs with manual setup is the same as it is with the Plus! Pack's Internet Setup Wizard.

 Manual setup on a LAN isn't much harder, but you may want your MIS department to do it. If not, you'll first need to install TCP/IP for your LAN adapter, not the Dial-Up Adapter. Second, you'll need to enter a Gateway in the TCP/IP Properties sheet.

Per Connection DNS Servers

 I'm puzzled that your IP address and DNS server have to be set in the Network applet, which means they apply to all Dial-Up connections. Suppose you have two PPP connections and each is assigned an IP address? Or each has its own DNS—is it fair to use the DNS address of one when you connect to the others?

Actually, you can assign these things on a per-connection basis. The natural place you enter these is indeed by calling up the Network Applet, highlighting `TCP/IP->Dial-Up Adapter`, and hitting `Properties`. That would set up global addresses used by every connection.

But you can also highlight a connection in the DUN folder, right-click, and pick `Properties`, then click `Server Type`, and then `TCP/IP settings. . .` (that hidden enough for you?). This is where you can enter settings for individual connections. But it's an all-or-nothing proposition. These settings are only used if you have blank settings in the Network applet, and in that case you must set them up for each and every connection.

Logon Scripts for CompuServe

A gent I know whose life is superfluidity
Took a job in CBS Continuity.

One night after too much Scotch paregoric,
He turned in a script just too prehistoric.

He was fired and said, as he read his doxology . . .
"I thought they would like my Paley-ontology."

—Paul W. White, Director of Special Events, CBS*

While the Internet Jumpstart Kit contains almost all the Plus! Pack Internet tools (it has the Internet Setup Wizard, the Browser and the Internet Mail server for Exchange), there is one Internet goody not included with the Jumpstart Kit because it is buried on the CD and available from the Microsoft Web site. It is also on Mom's companion CD! On the Windows CD, you'll find this scripting in the directory `\admin\apptools\dscript`. On Mom's CD it's in `\w95disks\admin\apptools\dscript`. To install, call up the `Add/Remove Programs` applet. Go to the `Windows Setup` tab and hit `Have Disk . . . .` Then Browse to the proper directory, hit `OK` a few times, and check the box next to the text `SLIP and Scripting for Dial-Up Networking`. If you've installed Plus!, it will install this scripting, and you don't need to go through the installation I just described.

In this section, I'll tell you how to set up a PPP connection if you have a CompuServe account and want to use it as your general purpose Internet provider. As you'll see it's very easy. On the next page Mao will tell you the more complicated things you need to do if you want to set up a more elaborate script for a third party Internet provider.

---

* William Paley was Chairman of CBS at the time.

Don't let the word *script* frighten you. Microsoft has included the script you need for CompuServe, so although you need the Plus! Pack, you don't need to do any programming. Here's what you do:

1. Get together the following pieces of information. The CompuServe telephone number that you want to use, your CompuServe I.D. number (something like 76123,4567), your password, and the name you want to give the Dial-Up connection you're going to make (for example, CIS-PPP).

2. If you've not yet run the Internet Setup Wizard or manually installed TCP/IP support, do that first. If you're not running the Setup wizard, open up `My Computer`, click on Dial-Up Networking, and then on New Connection. Either wizard will ask you for the name you want to give the connection and the telephone number. For this stage you'll need CompuServe's DNS numbers (you don't need a personal IP address; CompuServe assigns one on the fly each time you log on in PPP mode): `149.174.211.5` or `149.174.213.5`.

3. If you run the Internet Setup Wizard and CompuServe will be your only Internet provider, answer no to the question about using Internet mail. CompuServe lets you send mail to/from the Internet but doesn't use the SMNP protocol used by the Internet Mail Exchange service provider. Instead you'll need to set up CompuServe's Exchange service provider, which I discuss in Chapter 3.

4. Now, go to the Start Menu, go to `Programs/Accessories`, and look for an entry named `Dial-Up Scripting Tool` and run it.

5. You'll get the dialog shown in Figure 4-23. Highlight the CIS-PPP (or whatever you called it) on the Connections side and hit the `Browse` button. The dialog that pops up should show the folder `C:\Program Files\Accessories` and it should show all `.scp` files. One of them will be `cis.scp`. Select it, make sure the `Step through script` box is *not* checked and the `Start terminal...` is checked. Then hit `Apply` and `close`.

6. You're basically done. Double-click on the CIS-PPP icon in the Dial-Up Networking folder and you'll be asked to fill in user name and password. It will already have your name filled in as user name; that's wrong—you need to put your CompuServe user I.D. number in there. Hit Connect and you should be in business.

7. If you want CIS-PPP to be your default Internet provider, you'll need to call up the Internet applet—see the discussion of that later in this chapter.

Call me overly suspicious but I find it a might strange that the tools you need to turn CompuServe into a PPP provider on the same standing as The Microsoft Network are buried so deep on the CD and aren't included with Internet Jumpstart Kit where someone might think to look for them! Little nudge towards MSN, eh, Billy boy?

The Logon Scripting Language

If it's a good script I'll do it. And if it's a bad script, and they pay me enough, I'll do it.

—George Burns, *International Herald Tribune,* Nov. 9, 1988

Although it's true that some service providers have computers that are smart enough to log you on automatically when you dial in with Win95, in my experience a big percentage still make you type in your logon I.D., password, and usually a command like PPP or some such. That's why Win95 has a "Bring up terminal window after dialing" checkbox: Win95 has to step back after establishing the modem connection long enough to let you type in your I.D., password, and PPP.

Well, Scripting for Dial-Up Networking, which you can install following Sarah's instructions in the last section, does away with all of that mumbojumbo by allowing you to create automated logon scripts for any Dial-Up Networking connection, most particularly for dial-up access to the Net.

The easiest way to set up a logon script is to click on Start, then Help, then Index and bring up the Help topic "Automating a Dial-Up Networking Connection." I won't duplicate that information here, but I will show you the script I use for dialing in to my service provider. (My service provider prompts "username:" then "password:" then, after I'm logged on and the big computer says "annex:" I'm supposed to type in "ppp" and hit Enter.) Comments are preceded by a semi-colon.

```
; Mao's PPP logon script for SuperNet

proc main

    waitfor "username:" until 5 ;give it five seconds to
    stabilize

    if $FAILURE then

        goto BadConnection

    endif

    transmit $USERID + "^M" ;the connection's userid + Enter
```

```
    waitfor "password:" until 5 ;another five seconds for pword
    if $FAILURE then
        goto BadConnection
    endif
    transmit $PASSWORD + "^M"
    waitfor "annex:" until 20 ;20 seconds to actually log on
    if $FAILURE then
        goto BadConnection
    endif
    transmit "ppp^M"
    goto Bye        ;logged on
BadConnection:
    halt
Bye:
endproc
```

Basically you create the script using Notepad, then attach it to a particular Dial-Up Networking configuration by using a program called the Dial-Up Scripting Tool installed when you installed Plus! or you explicitly installed Scripting. You'll find it under the `Programs/Accessories` submenu of the Start Menu. If you're moderately comfortable with any Basic-type programming language, you'll find the scripting language easy to pick up — it's quite straightforward. If you installed Plus! details can be found in an eight-page file called `script.doc` in the `\Program Files\Plus!` folder. If you didn't install Plus!, there are details in a section of Help called Scripting Commands which is part of general Windows help. It's unfortunate that there is less help available if you haven't gotten Plus!

Here are four tips on using the scripting language:

1. If you want to look at more examples, check in the `\Program Files\` `Accessories` folder for `*.scp` files. I found those samples were a whole lot more complicated than what I wanted, but you may find them useful.

2. After you type in your program, save it to the `\Program Files\Accessories` folder with an `.scp` extension. That'll make it easier for Dial-Up Scripting Tool to find the script.

3. You want to disable the "Bring up terminal window after dialing" setting so you can test, and later run, your script. The manual logon mode just gets in the way. To get rid of it, in the Dial-Up Scripting Tool click Properties, then Configure, bring up the Options tab, and clear the "Bring up terminal window after dialing" checkbox.

4. The Dial-Up Scripting Tool has a great debug mode you can invoke (Figure 4-23). Just check Step Through Script and uncheck Start Terminal Screen Minimized. Debugging is pretty easy once you get the hang of it. Keep Notepad open with your `.scp` file showing, and try to logon—say, through Inbox. Rearrange the windows so you can see what's going on. Step through the script by pushing the Step button. When the script bombs (and it will!), make changes to the script in Notepad, click File, then Save, make changes to the Dial-Up Scripting Tool settings if necessary, click Apply, and try to log on again. When it's all working right, remember to uncheck Step Through Script and check Start Terminal Screen Minimized.

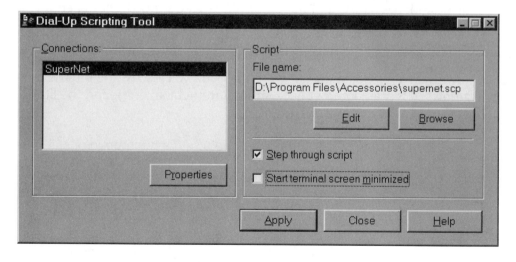

Figure 4-23. Dial-Up Scripting Tool in debug mode

Even if you're intimidated by the idea of writing a "real" program, give it a shot. You'll get the hang of it in no time.

Internet Tools

A century or so from now, observers looking back on the 1990s will consider the advent of the Internet and the World-Wide Web one of the great watersheds of history—comparable technologically to the invention of movable type, artistically to the Renaissance, and socially to the Declaration of Independence. You may think this assessment grandiose, but look around you: The great on-line body of individually authored and hyperlinked information that Ted Nelson envisioned decades ago as the Xanadu project is day by day crystallizing before our eyes. Tens of thousands of creative network citizens across the world are setting up their own information servers and joining the Web. In the process, those net citizens are completely bypassing the Establishment with its bureaucracies, class hierarchies, and power structures, not to mention the entire monolithic apparatus of the traditional publishing industry!

—Ray Duncan, *PC Magazine,* May 16, 1995

About 30 million users have access to Internet (as compared with fewer than 8 million users on all the big on-line services combined). Growth isn't at more than 100 percent, as it was for a few years, but it's certainly well into double digits. And the World-Wide Web's growth has been phenomenal. It too has slowed somewhat, but at the height of its growth in mid-1995, it was estimated that the number of "pages" on the Web was doubling every twenty-three days. Clearly, the Internet and its components are an important part of computing. Now that we've got you signed on, my gang will discuss the Internet's components, Windows 95's main Internet access tool (Internet Explorer), and the little Internet applets sprinkled around on your hard disk.

One has to take some of the Internet numbers with a huge grain of salt. Many of those 30 million users have email accounts only. And when a web site brags a million hits a day, that doesn't mean a million people visiting, since the counts typically include every page visited and count a page multiple times if the user's browser downloads it a second time when they return to it. Still 100,000 visitors a day and 5 million people browsing the Web are mind-numbing numbers.

The large numbers of users and sites and the variety of different information providers give the Internet something of an unruly nature. It will be a frequent occurrence that you'll click on a link on a Web page or request a file through the archie search engine and get a message that the resource you are looking for isn't available. This can have two different causes. First, the site you are searching for may have literally disappeared—the owners of the site may have stopped paying their bills to their service provider or the machine the site was on may be down, temporarily or permanently. When a piece of the net disappears, the pointers to it elsewhere on the net will long remain.

The second cause for unavailability is that there may be more users accessing the resource than the resource is able to handle. Sometimes, you'll get an explicit message from the resource telling you this but sometimes you'll just be unable to make the connection and not know why. Sometimes if there are too many users, performance just slows to a crawl. Speaking of performance, Web browsing is graphically intensive and that means large files. You won't find browsing at 9600 bps very pleasant. Some folks complain that anything less than 28,800 bps is unacceptable, but I've found 14,400 bps (while less than snappy) usually OK.

Net 102

> I've discovered the killer application that will establish Internet.
> No, it's not the World-Wide Web. It's email.

—Mom

So what can you do on the Internet? Here's a list of the main functions, listed roughly in the ranking of importance (according to Mom):

- email is short for electronic mail, not that anyone uses that term any more. There truly is a way to send messages to millions of other people, have them get them at their convenience, and transfer as cheaply to someone around the world as around the corner. Windows 95 supports email through Exchange (discussed in detail in Chapter 3) and, in particular, the Internet Jumpstart Kit adds Internet Mail support to Exchange for Internet Providers that use SMNP/POP3 servers, the standard on Internet.

- the World-Wide Web, aka the Web is a collection of information resources that are hyperlinked together. Providers produce one or more "home pages" of information with links to other pages that let you jump by pointing and clicking. There are literally millions of pages out there with useful information, varying from daily postings by *Time* magazine to access to parts of the Library of Congress. A high school student can not only locate information on hundreds of colleges, but often request an application while on the Web. Because of the links, you can wander from website to website searching and even sometimes enjoying. This is called "surfing the Web" or "surfing the net." Programs that let you surf the net are called Web Browsers. The Internet Jumpstart Kit includes Microsoft Internet Explorer, a full-featured Web Browser.

The Web truly is wonderful. If you have an idea of what you want to find, you can often get useful information quickly. But it is also the most overhyped service on the Internet. Random fooling can spend enormous gobs of time without much to show for it. That surfing the Web beats TV for entertainment is a negative statement about TV rather than a positive one about the Web.

- `ftp` short for File Transfer Protocol, the standard, er, protocol for transferring files over Internet. Actually, the name is used not so much for the protocol as for transferring files from special Internet nodes called "anonymous FTP sites." That name comes from the fact that you can log onto the nodes as a user called *anonymous,* with a password equal to your email address. You'll find software libraries, drivers from many vendors, and more at various `ftp` sites. You can do `ftp` transfer from Internet Explorer and Windows 95 also comes with a DOS (!) program called `ftp`.

- `archie` is the name given to search tools for files on FTP sites. Various archie sites are accessible via the Web and via Internet Explorer, as I'll explain.

- `telnet` is a protocol for remote login from one machine to another in dumb text mode. This is probably only relevant to you if you have an account on a UNIX-based network, if you get into MUDs (see the discussion of MUDs, following), or if you want to access a BBS system via Telnet. Windows 95 includes a GUI Telnet program that I'll discuss.

- `mailing lists` are an interesting hybrid between the discussion forums that you'll find on the on-line services and plain mail. Once you find out the source of the mailing list you subscribe to it (typically by sending email to an address that starts with `listserv@. . .` with text that says SUBSCRIBE), and it appears once a day in your mail box with all the messages for that day. Or you can ask the list server to send you messages individually as they come in. There is usually some process you have to go through to be authorized to add messages of your own to the list. When you subscribe, you'll get back a message telling you how to unsubscribe and usually providing other options. The `listserv` address is totally automated, so it is important you follow syntax directions precisely.

Some lists are moderated (someone authorizes which messages get passed on to the list) and some not. There are also private lists that are used to send messages out with no way for outsiders to submit their own messages—an example is the Winnews newsletter on Windows 95, put out by Microsoft. To subscribe to it, you send email to `enews99@microsoft.nwnet.com` with a blank subject line and message content consisting solely of SUBSCRIBE WINNEWS.

You don't need any special software to access mailing lists other than email software.

- `newsgroups`, aka `uunet` or `usenet`, are publicly posted groups of messages in forums that run the gamut from `rec.humor.funny` and `biz.jobs.offered` to `alt.tv.dinosaur.barney.die.die.die.` and `alt.sex.fetish.tickling`. As I'll explain, if your Internet Provider is MSN, you can use Internet Explorer for accessing Newsgroups, but you'll need some other software for Newsgroups if you're using an Internet provider other than MSN.

 `alt.sex.fetish.tickling` is for real and brings up the point that there are parts of Internet that are pretty raunchy. A kid who is looking can find pictures of naked ladies—and I do mean naked—in about five minutes. He can also do that at a local magazine stand, but he'd be more noticeable there. If your kids surf the net, they'll need some level of supervision.

- `gopher` is an older method than the World-Wide Web for dispersing information on the Internet. It involves text databases with fill-in-the-blank forms for searching. There is still a fair amount of information out there in gophers. As I'll explain, you can access gopher via Internet Explorer or via Telnet.

- `veronica*` is the name given to search tools for "gopherspace," that is, to try and locate a gopher with some particular information. Various veronica sites are accessible via the Web and so via Internet Explorer, as I'll explain.

- `chat`, aka `irc`, is short for Internet Relay Chat. It's what it sounds like—a CB simulator but text based. Windows 95 doesn't come with any software for IRC. You'll need third-party software for it. You'll find a shareware IRC program on Mom's CD.

- `MUD` is short for Multi-User Dungeons, Internet text-based games with elaborate rules. You log onto most MUDs via Telnet. Windows 95 includes a Telnet program. There are beginning to be Web-based GUI MUDs.

The Internet Applet

I think it is truly a wonderful thing that, through the Miracle of Computing, millions of people can read my column instead of leading productive lives.

—Dave Barry, commenting on the on-line posting of his column

---

* veronica = Very Easy Rodent Oriented Net-wide Index to Computerized Archives. Who ever said that computer people don't have warped senses of humor. Archie was a shortened version of archive, but then veronica and a less common jughead, both as acronyms, appeared.

I've explained how to set up a proper PPP signon to the Internet and I'm about to explain how to use various Internet applications, but how do you link the signon and the applications? One way is manual. You can start any Dial-Up connection by double-clicking its icon in the DUN folder. Or you can drag such an icon to the Desktop or a Start Menu subfolder to make a shortcut and you can launch that. If you have multiple Internet Dial-Up connections, even if you've chosen a preferred provider by the method I'll come to momentarily, you can override that choice by just starting some other provider and letting the logon finish before you start the Internet application.

When you install the Internet Jumpstart Kit, it adds an applet called `Internet` to Control Panel. You can use that (Figure 4-24) to set up autodial for the Internet by checking the appropriate box. If you use the Internet Setup Wizard, it will check the box for you, and you only want to know about this box in case you don't want the feature! In the drop-down you can choose which DUN connection is the one you want autodialed. Notice also the shortcuts to the New Connection Wizard and to the Connection Properties.

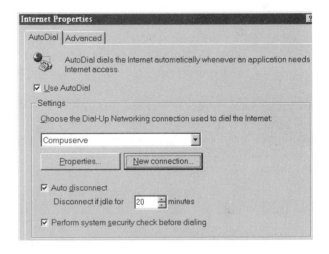

Figure 4-24. The Internet applet

If you configure this applet to `Use Autodial`, then whenever you start any Internet application, it first checks to see if you are connected to the Internet. If you are, it uses that connection. Otherwise, it requests that Windows 95 start up the provider you choose in the drop-down. It's all sort of magical.

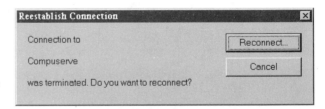

 Adding to the appearance of magic is the smarts that are built into Dial-Up Networking (Figure 4-25). If an Internet application has invoked an autodial connection, then if that connection is lost while the application is still running

Figure 4-25. Smart connections

you get the dialog on the top. And when you exit the application that initiated the connection, you get the dialog on the bottom.

 Internet aware applications can find out if you are connected to the net, request services from the net, and request autodial because they are using a standard API called Winsockets. These are implemented in the Windows 95 code library `winsock.dll`. The provider of the Winsockets API is often called a winsock.

 Before Windows 95, users had to get a third-party winsock or Internet application makers had to provide you with their own winsocks. The idea of the spec was to provide services to all comers. Winsocks are supposed to be interchangeable, but some application vendors built special dial-up features into their winsocks so that their programs wouldn't work with a generic winsock. The worst offender was Spry, whose product was the basis of CompuServe's browser. After the Windows 95 ship, *PC Week* had an article accusing Windows of tromping all over third-party winsocks when the problem was the third-party products violating the spirit of the winsock spec. For CompuServe, there are two solutions—you can move the CompuServe `winsock.dll` into the directory that CompuServe's browser is launched from or you can use the solution I discussed in "Logon Scripts for CompuServe" and use Netscape or Microsoft Internet Explorer.

Browsing the Web with Internet Explorer

That devilish Iron Horse, whose ear-rending neigh is heard throughout the town, has muddied the Boiling Spring with his foot, and he it is that has browsed off all the woods on Walden shore, that Trojan horse, with a thousand men in his belly, introduced by mercenary Greeks! Where is the country's champion, the Moore of Moore Hall, to meet him at the Deep Cut and thrust an avenging lance between the ribs of the bloated pest?

—Henry David Thoreau, *Walden,* 1854

Microsoft Internet Explorer (Figure 4-26) is available free with the Internet Jumpstart Kit and included with the Plus! Pack. Its basic function is to display pages from the World-Wide Web. You load it by double-clicking on The Internet icon. In the last section, I discussed how you link connecting to the Web and running a net aware program like this one.

Right off the bat you'll want to note two buttons in the toolbar that are mighty important. ⊠ will stop the downloading of the current page. You can tell that a page is still downloading because the windows flag in the upper-right corner stops waving when there is no download pending. You'll want to stop the page display if it is taking too long, if you see the next link you want to click on (although clicking on that link should stop the current download and start on the new page), or if the textual part of the page is your main interest, it's there and you want to abort the download of some large graphics.

 But remember that downloading goes on in the background. If you are going to be reading the text on a page, you may as well have the graphics download while you are reading that text than to have the computer twiddle its thumbs.

Figure 4-26. Wowser Browser

 Particularly if you are concerned about your access bill, note that you don't have to read that text on the spot while connected. You can save a page, either as plain text or in Web speak (known as HTML*). If saved as a `.htm` or `.html` file, you can later double-click on it and run Explorer off-line with the page loaded.

The other button to note right off is , which refreshes the current page. You'll want to do that if you earlier stopped the download and decide you want to finish it after all. You also need to know that Internet Explorer will cache recently accessed pages (even from recent sessions) on your disk and you may want to refresh a page you think has changed.

In this regard, the `Advanced` tab of the `View/Options. . .` dialog lets you determine how much disk space you'll dedicate to the cache and whether a page should be updated the first time it is hit on a session or if the cache should be used even for that first hit.

The cache is stored in `C:\Program Files\Plus!\Microsoft Internet\cache` as separate `.htm` files so even if you didn't explicitly save a page that you saw on-line and want to consult off-line, you are likely to find it in that folder; I'll explain later one efficient way to access that cache.

As you've no doubt seen, the addresses used by the Web are long and involved, and you aren't likely to want to type in explicit pages very often. In fact, you may never need to do so (or only need to do so if you read about an especially intriguing site). The main source of addresses will be links on pages to other pages. In Internet Explorer, links are shown in

---

* HTML = HyperText Markup Language

underlined blue if you haven't visited them recently and in underlined maroon if you have. You can change these colors on the `Appearence` tab of the `View/Options` menu choice. The initial page that you'll start with should clearly be a source of links—it is called the Start Page and defaults to `www.home.msn.com`, a Microsoft page. You can change this page in the `Start Page` tab of the same dialog. At any time, you can return to your start page by hitting 🏠 in the button bar.

One way of generating connections is to use one of the many Web sites that allow you to search the Web! My favorite is Yahoo. An imported version of Yahoo is linked to the default start page (this version can be seen in Figure 4-26). You might prefer reaching the original and placing it on the favorites menu, as I'll explain. Its address is `http://www.yahoo.com/search.html`. Yahoo is based at Stanford University.

Three other ways to access pages with Internet Explorer involve an extension of the Windows 95 notion of shortcuts to include Internet shortcuts. These files have the extension `url` in honor of the general names that you can place in a Browser address line: URL, pronounced "earl" and short for Universal Resource Locator.

First, whenever you see a link on a page, you can drag that link to your Desktop (or you can right-click and copy the link to clipboard and paste it to the Desktop or other location). You can also right-click on a non-shortcut part of a page, pick `Copy Shortcut`, and have a shortcut to the page (as opposed to the page pointed to by a link) placed on your Desktop. Later if you are off-line and click on such a shortcut, it will launch Internet Explorer and try to take you to the URL encapsulated in the shortcut.

Second, Internet Explorer has a favorites menu, a version of what some other browsers call a *hot list*. You can place Web sites on the hot list, pick one, and get taken to that site. While viewing a site, you can pick `Add to Favorites` from the `Favorites` menu and add an item there. There are two buttons that deal with Favorites, ⊞⊞ . The one on the right is the same as Add to Favorites and the one on the left is Open Favorites, where, as I'll explain, you can organize your Favorites.

The Internet Favorites have a Windows 95 twist—they are a folder-based menu system just like Start Menu. The menu system is based on `C:\windows\favorites`. Submenus of the Favorites menu correspond precisely to subfolders, and items are precisely the `.url` files in that folder. The `Add to Favorites` is a standard `File Save` dialog that lets you make new subfolders (i.e., submenus!) on the fly and place the new `.url` files in a subfolder if you wish. `Open Favorites` just opens the favorites folder in folder view (in Explorer mode if you are using Sarah's Smart Setup). You can use this mode to move/copy Internet shortcuts between the Desktop and Favorites menu system.

Unfortunately, `C:\windows\favorites` is also the directory that Microsoft Office uses for its favorites. Since Office's favorites items are likely to be shortcuts to `.doc` files and folders, they won't appear on the Internet Explorer favorites, but there will be confusion when `Open Favorites` is used.

The third method for accessing sites is a potentially huge list of previously visited sites stored as `.urls`. By default, the system stores three hundred sites, but that can be changed in the dialog shown in Figure 4-27. You can access this list from the `More history...` item on Internet Explorer's `File` menu, which opens the relevant directory (`C:\program files\plus!\microsoft Internet\history`) in folder view (in Explorer view if you use Sarah's Smart Setup).

 Such `.url` files typically take less than 200 bytes, so you might think that three hundred history items only used 60K of disk space. But the minimal size allotment can be a lot more than that. With a 512 MB–1 GB disk, each file takes a minimum of 16K so those 300 files take about 5 MB. With a compressed disk, that number will only be 150K.

 Until they wise up to its existence, a quick look at the `history` folder can be used to see where your kids have been net surfing.

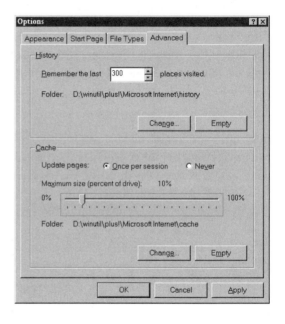

Figure 4-27. Internet Explorer advanced options

 Psst—kids, if you want to hide your tracks, just go to the `History` directory, sort on the Date modified column, and delete all the entries for the time you were on.

 Well, at least Igor didn't tell the kids about the file `GlobHist.htm` in the `History` directory. Load it into Internet Explorer (by double-clicking on it while you are off-line) and you get hyperlinks to large parts of the cache. This is a great way to access pages you've downloaded without having to go back on-line. `GlobHist.htm` is the last file in the `History` directory modified before Internet Explorer exits, so the quickest way to find it is to open the `History` folder in details view and click on the Modified column. It'll be at the top of the list. Double-click on it to load it into Internet Explorer.

I've not got a precise take on how Internet Explorer figures out which links to turn maroon, but it clearly has to do with some kind of interplay of this file, the whole `History` directory, and what's happened in the current session.

 You may be wondering what the `Global History` file and `History` folder have to do with the drop-down list associated to the text box just below the button bar labeled `Address:` or `Open:`. The answer is, not much! That's a list of the most recent addresses that you've explicitly typed in. It's stored in the Registry in the key `HKCU\Software\Microsoft\InternetExplorer\TypedURLs`. Unlike other most recently used type lists, this one does not use the MRUlist value entry scheme that I discussed in Chapter 3, "The Run Box and the Documents Menu."

 There's a good reason the MRU list scheme isn't used. This list is only used when Internet Explorer isn't running. That is, Internet Explorer reads the list from the Registry when it loads and then it writes it to the Registry when it exits. Since it often happens that there are lots of changes in the list, it is more efficient for Internet Explorer to directly read/write the entire list.

You'll want to check out the right-click context menus that are active when you are viewing an HTML document (whether on-line or a local document) in Internet Explorer, shown in Figure 4-28. You get different menus for the page as a whole, for links, and for graphics.

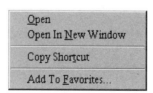

Figure 4-28. Web Page context menus

Especially noteworthy is the link command to `Open in a New Window` and the background command to `View Source` that can give you a quick lesson in what HTML is all about. Notice the `Set as Desktop Wallpaper` items. This saves the graphic (typically a `.jpg` or `.gif` file) as the Windows bitmap `C:\windows\Internet`

`Explorer Wallpaper.bmp`. Each time you save, the file is overwritten, so if you want to save a wallpaper, be sure to rename the file.

You can directly access the ability to save a file as `.bmp` by using the `Save Background As...` or `Save Picture As...` items and choosing `Bitmap (*.bmp)` from the `Save as type` drop-down. Since you can load any `.jpg` or `.gif` file from disk using Internet Explorer's File Open dialog, the program can serve as a file conversion utility. On the status bar, notice the little button . Placing the mouse cursor over that displays information about the current operation or page in a tooltip.

HTML understands text and two graphics types (`.gif` and `.jpg`). When a browser comes across another kind of file, it needs a program to open it—Netscape calls it a helper program. This is the standard issue of what program to use to open a particular kind of file, the problem that Windows usually solves with file associations. When Internet Explorer comes across a file it doesn't directly handle, it sees if there is an Open command associated to the extension of the file. If so, it pops up a dialog (Figure 4-29) offering to download the file and save it on disk or else to download it and open it in the associated program. In the latter case, it isn't "officially" saved in a file, although it will be saved in the cache directory. If there isn't a file type with Open that Internet Explorer can associate to the file, it pops up the dialog in Figure 4-30.

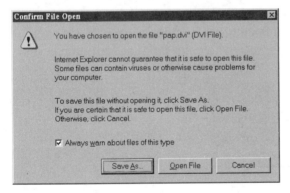

Figure 4-29. My kinda file

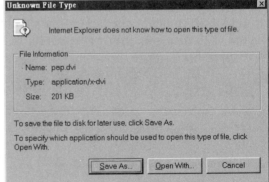

Figure 4-30. What the heck is this?!!

Most files you run across on the Web will have three character extensions, but if not, you can instead use their MIME* type to assign an application—or just use the `Open With...` in Figure 4-30 and it'll handle the MIME assignments automatically.

---

* MIME = multipurpose Internet mail extensions; it's the Internet equivalent of DOS/Windows extensions.

The war between Browsers is currently over various extensions of the basic HTML spec, most notably HTML 3.0, a specification still under development. Netscape has been the leader here. I'll discuss its Netscape Navigator program in the next chapter. Microsoft's Internet Explorer supports some of the fancier features—for example, colored background and forms—but not all of them. For example, there is no support for Netscape tables in version 1.0 (there is supposed to be support for Netscape Tables in the next version of Internet Explorer). What this means is that *most* home pages that say they require Netscape to read them will read fine in Internet Explorer.

One extension special to Internet Explorer is support for TrueType fonts. Microsoft has published a specification for home pages to add tags that its browser (and any other that wants to support it) can read. This is, of course, a Windows-centric extension since Xwindows UNIX systems don't understand TrueType.

Using Internet Explorer for Other Web Functions

The world still consists of two clearly divided groups: the English and the foreigners. One group consists of less than 50 million people; the other of 3,950 million. The latter group does not really count.

—George Mikes, *How to Be Decadent*

While the main function of a Web Browser is to interact with the World-Wide Web, other parts of the Internet are also accessible from a browser. One set of functions concerns hard links to Telnet and Exchange—some Web pages have links to call up a Telnet or mail program and Internet Explorer calls the right programs to accomplish that.

Another set concerns the use of non-`http` addresses. You've noticed that the URL addresses for web sites start with http,* as in `http://www.windows.microsoft.com`. But browsers understand other URL types, including anonymous ftp sites, as in `ftp://ftp.microsoft.com`, gopher sites like the Library of Congress at `gopher://marvel.loc.gov/11/locis`, local files like `file:C:\program files\plus!\Microsoft Internet\history\GlobHist.htm`, and Newsgroups, as in `news:comp.lang.basic.visual.misc`. That's right, file and news don't have a `//` after the colon and the others do.

---

* http = HyperText Transfer Protocol

Mail

Often a web page will have an Internet mail address in the color of link. Choosing that link is supposed to allow you to send mail to the address that is displayed. If you do this with Internet Explorer, it uses MAPI to launch the Exchange Mail Editor (or WordMail if that is the way you have Exchange configured) with the address filled in. The address will have a typical Internet format, e.g. `billg@microsoft.com`. Hit the 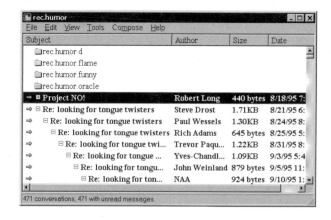 and that address will get recognized as an Internet SMNP address. Write the message. If you send mail to the Internet using Internet mail or MSN, just send it. If you use CompuServe, double-click on the name to bring up the mail properties and change the email type to CompuServe and add `Internet:` in front of `billg@microsoft.com` in the `E-mail address:` field.

If the new mail is Internet and Exchange is open, you can immediately send it because you are connected to the Internet. If the mail is MSN and your Internet service provider is MSN, again you can send it immediately. With CompuServe, you'll have to make a separate call later, even if you are on a PPP connection to CompuServe, since mail is not accessible via PPP.

Telnet

Some web links are supposed to call up Telnet applied to a particular address. Internet Explorer is hardwired to call up `telnet.exe` in `C:\windows` if you come across such a link.

Newsgroups

You can access Usenet Newsgroups from Internet Explorer if (and only if) your Internet provider is The Microsoft Network. Even if you are using another provider, as long as you've installed MSN, Internet Explorer will try to start it if you type in a `News:. . .` address. If you are on MSN, Internet Explorer drops into the background and opens up an MSN-style Explorer Window for threaded messages (Figure 4-31) similar to what it uses for its own bulletin boards. If you are using another Internet provider, you'll need another program for accessing newsgroups.

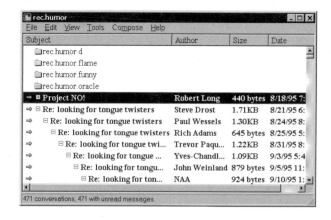

Figure 4-31. All the News that's fit to Group

By following this route, we can handle threading of messages and we can also control access to the seamier and steamier Newsgroups.

Archie and FTP

While Windows has its own DOS mode ftp program, you can also handle access to anonymous ftp sites from Internet Explorer. Some web pages will let you download software (for example, many of the Microsoft pages including PowerToys). Those essentially call up Internet Explorer's internal FTP to do the transfer. You can also directly type in an ftp address, such as `ftp://ftp.microsoft.com`, and meander through DOS-like directories (actually, they are most likely UNIX) looking for a needle in the haystack. The best way is to use an `archie`. You can search for possible web-accessible archies on yahoo; my favorite is `http://www-ns.rutgers.ed/htbin/archie`.

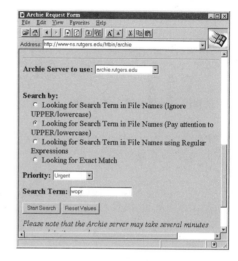

Figure 4-32. Archie Request Form

Once you get to the archie, you fill in the blanks, searching on filenames (Figure 4-32), and get back a list of results (Figure 4-33). The ftp site and filename are Web links. Double-click on the site and you get a directory to wander through. Double-click on the file. After a suitable confirmation (Figure 4-34), Internet Explorer just downloads it. Rather effortless location and downloading of files!

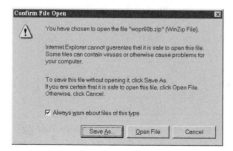

Figure 4-34. Download now?

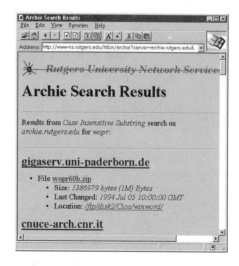

Figure 4-33. Archie results

This last sequence of screen shots shows the rather amorphous character of the Internet. Mao called up CompuServe's computers in Ohio and connected to an archie server in New Jersey and then double-clicked to download a file located in Germany! And he didn't need to be aware that he wasn't always in a single place.

Veronica and Gopher

Veronica is a search tool for Gopher databases. I've had the best luck with a gopher that lists veronica sites! Its URL is `gopher://veronica.scs.unr.edu/11/veronica`. Be aware that as gophers get replaced by websites, there are fewer veronicas around and they are often busy.

Other Internet Tools

While the main Internet tools will be Exchange and Internet Explorer (or some other browser), there are some other tools included with Windows 95. They aren't installed on the Start Menu, so you need to put them there or else enter them at the command line.

Telnet

Telnet means `C:\windows\telnet.exe`. This windows application (Figure 4-35) presents a fairly dumb terminal mode where you type in text commands and get text responses. It's important because there are still an awful lot of dumb terminal interfaces out there.

As you can see, there are some very simple options (Figure 4-36). You can change the background color and, through the fonts button, the foreground color. The terminal emulation is limited; most notably, what is often called ANSI-BBS (which gives colors and other fancy

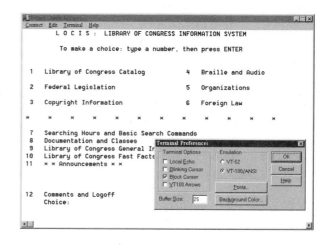

Figure 4-35. Telneting to the Library of Congress

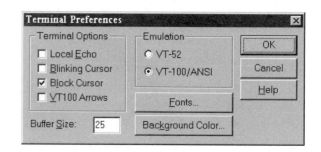

Figure 4-36. Telnet options

BBS screens) is missing.* With the advent of Telnet-accessible BBS this limitation will be important for some.

There is no support for keyboard translation and, in particular, on systems that don't understand `Backspace` but use `Del` for `Backspace`, you can't redefine `Backspace` to send a `Del`.

All the fonts available under the fonts button are fixed pitch, because terminal programs often assume you have fixed-width characters.

The most important setting is buffer size, which is given in lines. The default is twenty-five lines but I've run it under some circumstances at five hundred lines and the scrollback was wonderful. But this is a setting you need to change with care. Some terminal mode UNIX programs go bananas if they think your screen size is more than twenty-five lines. Telnet would be much more useful if you could assign a buffer size on a per-connection basis but you can't—it's global and you'll have to change it by hand.

The Windows 95 Telnet program is barely adequate for the occasional user of Telnet services. What they really should have done is set up Hyperterminal to allow Telnet connections. That would be a great solution (and one that has already been pioneered by ProComm and Qmodem—both of them comm programs that support Telnet connections).

FTP

Real men don't eat quiche and they use command line ftp utilities that show raw UNIX style directory listings and make them worry about the difference between `mode binary` and `mode ascii`. I can't imagine why. It's much better to use a browser to do ftp. But if you like to demonstrate your machismo or you get nostalgic for the `C>` prompt, it's there as `C:\windows\ftp.exe`.

---

* ANSI = American National Standards Institute. While the ANSI BBS spec is related to the ANSI spec for VT-100 terminals, they are distinct and the ANSI there doesn't mean that ANSI BBS colors are supported—they are not.

Well, remember that it's included with Windows 95 and Internet Explorer isn't, so you can bootstrap the process—use ftp to log into Microsoft's FTP site and download `msie??.exe`.

Nice theory, Billy, but one problem. Although `msie10.exe` was posted on Microsoft's Web site the day after Windows 95 shipped, a month later you still hadn't bothered to put it on your ftp site.

Miscellaneous

Here are one-line descriptions of little Internet applets you'll find in `C:\windows`:

- `arp`—displays and modifies the IP-to-Physical address translation tables used by address resolution protocol (ARP), whatever that is.

- `ping`—a diagnostic tool that sends packets to an IP address and waits for them to echo back.

- `route`—manipulates the network routing table. Keep your hands off of this unless you are a network guru.

- `tracert`—traces the connection route; more later.

- `winipcfg`—the only GUI program of the five, this displays the IP configuration in a window.

If you want to be awed at how the Internet works, open up a DOS window when you are connected to an Internet provider and type `tracert ftp.microsoft.com` at a DOS prompt. You'll be amazed at what a long route of nodes is taken.

Two uses of ping: If you want to see if you are connected to a TCP/IP network, find the numeric IP address of at least one node on the LAN and `ping` it—if it replies, at least your hardware is working. Second, if you suspect your DNS service isn't working but you want to confirm you are really on the Internet, type `ping 198.105.232.1`. That's the IP address of `ftp.microsoft.com`. If it pongs back, you know the connection is working.

Your WordPad or Mine?

Quotation . . . A writer expresses himself in words that have been used before because they give his meaning better than he can give it himself, or because they are beautiful or witty, or because he expects them to touch a cord of association in his reader, or because he wishes to show that he is learned and well read. Quotations due to the last motive are invariably ill-advised; the discerning reader detects it and is contemptuous; the undiscerning is perhaps impressed, but even then is at the same time repelled, pretentious quotations being the surest road to tedium.

—Henry W. Fowler, *A Dictionary of Modern English Usage*

 Oh, wow, I'm impressed by how well read and learned you guys are to have found that quote. But I find the quote kinda tedious, maybe even repulsive.

 ASCII files are ones that store pure text together with characters that indicate the ends of lines. There is no formatting information stored. Examples of ASCII files are your basic pre-Windows 95 configuration files (`autoexec.bat`, `win.ini`, etc.), `.ini` files for most Windows 3.x programs, and batch files.

Language source code (except for many flavors of BASIC) is also ASCII. That means that the ASCII file editor market is broken into two parts—ones intended for mere mortals and the programmer's editors with macro languages to warm the heart of a true code aficionado, compile from within options, and other goodies.

 So you need an ASCII editor to change your ASCII files. Windows 95 comes with, count 'em, four different programs that can manipulate ASCII files.

 You may be smart, Mao, but you can't count. Everyone knows that Windows comes with two such programs: Notepad and WordPad.

Besides Notepad and Wordpad, Windows 95 has a specialized program called *Sysedit* for editing your standard ASCII system files and there is a DOS-based editor called `edit` that is by far the best of the bunch!

Notepad will edit a single file at a time as long as the file isn't too large—once it is too large you get a message offering to load `WordPad`, which has no limit on the size files it will load—I tried a 20 MB ASCII file with WordPad and it did load, although `Ctrl+End` to get to the bottom of the file took a *long* time. Sysedit loads six files, but those are hard-coded as the four system files: `config.sys`, `autoexec.bat`, `win.ini`, and `system.ini`, plus `protocol.ini` and `msmail.ini`. The last two are left over from Windows for Workgroups, which shows how thoroughly Sysedit was overhauled for Windows 95. Sysedit also will only load these files if they aren't too large.

The limit for each program is about 50K (where that's the combined size allowed with Sysedit)—it is clearly related to the 64K data segment limit for 16-bit programs, so that shows these programs are not 32-bit. Most importantly, these programs acted flaky when the sizes were near the limits. Sysedit might load with `autoexec.bat` displayed as one long line and, in one case, it seemed to load a very large `config.sys` but only loaded part of it, so that when I edited and saved it, I lost 90 percent of the file! My strong advice is to only use Sysedit if the total size of your four system files is under 40K and only use Notepad on files under 40K in size.

Sysedit makes backups automatically with the extension `syd`, as in `config.syd`. Both programs will do simple searches backward or forward in the file, case-sensitive or not, as you choose. Both have single level undo. `Sysedit` has no on-line help, and its file menu has a `Print. . .` command—don't you believe the three dots; it prints the current file, no questions asked.

Notepad's `Print` command lets you put in date/time and filename into headers and footers using the special codes shown as follows:

&d	The current date
&p	Page numbers
&f	The current filename
&l	Text (following the code) to be aligned at the left margin
&r	Text (following the code) to be aligned at the right margin
&c	Text (following the code) to be centered between margins
&t	The current time

For example, to have a header with the date at the left margin, filename centered in the middle, and page number at the right, you would type `&l&d&c&f&rPage &p` in the header entry of the `File/Page Setup` menu dialog. These strings cannot be found in the Notepad on-line help, but they appear if you press ⍰ in the `File/Page Setup. . .` dialog and point at the word `Header`.

Notepad lets you add the date and time to a file from `Time/Date` item on the `Edit` menu. More interestingly, if you put `.LOG` on the first line of a file (it needs to be the only thing on the line, it must be the first line, it must start on the right, and it must be in all CAPS), Notepad will append the date/time to the bottom of the file every time you open it.

On Notepad's `Edit` menu is a toggle called `Word Wrap`. It wraps long lines at the word break closest to the right edge of the window, adjusting breaks as you resize the Notepad window. Use it with care, because you can forget it is on and save a file missing line breaks where you thought they were! Also, don't print with it on because `Print` does not wrap lines and you'll not realize what won't print if word wrap is on.

So what's missing? Here's a partial list:

1. The ability to open several files at once. It sure would be nice to have the MDI interface found in Sysedit available in Notepad

2. A most recently opened file list—for example have the file menu display the last three files that you opened and let you reopen by just picking

3. Search and Replace, as well as Search

4. Ability to handle very large files—at least to 300K

5. A Goto line number command and a status bar showing line numbers

6. Multilevel undo

7. The ability to insert a file

8. A word count

9. Memory via drop-down lists of previous choices of print headers and previous search strings

Not such a long list, but significant features. At least some of them are met with a program new to Windows 95 called `edit`. There has been an MS-DOS editor by that name since DOS 5, but that `edit` was a backdoor to a special mode of Qbasic where only the editor was active. This is a brand-new program that at least avoids some of the shortcomings just listed—you can load up to nine files, there is replace, it loads files with up to 65,280 lines, and line numbers are displayed in the status bar. But there is no undo at all, no file insertion (although you can load the second file and cut and paste), no Goto, no recently opened list and word count. `edit` is undoubtedly the best tool that Windows provides to edit ASCII files, but it is still nothing to rave about.

Millions of Windows users edit ASCII files each day. Is it so much to ask for a tool to do it that is halfway decent?

Write, Windows venerable word processing applet, has been retired and replaced by WordPad. In some ways, WordPad is an improvement. It will read Rich Text and Word `.doc` files. It's got a button bar and a ruler—through the `View/Options. . .` dialog you can turn them on or off independently for different file types among the four types that WordPad supports: Text, RTF, Word, and Write. Just as Write was a showcase for OLE 1.0, WordPad is a showcase for OLE 2.0—you can embed objects and have the native menus for the object appear when you are editing it. You can drop OLE scrap* onto the Desktop.

But when it comes to word processing features, WordPad is a step backward. The only supported tab stop is left, you can't justify paragraphs, and you can't insert page breaks, for example. WordPad will do for the occasional one page informal letter, but you'll need a real word processor if you intend to produce printed documents often.

WordPad's so-called support for Word `.doc` files is rather lacking. It gets royally confused by tables, doesn't show colored text, and otherwise is something of a mess. If you need to read `.doc` files, use the Word Viewer you'll find on Mom's CD.

Another Write feature missing in WordPad is the ability to load binary files. Write would load them, display their ASCII strings, and let you change them. WordPad won't let you load such files.

That was hardly a feature in Write—it was like giving someone a gun that tended to explode in the person's face if the trigger was pulled. The relative positions in a binary file are critical to the proper working of that file. With Write you could easily edit a string and inadvertently change its length, turning the binary file into junk or worse.

---

* I discussed OLE scrap in Chapter 2.

Draw, Pardner

Vigorous writing is concise. A sentence should contain no unnecessary words,
a paragraph no unnecessary sentences, for the same reason that a drawing should have no
unnecessary lines and a machine no unnecessary parts.

—William Strunk Jr. and E.B. White, *The Elements of Style*

Well, Paint actually. Microsoft Paint is a bitmap editor that is an improvement over the
Paintbrush program included with previous versions of Windows, but it is still pretty
limited. There are three functions that one wants to use bitmap manipulation programs for:
file conversion, bitmap editing, and bitmap creation. Paint is limited in all three areas!

The native format for Paint is Window Bitmap (.bmp). Indeed, it can only save in this
format. In principle, this is a loss from Windows 3.1's Paintbrush, which allowed saving in
.pcx format, but in practice, it isn't because that save was problem prone! The bare
Paintbrush can load two formats—.bmp and .pcx. However, it uses the same 32 bit import
filters as Office so when you install Office 95, Paint gains the ability to load (but not save
to) .tif, .gif, .tga and .jpg (see Figure 4-37).

Figure 4-37. Microsoft Paint

All you need to do is choose `All Files` in the Open dialog drop-down and pick one of these types and it gets converted to `.bmp`. This is useful if you have a file in one of these formats that you want to use as Wallpaper—you can save the file as a Windows Bitmap and use it as Wallpaper—Paint even has a menu choice to make that easy. You can reduce 24 color bitmaps to 256 color by using `File/Save As`, but there is no way to convert from color to gray-scale images.

Bitmap editing is the weakest of the elements of Paint. You can resize, skew, rotate, and mark a block to move it. But there are no serious selection tools and nothing to do with a selected area except to move it or copy it to the clipboard. In particular, there is no ability to crop a picture. There are no filters, not even a simple brighten/contrast.

Note the resize. Because it requires you to resize separately in the horizontal and vertical directions and uses percentages, it's a pain to work with, but you can use it to resize wallpaper. Note that 640 x 480 to 800 x 600 is 125 percent, 640 x 480 to 1024 x 768 is 160 percent, and 640 x 480 to 1024 x 768 is 128 percent.

On the creation/annotation side of things there is a good text tool (Figure 4-37; you right-click on the text entry box to invoke the font change dialog), and there is a curve tool and tools to draw polygon, rectangle, circle, and oval with the ability to draw a border only, a filled area, or an area with border. But anyone who has ever used a program like Fractal Painter will know that the creation tools are woefully limited.

So Paint does what it does with panache, but it is a pretty limited tool from any point of view.

C'mon guys, gimme a break. Of course Paint isn't serious competition for Hijaak on file conversion, Picture Publisher on bitmap editing, or Fractal Painter on bitmap creation, any more than WordPad is a competitor for Word. It's intended as a tool for users who want to futz a little with their wallpaper and little more. Oh, and it's part of the free screen capture program built into Windows 95, which you guys described in Chapter 2, "Keys to the Kingdom."

Little 'ns

> Listen to me, little fetus,
> Precious *homo incompletus,*
> As you dream your dreams placental
> Don't grow nothing accidental!

> —Poem by anonymous prospective father

The five miscellaneous applications discussed here are small applets, but each is useful in its own way.

Calculator

> It is wonderful when a calculation is made,
> how little the mind is actually employed in the discharge
> of any profession.

> —Samuel Johnson

The Windows calculator in its normal mode (Figure 4-38) is simplicity itself, but for a quick calculation it can be very handy since Edit/Copy instantly places the result of the calculation in the clipboard. The base calculator is a four-function with square roots and one memory location. It supports up to thirteen digits. It will shift into scientific notation if numbers get larger, but in this mode, there is no way to enter numbers in scientific notation.

Figure 4-38. Mild-mannered calculator

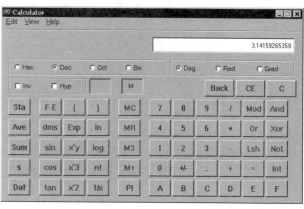

If you go to the View menu and switch from Standard to Scientific, you are switched to the impressive mode shown in Figure 4-39. This is both a programmer's calculator with binary and hex (even octal!) modes and a scientific calculator. For programming purposes, there are functions like xor, and the scientific part has the basic trigonometric and hyperbolic functions and their inverse functions. You can enter a number in

Figure 4-39. Calculator on steroids

scientific notation in this mode: enter the mantissa, hit the Exp button or the letter x, and then enter the exponent.

There is also a way to enter a series of numbers and get their average, sum, and standard deviation. You hit the Sta button, which opens a box that displays the data. Then you click on the calculator and enter the data. After each entry, you hit the Dat button or the keyboard's Ins key. You can clear an entry from the Stat box by highlighting it and hitting the CD button on the Statistic box. The Ave, Sum, and s buttons will then display in the average, sum, and standard deviation.

The calculator has keyboard shortcut entries for a wide variety of functions (see Figure 4-40). Remarkably, this information does not appear in a table in the help or documentation, but must be gleaned a key at a time from the context menu of the buttons!

Scientific							
sin	s	arcsin	is	sinh	hs	arcsinh	his
cos	o	arccos	io	cosh	ho	arccosh	hio
tan	t	arctan	it	tanh	ht	arctanh	hit
cot	tr	arccot	rit	coth	htr	arccoth	rhit
exp(N)	Nin	ln	n	log	l	n!	!
1/N	Nr	square	@	sqrt	i@	cube	#
pi	p	2*pi	ip	N^M	NyM=		
Memory		Statistics		Programmer's Functions			
MC	^L	STA	^S	And	&	RSH	i<
MR	^R	DAT	\<Ins\>	Or	|	int part	;
MS	^M	Ave	^A	Xor	^	frac part	i;
M+	^P	Sum	^T	Not	~	mod	%
		StdDev	^D	LSH	<		

Figure 4-40. Calculator keyboard shortcuts

In the table, the gray columns are functions and the white columns are keystrokes. For example, to compute the arctanh of the number displayed, you hit the keys h, i, and t in that order. In the table, ^L means Ctrl+L, and so on. <Ins> means the single Insert key. Cap N and M stand for entered numbers, so the table indicates that to compute N^M (i.e., N to the power M), you first enter N, then hit the y key, then enter M and hit the = key.

These are the keystrokes for Scientific mode. Remarkably, the designer of the calculator made the decision that while @ computes the square in scientific mode, it computes the square root in standard mode.

Folks are so used to seeing the number buttons on the screen, they tend to hit them with the mouse, but keyboard entry works for them. Use the numbers or the letters A–F for hex digits. Indeed, the apparently strange choice of o for cos is to avoid the conflict with the hex digit C.

The calculator is basically unchanged from Windows 3.x. The panel is now a solid gray, but otherwise, there is only one change—a bug fix! If you have the old Windows 3.1 calculator on your disk, run it (it'll run fine in Windows 95) and compute 2.01 – 2.00. Are you surprised that the answer is 0.00? Yeah, me too. This bug was apparently first pointed out to Microsoft during the early beta test phase of Windows 95 (then called Chicago) by a tester who thought it was a new bug. The reply he got was that the problem was already in the Windows 3.x calculator. They'd try to fix it, but since millions of 3.x users hadn't reported it, it wasn't a terribly high priority and might not get fixed. Then the Pentium coprocessor bug hit, and in the aftermath, *The Wall Street Journal* mentioned the Windows calculator bug on its front page. Whatya know—it was fixed in a day.

Charmap

The analysis of character is the highest human entertainment.

—Isaac Bashevis Singer, *New York Times,* Nov. 26, 1978

Charmap (Figure 4-41) displays the full character set of any font. You pick the font from the drop-down. You can press on a character to enlarge it for a better view, as I did here with the bomb. Double-clicking copies the characters to the copy box on the upper right. Hitting the Copy button then copies it to the clipboard. A simple but elegant application.

The problem, though, is in the way other Windows applications handle pastes from what Charmap puts on the clipboard. The letters are copied as straight text, but also as RTF text, which includes font information. There is no reason that an application shouldn't be able to get the font information when it is pasted in after a copy from Charmap. Word 7 passes in flying colors, but that's about it. All the other programs I tested in—Word Perfect, WordPad, Excel, Quattro Pro—failed to capture the font information, even if I did a Paste Special specifying RTF. Bah, humbug.

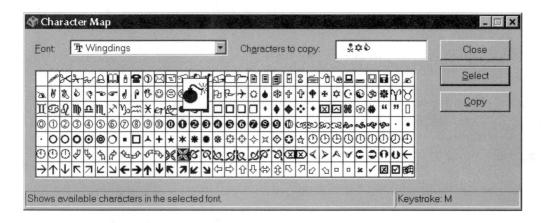

Figure 4-41. A great judge of character

Charmap must be a player in these problems, since these programs will copy formatted text between each other using RTF format.

So with most programs be prepared to have to select the text after you paste and pick the font again.

Clipboard Viewers

> A viewer who skips the advertising is the moral equivalent of a shoplifter.
>
> —Nicholas Johnson, Federal Communications Commission member

Included with Windows is not one but two programs for viewing the Clipboard—Clipboard Viewer( ) and Clipbook Viewer ( ), each with its own icon. But, as if to emphasize that you wouldn't want both, their executables normally have the same name (`clipbrd.exe`).

No part of Windows 95 is simple, is it? Here are the facts of the case and my theory of what is going on. If you look at Figure 4-42, where we list the files related to clipboard that are in the compressed libraries that are on the Windows CD and diskettes, you'll find that both clipboard (`clipbrd.*`) files and clipbook (`clipbook.*`) files are there. On the CD in the directory `\other\clipbook` there are files identical to the `clipbook.*` files, but with the names `clipbrd.*`. Moreover, there are directions on how to install the

Clipbook programs from `\other\clipbook`. The only theory I can come up with is that Microsoft forgot they'd put Clipbook in the base installation files.

Name	Size	CD File	Diskette File
clipbook.cnt	440	WIN95_02.CAB	WIN95_02.CAB
clipbook.exe	57,664	WIN95_02.CAB	WIN95_03.CAB
clipbook.hlp	20,029	WIN95_02.CAB	WIN95_03.CAB
clipbrd.cnt	411	WIN95_02.CAB	WIN95_02.CAB
clipbrd.exe	17,376	WIN95_02.CAB	WIN95_03.CAB
clipbrd.hlp	13,015	WIN95_02.CAB	WIN95_03.CAB
clipsrv.exe	16,608	WIN95_02.CAB	WIN95_03.CAB

Figure 4-42. Windows Installation Clipboard Files

Look at your `Programs\Accessories` submenu—if there isn't an entry for either Clipboard Viewer or Clipbook Viewer, you'll need to choose one or the other (I'll explain the differences below). To install Clipboard Viewer, go to the `Add/Remove Programs` applet, go to the `Windows Setup` tab, highlight `Accessories`, click on `Details`, click the box next to `Clipboard Viewer`, and go `OK`. If you have the Windows CD and want to install Clipbook or want to upgrade Clipboard to Clipbook on your system, again you'll need the `Windows Setup` tab, but this time click on `Have Disk. . .` and browse to the `\other\clipbook` directory on the CD, click on `clipbook.inf`, go `OK`, check off Clipbook Viewer, and `OK` again. If you do this and Clipboard Viewer was previously installed, the menu item for it is removed and replaced with one for Clipbook. The Clipboard programs are overwritten by the Clipbook programs that have the same name.

Both programs display what is currently on the Clipboard. Both have menus (called `Display` in Clipboard and `View` in Clipbook) that display the formats currently on the clipboard in black and the formats the supplying application has promised it will supply if requested to. These promised formats appear grayed out. You can display the black (but not the grayed out) formats by choosing them from the menu. Both programs have `File` menus that allow you to save the contents of the clipboard in a file with the extension of `.clp` and later open a saved `.clp` file. Both have a `Del` command in the `Edit` menu that lets you clear the Clipboard.

That's about as far as the Clipboard Viewer goes. Clipbook goes beyond it in two ways. First, it lets you save clipboard material into extra book pages that are always accessible to the program. These pages can be given names and later put back on the clipboard from within the Clipbook program. To put it back on the clipboard, you merely select the page and choose `Edit/Copy`. The juggling is a bit much, but it can be helpful if you have several large pieces of text or several bitmaps you want to reuse.

The second feature is that you can share Clipbook pages over a Network. When Mao started the research for this section, he found that he couldn't get it to work. The Clipbook help describes how to use the `Connect` item in the `File` menu to access remote Clipbooks. But Mao couldn't get a `Connect` item on his `File` menu no matter how hard he tried. Then he ran into Igor in the hall and mentioned it didn't work:

 Works great. I use it to send Erwin parts of my Hearts Tips books all the time.

 Hearts!! Games. Games. If you didn't play so many games, we might actually learn something around here. Get back to work!!!!

 Now, Mao. Igor is doing research for the games part of the book. Besides, he seems to have learned how to get Clipbook to work over a Network. Just run Hearts first.

Mom's right. Running Hearts will make the File menu and button bar for Clipbook blossom (Figure 4-43).

Button Bar and File Menu without NetDDE

Button Bar and File Menu with NetDDE running

Figure 4-43. You gotta have Hearts

But of course, we couldn't tell serious business users that the way to run Clipbook over a network is to first load hearts! There is another way besides running Hearts, and an explanation of why Hearts works. Both Hearts and Clipbook require Network DDE to work.

Under Windows for Workgroups, NetDDE was loaded in the StartUp group but since not that many users actually use NetDDE it is not automatic in Windows 95. We modified Hearts so that when it is loaded, it looks for NetDDE, and if it isn't there, it loads it. But, er, we forgot to fix Clipbook.

Bravo! Shows the right sense of priorities to put Hearts as more important than Clipbook.

Well, our scientific surveys show that a lot more users play Hearts over the network—on their lunch hour, of course—than use Clipbook.

You certainly fooled the Microsoft Product Support Services folks. They have a Knowledge Base article where they say that while this feature works in Windows 3.1, it doesn't in Windows 95. Gack—if even Microsoft Support can't get it right. . . . I guess they need to play Hearts more.

So you need to run the program `netdde` which is in the `C:\windows` directory. If you are using Clipbook over the network all the time, place a shortcut to `C:\windows\netdde.exe` in your StartUp folder. Otherwise, I'd suggest you replace the shortcut in the Start Menu that invokes Clipbook and change it to a shortcut to a batch file with the lines:

```
start C:\windows\netdde
start C:\windows\clipbrd
```

Once you've got the network stuff running, choosing `File\Connect` or clicking the correct button asks the name of the computer whose Clipbook you want to access. Once the connections are established, getting stuff from the remote Clipbook pages is as easy as from your local Clipbook. And whenever you run Clipbook, it will try to reestablish its prior connections.

If you need to share stuff across a network and don't want to start futzing with `netdde`, you can save a `.clp` file on a shared network drive and have the recipient open it in their own Clipboard or Clipbook Viewer.

While on the subject of Clipboard and Clipbook, they have a rather strange and remarkable feature. Look closely at Figure 4-44. On the left is an open dialog from Windows 3.1 Write (running under Windows 95); on the right is a dialog showing the same directories in Clipbook. Both are using the Windows 3.1 open dialog. But notice that the one on the right is displaying long filenames! It says `Program Files` and `Accessories` in place of `progra~1` and `access~1`. It's as if Microsoft were bragging, "See, we could do it if we wanted to."

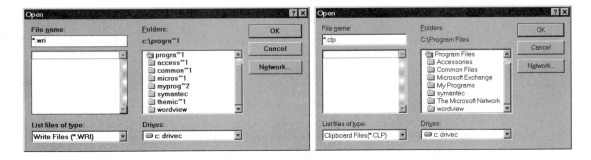

Figure 4-44. A Tale of Two Open Dialogs

Packager

> Adam and Eve ate the first vitamins, including the package.
>
> —Squibb Pharmaceutical ad

OLE data is most often embedded in documents as editable information viewed in its native format but sometimes it is displayed as an icon instead. For example, you can drag a shortcut (Windows `.lnk`, DOS `.pif`, Internet `.url`, or Microsoft Network `.mcc`) to a document or email message and have it embedded as an icon. This embedded icon and action is called a package.

The program Object Packager lets you edit the contents of a package or create a custom package yourself. You don't invoke this program from the Start Menu or command line because packages only make sense within the OLE client in which they are embedded. That means that you invoke Object Packager, either from the context menu of an embedded package (there is a submenu at the bottom of the context menu called `Package Object`—picking `Edit Package` will call up the Package in Object Packager) or you pick `Insert/Object` from the menu of an OLE client program and choose Package from the dialog and make your own package.

A package has three parts: the icon it displays in the client, the caption it displays, and the contents of the package. The caption is called a label by Packager. You get to change the label from the `Edit` menu, even though the icon is changeable only via the `Insert Icon. . .` button. I hate inconsistent interfaces that don't give you access to all choices through the menus, if that's where you happen to look.

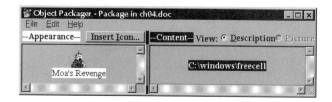

Figure 4-45. Packing it in

To add to the strangeness, there is a totally distinct way to change the icon and caption used in a package—from the context menu of the package itself, you can go to the Object Properties sheet and choose `Change Icon. . .` from the `View` tab. This choice also lets you change the label. Doing this doesn't replace the icon and label in the package itself, but just how they are displayed. You can shift back to the icon and label from the package via a radio button in the Object Properties sheet. I'm at a loss to understand why there are two different icons and two different labels stored with each package. Strange indeed.

The contents can be placed in a package by pasting it from the clipboard after you've clicked on the right side of the window—if the contents of the clipboard are from an OLE server, it is stored as an OLE object but if not then Package puts an OLE wrapper around it. Alternately, you can use the `Command Line. . .` item on the Edit menu to place a Run command line in the Package producing an instant command button.

Besides the obvious uses of editing packages and creating command buttons, Packager serves another need—there may be times you want to send an OLE object by email without it displaying, for example, an Excel spreadsheet fragment in a Word Mail document. You can Insert/Object/Package and paste the sheet into the package.

Resource Meter

> "Resource-constrained environment" [are] fancy Pentagon words
> that mean there isn't enough money to go around.

—Gen. John W Vessey Jr, Chairman, Joint Chiefs of Staff, *New York Times,* July 15, 1984

My favorite applet is the Resource Meter, a little step-ladder thing that sits in the "Notification Area" (down in the lower-right corner) and keeps track of Free System Resources, those fixed-size pools of memory that, when stressed, can bring all sorts of trouble. As long as the ladder is green, I'm in good shape. When I pass my mouse over the ladder, Resource Meter pops up a reading of the percentage of space left in each of the three Free System Resource pools, as you can see in Figure 4-46.

Figure 4-46. The Resource Meter in action

Resource Meter is automatically installed to your Start Menu's `Program/Accessories/System Tools` menu. If it is not, it must have been removed and can be reinstalled under the Details panel of the Accessories item of the `Windows Setup` tab of the `Add/Remove Programs` applet. In that panel it is called System Resource Monitor, even though *system* doesn't appear in the menu item or application caption. See Chapter 3 for instructions on how to install it in your StartUp group, my recommended place for it.

Two other related applets (available if you have the CD) that I'll not describe in detail are System Monitor and NetWatcher, both installable under the Details panel of the Accessories item of the `Windows Setup` tab of the `Add/Remove Programs` applet. System Monitor gives you reports in real time on all sorts of techie information, while NetWatcher will display information on which users are opening which files on your machine.

Multimediaaaaahhhhh

Television: a medium, so called because it is neither rare nor well done.

—Ernie Kovacs

There are four applets that appear on the `Programs/Accessories/Multimedia` submenu of the Start Menu. Two you may never need to start explicitly—media player is the application started when you double-click on an `.avi` or `.mid` file. CD Player starts automagically when you place an audio CD into the drive. If you've plugged a microphone into your sound card but it won't record, check out the section on the sound mixer.

Multimedia Player

> The media have just buried the last yuppie, a pathetic creature who had not heard the news
> that the great pendulum of public consciousness has just swung from Greed to Compassion
> and from Tex-Mex to meatballs.

> —Barbara Ehrenreich, *The Worst Years of Our Lives*

Multimedia Player is a powerful but simple application with the magical quality that it can
play media formats that didn't even exist when it was written. Basically, it is a shell around
MCI commands. I discussed the MCI spec in Chapter 2 in "Media Control Interface—Do
You Mean DeeDee Meyers?" You can load files with MCI drivers (for a default setup that
means video in `.avi` format, sound in `.wav` format, and MIDI in `.mid` and `.rmi`
formats) and then play them. Media Player is also the open command for videos and MIDI
files, so you'll call up Media Player if you double-click on an `.avi`, `.mid`, or `.rmi` file.
This mode is set to close when the clicked-on file is finished playing. The video player is a
stripped-down version with only the screen and not the controller. If you want to get the
controller, just double-click on the title bar of the playing `.avi`.

The Media Player controller (Figure 4-47)
has eleven buttons on it, many of them
standard VCR-type controls. The first
three (▌▌ ■ ▲) are play/pause, stop, and
eject (only works if you have CD audio
picked). The next four (|◄◄ ◄◄ ►► ►►|) go
to the start, a macro step back and forward

Figure 4-47. Media Player

and to the end. What I called a macro step
is precisely one-sixteenth of the total amount from start to finish. The buttons I said go to
start and finish only do that if there is no selected region. If there is a selection, then there
are four "marks"—file start, selection start, selection end, and file end and the outermost of
the set of four buttons go to the previous/next mark.

The last pair of larger buttons (▼ ▲) are for marking the start and end of a selection.
Finally, there are the tiny buttons (◄►►) to the right of the slider area. They move a single
frame for video and a fraction (1/128) of the total amount for sound files.

By using the `Edit/Copy Object` command you can copy a media file to the clipboard
and embed it in an application by pasting it in. For example, Figure 4-48 shows a video clip
embedded in Excel. Double-click on the embedded video and Media Player plays the clip.
Unlike my tests with Windows 3.1 applications several years ago, all the major applications
programs properly supported this feature.

You can control how the OLE clip appears and plays by setting some options in the `Edit/Options` menu of Media Player (Figure 4-49). You have to make the choices before you copy the clip to the clipboard. You get to choose if there is a simple slider control on playback or not. If there is, when not playing there is a caption and you get to choose that.

Note that if you drag a multimedia file from Explorer to Media Player, it will load and start playing so that an ideal way to check out the `avi` files on a CD ROM or a bunch of `wav` files is to place Explorer and Media Player side by side and drag the files over. If you drag over a file while another is playing, Media Player will stop the first and play the second.

Finally, if pasting a video clip as a full-size picture (as in Figure 4-48) seems a bit much, remember that you can use Object Packager to have it appear instead as an icon—see the discussion of Packager earlier in this chapter.

Figure 4-48. OLE videos

Sound Recorder

> One of the greatest sounds of them all—and to me it is a sound—is utter, complete silence.

—André Kostelanetz, *NY Journal-American,* Feb. 8, 1955

If you're here because you've plugged a mike into your sound card and you can't record, you're in the wrong place. Jump forward two sections to the discussion of the Mixer.

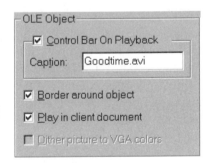

Figure 4-49. Controlling playback

Sound Recorder, as its name implies, is an applet that will record sound to a `wav` file. But it serves four other purposes.

- It provides information from the header of any `wav` file—the sample size, sample rate, and number of channels (mono vs. stereo). I described the meaning of this header data in "Riding the Perfect Wav" in Chapter 2.

- It provides a comprehensive sound conversion module.

- It can be used as an OLE server for `wav` file and is often a better alternative than Media Player for embedding sounds.

- It is a rudimentary sound editor.

Let's take them one at a time. You record sound by clicking the button with a red dot on it; but there is no menu option and no way of using the keyboard except multiple `Tab` and `Spacebar`.

The strangest one by far is one way of getting header information. To get the header information on a sound file, load it into Sound Recorder, and choose `Help/About` from the menu. The important part of that box is shown in Figure 4-50. Notice the fourth line, which says `PCM 22.050kHz, 8-bit, Mono`. There it is, the header information.

Figure 4-50. About Sound Recorder

Figure 4-51. File/Properties in Recorder

This has to rank as one of the weirdest tidbits in the Windows applets. Who had the idea of putting that information in the About box? Who'd normally expect to look there? Unlike the Windows 3.1, though, there is a more reasonable way of accessing information on the file. Go to the `Properties` item on the `File` menu, and you'll get a panel like that shown in Figure 4-51.

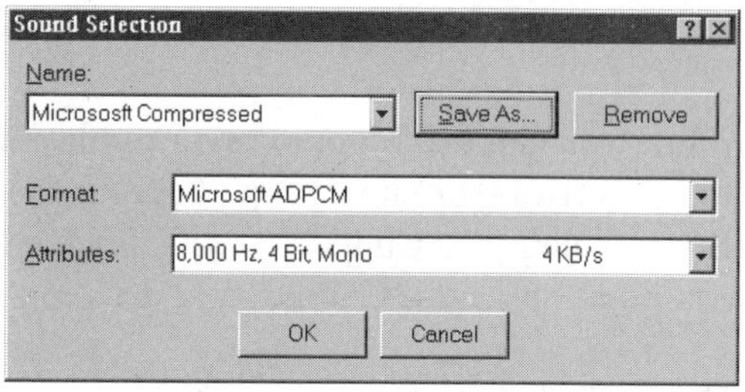

Notice the `Convert Now. . .` button in Figure 4-51. It leads to a dialog (Figure 4-52) where you can choose new properties and even a compression format to use. Obviously, converting from lower quality to higher won't magically improve the quality of the recording, but this will let you trade quality for file size. Also, if you use compression, the loss in quality may not be that severe. This conversion is pretty neat—too bad 99.9 percent of users won't have the foggiest idea it is here.

Figure 4-52. It's a sound conversion

To get OLE to work, just choose `Edit/Copy` from the Sound Recorder menus and paste into the client application. You'll see a loud speaker icon. Clicking on that will play the sound with no direct sign of Sound Recorder loading.

Sound editing is fairly limited. You can insert one `wav` file in another, mix two, increase/decrease volume and speed, reverse, and add echo. It's amusing to play some sounds in reverse—try it on The Microsoft Sound. What's missing from sound editing? The ability to deal with stereo channels, fade in and out, smoothing, and noise filtering, to name a few. Take a look at Sonic Foundry's `Sound Forge` (Voice: 608-256-3133) to see what a full-fledged sound editor can do. There's a working model on Mom's CD.

 What happens if you play `tada.wav` in reverse? Do you get a da-ta?

 No, adat, of course!

 Igor's right. It is data, after all!

 For sound conversion and recording, Media Player lets you give names to a combination of compression type and the other characteristics of the `.wav` file. It comes with three predefined types, all using standard uncompressed (PCM) format: CD Quality (44 KHz, 16 bit Stereo), Radio Quality (22 KHz, 8 bit Mono), and Telephone Quality (11 KHz, 8 bit, Mono). These schemes and any you may define are stored in the Registry Key `HKEY_CURRENT_USER\Software\Microsoft\Multimedia\Audio\WaveFormats`.

CD Player

One gets tired of the role critics are supposed to have in this culture: It's like being the piano player in a whorehouse; you don't have any control over the action going on upstairs.

—Robert Hughes, *Publishers Weekly,* Dec. 12, 1986

While you can use Media Player to play Audio CDs, Windows 95 includes a more flexible and powerful CD Player applet (Figure 4-53). Unless you change the option in the File Types dialog (see Chapter 3), this player will pop up and start playing automagically when you place an Audio CD into any drive on your system.

The controls to the right of the time display are of VCR type and similar to those in Media Player. I recommend you display the button bar (no, it's not under `Options` but under `View`). Tooltips will tell you about their functions, but I want to note two of them.

Figure 4-53. CD Player

 pops up a Play List where you can choose to play only some of the tracks and the order of play. It's here that you get to type in the Artist, CD Title, and Track names. These get stored in the file `cdplayer.ini` in the `C:\windows` directory in a section named with a seven-digit hexadecimal number. Every audio CD has a unique seven-digit number (a sort of digital ISBN for audio CDs), so once you've entered the information it gets remembered forever. Audio CDs using the new CD Plus format will have these fields on the CD, so you won't even need to fill this in once. I note that the format of the `.ini` file is so simple that it may be easier for you to get the CD I.D.s by adding, say, a Title and then put the other information in an ASCII editor.

 turns on support for multiple CD systems. If you have one of those multiple CD jukeboxes, you'll love this because it lets you place several CDs in the jukebox and have them played sequentially with the usual options of playing only some tracks in a user determined order. If you play sequentially, when the last track on one CD finishes the next CD is loaded in the jukebox and its first track is played.

You can configure the CD Player so the time displayed is any of the time elapsed on the track, the time remaining on the track, or the time remaining on the CD.

> If this program only placed an icon in the Notification Area for quick pause of playback when the phone rang, I'd truly love it.

> It's missing some of the neat features of a full-fledged CD player (like play list and multiple CD support) but Power Toys* FlexiCD has precisely the feature you covet Mom.

---

* I discuss the free Power Toys utilities in Chapter 5.

Sound Mixer and Volume Control

Political image is like mixing cement. When it's wet, you can move it around and shape it, but at some point it hardens and there's almost nothing you can do to reshape it.

—Walter F. Mondale

Windows comes with a volume control that works with most sound cards. Buried in the control is the input mixer, which you may need to be able to record with your microphone!

You'll find `Volume Control` on the `Programs\Accessories\Multimedia` submenu of Start Menu. More importantly, there is a checkbox labeled "`Show volume control on the Taskbar`" on the `Audio` page of the `Multimedia` applet in control panel.

Make sure that's checked and you'll have a loudspeaker icon in the Notification Area. Double-clicking that will bring up the Volume Control applet. That control is pretty much self-explanatory. There is a slider for master volume and typically separate sliders for CD, Wave and MIDI (called Synthesizer).

Now pick `Properties` from the `Options` menu. That will bring up a dialog like that in Figure 4-54, except the radio button will be on Playback. If your mike isn't working you may be tempted to check off the `Mic/Line` box in this Playback list that appears when you first call up this control. Instead, you need to click on the `Recording` radio button and then hit `OK`. That will bring up the Sound Mixer seen in Figure 4-55. This determines what input device is used and for the mike to work, you need to be sure that the select button in the panel labeled Mic/Line is checked.

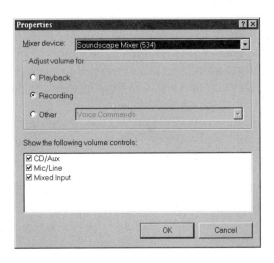

Figure 4-54. Accessing the Record Mixer

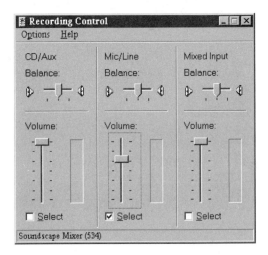

Figure 4-55. The Recording Mixer

You won't need the mixer often, so it is probably just as well that whenever you invoke the Volume control it pops up showing the Playback options.

One weird thing is that you can show a Mic/Line slider on the usual Volume Control (i.e. in Playback mode). Despite what you might think, it does not affect how you record. It only affects what would happen if you sent output through the mike jack (don't ask me how you'd do that!). To control the input volume, you need to shift to the Recording Mixer and adjust the slider there.

Da Games

Boss, you forgot da games.

Maybe I forgot the games, but Microsoft sure didn't. Each time a new version of Windows comes out they keep the old games, and this time they added one game for all users, a second for CD purchasers, and a third with Plus! It must give the State of Virginia (which banned Mine Sweeper from the offices of state employees) apoplexy. So that means you'll find:

- Solitaire (`C:\windows\sol.exe`)—The original Windows 3.0 game. Not a great game, but wizzy graphics.

- Mine Sweeper (`C:\windows\winmin.exe`)—The most habit-forming game known to humanity. Excuse me while I play a quick one. This was first introduced with Windows 3.1.

- Hearts (`C:\windows\mshearts.exe`)—This lets you set up multiple player games over the network. It was introduced as a demo of what NetDDE could do with Windows for Workgroups 3.11. Not the greatest computer hearts implementation. Card Shark Hearts is a lot better.

- FreeCell (`C:\windows\freecell.exe`)—The second most habit-forming game known to humanity. It was introduced with the win32s libraries, but made a little slicker for Windows 95.

- Hover (`\funstuff\hover\hover.exe` on the CD)—A maze and an action game at the same time.

- 3D Pinball (`C:\Program Files\Plus!\Pinball\pinball.exe` after you've installed Plus!)—Don't crash your hard disk while hitting the side of the pinball table!

 That FreeCell sure is addictive after an initial "this game is impossibly hard." I had a lot of fun with ole Mao over this 'un. With a little help from Sarah. I ran into Mao one day in the hall at Mom's and he said to me: "Well, Grasshopper, I finally understand what you find so fascinating about games. For a coupla weeks there I could hardly get any work done because I was sneaking in FreeCell games. I play sets of fifty, resetting the statistics after each set. I seem to have no trouble getting to about five in fifty, but can't push that down further." So says I, "Why would you want to push the number of wins down?" He explained that five was the number of losses, and he was regularly winning at least forty-five games. I think he sensed I was suspicious, so he took me to his office to show off his current statistics. Twenty-five straight—very impressive.

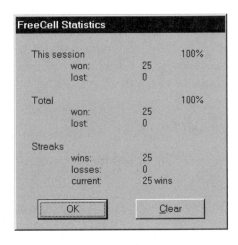

But I figured as a games player, I could do a lot better than that. Boy, did Mao's jaw drop when I took him into my office a week later and showed where I was at. He'd finally met a serious games player!!

Hehe. What I didn't tell him is that when I went to Sarah, she told me about the Registry key `HKEY_CURRENT_ USER\Software\ Microsoft\Windows\CurrentVersion\ Applets\FreeCell` and showed me how it all worked. I used Calc to figure out that 25,000 was 61A8 in Hex, which I needed, but it was easy. Mao still treats me with respect. Hehehe.

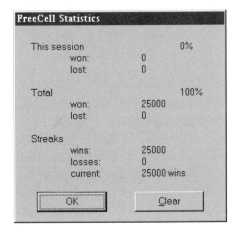

Act III, Scene 1. Kirk and Picard on horseback, on a lovely autumn afternoon.

Kirk: It just got so damn complicated I couldn't keep up.

Picard: Don't blame yourself, Captain. You only had one techie.

Kirk: It was harder for us. Got to the point where I couldn't fake the technical stuff.

Picard: When my writers fell into a technical hole, they brought in a touchy-feely solution.

Kirk: Not for us. Command Dot Com finally figured I was incompetent, so they promoted me.

Picard: So *that's* why I never made admiral.

Kirk: As long as they figure you still know enough to do real work, they won't let you go.

Picard: I always thought it was because they couldn't spell Jean Luc.

Kirk: Naw. Your name doesn't matter. Look what happened to Alec, er, Alex Trebec.

Picard: I guess he just had to read Jeopardy answers and pretend he knew 'em all along, eh?

Kirk: Precisely. You French Canadians have a leg up in this market anyway. It's the accent.

Picard: Are you sure the producers don't hate me because of my bald head?

Kirk: You gotta be kidding. Get a life. Or at least a rug.

 These three chapters take you beyond the foundation of Windows 95, and look at important ancillary topics - including the single most important Windows topic: how the hell do you keep on top of all this?

Don't assume that just because a utility or add-in program is available, it's worthwhile.
Utilities are meant to be problem solvers. If there's no problem,
chances are pretty good you don't need a solution.

—Barry Owen

 If you use a computer much, you owe it to yourself to get the tools that
make your interaction safe, pleasurable, and fun. Microsoft has done a
remarkable job of putting together a great set of tools in the base
operating system, but that doesn't change the fact that there are still lots
of places for other vendors to add value. I'm going to tell you about the
best of those tools that became available within a month after Windows 95 shipped.
No doubt others will appear. My gang will first summarize the built-in utilities, then talk
about utility add-ons from Microsoft, and finally turn to capsule reviews of some third-
party products.

Mom's Report Card

I don't know jokes; I just watch the government and report the facts.

—Will Rogers

 In order to understand what add-ons you need, it is useful to review the
utility components in Windows 95 and see how good they are compared
to third-party products. Here is my team's report card.

Function	Windows Program	Leading 3rd Party (Win 3.1)	Grade
Check the disk	ScanDisk	Norton Disk Doctor (NDW)	A–
Defrag Disk	Defrag	Norton Speed Disk (NDW)	A–
Anti-Virus	NONE	Dr. Solomon's, McAfee, Norton	F
Disk Compression	DriveSpace (3)	Stacker	A+
Backup	MS Backup	Norton Backup (NDW)	B
File Management	Explorer	PC Tools	A
File Viewing	Quickview	OutsideIn	C
Program Launching	StartMenu	NDW, Dashboard	A
Universal Email	Exchange	Email Connection	A
Fax	MS Fax	WinFax	A
Screen Saver	Display Applet Tab	After Dark	B
Bitmap Editor	Paint	Picture Publisher	C
Scheduler	System Agent (PLUS!)	NDW	A
System Reporting	Device Manager	CheckIt	A
Peer/Peer Networking	Client for MS Networks	Lantastic	A
Cable Connection	Direct Cable Connection	Laplink	A
Comm Program	HyperTerminal	ProComm	C
Web Browser	Internet Explorer (IJK)	Netscape Navigator	A–
Telnet	Telnet	ProComm	C
Remote Computing	Dial-Up Networking	Reach Out, PC Anywhere	B

A = comparable to best of breed; A– = close to best of breed; B = adequate for most; C = bare bones, only adequate for very light users. IJK = Internet Jumpstart Kit; NDW = Norton Desktop

Oh, Mom, I'm so proud. And my Mom is going to be so proud. Look at all those As! But Dad isn't going to be happy that I didn't get straight A+s.

That chart bodes ill for a lot of third-party vendors. The A+ for disk compression means that Stacker is not likely to survive (although the parent company with some newer utilities will)—indeed, it is likely we won't ever see a 32-bit version of Stacker. And the fact that the OS has a direct line into the guts of the system means that it will hard for the CheckIt's of the world to offer much beyond what is already in Device Manager.

Microsoft Presents

> She presents no beauty but the memory of beauty, sustained by cosmetics,
> clever lighting, good health and will power.

> —Dan Sullivan, *New York Times,* Oct. 4, 1968, talking about Marlene Dietrich

It may seem strange to include Microsoft prominently in a chapter that's supposed to tell you about utilities available from third parties, but some of the best add-ons for Windows 95 come from Microsoft in ways other than the Windows 95 CD (or diskettes).

The Plus! Pack

> If *A* is a success in life, then *A* equals *x* plus *y* plus *z.*
> Work is *x; y* is play; and *z* is keeping your mouth shut.

> —Albert Einstein, *Observer of London,* Jan. 15, 1950

The cynic would say that the Plus! Pack is just a way for Microsoft to pick another $50 from your pocket, or put differently, to charge $150 for an operating system that they make you think is only $100 because you get it in two installments. That isn't Microsoft's explanation, and I must say, except for the Internet Jumpstart Kit (which is available "for free" via other means), their argument does make sense.

Windows 95 will run on a 4 MB, 386 DX, straight VGA machine, as I'm fond of telling you. The Plus! Pack requires an 8 MB machine 486 with at least a 256-color display. That's why we didn't put it in the base product. And hey, making a few bucks on it keeps the stockholders happy.

Here, in brief, is what's in the Plus! Pack. You'll see that I've already talked about quite a bit of it:

- Drive Space 3, the enhanced Disk Compression software (discussed in Chapter 4)

- The Internet Jumpstart Kit, including the Internet Setup Wizard and Internet Explorer, as well as the Exchange client for Internet (SMNP) Mail (discussed in Chapter 4)

- The Scripting Tool for Dial-Up Networking (discussed in Chapter 4)

- The Remote Access Server for Dial-Up Networking (also discussed in Chapter 4)

- A Pinball game

- A scheduler called System Agent that lets you pick days and time to have ScanDisk and other programs run, including the Compression Agent—elegant, simple, and useful

- Antialiased screen fonts (the theory behind antialiasing is discussed in Chapter 2), full window drag (rather than just the outline of a window showing as you drag it)

- A spectacular set of 256 color icons used for drives, disks, and so on (in the file `cool.dll`)

- Desktop themes—professionally designed and correlated sets of wallpaper, colors, fonts, sounds, mouse pointers, icons, and a screen saver that you choose and modify through a special Control Applet (see Figure 5-1—some are listed as 256 color and some as 64K color)

Microsoft is to be commended for including the 64K Desktop themes. The current high-end machine with Pentium and coprocessed PCI video is capable of handling higher-color depths, and it is good for Microsoft to nudge us in that direction. Bravo!

It should be pointed out that if you are limited to 256 colors (and you want to avoid 64K colors—if you don't have coprocessed video, for example) you can still use the themes that claim they need 64K colors. It's important that you install the themes when in 256-color mode. If you install them in 64K mode and decide that, after all, you only want 256 colors, the

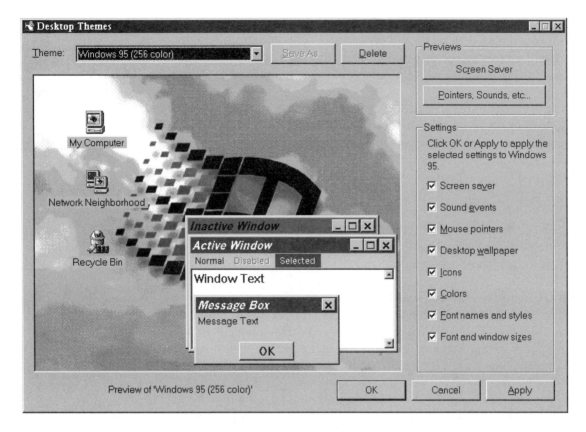

Figure 5-1. Desktop Themes

wallpaper won't look as good because it was installed for a 64K color system. But if you install the wallpaper in 256-color mode the wallpaper will look very good indeed. My favorites are the mystery theme and the screen saver called "Windows 95."

The Microsoft Office Shortcut Bar

> Personally, I can't see why it would be any less romantic to find a husband in a nice four-color catalogue than in the average downtown bar at happy hour.
>
> —Barbara Ehrenreich, *The Worst Years of Our Lives*

If you have Microsoft Office 95, you have two of the neatest "third-party" utilities around— the Microsoft System Information Utility and the Microsoft Office Shortcut Bar. The System Info program is the file `msinfo32.exe` in the directory `C:\Program Files\Common Files\MSInfo`. You can add it to the Start Menu if you wish or it can be invoked from the system menu of the Office Shortcut Bar. It provides information on general system properties, loaded programs and modules, fonts, OLE registered programs, and on things of specific interest to Office like a list of graphics converters.

The Shortcut Bar (Figure 5-2) is a quick launch bar that gives you handy buttons to start a number of your favorite applications. The bar allows you to display one strip of quick launch icons and have additional ones a click away. Five built-in strips are hardwired to read the folders (this assumes that you've installed Office with parent folder `C:\Msoffice`): `C:\windows\Desktop`, `C:\windows\favorites`, `C:\Msoffice\Office\MSN`; `C:\Start Menu\Programs` and `C:\Start Menu\Programs\Accessories`. Shortcuts are shown as buttons on the bar and subfolders as folders that opens in Folder view (rather than some kind of submenu).

Also, one additional bar is available for each subfolder of `C:\Msoffice\Office\Shortcut Bar`. In particular, Office comes with a subfolder of that folder, called `Office`. My own advice is to make a subfolder of that folder called `MyApps` and populate it with shortcuts to the items that you most want quick access to.

If you are running at 1024×768, there should be enough real estate to keep the toolbar on the right edge of the screen Always on Top. Otherwise, you'll have the usual problem trying to separate Desktop real estate needs from other needs.

You'll notice that MS couldn't resist giving the little extra push to MS Network, even here. Bah, humbug. Most of the built-in options are pretty lame, but if you roll your own subfolder of `C:\Msoffice\Office\Shortcut Bar`, you get considerable functionality.

In the last Windows 3.1 version of Office, the analog of the Shortcut Bar was called Microsoft Office Manager, which they said was called MOM for short. I notice that they've backed away from that. I bet they were afraid of Mom's lawyers.

Figure 5-2. The MS Office Shortcut Bar

Power Toys!

> If there hadn't been women we'd still be squatting in a cave eating raw meat,
> because we made civilization in order to impress our girl friends.
> And they tolerated it and let us go ahead and play with our toys.

> —Orson Welles

On the Microsoft Web site, there is a wondrous set of tools for power users called Power Toys! The full Web address (URL) is `http://www.microsoft.com/windows/software/powertoy.htm`. Or, if you go to any Microsoft top-level site and just look for Windows and then Free Software, you should find it. The introductory text on their Web page says that these are little utilities written by Windows 95 programmers when they "come in late at night, night after night, when everyone else is sound asleep." You are firmly warned that they are not supported by Microsoft, although most seem to have the Microsoft copyright. They seem to be a strange cross between focus group tests and beta tests of things that could wind up in the next version of Windows. No matter what they are, they are exceedingly useful and each is less than 30K and thus a very short download. The exact contents will likely change as they evolve, but to give you an idea of what is available, these things were around a month after Windows 95 shipped:

`Cabview`—This is an extension to Explorer. Once installed, Microsoft's `.cab` file, the compressed libraries that Microsoft products currently ship on (see Appendix E), have a special icon in Explorer views and when you click on them they open a folder like window displaying the files in the `.cab`. Moreover, from this view you can extract files you want.

`FlexiCD`—This is a basic but convenient replacement for the Audio CD Player that ships with Windows. It displays an icon in the notification area on the Taskbar. When an audio CD is inserted, you can start, pause, and restart playing by clicking on the icon on Taskbar.

`QuickRes`—This is another program that loads as an icon in the notification area of the Taskbar. It pops up and shows you supported screen resolutions and color depths and lets you change it on the fly! That's right—even though you have to reboot to change the color depth with the Display applet, with this gem, you can change color depth on the fly.

 One warning is that the install for these programs depends on the abilities of Windows Setup to process `.inf` files, and this part of Windows doesn't understand long filenames! That means the path to the files after you download has to contain directories that only have legal names under the old 8.3 scheme. If you place them in a directory called `Power Toys`, you'll get an error message when you try to install—even `PowerToys`, which is nine letters, won't work!! This is not a bug in Power Toys but in Windows 95 setup. Oh, how I love a nice bug in the mornin'.

Norton

> Like many businessmen of genius he learned that free competition was wasteful, monopoly efficient. And so he simply set about achieving that efficient monopoly.

—Mario Puzo, *The Godfather,* 1969

There has been an incredible concentration in the Windows utility market. Not only have a lot of small vendors gone out of business, but Symantec (the makers of the Norton products) bought Fifth Generation (Fastback and others) and Central Point (PC Tools) bought Executive Systems (Xtree). Still, there were two strong contenders—Norton and PC Tools—and users benefited enormously from the competition between them. And then, in the Spring of 1994, Symantec bought Central Point and, remarkably, the Justice Department let the sale go through. I'm still amazed at that.

Mom asked me to call my buddy Peter '95, the official spokesbaby for Symantec, to comment on these issues. Ole Pete is a strange kid. I don't see how he can drag around his sacks of moola if he always keeps his arms folded over his chest, but he somehow seems to manage. Maybe he's a Buddha or something with extra hands to go around or maybe it's just that his bag is so much smaller than mine he can tuck it under those folded arms. Anyhow, I asked Peter about the Justice gig and he said more or less (and mind you, I'm just telling you what Petie said, not that either I or the corporation I represent happen to agree . . .): "Well, we told them not to worry about us scampering monkeys getting together because there was this 500-pound gorilla in Redmond that we needed to deal with."

But while they may have fooled Justice, they understood quite well that they had an effective monopoly and did what monopolies have usually done—gouge the customer. Used to be you could get Norton Desktop *new* for about $120 and I'd seen PC Tools for Windows for as low as $89. Symantec split what had been in these products into three programs. To *upgrade* to all three costs about $120 and buying all three from scratch will set you back almost $300. And the three products combined have a lot missing that was in Norton Desktop: gone is the batch language, the backup, the wide array of file viewers, the ASCII editor, the icon editor, the fancy calculators, and the mini-PIM.

When Peter '95 heard what Rush said, he told me that people had to realize what a different ballgame Windows 95 was. The shift to a new API and 32 bits meant that there was a lot of complicated development work to be done. The Norton Utilities programming team may have produced fewer goodies, but it was twice the size. The upgrade was pricey because it wasn't an upgrade as much as a brand-new set of products.

The irony is that it is possible that Symantec could have been right when it told Justice about that 500-pound gorilla in Redmond. If users see the Plus! Pack for $39 and the Norton Utilities for $129, they may wonder why they are paying over three times the price. Norton may have wound up pricing its products into being power user toys, whereas they appealed to a broad market segment when they had Central Point to fight with.

Norton Navigator

Agriculture, manufactures, commerce, and navigation, the four pillars of our prosperity . . .

—Thomas Jefferson, *First Annual Message to Congress,* Dec. 8, 1801

The parts of Norton Desktop for Windows and PC Tools that dealt with file manipulation and program launching and a bunch of related utilities are sold as Norton Navigator. Rather than a replacement for the Windows shell, it's a vast enhancement of it. Among its components:

- `Norton Taskbar`—You can have multiple virtual Desktops, each represented by a separate thumbnail on the Taskbar.

- `Norton QuickMenu`—These are enhancements to the Start Menu, including a document list sorted by type and cascading history menu off the Run command.

- `Norton File Assist`—This adds three little buttons to the corner of the Common File dialogs next to the help and close buttons: ▣▣▣?✕. One is a drop-down of quite useful commands like copy, move, and compress (zip), one a drop-down list of documents recently opened or saved in the calling application, and one a drop-down list of directories recently accessed in this application.

- `Norton LFN Enabler`—Adds long filename support to programs using the Windows 3.1 common file dialogs.

- `Norton Explorer Extensions`—Adds a `Date` tab to file dialogs that lets you adjust any of the five dates or times associated to a file, and special menu items for files, folders, or drives, including copy, move, zip and uuencode.

- `Norton File Manager`—A replacement for Explorer with support for zips (shown as folders), for ftp (shown as folders), and for erased files. But in some ways, for example, automatic font installation, Explorer is better.

Norton Utilities

Norton sells a bunch of little (and not so little!) utilities in one package as the Norton Utilities:

- `Norton Protected Files and Unerase`—An erased file recovery system that supplements and enhances Recycle Bin. It saves copies of files deleted in DOS, deleted by programs and other files that don't go to the Recycle Bin, and you can set it to automatically empty itself of files order than a user defined period. Be warned that it can take up enormous gobs of space without you realizing it.

- `Norton Disk Doctor`—Long before DOS's chkdsk matured into ScanDisk, NDD was providing the smartest recovery from logical disk disasters.

- `Norton System Doctor`—Choose from a vast array of gauges (Figure 5-3) that display disk usage, memory usage, and a lot more. Any gauge can be set to trigger an alarm when something goes below a preset level or some danger is noticed (for example, disk integrity can be monitored with an offer to run NDD if an error is found).

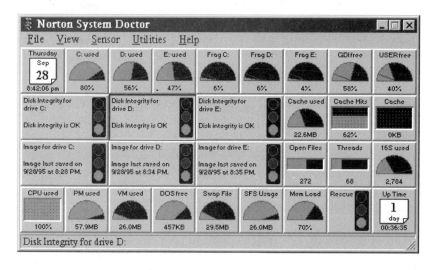

Figure 5-3. Norton System Doctor

- `Norton Rescue Disk`—Much more complete than the StartUp disk that Windows makes—this one usually requires multiple disks and saves the complete Registry and other important files.

- `Norton Image`—Saves backup copies of the FAT and other important system files.

- `Norton Space Wizard`—Searches out duplicated files, files with the extension `.bak`, and other space wasters.

- `Norton Speed Disk`—A disk defragger.

- `Norton System Information`—Provides a cornucopia of detailed information on system parameters; there's a copy of this on Mom's CD. See Appendix A.

- `Norton Disk Editor`—A low-level Hex editor that will even view the FAT and raw directories. You can run this only in DOS-exclusive mode.

 When Norton Protect Files are running, reports of free space by different utilities are vastly different. There's definitely something funny going on.

 The gauges are pretty and it is the best defragger around, but the level of the utilities built into Windows 95 is so good there is nothing even remotely compelling about the Norton Utilities. The "I gotta have it all" types will want this, but most users can pass.

 Unless the users really care about their data. Norton has gotten me out of a lot of scrapes in the past, and consistently, it has surpassed any other recovery tool on the market. I can't say that I've done serious tests on problems disks, but I can guarantee you that if I ever have a really serious disk disaster again, I'll reach for my Norton Disk Doctor before ScanDisk. Their track record just can't be ignored.

Norton Anti-Virus

Think of the earth as a living organism that is being attacked by billions of bacteria whose numbers double every forty years. Either the host dies, or the virus dies, or both die.

—Gore Vidal, *Observer of London,* Aug. 27, 1989

It's a cold, cruel world out there. Remember to wear your galoshes. And when computing, protect yourself against computer viruses. Don't be paranoid about them, but don't assume it couldn't happen to you. I doubt there is a 25-node network out there that has never been hit, and even many home users have. Alas, there are too many jerks out there who have nothing better to do than to prove their manhood (and it does appear that most virus writers disgrace the male side of the race) by writing some junk for poor users to trip over. The good news, though, is that most of these things are known or use known techniques that the good anti-virus programs can defend against.

There is no such thing as a harmless virus either, as the Windows disk 2 phenomenon showed. Some computer viruses do nothing more than propagate themselves by writing to a piece of the boot sector of diskettes that is normally empty. Harmless, right? Wrong! Because when Microsoft developed their new compressed format for diskettes to deliver programs on the least number of diskettes, they used this area on diskettes 2 and higher (diskette 1 had to be a standard type to start the programs that could read the new format!). A number of users were unaware they had a virus until they tried to install Windows and repeatedly got "Diskette 2 bad" messages because these diskettes had become infected. So all viruses are reprehensible.

DOS 6.x came with a virus scanner from Central Point, but Windows 95 doesn't. How come? Have viruses become unimportant? Ha! One consequence of the Norton/Central Point merger is that Microsoft could no longer play one off against the other, and so convince each of them to contribute components to the operating system. So there is no source of anti-virus software for Win 95. You're on your own.

At a minimum, get a copy of one of the virus scanners that are available for downloading and scan frequently. We expect that Mom's Bonus CD will have the Norton Scanner (see Appendix A). If you have the Plus! Pack, add a scanner to the programs run automatically while you sleep. Cheap insurance.

But unless you feel particularly insulated, you'll probably want to invest in one of the main anti-virus packages. Which means the ones from Norton, from McAffee, or from Dr. Solomon.

We use Norton here at Mom's because it was out first, but once Dr. Solomon is available (it wasn't before our deadline for the book, but should be out by the time you read this), we'll take a close look. The category is mature and you should do quite well with any of the programs, but Dr. Solomon's technical expertise is appealing.

Shell Enhancements or Replacements

The Windows 3.1 shell was weak enough that it spawned an entire industry of replacements. Windows 95 has a much stronger shell, but with millions of users, a lot of people will prefer something a little different. So there will be a market for replacement shells. We've already seen Norton Navigator, and I'll talk about Dashboard in a second.

These aren't replacements in the sense that there were shell replacements in Windows 3.1— these programs assume you'll still run with the system Taskbar and Explorer as your shell, so in a sense they are shell enhancements.

Not only are there sort-of replacements that are enhancements, there are programs that don't pretend to do anything but enhance. They use the fact that the Windows 95 shell is extensible so you can have an add-on that acts more as a part of Explorer than as a separate program. Hijaak for Windows 95 is the most extreme example of this—users can almost forget there is a third party providing the enhancements and think it's all a built-in part of Windows!

Yeah. Brilliant design, don't ya think?

Dashboard

No matter how hard you try, a Desktop interface will never be a desk.

—Gene Callahan

Dashboard sure has had trouble finding a corporate home, but you may want to give it one on your system. It started life as a product from HP, which planned a multiproduct software division. Dashboard did well in the reviews, and according to HP, it had over a million users, but HP couldn't quite figure out where software fit in. They closed down the division in the fall of 1994 and sold the product to Borland, who planned to use it as the centerpiece of a Simplicity division. But then a decision was made by the board to nudge Borland founder and CEO Philippe Kahn out of the CEO position. When the smoke cleared, Philippe had a new software company called Starfish Software (408-461-5800), and Borland had sold the new company Dashboard and Sidekick for an undisclosed amount.

The program squeezes an enormous amount into a small space (Figure 5-4) including:

Figure 5-4. Dashboard 95

- Launch tabs, which give you quick access to submenus of the Start Menu/Programs menu

- Quick Launch buttons for the Desktop, recent docs, and predefined or user-defined groups

- Quick Launch buttons for Explorer and other basic Windows programs

- A clock and calendar with alarms

- Multiple virtual Desktops

- Readout of memory usage, resources, and disk space

- A quick way to change printer drivers

- A quick casino game (not shown)

- A pseudo DOS window with a command line and run box with memory (not shown)

All this comes with an impressive amount of customization.

 It's impressive what gets packed into a small amount of Desktop space. Dashboard remains the king of the minimalist shells. But—and isn't there always a but?—given that the Taskbar and Start Menu also don't take much space and the Windows Run box now has memory, most users won't need what Dashboard offers.

QuickView Plus!

 Inso (312-329-0700) has a brilliant marketing shtick. They established their file viewer expertise with OutsideIn, a Windows 3.x product, and provided to Microsoft (at no cost, according to the grapevine) a set of very basic viewers for Explorer that I discussed in Chapter 3—the QuickView viewers. They offer a QuickView Plus with considerable greater functionality than the simple viewers they provided to Microsoft and with a considerably broader set of supported file types.

Figure 5-5 shows the same file viewed on the left in QuickView and on the right in QuickView Plus. The difference is in the button bar and menus. Four new critical buttons (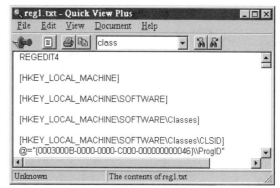) are added that allow you to print the file, copy selected text to the clipboard, and search for text backward or forward (the search text can be entered and/or recalled from a drop-down list). That's right—the viewers built into Windows 95 can do none of these functions.

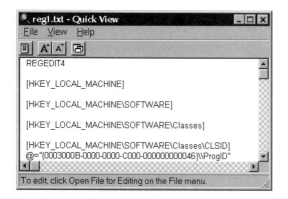

Figure 5-5. Two views, both Quick

QuickView Plus will view OLE-embedded objects in files and will view zips and files inside zips! It will even extract files from zips!

Besides this, QuickView Plus provides viewers for many, many more file types. The difference is especially dramatic for graphical file formats. Here's a partial list, with the types that are not supported in QuickView indicated with a *:

`Text and Word Processors:` .txt, .asc, .ini, .inf (ASCII text), .wri (Windows 3.x WRITE), .rtf (Rich Text Format), .sam (Ami, Ami Pro), .doc (Winword v1,2,6,7), .wps (Works Word Processing), .wpd (Word Perfect), .html *(web docs), uuencoded[†] docs*, word star docs * , xywrite docs * and dozens of old formats.

`Spreadsheets:` .xls (Excel 4 and 5, versions * 6 and 7), .wk1, .wks, .wk3, .wk4 (Lotus 1-2-3 v 1,2,3,4), .wq1, .wq2, .wb1 (Quattro Pro v4,5 for DOS, v1 for Windows; v2-6* for Windows), .mod (Multiplan), Enable *, Framework *

`Database formats:` .wdb (Works Database), .dbf *(dBase), .db * (Paradox), .mb * (Access)

`Graphics formats:` .bmp, .dib, .rle (Windows Bitmaps), .xlc (Excel 4 Chart), .cdr (Corel Draw, v4,5), .drw (Micrografx Draw), .wmf (Windows MetaFile), .ppt (Powerpoint, v 4, v* 5-7), .pre (Freelance), Harvard Graphics for DOS *, .gif * (CompuServe), .tif *, .pcx *, .tga *, .jpg *, .ico *, .cgm *, .wpg *, .dxf *

`Executable and Compressed Files:` .exe, .dll, .zip *, .tar *

WinZip

> I have not had major experience of talking with people once pronounced brain-dead,
> but I think we could be safe in saying he did not have great zip.

> —Sir Howard Smith, *Times of London,* Sept. 8, 1988, talking of Leonid Brezhnev

PKZIP has become a standard for compressed libraries of files—compression is typically 2 to 1 for text files, less for executable files, and much more for uncompressed multimedia/ graphics files and certain other files. For example, during the preparation of this book, where files had to be sent via email between Mom's branch offices, we dealt with graphic heavy Winword docs and typically had compression factors of at least 10 to 1 by zipping. As shown in Figure 5-6, some files had a compression factor of 30 to 1. You'll need a tool to unzip files that you download, but even more you'll need to compress files if you often send them by modem or on diskette.

The standard tool for dealing with zips among Mom's minions is WinZip (Niko Mak Computing; shareware, available from their Web site http://www.winzip.com/winzip). This is

---

[†] uuencode is a UNIX standard for converting binary files to ASCII only using characters below code 128 so that they can be passed through systems that only support 7-bit characters. Email from Internet systems often comes in uuencoded.

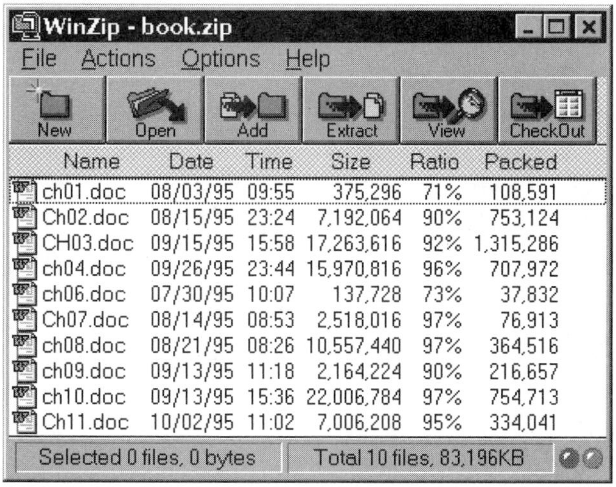

Name	Date	Time	Size	Ratio	Packed
ch01.doc	08/03/95	09:55	375,296	71%	108,591
Ch02.doc	08/15/95	23:24	7,192,064	90%	753,124
CH03.doc	09/15/95	15:58	17,263,616	92%	1,315,286
ch04.doc	09/26/95	23:44	15,970,816	96%	707,972
ch06.doc	07/30/95	10:07	137,728	73%	37,832
Ch07.doc	08/14/95	08:53	2,518,016	97%	76,913
ch08.doc	08/21/95	08:26	10,557,440	97%	364,516
ch09.doc	09/13/95	11:18	2,164,224	90%	216,657
ch10.doc	09/13/95	15:36	22,006,784	97%	754,713
Ch11.doc	10/02/95	11:02	7,006,208	95%	334,041

WinZip - book.zip

File Actions Options Help

New   Open   Add   Extract   View   CheckOut

Selected 0 files, 0 bytes   Total 10 files, 83,196KB

Figure 5-6. Winzippy-ity-do-dah

well integrated into Windows 95. Once you've installed WinZip, you can select any set of files in Explorer, right-click, and choose a menu item called Add to Zip, which WinZip has added. And, when you double-click on *.zip, file, it will open in WinZip (Figure 5-6).

The interface is simple and intuitive. You have lots of options, such as the ability to use supercompression (which typically decreases zip files by 10 percent and takes several times longer to compress). You do not need PKZIP to run WinZip—the zip compression and decompression is built in. WinZip also supports other compressed files like *.lhz, but there it just acts as a shell for DOS compression programs that you are required to have. You'll find WinZip on Mom's CD.

Hijaak 95

Hijaak from Inset Systems (800-203–740-2400) has long been synonymous with the best graphics format handling in the industry—an uncanny ability to deal with some of the weird variants that formats like .cgm and .tif come in. Their product for Windows 95 called Hijaak 95 is a wonderful set of shell extensions.

One is their icon handler, which displays thumbnails, as seen in Figure 5-7. It does this for the vast array of supported extensions including .ai, .cdr, .cgm, .drw, .emf, .eps, .gif, .jpg, .pcx, .tif, .ico, and .tga. And it does this without the performance hit that you get if you use Windows to display .bmp files (see "More Iconoclasms" in Chapter 11) because it saves the thumbnails on disk and does the updating in the background!

There is also a set of additions to the context menu of supported formats (Figure 5-8), including a full-blown conversion module that converts among raster formats, among vector formats, and from vector to raster. There is an extra tab added on the Property sheet of supported formats that gives details like resolution and color depth for raster files.

Figure 5-7. Hijaak thumbnails

 Hijaak does its magic by making extensive use of Windows 95 shell extensions. It not only adds its context menu and icon handler to its own file type but adds them to file types like Bitmap Image, which open with Paintbrush. It shows how powerful and flexible the shell extensions can be.

> HiJaak View
> HiJaak Print
> HiJaak Print Thumbnails
> HiJaak Update
> HiJaak Convert

Figure 5-8. Hijaak Context Menu

ClickFlick

The lovely woman-child Kaa was mercilessly chained to the cruel post of the warrior-chief Beast, with his barbarian tribe now stacking wood at her nubile feet, when the strong clear voice of the poetic and heroic Handsomas roared, "Flick your Bic, crisp that chick and you'll feel my steel through your last meal."

—Steve Garman, 1984 Winner of the Bulwer-Lytton Contest
for the worst opening sentence for a novel

ClickFlick (MiraTech, 800–330-9816) is a power user's power tool. The basic element of the program is the popbox, an elegant button box that pops up at the mouse cursor position when you hit the proper trigger. Triggers can be something like `Shift+Right Click`. Once you pop up the box, you flick the mouse and press the button—hence the program's name. Some buttons can be triggers for flyouts—other popboxes that appear somewhat like submenus. Figure 5-9 shows a popbox Mao built for Exchange with a flyout. The original popbox had a button marked Message in the lower-left corner. When the mouse moves over the corner, it expands to the four-button flyout shown here.

What makes ClickFlick so powerful is the array of possibilities that can be assigned to a button. It can be a key combination, a menu item from the underlying application, or even all the application menus made available to you without having to move the mouse up to the menu bar—look at the button marked App menu in Figure 5-9—that pops out a text list of the application's top level menus off of which the menus will cascade. There is even a professional version of ClickFlick that lets you assign buttons to macros written in a sophisticated Visual Basic–compatible language with a well-done recording option.

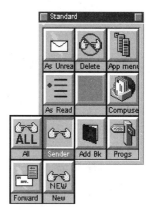

Figure 5-9. ClickFlick

 `Shift+Click` popups are a pain because of the `Shift`. ClickFlick is really wonderful with a three-button mouse like those from Logitech where you can assign the ClickFlick trigger to the middle button. I like this utility so much, I've gotten Logitech mice for all my machines so I have the middle button. And I've found I actually like the feel of the Logitech mice better than the Microsoft standard.

Take Command

> We were not born to sue, but to command.

> —William Shakespeare, *Richard II,* act 1, sc. 1

 Shakespeare? I thought it was Johnnie Cochran.

Some folks think GUI stuff is for the birds and pine for a smart command line. Others like GUIs fine but realize that a smart command line can sometimes be the most efficient way to accomplish certain file operations. The best-known replacement for `command.com` in the days of DOS was 4DOS. The same company, JP Software (800-368-8777), has come out with the ultimate pseudo-DOS for Windows—Take Command.

Take Command includes command recall, the ability to run DOS programs that only write to the console inside the Take Command window, the ability to launch DOS and Windows applications, color-code directories, a powerful batch language, and powerful ASCII viewer.

```
Take Command/Win95 - copy (*.dll) M:\temp            _ □ ✕
File  Edit  Apps  Options  Utilities  Help
Go  Quit  Toggle  Clear      26 chars       3 files 230k
☐hpu.dll                                16,384   11/04/94
☐INETMIB1.DLL                           50,512    7/11/95
☐MORICONS.DLL                           84,412    7/11/95
☐NDDEAPI.DLL                            14,032    7/11/95
☐NDDENB.DLL                             10,768    7/11/95
☒PLAYENU.DLL                            16,912   11/30/94
☐s32nav8.dll                           403,456    6/26/95
☒s32scani.dll                          104,448    6/26/95
☒siwnav32.dll                          113,152    6/26/95
☐VIEWENU.DLL                            17,536   11/30/94
☐WINSOCK.DLL                            42,080    7/11/95
◄                                                       ►
10/02/95  19:37:16   Load: 59%
```

Figure 5-10. For a smart command line, Take Command

 My favorite is the `select` command. If you type in `select copy (*.dll) M:\temp`, you'll get a screen like that shown in Figure 5-10, where you get to check off the files you want to have the command applied to. I'm a big fan of Take Command.

 I dunno. Take Command is a neat command line, but if you use doskey, with the new Start command and the other features in Windows 95's DOS boxes, the DOS command line is going to be enough for most users. But I guess that's what cockroach races are all about, isn't it Mao?

Internet Tools

> My problem lies in reconciling my gross habits with my net income.
>
> —Errol Flynn

Microsoft's Internet Tools are neat but there are literally hundreds of others available. I'll look briefly at two—the market leader browser from Netscape and a totally integrated package.

Netscape Navigator

Many attempts to communicate are nullified by saying too much.

—Robert Greenleaf, *Servant Leadership: A Journey into the Nature of Legitimate Power and Greatness*

 It's war—total, unconditional, take-no-prisoners war—out there and the territory that the participants want to conquer is your Desktop and the World-Wide Web. The protagonists are mighty Microsoft and startup Netscape. In 1994, Microsoft reported sales of $5,266,000,000 and net income of $1,307,000,000, while Netscape's sales were $696,000 and net income was **minus** $8,470,000. Truly, David versus Goliath. Who would you bet on? Before you answer, I should tell you who Wall Street was betting (and I do mean betting) on. Netscape (whose first half of 1995 sales had grown to just over $10 million) had an initial public offering (IPO) on August 9, 1995 that was one of the most spectacular in history. The offering price was $28/share but the stock opened at more than $50 (giving a killing to those with enough clout to get the initial offering) and went as high as $75 before settling down to about $60. The total value of the Netscape stock (the bulk of it owned by insiders—the IPO stock was about 15 percent of the total outstanding stock) is about $2 billion (Microsoft's is roughly $50 billion). Not bad for a small startup.

 *You're right, Mom. It sure is David versus Goliath. But Microsoft is the good-hearted David. It is estimated that about 80 percent of the people using the Web are using Netscape Navigator, and that in the first half of 1995, there were more than 4 million downloads of their program from their website and various echos of it. Microsoft, in the users service, ahem, offers its browser totally free of charge. Of course, you may pay a connect time charge to your Internet Provider, which could be, er, Microsoft. In a sense, Netscape is the most successful shareware program ever. You can download it free but unless you are a student or employee of an academic institution, you are supposed to buy Netscape after an initial trial.*

 Oh, poor little Microsoft fighting big Netscape. I know why you want to win this fight so badly. It has nothing to do with the Web as it existed in early 1995 and everything to do with what it is expected to become—a medium of commerce. You want to make a penny or two on each electronic purchase on the Web. Big bucks there, but you know if I were to bet, I'd pick Netscape. They have the market share. They've been the driving force behind most of the extensions of the HTML spec that controls what can be displayed on the Web. They're focusing on a lot more than browsers with a Web server, which has been their main source of income, and development tools to place full-blown applications on the Web.

They're being smart in offering free copies to the academic world, which still sets the pace on the Web, and they cover UNIX and Macs, not just Windows. Your solution, Billy, is too proprietary. Your browser is Windows only. Your server is going to be Windows NT. And Blackbird, your on-line development environment, is going to be linked to MSN, not the Web. I'd have thought you'd have learned the lesson long ago that proprietary solutions can't dislodge open ones.

Yeah, Rush, sure. That theory would say that UNIX should be beating Windows black and blue.

One evening as I was finishing up this chapter, I saw dramatically that it's a war out there. Earlier in the day, I'd downloaded the first beta version of Microsoft Internet Explorer version 2.0 from Microsoft's Web site. Then when I tried to run Netscape, I got a message about an expired beta and went to their site to download the latest beta of version 1.2, which I installed. Whatya know, with this version, I had a Netscape Navigator shortcut added directly to my Desktop. Every `.htm` file (saved web pages) on my Desktop had a Netscape icon instead of the one that Internet Explorer uses. I then installed the MS beta and, whatya know, my `.htm` files again had the MS Internet Explorer-related icon. Neither program asked me before it stole the `.htm` file type—they just did it. Sigh.

Figure 5-11. Netscape Navigator

If you do much web browsing and you don't have Navigator, you should check it out by downloading it from `http://home.netscape.com/`. It has a similar look (Figure 5-11) to Internet Explorer, not surprising since both are descendants of Mosiac, the first Web Browser.

While its handling of favorite places (which it calls bookmarks) isn't as natural to Windows as Internet Explorer's, it is functional.

Much of Navigator's magic is hidden from view in its ability to understand special kinds of tables and forms on the Web, its security, and more. Check it out.

Emissary

There are so many different components of the Internet that it can be confusing. The way Windows is set up, you need separate programs for mail, web browsing, and telnet. Although you can use the web browser for FTP, if you want to directly access directories in an anonymous FTP format, you need third-party software and yet another program. IRC requires still another program.

The integrated Internet application attempts to simplify this hodge-podge with a single program. I looked at Emissary (The Wollongong Group, 800-872-8649), the first of this genre of program, although several others should be out by the time this book is released. Emissary uses the Explorer metaphor (Figure 5-12) except that the tree this time has entries for Web Surfing, Mail, News, Files and Interactive. Files includes your local and network file tree to which ftp connections are added. Interactive means Telnet in this initial release (with IRC promised for later). The Telnet effortlessly supports ANSI BBS. If the integrated Internet application appeals to you, you'll want to look this one over.

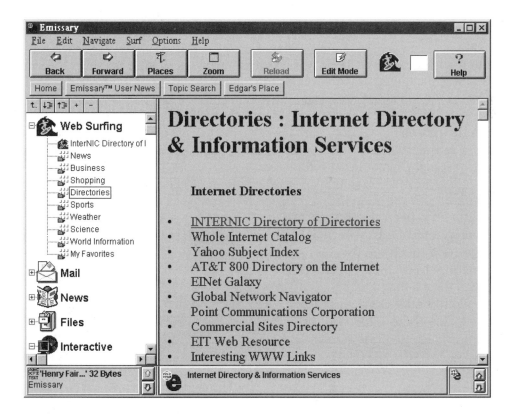

Figure 5-12. Using an Emissary to navigate and explore

Other Goodies

The morning after a death, we learned an avalanche of goodies about the renowned, some of which persuaded the reader that he should have cultivated the deceased in life.

—Jim Bishop, *New Jersey Daily Register,* June 11, 1980, speaking of
New York Times obituary writer Alden Whitman Shrewsbury

After Dark

Blemishes are hid by night and every fault forgiven; darkness makes any woman fair.

—Ovid, *Ars Amatoria*

 The makers of screen savers would have you believe that you need to get 'em to save your monitor from the dreaded burn in. That's a bunch of hooey. It was a problem with monochrome monitors, circa 1984. But hey, if it sold screen savers then, why not now? There's only one good reason to get a screen saver—because they are fun.

There's no doubt what the champ of the screen savers is—After Dark from Berkeley System (510-540-5535). From the lovely fish to the signature toasters to the—new with the Windows 95 version—flying toilets, their modules are imaginative, well drawn, and clever.

If you have modules from an old version, they'll work with the new one. Be sure to check out the randomizer module, which lets you make a new module that calls a collection of selected modules at random. Great, great fun.

 Probably no program in history has been pirated more than After Dark. I know that you have much too much integrity to do that. But do me a favor—if you have a friend who's been running a pirated After Dark—just as a short trial, of course—for, oh, the last two years, nudge 'em to become honest. OK?

Microangelo

I'd asked around 10 or 15 people for suggestions. . . . Finally one lady friend asked the right question, "Well, what do you love most?" That's how I started painting money.

—Andy Warhol, *Manhattan Inc,* Oct. 1984

Windows 95 supports (and the Plus! Pack uses!) several new formats beyond the 32 × 32 pixel, 16-color icon that was the Windows 3.x standard. That means that Windows 3.1 icon editors won't work on all icons and they won't read the 32-bit libraries that many icons are now packed in. Impact Software (909-590-8522) hasn't merely ported some Windows 3.1 tools—they've produced a powerful package of four programs you can use to organize all aspects of icons and cursors:

- `Microangelo Browser` lets you look through directories for icon libraries

- `Microangelo Librarian` (Figure 5-13) lets you view icons and make your own libraries with keywords assigned to icons.

- `Microangelo Studio` is an icon editing and creation tool.

- `Microangelo Animator` is an animated cursor browsing and editing tool.

Figure 5-13. Microangelo Librarian

These are all in a well-put-together, functional package. There are several special tools for editing 256-color icons that make what would be a complex task a pleasure. The Microangelo package is shareware—you'll find it on Mom's CD. (Animator is a registration bonus not available in the shareware version.)

ClickBook

The books we think we ought to read are poky, dull, and dry;
The books that we would like to read we are ashamed to buy;
The books that people talk about we never can recall;
And the books that people give us, oh, they're the worst of all.

—Carolyn Wells, *On Books*

ClickBook (Bookmaker Corp., 415-354-8161) is a gem that should be more widely known. It lets you print out in formats from booklets to simple two output pages to a page—accomplished by rotating the original pages, reducing, and printing in landscape mode. Saves a lot of trees.

ClickBook does its magic with a print driver that takes the output from a program and then passes it to a "real" printer driver. The program that you are printing from merrily sends its output assuming it's going a page at a time in portrait mode and then ClickBook transforms it into landscape mode and has it printed.

When I was writing this, ClickBook only had a Windows 3.1 version available, but it worked fine with Windows 95. A 32-bit version that uses Windows 95 dialogs should be out by the time this book goes through the production process.

Chapter 6

The Hard Stuff

> Grown up, and that is a terribly hard thing to do.
> It is much easier to skip it and go from one childhood to another.

—F. Scott Fitzgerald, *The Crack-up,* 1936

In this chapter Sarah looks at the hard side of Windows 95—what you need, what to buy, what's a waste, what works, what doesn't. It's a quick look at a difficult subject: instead of going into the nuances of all the pros and cons *(oy! the cons!)* of PC hardware, the chapter focuses on considerations unique to Windows 95. Mom summarizes it all in the last section, so even if you know everything there is to know about Win95 and hardware, be sure to check out Mom's Checklist at the end of the chapter.

Gotta Know It

> All knowledge is ambiguous.

—J. S. Habgood, Archbishop of York, *Observer,* 1991

This chapter assumes a nodding acquaintance with PCs and their innards. If you can point out a motherboard, and know a CPU from a RAM chip, you're in good shape.

But if you lack that kind of background, it's time to get up to speed. For a first course, check out Ron White's *PC/Computing—How Computers Work,* a gorgeous coffee-table book, illustrated by Timothy Edward Downs (ZD Press, 1993). Once you've seen the inner workings of your computer, try *The Underground Guide to PC Hardware* by Alfred Poor

(Addison-Wesley, 1995) for a thorough description of how the pieces fit together. They're remarkable books, both as tutorials and as references.

Ahem. You guys left out one of the best references on hardware, my own *PC Mom: The Mother of All PC Books* (Addison-Wesley, 1994). It doesn't have the depth on hardware of Ron's or Fred's books (because it talks about lots of other topics), but for the basic stuff you need for this chapter, it's ideal. And the next time you guys miss an opportunity to plug one of my books, I'll ground you for a week.

The Bottom Line on Component Upgrades

> We want beans, not goals.
>
> —Mexican Steelworkers' Banner, 1986 World Cup

It's depressing. So many people waste so much money every year on hardware upgrades that don't do squat. It's very, very rare that an upgrade to a faster processor or disk, or a swap of one board for another, will significantly improve your system's performance with Win95. Why? Because you can't feel any difference in processing power unless you can boost your *entire system's* performance by at least 25 percent—and even that thrill will fade in weeks, not months. When in doubt, don't throw good money after bad: wait until you can afford a new machine, then sell your old PC to some dolt who really believes he can upgrade it economically, or give it to your kids or the local school.

That said, a few single-component upgrades can breathe life into an aging Win95 PC:

- Bring the memory up to 8 MB. Even a 386—*especially* a 386—will run Win95 faster with a full 8 megs. You might even consider 16 MB of RAM if you have a 486 or better and don't plan on a total machine upgrade for the next year.

- If you have a local bus (PCI or VLB) machine, it undoubtedly has a local bus accelerated video card. Upgrading local bus video cards rarely breathes much new fire into a system's performance. But if you have an older machine with a clunker of a video card and no local bus, installing an accelerated video card can make a world of difference.

- If you have an old single-speed CD-ROM drive, and you notice the delay when working with interactive CDs, *and* you've maximized Win95's read-ahead cache (see Chapter 8) with insufficient effect, upgrading to a quad speed drive can bring new life to those CDs.

• If your modem still runs at 2400 or 9600 baud and your favorite on-line services support 14.4 or 28.8 Kbaud, upgrading your modem can pay for itself in a few months.

That's about it. Anything else and you've got "chump" written all over you.

Hey, Sarah! What, you nuts? There's a multibillion-dollar industry in upgrade parts! Did you forget to include the Overdrive processors, or the new 9 ms access hard drives? What about Fast and Wide SCSI, or 128-bit PCI video accelerators? C'mon! Get with the system.

Ah, my poor, deluded, occasionally-departed winged one. You've been listening to too much marketing hype. Why spend $500 on an Overdrive processor and get a 30 percent increase in overall system speed, when you can buy a whole new system for $1,500, sell the old one for $750—or, better yet, donate it to some worthy charity and deduct it off your taxes—and boost your performance by a factor of two or three? Why pay to get a hard drive with a faster access time rating, or a video card with a wider data bus, when there's no perceptible difference in speed? Sorry. To me, it doesn't make sense. Parts is parts. Upgrading components simply amounts to sliding down the wrong side of the price/performance curve.

Absolutely. Major technological advances occur with amazing frequency in this business. The problem stems from what I call the Frankenstein Syndrome. If Dr. Frankenstein sews a 20 percent stronger right leg on his monster, it won't run 20 percent faster. If he uses a 40 percent smarter brain, it won't work 40 percent harder. An 80 percent keener eye won't see 80 percent farther. Right, Igor? You know about these things.

Yetttttth mattther. Dr. FRAHN-ken-steeen spent his lifetime studying incremental upgrades and their effect on overall performance. That's why he had me take the body of an athlete, the brain of an academic, the eye of a newt . . . . *snort!*

Mao, knock it off. You're upsetting Igor. You know how painful these political flashbacks can be.

The point is valid, though. Super-charging one component of a Win95 PC, in general, won't improve overall system performance—the part you're concerned with—by much. Save your money and go for the big kahuna, not the little component upgrades. You may lose some serious bragging rights—nobody's going to be impressed by a puny 128K L-2 cache when 256K becomes the norm—but the effect is only temporary . . . and largely psychological.

But we all agree, the two exceptions to this dictum are more memory and an accelerated video card. Because those are upgrades that make a huge difference.

How Much Is That Hot-Diggity-Dog in the Window?

Plato and Aristotle were well-bred men, and like others, laughing with their friends:
and when they diverted themselves in making their laws and politics they did it playfully.
It was the least philosophic and least serious part of their lives.
The most philosophic was living peacefully and tranquilly.

—Blaise Pascal, *Pensées,* 1670

Are you thinking about buying a new Win95 PC? Yeah, aren't we all. Before you flip out that gold card, though, there are a few things you should know about PCs in general and Win95 PCs in particular. Like, if you upgrade from a 486DX/33 to a Pentium-100, what kind of performance improvement can you expect?

Mao and I put our heads together and came up with a chart (Figure 6-1) that should give you a first-approximation idea of the relative power of various kinds of computers when running Win95.

Here's how you read the chart. Say you're thinking of tossing away your old 486DX/33 and replacing it with a Pentium-90. According to this chart, the Pentium-90 should run Win95 about four times faster than your old machine. If you're thinking of getting rid of your Pentium-100 and replacing it with the first-generation "P6" machine, we think you'll see a 70 percent speed boost.

Several warnings pertain. First and foremost, the chart is based on "typical" systems for a particular processor: you can't replace the CPU chip in a 486 DX/33 system with a DX4/100 Overdrive chip, for example, and expect a threefold performance boost. On the other hand, if you have a typical 1993-vintage 486DX/33 and you replace it with a typical 1996-vintage DX4/100 system, you probably will see that big a difference. Remember that the main bottleneck with most Win95 multimedia products is *not* the processor.

Second, individual machines' performance can vary all over the place, with early, pioneering PCs often pulling up the rear. For example, the earliest Pentium-90 PCs run Win95 20 percent to 30 percent slower than the later machines. There's a settling-out period of four to six months after a new chip technology is introduced, when manufacturers poke and prod

	486 DX/33	486 DX2/66	DX4/ 100	Pentium 75	Pentium 90	Pentium 100	Pentium 120	Pentium 133	P6
386 DX/33	2X	4X	7X	8X	9X	10X	*	*	*
486 DX/33		80%	3X	4X	4X	5X	6X	*	*
486 DX2/66			80%	2X	2X	3X	3X	4X	*
DX4/100				NETPA	30%	50%	80%	2X	2.5X
Pentium 75					NETPA	NETPA	50%	70%	2X
Pentium 90						NETPA	NETPA	50%	2X
Pentium 100							NETPA	30%	70%
Pentium 120								NETPA	40%
Pentium 133									NETPA

NETPA = Not Enough to Spit At

* = So far off the scale it isn't worth worrying about

Figure 6-1. Relative PC muscle

and finally discover the best way to hook a machine together. Then other new technology comes along that, when retrofitted to the old chip, pushes the performance even higher.

Finally, these numbers represent a distillation of many different, often conflicting, sources. In particular, at the time this was written, we didn't have *any* production P6 machines capable of running Win95. Thus, your mileage may vary. But probably not by much.

What about non-Intel chips? All these companies say they have 486 work-alikes and Pentium-sortas. Are they any good? How do I tell where the non-Intel chips fall in the power pecking order?

As far as I'm concerned, non-Intel chips are just as good as the name-brand originals, once you figure out their numbering schemes and adjust for a bit of marketing hype. The Intel DX2/66 is about the same as an AMD 486 DX2/80, or a Cyrix or IBM DX2/80. The DX4/100 comes close to the AMD DX4/100 or /120, the Cyrix DX4/100, the NexGen Nx586-P80, or the Pentium-60 or -66 (neither of which I recommend because they run too hot). I'd also put the NexGen Nx586-P90 in the same class as the Pentium-75, and the Nx586-P100 near the Pentium-90.

Call me the cautious, nervous type but I figure there is enough to worry about in a system without taking a chance on a non-Intel processor. You know that most of the testing of software will be done on Intel-based systems.

As the official representative here of the infamous Wintel duopoly, I applaud your use of FUD.* Couldn't have done it better myself, Mom.

Once you've settled on a general type of machine, it's time to get down to specifics.

Narrowing the List

> Cherish forever what makes you unique,
> 'cuz you're really a yawn if it goes.

> —Bette Midler

While several considerations should enter into your final decision about which machine to buy—the manufacturer's reputation, for example, or the availability of maintenance contracts—there's one overarching factor in the search for the best PC for your money: performance. Why buy a Pentium-100 that runs like a DX4/100, when for the same amount of money (sometimes even less) you can get a real screamer?

The best way to measure performance is to do it yourself: figure out which applications you use the most, buy a stopwatch, and come up with a little test suite based on files you actually use. If you're a big word-processing user, time how long it takes to load a big document, scroll through it, and print it. If spreadsheets are your thing, time a recalc on a monster sheet. If you're a graphic artist, time the opening, redraw, and printing of your most horrendous picture.

Armed with times on your current machine, schlep your applications and that stopwatch down to the local computer store, install the app, run the benchmark, and see precisely how much faster it goes. Real data. Real application.

---

* FUD = Fear, Uncertainty, and Doubt; a marketing device honed to a science by IBM in the 1960s.

But make sure you delete the application and the data after you've run the benchmark.

Yeah, yeah, yeah. We wouldn't want the Software Publishing Association to bust your friendly local computer-store droid. By comparing real results from various machines, you'll get an idea of how much faster or slower your job will go in a typical working day. You'll see why any speed improvement under 25 percent or so really doesn't make that much difference in how much work you can get done. And you'll get a feel for how much money that new hardware adrenaline rush will cost.

But what about machines you can't test yourself? Say, mail-order PCs, or PCs in glued-tight cardboard boxes? How do you know how well those will work?

In a word, you don't. The closest substitute to a do-it-yourself benchmark test—and it's a poor substitute—is the Ziff Labs Winstone, which appears regularly in reviews carried by Ziff-Davis magazines (*PC Magazine, PC/Computing, Computer Shopper, Windows Sources,* and *PC Week*).

Most benchmarks (specInts and Winmarks and heaven-knows-what-all) try to draw conclusions about a PC's performance based on how quickly the PCs run routine, abstract tests: a PC that draws rectangles on the screen faster gets a higher score; one that transfers disk data across a bus faster gets a higher score; and never mind whether real Win95 users ever draw millions of rectangles or transfer blocks of gigabytes of data.

Abstract benchmarks don't tell you anything because you don't use components in a vacuum—a 50 percent faster disk transfer rate, say, will be totally imperceptible to any but a very small subset of Win95 users. Buying a PC based on component benchmarks is like trying to choose shoes by looking at the lengths of laces.

Some benchmarks (Intel's iComp comes to mind) are nothing more than marketing tools. Strip away all the mathematical gobbledy-gook and one fact comes through: they only exist to sell you hardware. Of course the P70 processor is 4.983 times as fast as the P60. Would you pay for anything less?

In contrast, Ziff Labs chose a strange approach to benchmarking when it developed the Winstone. They actually tried to measure what real Windows users do with real Windows machines, running real Windows applications. No two Windows users are alike, of course, and that ultimately is the Achilles Heel of the Winstone: your situation might be so far away from the Ziff Labs "profile" that the Winstone results may not apply to you at all.

The Winstone approach starts with dozens of the most-common Windows applications and automated scripts for testing the performance of each of those applications on a particular PC. Ziff Labs takes the individual applications' scores and combines them in a weird way. It starts by breaking the apps into categories—word processors, spreadsheets, drawing programs, utilities, and such—then applying a percentage to each category that matches their profile of the typical Windows user. For example, if they found that the typical users spend 38 percent of their time using word processors, 38 percent of the final Winstone score will be based on word-processor performance.

Then within each category, individual apps' scores are weighted depending on the market share of the app within the category. So if Ziff determines that 78 percent of all word-processing users run Word, 26 percent run WordPerfect, and 9 percent run WordPro, then 78 percent of the word-processing score is based on the Word results, 26 percent on WordPerfect's, and 9 percent on WordPro's.* The percentages are recalculated every time Ziff Labs updates the Winstone test.

So you see that even the Winstone must be regarded as an apples-and-oranges concoction, applicable to nobody in particular, but (perhaps arguably) more meaningful in the aggregate than abstract component testing.

One nice side-effect of Ziff's Winstone: a steep decline in cooking. A few years ago video card manufacturers spent obscene amounts of money "cooking" their hardware and software, so their products would run faster on the big magazines' abstract component tests. Hundreds of millions of dollars waited for the company whose imperceptibly faster board landed at the top of the latest magazine article's benchmarking tests. Actual performance for real Windows users took a distant back seat to the cooking exercises designed to run artificial tests ever faster.

Winstone changes the game just a bit. It's so complex that any attempt to cook its results will, most likely, lead to improved performance for real users. While video card makers will continue to cook as long as there are abstract component performance tests, the emphasis has switched from trying to fool often-naive individual consumers with fraudulent numbers to trying to sell boards to savvy PC companies.

---

* No, those aren't real numbers. Sheesh.

So keep your eyes on the bottom line, the Winstone, and ignore the benchmark numbers for individual components.

Multimedia Madness

For if the trumpet give an uncertain sound, who shall prepare himself to the battle?

—1 Corinthians 14:8.

The most remarkable development in hardware over the past few years is that the hardware needs for the home PC are now more substantial than for the office PC. The reason is simple—multimedia. In the next section you'll see this in the ever-changing multimedia PC spec that I discuss, but as preparation for what you want to buy, I asked my minions to get out their Ouija boards and look at some of the developing trends in video, sound, and CD. Of course, given the life of this book, I'm likely to have some egg on my face by the time you read this and know which of my predictions are wrong.

In **video,** the up-and-coming technology is MPEG.* Raw video overwhelms current computer technology. A minute of uncompressed full-speed video at $1024 \times 768 \times 24$ million colors requires 6 GB of data. The solution is to drop the number of colors, the size of the picture, and the number of frames per second. The result is the postage stamp, grainy, herky-jerky crap that computer fans ooh and aah over while real people scratch their heads, wondering why anyone raves at something that is so inferior to what you get from the tube. The solution is compression. While there are competing standards, it appears the industry is heading toward a particular compression scheme for video called MPEG. This allows full-screen, full-speed video, and even throws in improved audio.

MPEG requires considerable on-the-fly computing power to decompress data in real time as you are playing back the video. Traditionally, this has required a specialized MPEG chip available on expensive, specialized video boards, most notably, Sigma Design's RealMagic boards. Microsoft has purchased software MPEG technology that allows the playback of MPEG video on systems without specialized MPEG hardware. They have announced their intention of moving it into the operating system.

---

* Short for "Motion Picture Exhibition Group," er, "Experts Group," uh, "Exhibitionists Group"— knowing this is only significant if you play Trivial Pursuit.

It remains to be seen how rapidly MPEG will slide into Windows, especially given its CPU requirements—software MPEG needs at least a Pentium 90. I figure late 1996. That Pentium 90 requirement should warn you that software MPEG will be a resource hog . . . and it should suggest that MPEG hardware may still be a good idea for some.

Basically, this upcoming development suggests users shouldn't shell out $200 for a board that does little more than provide MPEG. But when hardware MPEG migrates to the video adapter or if it winds up on the motherboard, this will be a good thing to use to help you decide what brands to get.

CD capacities will take a leap upward. Soon you'll be able to buy CDs containing over 7 GB of data—more than a tenfold increase from the current 650 MB. The bad news is that your current CD drives won't read the new-format CDs. There is a standards war brewing, so if you rush out to embrace one format, you may find yourself like those folks who have betamax VCRs in their closets.

The bottom lines are two. Don't invest in a high-capacity format CD-ROM drive until you are sure who is winning the war; and bear in mind when you are buying current standard CD drives that the technology is going to be obsolete in a year or two!

CD Changers are clearly up-and-coming devices; they're currently included as standard equipment in Gateway's top-of-the-line machines. Changers allow you to put several CDs in a single magazine and (jukebox style) have one or another moved into the readable position. Each CD has its own drive letter and accessing a drive letter switches in that CD if it is not already loaded. Change times run about fifteen seconds.

These are a great convenience if you have several CDs you use regularly. With prices dropping, some users will find them irresistible. They are wonderful as a second CD device but not so attractive as your only CD drive because juggling the multi-CD magazines is a pain—more of a nuisance than fooling with CD caddies and much more of a pain than using a caddiless CD.

What You Need . . . and Don't

Oh ye gods, grant me this:
that I shall have little and need nothing.

—Apollonus of Tyana, ca. 30 A.D.

11th commandment—Covet not thy neighbor's Pentium.

—Heard on the Web

The Multimedia PC Working Group (commonly called MPC) has, over the years, established "standards" for multimedia PCs. Although you aren't bound to slavishly adhere to any of their recommended specifications, I thought it might be instructive for you to see how the definition of an "MPC PC" has changed over the years—and to see what multimedia software manufacturers are currently targeting as a standard machine (see Figure 6-2).

	MPC Level 1, 1991	**MPC Level 2, 1993**	**MPC Level 3, 1995**
Central Processor	386/16	486/25	Pentium-75
Memory	2 MB	4 MB	8 MB
Hard Drive	30 MB	160 MB	540 MB
CD	Single speed	Double speed	Quad speed
Audio	8 bit	16 bit	16 bit, wavetable
Video	None	None	MPEG-1 320 × 240 at 30 fps

Figure 6-2. MPC levels 1 to 3

I think MPC's new requirement for wavetable synthesis really puts the spec back on the map. It's an important part of any modern multimedia PC. (I discussed wavetable versus FM synthesis in Chapter 2.) Conversely, the MPEG-1 playback requirement (in a 320 × 240 pixel box, running at thirty frames per second) may be just a tad premature. Some people may be stampeded into buying MPEG video cards when, with just a bit of patience, they could use their existing hardware to slide down the technology curve. Software-based

MPEG—which doesn't require an expensive MPEG video card—is coming with a future version of Windows.

But remember that Microsoft's software MPEG requires at least a Pentium 90, which is why I recommend that if you're getting a new PC, get at least a Pentium 90.

So much for the theoretical. Let's get down to brass—uh, brassy—tacks.

In Chapter 1 I gave you my list of hardware requirements for running Windows 95. I'd like to go into a bit of detail here, assuming you're going to buy a new PC, and use it for running Windows 95 applications. If you don't understand all the technical terms here, don't worry. Just make sure that the person taking your order understands that you expect all this stuff.

Processor and Memory   Look for a Pentium (or "586") class processor, running at least 90 MHz on a PCI/ISA bus. Avoid anything marked EISA, MCA, or VLB. Make sure you have room left in the case for several new add-in cards, but don't pay extra for "upgradable" systems. You will want at least 128K of Level-2 ("L-2") memory cache. 256K is nice, but don't pay for any more than that. Some manufacturers claim that their faster main memory ("EDO RAM") eliminates the need for an L-2 cache, but I don't buy it. Get at least 8 MB of main memory, but don't pay extra for more than 16 MB.

Video   You will want a 17-inch or larger monitor with a dot pitch of 0.28 mm or less. (Before buying a behemoth, check and make sure your desk can hold it!) Your video card should connect to the PCI bus, have a driver made specifically for Windows 95, and be capable of running a resolution of 1024 $\times$ 768 with a minimum of 256 colors, at a refresh rate of 70 Hz or more.

Disks   Get at least 1 GB of hard disk space, on an Enhanced IDE ("EIDE") drive.* Make sure you have a 1.44 MB floppy drive, but don't bother with a 1.2 MB unless you absolutely know you need one. Splurge for a quad speed CD-ROM drive (connected via EIDE, SCSI, or a proprietary card; doesn't matter), but don't pay extra for anything faster than quad speed. Don't pay extra for SCSI unless you have a burning need for a scanner or high-capacity tape backup—and you have a high tolerance for pain. Caching EIDE controllers are also a waste of money; put the bucks in main memory, and let Win95 handle the cache.

---

* Also known as Fast-ATA. Don't let the terminology get you down. It's all marketing hype.

Audio   You'll want a Sound Blaster–compatible 16-bit sound card with Wavetable synthesis. Speakers are a black art; pick ones you like. Make sure the speakers have their own power: the power supply on most sound cards won't drive a wet noodle. Don't be afraid to shanghai an old stereo system and use it in place of "genuine" computer speakers, as long as you're sure the speakers are shielded, or they sit far enough away from your monitor so it doesn't go bananas.

The Rest   Find a keyboard you can live with, and a mouse that feels right. (Most cheapie keyboards and mice—the ones that come bundled with systems—are crap; buy good ones, and keep the old cheap ones as a backup.) Get an uninterruptable power supply (UPS) rated at 250 VA or more. If you need a modem, go straight for a 28.8 Kbaud ("V.34") external unit with a long warranty; don't bother with anything wimpier. PCI network interface cards are nice, but before you put out a lot of money on a fancy card, make sure that the main roadblock on your network isn't all the traffic; ISA interface cards may work just as well. Finally, spring for a small, cheap tape backup unit and a few pre-formatted tapes.

 Make sure that everything you buy is certified to work with Windows 95, but take it with a grain of salt. Plug 'n Play is nice, but it's going to take a while before all those peripherals really achieve the highest levels of Plug 'n Play enlightenment.

Most of all, don't skimp. Get everything you're likely to need for the next couple of years, and get it all installed when you buy the PC. If you have to wait to put the money together, wait. You'll save days of headache and tons of problems by getting your act together the first time.

The Transaction

> If you buy the cow take the tail into the bargain.

> —Thomas Fuller, *Gnomologia,* 1732

 When it comes time to buy that new machine, you have three options: get it from a local boutique computer store, fight off the crowds at the big discount chains, or order over the phone. Each option has advantages and disadvantages.

The Locals   Local stores can offer extensive help, before, during, and after your purchase. While you'll typically find a much smaller selection, and pay somewhat higher prices, than at the major discount stores, you're also more likely to find a salesperson who will take some time with you, make sure you get what you need, and help if something goes sour. The boutiques often service what they sell, too, and that can be a huge help . . . or a real disaster.

Superstores   The big chains—Computer City, Best Buy, Incredible Universe, Sam's Club, Price/Costco, and dozens of others—offer top products at prices that rival mail order. They also offer obsolete clunkers at prices that would make P.T. Barnum blush, and it's up to you to tell which is which. Often the chains carry products with weird model numbers, so it's almost impossible to tell if the machine you're looking at is the same one that was reviewed in last month's magazine article. That alone should give you pause. Big time.

A bit of advice on superstores, borne of much bitter personal experience.

- Don't assume that the product you see on the shelves is identical to a similar-sounding model, even if it's from the same manufacturer.

- Try to find a salesperson who will talk *with* you. (I dare you!) If a clerk can't converse in short, simple sentences that you can understand, assume he/she/it is trying to BS their way through the conversation.

- Once you've found such sales droids, stick with them. Buy from them. Pamper their egos. Call them for advice. But don't be too surprised if they up and quit in a month. Or a week. Superstores rarely pay enough to keep really knowledgeable techies happy.

- Make sure you get a no-questions-asked free return trial period, even if it only lasts forty-eight hours. (And I do mean free: none of this "restocking fee" garbage.) Take your new hardware home, install it immediately, and batter the living daylights out of it. If you have any misgivings, return it before the trial period ends. Ask questions later.

In many cases you'll find that the customers in superstores know the products better than the clerks. Don't be afraid to talk to strangers—*the stranger the better*—while shopping in a computer superstore.

Mail Order   Unless you're absolutely convinced that you need the one-on-one attention provided by boutiques or superstores, mail order is the only way to go. You'll consistently find the best products at the lowest prices by ordering over the phone. Of course, you have to know what you're doing, or at least be able to fake your way through it.

The best place to start your mail-order trek has to be *Computer Shopper,* the 500-pound-gorilla of the computer monthlies. Learn to use the index in the back, and brace yourself—the *Computer Shopper* experience, with hundreds of companies selling tens of thousands of products, can be overwhelming.

Just about any product you find reviewed in the major magazines will appear in *Computer Shopper,* with the latest features and prices in prominent display. Don't be intimidated. Pick up the phone and see if one of the mail-order companies can beat the best deal you find at a boutique or superstore. The money you save may be your own.

Repairs at mail-order companies differ from repairs at boutiques or superstores. If something goes wrong with your mail-order computer, you have to call the company and talk to their tech support people. They will try to step you through some simple diagnostics, and maybe a repair or two. Not until they have exhausted all reasonable possibilities will they issue you something called an RMA, or Return Merchandise Authorization, number. Almost every mail-order company requires an RMA number, prominently marked on the package, before they will accept any product for repair.

Horror stories for mail-order companies' repair services abound. But then again, so do horror stories with boutiques and superstores, which are less likely to be focused on one manufacturer's products. Will you get better service from a superstore, a boutique, or from a mail order company? I dunno.

Brand Names   If you go the mail-order route, the onus is on you to find the right system to fit your needs. It may help to discard some old prejudices. Some folks still believe that the only good PCs are ones manufactured by a "first-tier" company—say, IBM, or Apple, or maybe Compaq. That's simply not true: IBM, for example, has certainly had its fair share of clunkers. More than its fair share. Some people refuse to go beyond the "second-tier" of PC companies—maybe Dell, or Gateway 2000, or one of the other half-dozen or so largest firms. That's silly, too. Plenty of PC companies you've never heard of make and sell thousands of PCs every month.

Keep your options open. Small companies offer outstanding products, too, and the service and support to back them up. Watch the surveys in the major magazines: a company noted for its outstanding customer service this year may descend into repair hell a year from now, only to emerge as a paradigm of customer support a year later. It's happened before, and it will happen again.

Remember. Parts is parts.

Credit Cards   One enduring piece of advice when conducting computer transactions: use a credit card. Shun vendors who refuse to take credit cards. They're bad for you, and they're bad for the industry.

Why? Because a credit card is often the only recourse you have if the product you thought you bought isn't what you received. Rip-offs, both intentional and unintentional, abound in the computer biz. Don't set yourself up to be a victim.

Hard Times in Win9x

> All progress is based on a universal innate desire on the
> part of every organism to live beyond its income.

—Samuel Butler, *Note-Books,* ca. 1890

Several technologies with the potential to greatly increase Win95 processing speeds loom on the horizon. As is so often the case, the crystal ball is cloudy. Nonetheless, it would behoove you to keep an eye on some of the developments—and ignore others.

Bus Wars   In spite of several attempts to revive it, the VL-B local bus is a has-been, as are EISA and MCA. Only a putz would buy into those now. The up-and-comers: PCI, the local bus version you'll find on almost all Pentiums; Enhanced IDE (EIDE), which supports up to four devices (hard drives, and some CD and tape drives), usually on the motherboard; and good old ISA, the architecture that wouldn't die.

If you don't already have Enhanced IDE on your PC (simple check: can you connect four different hard drives?), installing an EIDE board, to the tune of about $50, would be an excellent idea.

SCSI continues to mutate (Fast SCSI, Ultra SCSI, Fast and Wide SCSI-2, SCSI-3, *ad nauseum*). Adaptec's ASPI driver makes SCSI easier than before, but you can still expect hassles with cable lengths, terminating resistors, manually configured addresses, and the rest of the SCSI madness. In spite of what you've read, there's no perceptible performance difference between an EIDE hard drive and a SCSI hard drive, and none of the new SCSI flavors will change that. Avoid SCSI unless you have no other choice.

I disagree, oh divine Sarah. I wouldn't consider a truly high-end PC without an Adaptec SCSI card. The best scanners are driven by SCSI, as are the best CD changer systems. While EIDE drive sizes are going up, truly huge drives still require SCSI, and to back up those huge drives you need SCSI tape. True, there are hassles, but they are getting fewer, and it appears Plug 'n Play may help more. On top of this, with SCSI connecting all these devices, it takes a single slot in your PC.

The Portly   Enhanced Parallel Ports (EPPs) are off to a stumbling start. Intended to speed the parallel connection and provide feedback from the peripheral to the PC, EPP instead bogged down in a morass of conflicting specs. Indeed, it seems the winner in the port wars may be a technologically more sophisticated design called the Enhanced Connection Port (ECP). Windows 95 supports both EPPs and ECPs but alas, most peripherals don't yet support them properly. It remains to be seen if HP can bring some sanity to the enhanced parallel port mess—and if HP doesn't do it, no other effort will have any impact.

Infrared ports (the "red eye" that eliminates the need for cables connecting your PC and, typically, your printer) leave much to be desired, too. As of this writing anyway, they're slow, error-prone, very sensitive to the location of both PC and printer, and dependent on unreliable drivers. The situation will improve, no doubt, but before buying one you should pay particular attention to speed and reliability concerns.

Serial ports, on the other hand, are due for a big breakthrough, probably playing out by the time you read this. Intel and Microsoft put their heads together and came up with a replacement for the slow, unwieldy, 1970s-vintage serial bus. The new Universal Serial Bus (USB) uses daisy-chained "hubs" to control serial devices—the keyboard, for example, may become a hub for a mouse, digitizer pad, magnetic card stripe reader, and joystick. The two serial ports on the back of your PC, the keyboard connector, microphone and speaker jacks, and joystick connector will all be replaced by a single plug that leads to a daisy chain of hubs.

USB can handle up to sixty-four devices, and can transmit data at a rated 12 MB per second (Mbps). That isn't as fast as some competing technologies (e.g., Apple's so-called "Fire Wire"), but it should be plenty good enough to handle typical serial devices.

Memory Skirmishes   Almost a dozen different kinds of new memory technologies are headed down the pike. One of them, Extended Data Out RAM or EDO RAM, appears poised to roll over the entire industry, as soon as enough manufacturing capacity comes on board. EDO RAM speeds up memory processes by 10 percent to 20 percent and costs no more than standard RAM.

Well, let's put it this way. It costs no more to manufacture than regular RAM. What these turkeys will charge for it is anybody's guess. When you decide to go with EDO RAM, you're stuck with it: All your memory upgrades have to be EDO RAM, too, and when manufacturers find a captive audience, they tend to, uh, unelasticize the price.

Keep an eye on something called Rambus RAM. The folks at Rambus may have found a novel way of rearranging both memory and the bus that controls it, and draw huge performance increases in the process.

Expect to see new, exotic forms of cache memory, too, but don't be swayed by the marketing hype. Pipelined-burst cache, for example, doesn't run any faster than the kind you'll find in most machines. Watch the Winstone ratings—if a manufacturer finds a significantly better kind of cache, it will show immediately in their machines' Winstones.

Video memory keeps changing, too, in the never-ending battle between price and performance. VRAM, current leader of the video memory pack, might soon give way to WRAM (Windows RAM) and SDRAM (Synchronous Dynamic RAM). Again, watch the Winstones.

Faster Communications   Fifteen years ago, at the dawn of the computer age, modem speed was 300 bits per second (bps). We are now at 28,800 bps, almost 100 times as fast. There seems to be a general consensus that we can't go much higher with ordinary phone lines (on the other hand, some pundits said that at 14,400 bps) and some folks have unacceptable error rates at 28,800 bps. On the other hand, pictures on the World-Wide Web—videos, sounds, and so on—cry out for higher bandwidth. You might say that with a 28,800 modem, you are on the Information Dirt Road.

Two technologies are being proposed to go beyond modems. The first is a special digital phone line called ISDN* and the second is direct connection using the technology that drives TV cable. ISDN out the box supports 64,000 bps and sometimes with special tricks you can get twice that if your software and the service provider's software support it and the wind is blowing in the right direction that day. ISDN is available now, although there may be a wait getting installation from your local phone company. Figure $150 installation for the phone line, $500 for the ISDN modem, and $20/month for a phone line that you can't use for anything but digital connections.

---

* ISDN = Integrated Services Digital Network; I don't think you need to know that, but I know you like to see what acronyms stand for and then forget them (which is fine with me).

Cable technology promises rates of 10 Mbps, a thirtyfold increase over the current 28,800 bps! When in place, Internet sites will be about as fast as a local hard disk! The first experiments with this cable technology are just beginning, and widespread availablity isn't predicted until 1997 *at the earliest.*

 It isn't the Internet connection possibilities that is driving the installation of the kind of two-way cables needed for speedy computer communications. The drive is the race for movies on demand. The bandwidths needed for that are awesome, and computers will go along for the ride. That suggests that the computer connection may not cost much more than the cost of the cable connection, but for now pricing is totally up in the air.

 The bottom line for home and small office user? By all means, be sure to upgrade to 28,800 bps modems that have drifted below $200 and should be soon around $100. Pass on ISDN. Why invest in specialized technology that will be obsolete in a year or three?

 Infoworld's Stewart Alsop says that users will be confused by cable technology used for computers so it will fail; he recommends ISDN.

 Absurd! It seems as if ISDN is being driven by some press folks so in love with the technology, they haven't done the arithmetic of 64,000 versus 10 million.

DSP and NSP   Digital Signal Processors and its Intel variant called Native Signal Processors will have a heavy impact on computing. This technology allows a single chip (or a part of a chip if Intel puts an NSP on the CPU!) to be programmed on the fly for lots of different peripheral functions like modems, sound cards, and hardware MPEG. Some IBM portables already have DSPs built in, but for now, the pricing is such they aren't very common. But they will become part of the motherboard before long and heavily affect what is included on the standard PC. However, the technology will just be there and shouldn't concern most users.

Mom's Checklist

> In the heat of battle,
> Do not forget thy list.

—Amok Singh, *My Years in the Horde*

 Here's a quick summary of what you *really* need to know about buying hardware for Windows 95.

☝ Don't upgrade components for the sheer halibut. A 25 percent speed increase in any single component of your PC won't feel like much, and even a 50 percent increase (except in video) probably won't have you doing cartwheels a week after the new hardware is installed.

☝ Take the chart in Figure 6-1: "Relative PC Muscle" and my list of "What you Need . . . and Don't" with you when you go shopping. How much more processing oomph will $100 buy? $500? Are you forgetting something? The charts tell all.

☝ Lots of companies, from hardware manufacturers to magazine publishers, want you to believe their benchmark numbers will reflect the way you work. Hogwash. If at all possible, take a stopwatch down to your local computer dealer and try the applications you'll be using. If you have to rely on published reports, trust the Winstone ratings you'll find in the various Ziff publications, and ignore all the other folderol. Only the Winstone relies on timed performance of real Windows applications, albeit under laboratory conditions.

☝ Shop around. Unless you really need the personal contact, try mail order. Start with the latest copy of *Computer Shopper.*

☝ Keep an open mind. Big household-name computer companies aren't necessarily any better—or any worse!—than the second- and third-tier manufacturers.

☝ Before you return something to a mail-order company, call and get an RMA number. Make sure it's clearly visible on the outside of the returned package.

☝ Never, ever, pay with anything but a credit card.

All this Polonius-like advice gives me a headache. Time for a light-bulb joke break:

Q: How many Californians does it take to change a light bulb?

A: Six. One to turn the bulb, one for support, and four to relate to the experience.

Q: How many Oregonians does it take to screw in a light bulb?

A: Five. One to change the bulb, and four more to chase off the Californians who have come up to relate to the experience.

Q: How many New Yorkers does it take to screw in a light bulb?

A1: None of your damn business!

A2: 50. 50? Yeah, 50! It's in the contract.

Chapter 7

Staying on Top

Driving that train*
High on Rogaine™

—Amok Singh, *On Reaching Middle Age in the Middle Ages,* ca. 1365

 A couple of decades ago, a technically savvy person who worked at it full-time could keep abreast of all the important changes in the computer industry. Maybe a decade ago, an individual stood a chance of keeping up by focusing exclusively on PCs. A few years ago, a really with-it techie might've been able to keep up on Windows developments, if he or she worked at it full time and kept to the major hardware and software vendors—but that was a stretch.

 Nowadays, you don't stand a chance of keeping on top of all the important developments in the Windows arena. Nobody does. The product has become too diverse, too complex, too omnipresent. Win95 applications alone will keep your head reeling—hell, staying abreast of the details in just *one* app can be quite a challenge. To top it off, if you specialize in Win95 you really need to know a lot about DOS and Windows 3.1, too!

 So, what's a mortal to do? Well, you need to read and study this book, of course. But beyond Mom's book, as I see it anyway, there's a three-prong attack that combines the best chance of keeping up, while extracting the least amount of time and money. That's what this short chapter is all about.

---

* Jerry Garcia, the embodiment of the '60s, died while we were writing this book. Rarely has such a genuine human being graced this planet. He'll be sorely missed. Wherever you are, Captain T, I hope they still let you drive that train.

Prong 1: Mags

The best offense is an offensive defense.

—Amok Singh, *My Life Among the Horde*, ca. 1218 A.D.

Magazines are the single best, fastest, least expensive way to keep up to date on Windows 95 and its fallout. If you subscribe, a magazine will cost $1.50 to $2.00 an issue—an incredible bang for your staying-up-to-date buck.

Aw, c'mon Mom. You know that the guys who wrote this book also write for magazines all the time—Woody's a contributing editor at *PC/Computing* and on-line with *Ziff-Davis Interactive*, Barry's a contributing editor at *PC Magazine*, and a frequent contributor to *PC/Computing*, and they both have long ties with Ziff. Could it be that they slipped you a little *baksheesh* to put the magazine plug up-front?

Who, *me*?

Who, *moi*?

Pssst . . . I'll let you in on a little magazine trick. New subscribers often get special deals. If you care about saving a few bucks, when you get a renewal notice, call up the 800-number of the card and ask for the mag's best rate for new subscribers. (You may or may not get quoted the best rate, but it's worth a shot.) After you have a quote for the best rate, tell them you want to renew and assume you can get the same rate. Usually you can. If you don't, you can always let your subscription lapse.

Jeeeez, Erwin. You'd cheat your own mother. Anyway, the biggest question is, which magazines? At the top of the list has to be *PC Magazine,* with its 10,000+ pages a year of comprehensive coverage. *PC Mag* has it all: first-look reviews, opinion columns, programming tool reviews, blockbuster features, programming columns, tips, and reviews of home software.

Don't plan on reading *PC Mag* cover-to-cover. The features are so comprehensive that unless you are currently in the market for whatever it is they're reviewing, you'll probably want to skim or skip. A good strategy is to skim the big reviews, read the introduction and the Editor's Choice box, and then store away the subject for when you're in the market. Six months from now, you'll remember where to look.

As for second choice . . . that's a tough one. There are several fine user mags out there with outstanding Windows coverage. Here are my favorites. And, to make sure that some of these mags' editors still talk to me after this book hits the stands, I'll list them in alphabetical order:

- *Computer Shopper* has excellent columnists and good, pithy reviews. The ads, of course, are something of a national treasure—whenever you've chosen what you're going to buy, *Shopper* is the place to find the best price. The only downside is that lifting it may give you a hernia. Good choice if your postal carrier works out.

- *PC/Computing* has traditionally done a superb job of condensing a lot of meat into a format suitable for the busy—generally business-oriented, or, dare I say "corporate"?—reader. Recently they've loosened their ties and developed a sense of humor, too. (So what was Penn Jillette, chopped liver?) Good place to catch Barry and Woody—and also a few people who really know what they're talking about.

- *Windows Magazine* remains one of the best all-around user-oriented, uh, Windows magazines ever produced. Strong, focused coverage every month, with tons of useful Windows tips.

- *Wired* magazine is one of Woody's favorites, and he threatened to quit if we didn't let him mention it here. *Wired* contains stories way beyond typical techie dreck. Sure to challenge some gray cells. Woody hopes to be cool enough to write for it some day, and has already purchased a smoking jacket and cravat in anticipation of his first accepted manuscript.

Wait a minute, Sarah. Whaddya, nuts? What about *Windows Sources*? It has good coverage of the Windows world. And *PC World*? They put out a good mag. What happened to *Byte,* fer heaven's sake?

I've been wondering that myself. But I'll stick to my guns, Rush. Between *PC Mag,* and one or two of the others—*Shopper, PC/C, Windows,* and *Wired*—most people will get all the news that's fit to print, and more than they'll be able to absorb in a month. Besides, at some point you have to stop getting your electronic information from dead trees.

Speaking of dead trees, don't forget the weeklies, boss!

Oh yes. *PC Week* and *Infoworld,* the two tabloid-size (and, some would argue, much too frequently tabloid-quality) weeklies remain excellent sources of up-to-the-minute news. I used to think that *Infoworld* was better, all around, but I'm changing my opinion, especially after the butcher job they foisted off as Win95 coverage. (In fact, I would've categorically changed my opinion already, except *PC Week* started running stories like, "Windows 95 won't run your old disk utility programs!" as if that were news. My, my, my, that Mr. Gates must be a terrible man to force us to use such long filenames. Gimme a break.) Brian Livingston's column in *Infoworld* is still required reading for Windows cognoscenti; on the basis of his column alone, I would recommend *Infoworld* over *PC Week.*

Of course the beauty of both **PC Week** and **Infoworld** is that they're "controlled circulation" magazines. In other words, they send you a questionnaire, and if they like your answers, you get the magazine free. If you lie your butt off ("What? Of *course* I have 37 LAN servers at home! Doesn't everybody?") they'll sign you up. For a **PC Week** application form call 609-461-2100; for *Infoworld,* 708-647-7925.

Hey, you two are way behind the times. All of this stuff is on the net. Check out *Infoworld'*s home page at http://www.infoworld.com, and *PC Week'*s tie-in with http://www.ziff.com. You get the stuff sooner, and you don't have to lie bad enough to make a politician blush. The full content of *PC Week* is also on Interchange, the on-line service from AT&T. Stop getting your electronic news from dead trees!

Prong 2: Conferences

Never burn bad incense before good gods.

—Chinese Proverb

Another excellent way to keep up with new developments is by attending trade shows and conferences—the traveling carnivals of the computer age. Many of them will reward a day or two of effort (and sore feet) with a large crop of fresh new ideas. In addition to the local trade shows held all over the world, there are three national shows—each quite unique—worthy of your consideration:

- Fall Comdex, held each November in Las Vegas, continues to be the mother of all computer shows. It's a zoo—Comdex strains Vegas' infrastructure well beyond the breaking point, and the locals seem to hate the geeks just as much as the geeks hate the vapid Vegas glitz—but it's the most information-dense experience in the industry.

- PC Expo, particularly the one in New York, held in late June, draws throngs of exhibitors with Fall Comdex–off-season wares. Emphasis is on corporate computing. High marks from almost everyone who attends, although it is crowded and a bit of a pain—*pain* being a nice term for New York in early summer.

- EEE ("E Cubed"), the Electronic Entertainment Expo, held in Los Angeles, is rapidly overtaking the Consumer Electronics Show as the place to see and be seen in consumer electronics. Very different slant from Comdex or PC Expo, but if you're into electronic toys of every imaginable description, EEE is your show.

Wait a minute! What about Spring Comdex, or PC Expo in Chicago? Or the biggest convention of any kind, CeBIT in Hanover? I mean, there are dozens of big conventions, every year, all over the world. You really missed the boat on this one, Mao.

Au contraire, oh dusty one. If you really wanted to go to all the major computer shows, you could probably go to one *every single day of the year.* For people who have to get real work done, Fall Comdex and PC Expo will keep you abreast of the industry with minimal down time better than any other pair of shows, and EEE can't be beat for electronic fun 'n games.

Of course, if you're seriously in the biz, the plethora of developers' conferences are crucial—if you can find one that covers your topic. (What, they don't have a conference yet for bald, overweight, word-processing template developers with webbed feet? It's only a matter of time. Hmmmmm . . . Sounds like a good candidate for a track at TechEd.)

Prong 3: Get On-line

Half the world does not know how the other half lives.

—Rabelais, *Pantagruel,* 1533

Way back in the hazy mist of pre-history, when the crew put together the original *Mother of All Windows Books,* there was absolutely no question that any serious Windows user needed to subscribe to CompuServe, to get specific Windows-related questions answered and to keep on top of the latest developments in Win-dom—at least, faster than the three-month lag time inherent in publishing magazines would allow. Let me tell you. Times have changed. While it's every bit as important as ever to get on-line, the choices for the Windows Wise are not nearly as straightforward as they once were.

Let me try to give you an idea of the services currently available from each of the major on-line choices. They are not mutually exclusive: many people will find that more than one service meets more than one part of their needs. Here are the major on-line alternatives, accurate as of press time, arranged in alphabetical order:

- **America Online,** once something of an underdog in the on-line arena, has emerged as a top-notch service for consumers. Although not as techy-heavy as CompuServe, AOL excels in entertainment topics and easy Internet access. Relatively few computer companies maintain a presence on AOL, but it's usually easy to get technical questions answered. AOL charges $9.95/month for the first five hours; extra hours are $2.95. (AOL was considering a heavy user pricing option, but it wasn't available at press time.)

- **CompuServe** still beats the competition in high-tech coverage. The largest libraries of software are on CompuServe; most major computer companies are directly available to answer your questions; and the people who haunt the forums are the most knowledgeable anywhere. The CIS standard plan runs $9.95/month for the first five hours; extra hours are $2.95. The heavy user plan is $24.95/month for the first twenty hours and $1.95 an hour after that.

- **Interchange,** from AT&T, hasn't drawn much of a following. Plagued by buggy software and cantankerous customer service, Ichange is still an on-line service in search of a niche. Both *The Washington Post* and Ziff-Davis maintain high profiles—indeed, to subscribe to Ichange, you must actually sign up with the *Post,* or Ziff, or one of the other content providers. Ziff writers appear frequently to answer questions. Interchange costs $4.95/month for the first five hours, but customers must also sign up with one of the content providers, for an additional $5 or so a month. Extra hours run $2.95.

- The **Internet** is really a world unto itself. Unmoderated newsgroups on technical subjects have, in recent years, become overwhelmed by large numbers of people seeking answers, with few knowledgeable responses. Moderated newsgroups fare better. By far the easiest way to start poking around Windows parts of the Net is by starting with one of the big Web index sites like http://www.yahoo.com, or even Microsoft's http://www.microsoft.com. Microsoft's "The Internet" icon puts you in http://www.home.msn.com. We've seen a lot of useful info at http://www.netex.net/hyper95/get/tricks.html. The Net is free, of course, once you get on. Local Service Providers range from $1 to $3 or more an hour.

- **Microsoft Network,** at this writing, is putting up a good fight along all fronts. You can, and should, expect the tech support on MSN to be sterling for any Windows-related questions. (Surprisingly, there are many who feel the best OS/2 support is on MSN as well!) While MSN lacks CompuServe's huge download libraries, and several major content providers (particularly in the entertainment industry) choose AOL over MSN hands-down, overall MSN is an excellent choice—providing it can keep up with demand. The standard plan is $4.95/month for the first three hours, and $2.50 for each additional hour. The heavy user plan costs $19.95/month for the first twenty hours, then $2.00 for each additional hour.

- **Prodigy** takes the cake when it comes to general "home" use, Gen-X entertainment, and games. It pulls up the rear for advanced technical support. Asking a tough Windows question on Prodigy is a lot like asking Monty Python about the meaning of life: you might get a correct answer (assuming one exists!), but you wouldn't want to bet the family jewels on it. The standard plan is $9.95/month for the first five hours, then $2.95 for each additional hour. The heavy user plan is $29.95/month for the first thirty hours, with extra hours also billed at $2.95.

All of the services have direct connections to the Net; the nature and flexibility of those connections change weekly.

Usage	AOL	CompuServe		Ichange	MS Network		Prodigy	
		Std	*Heavy*		*Std*	*Heavy*	*Std*	*Heavy*
3 hours/month	9.95	9.95	24.95	9.95	**4.95**	19.95	9.95	29.95
5 hours/month	**9.95**	**9.95**	24.95	**9.95**	**9.95**	19.95	**9.95**	29.95
10 hours/month	24.70	24.70	24.95	24.70	22.45	**19.95**	24.70	29.95
20 hours/month	54.20	54.20	24.95	54.20	47.45	**19.95**	54.20	29.95
30 hours/month	83.70	83.70	44.45	83.70	72.45	39.95	83.70	**29.95**
40 hours/month	113.20	113.20	63.95	113.20	97.45	59.95	113.20	**59.45**
50 hours/month	142.70	142.70	83.45	142.70	122.45	**79.95**	142.70	88.95

Figure 7-1. On-line service prices

Each service except the Net has different pricing plans, sign-up offers, giveaways including free access software, varying levels of support, and access/availability that can range from superb to dismal, often within the span of twenty-four hours. (The Net, of course, is free, has no software and no support, and requires an independent firm to give you access.)

Here, as of press time, are the fees being charged by the major services, at each of several levels of use (Figure 7-1). The cheapest option at each level is marked.

So you can see, just as there is no clear-cut content winner in the on-line service race, there is also no price leader. Pick and choose, I say, and let the best service gobble up all but one or two of the others!

Kirk: What's going on in the engine room, Mr. Scott?

Scott: I dunnae know, Captain, but I'm giving her all she's got!

Kirk: Wrong line, Scotty. We're orbiting on impulse power.

Scott: The dilithium crystals are drained, Captain.

Kirk: There's nothing wrong with the crystals, Scotty. What have you been drinking?

Scott: It'll take at least a week, Captain.

Kirk: Mr. Scott, must you always speak in cliches that rarely pertain to the topic at hand?

Scott: If we push her any harder, sir, she'll blow!

Kirk: What does it take to get a straightforward answer to a simple question, Engineer?

Scott: I cannae lie to ye, sir. Microsoft hired me to write user manuals.

 The next four chapters should give you a good idea of what Windows is really doing when you install it, when it starts, when it runs, and when it goes looking for settings. As far as I know, lots of this is previously undocumented, or, at best, scantily documented. It seems that the creators of Windows don't really want you to look under the hood—at least, not until you crash and burn miserably, get tech support on the phone, and have *them* tell you to manually set a Registry entry or dissect a startup log file. Anyway, here's our best take on what's going on beneath the surface, the result of months of banging away at Win95 and recording what did, and didn't, happen.

CHAPTER 8

Crank 'er Up

Everything unknown is taken to be magnificent.

—Tacitus, *Life of Agricola,* ca. 98

 This chapter tackles Setup and Startup, two terribly underdocumented parts of Windows 95. *Setup* refers to the entire installation process, from preparing your machine for a new Win95 installation to cleaning up the mess that Win95 so often leaves behind, as well as finding, installing, and deleting portions of Win95 as your predilection (or abject fear) may dictate. *Startup* refers to all the things that happen—and can and do go wrong—between the time you turn on your machine and the point when Windows's smiling face, the Desktop, appears.

 Actually, Sarah, Microsoft's *Windows Resource Kit* goes to extreme lengths to explain all the details of Setup. But the majority of the nitty-gritty is for network administrators. For example, the *WRK* covers "Push" server installation in amazing detail. What they've omitted is a straightforward, cookbook description of how the majority of us Windows users should approach Setup, and what we should do when things don't quite run to textbook perfection.

 Be strong and of good faith. The Windows 95 installer is incredibly robust: in fact, it may be singularly the most bullet-proof program I have ever used. So try not to jump outta your gourd when you get an awful error message and want to cry and curse the Redmondians at the same time. Even if you do succumb to crying, follow the instructions on the screen (or in this book) while the tears flow.

 If you've already installed Win95, and never expect to go through *that* experience again, skip down to the section called "MS Marines Are Looking for a Few Good Men." The latter part of this chapter contains lots of important information, including a bunch of tips for making Win95 work better. Don't miss it.

Deciding How to Install

> Let men decide firmly what they will not do,
> and they will be free to do vigorously what they ought to do.

—Mencius, *Discourses,* ca. 300 B.C.

Spend a little time up front deciding *how* you're going to install Windows 95, and you'll avoid a lot of last-minute panic decisions that might land you in hot water—or irreversibly create the kind of Win95 setup you don't really want.

Up-front decisions fall into four categories: which version of Win95 you should get; whether you should install it from DOS or an earlier version of Windows; where you should install to; and how much of Win95 you really need. The decisions are pretty straightforward for most people, once they're presented without the obscure terminology.

Which Win95?

First things first. Which flavor of Win95 should you buy? That's easy. Unless Win95 comes preinstalled on your PC, you almost certainly want to buy the Win95 upgrade, since it "upgrades" almost any version of DOS, Windows, or OS/2. In other words, unless you assembled your PC from a kit, you'll want the upgrade.

If you're buying a new PC with Win95 installed, insist on getting the Win95 CD. If you're upgrading and you have a CD drive, get the CD version of Win95: list prices for CD and 3.5-inch floppy versions are the same, so why spend all that time shuffling diskettes? Besides, the CD has extra goodies.

Hey, boss, don't forget da games! The CD includes a neato game called Hover, a politically correct shoot-em-up game without the gore. Fast, too.

If you have the CD version of Win95 and an extra 30 MB of free space on your hard drive, consider transferring all of the installation files from the CD to your hard drive. Once they're all copied, you can install from the hard drive and futz around with settings and adding/removing components of Win95 until you're happy with your installation. Then you can simply delete all the files. Transferring all the files is easy: using DOS or your current version of Windows,*

---

* The diskette version of Win95 contains nonstandard .CAB files that can't be copied by Windows 3.1. But you can copy them once Windows 95 is installed.

create a new directory (called, say, `winstall`), then copy all the files in the Win95 folder from the CD to that directory. Then, when you run Setup, do so from that directory.

Wait a minute! Wait a minute! You forgot the collector's edition . . . and, along with it, the coolest bit of Win95 trivia to hit the presses. You know how we put holograms on our boxes, to prevent blatant copying? Well, we found out rather quickly that the counterfeiters in China could duplicate almost any computer-generated image we could come up with, no sweat. But they had no end of trouble duplicating all the subtle curves and textures of a photograph— particularly a photograph of a human being. So we decided to use the picture of a baby, naked from the waist up, as the Win95 hologram. He looks a lot like me.

Hey, I saw that box. I'm shocked—*shocked!*—that you decided to use a picture of a half-naked baby to sell Windows. You have the morals of a Hollywood producer. Selling books is another story, of course.

Flattery will get you nowhere. Anyway, we had 3 million boxes printed up before the officials in one Middle Eastern country informed us that such a disgusting picture would never be permitted to enter their country. We went back to the printer, reshot the picture (of the same baby, who was much older by that time)—in a shirt, of course—and made our PC hologram, uh, P.C.

So, if you can find one of the original half-naked baby boxes, hold on to it! Some day it'll be as valuable as the original Windows 286 disks—the ones that shipped with the first version of EXCEL.

Where From?

Once you've got the goods, and you've ascertained that you have at least 30 MB of free disk space (the amount of space necessary for a typical install over Windows 3.1), you need to decide from where you will install. Uh, from whence you shall install. From. (Pardon my dangling participle.) It all boils down to a question of what operating system is running on your computer when you kick in the Win95 installer. You have six options:

• Install Win95 from DOS. If you choose this option, Win95 actually installs a minimal Windows 3.1 system (including SMARTDrive), then switches over to that system before proceeding with the full Win95 install. To use this option, start by reading the rest of this chapter, then get DOS cranked up, switch over to the drive that holds the Win95 CD (or diskette or `winstall` directory), type `setup`, and hit `Enter`. (Note: you can't install from a DOS box in Windows 3.1!)

- Install Win95 from Windows 3.x or Windows for Workgroups 3.11. If you have Windows 3.x or WFW 3.11 working on your machine, this is the way to go. Most upgraders will choose this option, and for good reason. As you'll see in a minute, it's probably the best way to make sure all your hardware works under Win95 the first time around. To install from Win31, read the rest of this chapter, then quit all your Windows programs and use File Manager to run `setup` on the CD (or diskette or `winstall` directory); or in Program Manager, click on File, then Run, navigate to `setup`, and click OK.

- Install Win95 from Win95. Already have Win95 running on your machine, but you're afraid that some of the system files are hosed? This might be the way to fix the problem. Run `setup` from the CD (or diskette or `winstall` directory), and specify that you want to reinstall Win95 to the same directory, the one that currently contains Win95. The installer will automatically verify all the Win95 system files and restore any that have been clobbered. Note that you can't use Win95 to install a brand-new copy of Win95 (i.e., into a different directory). The installer won't let you. If you want to create a brand-new copy of Win95 in a new directory, you'll have to install from the DOS prompt. (To get there from Win95, click Start, then Shut Down, click the Restart Computer in MS-DOS Mode? button, and OK.)

- Install Win95 from Windows NT, to create a multiboot (WinNT, DOS, Win95) system. Since Win95 won't recognize NT File System (NTFS) partitions on your hard disk, you need to set up at least one FAT partition and format it. Read the rest of this chapter. Then make sure WinNT is set up to dual boot. Use the dual-boot to get into DOS. (Do *not* boot to DOS from a floppy; if you do, you'll wipe out WinNT!) Switch over to the drive with the Win95 CD (or diskette or `winstall` directory), type `setup`, and `Enter`. Note that the Win95 installer isn't smart enough to pick up WinNT settings, so expect a rocky ride with any moderately unusual hardware. Also note that once you've installed Win95, running DOS from the WinNT multibooter is a bit convoluted: pick DOS from the multiboot menu, hit `F8` when the "Starting Windows 95 . . ." message appears, then pick Command Prompt Only (option 6) from the Win95 startup menu.

- Install Win95 from OS/2. This option requires some real *cojones,* as neither IBM nor Microsoft is going to be too happy about helping you make it work. Microsoft says you must first install MS-DOS (*not* PC-DOS), make sure you are running MS-DOS (presumably through dual boot), have at least one FAT partition, and run the Win95 install from DOS. From what we've seen the setup goes OK from PC-DOS, but if something goes kablooey, Microsoft probably won't help you, and IBM is likely to say, "Windows 95? What's that? We don' do no steeeenkin' Weeeendoze 95!" If you're running OS/2 boot manager, the Win95 install will wipe it out. You can restore OS/2 boot manager by running OS/2's FDISK, which is on the OS/2 boot disk. And, just as with Windows NT, do not boot an OS/2 machine with a DOS floppy and then install Windows 95—Win95 will wipe out OS/2.

If you want to be able to continue to easily boot into Win31 for a while or want to double-boot into OS/2 or Windows NT, look into *System Commander,* a well-done generic multiboot program from V Communications. You can phone (800) 648–8266.

• The sixth type of install is called a "Push" install, because it involves a network server "pushing" Win95 onto a networked machine. It's a topic unto itself, generally well beyond the scope of this book. If you're a network administrator struggling with a Push install, read the rest of this chapter, rub your lucky rabbit's foot, pour over Chapters 4, 5, and 6 of the *Windows Resource Kit,* stockpile a couple gallons of latte, and *(please!)* tread lightly on your users by implementing as few System Policy restrictions as possible. Remember that preventing users from choosing their own Windows wallpaper is as dumb as preventing office workers from putting family pictures in their cubicles. And remember what the movie *Easy Rider* had to say about Pushers.

Where To?

The next question is, install *to* what? Your new copy of Windows 95 has to live somewhere, and your choice of location can have many interesting— even devastating—ramifications. You have three options:

☞ Install Windows 95 on top of your current Windows 3.1 (or Windows for Workgroups 3.11) directory. Windows 95 removes a whole bunch of Windows 3.1 and DOS files, and sticks the new Win95 files in the old Win31 \windows directory. This isn't quite as final or as fatal as it may sound. Windows 95 actually compresses all the old files and saves them in a file called W95undo.dat, stored in the root of your boot disk. (I've heard of W95undo.dat files as small as 6 MB, but mine is a huge 26 MB.) If you should decide to uninstall Windows 95, the old files are restored. When you install this way, all the settings you have in old Windows .INI files are reflected in the Win95 Registry and all your old Program Manager groups get converted, so they appear on the Start/Programs menu in Win95.

☞ Install Win95 on top of your current version of Win95. This isn't so much an install as a refresh: Win95 scans the current system files and replaces any that appear to be damaged.

☞ Install Win95 to a brand new directory. There are two major advantages to this approach: Windows 95 doesn't get rid of any old files, so you can still boot to DOS and Windows 3.1; and the installation is "clean," so you can get rid of the junk that's been gradually accumulating in your Win31 \windows directory for all these years. But there are two significant disadvantages, as Mao will explain.

My advice is to do what Microsoft recommends, which is to install Windows 95 over the top of an existing Windows 3.1 system. If you have sufficient disk space, Windows will save the old systems files and you'll be able to uninstall Windows 95 if the urge should strike you. If you choose to install to a new directory, you get two small advantages but one huge disadvantage. The pluses: You can keep a double boot capability and more safely return to your pre-Win 95 state if you decide to. One minor disadvantage is that installing to a new directory takes a lot more disk space (figure on 10 to 15 MB extra, for a total of 40 MB space required for a "typical" installation). The whopper of a minus is that you'll have to reinstall every bloody Winapp, and most of your fonts, and you'll lose your program groups and any other customization you did. That's a bunch of powerful reasons for going with the default.

Yes, Mao, but you're forgetting one other factor. If you install to a new directory, it is a virgin install. As you've used Windows 3.x, you probably installed some stuff and got rid of it, but you were unable to do thorough uninstalls. So you probably have extra DLLs around, whole sections of your `win.ini` that are junk, and lots of flotsam and jetsam in your `\windows\system` directory. A fresh start is often the best thing—although, yes, there is the cost of reinstalling your applications. My bottom-line advice is to install over your Win31 installation if you've only been running Windows for a year or have a very simple setup. Do a clean install in a new directory if you've run Windows for more than two years or have a complicated setup.

Even if you decide to install into a new directory, run the install from within Windows 3.1, because if you run from DOS, Setup might not be able to find some of the real mode drivers it needs.

If your only interest is in double-booting Windows 3.1 and Windows 95, you're in luck: Win95 comes with its own double-boot feature. If you install Windows 95 in a new directory, the double-boot capability will be there automatically. To use it, simply hit `F8` within a couple of seconds of seeing the "Starting Windows 95 . . ." message flashing on your screen.* You'll be given several choices for starting modes; among them, `Previous version of MS-DOS` (option 8). Choose that option and your old `config.sys` and `autoexec.bat` run and you'll start up Windows 3.1 in no time at all if your old `autoexec.bat` ended in Windows 3.1.

---

* The precise amount of time, like many other startup options, can be modified by changing entries in a file called `msdos.sys`. We'll talk about `msdos.sys` a bit later in this chapter, then dissect it in detail in Chapter 9.

It isn't always quite that easy, of course. For example, my SoundBlaster doesn't work when I pop back into Win31; it bellyaches about some setting in `system.ini` that always seems to get screwed up when I install Win95, but by and large Win31 works fine.

Oh, and don't believe everything you hear about how hard it is to reinstall applications and re-form your groups, if you decide to install Win95 to a new directory. If you choose to install to a new directory, Setup will warn you that you'll lose all your Win31 groups and have to reinstall all software. That's only partially true. Sarah has found all sorts of tricks to ease the transition.

Right on. For example, if your old Win31 `\windows` and `\windows\system` directories are on your DOS `path=` (which you can set in `autoexec.bat`, the same as you did with earlier versions of DOS) any programs or DLLs required by existing Win31 programs will be found. Win95 is smart enough to look along the `path=` if it doesn't find the programs it needs in that new Win95 directory. Er, folder.

Besides, if you install to a new folder (or otherwise have some Windows 3.1 Program Manager Groups you need to convert for use under Win95), there is a program that will automate the conversion. It's called `grpconv.exe` and it's in the Windows 95 `\windows` directory. Er, folder. Running `grpconv /m` will start up the program and let you browse to pick a `.grp` file; alternatively, double-clicking on a `.grp` file will run `grpconv` on it. No matter if you run `grpconv` or double-click on `.grp` file, a subfolder of `C:\windows\start menu\programs` is created with the group name and each item of the group becomes a shortcut in that folder. That's precisely how Win95 converts groups when you install it in an existing Win31 `\windows` directory.

It's not just Program Manager groups. Windows programs usually convert just fine to run with a clean Win95. The only problems I've encountered are with application programs that look for `.ini` settings in the `\windows` directory, without searching the `path=`. If you know which `.ini` files a Win31 program uses, copying those `.ini` files from the Win31 `\windows` directory to the Win95 `\windows` directory (er, folder) may be enough to get the Win31 program running—in most cases, you won't have to reinstall the program at all. If the program supports OLE, it may pay to look for a file with extension `.reg` in its directory. If you find it, double-click on it and it should install the proper Registry settings into Windows 95.

Word for Windows 6.0 is one of those Win31 programs that gets persnickety about where its `.ini` file is located: it only looks in the `\windows` directory and refuses to look along the `path=`. If you install WinWord 6 under Win31, install Win95 to a fresh directory, and then run WinWord 6 under Win95, WinWord won't find its `winword6.ini` file, the one with all its customization settings. Start WinWord 6 under Win95 and it will look at the Win95 `\windows` directory for its `.ini` settings, instead of the old Win31 `\windows` directory.

Fortunately, the solution is pretty simple, once you know what's happening. Making WinWord 6 work with Win95 installed in a fresh directory takes two steps:

1. Make sure the Win31 `\windows` and `\windows\system` subdirectories are on the DOS `path=`. WinWord 6 needs a file called `SDM.DLL`, which is in the Win31 `\windows\system` subdirectory. By putting it on the path, Win95 will be able to find it when WinWord 6 comes looking for it. (If you don't want to put those subdirectories on the path, you can simply copy `SDM.DLL` from the Win31 `\windows` subdirectory to the Win95 `\windows` folder.)

2. To make sure all your customizing settings come through, copy `winword6.ini` from the Win31 `\windows` subdirectory to the Win95 `\windows` folder.

That's it. All the settings come across automatically, and WinWord 6 works just fine, no reinstallation required. I bet you'll find that most programs behave similarly.

If your purpose in a clean install is getting rid of junk, don't put the Win31 directories in your path. That defeats the purpose of the clean install. Systematically, try to get your programs running under Windows 95 as follows: first try moving `.ini` files for the program and try running the program. If a `.dll` program is missing, you'll probably get an explicit complaint and you can copy the `.dll`. Only if that fails do you need to reinstall the program. Once you've moved all the programs you want to keep and are sure you don't want to double-boot, you'll want to delete the Win31 `\windows` directory. My advice is: Once you first think it might be OK to run `deltree C:\windows`, wait a month and then do it. Mark it on your calendar. Go out and celebrate when you finally do!

How Much 95 Do You Need?

So by now you've probably decided you're going to install Windows 95 from Windows 3.1, and if you're a power user you'll probably install to a clean, new directory. (If you're a bit sheepish, though, you might've decided to install over the top of Windows 3.1. That's cool. *De gustibus non est disputandum,* eh wot?)

The last thing you must decide is *how much* of Windows 95 you want to install. The bare-bones size of Win95 will vary, depending on whether you are installing over the top of Win31 or Windows for Workgroups, or if you are installing to a brand new folder. Figure 8-1 lists the base sizes:

Type of Installation	Space for a Bare-Bones Install
Upgrade on top of Windows 3.1/3.11	20 MB
Upgrade on top of Windows for Workgroups 3.1/3.11	10 MB
Install into a clean directory	30 MB

Figure 8-1. Minimum "compact" disk space requirements

The Win95 installer will present you with three pre-fab options (Typical, Compact, and Portable), plus the opportunity to pick and choose from a list of the options you might want Custom. Figure 8-1 shows the size of a Compact installation. You have to add on all the additional space required by any options you choose.

Actually, the options aren't quite as simple as Microsoft would have you believe. The installer is quite clever in figuring out what kinds of hardware you have installed and modifying the default options accordingly. For example, if you choose the Compact option, and Win95 has determined that your machine has a modem installed, it will probably pick up "Dial-Up Networking" and "Direct Cable Connection," whereas modem-less machines won't get those on a Compact installation. There appear to be dozens, if not hundreds, of combinations, so use Mom's numbers as a guideline, not as a definitive statement.

Here's how the options shake out, listed in the order that you'll find the options if you choose a Custom installation, and then flip through to pick and choose your favorites. We tested this by using the Compact installation on a disk-poor PC with a modem; Portable installation on an older 486-class PC with a modem and sound card but no CD-ROM; and the Typical installation on an advanced multimedia machine with (detected) CD drive, sound card, modem, and network card, explicitly requesting both the Microsoft Network and Microsoft Fax. The sizes listed in Figure 8-2 (which can vary slightly from machine to machine!) are all from the Typical installation.

Option	Compact	Portable	Typical	Size
Accessibility (for physically disadvantaged)			Yes	0.4 MB
Accessories		Some	Some	
Briefcase		Yes	Yes	0.1 MB
Calculator		Yes	Yes	0.2 MB
Character Map				0.1 MB
Clipboard Viewer				0.1 MB
Desktop Wallpaper				0.7 MB
Document Templates			Yes	0.4 MB
Games				0.9 MB
Mouse Pointers				1.4 MB
Net Watcher				0.2 MB
Online User's Guide				7.8 MB
Paint			Yes	1.4 MB
Quick View				1.8 MB
Screen Savers		Some	Some	
Flying Windows		Yes	Yes	0.1 MB
Other Screen Savers				0.2 MB
System Monitor				0.2 MB
System Resource Meter				0.1 MB
Windows 95 Tour				2.5 MB
WinPopup (send messages on network)			Yes	0.1 MB
WordPad			Yes	1.4 MB
Communications	Some	Some	Some	
Dial-Up Networking	Yes	Yes	Yes	0.5 MB
Direct Cable Connection	Yes	Yes		0.5 MB
HyperTerminal		Yes	Yes	0.6 MB
Phone Dialer		Yes	Yes	0.2 MB
Disk Tools	Some	Some	Some	
Backup				1.2 MB
Defragmenter	Yes	Yes	Yes	0.3 MB
Disk Compression Tools	Yes	Yes	Yes	1.0 MB

Figure 8-2. Mom's installation component comparison

Option	Compact	Portable	Typical	Size
Microsoft Exchange				
MS Exchange	*	*	*	4.6 MB
MS Mail Client (uses Exchange)	*	*	*	0.6 MB
Microsoft Fax				
MS Fax (uses Exchange)	*	*	*	2.6 MB
MS Fax Viewer (uses Exchange)	*	*	*	0.5 MB
Multiple Language Support				†
Central European				
Cyrillic				
Greek				
Multimedia			Some	
Audio Compression			Yes	0.2 MB
CD Music Player			Yes	0.2 MB
Jungle Sound Scheme				3.4 MB
Media Player			Yes	0.3 MB
Musica Sound Scheme				0.7 MB
Robotz Sound Scheme				2.0 MB
Sample Sounds				0.7 MB
Sound Recorder			Yes	0.2 MB
Utopia Sound Scheme				1.0 MB
Video Compression			Yes	0.4 MB
Volume Control			Yes	0.2 MB
The Microsoft Network (uses Exchange)	*	*	*	2.6 MB

Figure 8-2 *(continued)*

---

* You're given the opportunity to install these portions of Windows 95 in a separate screen that invites you to install Microsoft Network, Microsoft Mail, and/or Microsoft Fax capabilities. If you choose any one of those, you also get the Microsoft Exchange software.

† Control Panel's Add/Remove Programs routine says Multiple Language Support takes 2.4 MB for one language; about 4.0 for two and 5.0 MB for all three.

As you'll see later in this chapter, this list does not include all the programs that ship with the CD—far from it! It's merely a list of all the options you'll find during a Custom installation, and/or later with the Add/Remove Programs applet in the Win95 Control Panel. For many of the more esoteric programs, you'll have to hunt through the CD and install manually. And some of the components that appear as installation options (e.g., disk compression and the defragger) disappear from the Add/Remove Program list after you're done with the installer, for reasons I don't begin to understand.

It should also be noted that the official, published list from Microsoft (in the *Windows Resource Kit*) is wrong, over and over again. Part of the problem, undoubtedly, lies in how the installer actually modifies the list of chosen (even available!) options, depending on whether any Win95 components have been installed previously, and depending on the hardware on the particular machine. Try it for yourself. You'll see.

I'm surprised that Typical installation doesn't include Quick View, which is often touted as one of Win95's big improvements; and the Clipboard Viewer and Backup, which almost everybody can use. I wouldn't even think of running Win95 without the System Resource Meter, and the System Monitor helps, too.

You forgot the games! Why doesn't the Typical installation include Microsoft's games? Free Cell, Hearts, Minesweeper, and Solitaire may not be the most awesome games on the planet, but they're all quite good . . . and they're free! Besides, they take up less than one megabyte of space, and even Windows novices—people who would have a hard time installing the games—would get a big kick out of them.*

It's more than just games. The Multimedia Sample Sounds include righteous MIDI files of excerpts from Bach's Brandenburg no. 3, Beethoven's Fifth and "Für Elise," "Dance of the Sugar-Plum Fairy," "Claire de Lune," "Hall of the Mountain King," and Mozart's Symphony no. 40. (If you explicitly elect to install them, they get copied to the Win95 `\windows\media` folder.) If you have a MIDI card, you really need to listen to these files.

---

* It's easy to claim your free games, even if you're still scared of blowing up your computer. Click on Start, then Settings, then Control Panel. Double-click on Add/Remove Programs. Click on the Windows Setup tab. Click Accessories, then the Details button. Make sure Games has a check mark beside it, and click OK. Click OK again. Now Windows 95 will ask you to insert a diskette or the CD in the appropriate drive. Do so. There. You just paid for this book!

Hey, wait a minute, fellas. Uh, ladies and fellas. You guys in the press have been roasting us 'Softies mercilessly for "program bloat"—the increased size of our programs, and how much disk real estate they demand. Now you're jabbing us for not including all your pet components in a Typical install! You can't have it both ways, guys.

Well, you've got a point, but it's not that simple. Some of the components that get installed are so poorly documented that most people probably don't even know they have 'em! For example, on a Typical install, if Win95 detects a network card, you'll automatically get a little "Accessory" called WinPopup. That WinPopup is so cool I can hardly stand it: with it I can send little messages to any person on my network, any machine, or all machines in a "broadcast." But to make it work, you have to manually make WinPopup start automatically every time Windows starts—and *there's no documentation on WinPopup* anywhere in the on-line Help file!

I prefer Winchat because it traces the entire conversation, but I guess that's beside the point at the moment; Winchat and WinPopup are described in Chapter 4. I can understand your frustration. Winchat, too, is not covered in the Win95 Help, and since it's not automatically copied from the Win95 CD to your hard disk, the contortions you have to go through to install it are pretty bizarre, too.

Microsoft is being super-conservative in how much hard disk space they say they use, just as the price of hard disks is falling through the cellar, *and* as disk compression technology (exemplified by Microsoft's own DriveSpace 3, which is part of Win95 and the Win95 Plus! Pack) has finally become rock-solid. When Windows 3.1 shipped, a 150 MB hard drive was a mark of luxury. Nowadays a doubled-up 850 MB drive, with an effective capacity of almost 2 GB, strikes me as rather pedestrian.

My advice? If you have 100 MB of free disk space, just go ahead and install everything. Think of it this way: hard disk space costs less than 20 cents per MB; half that if you use compression. If installing all of Win95 takes up an extra 70 MB, that's twenty bucks' worth of disk space—ten bucks if you use DriveSpace 3. Big highfalutin deal. Install everything. Live dangerously.

Preparing for Installation

To lead an untrained people into war is to throw them away.

—Confucius, *Analects,* ca. 500 B.C.

 Be prepared. That's where it's at. If you can follow all eight of Sarah's steps, covered in the next few pages, before you install Windows 95, you'll save yourself untold headaches during the process. An ounce of prevention is worth a pound of cure. Better safe than sorry. Look before you leap. In fair weather prepare for foul. Beware of Greeks bearing gifts. Ooops. Wrong aphorism.

 First a remark on what you don't need to do, or perhaps I should say, can't do! If you got the diskette version, you might want to exercise the safe computing lessons you learned long ago and make a backup copy of the diskettes. Sure there are—count 'em—thirteen diskettes but this is important stuff so you'd better go out, pick up a coupla ten packs of diskettes, and use diskcopy. Won't work. Oh, yeah, diskette 1 will copy fine, but not the others. In late 1994, Microsoft shifted over to a new format for diskettes that holds 1,716,224 bytes instead of the 1,457,664 bytes that standard 1.44 MB floppies hold. The problem is that to write this special format diskette takes special equipment so you won't be able to copy them. It is unfortunate that Microsoft went their own merry way on this.

 That extra 18 percent per diskette might not seem like much to you, but if we'd used normal diskettes instead of the new style we'd have needed fifteen diskettes per box instead of thirteen. That would mean a cost over the first year of Windows 95 sales of something like $5 million.

 A powerful argument, but that doesn't excuse the fact that until very recently, the installation instructions that came with most Microsoft packages told users to make a backup when they couldn't—you'd updated the diskette format but not the printed instructions. At least you've finally fixed that.

The files on the diskettes are also in a compressed format, so if you look at the third Windows 95 diskette, you'll find a single 1,716,224 byte file called `win95_03.cab`. That `cab` is short for *cabinet.* In Appendix E, I'll tell you more about the tool (called `extract.exe`) that comes with Windows for accessing cabinet files and I'll list the "real" contents of each diskette and each cabinet file on the CD.

Step 1: Double-Check the Chekhov list.

Equal exposure for Russians, I say. One last time, make sure your system is up to Win95 snuff. See Chapter 1 for a list of minimum requirements.

Step 2: Make a DOS emergency boot disk.

This one could save your PC's life, so listen up! If you don't have a boot disk, stick a clean diskette in the `a:` drive and type `format a: /s`. Copy across `autoexec.bat` and `config.sys` from your hard drive's root directory, and at a minimum `edit.com` and `qbasic.exe` from your `\dos` directory. You'll probably want to pack the diskette with `himem.sys` and `mouse.com` and any other programs that appear in `autoexec.bat` and `config.sys`.

Some older versions of DOS don't automatically copy `command.com` when you do a `format /s`, so make sure there's a `command.com` in the root directory of the emergency diskette.

If you already have an emergency boot disk, make sure it works! Stick it in your `a:` drive and hit your PC's Reset button. Make sure you know how to get Windows 3.1 started.

Step 3: Skin `autoexec.bat` **and** `config.sys`

The first hurdle you must clear to effect an easy Win95 installation is to clean up your `autoexec.bat` and `config.sys` files. If you're relatively comfortable with those two Files From Hell, hum a happy tune: once Windows 95 is installed, you may never need to touch them again. If you're a bit unsure of those two relics from a far sadder time, just follow along here and we'll teach you enough to go in and skin them alive.

As the commercial says, "They're germs. They deserve to die."

- Start by making backup copies. Using Windows 3.1 or DOS or whatever is handy, move over to your boot drive (normally `c:`), and make a copy of `autoexec.bat` called, oh, `autoexec.mom`; and make a copy of `config.sys` called `config.mom`.

- Now make sure Win95 doesn't get pointed in the wrong direction. Win95 is usually smart enough to find itself; but if there are vestiges of old Windows 3.1 flimflammery hanging around, Win95 can get confused. Open up `autoexec.bat` using Notepad in Win31, or Edit in DOS. If your `autoexec.bat` has either or both of these lines at the very end:

```
cd \windows
win
```

stick `REM` and a space in front of either or both lines, turning them into comments, effectively zapping them out. If they existed before, they should end up looking like this:

```
REM cd \windows
REM win
```

If you do `REM` out these lines but are installing to a new directory because you want to double-boot, be sure after the install to edit the file you'll find called `autoexec.dos` and remove the `REM` s. That'll be the `autoexec.bat` used when you dual boot to your old DOS.

- If the last line of your `autoexec.bat` calls another `.bat` file that contains those two lines, go into the other `.bat` file and `REM` the lines out.

- Close `autoexec.bat` (and any other open `.bat` files) and save changes.

- Using Notepad or Edit, open up `config.sys`. We need to get rid of EMM386's `highscan` parameter. If you have a line that looks like this:

```
device = emm386.exe 512 highscan
```

remove the `highscan` on the line. There may be many more parameters and worse-than-senseless things before or after `highscan`. Don't worry about them. Just zap the `highscan` and leave single spaces between the parameters.

- DOS 6.x let you specify multiple "configurations" in `config.sys`, using something called a `[Menu]` command, and let you choose among them when DOS started. Windows 95 still supports multiple configurations, in theory, but we've had nothing but headaches with them getting tangled up in Win95 setup. More than that, we can't think of one good reason to keep multiple DOS configurations in Windows 95. If your `config.sys` has a `[Menu]` command, pick the configuration you most often use and pare back `config.sys` to that single configuration.

- Finally, you'll want to get rid of your last drive setting. If your `config.sys` has a line that looks like this:

      lastdrive = e

remove the whole line. The letter on the end may be an `f` or a `z`, or just about anything. Don't worry about it. Zap out the entire line.

The kind of `lastdrive=` problem that can occur popped up on the system of my Master of the Sacred Texts. Said Master had a computer with a hard drive and CD set up by someone with `lastdrive=d` in `config.sys` to save a few bytes of low memory under DOS 6.2. The Master upgraded to Win95 and later installed a second hard disk. When he did, his CD-ROM was no longer seen by Windows 95! What had happened was that Win95 had moved the `lastdrive=` entry from `config.sys` and placed it in the Registry (key HKEY_LOCAL_MACHINE\ SOFTWARE\Microsoft\ Windows\ CurrentVersion\Setup with entry LastDrive set to "D"). I fixed him up, but it took forever to figure out what was going on.

- That's it for `config.sys`. Close it and save changes. Then reboot your machine entirely, to make sure you didn't screw up anything. You should be able to get into Windows 3.1 just like you normally do, except that you might have to type `win` and hit `Enter`. If there are problems, copy `autoexec.mom` back to `autoexec.bat` and `config.mom` to `config.sys`, and try again.

Step 4: Avoid memory lapses.

If you are running a third-party memory manager (for example, *QEMM* or *386max*), consider removing it before you try to install Windows 95. Otherwise, Win95 may set things up so it loads that manager for you every time you start Win95, but you don't want to do that! Running a Win31 version of *QEMM* or *386max* isn't likely to produce any problems, but you'll get no benefit and may lose memory.

The easiest way to remove QEMM if you are using it and DOS 6.x is to run DOS's `memmaker`. Just pop out to DOS and type `memmaker`. Don't even try to do anything fancy, optimize upper memory, or anything like that. Win95 will take care of everything later on. When `memmaker` is done, you should double-check `autoexec.bat` and remove QEMM's `dosdata` and `dos-up` programs by hand, if necessary.

Step 5: Check your hard drives.

 Windows 95 Setup is going to check your hard drives before it starts, looking for cross-linked files and the like. If Win95 setup finds errors, it's going to tell you that you need to run ScanDisk, and then it will stop running so you can comply. You may as well do it yourself before you run Setup for Windows 95.

To do so, exit Windows 3.1 and run ScanDisk. Run it on every one of your hard drives, not just the one that you are going to install Windows 95 to—because that's what Windows 95 setup is going to do.

It's probably a good idea to give your disks a real workout, defragment them, and just generally get your spinning platter house in order before the big Win95 installer hits.

Step 6: Back up, back up, back up.

 Ninety-nine times out of a hundred the Win95 installer works just fine. You may have to boot and reboot and cuss and kick your machine a few dozen times, but genuine data loss is so rare that you can safely ignore it, except . . .

Except when it happens to you, eh?

Don't be a chump. Back up. Back up. Back up. Every single file. Go out and buy a $150 tape drive if you have to: this is the perfect excuse to do what you should be doing every day anyway.

Step 7: Gather the stuff you'll need.

 Like most installers, the Windows 95 setup routines require you to enter some information. You'll need to know, uh, your name. ("Spiff, Citizen of the Univers" works just fine.) You can also enter a company name ("Spacely Sprockets," anybody?). If your PC is connected to a network, you'll need a logon ID and password—and if it's a Netware network, you can save yourself a lot of headache by entering your Netware ID and password correctly the first time.

Some of the other information is a bit more subtle. If you're connected to a network, you need to know your network workgroup name, and that name has to match your coworker's workgroup name precisely. You'll also need a unique node name for your PC. If you're going to set up Microsoft Fax to answer calls, you'll need an inbound phone number for your fax machine. If you're running Microsoft Mail, you'll need the path to your post office, your user name, and password. And you should know the manufacturer and "official" model name or number of every single piece of hardware in or attached to your PC. Dig out the old user manuals or receipts if you aren't absolutely sure; as a last resort, look for labels on the hardware itself.

Finally, you'll need one diskette that will fit in your `a:` drive. Everything on it will get wiped out, so don't use last year's tax return. That's about it.

Step 8: Brace yourself.

Whether you're installing from DOS, Windows 3.1, or Windows 95, you must first make sure all of your peripherals are working, and that you're connected to the network, if you have one. So reboot your machine afresh; bring up Windows 3.1 if you're going to be installing from it; test every single peripheral, including every disk drive, your modem, your printer, and especially your CD-ROM drive; then make sure your network connections are all working right.

Most important: turn off your screen saver. There's nothing worse than a crazy screen saver springing to life when you're trying to determine if your machine is frozen.

Now, hold your breath, pilgrim. It's time to take the big dive.

Setup Vérité

> It is no disgrace to start over. It is usually an opportunity.
>
> —George M. Adams

I have gone through gazillions of Win95 installs on many different machines and, while it can get a bit scary at times, invariably Windows 95 has always installed correctly. Every single time. Some of the icons' family members and associates can't say the same thing, but they tried to install before this book was ready and thus didn't have the advantage of Mom's sage advice and chicken soup.

In a nutshell, Windows 95 Setup takes a look at your system, figures out what parts of Win95 you need, then copies files and establishes preliminary hardware settings. After that it reboots, sets up some general items like Control Panel, and reboots a final time. During that final reboot, additional hardware drivers may get added. Invariably after the first or second reboot, Windows appears to get hung up in deep doo-doo. There may be a shift to text mode with a message about a fatal error. Or the hourglass pops up and stays and stays and stays, while Win95 drifts off to La-La Land. But just as invariably, when I reboot—by turning the PC off, then back on again, as specified in the Wizard screens—Setup recovered and got further in its process. On one machine the Setup Wizard crashed four times, and on each occasion I figured I'd bit the dust for good. But after those four extra reboots, Setup finished and the machine worked perfectly.

It's like I said at the beginning of the chapter. Be strong and of good faith. The Windows 95 installer is incredibly robust: in fact, it may be singularly the most bullet-proof program I have ever used.

The key to the Win95 installer's excellent non-self-destructiveness lies in several files that it creates and maintains as it's looking at your system. If the installer crashes once, it's smart enough to take a look at the log of its previous incarnation and skip over the step that hosed it the last time around. While it's true that this try-and-crash-but-live-to-try-again process can put gray hairs on the head of any PC user, it's a marvelously robust way to run an installer.

Let's step through a typical (which is to say, hassle-free) Win95 installation one screen at a time and see what's really going on. I ran this installation from Windows 3.1, using the CD version of Win95. Follow along as I explain the ins and outs of what appears on the screen.

Mao's Perfect Installation

From inside Windows 3.1, go into Program Manager, click File, then Run. Type the name of the drive (CD or diskette), then setup.

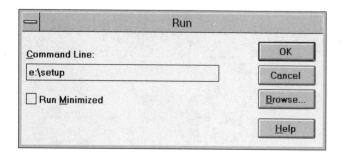

If you've already checked out all your drives by using ScanDisk, you can add the command line switch `/is` to keep the installer from checking again. If you know you have enough disk space, the `/id` switch will keep the installer from checking, too. It'll save a few minutes.

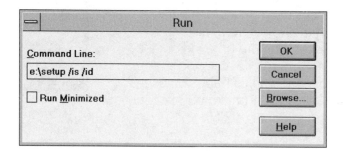

Yeah, yeah, yeah. You're cool, wired, and *very* good looking—not to mention intelligent—because you bought Win95.

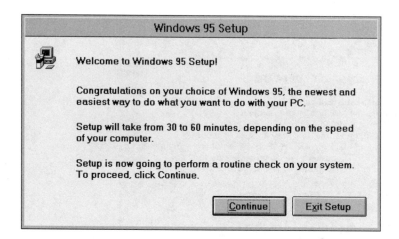

If you're very lucky, Setup will take a half hour. In most cases, I'd allow a leisurely afternoon (or a hectic evening) to get the beast installed and configured, and to get a good jump start on the Windows tour and tutorial.

If you did not use the /is and /id switches, this is what you'll see when the Installer runs ScanDisk. Allow several minutes—maybe more if you have a lot of hard disk space. Don't worry if the little magnifying glass pauses for a while.

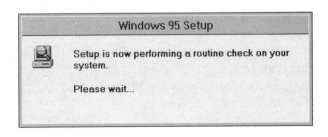

Satisfied that your hard disk isn't in danger of imminent demise, the Win95 Installer loads its Wizard and gets it started. If you're installing from DOS, the Installer actually sets up a minimal Win31 system before bringing out the Wizard. It's a watershed event. You can tell when it happens, as the white Win31 background in dialogs will suddenly shift to Win95 gray.

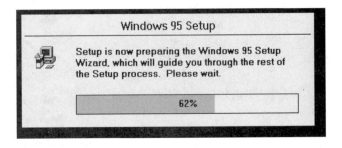

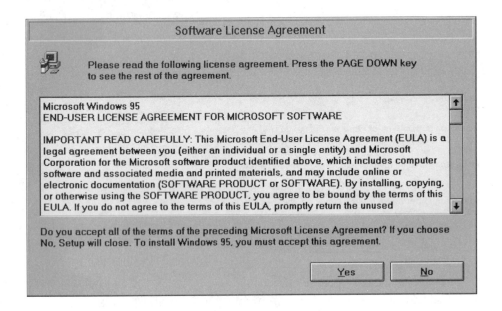

You'll be asked to accept the Microsoft End User Licensing Agreement (or EULA). It's a typical, unenforceable, one-sided "contract" that says you will only use one copy of

Win95 on one machine, you won't rent it out, and if your company goes bankrupt as a result of bugs in Win95, Microsoft only owes you the amount of the purchase price.* You know. The usual.

The Installer won't be able to update any files that are in use, so it would behoove you to close everything down. In practice, I've run some small programs while the Installer was running, but I wouldn't make a habit of it.

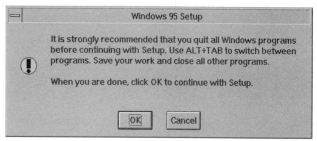

At last the Wizard appears, and your Win95 installation is almost underway. To proceed, click Next>. Note that you can exit at this point and nothing on your machine has been changed. Win95 starts keeping a log of all the choices you make, and the actions

---

* This is a personal—not a legal—opinion. If you have any questions, ask your lawyer, but be braced for the possibility that s/he may turn catatonic in laughter, and later sue you for loss of work time. Alternatively, you could try to hire Bill "Duke" Neukom and see what he says.

it takes in response to those choices, in a hidden file called `setuplog.txt`, which is stored in the root directory of your boot drive (e.g., `c:\setuplog.txt`).

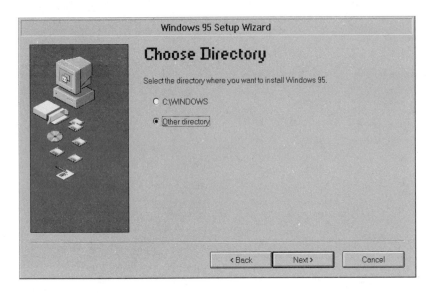

This is the single most important decision you will make during the installation. If you leave the top button checked, Win95 is installed over the top of your existing copy of Windows 3.x. If you click the lower button, Win95 will be installed to a new directory. For a detailed discussion, see "Where To?" earlier. (If you're a fairly knowledgeable Win31 user, you'll probably install a clean copy of Win95 to a new directory.)

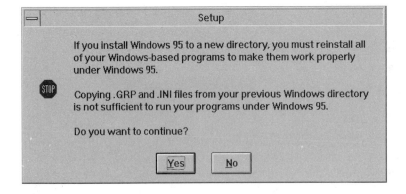

If you chose to install to a new directory, Win95 tries to scare you. You don't need to install all of your Win apps to make them work properly, you can reconstruct `.GRP` files with `GRPCNV`, and you can copy `.INI` files by, uh, copying `.INI` files. Don't let this little dialog box spook you.

If you chose to install Win95 in a new directory, this is where you type in the name of that directory. While Microsoft may recommend this only to "advanced users and system administrators," installing to a clean directory really isn't that difficult. And it gives you a chance to get rid of all the crap that's been accumulating in your old Win31 \windows directory.

The Win95 installer gets the new Windows folder started. (Yes! In spite of this dialog box's heading, at this point the location is destined to be a "folder," not a "directory"!)

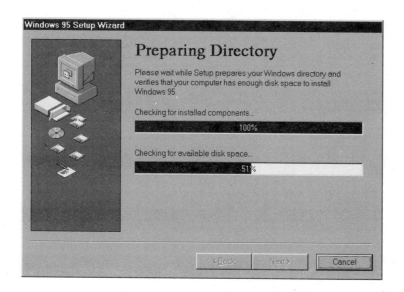

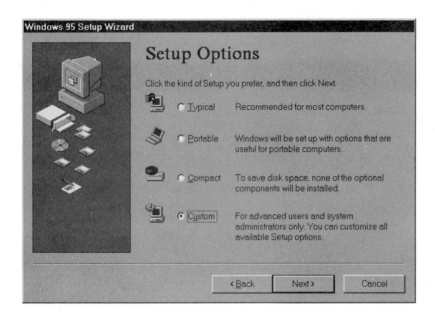

You can still cancel at this point and return to your old Win31 setup, without fear of being tossed into a weird half-Win31, half-Win95 twilight zone. (It can happen. Trust me. You don't want to be there.) I'll let you know when we reach the point of no return.

Now it's down to the nitty-gritty. If you're short on disk space, pick Portable or Compact. Otherwise, pick Custom. *Never choose Typical.* Why? Because all of the "Typical" choices are automatically selected when you choose Custom. By choosing Custom, then clicking `Next>`, you can see (later in the installation procedure) what Win95 wants to install on your system, then adjust the automatic choices as you see fit.

Time for a little breather. Once you've chosen your Setup option, the installer will probably ask you for your name, your company's name, and your product ID number. Make sure you use something for your name and your company's name that you can live with—it's virtually impossible to change once it's been entered, and that name can show up in the most embarrassing places.

The product ID number is on a hokey piece of paper in your Win95 box called a "Certificate of Authenticity." Yeah, sure. Authenticity. Anyway, as soon as you find the product ID number, get a permanent marker and write it on the label of your #1 installation diskette, or on the face (the printed side) of your installation CD. Two years from now when you've wiped out half your `\windows` directory or your hard disk has crashed, and the dog has desecrated your precious Certificate of Authenticity, you'll regret ever thinking of me as a dummy.

Now the installer switches gears, from asking you for information to analyzing the psyche of your PC itself. The `setup.log` file* contains information on everything you've chosen or typed up to this point. Attention now shifts to the part of installation called "Analyzing Your Computer." The file `msdet.inf` (located in your Win95 `\windows\inf` folder) comes to the forefront, guiding the way the installer goes spelunking through your PC. The results of its exploration are logged to a file called `detlog.txt`, which is in your boot drive's root directory. Er, folder. A separate file called `detcrash.log` contains detailed information about each installer attempt to reach out and touch something. That file is used if you land in the unfortunate position of requiring Safe Recovery—for if the installer's going to get hosed, this is where it's most likely to happen.

Follow along as we continue the perfect, hassle-free installation. Should your machine lock up while you're following in my footsteps, *don't panic.* Make sure that the screen is completely locked—the mouse doesn't move, the colorful Progress bars don't advance, the hard drives don't whirr, absolutely nothing happens—for a full five minutes. Time it with a watch. Only after you're completely sure the machine is toast should you follow the instructions on the screen to effect a recovery. (That means you physically turn off the machine— don't press `Ctrl+Alt+del`. Wait a minute or two, turn the machine back on, rerun Setup, go through the rigmarole of getting the Installation wizard going again, then click "Use Safe Recovery (Recommended)" on the Safe Recovery screen.) Sarah will continue with the scary part of the discussion in the next section, "What Can Go Wrong."

This is the "Analyzing" screen you'll see with a Custom install. The Win95 installer usually does a very good—even remarkable—job of detecting most common types of

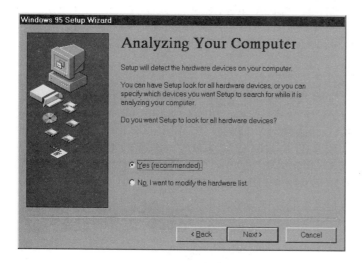

_____

* All of these files are dissected in Chapter 9.

hardware. You should only elect to modify the hardware list if you know for an absolute fact that a particular piece of hardware on your PC clobbers the analyzer every time—and you'd only know that if you've tried to run this analyzer over and over again and it's hung every time.

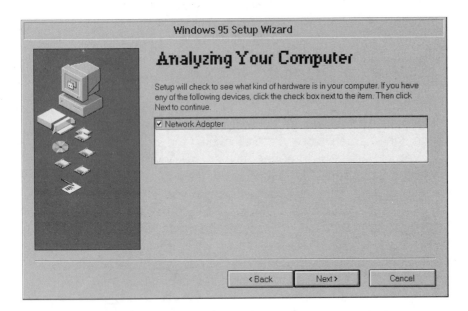

If you get a dialog box like this (which often appears on Typical installs, but only occasionally on Custom installs; I'm still not sure why), be sure you check each box that applies to your PC. The Seventh Ring of Install Hell awaits if you forget to check the CD-ROM box, then discover you only have the CD-ROM version of Win95 available to continue the installation.

The next dialog is the place the machine is most likely to hang up on you if it's going to. If everything stops for a span of five minutes, *don't panic.* Follow Sarah's steps in the next section to restart and proceed in Safe Recovery mode. Although you may feel lost, hangups at this point are quite normal, if not particularly reassuring. Oh. Don't trust that Progress bar. It can hop from 15 percent to 40 percent in a split second, then spend three or four minutes going from 96 percent to 97 percent.

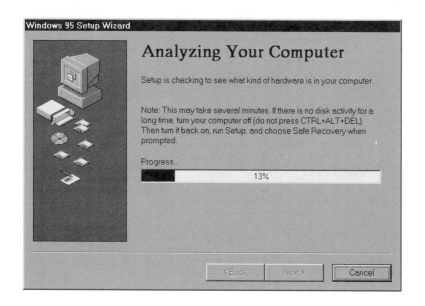

The next screen was added at the last minute: if you read a book about installing Win95 and it missed this screen, that's because the book was written based on an early beta-test version of Win95. Anyway, I'd recommend that you check the MS Network box if you have any interest in going on-line, and MS Fax if you have a modem. (MS Mail is only for folks attached to an MS Mail server.)

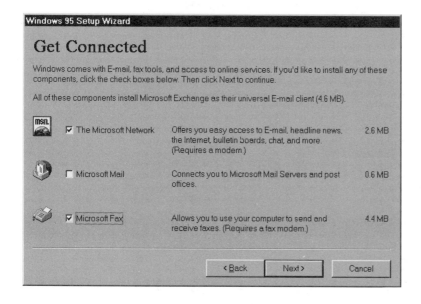

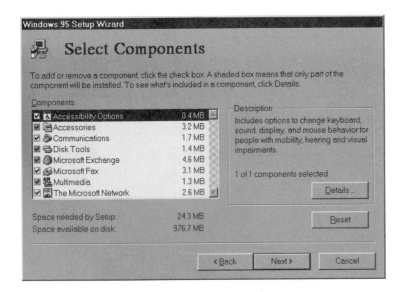

If you chose Custom installation, this is where you get to choose which components of Win95 will be installed on your machine. Note that the installer takes into account what kinds of hardware are installed on your machine before presenting you with this list, so the options you'll see may be different from the ones here. Don't sweat it if you forget something here. It's easy to Add or Remove components later.

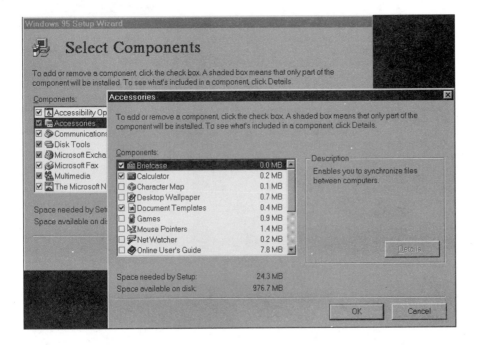

To pick specific components, click once on a category in the "Select Components" dialog, then click "Display." Choose whatever options you like. Components with only some options chosen appear with a check mark on a gray box. Pick all the options for a specific component by clicking on the component's box until you see a black check mark on a white box. It's a pain in the neck, but that's the only way Microsoft lets you do it.

Next, the wizard gives you a chance to make corrections to its choices for network protocols and dial-up networking capabilities. (In this particular case, I knew I would never need the "Client for Novell Networks," so I clicked on it once, clicked Remove, and it was gone.) If you're going to be on a network and you want other people on the network to be able to see your files and/or printer, click File and Printer Sharing right now.

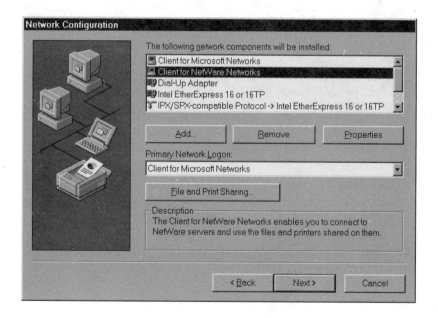

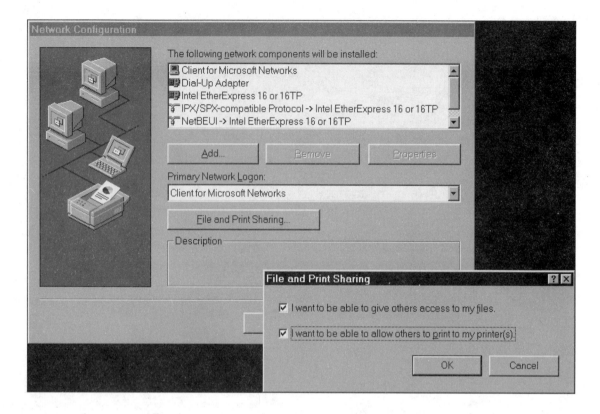

Setting up a Win95 peer-to-peer network is almost automatic, if you have the network hardware (interface cards, cable, and a hub, typically) working before you install Win95, and you remember to click this File and Printer Sharing button. If you forget, other people won't be able to "see" your computer on the network. If you forget to turn on sharing now, you can do it after installation by running the Network applet in the Win95 Control Panel.

The next dialog is where you need the precise name of your workgroup: other machines connected to your network have to use exactly the same workgroup name. In addition, the computer name must be unique within the workgroup. Be careful! You may be able to enter a computer name or workgroup name with spaces and odd characters, but some programs may go haywire trying to use them. Stick to simple names: letters and numbers.

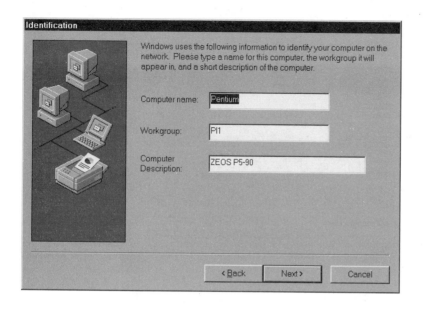

As something of a last hurrah in the "Analyzing" phase of a Custom installation, the Wizard lets you review which drivers it has chosen for your machine before they're actually put into use. In my experience, it rarely gets the Monitor right, stands at least a 50/50 chance of getting the Display right, and usually figures out all the rest. If you see something that's wrong (or something that *might* be wrong), click once on the offending setting and click Change.

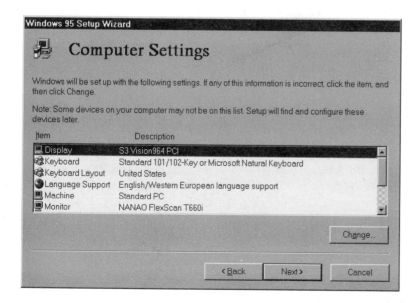

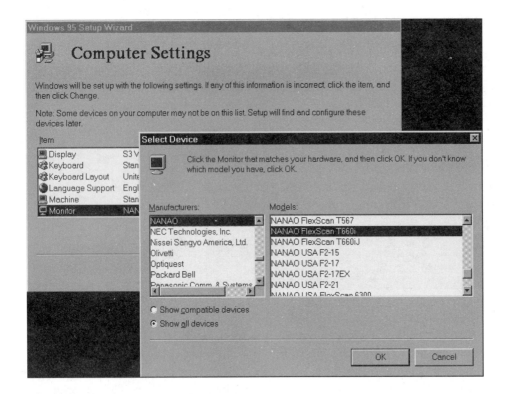

It's important that you get the settings right, even if the Wizard can't. If you slack off and pick a generic setting, your hardware won't work as well as it should. If you guess and pick the wrong variety ("Do I have a Wizbang or a Whizbang PCI?"), you might make it very difficult to start Win95 for the first time. So get 'em right: break out your owner's manual, or look at the labels on any iffy hardware. Call the manufacturer (but *not* Microsoft!) if you have any questions.

The last decision you have to make is the easiest. YES, you want a Startup Disk. You can actually cancel out of the Wizard at this point and return to Windows 3.1 as if nothing happened. But once you go beyond this point, Win95 is going to start infesting your machine, like some sort of flesh-eating bacteria. The Startup Disk is a major defense you have if something goes bump while your machine is in a precarious almost-Win95 state. DO IT!

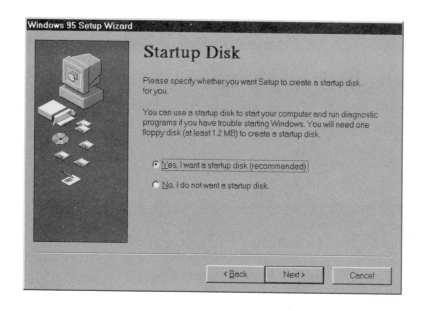

If you've made it this far without a hang, praise the WinGods: it's almost over, and the chances of major problems at this point are not great. At long, long last the Wizard is ready to get Win95 set up on your machine. After this screen you'll see several colorful but meaningless Progress bars and spend a lot of time watching as nothing much happens. Windows will reboot a couple of times, and you'll have to tell Win95 which time zone you live in.

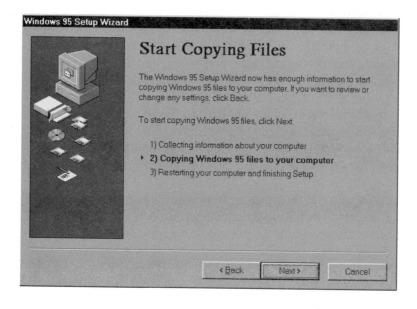

That's about it. After you twiddle your thumbs for a while, Win95 pops up on your machine and you can get down to business, cleaning up and fixing the many weird default values that Win95 insists on establishing. Would that all installs were this hassle-free!

Hey, if all installs were this easy, they wouldn't need us . . . . Remember the Full Employment Act of 95?

What Can Go Wrong

Success generally depends upon knowing how long it takes to succeed.

—C. L. de Montesquieu, *Pensées,* ca. 1750

Safe Recovery Mode

Far and away the most common installation problem is a lock-up when that "Analyzing Your Computer" dialog appears on the screen. If you suspect that the Win95 installer has dozed off, following a very simple series of steps will maximize your chances of getting your PC resuscitated. Follow them carefully.

- Make sure the machine is frozen but good. Move the mouse around and see if the pointer on the screen goes anywhere. Watch that Progress bar and see if another color block appears—it's entirely possible for an additional color block to appear long before the XX% status number increments. Look at the hard drive activity light and listen for any sign of life from your hard disk. And be aware of the fact that a screen saver (you *did* turn off the screen saver, didn't you?) can make the screen appear to be frozen while the installer is doing just fine, thank you.

- Once you're absolutely convinced that the machine has frozen, go get a clock or watch and *time it* for an additional five minutes. I've seen that screen sit there for three or four minutes without a breath of discernible activity, then suddenly start running like hell afire.

- If you're absolutely, totally convinced that the machine has passed into another realm, follow the instructions on the screen. To wit, turn the machine off. Don't hit `Ctrl+Alt+Del`. Don't push the reset button. Turn the power off.

- Now you need to get Win95 Setup running the same way it was running before. If you're running Setup from Win31 (the most likely situation), turn the PC back on, get Win31 running, click File, then Run, type `d:\setup` (using the appropriate drive letter) and run the Setup program again. If you're installing from DOS, turn the PC back on and run Setup from there. If you had originally booted from floppy, stick your boot disk in the `a:` drive and turn the PC back on. You get the idea.

- Sometimes you'll get weird text-only screens that warn you of all sorts of dire problems. If you see them, just navigate back out to DOS or choose in their menus to restart your machine. Then run Setup again. In every situation I've encountered, the installer comes up with a screen that looks like Figure 8-3.

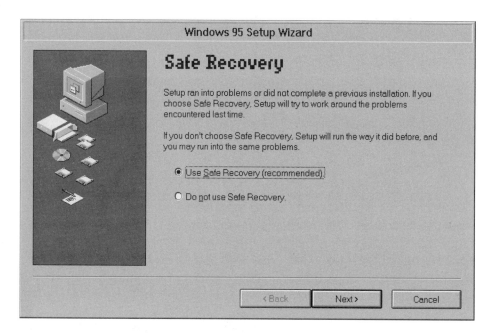

Figure 8-3. Safe recovery in the Install Wizard

- It's hard to imagine a situation where you'd want to bypass Safe Recovery. I imagine if the "Analyzing Your Computer" screen had frozen ten or fifteen times, you might be tempted to bypass Safe Recovery and manually specify which components you want the installer to look for. But in every case I've encountered, Safe Recovery has worked,

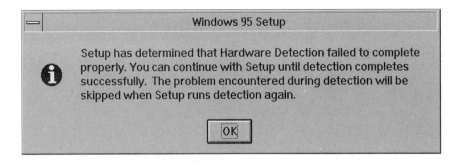

Figure 8-4. Safe recovery lands on its feet

sooner or later. (Yes, one machine did take four rounds of freezing and Safe Recovery. But such is life, eh?) If you choose Safe Recovery and click Next>, you will probably see a notice like that in Figure 8-4.

 At this point, the installer goes back into its "Analyzing Your Computer" routine and, while it may fail again, it will undoubtedly fail later down the road toward completion. The lock-ups during "Analyzing Your Computer" may put a few gray hairs on your head, but they always seen to come up aces.

Safe Mode

 The kinds of problems that really scare me are the ones that typically come at the end, when the installer is trying to reboot. They're unusual, and they make it sound like I've done irreparable harm to my machine. Fortunately, that's never been the case. I've seen a couple of different categories of problems, er, opportunities, that end in something called *Safe Mode*:

• Sometimes when the installer is trying to reboot, you'll see "Starting Windows 95 . . ." and then a text screen pops up with several options, among them "Start in Safe Mode," which is usually option 3. If you're given the choice, that's what you want to do.

• Sometimes you aren't given any choice at all, and Win95 starts in Safe Mode. (In spite of the similar names, starting Win95 in Safe Mode and rerunning the installer in Safe Recovery Mode are two entirely different things.) You'll know that you're in Safe Mode because the desktop will have "Safe Mode" in all four corners, and may or may not include any icons (see Figure 8-5). When Win95 is in Safe Mode, it runs slower than a snail in mud, so don't panic if things don't spring up quite the way they should.

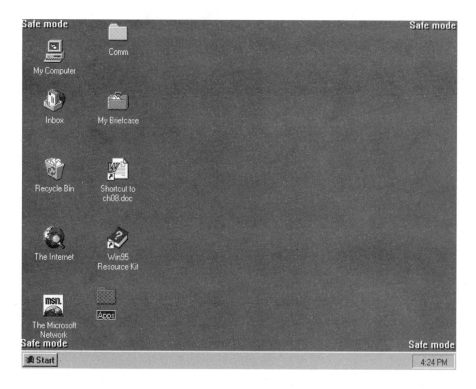

Figure 8-5. Starting Win95 in Safe Mode

- No need to panic. No matter how you got into Safe Mode, there's at least a 90 percent chance that simply clicking on Start, then Shut Down; picking the Restart the Computer button; and then clicking Yes will bring you back up in Windows 95. Something else they didn't tell you in Win95 school, eh?

- If you end up in Safe Mode again, you might have to play around with the settings in the Control Panel (click Start, then Settings, then Control Panel). The most likely suspect is your hardware configuration, so double-click on the System applet and bring up the Device Manager Tab. Click the Print button so you'll be able to restore things to their original settings. Then, one at a time, bring up the properties for each hardware component. If you can find any obvious sources for your problem, you may be able to change the driver using the \drivers folder on the setup CD. If that doesn't work, it's time to punt: you need to get Microsoft on the horn and plead your case. Pray for mercy.

Cat with a Cold

 Another problem you'll frequently encounter is a message from the installer that looks like Figure 8-6.

Figure 8-6. Cannot hail the .CAB

 It sounds so much more, uh, official, than, "You have a dirty CD," doesn't it? That's the problem, though. Take the CD out of the drive, blow on it or wipe it on your sleeve, or do whatever you usually do to clean a CD, stick it back in the drive, and click OK. If that doesn't solve the problem, get a can of compressed air and blow out the innards of the drive, and click OK again. If *that* doesn't work, get a CD-drive cleaning kit, even if you have to wait overnight to use it.

 I've seen some people who share their CD drive from their Windows for Workgroups machines and then attempt to install over the network from that shared drive. Sometimes when this happens they'll get random failure cases during the copying of the files. It seems that some versions of MSCDEX and/or CD drive firmware simply can't keep up with the constant reads that the Win95 Setup program attempts. In every case I've seen so far, it works to manually copy all of the files in the `\win95` directory from the shared CD drive over the network to the local machine, and then run the setup locally.

Biiiig Problem

 I hit one installation where I was just absolutely dead sure that the whole machine was tanked, and I'd only be able to salvage it for scrap metal. The fact that it happened on my main production machine while I was writing this book just added to the adrenaline rush. I walked around the house with clenched teeth for days. Fun and games.

I was installing Win95 to a new directory, from Win31, using the CD—precisely the way I recommend advanced Win31 users tackle the upgrade. Installation actually went quite well, almost all the way. I was more than halfway through "copying files" and way beyond the usual "Analyzing Your Computer" hangups. All of a sudden the screen went blank and a text message appeared: "Fatal Exception 0E." Ho-boy. Fatal Exception errors are very unusual, rogue errors that can appear almost anywhere at almost anytime; Microsoft tries to nail them down, but if the stuckee can't replicate the problem, there isn't much anybody can do.

Win95 will try to recover from a Fatal Exception if you push `Enter`. I did. It didn't. Faced with a complete meltdown, I hit the `Reset` button. The machine came back up with the text screen with Safe Mode as choice number 3. I picked 3, got the Safe Mode screen and . . . nothing. No Start button. No `My Computer` icon. Zip. Nada. Just Safe Mode in the four corners.

So I hit the `Reset` button. This time I chose "Run Previous Version of MS-DOS." You guessed it. Black screen. Nothing.

So I tried to boot with my brand-new Win95 startup diskette. (Yes, I did tell the installer to make a backup diskette.) I got to the `C:>` DOS prompt, moved to my old Win31 `\windows` directory, and typed `win`. DOS complained that it couldn't find `himem.sys`. I thought I might try to reinstall from DOS, so I moved over to my CD drive . . . and discovered that DOS couldn't find my CD drive. Undoubtedly it didn't have the right drivers loaded.

After swearing a bit and kicking a few things, I dug out my old DOS manuals and finally figured out that I could use `edit.com` on the startup diskette to create a new `config.sys` on the diskette, containing a line for `himem.sys`. You still with me?

With the quickie `himem.sys` in `config.sys` on the diskette, I could finally get Windows 3.1 running, but . . . you guessed it . . . Win31 couldn't "see" the CD, either. The right drivers weren't loaded. I was seriously considering cybercide.

To make a very long and sordid story short, I suddenly remembered that I had created a full Win31/DOS 6 emergency boot diskette, just as Mom recommended at the beginning of this chapter. I popped the boot diskette into the machine, booted into Win31, and ran Startup on the CD. The Win95 installer told me it detected an existing copy of Win95 on the machine, so I told it to "verify files." Bada-bing, bada-boom, Win95 was up and working in short order.

That install took almost an entire day. In fact, by the time Win95 was finally running, I was so burnt out I couldn't function—it may as well *have* taken all day. So when you read that putting Win95 on your machine will be a relatively painless thirty minutes, you can grin and say something like, "Yeah. Sure."

SCSI City

To date, I've only hit one machine that adamantly, absolutely refused to install Win95. It would go through all the motions, reboot just fine into Win95, set the time zone, then freeze at the very end of the "Converting Windows 3.1 program groups" phase.

We rebooted into Command Prompt mode (described at the end of this chapter), renamed all `*.grp` files in the Win31 `\windows` directory to `*.mom`, copied `system.1st` in the boot drive's root directory over the top of the Win95 `\windows\system.dat` file (a trick you'll read about in Chapter 9), and rebooted into Win95. Didn't work. The system still hung at the tail end of "Converting Windows 3.1 program groups."

We spoke at length with a fellow from the Microsoft campus, a guy who's in charge of tracing down weird install problems. At first he thought it was a corruption in upper memory. We tweaked and fiddled, but fifty-five minutes later got the same hang as all prior trials. Finally he went off line and got some peers to review the case; they figured it was a SCSI ID, cabling, or termination problem. In the old days, DOS didn't get real upset about SCSI details, but apparently Win95 sniffs out these types of subtle issues.

On this particular machine, the SCSI cable runs from the controller card to the NEC CD drive (not terminated) to the Conner hard drive (terminated). Here's what clued the Microsoft whiz in to this possible culprit: he noticed the NEC CD drive was running under Win95 in real mode (see "After the Installation," later in this chapter). We rerouted the cable to go from the card to the hard drive to the CD drive, left the IDs as is, and put the terminator on the CD drive. Bada-boom, bada-bing. Worked like a champ.

The moral of this story: If Win95 hangs for some reason and you can't figure out why, it may still be worthwhile to tweak and poke and prod, change SCSI routings or terminators, flip around DIP switches or jumper settings. Despite what you read in the supermarket tabloids, we are not yet in the Halcyon Land of Plug 'n Play.

The High Price of Nonsuccess

So what happens if you get this far and you can't solve the problem? Well, it's time to get on the phone to Windows tech support. (Their phone number is in the Win95 box.) Make sure you're sitting in front of your PC, and that you're prepared to talk civilly to somebody whose only purpose is to resolve your problem.

Although Microsoft's tech support policies change from time to time, the primary change with Win95 support seems particularly ominous. Microsoft will give you ninety days of free telephone support, as long as the support doesn't cover networking. As soon as a tech support person decides that your Win95 problem is really a Win95 networking problem, you'll be given the choice of hanging up and punting, or paying a robust $1.95/minute or $35 an incident to stay on the phone.

Hey, don't look at me that way. Tech support for these complex networking questions gets mighty expensive. We could do what IBM did, and sell an extra-cost package to add networking to the operating system. Instead, we gave it all away as part of Win95, and only charge people who need telephone support to get it working. Most of the time, the problem ends up being some other vendor's bug—so why should we swallow the expense?

Whoooooooaaaaa. Wait a minute. You aren't just talking about Netware bugs bringing down Win95 networking. The official Microsoft spokesperson also said that users will be charged from day one to resolve peer-to-peer Win95 networking problems, even when no software other than Win95 is involved. They even said they'd charge to resolve connection problems with The Microsoft Network!

I can't believe they're charging $35 for hookup support for The Microsoft Network. Users faced with that will just jump to CompuServe or America Online.

I can't believe we're charging $35 for hookup support for The Microsoft Network. Users faced with that will just jump to Compus . . . , er Compus . . . , er someplace else.

MS Marines Are Looking for a Few Good Men

> 'E isn't one o' the reg'lar line, nor 'e isn't one of the crew;
> 'E's a kind of a giddy harumfrodite—soldier and sailor too.

—Rudyard Kipling, *Soldier an' Sailor Too,* 1892

You gotta register, OK? I know you don't like the idea of becoming another bit in Microsoft's bucket. (They call the repository of all user information the "Regbase," short for "Registered User Database.") But it's for your own good. You'll only get tech support over the phone if you register. And you're likely to receive notices of bug fixes—cleverly disguised as upgrades—only if you're in the Regbase.

The easiest way to register is by using the on-line Registration wizard available at the end of Win95 installation, or by pushing the Online Registration button on the Welcome screen that pops up every time you start Windows.

What's that, you say? You got tired of the welcome messages and unchecked the box that says: `Show this Welcome Screen next time you start Windows` and now you want to do the on-line registration? No sweat. Click on Start, then Run, and type in `welcome`. Hit Enter. *Voilà*—the welcome screen will appear and you can proceed with Online Registration.

The Registration wizard collects information on you, your machine, and its applications. You can choose to include or exclude the machine and application information when you register. If you choose to send that information to us, we can use it to tailor offerings specific to you, your hardware, and your software. The whole thing is put in a file in your Win95 `\windows` folder called `reginfo.txt`. When you give the OK, the Registration wizard dials the phone and uploads the registration info—and *only* the info that you have approved—to Microsoft's computers.

Yeah. Tell me another one. You guys are really retrieving all that information so the Microsoft applications people can do marketing comparisons and target direct mailings. The database will be worth millions. Why is it Microsoft's business if I'm running Quattro Pro? I wouldn't have any problem with the whole Registration "Snooper" gig if the Operating Systems people were collecting that information to make the next version of Windows run better. By your own admission, though, you're using that info throughout Microsoft—and I'll bet the number-one use is in Applications marketing. Talk about exploiting a monopoly in one area for unfair advantage in other areas. Tell me, Billy95, are you going to make that information available to Microsoft's application competitors?

Hold on a minute, Rush. Microsoft played this game fair and square. They've said very specifically that they will use the information throughout Microsoft, for marketing purposes. They give people the option to withhold the information—in fact, Windows users have to *explicitly* grant their permission to send that information to Microsoft by pushing a couple of Yes buttons. They're *not* default buttons; you can't mindlessly click OK and accidentally send that info off to Redmond. If you don't want to give the info to Microsoft, just click NO! (Now, where have I heard that one before?)

Rush, you really are playing one card short of a full deck. How is this automatic registration any different than those low-tech paper registration cards that ask you all sorts of questions about other vendors' software you might be running? The only difference is that this actually makes it easier for the user.

Besides, this could be a whole lot of fun. What's to keep you from hacking `reginfo.txt` before sending it off? WordPad does a nifty job. Just wait until after the Registration Wizard has gathered all its information, then tackle `reginfo.txt` with WordPad before you click the button to dial the phone. Microsoft might be surprised to find a few lines like these in their database:

```
Operating System = None Of Your Business 95
Product Inventory 1 = Ronnie Does Redmond
Product Inventory 2 = Secret Schulman Decompiler
Product Inventory 3 = OS/2 Is Gonna Eat Yer Lunch!
Product Inventory 4 = Crash MS Regbase Virus
```

Just don't tell 'em where you got the idea, OK? Heh heh heh.

There was a huge brouhaha in the press and on the Net about Microsoft's "Snooper" Registration. Some guy posted a message on the Net saying Microsoft was transferring all sorts of illicit information from Win95 users' machines into their giant databases. Quite a conspiracy theory. *InfoWorld* spread the rumor, without actually verifying what data was being sent over the wires. That was unforgivable: it'd take the *InfoWorld* tech weenies in the labs all of ten minutes to figure out exactly what was being transmitted to Microsoft. Instead of checking their facts, *InfoWorld* just repeated the rumor—on its front page, no less. A real blot on the concept of computer "journalism." Oh well. I guess it sells magazines. *Et tu, Stu?*

After the Installation

> Who would be free, themselves must strike the blow.
>
> —Byron, *Childe Harold,* 1812

There's a sequence of steps you should take after installing Win95—steps that can make a big difference in how well Win95 works and how stable your system will be, particularly when running old (so-called 16-bit) Windows 3.1 applications.

Get Rid of Real Mode Drivers

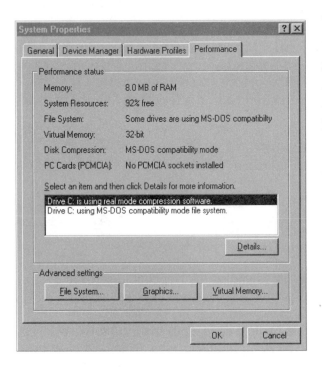

The worst antagonists to your Win95 system's performance fall under the general title of "real mode drivers." There's nothing particularly real about them: they were written to work with the old version of Windows—or even DOS. Captive to the lower regions of memory below the 640K line, they can't adapt to the greater freedom Win95 offers. Since they can't break free of their lower memory chains, Win95 has to handle them specially, and that special handling extracts a significant performance and stability penalty.

Figure 8-7. Vestiges of real mode

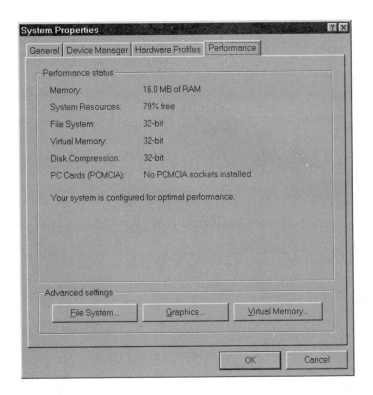

Figure 8-8. No real mode drivers

 There are cases where real mode drivers are necessary, particularly for older networks. Those network drivers must be loaded in `autoexec.bat` —you have no other choice—so they can kick in before Win95 takes over. If you discover a real mode network driver in `autoexec.bat`, after the Win95 installer does its things, you need to tread carefully when trying to get rid of it. Keep plenty of backups, and only make small, incremental changes, testing as you go along.

Real mode drivers are always loaded in either `config.sys` or `autoexec.bat`. You can tell if you have any real mode drivers infesting your Win95 system by clicking on Start, Settings, Control Panel, double-clicking on the System applet, and bringing up the Performance tab.

 If you have a real mode driver showing under the Performance tab, there's a real quick, easy way to see if the Win95 installer goofed and left the driver in when it isn't absolutely necessary: try booting with completely empty `autoexec.bat` and `config.sys` files. In the root directory of your boot disk (typically `c:\`), rename `autoexec.bat` to `autoexec.mao` and `config.sys` to `config.mao`. Then click Start, Shut Down (make sure the button says, "Shut Down the Computer?"), click OK, and when Win95 says, "It is now safe to shut off your computer," hit the PC's `Reset` button. When Win95 comes back up, take a look and see if everything is working. Pay particular attention to CD-ROM drives, scanners, and any oddball hardware. If everything works, thank your lucky stars and forget the old, now obsolete files.

If everything goes to hell, get running in DOS mode (use your startup diskette), rename `autoexec.mao` to `autoexec.bat` and `config.mao` to `config.sys`, and hit `Ctrl+Alt+Del` to restart Win95. Ah well. It was worth a try.

Paring down `autoexec` and `config`

 In fact, Mao, that trick is a good idea for *everybody*, whether they have real mode drivers showing on the Performance tab or not. Why? We're trying to get rid of those old dinosaurs! If you can make your system work with no `autoexec.bat` or `config.sys`, you're in the best of all possible situations. I strongly suggest that every first-time Win95 upgrader should try to boot with no `autoexec.bat` or `config.sys`. Strike a blow for progress.

Note that the Win95 installer automatically makes a copy of your old `autoexec.bat` and calls it `autoexec.dos`; it also makes a copy of the old `config.sys` as `config.dos`. If you push `F8` when booting and choose to "Run Previous Version of MS-DOS," the `.dos` files are used to get the machine going.

 If you can get Win95 to work without those hellish files, you can gradually add just a line or two to each, to solve very specific problems. What kinds of problems? Well, if you're well versed in the vagaries of those files, here are the kinds of things to look out for.

Win95 establishes the defaults in Figure 8-9 for settings that DOS used to get from `config.sys`:

```
dos=high                      files=60
device=himem.sys              lastdrive=z
device=ifshlp.sys             buffers=30
device=setver.exe             stacks=9,256
shell=command.com /p          fcbs=4
```

Figure 8-9. CONFIG.SYS 95

If you need to override one of the numbers in Figure 8-9, or add some esoteric switches to them, put a line in `config.sys`. For example, a `files=90` statement in `config.sys` will force Win95 to allocate ninety file handle buffers in DOS sessions.

In particular, if you have a (lousy, old) program that requires `emm386` with the `NOEMS` switch, you'll have to put a `device=emm386.exe noems` line in your `config.sys`. (Note that Win95 is smart enough to figure our that you're loading emm386, and automatically includes a `dos=umb` setting when it sees you loading `emm386`.)

Hey, I thought Win95 would get rid of all this DOS mumbo-jumbo. I mean, who cares if you're running `emm386`? And why should I have to futz around with a dumb text file to get a memory manager going? PCs these days are supposed to be smarter than that.

PCs are smarter than that. Unfortunately, people aren't. They're still running programs that were written three, five, even ten years ago—and those programs aren't so forgiving. All of these weird settings are in the interest of backward compatibility. If you don't want to bother with ten-year-old settings and obscure ten-year-old DOS concepts, don't use ten-year-old software!

If you're going to tackle a custom `config.sys` job (talk about living in the past!), the *Windows Resource Kit* contains a long list of files that should've been removed by the Win95 installer. In particular, Share, Smart Drive and any other disk caches, Mirror, and Fastopen should've been removed automatically. Don't put any of them back in. You should also manually remove any mouse-related `device=` entries; Win95 ignores them anyway.

If you're the kind of DOS junkie who loves to tweak the `command.com` command line, `config.sys` is child's play. Don't even bother with it. The real mother lode of `command.com` settings is in the property dialog. Look in Chapter 3.

Over on the `autoexec.bat` side, Win95 during startup automatically sets the variables `tmp` and `temp` to point to your Win95 `\windows\temp` folder, and variable `comspec` to point to the Win95 `\windows\command.com` file. (Note: the *Windows Resource Kit* is wrong here, too.) The `prompt=` is set to `$p$g`. Finally, it automatically adds the Win95 `\windows` and `\windows\command` folders to your `path=` statement.

If you should be possessed by an overwhelming desire to manually edit your `autoexec.bat` file, make sure that the first two folders to appear on your `path=` are the Win95 `\windows` and `\windows\command` folders. You can add just about anything after that. Dosshell, fastopen, mirror, share, Smart Drive (and any other disk caches), virus-checking software, and the command `win` should've been removed automatically. Don't put them back in. You should also manually remove any mouse entries.

 Microsoft warns against adding your Win31 `\windows` and `\windows\system` directories to the `path=`, if the Win31 directories still exist, but I've had the Win31 directories on my path for a long time now with nary a problem. Yet. Microsoft also advises that you leave your old DOS directory in the path. I don't, and it hasn't bitten me, either. Yet.

Set Up Sharing for Your Drives

If you're on a network, check that you can access shared resources on other machines. You may have figured that when you checked the box during setup to Allow File and Printer Sharing on your machine that you were making your resources available on the network but you weren't. That only turned on the potentiality of sharing. You'll need to go in and explicitly turn on sharing for resources that you want to share. Highlight the drive or directory you want to share in Explorer, right click, and pick Properties. There should be a Sharing tab (or pick Sharing . . . from the right click menu). See Figure 8-10.

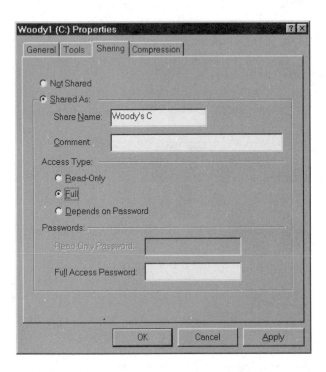

Figure 8-10. If you want Johnny to share his files with you, you'll have to share your files with him

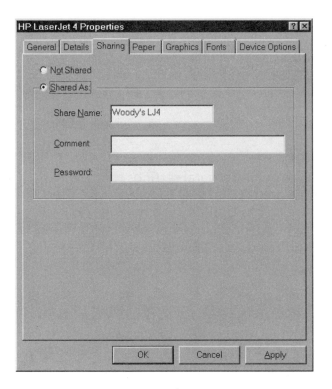

Figure 8-11. Printer sharing

If there is no Sharing tab in the Properties dialogs for Drives and Directories, File and Printer Sharing is not turned on. You'll need to do that by clicking the Network applet in Control Panel and clicking on the `File and Printer Sharing . . .` button in the Configuration tab.

To turn on Sharing for a Printer, find it in the Printer's folder and pick `Properties` or `Sharing . . .` from its right button menu; see Figure 8-11.

 You can tell if a drive is set to be shared by looking at it on the tree side in Explorer. Sharing is on for the drive if and only if there is a hand underneath the drive—sort of handing if off to someone!

These screen shots are what you'll see with for regular peer-to-peer sharing when you don't have a Novell or NT server around to perform authentication. If you're on a Novell or NT LAN and your system administrator has set those servers up properly, then you'll see a list of users on your network that you can then grant a variety of individual permissions. So it doesn't have to be the all-or-nothing aspect of allowing anyone with the proper password to access your shared files or printer.

Fix Weird Settings

When Win95 installs itself, it leaves behind several settings that are . . . strange. Billy95 says many of them are set that way to help novice users. That may be the case, and I'm sure he has Usability Lab numbers to back up his conclusions, but any user who spends much time at all with Win95 is bound to get confused and/or clobbered by some of this stuff. Here's my top-ten list of things you should change, immediately, before you try to get any work out of Win95.

👆 Change the size of the recycle bin to something sane. By default, Win95 sets aside 10 percent of the size of each drive for the Recycle Bin. For most people that's a bit excessive. Turn it back to 5 percent and you'll be just fine. Right-click on the Recycle Bin on your desktop, pick Properties, and bring up the Global tab. See Figure 8-12.

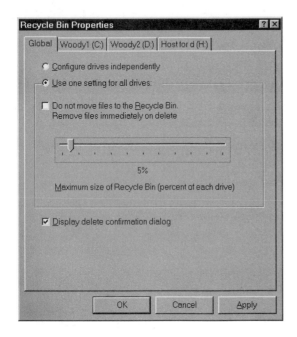

Figure 8-12. Recycle the Recycler

⚓ Force Explorer to show you everything, as explained in Chapter 3. Right-click on My Computer, pick Explore, click on View, then make sure both the Toolbar and Status Bar choices are checked. Then click View, click Options, and bring up the View tab. Make sure the Show All Files button is checked. Then check the Display the Full MS-DOS Path in the Title Bar, and uncheck Hide MS-DOS File Extensions for Types that Are Registered.

⚓ Change the keyboard repeat rate. I don't know why, but on many machines the repeater keys go into hyper-acceleration immediately after installing Win95: they're so fast you can't even begin to control, say, the Backspace key. Click on Start, then Settings, and Control Panel. Double-click on the Keyboard applet. Bring up the Speed tab (Figure 8-13). On my machine, I only have to nudge the Repeat rate slider a smidgen and the repeater keys suddenly start acting normally. Test the rate in the box and click OK when you're done.

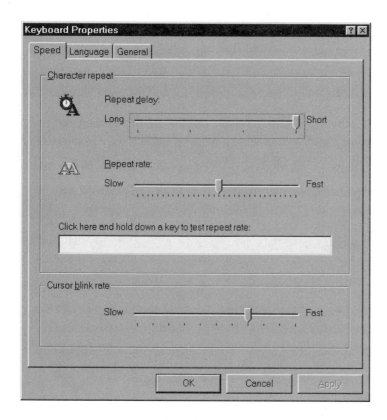

Figure 8-13. Keyboard Repeater

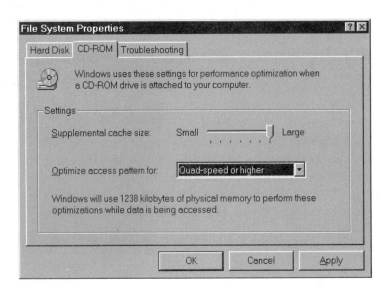

Figure 8-14. Set CD Cache

✎ Give your CD-ROM some breathing room. Click on Start, then Settings and Control Panel. Double-click on the System applet. Bring up the Performance tab, click File System, and bring up the CD-ROM tab (Figure 8-14). If you have 8 MB or more of memory and you use your CD driver rather commonly, maximize caching: set the cache size slider to Large and maximize for Quad-speed or higher.

Try to find *that* setting without a road map! Supposedly every human being on the planet knows every other one within six degrees of separation—a friend of a friend, and so on. Why does it take *seven* levels of clicking to adjust the lousy CD-ROM cache size to a level it should've been at in the first place?

✎ Win95 has a bad habit of not always identifying your video card and monitor correctly. I'm not sure why; could be a congenital defect. Check to be sure both of them are correct by clicking on Start, then Settings and Control Panel. Double-click on the Display applet. Bring up the Settings tab and click the Change Display Type button (Figure 8-15). Check and make sure your video card and monitor are correct. If they aren't, click the Change button and find them in the proffered lists.

If you have a Diamond Stealth 64 PCI video card, Win95 only identifies it as an "S3" (S3 being the manufacturer of the S3 964 chip that drives the Stealth 64 PCI). Unfortunately, the S3 driver has problems with the Stealth 64 PCI card. If you've seen a bunch of horizontal gray bars on the screen in 1024 _ 768 and higher resolutions, you'll know what I mean. (It's actually running in interlaced mode, if you can believe it!) Fortunately, the Stealth 64 PCI driver is on the Win95 CD, and it's easy to install from this point. Click Change, then click Have Disk. Point Windows to the `\drivers\display\diamond` folder on the Win95 CD. Click OK. The installer will kick in. When it asks you to insert the Win95 CD (!), point it to the `\Win95` folder on the CD. Take a look at Figure 8-15. It shows you what the real Diamond Stealth 64 PCI driver looks like. Oh how I love a nice bug in the mornin'.

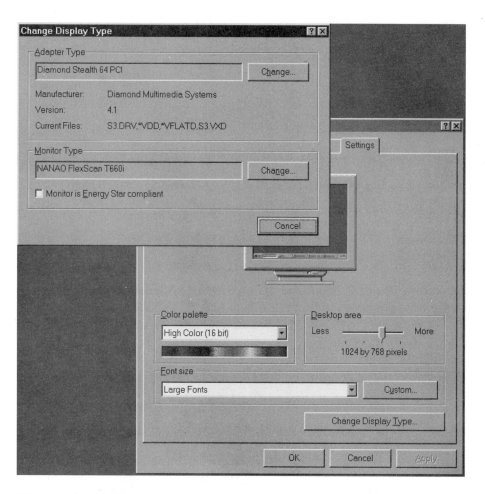

Figure 8-15. Diddling Display Type

The Win95 CD also contains updated drivers for the 8514 video card; the ATI mach 64 revision "CT" adapters (found on the Graphics Xpression and WinBoost PCI cards); several Diamond cards, including the Viper PCI and VLB (for more recent drivers, Diamond is on the Web at `http://www.diamondmm.com`); the Matrox MGA Millenium card; Number 9 (although it's not clear from their documentation which cards are affected); and a generic VGA driver that should be tried if Win95 won't boot with a very old VGA adapter. They're all in `\drivers\display`.

- If you have a sound card, double-check that Win95 selected your best MIDI driver (it misses the Sound Blaster AWE-32 MIDI driver, for example). To check, click on Start, then Settings and Control Panel. Double-click on the Multimedia applet. Bring up the MIDI tab. If you only have one option in the "Single Instrument" box, you only have one MIDI synthesizer and needn't worry about it.

- If you have more than one MIDI synthesizer to choose from, right-click on `My Computer` and pick Explore. Point Explorer at your Win95 `\windows\media` folder. If you installed Sample Sounds, you should have a bunch of MIDI files in there (all with an `.rmi` extension), including Beethoven's Fifth, which makes a good test.* Double-click on Beethoven's Fifth and play it. Then switch MIDI synthesizers by clicking on a new one. Click Apply. Play Beethoven's Fifth again. Choose the synthesizer you like best.

- If you are using Internet mail with any Service Provider other than the Microsoft Network, you need to set up Exchange to send Internet mail. The way the Internet mail client sets itself up is just plain dumb. See Chapter 3.

- For migration help with your Windows applications, and the latest Win95 info, get onto the Web and check out `http://www.windows.microsoft.com`. In particular, look around for a file called `win95app.hlp`.

- There are lots of useless files hanging around. If you don't use Microsoft Mail, you don't need the two Control Panel applets that only deal with MS Mail. Delete `wgpocpl.cpl` in the `\windows\system folder`. See Chapter 3 for details. And while you're at it, go into `\windows\help` and run the `.avi` files there by double-clicking on them. Do you really need those? If not, give 'em the heave-ho, too. If you've decided you'll never run your old version of DOS again, you can reclaim up to a whopping 27 MB of hard disk space by deleting `w95undo.dat` and `w95undo.ini` in the root directory of your boot drive.

---

*If you didn't install Sample Sounds, you may be able to find `canyon.mid` in your old Win31 `\windows` directory. Or you can always install the Sample Sounds by going back into Control Panel, double-clicking on the Add/Remove Programs applet, bringing up the Windows Setup tab, clicking on Multimedia, then Details, checking the Sample Sounds box, and clicking OK.

You should print a list of all your hardware settings—IRQs, I/O Ports, DMAs and much more, and keep it handy should the need ever arise. Click Start, Settings, Control Panel. Double-click on the System applet. Bring up the Device Manager tab and click Print. Choose "All Devices and System Summary." And to think, just a few years ago you could've paid $200 for a program that does less!

 Finally, I think everybody should use the trick in Chapter 3 to put a cascading list of all Control Panel applets on their Start Menu. And add System Resource Meter, as described in Chapter 4.

Fix ComXAutoAssign

Is not the whole world a vast house of assignation of which the filing system has been lost?

—Quentin Crisp, *The Naked Civil Servant*

 Some people set up their fax/modem so it will always answer the phone, receiving incoming faxes. If that's what you want to do, skip this section completely, and move on down to Ferreting More Goodies.

Open up `system.ini` in Notepad (or even better, run Sysedit). You're going to want to add a line that says

```
com1autoassign=2   or   com2autoasign=2
```

depending on whether your modem is on com port 1 or com port 2. First search on the string *"autoassign"* to check that there isn't already a line like that. Otherwise locate a line saying `[386Enh]`, go to its end, hit `Enter` and type in the autoassign line appropriate to your port.

What you've just done is turn off a weird Windows 95 default. Without this change, Windows treats multiple communication programs as follows: if you load a comm program and it uses the com port in any way, even to just initialize it upon startup, then you won't be able to have any other com program use the modem until you totally exit the first program. With the setting I just gave you, Windows 95 acts rationally—for example, you can load Exchange, use it, and then, keeping Exchange loaded, you can load and use WinCIM.

Of all the cockeyed things. Why make this default behavior so unfriendly? In a world where `ini` files are passé, how can Microsoft use `system.ini`?

It's not ideal, but I understand why Microsoft chose the default it did. This default (which is equivalent to `comXautoassign=0`) is the setting needed for FAXES in autoanswer mode. I guess the 'Softies decided that rather than give FAX receivers serious problems, they'd give other users a mild inconvenience. Still, a better solution would have been a checkbox in the modem properties sheet.

As to using `system.ini`, the `comXautoassign` setting was in Windows 3.x. All we've done is change the value used if the setting isn't present from 2 (the windows 3.x default) to 0. And consider this—if someone calls up tech support to complain, isn't it easier to have the complainer edit `system.ini` than to fool with Regedit?

Ferreting More Goodies

> All looks yellow to the jaundiced eye.
>
> —Alexander Pope, *Essay on Criticism,* 1711

The Win95 CD ships with dozens of programs that you'll never find if you don't know where to look. Some of them are marginally useful, but some of them quickly become favorites. Here's the crew's pick of the best, complete with instructions on how to find them, install them, and put them to good use. Amazing how no two of them install the same way, eh?

Oh. If you're instructed to install a program using the Control Panel's Add/Remove Programs applet, whether in this chapter or anyplace else in Win95dom, don't get fooled by the dialogs. You'll find a lot of stuff already checked—the stuff you've already installed. You might think that since you don't want to reinstall it, you should uncheck it, but if you do, Windows will happily uninstall the programs you've unchecked!

Hover

If you've got the Win95 CD, you already have one of the coolest first-person games ever invented. It's a maze game where you have to make your spacemobile catch all the flags before the enemy can capture its flags. Or something like that. It's called Hover, and installing it is so easy even I can do it.

Right-click on `My Computer`, pick Explorer. In Explorer, go over to the CD and look in the folder `\funstuff\hover` for a file called `hover.exe`. Now, by pushing the + signs, go to your Win95 `\windows` directory and expose a folder called `\windows\Start Menu\Programs\Accessories\Games`. Right-click on `hover.exe` and drag it to `\Games`. Pick Create Shortcut Here. Hover will now appear with the rest of your games: click Start, then Programs, then Accessories, then Games, and click Hover. Make sure the Win95 CD is in your CD drive, and you've got it made in the shade.

Windows Resource Kit

Microsoft's entire *Windows Resource Kit,* in Help file format, is on the Win95 CD. If you do a lot of detailed work with Win95, and have a piddling 7 MB of free disk space handy, it's well worth sticking a copy on your hard drive. Simply copy the CD files `\Admin\Reskit\Helpfile\Win95 rk.hlp` and `Win95rk.cnt` from the CD to a new folder on your hard drive. Then right-drag `Win95rk.hlp` onto the desktop, or into a convenient folder on your desktop, choosing Create Shortcut Here. Double-click on that icon, and the *WRK* springs to life.

CompuServe Mail Reader

If you're a big CompuServe user, Exchange at this point is all dressed up with nowhere to go. To get it talking with CompuServe, look in the Win95 CD's `\Drivers\Other\Exchange\Compusrv` folder. Yeah, they did a good job of hiding it. Just run `setup.exe` from there and you'll be all set. More information is in Chapter 3, in the section on Exchange.

WinPopup, WinChat

I get a big kick out of WinPopup. Any time I want to send a note to somebody on the network, I just push the button and away it goes. Complete installation instructions are in Chapter 4.

Clipbook Viewer

I would like to be able to recommend the Clipbook Viewer—which is supposed to let you organize the Clipboard and let other computers on the network get at info on your Clipboard—but it needs NetDDE to work right. See Chapter 4.

WordView

The WordPad application that's automatically installed with Win95 is pretty cool, but it won't accurately display relatively complex Word for Windows documents. If you want to be able to read and accurately print heavy-duty WinWord .`DOC`s, you should look at WordView, a free Word for Windows file viewer and printer that's on the Win95 CD. WordView takes up about 3 MB of disk space.

Microsoft let us distribute the latest version of WordView, here on my CD. (The one on the Win95 CD is a <i><sniff!></i> older version.) Check out Appendix A for details, Oh. If you've already installed the version of WordView that's on the Win95 CD, be sure to remove it by using the Control Panel's Add/Remove Programs applet before installing the latest from my CD.

Extract

Windows installs a DOS (!) program in the `C:\windows\command` directory called `extract.exe`. This can be used to generate directories of and extract files from the compressed `.cab` files that are on the distribution disk. Appendix E talks about this program and lists the contents of the various `.cab` files on the Windows 95 installation media. These lists will be invaluable if some component gets munged.

The Others

Looking for the Timex Datalink files, so you can run your wristwatch? I didn't think so. But they're on the Win95 CD, in the `\Datalink` folder. A performance improvement for Quicktime for Windows is in the `\Drivers\Other\Qtwfix` folder. Good luck. HP Ominbook 600 users should check `\Pcmcia\Hp` for a new driver. If you use a Compaq Prolinea or Deskpro with a LaserJet 4 or 5 or some Lexmark printers, look in `\printer\lpt` for a driver.

Oh. And be sure you check out Chapter 5 for a list of the delights that await you on the Web, with the Win95 Power Toys.

How Win95 Starts

The secrets of success are a good wife and a steady job.
My wife told me.

—Howard Nemerov, *Writer's Digest,* December 1988

It's very important that you understand the Win95 startup sequence, both to avoid and to recover from all sorts of very painful problems. Surprisingly, I've never seen the startup process described succinctly, in any books or manuals. So let's approach the sequence a little bit at a time.

Some people take the smallest nit-picking details very seriously. Microsoft insists that Windows 95 replaces DOS; that DOS has gone away. Andrew Schulman says that DOS is still there, alive and well and clunky as ever, and Microsoft is just trying to gloss over that fact with a lot of PR flak. Personally, I don't give a hairy rodent's posterior if Win95 is a floor wax or DOS is a dessert topping. *Wait! They're both!* I just had the icons translate as much of the technical gobbledygook as possible into real English, let the cow chips fall where they may. If you want to get into a theological debate, read the *Windows Resource Kit* for Microsoft's point of view, or *Unauthorized Windows 95* for Andrew's, and check back in with us when you know for sure how many angels can dance on the head of a pin.

BIOS Bootstrap

Win95 relies on the good old-fashioned BIOS bootstrap routine to get things going—if you don't have a Plug 'n Play BIOS, the routine is identical to the one you've been using for years, whether you knew it or not. "BIOS bootstrap" is just a fancy way of saying that there's a program inside your computer that runs whenever you turn it on. The program is responsible for checking memory (you'll see it counting off chunks of memory when you start the machine), possibly moving some system functions from slower to faster parts of memory (called "shadowing"), then verifying the existence and identity of your major peripherals. When it's done with the very low-level stuff, the bootstrapper looks for a boot diskette and, failing that, hands over control to a file called `io.sys`, which is essentially the DOS 7 part of Windows 95. (Microsoft calls `io.sys` "the Real-Mode Operating System that replaces MS-DOS" which, as far as I'm concerned, is the same thing as "the DOS part of Windows.")

If you do have a Plug 'n Play BIOS, it kicks in after the low-level check and resolves any configuration conflicts before loading and handing off control to `io.sys`.

If you have DoubleSpace or DriveSpace compressed hard drives, either `dblspace.bin` or `drvspace.bin` or both, as needed, are "pre-loaded" from the root folder of the boot directory. They're the real mode (i.e., old-fashioned DOS mode) drivers, but will ultimately be replaced by analogous VxDs, when Windows 95 is ready to run in protected mode.

Real Mode

 `io.sys` takes control of your machine. The first thing `io.sys` does is read a file of settings called `nmsdos.sys`. If you're an old DOS maven (or even a young one), you probably remember `msdos.sys` as one of those strange hidden files that's copied onto a diskette when you format it as a system diskette—and in the old days, that was true. Nowadays, though, `msdos.sys` is just a text file. It—like `io.sys`—sits in the root folder of your boot drive. And it's "hidden," so you may have to go into Explorer's View/Options/View Tab to check Show Hidden Files to see it. If you want to see what's inside it, double-click on it in Explorer and pick Notepad from the list that pops up (I'd recommend that you make sure the `Always use . . .` checkbox is *not* checked since there are so many other `.sys` files floating around, not all of them text files).

The action `io.sys` takes next depends entirely on the contents of `msdos.sys`. I'm going to assume that you installed Win95 to a clean, new directory, and that you therefore have settings in `msdos.sys` that look much like mine (in particular, that you have a setting of `BootMulti=1`). The implications of this and other `msdos.sys` settings will be covered in Chapter 9.

`io.sys` next puts the phrase "Starting Windows 95 . . ." up on your screen. From the moment that message hits the screen, you have two seconds* to push `F8` if you want to pick a nonstandard way of starting (say, going into Safe Mode, or booting to a DOS prompt). Mao will cover the nonstandard ways of starting later in this chapter.

When the two seconds are up, `io.sys` grabs the startup splash screen and sticks it on your monitor. It first looks in the root folder of your boot drive for a Windows bitmap (one that usually has the extension `.bmp` but not in this case!) called `logo.sys`. (Amazing how many different kinds of files are called `.sys`, eh?) Assuming the file is the right size (320 dots × 400 dots × 256 colors), `io.sys` uses it for the splash screen; otherwise `io.sys` uses a built-in bitmap—which just happens to be the flying Window splash screen you're probably used to. Windows itself doesn't come with a `logo.sys` but the Plus! Pack installs one. I'll talk about this and other splash screens in Chapter 9.

---

* In the next chapter, I'll explain how you can change setting in `msdos.sys` to increase that two-second pause or even arrange for the Startup Menu to always come up and wait for you.

`io.sys` next sets up the Registry (described in Chapters 2 and 11) from files `user.dat` and `system.dat` in the Win95 `\windows` folder. `io.sys` then looks in the folder specified by `WinBootDir=` in `msdos.sys` and loads the drivers `himem.sys`, `ifshlp.sys`, and `setver.sys` from that folder. `himem.sys` and `setver.sys` have their traditional roles as memory manager and adjuster of DOS version calls in older programs. The `ifs` in `ifshelp.sys` stands for "installable file system" and indicates the role of this driver as the first step in support for Windows 95 new file architecture.

`io.sys` next scans the `config.sys` file if there is one in the root directory of the boot drive. Settings in `config.sys` may override the settings already established by `io.sys` (see "Skin Your Autoexec," earlier in this chapter).

After establishing and then modifying `config.sys`-style settings, `io.sys` starts acting like `autoexec.bat`. If you're on a network it runs the equivalent of a `net start` command, then sets up all of these DOS environment variables, using the Win95 `\windows` directory as established by the `windir=` setting in `msdos.sys`:

```
TMP=C:\WINDOWS\TEMP
TEMP=C:\WINDOWS\TEMP
PROMPT=$p$g
winbootdir=C:\WINDOWS
PATH=C:WINDOWS;C:\WINDOWS\COMMAND
COMSPEC=C:\WINDOWS\COMMAND.COM
windir=C:\WINDOWS
```

 Note the capitalization here, which is documented incorrectly in the *Windows Resource Kit*. Also note that the *Windows Resource Kit* shows the wrong value for `COMSPEC=`.

io.sys next checks to see if there's an `autoexec.bat` file in the root folder of the boot directory. If there's an `autoexec.bat`, it loads the DOS command interpreter (the program that handles DOS commands, i.e., `command.com`), which better be in the location specified in `COMSPEC=`. io.sys then runs `autoexec.bat`, with the results showing on the monitor—that is, if something in `autoexec.bat` writes to the monitor, the splash screen gets yanked and the output from `autoexec` is displayed; if nothing in `autoexec` writes to the monitor, the splash screen stays up. `autoexec.bat` runs as it always does, possibly modifying the DOS environment variables established earlier and possibly loading real mode drivers. `command.com` is then unloaded.

When `autoexec.bat` finishes, `io.sys` puts the splash screen back up on the monitor. (If there is no `autoexec.bat`, the splash screen never went away.) It then enters its cocoon phase—the phase that `io.sys` enters as an ugly real-mode caterpillar, with Windows 95 emerging at the end, a full protected-mode butterfly.

 Or a vicious, horned Doom II Incubus spitting hell-fire. Perceptions vary. Take your pick.

`io.sys` loads a real-mode program called `win.com,` which then assembles the components of Windows 95 itself. The beginning of `win.com` is something of a bellwether point. You can tell Win95 to start in "Command Prompt Mode" (which looks and acts just as you would expect a "DOS 7" to act, with a `c:>` and the whole nine yards), then type in the command `win,` and get precisely the same behavior from that point onward that you'll see if you simply let `io.sys` load and run `win.com` all by itself.

 Actually, the command prompt ain't the *whole* nine yards, because there is no support for long filenames—which can be a problem if you are trying to use the command prompt for some subtle troubleshooting. I'd say about six and a half of the whole nine yards.

Among other things, `win.com` sets in motion a program called `vmm32.vxd,` which is charged with loading virtual device drivers (so-called VxDs—the programs that connect Win95 to the outside world). `vmm32.vxd` is a moshed-together bunch of VxDs that the Win95 Setup routine builds for each machine.

`vmm32.vxd` looks in the Registry key `HKEY_LOCAL_MACHINE\System\` `CurrentControlSet\Services\VxD,` and loads any VxDs it finds listed there. Then it scans the Registry for any other `StaticVxD=` entries and loads those virtual device drivers.

Next, `vmm32.vxd` opens up `system.ini` (!), if it exists in the Win95 `\windows` folder. It then loads any `device=` VxDs it finds in the `[386Enh]` section,* overwriting any existing VxDs with the same name. Finally, `vmm32.vxd` looks in the Win95 `\windows\system\vmm32` folder for any `.VXD` files, overwriting any previously encountered, similarly named VxDs with the files it finds there.

---

* And you thought you were done with `system.ini`! No way. Don't throw out those old Windows 3.1 books. The best source of unbiased info on `system.ini` and `win.ini` is the original *Mother of All Windows Books,* of course, ISBN 0-201-62708-6. If you can find it. The next best source of info is Microsoft Press' *Windows 3.1 Resource Kit.* Good luck. You'll need it.

One crucial component loaded by `vmm32.vxd` is the I/O Supervisor, which controls all input and output under Win95, including initialization of the devices during startup and ongoing file activities while Win95 is running. The I/O Supervisor sets up shop by looking in the Win95 `\windows\system\iosubsys` folders for drivers. Port drivers reside in `.PDR` files; Windows NT-style Miniport drivers are `.MPDs`; and other drivers may either be `.386` files (the designation used by Windows 3.1 drivers) or `.VXDs` designed to run with the I/O Supervisor.

Another crucial component loaded by `vmm32.vxd` is the Configuration Manager, which works with Plug 'n Play devices and Registry entries to figure out what is attached to your PC. As it sorts out the various conflicts, it has the I/O Supervisor initialize the peripherals, and your machine is almost ready to start.

Somewhere in here any real mode device drivers that aren't needed any longer are taken over, such as `drvspace.bin`. Their memory is reclaimed and made available again for the system to use elsewhere.

For you network buffs, the network redirectors get loaded at this point and initialize the lower-level network ("Ring 0") code on your machine. At this point they also asynchronously broadcast a machine addname to each of the protocols you have requested to be loaded. The system then pauses to wait for the acknowledgment of the addname (or a timeout occurs, whichever comes first). If you are running TCP/IP against a DHCP server, a dynamic IP address is assigned to your machine from the pool of available IP addressed at this point. Once your machine is available on the net (at these lower levels), any machine-level policies are downloaded from the appropriate secure Windows NT or Netware servers.

Then the main Windows components, the WinOoze, gets loaded: `kernel32.dll`, `krnl386.exe`, `gdi.exe`, `gdi32.exe`, `user.exe`, and `user32.exe`. Notice that both the old 16-bit and the new 32-bit versions make an appearance. Windows then checks the Registry entries for fonts. It then looks for additional fonts and other entries in `win.ini` (!), if it exists in the Win95 `\windows` folder, and updates the Registry accordingly.

Windows looks for a file called `winstart.bat` in the root folder of the boot drive. If it exists, Windows takes the splash screen off the monitor, loads `command.com`, and runs `winstart.bat`, just like any other `.BAT` file, with the results displayed on the monitor. Then `command.com` is unloaded. `win.com` does all the command interpretation in

Windows outside the DOS boxes. (If there is no `winstart`, the splash screen stays up and `command.com` is not loaded.) Commands in `winstart.bat` are different from commands in `autoexec.bat` in that programs loaded in `winstart.bat` are available for the Windows desktop and for Windows applications, but they are unloaded for any DOS session run over Windows.

The multiprotocol network route module `mprexe.exe` looks at the Registry's HKEY_LOCAL_MACHINE\SOFTWARE\Microsoft\Windows\CurrentVersion\ RunServices key to see if there are any programs that need to be started up before the user logs in, and then finally presents the logon screen to the user.

At that point, if you have enabled multiple-user logon, Win95 asks for your logon username and password. This is another choke point: all paths lead here, and then many things happen immediately after the username and password are validated. Let me try to get them in the right order.

1. After you enter your username/password combo, the system verifies the password, unlocks the master password file, and then attempts to log you onto each of the various networks you have loaded. Network authentication then occurs against any secure Windows NT and/or Netware servers you have on your network. If all is OK, you are granted access to the appropriate network resources that the system administrators have arranged for you—disks, printers, and whatnot.

2. Any user-level policies that a system administrator has entered are placed into effect. Then any network user-level Registry entries (the `user.dat` hive) are downloaded, merged into your PC's Registry, and placed into effect.

3. Next, Win95 processes any Netware logon scripts you might have.

4. Now Win95 looks in your Registry for the HKEY_LOCAL_MACHINE\SOFTWARE\ Microsoft\Windows\CurrentVersion\RunOnce key. It runs any programs found there, and *waits for the programs to finish* before it proceeds. If a RunOnce program requires user interaction, the program will sit on a completely blank screen—nothing else running, no Desktop, no Taskbar, nothing—waiting for the user to provide input.

5. It's a little hard to say precisely which of the following programs run in what order, but as far as I can tell, Win95 next runs any programs listed in `win.ini`'s `[windows]` section, `load=` line. (The `load=` programs run minimized.) Then it runs any programs on `win.ini`'s `run=` line. (The `run=` programs run "restored," or partial screen.) Then it runs any programs listed in the Registry's

HKEY_LOCAL_MACHINE\SOFTWARE\Microsoft\Windows\CurrentVersion\Run key. The Desktop is created and the Taskbar appears on the screen. All of these programs are run normally, in that they are started and allowed to multitask. They could complete in almost any order; that's why it's hard to tell exactly which ones run first.

6.   Next Win95 looks in the Registry's HKEY_CURRENT_USER\Software\Microsoft\Windows\CurrentVersion\Run key and runs any programs listed there. Then it looks in the HKEY_CURRENT_USER\Software\Microsoft\Windows\CurrentVersion\RunOnce key, and runs any programs listed. Unlike the HKEY_LOCAL_MACHINE RunOnce programs, the HKEY_CURRENT_USER RunOnce programs run just like any other program; they don't hold the machine hostage until finished, and they multitask with everything else.

7.   Finally, Win95 runs any programs located in the \Windows\Start Menu\Programs\Startup folder. It brings back up most folder windows that were open the last time Windows shut down, and hands control over to the user.

Nawww, it isn't that complicated, is it? Couldn't be. Hmmmmm . . . maybe it is . . .

Note that there are two `Run` keys in the Registry and two `RunOnce` keys. The paths to them look similar, but one pair starts from `HKEY_LOCAL_MACHINE` and is thus systemwide, affecting all users on that machine. The other pair starts from `HKEY_CURRENT_USER` and so is user-specific on systems with multiple user profiles. The `RunOnce` keys are called that because after the system finishes running the commands, they are removed from the Registry.

The two `RunOnce` keys behave very differently for a good reason. The one in `HKEY_LOCAL_MACHINE`, which prohibits any other programs from running until it is done, is there to allow an install program to reboot the system and be sure of regaining control. The one in `HKEY_CURRENT_USER` is there to allow a program to save its state when it is told Windows is shutting down, and then to restore that state upon a reboot.

Cool.

Lest you think that the parts that load the VxDs only load a VxD or two, I'd like to tell you about the logged boot that I ran on my machine. The log file that resulted was 24K bytes and more than 600 lines. Sixty VxDs, 7 `.drv`'s, 6 `exe/dll`'s and 8 `.fon` (bitmapped fonts) files were loaded.

Sixty VxDs. What a complicated architecture. Gotta be something wrong here!

Au contraire. Think of all the subsystems that need to be loaded. There are VxDs for keyboard, mouse, vfat, vcache, comm driver, disk stuff, network stuff, memory management, and a lot more.

That, as best we can tell, is the precise sequence of steps Win95 takes to get itself up and going in the morning. And to think, all I have to do is drag a comb across my head, scrape my teeth with a brush, walk downstairs, and pour some hot java.*

Andrew Schulman makes such a big deal about the appearance of `command.com` for processing `autoexec.bat` —the first chapter on *Unauthorized Windows 95* goes into detail—that I figured I'd try a little experiment. You can do it, too. I created an `autoexec.bat` that contains the command `mem /c /p`, and a `winstart.bat` that has the same command. I ran through a normal Win95 startup sequence, finishing with the command `mem /c /p` run from Win95's Start/Run line (*not* from a DOS box). Figure 8-16 shows what I found for conventional memory allocation, that is, the number of bytes below the 1 MB line that each module occupies.

Conclusions? Apparently `io.sys` calls itself `MSDOS`. Some would make much of that fact, but to me it's a bit of a yawner. Movement of "DOS" into upper memory obviously happens *after* autoexec runs. `command.com` is around to process `autoexec`; it's unloaded and then reloaded with parts in upper memory before `winstart` begins (in the `winstart` listing, `COMMAND` appears after `WIN` and `vmm32`); then it disappears entirely, presumably supplanted by `WIN`. Somehow `vmm32` rearranges itself just before Win95 kicks in. Many of the steps mentioned in this chapter were inferred from the results of this test. Not shown here: If I run `mem /c` from a DOS box, a 7,424 byte `COMMAND` gets loaded.

---

* Rush: Geez. Hot java in the morning? You go Web surfing early, doncha?

(All Sizes in bytes)	Size at autoexec time	Size at winstart time	Size inside Win95
MSDOS	128,368	18,464	18,464
HIMEM	1,120	1,120	1,120
IFSHLP	2,864	2,864	2,864
SETVER	832	832	832
COMMAND	10,386	7,520	Not loaded
WIN	Not loaded	3,568	3,568
vmm32	Not loaded	6,928	1,872

Figure 8-16. Lower memory residents during Startup

Nonstandard Ways of Starting

When two do the same thing it is never quite the same thing.

—Publilius Syrus, *Sententiæ*, ca 50 B.C.

Shifty Starts

Throughout Win95, holding down the Shift key while you start a program (sometimes even when you open a file!) usually means the typical Startup sequence gets bypassed. Win95 itself is no exception. There are, in fact, two different times during the Startup sequence when holding down the Shift key will work.

If you hold down the Shift key either before "Starting Windows 95 . . ." appears on the screen or within two seconds after the message appears, and you keep the Shift key down, you'll get a message flashed on the screen that says "Windows is bypassing your startup files." Startup progresses normally, but neither autoexec.bat nor config.sys get run. Similarly, winstart.bat is bypassed. You'll end up (after five minutes or so of heavy disk activity) in Safe Mode.

If you hold down the Shift key immediately after the network logon screen appears, Windows bypasses your \StartUp group.

Holding down the Shift key at any other point in the Startup process doesn't appear to have any effect.

F Key Express

 You may know that you can hit the F8 key shortly after the "Starting Windows 95 . . ." message appears on the screen, and be confronted with a large number of alternative ways of starting parts of Win95. Ends up that F8 isn't the only option. Let's take a look at all the F keys you can use, which options you have, and what they all accomplish. I'm going to assume your msdos.sys file looks as it would if you installed Win95 to a clean subdirectory—and that you haven't gone out of your way to delete any of the system files that Win95 creates. We'll have much more to say about all those files in the next chapter.

If you hit F8 within two seconds of the "Starting Windows 95 . . ." message appearing on the screen, you'll get the Win95 Startup Menu, Figure 8-17.

```
Microsoft Windows 95 Startup Menu
───────────────────────────────────────────────────────────

1.  Normal

2.  Logged (\BOOTLOG.TXT)

3.  Safe Mode

4.  Safe Mode with Network Support

5.  Step-by-step confirmation

6.  Command prompt only

7.  Safe mode command prompt only

8.  Previous version of MS-DOS

Enter a choice: 1

F5=Safe mode Shift+F5=Command prompt Shift+F8=Step-by-step
confirmation [N]
```

Figure 8-17. The full Win95 Startup Menu

If option number 8 doesn't appear in your Startup menu, it means that `msdos.sys` contains the line `BootMulti=0`; which probably means you installed Win95 over the top of Windows 3.1, and thus can't boot to your previous version of DOS (without a boot diskette, anyway). If option 4 doesn't appear in your Startup menu, it means `msdos.sys` does not contain the line `Network=1`, which probably means you don't have a network. We'll go over the many flavors of `msdos.sys` in Chapter 9.

1. `Normal` is the choice you want to make if you accidentally got into the Startup menu and want to get the hell out. It just tells Win95 to start the way it usually does.

2. `Logged (\BOOTLOG.TXT)` tells Win95 to start normally, but log each startup activity as it proceeds. The log is written to the file `bootlog.txt` in your boot drive's root folder. We'll be looking at `bootlog.txt` extensively in the next chapter. A more complicated way of accomplishing the same thing is to choose number 6 from this menu, wait until you get the `c:>` command prompt, and type `win /b` to start a boot log.

3. `Safe Mode` forces Win95 to start in, uh, Safe Mode, that weird quasi-Windows state (see Figure 8-5) that may or may not let you repair what ails your Windows. Safe Mode's greatest achievement—the fact that it will run just about anytime, even if your machine is on its last legs—is also its greatest shortcoming. In order to run in a crippled state, almost everything you might want to look at either doesn't work or works minimally. For example, the Control Panel System applet's Device Manager will tell you that, on every device, "Status is not available when Windows is running in Safe Mode." Hardly a comforting situation.

Safe Mode runs with generic mouse and keyboard drivers and standard VGA. That's about it. Your CD, for example, won't spin, your printer won't print, and your modem won't mo. Dem. While Safe Mode doesn't use many (if any!) settings from the Registry, you can get at Regedit while in Safe Mode, to modify aberrant Registry values.

The hard way to get to Safe Mode is to choose number 6 here, wait for the `c:>` prompt, and then type `win /d:m`. The easy way to get into Safe Mode next time is to reboot, look for the "Starting Windows 95 . . . ," and hit `F5`. Safe Mode has a more restrictive variant called Safe Mode Without Compression that bypasses the usual disk compression routines. The only way I found to get into that mode was by rebooting, waiting for "Starting Windows 95 . . ." to appear on the screen, then hitting `Ctrl+F5`.

4. `Safe Mode With Network Support`, as its name implies, is a more lenient variant of Safe Mode that includes network drivers. It suffers from the same fatal flaws as Safe Mode in general, although by using this option you can go into Network

Neighborhood and get connected. The hard way to get to Safe Mode With Network Support is to choose 6 here, wait for `c:>`, then type `win /d:n`. The easy way is to reboot, look for "Starting Windows 95 . . ." to flash on the screen, and hit `F6`.

5. `Step-by-step confirmation` boots into normal Windows 95, but it gives you the option to include or skip just about every step of the startup process—not just the traditional lines in `config.sys` and `autoexec.bat`. That can be very valuable if you've narrowed a startup problem down to one offensive component. It can also be very dangerous if you elect to exclude a crucial part of Win95.

I ran a test on Step-by-step confirmation and was quite impressed by the thoroughness of the choices offered. It really does seem to hit every component of the startup process, giving you the opportunity to run the command or pass it by. Here is a log of what Windows said:

```
Windows will prompt you to confirm each startup command
Load DoubleSpace drivers?
Process the system registry?
Create a startup log file (\BOOTLOG.TXT)?
Device = d:\windows\himem.sys?
Device = d:\windows\ifshlp.sys?
Device = d:\windows\setver.exe
Process your startup device drivers (Config.sys)?
Then it asked to run each line in config.sys
Process your startup command file (Autoexec.bat)?
Then it asked to run each line in autoexec.bat
WIN?
Load all Windows drivers?
If you choose yes, it loads all of them normally;
if you choose no, Win95 starts in Safe Mode
```

There's one odd part of Step-by-step confirmation that, uh, bugged me. It always seemed to run `winstart.bat`, no matter which choices I made. While it's true that few Windows users have a `winstart.bat` file, it's also true that those who do (often network users with weird connection problems) may need the Step-by-step process more than the average Win user.

If you want to run Step-by-step confirmation without going through the Startup menu, reboot. When "Starting Windows 95 . . ." appears on the screen, hit `Shift+F8`.

6. `Command prompt only` Oh, you diehard DOS fans. This option puts you in what amounts to DOS 7 mode, with a bare `c:>` prompt, on a wing and a prayer. It runs `config.sys` and `autoexec.bat`, and does everything else noted in the discussion about `io.sys` earlier, with two exceptions that I could find.

First, the lower memory situation at the command prompt is a bit strange, if you have no `config.sys` or `autoexec.bat`. Running a `mem /c /p` shows that `MSDOS` only takes up 18K of lower memory, which is great, but `DBLSPACE` occupies a whopping 109K. Second, the variable `windir=` is no longer in the DOS environment. Precisely as it should be.

Running in this mode you have access to some bare-bones functions for importing and exporting Registry entries. While you can't graphically get at the Registry directly from the command prompt, the limited capabilities may save your tail some day. If you get into those dire straits, take a look at Chapter 11, where we discuss `regedit` run in real mode.

 Surprisingly, there doesn't appear to be a "quick key" combination to get directly at the command prompt when "Starting Windows 95 . . ." appears on the screen. You have to hit `F8`, wait for the Startup menu to appear, then type 6. That's an odd oversight because speed demon DOS types seem to me to be the most likely to demand obscure key combinations to cut directly to their hallowed `c:>`.

7. `Safe mode command prompt only` is just about as bare-bones as you can get. Or would want to. This mode is a bit like Command Prompt Mode, except Win95 doesn't even look at your `config.sys` or `autoexec.bat` files. You get a `c:>` prompt, the same environment variables as in Command Prompt Mode, with `MSDOS` taking up 77K of lower memory, `DRVSPACE` (if you have compressed drives) taking another 109K, and `COMMAND` its 10K.

There *is* a quick combination into Safe Mode command prompt, though. When the "Starting Windows 95 . . ." line appears, hit `Shift+F5`.

8. `Previous version of MS-DOS` works slick as could be, providing you installed Win95 to a clean directory. When you choose this option, Win95 does the following in the root folder of the boot directory:

• Renames `autoexec.bat` (the current Win95 `autoexec` file) to `autoexec.w40`. Renames `autoexec.dos` (the copy of your original `autoexec.bat`, created back when you installed Win95) to `autoexec.bat`.

- Renames `config.sys` (the current Win95 `config` file) to `config.w40`. Renames `config.dos` (the copy of your original `config.sys`, created back when you installed Win95) to `config.sys`.

- Renames `command.com` (the Win95 command interpreter) to `command.w40`. Renames `command.dos` (the version of `command.com` that existed when you originally installed Win95, typically from DOS 5 or DOS 6) to `command.com`. Similarly, `mode.com` is renamed to `mode_dos.w40` and `mode.dos` is renamed to `mode.com`.

- Renames `msdos.sys` (the Win95 text file with startup settings) to `msdos.w40`. Renames `msdos.dos` (the program—*not* a text file— `msdos.sys` that existed when you originally installed Win95, typically from DOS 5 or DOS 6) to `msdos.sys`.

- Renames `io.sys` (the Win95 workhorse that gets Win95 started in the first place) to `winboot.sys`. Renames `io.dos` (the DOS 5 or DOS 6 program that existed when you originally installed Win95) to `io.sys`.

- Hands over control to the newly named `io.sys`, which in turn gets your old version of DOS running.

The quick key combination for running your previous version of DOS is to reboot, wait for "Starting Windows 95 . . ." to appear, then hit `F4`. Note once again that you have to be set up for dual booting (the mentioned files have to exist, with their proper names, and `msdos.sys` must contain the line `BootMulti=1`).

Once you're done with your DOS 5 or DOS 6 session, simply reboot the way you always have. Win95's shining face will greet you.

 The *Windows Resource Kit* says that Win95 `io.sys` is renamed to `io.w40`. T'ain't true. If you go looking for it, you won't find it . . . and therein lies a story. Oh, how I love a nice documentation bug in the morning'!

How Win95 Really Boots

> When you want to fool the world, tell the truth.

> —Otto von Bismarck

 Does this multiple boot stuff have you all confused? Yeah. Me, too. Like, how does Win95 mysteriously reappear after you've multi-booted to DOS 6, and then restarted the PC? *Something* has to go in there and swap out the DOS 6 `io.sys` with the Win95 `io.sys`, doesn't it? I sent our best no-nonsense icon to check it out.

 Not ta worry, Mom. It's all smoke 'n mirrors.

When a PC boots from a hard drive, it reads in the first record (called a "boot record") on the hard drive and hands control to the little program—the bootstrapper—located on that boot record. The bootstrapper, in turn, passes control over to a specific place on the hard drive that must contain all the programs necessary to bring the PC to life. The bootstrapper don't know nuthin' about filenames or any of that stuff. It just knows locations on the disk.

 In good ol' DOS, the boot record would always hand control over to a file called `io.sys`, which was always in the first data sector of the disk. When you made a "boot disk," you essentially put `io.sys` in the first data sector, thus ensuring that when the boot record handed off control, `io.sys` in particular and DOS in general would take over.

 But Win95 got tricky—it had to, if it was going to keep the ability to boot to either Win95 or to the previous version of DOS. Win95 has a file that can have either of two different names—`winboot.sys` or `io.sys`— depending on whether Win95 is running (when it's known as `io.sys`) or the previous version of DOS is running (when it's known as `winboot.sys`). The trick is that the file doesn't *move*.

 When Win95 installs itself, it creates a new boot record that points to that file-with-two-names. That means whenever your PC boots off the hard drive, control is passed to this file—whether it's called `io.sys` or `winboot.sys`, doesn't matter.

Oh. I get it now. When it comes to life, this program must look at one of the files that gets renamed, to see if DOS or Win95 was the last to run. I'd bet it looks at the first file on the disk. (At least, that would be one reasonable way to do it.) If the first file on the disk is called `io.dos`, the program knows that Win95 was the last operating system to run, that all is hunkey-dorey, and that processing can continue. But if it discovers that the first file is called `io.sys`, it knows that a previous version of DOS was the last operating system to run, and so it has to rename a whole bunch of files before it proceeds: `config.sys` has to be renamed `config.dos`; `config.w40` has to be renamed `config.sys`; similarly with `autoexec`, `command`, `msdos`, and `mode`.

Wait a minute! It can't be that simple, Mom. What if there's no older version of DOS on the PC? The first file on the disk could be almost anything. Oh, but you could get around *that* by. . . .

Details, details, details. Now you know how Win95 *really* wakes up in the morning: with an Excedrin-class headache.

Chapter 9

Techie Files, Techie Programs

As he knew not what to say,
he swore.

—Byron, *The Island,* 1823

 As you wend your way toward the Registry—and I just *know* that's what you're doing, reading these chapters sequentially in spite of all the warnings—the going gets tougher when you start talking about the files Win95 uses to store things, what's put in those files, and how certain fancy programs interact with the files.

 In this chapter we'll tackle files you can play with, and programs that will inevitably go kablooey when you do. The crazy part is that you may be forced to dig into these files some day, whether you want to or not. And at that point, I'll certainly understand if you use a word or two generally reserved for, oh, barroom brawls—or TV talk shows.

 Hey, boss. Don't forget to tell 'em that this is where they come to find out how to change the splash screens that Windows 95 uses—how they learn to replace the Windows logo that hogs the screen during bootup with a picture of their significant other . . . or Mom.

Setup

Doceo insanire omnes. *

—Horace, *Satires,* ca. 25 B.C.

---

* I teach that all men are crazy.

The key to the Win95 setup routine's wonderful robustness—or its infuriating inability to install on your machine, should you be so unfortunate—lies in the files Setup creates and uses to guide itself through the installation process. Those files can generally be divided into three types: the log files, which keep track of each step in the installation; the `.inf` files, which try to guide the installer, typically pointing it to correct drivers for identified hardware; and a whole bunch of miscellaneous files, some of which are totally inscrutable (to me anyway) and some of which can save your posterior if it becomes exposed.

LogView

 If you're going spelunking in your Windows 95 log files, and you have the Win95 CD, bring along a tool designed specifically for the job: a program called LogView (Figure 9-1).

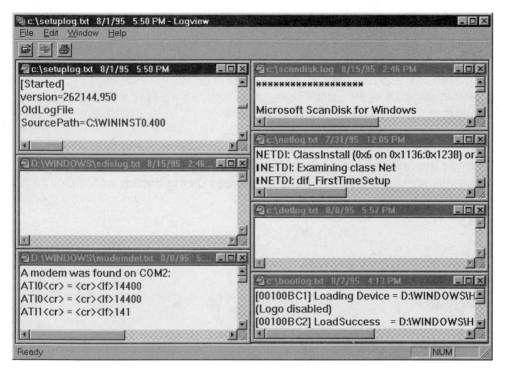

Figure 9-1. LogView

Drag and copy the file `logview.exe` from your CD's `\other\misc\logview` folder to someplace handy, like `\Program Files\Accessories`. Then right-click and drag it to the Win95 `\Windows\Start Menu\Programs\Accessories\System`

`Tools` folder, then pick Create Shortcut. I stick the shortcut there just because I like to navigate through five levels of cascading menus when working with high-powered tools.

Most log files and all `.INF` files are simple ASCII text files, arranged like a Windows 3.1 `.INI` file. Open up one of them and you'll find entries like this:

```
[Section]
Key1 = value
Key2 = value
```

Within a given section, there should be no duplicate keys. The ordering of sections within the file is not significant, nor is the ordering of keys within a section. For many other details on the precise way `.INI` files and their values are (generally) interpreted, see Chapter 8 of the original *Mother of All Windows Books,* ISBN 0-201-62708-6. If you've never dissected an `.INI` file, not to worry. You'll catch on real quick.

SETUPLOG.TXT

As the Win95 Setup wizard progresses through its steps, it maintains several log files. The first one to be created is called `setuplog.txt`. It resides in the root folder of your boot drive and serves several purposes. First, it's the repository of information for the Setup wizard—if you push a `<Back` button in one of the Wizard dialogs, the wizard can retrieve earlier information from `setuplog.txt`. Second, it provides a record of the early steps in installation—the part that comes before hardware detection—and then the later parts of installation, primarily the copying of files and booting of Win95 for the first time. If Setup crashes during the early or late stages, it's usually smart enough to read `setuplog.txt`, merge that information with the Registry if it exists, carry your good settings forward to the safe recovery stage, and avoid whatever it was that crashed you the first time. (We'll talk about hardware detection crashes when we discuss `detlog.txt` later.) Finally, and most important to us, `setuplog.txt` is designed to let *you* look at the results of Setup running on your machine—most likely to isolate a Setup problem, so you can bypass the problem spot during a hellacious installation.

Although the beginning of `setuplog.txt` looks more or less like an `.ini` file (with sections, keys, and values), the parts at the end are simple log entries, recorded when certain tasks have begun or ended. It's almost as if the Setup folks started out intent on building a real `.ini` file, then got lazy midway through. The log entries at the end are created sequentially—as things happen, Win95 Setup adds entries to the end of the file. A few notes about `setuplog.txt`:

- [Started] holds info about the Win95 version: the entry `version=262144,950` means you *are* running Win95; that's just the funny way Windows stores the version number 4.00.950.

- The Setup routine starts digesting entries from a file called `setup.inf`, located in the Win95 `\windows\inf` folder. The entire `\windows\inf` folder is hidden, so if you're looking for it with Explorer, you'll have to click on View, then Options, and check the Show All Files button. Among other things (including a few entries that look suspiciously like leftovers from the Win95 World Tour and something called the Microsoft Expo), `setup.inf` instructs the Setup routine to load *ninety* different `.inf` files, all located in the `\windows\inf` folder.

- "Normal" `.inf` files (and `setup.inf` is anything *but* normal) are described in Appendix C of the *Windows Resource Kit*. Try opening up `\windows\inf\keyboard.inf` to see what a real "normal" `.inf` file looks like.

system.1st

At the beginning of the Copy Files phase, the Setup routine backs up the Registry—copying `system.dat` to `system.da0` in the `\windows` folder (they're both hidden, read-only files), and `user.dat` to `user.da0`—and then, as best I can tell, makes *another* copy, called `system.new` and `user.new` (also hidden, read-only), in the root directory of the boot drive. (I think these two `.new` files are deleted later in the Setup process, if Win95 installs correctly, but I couldn't find any documentation about them.) Setup then creates the Startup Diskette.

Upon successful completion of the Copy Files phase, the Setup routine loads the Registry with its RunOnce program (the one that does the final configuration—setting Time Zones, moving Windows 3.1 groups to the Start Menu, building the initial Windows Help files, and the like; there's a description of RunOnce in Chapter 11). At this point, the Setup routine copies the Registry file `system.dat` (in the `\windows` folder) to the root of the boot drive, marking it hidden, read-only and system, and naming it `setup.1st`.

`system.1st` is as close to a clean Registry as your machine will ever see: if you somehow clobber both the Registry `.dat` files and their `.da0` backups, or if Win95 setup hangs when running the RunOnce program—a dilemma I've encountered on a bone-stock ALR 486—you may need `setup.1st` to restore things. Using `setup.1st` is *not* easy. You have to reboot with the F8 key (see Chapter 8) and get into Command Prompt Mode. Then you need to use the `attrib` command to change the hidden, read-only and system attributes on `setup.1st` and `\windows\setup.dat` (e.g., `attrib -h -r`

`-s` `setup.1st` Let's hear it for the DOS 7 command line, eh?) Finally, you need to copy `setup.1st` over the top of `\windows\setup.dat`. When you reboot into Win95, Windows will start in with the Setup RunOnce program, and you can proceed from there.

detlog.txt

While `setuplog.txt` is a real working file, `detlog.txt` can best be thought of as just another pretty face. The Setup routine uses `setuplog.txt` for all sorts of things; but `detlog.txt` only exists for humans to look at. And swear over. None of the hardware detection routines use any of the entries in `detlog.txt`. Although, amazingly, `detlog.txt` is marked by Win95 as system and hidden, so you'll have to futz with Explorer or the `attrib` command before you'll be able to look at it.

Windows creates a `detlog.txt` every time it runs its automatic hardware detection program, known to techies as `sysdetmg.dll`. You can choose to run that program if you pick "automatic detection" during Win95 setup. You can also run it if you pick "automatic detection" while using the Control Panel's Add/Remove Hardware applet (discussed in Chapter 10). `detlog.txt` makes no pretensions to being an `.ini` file or anything else. It's a straight, sequential ASCII text file that keeps a blow-by-blow log of all the steps `sysdetmg.dll` takes in trying to find and identify all your hardware.

The auto hardware detector maintains two generations of `detlog` files: `detlog.txt` and `detlog.old`. If the auto hardware detector discovers when it starts that it is running from inside the Setup routine while the Setup routine is in Safe Recovery Mode (see Chapter 7), it merely appends new hardware detection entries to the end of the existing `detlog.txt`. But if the auto hardware detector comes to life and finds it's running outside of Safe Recovery Mode, and it sees that there's an existing `detlog.txt` in the root directory of the boot drive, it renames that file `detlog.old` before creating a new, clean `detlog.txt`.

```
NewDanger: *:DETECTMITSUMI was crashed by *:DETECTSONYCD
LogDangerRes: new crash func. *:DETECTSONYCD
IO=310-313
```

Figure 9-2. detlog.txt logs a crash

That means, in general, if the auto hardware detection routines freeze, you can open up `detlog.txt`, take a look at the final entry (see Figure 9-2 for an example of a crash during detection of a CD-ROM drive), and have a pretty good idea of what was happening when the detector went belly up. *You* can. The *computer* doesn't; after all, `detlog.txt` is for human consumption only. Instead, every time `sysdetmg.dll` is about to try something the least bit likely to cause your system to lock up, it updates `detlog.txt`, then creates a binary file called `detcrash.log` in the root directory of the boot drive that says something like, "I'm about to try to find such-and-such hardware at thus-and-so location." If your system hangs during the detection and you restart in Safe Recovery Mode, `sysdetmg.dll` immediately looks for a `detcrash.log` file. If one exists, `sysdetmg.dll` is smart enough to fast-forward to the detection point that caused the hang, *skip over* the bad detection step—the one that locked up the machine—and continue with the next attempted detection in its list. That's the brilliance of auto hardware detection.

Would that the documentation were so brilliant. Don't trust what the *Windows Resource Kit* says about `detcrash.log`**. It's wrong, repeatedly.**

When the auto hardware detection completes successfully, it deletes any existing `detcrash.log,` but it preserves `detlog.txt`, in case you should ever need it.

If you're interested in a detailed definition of `detlog.txt` entries, look in Chapter 6 of the *Windows Resource Kit,* but to give you a taste of what's up, let's try this entry from my detlog on for size (Figure 9-3). We'll trace it all the way back to its origins, a key step missing in all the existing documentation.

```
Checking for: Motherboard Resources
Checking for: Keyboard
QueryIOMem: Caller=DETECTKBD, rcQuery=0
IO=60-60,64-64
GetKbdType: Keyboard ID=faab41
Detected: *PNP0303\0000 = [8] Standard 101/102-Key or
Microsoft Natural Keyboard
IO=60-60,64-64
IRQ=1
```

Figure 9-3. detlog.txt entries for the keyboard

As you can see, `sysdetmg.dll` gives you a full, almost-English-language analysis of what it is trying to find, and when it finds the hardware it's looking for, it tells you precisely what it found. (Bravo, Redmond!) In this case, it's looking for the keyboard by querying I/O locations 60 and 64. It detected a keyboard of the type PNP0303, which is a standard keyboard, using I/O locations 60 and 64, and IRQ 1. Cool.

You might think `sysdetmg.dll` is smart—but wait, it's even smarter than you think! This hardware detection stuff isn't hard-coded into the program. Instead, Microsoft designed it to be spoon-fed by a file called `msdet.inf`, which is located in your Win95 `\windows\inf` folder. For example, the line in `msdet.inf` that tells `sysdetmg.dll` to go out and search for a keyboard looks like this:

```
DetectKbd  =keyboard,keyboard.inf,BUS_ALL,RISK_VERYLOW,
```

The `BUS_ALL` value says that `DetectKbd` should be run for any (ISA, EISA, or MCA) bus machine. The `RISK_VERYLOW` value tells `sysdetmg.dll` that the chances of hanging the PC when running `DetectKbd` is, uh, very low. Moreover, the `keyboard.inf` value instructs `sysdetmg.dll` to look for details about detecting a keyboard in the file `keyboard.inf`, located in the Win95 `\windows\inf` folder. Buried down in `keyboard.inf`, you'll find entries that look like this:

```
[MS_KBD]
%*PNP0303.DeviceDesc% = PC_AT_Enh_Inst,*PNP0303
[PC_AT_Enh_Inst]
LogConfig = kbdlc
CopyFiles = MS_KBD_ENH_CopyFiles, KBD_VxDs
DelFiles = KBD_VxDs_Del
UpdateInis = PC_AT_Enh_Inis, Keyb.Common.Inis
AddReg=Keyb.Common.Reg
AddReg = MS_KBD_AddReg
```

Figure 9-4. keyboard.inf entries

which apparently tell `sysdetmg.dll` which VxD virtual device driver to use for this particular keyboard (it gets moshed into `\windows\system\vmm32.vxd`), and which entries to apply to the Registry. If you've ever wondered how the auto hardware detection routine figures out which VxDs and Registry entries are associated with a particular device, it's all buried here, down a couple of levels in huge `.inf` files.

netlog.txt

 As you might imagine, a big, tough part of auto hardware detection lies in figuring out what kind of network devices are attached to your computer, and which network protocols should be installed. The initial detection of network cards occurs during normal hardware detection, triggered by lines like this in `msdet.inf` that prompts `sysdetmg.dll` to look for an Intel EtherExpress card:

```
DetectEE16 =net,net.inf,BUS_ISA,RISK_DELICATE,
```

which tied in with a `net.inf` line like this:

```
*pnp812d=netee16.inf
```

to link to entries like this in `netee16.inf`:

```
[*PNP812D.ndi]
AddReg=*pnp812d.ndi.reg,EXP16.ndi.reg
LogConfig=*pnp812d.LogConfig
```

and resulted, on my machine, in a `detlog.txt` entry that looks like this:

```
Checking for: Intel EtherExpress 16 or 16TP Network Adapter
NCD: detecting net card *pnp812d
QueryIOMem: Caller=DETECTEE16, rcQuery=0
IO=300-30f
NetAvoidIO: 300-30f
QueryIOMem: Caller=DETECTEE16, rcQuery=0
IO=300-30f
DetFlags: 100000
Detected: *PNP812D\0000 = [11] Intel EtherExpress 16 or 16TP
IO=300-30f
IRQ=9
```

correctly identifying my EtherExpress 16 card, its I/O address, and IRQ. But wait! We aren't done yet . . . Network configuration is so hairy that, when the auto hardware detector encounters a network card or a modem, it starts (are you ready for this?) *yet another* log file, called `netlog.txt`, located in your boot drive's root directory, that records the details of installing services and protocols on the network card and "dial-up adapter."

This makes absolutely no sense, but while `detlog.txt` is marked as a hidden and system file, and thus takes some effort to peek at, `netlog.txt` has no restrictions at all. Why? Who knows.

Much as `msdet.inf` in the hidden `\windows\inf` folder provides information for detecting hardware, `netdet.ini` (note: not `.inf`!) in the wide-open `\windows` folder supplies information for identifying Netware installations and network programs such as WinFax Pro for Networks.

 If you're curious about the meaning of the various lines in `netlog.txt`, or if you're stuck with a network configuration problem that has you scanning `netlog.txt` for some insight, there's a very brief explanation of some of the entries in the *Windows Resource Kit,* Chapter 6. Sarah and I ran through our `netlog.txt` and found quite a few lines with undocumented actions, including several like these:

```
NETDI: Wrote p.ini:DriverName=nwlink$, sect: nwlink$
NETDI: Wrote p.ini:DriverName=NETBEUI$, sect: NETBEUI$
```

We were mighty perplexed—there's no `p.ini` on either of our machines—until, one day, Erwin noticed a few entries in the `\windows\protocol.ini` file on Sarah's machine that looked very suspicious:

```
[nwlink$]
DriverName=nwlink$
Frame_Type=4
cachesize=0
Bindings=EXP16$
[NETBEUI$]
DriverName=NETBEUI$
Lanabase=1
sessions=10
ncbs=12
Bindings=EXP16$
```

I'm convinced that these are the result of actions referred to by the `Wrote p.ini` entries in `netlog.txt`. Note that `protocol.ini`, much like `system.ini` and `win.ini`, can contain values that override Registry settings.

autoexec.bat and config.sys

Win95 Setup uses and modifies several other files. I talked about its modifications to `autoexec.bat` and `config.sys`, specifically to make those files peacefully coexist with Win95, in Chapter 8. But there's one modification I didn't mention then, just to keep from confusing an already cloudy situation.

Have you been wondering how the Win95 Setup routine figures out if it's starting out new, or if it's been restarted after the PC locked up? In the latter case, the Setup wizard needs to ask if you want to proceed in Safe Recovery Mode, thus bypassing whatever glitch caused Setup to fail in the first place. How does it know? The trick lies in modifications the Setup routine makes to `autoexec.bat` before it starts mucking around with your system.

To help manage all sorts of temporary setup-only files, Setup creates a temporary directory on your boot drive called `\wininst0.400`. If you've crashed and seen a strange directory sitting around with that name, it was left there by the Setup routine. When you start Setup, it sticks a DOS batch program called `suwarn.bat` in that temporary directory. `suwarn.bat`'s only purpose in life is to start Setup with a prompt asking the user if he or she wants to continue in Safe Recovery Mode.

The trick? Once `suwarn.bat` is in place, and before it does anything at all significant to your system, Setup puts these two lines at the beginning of your `autoexec.bat` file:

```
@if exist c:\wininst0.400\suwarn.bat call c:\wininst0.400\suwarn.bat

@if exist c:\wininst0.400\suwarn.bat del c:\wininst0.400\suwarn.bat
```

Those lines say, simply, if `suwarn.bat` exists, run it, and then delete it. If you restart your PC because it froze during a hardware detection phase, those two lines zip you back into Setup's Safe Recovery Mode. Ingeniously simple.

Chapter 8 in this book and Chapter 6 in the *Windows Resource Kit* cover most of the rest of the changes made to `autoexec.bat` and `config.sys` during Setup, with one exception: If you have DriveSpace installed, other changes made to `autoexec.bat` and `config.sys` are detailed in the file `\windows\drvspace.inf`. Worth checking.

system.ini and win.ini

If you ignored my advice and installed Win95 over the top of Windows 3.1, your `system.ini` and `win.ini` files are bound to be a jumbled mess. Chapter 6 of the *Windows Resource Kit* will tell you which entries are altered by the Setup routine. The rest of the garbage in those files may date back to three weeks before the beginning of time, and there's precious little you can do about it.

On the other hand, if you installed Win95 to a new directory, your `system.ini` and `win.ini` should look pretty much like typical Windows 3.1 versions.* `system.ini` has sections marked `[boot]`, `[keyboard]`, `[boot.description]`, `[386Enh]`, `[drivers]`, `[mci]`, and `[NonWindowsApp]`, all of which look like their Win31 brethren. `[Password Lists]` and `[drivers32]` are new, but self-explanatory. In `win.ini`, `[windows]`, `[Desktop]`, `[intl]`, `[FontSubstitutes]`, `[Compatibility]` (ten times its old size, with a similar purpose, but—surprise—none of these entries are migrated to the Registry; they're read on startup and somehow stored internally, outside the Registry), `[mci extensions]`, `[MCICompatibility]`, `[Extensions]`, `[Ports]`, `[embedding]`, `[PrinterPorts]`, `[Devices]`, and `[colors]` look much as they did under Win31. `[Compatibility32]` and `[ModuleCompatibility]` are two new sections, but they're self-explanatory, too.

There's one change that isn't obvious. In `win.ini` (whether you installed Win95 over the top of Win31, or you installed it into a new directory), there's a new entry that looks like this:

```
[Pscript.drv]
ATMWorkaround=1
```

No, it isn't a secret Microsoft plot to take over the Adobe Type Manager (ATM) world. It's just a flag that keeps earlier versions of ATM from clobbering the print driver. Apparently older versions of ATM write over a previously unclaimed part of the print driver. Win95 reclaimed that real estate as its own. `ATMWorkaround=1` lets the two live in détente.

Drat! And here I thought I had another good Microsoft conspiracy theory.

---

* At the risk of flagellating an expired equine, the original *Mother of All Windows Books,* ISBN 0-201-62708-6, covers these topics at length.

Startup

I saw "Hamlet, Prince of Denmark" played,
but now the old plays begin to disgust this refined age.

—John Evelyn, *Diary,* Nov. 26, 1661

 Another morass of files surround Win95's startup sequence. Two of them are particularly important, one for diagnosing problems, the other for allowing you to change some of Win95's startup behavior. Though this be madness, yet there is method in't . . .

bootlog.txt

 When you start Win95, you can tell it to produce a boot log by pressing `F8` immediately after the "Starting Windows 95 . . ." message appears, and then choosing option 2 from the Startup menu. The boot log, a simple text file called `bootlog.txt` (marked hidden and located in the root directory of the boot drive), contains hundreds of lines of detail about the Win95 startup process. A boot log is also produced automatically when you first boot Win95, at the tail end of the Setup sequence.

Actually, Windows maintains two generations of boot logs. If you tell Windows 95 that you want a boot log, and it discovers there's already a file called `bootlog.txt` in the root directory, that file is renamed `bootlog.prv` before Win95 creates a new `bootlog.txt`.

 Why `bootlog.prv`? I mean, all the other cycled-out files are called `.old`. I guess `.prv` must mean *previous.* Certainly is a strange inconsistency. And why on earth are both `bootlog.txt` and `bootlog.prv` marked hidden? Their only possible reason is to inform prying eyes of the progress of a Win95 boot. No doubt a foolish hobgoblin of Rush's mind.

The boot log contains a blow-by-blow description of what gets loaded and when, and if any problems were encountered in the process. If something goes seriously wrong when you try to start Win95, creating a boot log and then scanning the tail end of `bootlog.txt` may provide some insight into what went awry.

 The boot log starts by telling you if the real-mode drivers—typically `himem`, `ifshlp`, and `setver`—loaded properly. Then it tells you, one at a time, whether each of the dozens of virtual device drivers loaded correctly, and whether they initialized properly. After that the boot log notes loading of the system files like `gdi.exe` and `user.exe`, sound and communication drivers, system fonts, the mouse, keyboard and the like, and finally any installable drivers.

If your system starts acting very flakey—you can't get to a DoubleSpace drive, the mouse stops dead in its tracks, you start getting SHARE violations, or the print spooler suddenly croaks—it would be worth the effort to run a boot log and scan for the string "fail." Usually VxDs that fail to load do so for a good reason (e.g., they aren't needed or won't work on your machine), but occasionally a bit gets flipped in the .vxd file, causing a Load Failure. You may be able to revive a failed component by reconfirming the entire Win95 installation (just run Setup from diskette or CD) or by decompressing an appropriate file (see Appendix E).*

msdos.sys

This is the first-level hacker's file, the one dangled out for tire-kickers and weekend PC mechanics to modify. It contains a handful of settings that produce moderately interesting effects in the Win95 startup process. It's a simple .ini-style file, with sections, keys, and values—a far cry from the old DOS 6-and-earlier msdos.sys, which was an impenetrable binary file.

All the kick-butt Win95 power is in the Registry, of course. If you get a minor jolt out of rigging your msdos.sys, you're in for the, uh, rush of a lifetime when you twiddle the bits in your Registry. Patience. That's Chapter 11.

Let's start by taking off the training wheels. Right-click My Computer, pick Explorer. If you haven't already rigged Explorer to show all your files, click on View, then Options, make sure the Show All Files button is checked, and uncheck the Hide MS-DOS File Extensions for File Types That Are Registered box. Now go into the root directory of your boot drive (probably c:\), right-click on msdos.sys, and pick Properties. Clear the Hidden button. Click OK.

Up on the Explorer menu, click Edit, then Copy. Next click Edit, then Paste. If you scroll down to the bottom of the file list, you'll find a file called Copy of MSDOS.SYS. Right-click on it, pick Rename, and change the name to msdos.mom. Good. You now have a backup copy of msdos.sys with a short filename that's easy to get at from the DOS command line—just in case you screw up. A simple DOS command like

---

* Sometimes the fail is only because the vxd was loaded earlier. If you see a Load Failed line, check earlier in the log file and you'll probably find that the load succeeded.

```
copy c:\msdos.mom c:\msdos.sys
```

will return all your Win95 startup settings to their original upright positions.

 Time to see what you have to play with. Right-click on `msdos.sys`, pick Open With, make sure the Always Use This Program To Open This Kind of File box is cleared, scroll down, and double-click on Notepad. Along with a whole bunch of x-ed out lines, you should see some entries like those in Figure 9-5.

```
[Options]
BootGUI=1
BootMulti=1
Network=1
>>(all of those lines with x's)
[Paths]
WinDir=C:\WINDOWS
WinBootDir=C:\WINDOWS
HostWinBootDrv=H
UninstallDir=C:\
```

Figure 9-5. Sarah's msdos.sys

 Don't play around with the entries in the `[Paths]` section. Pointing `io.sys` (see Chapter 8) to the wrong directories for fundamental WinThings can lead to a severe case of indigestion—yours, of course. Think Hannibal Lector, *sans* fava beans.

 The *Windows Resource Kit* documents 16 settings for the `[Options]` section. Unfortunately, it doesn't get all of them right—and all the books and articles I've seen merely parrot the incorrect official documentation. Let me see if I can set the record straight. As best I can tell, this is exactly how the Win95 Startup routine* handles settings in `msdos.sys`:

Step 0. Startup reads the entire `msdos.sys` file from beginning to end, figures out which settings are in the file, and keeps track of all the settings. This is very different from the way typical `.ini` files are used—programs usually look up `.ini` file values only when they need 'em. If Startup doesn't like one of your settings, it'll give you an error message.

---

* It's really `io.sys`, but I'll call it the Startup routine so I don't sound so pretentious.

Step 1. Startup puts the message "Starting Windows 95 . . ." on the screen.

Step 2. Startup looks at the `BootMenu=` entry. If `BootMenu=1`, it immediately brings up the "Microsoft Windows 95 Startup Menu" and jumps down to **Step M1,** at the end of these steps. (One variation of the Startup Menu is shown here as Figure 9-6.)

Step 3. If there is no `BootMenu=` entry, or if `BootMenu=0`, Startup looks at the `BootKeys=` entry. If `BootKeys=0`, Startup bypasses the normal pause to wait for the user to hit `F8`, and jumps down to **Step 6.**

 If you can't get `F8` to work, chances are good some *furshlinger* system administrator or software vendor decided to make your PC "more secure" by adding the line `BootKeys=0` to your `msdos.sys`. You can flip 'em an electronic bird by simply modifying `msdos.sys` to get rid of the offensive line. (If Win95 has been jimmied so you can't edit `msdos.sys`, just boot from a floppy and edit the sucker in DOS mode.)

Step 4. If there is no `BootKeys=` entry, or if `BootKeys=1`, Startup begins monitoring for key presses. If it detects an `F8` (or any of the other shortcut keys that change the Startup sequence, including `F4`, `F5`, `F6`, and several `Shift+` and `Ctrl+` combinations; see Chapter 8), Startup brings up the "Microsoft Windows 95 Startup Menu" (or performs whatever action is dictated by the Startup shortcut keys) and skips to **Step M1.**

```
Microsoft Windows 95 Startup Menu

===================================

1. Normal
2. Logged (\BOOTLOG.TXT)
3. Safe Mode
4. Step-by-step confirmation
5. Command prompt only
6. Safe mode command prompt only
7. Previous version of MS-DOS
Enter a choice: 1
F5=Safe mode Shift+F5=Command prompt Shift+F8=Step-by-step
confirmation [N]
```

Figure 9-6. Startup Menu with Network=0, BootMulti=1, no timer

Step 5. Startup then looks for a `BootDelay=` setting, which specifies the number of seconds Startup is supposed to wait for an `F8` key press. If there is a `BootDelay=` setting, Startup waits the specified number of seconds. If there is no `BootDelay=` setting, Startup waits about two seconds.

 Note how the peculiarities in **Steps 4** and **5** will let you get into the Start Menu with an `F8`, even if `BootDelay=0`. As long as you're holding down the `F8` key before the message "Starting Windows 95 . . ." appears on the screen, the Start Menu will come up. (If you push `F8` too early, of course, the PC's own POST startup routine will gripe that the keyboard is stuck and start beeping at you like a Volkswagen with a grounded horn.) Moral of the story: the only way to really disable the `F8` and shortcut keys is to set `BootKeys=0`.

Step 6. Startup looks at the `Logo=` entry. If `Logo=0`, Startup does not put the startup logo (see `logo.sys`, below) on the screen. If there is no entry or `Logo=1`, the logo goes up.

 I'm not sure why, but one of the most-often-asked questions about earlier versions of Windows was, "How do I disable the startup screen?" (Remember `win : ?`) Some folks felt that splashing the Startup screen on the monitor somehow slowed down Windows' loading—when in fact the screen made at most a fraction-of-a-second difference. If you really want to disable the Startup screen in Win95, it's as easy as editing `msdos.sys` and putting the line `Logo=0` in the `[Options]` section. Before you do that, though, keep in mind that Win95 *does* take a long time to load, and many people—myself included—get antsy when they don't see anything but a dumb blinking cursor.

 The *Windows Resource Kit* says that setting `Logo=0` "also avoids hooking a variety of interrupts that can create incompatibilities with certain memory managers from other vendors." I don't know first-hand if that is true, but if it is, you've gotta ask yourself why people don't get rid of their incompatible memory managers! Dumb, dumb, dumb.

Step 7. Startup runs through `config.sys` and `autoexec.bat`, then checks the `BootGUI=` entry. If `BootGUI=0`, Startup dumps you out at the DOS 7 command prompt. As best I can tell, the net result is exactly the same as if you had hit `F8`, then chosen Command Prompt Only. (DOS environment variables and memory allocations appear to be identical.) When you're at the command prompt, you can type `win` to get Win95 started.

Step 8. That's all she wrote; `msdos.sys` is done. Startup continues in the usual way, loading things, running `winstart.bat` and the like, finally bringing up the Desktop and stepping out of the way, to let you go at it.

 Several settings in `msdos.sys` control the way the Startup routine handles the Startup menu. If you find yourself in the Startup menu—whether by hitting F8 at the right time, or using `BootMenu=1` in `msdos.sys`—these are the steps Startup takes:

Step M1. Startup figures out if it needs to put a timer on the Startup menu screen. (The timer controls how long Startup will show the screen, waiting for the user to type something, before taking off with the default action.) If Startup determines that it got to this point by user intervention (i.e., somebody pressed the F8 key), there's no timer, and the Startup menu will wait until hell freezes over for the user to type something. If Startup determines that it got to this point without user intervention (typically, `BootMenu=1`), it looks at the `BootMenuDelay=` setting and uses the indicated number of seconds for the timer. If there's no `BootMenuDelay=` setting, Startup uses 30 seconds.

Step M2. Startup determines which Startup Menu options are valid. Six options are always available: Normal, Logged, Safe Mode, Step-by-step confirmation, Command prompt only and Safe mode command prompt only. If `Network=1`, the option "Safe Mode with Network support" is added after "Safe Mode." (If `Network=0`, or there is no `Network=` entry, there's no such option.) If `BootMulti=1`, the option "Previous version of MS-DOS" is added to the end of the option list. (If `BootMulti=0` or there is no `BootMulti=` entry, there's no such option.) The result is a list of six, seven, or eight options.

Step M3. Startup determines if the user pushed one of two potentially invalid shortcut keys. If you pushed F4, which is the shortcut key for "Previous version of MS-DOS," and `BootMulti=0`—thus disabling the option—the Startup routine jumps back up to **Step 6,** above, and continues with a normal Startup. If Startup figures you pushed F6, the shortcut key for "Safe Mode with Networking," but finds the entry `Network=0`, it also kicks you out to **Step 6** and continues with a normal Startup. It's not nice to fool Mother Nature.

Step M4. The options are numbered sequentially (from 1 to 6, or 7, or 8, depending on the entries constructed in **Step M2),** and the Startup Menu appears on the screen, with a timer if appropriate (as determined in **Step M1).** See Figure 9-6.

Step M5. Startup looks for a `BootMenuDefault=` entry, and highlights the indicated number on the Startup Menu as the default choice. If the `BootMenuDefault=` number is less than one, or if there is no entry, option 1 is used as the default. If `BootMenuDefault=` is greater than the maximum number of options, the last option is used as the default.

Step M6. The user makes a choice, or the timer expires with a default option, and Startup continues as explained in Chapter 8. If option 1 is chosen, Startup effectively jumps back up to **Step 6,** above.

 The *Windows Resource Kit* documents a setting called `BootFailSafe=`. Hey, maybe it works on all the machines in Redmond, but I'll be quantumly expired if I can get it to work on any machine around here. I consistently receive "Invalid Entry in MSDOS.SYS" error messages whenever I try. Most of the documentation on `BootMenuDefault=` is all wrong, too.

The *WRK* also documents a setting called `BootWarn=`. Based on the description in the docs, I thought it might control the message you get when you boot into Win95 in Safe Mode—you know the one, "Windows is running in Safe Mode. This special diagnostic mode of Windows . . ." etc., etc. I also thought it might toss up a warning when you try to go into Safe Mode from the Start Menu. No dice. Couldn't get it to do anything.

There are several other documented settings shown in Chapter 6 of the *WRK*. `BootWin=` is supposed to disable Win95 as the operating system. I decided I'd rather drink hemlock than give that one a try and recommend you do likewise. `DblSpace=` is supposed to disable DoubleSpace; similarly for `DrvSpace=`. `Double-Buffer=` is supposed to be useful with double-buffered SCSI drives. And `LoadTop=` is supposed to disable loading DOS in upper memory, presumably for Netware compatibility. If you need any of those, consult the official documentation—and good luck.

ios.ini, ios.log

Several additional files control your Startup destiny.

 The startup routine, `io.sys`, uses the file `\windows\ios.ini` (also known as "The Safe Driver List") to determine if it can replace "safe" real-mode drivers with protected-mode drivers. If it decides to boot out a real-mode driver and replace it with a protected-mode driver, it writes a log of that action in `\windows\ios.log`. If you're getting strange driver problems, check the *Windows Resource Kit* for a description of the Safe Driver List entries.

Logon Password

If you don't see a network logon screen every time you start Windows 95, you can safely skip this part, and go on down to Changing the Splash Screen.

 Wish I had a nickel for every time I've been asked about logon passwords. While it's true that passwords help provide a more secure computing environment, it's also true that passwords provide the single simplest way to shoot yourself in the foot. If your PC is located in an area where just anybody can saunter in and log on, *and* you're connected to a network with sensitive data that isn't protected, you probably need a password. Otherwise . . . well, think about it.

Note that you can set up separate users on one machine—ideal for a home, where several family members want to use the same machine but maintain their own preferences for wallpaper, icons, and the like; or for an office with shared PCs—*without requiring passwords.* Simply make sure each user has a unique logon username, and Win95 will take care of the rest (see Chapter 3).

 Hey, my middle name is security. I know all about this game. Wherever there are passwords, you will find the single most common complaint is, "I forgot my password. How do I set it to something I'll remember?" Fortunately, Win95 comes with its own lock pick. You bypass logon security by deleting the *username*.pwl file. For example, if your logon username is *igor,* deleting the file \windows\igor.pwl and rebooting will let you log onto the machine as *igor,* and then you can change the password to anything you like. It's really that simple, although you may have to use the F8 Win95 startup trick to get to a command prompt and delete the file. The .pwl file isn't even marked Hidden or System, so a simple del command will zap it out. No wonder they call Win95 insecure. . .

 The file *username*.pwl contains all your system passwords, stored in a one-way encrypted format. ("One-way encrypted" means there's a validation program that takes the password you type into the computer, scrambles it, then compares the results of the scrambling with what's stored in the .pwl file. You can't go backwards; that is, you can't figure out the original password by looking at the scrambled entry in the .pwl file. As far as I know, nobody has cracked the Win95 one-way encryption routine.) If you delete *username*.pwl, you not only delete the logon password, but other system passwords as well, possibly including the passwords you need to get onto disk drives or printers on connected Win95 machines, passwords for Exchange (e.g., to log onto Microsoft Network), Netware passwords, and the password on Windows NT servers that aren't set up on your domain.

While we're on the subject of passwords . . . do you know how to bypass the Screen Saver password? The crew will talk about it more in Chapter 10, but the trick is that you have to hit the Reset button on your PC (or turn the power off, then back on again), log on with your username and password, and before the screen saver kicks in, right-click on the Desktop, pick Properties, then the Screen Saver tab, and uncheck the Password Protected box.

An INI Still?

> Old sacks want much patching.
>
> —Thomas Fuller, *Gnomologia,* 1732

Hard to believe, in this brave new world of Win95, that Windows itself continues to use old-fashioned `.ini` files. Microsoft has exhorted the programming troops to move on to the Registry, and leave the `.ini` files behind, all the while keeping a bunch of `.ini` files in its own closet. While some of them—notably `win.ini` and `system.ini`—have obviously been maintained for backward compatibility, and others are apparently used because Microsoft was too lazy to update old Win31 applications, a disturbingly large number of `.ini` files are attached to brand-new applets.

What amazes me about several of these files is that they appear to be simple *replacements* for working with the Registry, as all "good" Windows 95 programs should. In some cases it's unavoidable. But in other cases, there isn't any apparent reason for it.

Scandisk, for example, uses `\windows\command\scandisk.ini` to store settings for use when it's run in Command Prompt mode. The Registry isn't really available at that point, so it makes sense to store the settings in an `.ini` file. If you ask for Scandisk to keep a record of what it found, that log is stored in `scandisk.log`, in the root directory of your boot drive (usually `c:\`).

Why on earth is there a `wordpad.ini`? Or a `winhelp.ini`? Or a `telephon.ini`? Not to mention `dialer.ini`, `clpboard.ini`, `cdplayer.ini`, `exchng32.ini`, and `msmail.ini`? Those are all associated with programs that are brand new, or completely redesigned, for Windows 95. Winsock, the Windows "Sockets" routine for Internet SLIP/PPP access, apparently uses a file called `\windows\socket.ini` for its settings. I've already talked about `protocol.ini`, `netdet.ini`, and `ios.ini`.

Then there's `control.ini` and `winfile.ini`, apparently related to their Win31 cousins.

Some of those old files are still hanging around because other people have written Windows applications that scab off the old Win31 files to pick up settings. In other words, we have to keep the old files around so the Win31 programs don't break. A good example of that is the old Control Panel information file, `\windows\system\control.inf`, or `\windows\control.ini`. We also kept the old Program Manager info file, `\windows\progman.ini` and the old File Manager info file, `\windows\winfile.ini`, for precisely the same reason: If we did away with them, some old programs wouldn't run anymore.

Excuses, excuses. Get with the system, Redmond: get this stuff into the Registry, where it belongs. Why make us users chase all over hell's half-acre looking for simple settings? What's good for the goose and all that stuff.

Family Jewels

> None cuts a diamond but a diamond.
>
> —John Webster, *The Malcontent,* 1604

One of the most brilliant parts of Win95 is contained in a rarely noticed, hidden folder called `\windows\sysbckup`. That's where Win95 keeps copies of its family jewels, the programs and drivers that are so often clobbered by stupid application installation programs. You know the kind of installation program I'm talking about—the ones that insist on replacing vital Windows system files with older versions, without warning or even so much as a nod at the user.

In Figure 9-7 you can see the kind of error message that will appear if your Unidriver print driver, `unidrv.dll`, gets overwritten by some application's wayward installer. Figure 9-8 demonstrates what Win95 will tell you if the common dialog library, `commdlg.dll`, gets clobbered by a renegade installation program.

If you start getting weird error messages like these, or if you have another reason to believe some installer has overwritten your system files, compare the time and date stamps on those files (which usually reside in `\windows` or `\windows\system`) with the files in `\windows\sysbckup`. If you find that the version in `\windows\sysbckup` is newer than the offending file, copy the version from `\sysbckup` over the top of the out-of-date file.

Figure 9-7. Unidrv clobbered

 Actually, we don't advertise this a lot, but Win95 has some really advanced built-in smarts that may prevent those renegade programs from overwriting the family jewels in the first place. Win95 monitors certain types of installation programs to see if any of the files in \windows\sysbckup are clobbered by the installer. If Win95 finds that the installer has overwritten one of those files, we actually jump in and

Figure 9-8. Commdlg too

try to automatically change it back to the original version by copying from \windows\sysbckup. In those cases where we can't get the old versions reinstalled, we try to warn the user to use the Win95 setup disks to verify all files. Yet another example of Windows quietly trying to protect its users from the cruel, cold world.

Recycology

> Where the Devil can't go he sends his grandmother.
>
> —German Proverb

 As far as I know, nobody has documented what the Recycle Bin really entails. It took a while to figure out the details, but in the end Win95 Recycology is pretty simple. And some of the details might come in very handy, should you ever attempt to reconstruct a file that was accidentally deleted when you emptied the Recycle Bin.

As you know from Chapter 3, the Recycle Bin contains all deleted files from local hard disks. (Files on floppy are not placed in a Recycle Bin. Nor are files deleted from network drives. Diskette and network files are both "deleted" using the old-fashioned DOS tricks; for more details, see *The Mother of All PC Books*.) To restore a recycled file, simply double-click on the Desktop's Recycle Bin. To well and truly delete all the files in the Recycle Bin, go into the Recycle Bin, click File, and Empty Recycle Bin. That's the easy part.

Here's what's going on behind the scenes. Each logical hard drive on your system (including partitions on partitioned drives and hosts for compressed drives) contains a hidden system folder called `\recycled`. Any time you delete a file on a particular drive—that is, send a file on to "the Recycle Bin"—Windows actually moves the file to the `\recycled` folder on that drive.

When it's moved, the filename extension is retained, but the initial part of the name is changed to DD, followed by a number. For example, if the first file "deleted" on the `c:` drive is called `mydoc.doc`, it's moved and renamed to `c:\recycled\dd1.doc`. If the second "deleted" file is called `Some Program.lnk`, it's moved and renamed to `c:\recycled\dd2.lnk`. Note that the "deleted" files are not compressed or manipulated in any other way: they're simply moved to the appropriate `\recycled` folder, and renamed—a very fast operation, as only a few bytes need to be rewritten on disk.

 So where does Win95 store the original filenames? Good question. There's a file in every `\recycled` folder called `info`. That's it, just `info`. We didn't dig far enough into the structure of the file to figure out its precise format, but if you look at `info` with a hex viewer, you'll see that all of the original filenames and their paths are stored in `info`, in the event that Win95 needs the information to restore a recycled file.

Don't bother trying to find these folders or files with Win95's Explorer. As soon as you get into the `\recycled` folder, Explorer tosses a facade on the screen—much as it does with fonts—to hide all the inner workings from you. If you get as far as the `\recycled` folder in Explorer, you'll see a consolidated list of *all* "deleted" files in *all* the `\recycled` folders on your PC. It appears that Explorer looks in a file called `\recycled\Desktop.ini`, which has two lines like this:

```
[.ShellClassInfo]
CLSID={645FF040-5081-101B-9F08-00AA002F954E}
```

then uses the `CLSID` to look in the Registry for general Recycle Bin programs and settings.

The only way you'll be able to see what's really happening in your Recycle Bin is by using the DOS prompt to get into each drive's `\recycled` folder, and then using an editor like DOS's Edit to look inside the appropriate files.

 How can this information help you? Win95 "empties" the Recycle Bin by doing a plain old-fashioned DOS delete—in other words, it leaves the data intact, but changes the File Allocation Table. (Again, for details, see *The Mother of All PC Books*.) If you've emptied the Recycle Bin accidentally, and you're trying to restore a deleted file by using the old DOS undelete command, the files you want to look at were called dd*.*, where the filename extension matches the extension of the file you accidentally clobbered. The "emptied" Recycle Bin files were located in the appropriate drive's \recycled folder, uh, subdirectory. That should get you pointed in the right direction. Happy spelunking!

Changing the Splash Screens

> Vision is the art of seeing things invisible.
>
> —Jonathan Swift, *Thoughts on Various Subjects,* 1706

YO, READER! THIS IS THE PART YOU'RE LOOKING FOR! This is where you learn how to change the Startup splash screen. I *know* that's the only reason why you're reading this chapter. Well, I've got some good news for you. Not only is the screen easy to change, but you have all the tools you need to play around with it—draw your own, bring in scanned images, modify existing screens, touch-up, and paint to your heart's content, the whole ball of wax—right there on your disk, in bone-stock Win95. Complete details follow.

The Windows startup screen has become something of a geek Rorschach test. Some people report they can see a rampant horse in the vibrating blue clouds. Others claim it's BillG himself, striking a pose that would make Frank Zappa proud. Most of all, the screen Rorschach proves one thing: if you can see something in those clouds, you desperately need to get a life.

When Win95 starts, it looks in the root directory of your boot drive (typically, c:\) for a file called logo.sys. Win95 is very picky about that file: it has to be a bitmap, 320 dots wide by 400 dots high by 256 colors. If it finds a file matching those specifications, the file is used as the splash screen. If it doesn't find any file called logo.sys, it uses a file stored internally in io.sys, the one you're probably accustomed to seeing as the Win95 splash screen. If it does find a file called logo.sys, but that file doesn't match the 320 x 400 x 256 spec precisely, no splash screen will appear.

Chances are good that you don't have a logo.sys file in your root directory, unless you've installed the Plus! Pack. The Plus! Pack copies its own logo.sys file into the root directory when you install it. See Figure 9-9. Mom wasn't about to be outdone by those hacks in Redmond, so she put her own splash screen (Figure 9-10) in the MomStuff folder directory of this book's CD. Simply copy it to your boot disk's root directory (typically, c:\), and restart Windows.

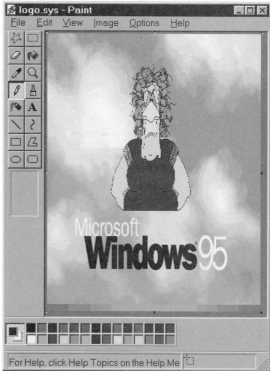

Figure 9-9. The Plus! Pack logo.sys   **Figure 9-10. The Mom Rules! logo.sys**

 When Win95 shuts down, it uses two different exit screens, both of them the standard 320 dots wide by 400 dots high by 256 colors. The first one, called `logow.sys`—the "Please wait while your computer shuts down" screen—must be located in the `\windows` folder. The second one, called `logos.sys`—"It's now safe to turn off your computer"—has to be in the `\windows` folder, too. See Figure 9-11 and Figure 9-12.

 If Win95 can't find those files, or they are of the wrong size, it puts a blinking cursor in the upper-left corner of a blank screen for the duration of time the screen would normally occupy. It's a very disconcerting image.

 As you can see, the Microsoft Paint application that ships with Windows 95 is reasonably suited for editing these `.sys` files. These are very odd-shaped files—they're taller than they are wide, whereas every screen I've ever used is wider than it is tall. Win95 stretches the pictures in the files horizontally when they appear as splash screens; the amount of stretch

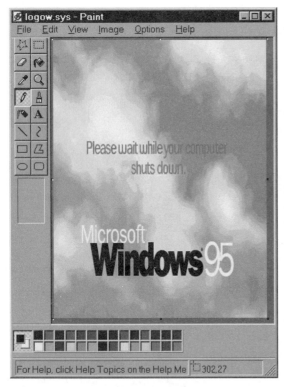

Figure 9-11. The exit screen logow.sys

Figure 9-12. The exit screen logos.sys

distortion varies depending on whether you're running at 640 x 480, 800 x 600, or 1024 x 768 resolution.

Here are my top tips for using Microsoft Paint to edit the splash `.sys` files:

- Make backup copies of the `logo*.sys` files before you start. (If worse comes to worst and you obliterate one, you can retrieve it from the Win95 installation `.cab` files; see Appendix E.)

- You may find it easier to start with `logow.sys` (or possibly `logos.sys`), and modify it, instead of trying to draw from scratch. Both of those files are already trimmed to 320 dots by 400 dots, so you don't need to worry about stretching or cropping.

- If you are working with a scanned image, or any lifelike artwork, start by using the Image/Stretch and Skew menu to scrunch the drawing by about 50 percent horizontally (or stretching it vertically by 200 percent). That maintains fairly lifelike proportions.

Remember, the picture you see in Microsoft Paint is *not* the image you'll end up seeing on the splash screen.

- If you don't start with `logow.sys` or `logos.sys`, you can adjust the drawing to the correct size by clicking on Image/Stretch and Skew to stretch or scrunch it. Once the drawing is approximately the right size, use Image/Attributes to trim it down or enlarge it to 320 by 400 Pels (i.e., pixels). Remember that the Attributes setting crops—it lops off the right or the bottom of the picture to match whatever size you specify.

- Try pulling in clip art or any image that MS Paint will accept. When you get the image scrunched the way you like it, select the image, use Edit/Copy to copy it to the clipboard, open up the `.sys` file, use Edit/Paste to paste the image on the splash screen, then immediately use the four-headed arrow to drag the image wherever you want to place it.

 We never did figure out a way to get the animated right-to-left crawler at the bottom of the splash screen to work. Even copying it from the bottom of the Plus! Pack's `logo.sys` (which is animated) didn't help. There's a bit of undocumented magic going on behind the scenes. So if you create your own screen, don't expect to see it move, unless you start with a screen like the one from the Plus! Pack that does move.

The Startup Disk

> They that are booted are not always ready.
>
> —George Herbert, *Outlandish Proverbs,* 1640

 When you originally install Win95, you have an opportunity to make a Startup disk. In addition, any time you feel like it, you can go into the Control Panel's Add/Remove Programs applet, select the Startup disk tab, and make an identical Startup disk.

 My, my, my. Aren't we being politically correct? What you're really talking about, Sarah, is what most people would call an emergency boot disk. In less squeamish days, DOS manuals and books would contain dire warnings, emphasized in neon red, that every user *needs* an emergency boot disk— preferably two—and that the disks should be kept handy in case the system goes crashing about the user's knees. Well, this is an emergency boot disk, and you do need one, just in case your system heads south in a hurry.

Whether you create the Emergen. . . uh, Startup disk during Windows 95 setup or from the Add/Remove Programs applet, here are the files that will be placed on your Startup disk. Note that the list in the *Windows Resource Kit* is wrong, repeatedly.

```
ATTRIB.EXE
CHKDSK.EXE
COMMAND.COM
DEBUG.EXE
DRVSPACE.BIN
EBD.SYS (hidden, 0 bytes)
EDIT.COM
FDISK.EXE
FORMAT.COM
IO.SYS (hidden)
MSDOS.SYS (hidden, read only)
REGEDIT.EXE
SCANDISK.EXE
SCANDISK.INI
SYS.COM
UNINSTAL.EXE
```

Figure 9-13. Contents of the Setup disk

 Those of you who are old enough to remember DOS 6 will recognize almost all of those files immediately.

- `attrib.exe` lets you change the hidden, system, and read-only attributes of files.

- `chkdsk.exe` is the old, familiar check-disk utility.

- `command.com` contains the DOS command interpreter.

- Hard to believe Microsoft would include the old line-oriented editor `debug.exe` on a fancy-schmancy twenty-first century emergency boot disk, but they do.

- `drvspace.bin` contains the DriveSpace disk compression routines.

- `ebd.sys`, the greatest enigma of the bunch, is a zero-byte, hidden file, that is nonetheless documented (!) as "Utility for the startup disk." It isn't, of course—it doesn't do a thing except sit there. One has to wonder if `ebd` stands for *emergency boot disk.*

- `edit.com` is a full screen text editor that has the look and feel of the old DOS 6 `edit.com`—but with one important difference. The DOS 6 `edit.com` was a 1 KB file that actually started Microsoft's old QuickBasic (QBasic) compiler in a special mode where only the editor worked. Now that QBasic has passed on and gone to add-on heaven, `edit.com` is a 69K file that is a stand-alone editor. The new edit's features are discussed in detail in Chapter 4.

- `fdisk.com`, perhaps the most dangerous utility ever created, is capable of partitioning (read: destroying) your hard drives with a slip of the fingers.

- `format.com` similarly lets you blast away an entire disk in nothing flat.

- `io.sys` and `msdos.sys`—the Win95 versions, mind you—are the central Win95 DOS routine and what amounts to its `.ini` file. (See Chapter 8.)

- I'll talk about `regedit.exe` in Chapter 11, where it's a Charles Atlas Windows app that lets you edit the Registry. The version here on the Setup disk, though, is a stunted DOS-mode Registry importer and exporter. If you ever have to rely on this DOS-mode version, you have my sympathy. For example, exporting the current Registry settings to a simple text file requires a monolithic command line that looks like this:

```
regedit /L:c:\windows\system.dat /R:c:\windows\user.dat /E c:\temp.txt
```

  If you screw up and get one space wrong, the whole thing goes kablooey. And once you get the command line right, you'll try to open up the text version of the Registry with `edit.com` only to discover that your mouse doesn't work because the Startup disk doesn't have a mouse driver . . . and when you finally *do* figure out the key strokes to bring in the file, you'll receive an error message like "Out of far memory." Far out. Welcome to the user-friendly world of Windows 95!

- `scandisk.exe` and `scandisk.ini` are the reliable, relatively modern DOS mode disk scanning utilities you've no doubt come to love, and its `.ini` file. Don't confuse this DOS Scandisk with the full-blown Windows Scandisk, which lives in a file called `scandskw.exe`.

- `sys.com` will transfer `io.sys`, `msdos.sys` and `command.com` to a disk. If you get your system really bollixed up, you might have to use this program to transfer copies of those files from the emergency disk to the hard disk.

- `uninstal.exe` is apparently the Win95 uninstaller. Running it should restore your old version of DOS. Personally, I don't have the guts to try it, and I would recommend strongly that you follow my lead in the chicken department.

 Note what's lacking on the emergency boot disk. There's no `config.sys` or `autoexec.bat`. There's no `win.ini` or `system.ini`. There are no mouse drivers, no CD-ROM drivers. There is no disk compression software outside of DriveSpace. There's no copy of the Registry. And on and on. This is one seriously deficient disk. In fact, if your only copy of Win95 is on CD-ROM, there isn't enough oomph in the default emergency boot disk to get you back to the Win95 Setup routine!

 Sooooo . . . break out a fresh new, formatted diskette. Put a sticker on it that says "Erwin's Emergency Boot Disk #2." Copy onto it `config.sys`, `autoexec.bat`, from your boot drive's root directory (if they exist), and every file mentioned in either of them, including drivers, TSRs, anything you need to read your compressed drives, and any weird files mentioned in `autoexec` or `config` that you've never heard of. (You don't want to copy those files onto the Emerg. . . uh, Startup disk, because you don't necessarily want `autoexec` or `config` to kick in on an emergency boot.)

Next, copy over `win.ini` and `system.ini` from your `\windows` folder. Finally— and it may take another empty diskette to hold all this gunk—copy over `system.dat` and `user.dat`, both from the `\windows` folder.

 Those aren't all the critical files on your machine, but if you have them, you at least stand a fighting chance of being able to get back up and running if, say, a cosmic ray hits your Registry and it flips a bit in the wrong place.

 I thought I'd be able to use the Win95 "Emergency Recovery Utility," `eru.exe`, found on the Win95 CD in the `\other\misc\eru` folder, to make extensive backups of all my important system files. After all, that's what the docs say it will do. No go. I tried over and over, and couldn't get that program to do anything.

CFGBACK—*Registry Backup*

> Live as on a mountain.
>
> —Marcus Aurelius, *Meditations*, ca. 170

 Although the `eru.exe` program doesn't seem to make system backups worth a hill of beans, the `cfgback.exe` program, which restricts itself to backing up and restoring the Registry, works just fine. It lets you keep up to nine levels of Registry backups, gives you a chance to identify those backups with full English-language descriptions, and as a bit of lagniappe, actually compresses the files for you.

The compressed files, with an extension of `.rbk`, get placed in the `\windows` folder. From there you can copy them to diskette for safekeeping.

You'll find `cfgback.exe` on this books' companion CD (see Appendix A), or on the Win95 distribution CD, in the `\other\misc\cfgback` folder.

 The only problem with `cfgback`? **Windows has to be running, and the** `.rbk` **files have to be in the** `\windows` **folder, for it to function. As such, it isn't suitable for an emergency boot disk. More's the pity.**

Bad Programs

> DOS always says, "Bad command or filename."
> That's so *negative*!
> Why can't Win95 say, "Most excellent command or filename, dude"?
>
> —Heard on the Net

 One of Win95's most brilliant capabilities lies in the trapping of old Windows applications known to cause problems under Win95, and *letting you do something about them.* The source of this magic lies in the Registry, in a key called (take a deep breath) `HKEY_LOCAL_MACHINE\System\ CurrentControlSet\Control\ SessionManager\CheckBadApps`. If you crank up the Registry (click Start, then Run, type Registry, hit Enter) and scan down to that key, you'll find a list of almost two hundred programs that are known to cause problems with Win95.

Should you try to run a program with one of the indicated names, you'll get a warning message like that shown in Figure 9-14. If you click on Help at that point, you'll see a full description of the known problems with that application, as in Figure 9-15. The Help message is tailored to this specific program, and following the tips in Help should get you going with the program (or at least should clue you in on its Win95 shortcomings!) in no time.

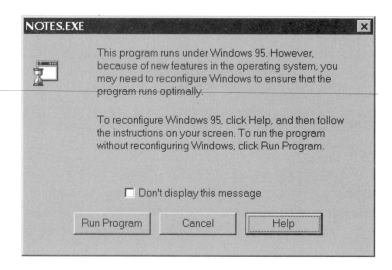

Figure 9-14. Naughty, naughty notes

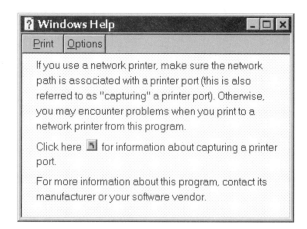

Figure 9-15. Helping notes reform

Figure 9-16. mkcompat in action

Speaking of bad programs and their reformation, Win95 ships with an application called `mkcompat.exe`, that lets you tell Windows how to fake out an older program that may have problems working with Windows 95.

To run `mkcompat.exe`, just click Start, then Run, type `mkcompat`, and hit `Enter`. You'll see the screen in Figure 9-16. Click on File, then Choose Program, and open whichever program has been giving you problems. Try clicking on some (or all!) of the boxes, clicking File, then Close, and running the application again. Win95 intercepts the program and applies whatever sleight-of-hand you specify. If you want to look at all the options available in `mkcompat`, click on File, then Advanced Options. You'll get a list that looks like Figure 9-17.

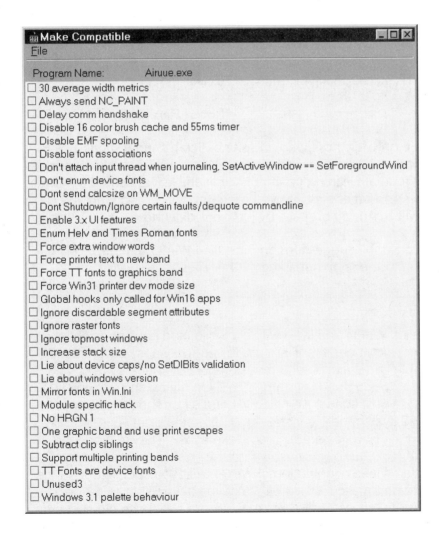

Figure 9-17: All the mkcompat options

How does it work? You won't believe it. Win95 stores a compatibility flag in `win.ini`! You'll get an entry that looks something like this:

```
[Compatibility]

AIRUUE=0x200000
```

and if you scan the Registry, you'll find that the program is never mentioned there. `mkcompat` simply manufactures `win.ini` `[Compatibility]` entries and merges them with whatever internal table Win95 generates at startup to keep track of those flags.

Cleaning Up

> 'Tis much, among the filthy, to be clean.
>
> —Robert Herrick, *Hesperides,* 1648

This section is only for those who, in spite of Sarah's suggestions in Chapter 8, installed Win95 over the top of Windows 3.1. While Windows 95 is pretty good at cleaning up after itself, it still leaves behind a number of Win31 files and other files that you probably don't need, and you can reclaim 10 MB to 40 MB of space by judicious deleting.

Those of you who followed Sarah's suggestions and installed Win95 to a new, clean subdirectory can skip down to the section marked "Other Files."

W95UNDO.DAT

If you've installed Win95 and lived with it a while, and have no intention of undoing the install to permanently return to your previous version of DOS, you may be able to reclaim an enormous amount of space by removing two files, `w95undo.dat` and `w95undo.ini`. On my machine, those two files take up *26 MB* of space. Admittedly, I had a horrendously huge Windows 3.1 and DOS 6.22 system before installing Win95, but I'll bet your `w95undo.dat` and `w95undo.ini` files are big, too. Take a look. They're hidden, read-only files in the root directory of your boot drive, typically `c:\`. They're created by Win95's installer if you install Win95 over the top of Win31, *and* you specify during the installation that you want to be able to remove Win95. If you have Explorer set up to show hidden files (click Tools/Options/ View), you'll be able to see those big suckers. Simply click on them and hit the `Del` key. They'll go to the Recycle Bin. Next time you empty the Recycle Bin, all vestiges will be gone.

Remember, this is an irreversible decision. If you delete these files and then decide to give up on Win95 sometime in the future, you'll have to wipe out most of your hard drive and reinstall DOS and Windows 3.1 from scratch. (Note, though, that removing the two files won't interfere with your dual-boot capabilities at all. They're compressed, archive files. Even with `w95undo.dat` and `w95undo.ini` long farmed out to the bit bucket, you can still hit `F8` on startup and "Boot to your previous version of DOS.") I have no idea why, but this tip doesn't seem to be mentioned in the Win95 on-line Help, the *Windows Resource Kit,* or any of the magazine articles I've seen. Odd.

Delectable Deletables

If you installed over Windows 3.1 or 3.11, Win95 doesn't delete files from several obsolete programs. Providing you use the Win95 replacements for these old programs, you can get rid of a bunch of old files.

• If you no longer use Win31's Terminal program—which has been superseded by Hyperterminal—you can delete `\windows\terminal.exe` and `terminal.hlp`

• If you never did use DOS 6/Windows 3.1's Backup program, or if you've started using Win95 Backup exclusively, you should first double-check and make sure that the new Win95 Backup program can read all your old tapes. (It should—but check anyway, OK?) If Win95 Backup can restore everything, you can delete the old Backup files, `\DOS\mwbackf.dll, mwbackr.dll, mwbackup.exe, mwbackup.hlp`, and `vfintd.386`.

• If you never did use DOS 6/Windows 3.1's anti-virus program, or if you've pretty much given up on it in favor of the new wave of anti-viral thingies, you can delete `\DOS\mwav.exe, mwav.hlp, mwavabsi.dll, mwavdlg.dll, mwavdos1.dll, mwavdrv.dll, mwavmgr.dll, mwavscan.dll, mwavsos.dll, mwavtree.dll` (which may not be on your machine), `mwavtsr.exe`, and `mwgrafic.dll`.

• If you don't use the old Win31 Calendar, Cardfile, Clock, or Recorder, delete `\windows\calendar.exe, calendar.hlp, cardfile.exe, cardfile.hlp, clock.exe, recorder.dll, recorder.exe`, and/or `recorder.hlp`. If you can't bear the thought of giving hard disk space to *<ugh!>* games, and you didn't install new versions of these games when you installed Win95, get rid of Hearts, which is files `\windows\cards.dll, mshearts.exe`, and `mshearts.hlp`; Minesweeper, files `winmine.exe` and `winmine.hlp`; and Solitaire, files `sol.exe` and `sol.hlp`. If you won't be using Help for Windows 3.1, you can get rid of the Help Glossary, `\windows\glossary.hlp`. If you won't be using the old Win31 Write application—which has been superseded by WordPad—get rid of its help file, `\windows\write.hlp`.

- If you installed over the top of Windows for Workgroups 3.11, and don't use the old Fax routines, delete `\windows\awcas.dll`, `awclass1.dll`, `awclass2.dll`, `awfaxio.dll`, `awfxprot.dll`, `awt30.dll`, `dllsched.dll`, `efaxpump.dll`, `efaxpump.ini`, `efaxrun.dll`, `faxcover.dll`, `faxmgr.exe`, `faxopt.dll`, `faxview.exe`, `ifkernel.dll`, `keyview.exe`, `lineariz.dll`, `msfax.hlp`, `netfax.dll`, `sigview.exe`, and `\windows\system\efaxdrv.drv`, `fax.cpl`, `faxnsp.dll`, and `faxstub.dll`.

- If you installed over the top of Windows for Workgroups 3.11, and don't use the old Microsoft Mail routines, delete `\windows\impexp.dll`, `mail.wri`, `msmail.exe`, `msmail.hlp`, and `wgpomgr.dll`. If you don't use Microsoft Mail at all (either the Win31 version or the Win95 version), go ahead and delete `msmail.ini` and `msmail.mmf`.

- If you installed over the top of Windows for Workgroups 3.11, and aren't keeping the old version of Schedule Plus (usually you would only do that for compatibility with other people in your workgroup who also use the old Workgroups version of Schedule Plus), you can delete `\windows\msremind.exe`, `mssched.dll`, `schedmsg.dll`, `schdplus.exe`, `schdplus.hlp`, `schdplus.ini`, `trnoff.dll`, and `trnsched.dll`.

That's not a complete list of all the worthless Win31 files that the Win95 installer leaves hanging around, but it's pretty close—and it's a very safe list, too, providing you meet the criterion mentioned. You should pick up 8 to 10 MB by deleting those files.

Psst, buddy. Wanna rub out some more files you won't need and get a payback of 7 MB? Just erase the `*.avi` files from `\windows\help`. See the discussion near the end of Chapter 3.

Other Files

> Moderation is a fatal thing;
> nothing succeeds like excess.
>
> —Oscar Wilde, *A Woman of No Importance,* 1893

 Windows 95 uses dozens—maybe hundreds—of additional files to go about its daily business. We couldn't begin to list them all, or define their functions. But a handful of files that don't fall into earlier categories could prove important to you, depending on your circumstances and position on the Win95 lifecycle.

`\windows\ShellIconCache` and `ttfCache` (both without filename extensions) are two important ones. As their names imply, Windows stores the most recent icons that the shell uses—like those for disk drives—in `ShellIconCache` and the most recently used TrueType fonts in `ttfCache`. The files' sole purpose seems to be to speed up reboot of the system. If you delete the files, Windows 95 will gladly recreate them the next time it starts; it just takes a little extra time. If some of your basic Desktop icons seem screwy, `ShellIconCache` may have become corrupted; try deleting it and rebooting. Also, if you've made a change that should've taken effect but didn't—for example, if you edit a `.dll` with icons in it and the changes don't "take" on the Desktop—try deleting `ShellIconCache` and see if the problem goes away.

 My favorites are the `\windows\system\color\*.icm` files, the ones that implement Image Color Matching. Although you shouldn't play around with those files manually, they're used to match colors when switching media: a red coming in from a scanner will look the same on the screen, and then look the same on paper or film when you print it out. It's a technology created by Kodak and licensed by Microsoft that translates among different devices' "color spaces" (and you thought computer geeks used weird terminology). Anyway, high-end image processing applications use these `.icm` files. Keep your hands off!

 Mom asked me to trace down a few other techy things, but we couldn't get the 'Softies to talk. They wouldn't take a carrot *or* a stick. Tough guys.

We never did find out what the `\windows\MOSusername.RHC` files contained, like `MOSIgor.RHC`. And the `suhdlog.dat` and `suhdlog.bak` files remain a mystery. Oh well. I guess any lady as classy as Win95 deserves to have a *few* secrets left.

 The fewer the better, as far as I'm concerned. This feminine mystique crap is way overblown.

Chapter 10

(Out of) Control Panel

So was their jolly whistle well y-wet.

—Geoffrey Chaucer, *Canterbury Tales*, 1386

This chapter concerns itself with the parts of the Control Panel that have not already been discussed. In particular, we're going to look at adding new hardware; Display properties and other settings (e.g., for the mouse, keyboard, and the joystick) that directly alter Registry values; and a handful of additional settings.

Oh, you're just softening us up for Chapter 11, the Registry chapter, aren't you Mom?

Very perceptive for a not-so-dumb dummy.

The crew will take on each of the twenty standard Control Panel applets, in turn, and show you how each one works. To get at the Control Panel, click Start, then Settings, then Control Panel. We want to encourage you to start poking around your Registry, if you haven't done so already. This is a nice, low-anxiety place to start learning Win95 Brain Surgery. To see the effect of Control Panel changes in the Registry, click on Start, then Run, type `regedit` and hit Enter. Then follow along in this chapter as we look at how Control Panel applets do their thing, and—halfway through the chapter, in the Screen Saver section, if you're brave enough—we actually go in and change a real, live setting. All together now. *Oooooooh. Aaaaaaaah.*

Chapter 3's first brush with Control Panel included the name of the `.cpl` file that each applet comes from. You need this name for shortcuts that launch a particular applet, even a particular tab on a particular applet. The syntax for such shortcuts is at the end of the section titled "A Fistful of Applets" in Chapter 3.

Abbreviations in the Belfry, er, Registry

> In order to speak short on any subject, think long.
>
> —H. H. Brackenridge, *Modern Chivalry,* 1792

 We're going to be seeing a lot of the Registry in this chapter. Just to get you in the mood, I'm going to start using two common abbreviations for Registry keys—they'll not only save me tons of typing, they'll save a few trees, too. If you look in the Registry, you'll find two keys used all the time: `HKEY_CURRENT_USER` and `HKEY_LOCAL_MACHINE`. Yep, they're always written in CAPITALS_LIKE_THAT. Well, my two time-saving, eye-saving, tree-saving abbreviations are these:

```
HKCU = HKEY_CURRENT_USER

HKLM = HKEY_LOCAL_MACHINE
```

I think you'll get accustomed to them both very quickly. I thank you. Your eyes thank you. My fingers thank you.

Accessibility Options

> Adversity reminds men of religion.
>
> —Livy, *History of Rome,* ca. 10

 In my opinion, the Accessibility Control Panel applet represents one of Microsoft's greatest achievements in Windows 95. While few people will use the options here, those who do will soon learn that somebody in Redmond cares about making computers usable by those with disabilities. Bravo.

Options include Sticky Keys, the ability to make Ctrl, Alt and Del "sticky", so you don't have to hold down one key while pressing another; Filter Keys which tells Win95 to "forgive" brief, presumably accidental, keystrokes; Toggle Keys, which makes the PC beep with different tones when Caps Lock, Num Lock, and Scroll Lock are turned on and off; Sound Sentry flashes the Windows title bar whenever the built-in speaker beeps; and Mouse Keys, which lets you use the number pad's arrow keys to move the cursor—it's described in Chapter 2.

Other settings are meant to feed information to applications, rather than changing Windows itself: Win95 controls a setting in the Registry, and programs are supposed to read that setting and respond to it. Show Sounds, for example, tells applications to substitute on-screen actions for sounds; High Contrast turns on a large-format, white-on-black mode that makes the screen easier to read for those with eyesight problems.

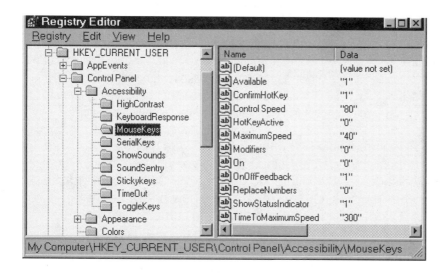

Figure 10-1. Mouse Keys in the Registry

If you've installed any of the Accessibility options, these settings are stored in the Registry key called HKCU\Control Panel\Accessibility.* If you've never poked around with the Registry before, now's a good time to try it (click Start/Run and type regedit). See the values called "On" or "Enable"? They're the ones that change when you change settings in the Accessibility applet.

I had a pretty rough time with High Contrast. Word, in particular, wouldn't go back into anything resembling normal condition when I turned off High Contrast. Fortunately, rebooting cleaned things up, but if Microsoft itself can't implement the options, it kinda makes you wonder, no?

---

* Remember, HKCU = HKEY_CURRENT_USER.

 *Add New Hardware*

Omnia mutantur, nihil interit. *

—Ovid, *Metamorphoses*, ca. 5

 Installing new hardware used to be such a joy. You had to check the vendor's documentation to see what IRQ settings are allowed, which I/O addresses would be taken, how many DMA channels were required, and which ones they might be. Then you had to take an inventory of what was in your computer, and (usually in a process of divination) figure out which IRQs, I/O addresses, and DMAs were available. If your new hardware needed a setting already taken by an installed component, you had to pull out *that* component and see if it could be changed.

 Nowadays, things are a little bit better. The hardware manufacturers are slowly getting their act together (although those of you with PCMCIA cards may violently disagree—and with good reason). Win95 has some native smarts that, when it works, can make installing new hardware a snap. When it doesn't work, though, you're back in the same old stew of IRQs, I/O addresses, and DMAs—although Win95 *will* give you an accurate inventory of occupied settings.

 The obvious solution is to throw away all of your old hardware and get nothing but the newest Win95-logo'd Plug 'n Play everything. Then, if your favorite piece of new hardware still won't install right, you can swear at Microsoft. That should make you feel better. Lots.

 Windows 95 offers two different ways to install new hardware. In one case, you tell Win95 what kind of hardware you're going to install, and it tells you which settings to use. You figure out how to get the settings straight on the new hardware, then physically install it. Win95 boots up, recognizes the hardware, and has it going in no time flat. That approach is good—in fact, I would say it's "preferred" for any hardware that isn't Plug 'n Play—if you understand IRQs, I/O locations, DMAs, and how to play with jumper switches, and futzing around with things doesn't drive you nuts.

If you're a little rusty on IRQs, I/O locations, and DMAs, there are plenty of books that will bring you up to speed. I'd be remiss if I didn't mention that *The Mother of All PC Books* has more than enough information on those topics to take you through just about any bout of Install Depression.

---

* The #1 rule of computer hardware: All things change; nothing perishes. So where's *your* old 1200-baud modem?

The other way to install new hardware—and *the* way to go with Plug 'n Play hardware—is to simply open up your computer and stick it in. Either Win95 will realize that it has a new piece of hardware or it won't. If it does realize there's something new, Win95 will bring up the Add New Hardware Wizard and step you through the configuration as best it can. In all cases with PnP hardware (at least in theory), and in some cases for non-PnP hardware, it'll recognize the hardware and install it for you without asking any questions. You should see some reassuring messages, though, about Windows 95 recognizing and installing the new hardware.

If it doesn't realize there's something new on board, you can kick-start the Add New Hardware Wizard by clicking on Start, then Options, then Control Panel and double-clicking the Add New Hardware applet. Whether Win95 realized it had new hardware or not, by using the Add New Hardware Wizard you stand a very good (but not perfect!) chance of getting the hardware installed properly and working in fairly short order. This is the better method for installing hardware if you don't care to learn about IRQs and all those senseless things, or if the thought of opening up the back of your computer makes you break out in a cold sweat. The upside: if it works, it's easy. The downside: if it doesn't work, you're probably best off returning the new hardware and getting your money back.

We're going to step you through the Add New Hardware Wizard twice, once using the "guru" method, once using the "naive" method. In both cases I'm going to install a new SoundBlaster AWE-32 sound board—a board that's far from the snarliest around, but one that nonetheless doesn't support Plug 'n Play, or anything resembling Plug 'n Play. If you're installing a new board, you're probably in pretty much the same boat.

Let's start with the guru. Take it away, Mao.

Guru Installation

So you just bought a shiny new SoundBlaster AWE-32 board and you're going to install it into your Windows 95 machine. You can tell an IRQ from a DMA (even if you aren't exactly sure what they are, or why they matter), you know that no two hardware devices can have the same IRQ number or use the same DMA channel, and you aren't intimidated by those little plastic and metal thingies called jumpers.

Well, the first good news is that the AWE-32 doesn't have any jumpers that you'll need to play with to get the sound going. So you can put away the needle-nose pliers. Fewer and fewer boards these days require you to make manual adjustments; most of them are software-adjustable.

Take a few minutes to look at your new board. Pet it (from outside the protective plastic wrapper, of course). Think good thoughts. Open up the manual and read about how good it's going to be. But don't crack open your PC just yet. Get Win95 running. Click on Start, Settings, Control Panel, and double-click Add New Hardware.

Panel 1. The Add New Hardware Wizard springs to life. Don't take that graphic on the left too seriously— your PC should be safely closed, Windows 95 should be running (note the conspicuous lack of sparks!), and the only entrails on your desk should be the new card, still in its protective wrapper, with the detritus from inside the box strewn out appropriately.

Panel 2. The Add New Hardware Wizard offers to detect new hardware for you. Since the Wizard isn't clairvoyant (wait for Windows 96!), that would be a little difficult. Simply click No and Next>. (By the way, this is one of the worst-behaved Win95 wizards. It doesn't remember your settings if you move Back! C'mon, Redmond. You folks can do better.)

Panel 3. Sometimes the choices in this panel aren't so obvious. For example, "Memory Technology Drivers" include Flash memory and SRAM cards; "multi-function adapters" include combo COM/LPT port cards, sound/SCSI cards, and the like. If you can't figure out the category, pick something reasonable and click Next>. ("Other Devices" actually lists all the available hardware.) You'll have an opportunity to backtrack with no untoward effect. I chose "sound, video and game controllers," of course.

Panel 4. Pick the manufacturer on the left, then pick the specific model on the right. If you don't find your hardware on the list, click `Back>` and try to find a better category. If you still can't find the hardware listed, look in the box your hardware came in. If it has a diskette clearly marked Windows 95 Driver, stick it in your diskette drive and click Have Disk. If there's no such diskette, or the only diskette in the box contains a Windows 3.1 driver, call the manufacturer and gripe. Real loud.

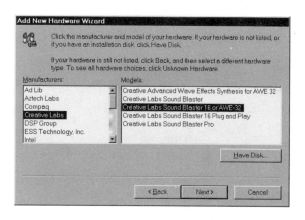

Panel 5. If Win95 detects no IRQ, I/O, or DMA conflicts, you'll get this message as an all-clear. If you get a screen like this, rejoice! You needn't futz with any settings at all—just install the card the way it came from the factory, and it should work right the first time. (Click on Details if you're hopelessly curious—or if the factory settings have somehow become jumbled, and you need to figure out what needs to be set to get 'em back.)

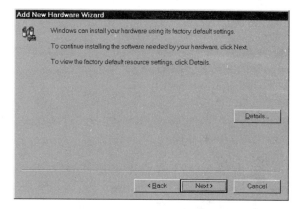

Panel 6. On the other hand, if Win95 detects a conflict (in this case, an IRQ overlap that I artificially induced by changing another card while you weren't looking), it warns you that you're going to have to change the hardware away from its factory default. More than that, though, it tells you exactly which settings you need for a clean installation. With these settings and the hardware's manual in hand, it should *(should!)* be relatively easy to pre-configure the board.

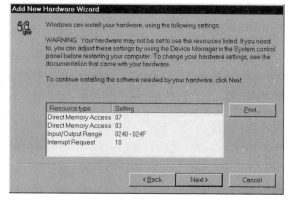

Panel 7. Okay, okay. I *know* you really wanted me to show you what's under the Details button in Panel 5. I was surprised to find that the factory default DMA settings (channels 1 and 5), which are both open on this machine, are good enough for the "all-clear" panel, Panel 5, but aren't the ones used in the "you gotta change the settings" panel, Panel 6. Somehow the Wizard doesn't find that the default DMA channels are both wide open—and thus tricks you into changing DMA channels on the card when it isn't absolutely necessary.

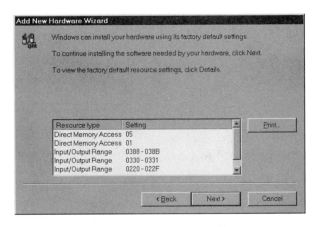

Panel 8. With this final panel, the Wizard is telling you that all you have to do is click Finish, shut down your machine, install the hardware per the manufacturer's instructions (possibly modifying the default settings, if the wizard found any conflicts), and turn the machine back on. With a little bit of luck, Win95 will detect the presence of the new hardware on startup and it'll suddenly be working—with no further effort on your part.

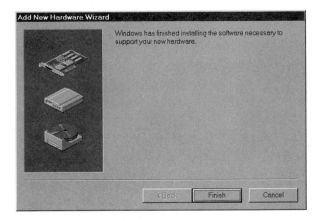

But just in case you're a little slow on the uptake, Win95 finishes with a flourish, telling you precisely what you need to do to get the hardware working. Bravo.

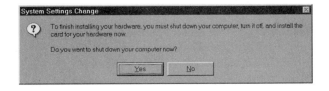

This precise installation worked like a champ on my machine. I stuck the card in my PC without modifying a thing. When I rebooted, Win95 informed me that it had detected new hardware—the "Creative Advanced Wave Effect Synthesis for AWE-32" mentioned at the top of Panel 4.

I'll bet you wondered why I didn't choose "Advanced Wave Effect Synthesis" in Panel 4, opting instead for "Creative Labs SoundBlaster 16 or AWE-32." It was mostly luck. But I had a hunch that I needed to install the more primitive-sounding "SoundBlaster 16 or AWE-32" before tackling the much more highfalutin "Advanced Wave Effect Synthesis." That was a good guess: Win95 loaded the additional software for AWE effects when I rebooted and took off. I hardly had a chance to blink. My AWE-32 runs like a-ringin' a bell—in orchestral 32-voice polyphonic sound.

What happens if you can't get your hardware to match the settings the Add New Hardware Wizard demands? Good question. I saw it happen once. It ends up that Windows 95 Help actually has a good troubleshooter that covers many possibilities, including the situation where the hardware you're installing can't conform to the Wizard's recommendation, and the possibility that you've run the Wizard twice for the same piece of hardware, creating two different entries in the Device Manager for one single physical piece of hardware. To get to the troubleshooter, click on Start, then Help. Pick Find. Type "hardware conflict." Click on Troubleshooting Hardware Conflicts, and follow the bouncing WinBall.

Naive Installation

Naive? Moi? Hey toots, I've been called a lot of things, but naive ain't among 'em. Anyway, Sarah talked me into trying to install the same board, in the same machine, by just sticking it in and seeing what happened.

I put the board in the PC and turned it on. Win95 didn't detect anything, so I clicked on Start, Settings, Control Panel, and double-clicked on the Add New Hardware applet. I was greeted by the same Add New Hardware Wizard that Mao hit.

So you figure I'm being paid to act dumb, eh? Don't laugh too hard. It's good work if you can get it. I get the same spiel about automatically detecting new hardware, except unlike Mao, I click Yes, I really do want Win95 to take care of all this IRQ DMA I/O crap for me. PDQ. UC? I click `Next>`.

Win95 just takes off. I'm sitting there watching the lights flash and listening to the hard drives whir. That Progress bar faked me out a couple of times—it goes real fast for a while, then sits forever in the same spot—but I remembered Sarah's Second Law of Progress Bars: don't panic unless they freeze for a full five minutes. Sarah's First Law of Progress Bars? Don't believe 'em. Forget the Second Law.

So I'm just sitting there, not doing a thing, when the Wizard pops up and says it's identified the new hardware. I pushed the Details button, so you could see the proof, but was there really any doubt? I clicked Finish, Windows went away for a few seconds, and all of a sudden the AWE-32 board is working fine. No reboot or anything. Most remarkable.

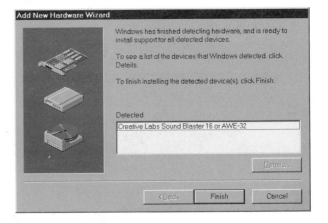

 Most (modern) hardware that I've tried to install has really gone just that easily. It's rare that I have to think about any of the old bugaboos: many of the demons that used to keep me from installing new hardware have somehow been exorcised. Quite a refreshing change.

One tiny problem with the AWE-32 board. When it's installed, the MIDI synthesizer somehow gets stuck on the old Yamaha OPL-3 synthesizer setting—you pay big bucks for a cool board, and the installer sets it up to run exclusively in first gear. To give your AWE-32 full voice, click on Start, Settings, Control Panel. Double-click on Multimedia. Click on the MIDI tab. Pick "Creative Advanced Wave Effects Synthesis for AWE-32" and OK all the way back out. Then go look for a `.MID` or `.RMI` file. Wondrous!

When Win95 performs a hardware autodetect, it maintains a file called `detlog.txt` with all the detection information. See Chapter 9 for details.

Many of the hardware settings are stored in and around Registry key `HKLM\System\CurrentControlSet\Services\Class`.* Again, feel free to use `regedit` to poke around there, but don't touch anything! I don't think *anybody* knows how all those entries are interconnected with the rest of the Registry.

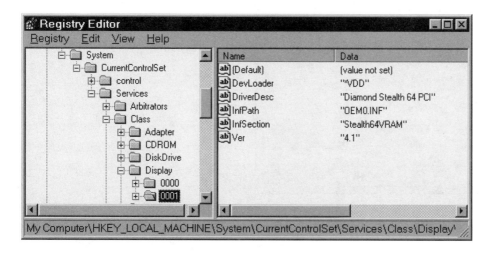

Figure 10-2. Where your display driver lives

Add/Remove Programs

The Add/Remove Programs wizard is covered at length in Chapter 3, in the section called "Software Installation."

---

* Remember, HKLM = HKEY_LOCAL_MACHINE.

Registry entries associated with the Remove Programs capability are located in `HKLM\`
`SOFTWARE\Microsoft\Windows\CurrentVersion\Uninstall`. The
`DisplayName` value shows up on the Add/Remove Programs list, and the
`UninstallString` value tells Win95 where the uninstall program for that particular
application resides. See how it works?

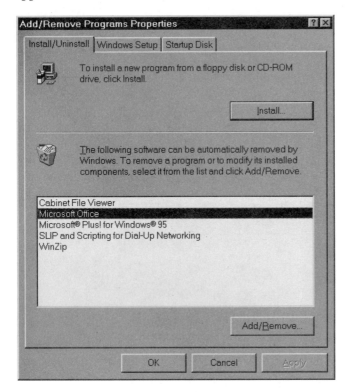

Figure 10-3. Mao's Add/Remove Programs list

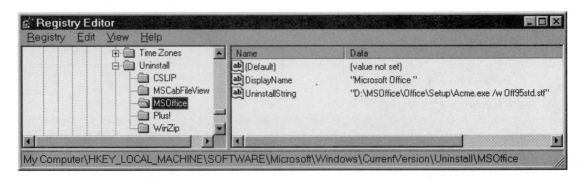

Figure 10-4. Source of the entries in Mao's list

 *Date/Time*

> Lost time is never found again,
> and what we call time enough always proves little enough.

—Benjamin Franklin, *Poor Richard's Almanac,* 1757

 By now you know all about that clock down in the lower right corner of your Win95 screen. Hold your mouse over the top of it and a ToolTip shows the date. Double-click on it and you'll get the Control Panel's Date/Time Properties dialog, same as if you picked the Date/Time applet from the Control Panel itself. From there you can set the time, date (Figure 10-5), and time zone (Figure 10-6). No biggie.

Now, let's take a look at some things I bet you *didn't* know.

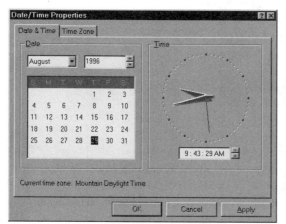

Figure 10-5. The Ho-Hum clock

Figure 10-6. The Cool clock

Windows 95 supports 51 different time zones; you can see them in the Registry key `HKLM\SOFTWARE\Microsoft\Windows\CurrentVersion\Time Zones` (Figure 10-7). With all the care that's obviously been lavished on the political sensibilities of various countries—including, for example, five *different* entries for GMT + 2 hours, which crosses the volatile Middle East—Win95's creators somehow missed Nepal, which has its own unique time zone.

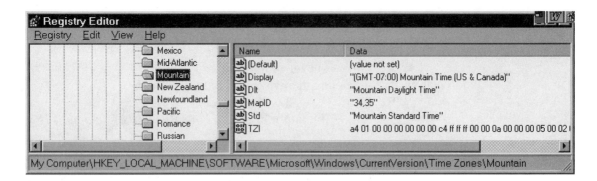

Figure 10-7. Time zones unveiled

While it's apparent that the time zone information stored in HKLM\SOFTWARE\
Microsoft\Windows\CurrentVersion\Time Zones makes its way into
HKLM\System\CurrentControlSet\control\ TimeZoneInformation
(see Figure 10-8)—you can actually see the TZI value in the former migrate to the
DaylightStart and StandardStart keys in the latter, for example—trying to
change any of these keys by hand is an invitation for disaster.

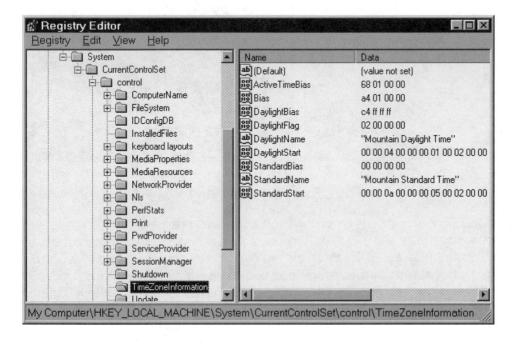

Figure 10-8. Time zone info at Mom Central

If you want to change the format of the date and time (say, you want a military-style 24-hour clock, or you want the date to appear as YY/MM/DD), you're in the wrong place. Take a look at the Regional Settings applet, described later.

 By the way, if the Windows 95 clock starts running fast, don't worry; you aren't going nuts. Mine does, too. I think it's a bug in the first release of the Plus! Pack's System Agent, or possibly in the DriveSpace 3 routines. I gain three or four minutes every night. Anyway, you'll find that restarting Win95 will reset your clock back to the correct time (or at least to the time maintained internally on your PC's motherboard—which may not be correct!). If you set the time with the Date/Time applet, your PC's motherboard clock will be set, too. Little-known fact: the world's most accurate time is always available, free except for long-distance charges, by calling the National Institute of Standards at 303-499-7111. You'll hear beeps and squawks, but every minute there's a real human voice that announces the Coordinated Universal Time. (Sounds better than Greenwich Mean, eh?)

 Display

The sense of sight is the keenest of all our senses.

—Cicero, *De oratore,* ca 80 B.C.

 The Control Panel's Display applet is accessible from two different locations: you can start up the Control Panel and double-click on Display; or you can right-click on a blank part of the Desktop and choose Properties. Either way, you'll get the screen shown in Figure 10-9. In this section we'll take a look at the (poorly named) Background, Screen Saver, Appearance, and Settings tabs. (Plus! is from Microsoft's Plus! Pack, which is! discussed in! chapter! 5!)

Background Tab

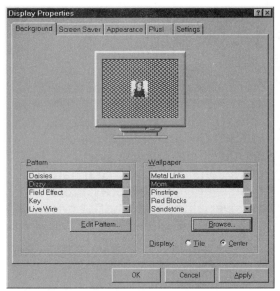

Figure 10-9. Display Properties/Background   **Figure 10-10. The resulting desktop**

 I always get confused by the difference between "Pattern" and "Wallpaper" —two rather meaningless terms for similar WinThings. Fortunately the preview offered under the Display applet's Background tab makes the differences pretty obvious when you're actually trying to put them to use. I finally figured out how they differ, conceptually, when I looked at the Registry entries. The settings are stored in the `HKCU\Control Panel\Desktop` key (Figure 10-11).

Apparently when Win95 draws the Desktop, it goes through a procedure something like this. First, it looks at the `Pattern` value in `HKCU\Control Panel\Desktop` and interprets the set of eight numbers there as a bit pattern. (If you've chosen no `Pattern`, the value is set to "`(None)`".) Sarah will talk about the patterns in a moment. Second, Win95 looks at the `Wallpaper` value to see if you've chosen a picture (`.bmp`, `.dib` or `.rle` files all work; `.pcx` and `.wmf` files do not). If you haven't chosen a Wallpaper, the value is simply "". Third, Win95 looks at the `TileWallpaper` value. If it's a `0`, the Wallpaper is centered on top of the Pattern. If it's a `1`, the Pattern is discarded completely, and the Wallpaper is duplicated so it covers the entire Desktop ("tiled," if you will), starting with an image in the upper-left corner. Finally, Win95 draws the icons, Taskbar, windows and the like on top of the Desktop.

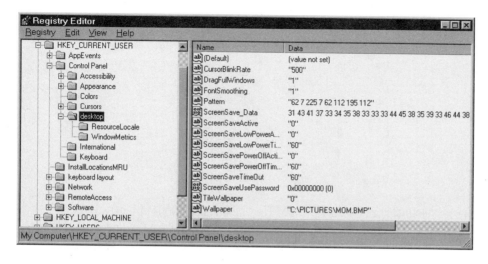

Figure 10-11. Desktop settings

 A "Pattern" is a collection of eight numbers, each between 0 and 255. The numbers correspond to the pixels that are marked. An easy way to see what's going on is to bring up the Desktop tab, pick a Pattern, then click Edit Pattern. For example, the Triangles pattern (Figure 10-12) looks like this:

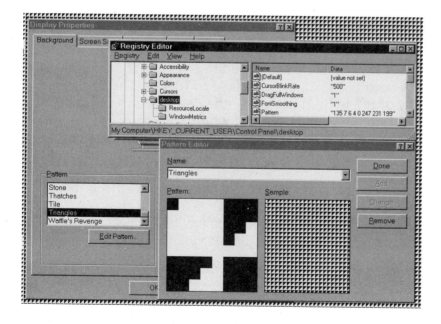

Figure 10-12. Triangle Pattern appears in the Registry

1	0	0	0	0	1	1	1
0	0	0	0	0	1	1	1
0	0	0	0	0	1	1	0
0	0	0	0	0	1	0	0
0	0	0	0	0	0	0	0
1	1	1	1	0	1	1	1
1	1	1	0	0	1	1	1
1	1	0	0	0	1	1	1

Each of those eight lines is interpreted as a binary number. The first number, 1000111 binary, is 135 in decimal. The second number, 0000111 binary, is 7. Then comes 6, 4, 0, 247 (take my word for it), 231, and 199. If you look at the Pattern value in Figure 10-12, you'll see how the Triangle Pattern is stored in the Registry. Neat, huh?

Believe it or not, the built-in Windows Patterns are tucked away in your Win95 \windows folder, in an old-fashioned .ini file called control.ini. There you'll find entries such as these:

```
[Patterns]
(None)=(None)
Triangles=135 7 6 4 0 247 231 199
```

If you want to distribute your own patterns, simply edit control.ini to add your favorites, and give the new control.ini to your circle of friends. The Registry contains no mention of any of the built-in patterns—the Registry only concerns itself with those sets of eight numbers, regardless of where they came from—so customizing your own control.ini is an easy, safe way to pass your patterns around.

Patterns are rather monotonous, single-color beasts, although it *is* rather surprising what can be done with a monochrome 8-x-8 bit array. Want to change the color of your pattern? You don't do that here. Look at the Desktop setting under the Appearance tab, described shortly.

Screen Saver Tab

The Screen Saver tab not only allows you to choose a screen saver, it also lets you set up password protection for screen savers in general, and it lets you control Energy Star power conservation signals sent from your PC to your monitor.

When you bring up the Display applet's Screen Saver tab, Win95 scans the Win95 `\windows` and `\windows\system` folders for any `*.scr` files. The names of those files (without their extensions) are presented in the Screen Saver scroll-down box. Win95 makes no allowances for screen savers located in other folders. If the `.scr` file you choose is a valid Win95 screen saver, the Preview button will work. If, in addition, the screen saver has user-adjustable properties, the Settings button comes to life. If the screen saver supports Win95 Password protection—and many old Windows 3.1 screen savers do not—the Password Protected Box becomes active.

While they may have some minor value as password protection devices, screen savers, of course, do absolutely nothing for your monitor. They're just for fun. Back in the days when screens were green, and advanced screens were amber, monitor burn-in was a problem. But ever since the late 1980s or so, monitors haven't been prone to burn-in. They have to be good. It's in their Contract with America.

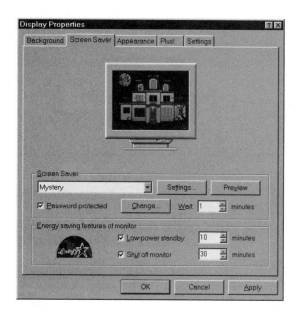

Figure 10-13. Screen Saver tab

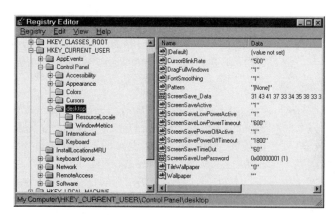

Figure 10-14. Screen Saver in the Registry

One of the weekly trade magazines made a big deal of the fact that typing Ctl+Alt+Del would bypass password "protection" on Windows 3.1 screen savers running under Windows 95. While that's literally true, at least for the screen savers that still work in Win95, the Win31 screen saver password "protection" was a complete joke to begin with. And if they had bothered to look here at the Screen Saver tab, where such things come to roost, they would've discovered the Password Protected Box grayed out. The moral of the story: don't rely on Win31 screen savers, particularly not for password protection. The .scr file format changed between Win31 and Win95, and programmers have to rewrite their screen savers to take advantage of all the hooks in the new world.

Win95 stores the settings you would expect (Screen Saver active, password required, time delays, and the like) in the Registry's HKCU\Control Panel\Desktop key. Even the password itself, one-way encoded in the value ScreenSave_Data, is here. *Except* the one thing you would most expect to be stored in the Registry—the name of the screen saver .scr file! To find the name of the current screen saver, you have to pop over to the Win95 \windows directory and look in system.ini's [boot] section for a line called scrnsave.exe=. Bizarre!

Not bizarre at all, my furry-faced fiend, er, friend. That's where the name of the screen saver was stored in Windows 3.1. If we had moved it, millions of people would've been disappointed (or worse!) when their favorite old screen saver or screen saver program didn't work. You don't understand how attached people become to their flying toasters.

The timeout settings under the Screen Saver tab are all measured in minutes, and if you play with them you'll discover that none can be set to less than one minute, or more than sixty minutes. Bummer. Some days I'd really like to set my screen saver to kick in quickly, and my monitor to power off at two or three hours. Guess what? You can do it. The timeout values in the Registry (ScreenSaveTimeOut, ScreenSavePowerOffTimeout and ScreenSaveLowPowerTimeout) are measured in seconds. All you have to do is change the setting manually—and subsequently avoid using the Screen Saver tab, which (if you click Apply or OK) will reset the numbers.

This is an excellent opportunity to edit your Registry, if you've never done so before. The setting is easy to find, and if you screw up you need only call up the Display applet's Screen Saver tab to make everything right. Start by bringing up the Screen Saver tab, picking a screen saver, and setting the wait time at one minute. Click OK. Now start Regedit, the Registry editor, by clicking Start, then Run, typing regedit, and hitting Enter. On the left, double-click on HKCU (that's HKEY_CURRENT_USER, remember?) then Control Panel, then Desktop. On the right, double-click on the value you want to change, in this case ScreenSaveTimeOut. You should get a box like Figure 10-15. Replace the old value of 60 (seconds) with 10, and click OK. Congratulations. You've just performed the Win95 equivalent of brain surgery. Now, restart your computer by clicking on Start, then Shut Down, picking the Restart the Computer? button, and clicking OK.

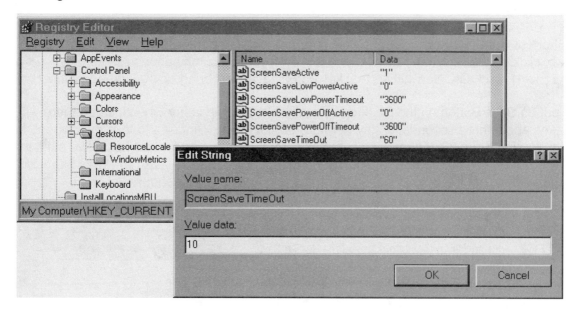

Figure 10-15. Screen Saver kicks in at 10 seconds

When you reboot, wait about ten seconds and your screen saver will kick in. Boom. Play with it a bit and you'll see that the screen saver does, indeed, work with a ten-second fuse. To restore everything to its old status, just right-click on the Desktop, pick Properties, bring up the Screen Saver tab, and make any changes you like.

You can run any Windows screen saver, even one that isn't your current one, by double-clicking on it in Explorer. The quickest way of checking out a bunch of screen savers is to sort Explorer on Type, look for Screen Saver, and double-click on 'em one at a time.

 Be sure to check out and use the right-click context menu for screen saver files. Not only is there the default Test item that double-clicking gets but there is a Configure choice and an Install choice that whisks you directly to the Screen Saver tab of the Display applet.

My favorite Stupid Desktop Trick has to be the screen saver hot foot. . . er, hot key—better known as da Boss Button. You know the scenario: the boss suddenly drops by and you're playing Leisure Suit Larry. If you have da Boss Button set up, a quick key combination gets rid of all the incriminating evidence and, before the boss has a chance to say, "Beach Blanket Babes from Beyond," you're suddenly sitting in front of a completely innocuous screen.

Go into Explorer, and right-click and drag any `.scr` file (like, oh, `Flying Windows.scr`) onto the Desktop. When you let go of the mouse button, pick "Create Shortcut Here." Right-click on the new shortcut, pick Properties, bring up the Shortcut tab, click on the Shortcut Key box, and hit whatever key combination you like (say, `Alt+F9`). Click OK. Now hitting that key combination will bring up the screen saver.

I put da Boss Button on the Desktop because it cranks up faster when located there—it takes about three seconds, on my Pentium-90, for Flying Windows to take over when I'm running Word 95. (Other, less complex screen savers start faster.) I could've put it in `\Windows\Start Menu` or any folder hanging off of `\Start Menu` (or `\Desktop` for that matter), but the hot key doesn't work as fast from those locations.

One last note on the Energy Star settings. If your monitor was identified as Energy Star compliant during Setup, the bottom area of the Screen Saver tab should be available for you to make changes to those settings. If you know your monitor supports the VESA Display Power Management Signaling specification, pop over to the Settings tab, click Change Display Type, and check the box marked Monitor is Energy Star Compliant.

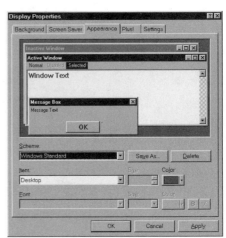

Figure 10-16. The Display Appearance tab

Appearance Tab

The Appearance tab lets you choose colors and fonts for just about everything that has to do with the Desktop, windows, and, uh, Windows. Settings that you choose under the Display tab (Figure 10-16) are stored in a shorthand form in the Registry's `HKCU\Control Panel\Appearance` key (Figure 10-17), with the actual working settings scattered more extensively in other parts of the Registry.

Figure 10-17. Appearance in the Registry

A *scheme* is just a collection of settings for everything from the Desktop color to the Active Title Bar's font size. Windows comes with a predefined collection of twenty-seven different schemes: you can see them by scrolling down the Schemes list on the Appearances tab or (easier) by looking at the Registry's HKCU\Control Panel\Appearances\ Schemes key. There are also schemes for mouse cursors and sounds.

As you create new schemes with the Save As . . . button on the Appearances tab (or delete them, for that matter, with the Delete button) the collection under the \Schemes key grows (or shrinks). In Figure 10-18, for example, I've created a new Appearance Scheme called Mom's Favorite Scheme by using the Save As . . . button. See how it appears under \Schemes?

Figure 10-18. Registry scheme-ing

There's nothing particularly magical about Schemes. At its core, an Appearance Scheme is really just a 500-byte collection of settings. You can see the odd assortment of numbers and ASCII characters that make up a Scheme by double-clicking in the Registry on the Scheme of your choice to bring up the Registry's edit box (Figure 10-19).

 The Item list on the Appearance tab contains eighteen Desktop Items—from "3D Objects" to "Desktop" to "Window"—that you can adjust from the Display applet. It probably won't surprise you to discover that these eighteen settings are just a small subset of all the Desktop settings maintained in the Registry.

Figure 10-19. Scheme in the raw

 I'll tell you what surprised me. I thought a scheme would hold settings for each of those eighteen Items. By choosing a scheme, I figured, all the eighteen Items would be set to values defined by the scheme. Not so. It ends up that a couple of the Items work independently of schemes: you can change the scheme till you're blue in the face, but never touch these Items' values. Weird.

Let me tell you what surprised *me.* This scheme and item folderol doesn't really mean anything. All they amount to is a pretty face painted on the top of the real, working settings: when Windows 95 goes to draw a screen, it couldn't care less what you've chosen for, say, the Desktop item, or the 3D Objects item. The *real* Appearance settings are in the Registry, stored in `HKCU\Control Panel\Desktop\WindowMetrics` (Figure 10-20) and `HKCU\Control Panel\Colors` (Figure 10-21) keys. These are the settings that actually affect how your screen appears—the schemes and items are mere biological window dressing for the binary-inhibited. You can control the appearance of your screen much more accurately by ditching the Display applet's Appearance Tab and editing the Registry entries by hand!

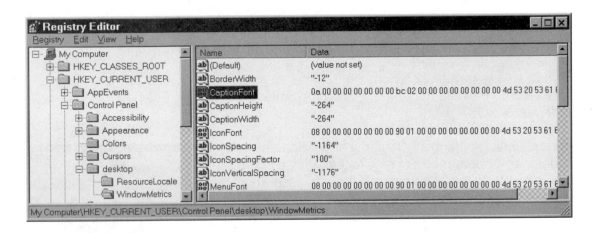

Figure 10-20. \WindowMetrics in the Registry

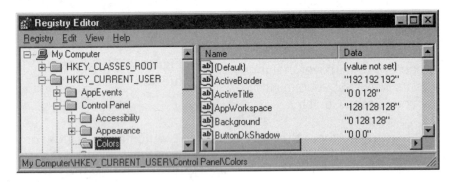

Figure 10-21. \Colors in the Registry

To see how changes in the eighteen items rippled down to the real working settings, I started by looking at those Registry settings with a pristine installation of the Windows Standard scheme—the default settings. Figure 10-22 shows what I found for the \WindowMetrics settings.

Registry Key	Default Value
BorderWidth	-12
CaptionFont	*
CaptionHeight	-216
CaptionWidth	-216
IconFont	*
IconSpacing	-1164
IconSpacingFactor	100
IconVerticalSpacing	-1176
MenuFont	*
MenuHeight	-216
MenuWidth	-216
MessageFont	*
ScrollHeight	-192
ScrollWidth	-192
Shell Icon BPP	16
Shell Icon Size	32
SmCaptionFont	*
SmCaptionHeight	-180
SmCaptionWidth	-180
StatusFont	*

Figure 10-22. Appearance Metrics

Although most of those values are primarily of interest to C programmers, the identity of the fonts can come in handy. The CaptionFont is what most people would call a window title font. For some unknown reason, though, it's also the font used in the Taskbar, and for the time in the Taskbar's notification area. (CaptionHeight, for what it's worth, controls not only the

---

* All default fonts are MS Sans Serif.

height of the window title area, but also the height of each line in the Taskbar area.) The `IconFont` is not only the font used for icon captions, as you might expect, it's also the internal font used for identifying folder contents, and by Explorer, Regedit, and other Windows apps. The `MenuFont` controls menus, including entries on the Start Menu (but not Start itself, which is in the `CaptionFont`). `MessageFont` only controls the text in a very few messages: most applications seem to ignore it. The only place I could find `SmCaptionFont` was in Microsoft Office's Shortcut bar, where it's used for a very brief time as the Shortcut bar is loaded. And the `StatusFont` not only controls the status bar in several Win95 applications, it's also used for Tooltips! Only Redmond knows why `StatusFont` is not used for the status bars in the MS Office applications. What's good for the goose, eh?

If you go to hack . . . uh, examine the Registry entries for these fonts, you'll find that the first two bytes are always the font's point size, expressed in hexadecimal. To change a 7-point font to 16-point, for example, change the first two bytes from 07 to 10.

Since Win95 uses the scalable Marlett font for the minimize/maximize/close buttons in the upper right corner of every window (see Chapter 2), those three buttons can automatically adjust their size, depending on changes in `CaptionHeight`. That's pretty cool, and sure beats the unscalable bitmaps used in older versions of Windows.

Next, to get our bearings before we started really messing up the Registry, I took a look at the `\Colors` settings, shown in Figure 10-23. These consist of a set of three numbers, representing red, green, and blue color intensities: 0 0 0 is black; 255 0 0 is bright red; 255 255 255 is white; and so on: color RGB values are discussed in Chapter 2.

Registry key	Default Value	Determines the color of:
ActiveBorder	192 192 192	Thin line inside border of resizable window with focus; thin line around Taskbar
ActiveTitle	0 0 128	Title bar of window with focus; this setting is ignored by MS Office applications
AppWorkspace	128 128 128	Background color in some apps (the "client area", e.g, if there is no open doc in Word, or if all docs are minimized; this is *not* the color behind Word docs in Page View)

Background	0 128 128	Desktop color; also primary color in Pattern
ButtonDkShadow	0 0 0	Extreme right and bottom of buttons
ButtonFace	192 192 192	Used all over Win95: face of buttons; dialog backgrounds; top & bottom areas of many Win apps; status bar background; Taskbar background; highlight around edges of menus; Toolbar backgrounds; scrollbar "thumb" (or "slider"); dithered with `ButtonHilight` for faces of "pushed" buttons, and for scrollbar itself
ButtonHilight	255 255 255	Extreme top and left of button; secondary color for Win app buttons and common dialog buttons; also used on dialog text boxes; many more less obvious uses
ButtonLight	223 223 223	Just below `ButtonHilight` on buttons
ButtonShadow	128 128 128	Just above `ButtonDkShadow` on buttons
ButtonText	0 0 0	Text on buttons; text on status bars; Taskbar icon captions; Taskbar time text; arrows on drop-down lists and scrollbars; primary color on Win app buttons and common dialog buttons
GrayText	128 128 128	Some old Windows 3.1 apps may use this color to indicate "grayed out" (not available) menu selections, but in Win95 "unavailable" menu selections use a ghosted font; primary use in Win95 is for the lines connecting folders in the tree side of Explorer-style windows
Hilight	0 0 128	Background of selected item in menu or in some Win apps; background of selected text in a text box and other Windows controls; also dithered with icon caption background color (`Background`: see **Desktop** Item, below) when icon has focus

HilightText	255 255 255	Text of selected item in menu or in some Win apps (e.g., Explorer); color of selected text in a text box and other Windows controls; also color of icon caption on Desktop when icon has focus
InactiveBorder	192 192 192	Thin line inside border of resizable window without focus; also used on Taskbar
InactiveTitle	128 128 128	Background of title bar of window without focus
InactiveTitleText	192 192 192	Text on title bar of window without focus
InfoText	0 0 0	Tooltip text in Win95, and the text of "tips" on buttons in such apps as Explorer, Paint, WordPad, and the Toolbar tips in the MS Office suite
InfoWindow	255 255 225	Tooltip background in Win95, and the background color of "tips" in Explorer, Paint, WordPad, and Office
Menu	192 192 192	Background of menu bar; background of menu items (including the Start Menu, but not the Start button itself)
MenuText	0 0 0	Text on menu bar and menu items (including the Start Menu, but not the Start button itself)
Scrollbar	192 192 192	Some old Win31 programs may use this for the main part of the scrollbar; I couldn't find it used anywhere in Win95. The main part of Win95 scrollbars are constructed by dithering ButtonFace and ButtonHilight.
TitleText	255 255 255	Text on title bar of window with focus (although the MS Office apps ignore this setting)
Window	255 255 255	Background of most Windows apps and Explorer-style icon windows; color of "page"

		in MS Office apps; background color for Windows controls, e.g., text boxes and list boxes . . . even radio buttons!
WindowFrame	0 0 0	Outermost right and bottom lines on some (not many) windows; outline for default pushbuttons; outline for Tooltips in MS Office apps
WindowText	0 0 0	Text within most applications; text and "+" and "–" boxes in Explorer; text in Windows dialog boxes; unselected text in text boxes and list boxes

Warning: you must restart Windows (at least "log on as a different user") to see the effect of changing these settings!

Figure 10-23. The Real Appearance Colors

 Armed with a guidebook of how the Registry settings start out, let's step through each of the eighteen Items in turn and see what changing them really will do to Windows. By the way, very little of this stuff is documented anywhere, as far as I know—and the little documentation I have seen is wrong, over and over again. Odd, considering how much interest there is in "personalizing" the Desktop.

This is a good time to go ahead and play with the Registry, if you like, although you'll have to reboot after making changes so they'll take. ("Close all Programs and Log on as a Different User" will do it.) If you get everything all bollixed, don't worry: bringing back the Display applet's Appearance tab and picking a scheme will reset all the settings. Well, almost all of them. I'll show you the two that stay "stuck."

The **3D Objects** item defines the background color (in the upper "Color" drop-down box) and the text color (in the lower "Color" drop-down box) of any standard Windows 3D control. Yes, both of those boxes are hot; make changes to each and you'll see. Since Win95 pretty much lives and dies with 3D objects—they appear everywhere from the Taskbar to the background of popular Windows apps—these settings can make a huge difference in Windows' appearance.

Behind the scenes, changing the 3D Objects background item really changes settings for *thirteen* different Registry entries: `Scrollbar`, `InactiveTitle`, `Menu`, `ActiveBorder`, `InactiveBorder`, `AppWorkspace`, `ButtonFace`, `ButtonShadow`, `GrayText`, `ButtonText`, `ButtonHilight`, `ButtonLight`, and `InfoWindow`.

I found the most wonderful thing when working with 3D Objects and background colors. The drop-down Color box has twenty entries, as usual. The first sixteen colors (reading left-to-right) in the drop-down list box are the standard RGB colors used since the very first PC descended from the Boca Raton heavens. The last one is fixed at the almost-gray with RGB = 160, 160, 164. But colors number 17, 18, and 19 will change depending on which color you've chosen for the 3D Objects background! Once you've chosen a color—which will become the `ButtonFace` color—Win95 automatically recalculates the twelve other colors and sticks them in the Registry. If you click on the Color drop-down box again, the `ButtonShadow` color is presented in the dialog as the new eighteenth color, and the `ButtonHilight` color is offered as the nineteenth color.

Because it takes over these three colors (recall that the 20 colors in the drop-down box are the 20 solid system colors on 256-color systems) on 256-color systems, Win95 can let you choose a dithered color (see Chapter 2) for 3D Objects backgrounds. If you pick a dithered color, the seventeenth color in the drop-down box becomes the solid color with RGB values identical to the color that used to be dithered! This is the only situation I know about where the Control Panel changes system colors on-the-fly.

If you change the font color in the 3D Objects item, down in the lower box on the Appearance tab, Win95 will change `IconFont` in addition to all the Registry settings mentioned earlier that were modified with the background change.

The **Active Title Bar** item, as you might imagine, changes the color, size, and font of the active title bar. Not unexpectedly, it changes the Registry `\WindowMetrics` entries for `CaptionFont`, `CaptionWidth`, `CaptionHeight`, and `smCaptionFont`, and the `\Colors` entries for `ActiveTitle` and `TitleText`. Ho-hum. It also changes the color `ButtonLight`, which, as you're about to see, is very common.

The **Active Window Border** item changes the `BorderWidth` (each unit of one on the Appearance tab seems to correspond to five pixels' thickness), and the `ActiveBorder` color, as expected. It also changes the color `ButtonLight`.

The **Application Background** item changes `AppWorkspace`. No surprises there. It also changes `ButtonLight`.

The **Caption Buttons** item not only lets you adjust the height of the "Minimize, Maximize, Exit" buttons in the upper-right corner of every window, it also controls the height of each line in the Taskbar, and the size of the icons in the Taskbar. It affects the Registry settings for `CaptionWidth` and `CaptionHeight`.

 The **Desktop** item controls the color of the Desktop (Registry entry `Background`), but it's a little more complicated than that. Each icon gets the Desktop color as a background to the caption: the color fills a small rectangular area surrounding the icon caption's text. If there's a tiled wallpaper (see Background tab, earlier in this chapter), or you have a wallpaper that fills the whole screen, the Desktop color only appears as background to the icons' text (Figure 10-25). If the wallpaper doesn't fill the whole screen and there's no Pattern (see Background tab), the Desktop color fills the Desktop, except for areas occupied by icons and the Taskbar. If there's a Pattern, the Desktop color is used for the "white" color in the Pattern, with black filling the other squares (Figure 10-26).

Changing the **Desktop** item will change the Registry `\Colors` value for `Background`. It also changes the color `ButtonLight` . . . but then again, what doesn't?

Figure 10-24. Icon, no Wallpaper, no Pattern

Figure 10-25. Icon with Wallpaper

Figure 10-26. Icon with Triangle Pattern

The **Icon** item lets you pick your icon size, and the icon captions' font and size. Changing the Item under the Appearances tab changes Registry entries `IconFont`, `IconSpacing`, `IconVerticalSpacing`, and `Shell Icon Size`. As noted earlier, `IconFont` is the font used not only for Desktop icons, but also for displaying folder contents, and in Explorer, Regedit, and other Windows apps.

 Want to change the color of your icon font? Well, as best I can tell—and, believe me, I tried—there's no way to do it! The font for a Desktop icon that doesn't have focus seems to be either white or black, depending on the `Background` color, and Windows appears to control the font's color, automatically, internally. When you click on an icon and it gets focus, it takes on the color called `HilightText`. That's the only human-adjustable icon caption color control I could find, either in the Control Panel or buried within the Registry itself. Considering how much control you have over every facet of Desktop appearance, this oversight seems bizarre.

Win95 generally has 32 x 32 pixel icons stored away for most applications. (The Plus! Pack also includes some 48 x 48 pixel icons.) If you choose a size of 32, you'll get good icons. Any other number, though, and what you'll see is a (usually ugly) automatically clipped-down version of what the icon should look like. Stick to size 32 and you'll be in good shape. Also, note that changing the size of the icon changes spacing in weird places—including the items on the Start Menu.

The **Icon Spacing (Horizontal)** and **Icon Spacing (Vertical)** items adjust the grid Win95 uses to rearrange icons on the Desktop. (They also adjust the grid used by Explorer windows with large icons.) The icons "snap to" the nearest grid location whenever you right-click on the Desktop and choose Line Up Icons; they'll fill in missing spots in the grid (from top to bottom, then left to right) if you click Arrange Icons, or leave Auto-Arrange Icons checked.

If you increase the **(Horizontal)** number, icons get more space stuck between them, from left to right. If you increase the **(Vertical)** number, they space out more from top to bottom. Unfortunately, when you get beyond that simplistic explanation, it isn't quite as simple as it sounds. And, in spite of what you may have read, these numbers have nothing to do with pixels, or anything else that makes a modicum of sense.

The problem lies in the way Windows measures distances on the screen. The Win95 *Software Development Kit* defines four different ways of measuring distances—and the fourth method, called Physical Device Space,* can in fact encompass many *more* ways of measuring distances. Personally, I don't pretend to understand it—and I'm not sure I trust anyone who says they do . . .

I sure wish Microsoft would find a way to present values to the user (or at least to me!) that bear some relationship to reality. When I'm working with the screen, I understand pixels. When I'm working with printed output, I understand inches—and, if coerced, will put up with centimeters and points. Anything more complicated than that falls into the category of "stuff the computer should figure out." These settings are among the worst offenders. Why doesn't Windows just let me pick how many icons I want to show on the screen? For years Word has had a slider "Insert Table" Toolbar button that

---

* Yes, Windows programming geeks talk that way . . . "Hey, Brad, hand me that quarter-physical-device-space-inch wrench. The one with the dented-logical-uh-page-space end." And you thought Ozzies talked funny. Here's a quick little test for hot-shot Win95-space programmers: I am using Large Fonts (125 pixels/inch), and set the Appearance Tab's **Icon Spacing (Horizontal)** to 60, and **(Vertical)** to 50. I then change to Small Fonts (96 pixels/inch) and reboot. What are the final values in the Registry for `IconSpacing` and `IconVertical Spacing`? And, based on those settings, how many icons will appear on my 1024 × 768 Desktop grid? *Bzzzzt.* Nope, you're wrong. Try it. You'll see.

accomplishes the same thing. If I change resolutions, I should be asked if I want to change the grid. Why must such simple things be so difficult?

 Anyway, the **(Horizontal)** and **(Vertical)** numbers you pick here under the Appearance tab are moshed together with the Windows 95 "Zoom" factor (which I'll talk about later under the Settings tab), and the result is stuck in the Registry settings `IconSpacing` and `IconVerticalSpacing`.

 I've found that my 1024 x 768 screen, running with Large Fonts, can pack ten icons across the screen with **(Horizontal)** set to 70. It will fit eleven icons across at 60, and twelve icons across at 50. With the **(Vertical)** number at 60, I get eight icons up and down; at 50, I get nine; and at 40 I get ten.

If I switch over to Small Fonts, I see one or two more icons across, and one more icon up-and-down. If I run a custom font (see the Settings tab discussion later) at 150 percent Zoom, I generally get one fewer icon than with the Large Fonts setting, in each direction.

 If your **(Horizontal)** and **(Vertical)** numbers get screwed up, make sure you have the size of font you want in the Settings tab, then flip over to the Appearance tab. Start with 60 for **(Horizontal)**, and 50 for **(Vertical)**, then right-click on the Desktop and pick Line Up Icons. Adjust the numbers until you get an icon arrangement you can live with.

These numbers are not stored in the Scheme. You can pick a new Scheme and **(Horizontal)** and **(Vertical)** will not change. Similarly, you can change **(Horizontal)** and **(Vertical)** without changing your Scheme. But **(Horizontal)** and **(Vertical)** numbers *do* change if you switch from Small Fonts to Large Fonts, or pick some custom "Zoom" factor under the Settings tab.

The **Inactive Title Bar** Item changes a whole lot more than the title of inactive windows (i.e., those without focus). In fact, it changes so much, I wonder if this isn't a bug. When you change **Inactive Title Bar,** the Registry's `CaptionWidth` and `CaptionHeight` values get changed, which affects the size of the title of *all* windows, inactive or not. The `CaptionFont` is changed, which not only affects all windows' captions, it also changes fonts in the Taskbar, including the time! In the `\Colors` section, it changes the `InactiveTitle` and `InactiveTitleText` colors, as well as `ButtonLight`.

The **Inactive Window Border** Item changes the `\WindowMetrics BorderWidth` setting—which, in turn, changes the size of the borders on *all* windows, whether they have focus or not—and the `InactiveBorder` color. And `ButtonLight`.

One of the few Appearance tab items that really does what it says it does, the **Menu** item adjusts the Registry's `MenuWidth` and `MenuHeight`, the `MenuFont`, and the colors `Menu` and `MenuText`. (And, of course, `ButtonLight`.) Remember that the Start Menu is a menu, too, and is thus affected by this setting. The Start Button itself is considered part of the Taskbar, so it escapes any **Menu** item changes. Let's hear it for Control Panel settings that do what they say they'll do. It's the American way.

In direct contrast, the next item, **Message Box,** changes all sorts of things—but probably not the things you were expecting! I thought **Message Box** would change the font used in message boxes. Well, it does, sorta. When you change the **Message Box** item, the Registry `\WindowMetrics` value for `MessageFont` changes. As noted earlier, that doesn't do much—very, very few Windows messages use the `MessageFont`. But it also changes the `\Colors` entry for `WindowText`, and *that* changes the color of just about everything inside Win95: text in Explorer and the other Win95 apps; the "default" color of text in all the MS Office apps, fer heaven's sake; the text in every standard Windows control (list boxes, text boxes, and the like); the body of Property Sheets; and so many more things I couldn't begin to list them all. This is one duplicitous setting. A good candidate for Rush's Beltway buddies.

What kinda cheap shot is that, from a guy whose species has been tormenting the Beltway for centuries? Sheeeesh. You want to see a duplicitous Appearance tab item, take a look at the next one. It's called **Palette Title,** but what the setting has to do with palettes is way beyond me. That setting just changes the Registry's `\WindowsMetric` values for `SmCaptionWidth` and `SmCaptionHeight` (which are always both set to the same number!), and the `SmCaptionFont`, which, as noted earlier, is used almost nowhere. In fact, the only place we could find it was in the title of the window that flashes by briefly as the MS Office Shortcut Bar gets loaded. That's it.

My species has been tormenting the Beltway? Whooa. You need a history lesson, me boy. Anyway, we're on a roll here. The next Appearance tab setting, called the **Scrollbar** item, should be indicted for false advertising. You'd expect it to control Scrollbars, but in fact it only changes the *size* of scrollbars, not their color. (To change the color, you'll have to experiment with **3D Objects** item. Good luck.) It affects the `\WindowsMetric` values for `ScrollHeight` and `ScrollWidth`—both always set to the same value—which in turn affect the size of scrollbars and the down arrows for drop-down list boxes and spin boxes, and at least a few MS Office Toolbar buttons (!).

My species hasn't done anything to the Beltway that an intrusive wimpy liberal Feminazi tree-hugging wetlands law enacted two hundred years ago couldn't have prevented. We could've made Washington safe for you roaches; then you would've had a chance to re-elect your own lying, crack-smoking felon to run the city. But enough of your problems. Look at this! The next Appearance tab Item is called **Selected Item,** and it changes stuff all over the place. It's supposed to control how selected menu items appear on the screen, but it changes the Registry's MenuHeight and MenuWidth settings, and the MenuFont—thus affecting all menus, including the Start Menu, whether anything is selected or not. It also changes Hilight and HilightText, thus doing what it's supposed to do with selected menu items and the color of icons with focus on the Desktop.

 Talk about weird side-effects. Changing the **ToolTips** Item on the Appearance tab changes the Registry's StatusFont. While StatusFont is used for the font in Win95 Desktop Tooltips and the "tips" attached to buttons in Explorer and Paint, among others, it is also used as the Status Bar font in some applications. The **ToolTips** Item also affects the Registry's InfoText and InfoWindows color settings, which are picked up in some applications and ignored in others.

The easiest way to explain all this is with a little table. Figure 10-27 shows what happens to several common Win95 applications and applets if you change the font and color in the **ToolTips** Item under the Appearance tab.

	"Tip" Font	"Tip" Font Color	"Tip" Background Color	Status Bar Font
Win95 Desktop	Changes	Changes	Changes	N/A
Explorer	Changes	Changes	Changes	Changes
Exchange	Changes	Changes	Changes	Changes
WordPad	Changes	Changes	Changes	No Change
Paint	Changes	Changes	Changes	No Change
Regedit	N/A	N/A	N/A	Changes
MS Office Apps	No Change	Changes	Changes	No Change

Figure 10-27. ToolTips Item changes

Several major Windows apps, like Hyperterminal, don't even have "tips"—and the Exchange mail editor doesn't even use the Status Bar, fer heaven's sake—so they aren't listed. Changing the **ToolTips** Item here has very inconsistent results, apparently depending on the phase of the moon, cosmic ray penetration, and the mood of the person who programmed the application you're using.

Finally, the **Window** Item on the Appearance tab lets you choose both a background color (in the upper box) and a foreground color (in the lower box) for nearly all applications in Windows 95. The upper box changes the Registry's \Color value for Window; the lower box changes WindowText. The Window value controls the default background color in most Windows apps—the "page" in MS Office applications, for example—as well as the background color in "My Computer" style icon boxes. It also controls the background of virtually all of Windows' built-in controls, like checkboxes, text boxes, unselected items in list boxes, and just about everything else except buttons. WindowText controls the default color of text in most applications, the color of text in dialog boxes, and unselected text in virtually all of Windows' built-in controls except buttons.

So much for the Appearance tab.

Somebody in Redmond really should go through the \WindowsMetric and \Colors keys and redesign things so each Desktop component has exactly one Registry value. This hunt-and-peck crap—where changes in, say, the color of the **Message Box** Item alters almost every character used in Win95—doesn't make any sense. And if MS will straighten out the mess, I'm sure some smart programmer somewhere will come up with a replacement for the Appearance tab that actually performs as advertised.

As Woody is fond of saying, if wishes were horses, then Hackers would ride.

Settings Tab

The final tab proffered by the Display applet is one marked, uh, Settings. (See Figure 10-28. They *pay* somebody to come up with these mnemonic terms, doncha think?) The Settings tab lets you alter your display: the drivers for your monitor and video card; the pixel resolution to be displayed on your screen; the maximum number of colors that can be displayed on the monitor simultaneously (commonly called the "color depth"); and the Win95 Desktop Zoom factor.

What's the Win95 Desktop Zoom factor? I don't see anything marked *Zoom* or *Factor*. Hey, Mao, Mom's fans from all over the world are going to call you on the carpet for this one. You blew it, big time.

Patience, my wooden grasshopper. The Font Size/Custom box you can see in Figure 10-28 really conceals an overall Win95 Zoom Factor—it has next to nothing to do with the Desktop's fonts, or their sizes. (You control those with the Appearance tab.) It's yet another example of WinObfuscation, a term I'm seriously considering having trademarked. I'll talk about the Win95 Zoom Factor at the end of this section, after we tackle the easy stuff.

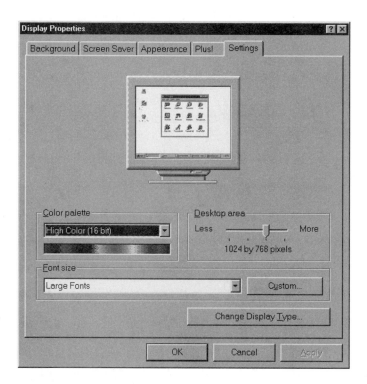

Figure 10-28. The Settings tab

The Color Palette lets you choose the maximum number of colors that your monitor can display simultaneously, from 16 colors, to 256 colors, and—if your video card can support it—High Color (16 bit) or True Color (24 bit). Once upon a time, using a larger palette would seriously reduce your video performance and effectively drag Windows to its knees. Nowadays, if you have an accelerated video card (and almost all new Win95 machines do), the performance penalty for more on-screen color generally isn't all that great.

Why would you want more color depth? It makes your display more lifelike and lively. Pictures that contain more than 256 colors are becoming increasingly common—the Plus! Pack, for example, contains several wallpaper images in High Color—and if you display those pictures with a palette of 256 (or, worse, 16) colors, the results are mighty underwhelming. See Chapter 2 for the definitive discussion of color palettes.

The next box, marked Desktop Area, controls the resolution you see on-screen. The minimum size (which results in the largest objects on-screen) is 640 × 480 pixels—effectively, Win95 generates 480 lines of 640 dots each, and those lines are more-or-less-evenly plastered on your monitor. Most people will try to put at least 800 × 600 pixels on their 15-inch or larger screens, simply because that lets them stuff more legible things (Desktop icons, Taskbar buttons, Toolbar buttons, text) on the screen. If you have a 17-inch screen, try 1024 × 768 pixels. And if you have a 21-inch or larger screen, the last thing you need is me trying to tell you what to do.

 There's a tradeoff here. The amount of memory on your video card limits the color depth you can display at any particular resolution. If you move the slider to turn resolution up to 1024 × 768 and suddenly the color depth flips from High Color to 256 color, you know that you've hit a limitation of your video card. Add more memory to the video card (*not* main memory inside your computer, but video memory!) to allow improved resolution and/or greater color depth.

Changing the color depth under the Settings tab will usually force you to reboot. Changing the resolution tab may or may not, depending on the agility of your video card. Microsoft's claim that Win95 lets you change screen resolution on the fly is technically accurate (at least in most cases) but—since most people change screen resolution about once a year—the "feature" itself is primarily useful in demos, where somebody is trying to convince you that Win95 is better than Win31. The Power Toys utilities discussed in Chapter 5 include one that lets you change color depth without rebooting.

 Skipping lightly over the Font Size box for the moment, you'll see a button that says Change Display Type. Every Win95 user should hit that button at least once, because chances are very good the Win95 installer didn't correctly identify your monitor. When you get the Change Display Type dialog (Figure 10-29), make sure the information in there is correct. If it's wrong—or if you have an updated video driver—hit the appropriate Change button. To pick the correct display, flip through the lists. To change the video driver, click Have Disk and follow the instructions. It's pretty easy, really.

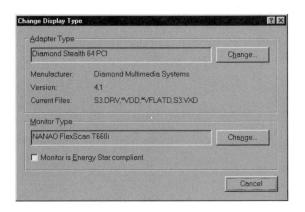

Figure 10-29. Pick a card, any card

That brings us to the Settings tab's Font Size/Custom box. In all of Windumb, this is one of the dumbest things. With one minor exception that Billy95 will explain momentarily, the Font Size/Custom box has nothing to do with Fonts, Font Sizes, or anything vaguely font-ish. It just controls the Windows Zoom Factor. A plain, simple Zoom Factor that affects everything in Windows except the icons (which look like hell if you try to zoom them).

 My guess is that Win95's designers were trying to avoid the concept of "Zoom," figuring it was too complex for, uh, dummies. Pardon me if I borrow one of Billy's favorite sayings, but that's *really stupid.* If you've ever used a moderately capable word processor, paint program, spreadsheet, or just about any Windows application, you've learned to work with Zoom. It's an easy concept to grasp and use. But Win95's creators felt Zoom was too complicated, I guess. In its place Microsoft concocted this grandiose story about Font Sizes and Rulers with no scale (see Figure 10-30, the Custom Font Size dialog box you get if you hit the Custom button), Large Fonts and Small Fonts and "pixels per inch" that have absolutely nothing to do with real inches, the kind you measure with a real ruler. It's artifice from beginning to end.

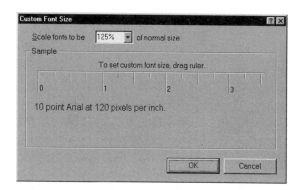

Figure 10-30. How do *you* spell Zoom?

 Sure, it's really sexy to click on that ruler in Figure 10-30 and drag it left and right—but Microsoft got the metaphor completely ass-backwards. There is no "inch" on a monitor. There's just pixels. What they *should* be showing you is how big or how small typical Desktop items will look as you change the Zoom factor: at a higher Zoom, dialog boxes look bigger; Desktop icon captions swell; the Taskbar holds fewer, but taller, buttons; 11-point text, say, in WordPad gets larger—as does text in everything else, from Explorer to the MS Office applications. As I mentioned in the Appearance tab discussion, the "snap-to" grid also adjusts itself, depending on the Zoom. Why not show all of that happening, instead of an expanding ruler juxtaposed on a slice of text that always measures "two"? Oy.

Okay, okay. Put down the brickbat. Dragging on the ruler is pretty intuitive—until you stop to think about it (just like the scrollbar behavior you talked about in Chapter 2). We couldn't call it Zoom because the icons *don't* zoom—they really deteriorate if we try to scale them to any size other than their hand-tuned original size. You guys are partially right, though. We showed the user our internal way of scaling things, instead of concentrating on stuff the user is interested in—how icon text fits into the Desktop grid, how big objects will appear in non-Zoomable applications, things like that. That ruler with the text line that's always "two" wide, with no indication of two *what*, was a master stroke, though. What can I say?

Well, you can start by 'fessing up about what's really happening with Large Fonts and Small Fonts. Those settings don't have anything to do with fonts, do they, Bill? Man, you've managed to fool me for a long, long time. The Large Fonts setting is just shorthand for "125% Zoom," isn't it? The Small Fonts is just shorthand for "100% Zoom." If you click the Custom button, you can pick from 75%, 100%, 125%, 150% and 200% Zoom settings; and 100% is precisely the same thing as Small Fonts, 125% is identical to Large Fonts. That's all there is to it, right?

Not quite, Mom, although I'll admit you're pretty close. The Zoom factor you choose in the Custom Font Size dialog (Figure 10-30) is translated into a number that we call Physical and Logical Dots Per Inch—a fancy term for *Zoom*, if you will. Those settings are stored in the Registry key HKLM\Config\ 0001\Display\Settings as DPILogicalX, DPILogicalY, DPIPhysicalX, and DPIPhysicalY. (All four numbers are identical.)

That's weird. All the \WindowMetrics settings we've seen so far are in HKCU\Control Panel. These Zoom factor Registry entries in HKLM are machine-wide settings and don't change if a different user logs onto the same machine.

Anyway, the one place where you're not quite right, Mom and Erwin, is that we *do* change the font based on the Zoom factor, although the visual consequences are admittedly small. If the user picks a Zoom factor of 100 percent or less (or, equivalently, chooses Small Fonts), Windows uses the VGA resolution fonts for MS Sans Serif (file sserife.fon). Since MS Sans Serif is the default font for all the Appearance tab settings, that effectively changes the font size, providing the user hasn't chosen a different font for things on the Desktop. So, even though our real reason for swapping out the .fon file was to get a better-looking hand-tuned font on the screen, in fact the Settings tab's Font Size/Custom box *does* change fonts.

Caught by a technicality. In fact, MS Serif is changed to VGA resolution, too, at Zoom factors of 100 percent or lower, as are Symbol, and the font called "Small Fonts." All of those settings are in the Registry key `HKLM\Config\0001\Display\Fonts`. The DOS fonts are changed, too, with a swap to VGA resolutions for `fonts.fon`, `fixedfon.fon`, and `oemfonts.fon`, which are all in `HKLM\Config\0001\Display\Settings`. Finally, there's a small change in the `DisplayParams` value in `HKLM\SOFTWARE\ Microsoft\Windows\CurrentVersion\MS-DOS Emulation`, presumably to change the appearance of the Lucida Console font in the DOS box.

Fonts

The Fonts Control Panel applet just opens a, uh, window onto Explorer's font routines. Fonts were discussed in Chapter 2. If you're getting your feet wet with the Registry, take a look at `HKLM\SOFTWARE\Microsoft\Windows\CurrentVersion\Fonts`.

Internet

The Internet applet gets installed by the Internet Jumpstart Kit (which is also included with the Plus! Pack). Look in Chapter 4 for a complete review.

Joystick

Windows 95 can handle up to two joysticks (or similar devices, such as digitizer tablets) simultaneously. Most *applications* only work with one, but that sad state of affairs seems to be improving. Win95 also accommodates three-dimensional motion and up to four buttons on each joystick. In short, Win95 can take almost anything current state-of-the-art game 'sticks demand, although it remains to be seen if Win95 will be up to handling VR helmets and other exotica.

 As a game lover, I'm the local expert on joysticks of course. If you haven't got a Joystick applet in Control Panel, your joystick isn't installed. Your sound card may have a joystick port on it but it may not install its own joystick drivers since it figures Windows has 'em. Anyhow, if you have a joystick port and joystick but no Joystick applet, go to the Add New Hardware applet, tell it No to the automatic installation, pick Sound Video and Game Controllers and at the next panel say that Microsoft is the vendor and the device is Gameport Joystick. After a reboot, the Joystick applet should be there.

The Joystick Properties dialog appears when you crank up the Control Panel's Joystick applet. While the current crop of Win95 joystick drivers will only support two joysticks running simultaneously, you can pre-configure up to four different 'sticks. The Joystick Selection drop-down list lets you choose from more than a dozen standard types (say, a 4-button flight yoke with throttle, or the Gravis Gamepad), or you can select (Custom) and tell Win95 about buttons, axes, features like a throttle, and even a VR hat (which we weren't able to test). While most older DOS-based games include their own calibration routines, Win95 games can take advantage of the Calibration Wizard looming behind the button marked "Calibrate."

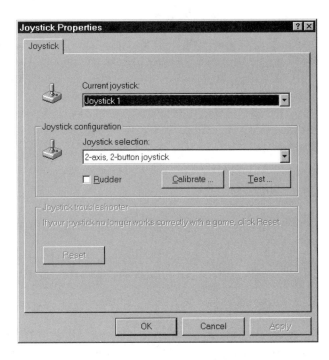

Everyone with a joystick should go through the Calibration Wizard at least once. The Wizard starts by having you center the joystick and push a button. (If all your buttons are on the stick itself, it can be a bit difficult to push the button without wiggling the stick. Good luck.) You're then instructed to move the joystick in full circles a few times, and hit a button again. Finally, you confirm the calibration by centering the stick again and pushing the button one last time.

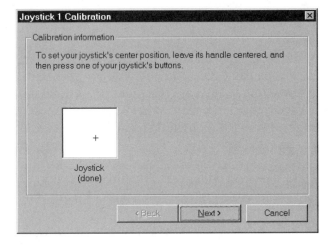

At the end of the calibration, you're given an opportunity to test the stick. (The same dialog pops up if you push the Test button in the original Joystick applet.) Obviously, you want to make sure the calibration worked correctly, that the cross-hairs sit in the middle of the Joystick box, and that you get a full range of movement with the 'stick. Not so obviously, though, you will probably be interested in discovering how Win95 maps the buttons on your joystick. One at a time, push each button on the 'stick and see which light flashes. You might be a bit surprised. At least, I was.

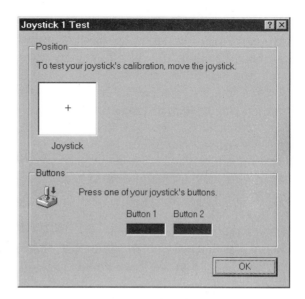

Joystick settings are scattered throughout the Registry, with the major repository of information about a 'stick's capabilities and calibration appearing in the keys `HKEY_ LOCAL_MACHINE\System\ Current ControlSet\control \Media Resources\joystick` and ... `\Media Resources \MediaExtensions\shellx\ AdvancedProperties\joystick`.

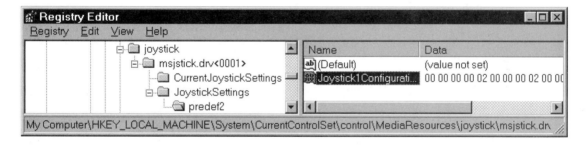

 If you run into a Windows 95 game that has problems recognizing your joystick, try bringing up the Control Panel's Joystick applet and push the Reset button. Will it work? Who knows. But it probably won't hurt. Oh. And recalibrate fairly often. Large swings in room temperature can affect 'stick calibration.

 *Keyboard*

Not only is the Keyboard applet in the Control Panel used to set keyboard response characteristics—repeat rate and delay until auto-repeat begins—but also the "insertion point" blink rate (yeah, this applet calls it a cursor, but the official term is "insertion point," i.e., the point at which text is inserted if you start typing), and the language settings for multi-key character composition support.

The Keyboard applet brings up the Keyboard Properties dialog, set on the Speed tab. Though it may be a little hard to tell from this dialog, you have a choice of four different pre-set delay values, and thirty-two different pre-set repeat rate values. There is no finer tuning: if "Short" is too short but the notch immediately to its left is too long, you're outta luck. Sometimes these settings get "stuck" (especially when you first install Win95), so before you go hog wild making adjustments, try nudging the slider one notch in either direction. See if you can live with the change you made by practicing in the indicated box. Remember that these settings apply to every well-behaved Windows app, including DOS boxes running under Windows 95.

The Keyboard Properties General tab is there to let you set up nonstandard keyboards, and those are mighty unusual. The General tab has a Change button that effectively "tunnels" to the Add New Hardware wizard's Keyboard routine. This Language tab lets you specify alternate languages: if you commonly switch languages, this box and the ability to specify hot keys for switching languages can be a godsend. (If you want to change layouts without changing languages, e.g., to specify a Dvorak layout for your U.S. English keyboard, click the Properties button.) *¡Cuidado! Achtung!* Don't count your multilingual chickens before they're hatched. Some applications are notorious for not recognizing all valid

key combinations in all the languages, while others "swallow" keystrokes unexpectedly. Extensive testing is in order.

If you have more than one Keyboard language installed, an icon appears in the Taskbar's notification area telling you which language is active. Click on that icon and you can switch languages without using the hot key.

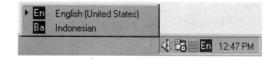

Keyboard repeat rates are stored in Registry key `HKCU\Control Panel\Keyboard`. The entry `KeyboardSpeed` ranges from `3` (which is shown as "Long" on the Speed Tab) to `0` (which is "Short"). The entry `KeyboardDelay` takes on values from `0` ("Slow" on the Speed Tab) to `31` ("Fast"). The cursor blink rate is in `HKCU\Control Panel\Desktop`, where the entry `CursorBlinkRate` goes from `1200` (which appears as "Slow" on the Speed Tab) to `200` ("Fast"). Manually adjusting the repeat rate entries beyond their prescribed bounds can have unpredictable effect on the rates (in other words, on reboot, Win95 changes them in ways I don't understand). Manually adjusting `CursorBlinkRate`, on the other hand, works fine.

Want to see the insertion point flicker like a firefly in heat? Try setting `CursorBlinkRate` *to 50. You'll have to restart your machine for the setting to take effect. Talk about Stupid Desktop Tricks.*

Mail and Fax

These are the Exchange settings. They're covered in Chapter 3, in the section on Exchange. If you're curious about the Registry connection, look at the key (hold your breath, now) `HKCU\Software\Microsoft\Windows Messaging Subsystem\Profiles\MS Exchange Settings`. Try saying that backward.

Microsoft Mail Postoffice

Just what the name suggests, this is for setting up and administering the Postoffice for the Microsoft Mail Workgroup edition that is included with Windows 95. It's covered in the section in Chapter 3 called Microsoft Mail Postoffice.

 *Modems*

> We are in great haste to construct a magnetic telegraph from Maine to Texas,
> but Maine and Texas, it may be, have nothing important to communicate.

—H. D. Thoreau, *Walden,* 1854

 If you don't have any modems currently installed and you crank up the Modems applet in the Control Panel (or try to do just about anything that requires a modem, from running the Welcome screen's On-Line Registration to sending a Fax), you'll be rocketed to the Install New Modem Wizard. This Wizard is pretty simple, so I won't bore you with the details. Basically, Windows has to figure out what AT command set your modem recognizes—an "AT command set" being the language your modem speaks when talking to your computer. So if you don't find your specific modem listed, pick one that's compatible with your modem, or pop over to the (Standard Modem Types) list and pick one that runs at the same speed. (Hint: almost all modems claim to be "Hayes Compatible" and that's equivalent to "Standard" in this list.)

Once a modem is installed, the Modems applet in the Control Panel will bring up the Modem Properties dialog. (You can get to the same screen from Control Panel's System applet.) Click on the Dialing Properties button here if you need to change your calling card number, outside access numbers, Tone/Pulse dialing, and the like. Most of that will only change if you're on the road. Ho-hum.

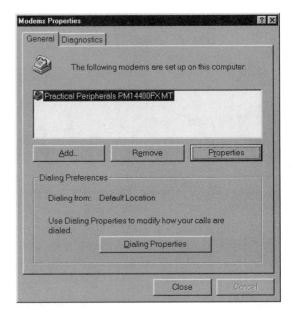

 Don't overlook the Properties button! If you have an 80486, Pentium, or faster machine, it's important that you click the Properties button here.

Down at the bottom of this dialog box is a setting that increased my throughput in Exchange by 15 percent when I finally figured out the real story. It's the Maximum Speed setting. Windows' on-line Help says you should pick "the maximum speed your modem can use," and that's horseradish. If you have an 80486,

Pentium, or faster machine,* you should crank this baby up as high as you can put it. Only back off if Exchange (or some other Win95 communications program) starts griping about bad packets—the telltale sign of a comm link trying to run too fast. Note that many comm packages won't use this setting, so you have to watch the results on Exchange and MS Network to see if it's set too high.

The Connection tab isn't very interesting. It's highly unlikely you'll want to change the 8N1 Data/Parity/Stop setting. You might turn off the Wait for Dial Tone Before Dialing box if you get stuck in a hotel room that's impossible to automatically dial out of. (You'd uncheck this box, dial the phone manually, then get the modem going.)

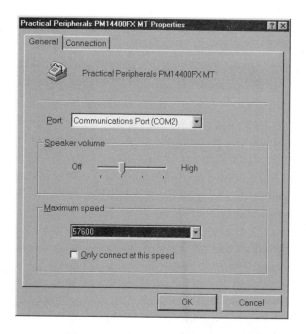

The interesting part of this tab lies behind the two boxes at the bottom: Port Settings, which was added to this dialog toward the end of the Windows 95 development cycle (thus, it isn't even mentioned in the *Windows Resource Kit*); and Advanced, which has one setting that just could save your tail some day.

The Port Settings button leads to this dialog box, called Advanced Port Settings (confusing the way they mixed the two buttons' names, eh?) that lets you control the effective size of the 16550's buffers. While there's no problem jacking up the Transmit Buffer size, be cautious with the

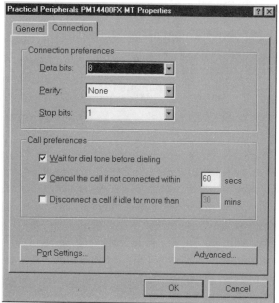

---

* I'm assuming that you also have a 16550 UART, the chip that allows for buffering of serial port data, which is highly likely if you have a newer machine with an external modem, or a fairly new internal modem. How to tell for sure? See the More Info dialog, coming up shortly.

Receive Buffer. Experiment, and
back off if you get too many errors.

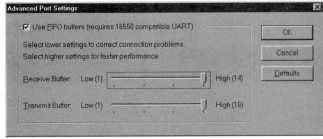

Beneath the Advanced button is this
Advanced Connection Settings
dialog. You should only change the
Error Control and Flow Control
settings if a knowledgeable sysop,
who is obviously in full possession
of his faculties (truly a *rara avis*),
holds a gun to your head. Anything you
type in Extra Settings is sent to the
modem after the AT command. The
important setting, Record a Log File,
causes Win95 to append a detailed log
of modem commands and responses to
`ModemLog.txt`, in the Win95
`\Windows` folder. Good debug
information, if you speak AT.

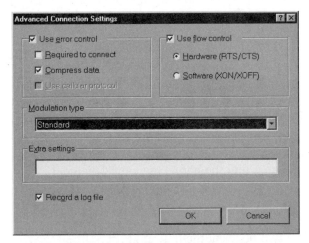

The Diagnostics tab in the Modems
applet leads to a button marked Help
(which brings up the Modem
Troubleshooter), and another button
mislabeled "More Info . . ." that actually
runs a full local-loop test of your modem.
Push that button and you'll get a complete
run of the AT command set, and the
results of that test are displayed in a box
here for you to compare with what your
modem manual says should be valid
results. Do you wonder if the modem is
responding correctly to all the
commands? This will tell you. It's also
the only place in all of Win95 that
divulges if you have a 16550 UART
installed! I have no idea why a diagnostic
routine this handy is buried down here in
Mudville, and why it's only accessible
through this torturous route.

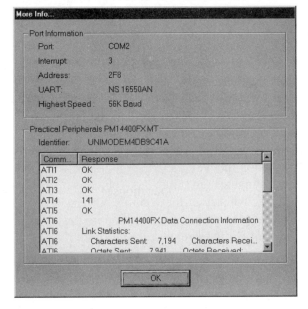

Information about the currently active modem is stored in the Registry key `HKLM\System\CurrentControlSet\Services\Class\Modem\0000`, with much of the important information crammed inscrutably into an entry called DCB. The *Windows Resource Kit* and *Device Developer's Kit* both have long, boring discussions of values listed under the . . . `\Class\Modem` key.

 Mouse

Quod movetur ab alio movetur. *

—Thomas Aquinas, *Summa Theologica,* ca. 1265

The big news in 95 mouse-ville is that the Win95 mouse drivers work both in Windows and in the DOS box. Like, big deal. But Microsoft made up for that decidedly yawn-inducing announcement with the Mouse applet's jack-in-the-box screen graphic that's used to tell you how sensitive the double-click setting has become—a wonderful metaphor understood immediately in almost any culture—and animated mouse cursors, which have a place on even the stodgiest Desktop.

When you double-click on the Mouse applet in Control Panel, you'll be greeted by the Mouse Properties dialog, Buttons tab. At the top you can swap the functions of the left and right mouse buttons. At the bottom you tell Win95 how quickly you have to click the mouse button to make two button clicks a "double-click." Test by clicking on the jack-in-the-box.

The Motion tab lets you set the pointer's speed (actually, its sensitivity to how you physically move your mouse) between "Slow" and "Fast." It also lets you show pointer trails (for improved visibility, typically on portables), and adjust them from "Short" to "Long." The General tab lets you change the mouse driver. Straightforward stuff.

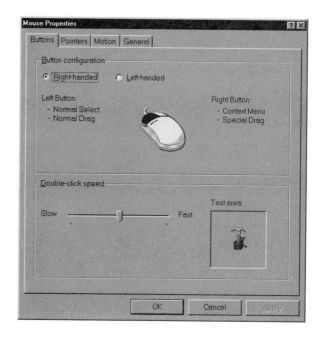

* That which moves is moved by another.

The Pointers tab lets you replace the built-in Windows pointers for everything from simple pointing to selection, the busy hourglass, resizing, and just about anything else you've ever seen. (Note that the Text Select pointer is not the same thing as an Insertion Point. As far as I can tell, the Insertion Point is implemented in hardware and can't be changed manually.) Many stationary pointers (`*.cur` files) and animated pointers (`*.ani`) await under the Browse button. Even if you *<sniff!>* wouldn't dream of putting something frivolous on your computer, consider using the Animated Hourglass mouse pointer Scheme. Often a frozen hourglass will be your first hint that the entire system has gone south.

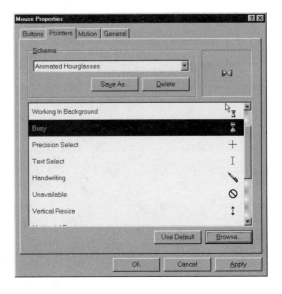

 Actually, you needn't use the whole Animated Hourglass scheme. The animated hourglasses, if you have them, are in files `\Windows\Cursors\appstart.ani` and `hourglas.ani`, and you can use them in any scheme by pushing the Browse button. If you installed Win95 from diskette, you probably don't have many mouse pointer or Scheme options: no problemo, we have them on my CD. (See Appendix A.) They're also available in file `mousep.exe` on the Microsoft Web site, `http://www.microsoft.com`. My CD also has a bunch of extra cursors for your computing pleasure—I especially like the Counter animated cursor for the Working in Background cursor.

If you installed Windows 95 from CD, you may be able to add more pointers and Schemes (in particular, the 3D Pointers Scheme, Standard (Large), and Standard (Extra Large)) by going into Control Panel's Add/Remove Programs applet, Windows Software tab, Accessories checkbox.

 When is a scheme not a scheme? Good question. Windows 95 has three different official "Schemes" that we could find: the Desktop scheme, used in the Display applet; the Mouse Pointer scheme, used here in the Mouse applet; and the Sound scheme, used in the Sound applet.* While they're all called "Schemes," they all behave very differently—and the differences have stung us more than once.

---

* There are many more parts of Win95 that look and behave much like schemes—the Country/Language choices in the Regional Settings applet, for example—but Microsoft doesn't call them schemes.

When I'm using a Desktop scheme and change one of the "Items" in the scheme (say, the Desktop's background color), Win95 responds by turning the box that holds the scheme name blank. That's great. It's a warning that I've changed something, and the scheme is no longer in full effect. The changes I made are put in the Registry, and all of it stays the same until I open the Display applet again. If I change to a new scheme, I'm prompted that the current scheme (the home-grown one I created) hasn't been saved and will be overwritten if I don't save it. I can actually redefine the built-in schemes by clicking Save As and carefully typing in the name of the scheme I want to overwrite, or by clicking on a built-in scheme and hitting Delete. That's all working the way it should. This method of handling schemes gives me a lot of flexibility, eliminates unnecessary constraints (e.g., it doesn't require me to give a name to a scheme I might not want to save), and protects me from myself.

The Sound scheme setup isn't quite as good, but I can live with it. If I change one of the Sounds in the scheme, the old scheme name still appears in the box, and I have to be careful not to overwrite a built-in scheme with one of my own devising.

The Mouse scheme is a completely different breed of vermin. If I change just one Item in a scheme, the whole scheme is overwritten, unless I'm very, very careful to assign it a new scheme name. There's no warning about it: change one Pointer and click OK, and the built-in scheme gets nuked, with nary a squeal of protest. Oh, how I love a little consistency in the mornin'.

The Registry settings that correspond to Mouse applet values are scattered around quite a bit.

On the Buttons tab, changing to a left-handed mouse puts the value `SwapMouseButtons=1` into the Registry key `HKCU\Control Panel\Mouse`.

The double-click speed is in `HKCU\Control Panel\Mouse`, where the setting "Slow" corresponds to a `DoubleClickSpeed` value of 900, which in turn means that Win95 will let you spend up to 900 milliseconds between clicks. The setting "Fast" corresponds to a `DoubleClickSpeed` value of 100, or at most one-tenth of a second between clicks. (Don't know about you, but I can't click that fast!)

Here's a fun undocumented setting. In addition to having time restrictions on a double-click—you have to click twice within the `DoubleClickTime` amount of time for it to be considered "double"—there are also space restrictions, which correspond to values for `DoubleClickHeight` and `DoubleClickWidth`. The rule is pretty simple: you must click twice within the `DoubleClickSpeed` amount of time, within a rectangle that is `DoubleClickHeight` pixels tall by `DoubleClickWidth` pixels wide. The odd part is that the two space restriction values are located in Registry key `HKCU\Control Panel\Desktop`, and not in `\Mouse`.

 If you're still a little green behind your Registry ears, try this. Don't worry, you won't hurt anything. (If you screw up, the settings will just be ignored.) Start by double-clicking in and around the Mouse applet's jack-in-the-box. Move the Double-click speed way down to Slow, and see how far you can move the mouse and still have a double-click "take." Not very far, true?

Okay. Let's change it. Get out of the Mouse applet. Click Start, Run, type `regedit`, hit Enter. Double-click `HKCU` (remember, that's shorthand for `HKEY_CURRENT_USER`), then double-click `Control Panel`, then double-click `Desktop`. Look at Figure 10-31.

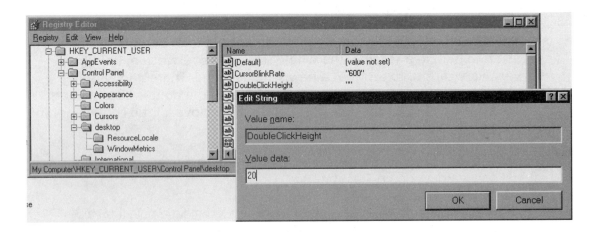

Figure 10-31. DoubleClickHeight enters the Registry

We want to add a string value, so click Edit, then New, then String Value. Type `DoubleClickHeight` (no spaces or anything) and hit Enter. Double-click on `DoubleClickHeight` and type in the value 20 (no quotes or anything). Hit Enter. Replicate those steps (Edit, New, String Value, type the name, Enter, double-click on the name, type the value, Enter) to put in a Value name called `DoubleClickWidth` with Value data of 20.

Want to see the effect of what you just did? Restart Windows (in Shut Down, click Close all programs and log on as a different user, if you have the option). Go into the Control Panel's Mouse applet. Move the double-click speed way down, and see how far you can move and still have a double-click "take." See that? You've just expanded the double-click area to 20 x 20 pixels, a square roughly the size of the front panel of the jack-in-the-box's box. Congratulations. You're well on your way to becoming a Registry pro.

To get rid of all the new stuff, just click once on `DoubleClickHeight` and hit the `Del` key, then click once on `DoubleClickWidth`, and hit the `Del` key.

 The cursor files used under the Pointers tab are stored away in `HKCU\Control Panel\Cursors`. The cursor files used in the Windows Standard scheme are apparently stored internally in Windows itself, as this key only lists cursors that differ from those used in the Windows Standard scheme.

 The schemes themselves appear in the worst jumbled-up Registry key I've ever seen. It's called `HKCU\Control Panel\Cursors\Schemes`. Instead of listing each scheme as a subkey of the `\Schemes` key, and then hanging the names of cursors as values off the individual scheme key (as, say, the Display applet does), this key has schemes and files and all sorts of inscrutable stuff crammed together. For example, the 3D Pointers value looks like this:

```
D:\WINDOWS\cursors\arrow_1.cur,D:\WINDOWS\cursors\help_1.cur
,D:\WINDOWS\cursors\wait_1.cur,D:\WINDOWS\cursors\busy_1.cur
,D:\WINDOWS\cursors\cross_1.cur,D:\WINDOWS\cursors\beam_1.cu
r,D:\WINDOWS\cursors\pen_1.cur,D:\WINDOWS\cursors\no_1.cur,D
:\WINDOWS\cursors\size4_1.cur,D:\WINDOWS\cursors\size3_1.cur
,D:\WINDOWS\cursors\size2_1.cur,D:\WINDOWS\cursors\size1_1.c
ur,D:\WINDOWS\cursors\move_1.cur,D:\WINDOWS\cursors\up_1.cur
```

I'd be tempted to call this the worst-designed Registry key in all of Windows 95. You Windows programmers and programmer wannabes should take a look, to see how *not* to manage a Registry entry. If you edit this key manually—heaven help ya!—be very careful to count the commas.

 The Motion tab has its own . . . idiosyncrasies. Registry settings for the mouse sensitivity (which the Motion tab calls Pointer Speed) are stored in the key `HKCU\Control Panel\Mouse`, in three separate values: `MouseSpeed`, `MouseThreshold1` and `MouseThreshold2`. The interaction of those three values can get pretty complicated.

Your mouse generates a hardware interrupt from time to time, and that interrupt tells your PC how far the mouse has moved, and in what direction. Microsoft discovered long ago that if you move your mouse slowly, you expect the cursor to move on the screen with great precision; conversely, if you move your mouse quickly, you expect some sort of acceleration to kick in, so the cursor flies across the screen much more rapidly. These three Registry entries control the amount of acceleration you experience, and how fast your mouse has to be moving—equivalently, how far it travels between hardware interrupts—before the acceleration kicks in.

- If `MouseSpeed` has a value of `0`, there is no acceleration. That's easy.

- If `MouseSpeed` has a value of `1`, Windows looks to see how many pixels your mouse has traveled between interrupts. If that number exceeds the value of `MouseThreshold1`, the first level of acceleration kicks in, and distances are doubled. For example, if your mouse has traveled 8 pixels since the last interrupt, `MouseSpeed` is `1`, and `MouseThreshold1` is, say, `6`, Windows will double the distance, and tell your applications that the mouse has actually traveled 16 pixels.

- If `MouseSpeed` has a value of `2`, again, Windows looks for the number of pixels traveled between interrupts. Just as in the previous case, if the number exceeds `MouseThreshold1`, the first level accelerator kicks in and the distance is doubled. In addition, if the number exceeds `MouseThreshold2`, the second accelerator kicks in and the distance is doubled again—so the application is told the mouse moved four times as far as it actually did.

For example, if `MouseSpeed` is `2`, `MouseThreshold1` is `4`, and `MouseThreshold2` is `12`, a movement of 2 pixels is reported as 2 pixels; if the mouse goes 8 pixels, the application thinks it went 16; and if the mouse really traveled 14 pixels, Windows would treat it as 56 pixels.

 Hey, Mao, all this Registry theory stuff is alright, I guess, as far as it goes, but are you sure you know what you're talking about? I mean, the Motion tab doesn't mention anything about `MouseSpeed` or `MouseThresholds`. The Pointer Speed box just has a little slider that stops in seven different positions, from "Slow" to "Fast."

Ah! My point exactly! The only way you can understand those seven positions and how they behave is by seeing the underlying Registry entries, and correlating those with some idea of how the mouse accelerators kick in. For example, the jump from position 4 to 5 is huge because the secondary acceleration after-burner kicks in, whereas the transition from position 3 to 4 is pretty subtle. The real scoop on Pointer Speed is in Figure 10-32.

Pointer Speed slider location	1	2	3	4	5	6	7
MouseSpeed	0	1	1	1	2	2	2
MouseThreshold1	N/A	10	7	4	4	4	4
MouseThreshold2	N/A	N/A	N/A	N/A	12	9	6

Figure 10-32. The truth on mouse acceleration

Finally, the Pointer Trails setting, a number between 2 and 7 that specifies the number of "ghosts" the mouse pointer will generate—corresponding to the six slider positions in the Pointer Trail box, where 2 is "Short" and 7 is "Long"—sits in Registry key HKLM\Config\ 0001\Display\Settings, the MouseTrails value. I have no idea why they stuck it there in the low rent district, with the resolution settings and system fonts.

 *Multimedia*

Our sweetest songs are those that tell of saddest thought.

—P. B. Shelley, *To a Skylark,* 1819

The Control Panel's Multimedia applet adjusts the settings for sound and video. Not particularly complex and not particularly glitzy, the applet holds few surprises.

When you start the Multimedia applet, the Audio tab presents itself. The Playback box simply specifies the sound card you want to use for everything except MIDI sound (see Chapter 2 for definitions). The Recording box determines the device you'll use to record—typically the recording part of your sound card. Click Customize and you can choose sampling frequencies and depth, and compression method.

The Video tab lets you pick full-screen or partial-screen playback. The CD Music tab tells Windows where to find your CD drive. The Advanced tab just tunnels into the Control Panel's System applet, starting at the Multimedia "device."

Surprisingly, Windows 95 has a bad habit of occasionally not picking the best MIDI

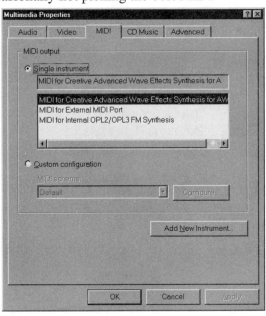

synthesizer. You can change the synthesizer, er, instrument, here under the MIDI tab. Pick a synthesizer, click Apply, then play a `.mid` or `.rmi` file by double-clicking on it. Choose the synthesizer you like best.

If you have a new MIDI instrument that you want to connect to your PC, click Add New Instrument and follow through with the MIDI Instrument Installation wizard.

Once you have new instruments defined, you can patch through to those instruments on specified MIDI channels by clicking Custom Configuration, then Configure, choosing the channel, clicking Change, and picking the instrument.

 General multimedia information is stored in Registry key `HKCU\Software\Microsoft\Multimedia`, with basic sound card information in `\SoundMapper`. Volume settings are in `HKCU\Software\Microsoft\Windows\CurrentVersion\Applets\Volume Control` with a key name equal to the name of the sound driver. There are other settings scattered throughout the Registry.

 *Network*

This applet is available from the Control Panel, of course. You may find it easier to get here, though, by right-clicking on Network Neighborhood and choosing Properties.

Repeating one of my tips from Chapter 3, when you install any networking capability at all—even a dial-up adapter, say, with no modem attached to your machine—the Shutdown dialog box gets the final entry, Close all programs and log on as a different user. That option alone is more than enough reason to hop in here and click Add, and pick Client for Microsoft Networks. Other than that, if you're looking at the Control Panel's Network applet, you probably want to do one of four things:

- To set up a simple network, cheap, read on.

- To figure out how to dial up your office PC from your house, or while you're on the road, look in Chapter 4. If your office network has an NT server or other network software that understands dialup, it can act as a server; otherwise you'll need to use the Plus! Pack to set up your office machine. The PC at the house (or on the road) just needs to be able to speak the right language over the modem. That's easy: if you don't have an entry on the Network applet's Configuration tab that says NetBEUI -> Dial-Up Adapter, click Add, click Protocol, click Add, on the left pick Microsoft, on the right pick NetBEUI and click OK back out. If there's still no NetBEUI -> Dial-Up Adapter line, click once on the Dial-Up Adapter line, click Properties, click the Bindings tab, and check the NetBEUI box. OK all the way back out. There. You're now ready to dial-in to your office computer.

- To figure out why your simple network isn't, uh, networking, go over the steps in this section, but don't get hung up on it. If you can't find the answer easily, click on Start, then Help, bring up the Find tab, and type "network trouble." You want the network troubleshooter. If that doesn't give you enough information, cross your fingers and dive into the *Windows Resource Kit.* Good luck.

- To get your PC to work with the big network at the office, contact the netdroids at the office. Troubleshooting Netware networks and Windows NT client/server networks falls way beyond the scope of this book . . . not to mention the fact that you're traveling in shark-infested waters that require very specialized navigation.

 Setting up a PC network has never been simpler than it is with Win95. It can literally take you less than an afternoon to put together a two-PC network, and share all the disk drives and printers between the two—if you know what you're doing. And there's the rub.

Start by getting the right hardware. Talk to somebody you trust at your local computer shop, or call a company like Cables To Go (voice 800-826-7904) that sells lots of computer cables and networking equipment. Tell them you need a cheap but 100 percent Intel EtherExpress-compatible setup to daisy-chain together two (or three or four . . .) Win95 PCs. They'll sell you a ThinNet rig, with a Network Interface Card (pronounced "nick") to go into each PC, a hunk of special co-ax known as ThinNet cable, T-connectors to connect the cable to the NIC, and terminators to cover the bare ends of the T-connectors, one each at the beginning and end of the cable.

When the package arrives, install the NICs in the PCs using the Add Hardware applet described earlier in this chapter. You can pick the guru or the naive method, as befits your technological self-image. Just get the cards installed; don't expect any heroics. Don't bother with any software that ships with the cards unless it's specifically designed for Windows 95 (and if the cards are 100 percent Intel EtherExpress-compatible, you won't need those diskettes anyway). Once the cards are installed, turn off the machines and daisy-chain the cable to the NICs, following the instructions that came in the package. When the cable is installed and you have the machines turned on, get on each PC in turn and pop into the Control Panel's Networking applet. If you get a message saying "your network is not set up properly," ignore it. Of course it isn't working properly . . . yet.

Start with the Configuration tab. It's important that you have four "components" installed; if any of them are missing, click Add and continue here with the next panel. Client for Microsoft Networks is a computer program that lets you communicate with the other Windows 95 PCs on your network. File and printer sharing for Microsoft Networks is another program that lets other people look at your disks, or print on your printer. Your NIC should have an entry with a weird green P next to it. Finally, you should have one of those loop-the-loop plug entries with NetBEUI -> pointing to the name of your NIC. Once you have all of those installed (clicking Add as necessary), make sure Primary Network Logon shows Client for Microsoft Networks; that forces Win95 to log you onto the network whenever you reboot your machine.

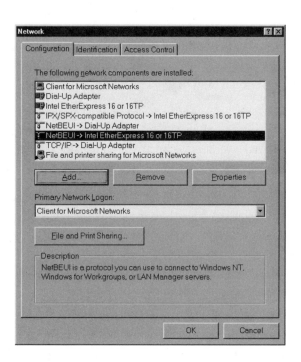

Any missing pieces in the Configuration tab are added by pushing the Add button there and working with this dialog. The descriptions at the bottom are confusing as hell, so ignore them. At the very least you need one Client (for Microsoft Networks), one Adapter (whichever NIC you have installed), one Protocol (NetBEUI hooked up to the NIC*) and one Service (File and printer sharing for Microsoft Networks). That's all.

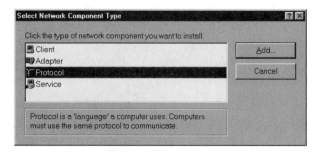

When you get back to the Configuration tab, don't forget to click the File and Printer Sharing button, and make sure both of these boxes are checked. These boxes just hook up your disks and printer to the network: they don't allow anybody in particular to use them. We'll cover that base in a bit.

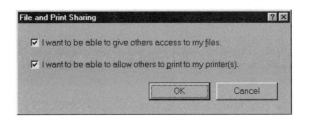

Once you have the Configuration tab complete—and it pays to spend some time on that tab, to make sure you get all the details right—move on to the Identification tab. The Computer Name box here has to have a name that's unique on the network: if you have two computers, they must have two different computer names. This is the name other people will use to get at the disks and printer attached to your computer. Avoid the temptation to be verbose; this name gets typed a lot. Also, limit yourself to simple letters and numbers, no spaces or other weird characters. Big networks can have more than one Workgroup. But since you're setting up a little network, you want to make sure everybody on the network has precisely the same Workgroup name in this box. The Description box can have anything you want.

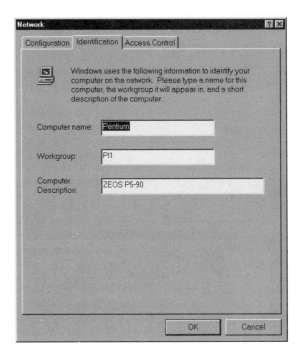

Finally, the Access Control tab lets you choose between allowing everybody equal access to your disks and printer or setting up specific access rules for each individual.

Note that "equal access" doesn't mean "free access." Once the network is going and you've chosen File and Print Sharing under the Configuration tab, you can specify passwords,

---

* NetBEUI is a simple Microsoft protocol for hooking together small networks. You can "bind" it manually to the NIC—creating a NetBEUI -> Network Card entry on the Configuration tab—if you have to, by going to the Configuration tab, clicking on the Adapter for the NIC, clicking Properties, selecting the Bindings tab, and checking the NetBEUI box.

read/write restrictions, and all sorts of things, down to the folder level. In Explorer, simply right-click on the folder or printer, and pick Sharing . . .

The Obtain list of users and groups from box will be gray unless you're connected to a network server.

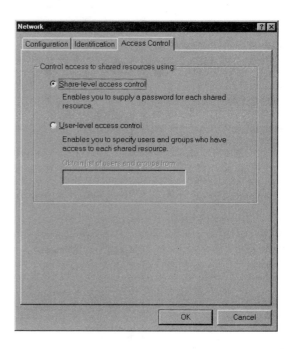

 If you're installing a new network from scratch, it's probably a good idea to reboot the machine once all of these settings are in place. After you've set up everything through the Network applet on all your computers, and rebooted all the machines, try clicking on Network Neighborhood and see if you can get a list of the other computers on your network.

 If you have problems finding other computers, the first thing to blame is the wires: go back and double-check all the connections. The second thing to blame is the Workgroup name: go back to each machine, look in the Network applet and make sure it's spelled precisely the same way on every one (and while you're at it, make sure the computer names are all different). If those all look good, pick one machine as a guinea pig and go through the network troubleshooter on that machine.

 Once all the machines are visible in Network Neighborhood, there's one *crucial* last step. You have to explicitly enable sharing for each drive (or folder) and each printer that you want accessible over the network. Go into Explorer, right-click on the disk or folder or printer you want to share, pick Sharing . . . , and select the level of sharing you feel comfortable with. Once sharing is enabled, other PCs on the network can get to the shared drivers (or folders) by simply clicking on them in Explorer's Network Neighborhood folder. They can also install your printer to work on their machines by double-clicking on the printer in Explorer's Network Neighborhood.

 There's a bit of a security issue here. If you let just anyone on the network into your data, well, you let *just anyone* on the network into your data. Once you've opened the gate, a nosey coworker or somebody walking by an unattended PC connected to your network would be able to look at the files that you've released. So think a bit about security before you open up your whole machine, and consider whether free access to your data is an altogether good thing.

 What about all those other things you have on the Configuration tab, Mao? They look mighty intimidating. Dial-Up adapters. IPX/SPX protocols. TCP/IP. Lots of alphabet soup.

 Yeah, it's too bad nobody translates this stuff into plain English. A dial-up adapter is a modem, or maybe a Direct Cable Connection (see Chapter 3)—in other words, a way to attach to other computers that isn't "on" all the time. The adapter entry in the Configuration tab is created automatically when you install DialUp Networking from the Add/Remove Programs applet.

IPX/SPX is the language ("protocol") Novell Netware uses for Netware computers to converse. I only have it installed on the off chance that I might try to dial in to a network someday that's running Netware. TCP/IP is the language of the Internet and most UNIX machines; that protocol was installed when I got my Web connection going.

NetBEUI is Microsoft's "little" network protocol; I had to make sure NetBEUI was "bound" to the "dial-up adapter" (translation: that my modem could speak NetBEUI) on my home computer so I could dial in to my PC at work. That's the Dial-Up Networking capability that Microsoft sells with the Plus! Pack. I had to install the Dial-Up Networking Server from the Plus! Pack on the machine at work, so it could answer the phone and do what I told it to do from home. Both of the machines used NetBEUI to communicate. In general, it doesn't hurt to install all three protocols, and having all of them available may come in handy some day.

 This really is amazing stuff. When it works, it's magic. You'll never put up with sneakernet again: printing on the group's laser printer, say, is just a point and a click away—as easy as printing on the printer right next to your computer.

 Bah! The Mac has had it for years.

Passwords

Chapter 3 discussed Passwords, including the way to set up multiple users for a single machine and the place in the Registry that's modified to adapt to more than one user.

If you're here because you want to get rid of that stupid logon screen—the one that asks you for a password every time you start Windows—the topic is covered in detail in Appendix F.

 *Printers*

I discussed the Printer applet in Chapter 3. The Control Panel's Printers icon just sweeps you off to the Printers Folder; there is no separate Printer applet.

In the Registry, if you want a list of all valid printers, take a look at the key `HKLM\System\CurrentControlSet\control\Print\Printers`. If you want the currently active printer, try `HKLM\Config\0001\System\ CurrentControlSet\Control\ Print\Printers`.

 Regional Settings

 This rather innocuous Control Panel applet serves up a goldmine of Registry entries. Although you'll find that Win95 uses the entries pretty consistently—change the format of the time in the Registry, say, and the clock in the Notification Area stands up and salutes—Windows apps in general are notorious for ignoring these settings. Some software developers who write the major apps don't even know they *exist,* the worst ignorance of all. So, while you might hope that changes made in this applet will ripple to all of your applications, don't be too surprised if you find out differently.

The first tab that appears in the Regional Settings applet is the, uh, Regional Settings tab. The drop-down list offers you a wide variety of choices (Nynorsk Norwegian, anybody?).

Think of these list entries as schemes—their primary purpose in life is to establish a whole bunch of settings, which you can later modify by clicking other tabs. Should you change the scheme in the list and then click on a tab, Win95 will effectively click "Apply" before proceeding to the tab. If you see a picture of this dialog in another book, it may have the country of choice highlighted on the map. The final, shipping product does not highlight countries, reportedly because of objections by the government of India. That's one sure way to pick out books written before Win95 was released. Ah, WinTrivia!

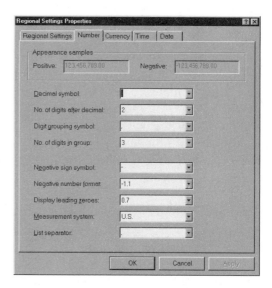

There's an amazing amount of intelligence built into the Number tab. If you choose a Country/Language combination in the Regional Settings list where number representations vary, the drop-down boxes will reflect the locally recognized alternatives. For example, choosing English (United States) will force the Number tab to show "." as the decimal symbol and "," as the digit grouping symbol. Yet the German choices allow either "." or "," as the decimal separator, and "," or "." as the digit grouping symbol—precisely the options widely used in German-speaking locales. Bravo! Also note that the measurement systems are now called "Metric" and "US"—not "English," as in earlier Windows versions.

The Currency tab is every bit as intelligent as the Number tab. For example, if you choose Sweden under the Regional Settings tab, the Currency tab will not only display the correct unit of currency (kr), as a default, Windows will position the symbol correctly—*after* the value (e.g., 3.50 kr). Undocumented fact: You can even type in a character number for the currency symbol by turning on the NumLock key, holding down Alt, and typing the four-digit character. This is important in places where fonts have single, nonstandard characters for the currency (e.g., some Spanish fonts have Pst as a single character for Pesetas; Portuguese fonts have a single Esc character for Escudos; Thai fonts have Bt in one character). Excellent work, Redmond!

Alas, after two panels of glory, Microsoft really fell down on the Time tab; it's full of bugs. The Time Sample box gives a pretty good indication of how the time will appear in, say, the Date/Time applet. The Time separator, AM and PM symbol all seem to work as you would expect. But the Time style box is all bollixed up. In general, you're supposed to construct a template of the time in this box: h stands for hour, mm for minute, ss for second, tt for the time symbol (AM/PM), H for hour on a 24-hour clock. You're also supposed to be able to put in text, using ' quotes to set it off. Try typing 'MOM time' hh:mm:ss tt in that box and hit Apply. See that? To clear out the mess, pick H:mm:ss, hit Apply, and then go back to hh:mm:ss tt, or whatever you like. Bummer.

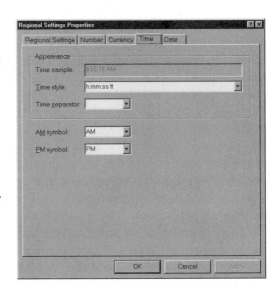

The final Tab in the Regional Settings applet, the Date Tab, lets you pick Windows' default formatting for dates. The Short Date format is used in Explorer and other WinApps. I couldn't find the Long Date format used anywhere. Undocumented fact: In Word 95, if you click on Insert, then Date, the first two options offered are the date in Short Date and Long Date formats, respectively. WordPad, on the other hand, is too lazy to bother checking for your settings.

While you're here, change the long date to get rid of one of the ds in dd. It should read dddd, MMMM d, yyyy. Not many people want to see leading zeroes on their dates!

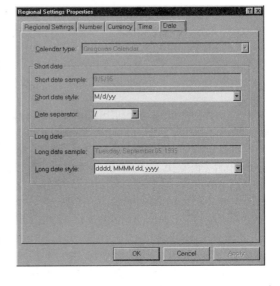

The Registry abounds with Regional settings. The full list of available Country/Language "Schemes" is located in HKLM\System\ CurrentControlSet\control\NIs\Locale. The Country/Language is identified in that key with a number: English (United States), for example, is number 00000409. The number of the currently selected

Country/Language appears in `HKCU\Control Panel\International` as the value `Locale`.

As best I can tell, the (disabled!) map highlighting information for each Country/Language is still there, in key `HKLM\SOFTWARE\Microsoft\Windows\CurrentVersion\NIs\LocaleMapIDs`. There are also keyboard layout settings linked to the Country-Language number, located in the key `HKLM\System\CurrentControlSet\control\keyboard layouts`.

 Though the Number, Currency, Time and Date settings associated with these Country/Language Schemes aren't stored anywhere in the Registry: they appear to be built into Windows itself, with parts stored in the file `\windows\inf\locale.inf`. That's really a shame, for at least two reasons. First, I can't assign unique settings to a Country/Language Scheme: If I change the currency symbol for Spanish (Modern) from Pst to $, the change "sticks" across languages—if I then switch to Portuguese (Standard), I want the currency symbol to switch over to Esc, but it stays at $. Bummer. Second, I can't create or distribute my own set of Country/Language schemes: Win95 wouldn't even know how to handle them.

 Sounds to me like Microsoft needs to rethink how it handles schemes in general. There are so many places where Win95 uses schemes, or something like schemes, but each one is handled in a different way, and switching among them can be very confusing. Uniform schemes, I say!

The Regional settings all appear in `HKCU\Control Panel\International`. If you have nothing in that key except `Locale`, it's because you haven't made any changes.

Taking the entries from the top of the Number tab dialog (and the default value under English (United States) Scheme), the Decimal symbol (.) is value `sDecimal`; number of digits after decimal (2) is `iDigits`; Digit grouping symbol (,) is `sThousand`; number of digits in group (3) is in `sGrouping`, but stored in a weird way (for example, a value of 5 is stored as 5;0—and I couldn't figure out what the semi-colon signified); Negative sign symbol (–) is `sNegativeSign`; Negative number format (1) is stored as a code in `iNegNumber`—0 is for the (1.1) format, 1 is for –1.1, 2 is for – 1.1 (with intervening space), 3 is for 1.1–, and 4 is for 1.1 – (with intervening space); Display leading zeroes (1) is a code in `iLZero`—0 for no leading zero, 1 for a single leading zero; Measurement system (1) is a code in `iMeasure`—0 for Metric, 1 for U.S.; and List separator (,) is in `sList`. The list separator is used internally within Win95 and rarely appears to the user.

The Currency tab settings: Currency symbol ($) in `sCurrency`; Position of currency symbol (0) is a code in `iCurrency`—0 for $1.00, 1 for 1.00 $, 2 for $ 1.00 (with intervening space), and 3 for 1.00 $ (with intervening space); Negative number format (0) is a code in `iNegCurr`—0 for ($1.00), 1 for –$1.00, 2 for $–1.00, 3 for $1.00–, 4 for (1.00$), 5 for –1.00$, 6 for 1.00–$, 7 for 1.00$–, (just in case you have to keep track, the preceding have no embedded spaces, and the following have one embedded space) 8 for – 1.00 $, 9 for –$ 1.00, 10 for 1.00 $–, 11 for $ 1.00–, 12 for $ –1.00, 13 for 1.00– $, 14 for ($ 1.00), and 15 for (1.00 $); Decimal symbol (.) is `sMonDecimalSep`; number of digits after decimal (2) is `iCurrDigits`; Digit grouping symbol is `sMonThousandSep`; and number of digits in group (3) is `sMonGrouping`, with the same strange format used in `sGrouping`, mentioned earlier.

Over on the Time tab, things are stranger. The Time style (h:mm:ss tt) setting translates into three Registry entries. One of them, `sTimeFormat`, contains the time format string, just as you see it. But a second entry, `iTLZero` appears with a value of 1 if the time format dictates that the time appear with a leading zero. And a third entry, `iTime`, appears with a value of 1 if the time format is for a 24-hour clock. The Time separator (:) is `sTime`. The AM symbol (AM) shows up as `s1159`, and the PM symbol (PM) is `s2359`.

What are you kvetching about? We had to put those entries in the Registry for compatibility purposes. Windows 3.1 set similar flags. Youse guys had the gall to document them in the original Mother of All Windows Books. Now everybody and his bro' uses the Win31 settings, and we had no choice but to maintain them.

<Gulp> The truth at all costs, says I. Rounding out the Regional Settings in the Registry, that Date tab has some more strange settings. `sShortDate` has the Short date formatting string (M/d/yy), just as it appears on the Date tab. In addition, though, `iDate` shows up with a 1 if the day is put ahead of the month, or 2 if the year appears before the month. The Date separator (/) is `sDate`. Finally, `sLongDate` has the Long date formatting string (dddd, MMMM dd, yyyy).

I really thought I was going crazy for a while, but it's just a bug. All of the changes you make manually to HKCU "take," as far as I can tell, when you go through the Shutdown routine marked Close all programs and log on as a different user. Except for these. *None* of the changes you make manually to keys in HKCU\Control Panel\International will "take" in Explorer unless you warm-boot the system.

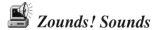

Zounds! Sounds

Lap me in soft Lydian airs.

—John Milton, *L'Allegro,* 1632

The Control Panel's Sounds applet is quite straightforward. In a nutshell, Windows and Windows apps make certain "events" available to the system—Starting Windows being the classic example, but also application-specific events, such as receiving a mail message. By using this applet, you can tell Win95 to play a particular `.wav` file whenever the event occurs. There are buttons to let you choose new sounds, and test play them before they're assigned to events. In the next chapter, I'll explain how to change the Registry to assign sounds to individual applications.

The only odd part of the applet is the way it handles Sound schemes. I talked about that extensively in the discussion on the Mouse applet. You have to be careful not to accidentally overwrite sounds in the built-in schemes—unless you really want to, of course!

Registry entries for sounds are stored in a rather bizarre hierarchy, even by Windows 95 standards. Default sounds (i.e., those that will play for any application) are in `HKCU\AppEvents\Schemes\Apps\.Default`. Sounds that play for Explorer events are in . . . `\Schemes\ Apps\Explorer`. Sounds that play for Media Player are in . . . `\Schemes\Apps\MPlayer`, and so on. Within each of those keys is a list of events that have been sound-enabled: `\Explorer`, for example, has the `\Explorer\EmptyRecycleBin` event; `\.Default` has `\.Default\SystemStart`, and many more. Underneath each of *those* keys is yet another group of keys, including at a minimum the Current sound and the Default sound. So, for example, the Empty Recycle Bin event has two keys, `\Explorer\ EmptyRecycleBin\ .Current` and `\Explorer\EmptyRecycleBin\.Default`. Each event key thus constructed has one value, the `(Default)` value, which is a pointer to the applicable `.wav` file.

Given that explanation, and the fact that the default sound for any recognized Windows event is to play the `ding.wav` file, would you care to guess the value of the key (deep breath): `HKCU\AppEvents\Schemes\Apps\ .Default\.Default\.Default (Default)`?

System

Ah, Tam! Ah, Tam! Thou'll get thy fairin';
In Hell they'll roast thee like a herrin'.

—Robert Burns, *Tam O'Shanter,* 1790

 Saving the best for last, the Control Panel's System applet must be considered the Mother of All Applets. Think of System as being a collection of the most advanced utilities ever created for Windows—or, if you prefer, as a set of velvet steps to the innermost circles of Windows Hell. You can get to the applet by either double-clicking on the System icon within the Control Panel, or by right-clicking on My Computer and choosing Properties.

 Woody let us print a copy of his System applet General tab in Figure 10-33, but only the top half: the bottom half contains the registration numbers that you'll need to get telephone support from Microsoft. Be careful not to let those get away too far!

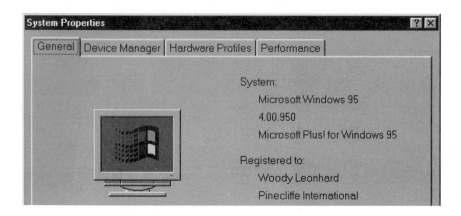

Figure 10-33. The System applet

The Device Manager tab lets you trace down all of your PC's resources. The Hardware Profiles tab sets up alternative "profiles," theoretically for PCs that change hardware frequently. Theoretically. The Performance tab lets you juggle with Win95's innards. Let's take each tab in turn.

Device Manager Tab

The Device Manager, which lurks under the Device Manager tab, is a marvelous "sniffer" application that—for the first time in the history of Windows, or even DOS—gives you a highly accurate view of what hardware sits inside, or is attached to, your PC. In addition, Device Manager lets you:

- look at and manually adjust IRQ, DMA and I/O address* assignments for every piece of hardware (except Plug 'n Play hardware, which theoretically never needs adjustment)

- tell Windows 95 to keep its hands off IRQ, DMA, and I/O addresses that you want to reserve for hardware that hasn't yet been installed

- see how devices are physically connected to the PC

- see what drivers are loaded for a particular piece of hardware

- find out if devices aren't working properly, or if they've been disabled by Windows or the hardware itself

- configure some of your ports and set other hardware options

- change drivers for any hardware device

- "hunt" for unused IRQs, DMAs, and I/O addresses

As Plug 'n Play hardware becomes more prevalent, the importance of Device Manager will diminish: when devices can change their IRQ, DMA, and I/O addresses under control of the PC, the need to futz with this stuff by hand will disappear. But as long as there are older devices that have to be configured by hand (typically with a pair of pliers and a Lilliputian jumper, but occasionally with software), and as long as some Plug 'n Play devices don't play as well as they should with their siblings, the Device Manager will remain one of the truly pivotal Windows utilities.

---

* While we'll look at many of the details shortly, the basic idea is pretty simple: there are a limited number of IRQs, DMAs, and I/O addresses available inside a PC; and no two hardware devices running at the same time can use the same IRQ, the same DMA, or the same I/O address. So, for example, if your modem uses IRQ number 3, and you install a sound card that also uses IRQ number 3, all hell will break loose. For a much more definitive explanation, see *The Mother of All PC Books*.

When you bring up the Device Manager tab, you'll find a complete list of the hardware within and attached to your PC, listed in alphabetical order by what Microsoft calls "Type." We'll dive into all the options available for examining those types in a moment, but for now, let's look at what you can do with "Computer," highlighted at the top. The Computer Type should probably be called Summary: Information you gather with Computer highlighted applies to the PC as a whole. We would've killed (or at least maimed) to get this kind of detailed Computer report just a couple of years ago. No third-party "sniffer" has ever come close to providing this amount of detail, or this level of accuracy.

With Computer highlighted, push Properties. You'll be treated to a complete list of assigned IRQs, or Interrupt Request Numbers, and the hardware device using each IRQ. (IRQs are numbered from 0 to 15, corresponding to the sixteen wires inside your computer that can force the central processor to interrupt its calculations and tend to outside business.) Watch out for duplicated IRQ numbers. Sometimes a device will get listed twice with the same IRQ (for example, my IDE Controller is listed twice with both IRQ 14 and IRQ 15), but if you have two different devices using the same IRQ, disaster may result.

Click the Input/Output radio button and you'll see a complete list of all the I/O Addresses used by your system and peripherals. (I/O Addresses are locations of external ports that devices use to communicate with the PC itself. If two different devices use the same I/O address, they can write all over each others' data.)

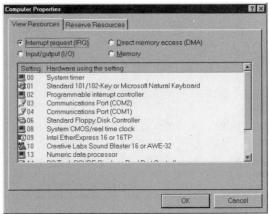

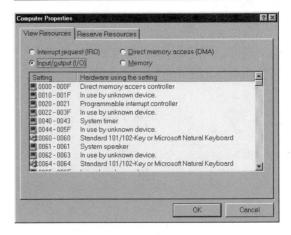

The addresses are listed in hexadecimal. This list isn't as useful as the preceding one for IRQs, simply because there are so many of the suckers, but the information contained here is vital to the hassle-free operation of any PC.

Click the Direct Memory Access (DMA) radio button and you'll see a complete list of used DMA channels. (DMA channels, numbered from 0 to 7, correspond to the eight different locations on the DMA Controller chip inside your PC that allow peripherals to send data, quickly, directly to the processor's main memory.)

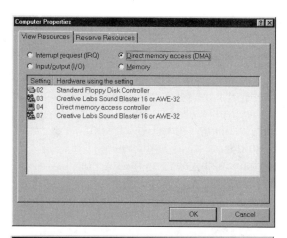

It's important that no two devices share the same DMA channel, so they don't end up clobbering each other when transferring data into memory.

Some specific locations in memory are set aside (or remapped) for video cards, and occasionally for other high-speed devices, in the region above 640K and below 1 MB— the so-called "Upper Memory Area." (And you thought Win95 got rid of that old-fashioned concept!) Click on the Memory radio button and you'll see which parts of upper memory have been set aside for those devices.

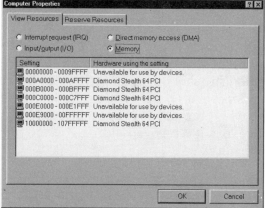

Bring up the Reserve Resources tab and you'll have an opportunity to set aside IRQs, DMAs, or I/O addresses—reserve them, so Win95 won't use them when it assigns resources in the Add New Hardware Wizard. To add new reservations, click the Add button here. If you try to reserve an IRQ, DMA, or I/O Address that's already in use, Win95 will warn you.

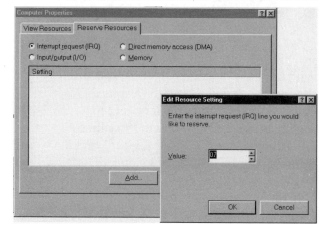

With Computer highlighted, hit the Print . . . button and you'll have a chance to print out a top-level summary of all assigned IRQs, DMAs, and I/O Addresses, in addition to Processor and BIOS information, a memory inventory, and information on your disk drives (none of which is available on-screen in Device Manager). It's a very valuable report, which you should store away somewhere . . . perhaps with your emergency boot disks.

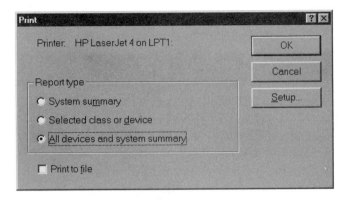

 I hate to be a wet blanket in the middle of this touchy-feely system sniffer nostalgia group-hug thing, but there are two different machines at Mom's place where the printed summary information is just plain wrong. The correct information appears on-screen, but somehow when it's translated into a printed report, on one machine one IRQ and two DMAs (all from the same card) are missing; on the other machine two IRQs and two DMAs (again, all on one card) are missing. Mom was as happy as a blind dog in a butcher shop when she saw her legacy sound card had its IRQs correctly identified on the screen—even if they *were* called "unknown device"—but she wasn't very happy at all when the printed report missed both of 'em. Watch out! That printed report is nice, but it'd be even nicer if it were accurate. Oh, how I love a nice bug in the mornin'!

 Those are the options available when the Computer "Type" is highlighted. Let's backtrack now, and see what else awaits under the Device Manager tab, when we look at individual devices.

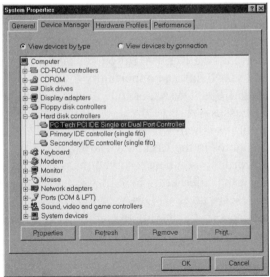

With the View devices by type radio button checked, you can look at the various logical groupings of hardware devices, and the actual devices installed on your machine. For example, under CDROM, you'll find the name of your CD-ROM drive; under Hard disk controllers you'll see the various kinds of hard disk controllers installed on your machine.

If you're curious about names and model numbers of hardware that came with your system, this is the place to start looking. There's a surprising amount of detail on everything from controller cards to exotic internal hardware, 'tho regrettably not much on generic hard drives, mice, or keyboards.

Click the View devices by connection button and Win95 will show you how it all hooks together. The internal logical connections show up on the screen: which devices are connected to what controllers, and how those fit onto the PC's bus. It's a very impressive view of the inside of your machine.

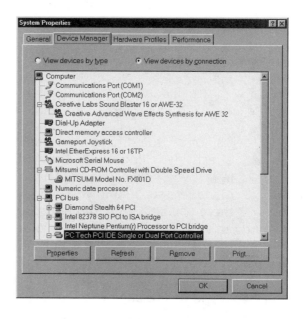

This screen is particularly valuable for verifying that the hardware you thought you bought is actually what you got. If you've ever wondered whether you have the Neptune chip set on your Pentium, or if that IDE hard drive controller really does go through the PCI bus, this display will show you in a snap.

Sometimes when Windows 95 detects that something is wrong, it will draw your attention to the potential problem by putting a yellow exclamation point on top of the device's icon. In this case, the IDE hard disk controller had been disabled, and Win95 alerted us by putting a yellow exclamation point on the PC Tech PCI Controller icon. We're not absolutely sure, but we think the PCI controller was disabled at the factory, in favor of the "Standard IDE/ESDI Hard Disk Controller" that appears next on the list. Win95 is also supposed to raise the yellow exclamation point flag if the resource settings you have listed for the device don't match the physical settings on the device itself.

If you have a yellow exclamation point and suspect there's a resource conflict—either the jumpers on the board don't match the settings Win95 has stored away, or two different devices are trying to get at the same IRQ, DMA or I/O address—Windows has a troubleshooter that may help. Click Start, then Help. Under the Find Tab, type conflict, and choose Troubleshooting Hardware Conflicts.

The Refresh button on the Device Manager tab tells Win95 to go back to the Registry and rebuild its list of all the devices and the resources they use. It does *not* force Win95 to scan for new hardware.

It's not all that difficult to install two copies of the same "device"—effectively telling Win95 that you have two keyboards, or two mice, when in fact you only have one. That's why the Remove button is on the Device Manager tab. Should you ever accidentally install the same device twice, there will be a repeated entry on the Device Manager tab. The challenge is to find out which, if either, of the two devices is installed properly (usually by clicking on the device, then clicking Properties, as we'll see in a moment). If you have a repeated entry here and can figure out which one is the correct one, select the wrong one and hit the Delete button. If both of them appear to be the same, flip a coin and delete one or the other.

If you accidentally remove a valid device, DON'T PANIC! Pick Cancel on the Device Manager tab, if you can. If not, just reboot. Windows 95 will often detect the hardware automatically the next time you reboot and may restore the old device without even telling you, much less asking your opinion. If the device appears to be well and truly gone, though, you'll have to go through the Add New Hardware Wizard to get it reinstalled (see Chapter 8).

Don't think if you remove what you think is a critical device like your display that Windows will refuse to run. It'll just shift to a generic driver. On one system I use, the display somehow got terribly confused and complained it was not correctly installed when I went to the Display applet. The only way I found to fix matters was to remove the display in Device Manager, reboot, and use Add New Hardware to have Windows reinstall the proper driver.

You can get a wealth of information about individual devices by double-clicking on the device in the Device Manager tab (or, equivalently, clicking the device once and clicking Properties). I'm going to step you through two rather different devices, a sound card and a COM port, to show you a few important details.

I chose the AWE-32 sound board because it uses quite a few resources, and sound boards are notorious for conflicts. This is the same sound board Mao installed with the Add New Hardware Wizard in Chapter 8. When you double-click on the sound board on the Device Manager tab, the Properties sheet for the board appears on the General tab. The Device Status box—arguably the only interesting thing on the tab—says that the device is working properly. Of course, Win95 isn't smart enough to know if it really *is* working properly. But if you see the "working properly" message, it means that there are no obvious resource conflicts, and that the device seems to be responding properly to inquiries from the PC (although for some devices a "proper" response is no response at all!).

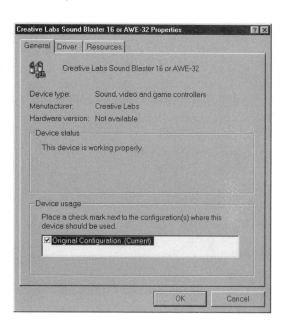

The AWE-32's Driver tab shows you the twelve *different* drivers Win95 needs to make the board work. This list is less important for the rote recital of driver names as it is for the help it lets you provide to tech support people. You can tell the techdroid on the phone which drivers are installed, with version number, in a matter of seconds. (Unfortunately, the File details box doesn't list the file size or date—which seems to be the only way some tech support people can track versions of their drivers. To get that info, you'll have to pop out to Explorer.)

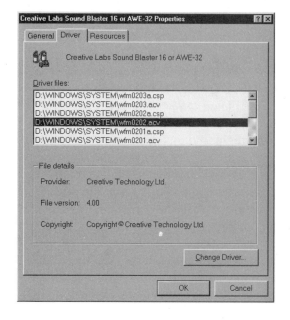

If you have a new driver, this is as good a place as any to install it. Click Change Drivers and follow the bouncing ball . . . you'll be transported to the Add New Hardware Wizard's Select a Driver box (see Chapter 8 for details).

The cantankerous part of the AWE-32's Properties sit beneath the Resources tab. As long as there are no conflicts, it's much, much easier to leave the Use automatic settings box checked. That gives Win95 maximum flexibility in assigning resources not only to this board, but to all the other devices in your system.

If there's a conflict, though, you'll have to uncheck the Use automatic settings box and try to find a compromise. Start by using the Basic Configuration list. Flip through the choices and see if any shows up with "No conflicts" in the Conflicting devices list. If that works, hit OK and you're done. If it doesn't work, though, you'll have to start hunting for settings. Pick an IRQ, DMA, or I/O Address and click the Change Settings button.

The Change Settings button leads to a dialog that lets you choose your resource (IRQ, DMA, or I/O Address) manually. Conflicts are clearly marked at the bottom of the dialog.

You might find that you can only get this device to work by changing the IRQ on another device. If that's the case, make the change here, then hop over to the other device and make the corresponding change to that device.

Win95 can do much of this adjudication automatically, but only if you leave the Use automatic settings box checked on the Resources tab!

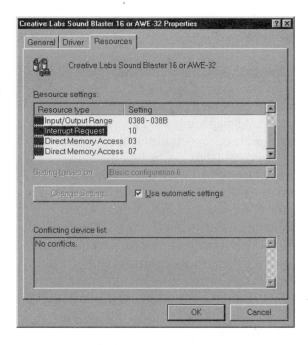

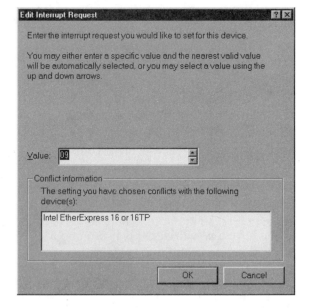

Once you find a group of settings that leaves all your devices conflict-free, your travails aren't yet over. In many cases you'll have to physically yank the board(s) out of your PC and change jumper settings or DIP switches. And the only guide you'll have there is the hardware's manual or tech support line. If you should find yourself in that position, keep two things in mind: doing the same thing was a *hell* of a lot harder before Windows 95; and, when Plug 'n Play really starts working, this will all be a not-so-fond memory.

I wanted to show you a COM port Properties sheet, simply because it has several important settings, and they bury this beast way down in about six levels of dialog boxes.

The easiest way to get here is to go to the Device Manager tab, clicking the View devices by connection radio button, choosing your modem's COM port (usually COM2), clicking Properties, then clicking the Port Settings tab.

I have no idea why, but Win95 insisted on capping this COM port back at 19,200 bits per second. That doesn't make any sense: regardless of the speed of the modem attached to the port, the port *itself* is capable of handling much more data. As you can see, I cranked it up to 57,600 bits per second, and seriously considered going higher.

I then clicked the Advanced button, when what to my wondering eyes should appear . . .

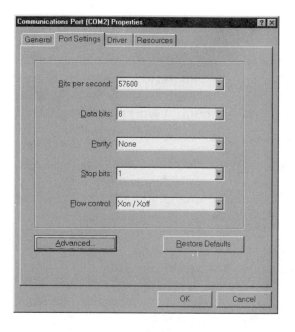

. . . but the Advanced Port Settings dialog Mao talked about when he discussed Control Panel's Modems applet! Sunuvagun. I made sure the 16550 UART was pegged at the high end for both transmit and receive, of course, and clicked OK.

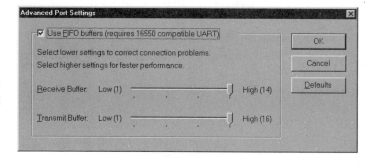

There are a few additional settings and oddities accessible from the Device Manager tab worth mentioning:

- CD-ROM drive entries let you choose whether to disable Auto-insert notification, which in turn can kill off Autoplay and Autorun.

- The Dial-Up Adapter device includes not only modems (as you would probably expect), but just about any networking connection that isn't permanent—it's a virtual device to provide networking capabilities in situations where you don't have a network card, where networking is accomplished, for example, via modem.

- If you have an "IO read data port for ISA Plug and Play enumerator" *(<whew!>)* device listed, take a look at its Resources Tab to make sure I/O space has been assigned to it.

Not all devices appear on the Device Manager tab. For example, my Colorado Memory Systems Jumbo 250 doesn't show up anywhere—even though it works just fine with Windows 95's backup routines. I have no idea why Win95 summarily skips some types of hardware.

Registry entries for these devices are located in various keys under HKLM, with \Enum being a favorite. I would strongly recommend against changing them manually inside the Registry. If you use the Device Manager to change an IRQ or other resource for some device, look for the changes to be reflected in a value called ForcedConfig.

Hardware Profiles Tab

Here's the concept. You have a portable PC with a docking station. You need to keep two completely different hardware profiles: one for the portable on the road, the other for the portable tethered to the station. The "Road" profile would include a small, 256-color monitor, a small keyboard with no number pad, and a single hard drive. The "Dock" profile would include a 21-inch monitor, a full-scale keyboard, and a 20 GB RAID-5 bank of hard drives. Every time you boot your PC, it asks if you want the "Road" or the "Dock" profile, and Win95 configures itself accordingly.

Here's the reality. Win95 needed this "profiling" capability anyway, to support Plug 'n Play. Since it was there anyway, they put a rather hokey people-interface on the front of it and turned it into a feature that many people might think they want, while few people could actually use. There aren't too many situations where you would *want* to manually create multiple hardware profiles, so you could choose from them when Win95 boots. Why?

- *The fancy new hardware doesn't need it.* If you have Plug 'n Play hardware, Win95 figures out what's working on-the-fly; there's no need to create a second hardware profile because the hardware is detected as soon as it's available.

- *Sometimes even old hardware doesn't need it.* If you have older hardware, Win95 still goes through a detection phase when it boots, and it's often smart enough to pull in the drivers and settings it needs for the hardware at hand.

The *Windows Resource Kit* says, "The only time Windows 95 prompts you for the name of a hardware profile is when two profiles are so similar that Windows 95 can't differentiate between them." In our experience it's unusual to have two real-world profiles so similar that manual intervention was necessary, yet so different that Win95 couldn't compensate on its own. Yes, you can create one profile for, oh, 640 × 480 resolution, and a second for 800 × 600, and have Win95 prompt you for your preferred profile every time you boot.

Given that caveat, creating multiple hardware profiles for very different hardware setups—say, a docked and an undocked portable—is easy. Here's how:

Start by installing drivers for all the hardware that you'll use for *all* your various profiles. Typically, that will involve using the Add Hardware Wizard to install every piece of hardware both on your portable and on your docking station.

Then, in Control Panel, double-click on System, and bring up the Hardware Profiles tab. You'll see the profile that includes all the hardware in both configurations listed as Original Configuration.

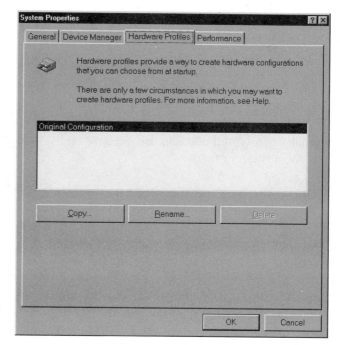

Click the button marked Copy. You'll be asked to provide a name for your new profile. You can use just about anything.

The new profile (which, at this point, is identical to the original profile) is listed under the Hardware Profiles tab. In the Registry, this second profile is identified by the key \0002. For example, where the original configuration information is stored in HKLM\Config\0001, the second Hardware Profile's config info is in HKLM\Config\0002, and so on.

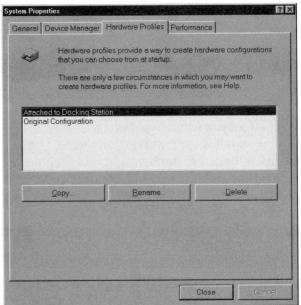

Finally, you need to go back to the Device Manager tab and, one at a time, double-click on each piece of hardware that you want to be included in separate Hardware Profiles. At the bottom of the General tab on each applicable device, you'll find two checkboxes. Check one or the other to differentiate the Hardware Profiles, or leave both checked to have the device available in both profiles.

In this example, the EtherExpress 16 card is installed in the docking station and not on the originally configured portable. Boxes have been checked accordingly.

The procedure for creating multiple hardware profiles for minor differences—say, one for 640 × 480 resolution, and another for 800 × 600 resolution—is similar. Just set up all your preferences for the one setting, go into the

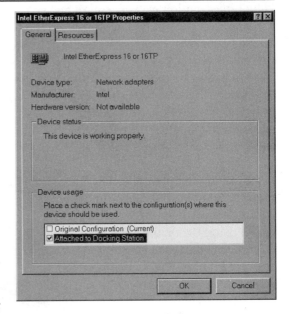

Hardware Profiles tab, and then hit Copy. Highlight the new profile and then go back and make the changes you want for the second profile. There's no "Save" button: Win95 remembers the last settings you establish for each chosen profile.

In theory, that's how you're supposed to set up Hardware Profiles. In practice, I haven't seen it do much more than behave as an admirable Win95 Parlor Trick. Chances are pretty good you won't want to go through the hassle.

Performance Tab

Windows 95 is so smart about optimizing performance in so many ways that it comes as a shock to many people when they discover that it's downright dumb about a few tuning points. The System applet's Performance tab lets you turn some of the oddball settings right—or shoot yourself in the foot, if you don't know what you're doing. It also lets you tone down Win95's performance, bit by bit, in case any problems you experience can be diminished by slowing things down.

Ha! Performance, they call it? Although there are a couple of performance options buried in this tab, the simple fact of the matter is that this is the Troubleshooting tab: this is where you go when Win95 is screwing up, to see if you can throttle back some of that wonderful performance, and get the bloody thing to simply *work*.

If you're not using any real-mode drivers, your Performance tab should look as clean as a hound's tooth. This particular machine is running 32-bit file and disk access (that's what "File system: 32-bit" means). It's also using the optimized Win95 routines for virtual memory and disk compression.

The phrase "Your system is configured for optimum performance" really means, "You don't have any real-mode drivers installed that are gumming up the works." There are still several points you should check before you're satisfied that your system is, indeed, configured for optimum performance.

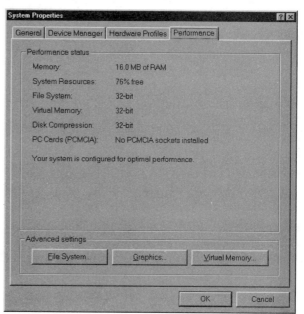

The next machine, on the other hand, is using a real-mode driver for disk access and one for disk compression—most likely old Stacker routines that weren't vetted by the

Win95 installer. The solution in this case is to contact the manufacturer for replacement 32-bit drivers, or to convert over to Win95 compression.

If you have any real-mode drivers, don't even bother with the rest of the Performance tab—the big performance boost you'll get is in zapping out those drivers. Fix the big problems before you tackle the little ones. Check Chapter 8 for several hints on how you might go about exorcising the 16-bit beasts.

If you push the Performance tab's Advanced settings/File System button, you'll find the Hard Disk tab. For Typical role of this machine, you get three choices: Network server allocates extra disk buffer space, at the possible expense of application work area; Desktop computer tries to strike a balance between applications and disk access; and Mobile system minimizes memory usage while increasing the frequency of buffer flushes (in case the battery gives out).

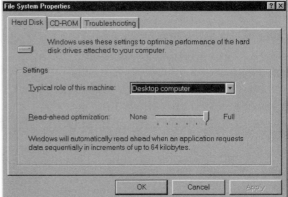

The CD-ROM tab brings up the entries for CDFS, the Win95 CD File System. If you use your CD frequently, I recommend you always crank up the Supplemental cache size, and that you adjust the Optimize access pattern for number depending on how much RAM is in your PC, as follows: If you have less than 8 MB, use single-speed (which creates a 64K cache); if you have 8 MB or more, quad-speed (which creates a 1238K cache). Extra CD cache space for multimedia apps makes a big difference.

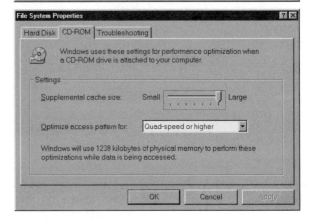

In spite of the dire warning on the Troubleshooting tab, checking any one of these boxes won't make your PC fritter away in a billowing cloud of smoke, although they will bog your machine down. Mostly, they're just increasingly unnecessary last-ditch ways of turning off advanced Windows features, primarily to accommodate old hardware and software that doesn't behave itself. For a full description of the various options, consult the *Windows Resource Kit.*

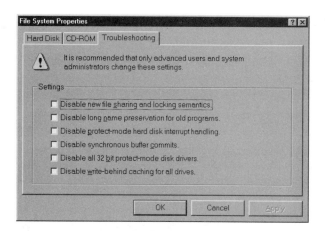

Back on the Performance tab, if you click the Graphics button, you'll have an opportunity to decrease your video system's performance, in pursuit of greater compatibility. Set the slider back one notch if you're having trouble with the video card's hardware cursor. Back two notches and you also move processing of bit block transfers from the video card to the PC. If you set it on None, you move all video acceleration functions from the video card back to the PC.*

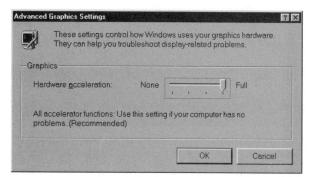

Finally, if you click the Virtual Memory button on the Performance tab, you'll be offered a chance to manually change the location and size of `win386.swp`, the Win95 swap file. In spite of the warning, there's absolutely nothing wrong with pointing Win95 to a drive that's faster or has more room than the drive Win95 automatically assigned to itself. Just be sure that the drive has enough room;

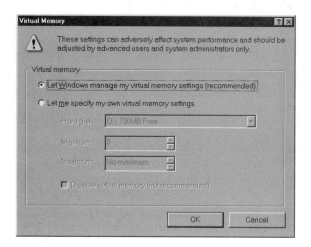

---

* If you find that setting this slider back makes your machine more stable, get on the phone and *scream* at your video card manufacturer.

running out of swap file space can be a deadly experience. If you leave the Maximum file size number alone, Win95 will know that it can grow as needs dictate; if you change it, Win95 will assume that you're specifying an absolute ceiling—which is not a good idea.

 Registry settings for the Hard Disk tab are in `HKLM\System\ CurrentControlSet\Control\FileSystem`, with values for `PathCache`, `NameCache`, `BufferIdleTimeout`, `BufferAgeTimeout`, and `VolumeIdleTimeout`—all of which are described at length in the *Windows Resource Kit*—plus the undocumented `ReadAheadThreshold` value, which tracks the size of the read-ahead buffer reported in the dialog.

The CD-ROM Tab affects Registry settings in `HKLM\System\CurrentControlSet\ control\FileSystem\CDFS`, with the undocumented values `CacheSize` (set by the "Optimize access patterns for" selection), and `Prefetch` and `PrefetchTail` (both of which are set by the Supplemental cache size slider).

The Troubleshooting tab puts new values in the Registry's `HKLM\System\ CurrentControlSet\Control\FileSystem` key. Full details are in the *Windows Resource Kit*. Those of you who remember struggling with the Windows 3.1 `.INI` file value called `VirtualHDIRQ` might want to look it up in the *WRK*. You'll get a kick out of reading about the old Emperor in his new Win95 clothes.

The *WRK* says that settings in the Graphics dialog are reflected in `win.ini` and `system.ini`. Sometimes I wonder what turnip truck these people fell out of. The settings are placed in `HKLM\Config\0001\Display\Settings`, in values `SwCursor`, `Mmio` and `SafeMode`.

On the other hand, the Virtual Memory settings are kept in `system.ini`! They're in the `[386Enh]` section, with entries such as these:

```
PagingDrive=D:

MinPagingFileSize=5120

MaxPagingFileSize=102400
```

Both of these numbers are bytes. If `MinPagingFileSize` is missing, Win95 assumes the paging file can shrink as small as it likes. If there is no `MaxPagingFileSize`, it can grow to fill the entire disk.

Chapter 11

Oh Registry, My Registry

We must make allowances for whoever does a thing first.

—Greek proverb

 Welcome to the graduate course on Windows 95. Your assignment for the next two hours is to learn enough about the structure and contents of the human brain to self-administer a pre-frontal lobotomy. I'm afraid that the campus bookstore hasn't yet received copies of the *Mother of All Anatomy Books,* so you'll have to make due with the *Bodily Resource Kit.* You'll note that the *BRK* spends twenty-five pages on "brain," six pages on "structure," one page on "lobes," and a paragraph on "pre-frontal" but sadly neglects to say anything about "lobotomy." That's okay. I'm sure you'll be able to pick it up once you get into the thick of things. Scalpels are available for your experimentation in the box marked Regedit.

 Ah, c'mon Mom. The Registry ain't *that* bad. Yeah, it's true that the Registry is Win95's brain. And, yeah, I'd have to admit that the *Windows Resource Kit* only spends twenty-five pages on the Registry. Hmmmm . . . Let me look in the book. There's six pages on HKEY_LOCAL_MACHINE, but, uh, oh I guess they only have one page on HKEY_CURRENT_USER don't they? How 'bout that. Hey. Where's the information on all the values? I mean, that's why you *have* a Registry, don't you?

 You're getting the idea. The deeper you look for information on the Registry, singularly the most important piece of Windows, the less there is to find. Microsoft would have you believe that the Registry need only be manipulated by very sophisticated users. But all too often when you ask Microsoft for tech support, the first question you hear is, "Do you know how to use Regedit?" The simple fact is that there are hundreds, if not thousands, of reasons why you might need to edit your Registry, and precious little documentation on how, or why, or what.

Mom rushes in where angels fear to tread, eh? You might think that this chapter is the place to start when pursuing Registry things. It isn't. A very large part of Chapter 10 was on the Registry—I just disguised it as a discussion of the Control Panel so you wouldn't freak out. If you're beginning with the Registry and want to learn more, or if you want to tweak anything contained in the Control Panel, start with Chapter 10.

Regedit

> The best partner for dice-playing is not a just man, but a good dice-player.

> —Plato, *The Republic,* ca. 370 B.C.

Ready to roll the dice? Excellent. We have some really good dice-players on Mom's crew, and we'll show you the in's and out's. Let's start by assuming that you've already seen the Registry and used `regedit` at least once. If you're completely green at editing the Registry, go back to Chapter 10 and start at the beginning. This is the Advanced Registry course, not Registry for Rush, OK?

Hey! Even Dummies need to learn how to use `redgedit`. You act like it's some big deal, but you and I both know that —as long as you're careful and make good backups—there's no reason why you shouldn't take your Registry into your own hands.

Keys, Values, Names, and Data

Let's start by taking a detailed look at `regedit` itself, and getting some of the (confusing!) terminology down. Click on Start, then Run, type `regedit,` and hit `Enter`. You'll see something like Figure 11-1. Click on a + sign and the entry expands. Double-click on a name in the right-hand panel, and the `regedit` edit box pops up, so you can change the value. Click once on almost anything and hit the `del` key to delete it. Click on Edit, then Find, and you can search for particular values or strings. You already know all that.

Now, to get the terminology straight, start by forgetting everything you've ever read about the Registry. (The *Windows Resource Kit* is confusing as hell.) Let's start with a clean slate. In Figure 11-1, every line in the left-hand box is called a *key.* Every line in the right-hand box is called a *value.* So, for example, the left-hand thing that appears as `HKEY_LOCAL_MACHINE\Network\Logon` is a key, and it has five values. The right-hand thing that appears as `username Mao` is one of those values.

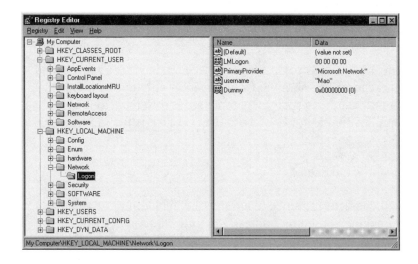

Figure 11-1. Regedit, top view

 Admittedly the terminology is a bit weird. (I, for one, tend to think of `username` as a part of the key, with `"Mao"` as the value—and I'll bet you do, too.) But we're talking about Official Microsoft Definitions here: any semblance to rationality is entirely coincidental. As you can see in Figure 11-1, the first part of the value (`Username` in this example) is called the *value name* and the second part of the value (`"Mao"` in this example) is called the *value data.* This terminology is an extreme example of techy obfuscation, but we'll stick with it to stay compatible with the official documentation.

 Look over on the key side of the fence. See how there are six high-level keys? They're called `HKEY_CLASSES_ROOT`, `HKEY_CURRENT_USER`, `HKEY_LOCAL_MACHINE`, `HKEY_USERS`, `HKEY_CURRENT_CONFIG`, and `HKEY_DYN_DATA`. For reasons that I'll discuss in the next section, we generally deal more often than not with just three of those keys: `HKEY_CLASSES_ROOT` (which I will abbreviate `HKCR`), `HKEY_CURRENT_USER` (abbreviated `HKCU`), and `HKEY_LOCAL_MACHINE` (abbreviated `HKLM`).

 Now look on the right side of Figure 11-1. See how the first Registry value name is listed as `(Default)`? That's a special value name: while you can change the `(Default)` value data—the part marked `(value not set)`—by double-clicking on `(Default)`, you cannot delete `(Default)`, and you cannot create a second `(Default)` value name. Every key (that is, every line on the left-hand side of `regedit`) has exactly one `(Default)` value (that is, one and only one `(Default)` value name on the right-hand side).

Every value has three parts: the value name, the type of data contained in the value (indicated by the icon to the left of the name), and the value data itself.

The other value names in Figure 11-1, LMLogon, PrimaryProvider, username and Dummy, show how value names can be just about any combination of letters or numbers, including spaces. Spaces are significant (Primary Provider is different from PrimaryProvider) but capitalization is not (PrimaryProvider is the same as primaryprovider).

There are three different flavors of value data:

- **string** value data are normal characters, numbers and the like, including just about any oddball character you can imagine, including quotes. The little 🔤 icon in regedit signifies that this value's data is string.

- **binary** value data is just a variable-length hexadecimal entry. Double-click on a value name and regedit shows you the value data both in hex and an ASCII translation. Cool. The 📟 icon in regedit signifies that this value's data type is either binary or dword (see next). When you overwrite binary data, be careful to make sure that you only overwrite the bytes you want to overwrite—because of the way the editor works, it's very easy to alter the size of a binary entry accidentally. Practice with it a couple of times and you'll see how it works.

- **dword** value data is the standard PC hex double-word. Programmers call a double-word (four bytes of data, with each byte containing two hex digits) a *dword*. It's usually interpreted as a number that can range from zero to FFFFFFFF hex—commonly written 0xFFFFFFFF. In decimal notation, that's zero to 4,294,967,295. Note how regedit shows both the hex (in 0x . . . . format) and decimal representations (in parenthesis) of every dword value. The only difference between a dword and a binary value is that the former has a fixed length of four bytes.

 (value not set) is a special, null value (er, value data) that only appears to be valid in (Default) entries; at least, I couldn't find it used with anything but (Default) entries. Although regedit puts the 🔤 icon in front of null values, (value not set) is *not* a character string. You can't search for it. If you use regedit's editor and type in the data (value not set), you'll get a string with that value, not a null! The only way I've found to reset a value to (value not set) is to click on (Default) and hit the del key.

Zero-length strings (often called "empty strings") show up in the regedit right-hand panel as a pair of quotes with nothing in between. While, technically, there is a difference between a zero-length string and a null (value not set) value data, in practice I haven't seen any difference in the way the two are treated in the Registry, or in Windows as a whole.

(`zero-length binary value`) is another special null value, this time for binary value data. Again, it is *not* a character string. You can assign the null (`zero-length binary value`) value to a binary entry by double-clicking on the value name and deleting everything in the `regedit` edit box.

 You're bound to ask, sooner or later, "What's the real meaning of those different types of value data?" Well, I hate to disillusion you, but there isn't any. Choice of a particular data type seems to be a reflection of what the programmer was feeling like on the day she decided to add the entry. One of the best examples of how the types get all jumbled sits in the Registry key that deals with window sizes and fonts, `HKCU\Control Panel\dekstop\ WindowMetrics`. If you look in there you'll find lots of numbers (e.g., the height of the title bar) stored as string data, and lots of strings (e.g., the names of fonts) stored as binary. And why are the `EditFlags` values—which are always four bytes long—stored in the Registry as binary data, instead of dword? Got me. Anybody who tells you that string data is for characters, and binary and dword data is for numbers, obviously hasn't spent much time in the Registry!

New Keys and Values

Adding new keys and values to the Registry is as simple as clicking on Edit, then New or, equivalently, right-clicking inside the `regedit` dialog. Following Explorer's folder metaphor, clicking on Edit, New, then Key will add a new key (that is, a left-hand entry in `regedit`) below the currently highlighted key. As soon as the new key is added, you'll notice that it has one automatically generated value attached to it with a value name of (`Default`) and value data of (`value not set`).

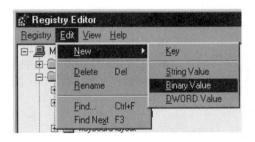

Figure 11-2. Regedit New

 While creating a new key is pretty easy and more-or-less intuitive, there's a trick to making the `regedit` approach to creating a new value rather easy. Start by clicking on the key you want to receive the new value then click on Edit, New, and choosing string, binary or dword. (Equivalently, you can right-click on the key and pick New, then string, binary or dword; or, you can simply right-click in the right-hand side of `regedit`, and pick New, then string, binary or dword.) The new value will have a name of New Value #1 (or #2, #3, etc.), and if you type immediately you'll overwrite the name.

Here's the trick: once you've typed in the new value name, hit Enter *twice.* That immediately brings up the `regedit` edit box, and typing in data at that point is easy. Every other method for typing in new data is a PITA.*

When you create a new value, the default value data varies, depending on what kind of value you've created:

- **string** value data starts out with a zero-length string.

- **binary** value data starts out as `(zero-length binary data)`.

- **dword** data starts out `00 00 00 00`, four bytes of zeroes.

In general, Windows will ignore new keys and values that you've typed in manually. There are lots of exceptions, though: for example, some Schemes (see Chapter 10) are established by sticking keys in the right place, in a process quite analogous to sticking folders in Win95's `\windows\Start Menu` folder to add new items to the Start Menu.

It's always safer to change keys associated with the Control Panel by playing with the Control Panel applets themselves, instead of `regedit`. Unfortunately, as discussed many times in Chapter 10, the Control Panel applets often fail to give you access to all the Registry settings. As the saying goes, necessity is a mother.

Don't delete keys willy-nilly, even if they have no values other than `(Default)`. In many cases, the mere existence of a key (even a value!) is important information for some part of Windows or an application.

Import/Export

`regedit` allows you to export all the values for a single key, or all the values for all the keys underneath a specific key, to a simple text file. (Except for the data in and under the key `HKEY_DYN_DATA`, which can't be exported under any circumstances.) To use the export capability, click on the key you want to export, then click Registry, and Export Registry File. Type in a file name for the exported file; Win95 will suggest you save it as a `.reg` file. The resulting file has entries for every value in the chosen key, plus the values of every key underneath the chosen key. To export the entire Registry, click on My Computer, then Registry, and Export Registry File. It's a real disk hog: A typical exported Registry will take 1 MB of space or more.

---

* Pain in the carapace. Another technical acronym you'll need for the test at the end of this chapter.

I recommend that you ignore Windows' suggestion and save exported Registry files with any extension *other* than `.reg`. `.txt` seems like a good choice, as you'll often want to look at and/or edit the resulting file. If you save the exported file as a `.reg`, accidentally double-clicking on it will immediately merge the file with the current Registry—a potentially hazardous happenstance.

If you export starting at the `HKLM\Network` key shown in Figure 11-1, you will get a text file that looks like Figure 11-3. (The key `HKLM\Network` has just one value, `(Default)` `(value not set)`.)

```
REGEDIT4

[HKEY_LOCAL_MACHINE\Network]

[HKEY_LOCAL_MACHINE\Network\Logon]
"PrimaryProvider"="Microsoft Network"
"LMLogon"=hex:00,00,00,00
"username"="Mao"
"Dummy"=dword:00000000
```

Figure 11-3. HKLM\Network .reg file

There are several points worth noting. See how the file starts with a line that says `REGEDIT4`? I'll talk about that line—hallmark of a `.reg` file—in the section on Merging `.reg` Files. Next, look at how the keys are handled. Each key appears on one line, in `[brackets]`, with the entire key between the brackets. While the Registry itself is hierarchical, a `.reg` file is just a straight, flat text file. The Registry's hierarchy is reflected in the key names. Also note that the `(Default)` `(value not set)` value doesn't create any entry at all in the `.reg` file. Finally, take a close look at how value names, string, binary and dword values appear in the `.reg` file. Looking at a raw `.reg` file can be a bit jarring at first, but give it some time and you'll come to appreciate the symmetry in the beast.

There are four odd values that appear in `.reg` files from time to time.

- While a `(Default)` `(value not set)` value doesn't appear in the `.reg` file at all, a `(Default)` `"some value"` entry generates a line that looks like this:

```
@="some value"
```

The @ sign apparently is used to take the place of a (Default) value name.

- Empty binary values look a bit odd, too. If your Registry has a ValueName (zero-length binary data) value, it shows up in the .reg file as:

```
"ValueName"=hex:
```

- Double-quotes in string value data are preceded by a backslash. For example, a value name of Test and value data of An "award winning" book appears in the .reg file as:

```
"Test"="An \"award winning\" book"
```

- Apparently because of the way double-quotes are treated, backslashes appear in the .reg file doubled. For example, a value name of Another Test and value data of c:\windows appears in the file as:

```
"Another Test"="c:\\windows"
```

While exporting with regedit covers a multitude of sins, importing with regedit is not very sophisticated. You tell regedit to import a file by clicking on Registry, then Import Registry File, and picking a file to import. regedit doesn't really import anything. It simply merges the selected .reg file with your Registry, the same as if you had double-clicked on the .reg file while in Explorer. I'll talk more about merging .reg files momentarily, in the section called "Merging .reg Files."

Regedit in DOS

A very different, command-line-only, version of regedit runs in DOS mode. You get none of the fancy graphics or regedit options that come for granted in the Windows 95 version. Still, there are times when the DOS regedit can save your butt.

A copy of the DOS regedit is on your emergency boot disk, so you can get at it by either booting from the emergency boot disk, or by hitting F8 on startup and choosing to start in DOS mode. As I explained in Chapter 9, you'd have to be crazy (or in a *very* tough spot) to use DOS regedit to export data from the Registry. The command line for a simple export of the whole Registry to temp.txt looks like this:

```
regedit /L:c:\windows\system.dat /R:c:\windows\user.dat /E c:\temp.txt
```

and if you miss one space or incorrectly type one letter, you're SOL.

Sometimes (usually when Windows goes belly-up after you've been manually screwing around with the Registry), you may have a `.reg` file on hand that will reset the Registry to its correct state. In such a case, get into DOS mode, move to your Win95 `\windows` folder, and try using a command line like this:

```
regedit c:\foo.reg
```

where `c:\foo.reg` is the `.reg` file that you want to merge into the Registry. In my experience, that works at least 90 percent of the time. If it doesn't work for you, type `regedit ?` for a list of all the parameters that DOS `regedit` will recognize—and good luck.

Care and Feeding of Da Registry

> Life is warfare, and the sojourn of a stranger in a strange land.
>
> —Marcus Aurelius, *Meditations*, ca. 170

Enough on `regedit` for the moment. No doubt you're wondering by now, what exactly *is* the Registry? The answer, it turns out, has an easy part and a hard part. Now that you've seen what the Registry really looks like, you're ready to understand both parts.

The Registry is a centrally maintained warehouse of information that programs—including Windows itself—use to store and retrieve information. Microsoft feels that allowing (even requiring!) programs to use a central warehouse is better than letting them store data ad-hoc: a central store is easier to manage, and can be much more efficient than the ad-hoc approach. On the flip side, though, storing all your eggs in one basket means that if the warehouse goes up in flames, all of Windows can, too. That's the easy part, the conceptual part, the part you already knew.

Microsoft, though, seems to want you to do what they say, not what they do. Not only are `win.ini` and `system.ini` still used for some data (see, for example, the discussion of "Media Control Interface—Do you mean DeeDee Meyers?" in Chapter 2), but a number of Windows 95 applets continue to use private `.ini` files instead of the Registry, for example `Exchang32.ini`, `dialer.ini`, `cdplayer.ini` and `telephon.ini`.

Physically, the Registry is an amalgam of data from two or three files,* plus a bunch of things that are created on-the-fly whenever Win95 gets going. And that's where things start getting complicated. Let me first explain which files are involved, and how they get mashed together to make the thing we call the Registry. Then I'll go into some detail about five methods you can use to change those files, when things go bump in the night. All five of these methods are in addition to `regedit,` of course, which can change Registry values (and the underlying files) from either Windows or DOS.

Registry Genesis

 The designers of the Registry had to take into account two conflicting sources of information when creating Registry entries:

• First is the information about a specific PC—what hardware exists, which ports are being used, what kind of printer is attached, and on and on. In a very broad sense, this information is stored in a file called `system.dat`, and becomes the Registry key `HKEY_LOCAL_MACHINE`.

• Second is the information about the currently-logged-on user—how the Desktop is laid out, which files were most recently used, how fast the mouse moves, and much more. Again in a very broad sense, this is stored in a file called `user.dat,` and becomes the Registry key `HKEY_CURRENT_USER`.

I waffled a bit in those descriptions because it isn't at all cut-and-dried. For example, I would've thought the system font—which can be changed with the Control Panel's Desktop applet, Appearance tab—should be a `user.dat` setting, like, oh, the active title bar's color. It isn't. For good technical reasons, the system font is a `system.dat` setting.

 In the simplest of all possible worlds—a PC with one hardware profile (see Chapter 10, System applet, Hardware Profiles tab) and a single user profile (see Chapter 3, Password applet, User Profiles tab)—the Registry is constructed from the files `system.dat` and `user.dat`, both in the Win95 `\windows` folder.

---

* If a network administrator has established network policies, there may be more than three files involved. These `.pol` files can get pretty hairy; since they're advanced networking files, they're mercifully beyond the scope of this book.

If the PC has more than one hardware profile, all of the information about the different profiles are stored in the file `\windows\system.dat`, and they are all accessible, regardless of which hardware profile may be in effect, with `regedit`. I'll talk more about hardware profiles and how their settings end up in `HKEY_DYN_DATA` in the section on `HKEY_DYN_DATA`. For now, suffice it to say that all the Registry's hardware information—regardless of which hardware profile may be in effect—resides in `system.dat`, and Win95 is smart enough to pick and choose which information it needs to build a Registry that accurately reflects the current hardware configuration.

 Constructing the Registry gets considerably more complicated if there is more than one user profile defined on a PC. Chapter 3 goes into considerable detail about how Win95 stores multiple profiles, and you should refer to the discussion there if you're in the dark. As a quick refresher, if there are two user profiles defined on a PC—say, one for logon I.D. *sarah,* and another for logon I.D. *mao*—there will be three `user.dat` files on the machine: a default one in the windows folder called `\windows\user.dat`; one for *sarah,* stored in her own windows profile folder, called `\windows\profiles\sarah\user.dat`, and one more for the user *mao,* called `\windows\profiles\mao\user.dat`.

If a user bypasses the normal logon sequence on a multiple-user profile PC (by, say, hitting the `Esc` key when presented with the logon screen), the Registry is constructed as it would be if there were only a single-user profile, that is, by combining `\windows\system.dat` with the file `\windows\user.dat`. In essence, `\windows\user.dat` is the "default" user data file, pressed into service when Win95 can't identify which user profile it should use.

On the other hand, if a user logs on normally to a multiple-user profile PC—say, *mao* logs on—the Registry is constructed by combining three files, not the normal two: `\windows\system.dat`, which provides the information for the Registry's `HKLM` key; `\windows\profiles\mao\user.dat`, which provides the information for the Registry's `HKCU` key; and `\windows\user.dat.`, which provides the information for a little-used key called `HKEY_USERS\.Default`.

 *That sounds a little convoluted, but it isn't, really. When a new user logs on, a personal copy of `\windows\user.dat` is placed in the user's `\windows\profiles` folder. (Or, equivalently, the user gets her own copy of `HKEY_USERS\.Default`, which becomes HKCU.) If the correct box is checked in the Passwords applet User Profiles tab, the user also gets her own, customizable `\Start Menu` and `\Desktop`, both located in the `\windows\profiles\username` folder. The Registry is modified to point to those new `\Start Menu` and `\Desktop` folders, so any changes made to the Desktop and Start Menu only affect the new user. Network administrators can set things up so the `user.dat` travels with the user on a network: if you log on from machine A, you'll get the same `user.dat` you'd get if you log on from machine B, so all of your settings travel along with you. It works pretty well.*

It doesn't work all that well. Among many other things, if *sarah* installs, oh, Office 95, the installer is smart enough to change Sarah's `\profiles\sarah\Start Menu`, so her Start Menu is updated to include all the new Office applications. That's fine. But the Office installer isn't smart enough to look for, much less change, *mao's* `\profiles\mao\`

`Start Menu`, so the next time Mao logs on, he won't have the applications on his menus, even though Office 95 is available on the machine. Contrariwise, if *sarah* makes changes to, oh, the Office Shortcut Bar, those changes will also show up when *mao* logs on. That isn't, strictly speaking, a Registry problem. But it's a big problem, nonetheless. The ability to customize menus and Desktops cuts both ways, and many users (including this one!) find it very confusing.

Copying .dat Files

Now that you know where the Registry bodies are buried, it probably won't surprise you to discover that keeping backups of the Registry `.dat` files is a tad more complicated than it would first appear.

Win95 maintains an automatic one-deep backup of all `.dat` files, naming them `.da0` (that's a zero): it makes a copy of `\windows\system.dat` and calls it `system.da0` and then it makes a copy of `\windows\user.dat` calling it `user.da0`. Then, presumably, you can restore a clobbered `system.dat`, say, by copying `system.da0` over the top of it.

The crucial piece of information missing in all the documentation is precisely *when* the `.da0` files are created. Without that piece of intelligence, you stand a good chance of making a bad situation worse by copying a screwy `user.da0`, say, over an almost OK `user.dat`. Mom and the crew conducted exhaustive experiments and came to the following conclusions:

- When you restart the computer (and you have to go all the way back out; logging on as a different user won't suffice), Win95 waits until *after* the first user logs on before it copies the current `\windows\system.dat` to `system.da0` and `\windows\user.dat` to `user.dao`. If you have Win95 set up so it doesn't require anybody to log on, the copy occurs sometime after `winstart.bat` runs but before the Taskbar appears.

- On a multiple-user profile system, when you restart the computer (again, you have to go all the way back out), `\windows\profile\username\user.dat` is only copied to `user.da0` for the first user to log onto the system. Backups are never made for any subsequent users.

Whoa! I didn't know that. You mean I have to be the first person to log onto the PC after a full warm boot for my user Registry settings to get backed up? That's obscene. Nobody warned me about that.

Yeah, as best we can tell, that's true. In fact, it's a little bit worse than that. If you set up a new user on your machine by "Logging on as a different user" and then typing in a new logon name, that new user won't *ever* get a .da0 file, unless at some time in the indeterminate future that user is the first one to log on after a full reboot.

You can also manually copy the .dat files any time you like, of course, and use those copies to restore the Registry to whatever status you like. If you'd like to keep close tabs on your Registry's status, consider using the Win95 program cfgback, described in Chapter 9.

Merging .reg Files

You now know that you can change Registry entries one at a time using regedit, or wholesale by copying over the system.dat or user.dat files. There's a third way to change the Registry that I want to cover before we get into the structure of Registry keys. You can change the Registry by using a .reg Registry merge file. I showed you a small-but-typical .reg file in Figure 11-3. Basically, a .reg file is just a simple text file that begins with the line REGEDIT4 and contains Registry keys in [brackets], with values following the keys. Running the .reg file (by double-clicking on it; right-clicking on it, and choosing Merge; or from inside regedit by clicking on Registry then Import Registry File) merges data from the .reg file into the Registry.

It isn't quite that simple, of course. We're talking Registry, here. If you expect simple, you're definitely in the wrong place. When Win95 merges a .reg file, it processes entries under each [key] as follows:

Step 1. Windows looks at the [key]. If that key starts with HKEY_DYN_DATA\, Windows spits out an error message and stops processing the .reg file. Ma Windows won't let you touch any Dynamic Data keys or values.

Step 2. If the key exists, Windows skips down to Step 4. If it does not exist, Windows tries to create a new key with that name.

Step 3. If the key starts with HKEY_CLASSES_ROOT\, HKEY_CURRENT_USER\, HKEY_LOCAL_MACHINE\, HKEY_USERS\, or HKEY_CURRENT_CONFIG\, a new key with the indicated name is created, and a value of (Default) (value not set) is entered for the key. If the key starts with anything other than one of those five established root names, you will *not* get an error message—in fact, you won't be notified of any problem at all—and the new key will *not* be created. Windows skips down the .reg file to the next key, and starts again at Step 1.

Step 4. If there are any values listed in the .reg file under the key, they're processed one by one. If a value name exists, the value data in the Registry is overwritten with whatever data appears in the .reg file. (Note that if the type of value data in the .reg file is different from the type of value data in the Registry, the Registry entry takes on the .reg file's data type—so if the Registry entry has, say, a binary zero and the .reg file has a character string "ABCD", the Registry entry is changed to be a character value, with data "ABCD".) If the value name does not exist, a new Registry value is created, based on the entry in the .reg file. Processing continues with the next key at Step 1.

 Wait a minute! If I read that right, you're saying that there's no way to construct a .reg file that deletes a key, deletes a value, or even renames a key or value. All you can do is add new keys under one of the politically correct five root keys, add values, or change value data. That's it. Ouch.

 Actually, Rush, it's worse than that. When merging .reg files, if Windows doesn't understand a particular line in the .reg file, it just ignores the problem and goes down to the next line, ultimately giving you the happy news that everything is well (Figure 11-4). Error messages are rare. Meaningful error messages are nonexistent.

Figure 11-4. The .reg **merge lie**

 Which leads me to one of my favorite bugs in all of Win. . .dumb. When Windows merges a .reg file, it looks at the first line of the file to make sure it says REGEDIT4. If you screw up that line just slightly—say, type REGEDIT 4, with a space—Win95 skips merging the whole file, but still gives you the Figure 11-4 message saying that everything has been merged successfully! Oh how I love a nice bug in the mornin'.

If you find that merging a `.reg` file doesn't do what you think it should, take a look at the file. Chances are good there's a quote missing, or a period in the wrong place, or a slightly misspelled name. Remember, when you're working with `.reg` files, you're working without a net.

`.inf` **and the Reg**

Those funny installation files I talked about in Chapter 9, the `.inf` files, can also manipulate Registry entries. They were set up that way to allow hardware manufacturers to put things in your Registry when you set up their hardware. Of course, you can take advantage of them, too, if you don't mind playing around with `.inf` files.

The *Windows Resource Kit* has a lengthy discussion of `.inf` files in Appendix C. Only one little problem: if you follow everything they say very carefully, you haven't a snowball's chance in hell of getting it to work. Some of the documentation errors are so egregious they'll keep you going in circles for days. At least they had Mom's crew tied up in knots for a long time, until they found a real, working `.inf` file that manipulates Registry entries, and then dissected it to figure out what would and would not work. (That file, in case you're interested, is `explore.inf`, and it's included in the Windows Power toys collection; it implements "Explore From Here.")

So let's shed a little light in this bastion of darkness. For our purposes, an `.inf` file can tell Win95 to add keys and/or values, or delete keys and/or values. An `.inf` file is a simple text file that looks a lot like an old-fashioned Windows 3.1 `.ini` file, with sections, keys, and the like. You "run" an `.inf` file by right-clicking on it and choosing Install. In our case, "Install" updates Registry entries. There's no error checking, no testing mode, no chance to see if the update proceeded without problem—indeed, there's no way to find out if the update even *ran,* except by examining contents of the Registry to see if they were changed. The syntax—at least the part of the syntax that I understand—is a bit strange, but that's par for the course.

Every `.inf` file (at least, every `.inf` file that works) starts with two lines:

```
[version]
signature="$CHICAGO$"
```

where `Chicago` can be uppercase or lowercase. Note that this is different from what the *WRK* says (that the `signature` must be `$Windows 95$`). The printed copy of the *WRK* (the dead tree version you spent $40 for) is wrong. Remarkably, the electronic version of the *WRK* (the one that comes free on the Win95 CD) is correct!

Every .inf file (at least, every .inf file that works by right-clicking and choosing Install) has a section that looks more or less like this:

```
[DefaultInstall]
AddReg = Some_Section
DelReg = Some_Other_Section
```

 Note that this is different from what the *WRK* says (that the Install section name has to be defined elsewhere in the .inf file, and that it can have any name). The *WRK* may well be right for many kinds of .inf files, but when it comes to the right-click install kind—the kind we're interested in—the *WRK* is wrong. For the .inf file to be installable with a right-click, you *must* use [DefaultInstall] as the name of the one and only Install section. (You 'Softies can see why if you look at the Registry key HKCR\inffile\shell\ install\ command, where DefaultInstall is clearly demanded.) Oh how I love a nice docbug in the morning.

The AddReg = line points to another section in the .inf file that contains a list of all keys and/or values that are to be added to the Registry. The DelReg = line points to another section in the .inf file that contains a list of all keys and/or values that are to be deleted from the Registry. An Add section might look something like this:

```
[Some_Section]
HKCR,txtfile\shell\SomeNewCommand\Command,,,"ZapIt.exe %1"
HKCU,AppEvents\Schemes\Apps\MyNewApp\Open\.Current,,,"tada.w av"
HKLM,Software\Microsoft\Windows\CurrentVersion\explorer\Tips ,50,,
"Always listen to your MOM!"
```

The general pattern for these entries is

```
MajorKey, Key, Value Name, Flags, Value Data
```

The MajorKey is one of the abbreviations

- HKCR, which is an abbreviation for HKEY_CLASSES_ROOT

- HKCU, which is an abbreviation for HKEY_CURRRENT_USER

- HKLM, which is an abbreviation for HKEY_LOCAL_MACHINE

we'll talk about later in this chapter. I have absolutely no idea what Flags means; couldn't find any details in any of the documentation, nor could I find any working examples.

The first line adds a new key to the Registry called HKEY_CLASSES_ROOT\txtfile\ shell\SomeNewCommand (assuming one does not already exist, of course). That key will have a (Default) value—all new keys get at least one value with that name—with (value not set) for data. In addition, there will be a second key set up called HKEY_CLASSES_ROOT\txtfile\shell\SomeNewCommand\Command, and it will have a (Default) value data of ZapIt.exe %1. You'll see in the section below on HKCR how that might be a valid entry, adding a new command to the right-click context menu for text files.

The second line adds the key HKEY_CURRENT_USER\AppEvents\Schemes\Apps\ MyNewApp\Open\.Current to the Registry, with a (Default) value data of tada.wav.

As you'll see later in the section on HKCU, this is a legitimate Registry entry that tells Windows to play the tada.wav sound every time an application called MyNewApp starts.

The third line shows how to add a new value to an existing key. In this case, Windows adds a value called 50 with data Always listen to your MOM! to the monstrously long-winded key HKEY_LOCAL_MACHINE\Software\Microsoft\Windows\ CurrentVersion\ explorer\Tips. As you'll see in the section on HKLM, this will put one new tip in the hopper to appear on your Windows startup/welcome screen.

A Delete section might look like this:

```
[Some_Other_Section]
HKCR,txtfile\shell\SomeNewCommand\Command
HKCU,AppEvents\Schemes\Apps\MyNewApp\Open\.Current,,,"tada.wav"
HKLM,Software\Microsoft\Windows\CurrentVersion\explorer\Tips ,
50,, "Always listen to your MOM!"
```

The first line deletes the key HKEY_CLASSES_ROOT\txtfile\shell\ SomeNewCommand\Command, but it leaves the key HKEY_CLASSES_ROOT\ txtfile\shell\SomeNewCommand intact.

The second line deletes the key HKEY_CURRENT_USER\AppEvents\ Schemes\Apps\MyNewApp\Open\.Current, but it leaves all keys above it intact.

This line also shows you that you can leave the extraneous garbage (`, , , "tada.wav"`) at the end of the line, and the key will still be deleted.

The third line only deletes the value named `50` from the `. . .\Tips` key. All the keys remain the same; specifying that a value be deleted does not delete the associated key, and again the extraneous garbage at the end is ignored.

As best I can tell, you can have any number of Add and Delete sections in the same `.inf` file, but if a single key or value appears in both an Add and a Delete section, heaven only knows whether the key or value will show up in the Registry after the `.inf` file is through running. Following is a perfectly legitimate Registry-manipulating `.inf` file, which will run on your machine. To run it, simply create a New text document, type this in, rename the file with an `.inf` extension, right-click on the file and pick Install.

```
[version]
signature="$Chicago$"

[DefaultInstall]
AddReg = MomLikesThis
DelReg = MomSaysGiveItTheHeaveHo

[MomLikesThis]
HKLM,Software\Microsoft\Windows\CurrentVersion\explorer\Tips ,
50,, "Always listen to your MOM!"

[MomSaysGiveItTheHeaveHo]
HKCU,AppEvents\Schemes\Apps\MyNewApp\Open\.Current
HKCR,txtfile\shell\SomeNewCommand\Command,,,"ZapIt.exe %1"
```

I believe all of this is previously undocumented.

The Mysterious Fifth

Think we've hit all the ways of changing the Registry? Well, there's one more way. Sometimes you'll go in with `regedit` and delete a key or a value. Then you'll come back a day later and the key or value has mysteriously reappeared. Change it or delete it, and a day or two later it comes back again. What could be happening?

Ends up that there's a small set of settings in `win.ini` that Win95 takes upon itself to post to the Registry every time Windows restarts. If you repeatedly delete or change an entry, and can't figure out why it's changing back, look first in your `win.ini`.

Note that these settings are *different* from the ones that are migrated from Win31 to Win95 during setup. They're also different from the settings that are intentionally maintained in `win.ini` for compatibility purposes. These settings are actually copied, wholesale, from `win.ini` to the Registry every time you start Windows.

Final Word on `.reg`

One last, crucial point, before you start poking around with your Registry. The *Windows Resource Kit,* and every book I've seen that discusses `.reg` files, would have you believe that you can save a complete backup of the current status of a key or group of keys by exporting a `.reg` file from `regedit`. Then, presumably, you can muck around with the key all you want and if you get in trouble, merging the `.reg` file back into the Registry will set everything right. Well, you now know that isn't entirely true. If you manually add a value to a key, for example, merging the old `.reg` file won't get rid of the value. If you rename a key, merging the `.reg` file won't remove the renamed key, it'll just restore the old key. In some cases—particularly when Win95 is looking for the presence of a key or a value— that can make a big difference. Using `.reg` files will *not* restore your Registry: to make a full and complete backup, you have to make a copy of the `system.dat,  user.dat` and `\profiles\username\ user.dat` files, and use them appropriately.

Alternatively, you can save a key to a `.reg` file, do whatever you like to that key in the Registry, then when you're ready to restore the key to its original status, manually delete the key before importing the `.reg` file back into the Registry. This approach leaves you hanging without a key for a while, so use it with extreme caution.

Some books strongly suggest that you *not* use `regedit` directly to change a value or key in the Registry. They insist that it's better to export a Registry key, make changes to the resulting `.reg` file, and then merge the changed key. I say balderdash. While it's certainly important to make backups of any key before changing it—and overall backups of the entire Registry from time to time, too—this slavish insistence on only editing a `.reg` text file is a crock.

Just for starters, as Erwin pointed out, you can't delete or rename keys or values using a `.reg` file: if you want to delete anything, you have to go in with `regedit` and do it manually. More than that, though, mucking around with the `"oops"="c:\\weird\\\".reg\\file\\\"format"` is a pain in the neck. Miss one of those dumb doubled-up backslashes, or type in a quote without a requisite backslash, and you'll not only screw up the Registry setting, the merge is so dumb you'll never even know something went wrong!

Besides, manually editing `.reg` files adds several extra steps to the process of editing the Registry—you have to export the key, use a text editor, then remerge the key—without giving you any benefit.

Working with `.reg` files is error-prone. It's slow. It's cumbersome. And it doesn't add any safety to the process. So why bother? Keep good backups, and use `regedit` directly.

Gettin' Around

> Whatever deceives seems to exercise a kind of magical enchantment.
>
> —Plato, *The Republic,* ca. 350 B.C.

It's taken me all this long to poke around the periphery of the Registry, and for that I apologize, but it's important that you know whence the Registry originates, and how you can safely change it. Now it's time to dive in with both feet.

You may find some of what follows rather rocky going. As is so often the case in Win95, there are dozens of new concepts you need to "get"—and for everything to make sense, you have to "get" them all at the same time. The Registry is a very complicated place. So take your time, and try to bite off small chunks. Make sure you have your computer handy, and follow along in `regedit` as we take a look.

The Registry, as mentioned earlier, consists of six major keys (I call them "root keys," but you can call 'em chicken soup if you like). Figure 11-5 shows you what those root keys look like, from `regedit`'s point of view. If you've read this far in Chapter 11, it probably won't surprise you one bit to discover that there's some real sleight-of-hand going on here. For openers, there are really just three root keys, and one of those three can't be changed at all by you. And therein lies a story . . .

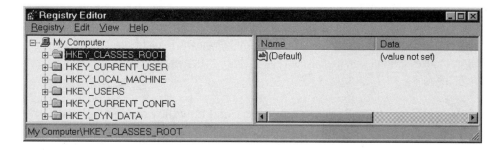

Figure 11-5. The root keys

Aliases

The root key HKEY_CURRENT_CONFIG is a sham. It's just an alias, a handy bit of shorthand, that points to the current configuration information in HKEY_LOCAL_MACHINE (or HKLM to the cognoscenti). If you have just one hardware profile, or if you have multiple hardware profiles but Win95 is currently using the first profile, the current configuration information is in HKLM\Config\0001 and HKEY_CURRENT_CONFIG is the same thing as HKLM\Config\0001. What do I mean by "the same thing"? Pop into regedit, and scroll down to HKLM\Confg\0001\Display. Double-click on (Default) and give it a value of "Mom says HI." Scroll down to

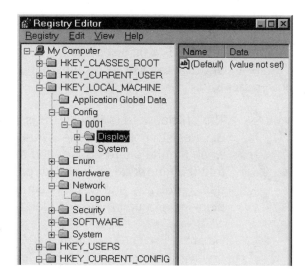

Figure 11-6. HKEY_CURRENT_CONFIG

HKEY_CURRENT_CONFIG\ Display. See how the value has been changed? Now single-click on (Default) and hit Del. The value data turns into (value not set), right? Scroll back to HKLM\Config\0001\Display. It's reverted to (value not set), yes?

Three of the root keys are really aliases for other keys. Microsoft set them up that way to make it easier for programmers to get in and out of frequently used parts of the Registry. For example, a program that makes changes to entries for the current hardware configuration could monkey around with HKLM, query the Registry to see which hardware profile is in use (it's almost always \0001), and then work directly with HKLM\Config\0001 (or whichever hardware profile happens to be in effect). Instead of requiring programmers to go through all that garbage, it's far, far simpler for the Registry to set up this pseudo-key called `HKEY_CURRENT_CONFIG` and just point it to `HKLM\Config\0001` (or whichever hardware profile happens to be in effect). That way, programmers need only monkey around with this aliased key `HKEY_CURRENT_CONFIG`, and the system will take care of the rest.

Let's take an eagle's-eye view of the Registry's root keys and how they are interrelated.

Classes

The root key `HKEY_CLASSES_ROOT` (also known as `HKCR`) is an alias for `HKLM\ SOFTWARE\ Classes`. It's a huge key; on Mom's machine there are more than four hundred sub-keys for this key alone. This is where Windows goes when it wants to associate a filename extension with a particular program, or a group of Windows objects with actions on those objects. When you double-click on a filename, run something with the Start/Run command, or right-click on just about anything, Windows checks this key to see what to do. I'll talk about `HKCR` extensively, as it harbors a very large percentage of Win95's cool power-user tricks.

The official word is that HKCR is essentially the same thing as the Windows 3.1 Registration Database. What a crock! There's plenty of stuff in `HKCR` that wasn't in the old RegBase, and there's plenty of stuff in the old RegBase that isn't in `HKCR`. It isn't like programs are looking for `HKCR`—they don't use `regedit`, and `HKCR` is simply an alias, an illusion created for humans plunking around in `regedit` and a shorthand for some programmers.

We actually put HKCR up at the top of `regedit` to make it easier for users to find the settings they'll want to look at most often. Not that I'm encouraging people to change their Registry settings manually, of course.

Current User

The `HKEY_CURRENT_USER` (HKCU) root key is also an alias. If there is only one user profile, it's an alias for `HKEY_USERS\.Default`. If the machine is set up for multiple-user profiles, it's an alias for the `HKEY_USERS\username` associated with the currently logged-on user, or, if the user bypassed the logon screen, `HKEY_USERS\.Default`.

HKCU was set up as an alias to keep programmers from having to constantly figure out which user is currently logged on to the machine.

Much information about Windows itself sits in the key `HKCU\Software\Microsoft\`
`Windows\CurrentVersion\` and the keys directly underneath it. I'll talk about `HKCU`
extensively in the rest of this chapter: it's a whole lot easier than constantly referring to "the
`HKEY_USERS` key for the currently logged-on user."

Speaking of convenience, why in the hell do I have to click down seven levels
in the Registry to get to the Windows settings? If Microsoft is going to insist
that it takes 7-level and 8-level keys to organize its own information (like,
say, `HKCU\Software\Microsoft\Windows\CurrentVersion\`
`Explorer\Streams\12`), the least they could do is provide easy ways to
get to the common fifth-level keys like `HKCU\Software\Microsoft\Windows\`
`CurrentVersion\`. There should be some sort of bookmark capability, or at least a
handful of common keys with icons on a toolbar, for heaven's sake.

Local Machine

HKEY_LOCAL_MACHINE (or HKLM), to a first approximation anyway, contains
information about the PC, the information stored in `system.dat`. I'll talk about `HKLM`
extensively later in this chapter, too.

The big key in `HKLM` is `HKLM\SOFTWARE\Microsoft\Windows\Current`
`Version`, which is roughly analogous to the `HKCU` key with the similar name, but
generally includes machine-dependent (instead of user-dependent) data.

Users

The root key HKEY_USERS has either one or two subkeys. On a single-user profile
machine, there's one subkey and it's called `HKEY_USERS\.Default` (note the period).
On a multiple-user profile machine where the currently active user bypassed the network
logon, there's only a `\.Default` subkey, too. On a multiple-user profile machine with a
logged on user, there's a `\.Default` subkey, plus one more subkey for the active user. The
name of the subkey is the same as the logon username of the user, which in turn is the same
as the name of the `\windows\profiles\username` folder.

Lots of sources, including the *WRK,* will tell you that there are
HKEY_USERS subkeys for all valid users. That isn't true, as a quick glance at
any multiple-user profile machine's `regedit` will confirm. If it were true,
you could go in and monkey around with other users' settings—a definite
no-no. Amazing how many books and articles just parrot the official
documentation, without even looking at the real world, eh?

I won't refer to HKEY_USERS very often, simply because the data you're most likely interested in changing sits inside the alias HKCU.

Current Configuration

Root key HKEY_CURRENT_CONFIG is another alias, as explained in Figure 11-6. It points to the currently active hardware profile, most commonly HKLM\Config\0001.

We won't be talking about HKEY_CURRENT_CONFIG in the rest of this chapter because none of the HKLM\Config\0001 information is particularly interesting, with one exception. If you're browsing quickly through the Registry to retrieve the name of the currently active printer (or writing a program that needs to find it, for that matter), and there's any chance the PC may have multiple hardware configurations, you should use HKEY_CURRENT_CONFIG to get the name, instead of HKLM\Config\0001.

Dynamic Data

 Quite probably the least-understood—or, equivalently, worst-documented—key of all, the third real root key HKEY_DYN_DATA contains information about the current hardware configuration (in the \Config Manager\Enum subkey), in addition to a whole slew of performance data (in \PerfStats).

 Why do you say it's the worst-documented key, Sarah? The *Windows Resource Kit* says HKEY_DYN_DATA "points to a branch of HKLM." Let me look in regedit. Oh, I see. It *doesn't* point to a branch of HKLM or anything else; it isn't an alias at all. The *WRK* makes a big deal out of the fact that this information isn't stored on disk—but it isn't the kind of stuff you'd want to keep from session to session anyway. Hmmmmm . . . I see what you mean.

 It's important to realize that the \Enum subkey here really does describe the machine in its current state—Plug 'n Play devices and all. \Enum is maintained dynamically. On startup, once the profile has been established, Win95 uses HKLM hardware information (generally stored in keys identified by \0000, for hardware that isn't dependent on the profile, or the profile number, such as \0001) to configure the machine, and all the information on the current configuration is transferred to HKEY_DYN_DATA.

As an example, Figure 11-7 shows the kind of information that's stored for your PC's Programmable Interrupt Controller. Since the PIC is always the same, regardless of hardware profile, its information is stored in a key named \0000. Similar information for, say, a monitor—which can be changed, based on hardware profile, is stored in keys named HKLM\Enum\Monitor\Default_Monitor\0001,

\0002, etc., where the number of keys depends on the number of hardware profiles defined on the machine.

Figure 11-8 shows how some of the PIC information has been shuffled to a different location in HKEY_DYN_DATA. Note, in particular, how the BootConfig value in HKLM has become the Allocation value in HKEY_DYN_DATA.

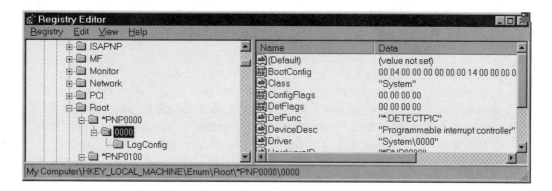

Figure 11-7. PIC info in HKLM

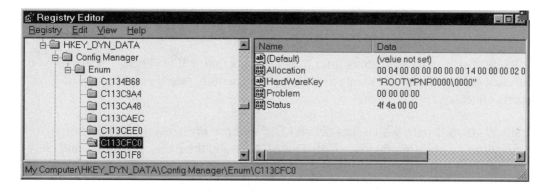

Figure 11-8. Same info in HKEY_DYN_DATA

Although you can't change any of the values in HKEY_DYN_DATA, the \Enum subkey is the ultimate place to go if you need the absolute truth on what Windows thinks is attached to your PC. By following the pointers there back to HKLM\Enum, where human-readable hardware descriptions await, you can tell precisely what hardware is active.

Now let's go through each of the big three root keys one at a time and see what kind of mischief we can get into.

HKCR

> Half the world knows not how the other half lives.

> —George Herbert, *Outlandish Proverbs,* 1640

The HKEY_CLASSES_ROOT key (or HKCR) is an alias for HKLM\SOFTWARE\Classes. It's a machine-related key, stored in system.dat, that doesn't vary depending on which user has logged on; and used to store information about file types, entries on right-click context menus, and some Property sheets.

 Wait a minute. You think I'm going to buy the Microsoft Party Line about system.dat containing all the data in HKLM, and user.dat storing all the data in HKCU? I don't believe it for a second. It's too clean, and Win95 is anything *but* clean. I bet, if you looked hard enough, you'd find some of the HKCU data in system.dat and some of the HKLM data in user.dat.

Orientation

 HKCR contains hundreds of entries. The sheer volume can be quite overwhelming, until you discover that there are really only six different kinds of entries:

- The HKCR* key, which contains links to commands that will (1) appear whenever you right-click on any file, or (2) create new Property sheet tabs when you bring up a Property sheet for any file;

- The HKCR\CLSID key, which lists "class I.D.s"—those mysterious 32-character identification numbers (commonly called CLSIDs)—and the icons, programs, and various settings associated with each CLSID;

- Hundreds of HKCR\.extension keys, identifiable by the period at the beginning of the subkey name, each of which associates that particular filename extension with a program I.D. (which I'll call a ProgID);

- Hundreds of HKCR\ProgID keys, which contain commands appropriate for the ProgID—such as Open, or Print—plus icons and occasional miscellaneous information pertaining to the ProgID.

- The HKCR\Unknown key, which behaves much like a HKCR\ProgID subkey, but applies to files with extensions that don't appear in HKCR; and

- The `HKCR\QuickView` key, which lists all the filename extensions for files with supported QuickView viewers.

The Plus! Pack also installs a unique key called `HKCR\MIME`, which stores MIME information about various file extensions. You can read about MIME in Chapter 4.

I'll get into details momentarily, but I want you to pause and consider one thing. Perhaps the single most brilliant part of the design of Win95 is its ability—even its *willingness*—to have programmers and users go in and change these settings. When you hear that Win95 has an "extensible shell," or when you read that a package has "Win95 shell extensions," or when you install a new software package and suddenly find that it has put its tentacles in all sorts of fancy places (right-click context menus, say, or Property sheets), this is where the magic originates.

Thank you, thank you. Actually, it took quite a leap of faith on the part of our developers to put these extensibility hooks into Win95, so developers can weave their new programs into the fabric of Windows itself, instead of patching onto the periphery with jackhammers and earthmovers. In the past we tended to build monolithic, insular systems, thinking that we were giving our users the best possible technology, and discouraging developers and advanced users from piddling around in places they didn't belong. What we found, though, was that developers and advanced users would hack into the bloody thing anyway. Taking a cue from our applications people (where WinWord was, arguably, the first significantly user-extensible Windows application), we decided that, this time around, we'd build Windows so it could be customized reliably by thousands of developers—thus, shell extensions like these.

That's a nice sales pitch, Billy95, but I think that what you really found was that you couldn't keep up with all the other developers. Microsoft doesn't have a monopoly on smarts, you know, and these other developers brought important new ideas to the party that Microsoft either didn't think about or decided not to implement. By giving them solid hooks into Win95 itself, Windows could start looking more like an easily extensible, customizable system, instead of an unstable deck of cards that threatened to collapse each time an outside developer had a great new idea.

Boys, boys, boys. Quit your bickering. The simple fact is that these HKCR keys give users and developers alike an unparalleled opportunity to customize the way Win95 works. I've already shown you, way back in Chapter 3, how a few changes to HKCR can turn the dumb way Win95 handles Explorer windows into a much smarter configuration. Now I'm going to show you the rest of the story.

\.extension **to** \ProgID **and Back**

 By far the large majority of entries in HKCR are HKCR\.extension subkeys that point to HKCR\ProgIDs, and the HKCR\ProgID subkeys themselves. The method Win95 uses to link extensions to ProgIDs is simplicity itself.

Take simple text files, the ones with a .txt extension. Figure 11-9 shows you how Win95 has associated the .txt extension with the ProgID called txtfile, using the (Default) value for the HKCR\.txt key. If you look in your Registry, you'll find the same association. (The Content Type value was put in the Registry by the Plus! Pack. You can follow its development through these screen shots, too.)

When Win95 needs to know what to do with a .txt file, it looks in HKCR for a key called HKCR\.txt. It then takes the (Default) value of that key and uses the value data to search for a ProgID—in this case, HKCR\txtfile. Figure 11-10 shows you what the txtfile ProgID entry in the Registry looks like.

Figure 11-9. .txt in Registry

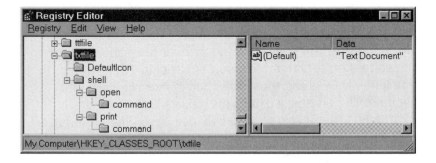

Figure 11-10. txtfile ProgID in Registry

Multiple HKCR\.extension keys may well point to the same ProgID. For example, unless you've done something to change it, if you look in your Registry you'll find that both HKCR\.bmp and HKCR\.pcx point to the ProgID Paint.Picture, which is the

ProgID for Microsoft Paint. Also note that the extensions need not be three characters long: they go from one character on up.

If you look at Figure 11-10, you'll see how the `HKCR\txtfile` key has two subkeys. The `HKCR\txtfile\DefaultIcon` key contains information Win95 uses to produce an icon (on the Desktop or in Explorer) for each file with the `.txt` extension. The `(Default)` value of this key follows the usual Win95 icon naming conventions, that is, it contains the name of a file containing an icon (generally, a `.dll`, `.exe`, or `.ico` file), and if the file has more than one icon in it, a number that points to which icon you've chosen. Icon numbers start at zero, so the value data `c:\windows\notepad.exe, 1` in this entry would signify the second icon in the file `notepad.exe`.

The `HKCR\txtfile\shell` key holds all the details Windows itself needs to handle `txtfiles`, and that gets a little complicated.

ProgIDs and File Types

If you open up Explorer, click on View, then Options, bring up the File Types tab, and scroll down to the Text Document line, you'll see something like Figure 11-11.

Every time you open the File Types dialog, it looks at all the entries in `HKCR` and builds a big table, listing all `HKCR\.extension` keys, their associated `HKCR\ProgID` keys, and a whole bunch of ancillary stuff. The Registered File Types list in Figure 11-11 is constructed in a rather complex way:

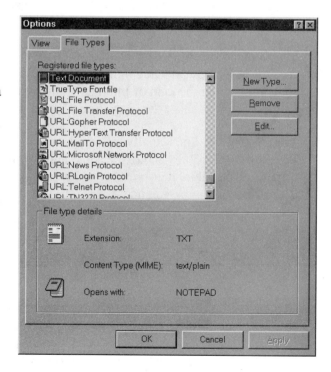

* Windows scans all the `HKCR\.extension` keys and keeps track of all the referenced ProgIDs. These are potential candidates for inclusion in the Registered File Types list box in Figure 11-11.

* Windows then looks at all the `HKCR\ProgID` keys that were referenced by `HKCR\.extension` keys. It

Figure 11-11. txtfile in File Types

collects the (Default) values associated with those keys. If the (Default) value data is (value not set), that particular HKCR\ProgID is ignored. Otherwise, the (Default) value data is used as a potential entry in the Registered File Types list box.

- Finally, Windows looks for values called EditFlags under each of the HKCR\ProgID keys. If it finds an EditFlags value name, the value data may force Windows to either include or exclude this particular key from the Registered File Types list box. For example, in this way, a ProgID like Drive appears on the list even though it has no associated extension. I'll discuss all the EditFlags in a section called, uh, Edit Flags, coming up in a bit.

 As you can see from Figure 11-10, the HKCR\txtfile key's (Default) value data is Text Document, and that's the entry that gets put in Figure 11-11's Registered File Types list box. If you look at the File Type Details box in Figure 11-11, you'll see that the File Types tab can tell you a few more things about the txtfile ProgID (although, surprisingly, the ProgID itself never appears):

- The Extension line tells you which HKCR\.extension keys point to HKCR\txtfile. In this case, HKCR\.txt is the only key that points to HKCR\txtfile.

- The Content Type (MIME) line comes from the Plus! Pack. It just displays the data of the Content Type value in the HKCR\.txt key, which is supposed to tell you something about the kind of Internet Multimedia Extensions data that would be included in a Net file with this extension. (See Chapter 4 for a discussion of MIME.)

- The Opens With line actually traces all the way down the HKCR\txtfile\shell\ open\command key and extracts the name of the program stored as that key's (Default) value. It also retrieves the icon associated with that program and displays it here. Pretty impressive, no?

 If you click once on Text Document, and then click Edit, you'll get something that looks like the Edit File Type box shown in Figure 11-12. I'll go into some detail on the Actions box momentarily, but first let's look at the less interesting features of the Edit File Type box:

- If you click on Change Icon, you'll have an opportunity to change the contents of the HKCR\txtfile\DefaultIcon key, which in turn affects the icon displayed in front of all txtfile files in Explorer or on the Desktop. Note in particular how you can only change the icon for the entire ProgID, and not for individual extensions.

- If you change Description of Type, you'll modify the (Default) value data for HKCR\txtfile, just as you would expect.

- The Content Type and Default Extension boxes merely let you choose from all the HKCR\.extension values that go into this ProgID. (Recall that Content Type is a value of the extension, not the ProgID, so there may be several of them.) Since txtfile has only one extension, HKCR\.txt, there is only one choice in each box.

- Down at the bottom, checking the Enable Quick View box puts a \Quickview subkey underneath the ProgID, in this case creating a HKCR\txtfile\Quickview key

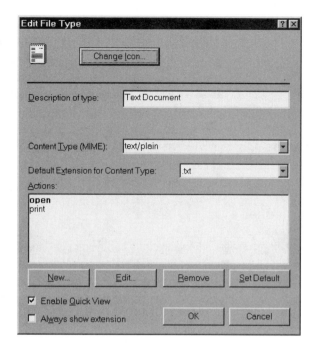

Figure 11-12. Edit txtfile

with a (Default) value data of *. (The * apparently tells the Quickviewer to look at the selected file.) The presence of the HKCR\txtfile\Quickview key, in turn, adds "Quick View" to the right-click Context menu for all txtfiles, as we'll see in a moment, in the section called Keys and Context Menus.

- The Always show extension box creates a value in the HKCR\txtfile key called AlwaysShowExt. Ends up that the data for that value doesn't matter—all that's important is the presence of the value. When Explorer finds a ProgID with an AlwaysShowExt value, it always shows the filename extension for that ProgID, even when the View/Options box marked "Hide MS-DOS file extensions for file types that are registered" box is checked. If you've ever wondered why .dll (ProgID = dllfile) and .sys files (ProgID = sysfile) always appear in Explorer with their filename extensions, look at their ProgID keys and you'll see that they have an AlwaysShowExt value. Note that AlwaysShowExt is a valid value for HKCR\ProgID keys only: if you put an AlwaysShowExt value in an HKCR\.extension key, it will have no effect. There's also a value called NeverShowExt that does precisely the opposite. (Look at HKCR\DocShortcut, HKCR\lnkfile, HKCR\piffile, and HKCR\ShellScrap for samples.) It has to be set manually.

For what it's worth, there's a value called `NoExtension` that is used for Briefcase files. If you look at `HKCR\.bfc\ShellNew\Config` you'll probably see a `NoExtension` value. Briefcases never have extensions. The `.bfc` entry here is a complete phantom. The only reason for its existence, as far as I can tell, is to provide a place for the `HKCR\.bfc\ShellNew` key, so "New Briefcase" will show up in the Desktop's right-click "New" menu. Apparently `NoExtension` was invented to keep this little kludge from confusing users. Oh, how I love a nice kludge in the mornin'!

So much for the easy parts of the Edit File Type dialog. Let's look at the tough one.

\shell

The Actions box here in the Edit File Type dialog puts a pretty, relatively easy to use face on one of the most powerful features of Win95. It lets you define new entries for the right-click context menus and, in some cases, lets you choose the "default" action—the one that Win95 takes when you double-click on a filename. To really understand what's going on, though—and to see how Win95 occasionally screws things up royally—you really have to see how changes here are reflected in the Registry.

Pick the first action in the alphabetical list, the one marked `open`, and click Edit. You should get a dialog similar to that in Figure 11-13.

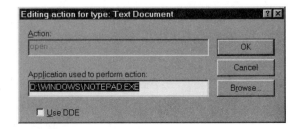

Figure 11-13. Open in File Types

See how the command `d:\windows\notepad.exe` in Figure 11-13 is translated into the similar (but different) command `d:\windows\notepad.exe %1` in the Registry, Figure 11-14? `%1` says to Windows, "Put the name of the current file right here before you run the command."

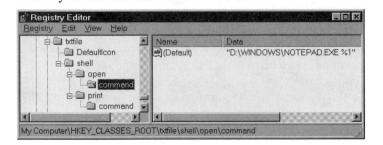

Figure 11-14. Open in the Registry

It's all automatic. Any command entered into the Editing action for type: dialog for a particular actionname gets a %1 stuck on the end, and the resulting command goes into the Registry's \shell\actionname\command key's (Default) value.

If you go back to the Edit File Type dialog, click on the print action, and click Edit; you'll see how the print action actually happens—with a /p command line switch fed to Notepad, as in Figure 11-15. The resulting Registry entry (Figure 11-16), once again, gets a %1 appended to it. That %1 is all well and good for some programs, but for others it can be the kiss of death. See the section called %1 Bugs later in this chapter.

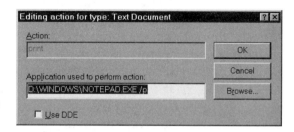

Figure 11-15. Print in File Types

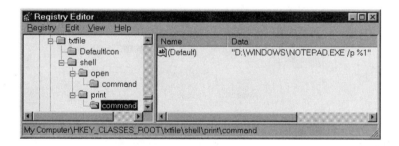

Figure 11-16. Print in the Registry

The "Use DDE" box you see at the bottom of Figure 11-13 and Figure 11-15 opens up an extended box that lets you enter Dynamic Data Exchange commands, which are placed in the \shell\actionname\ddeexec key and keys underneath it. (See Figures 11-17 and 11-18.)

The standard .doc file open command (ProgID = Word.Document.6) is implemented as a DDE command. If you have WinWord installed on your machine, look at the Explorer File Type called Microsoft Word Document and the key HKCR\Word.Document.6. Oh—in case you wondered, the /w switch on the WinWord command line starts Word without the Tip of the Day.

A thorough discussion of DDE is beyond the scope of this book, but suffice it to say that you can use DDE in many situations where a command line doesn't give you all the options you need to implement a particular action. Many more details are in *Windows 3.1 Programming for Mere Mortals,* by Woody Leonhard.

Far as I'm concerned, it's very odd that Explorer and the Registry only implement old-fashioned Dynamic Data Exchange, and not OLE Automation—which is infinitely more flexible and more stable, especially under Win95. Microsoft probably figured it would have to create an entire macro language to drive OLE Auto—or force people to buy Visual Basic 4, which would be a very popular decision, all the way from the front page of *InfoWorld* to the most obscure offices at the Justice Department. Oh well. Gotta leave something for Win00, I guess.

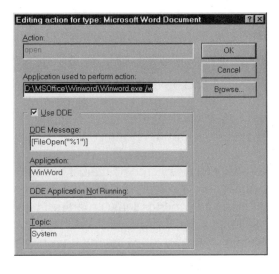

Figure 11-17. DDE in File Types

Before I leave the \shell discussion, I should mention that a very few HKCR\.extension keys have \shell subkeys hanging under them. (The \shell subkeys almost always go underneath HKCR\ProgID keys.) I've been told that these \shell subkeys exist for backward compatibility, notably for Microsoft's own PowerPoint (.pps) and Multimedia Viewer

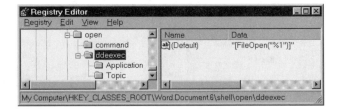

Figure 11-18. DDE in the Registry

(.mvb) files, and for other vendors' applications, including Paradox (.sdl) files, and others.

Default Action

Let me cap off the discussion of the things you can do with Explorer to change HKCR by looking at the so-called "default action" for ProgIDs. Move back to the Edit File Type box (Figure 11-12) for a moment. See how the open action name is highlighted? That's because open is the default action for txtfiles—if you double-click on a txtfile the open action is invoked; if you right-click on a txtfile, Open is highlighted. (See Figure 11-20, later.)

Most of the time, the default action for a ProgID key is open. Notable exceptions include audio files, where the default action is play. In general, you can change the default action for a ProgID by clicking the Action you want to become the default in the Edit File Type dialog, then clicking Set Default. (Sometimes Edit Flags will prevent you from doing so; see "Edit Flags," discussed later.)

 The new default action is stored in the `HKCR\ProgID\shell` key as the `(Default)` value. If the `(Default)` value data is `(value not set)` or an empty string, a default action of `open` is always assumed, if that action exists. If it does not exist, the default action is chosen from the other so-called canonical verbs (`print`, `explorer`, `find`, `openas`, and `properties`), if any of those exist. And if none of those exist, the first action, listed alphabetically, becomes the default action—although it isn't advertised as such on the Edit File Type dialog.

HKCR* **and** \unknown

Now that you know how the `HKCR\.extension` keys are related to `HKCR\ProgID` keys, these two should be pretty obvious. The `HKCR\*` key contains entries that apply to all files, regardless of their filename extension.

The `HKCR\Unknown` key contains entries that apply to files with extensions that do not have an `HKCR\.extension` key. Not surprisingly, the `HKCR\Unknown` key contains an `AlwaysShowExt` value, so Explorer will always show the unregistered filename extension. Its default action (and only action, for that matter) is `openas`. This is the only `openas` action that appears in the default Windows setup. When Windows encounters an `openas` command, it is translated to `Open With...` on the context menu.

 Many files without recognized extensions are ASCII text files. You might want to add an action for `HKCR\Unknown` called `notepad`.

Directory, Drive, Folder

 Files, files, files. All we've been talking about so far are files. Well, Windows does a lot more than files, and `HKCR` covers many non-file bases. Just for starters, `HKCR` has four `ProgID` keys that have nothing to do with files:

* `HKCR\Folder` contains information used whenever you right-click on a "virtual" folder, like My Computer, Network Neighborhood, Printers, or Dial-Up Networking, or bring up a Property sheet for a folder. (By "virtual" folder, I mean one that isn't physically a folder on a disk drive.) Actions are `explore`, which just cranks up Explorer, and `open`.

- HKCR\Drive holds information used when you right-click on a drive, or bring up a Property sheet for a drive. (More accurately, \Drive refers to root directories, including those on mapped drives.) The only action in a fresh Windows installation is find. (If you took Sarah's advice in Chapter 3 to make Explorer smart, open is also an action, as are several others if you followed all of Sarah's advice.) Windows has some built-in code that makes HKCR\Drive a daughter of HKCR\Folder, in the sense that whenever you do something that would use the contents of HKCR\Drive Registry keys, Windows behaves as if all the entries under the HKCR\Folder key were stuck under HKCR\Drive, too. So, for example, the explore action from HKCR\Folder shows up on the context menu when you right-click on a drive.

- HKCR\Directory has the settings for physical folders—or those things that used to be known, in pre-Win95 days, as directories. The only action is find—again, unless you followed along in Chapter 3, in which case you have find, open, and several others. Windows also treats HKCR\Directory as a daughter of HKCR\Folder.

- HKCR\AudioCD, similarly, has nothing to do with files. It has one action, play. Amazingly, though, in the Win95 hierarchy, HKCR\AudioCD is considered to be a daughter of HKCR\Drive (which, in turn, is a daughter of HKCR\Folder).

All this daughter key-cum-object-oriented inheritance would be very touching, if it were implemented worth a damn. As it stands, the only Registry inheritance is this obscure four-way interaction with Folder as the, uh, mother, Drive and Directory as the two daughters, and AudioCD hanging off Drive like a neglected stepsister. It's hard-coded into Windows; there's no way to set up your own inheritance schemes; it isn't documented anywhere. Worst of all, the "inheritance" doesn't obey any traditional inheritance rules: stick an open command in Folder, and another one in Drive, and they *both* show up on the context menu! Sheesh.

HKCR\CLSID

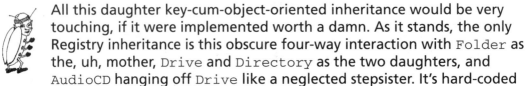

Perhaps the most important non-file part of HKCR revolves around treatment of class I.D.s, numbers that uniquely identify programs, commonly called CLSIDs. No doubt you've seen class I.D.s. They're written down as 32-hex characters, like this: {21ec2020-3aea-1069-a2dd-08002b30309d}, in an 8-4-4-4-12 pattern. Pretty hard to miss. Lots of Win95 tricks you'll see in books and magazines use CLSIDs, but the articles always seem to start mumbling when trying to explain *why* the tricks work. That's too bad, really, because the concept is pretty simple, and the implementation in Win95 isn't all that much more complicated.

Microsoft has set up a simple way for programmers to come up with a unique number, a unique CLSID, for each program they create. The procedure for getting the number isn't really important;* the important point is that each CLSID is unique, so Program A from Adams Amalgamated in Atlanta has a different number from Program D from Dubious Distribution in Dubuque, and both of those numbers are different from the hundred-plus numbers Microsoft has assigned to its hundred-plus programs in Win95.

You already know that when Win95 wants to figure out how to handle, oh, .txt files, it looks in the Registry for HKCR\.txt, and proceeds from that point. In a very similar manner, every time Win95 encounters a CLSID, it looks up the CLSID in HKCR\CLSID and runs the indicated program, which is usually a standard Windows .dll file.

What's a little bit different is the myriad ways Win95 can bump into a CLSID. Let me try to list all the ways I know about. (This is probably far from exhaustive.)

- A CLSID can appear as a filename extension. Just as the .txt extension triggers a look-up in the Registry for HKCR\.txt, a CLSID extension also triggers a look-up, in HKCR\CLSID. I haven't been able to get this to do anything interesting, but if you put the CLSID for a particular application (e.g., EXCEL) at the end of a filename, Explorer will show the file to be of that type (e.g., EXCEL Spreadsheet).

- A CLSID can appear as the filename extension for an entry on the Start Menu. This is the mechanism behind the trick for putting the Control Panel, Printers, or Dial-Up Networking fly-outs on the Start Menu, as described in Chapter 3. When your mouse goes over the Control Panel entry on the Start Menu, Win95 looks at the file name of the entry, strips off the CLSID filename extension, looks in HKCR\CLSID\{21ec2020-3aea-1069-a2dd-08002b30309d} and brings up the indicated program (from the InProcServer key), which is smart enough to say, "Oh! I'm on the Start Menu! I better show the Control Panel fly-out."

---

* Alright, you want the details, don't you? Inquisitive bugger. There's a program called guidgen.exe in the Win95 *Software Development Kit*. For some reason a different program called uuidgen.exe is included with the Win95 *Driver Development Kit*. When you run either program, it looks at the current machine's network card (which contains a unique number assigned by the board manufacturers), combines that information with the current day and time, and pops out a unique 32-hex-character number. The chances of any two different copies of guidgen.exe or uuidgen.exe running on two different machines coming up with the same CLSID are roughly equivalent to the chances of the Beatles getting back together and giving a free concert on top of the Apple building in January 2099, or the chances that Bill really knew all the lyrics of the Stones tune *Start It Up* before he bought the rights.

- A CLSID can appear as a value, or even a key, in the Registry. Take a look at Figure 11-19, a shot of HKCR*\shellex\PropertySheetHandlers, for examples of both. When Win95 is looking for a program in the Registry and hits a CLSID, it just jumps down to HKCR\CLSID and runs the indicated program. Programmers call this sort of setup a level of indirection.

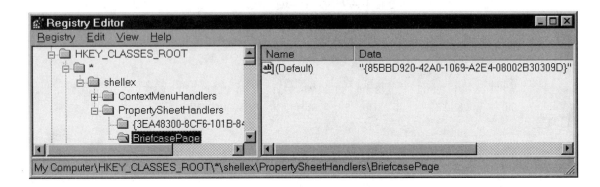

Figure 11-19. Dueling CLSIDs

- A CLSID can appear as the "extension" name of a folder. You didn't know folders could have extensions? Try this: right-click on the Desktop, pick New, Folder. Type in a name like this: mom.{21ec2020-3aea-1069-a2dd-08002b30309d}. Hit Enter. See how the CLSID for the Control Panel (the monstrosity that starts out {21. . .) turned this Plane-Jane folder into a copy of your Control Panel folder? (Go ahead and hit Del to get rid of the folder: don't worry, you won't delete any of the Control Panel applets.)

If you look at your HKCR\CLSID entries, by far the most common situation is for the CLSID itself to be assigned a name in the (Default) value, and for the key to have one or two subkeys, called \InprocServer and/or \InprocServer32. Those subkeys, more often than not, contain the names of programs called by Win95 to handle OLE with the named application.

 Why does this have to be so complicated? I mean, why use CLSIDs at all? Why not just put program names in there, and have Win95 use standard program names?

I can see three good reasons to use CLSIDs: they're a uniform way of approaching a potentially weird syntax (Can you imagine having a folder called `folderoll.c:\windows\program files\myapp.dll`?); they alleviate the problems with duplicate program names (what if two different companies come up with very different programs called `foobar.dll`?); and there's some potential for simplifying updates—to specify a new handler for a given CLSID, an installation program need only change the HKCR\CLSID entry, instead of trying to hopscotch throughout the entire Registry. Besides, OLE needs CLSIDs, so why not?

Keys and Context Menus

You've seen how the HKCR\.extension and HKCR\ProgID keys are constructed, and how parts of the keys can be maintained by Explorer's View/Options File Types tab. You've also seen how the HKCR\Folder, \Drive, and \Directory keys, interrelate, and how CLSIDs set up a single-level indirection, both within the Registry and out in the world of Win95 as a whole. Now let's take a look at how the keys and values change the way Win95 works.

When you right-click on a file, either in Explorer, or on the Desktop in general, Win95 creates a context menu like the one shown in Figure 11-20. In Chapter 3 I talked about the items on that menu below the first horizontal line—how Send To connects to the \windows\SendTo folder, and so on. Now you're in a position to see how the top items come into being.

When you right-click on a .txt file, Win95 looks in the Registry for HKCR\.txt. The (Default) value of the \.txt key is txtfile, so Win95 looks at HKCR\txtfile. In this example, the key HKCR\txtfile has three subkeys:

Figure 11-20. Right-click a .txt file

- HKCR\txtfile\DefaultIcon, which specifies the icon you see to the left of the .txt entry in Figure 11-20. (This key also controls which icon you see on the Desktop.) I'll talk more about DefaultIcon shortly.

- `HKCR\txtfile\QuickView`, with a single value of `(Default)`. I'm not sure what that entry does, because `.txt` is also listed under `HKCR\QuickView`, and *that* entry appears to control whether QuickView pops up for `.txt` files.

- `HKCR\txtfile\shell`, which has two subkeys, `HKCR\txtfile\shell\open` and `HKCR\txtfile\shell\print`. Since the single value in the `\open` key is `(Default) (value not set)`, Win95 uses the name of the key—open—as the first context menu choice. If `(Default)` had a value data other than `(value not set)`, that value data would've been used in place of "Open" on the context menu. Similarly, the single value in the `\print` key is `(Default) (value not set)`, so "Print" becomes the second entry on the menu.

In this example, `HKCR\txtfile\shell` has a value of `(Default) (value not set)`, so the default action—the one highlighted in the context menu, and the action that will be taken if the file is double-clicked—is set to "Open," as described earlier in the section called "Default Action."

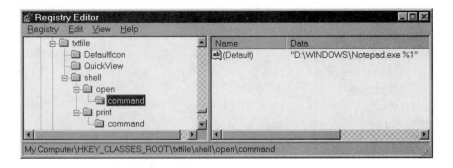

Figure 11-21. The txtfile Entry

This multiple use of `(Default)` can be confusing, so let me emphasize. There are two different ways `(Default)` is used to construct the context menu. The `(Default)` value for the `\shell` key determines what the default (highlighted) menu choice will be. The `(Default)` value for actions—which are always subkeys of `\shell`—determine the names of the actions on the context menu.

That's a big part of the story about the way Registry keys turn into context menu choices, but there are several more details. In the earlier section called Directory, Drive, Folder, I told you about the fledgling "inheritance" scheme Win95 establishes among the Registry's `HKCR\Folder`, `\Directory`, `\Drive`, and `\AudioCD` keys. Because of this inheritance, the context menu for `\Directory` includes all the menu items from

\Folder. The \AudioCD context menu includes all the menu items from \Drive; and the \Drive context menu, in turn, includes all the menu items from \Folder.

Also, the name that appears on the right-click context menu comes from the (Default) value for the action's key. For example, my Smart version of Windows assigns the key HKCR\Folder\shell\ open the (Default) value data FolderView. So, while Windows may think this is an open command, the user who right-clicks on a Folder actually sees a FolderView entry on the menu.

 That's generally true: if the HKCR\ProgID\shell key has a (Default) value (at least, one that isn't a blank string), the (Default) value data is used as the text on the context menu. Microsoft uses that for internationalization: HKCR\Directory\shell in Spanish Windows 95, for example, has a (Default) value data of Abrir, so Abrir appears on the context menu, where American Windows users would see Open.

 Wait a minute, wait a minute. Something's fishy here. You're telling me that when Win95 encounters a key with a name like \open, it's smart enough to capitalize the name, so the entry appears as Open on the context menu? I can buy that. But how does Win95 know to turn \find to Find . . .? And, how does it figure which characters on the menus should be underlined, making them accelerator keys? Where's all that stuff stored?

 I haven't the slightest idea. Some of the accelerator keys are specified by ampersands (&) in the (Default) values of the \shell\command keys—where the ampersand precedes the key that is to be underlined and become an accelerator, as is the general convention in Windows programming—but much of the accelerator key recognition must be built into Win95's core code, somehow.

It may have something to do with what the Windows *Software Development Kit* calls "canonical verbs," open, print, explorer, find, openas, and properties. (The *SDK* also lists printto as a canonical verb, but it never appears in context menus. printto is the default action taken when an object is dragged onto a printer icon. Thus, Windows can keep track of two different print actions for a given ProgID: the print action appears on the context menu; the printto action is for drag 'n drop.) I believe Windows uses the list of canonical verbs, in order, if no default action has been selected for a given ProgID. Several canonical verbs are "translated" before they appear on the context menu, with the strangest translation being openas to Open With . . .

\shellex

Time to let the other shoe drop. Many HKCR\ProgID keys—in addition to the HKCR* key and more than a few HKCR\CLSID keys—have subkeys called \shellex, a key name reserved by Windows 95 for so-called "shell extensions." That's a strange name for such a ubiquitous tool, really, because (as we'll see) bone-stock Win95 ships with hundreds of \shellex "extension" programs. Win95 shell extensions are not just for add-on software; Win95 itself uses them relentlessly.

\shellex programs are always referred to by their CLSIDs. If you look at Figure 11-22, you'll see just how. The \shellex subkey hangs off a HKCR\ProgID key, HKCR\CLSID\{. . .} key, or HKCR*. Then there's a subkey that describes the kind of shell extension. Finally, there's an application name set as a subkey, with a (Default) value that points to the CLSID of the associated program.

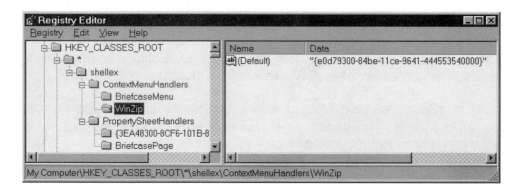

Figure 11-22. Variations on a \shellex theme

Those subkeys under \shellex control when Win95 runs the listed programs:

- \shellex\ContextMenuHandlers programs are run whenever the user right-clicks on a file, folder, drive, or directory with the given ProgID, an icon with the given CLSID, or—in the case of HKCR*\shellex\ContextMenuHandlers—any file at all. Win95 ships with many \ContextMenuHandlers. For example, HKCR\CLSID\{00028b00-0000-0000-c000-000000000046}\shelle x\ ContextMenuHandlers controls the contents of the context menu for The Microsoft Network's icon. The sharing option on drive context menus comes from the (Default) value data in HKCR\drive\shellex\ContextMenuHandlers.

Suppose your name is Mr. WinZip, and you want to write a Win95 program that hooks into all of Windows' file context menus: whenever a user right-clicks on a file, you want to have a choice on the context menu that says, oh, "Add to Zip," and if the user selects that choice you want Win95 to run your program, `myapp.dll`. How do you do that?

Well, if you're Mr. WinZip, you start by writing a special kind of program called a Context Menu Handler. The Context Menu Handler puts "Add to Zip" on the context menu, and it runs a program called `myapp.dll` if "Add to Zip" is chosen. Once you've created the Context Menu Handler, you run `guidgen.exe` to get a unique `CLSID`. Then you write an installer that puts your program's `CLSID`, along with a pointer to `myapp.dll` in `HKCR\CLSID`. Finally, the installer puts the `CLSID` in the `(Default)` value of the key `HKCR\*\shellex\ContextMenuHandlers`, just as you see in Figure 11-22.

- `\shellex\PropertySheetHandlers` programs are run whenever the user picks the associated Property sheet, typically (but not always) from the bottom of the context menu. Win95 also ships with many `\PropertySheetHandlers`. My favorite example is `HKCR\*\shellex\PropertySheetHandlers\{3ea48300-8cf6-101b-84fb-666ccb9bcd32}`. It's the program that looks at a file to see if it's an OLE compound document and, if so, displays the Property sheet for OLE compound docs. How do I know? Try a little experiment. Right-click on an OLE compound document, say a WinWord file (Figure 11-23). In `regedit`, click on `\PropertySheetHandlers` and export the key. Then delete the `{3ea48300` etc., etc., key. Bring up the Property sheet for the same file (Figure 11-24). See how the OLE Summary and Statistics tabs are missing? That's what a Property Sheet Handler does—manipulates the appearance of the Property sheet. (Be sure to restore the Registry by importing back the key!)

- `\shellex\CopyHookHandlers` programs are just like Context Menu Handlers, except they're fired up on a right-click, before Windows lets the user copy, move, delete, or rename a folder. The resulting context menu is manipulated by the Copy Hook Handlers programs, and Windows essentially asks the handler if it's OK to perform the requested action. You can see Copy Hook Handlers in the `HKCR\Directory` and `HKCR\Printers` keys.

- `\shellex\DragDropHandlers` programs are added to the context menu that pops up when you right drag and drop a file onto the object with the Drag Drop Handler. You can see Drag Drop Handlers in the `HKCR\Directory` and `HKCR\Printers` keys, too.

- `\shellex\DropHandlers` programs are called when something is dragged onto an object. For example, `HKCR\lnkfile` has a `\shellex\DropHandlers` program to let Win95 redirect files dropped onto a shortcut, so Win95 can act as if the file were dropped onto the program itself. You'll usually see `\DropHandlers` attached to data files—program files usually take care of their own drag 'n drop activities. The difference between a DragDropHandler and a DragHandler is that the former defines items that appear on the context menu that pops up when you right-drag and drop, while the latter defines actions that are taken when a drop is made with no menu involved.

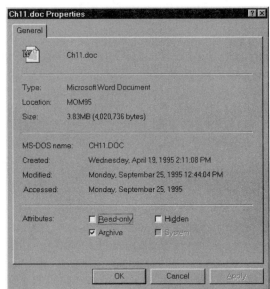

Figure 11-23. Doc with OLE Prop Handler   **Figure 11-24. Same doc, no Handler**

- `\shellex\IconHandlers` programs are run whenever Win95 needs to redraw an icon, either on the Desktop or in Explorer. `HKCR\lnkfile\shellex\IconHandlers`, for example, stores the `CLSID` of the program used by Win95 to help draw icons for shortcuts. Amazingly, the program does not draw the "arrow" on shortcuts—it draws the icon underneath! If you disable the `HKCR\lnkfile\shellex\IconHandlers` program, a shortcut icon that looks

  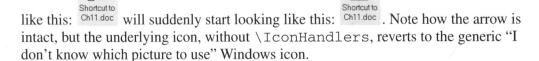

  like this: will suddenly start looking like this: . Note how the arrow is intact, but the underlying icon, without `\IconHandlers`, reverts to the generic "I don't know which picture to use" Windows icon.

- `\shellex\DataHandler` programs are run when Win95 transfers data between programs: the key's `CLSID` routine includes translators to handle unusual Clipboard data formats.

Some books will tell you that you can remove the shortcut arrow by removing the `IsShortcut` values from `HKCR\lnkfile` and `HKCR\piffile`. Although that certainly does get rid of the arrows, it might also have side effects (although, admittedly, I haven't hit any yet). You're probably far better off adjusting the `shell32.dll,29` value in `HKLM\S\M\W\CV\explorer\ShellIcons`, as I discuss later in the section called More Iconoclasms.

Keys and the Run Line

Since Win95, the Desktop and Explorer have this fantastic Default Action infrastructure, where the user can control precisely what gets executed, and how, when double-clicking on a particular file, you might assume that all of Win95 would take advantage of the Registry entries.

Well, you'd be wrong.

If you click on Start, then Run, type in the name of a file and hit `Enter`, you would think that Win95 would look in the Registry for the filename extension, wrap down to the `HKCR\ProgID` entry, pick the default action (specified in the `(Default)` value of the key or, if that is blank, Open or OpenAs). It doesn't.

Win95 behaves differently if you double-click on a file in Explorer or type the name of the file on the Start/Run line. Try it. Pick a little text file like, oh, `c:\netlog.txt`. Click on Start, then Run, type `c:\netlog.txt`, and hit `Enter`. See how it opens with Notepad? Good.

Now get Explorer going and double-click on `c:\netlog.txt`. See how it opens with Notepad, same as Start/Run? Let's reset the Default Action. Click on View, then Options, bring up the File Types tab, click Text Document, then Edit. Down at the bottom, click print and Set Default, then Close back out. Now double-click on `c:\netlog.txt`. It prints, right? That's as it should be.

Now click on Start, then Run, type `c:\netlog.txt` and hit `Enter`. Guess what? The Start/Run line ignored your choice for Default Action, reverting to the open entry, or equivalently the `HKCR\txtfile\open` key, regardless of what you've chosen.

That's true in general: Start/Run looks for an `\open` key and runs the program there, nevermind what you've established as your Default Action. Worse, if you have a default action but no `open` action at all, you get an error message if you try to run a file with the associated extension. Bad bug.

\ShellNew: Keys and the "New" Context Menu

When you right-click on the Desktop (or on an empty part of Explorer, or a folder window) and pick New, Win95 gives you an opportunity to create new files in a vast array of formats. All of the choices you see on the "New" context menu come from HKCR\.extension subkeys called \ShellNew.

For example, if you right-click on the Desktop and pick New, the first file type choice you'll see is for .txt files. That menu item appears because of the HKCR\.txt\ShellNew key. If you choose Text Document from the menu, Win95 will create a new .txt file and place it on the Desktop. The initial contents of that file are controlled by values under \ShellNew.

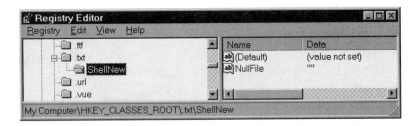

Figure 11-25. .txt\ShellNew Key

The names on the "new" context menu come from the (Default) value data of the HKCR\ProgID key associated with the specific HKCR\.extension containing the \ShellNew key. (Whew!) For example, HKCR\.txt has a \ShellNew key. When Win95 constructs the "new" context menu, it looks at the HKCR\.txt (Default) value and finds the associated ProgID, txtfile. Looking at HKCR\txtfile, Win95 finds its (Default) value data is Text Document, and sure enough, that's what's on the "new" context menu for a new .txt file.

When Win95 creates the new file, it looks for values in the \ShellNew key in this order:

- If there is a value named NullFile, Win95 creates an empty file; otherwise,

- If there is a value named FileName, Win95 creates a copy of the file listed in the value data and places that copy on the Desktop* (or within the folder, if the user right-clicked on a blank part of an open folder); otherwise,

---

* The FileName data need not include the full path of the "copy from" file if the file is located in the Win95 \windows\ShellNew directory.

- If there is a value named `Data`, Win95 takes the binary value data and creates a new file containing that binary data.

- If there is a value named `command`, Win95 runs the command, but only under certain circumstances. See the discussion at the end of this chapter called Word and the New Context Menu for details.

The new file is given a name of `New`, followed by the entry in the "new" context menu. For example, a new `Text Document` is called `New Text Document.txt`. Finally, once the new file with its new name sits on the Desktop, Win95 looks in the `\ShellNew` key for a value called `command`. If such a value exists, Win95 scans the command string data entry, replacing all `%1` occurrences with the name of the new file, and then runs the command.

 I was looking for Registry origins of the two menu entries at the top of Figure 11-26. I finally found the "New Shortcut" information stuffed under `HKCR\.lnk\ShellNew`—the `Command` value there is a bit unusual because it brings up the Shortcut wizard. I never did find the key for a new folder.

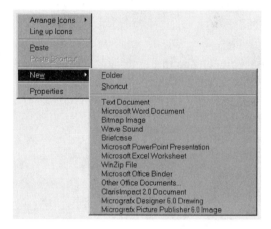

Figure 11-26. "New" context menu

 One of the nice implications of the `\ShellNew` key is that you can cut down the number of programs listed when you right-click the Desktop (Figure 11-26). Say you don't ever create new Wave Sounds, and you'd like to get that entry off the "New" context menu. It's easy. Get into `regedit`. Click on `HKCR`, scroll to `.wav`, right-click once on the `\HKCR\.wav\ShellNew` key. Pick Rename, and give it any name you like. Hit Enter. Now try the "New" context menu. See how the Wave Sound entry disappears? (You could delete the key, but by renaming it, you'll still have it around if you ever want to restore it. You could rename it to `REM ShellNew`, for example, if you're an REM fan.)

 I'll show you a really interesting way to use `\ShellNew` at the end of this chapter, and step you through some of its idiosyncrasies while I'm at it.

Edit Flags

 You're probably wondering about those mysterious Edit Flags I mentioned earlier, the ones that can force a particular ProgID to appear on—or disappear from—the Explorer File Types tab, and can keep you from changing the Default Action on a particular ProgID. Well, there are actually two different kinds of Edit Flags, those that are values of `HKCR\ProgID` keys, and those that are values of an action, two levels lower in the tree (e.g., `HKCR\batfile\ shell\open` on your system probably has an `EditFlags` value). Let's take a look at the higher level `HKCR\ProgID` keys' `EditFlags` first.

 Warning! Cuidado! Achtung! These flags are internal to the operating system. They may change in future versions of Windows. They are officially undocumented. Use at your own risk, and don't be surprised if you have to change them again when you change versions of Windows.

As you can see in Figure 11-27 and Figure 11-28, `EditFlags` is a value in `HKCR\ProgID` keys that consists of four bytes. The last two bytes are not used by the Explorer File Types tab; the third byte is associated with multimedia, but I'm not sure exactly how.

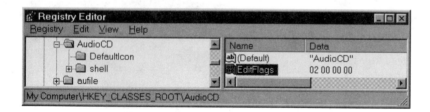

Figure 11-27. AudioCD Edit Flags

Figure 11-28. batfile Edit Flags

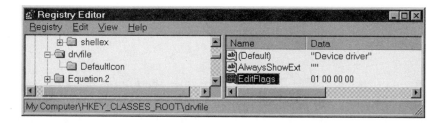

Figure 11-29. drvfile Edit Flags

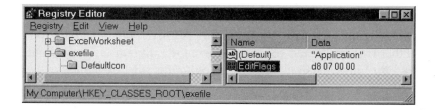

Figure 11-30. exefile Edit Flags

Many of the Edit Flags involve graying out buttons in two dialogs. The first dialog (Figure 11-11) is the one that appears when you pick the File Types tab in View/Options. The second dialog (Figure 11-12) is the one that appears when you pick the Edit. . . button from the first dialog. When I say "Such and so Edit Flag grays out the Edit button on the File Types dialog," I mean that if you click on a ProgID on this dialog, and the Edit Flag in the Registry for that ProgID is set to 1, the Edit button on this dialog will go gray—you won't be able to use it. When I say, "This other Edit Flag grays out the Remove button for the Edit File Types dialog," I mean that if you click on a ProgID in the first dialog and hit the Edit button, and the Edit Flag in the Registry for that particular ProgID is set to 1, the Remove button on the second dialog will go gray *no matter which action you pick in the second dialog.* I know that sounds complicated, but if you fiddle with the Edit Flags a couple of times, you'll see how it works.

To understand the meaning of the first two bytes, first expand them from hex to binary notation. (For example, a hex d is 13 in decimal, or 8+4+1, which translates to 1101 in binary. Remember that?) Like this:

> In Figure 11-27 02 00 hex expands to 0000 0010 0000 0000.
>
> In Figure 11-28 d0 04 hex expands to 1101 0000 0000 0100.
>
> In Figure 11-29 01 00 hex expands to 0000 0001 0000 0000.
>
> In Figure 11-30 d8 07 hex expands to 1101 1000 0000 0111.

Reading from left to right (which is *not* what programmers usually do, but if you aren't a programmer you'll find it a whole lot easier to follow), here is what a 1 in each of the 16-bit positions means:

Position 1 *The Remove button for the Edit File Type Actions dialog (see Figure 11-12) is grayed out.* Looking at the expanded Edit Flags just shown, you'll see that both batfile—which appears on the File Types tab as MS-DOS Application—and exefile—which appears as Application—have the Remove button grayed out. Go into Explorer and you'll see that's precisely what happens. There is one exception to this rule, explained shortly.

Position 2 *The Edit button for the Edit File Type Actions dialog is grayed out.* Again, if you look at Explorer, you'll find that batfile and exefile have the Edit buttons grayed out, which agrees with the binary Edit Flags. There is one exception to this rule, explained shortly.

Position 3 *The New button for the Edit File Type Actions dialog is grayed out.* I couldn't find this flag used anywhere in the Registry.

Position 4 *The Remove button on the File Types dialog (see Figure 11-11) for this ProgID is grayed out.* This keeps the user from removing the entire ProgID. In Explorer, both Application and MS-DOS Application have the Remove button grayed out, per the Edit Flags.

Position 5 *The Edit button on the File Types dialog for this ProgID is grayed out.* Prevents the user from adding to or changing any of the Actions, or the icon, for this ProgID. In Explorer, the Edit button for Application is grayed out, but MS-DOS Application is not.

Position 6 *The ProgID has an associated extension.* I couldn't find this flag used anywhere in the Registry.

Position 7 *Include in the File Types tab "Registered File Types" list.* Normally, a ProgID has to have an associated HKCR\.extension key to be eligible for listing. When this bit is 1, as it is with HKCR\drive for example, the ProgID is listed with the registered file types, whether it has an HKCR\.extension key or not.

Position 8 *Do not put on the Explorer File Types tab "Registered File Types" list.* drvfile, the ProgID for .drv driver files, shown in Figure 11-29, is one of those excluded from the list. If you look at the File Types tab, you won't see Device Driver listed, even though there is an associated extension.

Positions 9, 10 *Not used.*

Position 11 *In the Edit File Type Actions dialog box (refer to Figure 11-13), the Use DDE box is grayed out.*

Position 12 *In the Edit File Type Actions dialog box, the name of the* .exe *file in the Application to Perform Action box cannot be changed.*

Position 13 *In the Edit File Type Actions dialog box, the Application to Perform Action box is grayed out.*

Position 14 *The Set Default button in the Edit File Type Actions box is grayed out.* This is the case with `batfile`, where you're not allowed to change the default action from run (i.e., open) to print, unless you hack the Edit Flags—essentially, set this bit to 0. See the following, and Chapter 3, for details.

Position 15 *The Change Icon button in the Edit File Type dialog is grayed out.* I have no idea why Microsoft, in creating `exefile`, decided to turn on this bit *and* the one in position 5, which effectively prevents you from even getting to the Edit File Type dialog.

Position 16 *The Description of Type box in the Edit File Type dialog is grayed out.*

So now, you no doubt want to know about the exceptions to the rules for Position 1 and 2. This is where the lower-level `EditFlags` come in, the ones attached to `HKCR\ProgID\shell\action` keys, such as `HKCR\exefile\shell\open`. Any action with an `EditFlags` value can override the rules for Position 1 and 2, providing the data for the `EditFlags` value starts with 01. For example, if you create a new action for `exefiles` called `george`, and the key `HKCR\exefile\shell\george` contains a value called `EditFlags` with data 01 00 00 00, you will discover that the `george` action in the Edit File Type Actions dialog box will have both the Remove and Edit buttons available, even though the rest of the actions in that box have the two buttons grayed out.

In Figure 11-31, you can see the Edit Flags associated with the action `george`. In Figure 11-32, note how the Edit and Remove buttons are active for `george`, even though they're grayed out for all the other Actions. When you create a new action by pushing the New button here, a lower-level `EditFlags` value is automatically created for the new action, with the data 01 00 00 00. That means you will be able to edit your manually created action, even if all the other actions are grayed.

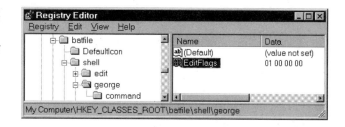

Figure 11-31. Lower-level Edit Flags

The ability to change your Edit Flags (and remove Win95's training wheels) is an important one. I've seen people—including some people who should know better— recommend that you change certain entries in the Registry manually because Explorer's View/Options File Types tab Edit capability for that particular ProgID is grayed out. **WRONG!** If any File Types key is grayed out, and that's preventing you from changing Win95 to work the way you want, your best solution is *never* to hack the Registry `\shell` keys directly. Your best solution is *always* to change the `EditFlags` for the ProgID that's causing you problems, and then using the File Types tab to make the changes you want. Why? Because once you've

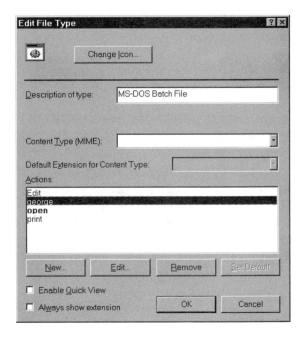

Figure 11-32. Overriding Edit Action

changed the `EditFlags` to let you in, making changes from the File Types dialog box is very easy—and (with the exception of the %1 Bug, coming up next) almost always consistent with what Windows 95 expects. The chances of making a bad mistake are greatly enhanced when you're tackling entries manually. Minimize your exposure by using the simplest possible and most robust tools—in this case the File Types dialog box—after you open up the forbidden parts of the Registry.

Don't screw around with the Edit Flags without understanding what you're up to! While you might want to zero out the bit in Position 2, which keeps you from changing the default action associated with some ProgIDs, you don't want to mess up, say, position 7 for Drive, as that would take it off the File Types list. A bit of caution is called for.

Oh, Mao! You don't have to be so damn conservative. I plunked around the Registry for a bit and came up with the list in Figure 11-33 of minimalist `EditFlags`, which you can use as long as you're cautious about how you change the `Open` action.

HKCR key	Minimalist `EditFlags`
\AudioCD	02 00 00 00
\AVIFile	00 00 00 00
\batfile	00 00 00 00
\comfile	00 00 00 00
\Directory	02 00 00 00
\dllfile	00 00 00 00
\Drive	02 00 00 00
\drvfile	00 00 00 00
\exefile	00 00 00 00
\file	02 00 00 00
\Folder	02 00 00 00
\lnkfile	00 00 00 00
\piffile	00 00 00 00
\sysfile	00 00 00 00
\vxdfile	00 00 00 00

Figure 11-33. Removing the Edit Flags training wheels

I think that may be the single most useful table for advanced Windows users in this whole book—or at least one of them. In fact, if you can remember to not turn the Open action into something weird (if you change the Open action for \exefile, for example, you might not be able to get regedit.exe to run!), I strongly recommend you go into your Registry right now and make all those changes. The power of the entire File Types shtick will be available to you, unfettered.

The basic rule is simple. To remove Windows's training wheels, use an `EditFlags` value of 02 00 00 00 for those few cases where you have a type that has no extension but you want to appear in the File Types list (that probably means exactly the four special built-in types and the type called \file added by Internet Explorer) and otherwise use 00 00 00 00.

%1 Bugs

Some Windows applications like Powerpoint are smart enough to take a command line like

```
powerpnt My Slide Show.ppt
```

and figure out that they should load the single file called My Slide Show.ppt. Other Windows applications (and I won't mention Word 95 by name) are too dumb to understand a command line that looks like

```
winword My Document.doc
```

and figure out that they're supposed to open up a single document called My Document.doc. Instead, when Word is confronted with that command line, it tries to open a file called My.doc, and then a file called Document.doc. Really smart for the flagship application of the world's largest software company, eh?

Nowhere is this bug more infuriating than in the creation of your own commands, using the File Types Action box "New" command. Win95 insists on sticking a %1 on the end of any command you create, and that can drive programs like Word batty.

 In Figure 11-34 you can see how I created a new command for Word documents called Open, Disable Auto Macros. It starts Word by running the WordBasic command DisableAutoMacros (that's what the /m means). In Figure 11-35, you can see how Win95 added a gratuitous %1 to the end of the command line.

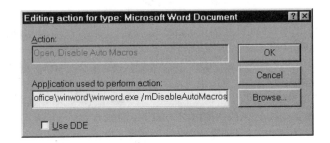

Figure 11-34. Word without %1

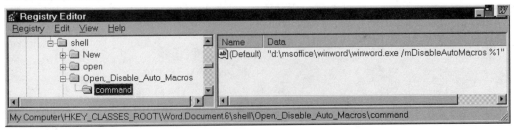

Figure 11-35. The gratuitous %1

If you right-click on a `.doc` file and pick Open, Disable Auto Macros, it works just great, as long as there are no spaces in the filename. Right-click on `AnyOldDocument.doc`, say, pick Open, Disable Auto Macros, and Word gets started with the command:

```
c:\msoffice\winword\winword.exe /mDisableAutoMacros AnyOldDocument.doc
```

which disables auto macros and loads `AnyOldDocument.doc`. Wunnerful, wunnerful. But what happens when you right-click on `Some Doc.doc` and pick Open, Disable Auto Macros? Word gets fed this command line:

```
c:\msoffice\winword\winword.exe /mDisableAutoMacros Some Doc.doc
```

and Word, in its infinite wisdom, tries to open `Some.doc` (giving you an error message) and `Doc.doc` (giving you another error message). Bummer.

Fortunately, the solution is quite simple. If you go into the Registry's `HKCR\Word.Document.6\shell\Open,_Disable_Auto_Macros\ command` key and change the value of `(Default)` to `c:\msoffice\winword\winword.exe /mDisableAutoMacros "%1"` (note the quotes!), Word works just fine. If you make that change, Word gets fed the command line

```
c:\msoffice\winword\winword.exe /mDisableAutoMacros "Some Doc.doc"
```

and all is right in the world. Amazing, no? Windows should automatically include the `"%1"`, of course, rather than just `%1`. Oh how I love a nice bug in the mornin'!

Where the Icons Come From

You can assign an icon to any ProgID, most easily by using the File Types tab, choosing the ProgID in question, hitting Edit, and then Change Icon. (You can do the same thing manually, by altering the `(Default)` value for the `HKCR\ProgID\DefaultIcon` key.) In the case of `.exe`, `.scr`, `.ico`, and `.ani` files and the like, Win95 extracts the icon from the file itself, of course.

But what does Windows 95 do for a picture—either on the Desktop, or in Explorer—when no icon has been provided? Ends up that Windows is pretty tricky on that score.

In Figure 11-36, I created a new icon on the Desktop and gave it an extension of `.foo`. Windows didn't know what to make of this new extension, so it punted for an icon. The icon you see there is the generic "I don't know what the hell to put on the screen" icon that Win95 uses when it's clueless in Seattle.

In Figure 11-37, you can see the icon for WordPad. You've seen it a million times. Now, if I right-click on `MyStuff.foo` and tell Win95 to Open it with WordPad, making sure that the box marked `Always use this program to open this type of file` is checked, Win95 automatically constructs an icon for `.foo` files that superimposes a scaled-down version of the WordPad icon and places it on top of a blank sheet of paper, per Figure 11-38. Pretty cool, eh? Many icons work this way: If you associate an

MyStuff.foo

Wordpad.exe

MyStuff.foo

Figure 11-36. Clueless   **Figure 11-37. WordPad**   **Figure 11-38. Clueless in WordPad**

Open action with the extension, a new icon is constructed superimposing a scaled-down version of the Open program's icon on top of a blank sheet of paper. Windows only does this if an explicit icon hasn't been assigned to the ProgID in the `DefaultIcon` value.

HKCU

> Mystery is the wisdom of blockheads.
>
> —Horace Walpole, Letter to Horace Mann, 1761

The Registry key `HKEY_CURRENT_USER` (or `HKCU`) contains user-specific information, stored in a `user.dat` file. It's actually an alias for `HKEY_USERS\username`, where `username` is the logon name of the currently logged-on user. In a single-user profile system, or when the user has bypassed logon by hitting the escape key, it's an alias for `HKEY_USERS\.Default`.

Orientation

HKCU has seven high-level subkeys. Although I don't claim to understand the details of many of them, as a first approximation, here is what those keys control:

- HKCU\AppEvents revolves around Application "Events"—the things that can trigger beeps, whoops, giggles, and fizzes. Mao talked about these oddly convoluted keys extensively in the Chapter 10 section on the Control Panel's Sound Applet, but I'll go into a little more detail momentarily, particularly for Windows applications.

- HKCU\Control Panel, as you might imagine, primarily deals with settings established and manipulated by the Control Panel. More than half of Chapter 10 discussed these keys. There are separate keys for \Accessibility (for details, look in Chapter 10 for the Control Panel's Accessibility applet), \Appearance (the Display applet), \Colors (also the Display applet), \Cursors (the Mouse applet), \International (mostly the Regional Settings applet), \Keyboard (the Keyboard applet), and \Mouse (the Mouse applet).

- HKCU\InstallLocationsMRU points to the places last used for installing Win95 components. I'll talk about it more in a moment.

- HKCU\keyboard layout has very little information in it; most of the keyboard settings are in HKCU\Control Panel\keyboard. Beats me why Microsoft constructed this separate key. HKCU\keyboard layout\preload\1 just contains the country code (see Chapter 10, Regional Settings applet). If multiple keyboard languages are chosen in the Keyboard applet's Language tab, they're listed as \1, \2, \3, and so on. The \toggle key apparently represents which key combination will switch among the languages.

- HKCU\Network contains some data on recently connected network drives. It's a jungle in there—but thankfully a *small* jungle if your network is simple.

- HKCU\RemoteAccess covers your Dial-Up Networking "connectoids" and all the details necessary to dial and connect to your dial-up services.

- HKCU\Software is a huge key that would take years to explore completely. In a nutshell, any software package that has user-specific settings (and most do) is supposed to put a subkey in here for the manufacturer, then subkeys off *that* subkey for each of its major products, and subkeys off *those* for each major revision of the software, and more subkeys off *those* for components. That's why you'll see entries like

`HKCU\Software\Pinecliffe\WOPR\95\Enveloper`. If you're trying to solve an application-specific problem, this is where you should start looking.

 In the rest of this chapter, I'll only look at the one `HKCU\Software` key called `HKCU\Software\Microsoft\Windows\CurrentVersion` (I'll give it the abbreviation `HKCU\S\M\W\CV`), and I'll only briefly touch on some of the hundreds of keys that live there. There's a similar key called `HKLM\Software\Microsoft\Windows\CurrentVersion` (or, much better, `HKLM\S\M\W\CV`), that controls Win95 settings that aren't specific to a single user. I'll talk about them in the section on `HKLM`.

Now let's take a look at some of the more interesting facets of `HKCU`.

Sounds

Any Windows program can have these events immortalized with song (or at least a `.wav` file): AppGPFault (the person who thought of that one must've been in a bizarre mood), Close, Maximize, MenuCommand, MenuPopup, Minimize, Open, RestoreDown, RestoreUp, SystemAsterisk (which sounds whenever a dialog box with an (I) Information symbol appears), SystemExclamation (for dialog boxes with ! exclamation points), SystemHand (for dialog boxes with Stop signs), and SystemQuestion (for dialog boxes with ? question marks).

Say you want the sound `c:\windows\tada.wav` to blast over your speakers every time you start the calculator. No problemo. In `regedit`, bring up `HKCU\AppEvents\Schemes\Apps`. Then add a key with a name that precisely matches your application's program name, in this case `\calc`. For a sound that corresponds to starting a program, use the `\Open` key and its subkey `\.Current` (for the currently active sound, of course). Finally, set the `HKCU\AppEvents\Schemes\Apps\calc\Open\.Current` key's (`Default`) value to `c:\windows.tada.wav`. That's all it takes.

You can do the same thing for other actions by replacing `\Open` in the key name by `\SystemAsterisk`, or any of the other events just mentioned. It's pretty impressive how you can customize things so thoroughly.

MRUs

Windows maintains several Most-Recently-Used lists. One of the lists you've no doubt encountered is the list of file specifications used in the Start/Find dialog: Win95 keeps track of which file spec strings you've looked for and lists them on the Find drop-down box (Figure 11-39).

The key `HKCU\S\M\W\CV\Explorer\Doc Find Spec MRU` contains the Find
MRU list. As you can see in Figure 11-40, the key contains a whole bunch of values with
value names that are letters of the alphabet, plus one value called `MRUList`. That's a
general pattern you'll find with every Win95 MRU list.

Win95 maintains the MRU list by changing the value data of `MRUList`. In Figure 11-40,
the data reads `hijcdfegab`, which is just shorthand for "the last-used document is stored
in value `h`; the next-most-recently-used is in value `i`; the next one is in `j`; and so on, down
to `b`."

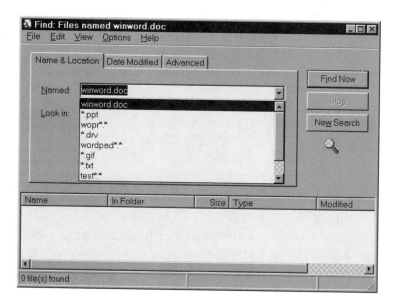

Figure 11-39. MRU Find Specifications

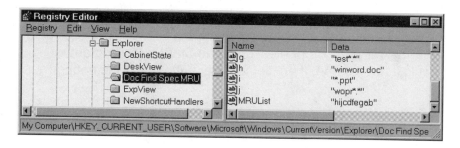

Figure 11-40. Where the Find Specs live

I talked about this in Chapter 3, but if you think about it for a minute, you can see why Microsoft used this simple method for keeping track of MRU lists. It's quite efficient. If you use the find criterion mentioned in value j, for example—the third-most-recently-used file specification—Win95 doesn't have to update the value data for j; it just has to move j to the front of MRUList. The time savings for any one MRU list isn't much, but if you multiply dozens of MRU lists, times hundreds of uses a day, it could become significant. Well, maybe not *that* significant, but it's still a cool way of handling MRUs.

The important thing to know about MRU lists is that you can get rid of them by deleting the single value called MRUList. In some cases (but not in this one), you'll also have to restart Windows—the Shutdown option "log on as a different user" is sufficient. In this particular case, deleting the MRUList value in Figure 11-40 will completely wipe out your Start/Find file spec list.

It's also important to know that, even when Win95 alphabetizes a list for you—as it does with the Start/Documents list—you can still retrieve all the information about most recently used items on the list, should you need it, by examining the appropriate MRUList value.

Speaking of the Start/Documents MRU list. That one follows the general pattern of Win95 MRU lists that you've been talking about, but it has an interesting twist: the entries in the MRU list don't point to the files themselves, but in fact point to *shortcuts* to those files maintained by Windows in the hidden folder called c:\windows\recent. If you want to wipe out the Start/Documents MRU list, you can either delete the HCKU\S\M\W\CV\ Explorer\RecentDocs key's MRUList value and restart Windows, just as you would with any other Win95 MRU list, or—much faster—simply delete all the files in c:\windows\recent. Without the shortcuts in the folder, Win95 doesn't know which files were most recently used.

Mao, you idiot! If you want to simply wipe out the whole list, you right-click on a blank part of the Taskbar, pick Properties, go to the StartMenu Program tab (where else would it be? <grin>), then hit the Clear button near the bottom!

In addition to the Start/Find file spec and Start/Documents lists, I've found these MRU lists in the Registry:

- The locations used to install Win95 components are in HKCU\InstallLocations MRU. You might want to go in and adjust this Registry key, but before you do check out the key HKLM\S\M\W\CV\Setup\SourcePath, covered later in this chapter. It's much more likely to be the key you want.

- The command lines used in the Start/Run box are in HKCU\S\M\W\CV\Explorer\ RunMRU. As discussed in Chapter 3's Explorering the Great Unknown, for some bizarre reason this is also the list used by Explorer in its Tools/GoTo menu.

- The data structures Explorer calls "Streams" (discussed under Streams, below) have an MRU list maintained in HKCU\S\M\W\CV\Explorer\StreamMRU. Win95 handles up to 29 streams by including values of a through z, {, } and |.

No doubt there are others.

Streams and Restoring the Desktop

Explorer uses twenty-nine separate temporary storage areas in the Registry that it calls Streams. They're located in the keys HKCU\S\M\W\CV\Explorer\Streams\0 through \28. I've been trying to figure out whether any interesting data is stored in the Streams, and I've only been able to come up with one likely candidate. But that one is so important that it's worth the hassle of wrangling with the entire key. One of the Streams holds all the information about the location of icons on your Desktop. (The actual objects on the Desktop are read from the folder \windows\Desktop and the HKLM\S\M\W\CV\explorer\Desktop\NameSpace key that I'll discuss later in this chapter.)

The problem with Streams is that they're never the same. Today, HKCU\S\M\W\CV\Explorer\ Streams\7 may hold the information about your Desktop icons; tomorrow it may be . . .\ Streams\23. I haven't figured out any way to nail down the number of the Stream, except by brute inspection. That's why Mao's Desktop Restoration Procedure is so klunky.

Klunky? Well, maybe so. But the fact is that I spend quite a bit of time and care arranging my Desktop, and I *hate* it when Win95 decides to rearrange my icons alphabetically in regimental rows—as it does frequently when I'm adding new user profiles, sometimes when screwing around with the Control Panel Desktop application, and always when I accidentally right-click on Desktop and pick Arrange Icons. Unfortunately, Windows doesn't have an automatic method for taking a snapshot of the Desktop and letting me restore the Desktop to my preferred arrangement: one accidental right-click and there's nothing I can do to say, "Undo, damned Spot!"

Here's my Restoration Procedure to store and restore Desktop:

1. Arrange Desktop however you like it, then (this is vital!) save your Desktop by either restarting Windows, or by clicking Start/ShutDown and clicking No.

2. Crank up `regedit`, and look for `HKCU\S\M\W\CV\Explorer\Streams`. Export the key to a text file. Then, with a text editor, go through the Streams one at a time. The Stream you want sticks out like a sore thumb: it has a ViewView key that's fifty or sixty lines long, where the rest of the ViewView keys are maybe two or three lines long.

3. Click on the appropriate Stream key name. For example, if you found `. . .\Streams\7` contains your Desktop icon information, click once on `. . .\Streams\7`. Click on Registry, then Export Registry File. Save the file as, oh, `c:\savedesk.reg`.

4. If your Desktop ever gets screwed up, bring up `regedit` again, and go over to the key called `HKLM\SOFTWARE\Microsoft\Windows\CurrentVersion\RunServicesOnce`. Change the value `(Default)` to have it run `regedit`, with the data `regedit c:\savedesk.reg`. Then restart Windows. *Boom!* Your old Desktop is restored.

 Pardon me, but that is seriously cool. Some day somebody will come up with a program that automates this stuff—maybe even lets you store alternate Desktop configurations, without going through the hassle of multiple user profiles—and make a fortune.

 The trick doesn't always work, particularly after a Spontaneous Desktop Meltdown. Streams primarily store the locations of Explorer windows. As you open more windows, Explorer has to decide which old Stream data to throw away. At some point, it can decide to throw away the icon location information. Gotcha! I call it Spontaneous Desktop Meltdown. Your Desktop self-combusts, rearranging all your icons in alphabetical order, throwing out all your careful tweaks.

Should you have a Spontaneous Desktop Meltdown, move a few icons around and Explorer will be forced to create a new Stream (with a new Stream number, natch). Then use the export trick to find the new Desktop icon Stream number. Finally, go in and change your `savedesk.reg` file so it restores to the correct Stream number, and import the modified `savedesk.reg` into the Registry.

Run and RunOnce

I talked about the HKCU\S\M\W\CV\Run and \RunOnce keys in Chapter 8, in the section on How Windows Starts. The important thing to realize: the programs stored in these keys are run *after* the user logs on (assuming the machine is set up for log on), and *only* for the current user (if somebody else logs on to the same machine, these programs are not run). There's a definitive list of all the \Runs in the discussion of HKLM, below.

\Shell Folders NOT!

The key HKCU\S\M\W\CV\Explorer\Shell Folders contains a cross-reference between folders with special meaning to Windows and their physical location on disk. For example, the value name Desktop has the data c:\windows\Desktop, telling Win95 that information about the Desktop can be found in the folder c:\windows\Desktop. Pretty simple.

The key also has values for Favorites, Fonts, NetHood, Personal ("My Documents"), Programs, Recent (shortcuts to the most recently used files), SendTo, Start Menu, Startup, and Templates (for the ShellNew templates).

Although it's true that you can change any of those locations by futzing around with this key—and several magazine articles recommend that you do so—the fact is that you're much better off simply changing the name of the folder in Explorer. If Explorer sees that you've renamed or moved the SendTo folder, for example, it's smart enough to alter this key so the SendTo value points to the folder's new location. And Explorer is smarter than you might be. For example, you might change the folder assigned to Start Menu without also adjusting the Startup folder but Explorer changes both if you change the name of the Start Menu folder in Explorer. Pretty slick.

Other HKCUs

Wonder where the various Microsoft installers pick up your name and company name? Take a look at HKCU\Software\Microsoft\MS Setup (ACME)\User Info. The information sent to Microsoft when you register Windows 95 on-line is duplicated in the key HKCU\Software\Microsoft\User information, and some installers may pick up information from that key. If you're paranoid about having a quick inventory of your system all in one place, ready for illicit sniffers, just delete this key.

I talked about the multimedia settings in HKCU\Software\Microsoft\Multimedia in Chapter 10, in the section on the Control Panel's Multimedia applet.

HKCU\S\M\W\CV\ settings span a huge range. Settings for many Win95 applets—Backup, Media Player, Paint, Resource Meter, Sound Recorder, Volume Control, WordPad, even regedit; as well as games—sit in the key HKCU\S\M\W\CV\Applets. Settings for the last use you made of Direct Cable Connection reside in HKCU\S\M\W\CV\DirectCable. Settings for the entire Windows Desktop, in addition to the Explorer application, reside in HKCU\S\M\W\CV\Explorer (but if you're looking for the list of Explorer startup tips—which, for some reason known only to Microsoft, apply to the whole machine, not a single user—you need to look at the machine-specific settings in HKLM\S\M\W\CV\Explorer). Internet Explorer settings live in HKCU\S\M\W\CV\Internet Settings, as you would probably expect, but they're also in HKCU\S\M\W\CV\Main, which I, for one, didn't expect, and in the enigmatically titled key HKCU\S\M\W\CV\Settings, as well as . . .\TypedURLs and just . . .\URL. I talked about those extensively in Chapter 4.

I'll talk about HKCU\S\M\W\CV\Policies later in this chapter, when I get into ultimate power users' tips. It's the key you use to hide some Desktop icons. (It's also the key that the network-oriented System Policy Editor works with, and that—thankfully—is beyond the scope of this book.)

If the animated window "explosion"—the edges that expand and contract when you maximize or minimize a window—bugs you, getting rid of the animation effect is easy. Add a string value to HKCU\Control Panel\Desktop\WindowsMetrics with the name MinAnimate and data 0. The zooms will no longer "trail" across the screen.

Finally, befitting so many things about Exchange, there are dozens of bizarre and completely inscrutable settings in and around the key HKCU\S\M\W\CV\Windows Message Subsystem\Profiles\MS Exchange Settings. This is only recommended if you speak HASL.*

HKLM

The key HKEY_LOCAL_MACHINE (or HKLM) contains information that pertains to the PC as a whole, from system.dat.

Orientation

The HKLM key has seven subkeys:

* HKLM\Config has entries for each hardware profile. On a single hardware profile machine (see the discussion of the System applet in Chapter 10), there's only one

---

* Hex as a Second Language.

subkey, called `HKLM\Config\0001`. On a multiple hardware profile PC, you'll also see `HKLM\Config\0002`, and so on. Each profile has just two subkeys, one called `\Display` that holds information about the system fonts and metrics (see the discussion of the Display applet in Chapter 10), and another called `\System` that— about ten levels down—finally tells you which printers are installed and which is active. That's the whole ball of wax.

- `HKLM\Enum` contains "bus enumerator" information—basically, a list of all the hardware that's installed on the machine (regardless of hardware profiles), descriptions, and resources like IRQ numbers, DMA channels, drive letters, and the like.

- A very strange subkey, `HKLM\hardware`, has information about the machine's floating point processor and the assignment of COM ports. That's all. The *Windows Resource Kit* says it's used by Hyperterminal.

- `HKLM\Network` contains the current user's username—that is, the username that will appear as the default the next time Windows restarts and puts the logon dialog up on the screen—as well as the PrimaryProvider entry.

- `HKLM\Security` concerns network security and is thus beyond the scope of this book. Thank heavens, 'cuz I couldn't figure out *what* these entries mean.

- `HKLM\SOFTWARE`, by contrast, is a gold mine of settings. I described the `HKEY_CLASSES_ROOT` alias, `HKLM\SOFTWARE\Classes`, earlier. Application software packages that have user-independent settings are supposed to put all of those settings here, listed by company name. A complete description of the hundreds of entries in `HKLM\SOFTWARE\Microsoft\Windows\Current Version` alone could probably fill another book this size. This is the mother lode for user-independent Registry entries.

- `HKLM\System` only has one subkey, `\CurrentControlSet`, but that subkey contains an impressive array of scary-looking entries. The *WRK* says this key is used during startup, but that's only part of the story: at the very least, some boilerplate text stored in `HKLM\System\CurrentControlSet\control\PerfStats` is used by the System Monitor (although the *WRK* is dead wrong in saying that the performance stats themselves live here). Stuff in this key finds its way into all sorts of nooks and crannies.

- For example, when Win95 determines which hardware profile is the active profile (usually on startup, but it can be changed manually with the Hardware Profiles tab), it sets the value `CurrentConfig` in the key `HKLM\System\CurrentControlSet\control\IDConfigDB` to the number of the currently active profile. (See Figure 11-41.) Although the HKLM\System key is fun to browse through, I haven't found any need to edit it directly and thus won't be talking much about it in the remainder of this chapter.

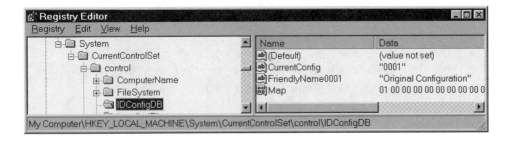

Figure 11-41. Current Hardware Profile

 There doesn't seem to be a whole lot of thought given to the structure of HKLM. Sometimes I really think these keys were put together with chewing gum and bailing wire, designed by committee, and reviewed by a random number generator. I mean, the name of the current printer for a single hardware profile machine is in the key HKLM\Config\0001\System\ CurrentControlSet\Control\Print\ Printers, in a value named Default— no, not the (Default) you've read about, the key's default value, but in a real-live value with a real-live value name of Default. And there's absolutely nothing else from \System on down the eight-deep chain of keys. C'mon, Redmond!

App Paths

Most of the interesting keys in HKLM live in HKLM\SOFTWARE\Microsoft\Windows\ Current Version, which I'll abbreviate HKLM\S\M\W\CV. It's a huge key, with hundreds of subkeys.

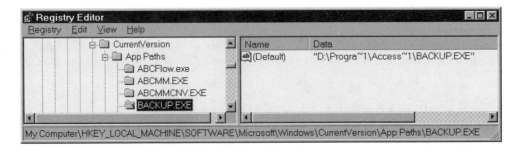

Figure 11-42. The Path to Backup

So how does Win95 find programs? Good question. As best I can tell, the Start/Run box looks for programs with names typed into the box in the following order:

1. In `c:\windows\system`;

2. In `c:\windows`;

3. In `c:\windows\command`;

4. If it still doesn't find the program, it looks along the DOS path, which was probably established in `autoexec.bat`.

5. If it doesn't find the program after all that, it looks in the Registry for a key called `HKLM\S\M\W\CV\App Paths\` and then the name of the program. For example, if the user types `test.bat` into the Start/Run box and `test.bat` isn't found in steps 1 through 4, Win95 looks for the key `HKLM\S\M\W\CV\App Paths\test.bat`. If it finds the key, Win95 *runs the program* listed in the `(Default)` value of the key.

Yes, you read that correctly. You might think that Windows would use the path information in the `(Default)` key to find the program, but you'd be wrong. In this example, if the key `HKLM\S\M\W\CV\App Paths\test.bat` had a `(Default)` value with the data `c:\windows\calc.exe`, and there was no `test.bat` in `\windows\system`, `\windows`, `\windows\command`, or along the DOS `path=`, Win95 would run the calculator, `calc.exe`. Go figger.

This is so that if you don't have an `autoexec.bat`, and hence, no MS-DOS `path=` set, you could still type `Excel` and the system would go out and find the correct version of Excel to execute (assuming, of course, that Excel properly registered itself when it was installed). Also, the `\AppPath` stuff works from the MS-DOS `start` command too. So `C:> start excel` would work just fine. We were very serious about making sure your system would work just fine if you had a zero-length `autoexec.bat` and `config.sys`.

I'll talk about a supremely cool way to use this key (for shortcuts in the Start/Run box) at the end of this chapter.

The `\App Paths\progname` key can have one more value, called `Path`, which sets the default path when the program in the `(Default)` value is run. All good Windows programs callable from the Start/Run box are supposed to register themselves in this set of keys.

This feature is only available for the new 32-bit Windows applications. Since all the old 16-bit apps share a common address space, there are no provisions to have a per-process environment like the one for 32-bit apps. In fact, the whole feature of per-app paths is implemented entirely in the shell with no changes to the underlying kernel!*

When Windows puts its program names in these keys, all the (Default) and Path values contain old-fashioned 8.3 filenames. Yet, when the Plus! Pack installs its programs, all the values contain new, full-length filenames. I have no idea why.

There is a good reason. Once upon a time, while we were developing Win95, there was an option to run Windows 95 with long filenames turned off, for compatibility with various disk utilities. Most of the programs that shipped with Windows 95 were designed to run in a long-name hostile environment, and hence their registry values were all 8.3 names since that was the only way we could guarantee that it would work in either mode. But it turned out that the non–long-filename systems made the system really cryptic to use (for example, c:\windows\Start Menu became c:\windows\startm~1). So we dropped this feature in one of the beta releases. The Plus! product team had the luxury of doing most of their development long after we punted on this feature, so they could assume that you would always have long filenames available on the local host volume.

Run, RunOnce, RunServices, RunServicesOnce

Here's the definitive list I promised of all the six \Run keys, and when, precisely, the programs mentioned in those keys' values actually run. This list is a little more detailed than the one in Chapter 8, on Startup, because you now know where all the bodies are buried.

1. The logo appears on the screen.

2. If there's a winstart.bat in the \windows directory, it runs and must complete before anything else happens.

---

* In case you programmers out there were curious about how it's actually implemented, when you run an application from the shell or the MS-DOS prompt, the shell simply reads the contents of this key, shoves it into the *lpvEnvironment* argument of the Create Process() API, and feeds it to the kernel. The kernel itself has no specific knowledge of per-app paths: it just gets this per-address space environment string from the shell.

3. `HKLM\S\M\W\CV\RunServices` and `HKLM\S\M\W\CV\RunServicesOnce` run after Windows is initialized, but before the logon screen appears. (All of the "Once" keys contain the names of programs that are run just once, then are deleted from the key. The plain "Run" keys, by contrast, contain the names of programs that are run every time Windows restarts.) Two oddities. First, the user may log on before the `\RunServices` and `\RunServicesOnce` programs complete, and if they do, the next programs in this list will get started. In other words, `\RunServices` and `\RunServicesOnce` are not show-stopper programs; they aren't required to complete before Windows continues. Second, if you shut down with the choice Close all programs and log on as a different user, all of the programs that were started with these two keys are shut down, but then they are *not* restarted as Windows comes back up again.*

4. The `HKLM\S\M\W\CV\RunOnce` programs start *and finish.* These are show-stopper programs: Windows will not proceed until all of the programs in this key have completed.

5. The `win.ini load=` and `run=` programs are started.

6. Then the `HKLM\S\M\W\CV\Run` programs are started.

7. Finally, the `HKCU\S\M\W\CV\Run` and `HKCU\S\M\W\CV\RunOnce` programs get started. All of these programs in Steps 5, 6 and 7 may finish asynchronously, at any time.

You now know nine different ways to run programs when Win95 starts. One of them is bound to do whatever you want.

Other HKLMs

You can control the default behavior of the MS-DOS Configuration Options described in the section of Chapter 3 called Setting Up the Penalty Box. Check out the keys stored underneath `HKLM\S\M\W\CV\MS-DOSOptions`, including `\CD-ROM`, `\Doskey`, `\DOSSettings` (for

---

* Billy: That's not the whole story. It's a security issue. Programmers need to be aware of the fact that, if the application calls the `SetServiceProcess()` API, then it will not be terminated when one user logs off. It also won't show up in the C-A-D dialog after that API is called. However, applications like that *must* be aware that there is only one security context systemwide in Windows 95. As a result, if User A logs in, whatever applications were started from that `\RunServices` key will inherit whatever network security privileges User A is allowed. When User B logs in, those network permissions are then changed out from under the service process to be those of User B.

DOS=HIGH, UMB and variants), \EMS, \Himem, \Lock (for direct disk access), \Mouse, \Net, \Smartdrv and \Vesa (for VLB support). These keys exist primarily to make it easier for hardware manufacturers to customize default Penalty Box settings on their systems, but you can use them, too.

The (Default) value for each key becomes the description in the Configuration Options box. Autoexec.Bat and Config.Sys values are strings that will appear in the Penalty Box's autoexec and config, respectively, if the key's box is checked in Configuration Options. The Order value controls the order of lines in the resulting autoexec and config—larger numbers are attached to keys with lines that appear toward the end of autoexec or config. The TipText value appears at the bottom of the Configuration Options box.

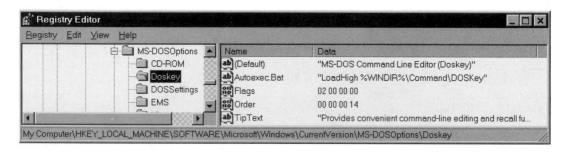

Figure 11-43. MS-DOSOptions Key

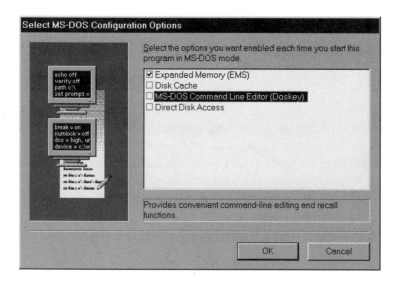

Figure 11-44. Configuration Options

The `Flags` values underneath these keys appear to control their appearance in the Advanced Settings dialog. As best I can tell, here are the valid value data for the first byte of the `Flags` value and what they imply in the Configuration Options box:

* 00 means that the key does not appear in the Configuration Options box.

* 02 means the key appears in the Configuration Options box, unchecked.

* 07 means the `Autoexec.Bat` or `Config.Sys` value appears in the default `autoexec` and/or `config`, in the Advanced Settings dialog, and there is no option for this key in the Configuration Options box.

* 1b means the key appears in the Configuration Options box, checked.

This one really bugs me. None of these settings are described in the Windows SDK or DDK. I'm convinced that Microsoft uses them as a cookie for the good developers and hardware vendors who kowtow to Microsoft's demands. Other vendors get to go pound sand.

HKLM has a handful of additional keys that may prove useful to you. For example, if you want to add your own pithy saying to the Windows welcome screen, just put new values in the key HKLM\S\M\W\CV\explorer\Tips.

But whatever you do, don't take some books' advice and change HKLM to start truncating long filenames. As it comes straight out of the box, Win95 changes long filenames into short filenames by cutting down the filename to six characters, then appending a tilde and a number to the name: `MyLongName.doc` becomes `mylong~1.doc`. The crew talked about that extensively in Chapter 2.

If you go to the key `HKLM\System\CurrentControlSet\Control\FileSystem` and add the value `NameNumericTail` with data 0, Windows will suddenly start truncating filenames: `MyLongName.doc` now becomes `mylongna.doc`.

What's wrong with that? Well, some programmers—including, as Billy explained earlier, the programmers who put together Windows 95—assumed that shortened names have tildes and wrote that assumption into their code. Don't ask me why, but they did. Anyway, `NameNumericTail` will break enough software that it just isn't worth the hassle.

There's a very useful key called `HKLM\S\M\W\CV\Setup\SourcePath` that I've modified on several machines. When Windows 95 needs an installation disk (either a floppy or the CD), it first looks at this key to see which drive letter it should first query. If Win95 finds the disk it wants in the path mentioned by this key, it just goes over there and snags what it needs, without even asking the user. For example, if you have your installation files copied to `c:\winstall`, and `\SourcePath` points there, you'll never hear a thing as Windows whooshes straight to the installation files. If it doesn't find the data it needs here, it pops up a dialog that lets the user browse and takes the information for the browse drop-down list from the key `HKCU\InstallLocationsMRU`.

The funny thing is that the `HKLM\S\M\W\CV\Setup\SourcePath` key is never updated. Even if you install Win95 components from a new location a hundred times, Win95 isn't smart enough to automatically look for that new location; it always hits you with the stupid browse dialog box. If you go in and manually change this key to point to the disk drive you use to install new Win95 components, Windows will never hit you with the browse dialog box again.

And that concludes the tutorial part of the chapter. Time to have some fun!

Registry Hacks, Ultimate Power Users' Tricks

Talk, talk, talk. It took you more than seventy pages to cover the basics. What I want to know is how I use this stuff to make Win95 cooler. You know, the best of the hacks.

It's important that you understand the basics and get the lay of the land before trying some of these advanced tricks. And, *oy!,* what tricks they are! Most books and mags extol the virtues of Send To. Well, sonny, this stuff is so advanced it puts Send To to shame.

The first big hack, of course, is my method for making Explorer "smart," as explained toward the end of Chapter 3. The second big hack is to go into HKCU and make Mom's modifications to take the training wheels off of the File Types tab, as she showed us in Figure 11-33. Now let's see what other mischief we can get into.

Renaming, Moving Desktop Icons

I'll bet the question I hear most often from advanced Win95 users is, "How do I get rid of the ^&%$#@! icons Win95 put on my Desktop?" Sometimes their language can be a little shocking, but it's hard not to sympathize with them. After all, My Computer is the kind of thing you'd expect to find on an 8-year-old's Desktop, but hardly the sort of power icon you'd want in the upper-left corner of, oh, the National Security Advisor's main screen, eh? Well, here's everything we've found about changing My Computer, Network Neighborhood, Recycle Bin, The Microsoft Network, Inbox, and Internet Explorer. The first two are a bit of a disappointment, but the rest succumb sooner or later to a coherent Registry attack.

I can't believe how hard it is to do this simple stuff. You can't drag the built-in Desktop icons to your own folders: you'll get shortcuts in the folders, with the icons still on the desktop. You can't delete them without a great deal of pain. Why doesn't Microsoft at *least* give me the option of consolidating all my communication-related icons into a single folder? Desktop real estate is precious. I hate to waste it on Politically Correct junk.

First the easy part. You know how to change the names of the Desktop icons, right? For any icon except the Recycle Bin, it's easy: just right-click on the offending icon and pick Rename. While it's true that some of the names are hardwired (for example, My Computer will show up in a few places, including the root of every key in `regedit`, even after you change the name on the Desktop icon), it's a good first start for getting rid of the most embarrassing aspect of the icons, their touchy-feely names. You can even "delete" the name on an icon entirely by simply renaming the icon with a single space.

If you just want to change the icon pictures for the Desktop icons, look for these keys:

To change this icon	Change `HKCR\CLSID\{this}\DefaultIcon`'s `(Default)` value
My Computer	`{20d04fe0-3aea-1069-a2d8-08002b30309d}`
Network Neighborhood	`{208d2c60-3aea-1069-a2d7-08002b30309d}`
Recycle Bin	`{645ff040-5081-101b-9f08-00aa002f954e}`
The Microsoft Network	`{00028b00-0000-0000-c000-000000000046}`
Inbox (Exchange)	`{00020d75-0000-0000-c000-000000000046}`
The Internet	`{fbf23b42-e3f0-101b-8488-00aa003e56f8}`

Figure 11-45. Where the Desktop icons are

To change the name of the Recycle Bin, go into `HKCR\CLSID\{645ff040-5081-101b-9f08-00aa002f954e}` and change the `(Default)` value data to whatever name you like. It's kinda funny because the right-click Rename option for all the other Desktop icons simply change the appropriate `CLSID`'s `(Default)` value. Hard to imagine what possessed Microsoft to not permit the same sort of right-click name change on the Recycle Bin, thus forcing you to manually hack the Registry.

If you want to move those icons around, the procedure is a bit tougher.

My Computer

Several books recommend that you get rid of your My Computer icon by going in to `HKCU\S\M\W\CV\Policies\Explorer` and adding a dword value called `NoDesktop`, setting it to 1. You can try that if you want to—on rebooting you won't see the My Computer icon—but I'd suggest you first consider poking out your eyes with a sharp stick.

Just as I was wrapping up his part of this book—the very last day of intense work on the Registry—I started fooling around with the `NoDesktop` value. Most of the time, when I set it to 1 and rebooted, I got either a completely blank screen (`Ctrl+Alt+Del` time) or just the Taskbar. Once, though, I crashed my whole system. Hosed it royal. When I reinstalled, every time Win95 started, it immediately crashed with a GPF in Explorer. It took me two full *days,* with our editor breathing fire for Mom's overdue book, to get back up and limping. Restoring my carefully made backup of the Registry (with `NoDesktop` set to 0) didn't help. I had to completely erase Win95 from my hard drive, and reinstall from DOS 6.2. True fact. Even now, I'm not back to full speed. While I can't swear it was all the fault of `NoDesktop`, I'm convinced the setting had something to do with my problems.

Which leads me to several important points. First, remember that merging an old copy of the Registry will *not* overwrite new values, like this `NoDesktop` value. You have to go into the `.reg` file and manually add a `"NoDesktop"=dword:0` line in the right place to remove the effects of a `NoDesktop` 1 setting. Failing that, you have to copy over old copies of `system.dat` and `user.dat`, making sure you put the old `user.dat` in the right place, if you have a multiple-user profile system.

Second, don't believe everything you read about the Registry, sonny, not even here in my book. What works for me today might not work for you tomorrow. A great deal of caution is called for. This stuff is way out on the bleeding edge. Don't play around with your Registry the day before a big assignment is due, OK? Anticipate some down time, and feel lucky if you escape unscathed.

Finally, a bit of advice from my friend, Dr. Ruthless: Don't play around with the Registry too much. Sex may be for Dummies—at least that's what the good doctor tells me— but playing with the Registry requires a keen mind and a deft hand. Play with it too much and you may go blind.

 I'm too chicken to get rid of My Computer completely: it seems to be too tightly tied into Windows itself. But I *do* know how to make it invisible, so you can't see it on the Desktop! The icon shown for My Computer on the Desktop is stored in the key HKCR\CLSID\{20d04fe0-3aea-1069-a2d8-08002b30309d}\DefaultIcon, in the (Default) value. You can put the name of any icon in there that you like, or use the filename,iconnumber convention (where filename contains more than one icon, and iconnumber is the number of the icon, the first icon being icon number zero; see Appendix B). For example, to use the sixth icon of c:\windows\moricons.dll, which is icon number five in the Windows counting method, set the value data for (Default) to c:\windows\moricons.dll,5.

 The coolest part of this is your ability to use "transparent" icons—ones that take on the underlying color of the Desktop itself. I've included a completely transparent icon on my CD, in the file screen.ico. If you assign the (Default) value of the HKCR\CLSID\{20d04fe0-3aea-1069-a2d8-08002b30309d} key to screen.ico (copy it to your hard disk first, of course), the My Computer icon will disappear entirely! If you then rename My Computer to a single space, you'll never see it again. Out of sight, out of mind. Outta sight!

Network Neighborhood

 If you want to get rid of the Network Neighborhood icon, get regedit going, hop over to HKCU\S\M\W\CV\Policies\Explorer and add a DWord value called NoNetHood, with data of 1. Reboot Windows, and Network Neighborhood is gone. As best I can tell, this NoNetHood setting prevents you from browsing the network to see what's on it—the Network Neighborhood icon on the Desktop disappears, of course, but so does the Network Neighborhood entry in Explorer and the Network Browse capability in File Open boxes and several wizards. Yet, NoNetHood does *not* prevent you from attaching to drives on the network, using UNCs. In addition, if you've told Win95 to automatically attach to the given resource on startup, the connection will be made. Thus, the major effect of NoNetHood is to curtail your searching ability—while your ability to attach to network resources stays intact. You can always retrieve Network Neighborhood, if you miss it, by simply removing the NoNetHood value, or setting it to 0.

This is an ideal way to get rid of the Network Neighborhood icon when you don't have a real network. If you install Direct Cable Connection, for example, Win95 puts the Network Neighborhood icon on your Desktop. If you took my advice and added a network protocol just to get the Close all programs . . . item on your Shutdown menu, Win95 put the Network Neighborhood icon on your Desktop. Hey, if you don't need it, nuke it.

Man, I tried and tried and couldn't figure out any other way to get rid of da Network Neighborhood icon, short of putting a transparent icon in the `DefaultIcon` value of `HKCR\CLSID\{208d2c60-3aea-1069-a2d7-08002b30309d}`, which is the CLSID for Network Neighborhood. Ideally, I'd like to establish a shortcut to Network Neighborhood that I can drag to a folder somewhere, so I can turn off the regular icon with `NoNetHood`. But as soon as the `NoNetHood` value takes effect, the shortcut gets cut off at the knees. If anybody ever cracks this one, I'd sure like to hear about it! I think the trick lies in figuring out precisely what the `%I` entries in `HKCR\CLSID\{208d2c60-3aea-1069-a2d7-08002b30309d}\shell\find\ddeexec` should be, but for the life of me I couldn't figure it out. . .

Recycle Bin

Unlike Network Neighborhood, the Recycle Bin is docile as could be. While you can't drag the Recycle Bin, per se, into a folder, you *can* create a fully functional clone of the Recycle Bin—and it's a real clone, identical to the original, including full drop functionality in drag 'n drop deleting—which can be moved anyplace you like. If you then delete the original Recycle Bin, this clone can take its place.

Right-click on the Desktop, pick New Folder. Type in the name `Zap.{645ff040-5081-101b-9f08-00aa002f954e}`. (The `Zap` part can be anything you like: whatever you type to the left of the period becomes the name of your new Recycle Bin.) Hit Enter. Test this new Zap Can out—move it into a folder; double-click on it to see the items in the Can; drop an unneeded file on top of it, and verify that the file was removed from its previous location and moved to the Can.

If the Zap Can works for you, delete the old Recycle Bin by going into `regedit`, looking for the key `HKLM\S\M\W\CV\explorer\Desktop\NameSpace\{645ff040-5081-101b-9f08-00aa002f954e}`, and deleting it. Restart Windows, and the old, rigid Recycle Bin is history.

If you just want to change the Recycle Bin icon, be aware of the fact that the Recycle Bin actually has two different icons in three keys, all stored in `HKCR\CLSID\{645ff040-5081-101b-9f08-00aa002f954e}`. The icon in the (Default) value's data is the icon that's currently shown on the screen. If you empty the Recycle Bin, the `empty` value gets moved into `(Default)`. If you then add anything at all to the Recycle Bin, the `full` value is moved into `(Default)`. Remember: two icons, three keys, and `full` doesn't mean "full," it means "not empty."

The Microsoft Network

Another easy one. Microsoft actually put a delete command on the right-click context menu for The Microsoft Network, shortly before Windows 95 shipped. Mom's crew calls this the Bingaman Switch.

Create a clone of The Microsoft Network icon by right-clicking on the Desktop, choosing New, then Folder,* and typing in a new name of MSN. `{00028b00-0000-0000-c000-000000000046}`. Again, you can type anything you like to the left of the period, and that will become the title of the new icon. Hit Enter. See how the picture turns to the MSN picture?

Double-check and make sure the icon works properly—double-click on it, mainly, and make sure it connects to MS Network. When you're satisfied that it's working properly, just right-click on the old The Microsoft Network icon and choose delete. For what it's worth, that delete option simply removes the key `HKLM\S\M\W\CV\explorer\Desktop\NameSpace\{00028b00-0000-0000-c000-000000000046}` from the Registry.

By the way, if you ever deleted your The Microsoft Network icon and think you might want to sign up to try MSN anyway, just follow the above instructions to create a new icon, and it'll work just like the old one.

Inbox

Changing the icon of the Exchange Inbox, if you have it, is pretty easy, too. Create a clone of the Inbox by right-clicking on the Desktop, choosing New, then Folder, and typing in a new name of Inbox. `{00020d75-0000-0000-c000-000000000046}` then hitting Enter. Test the new icon. When you're happy with it, get rid of the old icon by going into

---

* I have no idea why, but my inside sources in Redmond say you should use Folder, not Text Document, for all of these ersatz icons—even though Text Document seems to work just fine. Very strange. My sources, that is, not necessarily the advice.

regedit and deleting HKLM\S\M\W\CV\explorer\Desktop\NameSpace\
{00020d75-0000-0000-c000-000000000046}.

Internet Explorer

This icon is marked "The Internet." Moving it is easy, too. Create a clone by right-clicking on the Desktop, choosing New, Folder, and naming it Internet Explorer.
{fbf23b42-e3f0-101b-8488-00aa003e56f8}. When you're satisfied that it works correctly, delete HKLM\S\M\W\CV\explorer\Desktop\NameSpace\
{fbf23b42-e3f0-101b-8488-00aa003e56f8}. Piece o' cake.

More Iconoclasms

 By far the vast majority of icons used on the Desktop and in Explorer come from a file called shell32.dll. In Appendix B you can see a list of the icons stored in that file—they range from the familiar diskette and disk-drive icons to the shortcut arrow to just about every other icon you've seen Win95 use.

Ends up that there's a way to change the basic icons Win95 uses, by hacking yet another Registry entry. This one is in HKLM\S\M\W\CV\explorer\ShellIcons. If you do not yet have a key with that name, create it. This will be worth the effort. (If you already have a lot of values in a key with that name, they were probably put there by the Plus! Pack.) By changing values within this key, you can change the basic icons used by Windows itself. For example, if you prefer the big shortcut arrow shown in Figure 11-47 to the standard small shortcut arrow shown in Figure 11-46, one simple value in this key will change all the little arrows to big arrows, throughout Windows.

Figure 11-46. shell32.dll,29 Arrow   **Figure 11-47. shell32.dll,30 Arrow**

Windows numbers its icons internally. For example, it knows that the shortcut arrow is icon number 29. But before it actually paints an icon on the screen, it looks in this key to see if there's an "override." Thus, using this key, you can tell Windows, "Whenever you need to draw icon number 29, use this particular icon instead of the one you usually use."

Values within this key have the `shell32.dll` icon number as the value name, and the new file and icon number as the value data. For example, if you want to change the shortcut arrow from the small size (look in Appendix B and you'll see that's `shell32.dll,29`) to the big arrow (`shell32.dll,30`), you would set up a value in this key with the name `29` and the data `c:\windows\system\shell32.dll,30`. That tells Windows, "Whenever you need to draw icon number 29, use the icon `shell32.dll,30` instead of the one you usually use." If there is no value named `29`, Windows uses its default icon for the short arrow, `shell32.dll,29`. See how that works?

While the whole, illustrated list of `shell32.dll` icons is in Appendix B, Figure 11-48 gives a short list of the icons Windows uses most commonly.

What the icon is used for:	*Icon Number*
Default document icon	0
5.25" floppy	5
3.5" floppy	6
Tape drives	7
Local hard drives	8
Network hard drives	9
Disconnected network drive	10
CD ROM drive	11
Entire network in Network Neighborhood	13
Computer in Network Neighborhood	15
Printers in printer folder	16
Workgroups in Network Neighborhood	18
Superimposed for shared drives or directories	28
Superimposed for shortcuts	29

Figure 11-48. Important shell32.dll icons

Thus, if you want to change the icon used for Printers in the printer folder, you need to create a value in the `HKLM\S\M\W\CV\explorer\ShellIcons` key with the name `16` and data that points to the new icon.

You have to force Win95 to reconstruct the entire Desktop before changes in the `\ShellIcons` Registry key take effect. The simplest way to do that without restarting Windows is to right-click on the Desktop, choose Properties, pick the Appearance tab, choose Icon from the Item drop-down list, crank the Size up by 1, hit Apply, and then move the Size back down by 1, hitting OK all the way back out.

 Usually a .bmp file either on the Desktop or in Explorer will show a generic icon, one that signifies the file is a .bmp (see Figure 11-49). While Windows is smart enough to show you thumbnail sketches of the icons in .exe, .ico, .cur, and .ani files, it reverts to a generic icon for .bmps.

You can change that by (what else?) hacking the Registry. If you go into the key HKCR\Paint.Picture\DefaultIcon and change the (Default) value to have the data %1, your .bmp files will suddenly appear with thumbnails (Figure 11-50).

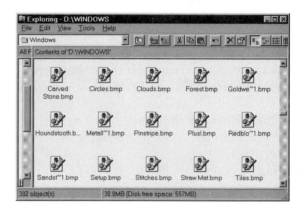

Figure 11-49. Generic .bmp Icons

 You better warn them about the side-effects of this change, Sarah. There's a reason why we didn't do this as the default in Windows 95 and left it to super sleuths to discover: showing .bmp thumbnails takes a significant performance hit. It's especially heinous when you open a floppy drive and Win95 has to scan all the .bmp files to extract thumbnails. Personally, I like the pretty pictures, but I didn't think our users would want to put up with the delays.

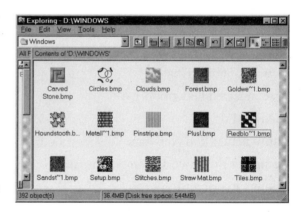

Figure 11-50. %1 .bmp Icons

Word and the New Context Menu

 I'm forever creating faxes. You'd think that the people in my small circle would be thoroughly wired by now, but noooooo: hardcopy email (also known as fax) still reigns supreme for many people. So I finally decided to bite the bullet and put a fax entry on my New context menu: that way I can right-click anywhere on the Desktop or in an Explorer window, pick New, then Fax from Mao, Ink. (Figure 11-51), and I'm magically transported into Word with a fax shell ready to go.

It ends up that I could've accomplished just about the same thing with a custom icon on my Desktop, but I wanted to give the New context menu a bit of a workout, and in the process see how hard it would really be to add a line to that menu.

You probably won't be surprised to know that it's a bit more difficult than I had imagined.

I started by looking at the \ShellNew discussion earlier in this chapter. That said, I would need to hang the \ShellNew key off an HKCR\.extension key, so I created a brand new extension called .MaoFax (Figure 11-52).

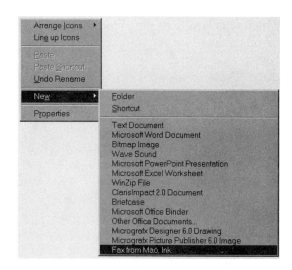

Figure 11-51. Invoice from Mao, Ink.

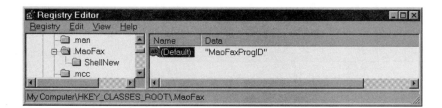

Figure 11-52. HKCR\.MaoFax

It's important to realize that .MaoFax is a dummy extension. I never intend to create any documents with that extension. I'm not going to use it in any way, except to trick the Registry into putting my invoices on the bottom of the New context menu. The .MaoFax extension has to point to a ProgID, using the (Default) value, so I invented a new ProgID called MaoFaxProgID (see Figure 11-52). Original, no?

The HKCR\.MaoFax\ShellNew key is the crucial entry (Figure 11-53). As discussed earlier in this chapter, that key can have any of several values. The one I wanted is the command value: it tells Win95 to run a command any time a New document of the indicated type gets created from the New context menu. In this case, the command value has the data:

```
d:\msoffice\winword\winword.exe /mCreateNewFax
```

which tells Win95 to start Word without a document and run the Word macro called `CreateNewFax`. As you probably guessed, the macro does all the work. It looks like this:

```
Sub MAIN

FileNew "d:\msoffice\templates\Letters & Faxes\Fax Wizard.wiz"
Dim fsa As FileSaveAs
GetCurValues fsa
fsa.Name = "d:\msoffice\winword\faxes\"
On Error Goto Bye
Dialog fsa
Bye:
End Sub
```

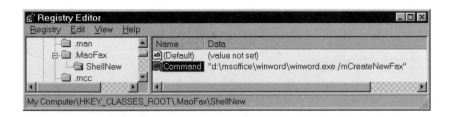

Figure 11-53. Mao's \ShellNew

I'm not going to try to turn you into a WordBasic maven here—if you feel so possessed, check out the *Hacker's Guide to Word for Windows**—but the macro is really pretty simple. (You can create one on your own machine by starting Word, clicking Tools, then Macro, typing `CreateNewFax`, clicking Create, typing in the macro as you see it, then clicking File, then Close. YES, you want to save changes.) The macro starts by running the Fax wizard that ships with Word (not my favorite wizard, but if you don't have a good fax template already, it'll do). Immediately after running the wizard and creating the new fax, the macro sets up a File Save As, forcing me to put the new invoice in the `\msoffice\winword\faxes` folder (which I created to hold my faxes), also forcing me to give it a unique, new name.

---

* Still the only source of unadulterated truth about Word and WordBasic, every serious Word user needs the *Hacker's Guide to Word for Windows,* 2nd Edition, by Woody Leonhard, Vince Chen, and Scott Krueger (Addison-Wesley, 1994), ISBN 0-201-40763-9. Shameless self-promotion provided by Woody.

That's the whole working part. Everything from this point on is just Windows dressing.

 I discovered a bunch of oddities about \ShellNew keys. First, as noted earlier, any HKCR\.extension key that has any hope of making it onto the New context menu must have an associated HKCR\ProgID; that's how Windows picks up the text that appears on the New context menu. You'll notice in Figure 11-54 how the text stored in the HKCR\MaoFaxProgID key's (Default) value ends up on the New context menu, in Figure 11-51.

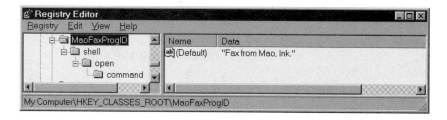

Figure 11-54. MaoFaxProgID

Second, it isn't enough to have an HKCR\ProgID key. If that was all I had, Windows wouldn't pick up the \ShellNew key and put an entry on the New context menu. In fact, it isn't enough to have an HKCR\MaoFaxProgID\shell key. I finally found out that I had to get all the way down to an HKCR\MaoFaxProgID\shell\open\ command key, and I had to put a valid program file in the (Default) value of that key before the \ShellNew would be recognized. Bizarre!

Third—and not totally unexpected—I found out that the contents of the (Default) value of the HKCR\MaoInvoiceProgID\shell\open\command key doesn't mean squat. Windows doesn't even look at it. If you check out Figure 11-55, you'll see that I used a command line that would run regedit, fer heaven's sake. Windows doesn't care. It just wants a valid program name.

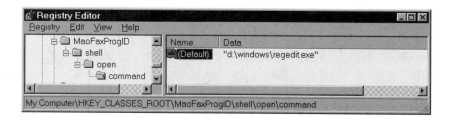

Figure 11-55. Dummy command

Those are odd, but this is a real bug. I tried to use the same trick to put the Windows calculator on the New context menu. I established a dummy extension, `.calc`, with `HKCR\.calc`'s `(Default)` value set to `CalcProgID`, and `HKCR\.calc\ShellNew`'s command value set to

`c:\windows\calc.exe`

Then I finished what Mao calls the "Windows dressing"—the stuff that Windows requires, but never really uses—by setting up `HKCR\CalcProgID` with `(Default)` value `Windows Calculator`, and a `HKCR\CalcProgID\shell\open\command` key with `(Default)` value of `c:\windows\regedit.exe`, just to give it a valid program name. Guess what? It didn't work! Even though it was entirely analogous to Mao's New Fax hack, and `Windows Calculator` appeared on the right-click New context menu, when I selected `Windows Calculator`, Windows did nothing.

I spent hours trying to figure out what was different, why Mao's Fax hack worked and my Calc hack didn't, until it suddenly struck me that Mao's `\ShellNew` command had a parameter on it—`/mCreateNewFax`—where my simple calc line did not. So I changed my `HKCR\.calc\ShellNew` key's command value to

`c:\windows\calc.exe ThisIsAUselessParameter`

and suddenly everything worked fine! Oh how I love a nice bug early in the mornin'!

 But that isn't a bug at all, Erwin. Remember how `\ShellNew` can have several different kinds of values, including `command`, but also `NullFile`, `FileName`, and `Data`—with all three of the latter creating new files without running any programs? We designed the `command` value so it would kick in if there was a parameter on the command line. That way a program could take control over the newly created file. We never intended to accommodate approaches like Mao's Fax hack. The New context menu, after all, was constructed as a means to create new files—not as an application launcher.

 If that's the case, your design was much too shortsighted. Why should the only user-extensible aspect of right-clicking on the Desktop be creation of new files? Why not open things up so right-clicking can launch programs, too?

Anyway, if you put the HKCR\.MaoFax key together just like this, you'll get a Mao Fax entry on your New context menu, and it'll work like a-ringin' a bell.

What did I learn from all of this? It's too much work! Use a Desktop icon: right-click, pick New, then Shortcut, and type in the command line

```
d:\msoffice\winword\winword.exe /mCreateNewFax
```

It's a lot easier.

I disagree, Mao. It's unfortunate that Microsoft made the placement of items on the New menu so hard, but once you make the effort, it is easier to have a menu item that works once you have even a tiny spot of Desktop free to right-click on, rather than being forced to search for an icon—not to mention waste all that Desktop real estate! You underestimate the coolness of your discovery.

Run Accelerators on the App Path

Here's my favorite Registry hack. I have a handful of programs that I'd like to "accelerate" in the Start/Run box. For example, instead of typing regedit in the Run box to run regedit, I'd like to set things up so that simply typing r and hitting Enter gets regedit going, for example, and typing w starts Word. Ends up, it ain't the least bit difficult.

If you go into HKLM\S\M\W\CV\App Paths and add a key called r.exe with a (Default) value that points to regedit (see Figure 11-56), Win95 will be smart enough to translate an r typed in the Start/Run box into the regedit command: when it doesn't find a file or program called r along its usual path, it looks in HKLM\S\M\W\CV\App Paths for the program and finds it here.

Similarly, an HKLM\S\M\W\CV\App Paths\w.exe key with a (Default) value pointing to Word will force Win95 to run Word whenever you type w in the Start/Run box. As you can see in Figure 11-57, you can even establish a starting path for an application in \App Paths by adding a value called Path to the appropriate key.

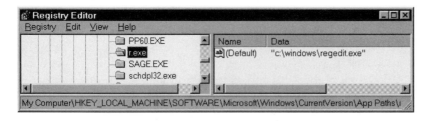

Figure 11-56. r turns to regedit

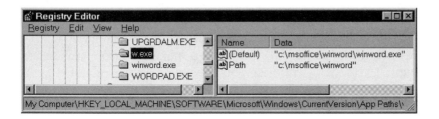

Figure 11-57. w turns to Word

 Watch out! Windows ignores `\App Paths` entries with `.bat`, or `.com` extensions. It's pretty weird: in the old DOS world, `.exe`, `.bat` and `.com` extensions were all considered when matching commands with filenames. Not so Win95: you must use an `.exe` extension in `\App Paths`.

 Good luck with the Registry! May it bring you as many hours of fun as it has to my crew. And keep your powder dry.

O Captain! my Captain! our fearful trip is done!
The ship has weather'd every rack, the prize we sought is won.
The port is near, the bells I hear, the people all exulting.

—Walt Whitman, *Leaves of Grass,* 1855

Act V, Scene 1. Bones is in Sick Bay talking to Kirk.

McCoy: We don't need appendices any more, Jim.

Kirk: But without sweetmeats, how can I vent my spleen in a properly Shakespearean way?

McCoy: *Oy gevalt.* Nobody likes that over-played stage crap anyway.

Kirk: My best Hamlet ever was in a T.J. Hooker episode…

McCoy: Jim, the only role you ever played worth a damn was Kirk.

Kirk: But, soft! what phaser through yonder window breaks?

McCoy: What is this? *King Lear Meets the Klingons*?

Kirk: Interesting idea. Wonder if Fox would buy that, too.

McCoy: In an age where George C. Scott does Postal Service ads, is anything *not* possible?

Kirk: I probably shouldn't recite any more. Copyright infringement and fair use, you know.

McCoy: Yeah. Next thing you know Shakespeare's great grand nephew will want royalties.

Kirk: Wonder if he renewed the copyright in time?

McCoy: If he did, Gates is probably after the rights.

 You got that right. Now you know why I haven't quoted from the Microsoft "Start It Up" commercial. Suffice it to say that the Rolling Stones had some very interesting lyrics toward the end of the song. Maybe Gerstner will follow Microsoft's lead and get the rights to "Louie Louie" for Notes 96. Anyway, this is where we stuck all the stuff that wouldn't fit in the rest of the book.

Mom, this Companion CD is so cool I can hardly believe it. There's enough here to keep a Windows maven poking through amazing stuff for days—even weeks.

It's more than just quantity. The quality of this collection beats the pants off any companion disk ever published in a computer book. Period. No matter what you do with, to, or for Windows, there's stuff on this disk that will suck you in.

And in addition to the Companion CD, which is bound into the back of this book, as the owner of a copy of *MOM95*, you are entitled to a copy of the Bonus CD—which includes another gargantuan array of top-notch software, plus the entire contents of this book in searchable Adobe Acrobat format—by calling 800-659-4696 (or 314-965-5630 outside the USA) and saying "I WANT MORE MOM!" There's a charge of $9.95 for shipping and handling ($14.95 outside the USA), and you can use any of the major credit cards.

Watch out! Many of the files on the CD are .drv, .dll, and system files. If you use Explorer to look for those files, you must tell Explorer to make them "visible." In Explorer, click on View, then Options, and make sure the Show All Files button is checked.

Orientation

In the rest of this chapter, I'll take you folder-by-folder through the companion CD, giving you a glimpse of the amazing goodies available there. We've got something for everybody, from the kids to the nerds to the wired to the peripatetic (not to mention the peripatetic wired nerd kids, too). At the end of the chapter, I'll also tell you about the highlights of the Bonus CD.

What You Can Do With It

The software on the Companion and Bonus CDs has been licensed specifically to Mom, and appears here by the good graces of the manufacturers. That means you, as the owner of a copy of *MOM95,* are entitled to use the software within the limitations described in the various `readme` and similar files accompanying each product. You are not authorized to distribute copies of the software, or sell it, or—in the case of Microsoft software, anyway, according to the contract they made Mom sign—give it away to organizations engaged in the unlawful production of weapons of mass destruction.

What's a Shareware?

Some of the software on the CD—and almost all of the software in the giant Public (software) Library Windows utility collection—is shareware. As you may know, shareware is the "try before you buy" approach to marketing software that lets you work with a full-blown version of a program before you spend the bucks to buy it.

 Different shareware authors have different restrictions—some limit the number of times you use the program, some disable portions of the program, others will only let you run it for 30 or 60 days—but the bottom line is the same: if you use a shareware product, pay for it. Many important improvements in PC products have originated in the shareware industry. By paying for the software you use, you help build this rich "gene pool" of new and innovative ideas, and not coincidentally keep some very smart people involved in finding new ways to solve your problems.

 It's more than that. The people who write shareware have shown an extraordinary amount of trust in *you:* they put their product out in the wild so you can see if it does what you want done. It's only fair that you reciprocate that trust by paying for the shareware you use. Lots of talented people rely on income from shareware to keep food on the table.

 If you use it, pay for it.

Nuff said.

The ZIP Thang

Many of the files on the CD are zipped, i.e., they have a file name extension of `.zip`. Mom's crew did that to cram even more on the CD than would otherwise be possible. A compressed `.zip` file has to be unZipped—creating one or more normal files—before it can be used.

There are two ways to unZip files. One is by using the free DOS command-line program called `unzip.exe`, which you will find on the Companion CD in the directory `\Pslutil`. It's a typical DOS program that requires lots of typing and futzing. Much better is to pick up (and register!) a Windows-based Zip program.

My favorite Windows-based Zip program is WinZip, and I put it in a special place on the CD, in the folder called `\Winzip`. Install it and take it for a ride. If you use WinZip, register! If you don't find it to your liking, try one of the other Zip programs in the `\Pslutil\Archive` folder. One of these zippers is bound to behave the way you want.

The Companion CD

Equi donati dentes non inspiciuntur. *

—St. Jerome, *On the Epistle to the Ephesians,* ca. 420 A.D.

Let's take a look at all the goodies you already have, in the Companion CD stuck to the back flap of this book.

Root Folder

The root folder has an update to one of the most popular packages I've ever included with my books. ProCD's Free Phone[†] and its companion, MapLinx, give you complete access to the entire 800-number directory in the USA—about 200,000 entries. This is the full commercial product, the

---

*Never look a gift horse in the mouth.

[†]Free Phone™ and Select Phone™ is republished with the permission of Pro CD 222 Rosewood Drive, Danvers, MA 01923, 508-750-0000. Listings copyright 1995 by AT&T and Pro CD. Software copyright 1995 Pro CD. All rights reserved. Pro CD also publishes a complete line of white & yellow page listing for the United States and Canada, including Select Phone, Home Phone, Business Phone, Canada Phone, ProCD Fax Book, and Home & Business Phone.

same as you'll find in computer stores for $39. To install Free Phone, just run `setupff.exe` in the root directory.

Give it a run and see how the newly updated search software works. I think you'll be impressed. Is it better than their number-one competitor, PhoneDisc? Hey! You get to try both of them (look at `\PhonDisc`). Decide for yourself! And don't forget to try MapLinx, with its Zip code and area code databases.

\Batutil

Alphabetically first (by no fault of its own), Batutil extends DOS in many useful ways. As I discussed in Chapter 3, DOS' batch language is a natural for running Windows apps, particularly because of the `start` command. Batutil gives your DOS batch files considerably greater flexibility and power than you get with DOS alone. Batutil is a shareware program developed by Barry Simon and Rick Wilson.

Yeah, *that* Barry Simon.

Batutil is bundled with a keyboard stuffer called Stackey. The `*.hlp` files for Batutil and Stackey are not Windows 95 help files—or even Windows help files. To load them, just include a `?` after the command name, e.g., `batutil ?` will load batutil help.

\Cursors

Here's an outstanding collection of more than 100 animated cursors (`*.ani` files) and another 100 or so static cursors (`*.csr` files) in the public domain. To use them, put Mom's CD in your CD drive, and copy the `.ani` and/or `.csr` files to your hard drive. Then bring up the Control Panel's Mouse applet, the Pointers Tab, click Browse, and point to the correct location on your hard drive. Seriously cool stuff.

These are in the public domain, so you don't have to pay anything extra to use them.

\Fdcd, \Fltdata

How often do you fly? If it's more than a few times a year, the Official Airline Guide's FlightDisk™ will make your life so much simpler, you'll wonder how you ever lived without it. With detailed information on more than 650,000 flights (yeah, you read that right) between 3,500 cities, FlightDisk brings the encyclopedic breadth of OAG's printed guides to your PC, and *you* get to give it a try right here on my CD.

The program itself presents you with drop-down lists for your city of origin and destination. You can choose dates, times, even a preferred airline, and you can either insist on direct flights or let the program figure out connecting flights. Once you've chosen the flights, you can call, fax or e-mail your travel agent to book the flight. And if you want, you can connect to OAG's FlightLine™ on-line system to grab the same up-to-the-minute pricing information and seat availability the airline Customer Reservations Services (CRS) representatives use (there's a transaction fee for using the on-line system).

Wait a minute. You're saying that when my travel agent tells me there's only one $99 seat available on Friday night from Los Angeles to Denver, I can go into *the same system he's using* and check to see if I can find something better? Wow. That's amazing. I guess the only thing I can't do with FlightDisk is book a seat.

There's a huge amount of ancillary information, too—everything from toll-free and local phone numbers for airlines and hotels to complete details on frequent traveler programs—that every traveler needs, on every trip. It's a one-disk survival kit.

Best of all, as a *MOM95* reader, you can get the most recent FlightDisk free. To receive your update, just call OAG at 800-342-5624 (or 708-574-6146 from outside the USA) and say "I'm a MOM Reader! I want promotional code 5AJC6!" You'll get a free 30-day trial subscription to FlightDisk. For your convenience, OAG will automatically send you an invoice reflecting the special *MOM95* price. If you are not completely satisfied, write CANCEL on the invoice, return it and owe nothing.

Here's the special *MOM95* subscription pricing, valid through the end of 1996:

3 month introductory offer

Worldwide Edition	$59 (regular value $75)
North American Edition	$49 (regular value $63)
European Edition - DOS only	$49 (regular value $63)

Save when you subscribe for a full year

Worldwide Edition $215 (regular value $299)

North American Edition $182 (regular value $252)

European Edition - DOS only $182 (regular value $252)

To install FlightDisk, just run `\Fdcd\setup.exe`.

Compose itineraries. Compare routings. Talk to your travel agent with all the details in hand, not just flight availability, but pricing, hotels, car rentals, the works. If your plans get screwed up (and whose don't?) you can look at all your alternatives with a click or two. This is one of the best programs—and best deals—ever to appear on one of my CDs.

Even if you always fly economy. Especially if you fly economy. Like me.

\Fonts

The folks at Bitstream let me give you this hand-picked collection of 20 top quality fonts, in Post Script and TrueType format. They're among Bitstream's most popular. As a *MOM95* owner, you are granted a license to use these fonts, free of charge; details are in the files `ps.txt` and `ttf.txt`. The files also tell you which fonts come in which `.ttf` or `.pf*` file: Bitstream loves to use intuitive file names, so the typeface Original Garamond Bold, say, lives in `tt0865m_.ttf`.

Here are the typefaces:

Cheltenham

Cheltenham Italic

Cheltenham Bold

Cheltenham Bold Italic

Cheltenham Bold Condensed

Chelthenham Bold Condensed Italic

Cheltenham Bold Extra Condensed

Original Garamond

Original Garamond Italic

Original Garamond Bold

Original Garamond Bold Italic

Snell

Snell Bold

SHOTGUN

SHOTGUN BLANKS

Engraver's Old English

Engraver's Old English Bold

Old Dreadful No. 7

♣▯·⊗⊠☑⌀✿○★♣★●●
(Commercial Pi)

◀▪■○○▢□☆#°′″∅±°′″℞

To install the TrueType fonts, bring up the Control Panel (Start/Settings/Control Panel), double-click on the Fonts applet, click File, then Install New Font, and point Windows at the `\Fonts\TrueType` folder on the CD.

Bitstream Typefaces courtesy of Bitstream, Inc, Cambridge MA USA. Phone 617-497-6222.

\Icons

A reprise from the original *CD-MOM* collection, you'll find over 4,000 `.ico` icons in this folder—surely including just the one you need for your particular shortcut or class of documents. They're in the public domain. (Details are in the file `allicons.doc`.)

The icons are stored in two different ways, for your convenience.

First, I put them in `.dll` files so you can copy them to your hard disk and use the Windows Browse buttons to get at all the pictures. To change the icon for a particular file name extension, bring up Explorer, click on View, then Options, bring up the File Types tab, click once on the class you'd like to change, click Edit, then Change Icon, click Browse, and point to the `.dll`. To change the icon on a shortcut, right-click, bring up Properties, then the Shortcut tab, click Change Icon, and then Browse.

Second, I put them in `.zip` files so you could move them around without worrying about consuming vast quantities of hard disk space. Remember, a little 760K file can take up 32K of space on an uncompressed hard drive—multiply 32K by 4,000 icons, and you can see why the `.zips` are more useful.

If you're using MicroAngelo (see the next section), you'll be able to use MicroAngelo's Librarian function to look in the `.dll` files and see each icon's name. Yet another reason to register MicroAngelo, eh?

The files break out like this:

- `appsicon` includes icons for general Windows appls, databases, integrated programs

- `charicon` has cartoon characters

- `comhdwic` has communications hardware icons

- `commicon` covers general communications

- `compicon` for computer icons

- `deskicon` has things you might find on a (physical) desktop

- `dosicon` is for DOS utilities

- `fileicon` has files and folders in mass profusion

- `finicon` covers financial stuff

- `flagicon` has flags

- `gameicon` covers computer-based and non-computer-based games

- `graficon` includes graphics icons and scanners

- `imagicon` has "images"

- `langicon` holds icons for computer languages

- `miscic01` and `miscic02` are "miscellaneous"

- `playicon` has mostly non-computer games

- `signicon` contains traffic and other signs

- `sprdicon` holds icons for spreadsheets

- `symbicon` includes a wide array of symbols

- `utilicon` covers utilities

- `winicon` is for Windows accessories and add-ons

- `wordicon` has icons for word processors and printing

- `writicon` includes books and writing implements

- `zipicon` contains icons for zip and compression programs

If you use one of these icons, make sure you copy the correct `.dll` file (or unZip the correct `.zip` file and copy the correct `.ico` file) to the hard disk before changing the icon. That will ensure Windows can find the icon, should it ever need to re-build the image.

There's a complete list of all the icons in these folders in the original *Mother of All Windows Books*. (It takes up almost 70 pages: we didn't have much room to spare in this edition, and opted to keep the cover price down!)

This isn't your only source of high-quality icons, by the way. Many of the 500 or so built-in Windows 95 icons are listed in Appendix B, and you can use them as easily as any others.

\MomStuff

 Here are the goodies I promised you, in various places throughout this book:

- The Mom logon screen, `logo.sys`. Rename the `logo.sys` that's currently in the root directory of your boot drive (usually `c:\`), then copy this `logo.sys` over. Next time you re-boot, my wonderful visage will beam upon you. No wisecracks, buster. I *have* to look like this. It's in my contract. What's your excuse?

- The message program, `mommess.exe`. Copy it to your `\windows` folder. While you're at it, check to make sure you have the Visual Basic 4.0 "runtime library" called `vb40032.dll` in your `\windows\system` folder. If it isn't there, `mommess` and other programs you'll acquire will need it, so copy the files called `vb40032.dll`, `olepro32.dll`, and `msvert40.dll` from here on the CD into `\windows\system`.

- `screen.ico` is the "transparent" icon you can use to make My Computer invisible on your Desktop. Look in Chapter 11 for details.

- `Welcom~1.doc` lists all the "Tips of the Day" you'll encounter when Win95 starts, as described in Chapter 2. Open the document with WordPad.

- `Win95f~1.doc` is an Excel spreadsheet that contains all the information about the contents of the Win95 distribution CD and diskettes, including detailed info on the components of the `.cab` files. See Appendix E for a digested version.

\MuAngelo

The product we used to perform most of the (considerable!) icon manipulation for this book, MicroAngelo does yeoman's work in the icon trades. Price ranges from $24.95 + s/h for the "Apprentice", which includes one add-on (I like Librarian best) to $59.95 for the whole she-bang. Run `setup.exe` to get going. The shareware version included with this book includes three of the four components. An animated cursor editor is included with the full registered version.

Mom appears courtesy of Mom, Inc., a joint venture of the NSA and Spacely Sprockets Amalgamated. All opinions expressed by the old biddy are strictly her own.

\PhonDisc

PhoneDisc has provided my readers with a huge, 200,000-entry database of all the computer companies (manufacturers, distributors, retailers, just about everybody) in the USA. It's an excellent chance to compare PhoneDisc's software with ProCD's (see Root Directory, above), and decide for yourself which of the two major CD-based telephone books *you* prefer.

To install PhoneDisc, just run `\PhonDisc\setup.exe`.

The information itself is mighty important, too, of course. Ever wonder how to get in touch with your video card manufacturer? All the numbers are right here. Give it a shot!

\Prowin

This is a data folder used by ProCD/Free Phone.

\PsLUtil

Nelson Ford and the other folks at Public (software) Library distribute a monthly CD including a huge assortment of shareware and freeware. This folder contains P(s)L's huge Windows utility shareware collection, up-to-date as of the time we went to press.

The folders are arranged as follows:

- `anti_vir` for anti-virus software
- `archive` contains archiving (e.g., Zip) utilities
- `copy_del` includes file copying, deleting and moving
- `desktool` has Desktop tools—clocks, calendars, notes
- `directry` contains directory utilities
- `disk_oth` for other disk and drive utilities
- `file_chg` includes file changing and conversion programs

PhoneDisc® is a registered trademark of Digital Directory Assistance, Inc.

- `file_oth` has other file utilities

- `filefind` is for file finders

- `fileman` contains file management routines

- `fileview` has file viewers

- `fmt_copy` is for disk formatters and copiers

- `harddisk` includes hard disk utilities

- `key_mous` contains keyboard, mouse and joystick utilities

- `opsys_ut` is an "all other" category for operating system utilities

- `security` covers passwords and encryption

- `sys_set` has system set-up and configuration analysis and testing programs

- `utl_sets` is for utilities bundled in sets

- `vid_util` contains video utilities, including screen blankers

Note that some of these utilities are specific to earlier versions of Windows, so a bit of discretion should be exercised. (None of the installers will hurt Windows 95, of course, but you could end up with a number of programs on your hard drive that don't really do much in Win95.)

To keep up with the latest in Windows 95 software, subscribe to the P(s)L monthly CD, for $19.95 per month + s/h. Contact: Public (software) Library, P.O. Box 35705, Houston, TX 77235-5705, voice 713-524-6394, fax 713-524-6398, CompuServe 71355,470.

\Sampler\ArcadeAm

Man, what a great multimedia sampler! The intro animation and Alcatraz game on Arcade America had me rolling in the aisles. Reminds me of home. Come to think of it, this *was* home.

Arcade America is the best walkin'-around adventure game since Sam 'n Max hit the road. Follow Joey (the, uh, corpulent, nose-picking butt-scratching anti-hero) as he stomps his way from a post-quake California to the rock scene in Woodstock. A laugh a minute. No. Make that ten laughs a minute. Big, deep, Joey-sized belly laughs.

Oh, and did I forget to mention? The *arcade* part is phenomenal, too, with a joystick or just on the keyboard. Hidden bonuses, slingshot zaps, even the patented Joey belly bounce, will keep your fingers twitching. One of the most addictive games I've ever played.

Figure A-1. Joey at the San Fran Bay

If you're working from the keyboard, make sure you get all the moves—not just the directional arrow keys, but X for jump, Z to shoot the slingshot, a double left or right arrow for the belly bounce, and a double up arrow for the pull.

Just run `setup.exe`. Enjoy!

\Sampler\ArcadeAm\Demo

We slipped this in at the last minute, so forgive me for how you have to hunt and peck to find it. Believe me, it's well worth scaling down several levels of folders to unearth this jewel.

What I have down in this folder is a collection of multimedia samplers for no fewer than *five* different 7th Level products:

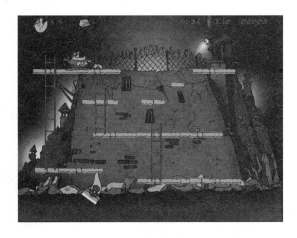

Figure A-2. Joey Jumps in Alcatraz

ArcadeAmerica™ from 7th Level, Inc.

- Take Your Best Shot, a bizarre multimedia sorta-game thingy, represented here by a Pong-like game with a dark twist—a disembodied head in the middle that yells "Ouch!" when the Pong Puck hits.

- TuneLand, an extraordinary collection of animated kids' songs. Both the music and the click-anywhere animation are first rate.

- The Great Word Adventure, starring Howie Mandel, which follows Lil' Howie (Figure A-3) and his progressively more difficult antics with synonyms, antonyms, and homonyms. (Hey, where's the nymonyms?)

Figure A-3. Great Word Adventure

- The Universe According to Virgil, wherein an eccentric, morphing science wonk with the voice of Charles Fleischer (a.k.a. Roger Rabbit) puts some fun and humor into a wide variety of science topics.

- And, of course, the big game from Monty Python's Compleat Waste of Time (Figure A-4). If you're a Python fan, you should have your head examined. If you *aren't* a Python fan, you should have your head examined. The big game is a sensitive, introspective, reserved tool for such self-examination, punctuated by the occasional offensive sound of exuberant bodily parts and the velvety crash of high caliber artillery shells encroaching on the odd half-naked nymphet. In other words, vintage Python, eh wot?

Figure A-4. Compleat Waste of Time

Spam. Spam. Spam. Spam. If you have the slightest bit of prurient interest left after battling the Win95 demons, you *have* to try the Python big game. To get the 7th Level working models going, take your mouse on an excursion to the Bureau of Sampler Silly Walks: navigate down to the `\Sampler\ArcadeAm\Demo` folder, and double-click on `demo.exe`.

\Sampler\FWFish

I included this multimedia sampler because it's really very different from most simulation games, and it gives you a chance to dig pretty deep into multimedia simulation if you've never tried it before. Animatek's Nature Collection Freshwater Fish puts you in the position of a public aquarium administrator attempting to pull together a big freshwater fish exhibit.

Figure A-5. Finny Friends in Freshwater Fish

The rules are fairly complicated—as with any good simulation, there are many things to learn, and in order to play you have to learn them all at once—but careful study of the Guide Book will take you through the paces. To install, run `\Sampler\Fwfish\setup.exe`.

If you know somebody who likes puzzles and tropical fish, this game is a dynamite combination, good for many fascinating hours of play.

\Sampler\Humongos

Long the innovators in Windows-based kids' games, Humongous Entertainment once again shows its technical prowess (not to mention extraordinary game design!) with Freddi Fish and the Case of the Missing Kelp Seeds, the first shipping Windows 95 Autorun CD. What does that mean, really? Just this: if you have a six-year-old who wants to play with

Freddi Fish, all she needs to do is pop the CD in the CD drive, and away she goes. No installation mumbo-jumbo. No inscrutable directions (inscrutable to either the parent or the kid). No hassle. Just pop it in and play.

I'm very proud to have four different multimedia samplers from Humongous, representing four of the finest multimedia titles ever produced:

Figure A-6. Freddi and the Starfish

- Freddi Fish and the Case of the Missing Kelp Seeds follows Freddi (the big fish in Figure A-6) and Luther (his little side-kick) as they look for Grandma Grouper's purloined seeds.

- Putt-Putt Saves the Zoo takes the famed purple speedster (Figure A-7) through Outback Al's Cartown Zoo. Kids help Putt-Putt save zoo animals in peril.

Figure A-7. Putt-Putt and the Penguins

- Let's Explore the Airport puts Buzzy, an inquisitive little, uh, bugger (Figure A-8), into the cockpit of a jet, all around the concourse, down in the baggage area, and everywhere else you can imagine in a busy airport.

- Let's Explore the Farm also follows Buzzy, this time around a working farm, with more than 200 different animals, a silo just begging to be explored, down a well.

 Humongous says these games are suitable for 3 to 8 year-olds. Personally, I think they're suitable for anybody who's old enough to push a mouse—and young enough to have fun. Gorgeous hand-drawn graphics. Engrossing, challenging, often educational games. A lively plot and strong action. And no reading required— all the text will be "read" aloud with the click of a button. There's a reason why Humongous keeps running away with all the kids software awards. Check it out!

Figure A-8. Buzzy Explores the Airport

Demos courtesy of Humongous Entertainment.

To install the demos, run `\Sampler\Humongos\install.exe`.

\Sampler\OSLO

The folks at Science for Kids have given me multimedia samplers of their two top science products. Suitable for kids from about 4 to 12 years (or even older), the OSLO adventures put a captivating spin on traditional—and all-too-often stodgy—science topics.

OSLO's Tools & Gadgets (just run `\Oslotg\oslotg.exe`) won *PC Magazine*'s Top 100 CD Award, not long ago. It encourages kids to use six simple tools (wheel, inclined plane, level, wedge, screw, and pully) to solve mechanical problems, in a very fun and lively way. (See Figure A-10.)

OSLO's World of Water (run `\Oslowow\oslowow.exe`) follows water in all its major states (liquid, steam, ice) over, under around and through the environment. There's a board game (Figure A-11) that uses water in the three states; a big, illustrated library of water-related science experiments; and a bunch of animated "Friends" who keep the action moving.

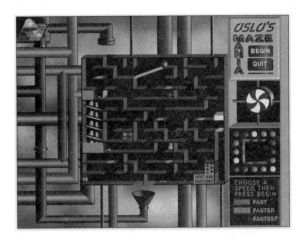

Figure A-10. OSLO Tools & Gadget Maze

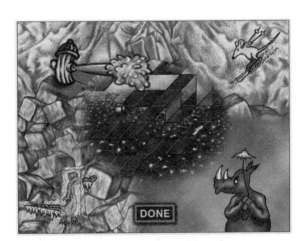

Figure A-11. OSLO WaterWorks Board Game

Both of the OSLO Adventures require Quicktime for Windows. If you try to run them and you get a message saying you must install Quicktime for Windows (or if you currently have a version of QTW earlier than 2.03), simply install Quicktime from the `\Oslo\Qtw` folder.

Adventures with OSLO™ Tools & Gadgets and Adventures with OSLO™ World of Water developed and published by Science for Kids™.

\SysInfo

Meet the Windows 95 incarnation of the classic Norton System Information package—better known, simply, as SysInfo. This is the full, working program, brought to Mom's readers by the good folks at Norton (who, not so incidentally, hope you'll also take a gander at their other fine Windows 95 products—SysInfo is part of the Norton Utilities package).

Running this program will bring you face-to-face with the updates to several classics—the latest version of the famous "Norton SI" Benchmarking number, for example. It'll also you show some of Norton's prowess in the new world of Win95. Take a look at the memory map, for example, where you'll see extensive reports on how much memory each of your programs occupies, how older libraries are being used, and much, much more.

My favorite is the Drive tab, where you can finally get a handle on space requirements for various programs, and see graphically once and for all whether that notorious disk hog of a program you're been running might really be a tiny suckling. Very useful stuff.

\W95Driv

This is the complete Windows 95 Driver Library, up-to-date as of the time we went to press. It contains more than a hundred drivers; some may be very important to you.

To install one of these drivers, bring up the Control Panel (Start/Settings/Control Panel), and double-click on the Add New Hardware icon. When the Wizard asks if you want Windows to detect new hardware, click No. Then pick the hardware that needs the new driver, click Have Disk, and point Windows over to the appropriate place on Mom's CD. The installer will take it from there.

\W95HCL

Here's the Hardware Compatibility List, the list of all the hardware that Microsoft tested while developing Win95, and an indication of which ones passed Redmond's muster. It also includes detailed information about the latest drivers available for the hardware. The information is presented in two different ways: a `.hlp` Help file for browsing, or an `.rtf` file for printing.

SysInfo™ by Symantec Corporation.

The Windows 95 Driver library provided courtesy of Microsoft.

The Windows 95 Hardware Compatibility list provided courtesy of Microsoft.

If you find a driver listed here as being "on-line", check first to see if the driver is in the \W95Driv. (It probably is.) Look for a file on the CD with the same name as the driver name, but with an .inf extension instead of .exe.

\W95Supp

If you picked up the 3.5-inch version of Windows 95 instead of the CD version, this is where you'll find all the files you missed—or at least, all the files Microsoft will send you if you return the sign-up card in the Windows package, requesting the Windows 95 Supplemental Disks.

To install any of these missing Windows 95 components:

- Quick View file viewers

- Character Map utility

- Net Watcher utility

- System Monitor utility

- Mouse Pointers

- CD Player utility

- Windows Tour

- Windows Online User's Guide

start the Control Panel (Start/Settings/Control Panel), double-click on the Add/Remove Programs applet and bring up the Windows Components tab. Click Have Disk, and point Windows to this folder on Mom's CD. The installer will go on from there.

To install any of these programs, look for the readme or similar .txt file in the indicated folder:

Configuration Backup Utility   OTHER\MISC\CFGBACK
Enhanced Print Troubleshooter   OTHER\MISC\EPTS

These programs provided courtesy of Microsoft.

Emergency Recovery Utility	OTHER\MISC\ERU
Log File Viewer	OTHER\MISC\LOGVIEW
Clipbook Viewer	OTHER\CLIPBOOK
Windows Chat	OTHER\CHAT
Old MS-DOS utilities	OTHER\OLDMSDOS
MSBACKUP from MS-DOS 6.x	OTHER\OLDMSDOS\MSBACKUP
Microsoft Diagnostics	OTHER\MSD
Windows 95 logo wallpaper	FUNSTUFF\PICTURES
Scripting for Dial-Up Networking	ADMIN\APPTOOLS\DSCRIPT
MS-DOS environment variables in Windows	ADMIN\APPTOOLS\ENVVARS
Long File Name Backup Utility	ADMIN\APPTOOLS\LFNBACK
System Policy Editor	ADMIN\APPTOOLS\POLEDIT
Password List Editor	ADMIN\APPTOOLS\PWLEDIT
Network Monitor Agent	ADMIN\NETTOOLS\NETMON
Remote Registry Service	ADMIN\NETTOOLS\REMOTREG

In many cases, you'll be instructed to use Add/Remove Programs for these components, too.

\W95UIG

Contains the complete contents of *The Windows Interface Guidelines for Software Design,* the definitive book on the Windows user interface. If you're curious about how the UI is supposed to work, this is the ultimate reference.

It's in `.hlp` Help file format, with contents identical to the book by the same name from Microsoft Press. (Retail: $39.95!)

\WinZip

 WinZip is, hands, down, my favorite Zip utility—and one of my favorite Windows utilities, period. Give it a try. You'll wonder how you ever lived without it. One of the great bargains in shareware: $29 registration from Nico Mak Computing, Inc., P.O. Box 919, Bristol, CT 06011, CompuServe 70056,241.

The Windows User Interface Guidelines Help file provided courtesy of Microsoft.

\Word95Vu

The Word for Windows viewer that ships with Windows 95 works. . . but just barely. Here's the latest, greatest version, from Microsoft. Much more accurate rendition of many different formatting details— particularly including tables—and (finally!) the chance to open more than one file simultaneously.

To create Word files, you'll still have to buy Word for Windows (or settle for the "baby" Word files produced by WordPad). But if you just want to look at them and print them, this is all you need. Run `setup.exe`, and you'll be installed in no time.

WinZip - book.zip					
File	Actions	Options	Help		
Name	Date	Time	Size	Ratio	Packed
ch01.doc	08/03/95	09:55	375,296	71%	108,591
Ch02.doc	08/15/95	23:24	7,192,064	90%	753,124
CH03.doc	09/15/95	15:58	17,263,616	92%	1,315,286
ch04.doc	09/26/95	23:44	15,970,816	96%	707,972
ch06.doc	07/30/95	10:07	137,728	73%	37,832
Ch07.doc	08/14/95	08:53	2,518,016	97%	76,913
ch08.doc	08/21/95	08:26	10,557,440	97%	364,516
ch09.doc	09/13/95	11:18	2,164,224	90%	216,657
ch10.doc	09/13/95	15:36	22,006,784	97%	754,713
Ch11.doc	10/02/95	11:02	7,006,208	95%	334,041
Selected 0 files, 0 bytes			Total 10 files, 83,196KB		

Figure A-12. WinZip in Action

\WorkModl\SndForge

A complete sound studio, under Windows. That's what Sound Forge delivers in this working model. The full Sound Forge product takes sound input from almost any conceivable source, manipulates the sounds in almost any conceivable manner, and produces output in almost any conceivable format (including blasting away on your speakers, using your sound card, of course). You'll be astounded by the capabilities of this program.

To install it, run `\WorkModl\SndForge\setup.exe`.

\WS_IRC

Caesar Samsi's Internet Relay Chat client for Windows appears here, in both shareware and freeware forms. Take a look at all the bells and whistles—an impressive array, indeed. Run `wsirc20.exe` to install. Then check the installed `readme.txt` file for registration and distribution information.

`Ws_IRC` presupposes that you have already installed Internet support, e.g., by running the Plus! Pack's Internet Setup Wizard.

The Word 95 Viewer provided courtesy of Microsoft.
Sound Forge by Sonic Foundry, Inc. Madison, WI.

The Bonus CD

He who tooteth not his own horn,
That same shall not be tooted.

—Political advice, Washington, DC, ca 1980

I have a second CD—the Mom Bonus CD—all ready for you, stuffed with all the stuff that didn't arrive in time for the Companion CD (the one stuck in the back of this book). What's on the CD? Well, how's this for starters:

- The complete text of this book, in Adobe Acrobat format, so you can search for the inimitable words and phrases from my crew wherever they may occur.

- The Adobe Acrobat viewer. (Ha! Bet you thought we'd forget that one!)

- Twenty *more* hand-picked Bitstream fonts: Bitstream Arrus (in 6 weights), Zapf Humanist (8 weights), Shelley (3 weights), Cooper Black (5 weights), Vineta, and Bitstream Holiday Pi.

- A bunch of working models—not little slide shows, mind you, but full-blown, working segments of important new Windows 95 products. At the moment we have products on tap from Knowledge Adventure and 7th Level, and a couple of others that are still top secret.

- And yet another fabulous collection of Windows 95 specific shareware and freeware.

I absolutely guarantee that you'll find Mom's Bonus CD to be an outstanding collection, worth many times its nominal price: just $9.95 inside the USA ($14.95 outside the USA), to cover Mom's costs for shipping and handling. One of the best values in the computer biz.

How to order? Easy. Pick up the phone and call 800-659-4696 or 314-965-5630. Alternatively, you can fax 314-966-1833, or e-mail 76711.1171@compuserve.com. If worse comes to worst, drop a line to Advanced Support Group, 11900 Grant Place, Des Peres, MO 63131 USA. All major credit cards, checks, money orders, and wampum accepted.

Mom's Icon Catalog

Windows 95 ships with an enormous number of very useful, extraordinarily well constructed icons—more than 500 of them—if you can only find them! They're scattered all over hell's half acre. This is my crew's attempt to bring most of the stock icons together in one place, so you stand a fighting chance of finding the icon you need.

To change the icon associated with a file name extension, go into Explorer's View/Options File Types tab, pick the extension, click Edit, and click the Change Icon button. To change icons on a shortcut, right-click on the shortcut, pick Properties, bring up the Shortcut tab, and click Change Icon. In either case you can click Browse, move to one of these files, select the icon you want, and click OK. In the Registry, you have to name the file and add the icon number: for example, `c:\windows\system\shell32.dll,3` will tell Windows to use icon number 3—which, in reality, is the *fourth* icon—in the file `shell32.dll`.

The numbers you see here are icon numbers, suitable for use in Registry entries. If there is a number with a blank icon, the icon is indeed blank—or "transparent" if you prefer.

Icons in c:\windows:

c:\windows\cdplayer.exe

| 0 | 1 |

c:\windows\clipbrd.exe[†]

| 0 | 1 | 2 | 3 | 4 | 5 |

[†] These are the icons available if you have installed Clipboard, not Clipbook. For a discussion of the difference, see Chapter 4.

c:\windows\defrag.exe

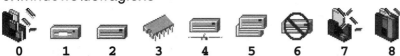

0   1   2   3   4   5   6   7   8

c:\windows\dialer.exe

0   1

c:\windows\directcc.exe

0   1   2   3   4   5

c:\windows\drvspace.exe

0   1   2   3   4   5   6   7

c:\windows\explorer.exe

0   1   2   3   4   5   6   7

c:\windows\expostrt.exe

0

c:\windows\faxcover.exe

0   1   2   3

c:\windows\faxview.exe

0   1   2

c:\windows\fontview.exe

0   1

c:\windows\freecell.exe

0

c:\windows\grpconv.exe

0   1

c:\windows\moreicons.dll

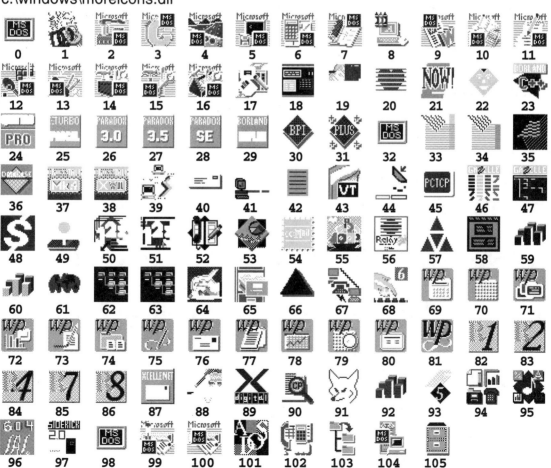

0   1   2   3   4   5   6   7   8   9   10   11

12   13   14   15   16   17   18   19   20   21   22   23

24   25   26   27   28   29   30   31   32   33   34   35

36   37   38   39   40   41   42   43   44   45   46   47

48   49   50   51   52   53   54   55   56   57   58   59

60   61   62   63   64   65   66   67   68   69   70   71

72   73   74   75   76   77   78   79   80   81   82   83

84   85   86   87   88   89   90   91   92   93   94   95

96   97   98   99   100   101   102   103   104   105

c:\windows\mplayer.exe

0 1 2 3 4 5 6

c:\windows\mshearts.exe

0

c:\windows\notepad.exe

0 1

c:\windows\package.exe

0

c:\windows\pbrush.exe

0

c:\windows\progman.exe

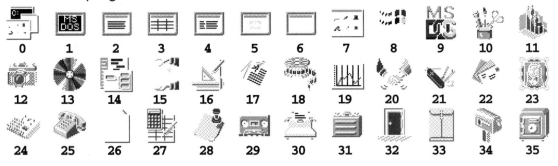

0 1 2 3 4 5 6 7 8 9 10 11

12 13 14 15 16 17 18 19 20 21 22 23

24 25 26 27 28 29 30 31 32 33 34 35

| 36 | 37 | 38 | 39 | 40 | 41 | 42 | 43 | 44 | 45 |

c:\windows\regedit.exe

| 0 | 1 | 2 |

c:\windows\sndrec32.exe

| 0 | 1 | 2 |

c:\windows\sndvol32.exe

| 0 | 1 | 2 | 3 | 4 |

c:\windows\sol.exe

| 0 |

c:\windows\sysmon.exe

| 0 |

c:\windows\taskman.exe

| 0 |

c:\windows\winfile.exe

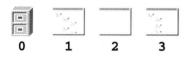

| 0 | 1 | 2 | 3 |

c:\windows\winipcfg.exe

0

c:\windows\winpopup.exe

0   1   2

c:\windows\winhlp32.exe

0   1   2

c:\windows\winmine.exe

0

c:\windows\write.exe

0

Icons in c:\windows\system

c:\windows\system\awfext32.dll

0   1   2   3   4

c:\windows\system\awfxcg32.dll

0   1   2   3   4

c:\windows\system\awfxex32.exe

| 0 | 1 | 2 | 3 | 4 | 5 | 6 | 7 | 8 | 9 | 10 | 11 |

c:\windows\system\awschd32.dll

0   1   2

c:\windows\system\awsnto32.exe

0   1

c:\windows\system\commdlg32.dll

| 0 | 1 | 2 | 3 | 4 | 5 | 6 | 7 | 8 | 9 | 10 | 11 |

c:\windows\system\deskcp16.dll

0

c:\windows\system\diskcopy.dll

0

c:\windows\system\fontext.dll

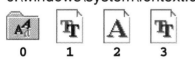

0   1   2   3

c:\windows\system\icmui.dll

0   1

c:\windows\system\iconlib.dll

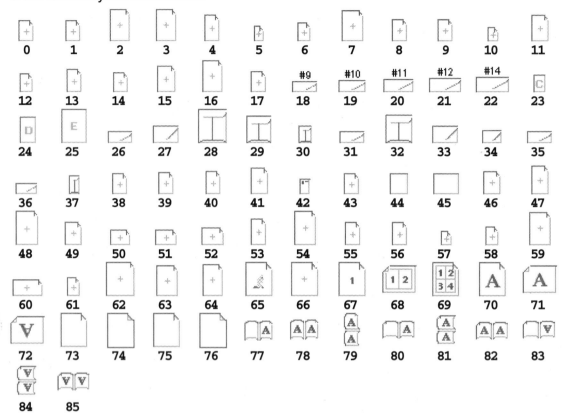

c:\windows\system\internat.exe

0

c:\windows\system\iosclass.exe

0   1

c:\windows\system\lights.exe

0   1   2   3   4

c:\windows\system\maincp16.dll

0   1

c:\windows\system\mapisp32.dll

0

c:\windows\system\mkcompat.exe

0

c:\windows\system\mmci.dll

0

c:\windows\system\modemui.dll

0   1   2   3

c:\windows\system\moscudll.dll

0

c:\windows\system\mprserv.dll

0   1   2

c:\windows\system\msacm.dll

0

c:\windows\system\msnexch.exe

0   1

c:\windows\system\msnp32.dll

0   1   2

c:\windows\system\mspcic.dll

0

c:\windows\msprint.dll

0

c:\windows\system\msvfw32.dll

0

c:\windows\system\pifmgr.dll

0   1   2   3   4   5   6   7   8   9   10   11

12   13   14   15   16   17   18   19   20   21   22   23

24   25   26   27   28   29   30   31   32   33   34   35

36   37

c:\windows\system\prodinv.dll

0

c:\windows\system\rasapi32.dll

0   1   2   3   4

c:\windows\system\regwiz.exe

0   1   2   3

c:\windows\system\rnaapp.exe

0   1   2

c:\windows\system\rnaui.dll

0   1   2   3   4

c:\windows\system\setup4.dll

0   1   2

c:\windows\system\setupx.dll

0   1   2   3   4   5   6   7   8   9   10   11

12   13   14   15   16   17

c:\windows\system\shell.dll

c:\windows\system\shell32.dll

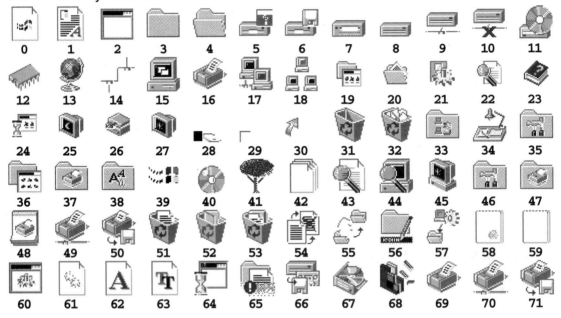

c:\windows\system\shscrap.dll

c:\windows\system\syncui.dll

c:\windows\system\sysedit.exe

0   1

c:\windows\system\systray.exe

0   1   2   3   4   5   6   7   8   9

c:\windows\system\tapi.dll

0   1   2

c:\windows\system\user.exe

0   1   2   3   4   5   6

c:\windows\system\wmsui32.dll

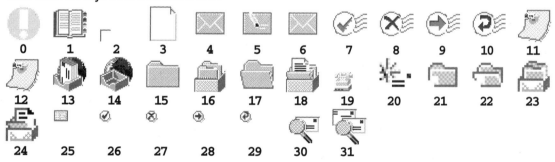

0   1   2   3   4   5   6   7   8   9   10   11

12   13   14   15   16   17   18   19   20   21   22   23

24   25   26   27   28   29   30   31

Plus Pack Icons

c:\windows\system\cool.dll

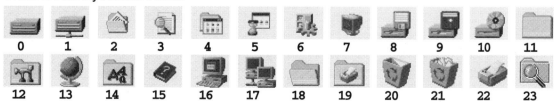

0   1   2   3   4   5   6   7   8   9   10   11

12   13   14   15   16   17   18   19   20   21   22   23

A

Adaptec, Inc.
691 South Milpitas Blvd.
Milpitas, CA 95035
SCSI Controllers
Sales: 408-945-8600
Tech Support: 800-959-7274, 408-945-2250
BBS: 408-945-7747

Addison-Wesley
One Jacob Way
Reading, MA 01867
Casa MOM
Corporate/Institutional Bulk Sales: 617-944-3700

America Online
8619 Westwood Center Dr.
Vienna, VA 22182-9806
Online service, diskette recycling
Sales: 800-827-6364

American Megatrends, Inc.
6145-F Northbelt Pkwy.
Norcross, GA 30071
Home of the AMI BIOS
Sales: 404-263-8181

American Power Conversion
132 Fairgrounds Road
P.O. Box 278
West Kingston, RI 02892
Uninterruptable Power Supplies
Sales: 800-800-4272
Tech Support: 401-789-5735

Apogee
3660 Broadway Blvd., Suite 235
Garland, TX 75043
Games
Sales: 214-271-2137

Apple Computer, Inc.
20525 Mariani Ave.
Cupertino, CA 95014
Computers, Software
Sales: 408-996-1010
Tech support: 800-767-2775
Compuserve: GO APPLE

Association of PC User Groups
To find a PC user group near you, call...
Locator Service: 914-876-6678

Association of Shareware Professionals
545 Grover Road
Muskegon, MI 49442-9427
The original shareware organization
CompuServe: GO ASP

AST Research Inc.
16215 Alton Pkwy.
Irvine, CA 92619-7005
Sales: 800-876-4278, 714-727-4141
Tech support: 800-727-1278
CompuServe: GO NVENA

ATI Technologies
3761 Victoria Park Ave.
Scarborough, Ontario M1W 3S2
Video boards
Sales: 905-882-2600
CompuServe: GO GRAPHAVEN

B

Bitstream, Inc.
215 First St.
Cambridge, MA 02142
Fonts
Sales: 800-223-3176, 617-497-6222
Fax: 617-868-4732
Tech Support: 617-497-7514
CompuServe: GO DTPVEN

Borland International, Inc.
100 Borland Way
Scotts Valley, CA 95067-0001
Turbo C, Paradox,dBase etc.
Sales: 800-331-0877, 408-438-8400
Tech support: 800-523-7070, 408-841-8180
Fax: 408-438-9119
CompuServe: GO BORLAND
BBS: 408-438-5780

Brøderbund
500 Redwood Blvd.
P.O. Box 6121
Novato, CA 94948-6121
Games, Educational Software
Sales: 415-382-4400, 800-521-6263
Fax: 415-382-4419

Brother International Corp.
8 Corporate Place
Piscataway, NJ 08855-0159
Printers
Sales: 800-284-4357, 210-981-0300
Parent Office: Brother Industries Ltd.
46-15, Ohsu, 3-chome
Naka-Ku
Nagoya 460, Japan

Byte Magazine
1 Phoenix Mill Lane
Peterborough, NH 03458
Byte Magazine
Subscriptions: 800-232-BYTE, 609-426-7676

C

Cables To Go
1501 Webster St.
Dayton, OH 45404
Mom's favorite source of oddball cables
Sales: 800-826-7904

Canon USA, Inc.
1 Canon Plaza
Lake Success, NY 11042
Printers, computers
Sales: 800-441-1313, 516-488-6700
Parent Office: Canon, Inc.
7-1, Nishi-Shinjuku, 2-chome
Shinjuku-Ku
Tokyo 163, Japan

Citizen American Corporation
PO Box 4003
2450 Broadway, Suite 600
Santa Monica, CA 90411-4003
Computers, Printers
Sales: 800-477-4683, 310-453-0614
Fax: 310-453-2814
Tech Support: 310-453-0614, exten. 464

Compaq Computer Corporation
P.O. Box 692000
Houston, TX 77269
Computers
Sales: 800-345-1518, 713-370-0670
Tech Support: 800-345-1518

Compton's NewMedia, Inc.
2320 Camino Vida Roble
Carlsbad, CA 92009
Lots of CD titles
Sales: 619-929-2500

Colorado Memory Systems
800 S. Taft Ave.
Loveland, CO 80537
Tape Backup
Sales: 800-845-7905, 303-669-6500
Fax: 303-667-0997

Tech Support: 800-845-7906
CompuServe: 71621,3022

CompuServe
5000 Arlington Centre Blvd.
P.O. Box 20212
Columbus, Ohio 43220
CompuServe Information Services
Sales/Support: 800-848-8990, 614-457-8600
CompuServe: GO FEEDBACK, GO WINCIM

Corel Systems Corporation
1600 Carling Ave.
Ottawa, Ontario, Canada K1Z 8R7
CorelDRAW
Sales: 800-836-DRAW, 613-728-8200
Fax: 613-761-9176
Tech Support: 613-728-1990
CompuServe: GO COREL

Corporate Assoc. Microcomputer Professionals
950 Skokie Blvd., Suite 310
Northbrook, IL 60062
A large for-profit PC user group
Info: 708-291-1360

Creative Labs, Inc.
131 South Maples Ave., #6
South San Francisco, CA 94080
SoundBlaster, Video Spigot
Sales: 408-428-6622
Tech Support: 415-742-6107

Davidson & Associates, Inc.
19840 Pioneer Ave.
Torrance, CA 90503
Educational Software
Sales: 310-793-0600, 800-545-7677
Fax: 310-793-0601

Dell Computer Corp.
9505 Arboretum Blvd.
Austin, TX 78759
Computers
Sales: 800-289-3355

Delrina Technology, Inc.
6830 Via Del Oro, Suite 240
San Jose, CA 95119
WinFax, PerForm
Sales: 800-268-6082, 408-363-2345
Fax: 408-363-2340
Tech Support: 416-441-0921
CompuServe: GO DELRINA

Diamond Computer Systems, Inc.
532 Mercury Dr.
Sunnyvale, CA 94086
Video cards
Sales/Tech Support: 408-736-2000
Fax: 408-730-5750
BBS: 408-730-1100
CompuServe: GO GRAPHBVEN

Digital Equipment Corporation (DEC)
146 Main St.
Maynard, MA 01754-2571
Computers
Sales: 800-332-4636, 508-493-5111
Fax: 508-841-6100
Tech Support: 800-354-9000
CompuServe: GO DEC

Discovery Channel
7700 Wisconsin Ave., 6th Floor
Bethesda, MD 20814
Edutainment
Sales: 301-986-1999, 800-762-2189

Epson America, Inc.
2780 Lomita Blvd.
Torrance, CA 90505
Printers, computers
Parent Office: Epson Corporation
80 Hirooka, Shiojiri-shi
Nagano 399-07, Japan

Everex Systems
901 Page Ave.
Fremont, CA 94538

Boards
Sales: 800-821-0806, 510-498-1111
Tech Support: 510-498-4411

Family PC
244 Main St.
Northampton, MA 01060-0929
Family PC Magazine
Subscriptions: 800-413-9749

Fujitsu America, Inc.
3055 Orchard Dr.
San Jose, CA 95134-2017
Printers, keyboards, disks
Sales: 408-432-1300
Parent Office: Fujitsu, Ltd.
6-1, Marunouchi, 1-chome
Chiyoda-Ku
Tokyo 100, Japan

Future Domain Corp.
2801 McGaw Ave.
Irvine, CA 92714
SCSI Boards
Sales: 714-253-0400
Fax: 714-253-0913

Future Vision
300 Airport Executive Park
Manuat, NY 10954
Multimedia Software
Sales: 914-426-0400
Fax: 914-426-2606

William H. Gates III
billg@microsoft.com
Gateway 2000, Inc.
610 Gateway Dr.
P.O. Box 2000
North Sioux City, SD 57049-2000

Computers
Sales: 800-846-2000, 605-232-2000
Tech Support: 800-846-2301
CompuServe: GO GATEWAY

Grolier Electronic Publishing
Sherman Turnpike
Danbury, CT 06816
Reference works
Sales: 203-797-3500

H

Hayes Microcomputer Products
5835 Peachtree Corners E
Norcross, GA 30092
Modems
Sales: 404-840-9200
Tech Support: 404-441-1617
BBS: 800-874-2937
CompuServe: GO HAYFORUM

Hewlett-Packard
974 East Arquez Ave.
Sunnyvale, CA 95086
Printers, Scanners
Sales: 408-720-3441, 800-554-1305, 800-752-0900
Fax: 408-720-4033
Tech Support: 408-720-4040
CompuServe: GO HP

Hitachi America, Ltd.
19530 Cabot Blvd.
Hayward, CA 94545
Sales: 510-785-9770
CD-ROM drives, memory
Parent Office: Hitachi Engineering Co., Ltd.
6 Kandu-Shurgadai, 4-chome
Chiyoda-Ku
Tokyo 101, Japan

Home Office Computing
411 Lafayette
New York, NY 10003
Home Office Computing Magazine
Subscriptions: 800-288-7812

Home PC
600 Community Drive
Manhasset, NY 11030
Home PC Magazine

Humongous Entertainment
16932 Woodinville-Redmond Rd NE
Suite 204
Woodinville, WA 98072
Games
Sales: 206-486-9258

I

IBM
Old Orchard Road
Armonk, NY 10504
Blue Three-Piece Suits
Sales: 800-336-5430, 800-426-333
Tech Support: 800-992-4777
IBM Personal Software Products
11400 Burnet Road
Austin, TX 78758
OS/2
Sales: 512-823-0000
CompuServe: GO IBMDESK

id Software
Town East Tower
18601 LBJ Freeway, Suite 615
Mesquite, TX 75150
Doom
Sales: 214-613-3589

Infoworld Publishing Company
155 Bouvet Road, Suite 800
San Mateo, CA 94402
Infoworld
Offices: 415-572-7341
Subscriptions: 708-647-7925

Inner Media, Inc.
60 Plain Road
Hollis, NH 03049
Collage Complete
Sales: 603-465-3216, 800-962-2949
Fax: 603-465-7195

Tech Support: 603-465-2696
CompuServe: 70444, 31

Inset Systems
71 Commerce Dr.
Brookfield, CT 06804
Hijaak
Sales: 800-374-6738, 203-740-2400
Fax: 203-775-5634
CompuServe: GO INSET

Intel Corporation
5200 N.E. Elam Young Pkwy.
Hillsboro, OR 97124
Chips, Cards
Sales: 800-538-3373
Fax: 800-458-6231
CompuServe: GO INTELFORUM

Intuit
PO Box 3014
Menlo Park, CA 94026
Quicken, Quickbooks, Turbo Tax
Sales: 415-322-0573, 415-852-9696
Tech Support: 800-624-8742
CompuServe: GO INTUIT

K

Knowledge Adventure
1311 Grand Central Ave.
Glendale, CA 91201
Edutainment
Sales: 818-246-4400
Fax: 818-246-5604

Knowledge Garden, Inc.
12-8 Technology Dr.
Setauket, NY 11733
KnowledgePro
Sales: 516-862-0600
CompuServe: GO WINAPB

L

The Learning Company
6493 Kaiser Dr.
Fremont, CA 94555
Educational Software
Sales: 510-792-2101, 800-852-2255
Fax: 510-792-9628

Woody Leonhard
Hack
woody@wopr.com, 72241.2125@compuserve.com

Living Books
(Broderbund/Random House)
160 Pacific Ave Mall, Suite 201
San Francisco, CA 94111
Edutainment
Sales: 415-352-5200

Logitech, Inc.
6505 Kaiser Dr.
Fremont, CA 94555
SoundMan, ScanMan, MouseMan, mice
Sales: 510-795-8500
CompuServe: GO LOGITECH

Lotus Development Corporation
(div. IBM)
55 Cambridge Pkwy.
Cambridge, MA 02142
*1-2-3, Ami Pro, Notes, cc:Mail, Freelance Graphics,
Improv*
Sales: 800-553-4270, 617-577-8500
Tech Support: 800-223-1662
CompuServe: GO LOTUS

Lucas Arts
P.O. Box 10307
San Rafael, CA 94912
Games
Sales: 415-721-3300
Fax: 415-721-3464
http://www.lucasarts.com

M

Macmillan New Media
124 Mt. Auburn St.
Cambridge, MA 02138
Multimedia CD-ROMs
Sales: 617-225-9023

Matrox
1055 St. Regis Blvd.
Dorval, Quebec, Canada H9P 2T4
Video boards
Sales: 514-685-2630, 514-685-2630
Fax: 514-685-2853

Maxis
2 Theater Square, Suite 230
Orinda, CA 94563
SimCity, SimEarth, RoboSport, Print Artist
Sales: 510-254-9700, 800-336-2947
Fax: 510-253-3736
Tech Support: 510-253-3755
CompuServe: GO GAMBPUB

Media Vision Inc.
3185 Laurelview Court
Fremont, CA 94538
Audio and Video Boards
Sales: 800-845-5870, 800-638-2807, 510-770-8600
Fax: 510-770-9592
Tech Support: 510-770-9905
CompuServe: GO MULTIVEN

MEI Micro Center
110 Steelwood Road
Columbus, OH 43212
High quality, cheap diskettes and QIC tapes
Sales: 800-634-3478
Fax: 614-486-6417

Micrografx, Inc.
1303 Arapaho
Richardson, TX 75081-2444
Draw, Designer, Picture Publisher, etc.
Sales: 214-234-1769, 800-733-3729
Tech Support: 214-234-2694
CompuServe: GO WINAPA

MicroProse
(div Spectrum Holobyte)
180 Lakefront Dr.
Hunt Valley, MD 21030-2245
Games
Sales: 410-771-0440

Microsoft Corporation
One Microsoft Way
Redmond, WA 98052-6399
Mutant Ninjas
Sales: 800-426-9400, 206-882-8080
Fax: 206-93-MS-FAX
Tech Support: 206-454-2030, 206-637-7098
BBS: 206-637-9009, 206-936-6735
CompuServe: GO MICROSOFT
http://www.microsoft.com

MIDISoft
P.O. Box 1000
15379 NE 90th St
Redmond, WA 98052
MIDISoft
Sales: 206-391-3610

Mindscape
(formerly Software Toolworks)
60 Leveroni Court
Novato, CA 94949
Games
Sales: 415-883-3000, 800-866-5967
Fax: 415-883-3303

Mitsubishi Electronics America
5665/5757 Plaza Drive
P.O. Box 6007
Cypress, CA 90630-0007
Monitors
Sales: 800-843-2515, 714-220-2500
Tech Support: 800-344-6352

Mom
Phone Home, Sonny

Claudette Moore
Moore Literary Agency
World's best agent

Multimedia World
501 Second St. #600
San Francisco, CA 94107

Multimedia World Magazine
Subscriptions: 800-766-3294
Fax: 415-882-0936

Nanao USA Corp.
23535 Telo Ave.
Torrance, CA 90503
Monitors that are works of art
Sales: 310-325-5202
Fax: 310-530-1679

National Computer Security Association (NCSA)
10 S. Courthouse Ave.
Carlisle, PA 17013
Who You Gonna Call?
Inquiries: 717-258-1816

National Cristina Foundation
42 Hillcrest Dr.
Pelham Manor, NY 10803
Distributes used computers to the needy
Sales: 914-738-7494

New Media
901 Mariner's Island Blvd.
Suite 365
San Mateo, CA 94404
New Media Magazine
Subscriptions: 609-786-4430

Novell, Inc.
122 East 1700 South
Provo, UT 84606
NetWare, DR-DOS
Sales: 800-453-1267, 800-NET-WARE,
801-429-7000
Fax: 801-429-3951
CompuServe: GO NOVLIB

Number Nine Computer Corporation
18 Hartwell Ave.
Lexington, MA 02173
Video boards
Sales: 617-674-0009
Fax: 617-674-2919

O

Orchid Technology
45365 Northport Loop, West
Fremont, CA 94538
Video cards
Sales: 800-7OR-CHID, 510-683-0300
Fax: 510-490-9312
Tech Support: 510-683-0323
BBS: 510-683-0327

P

Packard Bell, Inc.
9425 Canoga Ave.
Chatsworth, CA 91311
Computers
Sales: 818-886-9998
Fax: 818-773-9516
Tech Support: 800-733-4411, 818-886-2098
CompuServe: GO PACKARDBELL

Panasonic Industrial Co.
P.O. Box 1503
Secaucus, NJ 07094
Printers, computers
Sales: 201-348-7000
Parent Office: Matsushita Electric Co., Ltd.
1006, Kadona-City
Osaka 571, Japan

PC/Computing
Ziff-Davis Publishing Co.
950 Tower Lane, 20th Floor
Foster City, CA 94404
PC/Computing, the #1 monthly computer mag
Subscriptions: 800-365-2770, 303-447-9330
Offices: 415-578-7000
CompuServe: GO ZNT:PCCONTACT

PC Connection
6 Mill St.
Marlow, NH 03456
Mao's favorite source of computer supplies
Subscriptions: 800-800-0004, 603-446-0004
Fax: 603-446-7791

PC Magazine
Ziff-Davis Publishing Co.
One Park Ave.
New York, NY 10016
PC Magazine, the #1 computer mag
Subscriptions: 800-289-0429
Offices: 212-503-5446
CompuServe: GO ZNT:EDITORIAL
http://www.ziff.com

PC Techniques
7721 E. Gray Rd, Suite 204
Scottsdale, AZ 85260
PC Techniques Magazine
Subscriptions: 602-483-0192
CompuServe: 76711,470

PC Week
Ziff-Davis Publishing Co.
10 Presidents Landing
Medford, MA 02155
PC Week
Subscriptions: 609-461-2100
CompuServe: GO ZIFFNET

PC World
IDG Communications
501 Second St.
San Francisco, CA 94107
PC World magazine
Subscriptions: 800-234-3498, 303-447-9330
CompuServe: 74055,412

Pinecliffe International
Advanced Support Group
11900 Grant Place
Des Peres, MO 63131
WOPR—Woody's Office POWER Pack
Sales: 800-OK-WINWORD, 314-965-5630
Fax: 314-966-1833
Tech Support: 314-965-5630
http://www.wopr.com/wopr

PKWare, Inc.
9025 N. Deerwood Dr.
Brown Deer, WI 53223
PKZip
Sales: 414-354-8699
Fax: 414-354-8559
CompuServe: 75300,730

Pro CD, Inc.
222 Rosewood Dr.
Danvers, MA 01923
Phone CDs
Sales: 508-750-0000, 508-750-0110
Fax: 508-750-0060
http://www.procd.com

Public (software) Library—PsL
Nelson Ford
P.O. Box 35705
Houston, TX 77235-5705
Shareware disks
CardShark Hearts
Sales: 713-524-6394
Fax: 713-524-6398
CompuServe: 71355,470

Quarterdeck Office Systems
150 Pico Blvd.
Santa Monica, CA 90405
QEMM memory manager
Sales: 310-392-9851

Roland
7200 Dominion Circle
Los Angeles, CA 90040-0911
Sound cards, software
Sales: 213-685-5141

Rush
http://www.wopr.com/wopr

Igor Guido Salvatorre
http://www.wopr.com/wopr

Sarah Savant
http://www.wopr.com/wopr

Seagate Technologies
920 Disc Dr.
Scotts Valley, CA 95066
Disc Drives—probably 920 of 'em by now
Sales: 408-438-6550
Tech Support: 408-439-3244

Barry Simon
76004.1664@compuserve.com

Software Publishers Association
1730 M St. NW, Suite 700
Washington, DC 20036-4510
Software Anti-Piracy
Voice: 800-388-7478, 202-452-1600

Sonic Foundry
100 South Baldwin, Suite 204
Madison, WI 53703
Sound Forge
Sales: 608-256-3133
Fax: 608-256-7300

Sony Corp. of America
Business Products Division
1 Sony Dr.
Park Ridge, NJ 07656
Monitors, disk drives, computers
Sales: 201-930-1000, 800-222-SONY
Parent Office: Sony Corporation
6-7-35, Kitashinagawa
Shiagawa-Ku
Tokyo 141, Japan

Spectrum Holobyte
2490 Mariner Square Loop
Alameda, CA 94501
Games
Sales: 510-522-3584
Fax: 510-522-3587

SPRY
316 Occidental Ave S.
Suite 200
Seattle, WA 98104
Internet Software
Sales: 206-442-8231
http://www.spry.com

SuperNet
999 18th St.
Suite 2640
Denver, CO 80202
Igor's Internet Service Provider
Sales: 303-296-8202

Symantec
10201 Torre Ave.
Cupertino, CA 95014
Norton Desktop, Backup, AntiVirus, Actor, Q&A
Sales: 800-441-7234, 408-253-9600
Tech Support: 800-441-7234
CompuServe: GO SYMAPPS

Video Seven/Headland Technology
Video boards
Video Seven went out of business in July 1993

Western Digital
Hard drives
Sales: 800-228-6488
Tech Support: 714-932-0952
BBS: 714-753-1068

Windows Magazine
CMP Publications
600 Community Dr.
Manhasset, NY 11030
Windows Magazine
Offices: 516-562-5000
Subscriptions: 800-284-3584, 303-447-9330
CompuServe: 76520,2513

Windows Online Review
P.O. Box 1614
Danville, CA 94526-6614
Windows Online Review
Sales: 520-736-4376
BBS: 510-736-8343

Windows Sources
Ziff-Davis Publishing Co.
One Park Ave.
New York, NY 10016
Windows Sources magazine
Offices: 212-503-3500
Subscriptions: 800-365-3414, 303-447-9330
CompuServe: GO ZNT:WINSOURCES

Windows Tech Journal
Oakley Publishing
P.O. Box 70167
Eugene, OR 97401-0110
WinTech Journal
Subscriptions: 800-234-0386, 503-747-0800
Fax: 503-746-0071
CompuServe: GO CLMFORUM

Windows User Group/WUGNet
P.O. Box 1967
Media, PA 19063
Largest independent Windows user group
CompuServe: GO WUGNET

Windows Watcher
15127 NE 24th St.
Suite 344
Redmond, WA 98052-5549
Insider Magazine
Subscriptions: 206-881-7354
Fax: 206-883-1452

Wired
520 Third St.
Fourth Floor
San Francisco, CA 94107
The Incomparable Wired *Magazine*
Subscriptions: 800-SO-WIRED, 415-222-6200
http://www.hotwired.com

WordPerfect Corp.
(div. Novell Corp)
1555 North Technology Way
Orem, UT 84057-2399
WordPerfect, Presentations
Sales: 801-225-5000
Tech Support: 800-451-5151
Fax: 801-222-5077
BBS: 801-225-4444
CompuServe: GO WPUSERS

Appendix D

The Mother of All Windows File Type Lists

Here I'm going to tell you about the file types special to Windows and the extensions they use. The original *Mother of All Windows Books* has a more extensive list which I pared down to keep the cover price of this book lower.

I don't know why you are wasting our reader's time Mom. Extensions are passé, relics of a DOS era that has ended. Users no longer need to worry about arcane terms like .dll *and can think about more understandable names like* Application Extension. *That's why the default isn't to show extensions for registered file types.*

Gimme a break Billy. I refuse to think that it is any easier for users to understand MS-DOS Batch File than .bat. And it is harder for those who are used to the extensions. And what do you do when you look at files in an Open dialog set to display small icons? The long file type name is gone so if you've not turned extensions back on, you're forced to stare at cryptic icons to figure out the file type. This is progress—NOT. Nope, Mom's readers need to have a list like the one here.

Here's the extension list from *The Windows Interface Guidelines for Software Design:*

386	Windows virtual device driver
3GR	Screen grabber for MS-DOS–based applications
ACM	Audio compression manager driver
ADF	Administration configuration files
ANI	Animated pointer
AVI	Video clip
AWD	FAX viewer document
AWP	FAX key viewer
AWS	FAX signature viewer
BAK	Backed-up file
BAT	MS-DOS batch file

BFC	Briefcase*
BIN	Binary data file
BMP	Picture (Windows bitmap)
CAB	Windows Setup file
CAL	Windows Calendar file
CDA	CD audio track
CFG	Configuration file
CNT	Help contents
COM	MS-DOS-based application
CPD	FAX cover page
CPE	FAX cover page
CPI	International code page
CPL	Control Panel extension
CRD	Windows Cardfile document
CSV	Command-separated data file
CUR	Cursor (pointer)
DAT	System data file
DCX	FAX viewer document
DLL	Application extension (dynamic-link library)
DOC	WordPad document
DOS	MS-DOS file (also extension for NDIS2 net card and protocol drivers)
DRV	Device driver
EXE	Application
FND	Saved search
FON	Font file
FOT	Shortcut to font
GR3	Windows 3.0 screen grabber
GRP	Program group file

---

*As I explained in Chapter 11, this is a phony extension used to place Briefcase on the New menu. Real briefcases have no extension!

HLP	Help file
HT	HyperTerminalTM file
ICM	ICM profile
ICO	Icon
IDF	MIDI instrument definition
INF	Setup information
INI	Initialization file (configuration settings)
KBD	Keyboard layout
LGO	Windows logo driver
LIB	Static-link library
LNK	Shortcut
LOG	Log file
MCI	MCI command set
MDB	File viewer extension*
MID	MIDI sequence
MIF	MIDI instrument file
MMF	Microsoft Mail message file
MMM	Animation
MPD	Mini-port driver
MSG	Microsoft® Exchange mail document
MSN	Microsoft Network home base
NLS	Natural language services driver
PAB	Microsoft Exchange personal address book
PCX	Bitmap picture (PCX format)
PDR	Port driver
PF	ICM profile
PIF	Shortcut to MS-DOS-based application
PPD	PostScript® printer description file
PRT	Printer formatted file (result of Print to File option)

---

* MDB is an Access database but this is what the official MS documentation says. You'd think they'd know their own products, wouldn't you?

PST	Microsoft Exchange personal information store
PWL	Password list
QIC	Backup set for Microsoft Backup
REC	Windows Recorder file
REG	Application registration file
RLE	Picture (RLE format)
RMI	MIDI sequence
RTF	Document (rich-text format)
SCR	Screen saver
SET	File set for Microsoft Backup
SHB	Shortcut into a document
SHS	Scrap
SPD	PostScript printer description file
SWP	Virtual memory storage
SYS	System file
TIF	Picture (TIFF® format)
TMP	Temporary file
TRN	Translation file
TSP	Windows telephony service provider
TTF	TrueType® font
TXT	Text document
VBX	Microsoft Visual Basic® control file*
VER	Version description file
VXD	Virtual device driver
WAV	Sound wave
WPC	WordPad file converter
WRI	Windows Write document

---

*Interesting that they list VBXs but not the OCX OLE Custom Control which is the 32-bit replacement for VBXs.

Here are a few more that should certainly be on any list of Windows specific file extensions:

ANN	Windows Help annotations
BMK	Windows Help bookmarks
CLP	Saved Clipboard contents
DIB	Picture (Device Independent Bitmap)
EMF	Enhanced windows MetaFile
FTS	Full Text Search index for a Windows Help file
FTG	FTS Group
GID	Windows Help configuration file
HTM	aka HTML, HyperTextMarkup file used for World-Wide Web pages
MCC	Shortcut to the Microsoft Network
URL	Shortcut to an Internet Website
WMF	Windows MetaFile

'Twill be all one a thousand years hence.

—Jonathan Swift, *Polite Conversation,* 1738

If you ever figure you've clobbered a file and want to restore it directly from the Win95 distribution diskettes or the CD, this Appendix will tell you where to find the file and how to extract it. It's also useful if you want to retrieve files from the distribution diskettes or CD without first installing Windows 95, or if you need to grab one of those files from a PC that isn't running Win95.

If you want to install an entire subsystem of Windows, of course, you should go through the Control Panel's Add/Remove Programs applet. If you want to verify all the files on your PC, you should fire up the Setup program. But if you just want to snag a file or two, you're in the right place.

As far as we know, this is the only definitive listing of all files on the distribution diskettes and CD that you'll find anywhere. Just in case you want to perform your own analysis, there's an EXCEL spreadsheet called `Win95 File List.xls` on Mom's companion CD in the `\MomStuff` folder that includes all of this information, in an easily manipulable form, should you feel so possessed.

Trivia question of the day, preppies. I'll make it easy for you: the answer is, 83,034,996. The question? If you decompressed all the files in the Win95 distribution CD's compressed `.CAB` files, how many bytes would the files occupy?

Bonus question! How many files are missing from the distribution diskettes? Bzzzzt. An amazing 320 of 'em. And that doesn't include all the miscellaneous files—multimedia, extra drivers, and the like—that ship on the CD, outside the `.CAB` files. See why Mom recommended that you get the CD version?

From .CAB to File

Let the great world spin forever down the ringing grooves of changes.

—Alfred Tennyson, *Locksley Hall,* 1842

 Windows 95 is distributed as a bunch of compressed files called `.CAB` files—generally called *cabinets.* There are three parts to the Microsoft compression scheme. First, there's a new compression method that MS calls *Quantum.* Second, there's a method that MS calls *Diamond* for putting files into cabinets—possibly splitting a single file among two or more cabinets, on two or more diskettes. Third, there's a new scheme called *Distribution Media Format* or DMF, for physically formatting 1.44 MB diskettes in a nonstandard way, so they'll hold more data. Almost any diskette drive can read files from DMF-formatted diskettes. But you need very, very special equipment to write files onto DMF-formatted diskettes. That's why you can't copy most Microsoft distribution diskettes these days: your diskette drive can't write DMF-formatted diskettes.

 You'll notice that Quantum and Diamond sound a lot like the techniques used in PKZIP, but from Microsoft's point of view they have two distinct advantages. First, Quantum and Diamond are technologies that Microsoft owns: they don't suffer from the "not invented here" syndrome. Second, Unisys claims it patented one of the techniques used in PKZIP. It appears as if Quantum and Diamond don't rely on the same algorithm. So Microsoft is squeaky-clean.

 Cleaner than my mouse's tail. Heh heh heh.

 You called the compression scheme "Quantum"? I beg your pardon?

 Sticking the Win95 files in cabinets and using the infamous DMF maximizes MSFT,* an aspiration not without merit. Sticking the Win95 files in cabinets and using 2 MB-long cabinets on the distribution CD makes the installation program run faster. It also keeps confused novices from copying files straight off the CD and into their `\windows\command` directories, an aspiration

---

* MSFT = Microsoft's stock-market ticker symbol. Think of all the diskettes Microsoft doesn't have to buy because of Quantum, Diamond, and DMF. Think of profit margins. The stock's done pretty well, eh?

similarly not without merit. Unfortunately, using cabinets also makes it horrendously difficult for users like you and me to identify a file, find out which cabinet it occupies, extract it, and drop it where we want it.

The installer extracts Win95 files from the cabinets using a program called, uh, `extract`. It probably won't surprise you to discover that `extract` is a dumb DOS program, with a command line and no hope of a graphical interface. I guess Microsoft figures if you're smart enough to shoot yourself in the foot by decompressing individual files from the cabinets, you're probably smart enough to run `extract` from a command line. Bleccch.

You say Bleccch to the lowly DOS command line, but we would've had a devil of a time producing the tables in this chapter without it! Command lines hath their place. Besides, if you really want a GUI, take a look at PowerToys, which I discussed in Chapter 5. It includes a `.CAB` viewer shell extension. Just double-click on a `.CAB` file while in Explorer and the component files are immediately available: simply drag to extract and copy.

If you have Win95 installed, `extract` is located in the `\windows\command` folder (which is on your DOS path, so you don't need to maneuver around to run it from the DOS command line). If you don't have Win95 installed, it's in the `\WIN95` folder on the CD, or on diskette #1 in the root directory. As you probably know, diskette #1 of any Microsoft product that uses DMF is a normal, everyday diskette—you can read it, write to it, or copy from it just as you would any other diskette; thus, you can get at `extract` on the first diskette, if you're really up against a wall, by simply switching over to the diskette drive and typing `extract`.

When you run the `extract` command, typically from the Start/Run box or from an MS-DOS command prompt, you have several options, which are generally indicated thusly:

```
extract [/A][/E][/Y][/L Target_Directory] Cabinet_Name Files_To_Extract
```

Target_Directory is the place you want the extracted file(s) to go. If you don't specify one, Win95 sticks the extracted file in the current directory. It puts quotes around *Target_Directory* if it includes embedded spaces.

Cabinet_Name is the name of the `.CAB` file `extract` is supposed to look in.

Files_To_Extract is a list of files to extract, separated by blanks. You can use * and ?, the usual wild cards.

`/A` tells `extract` to look at all `.CAB` files beginning with the one called *Cabinet_Name*. For example, if you have the Win95 CD in drive `d:`, the command line

```
extract /A d:\WIN95\WIN95_04.CAB foo*.*
```

will extract all the `foo*.*` files in cabinets 4 through 17 (files `WIN95_04.CAB` through `WIN95_17.CAB`), placing them in the current directory.

`/E` is the same thing as using `*.*` for *Files_To_Extract*. For example, if you have the fourth diskette in drive `a:`, the command line

        extract /E /L c:\temp a:\WIN95_04.CAB

will extract all the files in the `WIN95_04.CAB` cabinet and place them in `c:\temp`.

`/Y` means "answer yes." Usually `extract` prompts the user before overwriting a file. If the `/Y` switch is used, it's as if the user answered "yes" to all those prompts.

There are two other forms of the `extract` command:

        extract /D Cabinet_Name [Files_To_List]

lists all the files in *Cabinet_Name* matching *Files_To_List*. If there is no *Files_To_List,* `extract` lists all the files in the cabinet.

        extract /C Cabinet_Name New_Directory

copies the cabinet called *Cabinet_Name* to the location *New_Directory*. For example, if you have Win95 diskette #7 in drive `a:` and you want to copy `WIN95_07.CAB` to `c:\temp,` this command will do it:

        extract /C a:\win95_07.cab c:\temp

Note that although you can generally copy `.CAB` files from diskette to hard drive, or hard drive to hard drive, there's no way using standard DOS or Windows commands to copy a large (bigger than 1.44 MB) `.CAB` file from a DMF-formatted diskette onto a "normal" diskette. They're just too big.

 The documentation on `extract` in the *Windows Resources Kit* is mighty hard to follow; I'm tempted to say that it's wrong, but I'm not sure I understand it well enough to pass judgment. Anyway, stick to what you see here and you'll be all right.

An example: You want to look at the file `mouse.txt,` which has info on Win95 mouse drivers, before installing Win95. You consult the list (following) and discover that `mouse.txt` is in the cabinet called `WIN95_03.CAB` (which is in the `\WIN95` folder, as is the file `extract`). To extract it from your CD on `e:` to `c:\temp,` you would run:

        e:\win95\extract /L c:\temp e:\WIN95\WIN95_03.CAB mouse.txt

Another example: You want to look at all the .txt files on your distribution diskettes before installing Win95, to see if they contain important installation information. (They do, they do!) Try this command line to extract all .txt files from .CAB files number 2 to 13, and put them in the directory c:\wintext:

```
a:\extract /A /L c:\wintext win95_02.cab *.txt
```

A Capital Idea

> Whatever deceives seems to exercise a kind of magical enchantment.

> —Plato, *The Republic,* ca. 350 B.C.

Watch out! Capitalization is important! Windows 95 contains fourteen files that appear, at first blush, to be duplicated—spelled once with all caps, spelled again all lowercase. Uppercase-named files are *not* the same as their lowercase brethren.

Take the file gdi.exe, for example. If you're a Windows 3.1 refugee, you'll recognize gdi.exe as being part of the "kernel" of Windows 3.1, one of the three main programs that, taken together, compose Windows 3.1 as we know it. Well, Windows 95 has *two different versions* of gdi.exe.

The first version of GDI.EXE (note the capitals: this first version is always referred to in all-caps), located in MINI.CAB on both the CD and the diskette versions of Win95, is a stunted GDI.EXE, size 149,456 bytes. Apparently, it contains just enough of the old Windows 3.1 gdi.exe to get the Win95 installer loaded and running.

The real gdi.exe (note the lowercase), the one that's normally run by Windows 95, takes up 312,208 bytes, and is located either in WIN95_03.CAB (if you have the CD) or WIN95_04.CAB (on the fourth diskette). If you think you zapped out your Win95 gdi.exe and want to restore it from diskette, make sure you retrieve gdi.exe, not GDI.EXE!

Here are the files that come in both uppercase and lowercase flavors. In all cases, the lowercase versions are the ones you want to restore Win95 files of the same name; the uppercase versions seem to be related exclusively to the Win95 installation routines.

Filename	Expanded File Size	Location on CD	Location on Diskettes
COMM.DRV	9,280	MINI.CAB	MINI.CAB
comm.drv	5,856	WIN95_03.CAB	WIN95_03.CAB
GDI.EXE	149,456	MINI.CAB	MINI.CAB
gdi.exe	312,208	WIN95_03.CAB	WIN95_04.CAB
KEYBOARD.DRV	7,568	MINI.CAB	MINI.CAB
keyboard.drv	12,688	WIN95_06.CAB	WIN95_06.CAB
KRNL386.EXE	75,490	MINI.CAB	MINI.CAB
krnl386.exe	124,416	WIN95_03.CAB	WIN95_04.CAB
LZEXPAND.DLL	9,936	MINI.CAB	MINI.CAB
lzexpand.dll	23,696	PRECOPY1.CAB	PRECOPY1.CAB
SERIFE.FON	57,936	MINI.CAB	MINI.CAB
serife.fon	57,952	WIN95_05.CAB	WIN95_06.CAB
SSERIFE.FON	64,544	MINI.CAB	MINI.CAB
sserife.fon	64,544	WIN95_05.CAB	WIN95_06.CAB
SYSTEM.DRV	2,304	MINI.CAB	MINI.CAB
system.drv	2,288	WIN95_03.CAB	WIN95_04.CAB
USER.EXE	264,016	MINI.CAB	MINI.CAB
user.exe	462,112	WIN95_03.CAB	WIN95_04.CAB
VER.DLL	9,008	MINI.CAB	MINI.CAB
ver.dll	9,008	PRECOPY2.CAB	PRECOPY2.CAB
VGA.DRV	73,200	MINI.CAB	MINI.CAB
vga.drv	52,064	WIN95_04.CAB	WIN95_05.CAB
VGAFIX.FON	5,360	MINI.CAB	MINI.CAB
vgafix.fon	5,360	WIN95_05.CAB	WIN95_06.CAB
VGAOEM.FON	5,168	MINI.CAB	MINI.CAB
vgaoem.fon	5,168	WIN95_05.CAB	WIN95_06.CAB
VGASYS.FON	7,280	MINI.CAB	MINI.CAB
vgasys.fon	7,296	WIN95_05.CAB	WIN95_06.CAB
WIN87EM.DLL	12,800	MINI.CAB	MINI.CAB
win87em.dll	11,904	WIN95_03.CAB	Win95_04.CAB

Figure 1: Uppercase vs. lowercase files

What's on the Diskettes

Here are the files on the thirteen-diskette version of Windows 95. Disk #1 contains the files listed under "Disk 1" following, in addition to `MINI.CAB` and `PRECOPY1.CAB` (the contents of which are listed separately). `PRECOPY2.CAB` and `WIN95_02.CAB` are both on the second diskette. After that, the `.CAB` files correspond to the diskettes directly, e.g., `WIN95_07.CAB` is on the seventh diskette.

A few files span two compressed `.CAB` "cabinets." When you try to `expand` those files, Windows 95 will prompt you to insert the second diskette and tell you which diskette to use. On multi-part files, this list shows you the first `.CAB` "cabinet" containing the file—which is also the diskette you should insert first when trying to `expand` the file.

Don't forget the fourteen files that differ only in capitalization, as described in the previous section!

Disk 1	NOMOUSE.DRV	netdet.ini	mf.inf	nettcc.inf
MINI .CAB	SYSTEM.DRV	rnasetup.dll	midi.inf	netcable.inf
PRECOPY1.CAB	VGA.DRV	setupx.dll	modems.inf	netprot.inf
WB16OFF.EXE	SOUND.DRV	shell.dll	monitor.inf	netgen.inf
SCANDISK.EXE	SERIFE.FON	suexpand.dll	monitor2.inf	netsock.inf
DOSSETUP.BIN	SSERIFE.FON	sysdetmg.dll	monitor3.inf	netamd.inf
WINSETUP.BIN	VGAFIX.FON	ver.dll	monitor4.inf	netdec.inf
DELTEMP.COM	VGAOEM.FON	verx.dll	mos.inf	netee16.inf
SAVE32.COM	VGASYS.FON	dskmaint.dll	motown.inf	netnice.inf
EXTRACT.EXE	SYSTEM.INI	win95bb.dll	msbase.inf	netnovel.inf
SCANPROG.EXE	WIN.INI	suwin.exe	msdet.inf	netoli.inf
SETUP.EXE		sufail.bat	msdisp.inf	netppp.inf
SMARTDRV.EXE	PRECOPY1.	sucheck.bat	msdos.inf	nethp.inf
XMSMMGR.EXE	CAB (Disk 1)	drvspace.bat	msfdc.inf	netsmc.inf
SCANDISK.PIF	command.com	dblspace.bat	mshdc.inf	netsmctr.inf
README.TXT	drvspace.bin	defrag.bat	msmail.inf	netxir.inf
SETUP.TXT	drvspace.sys	scandisk.bat	msmouse.inf	netibm.inf
	winboot.sys	copy.inf	msports.inf	netibmcc.inf
MINI.CAB	comctl31.dll	ren.inf	msprint.inf	netcpq.inf
(Disk 1)	commctrl.dll	del.inf	msprint2.inf	netsnip.inf
DOSX.EXE	kommctrl.dll	adapter.inf	mtd.inf	netcem.inf
USER.EXE	commdlg.dll	apm.inf	multilng.inf	cemmf.inf
GDI.EXE	complinc.dll	applets.inf	netcli.inf	mfosi.inf
KRNL386.EXE	lzexpand.dll	awfax.inf	netservr.inf	netosi.inf
LZEXPAND.DLL	msprint.dll	awupd.inf	netdef.inf	netbw.inf
MINIKBD.DLL	msprint2.dll	mscdrom.inf	netcli3.inf	netdlc.inf
WIN87EM.DLL	mstcp.dll	diskdrv.inf	net3com.inf	nodriver.inf
VER.DLL	netapi.dll	enable.inf	netsilc.inf	ole2.inf
COMM.DRV		icm.inf	nettdkp.inf	pcmcia.inf
KEYBOARD.DRV	PRECOPY2.	joystick.inf	netpci.inf	prtupd.inf
LMOUSE31.DRV	CAB (Disk 2)	keyboard.inf	netauxt.inf	scsi.inf
MSMOUS31.DRV	netdi.dll	locale.inf	netflex.inf	shell.inf
	netos.dll	machine.inf	netmadge.inf	shell2.inf

tapi.inf
timezone.inf
unknown.inf
vidcap.inf
wave.inf
wordpad.inf
rna.inf
net.inf
nettrans.inf
fonts.inf
precopy.inf
setupc.inf
setuppp.inf
winver.inf
layout.inf

WIN95_02. CAB (Disk 2)

format.com
sys.com
fdisk.exe
attrib.exe
edit.com
regedit.exe
scandisk.ini
debug.exe
chkdsk.exe
uninstal.exe
access.cpl
enable3.dll
accstat.exe
access.hlp
enable.vxd
enable2.vxd
enable4.vxd
clipbook.cnt
clipbrd.cnt
hypertrm.cnt
mspaint.cnt
packager.cnt
hticons.dll
hypertrm.dll
mfc30.dll
mfcd30.dll
mfcn30.dll
mfco30.dll
mspcx32.dll
msvcrt20.dll

WIN95_03. CAB (Disk 3)

calc.exe

clipbook.exe
clipbrd.exe
clipsrv.exe
hypertrm.exe
mspaint.exe
notepad.exe
packager.exe
pbrush.exe
sysedit.exe
write.exe
pcximp32.flt
clipbook.hlp
clipbrd.hlp
hypertrm.hlp
mspaint.hlp
packager.hlp
at&tma~1.ht
compus~1.ht
mcimai~1.ht
write32.wpc
rsrc16.dll
rsrc32.dll
rsrcmtr.exe
dialer.cnt
dialer.exe
dialer.hlp
3dblocks.bmp
clouds.bmp
forest.bmp
gator.bmp
mesh.bmp
sand.bmp
weave2.bmp
wordpad.cnt
mfcans32.dll
wordpad.exe
wordpad.hlp
mswd6_32.wpc
win.cnf
iosclass.dll
pifmgr.dll
winaspi.dll
wnaspi32.dll
bigmem.drv
mmsound.drv
sort.exe
ios.ini
winoa386.new
aspi2hlp.sys
himem.sys
apix.vxd
biosxlat.vxd
cdfs.vxd

cdtsd.vxd
cdvsd.vxd
disktsd.vxd
diskvsd.vxd
dosmgr.vxd
dosnet.vxd
dynapage.vxd
ebios.vxd
ifsmgr.vxd
int13.vxd
ios.vxd
pageswap.vxd
parity.vxd
qemmfix.vxd
reboot.vxd
v86mmgr.vxd
vcache.vxd
vcdfsd.vxd
vdef.vxd
vdmad.vxd
vfat.vxd
vfbackup.vxd
vfd.vxd
vkd.vxd
vmcpd.vxd
vmpoll.vxd
voltrack.vxd
vpicd.vxd
vsd.vxd
vtd.vxd
vtdapi.vxd
vxdldr.vxd
xlat850.bin
vga850.fon
vmm32.vxd
ntdll.dll
bamboo.bmp
bubbles.bmp
circles.bmp
egypt.bmp
halftone.bmp
hounds.bmp
pstripe.bmp
pyramid2.bmp
redtile.bmp
rivets2.bmp
thatch2.bmp
crtdll.dll
pkpd.dll
pkpd32.dll
license.hlp
desktop.ini
dosprmpt.pif

cmd640x.sys
cmd640x2.sys
config.txt
display.txt
exchange.txt
extra.txt
faq.txt
general.txt
hardware.txt
internet.txt
mouse.txt
msdosdrv.txt
msn.txt
network.txt
printers.txt
programs.txt
support.txt
tips.txt
necatapi.vxd
vpmtd.386
arrow.mpd
serialui.dll
umdm16.dll
umdm32.dll
comm.drv
unimdm.tsp
combuff.vxd
lpt.vxd
serenum.vxd
serial.vxd
unimodem.vxd

WIN95_04. CAB (Disk 4)

vcd.vxd
vcomm.vxd
vpd.vxd
desk.cpl
intl.cpl
main.cpl
maincp16.dll
sysdm.cpl
timedate.cpl
deskcp16.dll
powercfg.dll
ddeml.dll
dibeng.dll
mf3216.dll
systhunk.dll
toolhelp.dll
vdmdbg.dll
win32s16.dll
win87em.dll

system.drv
conagent.exe
gdi.exe
krnl386.exe
mkcompat.exe
redir32.exe
user.exe
redirect.mod
arial.ttf
arialbd.ttf
arialbi.ttf
ariali.ttf
cour.ttf
courbd.ttf
courbi.ttf
couri.ttf
times.ttf
timesbd.ttf
timesbi.ttf
timesi.ttf
wingding.ttf
vcond.vxd
vwin32.vxd
riched32.dll
defrag.exe
backup.cfg
backup.cnt
chiadi.dll
chikdi.dll
backup.exe

WIN95_05. CAB (Disk 5)

backup.hlp
qic117.vxd
vgafull.3gr
sxciext.dll
atim32.drv
atim64.drv
atim8.drv
chips.drv
cirrus.drv
cirrusmm.drv
compaq.drv
framebuf.drv
mga.drv
s3.drv
supervga.drv
tseng.drv
vga.drv
wd.drv
xga.drv
cpqmode.ini

cpqmon.ini
ati.vxd
chips.vxd
cirrus.vxd
compaq.vxd
mga.vxd
oak.vxd
s3.vxd
tseng.vxd
vdd.vxd
vflatd.vxd
video7.vxd
wd.vxd
xga.vxd
mscdex.exe
aha154x.mpd
aha174x.mpd
aic78xx.mpd
always.mpd
amsint.mpd
buslogic.mpd
dptscsi.mpd
fd16_700.mpd
fd8xx.mpd
mkecr5xx.mpd
mtmminip.mpd
ncr53c9x.mpd
ncrc700.mpd
ncrc710.mpd
ncrc810.mpd
ncrsdms.mpd
pc2x.mpd
slcd32.mpd
sparrow.mpd
sparrowx.mpd
spock.mpd
t160.mpd
t348.mpd
t358.mpd
tmv1.mpd
ultra124.mpd
ultra14f.mpd
ultra24f.mpd
wd7000ex.mpd
esdi_506.pdr
hsflop.pdr
rmm.pdr
scsiport.pdr
scsi1hlp.vxd
genfax.apd
awfax.cnt
faxcover.cnt
confdent.cpe

fyi.cpe
generic.cpe
urgent.cpe
awbmsc32.dll
awbtrv32.dll
awcapi32.dll
awcl1_32.dll
awcl2_32.dll
awcodc32.dll
awdcxc32.dll
awdevl16.dll
awdevl32.dll
awfaxp32.dll
awfext32.dll
awfmon32.dll
awfr32.dll
awfxab32.dll
awfxcg32.dll
awfxio32.dll
awfxrn32.dll
awkrnl32.dll
awlft332.dll
awlhut32.dll
awlinz32.dll
awlzrd32.dll
awnfax32.dll
awpwd32.dll
awramb32.dll
awrbae32.dll
awresx32.dll
awrndr32.dll
awschd32.dll
awsrvr32.dll
awt30_32.dll
awutil32.dll
awview32.dll
faxcodec.dll
rndsrv32.dll
wpsapd.dll
wpsunire.dll
wpsuni.drv
rcv0000.efx
awadpr32.exe
awfxex32.exe
awsnto32.exe
faxcover.exe
faxview.cnt
faxview.exe
faxview.hlp
awfax.hlp
awprt.hlp
faxcover.hlp
850.dat

synceng.dll
syncui.dll
vshare.vxd
8514fix.fon
8514oem.fon
8514sys.fon
app850.fon
coure.fon
courf.fon

WIN95_06. CAB (Disk 6)

dosapp.fon
modern.fon
serife.fon
seriff.fon
smalle.fon
smallf.fon
sserife.fon
sseriff.fon
symbole.fon
symbolf.fon
vgafix.fon
vgaoem.fon
vgasys.fon
marlett.ttf
symbol.ttf
freecell.cnt
mshearts.cnt
sol.cnt
winmine.cnt
cards.dll
freecell.exe
mshearts.exe
sol.exe
winmine.exe
freecell.hlp
mshearts.hlp
sol.hlp
winmine.hlp
audiocdc.hlp
ftsrch.dll
stem0409.dll
whlp16t.dll
whlp32t.dll
calc.cnt
drvspace.cnt
mouse.cnt
notepad.cnt
windows.cnt
winhlp32.cnt
winhelp.exe
winhlp32.exe

apps.hlp
calc.hlp
common.hlp
drvspace.hlp
edit.hlp
mfcuix.hlp
mouse.hlp
network.hlp
notepad.hlp
server.hlp
tty.hlp
windows.hlp
winhlp32.hlp
winnews.txt
regedit.cnt
31users.hlp
regedit.hlp
icm32.dll
icmui.dll
hp1200c.icm
hp1200ps.icm
hpsjtw.icm
kodakce.icm
mnb22g15.icm
mnb22g18.icm
mnb22g21.icm
mnebug15.icm
mnebug18.icm
mnebug21.icm
mnp22g15.icm
mnp22g18.icm
mnp22g21.icm
ps4079.icm
tpha200i.icm
tphaiii.icm
imm32.dll
msnfull.hlp
msnint.hlp
indicdll.dll
keyboard.drv
internat.exe
kbdbe.kbd
kbdbr.kbd
kbdca.kbd
kbdda.kbd
kbddv.kbd
kbdfc.kbd
kbdfi.kbd
kbdfr.kbd
kbdgr.kbd
kbdgr1.kbd
kbdic.kbd
kbdir.kbd

kbdit.kbd
kbdit1.kbd
kbdla.kbd
kbdne.kbd
kbdno.kbd
kbdpo.kbd
kbdsf.kbd
kbdsg.kbd
kbdsp.kbd
kbdsw.kbd
kbduk.kbd
kbdus.kbd
kbdusx.kbd
apps.inf
mapif0.cfg
mapif1.cfg
mapif2.cfg
mapif3.cfg
mapif4.cfg
mapif5.cfg
exchng.cnt
msfs.cnt
mapi.dll
mmfmig32.dll
mspst32.dll

WIN95_07. CAB (Disk 7)

wmsfr32.dll
exchng32.exe
exchng.hlp
msfs.hlp
mapif0l.ico
mapif0s.ico
mapif1l.ico
mapif1s.ico
mapif2l.ico
mapif2s.ico
mapif3l.ico
mapif3s.ico
mapif4l.ico
mapif4s.ico
mapif5l.ico
mapif5s.ico
mlcfg32.cpl
wgpocpl.cpl
cmc.dll
mapi32.dll
mapiu.dll
mapiu32.dll
mapix.dll
mapix32.dll
mlshext.dll

msfs32.dll
vlb32.dll
wgpoadmn.dll
wmsui32.dll
mapisp32.exe
mapisrvr.exe
ml3xec16.exe
mlset32.exe
scanpst.exe
scanpst.hlp
mapisvc.inf
mapirpc.reg
mapiwm.tpl
instbe.bat
msn.cnt
msnpss.cnt
800950.dat
ccapi.dll
ccei.dll
ccpsh.dll
confapi.dll
dataedcl.dll
dunzipnt.dll
findstub.dll
ftmapi.dll
homebase.dll
mcm.dll
mmvdib12.dll
mosabp32.dll
mosaf.dll
moscc.dll
moscfg32.dll
moscl.dll
moscomp.dll
moscudll.dll
mosfind.dll
mosmisc.dll
mosmutil.dll
mosrxp32.dll
mosshell.dll

WIN95_08. CAB (Disk 8)

mosstub.dll
mpccl.dll
msndui.dll
mvcl14n.dll
mvpr14n.dll
mvttl14c.dll
mvut14n.dll
prodinv.dll
saclient.dll
securcl.dll

svcprop.dll
treeedcl.dll
treenvcl.dll
ccdialer.exe
dnr.exe
ftmcl.exe
guide.exe
moscp.exe
mosview.exe
msnexch.exe
msnfind.exe
onlstmt.exe
regwiz.exe
signup.exe
textchat.exe
msn.hlp
msnbbs.hlp
msnchat.hlp
msnmail.hlp
msnpss.hlp
themic~1.msn
bbsnav.nav
dsnav.nav
guidenav.nav
dsned.ned
phone.pbk
state.pbk
msnver.txt
slenh.dll
power.drv
systray.exe
splitter.vxd
vgateway.vxd
vpowerd.vxd
modem.cpl
modemui.dll
mdmati.inf
mdmatt.inf
mdmaus.inf
mdmboca.inf
mdmcommu.inf
mdmcpi.inf
mdmcpq.inf
mdmdsi.inf
mdmexp.inf
mdmgatew.inf
mdmgen.inf
mdmgvc.inf
mdmhayes.inf
mdminfot.inf
mdmintel.inf
mdmintpc.inf
mdmmcom.inf

mdmmetri.inf
mdmmhrtz.inf
mdmmoto.inf
mdmmts.inf
mdmnokia.inf
mdmnova.inf
mdmosi.inf
mdmpace.inf
mdmpnb.inf
mdmpp.inf
mdmracal.inf
mdmrock.inf
mdmrock2.inf
mdmsier.inf
mdmsonix.inf
mdmspec.inf
mdmsupra.inf
mdmtdk.inf
mdmtelbt.inf
mdmti.inf
mdmtosh.inf
mdmusrcr.inf
mdmusrsp.inf
mdmusrwp.inf
mdmzoom.inf
mdmzyp.inf
mdmzyxel.inf
ppm.vxd
imaadp32.acm
msadp32.acm
msg711.acm
msgsm32.acm
tssoft32.acm
wfm0200.acv
wfm0201.acv
wfm0202.acv
wfm0203.acv
midimap.cfg
mplayer.cnt
sndvol32.cnt
soundrec.cnt
joy.cpl
mmsys.cpl
wfm0200a.csp
wfm0201a.csp
wfm0202a.csp
wfm0203a.csp
avicap.dll
avicap32.dll
avifil32.dll
avifile.dll
cspman.dll
dciman.dll

dciman32.dll
dispdib.dll
findmvi.dll
iccvid.dll
ir32_32.dll
mciole.dll
mmci.dll
mmmixer.dll
mmsystem.dll
msacm.dll
msacm32.dll
msmixmgr.dll
msrle32.dll
msvfw32.dll
msvidc32.dll
msvideo.dll
tsd32.dll
winmm.dll
azt16c.drv
azt16w.drv
es1488.drv
es1688.drv
es488.drv
es688.drv
essfm.drv
essmport.drv
essmpu.drv
mciavi.drv
mcicda.drv
mciseq.drv
mciwave.drv
midimap.drv
msacm.drv
msjstick.drv
msmpu401.drv
msopl.drv
mssblst.drv
mssndsys.drv
mvi401.drv
mvi514mx.drv
mvifm.drv

WIN95_09. CAB (Disk 9)

mviwave.drv
mvmixer.drv
mvproaud.drv
pa3dmxd.drv
sb16snd.drv
sbawe32.drv
sbfm.drv
mplayer.exe
sndrec32.exe

sndvol32.exe
mmdrv.hlp
mplayer.hlp
sndvol32.hlp
soundrec.hlp
general.idf
mvifm.pat
synthgm.sbk
mmtask.tsk
azt16.vxd
es1488.vxd
es1688.vxd
es488.vxd
es688.vxd
mmdevldr.vxd
msmpu401.vxd
msopl.vxd
mssblst.vxd
mssndsys.vxd
mvpas.vxd
sb16.vxd
sbawe.vxd
vjoyd.vxd
vmvid.vxd
vpasd.vxd
mssound.wav
pointer.dll
lmouse.drv
mouse.drv
pointer.exe
lmouse.vxd
msmouse.vxd
vmd.vxd
vmouse.vxd
ewrk3.dos
ewrk3.sys
ce2ndis3.vxd
cm2ndis3.vxd
ctndw.vxd
doskey.com
keyb.com
mode.com
more.com
choice.com
diskcopy.com
deltree.exe
drvspace.exe
emm386.exe
fc.exe
find.exe
label.exe
mem.exe
move.exe

nlsfunc.exe	socketsv.vxd	canon330.drv	aplwsel.spd	ib401917.spd
scandskw.exe	srammtd.vxd	canon800.drv	apple230.spd	ib401939.spd
setver.exe	msgsrv32.exe	canonlbp.drv	apple380.spd	ib402917.spd
share.exe	isapnp.vxd	cit24us.drv	aptolld1.spd	ib402939.spd
start.exe	sysclass.dll	cit9us.drv	aptollw1.spd	ibm20470.spd
subst.exe	cpqae05.exe	citoh.drv	ast__470.spd	ibm30505.spd
xcopy.exe	cpqae06.exe	dec24pin.drv	cp_ps241.spd	ibm31514.spd
xcopy32.exe	bios.vxd	dec3200.drv	cpper241.spd	ibm4039.spd
drvspace.inf	configmg.vxd	diconix.drv	cppmq151.spd	ibm4039p.spd
ansi.sys	eisa.vxd	epson9.drv	cppmq201.spd	ibm4079.spd
country.sys	lptenum.vxd	exprss24.drv	cppro518.spd	kdcolor1.spd
dblbuff.sys	pci.vxd	fuji24.drv	cppsnb10.spd	l100_425.spd
display.sys	addreg.exe	fuji9.drv	cppsx241.spd	l200_471.spd
keyboard.sys	spoolss.dll	ibm238x.drv	d2150_ms.spd	l300_471.spd
keybrd2.sys	winspl16.drv	ibm239x.drv	d2250_ms.spd	l500_493.spd
ramdrive.sys	winspool.drv	ibm5204.drv	datap462.spd	lh330__1.spd
drvspacx.vxd	spool32.exe	ibmppdsl.drv	dc1152_1.spd	lh530__1.spd
mrci2.vxd	spooler.vxd	jp350.drv	dc1152f1.spd	lh630__1.spd
cp_1252.nls	dmcolor.dll	kyocera.drv	dc2150p1.spd	lwnt_470.spd
cp_437.nls	finstall.dll	mantal24.drv	dc2250p1.spd	lwntx470.spd
cp_850.nls	iconlib.dll	mantal9.drv	dc5100_1.spd	mt_ti101.spd
locale.nls	pjlmon.dll	mtlite.drv	dccolor1.spd	n2090522.spd
unicode.nls	psmon.dll	nec24pin.drv	dcd11501.spd	n2290520.spd
compobj.dll	unidrv.dll	oki24.drv	dclf02_1.spd	n890_470.spd
ole2.dll	epson24.drv	oki9.drv	dclf02f1.spd	n890x505.spd
ole2conv.dll	escp2ms.drv	oki9ibm.drv	dcln03r1.spd	nccps401.spd
ole2disp.dll	hpdskjet.drv	olidm24.drv	dclps171.spd	nccps801.spd
ole2nls.dll	hppcl.drv	olidm9.drv	dclps321.spd	ncol_519.spd
ole32.dll	hppcl5ms.drv	p351sx2.drv	dclps401.spd	ncs29901.spd
oleaut32.dll	pscript.drv	paintjet.drv	dcps1721.spd	ncsw_951.spd
storage.dll	pscript.hlp	panson24.drv	dcps1761.spd	o5241503.spd
typelib.dll	unidrv.hlp	panson9.drv	dctps201.spd	o5242503.spd
stdole.tlb	pscript.ini	proprint.drv	dec3250.spd	oki830us.spd
stdole32.tlb	testps.txt	proprn24.drv	epl75523.spd	oki840us.spd
olecli.dll	finstall.hlp	ps1.drv	f71rx503.spd	oki850us.spd
olecli32.dll	hpcolor.dll	quietjet.drv	hp_3d522.spd	okol8701.spd
olesvr.dll	hpviol.dll	qwiii.drv	hp_3p522.spd	ol830525.spd
olesvr32.dll	hpvmon.dll	seiko24e.drv	hp1200c1.spd	ol840518.spd
mfcuia32.dll	hpvres.dll	seikosh9.drv	hp3si523.spd	ol850525.spd
mfcuiw32.dll	hpvui.dll	star24e.drv	hp4m_v4.spd	p4455514.spd
olecnv32.dll	deskjetc.drv	star9e.drv	hp4ml_v4.spd	pap54001.spd
oledlg.dll	hpvdjc.hlp	thinkjet.drv	hp4mp_v4.spd	pap54101.spd
	hpvcm.hpm	ti850.drv	hp4mv_v4.spd	phiipx.spd
WIN95_10.	hpdesk.icm	toshiba.drv	hp4plus4.spd	q2200_ms.spd
CAB (Disk 10)	bjc600.icm	tty.drv	hp4si_v4.spd	q2210_ms.spd
olethk32.dll	bjc800.icm	sf4029.exe	hpiid522.spd	q2220523.spd
mspcic.dll	hpclrlsr.icm	epsonsty.icm	hpiii522.spd	q800_ms.spd
carddrv.exe	hpxl300.icm	fonts.mfm	hpiip522.spd	q810_ms.spd
csmapper.sys	hpxl30ps.icm	a_pnt518.spd	hplj_31.spd	q810t_ms.spd
dbkvssd.vxd	qms10030.icm	aplw8101.spd	hplj_3d1.spd	q820_ms.spd
fls1mtd.vxd	brhj770.drv	aplwiif1.spd	hplj_3p1.spd	q820t517.spd
fls2mtd.vxd	brother9.drv	aplwiig1.spd	hpljp_v4.spd	q860pls2.spd
pccard.vxd	brothr24.drv	aplwntr1.spd	hppjxl31.spd	qcs1000.spd

qcs10503.spd
qcs30503.spd
qm1700_1.spd
qm2000_1.spd
qm825mr1.spd
qmps4101.spd
qms1725.spd
qms3225.spd
qms420.spd
qms45252.spd
qms860.spd
qms8p461.spd
qmscs210.spd
qmscs230.spd
skpsfa_1.spd
stls04ss.spd
stls08lp.spd
stls5ttu.spd
tim17521.spd
tim35521.spd
timlp232.spd
tk200172.spd
tk220171.spd
tkp200i2.spd
tkp220i1.spd
tkp2sdx1.spd
tkp300i1.spd
tkph4801.spd
tkphzr22.spd
tkphzr32.spd
triumph1.spd
triumph2.spd
u9415470.spd
vt600480.spd
wps_updt.dll
wpsmon.dll
wpsmon16.dll
hpplot.drv
hpplot.hlp
rasapi16.dll
rasapi32.dll

WIN95_11. CAB (Disk 11)

rnanp.dll
rnathunk.dll
rnaui.dll
directcc.exe
lights.exe
rnaapp.exe
logger.vxd
paralink.vxd
pppmac.vxd

spap.vxd
setup.bmp
setup4.dll
version.dll
runonce.exe
wininit.exe
winver.exe
clip.inf
ver.new
sulogo.sys
appstart.ani
hourglas.ani
progman.cnt
winfile.cnt
appwiz.cpl
comctl32.dll
comdlg32.dll
diskcopy.dll
docprop.dll
fontext.dll
linkinfo.dll
moricons.dll
panmap.dll
shell32.dll
shscrap.dll
winword.doc
winword2.doc
envoy.evy
control.exe
explorer.exe
fontreg.exe
fontview.exe
grpconv.exe
progman.exe
rundll.exe
rundll32.exe
taskman.exe
welcome.exe
winfile.exe
progman.hlp
winfile.hlp
control.inf
commdlg.new
shell.new
powerpnt.ppt
freelanc.pre
amipro.sam
bezier.scr
scrnsave.scr
ssflywin.scr
ssmarque.scr
ssmyst.scr
ssstars.scr

presenta.shw
shell.vxd
quattro.wb2
lotus.wk4
wordpfct.wpd
informs.wpf
wordpfct.wpg
wordpfct.wpw
excel.xls
excel4.xls
telephon.cpl
tapi.dll
tapi32.dll
tapiaddr.dll
tapiexe.exe
tapiini.exe
telephon.hlp
advapi32.dll
gdi32.dll
kernel32.dll
lz32.dll
user32.dll
wow32.dll
logos.sys
logow.sys
_pwmove.bat
dcamac.bin

WIN95_12. CAB (Disk 12)

eaglecaf.bin
eaglemac.bin
mdgmport.bin
ne3200.bin
netflx.bin
winpopup.cnt
netcpl.cpl
password.cpl
choosusr.dll
icmp.dll
inetmib1.dll
mpr.dll
mprserv.dll
msab32.dll
msnet32.dll
msnp32.dll
mspp32.dll
mspwl32.dll
msshrui.dll
nddeapi.dll
nddenb.dll
netapi32.dll
netbios.dll

nw16.dll
nwab32.dll
nwnet32.dll
nwnp32.dll
nwpp32.dll
pmspl.dll
rpcltc1.dll
rpcltc3.dll
rpcltc5.dll
rpcltc6.dll
rpclts3.dll
rpclts5.dll
rpclts6.dll
rpcns4.dll
rpcrt4.dll
sapnsp.dll
secur32.dll
svrapi.dll
winnet16.dll
winsock.dll
wnpp32.dll
wsock32.dll
am2100.dos
cpqndis.dos
dc21x4.dos
depca.dos
dncrwl02.dos
e100.dos
e20nd.dos
e21nd.dos
e22nd.dos
e30nd.dos
e31nd.dos
el59x.dos
elnk16.dos
elnk3.dos
elnkii.dos
elnkmc.dos
elnkpl.dos
epndis.dos
epro.dos
es3210.dos
evx16.dos
exp16.dos
hpfend.dos
hplan.dos
hplanb.dos
hplane.dos
hplanp.dos
i82593.dos
ibmtok.dos
irmatr.dos
ncc16.dos

ndis39xr.dos
ndis89xr.dos
ndis99xr.dos
ne1000.dos
ne2000.dos
ne3200.dos
netflx.dos
ni5210.dos
ni6510.dos
olitok16.dos
pcntnd.dos
pe2ndis.dos
pendis.dos
pro4.dos
pro4at.dos
slan.dos
smartnd.dos
smc_arc.dos
smc3000.dos
smc8000.dos
smc8100.dos
smc8232.dos
smc9000.dos
strn.dos
t20nd.dos
t30nd.dos
tccarc.dos
tcctok.dos
tlnk.dos
tlnk3.dos
ubnei.dos
ubneps.dos
msnet.drv
prorapm.dwn
arp.exe
ftp.exe
lmscript.exe
login.exe
mprexe.exe
msdlc.exe
nbtstat.exe
netdde.exe
netstat.exe
nwlscon.exe
nwlsproc.exe
odihlp.exe
pe3ndis.exe
ping.exe
route.exe
rpcss.exe
telnet.exe
tracert.exe
winipcfg.exe

winpopup.exe	octk16.sys	hpmca.vxd	pcntn3.vxd	vserver.vxd
wsasrv.exe	tdkcd02.sys	ibmtok.vxd	pe3ndis.vxd	wshtcp.vxd
telnet.hlp	afvxd.vxd	ibmtok4.vxd	perf.vxd	wsipx.vxd
winpopup.hlp	am1500t.vxd	irmatrac.vxd	proteon.vxd	wsock.vxd
winpopup.inf	cendis.vxd	msodisup.vxd	setp3.vxd	vdhcp.386
netware.ms	cpqndis3.vxd		smc8000w.vxd	vip.386
lmscript.pif	declan.vxd	**WIN95_13.**	smc80pc.vxd	vnbt.386
hosts.sam	e30n3.vxd	**CAB (Disk 13)**	smc8100w.vxd	vtcp.386
lmhosts.sam	e31n3.vxd		smc8232w.vxd	vtdi.386
dc21x4.sys	ee16.vxd	mssp.vxd	smc9000.vxd	protman.dos
e100.sys	el59x.vxd	ndis.vxd	snip.vxd	net.exe
e20n3.sys	elnk16.vxd	ndis2sup.vxd	socket.vxd	protman.exe
e21n3.sys	elnk3.vxd	netbeui.vxd	spendis.vxd	net.msg
e22n3.sys	elnkii.vxd	nice.vxd	t20n3.vxd	neth.msg
ee16.sys	elnkmc.vxd	nscl.vxd	t30n3.vxd	ndishlp.sys
ifshlp.sys	elpc3.vxd	nwlink.vxd	tctokch.vxd	unicode.bin
mdgmport.sys	epro.vxd	nwnblink.vxd	tlnk3.vxd	ega.cpi
ne1000.sys	filesec.vxd	nwredir.vxd	ubnei.vxd	iso.cpi
ne2000.sys	hpeisa.vxd	nwserver.vxd	vnetbios.vxd	
ne3200.sys	hpfend.vxd	nwsp.vxd	vnetsup.vxd	
netflx.sys	hpisa.vxd	octk32.vxd	vredir.vxd	
		otceth.vxd		

What's on the CD

These are the files on the distribution CD. They're all contained in the `\WIN95` folder. Once again, with respect to duplicated filenames, be aware of the difference between uppercase and lowercase names, as described earlier in this chapter.

In \WIN95 Folder (CD)	WIN95_04.CAB	USER.EXE	SYSTEM.INI	netos.dll
	WIN95_05.CAB	GDI.EXE	WIN.INI	netdet.ini
WIN95_10.CAB	WIN95_06.CAB	KRNL386.EXE		rnasetup.dll
DOSSETUP.BIN	WIN95_07.CAB	LZEXPAND.DLL	**PRECOPY1.**	setupx.dll
EXTRACT.EXE	WIN95_08.CAB	MINIKBD.DLL	**CAB (CD)**	shell.dll
MINI.CAB	WIN95_09.CAB	WIN87EM.DLL	command.com	suexpand.dll
PRECOPY1.CAB	DELTEMP.COM	VER.DLL	drvspace.bin	sysdetmg.dll
PRECOPY2.CAB	WIN95_11.CAB	COMM.DRV	drvspace.sys	
README.TXT	WIN95_12.CAB	KEYBOARD.DRV	winboot.sys	**PRECOPY2.**
SAVE32.COM	WIN95_13.CAB	LMOUSE31.DRV	comctl31.dll	**CAB (CD)**
SCANDISK.EXE	WIN95_14.CAB	MSMOUS31.DRV	commctrl.dll	ver.dll
SCANDISK.PIF	WIN95_15.CAB	NOMOUSE.DRV	kommctrl.dll	verx.dll
SCANPROG.EXE	WIN95_16.CAB	SYSTEM.DRV	commdlg.dll	dskmaint.dll
SETUP.EXE	WIN95_17.CAB	VGA.DRV	complinc.dll	win95bb.dll
SETUP.TXT	WINSETUP.BIN	SOUND.DRV	lzexpand.dll	suwin.exe
SMARTDRV.EXE	XMSMMGR.EXE	SERIFE.FON	msprint.dll	sufail.bat
SUHELPER.BIN		SSERIFE.FON	msprint2.dll	sucheck.bat
WB16OFF.EXE	**MINI.CAB**	VGAFIX.FON	mstcp.dll	drvspace.bat
WIN95_02.CAB	**(CD)**	VGAOEM.FON	netapi.dll	dblspace.bat
WIN95_03.CAB	DOSX.EXE	VGASYS.FON	netdi.dll	defrag.bat

scandisk.bat
copy.inf
ren.inf
del.inf
adapter.inf
apm.inf
applets.inf
awfax.inf
awupd.inf
mscdrom.inf
diskdrv.inf
enable.inf
icm.inf
joystick.inf
keyboard.inf
locale.inf
machine.inf
mf.inf
midi.inf
modems.inf
monitor.inf
monitor2.inf
monitor3.inf
monitor4.inf
mos.inf
motown.inf
msbase.inf
msdet.inf
msdisp.inf
msdos.inf
msfdc.inf
mshdc.inf
msmail.inf
msmouse.inf
msports.inf
msprint.inf
msprint2.inf
mtd.inf
multilng.inf
netcli.inf
netservr.inf
netdef.inf
netcli3.inf
net3com.inf
netsilc.inf
nettdkp.inf
netpci.inf
netauxt.inf
netflex.inf
netmadge.inf
nettcc.inf
netcable.inf
netprot.inf

netgen.inf
netsock.inf
netamd.inf
netdec.inf
netee16.inf
netnice.inf
netnovel.inf
netoli.inf
netppp.inf
nethp.inf
netsmc.inf
netsmctr.inf
netxir.inf
netibm.inf
netibmcc.inf
netcpq.inf
netsnip.inf
netcem.inf
cemmf.inf
mfosi.inf
netosi.inf
netbw.inf
netdlc.inf
nodriver.inf
ole2.inf
pcmcia.inf
prtupd.inf
scsi.inf
shell.inf
shell2.inf
tapi.inf
timezone.inf
unknown.inf
vidcap.inf
wave.inf
wordpad.inf
rna.inf
bkupprop.dll
cheyprop.dll
rplimage.dll
appletpp.inf
bkupagnt.inf
cheyenne.inf
decpsmw4.inf
mmopt.inf
shell3.inf
hpnetprn.inf
netcd.inf
netdca.inf
netsmc32.inf
netub.inf
netncr.inf
netracal.inf

netevx.inf
netznote.inf
nettulip.inf
netftp.inf
license.txt
net.inf
nettrans.inf
fonts.inf
precopy.inf
setupc.inf
setuppp.inf
winver.inf
layout.inf

Note: there is no WIN95_01.CAB

WIN95_02. CAB (CD)

format.com
sys.com
fdisk.exe
attrib.exe
edit.com
regedit.exe
scandisk.ini
debug.exe
chkdsk.exe
uninstal.exe
access.cpl
enable3.dll
accstat.exe
access.hlp
enable.vxd
enable2.vxd
enable4.vxd
clipbook.cnt
clipbrd.cnt
hypertrm.cnt
mspaint.cnt
packager.cnt
hticons.dll
hypertrm.dll
mfc30.dll
mfcd30.dll
mfcn30.dll
mfco30.dll
mspcx32.dll
msvcrt20.dll
calc.exe
clipbook.exe
clipbrd.exe
clipsrv.exe

hypertrm.exe
mspaint.exe
notepad.exe
packager.exe
pbrush.exe
sysedit.exe
write.exe
pcximp32.flt
clipbook.hlp
clipbrd.hlp
hypertrm.hlp
mspaint.hlp
packager.hlp
at&tma~1.ht
compus~1.ht
mcimai~1.ht
write32.wpc
rsrc16.dll
rsrc32.dll
rsrcmtr.exe
dialer.cnt
dialer.exe
dialer.hlp
3dblocks.bmp
clouds.bmp

WIN95_03. CAB (CD)

forest.bmp
gator.bmp
mesh.bmp
sand.bmp
weave2.bmp
wordpad.cnt
mfcans32.dll
wordpad.exe
wordpad.hlp
mswd6_32.wpc
win.cnf
iosclass.dll
pifmgr.dll
winaspi.dll
wnaspi32.dll
bigmem.drv
mmsound.drv
sort.exe
ios.ini
winoa386.new
aspi2hlp.sys
himem.sys
apix.vxd
biosxlat.vxd
cdfs.vxd

cdtsd.vxd
cdvsd.vxd
disktsd.vxd
diskvsd.vxd
dosmgr.vxd
dosnet.vxd
dynapage.vxd
ebios.vxd
ifsmgr.vxd
int13.vxd
ios.vxd
pageswap.vxd
parity.vxd
qemmfix.vxd
reboot.vxd
v86mmgr.vxd
vcache.vxd
vcdfsd.vxd
vdef.vxd
vdmad.vxd
vfat.vxd
vfbackup.vxd
vfd.vxd
vkd.vxd
vmcpd.vxd
vmpoll.vxd
voltrack.vxd
vpicd.vxd
vsd.vxd
vtd.vxd
vtdapi.vxd
vxdldr.vxd
xlat850.bin
vga850.fon
vmm32.vxd
ntdll.dll
bamboo.bmp
bubbles.bmp
circles.bmp
egypt.bmp
halftone.bmp
hounds.bmp
pstripe.bmp
pyramid2.bmp
redtile.bmp
rivets2.bmp
thatch2.bmp
crtdll.dll
pkpd.dll
pkpd32.dll
license.hlp
desktop.ini
dosprmpt.pif

cmd640x.sys
cmd640x2.sys
config.txt
display.txt
exchange.txt
extra.txt
faq.txt
general.txt
hardware.txt
internet.txt
mouse.txt
msdosdrv.txt
msn.txt
network.txt
printers.txt
programs.txt
support.txt
tips.txt
necatapi.vxd
vpmtd.386
arrow.mpd
serialui.dll
umdm16.dll
umdm32.dll
comm.drv
unimdm.tsp
combuff.vxd
lpt.vxd
serenum.vxd
serial.vxd
unimodem.vxd
vcd.vxd
vcomm.vxd
vpd.vxd
desk.cpl
intl.cpl
main.cpl
maincp16.dll
sysdm.cpl
timedate.cpl
deskcp16.dll
powercfg.dll
ddeml.dll
dibeng.dll
mf3216.dll
systhunk.dll
toolhelp.dll
vdmdbg.dll
win32s16.dll
win87em.dll
system.drv
conagent.exe
gdi.exe

krnl386.exe
mkcompat.exe
redir32.exe
user.exe

WIN95_04. CAB (CD)

redirect.mod
arial.ttf
arialbd.ttf
arialbi.ttf
ariali.ttf
cour.ttf
courbd.ttf
courbi.ttf
couri.ttf
times.ttf
timesbd.ttf
timesbi.ttf
timesi.ttf
wingding.ttf
vcond.vxd
vwin32.vxd
riched32.dll
defrag.exe
backup.cfg
backup.cnt
chiadi.dll
chikdi.dll
backup.exe
backup.hlp
qic117.vxd
vgafull.3gr
sxciext.dll
atim32.drv
atim64.drv
atim8.drv
chips.drv
cirrus.drv
cirrusmm.drv
compaq.drv
framebuf.drv
mga.drv
s3.drv
supervga.drv
tseng.drv
vga.drv
wd.drv
xga.drv
cpqmode.ini
cpqmon.ini
ati.vxd
chips.vxd

cirrus.vxd
compaq.vxd
mga.vxd
oak.vxd
s3.vxd
tseng.vxd
vdd.vxd
vflatd.vxd
video7.vxd
wd.vxd
xga.vxd
mscdex.exe
aha154x.mpd

WIN95_05. CAB (CD)

aha174x.mpd
aic78xx.mpd
always.mpd
amsint.mpd
buslogic.mpd
dptscsi.mpd
fd16_700.mpd
fd8xx.mpd
mkecr5xx.mpd
mtmminip.mpd
ncr53c9x.mpd
ncrc700.mpd
ncrc710.mpd
ncrc810.mpd
ncrsdms.mpd
pc2x.mpd
slcd32.mpd
sparrow.mpd
sparrowx.mpd
spock.mpd
t160.mpd
t348.mpd
t358.mpd
tmv1.mpd
ultra124.mpd
ultra14f.mpd
ultra24f.mpd
wd7000ex.mpd
esdi_506.pdr
hsflop.pdr
rmm.pdr
scsiport.pdr
scsi1hlp.vxd
genfax.apd
awfax.cnt
faxcover.cnt
confdent.cpe

fyi.cpe
generic.cpe
urgent.cpe
awbmsc32.dll
awbtrv32.dll
awcapi32.dll
awcl1_32.dll
awcl2_32.dll
awcodc32.dll
awdcxc32.dll
awdevl16.dll
awdevl32.dll
awfaxp32.dll
awfext32.dll
awfmon32.dll
awfr32.dll
awfxab32.dll
awfxcg32.dll
awfxio32.dll
awfxrn32.dll
awkrnl32.dll
awlft332.dll
awlhut32.dll
awlinz32.dll
awlzrd32.dll
awnfax32.dll
awpwd32.dll
awramb32.dll
awrbae32.dll
awresx32.dll
awrndr32.dll
awschd32.dll
awsrvr32.dll
awt30_32.dll
awutil32.dll
awview32.dll
faxcodec.dll
rndsrv32.dll
wpsapd.dll
wpsunire.dll
wpsuni.drv
rcv0000.efx
awadpr32.exe
awfxex32.exe
awsnto32.exe
faxcover.exe
faxview.cnt
faxview.exe
faxview.hlp
awfax.hlp
awprt.hlp
faxcover.hlp
850.dat

synceng.dll
syncui.dll
vshare.vxd
8514fix.fon
8514oem.fon
8514sys.fon
app850.fon
coure.fon
courf.fon
dosapp.fon
modern.fon
serife.fon
seriff.fon
smalle.fon
smallf.fon
sserife.fon
sseriff.fon
symbole.fon
symbolf.fon
vgafix.fon
vgaoem.fon
vgasys.fon
marlett.ttf
symbol.ttf
freecell.cnt
mshearts.cnt
sol.cnt
winmine.cnt
cards.dll
freecell.exe
mshearts.exe
sol.exe
winmine.exe
freecell.hlp
mshearts.hlp
sol.hlp
winmine.hlp
audiocdc.hlp
ftsrch.dll
stem0409.dll
whlp16t.dll
whlp32t.dll
calc.cnt
drvspace.cnt
mouse.cnt
notepad.cnt
windows.cnt
winhlp32.cnt
winhelp.exe
winhlp32.exe
apps.hlp
calc.hlp
common.hlp

drvspace.hlp
edit.hlp
mfcuix.hlp
mouse.hlp
network.hlp
notepad.hlp
server.hlp
tty.hlp
windows.hlp

WIN95_06. CAB (CD)

winhlp32.hlp
winnews.txt
regedit.cnt
31users.hlp
regedit.hlp
icm32.dll
icmui.dll
hp1200c.icm
hp1200ps.icm
hpsjtw.icm
kodakce.icm
mnb22g15.icm
mnb22g18.icm
mnb22g21.icm
mnebug15.icm
mnebug18.icm
mnebug21.icm
mnp22g15.icm
mnp22g18.icm
mnp22g21.icm
ps4079.icm
tpha200i.icm
tphaiii.icm
imm32.dll
msnfull.hlp
msnint.hlp
indicdll.dll
keyboard.drv
internat.exe
kbdbe.kbd
kbdbr.kbd
kbdca.kbd
kbdda.kbd
kbddv.kbd
kbdfc.kbd
kbdfi.kbd
kbdfr.kbd
kbdgr.kbd
kbdgr1.kbd
kbdic.kbd

kbdir.kbd
kbdit.kbd
kbdit1.kbd
kbdla.kbd
kbdne.kbd
kbdno.kbd
kbdpo.kbd
kbdsf.kbd
kbdsg.kbd
kbdsp.kbd
kbdsw.kbd
kbduk.kbd
kbdus.kbd
kbdusx.kbd
apps.inf
mapif0.cfg
mapif1.cfg
mapif2.cfg
mapif3.cfg
mapif4.cfg
mapif5.cfg
exchng.cnt
msfs.cnt
mapi.dll
mmfmig32.dll
mspst32.dll
wmsfr32.dll
exchng32.exe
exchng.hlp
msfs.hlp
mapif0l.ico
mapif0s.ico
mapif1l.ico
mapif1s.ico
mapif2l.ico
mapif2s.ico
mapif3l.ico
mapif3s.ico
mapif4l.ico
mapif4s.ico
mapif5l.ico
mapif5s.ico
mlcfg32.cpl
wgpocpl.cpl
cmc.dll
mapi32.dll
mapiu.dll
mapiu32.dll
mapix.dll
mapix32.dll
mlshext.dll
msfs32.dll

vlb32.dll
wgpoadmn.dll
wmsui32.dll

WIN95_07. CAB (CD)

mapisp32.exe
mapisrvr.exe
ml3xec16.exe
mlset32.exe
scanpst.exe
scanpst.hlp
mapisvc.inf
mapirpc.reg
mapiwm.tpl
instbe.bat
msn.cnt
msnpss.cnt
800950.dat
ccapi.dll
ccei.dll
ccpsh.dll
confapi.dll
dataedcl.dll
dunzipnt.dll
findstub.dll
ftmapi.dll
homebase.dll
mcm.dll
mmvdib12.dll
mosabp32.dll
mosaf.dll
moscc.dll
moscfg32.dll
moscl.dll
moscomp.dll
moscudll.dll
mosfind.dll
mosmisc.dll
mosmutil.dll
mosrxp32.dll
mosshell.dll
mosstub.dll
mpccl.dll
msndui.dll
mvcl14n.dll
mvpr14n.dll
mvttl14c.dll
mvut14n.dll
prodinv.dll
saclient.dll
securcl.dll

svcprop.dll
treeedcl.dll
treenvcl.dll
ccdialer.exe
dnr.exe
ftmcl.exe
guide.exe
moscp.exe
mosview.exe
msnexch.exe
msnfind.exe
onlstmt.exe
regwiz.exe
signup.exe
textchat.exe
msn.hlp
msnbbs.hlp
msnchat.hlp
msnmail.hlp
msnpss.hlp
themic~1.msn
bbsnav.nav
dsnav.nav
guidenav.nav
dsned.ned
phone.pbk
state.pbk
msnver.txt
slenh.dll
power.drv
systray.exe
splitter.vxd
vgateway.vxd
vpowerd.vxd
modem.cpl
modemui.dll
mdmati.inf
mdmatt.inf
mdmaus.inf
mdmboca.inf
mdmcommu.inf
mdmcpi.inf
mdmcpq.inf
mdmdsi.inf
mdmexp.inf
mdmgatew.inf
mdmgen.inf
mdmgvc.inf
mdmhayes.inf
mdminfot.inf
mdmintel.inf
mdmintpc.inf

mdmmcom.inf
mdmmetri.inf
mdmmhrtz.inf
mdmmoto.inf
mdmmts.inf
mdmnokia.inf
mdmnova.inf
mdmosi.inf
mdmpace.inf
mdmpnb.inf
mdmpp.inf

WIN95_08. CAB (CD)

mdmracal.inf
mdmrock.inf
mdmrock2.inf
mdmsier.inf
mdmsonix.inf
mdmspec.inf
mdmsupra.inf
mdmtdk.inf
mdmtelbt.inf
mdmti.inf
mdmtosh.inf
mdmusrcr.inf
mdmusrsp.inf
mdmusrwp.inf
mdmzoom.inf
mdmzyp.inf
mdmzyxel.inf
ppm.vxd
imaadp32.acm
msadp32.acm
msg711.acm
msgsm32.acm
tssoft32.acm
wfm0200.acv
wfm0201.acv
wfm0202.acv
wfm0203.acv
midimap.cfg
mplayer.cnt
sndvol32.cnt
soundrec.cnt
joy.cpl
mmsys.cpl
wfm0200a.csp
wfm0201a.csp
wfm0202a.csp
wfm0203a.csp
avicap.dll

avicap32.dll
avifil32.dll
avifile.dll
cspman.dll
dciman.dll
dciman32.dll
dispdib.dll
findmvi.dll
iccvid.dll
ir32_32.dll
mciole.dll
mmci.dll
mmmixer.dll
mmsystem.dll
msacm.dll
msacm32.dll
msmixmgr.dll
msrle32.dll
msvfw32.dll
msvidc32.dll
msvideo.dll
tsd32.dll
winmm.dll
azt16c.drv
azt16w.drv
es1488.drv
es1688.drv
es488.drv
es688.drv
essfm.drv
essmport.drv
essmpu.drv
mciavi.drv
mcicda.drv
mciseq.drv
mciwave.drv
midimap.drv
msacm.drv
msjstick.drv
msmpu401.drv
msopl.drv
mssblst.drv
mssndsys.drv
mvi401.drv
mvi514mx.drv
mvifm.drv
mviwave.drv
mvmixer.drv
mvproaud.drv
pa3dmxd.drv
sb16snd.drv
sbawe32.drv

sbfm.drv
mplayer.exe
sndrec32.exe
sndvol32.exe
mmdrv.hlp
mplayer.hlp
sndvol32.hlp
soundrec.hlp
general.idf
mvifm.pat
synthgm.sbk
mmtask.tsk
azt16.vxd
es1488.vxd
es1688.vxd
es488.vxd
es688.vxd
mmdevldr.vxd
msmpu401.vxd
msopl.vxd
mssblst.vxd
mssndsys.vxd
mvpas.vxd
sb16.vxd
sbawe.vxd
vjoyd.vxd
vmvid.vxd
vpasd.vxd
mssound.wav
pointer.dll
lmouse.drv
mouse.drv
pointer.exe
lmouse.vxd
msmouse.vxd
vmd.vxd
vmouse.vxd
ewrk3.dos
ewrk3.sys
ce2ndis3.vxd
cm2ndis3.vxd
ctndw.vxd
doskey.com
keyb.com
mode.com
more.com
choice.com
diskcopy.com
deltree.exe
drvspace.exe
emm386.exe
fc.exe

find.exe
label.exe
mem.exe

WIN95_09. CAB (CD)

move.exe
nlsfunc.exe
scandskw.exe
setver.exe
share.exe
start.exe
subst.exe
xcopy.exe
xcopy32.exe
drvspace.inf
ansi.sys
country.sys
dblbuff.sys
display.sys
keyboard.sys
keybrd2.sys
ramdrive.sys
drvspacx.vxd
mrci2.vxd
cp_1252.nls
cp_437.nls
cp_850.nls
locale.nls
unicode.nls
compobj.dll
ole2.dll
ole2conv.dll
ole2disp.dll
ole2nls.dll
ole32.dll
oleaut32.dll
storage.dll
typelib.dll
stdole.tlb
stdole32.tlb
olecli.dll
olecli32.dll
olesvr.dll
olesvr32.dll
mfcuia32.dll
mfcuiw32.dll
olecnv32.dll
oledlg.dll
olethk32.dll
mspcic.dll
carddrv.exe

csmapper.sys
dbkvssd.vxd
fls1mtd.vxd
fls2mtd.vxd
pccard.vxd
socketsv.vxd
srammtd.vxd
msgsrv32.exe
isapnp.vxd
sysclass.dll
cpqae05.exe
cpqae06.exe
bios.vxd
configmg.vxd
eisa.vxd
lptenum.vxd
pci.vxd
addreg.exe
spoolss.dll
winspl16.drv
winspool.drv
spool32.exe
spooler.vxd
dmcolor.dll
finstall.dll
iconlib.dll
pjlmon.dll
psmon.dll
unidrv.dll
epson24.drv
escp2ms.drv
hpdskjet.drv
hppcl.drv
hppcl5ms.drv
pscript.drv
pscript.hlp
unidrv.hlp
pscript.ini
testps.txt
finstall.hlp
hpcolor.dll
hpviol.dll
hpvmon.dll
hpvres.dll
hpvui.dll
deskjetc.drv

WIN95_10. CAB (CD)

hpvdjc.hlp
hpvcm.hpm
hpdesk.icm

bjc600.icm
bjc800.icm
hpclrlsr.icm
hpxl300.icm
hpxl30ps.icm
qms10030.icm
brhj770.drv
brother9.drv
brothr24.drv
canon330.drv
canon800.drv
canonlbp.drv
cit24us.drv
cit9us.drv
citoh.drv
dec24pin.drv
dec3200.drv
diconix.drv
epson9.drv
exprss24.drv
fuji24.drv
fuji9.drv
ibm238x.drv
ibm239x.drv
ibm5204.drv
ibmppdsl.drv
jp350.drv
kyocera.drv
mantal24.drv
mantal9.drv
mtlite.drv
nec24pin.drv
oki24.drv
oki9.drv
oki9ibm.drv
olidm24.drv
olidm9.drv
p351sx2.drv
paintjet.drv
panson24.drv
panson9.drv
proprint.drv
proprn24.drv
ps1.drv
quietjet.drv
qwiii.drv
seiko24e.drv
seikosh9.drv
star24e.drv
star9e.drv
thinkjet.drv
ti850.drv

toshiba.drv
tty.drv
sf4029.exe
epsonsty.icm
fonts.mfm
a_pnt518.spd
aplw8101.spd
aplwiif1.spd
aplwiig1.spd
aplwntr1.spd
aplwsel.spd
apple230.spd
apple380.spd
aptolld1.spd
aptollw1.spd
ast__470.spd
cp_ps241.spd
cpper241.spd
cppmq151.spd
cppmq201.spd
cppro518.spd
cppsnb10.spd
cppsx241.spd
d2150_ms.spd
d2250_ms.spd
datap462.spd
dc1152_1.spd
dc1152f1.spd
dc2150p1.spd
dc2250p1.spd
dc5100_1.spd
dccolor1.spd
dcd11501.spd
dclf02_1.spd
dclf02f1.spd
dcln03r1.spd
dclps171.spd
dclps321.spd
dclps401.spd
dcps1721.spd
dcps1761.spd
dctps201.spd
dec3250.spd
epl75523.spd
f71rx503.spd
hp_3d522.spd
hp_3p522.spd
hp1200c1.spd
hp3si523.spd
hp4m_v4.spd
hp4ml_v4.spd
hp4mp_v4.spd
hp4mv_v4.spd
hp4plus4.spd

hp4si_v4.spd
hpiid522.spd
hpiii522.spd
hpiip522.spd
hplj_31.spd
hplj_3d1.spd
hplj_3p1.spd
hpljp_v4.spd
hppjxl31.spd
ib401917.spd
ib401939.spd
ib402917.spd
ib402939.spd
ibm20470.spd
ibm30505.spd
ibm31514.spd
ibm4039.spd
ibm4039p.spd
ibm4079.spd
kdcolor1.spd
l100_425.spd
l200_471.spd
l300_471.spd
l500_493.spd
lh330__1.spd
lh530__1.spd
lh630__1.spd
lwnt_470.spd
lwntx470.spd
mt_ti101.spd
n2090522.spd
n2290520.spd
n890_470.spd
n890x505.spd
nccps401.spd
nccps801.spd
ncol_519.spd
ncs29901.spd
ncsw_951.spd
o5241503.spd
o5242503.spd
oki830us.spd
oki840us.spd
oki850us.spd
okol8701.spd
ol830525.spd
ol840518.spd
ol850525.spd
p4455514.spd
pap54001.spd
pap54101.spd
phiipx.spd
q2200_ms.spd
q2210_ms.spd

q2220523.spd
q800_ms.spd
q810_ms.spd
q810t_ms.spd
q820_ms.spd
q820t517.spd
q860pls2.spd
qcs1000.spd
qcs10503.spd
qcs30503.spd
qm1700_1.spd
qm2000_1.spd
qm825mr1.spd
qmps4101.spd
qms1725.spd
qms3225.spd
qms420.spd
qms45252.spd
qms860.spd
qms8p461.spd
qmscs210.spd
qmscs230.spd
skpsfa_1.spd
stls04ss.spd
stls08lp.spd
stls5ttu.spd
tim17521.spd
tim35521.spd
timlp232.spd
tk200172.spd
tk220171.spd
tkp200i2.spd
tkp220i1.spd
tkp2sdx1.spd
tkp300i1.spd
tkph4801.spd
tkphzr22.spd
tkphzr32.spd
triumph1.spd
triumph2.spd
u9415470.spd
vt600480.spd
wps_updt.dll
wpsmon.dll
wpsmon16.dll
hpplot.drv
hpplot.hlp
rasapi16.dll
rasapi32.dll
rnanp.dll
rnathunk.dll
rnaui.dll
directcc.exe
lights.exe

rnaapp.exe
logger.vxd
paralink.vxd
pppmac.vxd
spap.vxd
setup.bmp
setup4.dll
version.dll
runonce.exe
wininit.exe
winver.exe
clip.inf
ver.new
sulogo.sys
appstart.ani
hourglas.ani
progman.cnt
winfile.cnt
appwiz.cpl
comctl32.dll
comdlg32.dll
diskcopy.dll
docprop.dll
fontext.dll
linkinfo.dll
moricons.dll
panmap.dll
shell32.dll
shscrap.dll
winword.doc
winword2.doc
envoy.evy
control.exe
explorer.exe

WIN95_11. CAB (CD)

fontreg.exe
fontview.exe
grpconv.exe
progman.exe
rundll.exe
rundll32.exe
taskman.exe
welcome.exe
winfile.exe
progman.hlp
winfile.hlp
control.inf
commdlg.new
shell.new
powerpnt.ppt
freelanc.pre
amipro.sam

bezier.scr
scrnsave.scr
ssflywin.scr
ssmarque.scr
ssmyst.scr
ssstars.scr
presenta.shw
shell.vxd
quattro.wb2
lotus.wk4
wordpfct.wpd
informs.wpf
wordpfct.wpg
wordpfct.wpw
excel.xls
excel4.xls
telephon.cpl
tapi.dll
tapi32.dll
tapiaddr.dll
tapiexe.exe
tapiiini.exe
telephon.hlp
advapi32.dll
gdi32.dll
kernel32.dll
lz32.dll
user32.dll
wow32.dll
logos.sys
logow.sys
_pwmove.bat
dcamac.bin
eaglecaf.bin
eaglemac.bin
mdgmport.bin
ne3200.bin
netflx.bin
winpopup.cnt
netcpl.cpl
password.cpl
choosusr.dll
icmp.dll
inetmib1.dll
mpr.dll
mprserv.dll
msab32.dll
msnet32.dll
msnp32.dll
mspp32.dll
mspwl32.dll
msshrui.dll
nddeapi.dll
nddenb.dll

netapi32.dll
netbios.dll
nw16.dll
nwab32.dll
nwnet32.dll
nwnp32.dll
nwpp32.dll
pmspl.dll
rpcltc1.dll
rpcltc3.dll
rpcltc5.dll
rpcltc6.dll
rpclts3.dll
rpclts5.dll
rpclts6.dll
rpcns4.dll
rpcrt4.dll
sapnsp.dll
secur32.dll
svrapi.dll
winnet16.dll
winsock.dll
wnpp32.dll
wsock32.dll
am2100.dos
cpqndis.dos
dc21x4.dos
depca.dos
dncrwl02.dos
e100.dos
e20nd.dos
e21nd.dos
e22nd.dos
e30nd.dos
e31nd.dos
el59x.dos
elnk16.dos
elnk3.dos
elnkii.dos
elnkmc.dos
elnkpl.dos
epndis.dos
epro.dos
es3210.dos
evx16.dos
exp16.dos
hpfend.dos
hplan.dos
hplanb.dos
hplane.dos
hplanp.dos
i82593.dos
ibmtok.dos
irmatr.dos

ncc16.dos
ndis39xr.dos
ndis89xr.dos
ndis99xr.dos
ne1000.dos
ne2000.dos
ne3200.dos
netflx.dos
ni5210.dos
ni6510.dos
olitok16.dos
pcntnd.dos
pe2ndis.dos
pendis.dos
pro4.dos
pro4at.dos
slan.dos
smartnd.dos
smc_arc.dos
smc3000.dos
smc8000.dos
smc8100.dos

WIN95_12. CAB (CD)

smc8232.dos
smc9000.dos
strn.dos
t20nd.dos
t30nd.dos
tccarc.dos
tcctok.dos
tlnk.dos
tlnk3.dos
ubnei.dos
ubneps.dos
msnet.drv
prorapm.dwn
arp.exe
ftp.exe
lmscript.exe
login.exe
mprexe.exe
msdlc.exe
nbtstat.exe
netdde.exe
netstat.exe
nwlscon.exe
nwlsproc.exe
odihlp.exe
pe3ndis.exe
ping.exe
route.exe
rpcss.exe

telnet.exe
tracert.exe
winipcfg.exe
winpopup.exe
wsasrv.exe
telnet.hlp
winpopup.hlp
winpopup.inf
netware.ms
lmscript.pif
hosts.sam
lmhosts.sam
dc21x4.sys
e100.sys
e20n3.sys
e21n3.sys
e22n3.sys
ee16.sys
ifshlp.sys
mdgmport.sys
ne1000.sys
ne2000.sys
ne3200.sys
netflx.sys
octk16.sys
tdkcd02.sys
afvxd.vxd
am1500t.vxd
cendis.vxd
cpqndis3.vxd
declan.vxd
e30n3.vxd
e31n3.vxd
ee16.vxd
el59x.vxd
elnk16.vxd
elnk3.vxd
elnkii.vxd
elnkmc.vxd
elpc3.vxd
epro.vxd
filesec.vxd
hpeisa.vxd
hpfend.vxd
hpisa.vxd
hpmca.vxd
ibmtok.vxd
ibmtok4.vxd
irmatrac.vxd
msodisup.vxd
mssp.vxd
ndis.vxd
ndis2sup.vxd
netbeui.vxd

nice.vxd
nscl.vxd
nwlink.vxd
nwnblink.vxd
nwredir.vxd
nwserver.vxd
nwsp.vxd
octk32.vxd
otceth.vxd
pcntn3.vxd
pe3ndis.vxd
perf.vxd
proteon.vxd
setp3.vxd
smc8000w.vxd
smc80pc.vxd
smc8100w.vxd
smc8232w.vxd
smc9000.vxd
snip.vxd
socket.vxd
spendis.vxd
t20n3.vxd
t30n3.vxd
tctokch.vxd
tlnk3.vxd
ubnei.vxd
vnetbios.vxd
vnetsup.vxd
vredir.vxd
vserver.vxd
wshtcp.vxd
wsipx.vxd
wsock.vxd
vdhcp.386
vip.386
vnbt.386
vtcp.386
vtdi.386
protman.dos
net.exe
protman.exe
net.msg
neth.msg

WIN95_13. CAB (CD)

ndishlp.sys
unicode.bin
ega.cpi
iso.cpi
netwatch.cnt
charmap.exe
arrow_m.cur

beam_1.cur
beam_l.cur
beam_m.cur
busy_1.cur
busy_l.cur
busy_m.cur
cross_1.cur
cross_l.cur
cross_m.cur
help_1.cur
help_l.cur
help_m.cur
move_1.cur
move_l.cur
move_m.cur
no_1.cur
no_l.cur
no_m.cur
pen_1.cur
pen_l.cur
pen_m.cur
size1_1.cur
size1_l.cur
size1_m.cur
size2_1.cur
size2_l.cur
size2_m.cur
size3_1.cur
size3_l.cur
size3_m.cur
size4_1.cur
size4_l.cur
size4_m.cur
up_1.cur
up_l.cur
up_m.cur
wait_1.cur
wait_l.cur
wait_m.cur
debmp.dll
dehex.dll
demet.dll
dess.dll
dewp.dll
msviewut.dll
sccview.dll
vsami.dll
vsasc8.dll
vsbmp.dll
vsdrw.dll
vsexe2.dll
vsflw.dll
vsmp.dll
vsmsw.dll

vspp.dll
vsrtf.dll
vsw6.dll
vswk4.dll
vswks.dll
vswmf.dll
vsword.dll
vswork.dll
vswp5.dll
vswp6.dll
vswpf.dll
vsxl5.dll
quikview.exe
sysmon.cnt
netwatch.hlp
sysmon.hlp
mullang.inf
larial.ttf
larialbd.ttf
larialbi.ttf
lariali.ttf
lcour.ttf
lcourbd.ttf
lcourbi.ttf
lcouri.ttf
ltimes.ttf
ltimesbd.ttf
ltimesbi.ttf
ltimesi.ttf
cp_1250.nls
cp_1251.nls
cp_1253.nls
cp_737.nls
cp_852.nls
cp_866.nls
cp_869.nls
kbdbll.kbd
kbdblr.kbd
kbdbul.kbd
kbdcz.kbd
kbdcz1.kbd
kbdgk.kbd
kbdgk220.kbd
kbdgk319.kbd
kbdgl220.kbd
kbdgl319.kbd
kbdhu.kbd
kbdhu1.kbd
kbdpl.kbd
kbdpl1.kbd

kbdru.kbd
kbdru1.kbd
kbdsv.kbd
cdplayer.cnt
avwin.dll
avcapt.drv
mcipionr.drv
mcivisca.drv
cdplayer.exe
cdplayer.hlp
avwin.ini
canyon.mid
passport.mid
bachsb~1.rmi
beetho~2.rmi

WIN95_14. CAB (CD)

claire~1.rmi
danceo~2.rmi
fureli~1.rmi
hallof~2.rmi
mozart~2.rmi
avvxp500.vxd
chimes.wav
chord.wav
ding.wav
jungle~1.wav
jungle~2.wav
jungle~3.wav
jungle~4.wav
jungleas.wav
junglecl.wav
junglecr.wav
junglede.wav
jungleer.wav
jungleex.wav
junglema.wav
jungleme.wav
junglemi.wav
jungleop.wav
junglequ.wav
junglere.wav
junglewi.wav

WIN95_15. CAB (CD)

musica~1.wav
musica~2.wav
musica~3.wav

musica~4.wav
musicaas.wav
musicacl.wav
musicacr.wav
musicade.wav
musicaer.wav
musicaex.wav
musicama.wav
musicame.wav
musicami.wav
musicaop.wav
musicaqu.wav
musicare.wav
musicawi.wav
robotz~1.wav
robotz~2.wav
robotz~3.wav
robotz~4.wav
robotzas.wav
robotzcl.wav
robotzcr.wav
robotzde.wav
robotzer.wav
robotzex.wav
robotzma.wav
robotzme.wav
robotzmi.wav
robotzop.wav
robotzqu.wav
robotzre.wav
robotzwi.wav
tada.wav
utopia~1.wav
utopia~2.wav
utopia~3.wav
utopia~4.wav
utopiaas.wav
utopiacl.wav
utopiacr.wav
utopiade.wav
utopiaer.wav
utopiaex.wav

WIN95_16. CAB (CD)

utopiama.wav
utopiame.wav
utopiami.wav
utopiaop.wav
utopiaqu.wav

utopiare.wav
utopiawi.wav
closewin.avi
dragdrop.avi
explorer.avi
find.avi
movewin.avi
paste.avi
scroll.avi
sizewin.avi
taskswch.avi
whatson.avi
w_over.cnt
overview.hlp
hpjahlp.cnt
jetadmin.cpl
decpsmw4.dll
hpalerts.dll
hparrkui.dll
hpcola.dll
hpdmipx.dll
hpjd.dll
hpjdcom.dll
hpjdmon.dll
hpjdnp.dll
hpjdpp.dll
hpjdui.dll
hpjdund.dll
hpnetsrv.dll
hpnw416.dll
hpnw432.dll
hpnwpsrv.dll
hpnwshim.dll
hppjl.dll
hppjlext.dll
hpprarrk.dll
hpprntr.dll
hpprrush.dll
hpprui.dll
hprushui.dll
hpsnmp.dll
hptabs.dll
hptrbit.dll
hpvbit.dll
hpwiz.dll
hppropty.exe
jetadmin.exe
decpsmw4.hlp
hpjdund.hlp
hpprarrk.hlp

hpprntr.hlp
jetadmin.hlp
d17_ms.spd
d1712_ms.spd
d176_ms.spd
d20_ms.spd
d32_ms.spd
d40_ms.spd
d5100_ms.spd
expostrt.exe

WIN95_17. CAB (CD)

expo.hlp
arrow_1.cur
arrow_l.cur
w_tour.cnt
tourani.dll
tourstr.dll
tourutil.dll
vbrun300.dll
tour.exe
threed.vbx
vsqpw2.dll
filexfer.cnt
fte.dll
filexfer.exe
vvexe32.exe
filexfer.hlp
mdmvv.inf
wsvv.vxd
nwrpltrm.com
bkupnet.dll
instl50.dll
instl51.dll
arcsrv32.exe
bkupagnt.exe
netwatch.exe
pcsa.exe
select.exe
setmdir.exe
snapshot.exe
sysmon.exe
dllndis.new
dllndist.new
srm.new
rplboot.sys
deccore.vxd
declicl.vxd
snapshot.vxd

Alphabetical File List

If you know the name of the file you want to extract but can't figure out where to find it, this list is for you. The list may also come in handy if you find yourself wondering precisely what is and isn't on the diskettes. Again, before you start copying willy-nilly, make sure you understand the difference between files with identical names—one capitalized and the other lowercase. The difference is explained earlier in this chapter.

File	Size	CD Location	Disk Location	File	Size	CD Location	Disk Location
_pwmove.bat	576	WIN95_11.CAB	WIN95_11.CAB	aptolld1.spd	15,105	WIN95_10.CAB	WIN95_10.CAB
31users.hlp	47,506	WIN95_06.CAB	WIN95_06.CAB	aptollw1.spd	14,580	WIN95_10.CAB	WIN95_10.CAB
3dblocks.bmp	2,754	WIN95_02.CAB	WIN95_03.CAB	arcsrv32.exe	168,448	WIN95_17.CAB	(Not on diskette)
800950.dat	10,098	WIN95_07.CAB	WIN95_07.CAB	arial.ttf	65,412	WIN95_04.CAB	WIN95_04.CAB
850.dat	524	WIN95_05.CAB	WIN95_05.CAB	arialbd.ttf	66,952	WIN95_04.CAB	WIN95_04.CAB
8514fix.fon	10,992	WIN95_05.CAB	WIN95_05.CAB	arialbi.ttf	73,984	WIN95_04.CAB	WIN95_04.CAB
8514oem.fon	12,288	WIN95_05.CAB	WIN95_05.CAB	ariali.ttf	62,968	WIN95_04.CAB	WIN95_04.CAB
8514sys.fon	9,600	WIN95_05.CAB	WIN95_05.CAB	arp.exe	19,536	WIN95_12.CAB	WIN95_12.CAB
a_pnt518.spd	7,098	WIN95_10.CAB	WIN95_10.CAB	arrow.mpd	34,848	WIN95_03.CAB	WIN95_03.CAB
access.cpl	57,344	WIN95_02.CAB	WIN95_02.CAB	arrow_l.cur	766	WIN95_17.CAB	(Not on diskette)
access.hlp	34,923	WIN95_02.CAB	WIN95_02.CAB	arrow_l.cur	766	WIN95_17.CAB	(Not on diskette)
accstat.exe	24,576	WIN95_02.CAB	WIN95_02.CAB	arrow_m.cur	766	WIN95_13.CAB	(Not on diskette)
adapter.inf	4,788	PRECOPY2.CAB	PRECOPY2.CAB	aspi2hlp.sys	1,105	WIN95_03.CAB	WIN95_03.CAB
addreg.exe	14,336	WIN95_09.CAB	WIN95_10.CAB	ast__470.spd	4,436	WIN95_10.CAB	WIN95_10.CAB
advapi32.dll	13,824	WIN95_11.CAB	WIN95_11.CAB	at&tma~1.ht	829	WIN95_02.CAB	(Not on diskette)
afvxd.vxd	25,402	WIN95_12.CAB	WIN95_12.CAB	ati.vxd	25,737	WIN95_04.CAB	WIN95_05.CAB
aha154x.mpd	8,592	WIN95_04.CAB	WIN95_05.CAB	atim32.drv	94,768	WIN95_04.CAB	WIN95_05.CAB
aha174x.mpd	5,040	WIN95_05.CAB	WIN95_05.CAB	atim64.drv	66,336	WIN95_04.CAB	WIN95_05.CAB
aic78xx.mpd	23,824	WIN95_05.CAB	WIN95_05.CAB	atim8.drv	128,800	WIN95_04.CAB	WIN95_05.CAB
always.mpd	13,600	WIN95_05.CAB	WIN95_05.CAB	attrib.exe	15,252	WIN95_02.CAB	WIN95_02.CAB
am1500t.vxd	22,631	WIN95_12.CAB	WIN95_12.CAB	audiocdc.hlp	8,651	WIN95_05.CAB	WIN95_06.CAB
am2100.dos	11,105	WIN95_11.CAB	WIN95_12.CAB	avcapt.drv	24,336	WIN95_13.CAB	(Not on diskette)
amipro.sam	4,570	WIN95_11.CAB	WIN95_11.CAB	avicap.dll	72,272	WIN95_08.CAB	WIN95_08.CAB
amsint.mpd	13,264	WIN95_05.CAB	WIN95_05.CAB	avicap32.dll	59,904	WIN95_08.CAB	WIN95_08.CAB
ansi.sys	9,719	WIN95_09.CAB	WIN95_09.CAB	avifil32.dll	88,064	WIN95_08.CAB	WIN95_08.CAB
apix.vxd	29,404	WIN95_03.CAB	WIN95_03.CAB	avifile.dll	109,424	WIN95_08.CAB	WIN95_08.CAB
aplw8101.spd	22,106	WIN95_10.CAB	WIN95_10.CAB	avvxp500.vxd	11,860	WIN95_14.CAB	(Not on diskette)
aplwiif1.spd	19,120	WIN95_10.CAB	WIN95_10.CAB	avwin.dll	41,344	WIN95_13.CAB	(Not on diskette)
aplwiig1.spd	15,266	WIN95_10.CAB	WIN95_10.CAB	avwin.ini	8,622	WIN95_13.CAB	(Not on diskette)
aplwntr1.spd	8,913	WIN95_10.CAB	WIN95_10.CAB	awadpr32.exe	9,728	WIN95_05.CAB	WIN95_05.CAB
aplwsel.spd	13,016	WIN95_10.CAB	WIN95_10.CAB	awbmsc32.dll	10,240	WIN95_05.CAB	WIN95_05.CAB
apm.inf	2,578	PRECOPY2.CAB	PRECOPY2.CAB	awbtrv32.dll	5,120	WIN95_05.CAB	WIN95_05.CAB
app850.fon	44,320	WIN95_05.CAB	WIN95_05.CAB	awcapi32.dll	9,216	WIN95_05.CAB	WIN95_05.CAB
apple230.spd	5,681	WIN95_10.CAB	WIN95_10.CAB	awcl1_32.dll	22,528	WIN95_05.CAB	WIN95_05.CAB
apple380.spd	6,046	WIN95_10.CAB	WIN95_10.CAB	awcl2_32.dll	24,064	WIN95_05.CAB	WIN95_05.CAB
appletpp.inf	22,326	PRECOPY2.CAB	(Not on diskette)	awcodc32.dll	24,576	WIN95_05.CAB	WIN95_05.CAB
applets.inf	45,231	PRECOPY2.CAB	PRECOPY2.CAB	awdcxc32.dll	6,144	WIN95_05.CAB	WIN95_05.CAB
apps.hlp	58,872	WIN95_05.CAB	WIN95_06.CAB	awdevl16.dll	7,248	WIN95_05.CAB	WIN95_05.CAB
apps.inf	62,339	WIN95_06.CAB	WIN95_06.CAB	awdevl32.dll	6,656	WIN95_05.CAB	WIN95_05.CAB
appstart.ani	8,274	WIN95_10.CAB	WIN95_11.CAB	awfax.cnt	1,912	WIN95_05.CAB	WIN95_05.CAB
appwiz.cpl	63,488	WIN95_10.CAB	WIN95_11.CAB	awfax.hlp	58,931	WIN95_05.CAB	WIN95_05.CAB

File	Size	CD Location	Disk Location	File	Size	CD Location	Disk Location
awfax.inf	19,824	PRECOPY2.CAB	PRECOPY2.CAB	bkupprop.dll	40,960	PRECOPY2.CAB	(Not on diskette)
awfaxp32.dll	116,736	WIN95_05.CAB	WIN95_05.CAB	brhj770.drv	13,648	WIN95_10.CAB	WIN95_10.CAB
awfext32.dll	123,392	WIN95_05.CAB	WIN95_05.CAB	brother9.drv	16,464	WIN95_10.CAB	WIN95_10.CAB
awfmon32.dll	15,360	WIN95_05.CAB	WIN95_05.CAB	brothr24.drv	32,528	WIN95_10.CAB	WIN95_10.CAB
awfr32.dll	35,840	WIN95_05.CAB	WIN95_05.CAB	bubbles.bmp	2,118	WIN95_03.CAB	WIN95_03.CAB
awfxab32.dll	49,152	WIN95_05.CAB	WIN95_05.CAB	buslogic.mpd	8,144	WIN95_05.CAB	WIN95_05.CAB
awfxcg32.dll	116,224	WIN95_05.CAB	WIN95_05.CAB	busy_1.cur	766	WIN95_13.CAB	(Not on diskette)
awfxex32.exe	74,240	WIN95_05.CAB	WIN95_05.CAB	busy_l.cur	766	WIN95_13.CAB	(Not on diskette)
awfxio32.dll	44,032	WIN95_05.CAB	WIN95_05.CAB	busy_m.cur	766	WIN95_13.CAB	(Not on diskette)
awfxrn32.dll	49,152	WIN95_05.CAB	WIN95_05.CAB	calc.cnt	508	WIN95_05.CAB	WIN95_06.CAB
awkrnl32.dll	27,136	WIN95_05.CAB	WIN95_05.CAB	calc.exe	59,392	WIN95_02.CAB	WIN95_03.CAB
awlft332.dll	34,304	WIN95_05.CAB	WIN95_05.CAB	calc.hlp	31,886	WIN95_05.CAB	WIN95_06.CAB
awlhut32.dll	13,312	WIN95_05.CAB	WIN95_05.CAB	canon330.drv	29,104	WIN95_10.CAB	WIN95_10.CAB
awlinz32.dll	32,256	WIN95_05.CAB	WIN95_05.CAB	canon800.drv	10,000	WIN95_10.CAB	WIN95_10.CAB
awlzrd32.dll	8,192	WIN95_05.CAB	WIN95_05.CAB	canonlbp.drv	80,864	WIN95_10.CAB	WIN95_10.CAB
awnfax32.dll	34,304	WIN95_05.CAB	WIN95_05.CAB	canyon.mid	20,861	WIN95_13.CAB	(Not on diskette)
awprt.hlp	8,679	WIN95_05.CAB	WIN95_05.CAB	carddrv.exe	27,296	WIN95_09.CAB	WIN95_10.CAB
awpwd32.dll	20,480	WIN95_05.CAB	WIN95_05.CAB	cards.dll	148,528	WIN95_05.CAB	WIN95_06.CAB
awramb32.dll	11,264	WIN95_05.CAB	WIN95_05.CAB	ccapi.dll	29,696	WIN95_07.CAB	WIN95_07.CAB
awrbae32.dll	8,192	WIN95_05.CAB	WIN95_05.CAB	ccdialer.exe	22,016	WIN95_07.CAB	WIN95_08.CAB
awresx32.dll	26,624	WIN95_05.CAB	WIN95_05.CAB	ccei.dll	13,312	WIN95_07.CAB	WIN95_07.CAB
awrndr32.dll	6,144	WIN95_05.CAB	WIN95_05.CAB	ccpsh.dll	13,824	WIN95_07.CAB	WIN95_07.CAB
awschd32.dll	46,592	WIN95_05.CAB	WIN95_05.CAB	cdfs.vxd	58,620	WIN95_03.CAB	WIN95_03.CAB
awsnto32.exe	35,328	WIN95_05.CAB	WIN95_05.CAB	cdplayer.cnt	643	WIN95_13.CAB	(Not on diskette)
awsrvr32.dll	13,824	WIN95_05.CAB	WIN95_05.CAB	cdplayer.exe	88,064	WIN95_13.CAB	(Not on diskette)
awt30_32.dll	33,280	WIN95_05.CAB	WIN95_05.CAB	cdplayer.hlp	20,579	WIN95_13.CAB	(Not on diskette)
awupd.inf	2,191	PRECOPY2.CAB	PRECOPY2.CAB	cdtsd.vxd	13,883	WIN95_03.CAB	WIN95_03.CAB
awutil32.dll	40,448	WIN95_05.CAB	WIN95_05.CAB	cdvsd.vxd	14,962	WIN95_03.CAB	WIN95_03.CAB
awview32.dll	11,264	WIN95_05.CAB	WIN95_05.CAB	ce2ndis3.vxd	38,352	WIN95_08.CAB	WIN95_09.CAB
azt16.vxd	24,214	WIN95_08.CAB	WIN95_09.CAB	cemmf.inf	35,608	PRECOPY2.CAB	PRECOPY2.CAB
azt16c.drv	42,080	WIN95_08.CAB	WIN95_08.CAB	cendis.vxd	22,617	WIN95_12.CAB	WIN95_12.CAB
azt16w.drv	43,664	WIN95_08.CAB	WIN95_08.CAB	charmap.exe	14,752	WIN95_13.CAB	(Not on diskette)
bachsb~1.rmi	144,902	WIN95_13.CAB	(Not on diskette)	cheyenne.inf	1,657	PRECOPY2.CAB	(Not on diskette)
backup.cfg	23,834	WIN95_04.CAB	WIN95_04.CAB	cheyprop.dll	11,792	PRECOPY2.CAB	(Not on diskette)
backup.cnt	1,189	WIN95_04.CAB	WIN95_04.CAB	chiadi.dll	16,384	WIN95_04.CAB	WIN95_04.CAB
backup.exe	820,224	WIN95_04.CAB	WIN95_04.CAB	chikdi.dll	15,360	WIN95_04.CAB	WIN95_04.CAB
backup.hlp	33,018	WIN95_04.CAB	WIN95_05.CAB	chimes.wav	15,932	WIN95_14.CAB	(Not on diskette)
bamboo.bmp	590	WIN95_03.CAB	WIN95_03.CAB	chips.drv	25,328	WIN95_04.CAB	WIN95_05.CAB
bbsnav.nav	214,528	WIN95_07.CAB	WIN95_08.CAB	chips.vxd	18,590	WIN95_04.CAB	WIN95_05.CAB
beam_1.cur	766	WIN95_13.CAB	(Not on diskette)	chkdsk.exe	27,248	WIN95_02.CAB	WIN95_02.CAB
beam_l.cur	766	WIN95_13.CAB	(Not on diskette)	choice.com	5,175	WIN95_08.CAB	WIN95_09.CAB
beam_m.cur	766	WIN95_13.CAB	(Not on diskette)	choosusr.dll	22,016	WIN95_11.CAB	WIN95_12.CAB
beetho~2.rmi	92,466	WIN95_13.CAB	(Not on diskette)	chord.wav	24,994	WIN95_14.CAB	(Not on diskette)
bezier.scr	15,872	WIN95_11.CAB	WIN95_11.CAB	circles.bmp	190	WIN95_03.CAB	WIN95_03.CAB
bigmem.drv	9,962	WIN95_03.CAB	WIN95_03.CAB	cirrus.drv	57,632	WIN95_04.CAB	WIN95_05.CAB
bios.vxd	32,841	WIN95_09.CAB	WIN95_10.CAB	cirrus.vxd	16,950	WIN95_04.CAB	WIN95_05.CAB
biosxlat.vxd	18,077	WIN95_03.CAB	WIN95_03.CAB	cirrusmm.drv	35,344	WIN95_04.CAB	WIN95_05.CAB
bjc600.icm	12,504	WIN95_10.CAB	WIN95_10.CAB	cit24us.drv	40,544	WIN95_10.CAB	WIN95_10.CAB
bjc800.icm	12,684	WIN95_10.CAB	WIN95_10.CAB	cit9us.drv	29,184	WIN95_10.CAB	WIN95_10.CAB
bkupagnt.exe	61,952	WIN95_17.CAB	(Not on diskette)	citoh.drv	5,360	WIN95_10.CAB	WIN95_10.CAB
bkupagnt.inf	2,893	PRECOPY2.CAB	(Not on diskette)	claire~1.rmi	27,940	WIN95_14.CAB	(Not on diskette)
bkupnet.dll	39,936	WIN95_17.CAB	(Not on diskette)	clip.inf	2,213	WIN95_10.CAB	WIN95_11.CAB

File	Size	CD Location	Disk Location	File	Size	CD Location	Disk Location
clipbook.cnt	440	WIN95_02.CAB	WIN95_02.CAB	cp_866.nls	7,316	WIN95_13.CAB	(Not on diskette)
clipbook.exe	57,664	WIN95_02.CAB	WIN95_03.CAB	cp_869.nls	7,240	WIN95_13.CAB	(Not on diskette)
clipbook.hlp	20,029	WIN95_02.CAB	WIN95_03.CAB	cp_ps241.spd	16,062	WIN95_10.CAB	WIN95_10.CAB
clipbrd.cnt	411	WIN95_02.CAB	WIN95_02.CAB	cpper241.spd	16,432	WIN95_10.CAB	WIN95_10.CAB
clipbrd.exe	17,376	WIN95_02.CAB	WIN95_03.CAB	cppmq151.spd	17,878	WIN95_10.CAB	WIN95_10.CAB
clipbrd.hlp	13,015	WIN95_02.CAB	WIN95_03.CAB	cppmq201.spd	19,463	WIN95_10.CAB	WIN95_10.CAB
clipsrv.exe	16,608	WIN95_02.CAB	WIN95_03.CAB	cppro518.spd	5,794	WIN95_10.CAB	WIN95_10.CAB
closewin.avi	410,588	WIN95_16.CAB	(Not on diskette)	cppsnb10.spd	9,343	WIN95_10.CAB	WIN95_10.CAB
clouds.bmp	307,514	WIN95_02.CAB	WIN95_03.CAB	cppsx241.spd	8,806	WIN95_10.CAB	WIN95_10.CAB
cm2ndis3.vxd	22,109	WIN95_08.CAB	WIN95_09.CAB	cpqae05.exe	7,954	WIN95_09.CAB	WIN95_10.CAB
cmc.dll	6,304	WIN95_06.CAB	WIN95_07.CAB	cpqae06.exe	7,288	WIN95_09.CAB	WIN95_10.CAB
cmd640x.sys	24,626	WIN95_03.CAB	WIN95_03.CAB	cpqmode.ini	52,899	WIN95_04.CAB	WIN95_05.CAB
cmd640x2.sys	20,901	WIN95_03.CAB	WIN95_03.CAB	cpqmon.ini	41,810	WIN95_04.CAB	WIN95_05.CAB
combuff.vxd	10,401	WIN95_03.CAB	WIN95_03.CAB	cpqndis.dos	16,955	WIN95_11.CAB	WIN95_12.CAB
comctl31.dll	46,480	PRECOPY1.CAB	PRECOPY1.CAB	cpqndis3.vxd	31,837	WIN95_12.CAB	WIN95_12.CAB
comctl32.dll	182,272	WIN95_10.CAB	WIN95_11.CAB	cross_1.cur	766	WIN95_13.CAB	(Not on diskette)
comdlg32.dll	92,672	WIN95_10.CAB	WIN95_11.CAB	cross_l.cur	766	WIN95_13.CAB	(Not on diskette)
COMM.DRV	9,280	MINI.CAB	MINI.CAB	cross_m.cur	766	WIN95_13.CAB	(Not on diskette)
comm.drv	5,856	WIN95_03.CAB	WIN95_03.CAB	crtdll.dll	161,280	WIN95_03.CAB	WIN95_03.CAB
command.com	92,870	PRECOPY1.CAB	PRECOPY1.CAB	csmapper.sys	13,390	WIN95_09.CAB	WIN95_10.CAB
commctrl.dll	48,112	PRECOPY1.CAB	PRECOPY1.CAB	cspman.dll	17,776	WIN95_08.CAB	WIN95_08.CAB
commdlg.dll	97,936	PRECOPY1.CAB	PRECOPY1.CAB	ctndw.vxd	50,775	WIN95_08.CAB	WIN95_09.CAB
commdlg.new	88,544	WIN95_11.CAB	WIN95_11.CAB	d17_ms.spd	94	WIN95_16.CAB	(Not on diskette)
common.hlp	22,233	WIN95_05.CAB	WIN95_06.CAB	d1712_ms.spd	99	WIN95_16.CAB	(Not on diskette)
compaq.drv	82,080	WIN95_04.CAB	WIN95_05.CAB	d176_ms.spd	98	WIN95_16.CAB	(Not on diskette)
compaq.vxd	17,913	WIN95_04.CAB	WIN95_05.CAB	d20_ms.spd	99	WIN95_16.CAB	(Not on diskette)
complinc.dll	43,504	PRECOPY1.CAB	PRECOPY1.CAB	d2150_ms.spd	89	WIN95_10.CAB	WIN95_10.CAB
compobj.dll	30,976	WIN95_09.CAB	WIN95_09.CAB	d2250_ms.spd	89	WIN95_10.CAB	WIN95_10.CAB
compus~1.ht	829	WIN95_02.CAB	(Not on diskette)	d32_ms.spd	94	WIN95_16.CAB	(Not on diskette)
conagent.exe	14,596	WIN95_03.CAB	WIN95_04.CAB	d40_ms.spd	94	WIN95_16.CAB	(Not on diskette)
confapi.dll	23,552	WIN95_07.CAB	WIN95_07.CAB	d5100_ms.spd	93	WIN95_16.CAB	(Not on diskette)
confdent.cpe	4,357	WIN95_05.CAB	WIN95_05.CAB	danceo~2.rmi	20,906	WIN95_14.CAB	(Not on diskette)
config.txt	17,752	WIN95_03.CAB	WIN95_03.CAB	dataedcl.dll	12,800	WIN95_07.CAB	WIN95_07.CAB
configmg.vxd	85,613	WIN95_09.CAB	WIN95_10.CAB	datap462.spd	5,593	WIN95_10.CAB	WIN95_10.CAB
control.exe	2,112	WIN95_10.CAB	WIN95_11.CAB	dbkvssd.vxd	18,639	WIN95_09.CAB	WIN95_10.CAB
control.inf	2,497	WIN95_11.CAB	WIN95_11.CAB	dblbuff.sys	2,100	WIN95_09.CAB	WIN95_09.CAB
copy.inf	33,338	PRECOPY2.CAB	PRECOPY2.CAB	dblspace.bat	403	PRECOPY2.CAB	PRECOPY2.CAB
country.sys	27,094	WIN95_09.CAB	WIN95_09.CAB	dc1152_1.spd	9,476	WIN95_10.CAB	WIN95_10.CAB
cour.ttf	98,872	WIN95_04.CAB	WIN95_04.CAB	dc1152f1.spd	11,025	WIN95_10.CAB	WIN95_10.CAB
courbd.ttf	84,360	WIN95_04.CAB	WIN95_04.CAB	dc2150p1.spd	9,072	WIN95_10.CAB	WIN95_10.CAB
courbi.ttf	85,152	WIN95_04.CAB	WIN95_04.CAB	dc21x4.dos	46,573	WIN95_11.CAB	WIN95_12.CAB
coure.fon	23,424	WIN95_05.CAB	WIN95_05.CAB	dc21x4.sys	35,328	WIN95_12.CAB	WIN95_12.CAB
courf.fon	31,744	WIN95_05.CAB	WIN95_05.CAB	dc2250p1.spd	13,611	WIN95_10.CAB	WIN95_10.CAB
couri.ttf	82,092	WIN95_04.CAB	WIN95_04.CAB	dc5100_1.spd	29,406	WIN95_10.CAB	WIN95_10.CAB
cp_1250.nls	9,124	WIN95_13.CAB	(Not on diskette)	dcamac.bin	40,742	WIN95_11.CAB	WIN95_11.CAB
cp_1251.nls	6,868	WIN95_13.CAB	(Not on diskette)	dccolor1.spd	4,545	WIN95_10.CAB	WIN95_10.CAB
cp_1252.nls	9,194	WIN95_09.CAB	WIN95_09.CAB	dcd11501.spd	9,656	WIN95_10.CAB	WIN95_10.CAB
cp_1253.nls	6,856	WIN95_13.CAB	(Not on diskette)	dciman.dll	6,928	WIN95_08.CAB	WIN95_08.CAB
cp_437.nls	9,522	WIN95_09.CAB	WIN95_09.CAB	dciman32.dll	5,632	WIN95_08.CAB	WIN95_08.CAB
cp_737.nls	6,600	WIN95_13.CAB	(Not on diskette)	dclf02_1.spd	9,552	WIN95_10.CAB	WIN95_10.CAB
cp_850.nls	9,826	WIN95_09.CAB	WIN95_09.CAB	dclf02f1.spd	10,914	WIN95_10.CAB	WIN95_10.CAB
cp_852.nls	9,618	WIN95_13.CAB	(Not on diskette)	dcln03r1.spd	3,851	WIN95_10.CAB	WIN95_10.CAB

File	Size	CD Location	Disk Location	File	Size	CD Location	Disk Location
dclps171.spd	10,167	WIN95_10.CAB	WIN95_10.CAB	docprop.dll	17,408	WIN95_10.CAB	WIN95_11.CAB
dclps321.spd	10,876	WIN95_10.CAB	WIN95_10.CAB	dosapp.fon	44,304	WIN95_05.CAB	WIN95_06.CAB
dclps401.spd	6,908	WIN95_10.CAB	WIN95_10.CAB	doskey.com	15,431	WIN95_08.CAB	WIN95_09.CAB
dcps1721.spd	18,566	WIN95_10.CAB	WIN95_10.CAB	dosmgr.vxd	106,862	WIN95_03.CAB	WIN95_03.CAB
dcps1761.spd	18,213	WIN95_10.CAB	WIN95_10.CAB	dosnet.vxd	13,912	WIN95_03.CAB	WIN95_03.CAB
dctps201.spd	7,935	WIN95_10.CAB	WIN95_10.CAB	dosprmpt.pif	545	WIN95_03.CAB	WIN95_03.CAB
ddeml.dll	32,240	WIN95_03.CAB	WIN95_04.CAB	DOSSETUP.BIN	72,246	\WIN95 folder	Diskette 1 Root
debmp.dll	21,504	WIN95_13.CAB	(Not on diskette)	DOSX.EXE	32,682	MINI.CAB	MINI.CAB
debug.exe	20,522	WIN95_02.CAB	WIN95_02.CAB	dptscsi.mpd	12,000	WIN95_05.CAB	WIN95_05.CAB
dec24pin.drv	12,048	WIN95_10.CAB	WIN95_10.CAB	dragdrop.avi	306,608	WIN95_16.CAB	(Not on diskette)
dec3200.drv	14,192	WIN95_10.CAB	WIN95_10.CAB	drvspace.bat	329	PRECOPY2.CAB	PRECOPY2.CAB
dec3250.spd	11,669	WIN95_10.CAB	WIN95_10.CAB	drvspace.bin	71,287	PRECOPY1.CAB	PRECOPY1.CAB
deccore.vxd	15,062	WIN95_17.CAB	(Not on diskette)	drvspace.cnt	822	WIN95_05.CAB	WIN95_06.CAB
declan.vxd	27,213	WIN95_12.CAB	WIN95_12.CAB	drvspace.exe	336,736	WIN95_08.CAB	WIN95_09.CAB
declicl.vxd	36,587	WIN95_17.CAB	(Not on diskette)	drvspace.hlp	23,816	WIN95_05.CAB	WIN95_06.CAB
decpsmw4.dll	369,664	WIN95_16.CAB	(Not on diskette)	drvspace.inf	1,121	WIN95_09.CAB	WIN95_09.CAB
decpsmw4.hlp	235,199	WIN95_16.CAB	(Not on diskette)	drvspace.sys	15,831	PRECOPY1.CAB	PRECOPY1.CAB
decpsmw4.inf	2,436	PRECOPY2.CAB	(Not on diskette)	drvspacx.vxd	54,207	WIN95_09.CAB	WIN95_09.CAB
defrag.bat	339	PRECOPY2.CAB	PRECOPY2.CAB	dskmaint.dll	189,456	PRECOPY2.CAB	PRECOPY2.CAB
defrag.exe	241,600	WIN95_04.CAB	WIN95_04.CAB	dsnav.nav	31,744	WIN95_07.CAB	WIN95_08.CAB
dehex.dll	8,192	WIN95_13.CAB	(Not on diskette)	dsned.ned	36,864	WIN95_07.CAB	WIN95_08.CAB
del.inf	36,793	PRECOPY2.CAB	PRECOPY2.CAB	dunzipnt.dll	94,720	WIN95_07.CAB	WIN95_07.CAB
DELTEMP.COM	496	\WIN95 folder	Diskette 1 Root	dynapage.vxd	26,982	WIN95_03.CAB	WIN95_03.CAB
deltree.exe	19,019	WIN95_08.CAB	WIN95_09.CAB	e100.dos	22,192	WIN95_11.CAB	WIN95_12.CAB
demet.dll	40,448	WIN95_13.CAB	(Not on diskette)	e100.sys	39,424	WIN95_12.CAB	WIN95_12.CAB
depca.dos	15,593	WIN95_11.CAB	WIN95_12.CAB	e20n3.sys	14,256	WIN95_12.CAB	WIN95_12.CAB
desk.cpl	8,704	WIN95_03.CAB	WIN95_04.CAB	e20nd.dos	16,332	WIN95_11.CAB	WIN95_12.CAB
deskcp16.dll	83,472	WIN95_03.CAB	WIN95_04.CAB	e21n3.sys	15,328	WIN95_12.CAB	WIN95_12.CAB
deskjetc.drv	181,840	WIN95_09.CAB	WIN95_10.CAB	e21nd.dos	8,832	WIN95_11.CAB	WIN95_12.CAB
desktop.ini	67	WIN95_03.CAB	WIN95_03.CAB	e22n3.sys	31,744	WIN95_12.CAB	WIN95_12.CAB
dess.dll	36,352	WIN95_13.CAB	(Not on diskette)	e22nd.dos	10,512	WIN95_11.CAB	WIN95_12.CAB
dewp.dll	48,128	WIN95_13.CAB	(Not on diskette)	e30n3.vxd	31,636	WIN95_12.CAB	WIN95_12.CAB
dialer.cnt	552	WIN95_02.CAB	WIN95_03.CAB	e30nd.dos	16,002	WIN95_11.CAB	WIN95_12.CAB
dialer.exe	63,240	WIN95_02.CAB	WIN95_03.CAB	e31n3.vxd	31,636	WIN95_12.CAB	WIN95_12.CAB
dialer.hlp	19,193	WIN95_02.CAB	WIN95_03.CAB	e31nd.dos	8,031	WIN95_11.CAB	WIN95_12.CAB
dibeng.dll	201,136	WIN95_03.CAB	WIN95_04.CAB	eaglecaf.bin	26,880	WIN95_11.CAB	WIN95_12.CAB
diconix.drv	5,136	WIN95_10.CAB	WIN95_10.CAB	eaglemac.bin	26,880	WIN95_11.CAB	WIN95_12.CAB
ding.wav	11,586	WIN95_14.CAB	(Not on diskette)	ebios.vxd	17,993	WIN95_03.CAB	WIN95_03.CAB
directcc.exe	60,416	WIN95_10.CAB	WIN95_11.CAB	edit.com	69,886	WIN95_02.CAB	WIN95_02.CAB
diskcopy.com	21,959	WIN95_08.CAB	WIN95_09.CAB	edit.hlp	10,790	WIN95_05.CAB	WIN95_06.CAB
diskcopy.dll	15,872	WIN95_10.CAB	WIN95_11.CAB	ee16.sys	16,896	WIN95_12.CAB	WIN95_12.CAB
diskdrv.inf	765	PRECOPY2.CAB	PRECOPY2.CAB	ee16.vxd	23,129	WIN95_12.CAB	WIN95_12.CAB
disktsd.vxd	16,478	WIN95_03.CAB	WIN95_03.CAB	ega.cpi	58,870	WIN95_13.CAB	WIN95_13.CAB
diskvsd.vxd	10,094	WIN95_03.CAB	WIN95_03.CAB	egypt.bmp	582	WIN95_03.CAB	WIN95_03.CAB
dispdib.dll	6,992	WIN95_08.CAB	WIN95_08.CAB	eisa.vxd	13,669	WIN95_09.CAB	WIN95_10.CAB
display.sys	17,175	WIN95_09.CAB	WIN95_09.CAB	el59x.dos	17,430	WIN95_11.CAB	WIN95_12.CAB
display.txt	15,954	WIN95_03.CAB	WIN95_03.CAB	el59x.vxd	48,710	WIN95_12.CAB	WIN95_12.CAB
dllndis.new	14,757	WIN95_17.CAB	(Not on diskette)	elnk16.dos	9,792	WIN95_11.CAB	WIN95_12.CAB
dllndist.new	16,588	WIN95_17.CAB	(Not on diskette)	elnk16.vxd	29,379	WIN95_12.CAB	WIN95_12.CAB
dmcolor.dll	18,272	WIN95_09.CAB	WIN95_10.CAB	elnk3.dos	15,519	WIN95_11.CAB	WIN95_12.CAB
dncrwl02.dos	35,647	WIN95_11.CAB	WIN95_12.CAB	elnk3.vxd	30,773	WIN95_12.CAB	WIN95_12.CAB
dnr.exe	3,584	WIN95_07.CAB	WIN95_08.CAB	elnkii.dos	11,322	WIN95_11.CAB	WIN95_12.CAB

File	Size	CD Location	Disk Location	File	Size	CD Location	Disk Location
elnkii.vxd	31,325	WIN95_12.CAB	WIN95_12.CAB	faxcodec.dll	14,336	WIN95_05.CAB	WIN95_05.CAB
elnkmc.dos	9,542	WIN95_11.CAB	WIN95_12.CAB	faxcover.cnt	653	WIN95_05.CAB	WIN95_05.CAB
elnkmc.vxd	28,787	WIN95_12.CAB	WIN95_12.CAB	faxcover.exe	191,488	WIN95_05.CAB	WIN95_05.CAB
elnkpl.dos	17,116	WIN95_11.CAB	WIN95_12.CAB	faxcover.hlp	15,185	WIN95_05.CAB	WIN95_05.CAB
elpc3.vxd	29,785	WIN95_12.CAB	WIN95_12.CAB	faxview.cnt	204	WIN95_05.CAB	WIN95_05.CAB
emm386.exe	125,495	WIN95_08.CAB	WIN95_09.CAB	faxview.exe	166,912	WIN95_05.CAB	WIN95_05.CAB
enable.inf	2,971	PRECOPY2.CAB	PRECOPY2.CAB	faxview.hlp	12,186	WIN95_05.CAB	WIN95_05.CAB
enable.vxd	43,197	WIN95_02.CAB	WIN95_02.CAB	fc.exe	20,494	WIN95_08.CAB	WIN95_09.CAB
enable2.vxd	25,154	WIN95_02.CAB	WIN95_02.CAB	fd16_700.mpd	10,736	WIN95_05.CAB	WIN95_05.CAB
enable3.dll	6,160	WIN95_02.CAB	WIN95_02.CAB	fd8xx.mpd	8,352	WIN95_05.CAB	WIN95_05.CAB
enable4.vxd	21,629	WIN95_02.CAB	WIN95_02.CAB	fdisk.exe	59,128	WIN95_02.CAB	WIN95_02.CAB
envoy.evy	293	WIN95_10.CAB	WIN95_11.CAB	filesec.vxd	23,025	WIN95_12.CAB	WIN95_12.CAB
epl75523.spd	7,376	WIN95_10.CAB	WIN95_10.CAB	filexfer.cnt	342	WIN95_17.CAB	(Not on diskette)
epndis.dos	19,230	WIN95_11.CAB	WIN95_12.CAB	filexfer.exe	48,128	WIN95_17.CAB	(Not on diskette)
epro.dos	16,995	WIN95_11.CAB	WIN95_12.CAB	filexfer.hlp	14,007	WIN95_17.CAB	(Not on diskette)
epro.vxd	25,152	WIN95_12.CAB	WIN95_12.CAB	find.avi	488,492	WIN95_16.CAB	(Not on diskette)
epson24.drv	25,168	WIN95_09.CAB	WIN95_10.CAB	find.exe	6,658	WIN95_08.CAB	WIN95_09.CAB
epson9.drv	31,776	WIN95_10.CAB	WIN95_10.CAB	findmvi.dll	5,728	WIN95_08.CAB	WIN95_08.CAB
epsonsty.icm	12,628	WIN95_10.CAB	WIN95_10.CAB	findstub.dll	10,752	WIN95_07.CAB	WIN95_07.CAB
es1488.drv	43,936	WIN95_08.CAB	WIN95_08.CAB	finstall.dll	188,848	WIN95_09.CAB	WIN95_10.CAB
es1488.vxd	18,072	WIN95_08.CAB	WIN95_09.CAB	finstall.hlp	21,491	WIN95_09.CAB	WIN95_10.CAB
es1688.drv	50,128	WIN95_08.CAB	WIN95_08.CAB	fls1mtd.vxd	3,706	WIN95_09.CAB	WIN95_10.CAB
es1688.vxd	22,168	WIN95_08.CAB	WIN95_09.CAB	fls2mtd.vxd	3,810	WIN95_09.CAB	WIN95_10.CAB
es3210.dos	14,544	WIN95_11.CAB	WIN95_12.CAB	fontext.dll	105,984	WIN95_10.CAB	WIN95_11.CAB
es488.drv	36,976	WIN95_08.CAB	WIN95_08.CAB	fontreg.exe	6,656	WIN95_11.CAB	WIN95_11.CAB
es488.vxd	18,071	WIN95_08.CAB	WIN95_09.CAB	fonts.inf	24,626	PRECOPY2.CAB	PRECOPY2.CAB
es688.drv	47,008	WIN95_08.CAB	WIN95_08.CAB	fonts.mfm	95,719	WIN95_10.CAB	WIN95_10.CAB
es688.vxd	19,607	WIN95_08.CAB	WIN95_09.CAB	fontview.exe	36,352	WIN95_11.CAB	WIN95_11.CAB
escp2ms.drv	23,200	WIN95_09.CAB	WIN95_10.CAB	forest.bmp	66,146	WIN95_03.CAB	WIN95_03.CAB
esdi_506.pdr	23,758	WIN95_05.CAB	WIN95_05.CAB	format.com	40,135	WIN95_02.CAB	WIN95_02.CAB
essfm.drv	17,920	WIN95_08.CAB	WIN95_08.CAB	framebuf.drv	16,752	WIN95_04.CAB	WIN95_05.CAB
essmport.drv	9,904	WIN95_08.CAB	WIN95_08.CAB	freecell.cnt	196	WIN95_05.CAB	WIN95_06.CAB
essmpu.drv	8,240	WIN95_08.CAB	WIN95_08.CAB	freecell.exe	28,560	WIN95_05.CAB	WIN95_06.CAB
evx16.dos	11,299	WIN95_11.CAB	WIN95_12.CAB	freecell.hlp	11,618	WIN95_05.CAB	WIN95_06.CAB
ewrk3.dos	9,509	WIN95_08.CAB	WIN95_09.CAB	freelanc.pre	12,701	WIN95_11.CAB	WIN95_11.CAB
ewrk3.sys	24,064	WIN95_08.CAB	WIN95_09.CAB	fte.dll	53,248	WIN95_17.CAB	(Not on diskette)
excel.xls	5,632	WIN95_11.CAB	WIN95_11.CAB	ftmapi.dll	66,048	WIN95_07.CAB	WIN95_07.CAB
excel4.xls	1,518	WIN95_11.CAB	WIN95_11.CAB	ftmcl.exe	46,592	WIN95_07.CAB	WIN95_08.CAB
exchange.txt	7,072	WIN95_03.CAB	WIN95_03.CAB	ftp.exe	37,520	WIN95_12.CAB	WIN95_12.CAB
exchng.cnt	1,639	WIN95_06.CAB	WIN95_06.CAB	ftsrch.dll	231,936	WIN95_05.CAB	WIN95_06.CAB
exchng.hlp	100,371	WIN95_06.CAB	WIN95_07.CAB	fuji24.drv	32,176	WIN95_10.CAB	WIN95_10.CAB
exchng32.exe	20,240	WIN95_06.CAB	WIN95_07.CAB	fuji9.drv	12,224	WIN95_10.CAB	WIN95_10.CAB
exp16.dos	10,478	WIN95_11.CAB	WIN95_12.CAB	fureli~1.rmi	21,312	WIN95_14.CAB	(Not on diskette)
explorer.avi	872,208	WIN95_16.CAB	(Not on diskette)	fyi.cpe	4,473	WIN95_05.CAB	WIN95_05.CAB
explorer.exe	204,288	WIN95_10.CAB	WIN95_11.CAB	gator.bmp	32,850	WIN95_03.CAB	WIN95_03.CAB
expo.hlp	9,079	WIN95_17.CAB	(Not on diskette)	GDI.EXE	149,456	MINI.CAB	MINI.CAB
expostrt.exe	33,280	WIN95_16.CAB	(Not on diskette)	gdi.exe	312,208	WIN95_03.CAB	WIN95_04.CAB
exprss24.drv	15,152	WIN95_10.CAB	WIN95_10.CAB	gdi32.dll	131,072	WIN95_11.CAB	WIN95_11.CAB
extra.txt	2,685	WIN95_03.CAB	WIN95_03.CAB	general.idf	654	WIN95_08.CAB	WIN95_09.CAB
EXTRACT.EXE	46,656	\WIN95 folder	Diskette 1 Root	general.txt	17,965	WIN95_03.CAB	WIN95_03.CAB
f71rx503.spd	5,476	WIN95_10.CAB	WIN95_10.CAB	generic.cpe	5,935	WIN95_05.CAB	WIN95_05.CAB
faq.txt	40,378	WIN95_03.CAB	WIN95_03.CAB	genfax.apd	15,624	WIN95_05.CAB	WIN95_05.CAB

File	Size	CD Location	Disk Location	File	Size	CD Location	Disk Location
grpconv.exe	33,280	WIN95_11.CAB	WIN95_11.CAB	hplane.dos	17,936	WIN95_11.CAB	WIN95_12.CAB
guide.exe	110,080	WIN95_07.CAB	WIN95_08.CAB	hplanp.dos	12,640	WIN95_11.CAB	WIN95_12.CAB
guidenav.nav	40,960	WIN95_07.CAB	WIN95_08.CAB	hplj_31.spd	9,632	WIN95_10.CAB	WIN95_10.CAB
halftone.bmp	190	WIN95_03.CAB	WIN95_03.CAB	hplj_3d1.spd	14,102	WIN95_10.CAB	WIN95_10.CAB
hallof~2.rmi	38,444	WIN95_14.CAB	(Not on diskette)	hplj_3p1.spd	11,136	WIN95_10.CAB	WIN95_10.CAB
hardware.txt	21,548	WIN95_03.CAB	WIN95_03.CAB	hpljp_v4.spd	14,100	WIN95_10.CAB	WIN95_10.CAB
help_1.cur	766	WIN95_13.CAB	(Not on diskette)	hpmca.vxd	43,588	WIN95_12.CAB	WIN95_12.CAB
help_l.cur	766	WIN95_13.CAB	(Not on diskette)	hpnetprn.inf	5,297	PRECOPY2.CAB	(Not on diskette)
help_m.cur	766	WIN95_13.CAB	(Not on diskette)	hpnetsrv.dll	15,872	WIN95_16.CAB	(Not on diskette)
himem.sys	32,935	WIN95_03.CAB	WIN95_03.CAB	hpnw416.dll	1,431	WIN95_16.CAB	(Not on diskette)
homebase.dll	58,368	WIN95_07.CAB	WIN95_07.CAB	hpnw432.dll	18,944	WIN95_16.CAB	(Not on diskette)
hosts.sam	728	WIN95_12.CAB	WIN95_12.CAB	hpnwpsrv.dll	21,504	WIN95_16.CAB	(Not on diskette)
hounds.bmp	470	WIN95_03.CAB	WIN95_03.CAB	hpnwshim.dll	27,648	WIN95_16.CAB	(Not on diskette)
hourglas.ani	12,144	WIN95_10.CAB	WIN95_11.CAB	hppcl.drv	202,992	WIN95_09.CAB	WIN95_10.CAB
hp_3d522.spd	9,435	WIN95_10.CAB	WIN95_10.CAB	hppcl5ms.drv	525,856	WIN95_09.CAB	WIN95_10.CAB
hp_3p522.spd	7,743	WIN95_10.CAB	WIN95_10.CAB	hppjl.dll	18,944	WIN95_16.CAB	(Not on diskette)
hp1200c.icm	12,716	WIN95_06.CAB	WIN95_06.CAB	hppjlext.dll	168,448	WIN95_16.CAB	(Not on diskette)
hp1200c1.spd	12,334	WIN95_10.CAB	WIN95_10.CAB	hppjxl31.spd	14,442	WIN95_10.CAB	WIN95_10.CAB
hp1200ps.icm	24,600	WIN95_06.CAB	WIN95_06.CAB	hpplot.drv	66,976	WIN95_10.CAB	WIN95_10.CAB
hp3si523.spd	9,365	WIN95_10.CAB	WIN95_10.CAB	hpplot.hlp	10,119	WIN95_10.CAB	WIN95_10.CAB
hp4m_v4.spd	14,273	WIN95_10.CAB	WIN95_10.CAB	hpprarrk.dll	7,680	WIN95_16.CAB	(Not on diskette)
hp4ml_v4.spd	12,236	WIN95_10.CAB	WIN95_10.CAB	hpprarrk.hlp	26,913	WIN95_16.CAB	(Not on diskette)
hp4mp_v4.spd	12,605	WIN95_10.CAB	WIN95_10.CAB	hpprntr.dll	36,864	WIN95_16.CAB	(Not on diskette)
hp4mv_v4.spd	18,906	WIN95_10.CAB	WIN95_10.CAB	hpprntr.hlp	81,937	WIN95_16.CAB	(Not on diskette)
hp4plus4.spd	12,996	WIN95_10.CAB	WIN95_10.CAB	hppropty.exe	30,720	WIN95_16.CAB	(Not on diskette)
hp4si_v4.spd	14,880	WIN95_10.CAB	WIN95_10.CAB	hpprrush.dll	7,680	WIN95_16.CAB	(Not on diskette)
hpalerts.dll	21,504	WIN95_16.CAB	(Not on diskette)	hpprui.dll	246,784	WIN95_16.CAB	(Not on diskette)
hparrkui.dll	45,056	WIN95_16.CAB	(Not on diskette)	hprushui.dll	24,576	WIN95_16.CAB	(Not on diskette)
hpclrlsr.icm	12,176	WIN95_10.CAB	WIN95_10.CAB	hpsjtw.icm	6,514	WIN95_06.CAB	WIN95_06.CAB
hpcola.dll	105,984	WIN95_16.CAB	(Not on diskette)	hpsnmp.dll	152,064	WIN95_16.CAB	(Not on diskette)
hpcolor.dll	18,496	WIN95_09.CAB	WIN95_10.CAB	hptabs.dll	41,472	WIN95_16.CAB	(Not on diskette)
hpdesk.icm	12,956	WIN95_10.CAB	WIN95_10.CAB	hptrbit.dll	5,632	WIN95_16.CAB	(Not on diskette)
hpdmipx.dll	25,088	WIN95_16.CAB	(Not on diskette)	hpvbit.dll	11,264	WIN95_16.CAB	(Not on diskette)
hpdskjet.drv	90,560	WIN95_09.CAB	WIN95_10.CAB	hpvcm.hpm	13,623	WIN95_10.CAB	WIN95_10.CAB
hpeisa.vxd	35,629	WIN95_12.CAB	WIN95_12.CAB	hpvdjc.hlp	17,166	WIN95_10.CAB	WIN95_10.CAB
hpfend.dos	14,299	WIN95_11.CAB	WIN95_12.CAB	hpviol.dll	25,216	WIN95_09.CAB	WIN95_10.CAB
hpfend.vxd	39,494	WIN95_12.CAB	WIN95_12.CAB	hpvmon.dll	13,280	WIN95_09.CAB	WIN95_10.CAB
hpiid522.spd	8,617	WIN95_10.CAB	WIN95_10.CAB	hpvres.dll	21,072	WIN95_09.CAB	WIN95_10.CAB
hpiii522.spd	7,581	WIN95_10.CAB	WIN95_10.CAB	hpvui.dll	49,104	WIN95_09.CAB	WIN95_10.CAB
hpiip522.spd	7,288	WIN95_10.CAB	WIN95_10.CAB	hpwiz.dll	24,576	WIN95_16.CAB	(Not on diskette)
hpisa.vxd	43,588	WIN95_12.CAB	WIN95_12.CAB	hpxl300.icm	12,700	WIN95_10.CAB	WIN95_10.CAB
hpjahlp.cnt	3,386	WIN95_16.CAB	(Not on diskette)	hpxl30ps.icm	24,596	WIN95_10.CAB	WIN95_10.CAB
hpjd.dll	5,152	WIN95_16.CAB	(Not on diskette)	hsflop.pdr	18,998	WIN95_05.CAB	WIN95_05.CAB
hpjdcom.dll	48,640	WIN95_16.CAB	(Not on diskette)	hticons.dll	20,480	WIN95_02.CAB	WIN95_02.CAB
hpjdmon.dll	8,704	WIN95_16.CAB	(Not on diskette)	hypertrm.cnt	910	WIN95_02.CAB	WIN95_02.CAB
hpjdnp.dll	12,288	WIN95_16.CAB	(Not on diskette)	hypertrm.dll	326,144	WIN95_02.CAB	WIN95_02.CAB
hpjdpp.dll	48,640	WIN95_16.CAB	(Not on diskette)	hypertrm.exe	6,144	WIN95_02.CAB	WIN95_03.CAB
hpjdui.dll	116,224	WIN95_16.CAB	(Not on diskette)	hypertrm.hlp	21,473	WIN95_02.CAB	WIN95_03.CAB
hpjdund.dll	23,552	WIN95_16.CAB	(Not on diskette)	i82593.dos	10,279	WIN95_11.CAB	WIN95_12.CAB
hpjdund.hlp	57,660	WIN95_16.CAB	(Not on diskette)	ib401917.spd	9,076	WIN95_10.CAB	WIN95_10.CAB
hplan.dos	15,470	WIN95_11.CAB	WIN95_12.CAB	ib401939.spd	10,431	WIN95_10.CAB	WIN95_10.CAB
hplanb.dos	11,744	WIN95_11.CAB	WIN95_12.CAB	ib402917.spd	10,784	WIN95_10.CAB	WIN95_10.CAB

File	Size	CD Location	Disk Location	File	Size	CD Location	Disk Location
ib402939.spd	12,152	WIN95_10.CAB	WIN95_10.CAB	jungleas.wav	89,126	WIN95_14.CAB	(Not on diskette)
ibm20470.spd	12,116	WIN95_10.CAB	WIN95_10.CAB	junglecl.wav	143,914	WIN95_14.CAB	(Not on diskette)
ibm238x.drv	15,024	WIN95_10.CAB	WIN95_10.CAB	junglecr.wav	175,146	WIN95_14.CAB	(Not on diskette)
ibm239x.drv	30,560	WIN95_10.CAB	WIN95_10.CAB	junglede.wav	140,330	WIN95_14.CAB	(Not on diskette)
ibm30505.spd	5,825	WIN95_10.CAB	WIN95_10.CAB	jungleer.wav	166,954	WIN95_14.CAB	(Not on diskette)
ibm31514.spd	4,586	WIN95_10.CAB	WIN95_10.CAB	jungleex.wav	147,754	WIN95_14.CAB	(Not on diskette)
ibm4039.spd	12,095	WIN95_10.CAB	WIN95_10.CAB	junglema.wav	169,010	WIN95_14.CAB	(Not on diskette)
ibm4039p.spd	15,322	WIN95_10.CAB	WIN95_10.CAB	jungleme.wav	74,026	WIN95_14.CAB	(Not on diskette)
ibm4079.spd	6,451	WIN95_10.CAB	WIN95_10.CAB	junglemi.wav	169,010	WIN95_14.CAB	(Not on diskette)
ibm5204.drv	19,216	WIN95_10.CAB	WIN95_10.CAB	jungleop.wav	129,578	WIN95_14.CAB	(Not on diskette)
ibmppdsl.drv	25,920	WIN95_10.CAB	WIN95_10.CAB	junglequ.wav	145,446	WIN95_14.CAB	(Not on diskette)
ibmtok.dos	10,112	WIN95_11.CAB	WIN95_12.CAB	junglere.wav	159,782	WIN95_14.CAB	(Not on diskette)
ibmtok.vxd	39,250	WIN95_12.CAB	WIN95_12.CAB	junglewi.wav	474,238	WIN95_14.CAB	(Not on diskette)
ibmtok4.vxd	35,086	WIN95_12.CAB	WIN95_12.CAB	kbdbe.kbd	611	WIN95_06.CAB	WIN95_06.CAB
iccvid.dll	77,824	WIN95_08.CAB	WIN95_08.CAB	kbdbll.kbd	403	WIN95_13.CAB	(Not on diskette)
icm.inf	2,049	PRECOPY2.CAB	PRECOPY2.CAB	kbdblr.kbd	403	WIN95_13.CAB	(Not on diskette)
icm32.dll	140,288	WIN95_06.CAB	WIN95_06.CAB	kbdbr.kbd	613	WIN95_06.CAB	WIN95_06.CAB
icmp.dll	6,496	WIN95_11.CAB	WIN95_12.CAB	kbdbul.kbd	403	WIN95_13.CAB	(Not on diskette)
icmui.dll	22,016	WIN95_06.CAB	WIN95_06.CAB	kbdca.kbd	621	WIN95_06.CAB	WIN95_06.CAB
iconlib.dll	77,712	WIN95_09.CAB	WIN95_10.CAB	kbdcz.kbd	804	WIN95_13.CAB	(Not on diskette)
ifshlp.sys	3,708	WIN95_12.CAB	WIN95_12.CAB	kbdcz1.kbd	796	WIN95_13.CAB	(Not on diskette)
ifsmgr.vxd	165,029	WIN95_03.CAB	WIN95_03.CAB	kbdda.kbd	603	WIN95_06.CAB	WIN95_06.CAB
imaadp32.acm	18,944	WIN95_08.CAB	WIN95_08.CAB	kbddv.kbd	398	WIN95_06.CAB	WIN95_06.CAB
imm32.dll	6,144	WIN95_06.CAB	WIN95_06.CAB	kbdfc.kbd	693	WIN95_06.CAB	WIN95_06.CAB
indicdll.dll	5,120	WIN95_06.CAB	WIN95_06.CAB	kbdfi.kbd	610	WIN95_06.CAB	WIN95_06.CAB
inetmib1.dll	50,512	WIN95_11.CAB	WIN95_12.CAB	kbdfr.kbd	574	WIN95_06.CAB	WIN95_06.CAB
informs.wpf	2,274	WIN95_11.CAB	WIN95_11.CAB	kbdgk.kbd	520	WIN95_13.CAB	(Not on diskette)
instbe.bat	2,456	WIN95_07.CAB	WIN95_07.CAB	kbdgk220.kbd	499	WIN95_13.CAB	(Not on diskette)
instl50.dll	66,192	WIN95_17.CAB	(Not on diskette)	kbdgk319.kbd	495	WIN95_13.CAB	(Not on diskette)
instl51.dll	66,192	WIN95_17.CAB	(Not on diskette)	kbdgl220.kbd	539	WIN95_13.CAB	(Not on diskette)
int13.vxd	9,934	WIN95_03.CAB	WIN95_03.CAB	kbdgl319.kbd	569	WIN95_13.CAB	(Not on diskette)
internat.exe	12,800	WIN95_06.CAB	WIN95_06.CAB	kbdgr.kbd	547	WIN95_06.CAB	WIN95_06.CAB
internet.txt	3,277	WIN95_03.CAB	WIN95_03.CAB	kbdgr1.kbd	547	WIN95_06.CAB	WIN95_06.CAB
intl.cpl	48,640	WIN95_03.CAB	WIN95_04.CAB	kbdhu.kbd	786	WIN95_13.CAB	(Not on diskette)
ios.ini	10,398	WIN95_03.CAB	WIN95_03.CAB	kbdhu1.kbd	501	WIN95_13.CAB	(Not on diskette)
ios.vxd	68,289	WIN95_03.CAB	WIN95_03.CAB	kbdic.kbd	670	WIN95_06.CAB	WIN95_06.CAB
iosclass.dll	9,744	WIN95_03.CAB	WIN95_03.CAB	kbdir.kbd	509	WIN95_06.CAB	WIN95_06.CAB
ir32_32.dll	193,024	WIN95_08.CAB	WIN95_08.CAB	kbdit.kbd	424	WIN95_06.CAB	WIN95_06.CAB
irmatr.dos	59,448	WIN95_11.CAB	WIN95_12.CAB	kbdit1.kbd	518	WIN95_06.CAB	WIN95_06.CAB
irmatrac.vxd	41,075	WIN95_12.CAB	WIN95_12.CAB	kbdla.kbd	575	WIN95_06.CAB	WIN95_06.CAB
isapnp.vxd	18,817	WIN95_09.CAB	WIN95_10.CAB	kbdne.kbd	635	WIN95_06.CAB	WIN95_06.CAB
iso.cpi	49,754	WIN95_13.CAB	WIN95_13.CAB	kbdno.kbd	610	WIN95_06.CAB	WIN95_06.CAB
jetadmin.cpl	7,680	WIN95_16.CAB	(Not on diskette)	kbdpl.kbd	774	WIN95_13.CAB	(Not on diskette)
jetadmin.exe	693,760	WIN95_16.CAB	(Not on diskette)	kbdpl1.kbd	528	WIN95_13.CAB	(Not on diskette)
jetadmin.hlp	285,953	WIN95_16.CAB	(Not on diskette)	kbdpo.kbd	593	WIN95_06.CAB	WIN95_06.CAB
joy.cpl	51,200	WIN95_08.CAB	WIN95_08.CAB	kbdru.kbd	473	WIN95_13.CAB	(Not on diskette)
joystick.inf	2,830	PRECOPY2.CAB	PRECOPY2.CAB	kbdru1.kbd	403	WIN95_13.CAB	(Not on diskette)
jp350.drv	73,440	WIN95_10.CAB	WIN95_10.CAB	kbdsf.kbd	615	WIN95_06.CAB	WIN95_06.CAB
jungle~1.wav	336,938	WIN95_14.CAB	(Not on diskette)	kbdsg.kbd	727	WIN95_06.CAB	WIN95_06.CAB
jungle~2.wav	142,888	WIN95_14.CAB	(Not on diskette)	kbdsp.kbd	592	WIN95_06.CAB	WIN95_06.CAB
jungle~3.wav	145,450	WIN95_14.CAB	(Not on diskette)	kbdsv.kbd	781	WIN95_13.CAB	(Not on diskette)
jungle~4.wav	184,872	WIN95_14.CAB	(Not on diskette)	kbdsw.kbd	610	WIN95_06.CAB	WIN95_06.CAB

File	Size	CD Location	Disk Location	File	Size	CD Location	Disk Location
kbduk.kbd	430	WIN95_06.CAB	WIN95_06.CAB	ltimesbd.ttf	177,800	WIN95_13.CAB	(Not on diskette)
kbdus.kbd	398	WIN95_06.CAB	WIN95_06.CAB	ltimesbi.ttf	166,456	WIN95_13.CAB	(Not on diskette)
kbdusx.kbd	794	WIN95_06.CAB	WIN95_06.CAB	ltimesi.ttf	176,736	WIN95_13.CAB	(Not on diskette)
kdcolor1.spd	5,725	WIN95_10.CAB	WIN95_10.CAB	lwnt_470.spd	6,427	WIN95_10.CAB	WIN95_10.CAB
kernel32.dll	411,136	WIN95_11.CAB	WIN95_11.CAB	lwntx470.spd	6,379	WIN95_10.CAB	WIN95_10.CAB
keyb.com	19,927	WIN95_08.CAB	WIN95_09.CAB	lz32.dll	5,632	WIN95_11.CAB	WIN95_11.CAB
KEYBOARD.DRV	7,568	MINI.CAB	MINI.CAB	LZEXPAND.DLL	9,936	MINI.CAB	MINI.CAB
keyboard.drv	12,688	WIN95_06.CAB	WIN95_06.CAB	lzexpand.dll	23,696	PRECOPY1.CAB	PRECOPY1.CAB
keyboard.inf	6,953	PRECOPY2.CAB	PRECOPY2.CAB	machine.inf	30,827	PRECOPY2.CAB	PRECOPY2.CAB
keyboard.sys	34,566	WIN95_09.CAB	WIN95_09.CAB	main.cpl	67,584	WIN95_03.CAB	WIN95_04.CAB
keybrd2.sys	31,942	WIN95_09.CAB	WIN95_09.CAB	maincp16.dll	22,096	WIN95_03.CAB	WIN95_04.CAB
kodakce.icm	24,416	WIN95_06.CAB	WIN95_06.CAB	mantal24.drv	34,160	WIN95_10.CAB	WIN95_10.CAB
kommctrl.dll	154,880	PRECOPY1.CAB	PRECOPY1.CAB	mantal9.drv	22,992	WIN95_10.CAB	WIN95_10.CAB
KRNL386.EXE	75,490	MINI.CAB	MINI.CAB	mapi.dll	441,088	WIN95_06.CAB	WIN95_06.CAB
krnl386.exe	124,416	WIN95_03.CAB	WIN95_04.CAB	mapi32.dll	592,896	WIN95_06.CAB	WIN95_07.CAB
kyocera.drv	30,608	WIN95_10.CAB	WIN95_10.CAB	mapif0.cfg	797	WIN95_06.CAB	WIN95_06.CAB
l100_425.spd	5,825	WIN95_10.CAB	WIN95_10.CAB	mapif0l.ico	766	WIN95_06.CAB	WIN95_07.CAB
l200_471.spd	7,838	WIN95_10.CAB	WIN95_10.CAB	mapif0s.ico	766	WIN95_06.CAB	WIN95_07.CAB
l300_471.spd	7,845	WIN95_10.CAB	WIN95_10.CAB	mapif1.cfg	799	WIN95_06.CAB	WIN95_06.CAB
l500_493.spd	7,843	WIN95_10.CAB	WIN95_10.CAB	mapif1l.ico	766	WIN95_06.CAB	WIN95_07.CAB
label.exe	9,260	WIN95_08.CAB	WIN95_09.CAB	mapif1s.ico	766	WIN95_06.CAB	WIN95_07.CAB
larial.ttf	138,332	WIN95_13.CAB	(Not on diskette)	mapif2.cfg	3,989	WIN95_06.CAB	WIN95_06.CAB
larialbd.ttf	139,284	WIN95_13.CAB	(Not on diskette)	mapif2l.ico	766	WIN95_06.CAB	WIN95_07.CAB
larialbi.ttf	159,720	WIN95_13.CAB	(Not on diskette)	mapif2s.ico	766	WIN95_06.CAB	WIN95_07.CAB
lariali.ttf	139,172	WIN95_13.CAB	(Not on diskette)	mapif3.cfg	795	WIN95_06.CAB	WIN95_06.CAB
layout.inf	51,173	PRECOPY2.CAB	PRECOPY2.CAB	mapif3l.ico	766	WIN95_06.CAB	WIN95_07.CAB
lcour.ttf	168,792	WIN95_13.CAB	(Not on diskette)	mapif3s.ico	766	WIN95_06.CAB	WIN95_07.CAB
lcourbd.ttf	174,376	WIN95_13.CAB	(Not on diskette)	mapif4.cfg	787	WIN95_06.CAB	WIN95_06.CAB
lcourbi.ttf	179,848	WIN95_13.CAB	(Not on diskette)	mapif4l.ico	766	WIN95_06.CAB	WIN95_07.CAB
lcouri.ttf	187,948	WIN95_13.CAB	(Not on diskette)	mapif4s.ico	766	WIN95_06.CAB	WIN95_07.CAB
lh330__1.spd	13,705	WIN95_10.CAB	WIN95_10.CAB	mapif5.cfg	826	WIN95_06.CAB	WIN95_06.CAB
lh530__1.spd	13,953	WIN95_10.CAB	WIN95_10.CAB	mapif5l.ico	766	WIN95_06.CAB	WIN95_07.CAB
lh630__1.spd	12,216	WIN95_10.CAB	WIN95_10.CAB	mapif5s.ico	766	WIN95_06.CAB	WIN95_07.CAB
license.hlp	26,905	WIN95_03.CAB	WIN95_03.CAB	mapirpc.reg	11,971	WIN95_07.CAB	WIN95_07.CAB
license.txt	12,922	PRECOPY2.CAB	PRECOPY2.CAB	mapisp32.exe	7,488	WIN95_07.CAB	WIN95_07.CAB
lights.exe	32,768	WIN95_10.CAB	WIN95_11.CAB	mapisrvr.exe	24,272	WIN95_07.CAB	WIN95_07.CAB
linkinfo.dll	13,824	WIN95_10.CAB	WIN95_11.CAB	mapisvc.inf	4,993	WIN95_07.CAB	WIN95_07.CAB
lmhosts.sam	3,691	WIN95_12.CAB	WIN95_12.CAB	mapiu.dll	5,440	WIN95_06.CAB	WIN95_07.CAB
lmouse.drv	7,984	WIN95_08.CAB	WIN95_09.CAB	mapiu32.dll	4,384	WIN95_06.CAB	WIN95_07.CAB
lmouse.vxd	69,231	WIN95_08.CAB	WIN95_09.CAB	mapiwm.tpl	4,136	WIN95_07.CAB	WIN95_07.CAB
LMOUSE31.DRV	12,928	MINI.CAB	MINI.CAB	mapix.dll	4,448	WIN95_06.CAB	WIN95_07.CAB
lmscript.exe	4,785	WIN95_12.CAB	WIN95_12.CAB	mapix32.dll	6,000	WIN95_06.CAB	WIN95_07.CAB
lmscript.pif	995	WIN95_12.CAB	WIN95_12.CAB	marlett.ttf	17,412	WIN95_05.CAB	WIN95_06.CAB
locale.inf	40,671	PRECOPY2.CAB	PRECOPY2.CAB	mciavi.drv	67,520	WIN95_08.CAB	WIN95_08.CAB
locale.nls	127,912	WIN95_09.CAB	WIN95_09.CAB	mcicda.drv	12,800	WIN95_08.CAB	WIN95_08.CAB
logger.vxd	11,637	WIN95_10.CAB	WIN95_11.CAB	mcimai~1.ht	829	WIN95_02.CAB	(Not on diskette)
login.exe	12,135	WIN95_12.CAB	WIN95_12.CAB	mciole.dll	5,584	WIN95_08.CAB	WIN95_08.CAB
logos.sys	129,078	WIN95_11.CAB	WIN95_11.CAB	mcipionr.drv	13,712	WIN95_13.CAB	(Not on diskette)
logow.sys	129,078	WIN95_11.CAB	WIN95_11.CAB	mciseq.drv	18,672	WIN95_08.CAB	WIN95_08.CAB
lotus.wk4	2,448	WIN95_11.CAB	WIN95_11.CAB	mcivisca.drv	95,776	MINI_13.CAB	(Not on diskette)
lpt.vxd	35,479	WIN95_03.CAB	WIN95_03.CAB	mciwave.drv	22,016	WIN95_08.CAB	WIN95_08.CAB
lptenum.vxd	17,179	WIN95_09.CAB	WIN95_10.CAB	mcm.dll	99,840	WIN95_07.CAB	WIN95_07.CAB
ltimes.ttf	184,328	WIN95_13.CAB	(Not on diskette)	mdgmport.bin	51,350	WIN95_11.CAB	WIN95_12.CAB

File	Size	CD Location	Disk Location	File	Size	CD Location	Disk Location
mdgmport.sys	41,616	WIN95_12.CAB	WIN95_12.CAB	mfcn30.dll	15,872	WIN95_02.CAB	WIN95_02.CAB
mdmati.inf	12,865	WIN95_07.CAB	WIN95_08.CAB	mfco30.dll	133,392	WIN95_02.CAB	WIN95_02.CAB
mdmatt.inf	29,686	WIN95_07.CAB	WIN95_08.CAB	mfcuia32.dll	5,632	WIN95_09.CAB	WIN95_09.CAB
mdmaus.inf	35,436	WIN95_07.CAB	WIN95_08.CAB	mfcuiw32.dll	4,096	WIN95_09.CAB	WIN95_09.CAB
mdmboca.inf	23,455	WIN95_07.CAB	WIN95_08.CAB	mfcuix.hlp	13,101	WIN95_05.CAB	WIN95_06.CAB
mdmcommu.inf	25,304	WIN95_07.CAB	WIN95_08.CAB	mfosi.inf	7,288	PRECOPY2.CAB	PRECOPY2.CAB
mdmcpi.inf	33,941	WIN95_07.CAB	WIN95_08.CAB	mga.drv	110,528	WIN95_04.CAB	WIN95_05.CAB
mdmcpq.inf	40,135	WIN95_07.CAB	WIN95_08.CAB	mga.vxd	9,818	WIN95_04.CAB	WIN95_05.CAB
mdmdsi.inf	37,416	WIN95_07.CAB	WIN95_08.CAB	midi.inf	5,315	PRECOPY2.CAB	PRECOPY2.CAB
mdmexp.inf	37,676	WIN95_07.CAB	WIN95_08.CAB	midimap.cfg	1	WIN95_08.CAB	WIN95_08.CAB
mdmgatew.inf	23,617	WIN95_07.CAB	WIN95_08.CAB	midimap.drv	16,976	WIN95_08.CAB	WIN95_08.CAB
mdmgen.inf	33,192	WIN95_07.CAB	WIN95_08.CAB	MINIKBD.DLL	1,300	MINI.CAB	MINI.CAB
mdmgvc.inf	47,472	WIN95_07.CAB	WIN95_08.CAB	mkcompat.exe	33,792	WIN95_03.CAB	WIN95_04.CAB
mdmhayes.inf	42,229	WIN95_07.CAB	WIN95_08.CAB	mkecr5xx.mpd	53,264	WIN95_05.CAB	WIN95_05.CAB
mdminfot.inf	28,232	WIN95_07.CAB	WIN95_08.CAB	ml3xec16.exe	6,367	WIN95_07.CAB	WIN95_07.CAB
mdmintel.inf	17,067	WIN95_07.CAB	WIN95_08.CAB	mlcfg32.cpl	42,768	WIN95_06.CAB	WIN95_07.CAB
mdmintpc.inf	26,967	WIN95_07.CAB	WIN95_08.CAB	mlset32.exe	24,336	WIN95_07.CAB	WIN95_07.CAB
mdmmcom.inf	23,124	WIN95_07.CAB	WIN95_08.CAB	mlshext.dll	12,048	WIN95_06.CAB	WIN95_07.CAB
mdmmetri.inf	4,576	WIN95_07.CAB	WIN95_08.CAB	mmci.dll	13,536	WIN95_08.CAB	WIN95_08.CAB
mdmmhrtz.inf	30,549	WIN95_07.CAB	WIN95_08.CAB	mmdevldr.vxd	11,844	WIN95_08.CAB	WIN95_09.CAB
mdmmoto.inf	36,008	WIN95_07.CAB	WIN95_08.CAB	mmdrv.hlp	9,584	WIN95_08.CAB	WIN95_09.CAB
mdmmts.inf	22,953	WIN95_07.CAB	WIN95_08.CAB	mmfmig32.dll	268,176	WIN95_06.CAB	WIN95_06.CAB
mdmnokia.inf	2,972	WIN95_07.CAB	WIN95_08.CAB	mmmixer.dll	5,152	WIN95_08.CAB	WIN95_08.CAB
mdmnova.inf	12,342	WIN95_07.CAB	WIN95_08.CAB	mmopt.inf	37,061	PRECOPY2.CAB	(Not on diskette)
mdmosi.inf	9,964	WIN95_07.CAB	WIN95_08.CAB	mmsound.drv	3,104	WIN95_03.CAB	WIN95_03.CAB
mdmpace.inf	26,351	WIN95_07.CAB	WIN95_08.CAB	mmsys.cpl	193,024	WIN95_08.CAB	WIN95_08.CAB
mdmpnb.inf	33,251	WIN95_07.CAB	WIN95_08.CAB	mmsystem.dll	103,248	WIN95_08.CAB	WIN95_08.CAB
mdmpp.inf	25,055	WIN95_07.CAB	WIN95_08.CAB	mmtask.tsk	1,168	WIN95_08.CAB	WIN95_09.CAB
mdmracal.inf	25,804	WIN95_08.CAB	WIN95_08.CAB	mmvdib12.dll	53,248	WIN95_07.CAB	WIN95_07.CAB
mdmrock.inf	62,394	WIN95_08.CAB	WIN95_08.CAB	mnb22g15.icm	59,564	WIN95_06.CAB	WIN95_06.CAB
mdmrock2.inf	50,109	WIN95_08.CAB	WIN95_08.CAB	mnb22g18.icm	59,564	WIN95_06.CAB	WIN95_06.CAB
mdmsier.inf	9,208	WIN95_08.CAB	WIN95_08.CAB	mnb22g21.icm	59,564	WIN95_06.CAB	WIN95_06.CAB
mdmsonix.inf	23,370	WIN95_08.CAB	WIN95_08.CAB	mnebug15.icm	59,964	WIN95_06.CAB	WIN95_06.CAB
mdmspec.inf	11,458	WIN95_08.CAB	WIN95_08.CAB	mnebug18.icm	59,964	WIN95_06.CAB	WIN95_06.CAB
mdmsupra.inf	15,275	WIN95_08.CAB	WIN95_08.CAB	mnebug21.icm	59,964	WIN95_06.CAB	WIN95_06.CAB
mdmtdk.inf	5,864	WIN95_08.CAB	WIN95_08.CAB	mnp22g15.icm	59,980	WIN95_06.CAB	WIN95_06.CAB
mdmtelbt.inf	31,377	WIN95_08.CAB	WIN95_08.CAB	mnp22g18.icm	59,980	WIN95_06.CAB	WIN95_06.CAB
mdmti.inf	5,861	WIN95_08.CAB	WIN95_08.CAB	mnp22g21.icm	59,980	WIN95_06.CAB	WIN95_06.CAB
mdmtosh.inf	45,577	WIN95_08.CAB	WIN95_08.CAB	mode.com	29,191	WIN95_08.CAB	WIN95_09.CAB
mdmusrcr.inf	50,070	WIN95_08.CAB	WIN95_08.CAB	modem.cpl	52,096	WIN95_07.CAB	WIN95_08.CAB
mdmusrsp.inf	44,991	WIN95_08.CAB	WIN95_08.CAB	modems.inf	1,773	PRECOPY2.CAB	PRECOPY2.CAB
mdmusrwp.inf	50,051	WIN95_08.CAB	WIN95_08.CAB	modemui.dll	27,504	WIN95_07.CAB	WIN95_08.CAB
mdmvv.inf	33,304	WIN95_17.CAB	(Not on diskette)	modern.fon	7,968	WIN95_05.CAB	WIN95_06.CAB
mdmzoom.inf	16,156	WIN95_08.CAB	WIN95_08.CAB	monitor.inf	37,649	PRECOPY2.CAB	PRECOPY2.CAB
mdmzyp.inf	23,916	WIN95_08.CAB	WIN95_08.CAB	monitor2.inf	55,766	PRECOPY2.CAB	PRECOPY2.CAB
mdmzyxel.inf	9,166	WIN95_08.CAB	WIN95_08.CAB	monitor3.inf	56,254	PRECOPY2.CAB	PRECOPY2.CAB
mem.exe	32,082	WIN95_08.CAB	WIN95_09.CAB	monitor4.inf	42,030	PRECOPY2.CAB	PRECOPY2.CAB
mesh.bmp	36,182	WIN95_03.CAB	WIN95_03.CAB	more.com	10,471	WIN95_08.CAB	WIN95_09.CAB
mf.inf	7,887	PRECOPY2.CAB	PRECOPY2.CAB	moricons.dll	84,412	WIN95_10.CAB	WIN95_11.CAB
mf3216.dll	30,720	WIN95_03.CAB	WIN95_04.CAB	mos.inf	46,923	PRECOPY2.CAB	PRECOPY2.CAB
mfc30.dll	322,832	WIN95_02.CAB	WIN95_02.CAB	mosabp32.dll	107,520	WIN95_07.CAB	WIN95_07.CAB
mfcans32.dll	133,904	WIN95_03.CAB	WIN95_03.CAB	mosaf.dll	24,576	WIN95_07.CAB	WIN95_07.CAB
mfcd30.dll	55,808	WIN95_02.CAB	WIN95_02.CAB	moscc.dll	47,616	WIN95_07.CAB	WIN95_07.CAB

File	Size	CD Location	Disk Location	File	Size	CD Location	Disk Location
moscfg32.dll	15,360	WIN95_07.CAB	WIN95_07.CAB	mshearts.exe	122,240	WIN95_05.CAB	WIN95_06.CAB
moscl.dll	36,864	WIN95_07.CAB	WIN95_07.CAB	mshearts.hlp	11,661	WIN95_05.CAB	WIN95_06.CAB
moscomp.dll	149,504	WIN95_07.CAB	WIN95_07.CAB	msjstick.drv	7,744	WIN95_08.CAB	WIN95_08.CAB
moscp.exe	69,632	WIN95_07.CAB	WIN95_08.CAB	msmail.inf	36,068	PRECOPY2.CAB	PRECOPY2.CAB
moscudll.dll	21,504	WIN95_07.CAB	WIN95_07.CAB	msmixmgr.dll	1,264	WIN95_08.CAB	WIN95_08.CAB
mosfind.dll	25,600	WIN95_07.CAB	WIN95_07.CAB	MSMOUS31.DRV	10,672	MINI.CAB	MINI.CAB
mosmisc.dll	9,216	WIN95_07.CAB	WIN95_07.CAB	msmouse.inf	13,322	PRECOPY2.CAB	PRECOPY2.CAB
mosmutil.dll	26,624	WIN95_07.CAB	WIN95_07.CAB	msmouse.vxd	15,804	WIN95_08.CAB	WIN95_09.CAB
mosrxp32.dll	56,832	WIN95_07.CAB	WIN95_07.CAB	msmpu401.drv	8,704	WIN95_08.CAB	WIN95_08.CAB
mosshell.dll	182,784	WIN95_07.CAB	WIN95_07.CAB	msmpu401.vxd	12,972	WIN95_08.CAB	WIN95_09.CAB
mosstub.dll	7,680	WIN95_07.CAB	WIN95_08.CAB	msn.cnt	13,392	WIN95_07.CAB	WIN95_07.CAB
mosview.exe	55,296	WIN95_07.CAB	WIN95_08.CAB	msn.hlp	17,780	WIN95_07.CAB	WIN95_08.CAB
motown.inf	47,846	PRECOPY2.CAB	PRECOPY2.CAB	msn.txt	4,111	WIN95_03.CAB	WIN95_03.CAB
mouse.cnt	509	WIN95_05.CAB	WIN95_06.CAB	msnbbs.hlp	52,454	WIN95_07.CAB	WIN95_08.CAB
mouse.drv	7,712	WIN95_08.CAB	WIN95_09.CAB	msnchat.hlp	28,695	WIN95_07.CAB	WIN95_08.CAB
mouse.hlp	16,577	WIN95_05.CAB	WIN95_06.CAB	msndui.dll	25,600	WIN95_07.CAB	WIN95_08.CAB
mouse.txt	5,532	WIN95_03.CAB	WIN95_03.CAB	msnet.drv	7,072	WIN95_12.CAB	WIN95_12.CAB
move.exe	27,235	WIN95_09.CAB	WIN95_09.CAB	msnet32.dll	60,416	WIN95_11.CAB	WIN95_12.CAB
move_1.cur	766	WIN95_13.CAB	(Not on diskette)	msnexch.exe	17,408	WIN95_07.CAB	WIN95_08.CAB
move_1.cur	766	WIN95_13.CAB	(Not on diskette)	msnfind.exe	52,224	WIN95_07.CAB	WIN95_08.CAB
move_m.cur	766	WIN95_13.CAB	(Not on diskette)	msnfull.hlp	107,361	WIN95_06.CAB	WIN95_06.CAB
movewin.avi	754,922	WIN95_16.CAB	(Not on diskette)	msnint.hlp	32,773	WIN95_06.CAB	WIN95_06.CAB
mozart~2.rmi	18,130	WIN95_14.CAB	(Not on diskette)	msnmail.hlp	48,932	WIN95_07.CAB	WIN95_08.CAB
mpccl.dll	87,040	WIN95_07.CAB	WIN95_08.CAB	msnp32.dll	67,584	WIN95_11.CAB	WIN95_12.CAB
mplayer.cnt	1,042	WIN95_08.CAB	WIN95_08.CAB	msnpss.cnt	246	WIN95_07.CAB	WIN95_07.CAB
mplayer.exe	147,968	WIN95_08.CAB	WIN95_09.CAB	msnpss.hlp	34,974	WIN95_07.CAB	WIN95_08.CAB
mplayer.hlp	26,940	WIN95_08.CAB	WIN95_09.CAB	msnver.txt	4	WIN95_07.CAB	WIN95_08.CAB
mpr.dll	40,448	WIN95_11.CAB	WIN95_12.CAB	msodisup.vxd	23,897	WIN95_12.CAB	WIN95_12.CAB
mprexe.exe	12,800	WIN95_12.CAB	WIN95_12.CAB	msopl.drv	17,952	WIN95_08.CAB	WIN95_08.CAB
mprserv.dll	119,296	WIN95_11.CAB	WIN95_12.CAB	msopl.vxd	13,462	WIN95_08.CAB	WIN95_09.CAB
mrci2.vxd	46,746	WIN95_09.CAB	WIN95_09.CAB	mspaint.cnt	1,978	WIN95_02.CAB	WIN95_02.CAB
msab32.dll	61,952	WIN95_11.CAB	WIN95_12.CAB	mspaint.exe	311,808	WIN95_02.CAB	WIN95_03.CAB
msacm.dll	53,552	WIN95_08.CAB	WIN95_08.CAB	mspaint.hlp	43,620	WIN95_02.CAB	WIN95_03.CAB
msacm.drv	21,872	WIN95_08.CAB	WIN95_08.CAB	mspcic.dll	36,400	WIN95_09.CAB	WIN95_10.CAB
msacm32.dll	91,648	WIN95_08.CAB	WIN95_08.CAB	mspcx32.dll	32,256	WIN95_02.CAB	WIN95_02.CAB
msadp32.acm	17,920	WIN95_08.CAB	WIN95_08.CAB	msports.inf	9,510	PRECOPY2.CAB	PRECOPY2.CAB
msbase.inf	58,621	PRECOPY2.CAB	PRECOPY2.CAB	mspp32.dll	17,920	WIN95_11.CAB	WIN95_12.CAB
mscdex.exe	25,473	WIN95_04.CAB	WIN95_05.CAB	msprint.dll	55,872	PRECOPY1.CAB	PRECOPY1.CAB
mscdrom.inf	951	PRECOPY2.CAB	PRECOPY2.CAB	msprint.inf	46,309	PRECOPY2.CAB	PRECOPY2.CAB
msdet.inf	21,472	PRECOPY2.CAB	PRECOPY2.CAB	msprint2.dll	48,128	PRECOPY1.CAB	PRECOPY1.CAB
msdisp.inf	40,877	PRECOPY2.CAB	PRECOPY2.CAB	msprint2.inf	37,350	PRECOPY2.CAB	PRECOPY2.CAB
msdlc.exe	31,284	WIN95_12.CAB	WIN95_12.CAB	mspst32.dll	386,560	WIN95_06.CAB	WIN95_06.CAB
msdos.inf	10,998	PRECOPY2.CAB	PRECOPY2.CAB	mspwl32.dll	15,360	WIN95_11.CAB	WIN95_12.CAB
msdosdrv.txt	42,205	WIN95_03.CAB	WIN95_03.CAB	msrle32.dll	11,264	WIN95_08.CAB	WIN95_08.CAB
msfdc.inf	3,657	PRECOPY2.CAB	PRECOPY2.CAB	mssblst.drv	40,848	WIN95_08.CAB	WIN95_08.CAB
msfs.cnt	1,221	WIN95_06.CAB	WIN95_06.CAB	mssblst.vxd	17,562	WIN95_08.CAB	WIN95_09.CAB
msfs.hlp	34,832	WIN95_06.CAB	WIN95_07.CAB	msshrui.dll	74,752	WIN95_11.CAB	WIN95_12.CAB
msfs32.dll	402,944	WIN95_06.CAB	WIN95_07.CAB	mssndsys.drv	39,728	WIN95_08.CAB	WIN95_08.CAB
msg711.acm	10,240	WIN95_08.CAB	WIN95_08.CAB	mssndsys.vxd	28,400	WIN95_08.CAB	WIN95_09.CAB
msgsm32.acm	25,088	WIN95_08.CAB	WIN95_08.CAB	mssound.wav	135,876	WIN95_08.CAB	WIN95_09.CAB
msgsrv32.exe	10,192	WIN95_09.CAB	WIN95_10.CAB	mssp.vxd	21,657	WIN95_12.CAB	WIN95_13.CAB
mshdc.inf	12,267	PRECOPY2.CAB	PRECOPY2.CAB	mstcp.dll	26,832	PRECOPY1.CAB	PRECOPY1.CAB
mshearts.cnt	206	WIN95_05.CAB	WIN95_06.CAB	msvcrt20.dll	253,952	WIN95_02.CAB	WIN95_02.CAB

File	Size	CD Location	Disk Location	File	Size	CD Location	Disk Location
msvfw32.dll	129,536	WIN95_08.CAB	WIN95_08.CAB	ncrsdms.mpd	25,056	WIN95_05.CAB	WIN95_05.CAB
msvidc32.dll	30,208	WIN95_08.CAB	WIN95_08.CAB	ncs29901.spd	6,713	WIN95_10.CAB	WIN95_10.CAB
msvideo.dll	113,664	WIN95_08.CAB	WIN95_08.CAB	ncsw_951.spd	8,307	WIN95_10.CAB	WIN95_10.CAB
msviewut.dll	147,968	WIN95_13.CAB	(Not on diskette)	nddeapi.dll	14,032	WIN95_11.CAB	WIN95_12.CAB
mswd6_32.wpc	164,352	WIN95_03.CAB	WIN95_03.CAB	nddenb.dll	10,768	WIN95_11.CAB	WIN95_12.CAB
mt_ti101.spd	3,853	WIN95_10.CAB	WIN95_10.CAB	ndis.vxd	99,084	WIN95_12.CAB	WIN95_13.CAB
mtd.inf	1,891	PRECOPY2.CAB	PRECOPY2.CAB	ndis2sup.vxd	23,744	WIN95_12.CAB	WIN95_13.CAB
mtlite.drv	8,304	WIN95_10.CAB	WIN95_10.CAB	ndis39xr.dos	34,880	WIN95_11.CAB	WIN95_12.CAB
mtmminip.mpd	21,968	WIN95_05.CAB	WIN95_05.CAB	ndis89xr.dos	35,160	WIN95_11.CAB	WIN95_12.CAB
mullang.inf	11,024	WIN95_13.CAB	(Not on diskette)	ndis99xr.dos	38,251	WIN95_11.CAB	WIN95_12.CAB
multilng.inf	25,665	PRECOPY2.CAB	PRECOPY2.CAB	ndishlp.sys	6,140	WIN95_13.CAB	WIN95_13.CAB
musica~1.wav	21,816	WIN95_15.CAB	(Not on diskette)	ne1000.dos	14,020	WIN95_11.CAB	WIN95_12.CAB
musica~2.wav	8,288	WIN95_15.CAB	(Not on diskette)	ne1000.sys	18,432	WIN95_12.CAB	WIN95_12.CAB
musica~3.wav	12,490	WIN95_15.CAB	(Not on diskette)	ne2000.dos	13,964	WIN95_11.CAB	WIN95_12.CAB
musica~4.wav	12,054	WIN95_15.CAB	(Not on diskette)	ne2000.sys	18,256	WIN95_12.CAB	WIN95_12.CAB
musicaas.wav	28,338	WIN95_15.CAB	(Not on diskette)	ne3200.bin	4,096	WIN95_11.CAB	WIN95_12.CAB
musicacl.wav	45,816	WIN95_15.CAB	(Not on diskette)	ne3200.dos	33,582	WIN95_11.CAB	WIN95_12.CAB
musicacr.wav	10,272	WIN95_15.CAB	(Not on diskette)	ne3200.sys	19,152	WIN95_12.CAB	WIN95_12.CAB
musicade.wav	6,262	WIN95_15.CAB	(Not on diskette)	nec24pin.drv	23,424	WIN95_10.CAB	WIN95_10.CAB
musicaer.wav	20,344	WIN95_15.CAB	(Not on diskette)	necatapi.vxd	9,929	WIN95_03.CAB	WIN95_03.CAB
musicaex.wav	9,584	WIN95_15.CAB	(Not on diskette)	net.exe	375,962	WIN95_12.CAB	WIN95_13.CAB
musicama.wav	8,608	WIN95_15.CAB	(Not on diskette)	net.inf	21,393	PRECOPY2.CAB	PRECOPY2.CAB
musicame.wav	8,186	WIN95_15.CAB	(Not on diskette)	net.msg	109,229	WIN95_12.CAB	WIN95_13.CAB
musicami.wav	7,800	WIN95_15.CAB	(Not on diskette)	net3com.inf	31,895	PRECOPY2.CAB	PRECOPY2.CAB
musicaop.wav	43,096	WIN95_15.CAB	(Not on diskette)	netamd.inf	19,762	PRECOPY2.CAB	PRECOPY2.CAB
musicaqu.wav	11,932	WIN95_15.CAB	(Not on diskette)	netapi.dll	106,960	PRECOPY1.CAB	PRECOPY1.CAB
musicare.wav	20,596	WIN95_15.CAB	(Not on diskette)	netapi32.dll	4,096	WIN95_11.CAB	WIN95_12.CAB
musicawi.wav	49,026	WIN95_15.CAB	(Not on diskette)	netauxt.inf	153	PRECOPY2.CAB	PRECOPY2.CAB
mvcl14n.dll	112,128	WIN95_07.CAB	WIN95_08.CAB	netbeui.vxd	45,756	WIN95_12.CAB	WIN95_13.CAB
mvi401.drv	12,640	WIN95_08.CAB	WIN95_08.CAB	netbios.dll	6,656	WIN95_11.CAB	WIN95_12.CAB
mvi514mx.drv	38,432	WIN95_08.CAB	WIN95_08.CAB	netbw.inf	4,152	PRECOPY2.CAB	PRECOPY2.CAB
mvifm.drv	41,232	WIN95_08.CAB	WIN95_08.CAB	netcable.inf	25,234	PRECOPY2.CAB	PRECOPY2.CAB
mvifm.pat	7,188	WIN95_08.CAB	WIN95_09.CAB	netcd.inf	30,838	PRECOPY2.CAB	(Not on diskette)
mviwave.drv	19,760	WIN95_08.CAB	WIN95_09.CAB	netcem.inf	2,810	PRECOPY2.CAB	PRECOPY2.CAB
mvmixer.drv	59,568	WIN95_08.CAB	WIN95_09.CAB	netcli.inf	16,390	PRECOPY2.CAB	PRECOPY2.CAB
mvpas.vxd	8,898	WIN95_08.CAB	WIN95_09.CAB	netcli3.inf	28,011	PRECOPY2.CAB	PRECOPY2.CAB
mvpr14n.dll	51,712	WIN95_07.CAB	WIN95_08.CAB	netcpl.cpl	5,312	WIN95_11.CAB	WIN95_12.CAB
mvproaud.drv	26,128	WIN95_08.CAB	WIN95_09.CAB	netcpq.inf	6,816	PRECOPY2.CAB	PRECOPY2.CAB
mvttl14c.dll	77,312	WIN95_07.CAB	WIN95_08.CAB	netdca.inf	16,782	PRECOPY2.CAB	(Not on diskette)
mvut14n.dll	10,240	WIN95_07.CAB	WIN95_08.CAB	netdde.exe	54,992	WIN95_12.CAB	WIN95_12.CAB
n2090522.spd	5,925	WIN95_10.CAB	WIN95_10.CAB	netdec.inf	20,208	PRECOPY2.CAB	PRECOPY2.CAB
n2290520.spd	5,227	WIN95_10.CAB	WIN95_10.CAB	netdef.inf	10,275	PRECOPY2.CAB	PRECOPY2.CAB
n890_470.spd	5,472	WIN95_10.CAB	WIN95_10.CAB	netdet.ini	7,885	PRECOPY1.CAB	PRECOPY2.CAB
n890x505.spd	5,483	WIN95_10.CAB	WIN95_10.CAB	netdi.dll	282,832	PRECOPY1.CAB	PRECOPY2.CAB
nbtstat.exe	33,371	WIN95_12.CAB	WIN95_12.CAB	netdlc.inf	12,788	PRECOPY2.CAB	PRECOPY2.CAB
ncc16.dos	42,802	WIN95_11.CAB	WIN95_12.CAB	netee16.inf	22,103	PRECOPY2.CAB	PRECOPY2.CAB
nccps401.spd	3,403	WIN95_10.CAB	WIN95_10.CAB	netevx.inf	2,634	PRECOPY2.CAB	(Not on diskette)
nccps801.spd	4,658	WIN95_10.CAB	WIN95_10.CAB	netflex.inf	7,168	PRECOPY2.CAB	PRECOPY2.CAB
ncol_519.spd	4,563	WIN95_10.CAB	WIN95_10.CAB	netflx.bin	110,720	WIN95_11.CAB	WIN95_12.CAB
ncr53c9x.mpd	11,120	WIN95_05.CAB	WIN95_05.CAB	netflx.dos	78,996	WIN95_11.CAB	WIN95_12.CAB
ncrc700.mpd	9,920	WIN95_05.CAB	WIN95_05.CAB	netflx.sys	30,992	WIN95_12.CAB	WIN95_12.CAB
ncrc710.mpd	10,352	WIN95_05.CAB	WIN95_05.CAB	netftp.inf	4,125	PRECOPY2.CAB	(Not on diskette)
ncrc810.mpd	10,848	WIN95_05.CAB	WIN95_05.CAB	netgen.inf	4,039	PRECOPY2.CAB	PRECOPY2.CAB

File	Size	CD Location	Disk Location	File	Size	CD Location	Disk Location
neth.msg	73,275	WIN95_12.CAB	WIN95_13.CAB	nwlscon.exe	13,824	WIN95_12.CAB	WIN95_12.CAB
nethp.inf	10,111	PRECOPY2.CAB	PRECOPY2.CAB	nwlsproc.exe	71,680	WIN95_12.CAB	WIN95_12.CAB
netibm.inf	17,817	PRECOPY2.CAB	PRECOPY2.CAB	nwnblink.vxd	46,653	WIN95_11.CAB	WIN95_13.CAB
netibmcc.inf	19,419	PRECOPY2.CAB	PRECOPY2.CAB	nwnet32.dll	21,504	WIN95_11.CAB	WIN95_12.CAB
netmadge.inf	25,842	PRECOPY2.CAB	PRECOPY2.CAB	nwnp32.dll	77,312	WIN95_11.CAB	WIN95_12.CAB
netncr.inf	16,525	PRECOPY2.CAB	(Not on diskette)	nwpp32.dll	43,008	WIN95_11.CAB	WIN95_12.CAB
netnice.inf	3,808	PRECOPY2.CAB	PRECOPY2.CAB	nwredir.vxd	123,963	WIN95_12.CAB	WIN95_13.CAB
netnovel.inf	22,774	PRECOPY2.CAB	PRECOPY2.CAB	nwrpltrm.com	28	WIN95_17.CAB	(Not on diskette)
netoli.inf	21,733	PRECOPY2.CAB	PRECOPY2.CAB	nwserver.vxd	130,636	WIN95_12.CAB	WIN95_13.CAB
netos.dll	24,400	PRECOPY1.CAB	PRECOPY2.CAB	nwsp.vxd	14,438	WIN95_12.CAB	WIN95_13.CAB
netosi.inf	3,811	PRECOPY2.CAB	PRECOPY2.CAB	o5241503.spd	4,264	WIN95_10.CAB	WIN95_10.CAB
netpci.inf	11,080	PRECOPY2.CAB	PRECOPY2.CAB	o5242503.spd	5,136	WIN95_10.CAB	WIN95_10.CAB
netppp.inf	2,883	PRECOPY2.CAB	PRECOPY2.CAB	oak.vxd	14,476	WIN95_04.CAB	WIN95_05.CAB
netprot.inf	12,890	PRECOPY2.CAB	PRECOPY2.CAB	octk16.sys	85,504	WIN95_12.CAB	WIN95_12.CAB
netracal.inf	8,055	PRECOPY2.CAB	(Not on diskette)	octk32.vxd	72,655	WIN95_12.CAB	WIN95_13.CAB
netservr.inf	12,223	PRECOPY2.CAB	PRECOPY2.CAB	odihlp.exe	4,197	WIN95_12.CAB	WIN95_12.CAB
netsilc.inf	7,524	PRECOPY2.CAB	PRECOPY2.CAB	oki24.drv	40,848	WIN95_10.CAB	WIN95_10.CAB
netsmc.inf	36,024	PRECOPY2.CAB	PRECOPY2.CAB	oki830us.spd	5,830	WIN95_10.CAB	WIN95_10.CAB
netsmc32.inf	2,593	PRECOPY2.CAB	(Not on diskette)	oki840us.spd	6,899	WIN95_10.CAB	WIN95_10.CAB
netsmctr.inf	4,543	PRECOPY2.CAB	PRECOPY2.CAB	oki850us.spd	7,028	WIN95_10.CAB	WIN95_10.CAB
netsnip.inf	8,345	PRECOPY2.CAB	PRECOPY2.CAB	oki9.drv	18,336	WIN95_10.CAB	WIN95_10.CAB
netsock.inf	3,155	PRECOPY2.CAB	PRECOPY2.CAB	oki9ibm.drv	48,720	WIN95_10.CAB	WIN95_10.CAB
netstat.exe	23,776	WIN95_12.CAB	WIN95_12.CAB	okol8701.spd	10,570	WIN95_10.CAB	WIN95_10.CAB
nettcc.inf	16,149	PRECOPY2.CAB	PRECOPY2.CAB	ol830525.spd	5,551	WIN95_10.CAB	WIN95_10.CAB
nettdkp.inf	4,828	PRECOPY2.CAB	PRECOPY2.CAB	ol840518.spd	6,641	WIN95_10.CAB	WIN95_10.CAB
nettrans.inf	37,248	PRECOPY2.CAB	PRECOPY2.CAB	ol850525.spd	6,651	WIN95_10.CAB	WIN95_10.CAB
nettulip.inf	1,980	PRECOPY2.CAB	(Not on diskette)	ole2.dll	39,744	WIN95_09.CAB	WIN95_09.CAB
netub.inf	13,101	PRECOPY2.CAB	(Not on diskette)	ole2.inf	25,550	PRECOPY2.CAB	PRECOPY2.CAB
netware.ms	1,632	WIN95_12.CAB	WIN95_12.CAB	ole2conv.dll	57,328	WIN95_09.CAB	WIN95_09.CAB
netwatch.cnt	391	WIN95_13.CAB	(Not on diskette)	ole2disp.dll	169,440	WIN95_09.CAB	WIN95_09.CAB
netwatch.exe	63,488	WIN95_17.CAB	(Not on diskette)	ole2nls.dll	153,040	WIN95_09.CAB	WIN95_09.CAB
netwatch.hlp	12,339	WIN95_13.CAB	(Not on diskette)	ole32.dll	557,664	WIN95_09.CAB	WIN95_09.CAB
network.hlp	88,385	WIN95_05.CAB	WIN95_06.CAB	oleaut32.dll	232,720	WIN95_09.CAB	WIN95_09.CAB
network.txt	18,538	WIN95_03.CAB	WIN95_03.CAB	olecli.dll	82,944	WIN95_09.CAB	WIN95_09.CAB
netxir.inf	24,805	PRECOPY2.CAB	PRECOPY2.CAB	olecli32.dll	12,288	WIN95_09.CAB	WIN95_09.CAB
netznote.inf	3,831	PRECOPY2.CAB	(Not on diskette)	olecnv32.dll	40,576	WIN95_09.CAB	WIN95_09.CAB
ni5210.dos	10,472	WIN95_11.CAB	WIN95_12.CAB	oledlg.dll	112,640	WIN95_09.CAB	WIN95_09.CAB
ni6510.dos	11,070	WIN95_11.CAB	WIN95_12.CAB	olesvr.dll	24,064	WIN95_09.CAB	WIN95_09.CAB
nice.vxd	22,609	WIN95_12.CAB	WIN95_13.CAB	olesvr32.dll	6,144	WIN95_09.CAB	WIN95_09.CAB
nlsfunc.exe	6,940	WIN95_09.CAB	WIN95_09.CAB	olethk32.dll	79,424	WIN95_09.CAB	WIN95_10.CAB
no_1.cur	766	WIN95_13.CAB	(Not on diskette)	olidm24.drv	24,176	WIN95_10.CAB	WIN95_10.CAB
no_l.cur	766	WIN95_13.CAB	(Not on diskette)	olidm9.drv	33,232	WIN95_10.CAB	WIN95_10.CAB
no_m.cur	766	WIN95_13.CAB	(Not on diskette)	olitok16.dos	55,710	WIN95_11.CAB	WIN95_12.CAB
nodriver.inf	2,572	PRECOPY2.CAB	PRECOPY2.CAB	onlstmt.exe	74,240	WIN95_07.CAB	WIN95_08.CAB
NOMOUSE.DRV	416	MINI.CAB	MINI.CAB	otceth.vxd	39,827	WIN95_12.CAB	WIN95_13.CAB
notepad.cnt	571	WIN95_05.CAB	WIN95_06.CAB	overview.hlp	255,760	WIN95_16.CAB	(Not on diskette)
notepad.exe	34,304	WIN95_02.CAB	WIN95_03.CAB	p351sx2.drv	19,040	WIN95_10.CAB	WIN95_10.CAB
notepad.hlp	11,708	WIN95_05.CAB	WIN95_06.CAB	p4455514.spd	6,481	WIN95_10.CAB	WIN95_10.CAB
nscl.vxd	23,606	WIN95_12.CAB	WIN95_13.CAB	pa3dmxd.drv	53,200	WIN95_08.CAB	WIN95_09.CAB
ntdll.dll	5,632	WIN95_03.CAB	WIN95_03.CAB	packager.cnt	940	WIN95_02.CAB	WIN95_02.CAB
nw16.dll	6,528	WIN95_11.CAB	WIN95_12.CAB	packager.exe	65,024	WIN95_02.CAB	WIN95_03.CAB
nwab32.dll	25,600	WIN95_11.CAB	WIN95_12.CAB	packager.hlp	23,529	WIN95_02.CAB	WIN95_03.CAB
nwlink.vxd	51,001	WIN95_12.CAB	WIN95_13.CAB	pageswap.vxd	13,905	WIN95_03.CAB	WIN95_03.CAB

File	Size	CD Location	Disk Location	File	Size	CD Location	Disk Location
paintjet.drv	7,664	WIN95_10.CAB	WIN95_10.CAB	proprint.drv	12,192	WIN95_10.CAB	WIN95_10.CAB
panmap.dll	20,480	WIN95_10.CAB	WIN95_11.CAB	proprn24.drv	11,120	WIN95_10.CAB	WIN95_10.CAB
panson24.drv	31,312	WIN95_10.CAB	WIN95_10.CAB	prorapm.dwn	24,734	WIN95_12.CAB	WIN95_12.CAB
panson9.drv	28,000	WIN95_10.CAB	WIN95_10.CAB	proteon.vxd	38,995	WIN95_12.CAB	WIN95_13.CAB
pap54001.spd	4,128	WIN95_10.CAB	WIN95_10.CAB	protman.dos	22,810	WIN95_12.CAB	WIN95_13.CAB
pap54101.spd	7,607	WIN95_10.CAB	WIN95_10.CAB	protman.exe	14,952	WIN95_12.CAB	WIN95_13.CAB
paralink.vxd	23,105	WIN95_10.CAB	WIN95_11.CAB	prtupd.inf	20,851	PRECOPY2.CAB	PRECOPY2.CAB
parity.vxd	9,801	WIN95_03.CAB	WIN95_03.CAB	ps1.drv	13,856	WIN95_10.CAB	WIN95_10.CAB
passport.mid	23,165	WIN95_13.CAB	(Not on diskette)	ps4079.icm	24,348	WIN95_06.CAB	WIN95_06.CAB
password.cpl	37,376	WIN95_11.CAB	WIN95_12.CAB	pscript.drv	393,200	WIN95_09.CAB	WIN95_10.CAB
paste.avi	1,011,692	WIN95_16.CAB	(Not on diskette)	pscript.hlp	20,439	WIN95_09.CAB	WIN95_10.CAB
pbrush.exe	4,608	WIN95_02.CAB	WIN95_03.CAB	pscript.ini	328	WIN95_09.CAB	WIN95_10.CAB
pc2x.mpd	4,304	WIN95_05.CAB	WIN95_05.CAB	psmon.dll	28,672	WIN95_09.CAB	WIN95_10.CAB
pccard.vxd	77,661	WIN95_09.CAB	WIN95_10.CAB	pstripe.bmp	578	WIN95_03.CAB	WIN95_03.CAB
pci.vxd	24,535	WIN95_09.CAB	WIN95_10.CAB	pyramid2.bmp	198	WIN95_03.CAB	WIN95_03.CAB
pcmcia.inf	10,079	PRECOPY2.CAB	PRECOPY2.CAB	q2200_ms.spd	79	WIN95_10.CAB	WIN95_10.CAB
pcntn3.vxd	35,461	WIN95_12.CAB	WIN95_13.CAB	q2210_ms.spd	79	WIN95_10.CAB	WIN95_10.CAB
pcntnd.dos	50,400	WIN95_11.CAB	WIN95_12.CAB	q2220523.spd	7,328	WIN95_10.CAB	WIN95_10.CAB
pcsa.exe	23,299	WIN95_17.CAB	(Not on diskette)	q800_ms.spd	78	WIN95_10.CAB	WIN95_10.CAB
pcximp32.flt	26,624	WIN95_02.CAB	WIN95_03.CAB	q810_ms.spd	78	WIN95_10.CAB	WIN95_10.CAB
pe2ndis.dos	30,721	WIN95_11.CAB	WIN95_12.CAB	q810t_ms.spd	84	WIN95_10.CAB	WIN95_10.CAB
pe3ndis.exe	23,506	WIN95_12.CAB	WIN95_12.CAB	q820_ms.spd	78	WIN95_10.CAB	WIN95_10.CAB
pe3ndis.vxd	30,811	WIN95_12.CAB	WIN95_13.CAB	q820t517.spd	5,699	WIN95_10.CAB	WIN95_10.CAB
pen_1.cur	766	WIN95_13.CAB	(Not on diskette)	q860pls2.spd	11,333	WIN95_10.CAB	WIN95_10.CAB
pen_l.cur	766	WIN95_13.CAB	(Not on diskette)	qcs1000.spd	10,440	WIN95_10.CAB	WIN95_10.CAB
pen_m.cur	766	WIN95_13.CAB	(Not on diskette)	qcs10503.spd	4,763	WIN95_10.CAB	WIN95_10.CAB
pendis.dos	22,266	WIN95_11.CAB	WIN95_12.CAB	qcs30503.spd	4,786	WIN95_10.CAB	WIN95_10.CAB
perf.vxd	22,583	WIN95_12.CAB	WIN95_13.CAB	qemmfix.vxd	9,787	WIN95_03.CAB	WIN95_03.CAB
phiipx.spd	3,458	WIN95_10.CAB	WIN95_10.CAB	qic117.vxd	57,437	WIN95_04.CAB	WIN95_05.CAB
phone.pbk	41,369	WIN95_07.CAB	WIN95_08.CAB	qm1700_1.spd	8,236	WIN95_10.CAB	WIN95_10.CAB
pifmgr.dll	82,816	WIN95_03.CAB	WIN95_03.CAB	qm2000_1.spd	8,620	WIN95_10.CAB	WIN95_10.CAB
ping.exe	12,128	WIN95_12.CAB	WIN95_12.CAB	qm825mr1.spd	8,006	WIN95_10.CAB	WIN95_10.CAB
pjlmon.dll	12,288	WIN95_09.CAB	WIN95_10.CAB	qmps4101.spd	7,238	WIN95_10.CAB	WIN95_10.CAB
pkpd.dll	48,880	WIN95_03.CAB	WIN95_03.CAB	qms10030.icm	24,716	WIN95_10.CAB	WIN95_10.CAB
pkpd32.dll	11,776	WIN95_03.CAB	WIN95_03.CAB	qms1725.spd	9,083	WIN95_10.CAB	WIN95_10.CAB
pmspl.dll	26,608	WIN95_11.CAB	WIN95_12.CAB	qms3225.spd	9,873	WIN95_10.CAB	WIN95_10.CAB
pointer.dll	55,152	WIN95_08.CAB	WIN95_09.CAB	qms420.spd	8,507	WIN95_10.CAB	WIN95_10.CAB
pointer.exe	37,344	WIN95_08.CAB	WIN95_09.CAB	qms45252.spd	10,650	WIN95_10.CAB	WIN95_10.CAB
power.drv	1,920	WIN95_07.CAB	WIN95_08.CAB	qms860.spd	7,717	WIN95_10.CAB	WIN95_10.CAB
powercfg.dll	12,800	WIN95_03.CAB	WIN95_04.CAB	qms8p461.spd	5,395	WIN95_10.CAB	WIN95_10.CAB
powerpnt.ppt	12,288	WIN95_11.CAB	WIN95_11.CAB	qmscs210.spd	7,933	WIN95_10.CAB	WIN95_10.CAB
ppm.vxd	18,458	WIN95_08.CAB	WIN95_08.CAB	qmscs230.spd	8,673	WIN95_10.CAB	WIN95_10.CAB
pppmac.vxd	135,264	WIN95_10.CAB	WIN95_11.CAB	quattro.wb2	4,017	WIN95_11.CAB	WIN95_11.CAB
precopy.inf	2,538	PRECOPY2.CAB	PRECOPY2.CAB	quietjet.drv	5,776	WIN95_10.CAB	WIN95_10.CAB
presenta.shw	461	WIN95_11.CAB	WIN95_11.CAB	quikview.exe	20,992	WIN95_13.CAB	(Not on diskette)
printers.txt	16,199	WIN95_03.CAB	WIN95_03.CAB	qwiii.drv	17,648	WIN95_10.CAB	WIN95_10.CAB
pro4.dos	29,090	WIN95_11.CAB	WIN95_12.CAB	ramdrive.sys	12,663	WIN95_09.CAB	WIN95_09.CAB
pro4at.dos	33,770	WIN95_11.CAB	WIN95_12.CAB	rasapi16.dll	1,632	WIN95_10.CAB	WIN95_10.CAB
prodinv.dll	72,192	WIN95_07.CAB	WIN95_08.CAB	rasapi32.dll	147,456	WIN95_10.CAB	WIN95_10.CAB
progman.cnt	919	WIN95_10.CAB	WIN95_11.CAB	rcv0000.efx	5,378	WIN95_05.CAB	WIN95_05.CAB
progman.exe	113,456	WIN95_11.CAB	WIN95_11.CAB	README.TXT	7,302	\WIN95 folder	Diskette 1 Root
progman.hlp	24,466	WIN95_11.CAB	WIN95_11.CAB	reboot.vxd	22,127	WIN95_03.CAB	WIN95_03.CAB
programs.txt	35,070	WIN95_03.CAB	WIN95_03.CAB	redir32.exe	13,312	WIN95_03.CAB	WIN95_04.CAB

File	Size	CD Location	Disk Location	File	Size	CD Location	Disk Location
redirect.mod	4,313	WIN95_04.CAB	WIN95_04.CAB	runonce.exe	11,264	WIN95_10.CAB	WIN95_11.CAB
redtile.bmp	578	WIN95_03.CAB	WIN95_03.CAB	s3.drv	57,632	WIN95_04.CAB	WIN95_05.CAB
regedit.cnt	544	WIN95_06.CAB	WIN95_06.CAB	s3.vxd	17,087	WIN95_04.CAB	WIN95_05.CAB
regedit.exe	120,320	WIN95_02.CAB	WIN95_02.CAB	saclient.dll	29,184	WIN95_07.CAB	WIN95_08.CAB
regedit.hlp	18,338	WIN95_06.CAB	WIN95_06.CAB	sand.bmp	32,854	WIN95_11.CAB	WIN95_12.CAB
regwiz.exe	176,640	WIN95_07.CAB	WIN95_08.CAB	sapnsp.dll	9,216	WIN95_11.CAB	WIN95_12.CAB
ren.inf	7,703	PRECOPY2.CAB	PRECOPY2.CAB	SAVE32.COM	920	\WIN95 folder	Diskette 1 Root
riched32.dll	178,176	WIN95_04.CAB	WIN95_04.CAB	sb16.vxd	54,363	WIN95_08.CAB	WIN95_09.CAB
rivets2.bmp	194	WIN95_03.CAB	WIN95_03.CAB	sb16snd.drv	46,000	WIN95_08.CAB	WIN95_09.CAB
rmm.pdr	13,229	WIN95_05.CAB	WIN95_05.CAB	sbawe.vxd	40,014	WIN95_08.CAB	WIN95_09.CAB
rna.inf	10,611	PRECOPY2.CAB	PRECOPY2.CAB	sbawe32.drv	23,216	WIN95_08.CAB	WIN95_09.CAB
rnaapp.exe	25,600	WIN95_10.CAB	WIN95_11.CAB	sbfm.drv	4,128	WIN95_08.CAB	WIN95_09.CAB
rnanp.dll	11,776	WIN95_10.CAB	WIN95_11.CAB	scandisk.bat	152	PRECOPY2.CAB	PRECOPY2.CAB
rnasetup.dll	5,408	PRECOPY1.CAB	PRECOPY2.CAB	SCANDISK.EXE	134,738	\WIN95 folder	Diskette 1 Root
rnathunk.dll	5,120	WIN95_10.CAB	WIN95_11.CAB	scandisk.ini	7,270	WIN95_02.CAB	WIN95_02.CAB
rnaui.dll	54,272	WIN95_10.CAB	WIN95_11.CAB	SCANDISK.PIF	995	\WIN95 folder	Diskette 1 Root
rndsrv32.dll	31,232	WIN95_05.CAB	WIN95_05.CAB	scandskw.exe	4,608	WIN95_09.CAB	WIN95_09.CAB
robotz~1.wav	249,570	WIN95_15.CAB	(Not on diskette)	SCANPROG.EXE	4,438	\WIN95 folder	Diskette 1 Root
robotz~2.wav	71,868	WIN95_15.CAB	(Not on diskette)	scanpst.exe	264,384	WIN95_07.CAB	WIN95_07.CAB
robotz~3.wav	49,578	WIN95_15.CAB	(Not on diskette)	scanpst.hlp	14,135	WIN95_07.CAB	WIN95_07.CAB
robotz~4.wav	109,688	WIN95_15.CAB	(Not on diskette)	sccview.dll	32,256	WIN95_13.CAB	(Not on diskette)
robotzas.wav	70,426	WIN95_15.CAB	(Not on diskette)	scrnsave.scr	9,728	WIN95_11.CAB	WIN95_11.CAB
robotzcl.wav	94,818	WIN95_15.CAB	(Not on diskette)	scroll.avi	1,510,732	WIN95_16.CAB	(Not on diskette)
robotzcr.wav	54,150	WIN95_15.CAB	(Not on diskette)	scsi.inf	35,741	PRECOPY2.CAB	PRECOPY2.CAB
robotzde.wav	44,546	WIN95_15.CAB	(Not on diskette)	scsi1hlp.vxd	19,189	WIN95_05.CAB	WIN95_05.CAB
robotzer.wav	49,284	WIN95_15.CAB	(Not on diskette)	scsiport.pdr	23,133	WIN95_05.CAB	WIN95_05.CAB
robotzex.wav	30,194	WIN95_15.CAB	(Not on diskette)	secur32.dll	25,088	WIN95_11.CAB	WIN95_12.CAB
robotzma.wav	74,722	WIN95_15.CAB	(Not on diskette)	securcl.dll	15,360	WIN95_07.CAB	WIN95_08.CAB
robotzme.wav	13,920	WIN95_15.CAB	(Not on diskette)	seiko24e.drv	31,376	WIN95_10.CAB	WIN95_10.CAB
robotzmi.wav	150,442	WIN95_15.CAB	(Not on diskette)	seikosh9.drv	18,736	WIN95_10.CAB	WIN95_10.CAB
robotzop.wav	81,390	WIN95_15.CAB	(Not on diskette)	select.exe	240,322	WIN95_17.CAB	(Not on diskette)
robotzqu.wav	79,002	WIN95_15.CAB	(Not on diskette)	serenum.vxd	19,899	WIN95_03.CAB	WIN95_03.CAB
robotzre.wav	119,134	WIN95_15.CAB	(Not on diskette)	serial.vxd	18,572	WIN95_03.CAB	WIN95_03.CAB
robotzwi.wav	275,950	WIN95_15.CAB	(Not on diskette)	serialui.dll	12,032	WIN95_03.CAB	WIN95_03.CAB
route.exe	23,696	WIN95_12.CAB	WIN95_12.CAB	SERIFE.FON	57,936	MINI.CAB	MINI.CAB
rpcltc1.dll	8,192	WIN95_11.CAB	WIN95_12.CAB	serife.fon	57,952	WIN95_05.CAB	WIN95_06.CAB
rpcltc3.dll	7,584	WIN95_11.CAB	WIN95_12.CAB	seriff.fon	81,744	WIN95_05.CAB	WIN95_06.CAB
rpcltc5.dll	9,200	WIN95_11.CAB	WIN95_12.CAB	server.hlp	22,948	WIN95_05.CAB	WIN95_06.CAB
rpcltc6.dll	8,128	WIN95_11.CAB	WIN95_12.CAB	setmdir.exe	57,209	WIN95_17.CAB	(Not on diskette)
rpclts3.dll	9,168	WIN95_11.CAB	WIN95_12.CAB	setp3.vxd	31,838	WIN95_12.CAB	WIN95_13.CAB
rpclts5.dll	10,736	WIN95_11.CAB	WIN95_12.CAB	setup.bmp	38,462	WIN95_10.CAB	WIN95_11.CAB
rpclts6.dll	9,696	WIN95_11.CAB	WIN95_12.CAB	SETUP.EXE	5,184	\WIN95 folder	Diskette 1 Root
rpcns4.dll	30,832	WIN95_11.CAB	WIN95_12.CAB	SETUP.TXT	34,612	\WIN95 folder	Diskette 1 Root
rpcrt4.dll	202,240	WIN95_11.CAB	WIN95_12.CAB	setup4.dll	6,240	WIN95_10.CAB	WIN95_11.CAB
rpcss.exe	81,644	WIN95_12.CAB	WIN95_12.CAB	setupc.inf	55,858	PRECOPY2.CAB	PRECOPY2.CAB
rplboot.sys	1,536	WIN95_17.CAB	(Not on diskette)	setuppp.inf	4,242	PRECOPY1.CAB	PRECOPY2.CAB
rplimage.dll	23,040	PRECOPY2.CAB	(Not on diskette)	setupx.dll	355,136	PRECOPY1.CAB	PRECOPY2.CAB
rsrc16.dll	1,312	WIN95_02.CAB	WIN95_03.CAB	setver.exe	18,939	WIN95_09.CAB	WIN95_09.CAB
rsrc32.dll	4,608	WIN95_02.CAB	WIN95_03.CAB	sf4029.exe	108,544	WIN95_10.CAB	WIN95_10.CAB
rsrcmtr.exe	15,360	WIN95_02.CAB	WIN95_03.CAB	share.exe	10,304	WIN95_09.CAB	WIN95_09.CAB
rundll.exe	4,912	WIN95_11.CAB	WIN95_11.CAB	shell.dll	41,600	PRECOPY1.CAB	PRECOPY2.CAB
rundll32.exe	8,192	WIN95_11.CAB	WIN95_11.CAB	shell.inf	48,580	PRECOPY2.CAB	PRECOPY2.CAB

File	Size	CD Location	Disk Location	File	Size	CD Location	Disk Location
shell.new	116,144	WIN95_11.CAB	WIN95_11.CAB	SOUND.DRV	3,440	MINI.CAB	MINI.CAB
shell.vxd	78,964	WIN95_11.CAB	WIN95_11.CAB	soundrec.cnt	1,023	WIN95_08.CAB	WIN95_08.CAB
shell2.inf	46,936	PRECOPY2.CAB	PRECOPY2.CAB	soundrec.hlp	24,895	WIN95_08.CAB	WIN95_09.CAB
shell3.inf	7,272	PRECOPY2.CAB	(Not on diskette)	spap.vxd	9,908	WIN95_10.CAB	WIN95_11.CAB
shell32.dll	817,664	WIN95_10.CAB	WIN95_11.CAB	sparrow.mpd	16,960	WIN95_05.CAB	WIN95_05.CAB
shscrap.dll	24,576	WIN95_10.CAB	WIN95_11.CAB	sparrowx.mpd	18,944	WIN95_05.CAB	WIN95_05.CAB
signup.exe	202,752	WIN95_07.CAB	WIN95_08.CAB	spendis.vxd	17,996	WIN95_12.CAB	WIN95_13.CAB
size1_1.cur	766	WIN95_13.CAB	(Not on diskette)	splitter.vxd	2,596	WIN95_07.CAB	WIN95_08.CAB
size1_l.cur	766	WIN95_13.CAB	(Not on diskette)	spock.mpd	5,280	WIN95_05.CAB	WIN95_05.CAB
size1_m.cur	766	WIN95_13.CAB	(Not on diskette)	spool32.exe	20,992	WIN95_09.CAB	WIN95_10.CAB
size2_1.cur	766	WIN95_13.CAB	(Not on diskette)	spooler.vxd	27,196	WIN95_09.CAB	WIN95_10.CAB
size2_l.cur	766	WIN95_13.CAB	(Not on diskette)	spoolss.dll	91,136	WIN95_09.CAB	WIN95_10.CAB
size2_m.cur	766	WIN95_13.CAB	(Not on diskette)	srammtd.vxd	3,202	WIN95_09.CAB	WIN95_10.CAB
size3_1.cur	766	WIN95_13.CAB	(Not on diskette)	srm.new	5,329	WIN95_17.CAB	(Not on diskette)
size3_l.cur	766	WIN95_13.CAB	(Not on diskette)	SSERIFE.FON	64,544	MINI.CAB	MINI.CAB
size3_m.cur	766	WIN95_13.CAB	(Not on diskette)	sserife.fon	64,544	WIN95_05.CAB	WIN95_06.CAB
size4_1.cur	766	WIN95_13.CAB	(Not on diskette)	sseriff.fon	89,680	WIN95_05.CAB	WIN95_06.CAB
size4_l.cur	766	WIN95_13.CAB	(Not on diskette)	ssflywin.scr	14,336	WIN95_11.CAB	WIN95_11.CAB
size4_m.cur	766	WIN95_13.CAB	(Not on diskette)	ssmarque.scr	18,944	WIN95_11.CAB	WIN95_11.CAB
sizewin.avi	832,222	WIN95_16.CAB	(Not on diskette)	ssmyst.scr	20,992	WIN95_11.CAB	WIN95_11.CAB
skpsfa_1.spd	33,024	WIN95_10.CAB	WIN95_10.CAB	ssstars.scr	15,872	WIN95_11.CAB	WIN95_11.CAB
slan.dos	13,578	WIN95_11.CAB	WIN95_12.CAB	star24e.drv	63,088	WIN95_10.CAB	WIN95_10.CAB
slcd32.mpd	31,632	WIN95_05.CAB	WIN95_05.CAB	star9e.drv	38,160	WIN95_10.CAB	WIN95_10.CAB
slenh.dll	16,512	WIN95_07.CAB	WIN95_08.CAB	start.exe	9,216	WIN95_09.CAB	WIN95_09.CAB
smalle.fon	24,352	WIN95_05.CAB	WIN95_06.CAB	state.pbk	851	WIN95_07.CAB	WIN95_08.CAB
smallf.fon	19,632	WIN95_05.CAB	WIN95_06.CAB	stdole.tlb	5,532	WIN95_09.CAB	WIN95_09.CAB
smartnd.dos	88,809	WIN95_11.CAB	WIN95_12.CAB	stdole32.tlb	7,168	WIN95_09.CAB	WIN95_09.CAB
SMARTDRV.EXE	45,145	\WIN95 folder	Diskette 1 Root	stem0409.dll	7,168	WIN95_05.CAB	WIN95_06.CAB
smc_arc.dos	20,327	WIN95_11.CAB	WIN95_12.CAB	stls04ss.spd	4,779	WIN95_10.CAB	WIN95_10.CAB
smc3000.dos	12,271	WIN95_11.CAB	WIN95_12.CAB	stls08lp.spd	4,832	WIN95_10.CAB	WIN95_10.CAB
smc8000.dos	35,584	WIN95_11.CAB	WIN95_12.CAB	stls5ttu.spd	4,938	WIN95_10.CAB	WIN95_10.CAB
smc8000w.vxd	36,959	WIN95_12.CAB	WIN95_13.CAB	storage.dll	4,208	WIN95_09.CAB	WIN95_09.CAB
smc80pc.vxd	28,765	WIN95_12.CAB	WIN95_13.CAB	strn.dos	41,946	WIN95_12.CAB	WIN95_12.CAB
smc8100.dos	62,496	WIN95_11.CAB	WIN95_12.CAB	subst.exe	17,904	WIN95_09.CAB	WIN95_09.CAB
smc8100w.vxd	71,773	WIN95_12.CAB	WIN95_13.CAB	sucheck.bat	816	PRECOPY2.CAB	PRECOPY2.CAB
smc8232.dos	31,232	WIN95_12.CAB	WIN95_12.CAB	suexpand.dll	9,936	PRECOPY1.CAB	PRECOPY2.CAB
smc8232w.vxd	28,767	WIN95_12.CAB	WIN95_13.CAB	sufail.bat	751	PRECOPY2.CAB	PRECOPY2.CAB
smc9000.dos	17,184	WIN95_12.CAB	WIN95_12.CAB	SUHELPER.BIN	1,472	\WIN95 folder	(Not on diskette)
smc9000.vxd	29,433	WIN95_12.CAB	WIN95_13.CAB	sulogo.sys	129,078	WIN95_10.CAB	WIN95_11.CAB
snapshot.exe	6,122	WIN95_17.CAB	(Not on diskette)	supervga.drv	52,320	WIN95_04.CAB	WIN95_05.CAB
snapshot.vxd	13,884	WIN95_17.CAB	(Not on diskette)	support.txt	24,482	WIN95_03.CAB	WIN95_03.CAB
sndrec32.exe	105,472	WIN95_08.CAB	WIN95_09.CAB	suwin.exe	352,608	PRECOPY2.CAB	PRECOPY2.CAB
sndvol32.cnt	392	WIN95_08.CAB	WIN95_08.CAB	svcprop.dll	11,264	WIN95_07.CAB	WIN95_08.CAB
sndvol32.exe	54,784	WIN95_08.CAB	WIN95_09.CAB	svrapi.dll	13,312	WIN95_11.CAB	WIN95_12.CAB
sndvol32.hlp	11,120	WIN95_08.CAB	WIN95_09.CAB	sxciext.dll	98,144	WIN95_04.CAB	WIN95_05.CAB
snip.vxd	27,217	WIN95_12.CAB	WIN95_13.CAB	symbol.ttf	60,096	WIN95_05.CAB	WIN95_06.CAB
socket.vxd	27,217	WIN95_12.CAB	WIN95_13.CAB	symbole.fon	56,336	WIN95_05.CAB	WIN95_06.CAB
socketsv.vxd	9,806	WIN95_09.CAB	WIN95_10.CAB	symbolf.fon	80,928	WIN95_05.CAB	WIN95_06.CAB
sol.cnt	157	WIN95_05.CAB	WIN95_06.CAB	synceng.dll	55,296	WIN95_05.CAB	WIN95_05.CAB
sol.exe	171,392	WIN95_05.CAB	WIN95_06.CAB	syncui.dll	151,040	WIN95_05.CAB	WIN95_05.CAB
sol.hlp	10,145	WIN95_05.CAB	WIN95_06.CAB	synthgm.sbk	34,832	WIN95_08.CAB	WIN95_09.CAB
sort.exe	25,802	WIN95_03.CAB	WIN95_03.CAB	sys.com	13,239	WIN95_02.CAB	WIN95_02.CAB

File	Size	CD Location	Disk Location	File	Size	CD Location	Disk Location
sysclass.dll	12,880	WIN95_09.CAB	WIN95_10.CAB	tips.txt	28,617	WIN95_03.CAB	WIN95_03.CAB
sysdetmg.dll	318,304	PRECOPY1.CAB	PRECOPY2.CAB	tk200172.spd	17,049	WIN95_10.CAB	WIN95_10.CAB
sysdm.cpl	221,776	WIN95_03.CAB	WIN95_04.CAB	tk220171.spd	9,742	WIN95_10.CAB	WIN95_10.CAB
sysedit.exe	19,488	WIN95_02.CAB	WIN95_03.CAB	tkp200i2.spd	18,748	WIN95_10.CAB	WIN95_10.CAB
sysmon.cnt	263	WIN95_13.CAB	(Not on diskette)	tkp220i1.spd	11,782	WIN95_10.CAB	WIN95_10.CAB
sysmon.exe	65,024	WIN95_17.CAB	(Not on diskette)	tkp2sdx1.spd	18,614	WIN95_10.CAB	WIN95_10.CAB
sysmon.hlp	10,558	WIN95_13.CAB	(Not on diskette)	tkp300i1.spd	21,941	WIN95_10.CAB	WIN95_10.CAB
SYSTEM.DRV	2,304	MINI.CAB	MINI.CAB	tkph4801.spd	10,995	WIN95_10.CAB	WIN95_10.CAB
system.drv	2,288	WIN95_03.CAB	WIN95_04.CAB	tkphzr22.spd	19,639	WIN95_10.CAB	WIN95_10.CAB
SYSTEM.INI	358	MINI.CAB	MINI.CAB	tkphzr32.spd	27,202	WIN95_10.CAB	WIN95_10.CAB
systhunk.dll	16,432	WIN95_03.CAB	WIN95_04.CAB	tlnk.dos	12,426	WIN95_12.CAB	WIN95_12.CAB
systray.exe	26,112	WIN95_07.CAB	WIN95_08.CAB	tlnk3.dos	10,896	WIN95_12.CAB	WIN95_12.CAB
t160.mpd	11,104	WIN95_05.CAB	WIN95_05.CAB	tlnk3.vxd	52,627	WIN95_12.CAB	WIN95_13.CAB
t20n3.vxd	63,935	WIN95_12.CAB	WIN95_13.CAB	tmv1.mpd	12,048	WIN95_05.CAB	WIN95_05.CAB
t20nd.dos	37,939	WIN95_12.CAB	WIN95_12.CAB	toolhelp.dll	12,112	WIN95_03.CAB	WIN95_04.CAB
t30n3.vxd	64,027	WIN95_12.CAB	WIN95_13.CAB	toshiba.drv	10,880	WIN95_10.CAB	WIN95_10.CAB
t30nd.dos	45,388	WIN95_12.CAB	WIN95_12.CAB	tour.exe	339,456	WIN95_17.CAB	(Not on diskette)
t348.mpd	11,584	WIN95_05.CAB	WIN95_05.CAB	tourani.dll	967,104	WIN95_17.CAB	(Not on diskette)
t358.mpd	13,984	WIN95_05.CAB	WIN95_05.CAB	tourstr.dll	9,568	WIN95_17.CAB	(Not on diskette)
tada.wav	27,516	WIN95_15.CAB	(Not on diskette)	tourutil.dll	638,528	WIN95_17.CAB	(Not on diskette)
tapi.dll	161,712	WIN95_11.CAB	WIN95_11.CAB	tpha200i.icm	24,844	WIN95_06.CAB	WIN95_06.CAB
tapi.inf	1,046	PRECOPY2.CAB	PRECOPY2.CAB	tphaiii.icm	24,804	WIN95_06.CAB	WIN95_06.CAB
tapi32.dll	11,776	WIN95_11.CAB	WIN95_11.CAB	tracert.exe	9,056	WIN95_12.CAB	WIN95_12.CAB
tapiaddr.dll	20,616	WIN95_11.CAB	WIN95_11.CAB	treeedcl.dll	17,408	WIN95_07.CAB	WIN95_08.CAB
tapiexe.exe	1,784	WIN95_11.CAB	WIN95_11.CAB	treenvcl.dll	16,384	WIN95_07.CAB	WIN95_08.CAB
tapiini.exe	7,632	WIN95_11.CAB	WIN95_11.CAB	triumph1.spd	2,185	WIN95_10.CAB	WIN95_10.CAB
taskman.exe	28,672	WIN95_11.CAB	WIN95_11.CAB	triumph2.spd	3,260	WIN95_10.CAB	WIN95_10.CAB
taskswch.avi	425,742	WIN95_16.CAB	(Not on diskette)	tsd32.dll	17,408	WIN95_08.CAB	WIN95_08.CAB
tccarc.dos	19,972	WIN95_12.CAB	WIN95_12.CAB	tseng.drv	28,864	WIN95_04.CAB	WIN95_05.CAB
tcctok.dos	24,954	WIN95_12.CAB	WIN95_12.CAB	tseng.vxd	14,531	WIN95_04.CAB	WIN95_05.CAB
tctokch.vxd	37,616	WIN95_12.CAB	WIN95_13.CAB	tssoft32.acm	8,704	WIN95_08.CAB	WIN95_08.CAB
tdkcd02.sys	24,224	WIN95_12.CAB	WIN95_12.CAB	tty.drv	31,152	WIN95_10.CAB	WIN95_10.CAB
telephon.cpl	33,272	WIN95_11.CAB	WIN95_11.CAB	tty.hlp	11,606	WIN95_05.CAB	WIN95_06.CAB
telephon.hlp	7,315	WIN95_11.CAB	WIN95_11.CAB	typelib.dll	177,856	WIN95_09.CAB	WIN95_09.CAB
telnet.exe	66,672	WIN95_12.CAB	WIN95_12.CAB	u9415470.spd	4,900	WIN95_10.CAB	WIN95_10.CAB
telnet.hlp	24,099	WIN95_12.CAB	WIN95_12.CAB	ubnei.dos	24,930	WIN95_12.CAB	WIN95_13.CAB
testps.txt	2,640	WIN95_09.CAB	WIN95_10.CAB	ubnei.vxd	31,311	WIN95_12.CAB	WIN95_12.CAB
textchat.exe	53,248	WIN95_07.CAB	WIN95_08.CAB	ubneps.dos	20,257	WIN95_12.CAB	WIN95_12.CAB
thatch2.bmp	182	WIN95_03.CAB	WIN95_03.CAB	ultra124.mpd	4,912	WIN95_05.CAB	WIN95_05.CAB
themic~1.msn	4	WIN95_07.CAB	(Not on diskette)	ultra14f.mpd	4,624	WIN95_05.CAB	WIN95_05.CAB
thinkjet.drv	6,752	WIN95_10.CAB	WIN95_10.CAB	ultra24f.mpd	4,256	WIN95_05.CAB	WIN95_05.CAB
threed.vbx	64,432	WIN95_17.CAB	(Not on diskette)	umdm16.dll	1,952	WIN95_03.CAB	WIN95_03.CAB
ti850.drv	5,056	WIN95_10.CAB	WIN95_10.CAB	umdm32.dll	6,144	WIN95_03.CAB	WIN95_03.CAB
tim17521.spd	7,063	WIN95_10.CAB	WIN95_10.CAB	unicode.bin	3,279	WIN95_13.CAB	WIN95_13.CAB
tim35521.spd	8,179	WIN95_10.CAB	WIN95_10.CAB	unicode.nls	34,676	WIN95_09.CAB	WIN95_09.CAB
timedate.cpl	49,152	WIN95_03.CAB	WIN95_04.CAB	unidrv.dll	197,024	WIN95_09.CAB	WIN95_10.CAB
times.ttf	85,240	WIN95_04.CAB	WIN95_04.CAB	unidrv.hlp	15,343	WIN95_09.CAB	WIN95_10.CAB
timesbd.ttf	83,228	WIN95_04.CAB	WIN95_04.CAB	unimdm.tsp	28,896	WIN95_03.CAB	WIN95_03.CAB
timesbi.ttf	77,080	WIN95_04.CAB	WIN95_04.CAB	unimodem.vxd	41,598	WIN95_03.CAB	WIN95_03.CAB
timesi.ttf	79,672	WIN95_04.CAB	WIN95_04.CAB	uninstal.exe	76,496	WIN95_02.CAB	WIN95_02.CAB
timezone.inf	46,060	PRECOPY2.CAB	PRECOPY2.CAB	unknown.inf	462	PRECOPY2.CAB	PRECOPY2.CAB
timlp232.spd	17,135	WIN95_10.CAB	WIN95_10.CAB	up_1.cur	766	WIN95_13.CAB	(Not on diskette)

File	Size	CD Location	Disk Location	File	Size	CD Location	Disk Location
up_l.cur	766	WIN95_13.CAB	(Not on diskette)	VGASYS.FON	7,280	MINI.CAB	MINI.CAB
up_m.cur	766	WIN95_13.CAB	(Not on diskette)	vgasys.fon	7,296	WIN95_05.CAB	WIN95_06.CAB
urgent.cpe	4,345	WIN95_05.CAB	WIN95_05.CAB	vgateway.vxd	42,749	WIN95_07.CAB	WIN95_08.CAB
USER.EXE	264,016	MINI.CAB	MINI.CAB	vidcap.inf	2,158	PRECOPY2.CAB	PRECOPY2.CAB
user.exe	462,112	WIN95_03.CAB	WIN95_04.CAB	video7.vxd	14,938	WIN95_04.CAB	WIN95_05.CAB
user32.dll	44,544	WIN95_11.CAB	WIN95_11.CAB	vip.386	62,614	WIN95_12.CAB	WIN95_13.CAB
utopia~1.wav	86,798	WIN95_15.CAB	(Not on diskette)	vjoyd.vxd	20,590	WIN95_08.CAB	WIN95_09.CAB
utopia~2.wav	2,692	WIN95_15.CAB	(Not on diskette)	vkd.vxd	45,371	WIN95_03.CAB	WIN95_03.CAB
utopia~3.wav	5,120	WIN95_15.CAB	(Not on diskette)	vlb32.dll	42,496	WIN95_06.CAB	WIN95_07.CAB
utopia~4.wav	15,372	WIN95_15.CAB	(Not on diskette)	vmcpd.vxd	13,973	WIN95_03.CAB	WIN95_03.CAB
utopiaas.wav	95,708	WIN95_15.CAB	(Not on diskette)	vmd.vxd	9,815	WIN95_08.CAB	WIN95_09.CAB
utopiacl.wav	4,616	WIN95_15.CAB	(Not on diskette)	vmm32.vxd	411,132	WIN95_03.CAB	WIN95_03.CAB
utopiacr.wav	5,824	WIN95_15.CAB	(Not on diskette)	vmouse.vxd	32,815	WIN95_08.CAB	WIN95_09.CAB
utopiade.wav	9,946	WIN95_15.CAB	(Not on diskette)	vmpoll.vxd	30,931	WIN95_03.CAB	WIN95_03.CAB
utopiaer.wav	24,596	WIN95_15.CAB	(Not on diskette)	vmvid.vxd	16,030	WIN95_08.CAB	WIN95_09.CAB
utopiaex.wav	13,026	WIN95_15.CAB	(Not on diskette)	vnbt.386	95,969	WIN95_12.CAB	WIN95_13.CAB
utopiama.wav	14,922	WIN95_16.CAB	(Not on diskette)	vnetbios.vxd	27,221	WIN95_12.CAB	WIN95_13.CAB
utopiame.wav	3,462	WIN95_16.CAB	(Not on diskette)	vnetsup.vxd	19,129	WIN95_12.CAB	WIN95_13.CAB
utopiami.wav	14,990	WIN95_16.CAB	(Not on diskette)	voltrack.vxd	18,494	WIN95_03.CAB	WIN95_03.CAB
utopiaop.wav	10,760	WIN95_16.CAB	(Not on diskette)	vpasd.vxd	21,094	WIN95_08.CAB	WIN95_09.CAB
utopiaqu.wav	13,084	WIN95_16.CAB	(Not on diskette)	vpd.vxd	22,618	WIN95_03.CAB	WIN95_04.CAB
utopiare.wav	98,330	WIN95_16.CAB	(Not on diskette)	vpicd.vxd	46,543	WIN95_03.CAB	WIN95_03.CAB
utopiawi.wav	156,760	WIN95_16.CAB	(Not on diskette)	vpmtd.386	5,668	WIN95_03.CAB	WIN95_03.CAB
v86mmgr.vxd	95,387	WIN95_03.CAB	WIN95_03.CAB	vpowerd.vxd	19,669	WIN95_07.CAB	WIN95_08.CAB
vbrun300.dll	398,416	WIN95_17.CAB	(Not on diskette)	vredir.vxd	140,343	WIN95_12.CAB	WIN95_13.CAB
vcache.vxd	19,566	WIN95_03.CAB	WIN95_03.CAB	vsami.dll	48,640	WIN95_13.CAB	(Not on diskette)
vcd.vxd	23,939	WIN95_03.CAB	WIN95_04.CAB	vsasc8.dll	17,920	WIN95_13.CAB	(Not on diskette)
vcdfsd.vxd	22,408	WIN95_03.CAB	WIN95_03.CAB	vsbmp.dll	24,064	WIN95_13.CAB	(Not on diskette)
vcomm.vxd	32,638	WIN95_03.CAB	WIN95_04.CAB	vsd.vxd	5,721	WIN95_03.CAB	WIN95_03.CAB
vcond.vxd	53,438	WIN95_04.CAB	WIN95_04.CAB	vsdrw.dll	29,184	WIN95_13.CAB	(Not on diskette)
vdd.vxd	73,592	WIN95_04.CAB	WIN95_05.CAB	vserver.vxd	108,264	WIN95_12.CAB	WIN95_13.CAB
vdef.vxd	9,768	WIN95_03.CAB	WIN95_03.CAB	vsexe2.dll	38,400	WIN95_13.CAB	(Not on diskette)
vdhcp.386	27,961	WIN95_12.CAB	WIN95_13.CAB	vsflw.dll	64,512	WIN95_13.CAB	(Not on diskette)
vdmad.vxd	41,844	WIN95_03.CAB	WIN95_03.CAB	vshare.vxd	14,926	WIN95_05.CAB	WIN95_05.CAB
vdmdbg.dll	4,096	WIN95_03.CAB	WIN95_04.CAB	vsmp.dll	25,088	WIN95_13.CAB	(Not on diskette)
VER.DLL	9,008	MINI.CAB	MINI.CAB	vsmsw.dll	33,792	WIN95_13.CAB	(Not on diskette)
ver.dll	9,008	PRECOPY2.CAB	PRECOPY2.CAB	vspp.dll	37,376	WIN95_13.CAB	(Not on diskette)
ver.new	12,144	WIN95_10.CAB	WIN95_11.CAB	vsqpw2.dll	86,016	WIN95_17.CAB	(Not on diskette)
version.dll	6,656	WIN95_10.CAB	WIN95_11.CAB	vsrtf.dll	34,816	WIN95_13.CAB	(Not on diskette)
verx.dll	14,768	PRECOPY2.CAB	PRECOPY2.CAB	vsw6.dll	43,520	WIN95_13.CAB	(Not on diskette)
vfat.vxd	57,917	WIN95_03.CAB	WIN95_03.CAB	vswk4.dll	78,848	WIN95_13.CAB	(Not on diskette)
vfbackup.vxd	16,831	WIN95_03.CAB	WIN95_03.CAB	vswks.dll	35,328	WIN95_13.CAB	(Not on diskette)
vfd.vxd	5,857	WIN95_03.CAB	WIN95_03.CAB	vswmf.dll	28,160	WIN95_13.CAB	(Not on diskette)
vflatd.vxd	7,723	WIN95_04.CAB	WIN95_05.CAB	vsword.dll	64,512	WIN95_13.CAB	(Not on diskette)
VGA.DRV	73,200	MINI.CAB	MINI.CAB	vswork.dll	28,672	WIN95_13.CAB	(Not on diskette)
vga.drv	52,064	WIN95_04.CAB	WIN95_05.CAB	vswp5.dll	43,008	WIN95_13.CAB	(Not on diskette)
vga850.fon	5,232	WIN95_03.CAB	WIN95_03.CAB	vswp6.dll	51,712	WIN95_13.CAB	(Not on diskette)
VGAFIX.FON	5,360	MINI.CAB	MINI.CAB	vswpf.dll	27,136	WIN95_13.CAB	(Not on diskette)
vgafix.fon	5,360	WIN95_05.CAB	WIN95_06.CAB	vsxl5.dll	81,408	WIN95_13.CAB	(Not on diskette)
vgafull.3gr	14,624	WIN95_04.CAB	WIN95_05.CAB	vt600480.spd	1,969	WIN95_10.CAB	WIN95_10.CAB
VGAOEM.FON	5,168	MINI.CAB	MINI.CAB	vtcp.386	47,377	WIN95_12.CAB	WIN95_13.CAB
vgaoem.fon	5,168	WIN95_05.CAB	WIN95_06.CAB	vtd.vxd	31,684	WIN95_03.CAB	WIN95_03.CAB

File	Size	CD Location	Disk Location	File	Size	CD Location	Disk Location
vtdapi.vxd	18,546	WIN95_03.CAB	WIN95_03.CAB	winmine.exe	24,176	WIN95_05.CAB	WIN95_06.CAB
vtdi.386	5,687	WIN95_12.CAB	WIN95_13.CAB	winmine.hlp	9,133	WIN95_05.CAB	WIN95_06.CAB
vvexe32.exe	10,240	WIN95_17.CAB	(Not on diskette)	winmm.dll	49,152	WIN95_08.CAB	WIN95_08.CAB
vwin32.vxd	54,497	WIN95_04.CAB	WIN95_04.CAB	winnet16.dll	2,000	WIN95_11.CAB	WIN95_12.CAB
vxdldr.vxd	35,112	WIN95_03.CAB	WIN95_03.CAB	winnews.txt	1,056	WIN95_06.CAB	WIN95_06.CAB
w_over.cnt	1,722	WIN95_16.CAB	(Not on diskette)	winoa386.new	61,680	WIN95_03.CAB	WIN95_03.CAB
w_tour.cnt	144	WIN95_17.CAB	(Not on diskette)	winpopup.cnt	403	WIN95_11.CAB	WIN95_12.CAB
wait_1.cur	766	WIN95_13.CAB	(Not on diskette)	winpopup.exe	27,600	WIN95_12.CAB	WIN95_12.CAB
wait_l.cur	766	WIN95_13.CAB	(Not on diskette)	winpopup.hlp	11,591	WIN95_12.CAB	WIN95_12.CAB
wait_m.cur	766	WIN95_13.CAB	(Not on diskette)	winpopup.inf	1,932	WIN95_12.CAB	WIN95_12.CAB
wave.inf	62,619	PRECOPY2.CAB	PRECOPY2.CAB	WINSETUP.BIN	159,504	\WIN95 folder	Diskette 1 Root
WB16OFF.EXE	537	\WIN95 folder	Diskette 1 Root	winsock.dll	42,080	WIN95_11.CAB	WIN95_12.CAB
wd.drv	21,680	WIN95_04.CAB	WIN95_05.CAB	winspl16.drv	3,552	WIN95_09.CAB	WIN95_10.CAB
wd.vxd	18,328	WIN95_04.CAB	WIN95_05.CAB	winspool.drv	18,944	WIN95_09.CAB	WIN95_10.CAB
wd7000ex.mpd	4,448	WIN95_05.CAB	WIN95_05.CAB	winver.exe	3,632	WIN95_10.CAB	WIN95_11.CAB
weave2.bmp	4,678	WIN95_03.CAB	WIN95_03.CAB	winver.inf	56,062	PRECOPY2.CAB	PRECOPY2.CAB
welcome.exe	16,384	WIN95_11.CAB	WIN95_11.CAB	winword.doc	4,608	WIN95_10.CAB	WIN95_11.CAB
wfm0200.acv	13,456	WIN95_08.CAB	WIN95_08.CAB	winword2.doc	1,769	WIN95_10.CAB	WIN95_11.CAB
wfm0200a.csp	2,238	WIN95_08.CAB	WIN95_08.CAB	wmsfr32.dll	211,456	WIN95_06.CAB	WIN95_07.CAB
wfm0201.acv	5,184	WIN95_08.CAB	WIN95_08.CAB	wmsui32.dll	877,568	WIN95_06.CAB	WIN95_07.CAB
wfm0201a.csp	6,776	WIN95_08.CAB	WIN95_08.CAB	wnaspi32.dll	16,384	WIN95_03.CAB	WIN95_03.CAB
wfm0202.acv	9,056	WIN95_08.CAB	WIN95_08.CAB	wnpp32.dll	13,824	WIN95_11.CAB	WIN95_12.CAB
wfm0202a.csp	9,004	WIN95_08.CAB	WIN95_08.CAB	wordpad.cnt	1,920	WIN95_03.CAB	WIN95_03.CAB
wfm0203.acv	9,056	WIN95_08.CAB	WIN95_08.CAB	wordpad.exe	183,296	WIN95_03.CAB	WIN95_03.CAB
wfm0203a.csp	9,004	WIN95_08.CAB	WIN95_08.CAB	wordpad.hlp	28,422	WIN95_03.CAB	WIN95_03.CAB
wgpoadmn.dll	81,168	WIN95_06.CAB	WIN95_07.CAB	wordpad.inf	10,491	PRECOPY2.CAB	PRECOPY2.CAB
wgpocpl.cpl	32,528	WIN95_06.CAB	WIN95_07.CAB	wordpfct.wpd	30	WIN95_11.CAB	WIN95_11.CAB
whatson.avi	745,920	WIN95_16.CAB	(Not on diskette)	wordpfct.wpg	57	WIN95_11.CAB	WIN95_11.CAB
whlp16t.dll	3,888	WIN95_05.CAB	WIN95_06.CAB	wordpfct.wpw	1,371	WIN95_11.CAB	WIN95_11.CAB
whlp32t.dll	10,240	WIN95_05.CAB	WIN95_06.CAB	wow32.dll	4,096	WIN95_11.CAB	WIN95_11.CAB
win.cnf	22,679	WIN95_03.CAB	WIN95_03.CAB	wps_updt.dll	462,848	WIN95_10.CAB	WIN95_10.CAB
WIN.INI	165	MINI.CAB	MINI.CAB	wpsapd.dll	8,672	WIN95_05.CAB	WIN95_05.CAB
win32s16.dll	3,200	WIN95_03.CAB	WIN95_04.CAB	wpsmon.dll	13,312	WIN95_10.CAB	WIN95_10.CAB
WIN87EM.DLL	12,800	MINI.CAB	MINI.CAB	wpsmon16.dll	8,080	WIN95_10.CAB	WIN95_10.CAB
win87em.dll	11,904	WIN95_03.CAB	Win95_04.CAB	wpsuni.drv	145,456	WIN95_05.CAB	WIN95_05.CAB
win95bb.dll	342,640	PRECOPY2.CAB	PRECOPY2.CAB	wpsunire.dll	16,896	WIN95_05.CAB	WIN95_05.CAB
winaspi.dll	3,536	WIN95_03.CAB	WIN95_03.CAB	write.exe	5,120	WIN95_02.CAB	WIN95_03.CAB
winboot.sys	223,148	PRECOPY1.CAB	PRECOPY1.CAB	write32.wpc	62,464	WIN95_02.CAB	WIN95_03.CAB
windows.cnt	13,743	WIN95_05.CAB	WIN95_06.CAB	wsasrv.exe	6,960	WIN95_12.CAB	WIN95_12.CAB
windows.hlp	519,340	WIN95_05.CAB	WIN95_06.CAB	wshtcp.vxd	5,816	WIN95_12.CAB	WIN95_13.CAB
winfile.cnt	2,169	WIN95_10.CAB	WIN95_11.CAB	wsipx.vxd	14,521	WIN95_12.CAB	WIN95_13.CAB
winfile.exe	155,408	WIN95_11.CAB	WIN95_11.CAB	wsock.vxd	15,522	WIN95_12.CAB	WIN95_13.CAB
winfile.hlp	43,833	WIN95_11.CAB	WIN95_11.CAB	wsock32.dll	66,560	WIN95_11.CAB	WIN95_12.CAB
wingding.ttf	71,196	WIN95_04.CAB	WIN95_04.CAB	wsvv.vxd	92,244	WIN95_17.CAB	(Not on diskette)
winhelp.exe	2,416	WIN95_05.CAB	WIN95_06.CAB	xcopy.exe	3,878	WIN95_09.CAB	WIN95_09.CAB
winhlp32.cnt	930	WIN95_05.CAB	WIN95_06.CAB	xcopy32.exe	40,960	WIN95_09.CAB	WIN95_09.CAB
winhlp32.exe	306,688	WIN95_05.CAB	WIN95_06.CAB	xga.drv	12,864	WIN95_04.CAB	WIN95_05.CAB
winhlp32.hlp	27,507	WIN95_06.CAB	WIN95_06.CAB	xga.vxd	20,151	WIN95_04.CAB	WIN95_05.CAB
wininit.exe	40,801	WIN95_10.CAB	WIN95_11.CAB	xlat850.bin	407	WIN95_03.CAB	WIN95_03.CAB
winipcfg.exe	38,912	WIN95_12.CAB	WIN95_12.CAB	XMSMMGR.EXE	14,144	\WIN95 folder	Diskette 1 Root
winmine.cnt	168	WIN95_05.CAB	WIN95_06.CAB				

Appendix F

Haaaaaaalp

I am a fool by profession.

—Robert Burns, *The Jolly Beggars,* 1785

In this short chapter we won't try to answer your every question. Instead, we'll try to give very succinct answers to a handful of very difficult questions—the questions that the crew and I seem to hear over and over again.

We'll also try to pass along a little bit of our hard-won experience, in the hope that it may pull you out of a tight spot some day.

Windows 95 is still enough of a black box that, occasionally, things happen that *I* sure don't understand. Cosmic rays. Rampant gremlins. Who knows? But usually you can get up and running—even running well— by staying calm and working through the problem.

So think of this chapter as a second line of defense. A large portion of the questions most people have about Windows can be solved by simply understanding what's going on—the provenance of all that precedes this appendix. That's your first, best line of defense. A few things, though, take a bit of black magic, and that's what we'll provide here.

In other words, this is where you should look when you're ready to stick your fist through the monitor.

Win95 Won't Install

I've heard of two machines that absolutely, adamantly refused to install Windows 95. I'm not talking about your garden-variety failure to recognize hardware, or a multiple boot-to-safe-mode hair raiser—all of that stuff is covered in great detail in Chapter 8. I mean a full-blown dead on arrival PC.

PnP Doesn't and Won't

The first DOA PC would behave itself all the way through a normal installation, until it got to the point where the user was supposed to identify their time zone—way, way down the line, as installation procedures go. At that point the PC would freeze completely. The PC's owner tried and tried and tried. He wiped the hard drives clean. He tried to install from Windows 3.1. He tried to install from DOS. He tried to install from Outer Mongolia. He tried to install with a new video board. He tried to install with a new network board. He tried to install with a new Ouija Board. Nothing worked.

That poor PC was examined thoroughly by the manufacturer, by several companies that provided parts to the manufacturer, and ultimately even by Microsoft. Everybody pointed fingers at everybody else: software people said it was hardware; hardware people said it was other hardware; firmware people stood in the middle and said they were all wrong. You know the tune.

Ultimately the owner figured out the problem. The machine had a nifty, fast SCSI controller for the machine's hard drives. It had a nifty, new feature called Plug 'n Play: if you set the jumpers one way, the controller was fully Plug 'n Play compatible; if you set the jumpers the other way, Plug 'n Play was disabled. The controller had been tested under Win95 ten ways from Tuesday, with no reported problems.

The problem? That controller's Plug 'n Play didn't quite meet spec. As long as it was set up for Plug 'n Play—and it worked great under Windows 3.1 with Plug 'n Play enabled!—you didn't stand a snowball's chance in hell of getting the controller to run under Win95. A quick switch of the jumpers to "dumb" mode, and Win95 installed immediately, the controller was identified automatically and set up with all the requisite drivers, and the owner was one recently-happy camper.

Why did the PC freeze when the user was setting up time zones, fer heaven's sake? Who knows? But it did. Reliably. Dozens and dozens of times. The moral of this story: if you can't install Win95 and all else fails, try to "dumbify" any fancy hardware. It just might work. And if you can narrow down the source of the problem, you can (1) slowly restore the hardware's functionality, a step at a time, watching to see when it goes kaboom, and/or (2) scream bloody murder at the manufacturer and demand a compatible piece of hardware. Personally, I prefer the latter approach, as it's the only way recalcitrant hardware manufacturers will be brought to justice.

A Real Virus

All the learned sages in the previous example would, from time to time, start muttering things about viruses and how the DOA PC must've been infected—if not possessed. Well, the simple fact is that viruses don't work that way. (At least, none of the viruses I've seen or read about work that way.) They don't freeze your machine suddenly when you're trying to install Win95.

Except . . . except . . .

We found out that there is a virus that can stop a Win95 install dead in its tracks. It's a common boot-sector virus that people rarely discover until they're installing software—any software, including Windows 95—from our special high-density disks. The virus infects the boot sector of every diskette put in the diskette drive. So when somebody installs Windows 95, this virus infects the first install diskette, which is a normal 1.44 MB diskette. When the user puts the second diskette into the machine, though, the virus tries to write to the boot sector— and discovers that it can't write to one of our specially formatted high-density diskettes. The machine locks up just after diskette #2 is inserted.

Several people on-line have hinted that the real problem lies in a virus distributed on the Windows 95 diskettes. I'm here to tell you that—much as I enjoy a good conspiracy theory—this one is pure bull. The virus is real, and if your machine locks up immediately after inserting the second Win95 installation diskette, the virus was on your machine before you started the installation. You should actually be <gulp> grateful to Microsoft for catching this one.

The best solution? If your machine locks up immediately after you put the second installation diskette in the drive (for Windows 95, or any of the Office 95 products for that matter), turn off your machine, do not put any more diskettes in the drive, and call Microsoft immediately: 800-426-9400 in the USA; your local Microsoft office outside the USA. Tell them that you have the "second install disk virus" and have one of the 'Softies check the Microsoft Knowledge Base for the latest information on how to remove it. If the person on the other end of the phone doesn't know what you're talking about, get somebody else.

Hardware on the Flipside

Many people get very upset when they find that their hardware isn't correctly identified during the installation phase, but then gets picked up when Windows boots for the first time. It seems weird, but that's how Win95 identifies some things. My Sound Blaster AWE 32, for example, isn't identified during the hardware detection phase, but it's always picked up when I boot for the first time—when Windows says it has "identified new hardware."

If you don't get your hardware identified the first time around, don't sweat it.

If All Else Fails

Oh. The second DOA PC? I never did figure out what was wrong with it. I went through all the steps in Chapter 8 and even tried to decipher the log files described in Chapter 9. No luck.

Granted, it was a 386/33 with 4 MB of memory and kind of nearing the end of its useful Windows life anyway. I talked the owner into donating it to his daughter's school and taking a tax write-off. The school appreciated it. The guy went out and bought a Pentium, with Windows 95 preinstalled. We all saved hours— no, days, if not *weeks*—of agony. Everybody made out on that deal.

The moral? Sometimes it just ain't worth the effort. I know you don't want to read that, but it's true. How much is your time worth? $20 an hour? $50? When you're wrestling with a bad Win95 install, you should qualify for hazardous duty pay, too. New machines are incredibly cheap, and much more powerful than what you have right now. Others—schools, charities, Boy Scout troops—can put that old hardware to good use, and you can claim the tax deduction if you itemize. Why bother?

Win95 Won't Start

Windows offers a huge array of methods to decipher how and why a machine won't boot. They're covered in detail in Chapters 8 and 9.

I had one little tip, though, that's so easy you might overlook it. If I ever have trouble booting Windows 95, the first thing I do is restart the machine with an old DOS boot disk, then hop over to the root directory of my boot drive (typically, `c:\`), rename both `autoexec.bat` and `config.sys`, and try to bring up Win95. That doesn't work every time, but when it does, the problem— generally a weird line stuck in `autoexec` or `config` by a pre-Win95 installation program—is usually pretty easy to identify and fix.

My big tip is to take the log files described in Chapter 9 with a grain of salt. It's easy to get freaked out by a line in a log file that says Load Failed or some such. I've done it myself. Often, though, you'll find that such scary-sounding lines are quite normal. In particular, if a specific driver was already loaded (as indicated by an earlier line in the log file), it's quite natural for a second attempt to load the same driver to fail. Don't come to any hasty conclusions.

But why would Windows try to load something that's already loaded? Doesn't make any sense to me.

It can happen when more than one setting forces a library to be loaded. It's more efficient to have the load process itself trap the fact that the library is already loaded once, than to keep track of how many settings want to load something.

Weird Hardware Problems

I'd guess that well over three-quarters of the strange hardware problems I've encountered were solved with the aid of a standard Windows Help "Troubleshooter" list. They can be very valuable, and you should learn to rely on them.

There are two problems with Troubleshooters.

First, they can be absolutely impossible to find, if you always use the Windows Help "Find" tab: the people/programs who put together the "find" search words for Windows Help never seem to speak the same language I do. I've discovered the hard way that there's only one way to find a Troubleshooter when a piece of hardware isn't working right. I go over to the Help "Index" tab and look up troubleshooting. That brings up a couple of dozen entries, but I can usually figure out which one applies to the problem I'm having.

Second, they're very narrow. Often the Troubleshooter will solve a specific problem that's very close to the problem you've encountered, but it takes a little leap of faith to branch out and poke some things not explicitly mentioned in the Troubleshooter. You should never be afraid to try something slightly different from what appears in a Troubleshooter: just take good notes, and if you screw up, retrace your steps to set it aright.

Hey, Microsoft! You want to do something *important* with my $89? Beef up the Troubleshooters! Make them more flexible and more comprehensive. I don't want any of that fancy-schmancy BS like the "English language" help in the Office products. You know, the Help that's supposed to read my mind when I type in a question like "How do I center a paragraph?" or "Why the hell did I buy this package?". What I *really* want is some simple, step-by-step stuff that pulls me out when I'm up to my keester in hungry 'gators. I WANT MORE TROUBLESHOOTERS!

Lost CD Drive

I've seen this one happen a dozen times. Your Win95 installation goes perfectly. Applications work just great. You reboot and re-organize things a dozen times. All of a sudden, and for no apparent reason, one morning you boot up Windows 95 and your CD-ROM drive is dead. Explorer doesn't have an icon for it. The System applet doesn't mention it. Put an Autorun CD in the drive and it doesn't run.

I don't know why it happens, but it does.

Fortunately, the solution is very easy if you have your old DOS `autoexec.bat` and `config.sys` files lying around. (Remember how Mom warned you to keep copies of them, back in Chapter 8?) What you want to do is start Win95 with your old "real mode" drivers working—the ones that are enshrined in the old `autoexec.bat` and `config.sys`. You do that by simply copying the old `autoexec` and `config` to the root directory of your boot drive (typically `c:\`)—making sure that you keep copies of any existing `autoexec` and `config`, of course, and rebooting into win95.

I don't know why, but if you start Win95 with the real mode drivers going, it suddenly realizes there's a CD-ROM drive, and everything starts working again. You only have to boot once: you can then remove the old `autoexec` and `config` (possibly replacing them by the copies you just saved), reboot, and you're as good as new.

If you ever figure that you want to keep the old CD-ROM drive information from your old `autoexec.bat` and `config.sys` in your Windows 95 boot sequence, you need to copy several lines from the old `autoexec` and `config` to the new one. In `config`, look for a `device=` line with the letters `cd` in it and, if you have a SCSI card, another `device=` line with `aspi` in it. In `autoexec`, look for a line with `mscdex`. Copy those lines into your new `autoexec` and `config`, and Windows will always be forced to recognize your CD-ROM drive.

 I hit another odd situation that made Win95 suddenly unable to recognize a CD-ROM drive. It was a Windows 3.1 machine set up with a single hard drive, `c:`, and a single CD-ROM drive, `d:`. The owner upgraded to Win95, and everything worked fine. One day he installed a second hard drive. Sure enough, Win95 recognized his new hard drive as `d:`, but it adamantly refused to recognize the CD-ROM drive!

We finally tracked down the problem (and it wasn't easy, believe me!). Back in Windows 3.1, he had a `lastdrive=d` line in `config.sys`, to save a little lower memory space. When he upgraded to Windows 95, that `lastdrive` setting was copied into the Win95 Registry, *and it stuck!* Win95 absolutely, positively refused to recognize any drives beyond the letter `d:`.

The solution was quite simple. I constructed a one-line `config.sys` saying simply `lastdrive=z`. I rebooted Windows 95 once. It picked up the new setting. Then I got rid of the `config.sys`. From that point on, Win95 would recognize the missing CD.

CD Drive Letter

 What, you have a hundred programs set up to look for CDs on drive `f:` and Windows 95 insists on making it drive `e:`? Join the club. Fortunately, changing it is very easy.

Crank up Control Panel (Start/Settings/Control Panel), double click on the System applet, and bring up the Device Manager tab. Pick your CD-ROM drive from the list and click Properties, then Settings. Down where it says Reserved Drive Letter, put your desired drive letter in *both* the Start Drive Letter and End Drive Letter boxes. OK all the way out.

Next time you reboot, your CD-ROM drive letter will be reset, permanently.

Enhanced Parallel Port

 I got a big kick out of the journalist writing for one of the big weaklies who was so disgusted with Win95 because he manually installed Enhanced Parallel Port support for his printer, and everything locked up.

Word of warning to the clueless: there's a reason why you have to manually shoot yourself in the foot, er, manually install Enhanced Parallel Port support in Windows 95. *It doesn't work!* At least a couple of months after Windows 95 shipped, only a very few, very obscure printers hanging off a very few PCs could operate at all with EPP. Yeah, the printers all say they support EPP. Yeah, the PC makers say they support EPP. Well, the manufacturers speak with forked Centronics cable. The fact is that there's never been a stable enough combination of PC and printer to nail the EPP spec down solid, and Microsoft wrote to the spec—not to the vagaries of the existing hardware.

Look for EPP and other advanced Win95 features (Fax on Demand comes to mind immediately) to be implemented sporadically. And remember that you can always tell the pioneers by the arrows in their backs.

Weird Software Problems

Several software problems can be solved by the Windows Troubleshooters, and my comments about them in the previous section apply here, too.

Import Filters

If you installed Win95 into a clean, new directory (as Mom recommends), you may have a few settings in your old Windows 3.1 `win.ini` file that need to be copied to the new Windows 95 `win.ini` (and, no, I *don't* mean you have to put the entries in the Win95 Registry).

I hit this problem when trying to insert pictures into WinWord documents shortly after installing Windows 95. Word complained that it didn't have an import filter for the picture—when I knew darn good and well that I have import filters for `.tif`, `.bmp`, `.pcx`, and almost any other picture file format you can mention.

Ends up that the solution was in `win.ini`. I had to copy the `[MS Graphic Import Filters]` section, including all the entries underneath that line, from my Windows 3.1 `win.ini` to my Windows 95 `win.ini`. While i was at it, I also copied over the `[MS Proofing Tools]`, `[MS Text Converters]`, and `[MSWord Text converters]` sections, and their contents. I restarted Windows 95 and everything worked fine.

I was tempted to copy over the [extensions] section, too, but decided against it. That's the section used for Object Linking and Embedding 1.0—the old, notorious OLE, the one that had trouble walking and chewing gum at the same time. I finally figured that the old OLE was so unstable that I really didn't want any vestiges of it hanging around in my new Win95/OLE 2 world. And I haven't regretted the decision.

DOS Weenie Weirdness

Come on, confess. You know a DOS Weenie, don't you? Somebody who just has to flip out to the old DOS command prompt to do something, every now and then. Hey, it's hard to forget your upbringing.

DOS Weenies will be glad to know that they can extend the DOS command line to hold more than 127 characters—a necessity, sooner or later, when dealing with long file names. It's pretty easy. You just need the line:

```
shell=c:\windows\command.com /u:250
```

in your config.sys. To quote from Microsoft's official Knowledge Base article:

> *With the command-line character limitation set to its maximum, filenames are limited to 250 characters minus the number of characters in the command line. For example, if the command line reads*
>
> ```
> copy con "<long filename>"
> ```
>
> *the maximum length of the <long filename> is 244 characters (that is, 250 minus the 11 characters of the command line).*

 250 minus 11 is 244, eh? Now you know how they do arithmetic in the Land of Nod. Maybe that's how Bill ties his accountants up in knots.

Exchange

Microsoft's Exchange is a basket case. As the saying goes, it's the worst email client, except for all the others.*

While Exchange is covered at length in Chapter 3—and you'd be crazy to try to put it to work without consulting that chapter at length—there are two things you *must* know about Exchange before you can even think about using it. I'm going to repeat them here because they're so important.

- Yes, there is a way to add the name from an inbound email message to your address book. Right-click on the Sender's name, even though it appears in black on a gray background, the traditional "dead field" indicator for all Windows applications. Pick Add to Address Book. Then immediately flip over to the Address Book to make sure Exchange added it correctly.

- Yes, there is a way to send your outbound Internet mail via your usual Internet service provider. Unless you change it, Exchange always, uh, assumes you want to send outbound Internet mail via Microsoft Network, and it will adamantly refuse to send Internet mail via any other carrier. The trick is to click on Tools, then Options, bring up the Delivery tab, and make sure "Internet Mail" in the lower box appears before "The Microsoft Network Online Service." Click the up and down arrows to adjust correctly. You'll have to restart Exchange for the change to "take."

Some day Exchange will be ready for prime time. I, for one, can't wait.

Odds 'n Ends

Here's a little grab-bag of questions I've encountered while struggling with Windows 95. Hope some of them ring a bell with you.

---

*Truth be told, Barry and Woody use Exchange every day, and have come to rely on it almost as much as they rely on their PCs. But they hate it! Oy, do they hate it . . .

Getting Rid of the Logon Screen

Do you have a stand-alone machine, one that doesn't ever connect to a network? Are you tired of seeing that stupid logon screen every time you boot Windows 95? Yeah. Me, too. Here's how you give it the deep-six:

- In Control Panel (Start/Settings/Control Panel), double-click on the Network applet. Change the Primary Network Logon setting to Windows Logon. Click OK, and Windows will restart.

- Log on the usual way, then go back into Control Panel, double-click on the Passwords applet, and click Change Windows Password. Where it says Old password: type your old password. Leave the boxes marked New password: and Confirm new password: blank.

- That's it. Next time you restart Windows, your logon screen is long gone.

To bring the logon screen back, just pop into the Passwords applet and give yourself a password. That's all it takes.

Restoring Obliterated Icons

As I mentioned in Chapter 9, sometimes icon pictures get . . . weird. They'll change colors, or develop black Icon Ebola blotches. If that should ever happen to you, look in your \windows folder for a hidden file called ShellIconCache. That's it. No extension or anything. Delete that file and restart Windows. Your icons should return to their normal state.

I Forgot My Password

Windows 95 isn't well known for its superb security, and this is one place where that lack really helps. As long as you're a legitimate user, of course.

If you ever forget your password, you'll have to get Windows—or at least DOS—going first. (In general, you can reboot normally, then hit the Esc key when confronted with the logon screen. In rare circumstances, you may have to boot from a floppy disk.)

Next you want to look in the \windows folder for a .pwl file. If your logon i.d. is mao, for example, you want to find mao.pwl. Generally, the file isn't even marked as a Hidden or System file, but if somebody has been screwing around—trying to hide the file, say, from prying eyes—and you're using DOS mode, you may have to use the `attrib` command (on your emergency boot disk) to turn off Hidden and/or System.

Finally, delete the file. That's all it takes. Reboot Windows 95, type in your logon i.d. and a new password, and you're on your way.

The downside to all of this is that you lose all your passwords—including, say, your on-line service logon passwords. So make sure you can stand the cure before you implement it!

And that ends another edition of *As the Mom Turns.* . . .

Stay Tuned!

You can't keep a good icon down.

INDEX

@ (at symbol), 129
" (double quotes), 98–99, 131
: (colon), 427
; (semicolon), 318, 413

16-bit programming, 13–14, 75
32-bit programming, 10, 39
  basic description of, 13–14
  drivers and, 104
  version of ClickBook, 482
3D Objects, 657–59, 662
3D Pinball, 456

A

Accelerator keys, 47–48, 61–63, 797–98. *See also*
  Hotkeys; Shortcuts
Accented letters, 131
access.cpl, 265
Accessibility packages, 64
Acrobat Distiller, 142–43
Acrobat Exchange, 142–43
Acrobat Reader, 142–43
ActiveBorder, 654
ActiveTitle, 654
Adapters, basic description of, 173
Add New Hardware Wizard, 632–40, 672, 685,
  702, 707
Add Printer Wizard, 271, 273
Add/Remove Programs applet, 33, 88, 268–70,
  341, 617–20, 639–40
Address Book, 175–77, 328
  basic description of, 311–12, 315–18
  MS Mail and, 339
  profiles and, 356
  Viewer, 317
Adobe Acrobat, 142
Adobe Designer, 118
Adobe Illustrator, 112, 118
Adobe Photoshop, 112–13
Adobe Type Manager (ATM), 138–40, 601
Advanced Configuration dialog, 306
Advanced Program Settings dialog, 285

After Dark, 458, 480
Aldus, 80, 82
Allocation units, 373
AlwaysShowExt, 188, 743
America Online (AOL), 176, 354, 402, 510, 512,
  557
Ami Pro, 81–83
Analyzing screen, 541–44, 547, 551–52, 555
Animated cursors, 34, 481–82, 677–78
Animated Hourglass scheme, 677–78
ANN files, 366–67, 369
Annotations, 366–67, 369
ANSI (American National Standards Institute),
  131–32, 145, 432
ansi.sys, 298
Antialiasing, 114–16, 460
Antivirus software, 37–38, 98–99, 458, 467–68,
  625
AOL (America Online), 176, 354, 402, 510, 512,
  557
API (application programming interface), 103,
  167
APM (Advanced Power Management), 186
Appearance tab, 154, 155
Append, 80
Apple Computer, 17, 106, 113, 497. *See also*
  Macintosh
Applet Property Sheets, 264
Application Bar, 43
Application descriptions, 236
Application identifier keys, 236
Application key, 62–63
apps.inf, 294–95
appwiz.cpl, 265
AppWorkspace, 654
archie, 418, 429–30
Arial fonts, 119–21, 123, 127–28, 139
ARP (address resolution protocol), 433
Artificial intelligence, use of the term, 22
Ascender, definition of, 121
ASCII format, 22, 96–97, 105, 221, 651
  character set, 129–33, 136, 285
  converting .doc files into, 251–52

ASCII format *(continued)*
  e-mail and, 329
  file compare utilities and, 299
  file compression and, 165
  files, opening, 244
  files, printing, 276
  help files and, 368
  Phone Dialer and, 397
  PIF files and, 281
  QuickView Plus and, 472
  RTF format and, 320
  text viewers, 241
  as a universal format, 142
  WordPad and, 433–36
Ashton Tate, 21
Associations, configuring, 235–63
AT&T, 511
AT command, 674
ATM (Adobe Type Manager), 138–40, 601
At symbol (@), 129
attrib command, 88, 145, 594
attrib.exe, 299, 618
Audio. *See* Audio CDs; Sound
Audio CDs. *See also* Sound
  autoplay of, disabling, 248–50
  Control Panel settings for, 684
Autodesk Animator, 113, 163
autoexec.bat, 16, 225, 303–9, 434, 782
  absence of, from emergency boot disks, 620
  DriveSpace and, 600
  io.sys and, 577–78
  Win95 installation and, 520, 529–31, 561–64, 577–78, 582–88
autoexec.dos, 308
autoexec.mom, 529–31
autoexec.w40, 586
Autohide feature, 183–84
Autorun, 32, 249–50
AVI files, 113, 163, 371, 448

B

Background tab, 293, 644–46
Backup systems, 88, 382–83, 458, 524, 621, 625
Bandwidth, 500
Baseline, definition of, 121
Batch language, 250, 300–301
Benchmarks, 489–91
Berkeley Systems, 480

Beta testing, 543
Bezier curves, 112
BIOS, 108, 575–76
Bitmaps
  basic description of, 111–14
  the clipboard and, 79
  copying current windows as, 60
  as the native format for Paint files, 437–38
  saving files as, 425–26
  scalable graphics vs., 114
  sound files and, comparison of, 157
Bits, definition of, 13
BMP files. *See* Bitmaps
Boldface font
  definition of, 119
  tips for using, 137
Booting. *See also* Rebooting
  basic description of, 575–90, 602–10
  device drivers and, 35
  emergency boot disks, 529–31, 555, 617–20, 720
  nonstandard, 583–88
  Plug n' Play and, 107
  step-by-step confirmation, 586
  while holding down an F key, 584–88, 594, 625
bootlog.prv, 602
bootlog.txt, 585, 602–3
Borders, window, basic description of, 45
Borland, 21, 82, 469
Briefcase, 392–95, 524
Brooklyn Bridge (program), 388
Browse button, 93
"Browse for file" capability, 68
Browsers. *See* Web browsers
budget.xls, 395
Bug(s), 108–10, 766–67. *See also* Errors; GPFs
    (General Protection Faults)
  clock and, 643
  Exchange and, 316
  fax transmissions and, 348
  First Name bug, 316
  handling fonts and, 148–49
  help and, 361, 365
  INF files and, 99
  liability for, licensing agreements and, 536–37
  New context menu and, 796
  screen settings and, 292
  Send To menu and, 258
  Start Menu and, 215

Errors *(continued)*
  technical support and, 557
  UMB memory support and, 308
Bus, 498–501
BUS_ALL, 597
Button bar. *See* Toolbar
ButtonDkShadow, 655
ButtonFace, 655
ButtonHilight, 655
ButtonLight, 655, 661
ButtonShadow, 655
ButtonText, 655
Byte, definition of, 13

C

Cabinet, 529
Cables, parallel, 389
Cables To Go, 685
Cabview, 463
calc.exe, 92–93
Calculator, 43, 439–41, 524
Calibration Wizard, 670–71
calllog.txt, 397
Canopus forum (CompuServe), 15
canyon.mid, 570
Capitalization, 126, 137
CaptionHeight, 661
CaptionWidth, 661
Cardfile, 37
CD icons, 232
CD Player, 170, 249, 448, 452–53
cdplayer.exe, 249
CD-ROMs, 6–7, 20, 170–71, 379, 568
  Autorun and, 32, 249–50
  Control Panel settings and, 700, 706, 710–12
  drives for, dirty, 554
  enhanced support for, 32
  hardware upgrades and, 484–85, 490–92, 494
  Media Player and, 450
  penalty boxes and, 303–4, 307, 308–9
  sound and, 158
  Win95 installation and, 523, 533, 542, 554, 568
CeBIT, 509
Central Point, 21, 464, 468
Certificate of Authenticity, 540–41
cfgback.exe, 621
CGA text mode, 153
CGM files, 112, 113, 207, 472

Character sets. *See* Charmap
  ANSI, 131–32, 145
  ASCII, 129–33, 136, 285
  basic description of, 129–33
  IBM, 129–30, 132, 285
Charmap, 132, 441–42, 524
Chat, basic description of, 419
Check boxes, basic description of, 52
CheckIn, 459
CheckIt, 12, 458
checkup.bat, 248
chkdsk.exe, 618
Claris, 19, 184
Click and drag, basic description of, 44
ClickBook, 482
ClickFlick, 474–75
Clip art, 113, 445
Clipboard
  basic description of, 78–80, 199
  copying/pasting to, 49, 60–61, 78–80, 205
  DOS sessions and, 291
  viewing, 62, 78–79, 442–46, 524, 574
Clipbook, 444–46
Clock, 4–5, 182, 625, 641–43
Close button, 43
Closing applications, 44, 48, 49
  Close Program dialog and, 3
  keystroke combination for, 60
clouds.mid, 235
CLSIDs, 228, 748–51, 756
Clusters
  basic description of, 373
  disk tools and, 373–81
CMC (Common Message Calls), 177
Cmdline, 284
CMS (Colorado Memory Systems), 382, 706
COGs (cost of goods), 361
Colon (:), 427
Color
  CYMK color, 149–50
  displays, basic description of, 110–18, 650–64
  dithered, 152
  in e-mail messages, 329
  file compression and, 164
  icons, 460
  matching, 627
  palettes, 149–52, 665–66
  picker, 72
  rasterization and, 114–16

Color *(continued)*
  RGB color, 149, 151, 153, 155
  systems, 367, 460–61, 627
Columns dialog, 320–21
COM (Common Object Model), 15, 35, 84
Combo controls, 53
Comdex, 509
Command buttons, basic description of, 51–54
command.com, 200, 475, 618
  io.sys and, 577
  Win95 installation and, 563, 577, 582, 588
Command message interface, 167–68
Command Prompt mode, 556, 594, 610
Command string interface, 167–68
comm drivers, 39
Common dialogs. *See also* specific dialogs
  basic description of, 71–76
  Microsoft Office and, 222
Common Print dialog, 48
Compose menu, 346
Compression, 441, 460, 621. *See also*
DriveSpace
  fonts and, 143
  graphics files and, 112
  OLE and, 82
  pasting text and, 80
  QuickView Plus and, 472
Compression Agent, 460
CompuServe, 15, 33, 111, 143, 176, 557, 573
  Exchange and, 312, 315, 328–34, 354–56
  fax transmissions and, 354
  as a general-purpose PPP provider, 402
  Internet Explorer and, 428
  logon scripts for, 411–16, 420
  prices, 402, 510
  Web browser, 420
Computers
  choosing, narrowing your list for, 488–91
  choosing a vendor to buy from, 495–98
  upgrading, overview of, 484–88
Computer Shopper, 496–97, 502, 507
COMSPEC, 306
ComXAutoAssign, 571–72
Conferences, 509–10
config.dos, 587
config.sys, 16, 97, 199, 225, 298–309, 434, 583, 782
  absence of, from emergency boot disks, 620
  DriveSpace and, 600

io.sys and, 577
  Win95 installation and, 520, 529–31, 555, 561–64, 577, 583, 586–88
config.w40, 587
config.wos, 304–5
Configurations Options box, 782–83
Configuration tab, 686–87
Contents tab, 369–71
Context menus, 29–30, 32
  accessing, 61, 62, 84
  basic description of, 67–68, 181–82
  configuring, 235–63
  creating shortcuts and, 36
  Notification Area and, 185
  Registry and, 751–53, 758, 792–97
control.ini, 646
Control Panel, 264–311, 629–712
  Accessibility applet, 630–31
  Add New Hardware applet, 632–40, 672, 685, 702, 707
  Add/Remove Programs applet, 33, 88, 268–70, 341, 617–20, 639–40
  Appearance tab, 646, 650–64
  applets, shortcuts to, 36
  Background tab, 644–46
  CD-ROM settings, 568, 710–12
  color settings, 151, 153, 643–69
  Date/Time settings, 641–43
  Desktop applet, 773
  Device Manager tab, 708
  Display applet, 643–69
  Hardware Profiles tab, 706–9
  Internet applet, 420, 669
  Joystick applet, 669–71
  Keyboard applet, 671–73
  Modems applet, 674–77
  Mouse applet, 276, 677–83
  Multimedia applet, 160, 166, 168, 683–84
  Network applet, 173, 684–89
  opening, 62
  Performance tab, 709–12
  profiles and, 356
  Regional Settings applet, 690–94
  Screen Saver tab, 647–50
  Settings tab, 664–69
  shortcut to, creating, 226–28
  Sounds applet, 695
  Start Menu and, 210–211, 212
  System applet, 696–712

Control Panel *(continued)*
  turning MouseKeys on in, 64
  User Profiles and, 276
  Win95 installation and, 534, 568–72
Conversion
  of DOC files, 251–52
  of graphics files, 116–17
cool.dll, 460
Copying
  to the clipboard, 49–50, 60–61, 78–80, 199,
    205, 291
  DAT files, 724–25
  diskettes, 200
  files, 197, 198, 205, 724–25
Copyright character, 132
CORBA (Common Object Request Broker
    Architecture), 84
CorelDRAW!, 81–82, 112, 118, 142, 472
CPL files, 265, 239, 629
CPUs (central processing units), 111, 701
  Pentium, 460, 485–88
  speed of, basic description of, 13
  system requirements and, 6–8, 485–88
  upgrading, 485–88, 494
Crashes, 15, 540. *See also* Bugs; Errors
  basic description of, 108–10
  detlog.txt and, 593, 595–96
  disk tools and, 375
Create Fax Wizard, 352
Create Shortcut Wizard, 90–91
Credit cards, 386, 498
ctomao.pwl, 278
Ctrl+Alt+Del, 2–3, 110, 225, 280, 541, 550, 562,
    648, 786
CUI (Common User Interface), 71
Currency characters, 131
Currency tab, 691, 694
Cursors, animated, 34, 481–82, 677–78
Customer support, Microsoft, cost of, 407, 557
Cut button, 55
CVF files, 381
CYMK color, 149–50

D

daily.xls, 80–81
Dashboard, 469–70
Date/time settings, 219–20, 265, 642–43, 692
dBase, 21

dblspace.sys, 381
DCC (Direct Cable Connection), 299–300,
    388–91, 394–95, 689
  quality of, grading of, 458
  Win95 installation and, 523, 524
DDE (Dynamic Data Exchange), 215, 217, 221,
    745–46
  clipboard and, 78, 80–81
  configuring context menus and, 240
  links, manual/automatic, 81
  OLE and, 83
debug.exe, 618
Debug mode, 415
Debug utility, 299
Defrag, 524
  basic description of, 375–78
  quality of, grading of, 458
Deleting
  clipboard contents, 442
  current selections, 50
  e-mail messages, 319, 323
  files, 74, 197, 202, 225–26
  icons, 86–87
Dell Computer, 497
Descender, definition of, 121
desk.cpl, 265
Desktop, 650–64
  accessing, by hitting the Backspace key, 86,
    87
  accessing, with all windows gone, 181
  Background tab and, 644–46
  basic description of, 26–32, 230–35
  common dialogs and, 71–76
  "hidden" directories in, 87–89
  icons, manipulating, 231–32, 785–92
  themes, 460–61
  storing/restoring, 773–74
  tips, 182, 232–33
  User Profiles and, 278–79
  working with folders and, 34–37
  Zoom factor, 664–69
desktop.ini, 392
Details button, 55
detcrash.log, 541, 596
detlog.txt, 541, 593, 595–97, 639
devicehigh, 309
Device Manager, 458, 459, 696–706, 708
Dialog(s). *See also* Dialogs (listed by name)
  basic description of, 50–54, 71–76

Dialog(s) *(continued)*
  common, 71–76, 222
  frames, 52
  tab order sets, 54
Dialogs (listed by name). *See also* Dialogs
  Advanced Configuration dialog, 306
  Advanced Program Settings dialog, 285
  Columns dialog, 320–21
  Common Print dialog, 48
  Edit Actions dialog, 240–41
  Edit File Type Actions dialog, 284
  Edit File Types dialog, 239, 744–47
  File Open dialog, 74, 87, 93
  File Types dialog, 236–42, 250, 258, 452
  Find Options dialog, 365–66
  Open dialogs, 33, 72–74, 230, 243–46
  Tools/Options dialog, 319, 335
  View/Option dialog, 88
Dial-Up Networking (DUN), 86, 226, 460,
    706
  basic description of, 33, 384–92
  DNS servers and, 410–11
  Internet applet and, 420–21
  Internet Setup Wizard and, 404
  logon scripts and, 411–15
  Microsoft Mail and, 336
  protocols and, 689
  quality of, grading of, 458
  shortcuts and, 91, 223
  terminology, 173–74
  Win95 installation and, 523–25
Digital Research, 20
dir command, 88, 93, 101, 144, 145, 286, 297
Direct Audio, 33
Direct Cable Connection, 299–300, 388–91,
    394–95, 689
  quality of, grading of, 458
  Win95 installation and, 523, 524
Direct Draw, 33
Directories. *See also* Folders
  directory trees and, 193–94
  basic description of, 34–37, 85–87
  fax transmissions and, 350–51
  "hidden," 87–89
  HKCR and, 747–48
  listings for, printing, 253–54
  property sheets and, 194–96
  shortcuts and, 90–94
  storing long filenames in, 101

the "two directory conundrum" and, 204–6
  Win95 installation and, 519–20, 523, 539–40
dirlist.bat, 254
dir.reg, 262
dir.txt, 260, 261
Diskedit, 101
Diskettes. *See* Floppy disks
Disk(s). *See also* Floppy disks; Hard disks
  emergency boot, 529–31, 555, 617–20, 720
  tools, 373–81
Display applet, 458, 643–69
Dithered color, 152
DLLs (Dynamic Link Libraries), 12–13, 35,
    520–22, 749
DMA (Direct Memory Access), 106, 697, 699–
    700, 702, 704, 632, 636
DNS (Domain Name Server), 405, 410–11, 433
DOC files, 71, 83, 766–67
  converting, 251–52
  WordPad and, 436
Documents menu, 221–23
DOS (Disk Operating System). *See also*
DOS sessions; MS-DOS
  attrib command, 88, 145, 594
  Backup, 382–83
  batch files, 300–301
  character sets and, 133
  commands, overview of, 295–301
  common dialogs and, 71
  communications drivers and, 33
  copy command, 298
  deltree command, 297
  dir command, 88, 93, 101, 144, 145, 286, 297
  doskey command, 11, 297
  downloading files and, 39
  drag and drop capabilities and, 68
  edit command, 296
  emergency boot disks, 529–31, 555, 617–20,
    720
  exclusive mode, 101, 285, 300–309
  executable files, 31, 35
  FAT (File Allocation Table) system, 196, 374,
    467, 518
  FileFind and, 217–21
  filenames, 96, 97, 99–100
  fonts and, 143, 285–88
  help command, 295
  hidden directories and, 88
  integration with, 10–12, 16–17, 21

DOS sessions *(continued)*
 keystroke combinations and, 59
 Local-DOS actions and, 253
 maximized windows and, 43
 mem command, 295
 move command, 100, 298, 391
 pasting names of files into, 199
 PIF files and, 88, 91, 100, 266, 284
 printer installation and, 272
 PrintScreen and, 60–61
 problems with, 280–81
 ScanDisk and, 377
 screen settings and, 291–93
 start command, 296
 toolbars and, 290–91
 UNC pathnames and, 391
 VxDs and, 104
 Win95 installation and, 517, 521, 529–32, 536,
  551, 555–56, 562–64, 570, 575–83, 589–90
 xcopy command, 297
dosapp.fon, 286
dosapps.inf, 282
DOS.pif, 266
dosprmpt.pif, 281
DOS sessions. *See also* DOS (Disk Operating
 System)
 button bar in, 32
 character sets and, 130
 deleting files in, 38
 DriveSpace and, 378
 memory settings and, 289–90
 toggling between full-screen sessions and, 60
dosstart.bat, 303
DoubleSpace, 603
Drag and drop, 68–71, 197–98
Draw, 437–38
Drive context menu, 255
drive.reg, 262
drive.txt, 261
Drivers, 33, 35, 39. *See also* VxDs (virtual device
 drivers)
 basic description of, 102–5
 MCI, 167–68
 printer, 103–4, 611
 real mode, 560–61
DriveSpace, 3, 36, 165, 309–10, 387–91, 527, 460,
 600
drvspace.bin, 200, 309, 381, 618–19
drvspace.sys, 381

DSP (Digital Signal Processors), 500
dumbwin.reg, 261, 263
DUN. *See* Dial-Up Networking (DUN)

E

Easter Eggs, 234–35
ECP (Enhanced Connection Port), 107–8, 499
edb.sys, 618–19
Edit Actions dialog, 240–41
edit.com, 529, 555, 618–19
Edit File Type Actions dialog, 284
Edit File Types dialog, 239, 744–47
Edit Flags, 188, 241, 263, 742, 760–65
Edit menu, 32, 434–35, 442
 clipboard and, 79
 DDE and, 80–81
 items, list of, 49–50
Edit Start menu, 214–15
E-mail. *See also* Address Book; Exchange
 addresses, assigned by Internet Service Pro-
  viders, 405–6
 addresses, using easy to remember, 405
 basic description of, 326–35, 417
 Internet Explorer and, 428
 reading/composing, 326–31
 sending/receiving, 331–35, 408–9
 trouble retrieving, 408–9
email.dot, 326
Em dashes, 125, 131–32, 136
Emergency boot disks, 529–31, 555, 617–20, 720
EMF (Enhanced MetaFile Format), 104, 112, 207,
 275
Emissary, 479
emm386, 307, 530, 563
EMM386 driver, 307
EMS memory, 306, 307–8
Enable Quick View check box, 240–41
Encapsulated Postscript, 112
EnCarta, 170
Encryption, 325, 355
En dashes, 125, 131–32, 136
Energy Star settings, 650
Envoy, 143
EPPs (Enhanced Parallel Ports), 499
EPS files, 112
Error(s). *See also* Bugs; Crashes
 "bad programs" and, 621–24
 decoding, 554

Error(s) *(continued)*
  Fatal Exception, 555
  fax transmissions and, 354
  information, saving, 109
  long pathnames and, 100
  protection violation, 109
  ScanDisk and, 247
  Setup and, 611–12
EULA (End User Licensing Agreement),
    536–37
Excel, 3, 300, 517, 749
  Charmap and, 441
  clipboard and, 78
  DDE and, 80–81
  pasting text from, 79–80
  QuickView Plus and, 472
Exchange, 8, 33, 175–76, 428, 673. *See also*
    Address Book; E-mail
  accessing, 49
  applet in the Internet Jump Start kit, 266
  basic description of, 310–60
  Explorer and, 209
  fax transmissions and, 340–55
  improving your delivery with, 339–40
  Internet Explorer and, 427
  modem settings and, 674–77
  multiple message stores and, 358–60
  Notification area and, 186
  organizing your mail in, 318–25
  profiles, 355–58
  quality of, grading of, 458
  reading/composing mail with, 326–31
  sending/receiving mail with, 331–35
  toolbar, 56
  Win95 installation and, 525, 571
Exchange Server, 175, 324
Exclusive mode. *See* Penalty boxes
EXE files, 35, 90, 281
Executive Systems, 464
Exit command, 49
Explorer, 100, 56, 255, 337
  basic description of, 187–210
  command line, 201–2
  common controls and, 74, 75, 76–78
  configurations of, 28–30
  DDE and, 80
  default options, 188

directory trees and, 193–94
displaying files/file extensions in, 23, 93, 189,
    567, 603, 743
Documents menu and, 221–23
dragging and dropping files in, 68–71, 197–98
errors and, 109
File/New dialog, 23, 24
filtering and, 190–93
Fonts folder and, 144
"hidden" directories and, 87–89
limitations of, 208–10
organizing e-mail and, 320
property sheets and, 194–96
quality of, grading of, 458
renaming files in, 32, 189, 197–98
selection techniques for, 58
shortcuts and, 90, 203
sorting and, 190–93
Start Menu and, 212–14
tips, 202–3
views in, 190–93, 202, 208
working with folders and, 36, 37, 85–87
explorer.exe, 191–92, 195
Extract, 574
extract.exe, 529, 574

F

Fastback, 464
Fast Find, 221
FAT (File Allocation Table), 196, 374, 467, 518, 613
Favorite Dirs folder, 233
Favorites folder, 75, 93–94, 95
Favorites menu, 423–24
Fax transmission(s), 104, 175, 266, 458
  Address Book and, 316
  cover sheets for, 351–53
  Exchange and, 312–14, 316, 318, 331, 340–55
  file transfers and, 354–55
  New context menu and, 792–97
  quality of, grading of, 458
  Request a Fax feature and, 349
  Send To menu and, 257
  Win95 installation and, 340–46, 523, 525, 533,
    572
fc.exe, 210, 299
Fdisk, 299, 518

fdisk.exe, 618–19

Fifth Generation, 464

File compression, 441, 460, 621. *See also*
    DriveSpace
    fonts and, 143
    graphics files and, 112
    OLE and, 82
    pasting text and, 80
    QuickView Plus and, 472

File extensions. *See also* File extensions
    (listed by name)
    displaying, in the Explorer, 23, 93, 189, 567,
      603, 743
    dropping, from filenames, 23–24
    handling, with File Manager, 245
    retention of, when a file is moved, 613
    supported by Quick View, 206–7

File extensions (listed by name)
    .cvf, 381
    .fax, 350
    .foo, 768
    .inf, 88, 99, 269–70
    .lnk, 35, 89, 92, 188
    .mcc, 92
    .mid, 156
    .pab, 175
    .pst, 175
    .rbk, 621
    .rmi, 570
    .shb, 84
    .shs, 84
    .ttf, 144
    .url, 92

File Find, 217–21, 323

File Maker Pro, 184

File Manager, 28, 58, 229, 245–46

File menu, 36, 444
    creating new documents and, 199
    items, list of, 48–49
    renaming files and, 198

Filenames. *See also* File extensions
    forbidden characters in, 96
    long, support for, 36, 74–75, 96–102
    UNC (Universal Naming Convention), 174

File Open dialog, 74, 87, 93

File Types dialog, 236–42, 250, 258, 452

File Viewers, 206–8

Find and Replace, 50, 72

Find Options dialog, 365–66

Find Setup Wizard, 364

findfast.cpl, 267

Fixed-pitch fonts, 122–23

F keys, booting while holding down, 584–88, 594,
    625

FLC files, 113, 163

FlexiCD, 249, 463

Floppy disks
    briefcases and, 392–93
    copying, 200
    emergency boot disks, 529–31, 555, 720
    file compression and, 200
    formatting, 200
    installation and, 268, 528–31

Folders. *See also* Folder view; specific folders
    basic description of, 34–37, 85–87
    HKCR and, 747–48
    shortcuts and, 90–94

folder.txt, 260, 261

Folder view, 190–93, 208
    briefcases and, 393–94
    Setup and, 259
    that looks like Program Manager, 229
    viewing folder hierarchy in, 254–55

FON files, 145, 286

Font(s)
    antialiasing and, 115–16
    applet, in the Internet Jump Start kit, 265
    basic description of, 118–23
    boldface, 119, 137
    caches, 139, 140
    Control Panel settings for, 667–69
    Desktop, 650–64
    in e-mail messages, 329
    Font Pack and, 140–42
    Fonts folder and, 128, 144–49
    Font tab and, 285–88
    help for, 367
    installing/removing, 146–49
    italics, 55, 119, 137
    overview of, 118–46
    printers and, 274
    scalable graphics and, 113–14
    tips for using, 133–37
    tools, 143–46

Font Minder, 142
fontview.exe, 145
Foreground settings, 293
Foreign languages, 132–33, 145, 672–73, 691–93.
  See also Character sets
format.com, 618–19
FoxPro, 21
Fractal Painter, 112, 438
Fraction characters, 131
Freecell, 36, 455, 456, 526
FSR (Free System Resources), 2, 32
FTG files, 369–70
FTP (File Transfer Protocol), 210, 418, 429–30,
  432–33, 479
FTS files, 369–70

G

Games, 33, 171–72, 524, 526
  Advanced Program Settings dialog and, 285
  basic description of, 455–56
  Start Menu and, 215
  VESA spec and, 307
Games folder, 220
gdi32.dll, 13, 14
gdi32.exe, 579
gdi.exe, 579, 602
General tab, 335, 358, 696, 703
Generic files, editing, 250
GID files, 368–70
GIF files, 111, 165, 188, 207–8, 244, 425–26
Global keystrokes, 59–61
Go to . . . feature, 203
gopher, 419
GPFs (General Protection Faults), 100
Graphics. *See also* Bitmaps; Paint
  display, basic description of, 110–18
  files, converting, 116–17
  scalable, 113–14
GrayText, 655
GRP files, 90, 521, 539
GUI (graphical user interface), 71

H

Hanging indents, 125
Hard disk(s)
  allocation of space on, 299, 373–74
  space, recommendations for, 494

Harvard Graphics for DOS, 472
Header controls, 77
Hearts, 444, 455, 526
Help, 33, 55, 210. *See also* WRK (Windows
  Resource Kit)
  basic description of, 360–71
  context-sensitive, 55
  DOS, 284
  "esoteric," 366–67
  information on ordering parallel cables in,
    389
  logon scripts and, 414
  topics, accessing, 62
Hewlett Packard (HP), 22–23, 82, 103, 469,
  574
  Admin hardware, 265
  printers, 115
Hi Color driver, 152
Hidden directories, 87–89
High Contrast, 631
Hijaak, 104, 117, 472–73
Hilight, 655, 663
HilightText, 656, 659, 663
himem, 602
Hinting, 138–39
HLS color, 149, 151
Hotkeys, 216–217, 221, 317, 649. *See also*
  Shortcuts
Hourglass cursor, 678
Hover, 455, 573
HSB color, 149–51
HTML (HyperText Markup Language), 422,
  425–27
Hyperterminal, 396, 458, 524, 625

I

IBM (International Business Machines), 11, 84,
  106, 134, 159, 281, 336. *See also* OS/2
  brand name recognition and, 497
  character sets, 129–30, 132, 285
  keyboards, 63
  portables, with DSPs built in, 500
  processors, 487
IconFont, 659–60
Icons. *See also* specific icons
  assigning, to ProgIDs, 767–68
  Control Panel settings for, 659–60
  deleting, 627

Icons (continued)
  launchable, 27, 30
  renaming/moving, 785–92
  that represent disk drives, adding, 231–32
  shell32.dll and, 790–92
  toolbar, twenty-four standard, 55–56
  transparent, 787
IconSpacing, 659–60
IconVerticalSpacing, 659–60
Idle sensitivity setting, 293
ID numbers, product, 540–41
IJK (Internet Jump Start Kit), 242, 265, 332, 404,
    409, 411, 460
  basic description of, 400–403
  Internet applet and, 420
  quality of, grading of, 458
Illegal operations, rebooting after, 109
Image Editor, 111–12
Impact Software, 481
Importing/exporting, key values with regedit,
    718–20
InactiveBorder, 656, 661
InactiveTitle, 656
InactiveTitleText, 656
Inbox icon, 26, 35, 86, 789–90
inetcpl.cpl, 266
INF files, 88, 99, 463, 593, 727–30
InfoCenter, 323
InfoText, 656
InfoWindow, 656
infshlp, 602
INI files, 98, 105, 521–22, 539, 593, 610
Insert Date/Time icon, 56
Ins key, 64
Installation, 5–8, 268–76. See also Setup
  choosing Win95 versions before, 516–17
  Compact, 523
  Custom, 523, 526, 540–42, 544, 547
  decoding errors and, 554
  drivers and, 104
  fonts and, 146–49
  options, choosing, 516–22
  of peripheral devices, Add New Hardware Wiz-
    ard and, 632–40
  Portable, 523
  preparing for, 528–33
  printers and, 270–76
  Safe Mode and, 552–56, 583, 585–87
  Safe Recovery mode and, 541–42, 550–52

  sound card, 632–40
  things to do after, 560–66
  Typical, 523–26, 540
  uninstall procedure and, 33, 268–70
install.exe, 268
Interchange, 511–12
Interlink, 388
interlnk.exe, 299–300
International MIDI Association, 162
Internet. See also Internet Explorer;
Internet Mail; Internet Setup Wizard
  applet, 419–21
  icon, 87
  Service providers, 510–12
  shortcuts to, 36, 95
  tools, 413–33, 476–77
  tutorials, 401–2, 417–19
Internet Explorer, 95, 208, 460, 509
  basic description of, 421–23
  icon, modifying, 790
  Netscape Navigator and, 478
Internet Mail, 175, 331–32, 334, 340, 406,
    409
Internet Setup Wizard, 400–402, 409, 460
  basic description of, 403–6
  problems getting connected with, 406–7
intersvr.exe, 299–300
intl.cpl, 267
I/O Supervisor, 579
io.sys, 200, 575–83, 588, 589–90, 604,
    618–19
io.w40, 588
ios.ini, 608
ios.log, 608
IP (Internet Protocol) addresses, 405, 412,
    433
IPX/SPX, 173, 389, 689
IRC (Internet Relay Chat), 419
Iris, 82
IRS (Internal Revenue Service), 143
ISA interface cards, 495
ISDN (Integrated Services Digital
Network), 500
Italic font, 55, 119, 137

J

joy.cpl, 266
Joystick, 266, 669–71

JPG files, 111, 165, 208, 425–26, 472
Justification, 126

K

kernel32.dll, 13, 14, 579
Kerning, definition of, 124–25
Keyboard
    applets, 266, 671–73
    menu selections with, 47–48
    Microsoft Natural, 61–63, 265
    numeric keypad, 64–66, 132
    repeat rate, 567
    scrolling with, 46
    shopping for, 495
killos2.exe, 15
krnl386.exe, 579

L

LAN connections, 336, 338, 347, 384–88
    central role of, 383–84
    Internet Jump Start Kit, 400
    Internet Setup Wizard and, 406
    ping and, 433
Languages, foreign, 132–33, 145, 672–73,
    691–93. *See also* character sets
Lantastic, 458
Laplink, 388, 389, 458
Laptop computers, numeric keypads and, 66
Large icons button, 55
LaserWriter, 127
Launchable icons/shortcuts, 27, 30
Leading, definition of, 122
Legacy hardware, 107
Lempel-Ziv algorithm, 165
LFN directory files, 101–2
Licensing agreements, 536–37
Ligatures, 126
List View controls, 55, 77
LNK files, 35, 89, 90, 92, 93, 246
loadhigh, 307, 309
logo.sys, 576, 614–17
Logon scripts, 411–15
LogView, 592–601
logview.exe, 592–601
Lotus
    Lotus 1-2-3, 20–21, 472

Lotus Notes, 20–21, 175–76, 311, 324–25
    OLE and, 82

M

Macintosh, 17, 19, 21, 478. *See also* Apple
    Computer
    folders, 34
    keystrokes, 50
    sound features, 156
Macros, 766–67
    converting DOC files and, 251–52
    Exchange and, 326
Magazines, computer, 506–8
Mailing lists, basic description of, 418
Mail-order companies, 496–97
main.cpl, 265–67
MAPI (Messaging API), 104, 175–77, 312–14, 428
marlett.ttf, 128
Maximize button, 43–44
MaxPagingFileSize, 712
MCC files, 92
mciSendCommand, 167
MDI (multiple document interface), 435
Media Player, 167–69, 449–50, 452, 525
Media Studio Pro, 164
mem command, 295
memmaker.exe, 298–99
Memory
    640K barrier, 289, 307, 560
    Backup and, 382–83
    CD-ROMs and, 170
    the clipboard as a area of, 78
    consumed by shortcuts, 36
    consumed by sound files, 156–57
    DOS exclusive mode and, 303
    fonts and, 133, 139, 140
    managers, removing, 531
    new technologies and, 499–500
    penalty boxes and, 305
    random-access (RAM), 6–8, 111, 499–500, 710
    rebooting and, 224–25
    requirements, 6–8, 15–16, 484–86, 494
    settings, 288–90
    UMB memory, 305–9
    video (VRAM), 500
    Win95 installation and, 523, 527–28, 531–32
    WordPad and, 434

Menu(s). *See also* specific menus
  basic description of, 42, 47–50
  toggled items on, 48
  tree-based, 94–95
MenuFont, 654
MenuHeight, 662, 663
MenuText, 656
MenuWidth, 662, 663
Message aware applications, 176
MessageFont, 654
Message Store, 176
Metaphor, 82
MGS (Microsoft Goody
Specification), 219
Microangelo, 481–82
Micrografx, 82, 112, 472
Microsoft
  Natural Keyboard, 61–63, 265
  technical support, cost of, 407, 557
  Web site, 463, 478, 678
Microsoft Mail, 266, 312, 335–39, 543, 570, 673
Microsoft Network. *See* MSN (Microsoft Net-
  work)
Microsoft Office, 21, 38, 221, 267
  Application Bar, 43
  common dialogs and, 222
  converting graphics file and, 117
  Exchange and, 326
  Favorites folder and, 95
  File dialogs in, 75
  fonts and, 142
  pasting text and, 79–80
  shortcuts and, 93–94, 461–63
MIDI (Musical Instrument Digital Interface), 33,
  156–63, 168–69, 449, 454, 526, 570, 683–84
midseq.drv, 169
MIME (Multipurpose Internet Mail Extensions),
  242, 329, 426, 739, 742
Mine Sweeper, 455, 526
Minimize button, 43
MinPagingFileSize, 712
Minus key, 64
MiraTech, 474–75
mkcompat.exe, 623–24
mlcfg32.cpl, 266, 570
mmsys.cpl, 265–67
mode.dos, 588
mode_dos.w40, 588

Modem(s), 6–7, 33, 266, 342–51, 354
  Control Panel settings for, 674–77, 705–6
  file transfers and, 397–98
  problems with, 406
  speeds, 500–501
  TCP/IP and, 409–10
  Win95 installation and, 523, 533
modem.cpl, 266
Monitors. *See also* Screens
  io.sys and, 576
  shopping for, 494
Mosaic, 478
Motion Tab, 677
Mouse
  applet, in the Internet Jump Start kit, 266
  Control Panel settings for, 677–83
  DOS sessions and, 293
  double clicking, avoiding the need for,
    24–25
  keys, in the Registry, 631
  making menu choices with, 29–30
  Mousekeys and, 64–66
  pointers, changes in, over window borders,
    45
  right clicking, 29–30, 61, 67–68
  shopping for, 495
  software, 63
  system requirements and, 6–7
move command, 100, 298, 391
MOV files, 113, 163
MPC (Multimedia PC Working Group), 493–94
MPEG files, 165, 172, 491–94, 500
MRUlist, 222–23
MRUs (Most Recently Used Lists), 222–23,
  770–73
MSCDEX, 170, 300, 554
MS-DOS, 11, 518. *See also* DOS (Disk Operating
  System)
  batch files, 241
  exclusive mode, 300, 302–9
  restarting Windows and, 226
  WordPad and, 435
msdet.inf, 541, 597, 598–99
msdos.dos, 588
msdos.sys, 200, 520, 576, 585, 588, 603–8,
  618–19
msie10.exe, 400
msmail.ini, 434

MSN (Microsoft Network), 8, 33, 92, 389
  Control Panel settings for, 684–89
  downloading from, 100
  Exchange and, 312, 314, 329, 333, 334, 340
  hookup support for, charges for, 557
  icon, 26, 35, 86–87, 789
  Internet Explorer and, 428
  Internet Setup Wizard and, 404
  MAPI and, 175
  rates, 511–12, 557
  shortcuts and, 36
  Win95 installation and, 399–400, 523, 543,
    557, 570
MUD (Multi-User Dungeons), 419
Multimedia. *See also* Graphics; Sound;
    Video
  applets, 448–55, 683–84
  hardware for, 491–95
  use of the term, 22
Multimedia Properties tab, 166
Multiple User Profiles, 276–80
Multitasking, 10, 39
Multithreading, 10
My Computer, 26, 35, 230, 385
  basic description of, 85–87
  Control Panel and, 264
  fonts and, 143–44
  Properties choice on, 67–68
  renaming/moving, 785–92
  shortcuts and, 226
My Computer folder, 90
MyNewApp, 729

N

NetBEUI, 173, 389, 685–89
netcpl.cpl, 266
NetDDE, 445
netdet.ini, 598
netfax2.inf, 350
netfax2.q, 350
netfax2.sta, 350
nethood subdirectory, 88
netlog.txt, 598–600
Netscape Navigator, 143, 426–27, 458,
    476–78
NetWatcher, 448
Network Neighborhood, 35, 73
  basic description of, 86, 310

icon, deleting, 787–88
  location of, on the Win95 Desktop, 26
  shortcuts and, 91
NeverShowExt, 188
New Connection Wizard, 420
New context menu, 792–97
New Fax Wizard, 347
New menu, 199
New Profile Wizard, 356
newsgroups, 419, 428–29
New Wave, 22–23, 82
NICs (Network Interface Cards), 685
Niko Mak Computing, 472
Nintendo, 171
nmsdos.sys, 576
NoDesktop, 786
Norton Navigator, 74–75, 196, 206, 210, 465–66,
    469
Norton Utilities, 21, 38, 101, 197, 465–69
  Norton Backup, 458
  Norton Desktop, 27, 464–65
  Norton Disk Doctor, 458, 466
  Norton Disk Editor, 306
  Norton Virus Scan, 98–99, 376
Notepad, 25, 98, 109, 236, 244, 246
  help and, 370
  logon scripts and, 415
  Win95 installation and, 530, 571
  WordPad and, 433
notepad.exe, 244, 744
Notification Area
  basic description of, 181, 184–87
  CD Player and, 453
  context menus and, 185
  Sound Mixer and, 454
Novell, 84, 173, 177, 336, 445, 566, 689
NSP (Native Signal Processors), 500
NullFile, 759, 796
Numeric keypad, 64–66, 132

O

Object-oriented, use of the term, 22
Object Packager, 446–47, 450
OCR (optical character recognition), 349, 354
ODBC (Open Database Connectivity), 267
OLE (object linking and embedding), 23, 84, 105,
    436, 462
  acronyms related to, 83–84

OLE (object linking and embedding) *(continued)*
  automation, 80, 746
  basic description of, 81–84
  clipboard and, 78
  Exchange and, 236, 321, 330, 352
  Media Player and, 450
  object commands, 49
  Object Packager and, 446–47, 450
  QuickView Plus and, 471
  scrap, shortcuts to, 36
  shortcuts and, 91
  WAV files and, 451–52
Open dialogs, 33, 72–74, 230, 243–46
Orphans, 126
OS/2, 4–5, 10–12, 15, 17, 204
  keystrokes, 50
  vs. Windows 95, 20–21, 39
  Win95 installation and, 518
Outbox folder, 330
OutsideIn, 458, 471

P

P6 processor, 687
PAB files, 315, 317
PageMaker, 142
Page Setup, 72
Paint, 112, 117, 352, 391, 524
  basic description of, 437–38
  editing SYS files with, 616–17
  quality of, grading of, 458
  screen capture and, 61
Panose numbers, 127
Paradox, 472
Password(s), 355, 387–88
  Control Panel settings for, 690
  e-mail and, 325, 408
  files, master, 580
  logon, 403, 405, 413, 609–10
  password.cpl and, 267
  profiles and, 276, 278, 355
Paste button, 55
Paste command, 50
Paste Link, 80–81
Paste Special, 79
Pasting. *See also* Copying
  to the clipboard, 49, 60–61, 78–80, 205
  text from Excel, 79–80
Patterns, 645–47

PC Anywhere, 458
PC Expo, 509
PC Paintbrush, 111
PC Tools, 246, 458, 464, 465
PCX files, 82–83, 111–12, 117, 207, 244, 472
PDF (portable document format), 142–43
PDLs (Personal Distribution Lists), 314, 318
Penalty boxes, 226, 285, 782
  basic description of, 301–9
  DriveSpace and, 309
  setting up, 305–7
Pentium processors, 460, 485–88
Phone Dialer, 396–97, 524
PhotoFinish, 83
Photographs, scanning in, 113
PhotoMagic, 115
Picture Publisher, 81–83, 112–13, 438, 458
PIF files, 31, 88, 91, 100, 144, 238
  apps.inf and, 294–95
  basic description of, 281–85
  penalty boxes and, 303
PIF Program tab, 283–85
PIMs (personal information managers), 177, 311
Pinball game, 460
ping, 433
p.ini, 599–600
Pixels, 110–18
PKZIP, 355, 472–73
Plug n' Play, 32, 556, 575
  basic description of, 106–8
  Control Panel settings and, 632–33, 697
Plus! Pack, 33, 36, 85–87, 364, 388, 409
  antialiasing and, 115
  basic description of, 459–61
  character sets and, 130
  color palettes and, 152
  CompuServe and, 402
  Dial-Up Networking and, 386
  disk tools and, 376–77, 381
  Display applet and, 267
  Exchange and, 332, 333
  File Type Details panel, 242
  fonts and, 142, 285–88
  Internet Jump Start Kit and, 332
  Internet Setup Wizard and, 404–5
  logo.sys in, 614
  MAPI and, 175
  ProgIDs and, 238
  quality of, grading of, 458

Plus! Pack *(continued)*
    shortcuts and, 92
    System Agent, 98–99, 376–77
pointer32.dll, 63
pointer.dll, 63
pointer.exe, 63
Points, definition of, 121–22
POL files, 279, 722
POP3 (Post Office Protocol -Version 3), 331
Portable documents, 142–43
PostScript fonts, 112, 125, 127–28, 138
POTS (Plain Old Telephone Service), 177
Powerpoint, 80, 472, 766
Power Toys, 184–85, 205, 209, 258, 463–64
Printer(s), 267, 353–54, 533, 546. *See also*
    Printing
    drivers, 103–4, 611
    resolution, 103, 110, 113
    settings, 49, 72, 76, 270–76, 690
    sharing, 564–65
    spooling, 33, 88, 186, 274–75
    troubleshooting, 274
Printers folder, 62, 91, 210–11, 226, 270–76
Printing. *See also* Printers
    common dialogs and, 72, 76
    directory listings, 253
    documents, File menu command for, 48
    fonts, 145
    gray-scale, 115
    WordPad and, 434–35
PrintScreen, 60–61
ProComm, 354, 432, 458
Prodigy, 176, 402, 511–12
Product ID numbers, 540–41
Profiles, 276–80, 355–58, 706–9
ProgIDs, 221, 236–38, 241
    default action for, 746–47, 753
    Open With dialog and, 243–46
    Registry and, 740–48, 753, 764, 767–68
progman.exe, 229
Program Manager, 27, 82, 209, 215
    hotkeys, 216
    PIF files and, 281
    Windows 95 version of, 228–29
Progress buttons, 53
prompt.pif, 282
Properties button, 55
Properties menu selection, 67–68

Property sheets, 31–32, 194–96
Proportional fonts, 123
protocol.ini, 434, 600
Protocols
    basic description of, 173–74
    FTP, 210, 429–30, 432–33, 418, 479
    Hyperterminal and, 396
    SMTP, 329, 331, 340, 412, 428, 460
    TCP/IP, 33, 173–74, 409–10, 412, 433, 579
    Zmodem, 396
PST files, 323
PWL files, 279

Q

Qbasic (Quick Basic), 37, 284, 294–95, 300
QEMM, 531–32
Qmodem, 432
Quattro Pro, 79–80, 441
Quicken, 21
QuickRes, 463
QuickTime, 113, 163, 168
QuickView, 73, 240–41, 471–72, 524, 526
    basic description of, 206–8
    quality of, grading of, 458
Quotes ("), 98–99, 131

R

Radio buttons, 52–53
Raised caps, 125
RAM (random-access memory), 6–8, 111,
    499–500, 710
RAS (Remote Access Server), 386–87
Rasterization, 111, 113–14, 117–18, 138–39
Reach Out, 458
Real mode, 560–61, 575–83
Reality Lab, 172
RealMagic, 491
Rebooting, 4, 277. *See also* Booting
    after errors, 109
    cold, 224
    warm, 225
Recording Mixer, 454–55
Recycle Bin, 38, 197–99, 209, 279
    deleting files and, 74
    dragging shortcuts to, 148–49
    Exchange and, 319

Recycle Bin *(continued)*
  icon, 26, 35, 86, 788–89
  recovering files from, 466
  Setup and, 566–67, 612–14
Redo button, 55
Refresh features, 422
Regedit, 105, 235, 241, 246, 248. *See also*
    Registry
  basic description of, 713–21
  importing/exporting key values with,
    718–20
  merging REF files and, 725–27
  Setup and, 260, 261
regedit.exe, 618–19
reginfo.txt, 558–59
Registration Wizard, 558–59
Registry, 85–89, 581. *See also* Regedit
  adding new keys and values to, 717–18
  aliases and, 733–34
  app paths and, 778–80
  Appearance settings in, 652
  Backup and, 383
  basic description of, 105–6, 713–98
  binary backup of, 259–60
  briefcases and, 392
  CLSIDs and, 228
  color palettes and, 155
  design of, 722–24
  DoubleClickHeight in, 680
  Edit Flags in, 241
  fonts and, 128, 129, 144, 147
  games and, 456
  getting used to working with, 260
  help and, 367
  INF files and, 727–30
  keys, abbreviations for, 630
  MCI types in, 168
  merging REF files and, 725–27
  MRUs and, 770–73
  power users' tricks for, 784–85
  ProgIDs and, 740–48
  root keys in, basic description of, 732–34
  ScanDisk and, 248
  Screen Saver tab and, 648–49
  Setup and, 594, 597, 603, 610
  vmm32.vxd and, 578–79
Relogging Windows, 225–26
Repeat command, 50

Replace button, 55
report.doc, 80–81
Resource Meter, 186, 447–448
Restarting Windows option, 223–24, 225
Restore button, 44
RET (resolution enhancement technology), 115
RGB color, 149, 151, 153, 155
RIFF (Resource Interchange File Format), 156,
    163
Right click menus. *See* Context menus
RLE (Run Length Encoding), 165
RMA (Return Merchandise
  Authorization), 497
RMI files, 449
Root folder menu, 94–95
RTF (Rich Text Format), 319–20, 329, 436
  Charmap and, 441
  QuickView Plus and, 472
Rules, definition of, 125
Run box, 221–23
RunOnce, 581, 594, 595, 775, 780–81

S

Safe Mode, 552–56, 583, 585–87, 607
Safe Recovery mode, 541–42, 550–52, 600
sarah.txt, 261–62
SaveAsText macro, 252
Save password checkbox, 387–88
Saving
  documents, menu selections for, 48, 49,
    221–223
  e-mail messages, 360
  error information, 109
  file find searches, 220–21
  with the Save As action, 48, 72, 230
Scalable graphics/fonts, 113–14, 120, 122, 128,
    138
ScanDisk, 196, 247–48, 254, 373, 458, 460, 466,
    532, 535–36
  accessing, 67
  basic description of, 375–78
  emergency boot diskettes and, 618–19
  property sheets and, 31
  scandisk.exe and, 377, 618–19
  scandisk.ini and, 618–19
  scandisk.log and, 610
SCC (System Compatibility Corporation), 207

SCP files, 414–15
Screen(s). *See also* Monitors
   capture, 60–61
   measuring distances on, 660
   resolution, 31, 33, 110, 114–16, 215, 616, 666
   savers, 26, 31, 458, 480, 524, 647–50
   settings, in the Screen tab, 291–93
   Shortcut Bar and, 462
   size, 183, 285–86
   splash, 614–17, 606, 609
ScreenSaveTimeOut, 649
Scripts, logon, 411–15
Scroll arrows, 24–25
Scrollbar
   basic description of, 45–46
   Control Panel settings and, 662
   four parts of, 46
   Registry key for, 656
SCSI, 308, 498–499, 556
SDM.DLL, 522
SDRAM (Synchronous Dynamic RAM), 500
Security, 325, 688. *See also* Passwords
Semicolon (;), 318, 413
SendTo directory, 279
SendTo folder, 775
SendTo menu, 73, 95, 256–58
Setup, 9, 99, 268–69, 463. *See* Installation
   basic description of, 258–63, 533–50,
     591–601
   cleaning up after, 624–26
   Copy Files phase, 594
   Explorer and, 190–92, 203
   Power Toys! and, 463
   quick install and, 250–51
   Setup Wizard and, 593
   video files and, 166
setup.exe, 268
setup.inf, 594
setuplog.txt, 538, 593–94, 595
setver, 602
SHARE violations, 603
Sharing files/printers, 564–65
shell32.dll, 100, 790–92
Shell enhancements, 469–76
ShellIconCache, 89, 627
Shell Identifier keys, 237
shellname, 229–30
ShellNew, 88, 246

Shift key, holding down, while
   starting, 583–84
Shortcuts. *See also* Accelerator keys; Hotkeys
   basic description of, 35–36, 89–94
   DOS sessions and, 294
   Shortcut Bar and, 461–63
Shut Down option, 27, 223–226, 280, 694
Sigma Design, 491
Signatures, digital, 325
Size, font, definition of, 119
Sliders, 46, 47, 53
SMARTDrive, 517, 563
smartwin.reg, 263
SMTP (Simple Mail Transfer Protocol), 329, 331,
   340, 412, 428, 460
Snap To, 63
"Snooper" Registration, 596
Solitaire, 455, 526
Sonic Foundry, 158, 452
Sound(s). *See also* Multimedia
   applet, 266, 267
   cards, 6–7, 156, 158, 160–61, 308–9, 495, 570,
     632–40
   Control Panel settings for, 695
   MIDI files and, 33, 156–63, 168–69, 449, 454,
     526, 570, 683–84
   mono/stereo parameters, 157–58
   overview of, 156–63
   sample, 157–58, 570
   scheme setup, 678–79
Sound Blaster, 156, 158, 160–61, 309, 495
Sound Forge, 452
Sound Mixer, 454–55
Sound Recorder, 450–52, 525
Space bar, toggling a check box with, 52
Spin buttons, 53
Stability, 4, 15. *See also* Crashes
Stacker, 458, 459
Starfish Software, 470
Start button, 27, 181, 210–11
   context menus and, 67–68
   Control Panel settings and, 662
Start Menu, 27, 30, 106, 210–29
   accessing, 62, 63, 59
   Backup and, 382–83
   basic description of, 37
   configuring, 211–216
   DDE and, 80

Start Menu *(continued)*
    Document command, 88
    FileFind and, 217–21
    help and, 371
    logon scripts and, 414
    quality of, grading of, 458
    Run box, 203, 239
    tips, 226–28
    as a tree-based menu, 94–95
    User Profiles and, 276–79
Startup, 291–93. *See also* Booting
    basic description of, 602–10
    disks (emergency boot disks), 529–31, 555,
        617–20
    splash screens at, 614–17, 606, 609
StartUp Disk tab, 269
Status bar, basic description of, 45
Streams, 773–74
Style, font, definition of, 119
Submenus
    basic description of, 47–50
    cascading, 47
    grayed-out choices on, 47
SUM formula, 79
suwarn.bat, 600
Symantec, 464–65
symbols
    @ (at symbol), 129
    " (double quotes), 98–99, 131
    : (colon), 427
    ; (semicolon), 318, 413
sys.com, 618, 620
sysbckup subdirectory, 88
sysdetmg.dll, 595–98
sysdm.cpl, 265, 267
Sysedit, 433, 434, 571
system.1st, 594–95
System Agent, 458, 460
system.bac, 260
system.da0, 89, 594–95, 724
system.dat, 89, 259–60, 383, 594–95, 722–23
system.ini, 169, 434, 521, 571–72, 578, 601, 610,
    721
    absence of, from emergency boot disks, 620
    virtual memory settings in, 712
System menu, displaying, 44, 60
System Monitor, 26–27, 184, 448
system.new, 594–95

T

Tabbed dialogs, basic description of, 53
tada.wav, 729
Take Command, 475–76
TAPI (Telephony API), 175–77, 265, 396
Taskbar, 5, 8, 25–27
    basic description of, 27, 44–45, 179–87
    button, 25, 26, 44
    context menus and, 67–68
    Control Panel settings and, 662
Taskbar Properties menu, 181–82
Taskbar Properties sheet, 211, 213
Task Manager, 25, 63, 187
Taskman.exe, 187
TCP/IP (Transmission Control Protocol/Internet
    Protocol), 33, 173–74, 409–10, 412, 433, 579
Technical support, Microsoft, cost of, 407, 557
Telnet
    Emissary and, 479
    quality of, grading of, 458
    using, 427–28, 430–41
Terminal, 396, 625
terminal.exe, 625
terminal.hlp, 625
Termination setting, 293
TIFF (Tagged Image File Format), 111–12, 117,
    118, 188, 207, 244, 472, 473
timedate.cpl, 265
Timex Datalink files, 574
Time zones, 5, 594, 641–43
Title bar, basic description of, 43–44
TitleText, 656
Toolbars, 45, 60
    basic description of, 54–56
    DOS sessions and, 290–91
    dragging a item to a running application on,
        71
    Exchange and, 321–22, 330
Tools menu, 321–22
Tools/Options dialog, 319, 335
Tooltips, 56–57, 184, 452, 663
Topview, 281
topwin.exe, 218
Tracking, definition of, 124
Trademark character, 131, 132
Traveling Software, 388
Tree-based menus, 94–95

Tree View controls, 77
True Color driver, 152
ttfcache, 89, 627
TTF files, 144–49
Turbo Tax for Windows, 8
TXT files, 236
Typeface, definition of, 119

U

UARTs, 33
Ulead, 164
UMB memory, 305–9
UNC (Universal Network Connections)
  pathnames, 33, 73, 219, 391
  fax transmissions and, 350
  MS Mail and, 338
  Network Neighborhood and, 310
Undelete program, 38
Underline button, 55
Undo feature, 32, 59, 55
Unicode, 132–33
unidriver, 103–4
unidrv.dll, 611
Uninstall feature, 33, 268–70, 618, 620
Univeral Cable Modems, 389
UNIX, 39, 97, 319, 401
  Exchange and, 335
  ftp and, 432
  Netscape Navigator and, 478
Upgrades
  checklist for, 502–3
  component, 484–86, 494
  processor, 485–88, 494
  "rule of three" for, 1–5
UPS (uninterruptable power supply), 495
URLs (Universal Resource Locators), 92, 95
  basic description of, 423–24
  for the Microsoft Web site, 400
Usability testing, 24–25
user32.dll, 13, 14
user32.exe, 579
user.bac, 260
user.da0, 89, 278, 724
user.dat, 89, 259–60, 278, 383, 594–95, 722–24, 731
user.exe, 579, 602

User-friendly, use of the term, 22
username.pwl, 609
user.new, 594–95
User Profiles, 276–280

V

Verbs, "canonical," 753
Veronica, 419, 430
VESA spec, 307
Video, 6–7. *See also* Multimedia
  cards, 484–86, 569–70, 666
  files, 113, 163–71
  surround, 172
View menu, 77, 146
View/Option dialog, 88
Virus checking, 37–38, 98–99, 458, 467–68, 564, 625
Visio, 112, 353
Visual Basic, 168, 300
vmm32, 582–83
vmm32.vxd, 578–79
VoiceView modems, 397
Volume control, 185
VRAM (video memory), 500
VxDs (virtual device drivers), 15, 32, 35, 578–79, 581–82
  basic description of, 104
  bootlog.txt and, 602–3
  sysdetmg.dll and, 597

W

w95undo.dat, 570, 624–25
w95undo.ini, 570, 624–25
Wallpaper, 31, 111, 425–26, 438, 460, 524, 644–46
Wave Mapper, 21, 167
WAV files, 156–63, 166, 450–52
Web browsers
  basic description of, 417
  fonts and, 143
  Internet Explorer, 95, 208, 421–23, 460, 478, 509, 790
  MIME systems and, 242
  Mosaic, 478
  Netscape Navigator, 143, 426–27, 458, 476–78

Weight, font, definition of, 119
Welcome.doc, 180
Welcome messages, disabling, 180
wgpocpl.cpl, 266, 570
What is this? button, 55, 61
Wildcard characters, 96, 217
win386.swp, 711
win95app.hlp , 570
Win95rk.cnt, 573
Win95rk.hlp, 573
winboot.sys, 588, 589
WinChat, 398–99, 527, 573
WinCIM, 332, 571
win.com, 578, 579
win.ini, 147, 169, 218, 222, 601, 610, 721,
   731
   absence of, from emergency boot disks,
      620
   installation and, 520, 579, 580
Windowed DOS sessions. *See* DOS sessions
WindowFrame, 657
WindowMetrics, 661
Windows 1.0, 11
Windows 2.x, 11, 50
Windows 3.1, 2–5, 8, 15–16
   applications, not included in Windows 95,
      37–38
   bitmapped fonts in, 286
   color in, 155
   common dialogs, 72, 74–75, 446
   Control Panel, 264
   CPL files, 267
   drivers, 103–4
   help engine, 361
   icon editors, 481
   performance of, vs. Windows 95, 39
   PIF files and, 281
   Setup and, 225–26
   Win95 installation and, 6, 331, 519–28, 536,
      540, 555
Windows 3.x, 2–5, 8, 15, 76, 230
   Control Panel, 264
   keystrokes, 58, 60
   long filenames and, 99
   mouse software, 63
   processing speed of, 13
   Program Manager, 90, 209, 215–17, 281

   the Wave Mapper scandal and, 21
   Win95 installation and, 38, 518, 520
   window captions and, 44
windows.cnt, 370–71
Windows for Workgroups, 38–39, 387, 445
   Setup and, 226
   stability of, 4
   Win95 installation and, 518, 523
   WordPad and, 434
Windows key, 61–63
Windows Metafile Format, 112
Windows NT, 4–5, 15, 518
   Netscape Navigator and, 478
   networking and, 173, 387
   performance of, vs. Windows 95, 39
WindowText, 657
windstart.bat, 579
Windstone ratings, 502
WinFax, 458
WinG, 33, 172
winhelp.ini, 610
WinPopUp, 398–99, 527, 573
Winsock, 174, 420
winstart.bat, 225, 303, 580, 582–83, 607, 724,
   780–81
Winstone test, 489–90
Winword (Word for Windows), 25, 80, 207. *See
   also* DOC files
   batch language and, 300–301
   Charmap and, 441
   Customize Toolbar mode in, 322
   DDE and, 81
   Exchange and, 314, 322, 326–27
   fax transmissions and, 353–55, 792–97
   filenames and, 98
   the Free System Resources problem and, 3
   keystrokes, 61
   links, manual/automatic, 81
   OLE and, 81, 84
   pasting text and, 80
   QuickView Plus and, 472
   right-dragging files to, 70
   shortcuts and, 91
   slider in, 47
   toolbars, 57
   Win95 installation and, 521–22
   WordPad and, 436

Winzip, 237, 355, 472–73
Wizards. *See also* Internet Setup Wizard
  Add New Hardware Wizard, 632–40, 672, 685,
    702, 707
  Add Printer Wizard, 271, 273
  Calibration Wizard, 670–71
  Create Fax Wizard, 352
  Create Shortcut Wizard, 90–91
  Find Setup Wizard, 364
  New Connection Wizard, 420
  New Fax Wizard, 347
  New Profile Wizard, 356
  Registration Wizard, 558–59
  Setup Wizard, 593
WNF files, 112
Wollongong Group, 479
Word for Windows. *See* Winword (Word for
  Windows)
WordMail, 326–27, 330, 345, 428
WordPad, 56, 60, 84, 199, 433–36, 768
  Charmap and, 441
  filenames and, 98
  fonts and, 128
  pasting text and, 80
  Setup and, 262
  Win95 installation and, 524, 559
wordpad.ini, 610
WordPerfect, 21, 207
WordPro, 490
WordView, 207, 574
Word Wrap, 435
World Wide Web. *See also* Internet; Web
  browsers
  basic description of, 417–18
  browsing, 421–27

the Microsoft Web site on, 463, 478, 678
  transmission speeds and, 500
WPG files, 112, 207, 472
WPOffice Editor, 295
WRAM (Windows RAM), 500
Write, 246, 436, 472
WRK (Windows Resource Kit), 102, 727–28, 731,
  726
  basic description of, 573
  Control Panel settings and, 685, 707, 711, 712
  detcrash.log documentation, 596
  INF file documentation, 594, 727–28
  netlog.txt documentation, 598
  Startup documentation, 604, 606, 608
  system.ini documentation, 601
  Win95 installation and, 515, 519, 526, 563, 573,
    575, 577, 588
  win.ini documentation in, 601

X

xcopy, 297, 391
Xerox PARC, 17
Xtree, 464

Y

Yahoo, 423

Z

Zero-length strings, 716–17
Ziff Labs, 489–90
ZIP files, 165, 210
Zmodem protocol, 396

DON'T TOUCH THAT CD!

. . . until you've ordered the second,
Bonus CD in my official two-CD set.

Listen up, sonny. There's a whole bunch of stuff that we couldn't ship with the book. Some of it - like the full text of this book, in searchable, Adobe Acrobat format—wasn't ready in time to be bound into the back of the book.

Besides, the only way we could keep the cover price of *The Mother of All Windows 95 Books* down to US$39.95 was to limit it to one CD. Consider that the original *CD-MOM: The Mother of All Windows Books* listed for $49.95. So you only get one CD, but you save ten smackers. You oughtta be down on your knees right now, kissing my feet for that one. Other Moms would've said, "Let 'em eat cake." But not this one.

What, you don't want to kiss my feet? Alright. I know how you can blow that ten bucks right now. Grab your Mastercard, Visa, or Amex, and make sure you have $9.95 left on your credit limit. Pick up the phone, dial 800-659-4696, and say, "I WANT MORE MOM!" (Outside the USA call 314-965-5630 and be prepared to pay $14.95.) For the price of three café lattes, give or take, you'll get:

- The entire contents of this book in Acrobat format.
- The Acrobat reader.
- 20 more Bitstream fonts.
- Lots and lots of additional goodies, some of which are still top secret.*

In addition, you'll get my world-famous lifetime moneyback guarantee: if the Bonus CD doesn't live up to your expectations—doesn't matter what you expected, or why—simply return it to Mom's Advanced Support Group, 11900 Grant Place, Des Peres, MO 63131, and you'll get a full and immediate refund. Period.

How can you lose?

---

* Rush: Top secret my foot. You still haven't gotten it all together, have you Mom? But I'm sure you'll put together lots of neat goodies while the book is at the printer. Or else . . .

END-USER LICENSE AGREEMENT FOR MICROSOFT SOFTWARE

IMPORTANT—READ CAREFULLY: This Microsoft End-User License Agreement ("EULA") is a legal agreement between you (either an individual or a single entity) and Microsoft Corporation for the Microsoft software accompanying this EULA, which includes computer software and associated media and printed materials, and may include "online" or electronic documentation ("SOFTWARE PRODUCT" or "SOFTWARE"). By opening the sealed packet(s) OR exercising your rights to make and use copies of the SOFTWARE PRODUCT, you agree to be bound by the terms of this EULA. If you do not agree to the terms of this EULA, promptly return this package to the place from which you obtained it.

SOFTWARE PRODUCT LICENSE
The SOFTWARE PRODUCT is protected by copyright laws and international copyright treaties, as well as other intellectual property laws and treaties. The SOFTWARE PRODUCT is licensed, not sold.

1. GRANT OF LICENSE. Microsoft grants to you a nonexclusive, royalty-free right to make and use an unlimited number of copies of the SOFTWARE PRODUCT, provided that each copy shall be a true and complete copy, including all copyright and trademark notices. If required in the printed material accompanying the SOFTWARE PRODUCT, you agree to display the designated patent notices on the packaging and in the README file of your software product.

2. COPYRIGHT. All title and copyrights in and to the SOFTWARE PRODUCT (including but not limited to any images, photographs, animations, video, audio, music, text, and "applets," incorporated into the SOFTWARE PRODUCT), the accompanying printed materials, and any copies of the SOFTWARE PRODUCT, are owned by Microsoft or its suppliers. The SOFTWARE PRODUCT is protected by copyright laws and international treaty provisions. Therefore, you must treat the SOFTWARE PRODUCT like any other copyrighted material except that you may either (a) make one copy of the SOFTWARE PRODUCT solely for backup or archival purposes, or (b) install the SOFTWARE PRODUCT on a single computer provided you keep the original solely for backup or archival purposes.

3. OTHER RESTRICTIONS. This EULA is your proof of license to exercise the rights granted herein and must be retained by you. You may not reverse engineer, decompile, or disassemble the SOFTWARE PRODUCT, except and only to the extent that such activity is expressly permitted by applicable law notwithstanding this limitation.

LIMITED WARRANTY
NO WARRANTIES. Microsoft expressly disclaims any warranty for the SOFTWARE PRODUCT. The SOFTWARE PRODUCT and any related documentation is provided "as is" without warranty of any kind, either express or implied, including, without limitation, the implied warranties or merchantability, fitness for a particular purpose, or noninfringement. The entire risk arising out of use or performance of the SOFTWARE PRODUCT remains with you.

NO LIABILITY FOR CONSEQUENTIAL DAMAGES. In no event shall Microsoft or its suppliers be liable for any damages whatsoever (including, without limitation, damages for loss of business profits, business interruption, loss of business information, or any other pecuniary loss) arising out of the use of or inability to use this Microsoft product, even if Microsoft has been advised of the possibility of such damages. Because some states/jurisdictions do not allow the exclusion or limitation of liability for consequential or incidental damages, the above limitation may not apply to you.

U.S. GOVERNMENT RESTRICTED RIGHTS
The SOFTWARE PRODUCT is provided with RESTRICTED RIGHTS. Use, duplication, or disclosure by the Government is subject to restrictions as set forth in subparagraph (c)(1)(ii) of The Rights in Technical Data and Computer Software clause at DFARS 252.227-7013 or subparagraphs (c)(1) and (2) of the Commercial Computer Software-Restricted Rights at 48 CFR 52.227-19, as applicable. Manufacturer is Microsoft Corporation/One Microsoft Way/Redmond, WA 98052-6399.

MISCELLANEOUS
If you acquired this product in the United States, this EULA is governed by the laws of the State of Washington.

If this product was acquired outside the United States, then local laws may apply.

Should you have any questions concerning this EULA, or if you desire to contact Microsoft for any reason, please contact the Microsoft subsidiary serving your country, or write:

    Microsoft Office Compatible Program
    One Microsoft Way
    Redmond, WA 98052-6399.

8/95